MASTER VISUALLY®

by Elaine Marmel

Visual®

Excel® 2007

Wiley Publishing, Inc.

Master VISUALLY® Excel® 2007

Published by
Wiley Publishing, Inc.
10475 Crosspoint Boulevard
Indianapolis, IN 46256
www.wiley.com

Published simultaneously in Canada

Library of Congress Control Number: 2008920773

ISBN: 978-0-470-18170-6

Manufactured in the United States of America

10 9 8 7 6 5 4 3 2 1

Trademark Acknowledgments

Contact Us

For general information on our other products and services please contact our Customer Care Department within the U.S. at 800-762-2974, outside the U.S. at 317-572-3993 or fax 317-572-4002.

For technical support please visit www.wiley.com/techsupport.

WILEY

U.S. Sales

Contact Wiley at (800) 762-2974 or fax (317) 572-4002.

Praise for Visual Books...

"If you have to see it to believe it, this is the book for you!"

—PC World

"A master tutorial/reference — from the leaders in visual learning!"

—Infoworld

"A publishing concept whose time has come!"

—The Globe and Mail

"Just wanted to say THANK YOU to your company for providing books which make learning fast, easy, and exciting! I learn visually so your books have helped me greatly — from Windows instruction to Web development. Best wishes for continued success."

—Angela J. Barker (Springfield, MO)

"I have over the last 10–15 years purchased thousands of dollars worth of computer books but find your books the most easily read, best set out, and most helpful and easily understood books on software and computers I have ever read. Please keep up the good work."

—John Gatt (Adamstown Heights, Australia)

"You're marvelous! I am greatly in your debt."

—Patrick Baird (Lacey, WA)

"I am an avid fan of your Visual books. If I need to learn anything, I just buy one of your books and learn the topic in no time. Wonders! I have even trained my friends to give me Visual books as gifts."

—Illona Bergstrom (Aventura, FL)

"I have quite a few of your Visual books and have been very pleased with all of them. I love the way the lessons are presented!"

—Mary Jane Newman (Yorba Linda, CA)

"Like a lot of other people, I understand things best when I see them visually. Your books really make learning easy and life more fun."

—John T. Frey (Cadillac, MI)

"Your Visual books have been a great help to me. I now have a number of your books and they are all great. My friends always ask to borrow my Visual books — trouble is, I always have to ask for them back!"

—John Robson
(Brampton, Ontario, Canada)

"I write to extend my thanks and appreciation for your books. They are clear, easy to follow, and straight to the point. Keep up the good work! I bought several of your books and they are just right! No regrets! I will always buy your books because they are the best."

—Seward Kollie (Dakar, Senegal)

"What fantastic teaching books you have produced! Congratulations to you and your staff."

—Bruno Tonon (Melbourne, Australia)

"Thank you for the wonderful books you produce. It wasn't until I was an adult that I discovered how I learn — visually. Although a few publishers claim to present the materially visually, nothing compares to Visual books. I love the simple layout. Everything is easy to follow. I can just grab a book and use it at my computer, lesson by lesson. And I understand the material! You really know the way I think and learn. Thanks so much!"

—Stacey Han (Avondale, AZ)

"The Greatest. This whole series is the best computer-learning tool of any kind I've ever seen."

—Joe Orr (Brooklyn, NY)

July 05

Credits

Project Editor
Timothy J. Borek

Acquisitions Editor
Jody Lefevere

Copy Editor
Marylouise Wiack

Technical Editor
Diane Koers

Editorial Manager
Robyn Siesky

Business Manager
Amy Knies

Sr. Marketing Manager
Sandy Smith

Manufacturing
Allan Conley
Linda Cook
Paul Gilchrist
Jennifer Guynn

Book Design
Kathie Rickard

Project Coordinator
Erin Smith

Layout
Carrie A. Cesavice
Andrea Hornberger
Jennifer Mayberry

Screen Artist
Jill Proll

Illustrator
Ronda David-Burroughs

Proofreader
Broccoli Information Management

Quality Control
Todd Lothery

Indexer
Valerie Haynes Perry

Special Help
Sarah Hellert

Vice President and Executive Group Publisher
Richard Swadley

Vice President and Publisher
Barry Pruett

Composition Director
Debbie Stailey

About the Author

Elaine Marmel is President of Marmel Enterprises, LLC, an organization which specializes in technical writing and software training. Elaine spends most of her time writing; she has authored and co-authored over 50 books about Microsoft Project, Microsoft Excel, QuickBooks, Peachtree, Quicken for Windows, Quicken for DOS, Microsoft Word for Windows, Microsoft Word for the Mac, Windows 98, 1-2-3 for Windows, and Lotus Notes. From 1994 to 2006, she also was the contributing editor to monthly publications *Peachtree Extra* and *QuickBooks Extra*.

Elaine left her native Chicago for the warmer climes of Arizona (by way of Cincinnati, OH; Jerusalem, Israel; Ithaca, NY; Washington, D.C. and Tampa, FL), where she basks in the sun with her PC, her dog Josh, and her cats, Cato, Watson, and Buddy, and sings barbershop harmony with the 2006 International Championship Scottsdale Chorus.

Author's Acknowledgments

No book is the product of a single individual, and there are many folks to thank. I'd like to thank my friend and colleague, Diane Koers, technical editor extraordinaire; as always Diane, it was delightful to work with you and you kept me smiling. I'd also like to thank Jody Lefevere for giving me the privilege of writing this book and for being flexible on my due dates when I got sick. Thanks to Tim Borek for managing the writing process and making it so easy for me. Thanks to Marylouise Wiack for helping to keep me gramatically correct. And thanks to all those folks in Composition Services who worked hard to make the book attractive.

PART I Excel Basics

1) Getting Started with Excel
2) Managing Workbooks
3) Formatting Cells

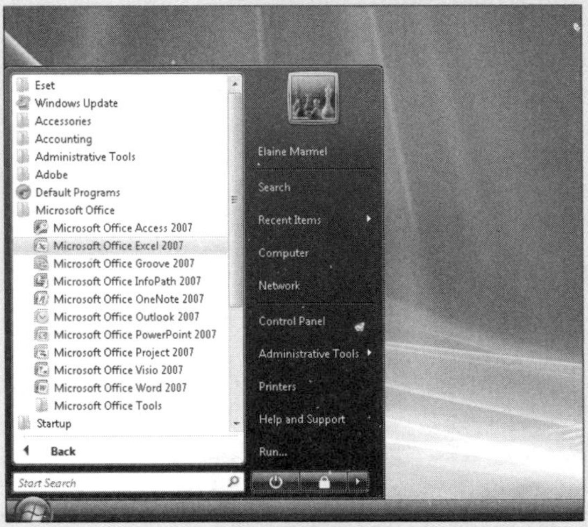

PART III Calculating Data

10) Performing Basic Math
11) Working with Common Formulas
12) Mastering Date and Time Formulas
13) Working with Financial Formulas
14) Working with Lookup Formulas
15) Applying Reference, Information, and Text Formulas
16) Working with Logical and Error Trapping Formulas
17) Analyzing Tabular Information with Functions
18) Analyzing Formulas and Worksheets

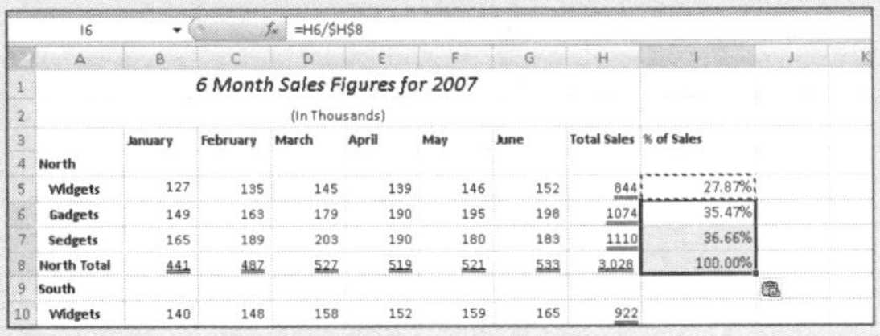

PART II Designing Worksheets

4) Editing Worksheets
5) Proofreading a Worksheet
6) Adjusting Worksheets
7) Managing Workbook Structure
8) Working with Views
9) Printing Worksheet Information

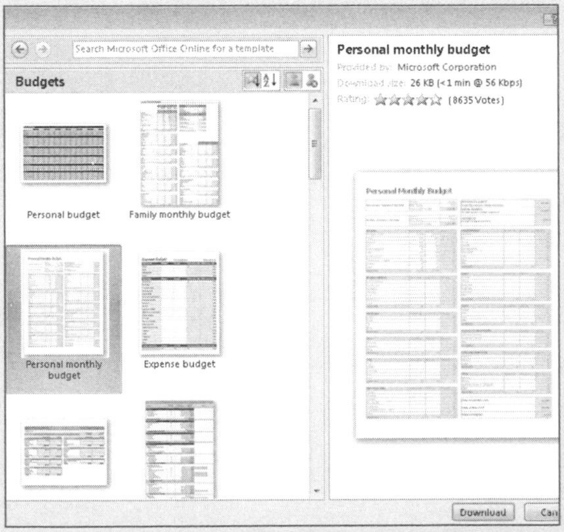

PART IV Mastering Excel Charts

19) Discovering Chart Basics
20) Changing Chart Layout Details
21) Formatting Charts
22) Working with Graphic Elements

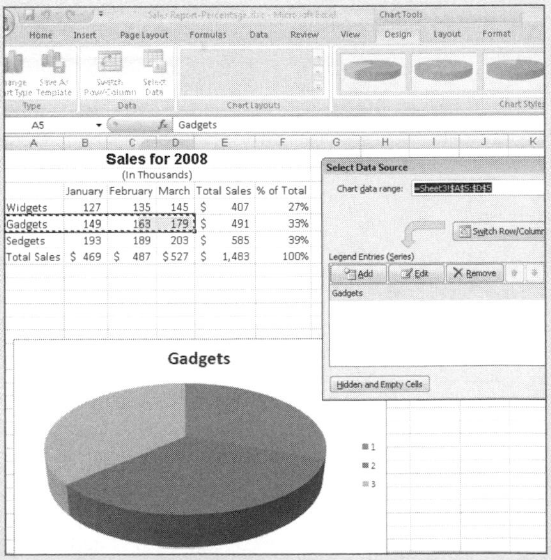

WHAT'S INSIDE

PART V Analyzing Data

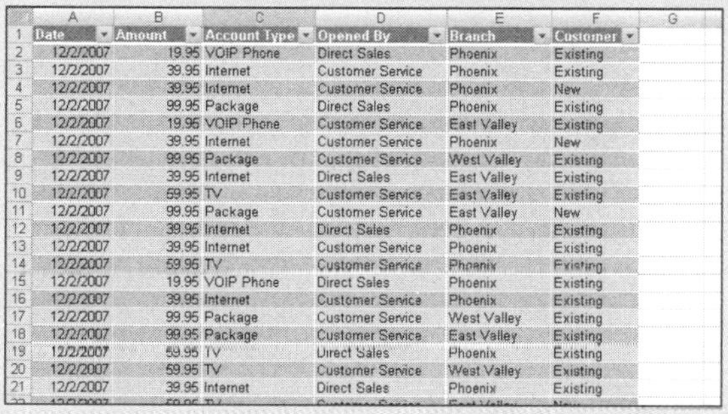

PART VI Customizing the Excel Environment

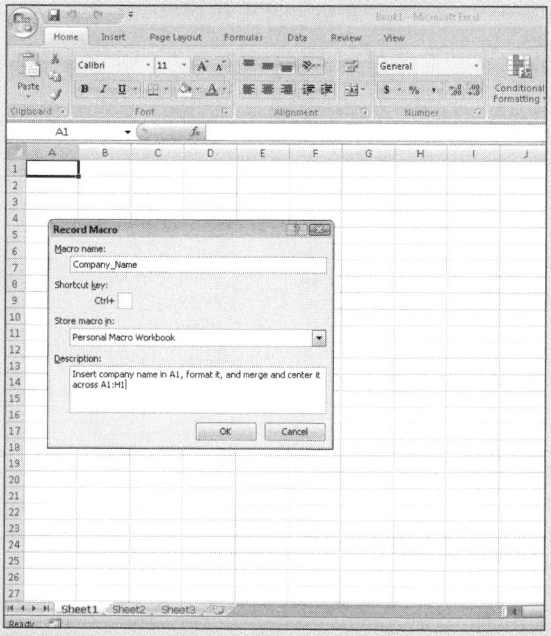

PART VII Using Excel in Collaboration with Others

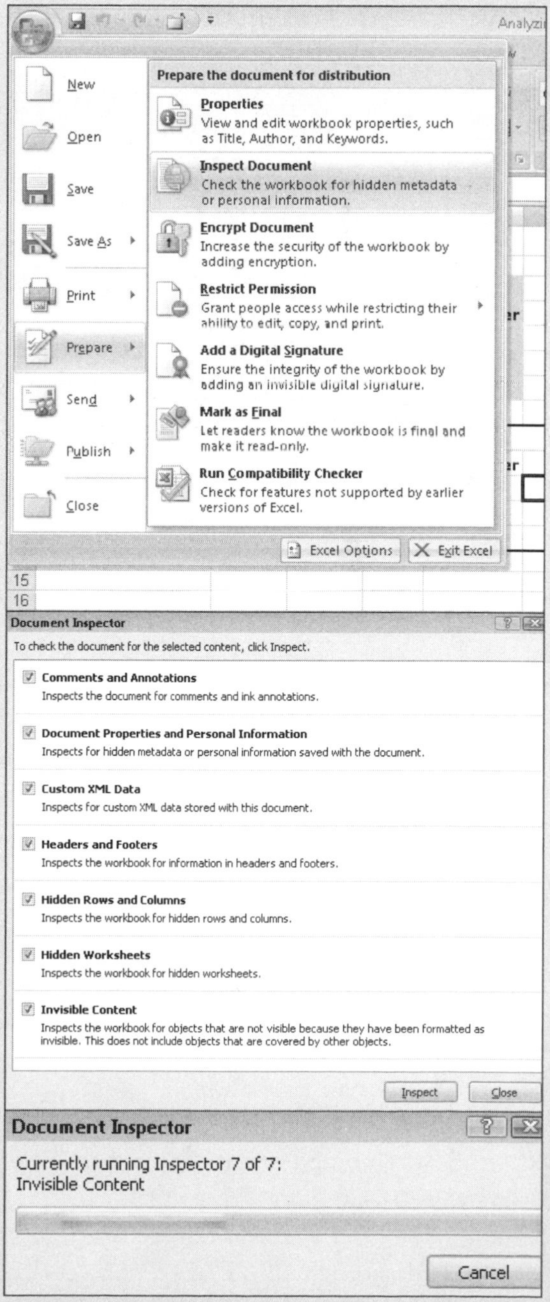

PART I Excel Basics

❶ Getting Started with Excel

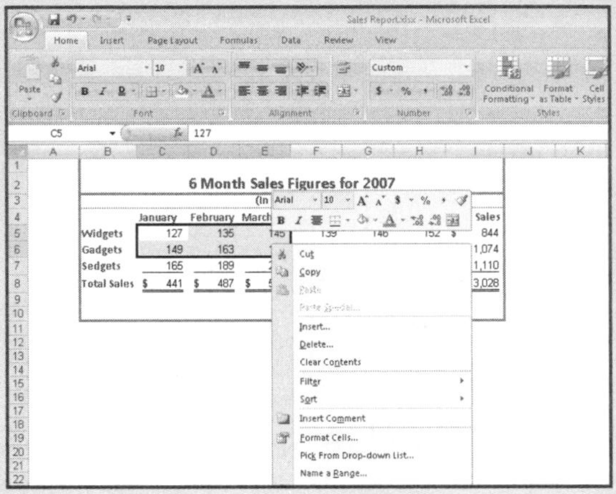

❷ Managing Workbooks

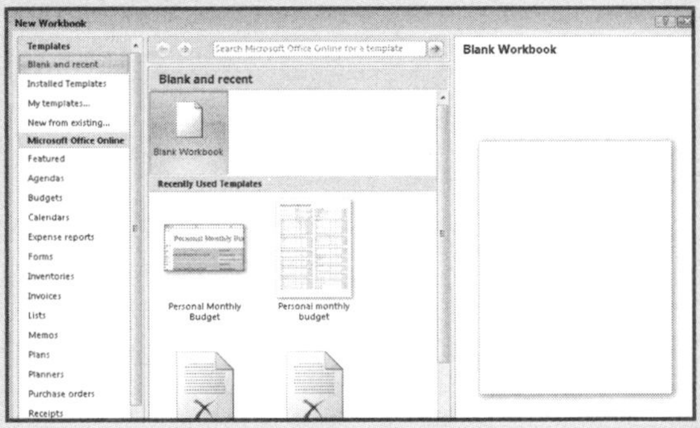

❸ Formatting Cells

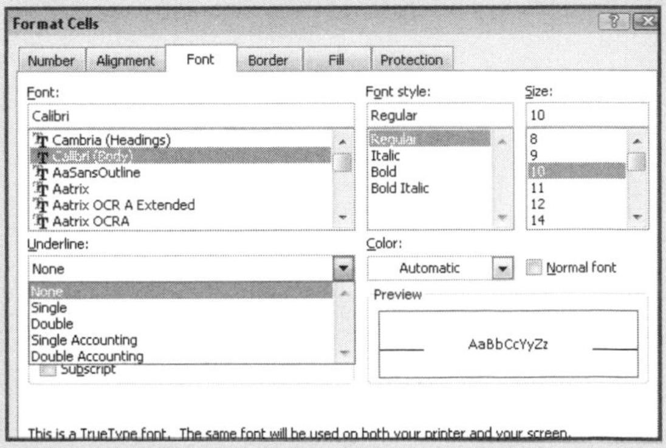

TABLE OF CONTENTS

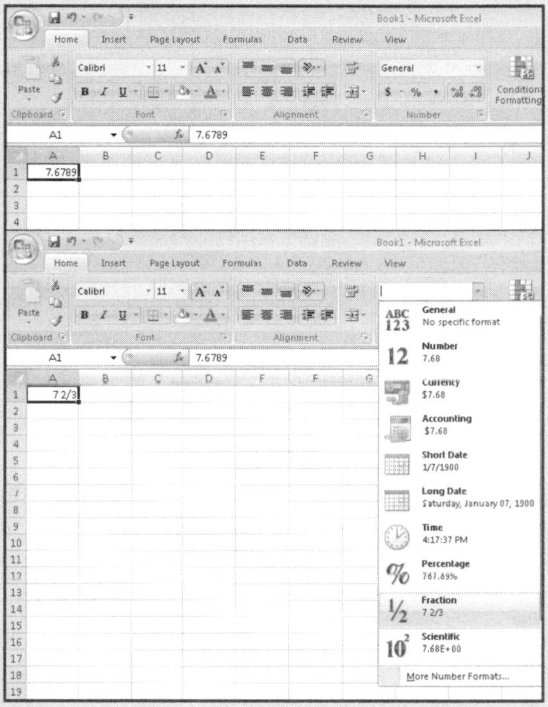

PART II Designing Worksheets

4 Editing Worksheets

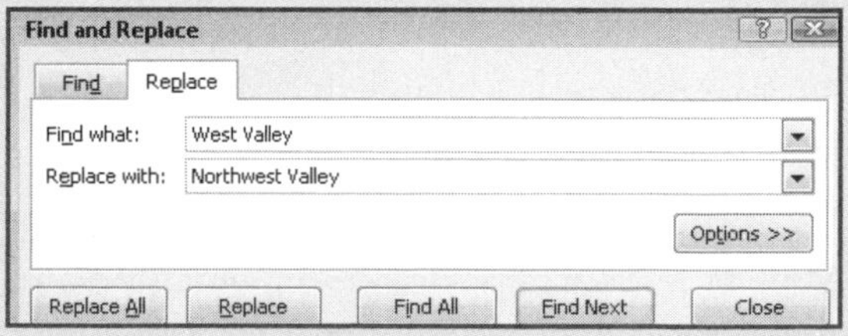

5 Proofreading a Worksheet

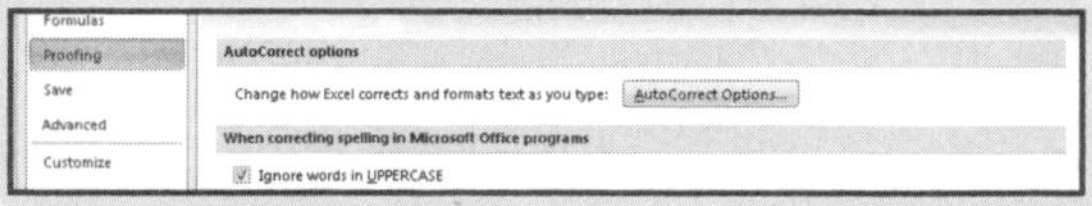

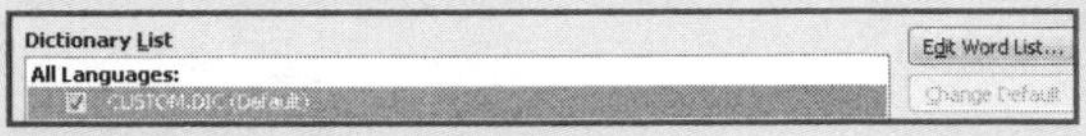

6 Adjusting Worksheets

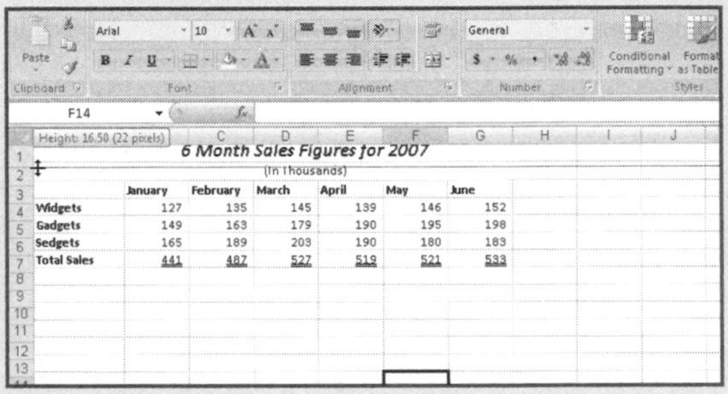

7 Managing Workbook Structure

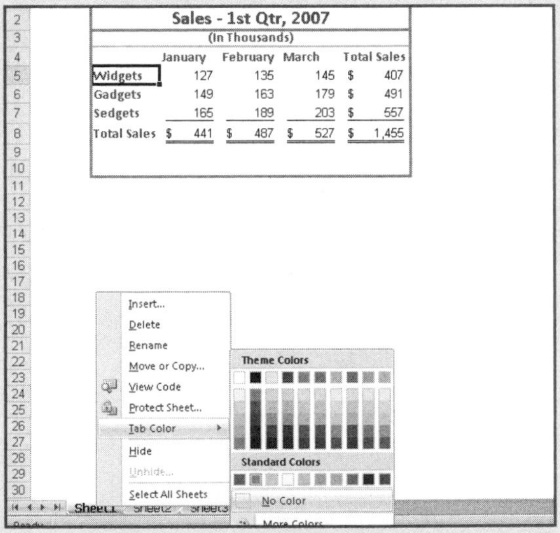

8 Working with Views

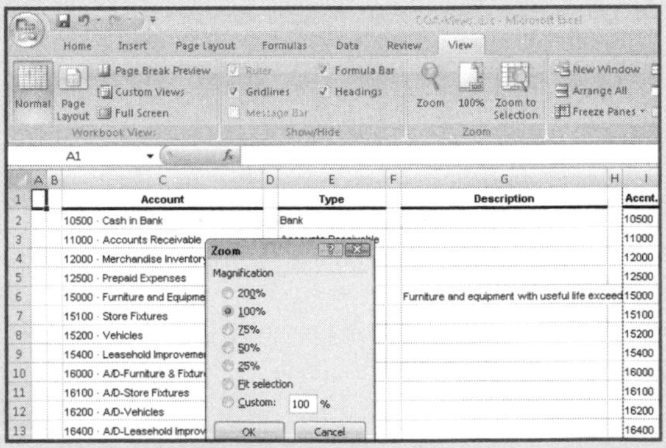

TABLE OF CONTENTS

9 Printing Worksheet Information

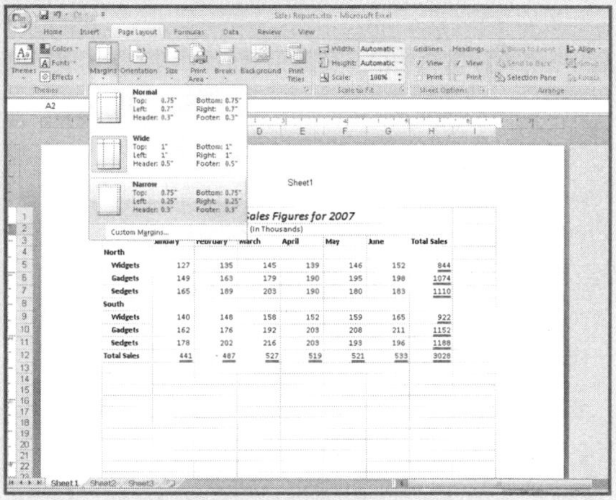

PART III Calculating Data

10 Performing Basic Math

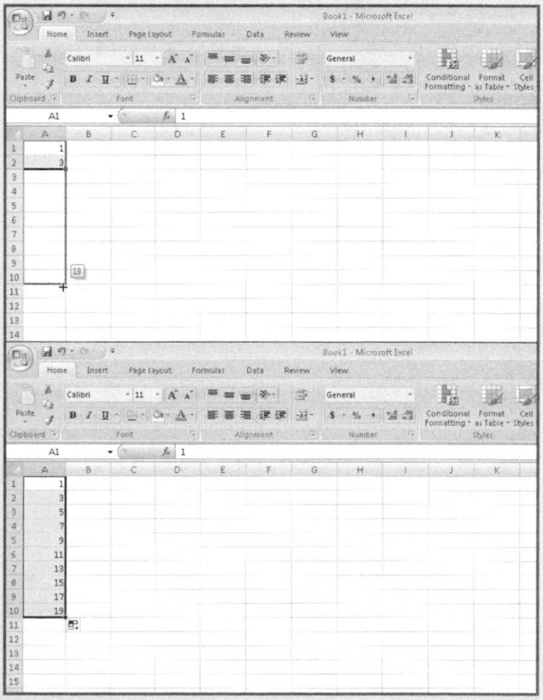

⑪ Working with Common Formulas

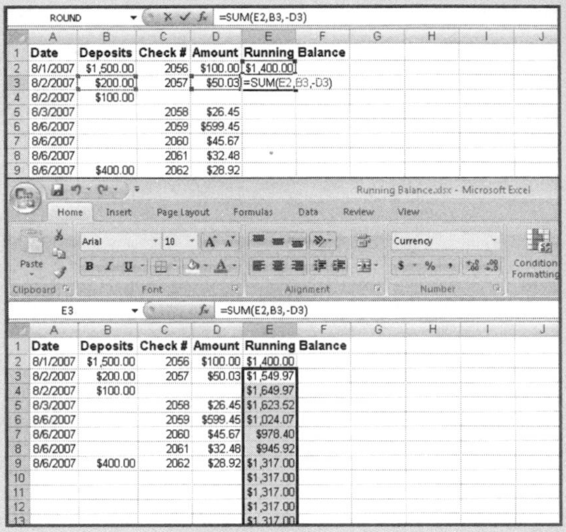

⑫ Mastering Date and Time Formulas

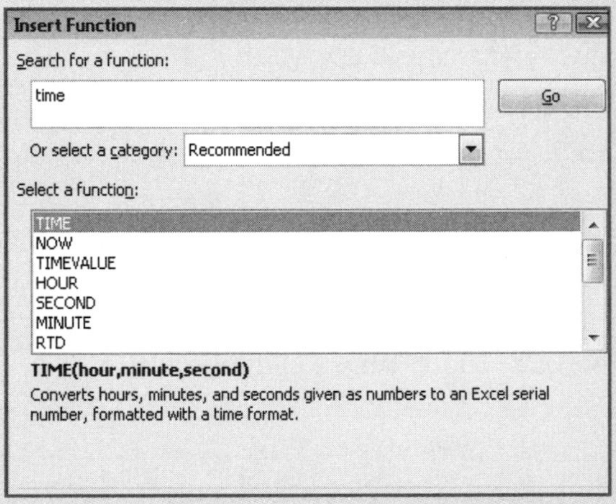

⑬ Working with Financial Formulas

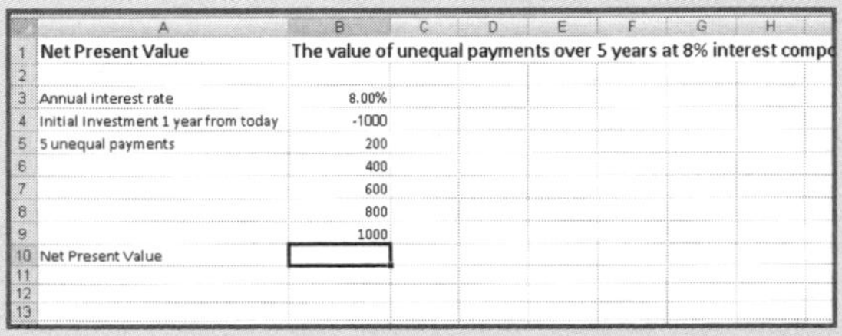

TABLE OF CONTENTS

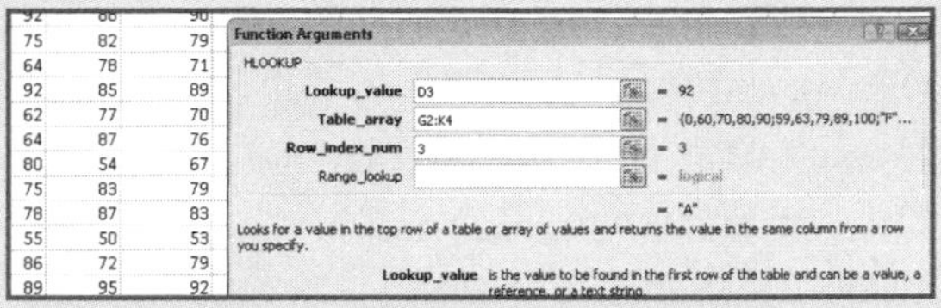

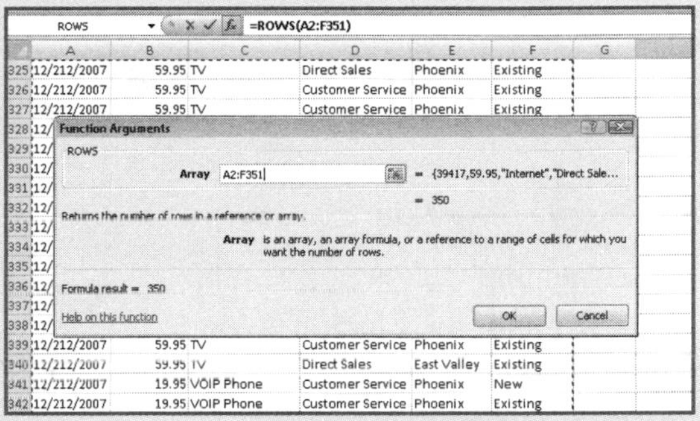

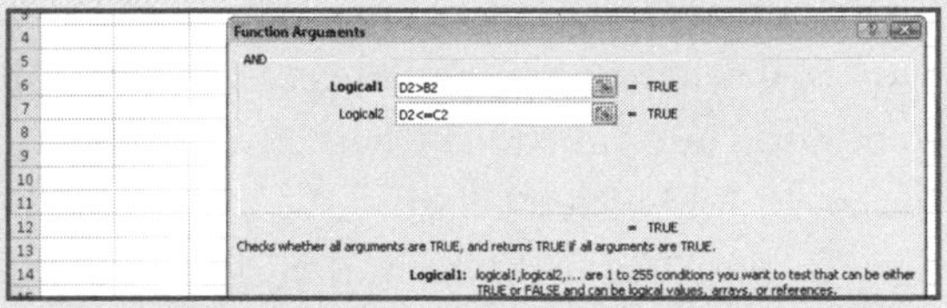

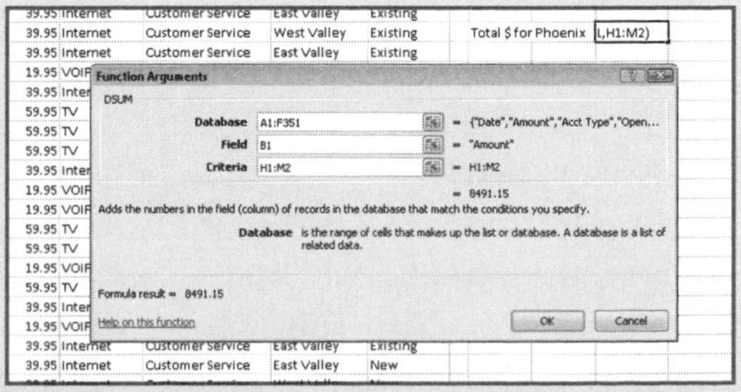

18 Analyzing Formulas and Worksheets

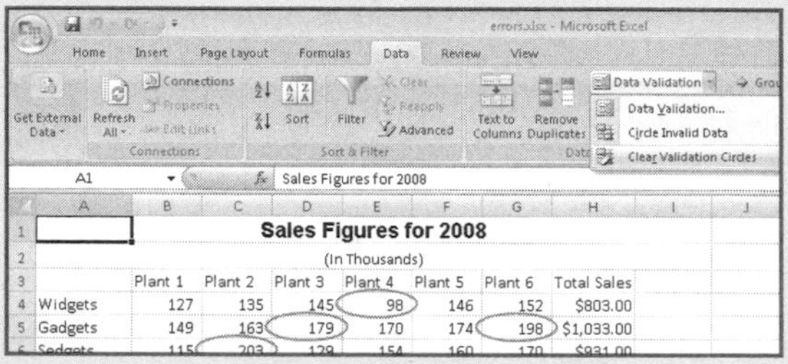

PART IV Mastering Excel Charts

19 Discovering Chart Basics

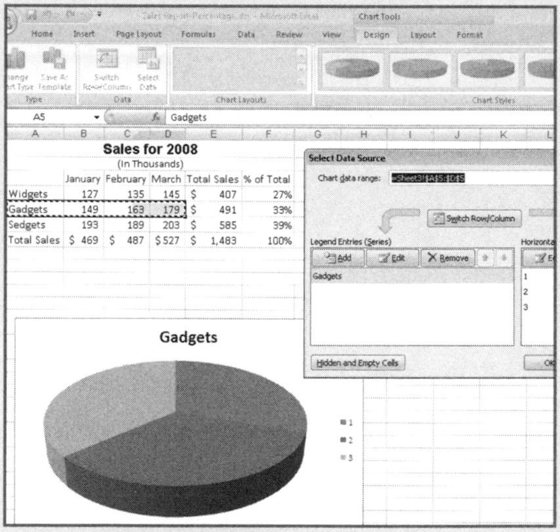

20 Changing Chart Layout Details

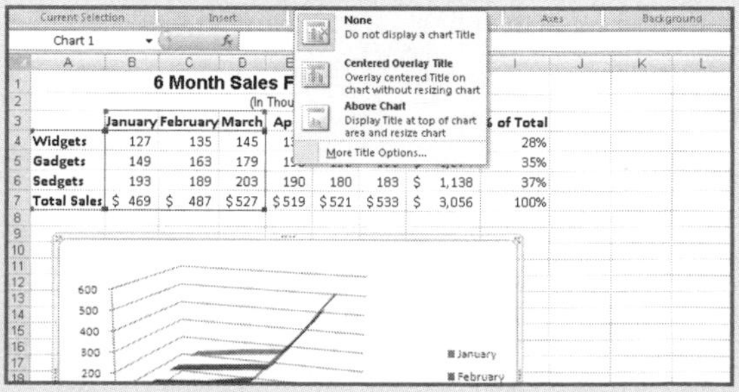

TABLE OF CONTENTS

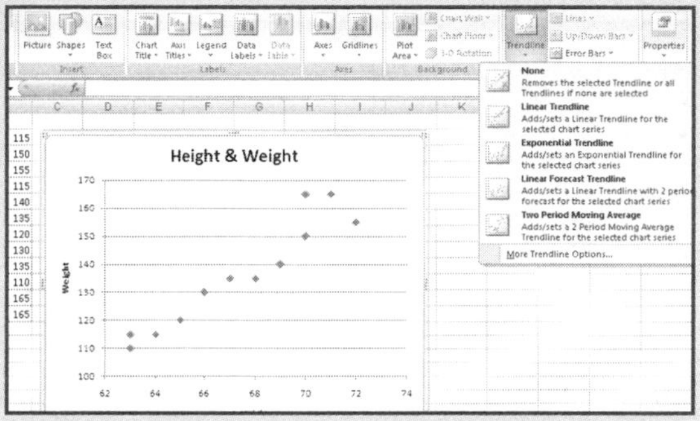

㉑ Formatting Charts

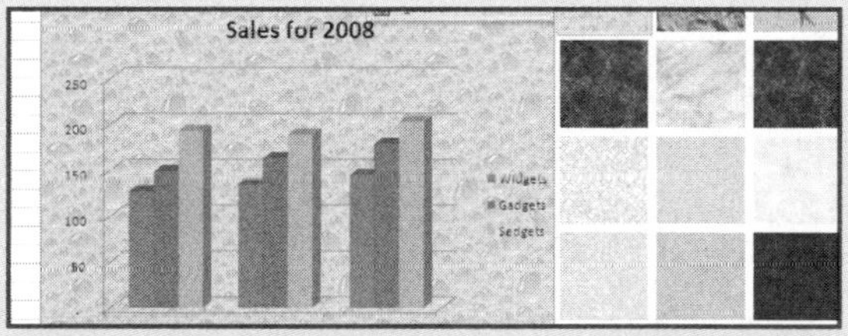

㉒ Working with Graphic Elements

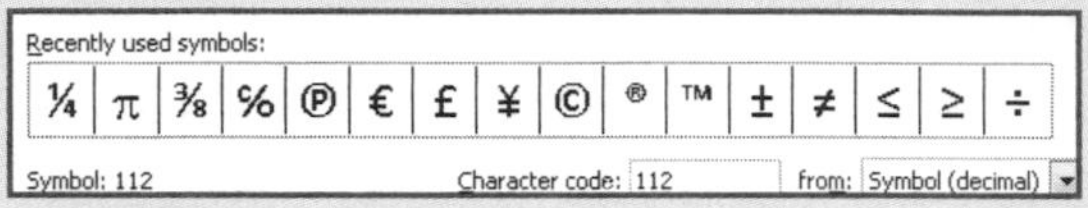

PART V Analyzing data

23 Working with Tables

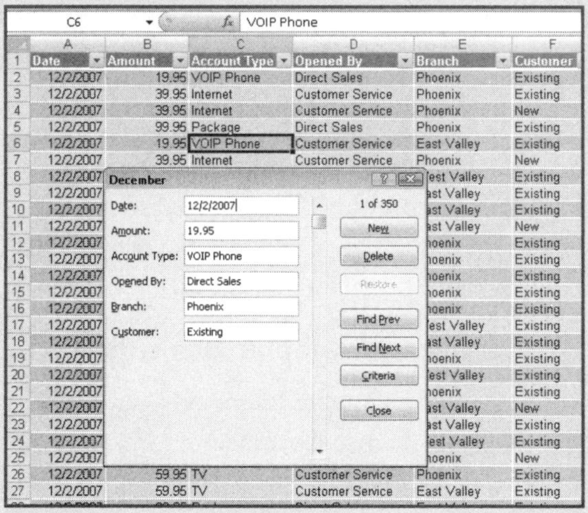

24 Summarizing Data with PivotTables and PivotCharts

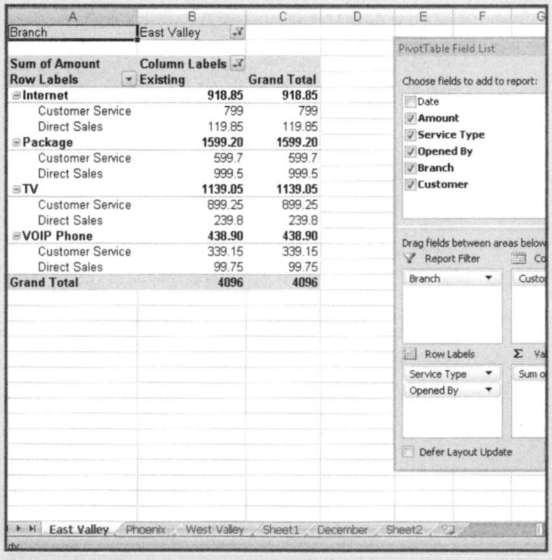

TABLE OF CONTENTS

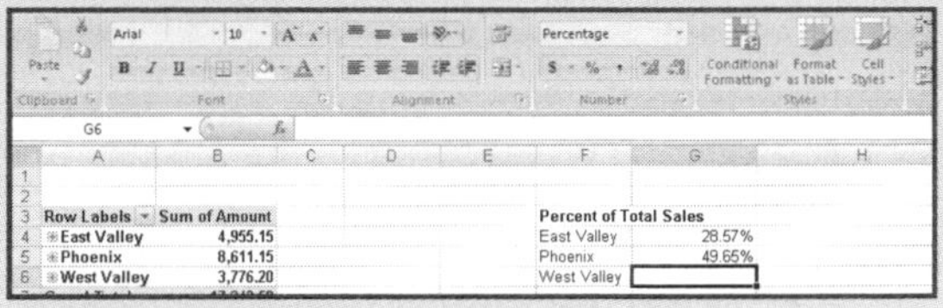

㉕ Visually Analyzing Data

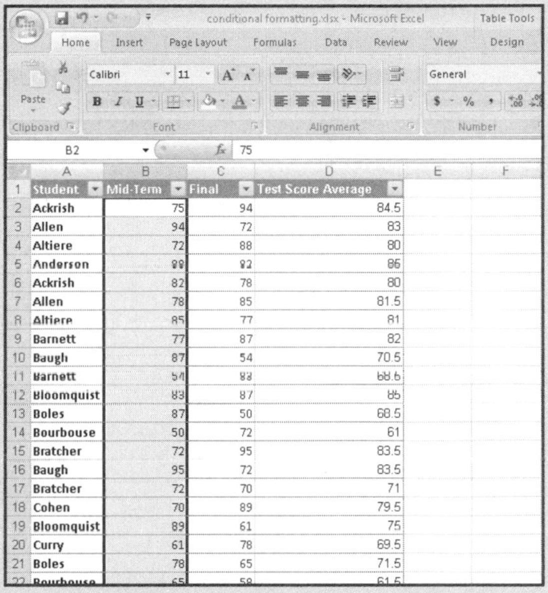

㉖ Linking and Consolidating Worksheets

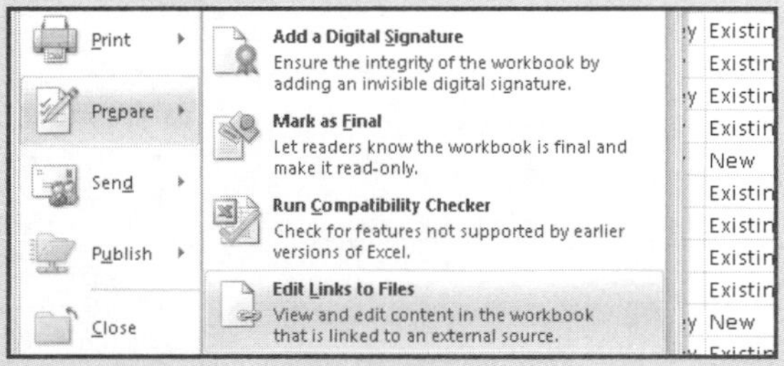

㉗ Performing What-If Analysis

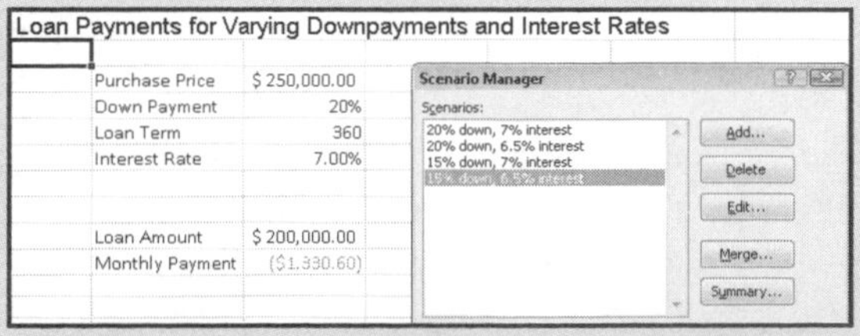

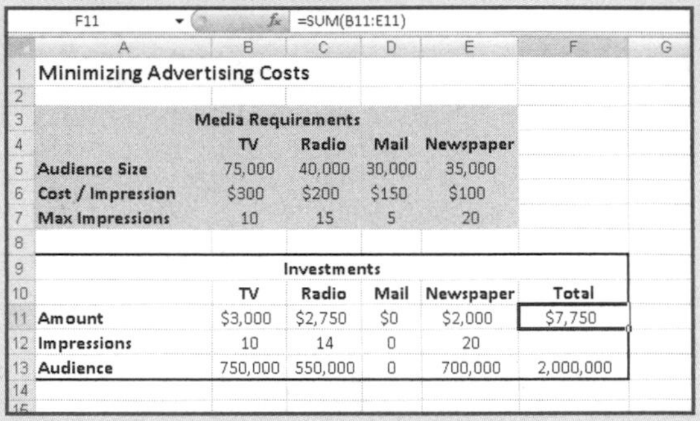

28 Performing Advanced Statistical Analysis

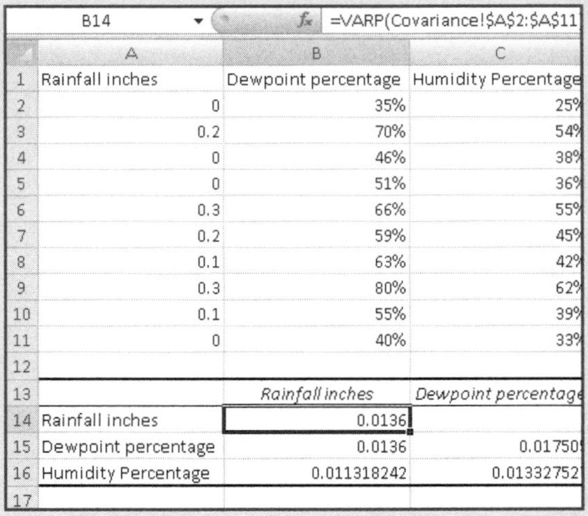

PART VI Customizing the Excel Environment

29 Working with Macros

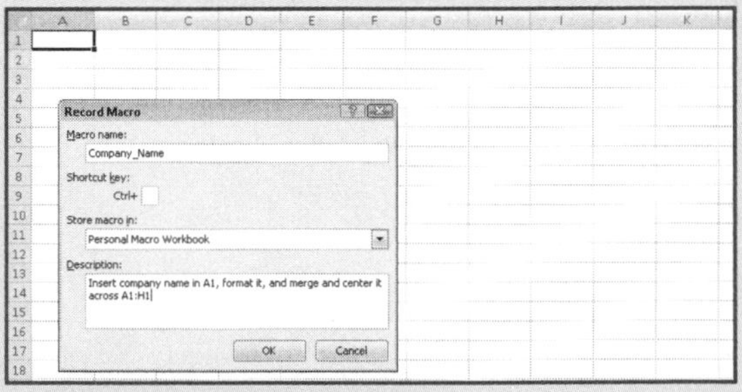

TABLE OF CONTENTS

30 Changing Excel Behavior

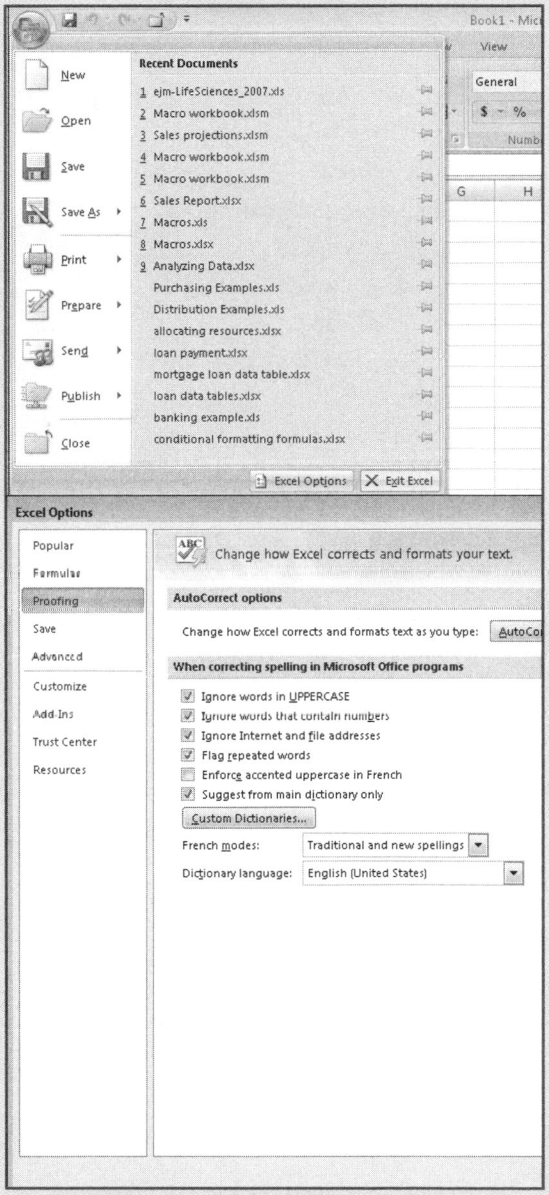

PART VII Using Excel in Collaboration with Others

31 Using Workbooks in a Multi-User Environment

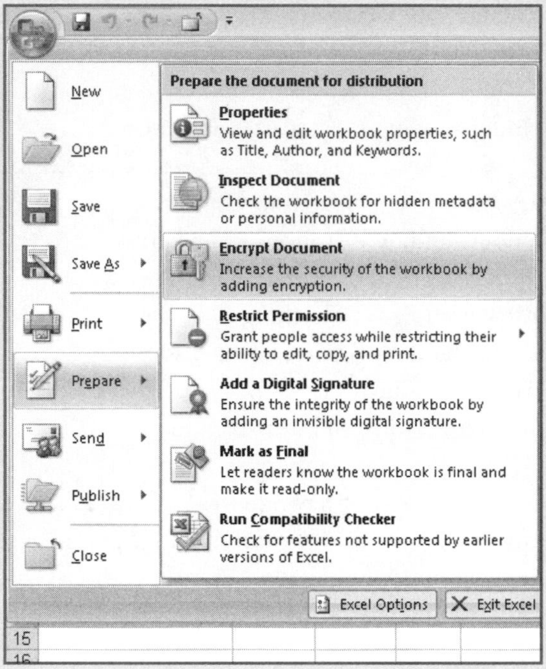

TABLE OF CONTENTS

32 Sharing Excel Data with Other Programs

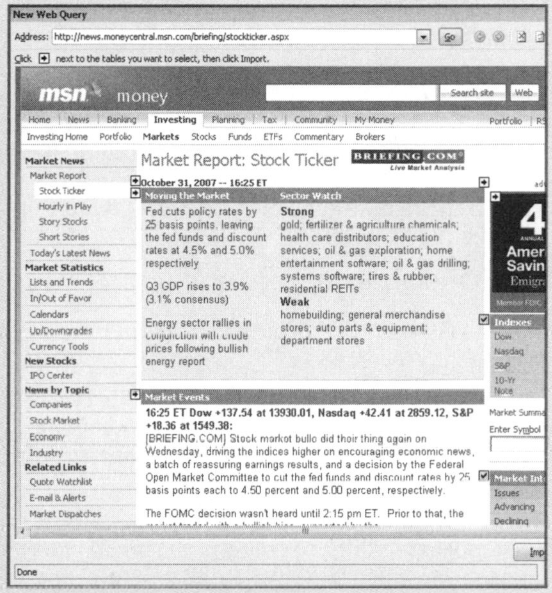

Appendix

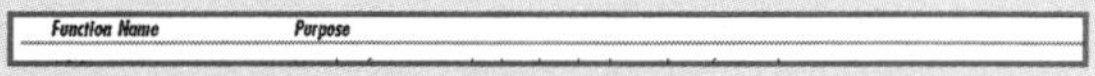

How to Use this Master VISUALLY Book

Do you look at the pictures in a book or newspaper before anything else on a page? Would you rather see an image than read how to do something? Search no further. This book is for you. Opening *Master VISUALLY Excel 2007* allows you to read less and learn more about the Excel program.

Who Needs This Book

This book is for a reader who has never used this particular technology or software application. It is also for more computer literate individuals who want to expand their knowledge of the different features that Excel 2007 has to offer.

Book Organization

Master VISUALLY Excel 2007 has 32 chapters and is divided into seven parts.

Part I, "Excel Basics," helps you master the basics of working with Excel, including understanding and navigating the Excel window, opening and saving workbooks, and formatting cells.

Part II, "Designing Worksheets," moves you past basic workbook operations to edit and proofread worksheets, manage worksheet and workbook structure, and view and print worksheets.

Part III, "Calculating Data," takes you into the heart of Excel's strength by introducing you to many of the formulas and functions available in Excel.

Part IV, "Mastering Excel Charts," shows you how to visually display numeric data using charts — an approach that often helps your reader better understand the information you are presenting. This part also shows you how to include graphic elements in worksheets to help you make your point.

Part V, "Analyzing Data," shows you how to use tables, PivotTables and PivotCharts, conditional formatting, and what-if analysis to analyze data, and also introduces advanced statistical analysis features available in Excel.

Part VI, "Customizing the Excel Environment," helps you make Excel work the way you are most comfortable.

Part VII, "Using Excel in Collaboration with Others," introduces you to the ways in which you can use Excel when you work in a workgroup.

Chapter Organization

This book consists of sections, all listed in the book's table of contents. A *section* is a set of steps that show you how to complete a specific computer task.

Each section, usually contained on two facing pages, has an introduction to the task at hand, a set of full-color screen shots and steps that walk you through the task, and a set of tips. This format allows you to quickly look at a topic of interest and learn it instantly.

Chapters group together three or more sections with a common theme. A chapter may also contain pages that give you the background information needed to understand the sections in a chapter.

What You Need to Use This Book

To master the techniques shown in this book, you need a PC capable of running Windows XP or Windows Vista and Microsoft Office Excel 2007.

Using the Mouse

This book uses the following conventions to describe the actions you perform when using the mouse:

Click

Press your left mouse button once. You generally click your mouse on something to select something on the screen.

Double-click

Press your left mouse button twice. Double-clicking something on the computer screen generally opens whatever item you have double-clicked.

HOW TO USE THIS BOOK

Right-click

Press your right mouse button. When you right-click anything on the computer screen, the program displays a shortcut menu containing commands specific to the selected item.

Click and Drag, and Release the Mouse

Move your mouse pointer and hover it over an item on the screen. Press and hold down the left mouse button. Now, move the mouse to where you want to place the item and then release the button. You use this method to move an item from one area of the computer screen to another.

The Conventions in This Book

A number of typographic and layout styles have been used throughout *Master VISUALLY Excel 2007* to distinguish different types of information.

Bold

Bold type represents the names of commands and options that you interact with. Bold type also indicates text and numbers that you must type into a dialog box or window.

Italics

Italic words introduce a new term and are followed by a definition.

Numbered Steps

You must perform the instructions in numbered steps in order to successfully complete a section and achieve the final results.

Bulleted Steps

These steps point out various optional features. You do not have to perform these steps; they simply give additional information about a feature.

Indented Text

Indented text tells you what the program does in response to you following a numbered step. For example, if you click a certain menu command, a dialog box may appear, or a window may open. Indented text may also tell you what the final result is when you follow a set of numbered steps.

Notes

Notes give additional information. They may describe special conditions that may occur during an operation. They may warn you of a situation that you want to avoid, for example, the loss of data. A note may also cross reference a related area of the book. A cross reference may guide you to another chapter, or another section within the current chapter.

Icons and Buttons

Icons and buttons are graphical representations within the text. They show you exactly what you need to click to perform a step.

You can easily identify the tips in any section by looking for the Master It icon. Master It offers additional information, including tips, hints, and tricks. You can use the Master It information to go beyond what you have learned in the steps.

1 Getting Started with Excel

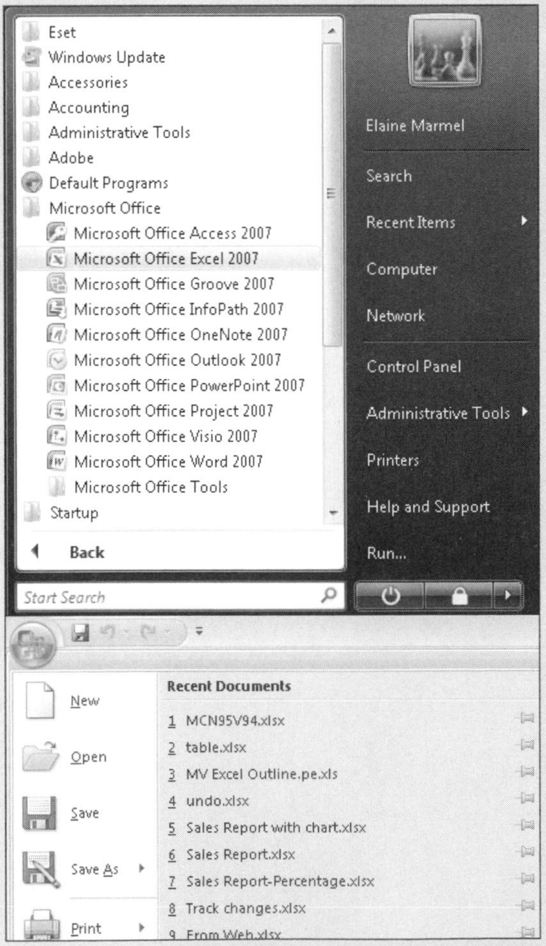

2 Managing Workbooks

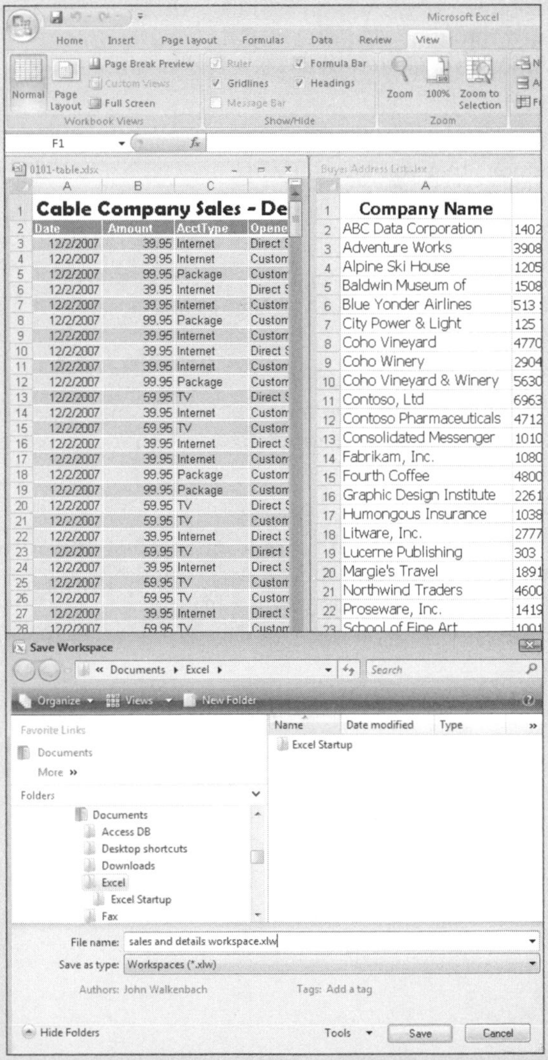

PART I
EXCEL BASICS

3 Formatting Cells

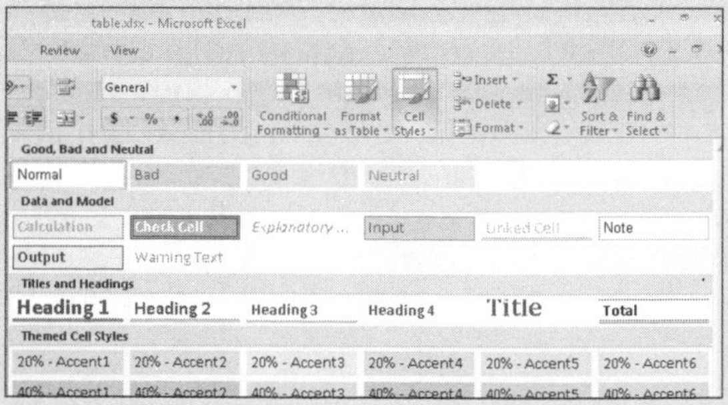

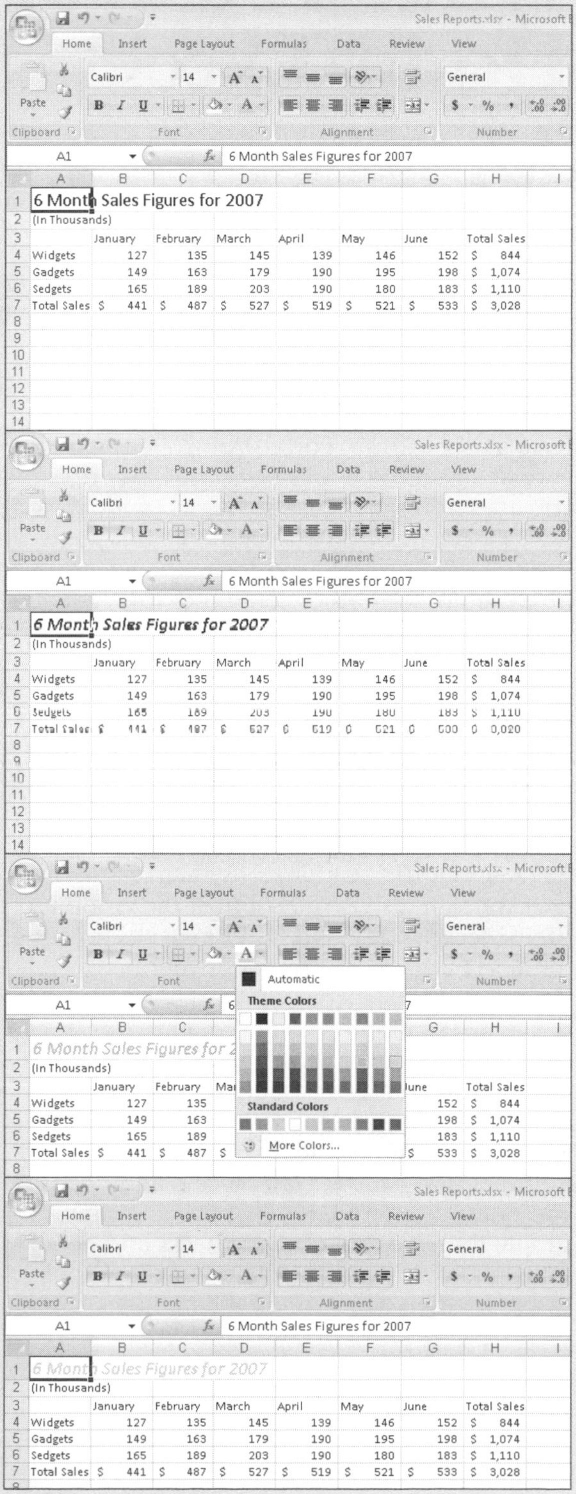

What You Can Do in Excel

Microsoft Excel is one of the world's most popular spreadsheet programs. You could create worksheets on ledger paper and use a calculator, or draw charts on graph paper, but Excel makes these tasks and others related to managing numeric information easier. You can use the program to create worksheets, databases, and charts. Without a doubt, you could perform the following functions manually, but you can use Excel to make them easier.

Lay Out a Worksheet

When you sit down to develop a worksheet with a pencil and ledger paper, you do not always have all the information to complete the design and layout of the worksheet. Ideas may occur to you after you sketch the layout of your worksheet. After you are finished jotting down the column headings and the row headings, you might think of another column or row that you did not include. If you are working with pencil and paper, restructuring the layout of a worksheet can be tedious and time-consuming. With Excel, you can easily insert columns and rows and move information from one location to another.

Calculate Numbers

Think about the tasks involved in managing your checkbook register. You subtract the amount of each check written and add the deposits to the running balance. You then use your bank statement to balance your checkbook, and it is not at all uncommon to find math errors in your checkbook. So, you must then recalculate the numbers in your checkbook register and jot down the new answers. If you set up an Excel workbook for the same tasks, you can use formulas that subtract checks and add deposits. You enter the formulas only once and simply supply the amounts of your checks and deposits, much as you record them in your checkbook register. When you change the numbers in the workbook, Excel uses the formulas to recalculate the information in your workbook and instantly gives you the new answers — in most cases without the associated math errors.

Organize, Sort, and Filter Lists

You can create tables to organize your data in lists. For example, you can create inventory lists, employee lists, customer lists, student grade lists, and sales records. In Excel, you can add, delete, sort, search, and display records in the list as often as required to maintain the list. You can sort data on the worksheet alphabetically and numerically in ascending or descending order. For example, you can sort sales records in chronological order by dates. You can also use the AutoFilter feature to quickly find information that meets a specific criterion or to find the top or bottom ten values in the list without sorting.

View Data

When working with a large worksheet on ledger paper, such as a financial statement, you might have to use a ruler to compare figures on a far portion of the worksheet. You might even find yourself folding the ledger paper to bring the columns you want to compare close together. In Excel, you can split the worksheet into two or four panes to view distant figures side by side. That way, you can easily see the effects of asking "what happens when I change this value?" to project changes. You can also temporarily hide intermediary columns so that distant figures appear right next to each other as you work.

Make Editing Changes

To correct a mistake on ledger paper, you have to use an eraser, or you have to reconstruct the entire worksheet. With Excel, you can overwrite data in any cell in your worksheet. You can also delete data quickly, in one cell or a group of cells. And, when you accidentally make mistakes that overwrite original data while using Excel, you do not have to retype or reconstruct information. Instead, you can just restore the data using the Undo button.

Check Spelling

No more manually proofreading your work. When you use Excel's AutoCorrect feature, Excel corrects commonly made mistakes as you type — and you can add your own personal set of "common typos" to the list. In addition, before you print, you can run a spell check to search for misspellings. If you are a poor typist, this feature enables you to concentrate on calculating your numbers while Excel catches spelling errors.

Make Formatting Changes

Excel easily enables you to align data in cells; center column headings across columns; adjust column width; and display numbers with dollar signs, commas, and decimal points. You can experiment with the settings until the worksheet appears the way that you want it; then you can print it. You can boldface, italicize, and underline data, and change fonts and font sizes. Excel also lets you shade cells, add borders, and apply styles to improve the appearance of a worksheet.

Preview Before Printing

You can preview your worksheet to see how it will look when you print it. You also can add headers and footers and adjust page breaks before you print.

Chart Numeric Data

Numbers form the foundation of charts. Manually creating charts is time-consuming and takes some artistic skill. In Excel, creating charts is quick and easy. You can track the sales trends of several products with a chart. You also can make as many "what if?" projections as you want in the worksheet by increasing and decreasing the numbers used in the chart; as you change the numbers in the worksheet, Excel instantly updates the chart. Excel's charts let you simultaneously view the sales trends in a picture representation on-screen and the numbers in the worksheet, making your sales forecasting more efficient.

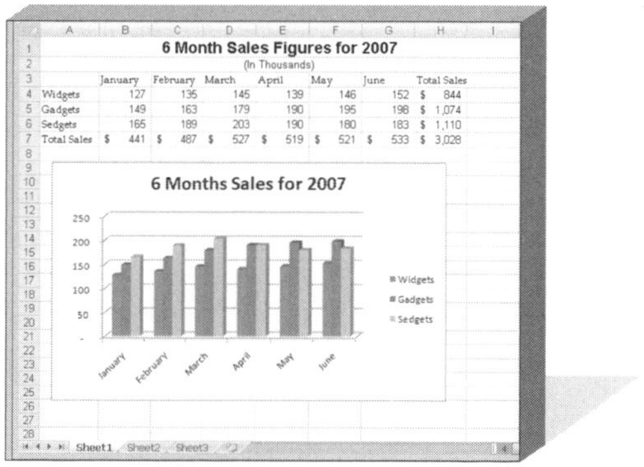

Start and Close Excel

You can start the Excel program using the Windows Start menu. When you open the Start menu, a search field appears at the bottom and the All Programs choice appears immediately above the search field. Once you select All Programs, Windows displays folders that contain the programs installed on your computer. The shortcut to start Excel appears in the Microsoft Office folder. After you select Excel from the Microsoft Office folder several times, it will appear on the Start menu in the list of recently opened files. You can select Microsoft Office Excel 2007 from that list to open the program. If you use Excel regularly, you may want to pin Excel to the Start menu or create a desktop shortcut for it so that you can open it more quickly.

You can close Excel using a command on the Office menu, or you can use the Close button in the upper-right corner of the Excel window. Excel behaves differently, depending on the method you choose to close the program, the number of workbooks you have open, and whether you have made changes to any of the open workbooks.

Start and Close Excel

Start Excel

1. Click Start.

   The Start menu appears.

2. Click All Programs.

- All Programs changes to Back.

3. Click Microsoft Office.

   - The list of installed Microsoft Office programs appears.

4. Click Microsoft Office Excel 2007.

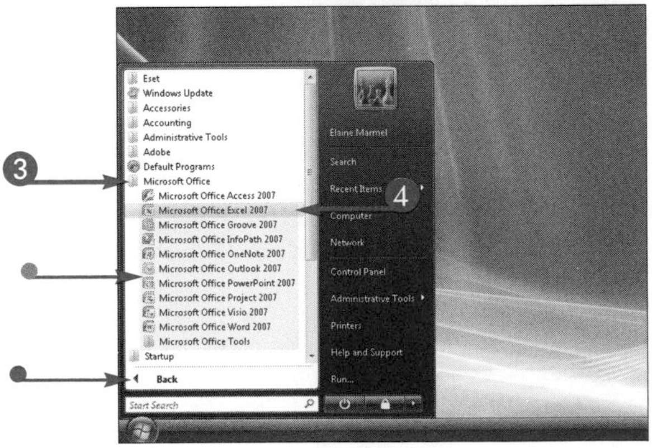

The main window for Excel appears.

The cell pointer (✚) appears as you move the mouse over cells in the worksheet. You use the cell pointer to select cells.

Note: *See Chapter 4 for details on selecting cells.*

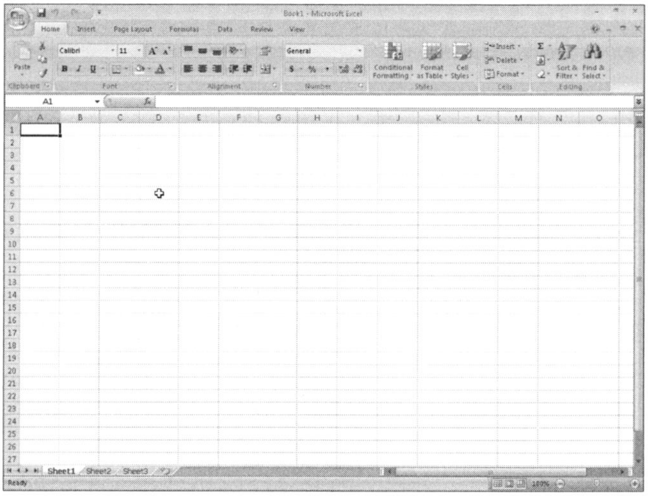

Close Excel

1. Click the Microsoft Office button (◙).
2. Click Exit Excel.

Excel closes all open workbooks.

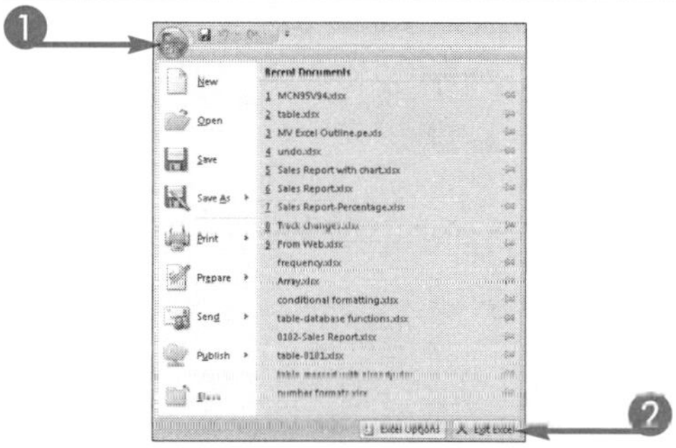

MASTER IT

Does Excel prompt me to save before closing the program?

▼ If you have not made any changes to the workbook, Excel closes without prompting you to take any further action. However, if you have made changes to an open workbook, Excel prompts you to save the workbook. After you respond to the prompt, Excel closes, regardless of whether you save the workbook.

Can I click the X in the upper-right corner to close Excel?

▼ Yes, but, if you have more than one workbook open, Excel closes only the active workbook, instead of the program. You must click the X in the upper-right corner of each open workbook. When you click the X while viewing the last open workbook, both the workbook and the program close. Before Excel closes any workbook you have changed, Excel prompts you to save the workbook.

What happens if I pin Excel to the Start menu?

▼ Excel always appears on the left side of the Start menu, above the list of recently opened files. Right-click the Excel icon and click Pin to Start Menu.

How do I create a desktop shortcut.

▼ To create a desktop shortcut for Excel, right-click the Excel icon, click Send To, and then click Desktop (Create Shortcut).

Understanding the Excel Screen

Each time you open Excel, you see a new workbook named Book1 that contains three worksheets.

Ⓐ Title Bar
Displays the name of the workbook and the name of the program.

Ⓑ Office Button
Opens a menu containing commands related to file operations such as Save and Print.

Ⓒ Quick Access Toolbar
By default, contains buttons that enable you to save, undo your last action, and redo your last action. You can also add buttons to this toolbar; see Chapter 30 for details.

Ⓓ Ribbon
Contains most Excel commands, organized on tabs. See the section, "Understanding the Ribbon," for details.

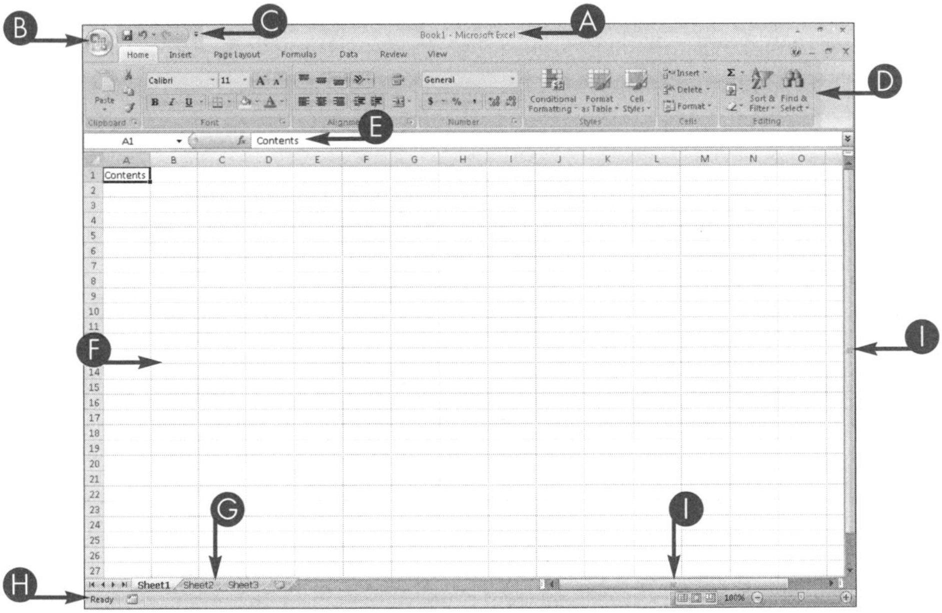

Ⓔ Formula Bar
Made up of three parts, the Formula Bar contains the Name box, buttons that pertain to entering data, and the contents of the currently selected cell.

Ⓕ Worksheet Area
The place where you enter information into Excel, divided into rows and columns.

Ⓘ Scroll Bars
Enable you to view more rows and columns of the worksheet.

Ⓗ Status Bar
Displays Excel's current mode, such as Ready or Edit, and identifies any special keys you press, such as CAPS LOCK. The Status Bar also contains View buttons that you can use to switch views, and a Zoom control to help you zoom in or zoom out. See Chapter 8 for more information on views and zooming.

Ⓖ Worksheet Tabs
Tabs that identify the worksheet on which you are currently working. You can switch worksheets by clicking a worksheet tab.

Learn Excel Terminology

When you learn anything new, you need to learn its terminology. Presented below are a series of terms you need to know as you work with Excel.

Workbook

A *workbook* is a file in which you store your data. Think of a workbook as a three-ring binder. Each workbook contains at least one worksheet, and a new workbook contains three worksheets, named Sheet1, Sheet2, and Sheet3. People use worksheets to organize, manage, and consolidate data. You can have as many worksheets in a workbook as the memory on your computer permits.

Worksheet

A *worksheet* is a grid of columns and rows. Each Excel workbook contains 1,048,576 rows and 16,384 columns. Each column is labeled using a letter of the alphabet; the column following column Z is column AA, followed by AB, and so on. The last column in any worksheet is column XFD. Each row is labeled using a number, starting with row 1 and ending with row 1,048,576.

Cell

A *cell* is the intersection of a row and a column. Each cell in a worksheet has a unique name called a *cell address*. A cell address is the designation formed by combining the column and row names in column/row order. For example, the cell at the intersection of column A and row 8 is called cell A8, and A8 is its cell address.

Cell Pointer

✥ The *cell pointer* appears as you move the mouse over cells in the worksheet. You use the cell pointer to select cells in the worksheet.

Currently Selected Cell

You click a cell to select it. Excel identifies the currently selected cell, also called the *active cell*, by surrounding it with a bold, black box containing a small, black square in the lower-right corner. That small, black square is called the *Fill handle*; you can read more about the Fill handle in Chapter 10.

Range

The term *range* refers to a group of cells. A range can be any rectangular set of cells. To identify a range, you use a combination of two cell addresses: the address of the cell in the upper-left corner of the range, and the address of the cell in the lower right corner of the range. A colon (:) separates the two cell addresses. For example, the range A2:C4 includes the cells A2, A3, A4, B2, B3, B4, C2, C3, and C4.

Formula Bar

The *Formula Bar* is made up of three parts. At the left edge of the Formula Bar, the Name box displays the location of the currently selected cell.

The Cell Contents area appears on the right side of the Formula Bar and displays the information stored in the currently selected cell. If a cell contains a formula, the formula appears in the Cell Contents area, while the formula's result appears in the active cell. If the active cell contains a very long entry, you can use ⌄ at the right edge of the Cell Contents area to expand the size of the Cell Contents area vertically.

Between the Name box and the Cell Contents area, buttons appear that help you enter information. Before you start typing in a cell, only the Function Wizard button (fx) appears, as described in Part III; you can use this button to help you enter Excel functions. Once you start typing, two more buttons appear; click ✓ to accept the entry as it appears in the Cell Contents area, or click ✗ to reject any typing and return the cell's contents to the way they appeared before you began typing.

Understanding the Ribbon

To accomplish tasks in Excel, you use commands that appear on the Ribbon. New to Excel 2007, the Ribbon fundamentally changes the way you work in Excel compared to earlier versions of Excel. You no longer open menus to find commands; buttons for commands appear on the Ribbon. By default, the Ribbon contains the commands most commonly used to complete an Excel task. Do not worry if you do not find a particular command on the Ribbon; it is still available and, if you use it often, you can add it to the Quick Access Toolbar, which appears at the top of the Ribbon. See Chapter 30 for details on customizing the Quick Access Toolbar.

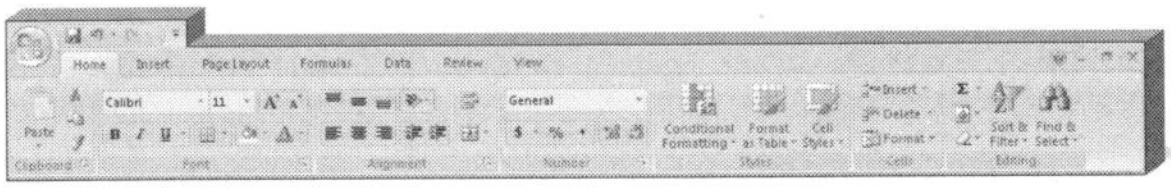

On the Ribbon, in addition to the Office Button ( ) and the Quick Access Toolbar, you find tabs, which take the place of menus in Excel 2007. Each tab contains a collection of buttons that you use to perform a particular action. On each tab, commands are grouped together. For example, on the Home tab, you find seven groups: Clipboard, Font, Alignment, Number, Styles, Cells, and Editing. In the lower-left corner of some groups, you see a dialog box launcher icon ( ) that you can click to see additional options that you can set for the group.

By default, the Ribbon contains seven tabs, as described in the following table.

Tabs on the Ribbon

Tab	*Purpose*
Home	This tab helps you format and edit a worksheet.
Insert	This tab helps you add elements such as tables, charts, PivotTables, hyperlinks, headers, and footers.
Page Layout	This tab helps you set up a worksheet for printing, by setting elements such as margins, page size and orientation, and page breaks.
Formulas	This tab helps you add formulas and functions to a worksheet.
Data	This tab helps you import and query data, outline a worksheet, sort and filter information, validate and consolidate data, and perform What-If analysis.
Review	This tab helps you proof a worksheet for spelling errors, and also contains other proofing tools. From this tab, you can add comments to a worksheet, protect and share a workbook, and track changes that others make to the workbook.
View	This tab helps you view your worksheet in a variety of ways. You can show or hide worksheet elements such as gridlines, column letters, and row numbers. You can also zoom in or out.

In addition to these seven tabs, Excel displays *contextual tabs*, which are tabs that appear because you are performing a particular task. For example, when you select a chart in a workbook, Excel adds the Chart Tools tab behind the View tab. The Chart Tools tab contains three tabs of its own: Design, Layout, and Format. As soon as you select something other than the chart in the workbook, the Chart Tools tab and its three sub-tabs disappear.

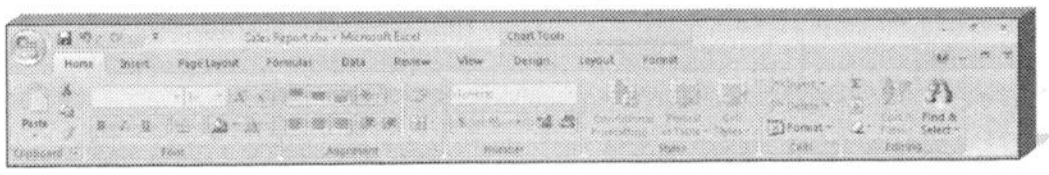

To use the commands on the Ribbon, you simply click a button. If you prefer to use a keyboard, you can press the Alt key; Excel displays keyboard characters that you can press to select , tools on the Quick Access Toolbar, and tabs on the Ribbon. If you press a key to display a tab on the Ribbon, Excel then displays all the keyboard characters you can press to select a particular command on the Ribbon.

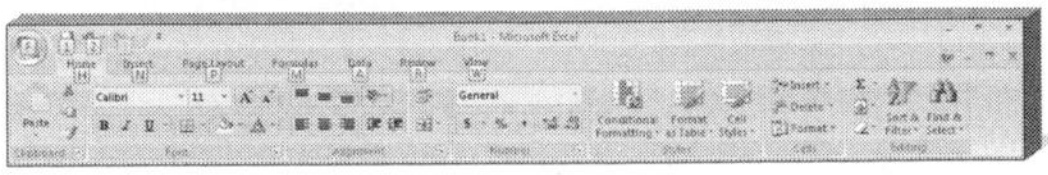

Work with the Mini Toolbar and Context Menu

You can use the Mini Toolbar and the Context menu to help you quickly format text without switching to the Home tab. The Mini Toolbar and the Context menu contain a combination of the most commonly used commands available in the Clipboard, Font, Alignment, and Number groups on the Home tab.

The Mini Toolbar and the Context menu always appear together when you work with shapes, text boxes, WordArt, or cells containing text or numbers.

The Mini Toolbar does not appear when you work with pictures, charts, Clip Art, or SmartArt.

The buttons that appear on the Mini Toolbar do not change; you always see the same set of buttons. However, the commands that appear on the Context menu, also called a shortcut menu, change depending on the cells or object with which you are working. That is, Excel displays only those commands on the Context menu that are relevant to the cells or object you select; this is how the Context menu got its name.

Work with the Mini Toolbar and Context Menu

1. Select a cell or range of cells.

Note: *See Chapter 4 for details on selecting cells.*

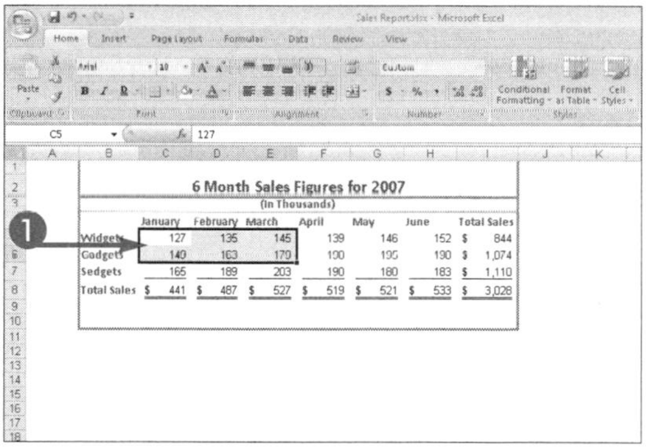

2. Right-click the selection.

   - The Mini Toolbar appears above the Context menu.

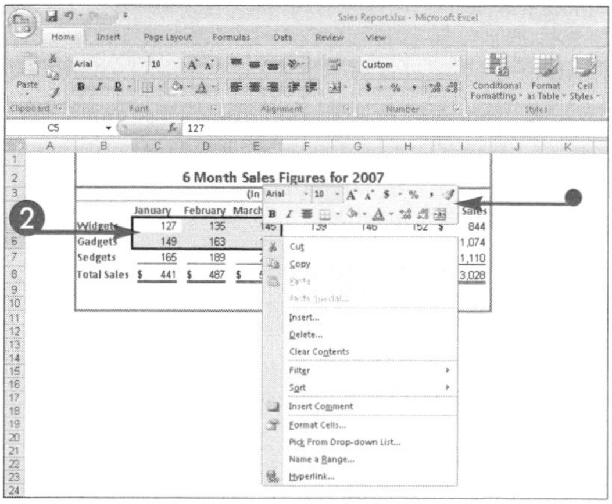

Enter Information

You can quickly and easily type text and numbers into your worksheet. Most people use Excel primarily to accomplish math-related tasks, and supplying text labels for the numbers you enter provides meaning to those tasks. Although you can type information into a worksheet in any order, some people find it easier to type labels first, because it helps them identify the correct place for corresponding numbers.

You enter text using your keyboard, and you can enter numbers using either the number keys above the letters on your keyboard or the number pad to the right of the letters on your keyboard. To use the numbers on the number pad, you can press the Num Lock key.

By default, when you enter *text* into a cell, Excel left-aligns it in the cell and assigns it a General format. When you enter a *number* into a cell, Excel right-aligns it in the cell and assigns it a General format. Excel also recognizes some dates that you type; as a result, it right-aligns them in cells and formats them as dates. Information in a selected cell appears both in the cell and in the Formula Bar. For more information on formats, see Chapter 3.

Enter Information

Enter Text

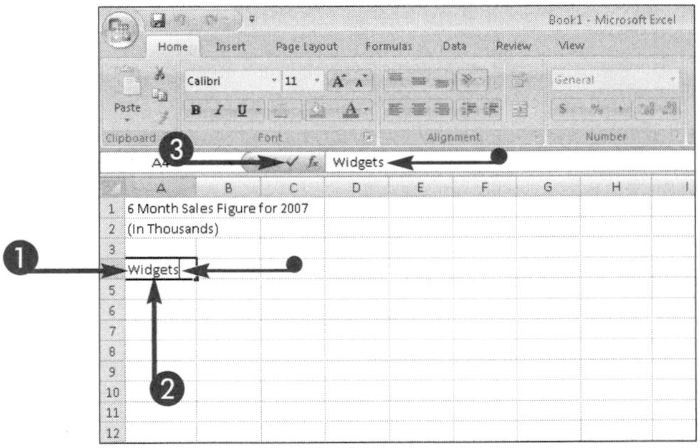

1. Click a cell to select it.

Note: *See Chapter 4 for details on selecting cells.*

2. Type text.

   - As you type, the information appears both in the cell and in the Formula Bar.

3. Click ☑.

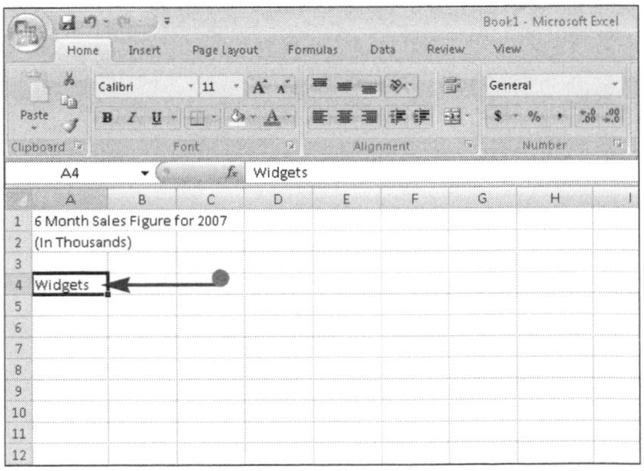

   - The cell pointer remains in the cell you selected in Step 1, and the text you typed appears left aligned.

4. Repeat Steps 1 to 3 to enter other text labels.

Enter Numbers

1. Select a cell and type a number.
2. Press Enter.
   - The number you typed appears right aligned in the cell you selected in Step 1.
   - The cell pointer moves down one row.
3. Repeat Steps 1 and 2 to enter other numbers.

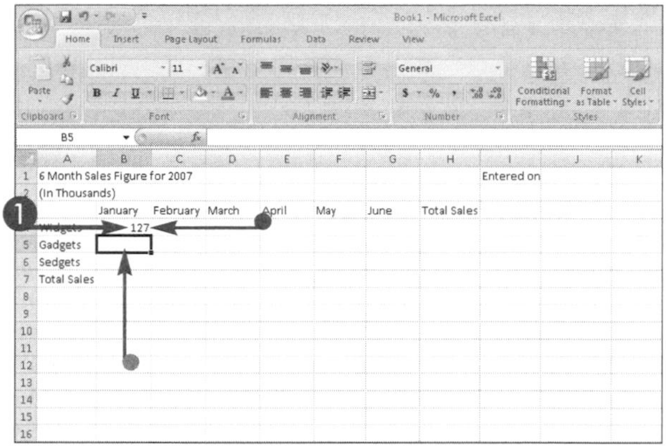

Enter Dates

1. Select a cell.
2. Type a date in mm-dd-yy format, separating the parts of the date with either dashes (-) or slashes (/).
3. Press Enter.
   - The date you typed appears right aligned in the cell you selected in Step 1.
   - The cell pointer moves down one row.
4. Repeat Steps 1 to 3 to enter other numbers.

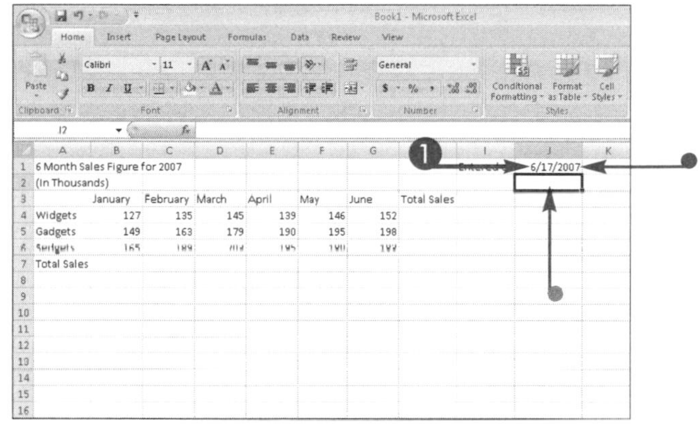

MASTER IT

Can I edit or delete the information that I type in a cell?

▼ Yes. You can edit the information either as you type it or after you type it by pressing the F2 key on your keyboard to switch to Edit mode. To edit as you type, just press F2. To edit after you type, click the cell to select it and then press F2. To change an entry completely, enter new information as described in this section. To delete all of the information in a cell, select the cell and press Delete. To delete both information and cell formatting, see Chapter 3.

Why does my label in cell A1 appear truncated while my label in cell B1 seems to occupy both cells B1 and C1?

▼ The information in both cells exceeds their column widths. When an empty cell such as C1 appears beside a cell containing an over-large entry such as B1, information seems to occupy both cells. However, Excel actually stores all of the information in cell B1; look at the Formula Bar as you select cell B1 and then cell C1. The information in B1 is also hiding part of the over-large entry in A1. To view all of an over-large entry on the worksheet, widen the column. See Chapter 6 for details.

Undo and Redo

You can use the Undo feature in Excel to recover from editing mistakes that might otherwise force you to re-enter data. The Undo feature in Excel is cumulative, meaning that Excel keeps track of all of the actions you take until you close the program. When you use the Undo feature, Excel begins by reversing the effects of the last action you took. If you undo four times, Excel reverses the effects of the last four actions you took in the order you took them. For example, suppose that you edit a text label and remove some characters. If you undo the action, Excel reinserts those characters.

The Redo feature works like the Undo feature, but in reverse. After you undo an action, you can redo it. If you undo several actions in a row, you can redo all of them, in the order you undid them. For example, if you undo typing and then the effects of resizing a column, when you use the Redo feature, Excel first restores the effects of resizing the column. If you then immediately use the Redo feature again, Excel restores the typing.

Undo and Redo

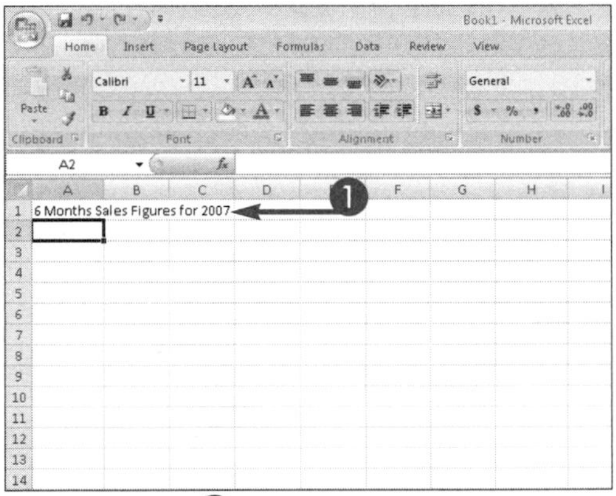

1. Perform an action.

   In this example, text is typed.

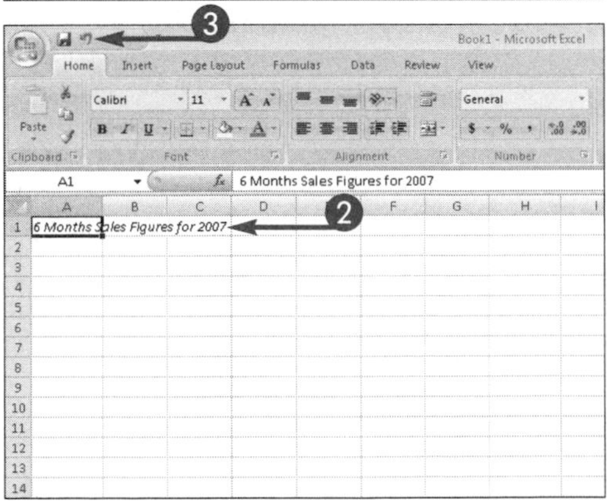

2. Perform another action.

   In this example, italics are added.

Note: *See Chapter 3 for details on adding italics.*

3. Click the Undo button ( ).

- Excel reverses the last action.

In this example, Excel removes italics.

If you click Undo again in this example, Excel removes the text.

4 Click the Redo button ( ).

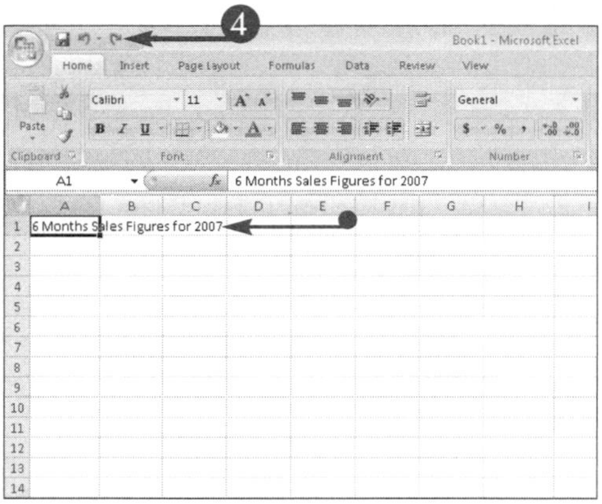

- Excel reverses the effect of undoing by adding back your last action. In this example, Excel reapplies italics.

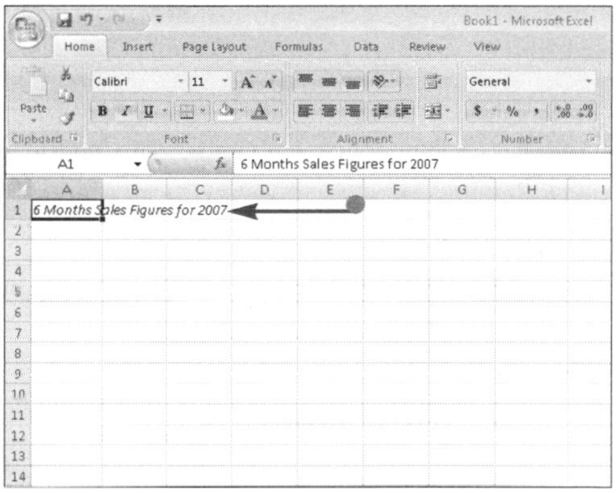

MASTER IT

Can I undo more than one action at a time?

▼ Yes. Click beside to display the list of actions you can undo. Click the oldest action you want to undo, and Excel undoes all of the actions from the oldest one you select to the latest, showing you the worksheet at the point in time before you took any of those actions.

Can I redo more than one action at a time.

▼ Yes. The Redo feature works the same way as the Undo feature. To be able to redo more than one action at a time, you must undo multiple actions before you redo. Then, click beside to display a list of actions you can redo. Click the oldest action, and Excel redoes all of the actions from the oldest to the latest.

Why is the Redo button unavailable when the Undo button is available?

▼ Excel keeps track of all actions you take in all open workbooks and makes those actions available to undo until you close Excel. The button will not be available unless there are actions to redo, and actions to redo do not become available until you undo an action. If you then click to redo the action you undid, then becomes unavailable because there are no more actions to redo.

Move Around in a Worksheet

You can use arrow keys to move around a worksheet, moving the cell pointer up, down, left, or right one cell at a time. If you hold down an arrow key, Excel moves the cell pointer repeatedly in the direction designated by the arrow key. You can also move one screen at a time using the Page Up and Page Down keys.

To quickly move to the first or last cell in a range, you can take advantage of the End key. You use the End key in combination with the arrow keys to move the cell pointer to the top or bottom cell in a column, or the left or right cell in a row. When you use the End key, Excel displays "End Mode" on the Status Bar to alert you that the cell pointer will move to the first or last cell in the direction of the arrow key you use.

When you know the address of the cell in which you want to work, you can move directly to that cell using the Go To dialog box.

Move Around in a Worksheet

❶ Click a cell.

- Excel displays the cell pointer in that cell.

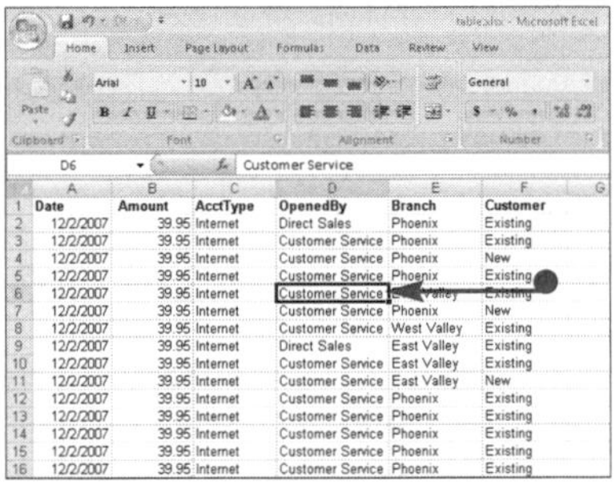

❷ Press the right-arrow key on the keyboard.

- Excel moves the cell pointer one column to the right.

You can press any arrow key to move the cell pointer one cell in that direction.

You can press and hold an arrow key to repeatedly move the cell pointer in that direction.

❸ Press the End key.

- The Status Bar displays "End Mode."

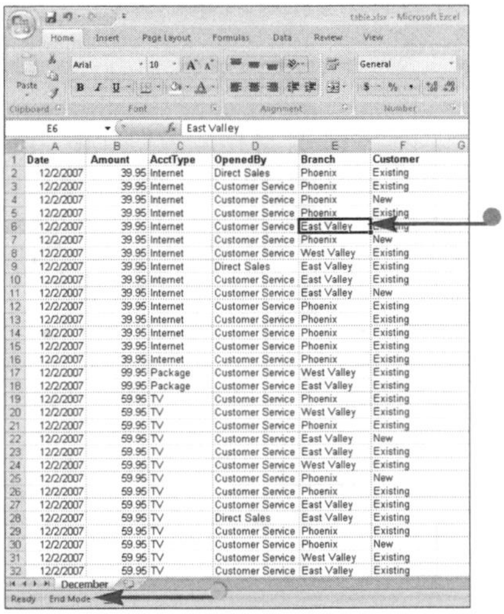

4 Press the up-arrow key.

- Excel moves the cell pointer to the first cell in the column containing information.

You can use the End key with any arrow key to move to the first or last cell in the row or column containing information.

You can press Ctrl+Home to move to cell A1.

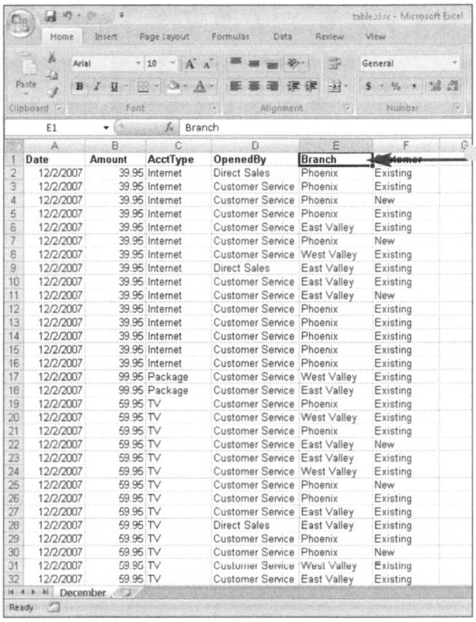

5 Press F5.

The Go To dialog box appears.

6 Type a cell address.

7 Click OK.

Excel moves the cell pointer to the address you typed.

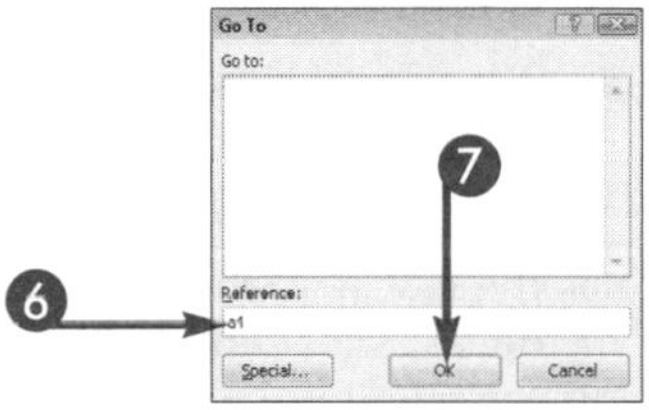

MASTER IT

What happens if I click the Special button in the Go To dialog box?

▼ Excel displays the Go To Special dialog box, where you can set special conditions for Excel to use to go to a particular cell. For example, if you select the Comments option, Excel selects all cells that contain comments. If you select the Formulas option, Excel selects all cells that contain formulas.

Where does Excel place the cell pointer when I move a screen at a time?

▼ The cell pointer remains in the same relative position on the screen when you press the Page Up or Page Down keys. For example, if D10 is the active cell while viewing rows 1 to 27 and you press the Page Down key, then Excel displays D37 as the active cell. However, the cell pointer does not move if you click in the horizontal scroll bar.

What happens when I press the Page Down key?

▼ Excel displays the next page of rows. For example, if you are viewing rows 1 to 27 on one screen and you press the Page Down key, then Excel displays rows 28 to 54.

Is there an easy way to move one screen to the right or left?

▼ Yes. You can click a blank area in the horizontal scroll bar that runs across the bottom of the screen.

Move Around in a Workbook

You can move between the worksheets in a workbook using the tabs and controls at the bottom of the Excel screen. By default, a workbook contains at least three worksheets and you can switch between them. If your workbook contains more than three worksheets, it is possible that the tabs for all worksheets will not be visible at all times. You can use the controls to the left of the worksheet tabs to scroll through hidden worksheets. The first and last controls scroll all of the worksheet tabs to display the first and last worksheets, respectively. The middle controls scroll to display the next worksheet tab in the direction of the control's arrow.

MASTER IT

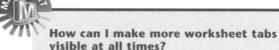

How can I make more worksheet tabs visible at all times?

▼ Resize the horizontal scroll bar by moving the mouse pointer over the left edge of the horizontal scroll bar. When the resizing mouse pointer (⟛) appears, click and drag to the right. Excel makes more space available for worksheet tabs and less for the horizontal scroll bar.

Move Around in a Workbook

1. Open a workbook.
   - Excel displays the first worksheet in the workbook or the last sheet you viewed before saving the workbook.
2. Click a worksheet tab.

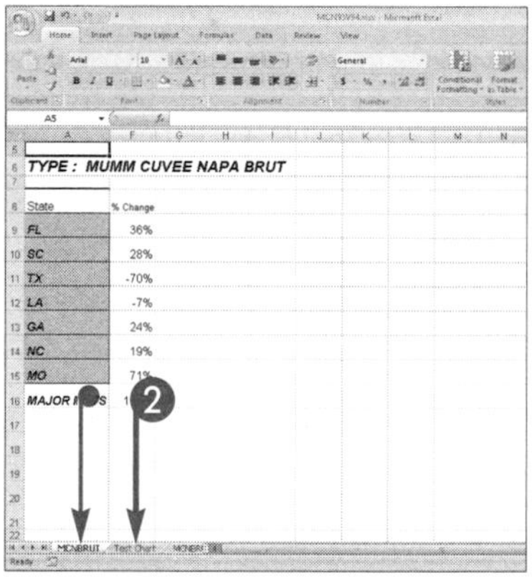

- Excel displays that worksheet.
- To display additional worksheet tabs, you can click these controls.

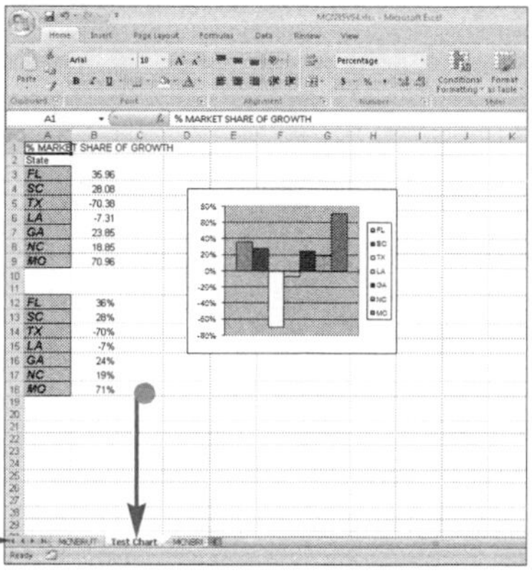

Manage the Status Bar

You can add elements to, or remove elements from, the Status Bar to display many different types of information. When you open a blank workbook, the Status Bar displays the cell mode, the macro recording state, the View shortcuts, the zoom factor, and the zoom slider. The Status Bar is actually set to display a wide variety of information, if conditions are right to display the information. For example, if you press the Scroll Lock key on the keyboard, Excel displays the state of the Scroll Lock key on the Status Bar.

The cell mode that appears by default in all workbooks switches between four states. *Ready mode* is a general state, and the state that appears when no other state is appropriate. *Enter mode* appears as soon as you start typing in a cell, and Excel returns to Ready mode after you press Enter to store the information in the cell. When you edit any cell entry, *Edit mode* appears on the Status Bar. *Point mode* appears on the Status Bar when you point to cells that you want to include while setting up a formula.

Manage the Status Bar

1. Right-click the Status Bar.
   - Excel displays the Customize Status Bar menu. Each item with a check mark (✓) beside it will appear on the Status Bar under appropriate conditions.
2. Click an item that does not contain ✓.

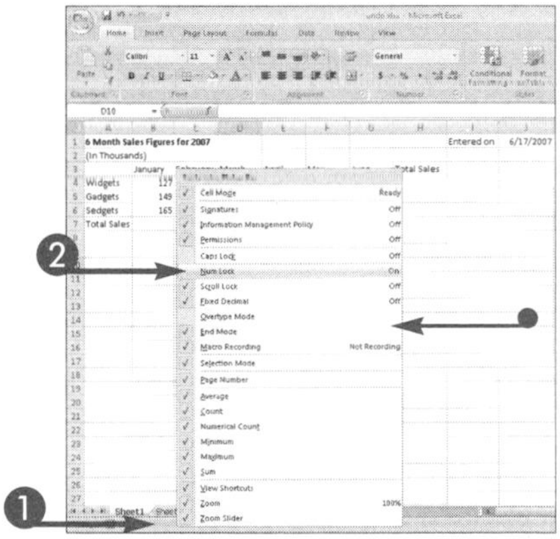

   - Excel can now include that item on the Status Bar.
   - If appropriate conditions exist, the item appears immediately on the Status Bar.
3. Click anywhere on the worksheet to hide the Status Bar menu.

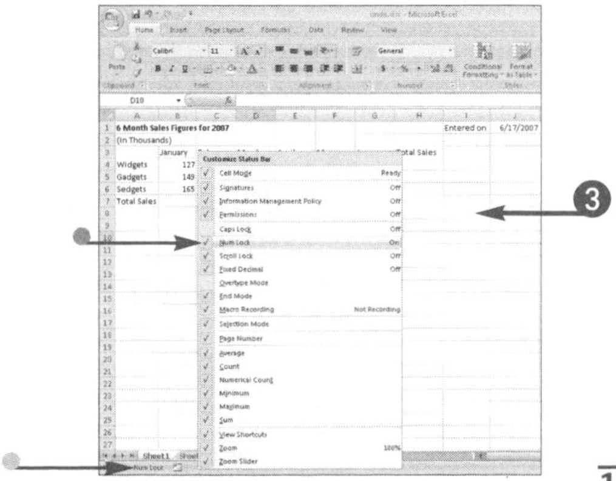

Save a Workbook

You can save your workbook so that you can use it at another time in Excel 2007. Excel 2007 uses a new file format that is XML-based. The new file format reduces the size of a workbook, which improves the likelihood of recovering information if a file becomes corrupted.

By default, Excel saves new workbooks in the new file format, assigning an extension of .xlsx to the workbook. However, if you open a workbook created in Excel 97-2003, make changes, and save the workbook, Excel assumes that you want to save the file in Excel 97-2003 format with a file extension of .xls.

To help you work with others who have not yet upgraded to Excel 2007, you can save a copy of an Excel 2007 workbook in Excel 97-2003 format. Saving an Excel 2007 workbook as an Excel 97-2003 workbook does not affect the Excel 2007 file, but the Compatibility Checker dialog box may appear and indicate that the workbook contains features that are not supported by Excel 97-2003. The Compatibility Checker dialog box also indicates that Excel 2007 will convert those features to the closest available format.

Save a Workbook

Save an Excel 2007 Workbook

1. Click the Office button.
2. Click Save.

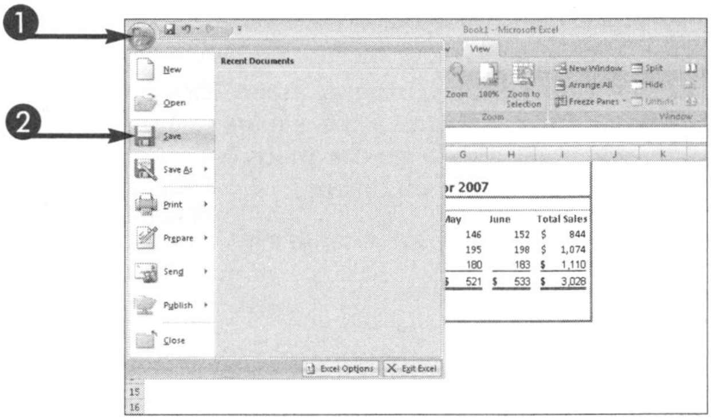

The Save As dialog box appears.

- The Save As Type drop-down menu shows Excel Workbook (*.xlsx).

3. Type a name for the workbook here.
   - You can click here to select a folder in which to save the workbook.
   - You can click here to create a new folder for the workbook.

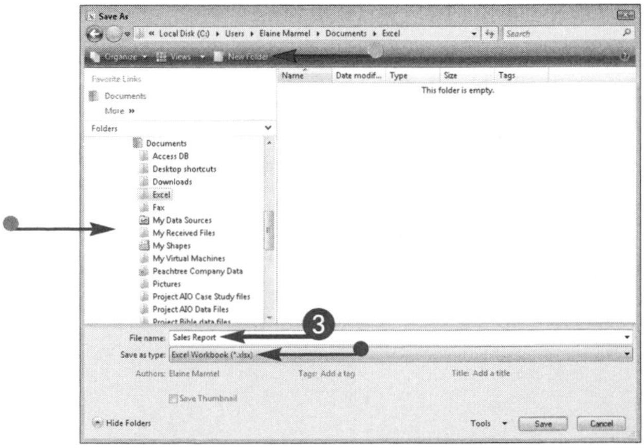

Save a Workbook in Excel 97-2003 format

1. Click .
2. Click Save As.
3. Click Excel 97-2003 Workbook.

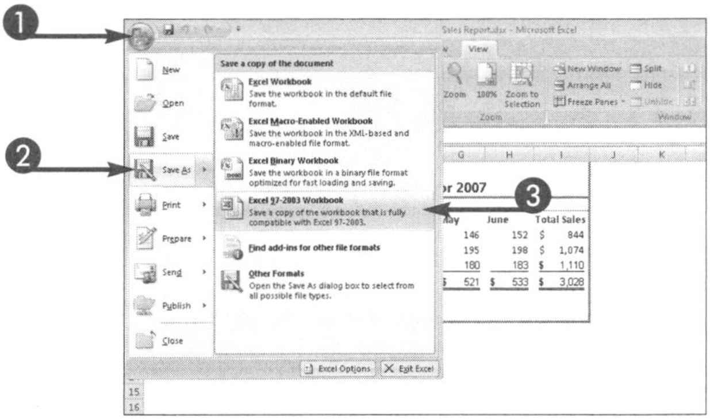

The Save As dialog box appears.

- The Save As Type drop-down menu shows Excel 97-2003 Workbook (*.xls).

4. Type a name for the workbook here.

- You can click here to select a folder in which to save the workbook.
- You can click here to create a new folder for the workbook.

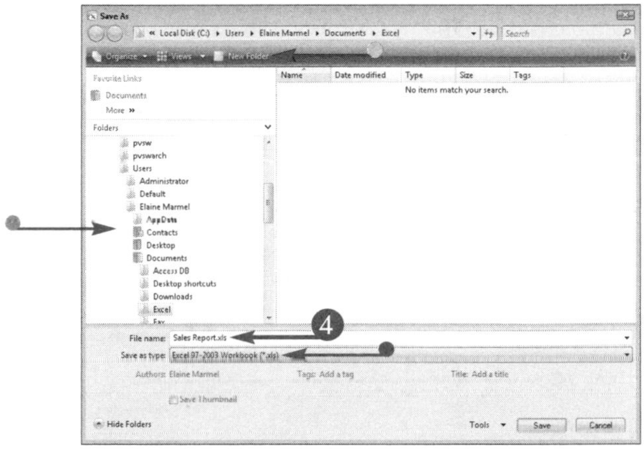

MASTER IT

Is there a quick way to save a workbook?

▼ Yes. After you save a workbook for the first time, you can click the Save button ( ) on the Quick Access Toolbar to save it again. Excel assumes that you want to use the same filename for the workbook and save the workbook in the same folder, and so Excel does not display the Save As dialog box.

Can I save my workbook in portable document format?

▼ By installing an add-in from Microsoft, you can save Excel workbooks in PDF or XPS format. The PDF (portable document format) file format comes from Adobe and is widely used because documents saved in this format retain visual formatting and can be opened using Adobe's free Acrobat Reader program. The XPS (XML paper specification) file format is new from Microsoft and works the same way that PDF files work.

How do I install the add-in to be able to save Excel workbooks in PDF or XPS format?

▼ Click and then click Save As. On the menu that appears, click Find Add-Ins For Other File Formats. Excel Help opens. When you click the "Install and Use the Save as PDF or XPS Add-In from Microsoft" link, Excel displays a help topic that includes a link to an Internet page that provides instructions for downloading and installing the add-in.

Open a Workbook

You can display workbooks on-screen that you previously saved so that you can continue working on them or print them. To open a workbook, you choose from a list of available workbooks in the folder that you select. By default, Excel displays all workbooks created by Excel 2007 and Excel 97 to 2003.

When you use Excel 2007 under Windows Vista, the appearance of the Open dialog box differs from the one you see when using Excel 2007 under Windows XP. In Windows Vista, you select the folder containing the file you want to open from the Navigation pane that appears on the left side of the dialog box. When you select a folder, the files it contains appear in the pane on the right side of the dialog box. By default, in the Navigation pane, Excel selects the folder you designate as the Default File Location when you set Excel options. See Chapter 30 for details on setting the Default File Location. If you select a different folder, Excel continues to select that folder until you select another folder or close Excel. In this section, you see the version of the Open dialog box as it appears under Windows Vista.

Open a Workbook

Open Excel Workbooks

1. Click [Office button].
2. Click Open.

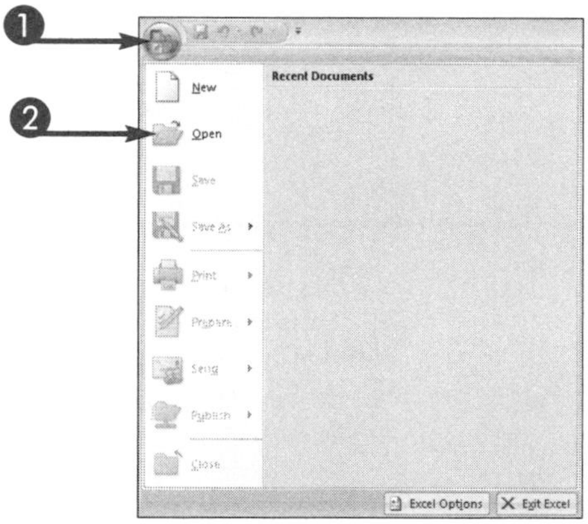

- The Open dialog box appears.

3. Click here to navigate to the folder containing the workbook you want to open.
   - When you click a folder, the files in it appear here.

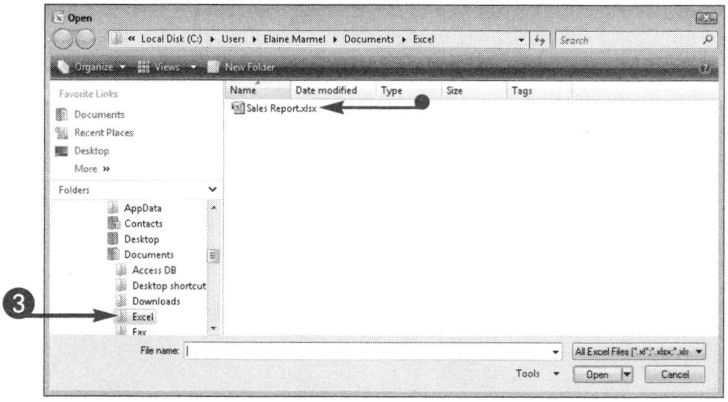

4 Click the workbook you want to open.

- The filename appears here.

5 Click Open.

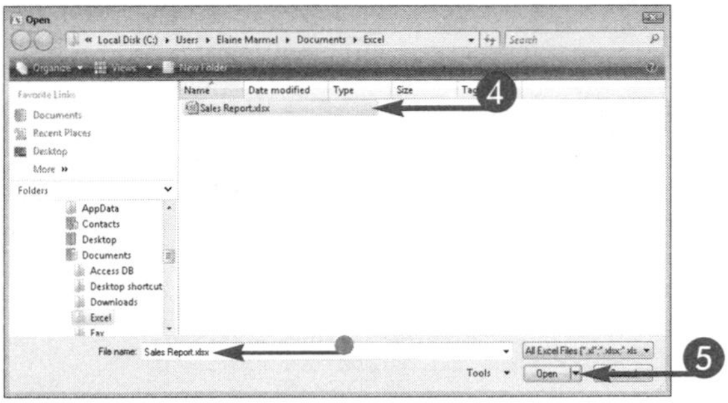

The workbook appears on-screen.

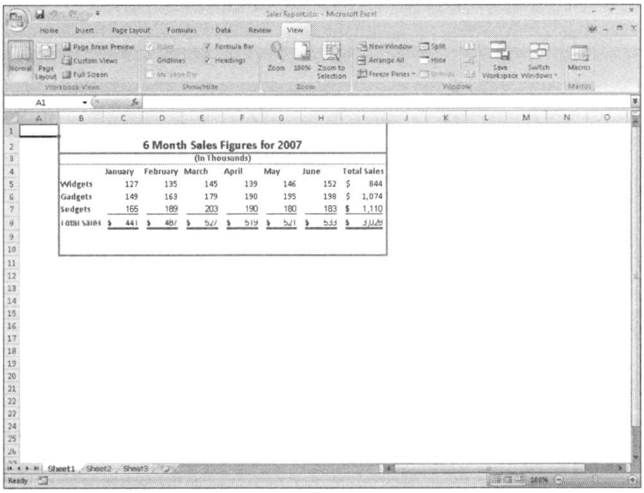

MASTER IT

How many workbooks can I open at one time?

▼ As many as memory permits. You can select all of the workbooks you want to open simultaneously in the Open dialog box, and Excel opens them in the order they appear in the Open dialog box. To select multiple workbooks that do not appear contiguously in the Open dialog box, press and hold Ctrl as you click each filename. If the workbooks are listed contiguously, you can press and hold Shift as you click the first workbook and the last workbook you want to open.

Is there a quick way to open a file I just closed?

▼ Yes. You can use the Recent Documents list that appears when you click [Office button]. Excel displays the names of the most recently opened workbooks. You can set Excel options to list up to 50 of the most recently opened workbooks when you click [Office button].

What should I do if I cannot remember where I saved the Excel workbook I want to open?

▼ Click the Start button. In the Start Search field, begin to type the name of the workbook. When you see the workbook you want to open, click it.

continued

Open a Workbook *(Continued)*

Excel provides options on the Open button that you can use when you open workbooks. For example, you can open a workbook in a read-only state, which means that you can look at the information in the workbook but not save changes to it. You can also open a workbook as a copy of the original. Then, you can work with the copy without disturbing the original workbook. You can open and repair workbooks when they are damaged. Using this option, you can attempt to recover information in the workbook.

You can open a wide variety of other kinds of files in addition to Excel workbooks. For example, you can open Web pages, XML files, text files, comma-separated value files, or tables created in Access, just to name a few. When you open a file that is not a workbook, Excel's behavior changes, depending on the type of file you open. In Chapter 32, you see what happens in Excel when you import a text or comma-separated value file into Excel. In this section, you see what happens when you open a table created in Access.

Open a Workbook *(continued)*

Open a File in Another Format

1. Click [Office button].
2. Click Open.

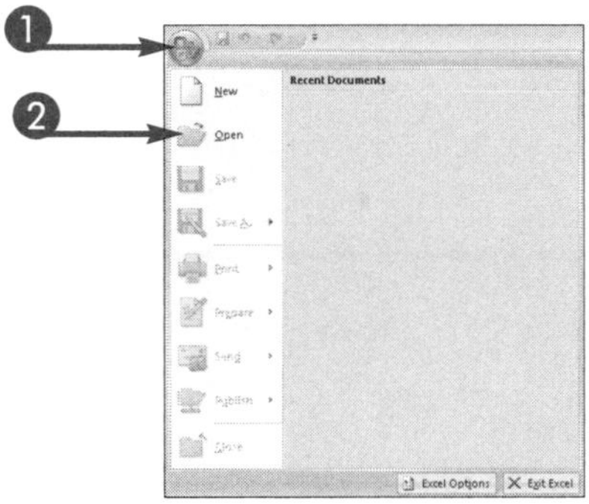

The Open dialog box appears.

3. Click here to navigate to the folder containing the file you want.
   - The files in the folder appear here.
4. Click here to display the types of files you can open.
5. Click to select a file type.

   This example uses an Access file.

- Files of the type you select appear here.

6 Click the file you want to open.

- The filename appears here.

7 Click Open.

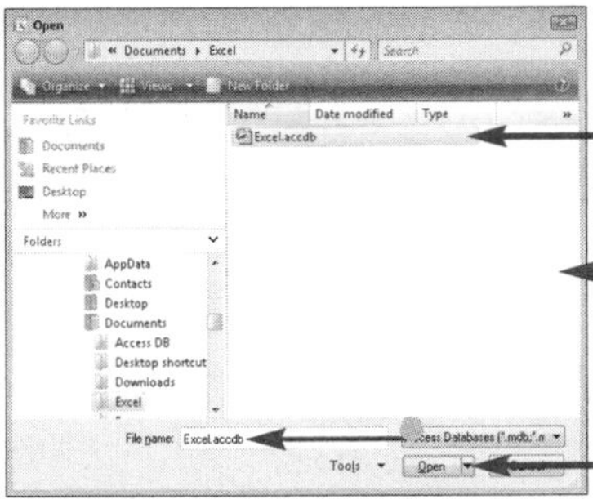

The file appears on-screen.

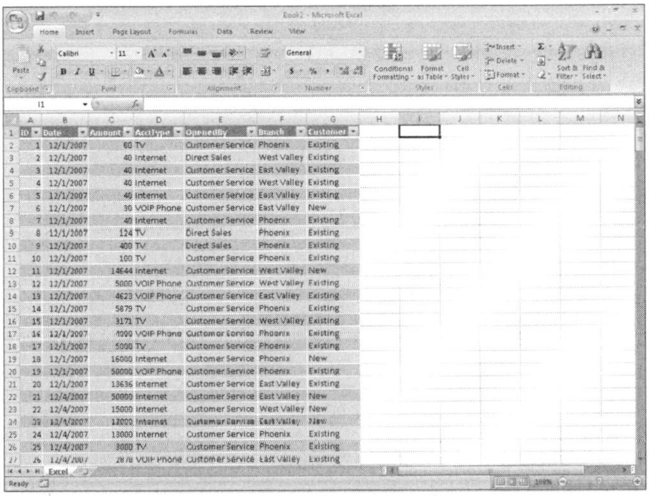

What are comma-separated files?

▼ Comma-separated files contain all information about a particular entry on one line, with each piece of information separate by commas. For example, if you stored an address book in a comma-separated file, each line would contain all the information about one addressee, and the addressee's name, address, city, state, and Zip code would be separated by commas. You can typically open a comma-separated file in Windows Notepad.

What are text files?

▼ Text files are like comma-separated files in that they contain all of the information about a particular entry on one line. However, in a text file, the information is separated by some character other than a comma. For example, if you open a text file in Windows Notepad, you might see the information separated by spaces or tabs.

When I use Excel to open a file created in Access, why does a dialog box appear after Step 6 before the file appears on-screen?

▼ If your Access file contains more than one table, Excel needs to know which table you want to open. Therefore, before opening the file, Excel displays the Select Table dialog box, from which you must select a table and then click OK.

Convert an Excel 97-2003 Workbook to an Excel 2007 Workbook

You can convert existing Excel workbooks to the new Excel 2007 format. You do not need to convert an Excel workbook that uses an older format to the Excel 2007 format to open and edit the workbook. When you open a workbook formatted in an older version of Excel, Excel 2007 displays the workbook's title along with the words "Compatibility Mode." You can edit the workbook using all of the tools available in Excel 2007. However, if you try to save the workbook, you may see a message from Excel's Compatibility Checker feature that indicates that the workbook now contains features available only in Excel 2007. If you want to retain all of the editing that you have done, you should convert the file.

During the conversion process, Excel also saves your workbook. As a result, if you see a Compatibility Checker dialog box when you try to save a workbook created in an older version of Excel but edited in Excel 2007, you can cancel the Compatibility Checker and use the steps in this section to convert the workbook to Excel 2007 format.

Convert an Excel 97-2003 Workbook to an Excel 2007 Workbook

1. Open a workbook created in a version of Excel older than Excel 2007.

Note: *See the section, "Open Workbooks," earlier in this chapter for details.*

- In the title bar, Excel 2007 indicates that the workbook is open in Compatibility Mode.

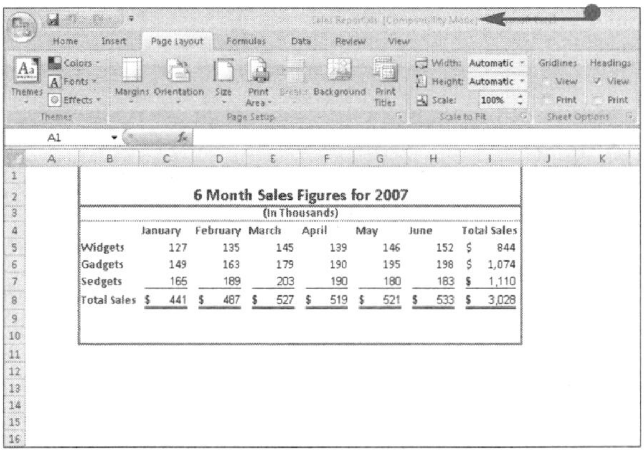

2. Click .
3. Click Convert.

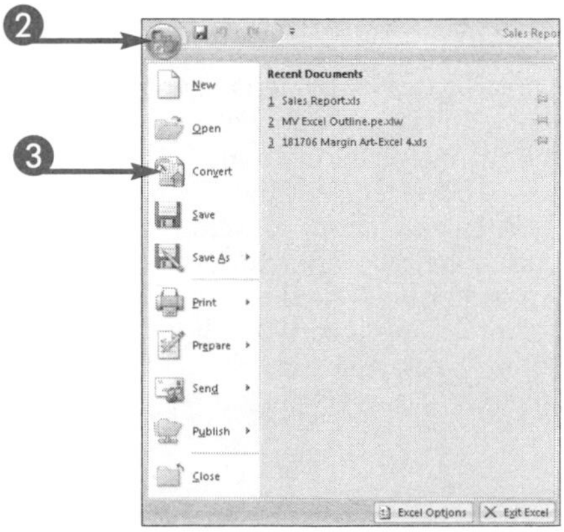

Excel displays a message indicating that it will convert the workbook to the newest file format.

4 Click OK.

Excel displays a message indicating that conversion was successful and that you must close and reopen the workbook.

- Excel also changes the filename extension to .xlsx.

5 Click Yes.

Excel closes and reopens the workbook.

"Compatibility Mode" no longer appears in the title bar.

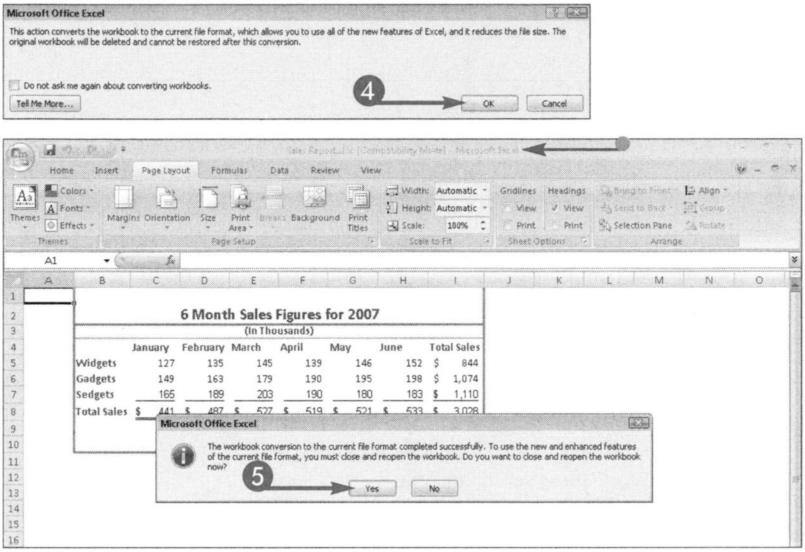

What kinds of compatibility issues can I expect?

▼ You may experience issues that cause a significant loss of functionality, including situations where you would lose data if you saved to an older format. For example, the number of rows and columns in Excel 2007 exceeds the size of worksheets in older versions. If your workbook contains data outside the range of available cells in the older version, that data will be lost. You may also experience issues that cause a minor loss of fidelity. For example, your workbook may contain formatting such as even or first page headers or footers that only Excel 2007 supports. Older versions of Excel do not display these headers or footers.

The Convert option does not appear when I click . Why not?

▼ The workbook you are viewing is already in Excel 2007 format, with a filename extension of .xlsx. The Convert option appears on the Office menu only when you are viewing a workbook created in an older version of Excel and working in Compatibility Mode.

What versions of Excel workbooks can I convert?

▼ You can convert files from all versions of Excel prior to Excel 2007, including Excel 2.1 worksheets, Excel 3.0 worksheets, Excel 4.0 worksheets and workbooks, Excel 5.0/95 workbooks, and Excel 97-2003 workbooks. Just open any of these files and follow the steps in this section.

Start a New Workbook

Although a new, blank workbook appears by default when you open Excel, you do not need to close and reopen Excel to start a new workbook. If you prefer, you can use a variety of templates as the foundation for an Excel workbook. Templates are workbooks that contain predefined information and settings that you can use so that you do not need to create the settings yourself. Excel installs some commonly used templates when you install the program. Other templates are available to download from Microsoft's Web site. You can read about creating a workbook using an online template that you download in Chapter 4.

All workbooks, including the blank workbook that appears when you start Excel, are based on a template. You cannot change the default settings in the blank workbook, but you can create your own version of the default blank workbook that Excel opens instead of the original default blank workbook. For example, you may prefer a different font and font size for all new workbooks. You can make your settings permanent so that, each time you start Excel, Excel opens a blank workbook that uses your font and font size.

Start a New Workbook

1. Click .
2. Click New.

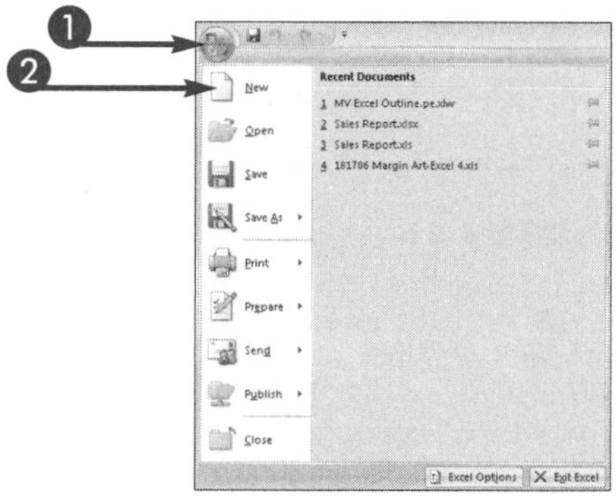

The New Workbook dialog box appears.

- Categories of templates appear here.
- Templates in the selected category appear here.
- A preview of the selected template appears here.

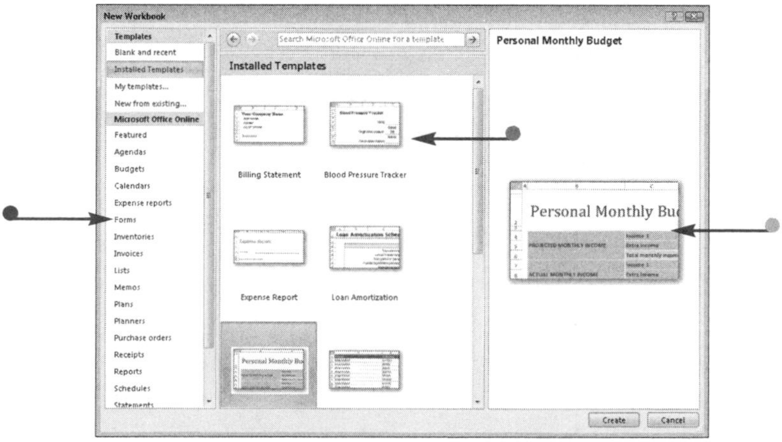

3. Click a category in the Templates list.
4. Click a template.
5. Click Create.

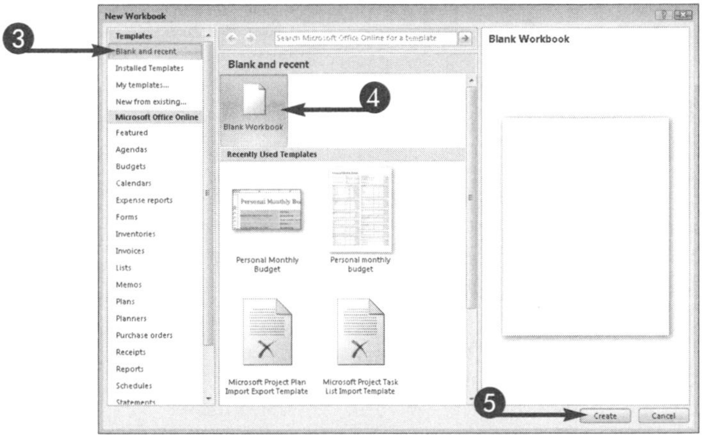

A new workbook appears on-screen.

You can edit this workbook the same way you edit any workbook.

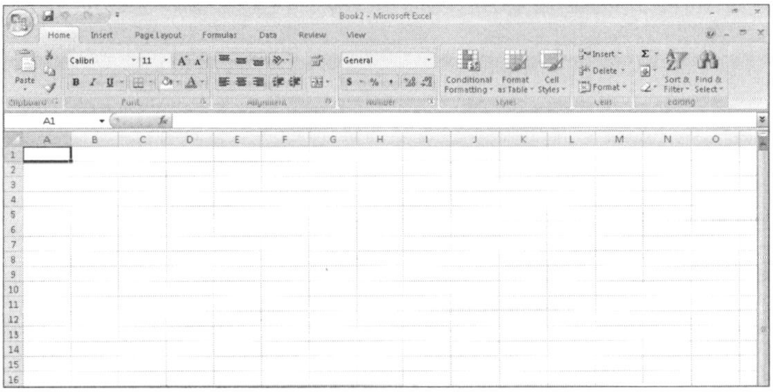

MASTER IT

Is there a way to modify the settings displayed by the default blank workbook?

▼ You cannot modify the default blank workbook because it exists in memory only. However, you can create a blank workbook, not a template, that uses your settings and have Excel always open that workbook when you start Excel. Set up the workbook and save it to a particular folder, such as C:\users\username\Documents\Excel Startup. Then, in Excel, click and click Excel Options. In the Excel Options dialog box, click Advanced and scroll down to the General section. Type the pathname containing your workbook in the At Startup, Open All Files In box. When you next open Excel, your workbook appears.

Can I open Excel without a blank workbook?

▼ Yes. Click Start and type **excel.exe** in the Start Search field. Right-click the file that appears, click Send To, and click Desktop (Create Shortcut). Display your desktop, right-click the new shortcut, and click Properties. At the end of the line in the Target field, add a space and type **/e**. Click OK and open Excel using that shortcut.

If I just want a new blank workbook, is there a faster way to open one?

▼ Yes. Using a keyboard shortcut, you can bypass the Office menu and the New Workbook dialog box. While viewing any open workbook, press Ctrl+N. Excel displays a new blank workbook without showing you the New Workbook dialog box.

Switch between Workbooks

You can have more than one workbook open at the same time and switch between the workbooks as you work. In fact, the number of workbooks you can have open at the same time is limited only by the amount of memory in your computer.

It is not uncommon to need to use more than one workbook at the same time. Often one workbook contains information that you want to copy and paste into another workbook. You may also need to create formulas that combine data from a worksheet in one workbook with another worksheet in a different workbook. Or you may need to link workbooks so that Excel updates the information in one workbook when you make a change in the other workbook. Creating formulas using data from different workbooks and linking workbooks is easiest if all of the workbooks that you need to link are open at the same time. See Chapter 10 for more information on creating formulas using data from different workbooks. See Chapter 26 for more information on linking workbooks.

You can switch between open workbooks using Excel features or using the Windows taskbar.

Switch between Workbooks

Switch Workbooks using Excel

1. Click the View tab.
2. Click Switch Windows.

   A list of all open workbooks appears.

3. Click the workbook you want to view.

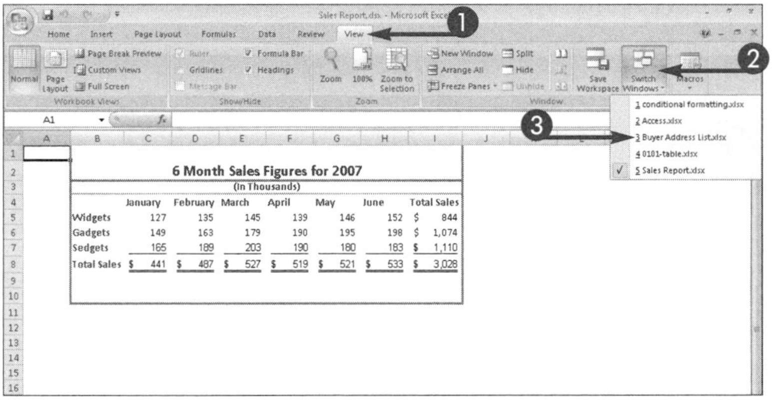

The selected workbook appears.

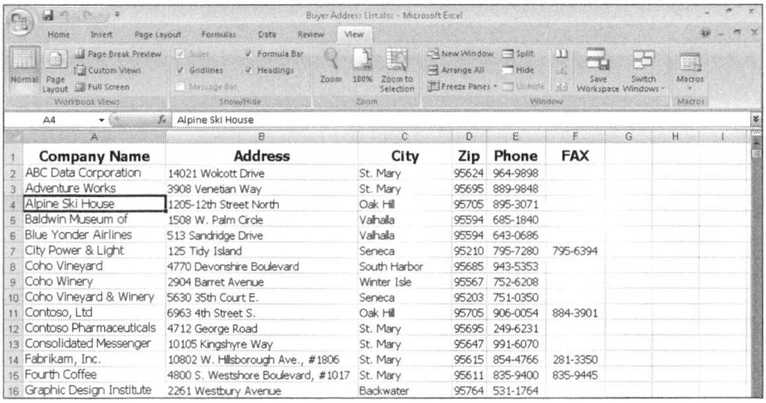

Switch documents using the Windows taskbar

1. Open all the workbooks you want to work with.

Note: To open a workbook, see the section, "Open Workbooks."

- Each open workbook appears as a button on the Windows taskbar.

2. Click the button of the workbook you want to view.

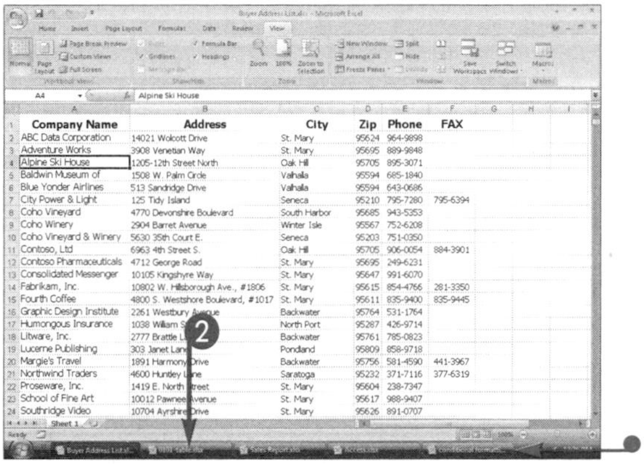

The workbook appears on-screen.

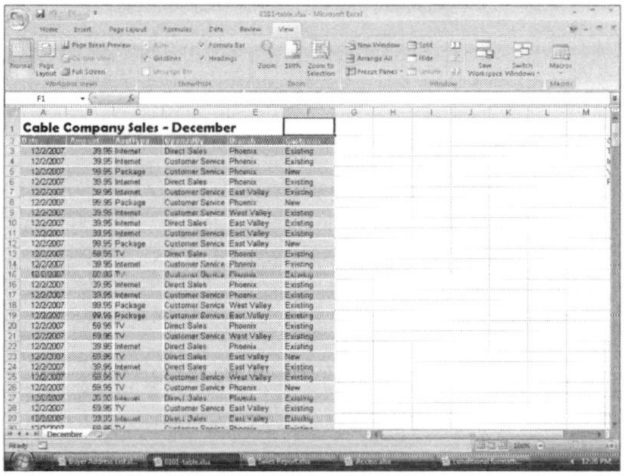

Why do I not see windows for each Excel workbook in the Windows taskbar?

▼ Excel options may not be set to display workbooks in the Windows taskbar. Click   and then click Excel Options. Click Advanced in the left pane and scroll down to the Display section. Click Show All Windows in the Taskbar (☐ changes to ☑). Click OK. You should now see buttons in the Windows taskbar for all open workbooks.

Why do I see only one button on the Windows taskbar when I have several workbooks open?

▼ The Windows taskbar displays buttons for all open documents in any program and has a limited amount of space to display those buttons. To make space, the Windows taskbar groups open documents from the same program on a single button. If you click that button, Windows displays a list of the open documents for that program, and you can click one to view it.

My Windows taskbar appears only when I press the Windows key on my keyboard. How can I display it all the time?

▼ To display the Windows taskbar all the time, right-click a blank area of the Windows taskbar and click Properties. In the Taskbar and Start Menu Properties dialog box, on the Taskbar tab, click Keep the Taskbar on Top of Other Windows (☐ changes to ☑). Click OK. The Windows taskbar should remain visible at all times.

Work with Workspaces

You can save arrangements of Excel workbook windows using a workspace. Saving a workspace is particularly useful when you work with several workbooks at one time. You may have different visual and print settings for each workbook and, if you spend time setting up the workbooks to work with them simultaneously, saving a workspace can save you time. When you save a workspace, you create a special type of Excel file that contains information about the open workbooks. You can then reopen the workspace the next time you want to work with the same set of workbooks, and Excel displays all of the workbooks, arranged just as you had them when you created the workspace.

A workspace file stores print information and visual information about the open workbooks. For example, a workspace stores print information such as print area information, headers, footers, margins, and page orientation. For visual information, a workspace stores magnification settings, window placement on-screen, whether the scroll bars appear, whether sheet tabs appear, whether row numbers and column letters appear, and whether gridlines appear, among other visual elements. Workspace files do not contain actual data stored in the workbooks.

Work with Workspaces

Save a Workspace

1. Set up the workbooks you want to include in the workspace.
2. Click the View tab.
3. Click Save Workspace.

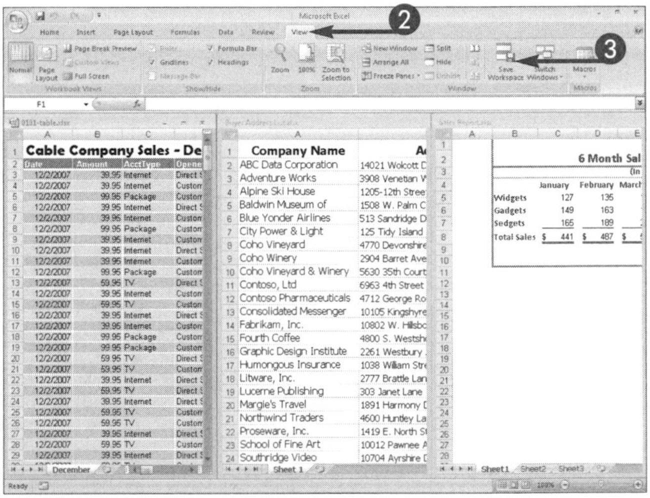

The Save Workspace dialog box appears.

4. Type a name for the workspace.
   - Excel automatically selects Workspaces (*.xlw) in the Save as Type drop-down menu.
5. Click Save.

   Excel saves the workspace.

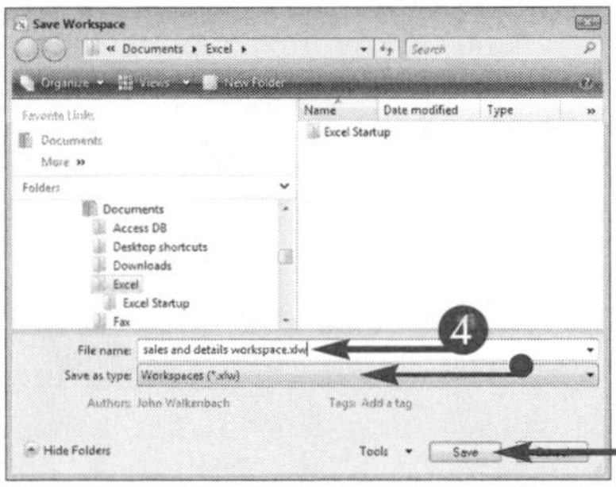

Open a Workspace

1. Click [Office Button].
2. Click Open.

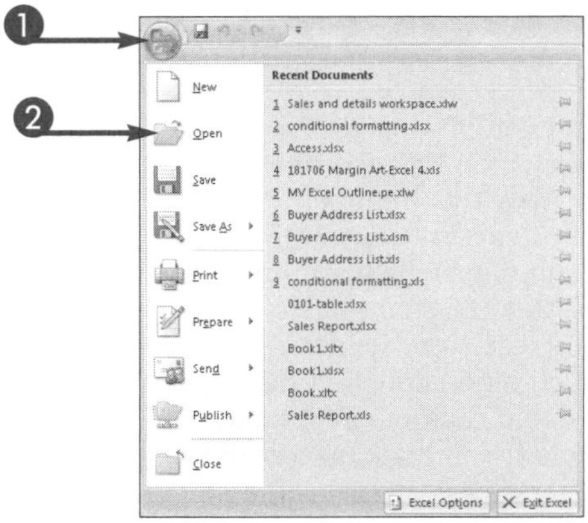

The Open dialog box appears.

3. Click here to select Workspaces from the types of files you can open.
4. Click the workspace file you want to open.
   - The filename appears here.
5. Click Open.

Excel displays the workspace.

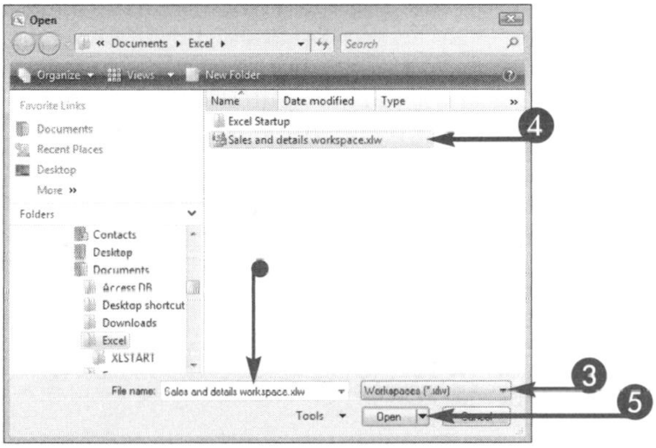

MASTER IT

My co-worker, who also uses Excel 2007, could not use the Excel workspace that I sent to them. Why not?

▼ A workspace file contains only certain information about the workbooks that you have open at the time you create the workspace. The workspace file stores print area information for each open workbook and visual display settings such as how you have the workbooks arranged on-screen. However, the workspace file does not store the actual data in each workbook. For someone else to use a workspace file that you create, you must give them the workspace and all of the workbooks included in the workspace.

Is there a list of the display-related elements that I can save in a workspace?

▼ Yes. Click [Office Button] and then click Excel Options. In the Excel Options dialog box, click Advanced. Scroll down and review the options in the Display section, the Display Options for this Workbook section, and the Display Options for this Worksheet section. You can store any of these settings in a workspace as long as you save the settings in the workbook. For example, you can hide gridlines for one workbook in a workspace, but you must save that setting in the workbook as well as the workspace. When you open the workbook alone or in the workspace, it will not display gridlines.

Add Properties to a Workbook

If you use the Document Information Panel to enter overview information that describes a workbook, you can view that information in the Open dialog box before you actually open the workbook to help you determine whether it is the workbook that you want to open. You can store the name of the person who created the workbook, a workbook title and subject, a description of the workbook and keywords, and category information. Excel fills in the Status field if you mark the workbook as final. See Chapter 31 for details on marking a workbook as final.

If you store keywords for a workbook, they appear in the Tags column of the Open dialog box when you view the details of the folder's contents. You can also use the Search Bar on the Start menu to search for a workbook using data stored in the Document Information Panel.

MASTER IT

Is there a way to view and store more details about a workbook?

▼ Yes. You can click Document Properties and then click Advanced Properties to display the Properties dialog box, which contains five tabs of information. On the Custom tab, you can add fields of information that you want to store.

Add Properties to a Workbook

1. Click ⓘ.
2. Click Prepare.
3. Click Properties.

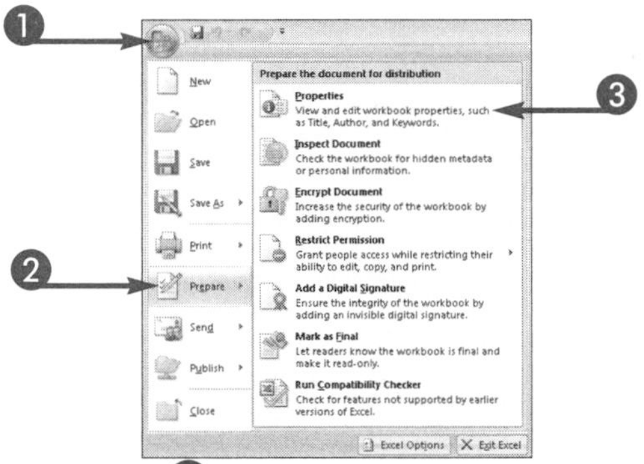

Excel displays the Document Information Panel.

4. Fill in any information that you want to store with the document.
   - If you store more than one keyword, you need to separate them with commas.
5. Click here to hide the document information.
6. Click here to save the workbook with the document information.

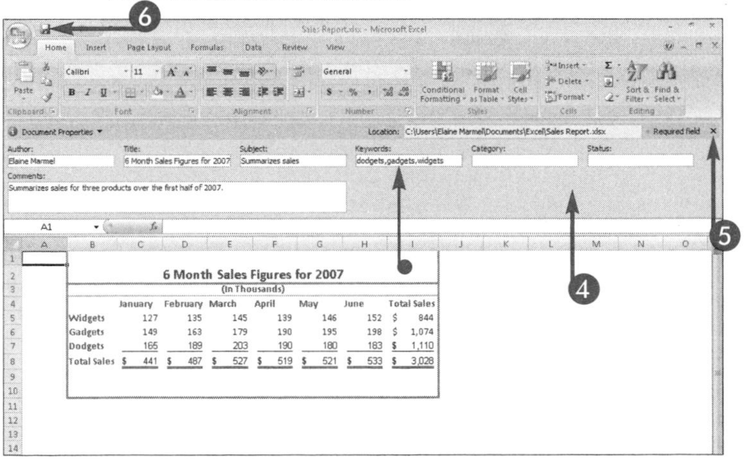

Close a Workbook

When you finish working with a workbook, you can close it. What you see after you close a workbook depends on whether you have more than one workbook open. If you have only one workbook open and you close it, Excel displays a blank window like the one you see in this section. If you have multiple workbooks open and you close one workbook, Excel displays one of the remaining open workbooks.

When you close a workbook, Excel prompts you to save the workbook only if you have made changes that you have not saved. If you have made no changes to a workbook and you tell Excel to close it, you do not see a prompt about saving the workbook and you can safely assume that all changes were saved previously.

MASTER IT

Is there a way to close a workbook without using the Office menu?

▼ Yes. You can click the X that appears on the same row as the tabs on the Ribbon. If you have more than one workbook open, you can click the X in the upper-right corner of the screen, which closes both your workbook and Excel if you have only one workbook open.

Close a Workbook

1. Click [Office button].
2. Click Close.

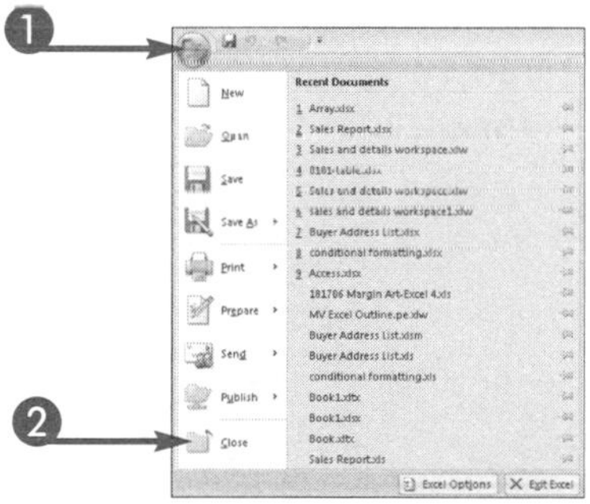

- Excel removes the workbook from the screen.
- If you made changes and did not save them, Excel prompts you to save them before it closes the workbook.
- If another workbook is open, Excel displays that workbook.

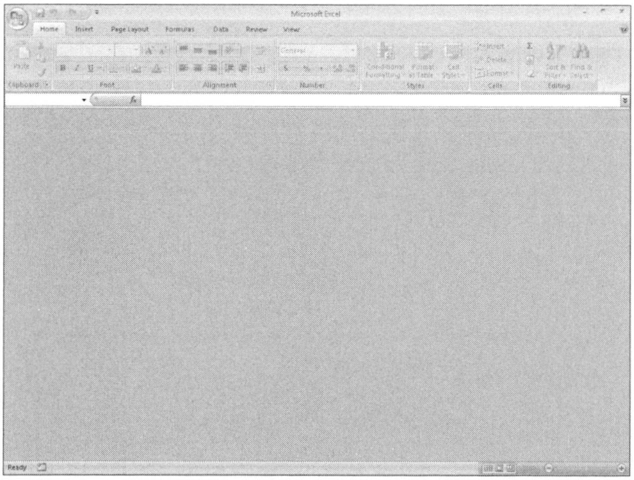

Change Fonts or Font Size

You can change the font face and font size in your workbook. By default, each workbook that you create in Excel 2007 uses a new, sans-serif font called Calibri and the size is set at 11 points. You can select from a wide variety of serif and sans-serif fonts that are TrueType fonts and will print as they appear on-screen. Serif font faces contain short lines stemming from the bottoms of the letters, while sans-serif font faces do not contain these short lines.

You can change the font and font size for a single cell or selected cells, or for an entire worksheet. As you make changes, Excel shows you a preview of the way information in the cells you select will appear.

It is possible that you will need to change the font face or the font size almost every time you create a new workbook. If you find that the Calibri font face or its size do not work for you most of the time, you can change the default font face or size so that each new workbook you create uses a font face and size of your choice.

Change Fonts or Font Size

Make changes for a selection

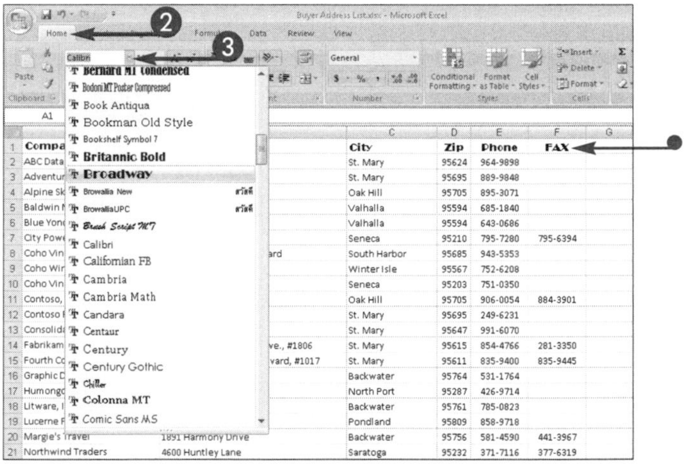

1. Select the cell or range for which you want to change font faces or sizes.

Note: *See Chapter 4 for details on selecting cells.*

2. Click the Home tab.
3. Click ▾ to display the list of available fonts.
   - As you pass the mouse pointer over a font, Excel displays the selected cells in that font.
4. Click a font.

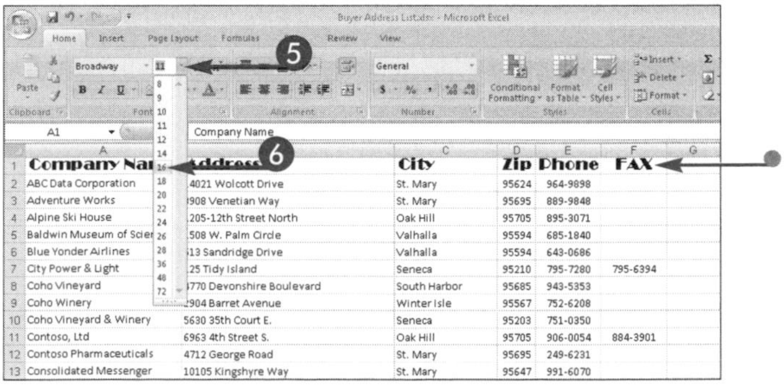

- Excel applies the font to the selection.

5. Click ▾ to display the list of available font sizes.

   As you pass the mouse pointer over a font size, Excel displays the selected cells in that font size.

6. Click a font size.

   Excel applies the font size to the selection.

Change the Defaults

1. Click [icon].
2. Click Excel Options.

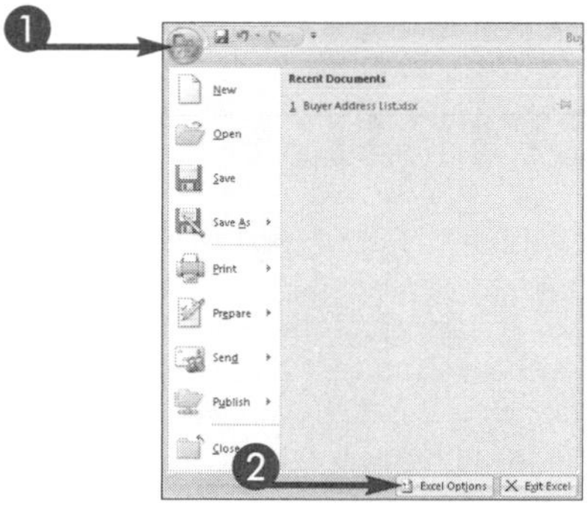

3. Click Popular.
4. Click [▼] to select a font from the list of available fonts.
5. Click [▼] to select a size from the list of available font sizes.
6. Click OK.

   Each new workbook will use the font and font size you selected.

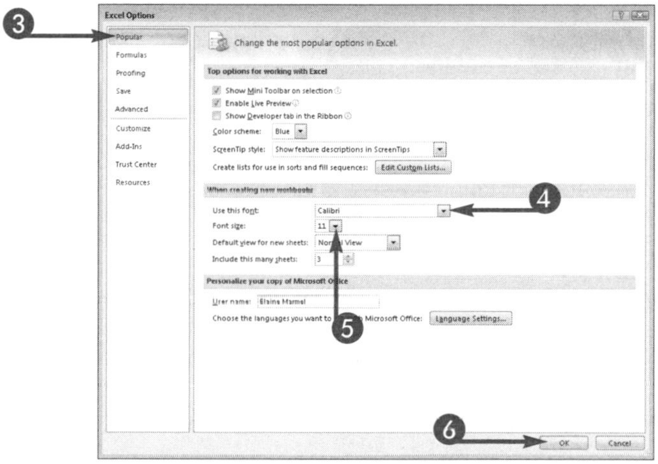

MASTER IT

When should I use a serif font face and when should I use a sans-serif font face?

▼ The lines provided by serif font faces make them ideal for reading because the lines help guide the eye along the text. If you pay close attention, you will notice that most books and newspaper articles use serif fonts such as Times New Roman. In contrast, sans-serif fonts — Arial being among the most popular — work very well for headlines because they tend to catch the eye. Headings in books and newspaper headlines typically use sans-serif fonts.

Is there another way to change the font and font size?

▼ You may want to use the Font tab of the Format Cells dialog box, which enables you to change not only the font face and size but also apply a font style, add font effects, and change the color of the text. Click [icon] in the Font group on the Home tab of the Ribbon to open the Format Cells dialog box to the Font tab. For details on working with font styles, font colors, and font effects, see the next three sections in this chapter.

Apply Boldface, Italics, or Underlining

You can enhance text in a cell by applying a font style such as boldface, italics, or underlining to the text. Applying a font style to enhance text helps call attention to the text and can improve the appearance of your worksheet. However, the old adage, "Too much of a good thing is no good," holds true. Font styles are most effective when used sparingly. If you apply font styles such as boldface to too many cells, the impact of the enhancement can be lost in a sea of boldface cells.

You can apply more than one font style to a selection. For example, you can apply both boldface and italics to the text in a single cell. You also can apply single underlining or double underlining to a cell from the Ribbon.

MASTER IT

How do I choose between single underlining and double underlining?

▼ On the Ribbon, you can click ▾ beside the Underline button (U). Excel displays a drop-down menu that contains two choices: Underline and Double Underline. Choose Underline for a single underline. Excel also supports accounting underlining; for details, see the section, "Apply Font Effects," later in this chapter.

Apply Boldface, Italics, or Underlining

1. Select the cell or range to which you want to apply a font style.

Note: *See Chapter 4 for details on selecting cells.*

2. Click the Home tab.
3. Click the appropriate button on the Ribbon.

   You can click more than one font style button.

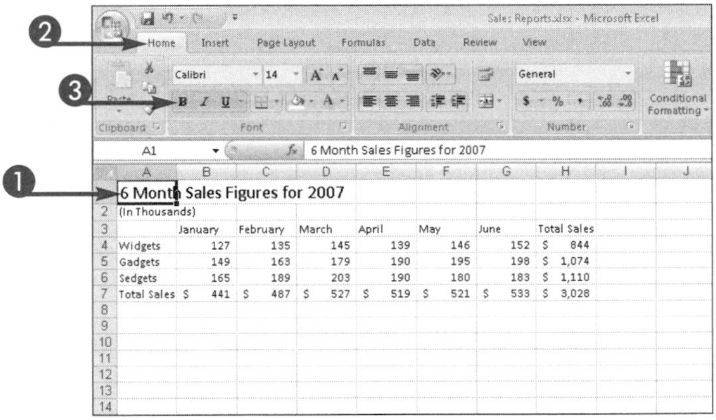

- Excel applies the font style to the selected cells.
- The buttons you click on the Ribbon appear pressed.

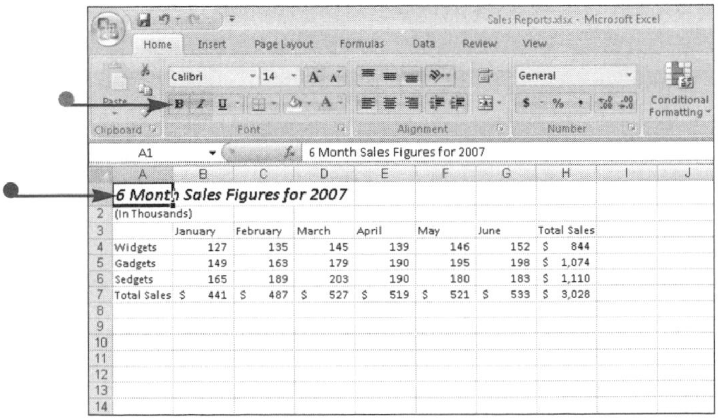

Change Font Color

You can change the color of text in cells to enhance the appearance of your worksheet. Color is effective when you view your workbook on-screen, save it to a PDF or XPS file, or print it using a color printer; however, applying color when you intend to print a workbook to a non-color printer can make reading more difficult.

You can select any of ten standard colors or ten theme colors. Each theme color also offers you five variations of the theme color, ranging from 80 percent lighter than the main theme color to 50 percent darker than the main theme color. As a result, you can select a color from 60 possible theme colors.

MASTER IT

What can I do if I do not see the color I want?

▼ You can click More Colors at the bottom of the Colors drop-down list to display the Colors dialog box. Use the Standard tab to select a standard color; just click the color and click OK. If none of the standard colors appeal to you, use the Custom tab to select from many shades of the same color.

Change Font Color

1. Select the cell or range for which you want to change the font color.

Note: *See Chapter 4 for details on selecting cells.*

2. Click the Home tab.
3. Click ▾ to display the list of available font colors.

   As you pass the mouse pointer over a color, Excel displays the text in the selected cells in that color.

4. Click a color.

- Excel applies the color to the text in the selected cells.

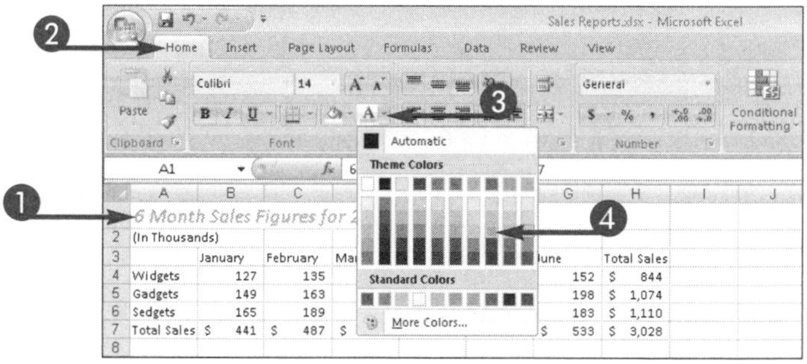

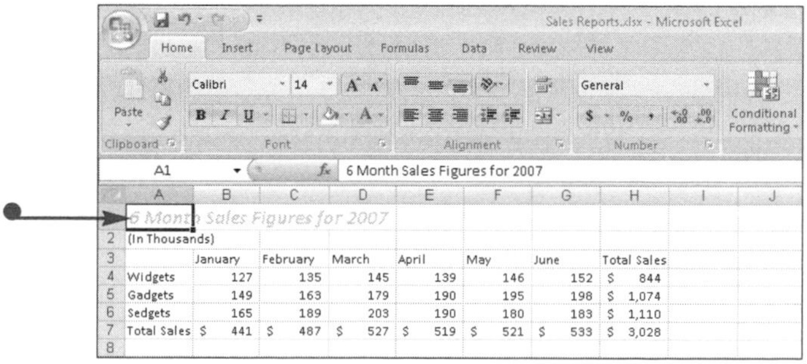

Apply Font Effects

You can apply a variety of special font effects to text in cells. For example, you can assign superscript notation to a cell to represent a trademark. You can apply a subscript to a cell as part of a mathematical formula. Superscripting and subscripting reduce the size of the information and then adjust its vertical position so that it appears slightly above or below the line on which regular-sized information appears.

You can apply strikethrough to indicate that information should be deleted. When you apply strikethrough, Excel draws a line through the middle of the text.

You can also apply four different styles of underlining to selected cells. Two of those underline styles, single and double, are available directly from the Ribbon; see the section, "Apply Boldface, Italics, or Underlining," for details on applying these types of underlining styles. When you use the accounting variation of underlining, Excel adds a bit more space between the underline and the text than if you use the regular underlining styles.

To apply the accounting variation of underlining along with the strikethrough, superscript, or subscript font effects, you can use the Format Cells dialog box.

Apply Font Effects

1. Select the cells to which you want to apply effects.

Note: *See Chapter 4 for details on selecting cells.*

2. Click the Home tab.
3. Click in the Font group.

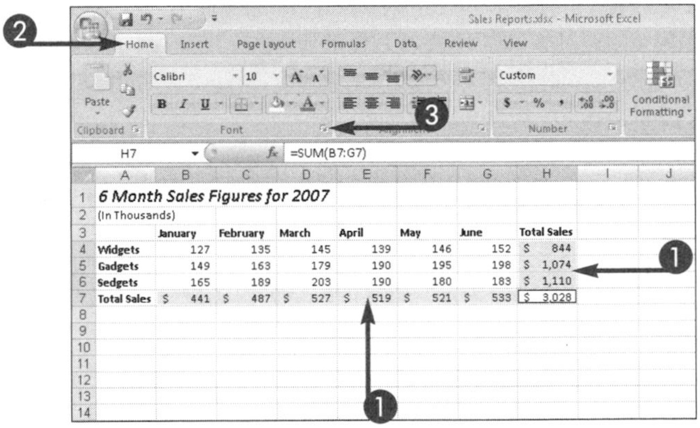

The Format Cells dialog box appears.

4. Click the Font tab.

- You can click here (☐ changes to ☑) to apply the strikethrough font effect.
- You can click here (☐ changes to ☑) to apply the superscript font effect.
- You can click here (☐ changes to ☑) to apply the subscript font effect.

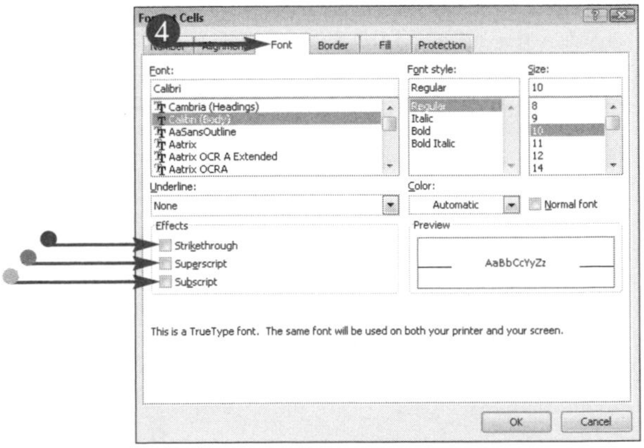

- You can click ▾ to select an underline effect from the list.

5 Click OK.

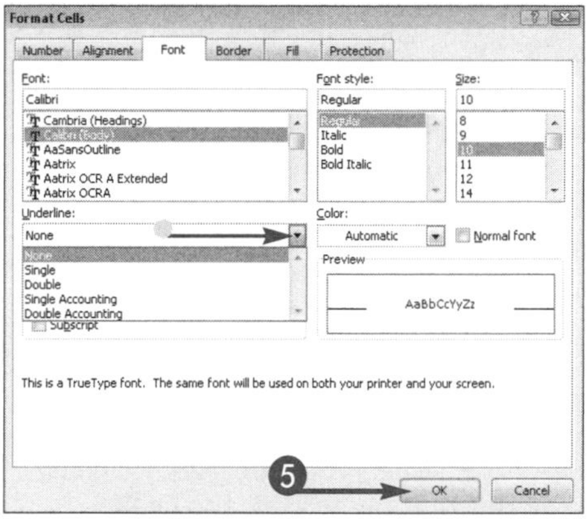

Excel applies the chosen effects to the selected cells.

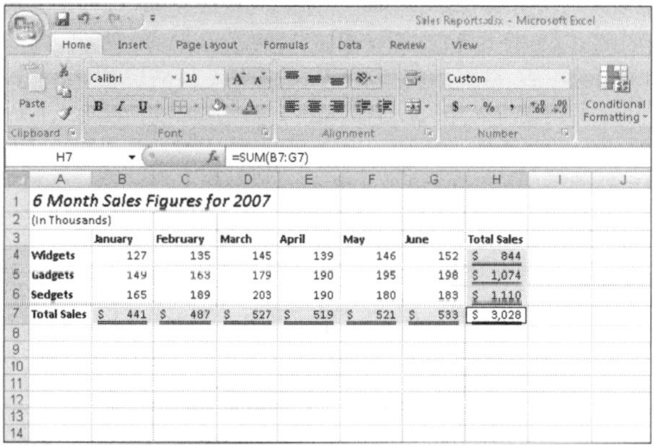

MASTER IT

Excel applies the effects you selected to the selected cells. Can I superscript only some text in a cell?

▼ Yes. Select the cell, press F2 to edit it, and click and drag to select just that portion of the text in the cell that you want to superscript. Then follow the steps in this section. When you finish, press Enter to save the contents of the cell. Excel applies the superscript font effect to only the text you selected in the cell.

How can I select two ranges of cells so that I can apply the same font effect to all of them?

▼ Click and drag to select the first set of cells. Then, press and hold Ctrl as you click and drag to select the second set of cells. Excel adds the second selection to the first selection. You can add a third selection using the same technique.

When should I use Single Accounting underlining versus Double Accounting underlining?

▼ Accounting practices dictate that you use Single Accounting underlining to indicate that you are performing a mathematical operation on the numbers above the underline. They dictate that you use Double Accounting underlining to identify a number as the result of the mathematical operation. Apply Double Accounting underlining to totals.

Assign a Number Format

You can assign a Number format to a cell to add a decimal point followed by two zeros, and, if appropriate, a comma to separate thousands in the number in the cell. Applying the Number format to a cell changes the appearance of the cell on the worksheet but does not change the number stored in the cell.

When performing calculations, Excel uses the value stored in the cell, not the number that appears on the worksheet. For example, when you type 123.45 in cell A1 and then apply the Number format, the cell's appearance does not change. However, if cell A1 contains 123.456, Excel changes the appearance of the number in the worksheet to 123.46, rounding cell A1. But, if you use cell A1 in a calculation, Excel uses 123.456, the value stored in the cell, instead of 123.46, the value that appears in the worksheet.

MASTER IT

Can I control the number of decimal places Excel uses for the Number format?

▼ Yes. You can use the Increase Decimal button ( ) and the Decrease Decimal button ( ) to display anywhere between 0 and 30 decimal places. You can also click the Comma Style button ( ) to have Excel use commas to separate groups of thousands.

Assign a Number Format

1. Click a cell containing a number.
2. Click the Home tab.
   - The number appears in the cell and in the Formula Bar.
   - Excel assigns the number a General format.

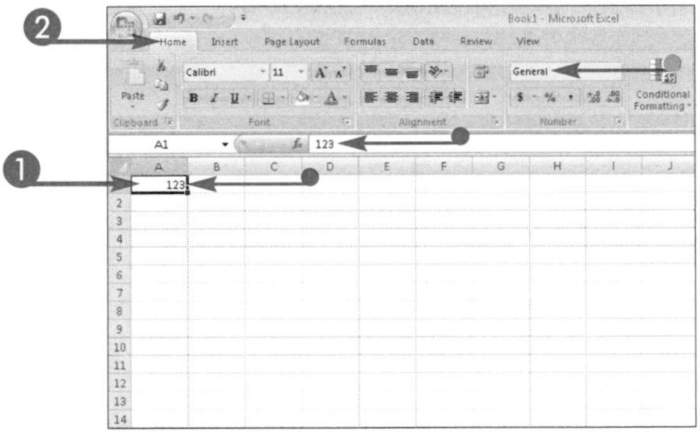

3. Click .
4. Click Number.
   - Excel adds a decimal point and two zeros to the number.
   - Excel changes the appearance only in the cell, not in the Formula Bar.

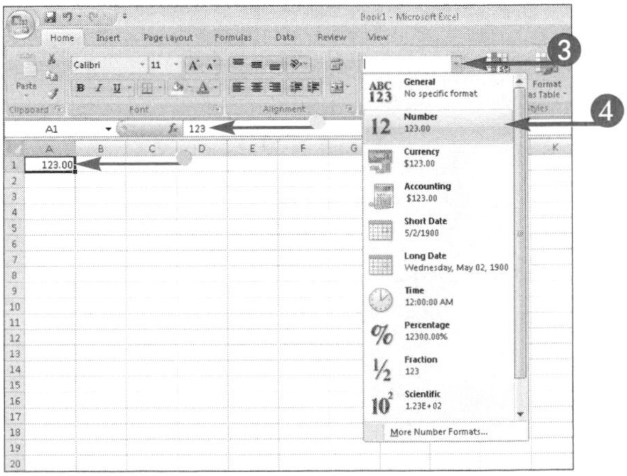

Assign a Currency Format

To represent money, you can assign a Currency format to a cell to add a dollar sign, a decimal point followed by two zeros, and, if appropriate, a comma to separate thousands in the number in the cell. Applying the Currency format to a cell changes the appearance of the cell on the worksheet but does not change the number stored in the cell.

When performing calculations, Excel uses the value stored in the cell, not the number that appears on the worksheet. For example, if you type 123.456 in cell A1 and then apply the Currency format, Excel adds the dollar sign and changes the appearance of the number in the worksheet to $123.46, rounding cell A1 in the process. However, if you use cell A1 in a calculation, Excel uses 123.456, the value stored in the cell, not the rounded value that appears in the worksheet.

MASTER IT

Can I replace the dollar sign with another currency symbol?

▼ Yes. From the Number tab of the Format Cells dialog box, you can replace the dollar sign with another symbol of your choice. You can also control the number of decimal places that Excel displays and the way Excel displays negative numbers. Select the cell and click ▣ in the Number group.

Assign a Currency Format

1. Click a cell containing a number.
2. Click the Home tab.
   - The number appears in the cell and in the Formula Bar.
   - Excel assigns the number a General format.

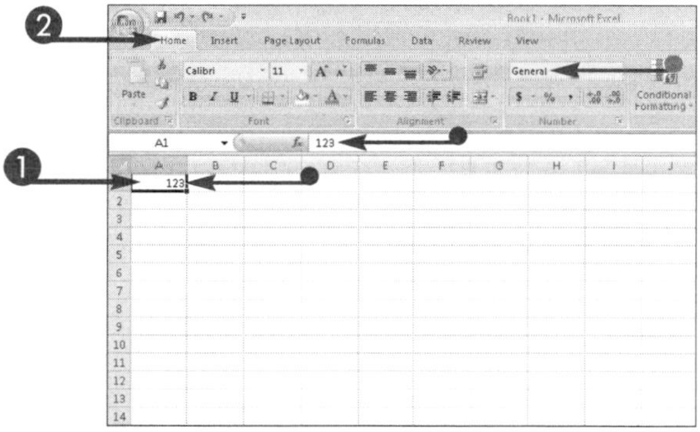

3. Click ▣.
4. Click Currency.
   - Excel adds a dollar sign, a decimal point, and two zeros to the number in the worksheet.
   - Excel changes the appearance only in the cell, not in the Formula Bar.

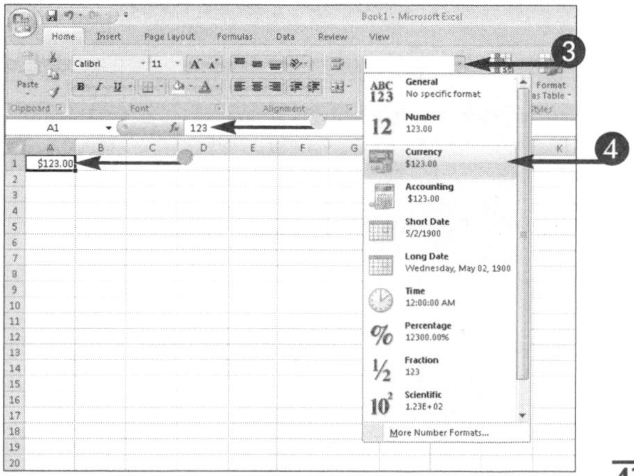

Assign an Accounting Format

To retain accounting standards for appearance, you can apply the Accounting format to a cell. Like the Currency format, the Accounting format adds a dollar sign, a decimal followed by two zeros, and, if appropriate, a comma to separate thousands in the number in the cell. However, accounting standards prefer to line up dollar signs and decimal points in columns of numbers. To achieve this, the dollar sign appears left-justified while the rest of the number appears right-justified. Also, typically, on financial statements, only the first number and the column total display a dollar sign.

Applying the Accounting format to a cell changes the appearance of the cell on the worksheet but does not change the number stored in the cell. When performing calculations, Excel uses the value stored in the cell, not the number that appears on the worksheet. For example, if you type 123.456 in cell A1 and then apply the Accounting format, Excel adds the dollar sign and changes the appearance of the number in the worksheet to display $123.46, rounding cell A1 in the process. However, if you use cell A1 in a calculation, Excel uses 123.456, the value stored in the cell, not the rounded value that appears in the worksheet.

Assign an Accounting Format

1. Click a cell containing a number.
2. Click the Home tab.
   - The number appears in the cell and in the Formula Bar.
   - Excel assigns the number a General format.

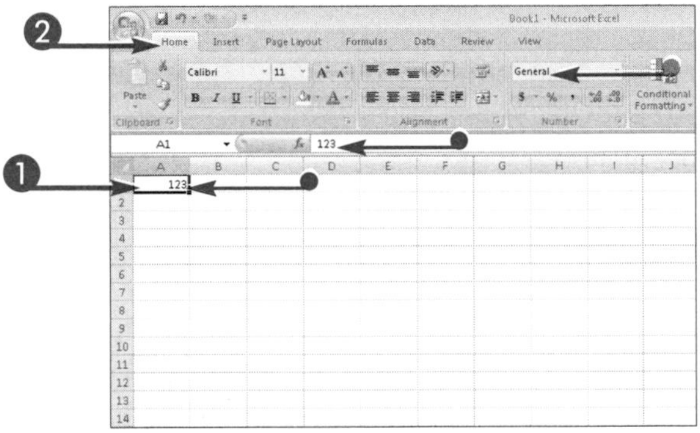

3. Click ▾.
4. Click Accounting.
   - Excel adds a left-justified dollar sign, a decimal point, and two zeros to the number in the worksheet.
   - Excel changes the appearance only in the cell, not in the Formula Bar.

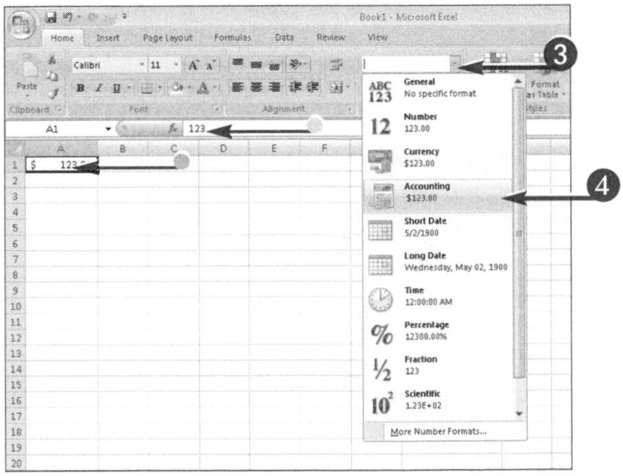

Assign a Short Date Format

You can type numbers and format their appearance as dates. Excel treats dates as serial numbers so that you can easily perform calculations using dates. The serial number 1 corresponds to January 1, 1900, the serial number 2 corresponds to January 2, 1900, and so on. Excel supports serial dates up to 2,958,465, which corresponds to December 31, 9999. When you assign the Short Date format to a cell, Excel displays the date using the format that matches the Short Date format stored in the Regional and Language Options dialog box.

You can also type dates directly into a cell. If you use a format that corresponds to the date formats stored in the Windows Regional and Language Options dialog box, Excel automatically assigns a date format to the cell and displays the date format in both the cell and the Formula Bar. However, in the background, Excel converts the date to its serial value for calculations.

MASTER IT

The serial number 1 corresponds to January 1, 1904 in a workbook I received from an Excel for Mac user. Why does this occur?

▼ Excel for Mac bases serial dates on 1904 instead of 1900. Excel for Windows supports both for compatibility. You can change the date system for the workbook by changing Excel options. For more information, see Chapter 30.

Assign a Short Date Format

1. Click a cell containing a number.
2. Click the Home tab.
   - The number appears in the cell and in the Formula Bar.
   - Excel assigns the number a General format.

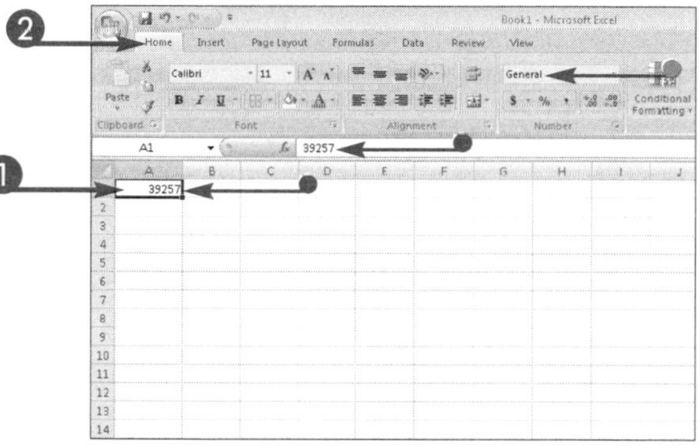

3. Click ▾.
4. Click Short Date.
   - Excel displays a date format in the worksheet.
   - Excel also changes the appearance in the Formula Bar.

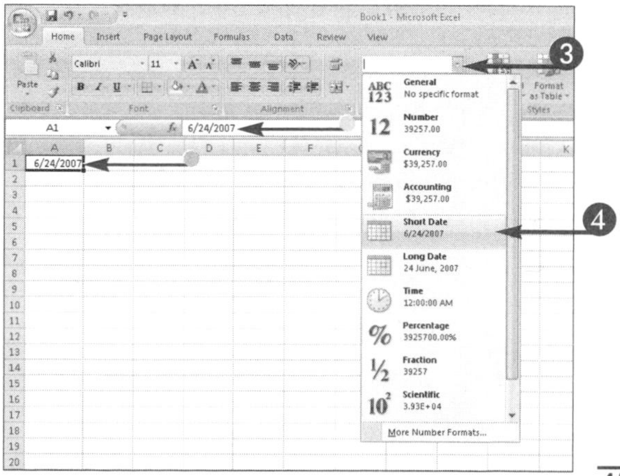

Assign a Long Date Format

You can type numbers and format their appearance as dates. When you assign the Long Date format to a cell, Excel displays the date using the format that matches the Long Date format stored in the Regional and Language Options dialog box.

Although this section shows you how to apply a Long Date format to an existing number, you can also type dates directly into a cell. If you use a format that corresponds to the date formats stored in the Regional and Language Options dialog box, Excel automatically assigns a date format to the cell and displays the Long Date format in the worksheet and the Short Date format in the Formula Bar.

If you type a date in a format that Windows does not recognize as a date, Excel does not treat the entry as a date. For example, suppose that your regional settings show the Long Date format as dd MMMM, yyyy. Excel expects you to enter June 24, 2007 as 24-Jun-2007. If you enter June 24, 2007, Excel applies a General format and does not treat the date as a date. You will therefore not be able to use the date in calculations.

Assign a Long Date Format

1. Click a cell containing a number.
2. Click the Home tab.
   - The number appears in the cell and in the Formula Bar.
   - Excel assigns the number a General format.

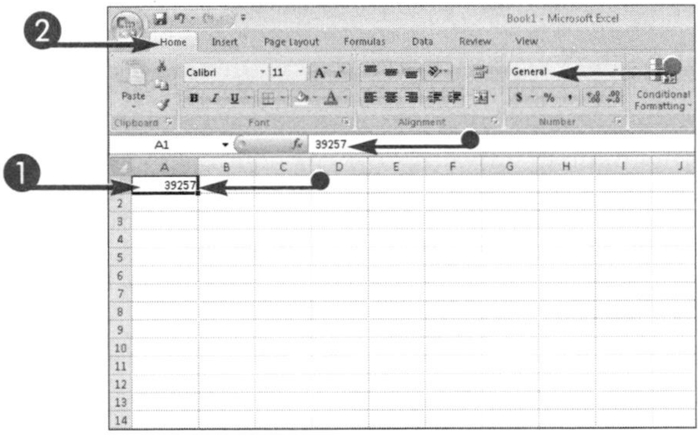

3. Click ▾.
4. Click Long Date.
   - Excel displays a date format in the worksheet.
   - Excel displays the Short Date format in the Formula Bar.

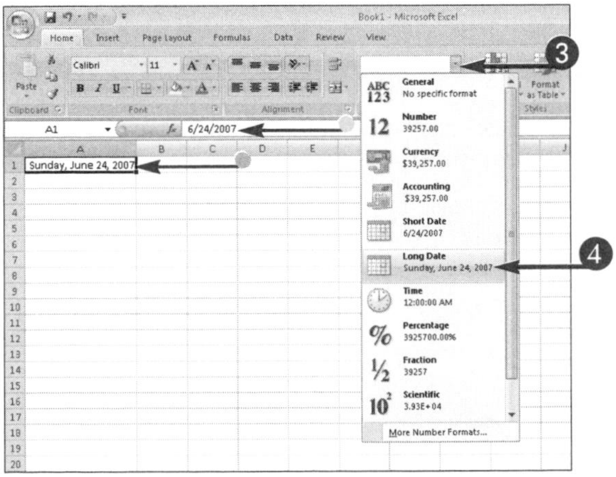

Assign a Time Format

You can type numbers and format their appearance as times. Excel displays the time using the format that matches the Time format stored in the Regional and Language Options dialog box.

Excel treats any decimal value between 0 and 1 that you enter as a serial number to make it easy for you to perform calculations using dates. The serial number 0 corresponds to midnight, the serial number .00001 corresponds to 12:00:01 AM, and the serial number .99999 corresponds to 11:59:59 PM. When you assign the Time format to a cell, Excel displays the date using the format that matches the Time format stored in the Regional and Language Options dialog box.

If you apply a time format to a number larger than 1 that also includes decimals, such as 1.2345, then Excel displays a combination of the date and time corresponding to the number.

MASTER IT

When I enter a time, why does Excel fill the cell with number signs (#) instead of displaying the time?

▼ The column containing the cell is not wide enough for Excel to display the time. You can easily widen the column to display the time. See Chapter 6 for more details.

Assign a Time Format

1. Click a cell containing a number.
2. Click the Home tab.
   - The number appears in the cell and in the Formula Bar.
   - Excel assigns the number a General format.

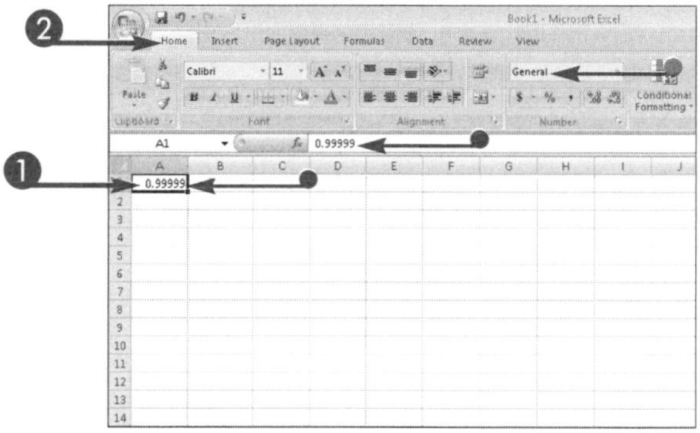

3. Click ▾.
4. Click Time.
   - Excel displays the Time format in the worksheet.
   - Excel also displays the Time format in the Formula Bar.

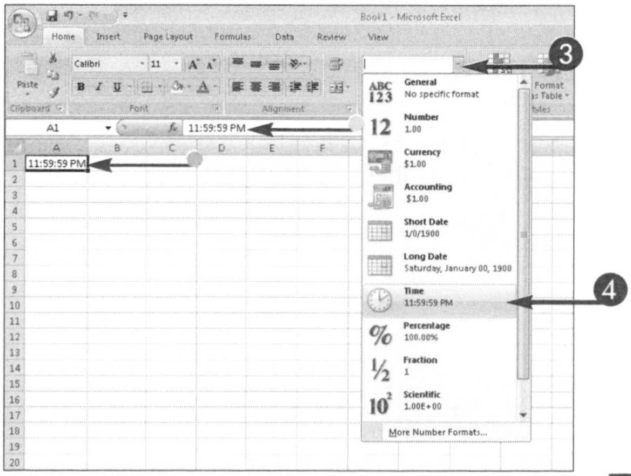

Assign a General Format

To assign the default formatting that Excel assigns initially to all cells, you can apply the General format. When you use the General format, Excel displays the number as you enter it, with the following exceptions:

- Excel drops any trailing zeros in whole numbers, or leading zeros; for example, Excel stores both 0123 and 123.00 as 123.
- Excel inserts a leading zero before a decimal without a whole number; for example, Excel stores .123 as 0.123.
- Excel truncates decimal places when a number contains too many digits to display using the current column width.
- Excel converts whole numbers to scientific notation when the number contains too many digits to display using the current column width.

In most cases, the Formula Bar displays the General format, while the worksheet displays the new format. You can reinstate the initial cell formatting by reassigning the General format so that both the worksheet and the Formula Bar display the General format.

You can also apply the General format to a cell containing a date or a time to display the serial number associated with a date or a time.

Assign a General Format

1. Click a cell formatted using any format other than General.
2. Click the Home tab.
   - The number's underlying format appears in the Formula Bar.

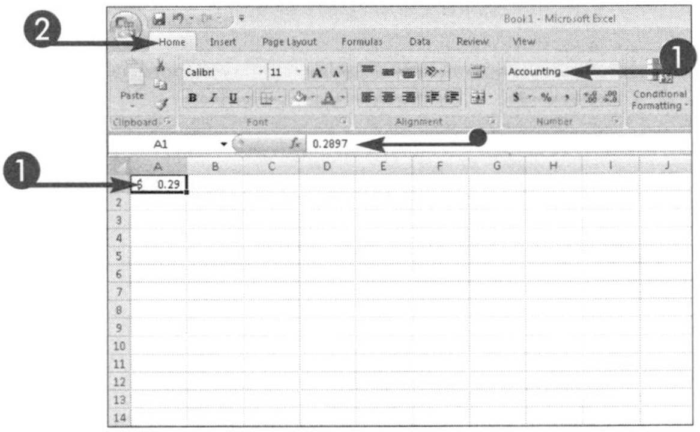

3. Click ▾.
4. Click General.
   - Excel displays the General format in both the worksheet and the Formula Bar.

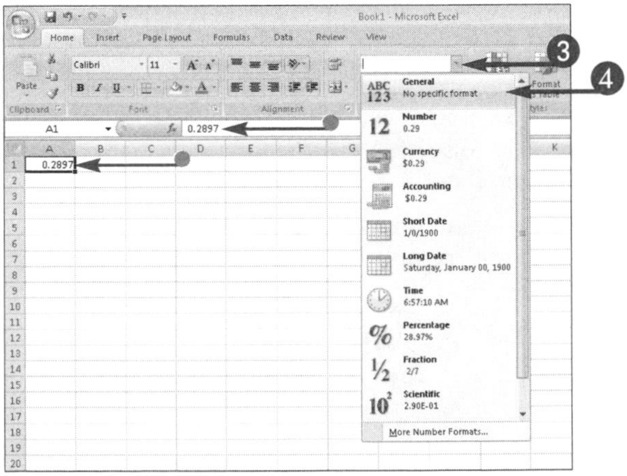

Assign a Percentage Format

You can display a decimal number between 0 and 1 as a percentage. For example, you may want to show the percentage of total sales associated with each product that you sell. In the worksheet, Excel moves the decimal point two places to the right, rounds the number to display only two decimal places to the right of the decimal point, and displays a percentage sign (%) at the end of the number. In the Formula Bar, Excel moves the decimal point two places to the right and displays a percentage sign at the end of the number, but retains all of the digits of the original number.

When you add up a series of numbers formatted as percentages, Excel uses the value shown in the Formula Bar. Due to rounding, you may think that Excel has added the numbers incorrectly, but if you increase the number of decimal places that display, you will find that Excel has added the numbers correctly.

MASTER IT

Can I assign a percentage format to a number greater than 1?

▼ Yes. Excel allows you to apply the format, but the value is meaningless, because 1 represents 100 percent. For example, you cannot sell more than 100 percent of the products you own.

Assign a Percentage Format

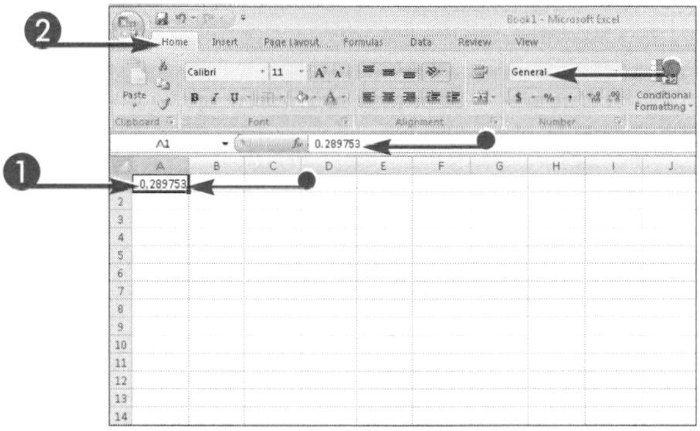

1. Click a cell containing a number between 0 and 1.
2. Click the Home tab.
   - The number appears in the cell and in the Formula Bar.
   - Excel assigns the number a General format.

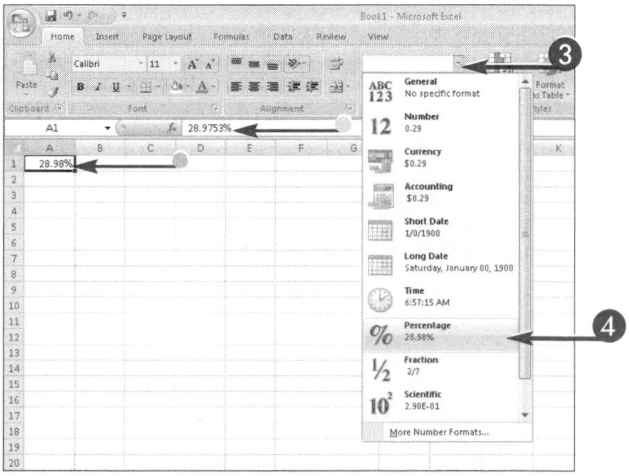

3. Click ▾.
4. Click Percentage.
   - Excel displays the Percentage format in the worksheet.
   - Excel also displays the Percentage format in the Formula Bar, but retains all of the original decimal places.

Assign a Fraction Format

You can display the contents of a cell as a fraction. In the worksheet, Excel displays the fractional equivalent of the value displayed in the Formula Bar. By default, Excel rounds the value in the cell to display one-digit fractions. For example, if you format .5342 as a fraction, Excel displays 1/2 in the cell. You can change the number of digits Excel displays in the fraction to either two or three digits. For example, if you set the display to two-digit fractions for .5432, then Excel displays 39/73, and if you set the display to three digits, then Excel displays 164/307.

When you add up a series of numbers formatted as fractions, Excel uses the value shown in the Formula Bar. Due to rounding, you may think that Excel has added the numbers incorrectly, but, if you reformat the numbers using the General format, you will find that Excel has added the numbers correctly.

MASTER IT

Why does January 2 appear as 2-Jan when I type 1/2 in cell A1?

▼ Unless you format cell A1 as a fraction, Excel assumes that you are entering a date and matches your entry to the closest date format stored in the Regional and Language Options dialog box.

Assign a Fraction Format

1. Click a cell containing a number.
2. Click the Home tab.
   - The number appears in the cell and in the Formula Bar.
   - Excel assigns the number a General format.

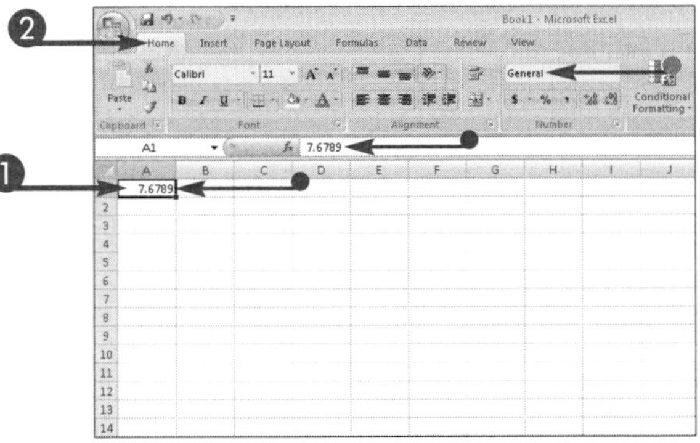

3. Click .
4. Click Fraction.
   - Excel displays a fraction form of the number in the worksheet.
   - Excel displays the decimal format of the number in the Formula Bar, retaining all of the original decimal places.

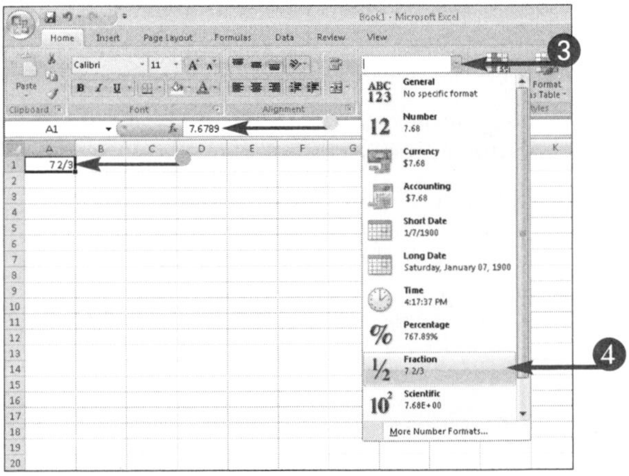

Assign a Scientific Format

You can display a number using the Scientific format. When you use the Scientific format, Excel displays the number using exponential notation. Exponential notation provides a shorthand way for scientists to write a large number such as 456,000,000 using fewer characters. In scientific notation, 456,000,000 would appear as 4.56 x 10^8 or 4.56E+08. Excel uses the second format.

A number in scientific notation has three parts. The first part, the coefficient, must always be greater than or equal to 1 and less than 10. For example, 4.56 is the coefficient in 4.56E+08. The second part, the base, must always be 10 in scientific notation. In the format Excel uses, 10 does not appear but is implied. The third part is called the exponent. In 4.56E+08, 8 is the exponent. To write a number in scientific notation, you create the coefficient by placing the decimal after the first non-zero digit. You retain the first two values to the right of the decimal point and represent all the rest of the values with an exponent. To find the exponent, count the number of places from the decimal to the end of the number. In 456,000,000 there are eight places after the first digit of 4, and so, the exponent is 8.

Assign a Scientific Format

1. Click a cell containing a number.
2. Click the Home tab.
   - The number appears in the cell and in the Formula Bar.
   - Excel assigns the number a General format.

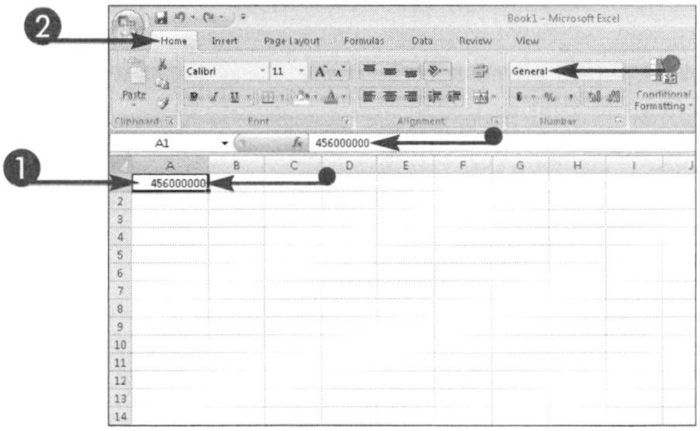

3. Click ▾.
4. Click Scientific.
   - Excel displays the number in scientific notation in the worksheet.
   - Excel displays the original form of the number in the Formula Bar.

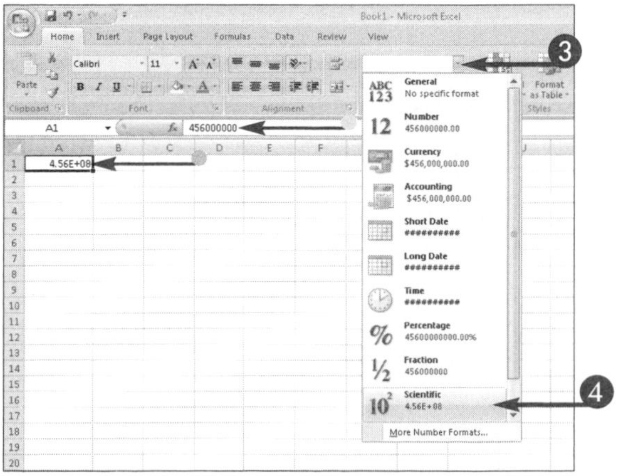

Assign a Text Format

If you have numbers in a worksheet that you do not want to include in calculations, you can format them as text. For example, suppose that your worksheet includes information about inventory parts that you sell, and your part numbers are exactly that — numbers. However, they are not numbers that you want to include in calculations. You can format them as text, as Excel does not perform mathematical calculations on the cells that use the Text format.

Before you format a cell using the Text format, any number in the cell appears right-aligned because Excel right-aligns numbers in cells by default. Similarly, Excel left-aligns text in cells by default. As a result, when you apply the Text format to a number, Excel left-aligns the number in the cell. You can use this alignment as a visual cue that a cell has been formatted using the Text format. Again, this left-alignment would work very well in the example workbook where you happen to use part numbers and those part numbers do not represent numerical values.

This section shows you how to apply a text format after you type a number, but you can also apply the format before you type.

Assign a Text Format

1 Click a cell containing a number that you want to format as text.

The number appears right-aligned in the cell.

2 Click the Home tab.

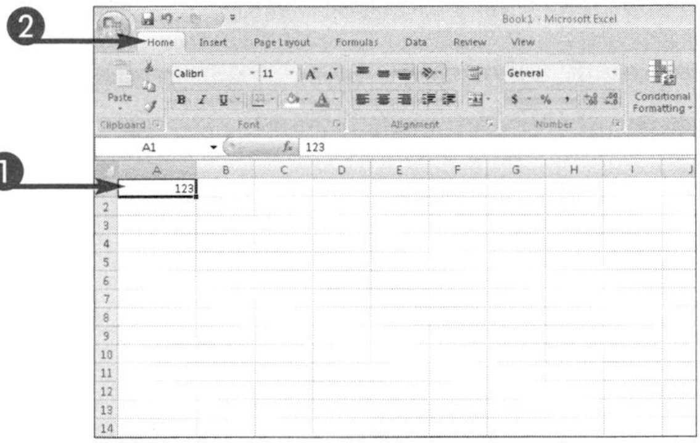

3 Click ▾.

4 Click More Number Formats.

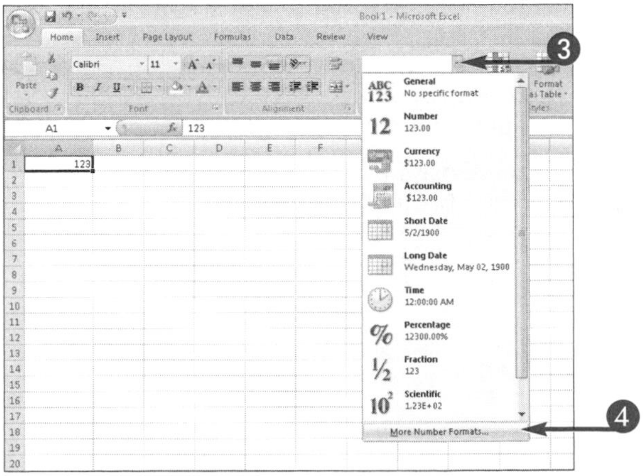

The Format Cells dialog box appears.

5 Click the Number tab.

6 Click Text.

7 Click OK.

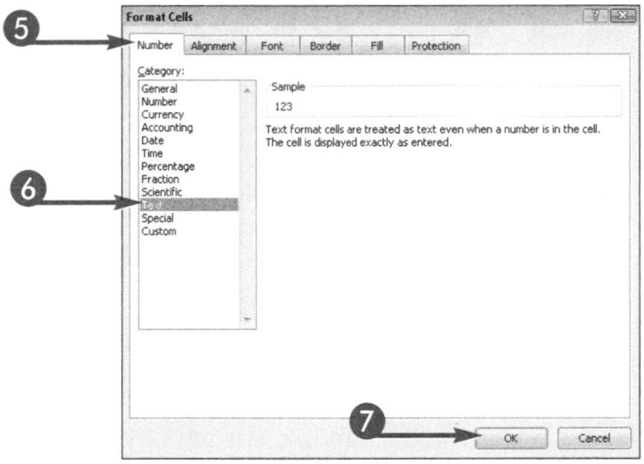

- Excel formats the number in the selected cell as text.
- The number appears left-aligned in the worksheet.
- The number's appearance does not change in the Formula Bar.

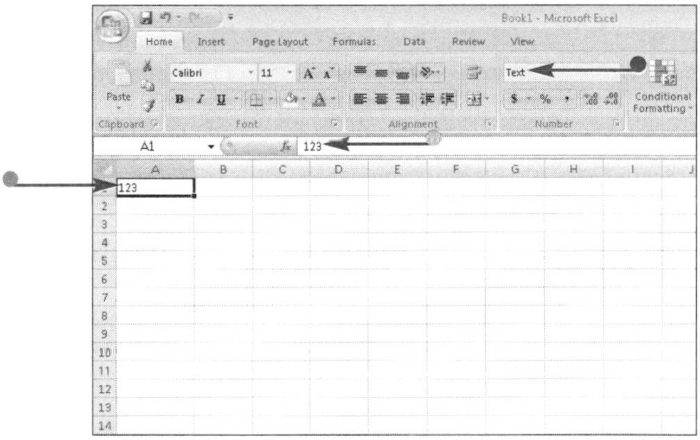

MASTER IT

Can I change the format of a number from text back to a numeric format?

▼ If the number was originally entered as a number, you can simply select a numeric format; Excel starts treating the cell contents as a value and includes it in calculations. However, if the number was not entered as a number, selecting a numeric format will not help. Instead, you must change the text to a numeric value. This situation often occurs when you import data into Excel. See Chapter 15 for details on changing text to values.

Can I include decimal points in numbers formatted as text?

▼ Yes, but you must type the decimal in the number because the Text format does not affect decimal points in any way. When you store a number containing decimal places as text, Excel assumes that you made a mistake and meant to store the number as a number; as a result, Excel displays a Smart Tag. When you point the mouse at the Smart Tag, Excel tells you that the cell contains a number stored as text. You can click the Smart Tag and, from the options displayed, select Ignore Error.

Assign a Special Format

You can use any of Excel's four Special formats to format numbers as five-digit Zip codes, nine-digit Zip codes, phone numbers, or social security numbers. These useful formats can save you from having to type special characters such as parentheses and dashes that are required in these formats.

Suppose that you type a four-digit number, such as 1234, into a cell and then apply a Special format. In the Formula Bar, the number's appearance does not change. What happens in the worksheet depends on the Special format you select:

- If you select the five-digit Zip code Special format, Excel displays a leading zero before the four digits, formatting the number to look like 01234, a five-digit Zip code.
- If you select the nine-digit Zip code Special format, Excel displays five zeros and then a dash followed by the four digits you typed, formatting the number to look like 00000-1234, a nine-digit Zip code.
- If you select the phone number Special format, Excel displays -1234, treating your number like the last four digits of a phone number.
- If you select the Social Security number Special format, Excel adds five zeros and two dashes, formatting the number to look like 000-00-1234, a social security number.

Assign a Special Format

1. Click a cell containing a number that you want to format.
2. Click the Home tab.

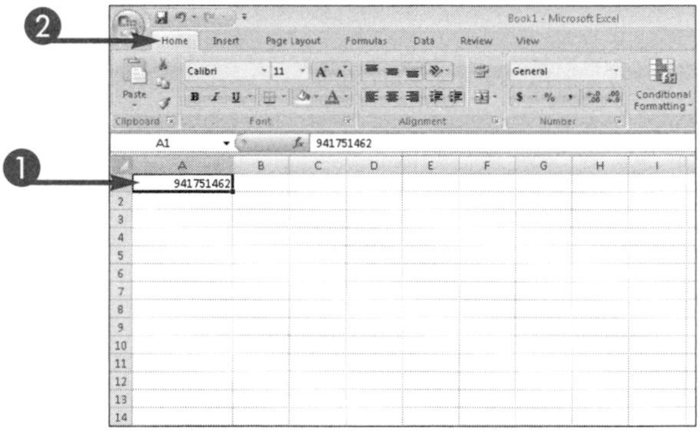

3. Click ▾.
4. Click More Number Formats.

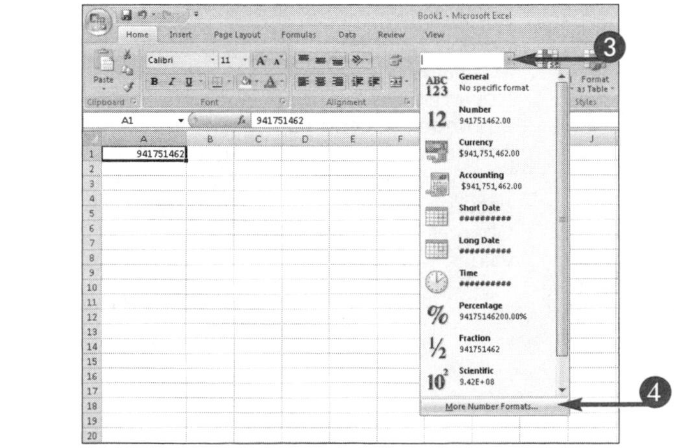

The Format Cells dialog box appears.

5 Click the Number tab.

6 Click Special.

7 Click a format.

8 Click OK.

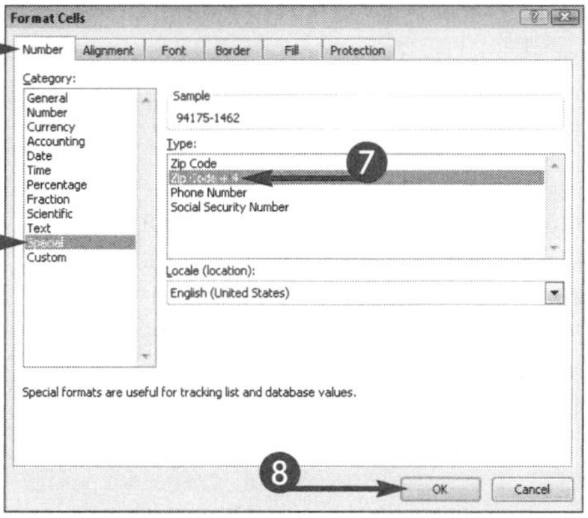

- Excel formats the number in the selected cell.
- Excel adjusts the column width for the format, if necessary, and the number appears right-aligned in the worksheet.
- The number's appearance does not change in the Formula Bar.

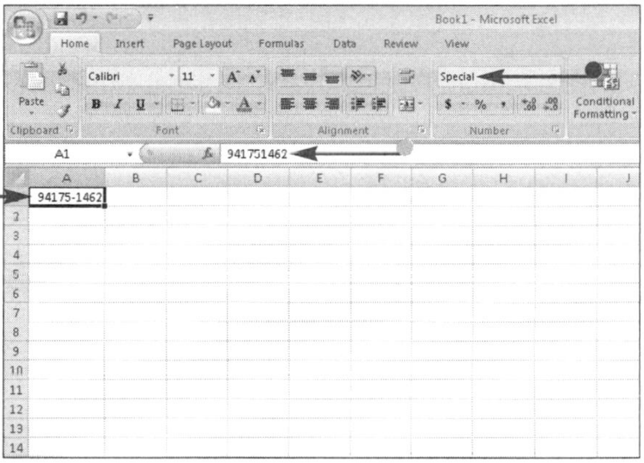

MASTER IT

If I supply a ten-digit phone number, how does Excel display the number?

▼ Using the English (United States) locale format, Excel displays the first three digits, the area code, in parentheses, and includes a space before displaying the next three digits. Excel then inserts a dash and displays the last four digits. As a result, a phone number of 1234567890 appears as (123) 456-7890.

If I include the leading 1 before a ten-digit phone number, how does Excel display the number?

▼ Excel does not recognize an 11-digit phone number. If you include a leading 1 in the English (United States) locale format, Excel adds the leading 1 into the area code portion of the number, which appears in parentheses. As a result, your area code will appear to be four digits in length.

What is the Locale list for?

▼ Different locales have different Special formats. For example, a Canadian phone number Special format does not display the area code in parentheses followed by a space like a United States phone number Special format does. The English (Canada) locale also has a Social Insurance Number format that the English (United States) locale does not.

Assign a Custom Format

When you cannot find a number format that matches your needs, you can create your own custom format. For example, suppose that you need to enter a series of part numbers in a workbook. Your part numbers are all preceded by an alphabetic prefix, and the alphabetic prefix represents a certain group of parts; as a result, several part numbers will have the same prefix. You can save some typing if you create a Custom format that applies the prefix to numbers that you enter. Then, you enter only the numeric portion of the number. When you apply the Custom format, Excel adds the alphabetic prefix for you.

You can type the Custom format to create it, or you can use an existing format as a model and modify it to suit your needs. Excel uses characters as placeholders. For example, #, 0, and ? all represent a digit placeholder. The # sign displays only significant zeros. The 0 character displays insignificant zeros if a number has fewer numbers than zeros. The ? character adds spaces for insignificant zeros on each side of the decimal point to help align decimal points. An underscore (_) leaves a space in the format.

Assign a Custom Format

1. Click a cell containing a number that you want to format.
2. Click the Home tab.
3. Click ▾.
4. Click More Number Formats.

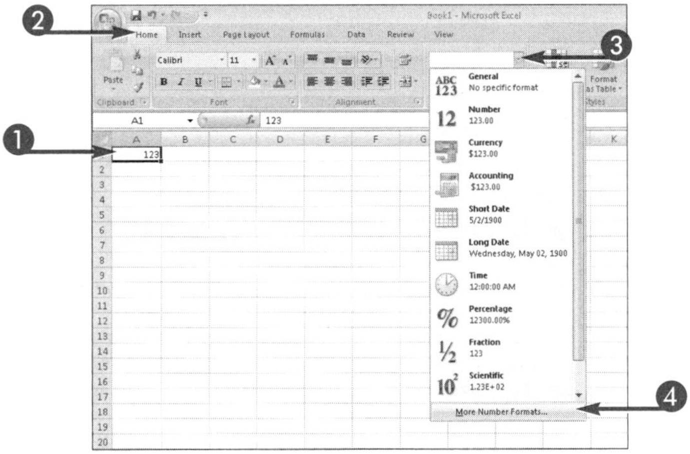

The Format Cells dialog box appears.

5. Click the Number tab.
6. Click the category that most closely matches the format you need.

   If no format matches, you can click General.

7. Click Custom.

- In the Type list box, Excel fills in placeholder characters for the format you selected in Step 6.

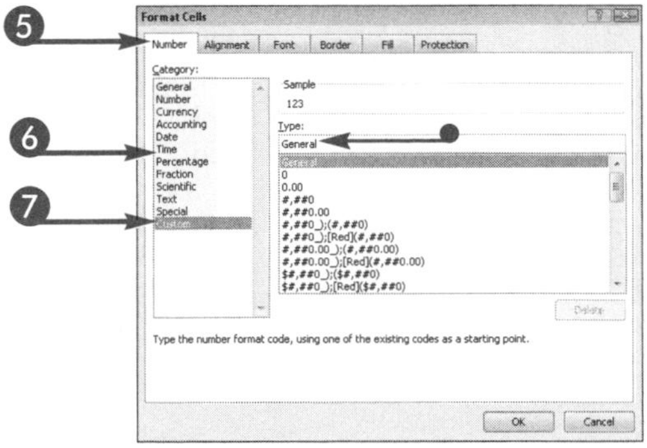

8. Modify the characters in the Type field to represent your format.
9. Click OK.

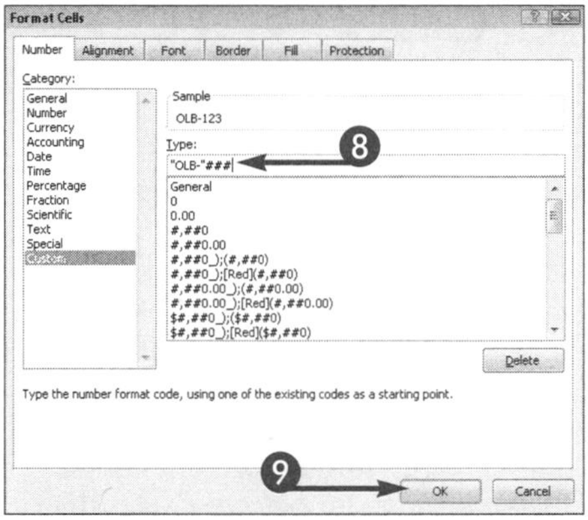

- Excel assigns the Custom format to the selected cell.
- Excel adjusts the column width for the format, if necessary, and the number appears right-aligned in the worksheet.

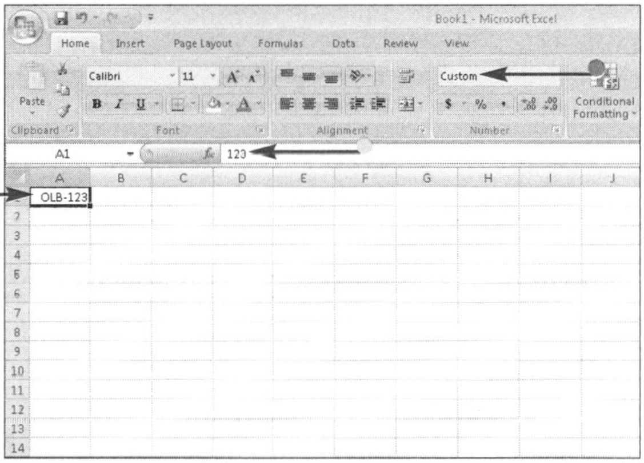

MASTER IT

The number's appearance does not change in the Formula Bar. What happens if I include a dollar sign ($) in a Custom format?

▼ Excel displays the actual character when you include a dollar sign ($), a dash (-), a plus sign (+), parentheses (), a slash (/), or a colon (:) in a Custom format. You can include fixed text in a Custom format if you enclose the text in quotation marks.

Can I use a Custom format that I create in any workbook?

▼ Yes. Excel stores the Custom format in the workbook where you create it. However, you can copy a cell that uses the format from the workbook in which you created the format to another workbook, and Excel adds the Custom format to the other workbook.

How do I create a Custom format that distinguishes between positive and negative numbers?

▼ Your Custom format can have up to four sections so that the format can accommodate positive numbers, negative numbers, zero values, and text. Create the format for each section and end the section with a semicolon. When you create two sections for your Custom format, Excel applies the first section to positive numbers and zeros, and the second section to negative numbers.

Fill Cells with Color

You can add color to the background of cells to call attention to those cells. Color is effective when you view your workbook on-screen, save it to a PDF or XPS file, or print it using a color printer. However, applying color when you intend to print a workbook to a non-color printer can make reading more difficult.

You can select any of ten standard colors or ten theme colors. Each theme color also offers you five variations of the theme color, ranging from 80 percent lighter than the main theme color to 50 percent darker than the main theme color. As a result, you can select a color from 60 possible theme colors. Once you select a color, it appears on the Fill Color button, and so you can quickly apply the color again.

MASTER IT

If I want to use a black-and-white printer, is there a way to call attention to a cell?

▼ Yes. You can add a pattern to the cell background. Click ◰ in the Font group to display the Format Cells dialog box. Click the Fill tab and then click the Pattern Style ▾ to select a pattern. Be sure that you select a light pattern that will not make the text in the cell illegible.

Fill Cells with Color

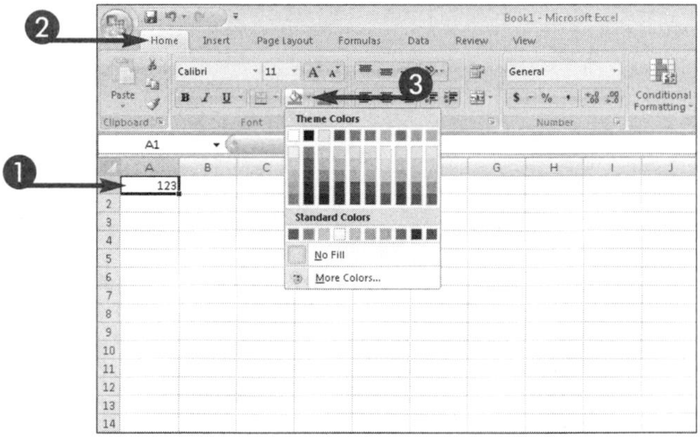

❶ Select the cells that you want to fill with color.

***Note:** See Chapter 4 for details on selecting cells.*

❷ Click the Home tab.

❸ Click ▾ to display the list of available colors.

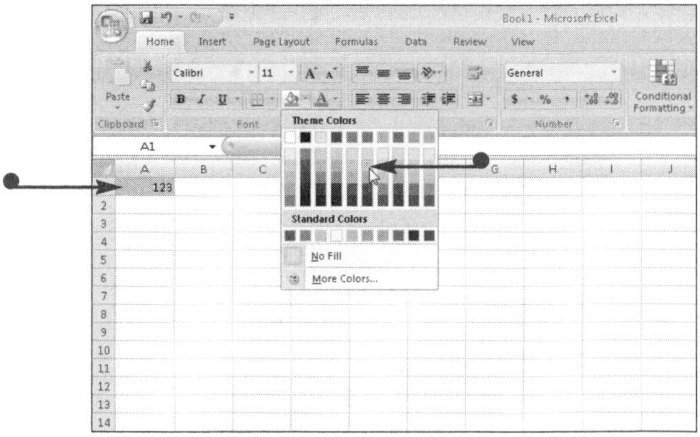

- As you pass the mouse pointer over a color, Excel fills the selected cells with that color.

❹ Click a color.

Excel applies the color to the selected cells.

The color you select remains on the Fill Color button (🖌) so that you can just click the button to apply the color to another cell.

Indent Text within Cells

You can indent characters in cells to help improve readability in a worksheet. For example, suppose that you have a worksheet that shows sales for two regions, North and South, for three products. If you indent the product names underneath the region name, the worksheet will be easier to read.

Each time you indent the contents of a cell, Excel indents the contents from the left edge of the cell by one character. You can increase the indentation repeatedly, as well as decrease the indentation.

You can indent cells containing numbers. If you do, Excel changes the right alignment of the number and moves it so that it appears one character from the left edge of the cell. Numbers in columns do not appear aligned, and so you should exercise caution if you decide to indent cells containing numbers.

MASTER IT

If I indent a cell containing a number, does Excel stop treating the number as a value?

▼ No, Excel continues to treat the number as a number, and you can use the number in calculations. Only the number's appearance in the worksheet changes. Its appearance in the Formula Bar remains the same.

Indent Text within Cells

1. Select the cells that you want to indent.

Note: *See Chapter 4 for details on selecting cells.*

2. Click the Home tab.
3. Click the Increase Indent button (▤).

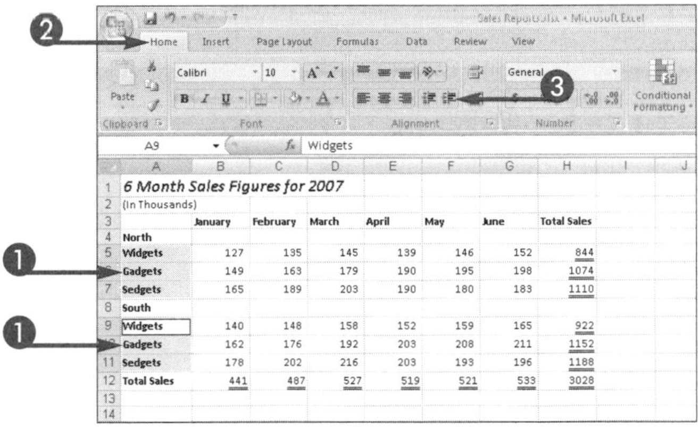

- Excel indents the text in the selected cells by one character.
- You can click the Decrease Indent button (▤) to move text closer to the left edge of the cell.

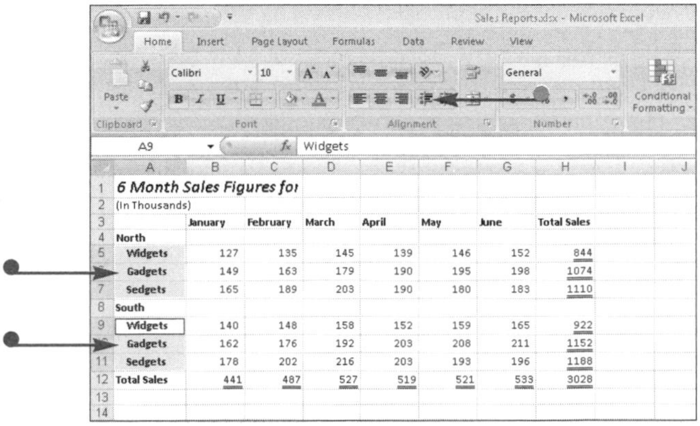

Align Cell Content Vertically

If your workbook contains cells that are taller than normal, you can align the information in a cell with the top or bottom edge of the cell, or you can align the information so that it appears centered between the top and bottom of the cell. You can also set a vertical alignment that justifies text or distributes text evenly in the allotted vertical space of the cell.

Aligning information vertically in a cell provides a pleasing aesthetic effect. You will not notice any difference in appearance if you vertically align text in a row that is not taller than normal, because Excel has no vertical space over which to align the text. To change the height of a row, see Chapter 6.

MASTER IT

How can I set a vertical alignment that justifies text in the cell?

▼ You can select the cell and use settings in the Format Cells dialog box. Click the dialog box launcher in the Alignment group to open the Format Cells dialog box. Click the Alignment tab and then click the drop-down arrow beside the Vertical box to select Justify. Then click OK. To set a vertical alignment that distributes text evenly in the cell, select Distributed instead of Justify.

Align Cell Content Vertically

1. Click the cell you want to align.
2. Click the Home tab.
3. Click a vertical alignment button.

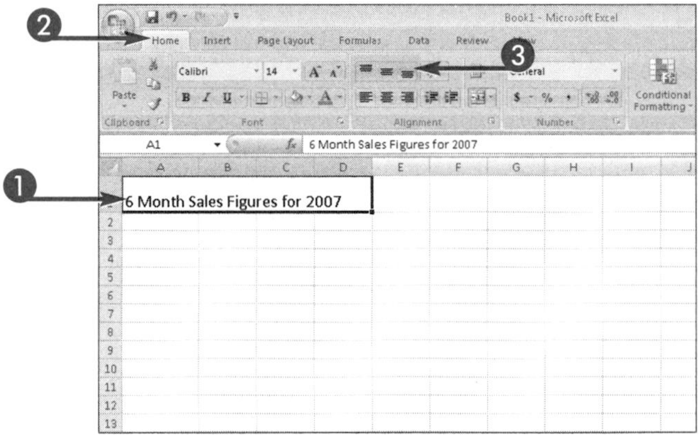

- You can click the Bottom Align button to align the information with the bottom of the cell.
- You can click the Middle Align button to align the information with the middle of the cell.
- You can click the Top Align button to align the information with the top of the cell.

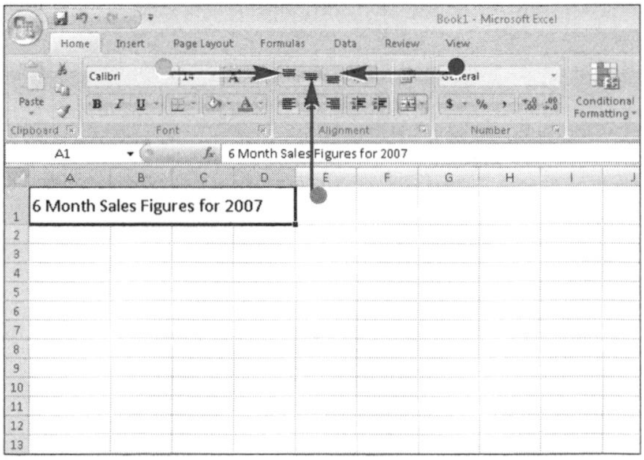

Align Cell Content Horizontally

If the information in a particular cell does not fill the cell, you can use buttons on the Ribbon to align the information to the left or right side of the cell, or center the information horizontally in the cell. You can also use the Format Cells dialog box to set horizontal alignments that justify the information between the right and left edges of the cell, center information over a selection of columns, or distribute the information across a selection of columns. If you choose General alignment, Excel aligns numbers on the right and text on the left edge of cells.

If the information fills the cell's width, you will not notice the effect of aligning horizontally. To see the effect, you can make cells in a column wider; see Chapter 6 for details.

MASTER IT

Is there an easy way to center text within a single cell?

▼ Yes. You can use the alignment buttons on the Ribbon to quickly align text. Click the Align Text Left button () to align text with the left edge of a cell. Click the Center Text button () to center text within a cell. Click the Align Text Right button () to align text with the right edge of a cell.

Align Cell Content Horizontally

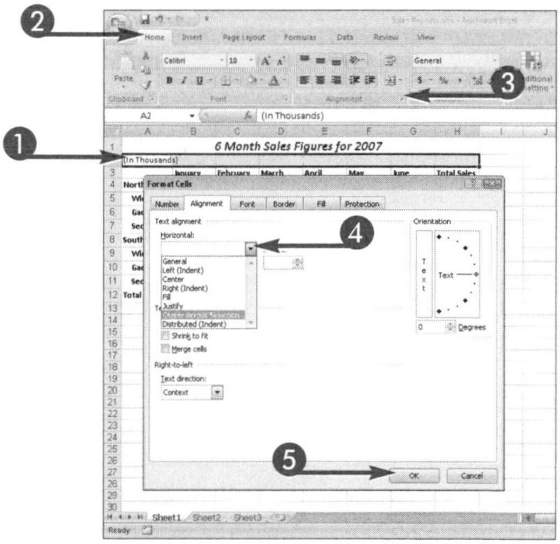

1. Select the cell you want to align.

   To center across columns, you should also select the cells in those columns.

Note: See Chapter 4 for details on selecting cells.

2. Click the Home tab.
3. Click the dialog box launcher for the Alignment group.

   The Format Cells dialog box appears.

4. Click the drop-down arrow to select an alignment.
5. Click OK.

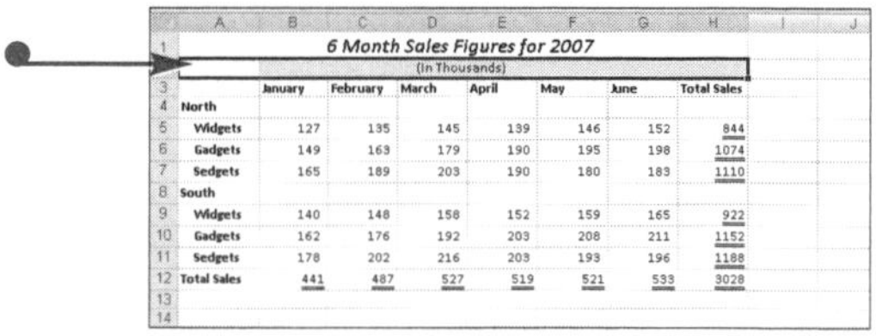

- Excel aligns the selection horizontally.

Wrap Text within Cells

If you have a lot of text to store in a single cell, you can wrap the text to make it appear on several lines within the cell. Suppose that you have a lot of text to store in cell A1. You have so much text, in fact, that the information spills over not only into cell B1, but also into cells C1 to K1. However, you also want to store information in cells B1 to K1, and so the long line of text will appear truncated on your worksheet unless you widen column A. But, making column A excessively wide will also make editing and printing your worksheet difficult.

To solve this problem, Excel wraps text to fit in one cell within the width of the column. Using the Wrap Text feature enables you to display all of the text in a paragraph-like form in a single cell without reducing the size of the text.

MASTER IT

Is there a way to make the text wrap but not into so many skinny lines?

▼ Yes. You can make the column wider, and Excel redistributes the wrapped text to fit within the wider space. The wrapped text will resemble a paragraph. For details on making a column wider, see Chapter 6.

Wrap Text within Cells

1. Click the cell containing the text you want to wrap.
2. Click the Home tab.
3. Click the Wrap Text button (▤).

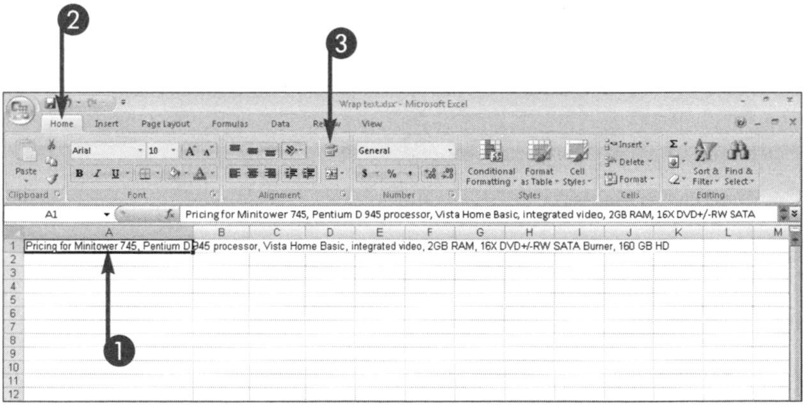

- Excel wraps the text onto several lines within the width of the column.

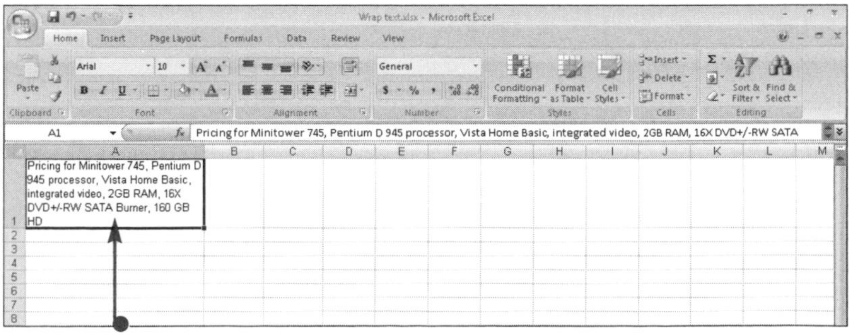

Shrink Text within Cells

If the text you need to fit in a cell spills slightly over, you can shrink the size of the text. For example, suppose that you have just enough text in cell A1 that two or three characters spill over into cell B1. If you shrink the text, you can fit all of the text into cell A1.

The Shrink Text feature reduces the size of the text in a selected cell just enough to fit the text into the cell. Although you can manually change the font size of the selected cell, you would need to guess the correct size. You can use the Shrink Text feature to take the guesswork out of reducing the text.

The Shrink Text feature does not work well if the text spills over the right edge of the cell by more than a few characters, because the shrunken text will become illegible unless you use a magnifying glass.

MASTER IT

If I do not want to shrink the text and I do not want to wrap the text, what else can I do?

▼ You can make the column wide enough to accommodate the text within the cell. For details on making a column wider, see Chapter 6.

Shrink Text within Cells

1. Click the cell containing the text you want to reduce in size.
2. Click the Home tab.
3. Click ▣ for the Alignment group.

   The Format Cells dialog box appears.
4. Click here (☐ changes to ☑).
5. Click OK.

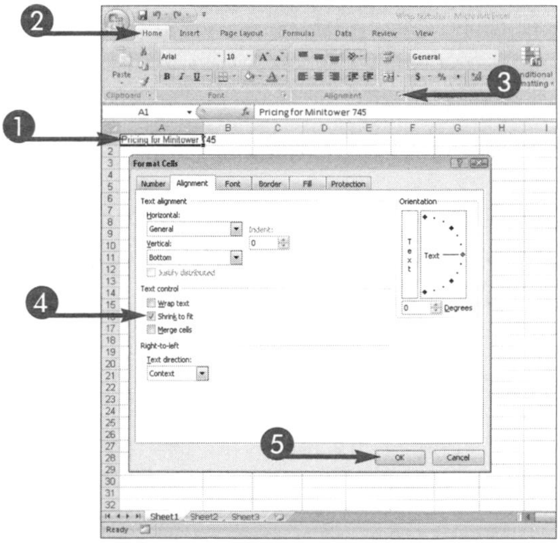

- Excel shrinks the information to fit within the cell.

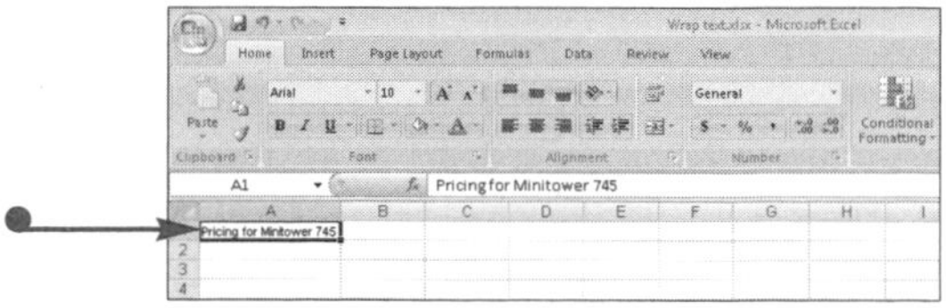

Rotate Text in Cells

You can rotate text within cells so that the text displays at various angles. Rotated text often works well on column headings, enhancing the appearance of your information by providing some novel variety.

From the Ribbon, you can rotate text 45 degrees counterclockwise or clockwise. You can also display text vertically within a cell instead of the usual horizontal display, and you can rotate text on its side so that it reads up or down instead of left to right.

You can control text orientation to a greater degree in the Format Cells dialog box. From the Alignment tab of the Format Cells dialog box, you can rotate text counterclockwise or clockwise by a degree that you designate, rather than the standard 45 degrees available on the Ribbon. You can also set text orientation to display text vertically within a cell like you can on the Ribbon.

The Format Cells dialog box contains another less commonly used orientation-related setting that enables you to set the direction of text so that it reads from left to right or right to left. This setting is used for languages such as Hebrew, which is read from right to left.

Rotate Text in Cells

Apply Basic Orientation

1. Click the cell containing the text you want to rotate.
2. Click the Home tab.
3. Click the Orientation button (⟋).
   - Excel displays the orientation choices.
4. Click an orientation.

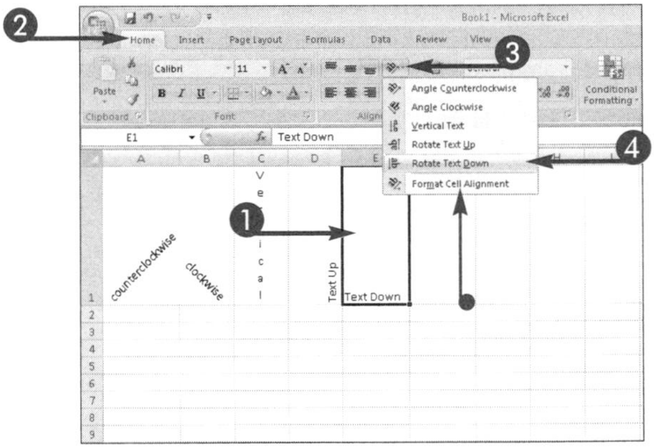

- Excel orients the text in the selected cell.

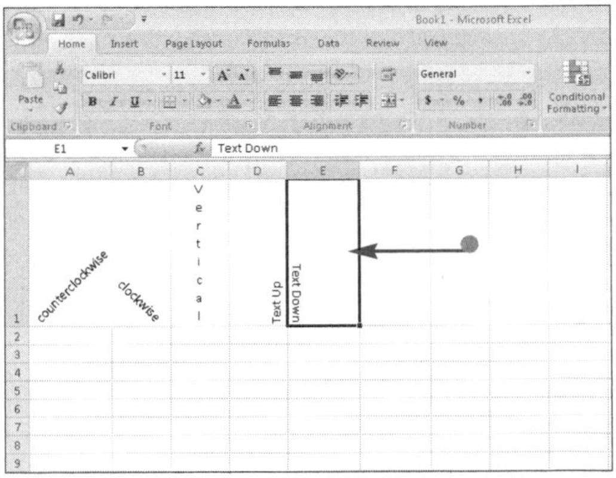

Control Orientation

1. Select the cell or cells containing the text you want to rotate.
2. Click the Home tab.
3. Click ▣ for the Alignment group.

   The Format Cells dialog box appears.
4. Type a degree of orientation here.
5. Click OK.

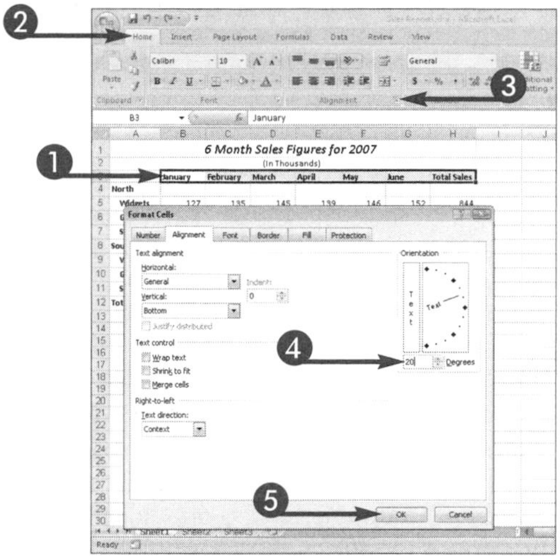

- Excel rotates the text in the selected cells by the amount you specified.

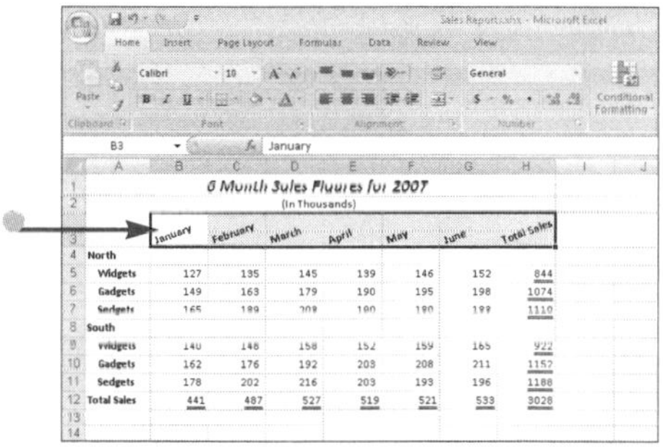

MASTER IT

Is there a way to use the dial in the Orientation section to set orientation?

▼ Yes, you can drag the pointer instead of typing degrees. When you type **0** in the Degrees field, the pointer appears horizontal. Dragging the pointer up sets a positive number in the Degrees field and results in text being rotated counterclockwise. Dragging it down sets a negative number in the Degrees field and results in text being rotated clockwise. You can also click the box in which "Text" appears vertically to set a vertical orientation for the text in the selected cell.

Why does nothing happen when I test the Right-to-Left Text Direction feature?

▼ This feature does not work unless you have language drivers installed on your computer that support a text direction other than the standard one for your version of Excel. For example, if you are using the English-language version of Excel, then you must install a language driver such as the Hebrew language driver to be able to change the text direction from left to right to right to left. You install language drivers using the same disc you used to install Excel.

Add Borders to Cells

You can display borders around cells to call attention to those cells. Excel enables you to select cells and then display a bottom, top, left, or right border, or you can display a border around all sides of the selected cells, which results in a grid-like display. You can also display a thin or thick border around the outside of the selected cells, effectively placing a box around the group of cells.

Excel also provides you with special options for bottom borders and both top and bottom borders. You can apply a double border or a thick border to the bottom of the selection, and you can combine a thin top border with a thin, thick, or double bottom border.

When you apply any of these borders, you should first select the cells around which you want to place them. Excel also enables you to draw borders by clicking and dragging. You can draw a thin outside border around cells, or you can draw a border grid through cells to display a border around all sides of the cells.

You can control the color and style of the border line that you add, whether you select cells and add a border or draw a border.

Add Borders to Cells

Apply a Border

1. Select the cells around which you want to place borders.

Note: See Chapter 4 for details on selecting cells.

2. Click the Home tab.
3. Click ▾ to display the borders you can apply.
4. Click a border.

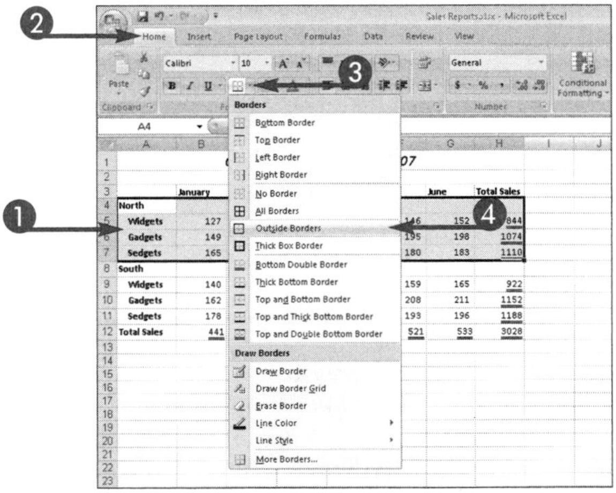

- Excel applies the border to the selected cells.

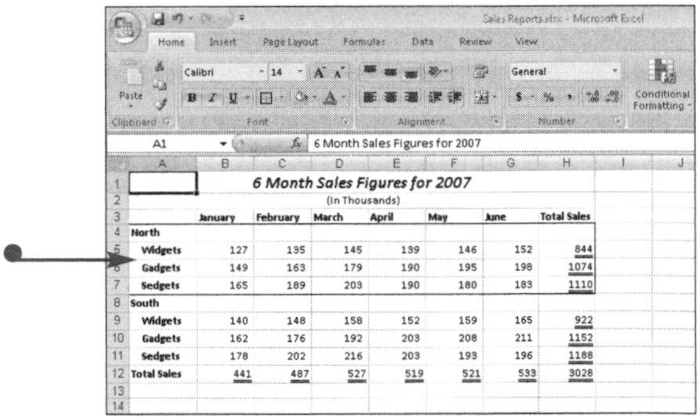

Draw a Border

1. Click the Home tab.
2. Click ▾ to display the borders you can apply.
3. Click Draw Border.

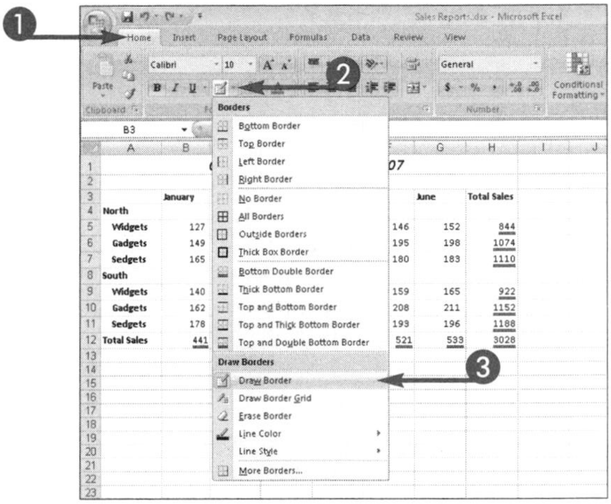

- The mouse pointer changes to ✎.

4. Click and drag through cells to draw a border around them.
5. Click the Draw Border Line button ( ) to stop drawing borders.

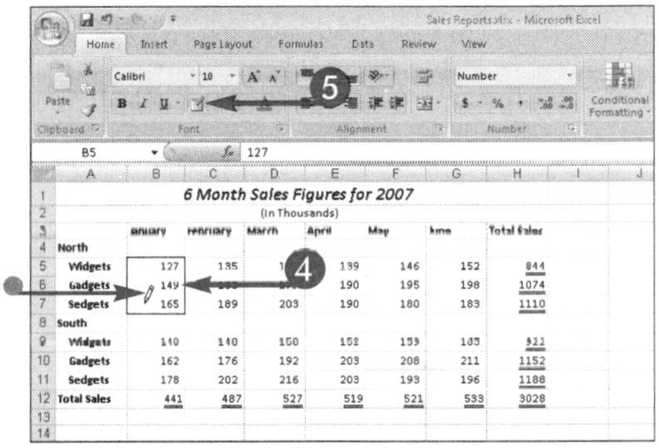

MASTER IT

How can I remove a border that I added to a cell?

▼ You can click the Home tab, then click ▾ beside , and then click Erase Border. Then click and drag over the cells that contain the border. When you release the mouse button, the border will be gone. You can also select the cells that have borders, click ▾ beside , and then click No Border.

Why does the appearance of the button I click to select a border keep changing?

▼ On the button, Excel displays the border that you last selected. When you make another selection from the drop-down menu that appears when you click ▾ beside the button, Excel changes the face of the button to match your latest selection. If you pause the mouse pointer over the button, you will notice that the tip you see matches the current version of the button face.

Is there a difference between All Borders and Draw Border Grid?

▼ There is no difference in the end result, because Excel displays borders around all sides of the cells involved. The difference lies in the method you use to apply the border. To use All Borders, you follow the steps in the subsection, "Apply a Border." To use Draw Border Grid, you follow the steps in the subsection, "Draw a Border."

Apply a Style

You can apply predefined styles to cells to enhance their appearance. Styles are collections of settings that often include font, font size, font color, cell background color, and cell borders. Excel displays predefined styles in a gallery divided into four groupings, but you can apply a style from any group, even if your selection does not match the group's characteristics.

From Excel's first group, you can apply styles to characterize cells as normal, bad, good, or neutral. From Excel's second group, you can apply styles to identify a cell's content as a calculation, input, output, explanatory, warning text, or a note. Using the styles in this group, you can also identify a cell as being linked to another cell or checking the content of another cell.

Excel's third group of styles is appropriate for cells that contain headings for titles in your worksheet. From Excel's fourth group, you can apply themed cell styles. You can select any of six theme colors. Each theme color also offers you four variations of the theme color, ranging from lighter to darker shades of the theme's color. As a result, you can select from 24 possible theme colors.

Apply a Style

1. Select the cells to which you want to apply a style.

Note: *See Chapter 4 for details on selecting cells.*

2. Click the Home tab.
3. Click Cell Styles to display the styles in the Style Gallery that you can apply.
4. Move the mouse pointer over a style.

   Excel displays a live preview of the selected text in that style.

5. Click a style.
   - Excel displays the selected cells in the style.

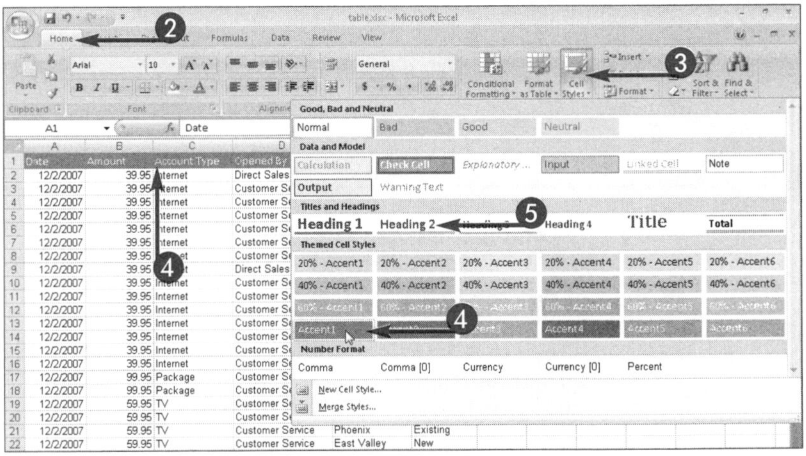

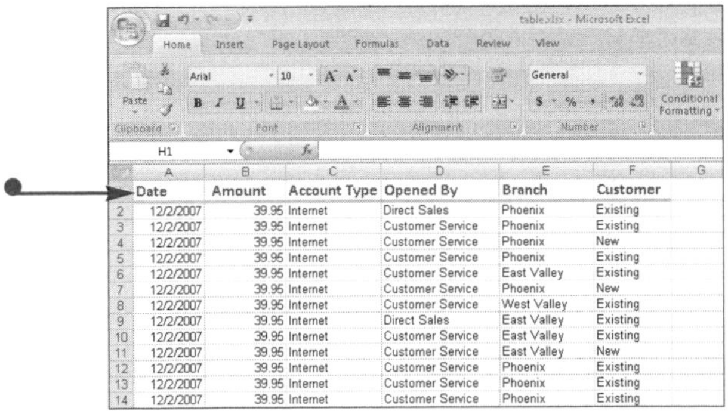

Create a Style

If you do not find a style in the Style Gallery that suits your needs, you can create a style of your own and add it to the Style Gallery. Although you can specify all of the style's settings when you create it, you will find it easiest to create a new style by applying all the formatting you want in the style to a cell in your worksheet. Then you can use the cell you formatted as the model for the style.

When you create a style, you can include any of the formatting available in the Format Cells dialog box, including font, font size, font color, cell background color, alignment, orientation, and borders.

MASTER IT

When I create a new style, is it available in all workbooks?

▼ No, Excel stores the style only in the workbook in which you created it. You can make the style available in another workbook by copying a cell formatted with the style into the other workbook. If you have many styles that you want to make available, you can also merge styles. See Chapter 7 for details on merging styles.

Create a Style

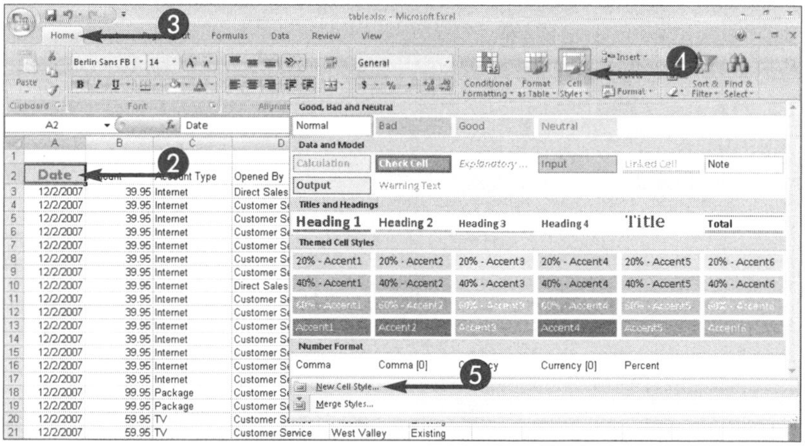

1. Format a cell using the cell formatting techniques described throughout this chapter.
2. Click the cell containing the formatting you want to save in a style.
3. Click the Home tab.
4. Click Cell Styles.
5. Click New Cell Style.

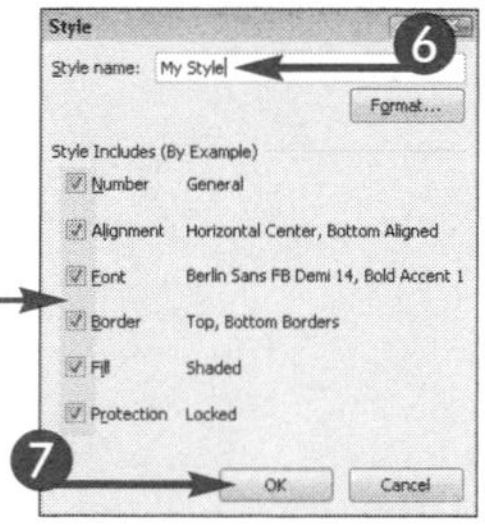

The Style dialog box appears.

- The check boxes beside all formatting options contain check marks (☑).

6. Type a name for the new style.
7. Click OK to save the style in the Style Gallery.

Copy Formatting

You can copy all of the formatting from one cell to another cell. For example, suppose that you need to apply special formatting to several cells in your workbook but you know that you will not need to use the formatting in the future. In this case, you really do not need to create a style. However, you can apply all of the formatting to a single cell and then use the Format Painter to copy the formatting from the cell that contains the formatting to the other cells that need it.

The cell containing the formatting can include any of the formatting available in the Format Cells dialog box, including font, font size, font color, font style, cell background color, alignment, orientation, and borders. For details on applying any of these formats, see the appropriate section in this chapter.

MASTER IT

Is there a way to turn on the Format Painter and leave it on so that I can apply the formats to several cells?

▼ Yes. You can double-click . When you move the mouse pointer into the worksheet area, the button appears pressed in the Ribbon. Click as many cells as you want. When you finish applying the formatting, click again to turn off the Format Painter.

Copy Formatting

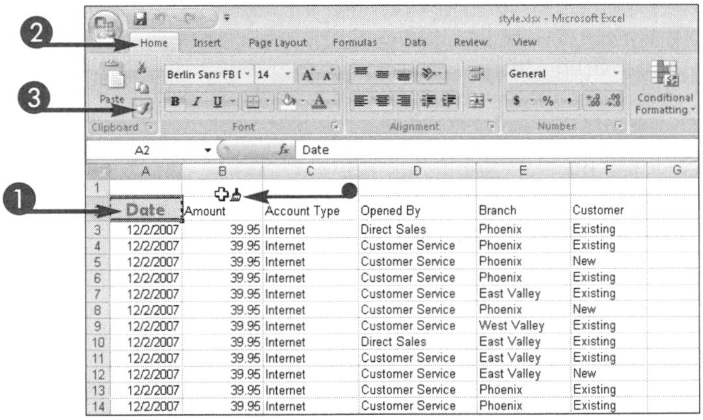

1. Click the cell containing the formatting you want to copy.
2. Click the Home tab.
3. Click the Format Painter button ().
   - The mouse pointer changes to the Format Painter pointer ().

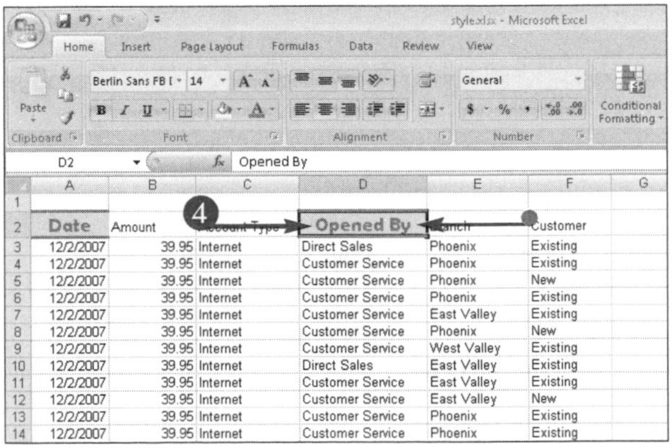

4. Click the cell to which you want to copy formatting.
   - Excel copies the formatting from the cell you selected in Step 1 to the cell you selected in Step 4.

Clear Formatting

You can clear the formatting applied to the cell, the contents of the cell, any comments you assigned to the cell, or all of these elements. Clearing a cell is useful when you want to return the cell to its original state in Excel and you do not want to apply all of Excel's original formats manually.

Although you can delete the contents of a cell by pressing Delete, this action does not affect the formatting applied to the cell, and any future entries you make in the cell will use the formatting applied to the cell. You may also not want to delete the cell's contents but you may want to return the cell's formatting to its original state. Finally, the information and formatting in a cell may still be appropriate, but the comments may no longer apply.

MASTER IT

What is a comment?

▼ Comments are most useful when you intend to share a workbook. You can use comments to call attention to or point out information about particular cells to others who use the workbook. See Chapter 31 for details on adding comments to cells.

Clear Formatting

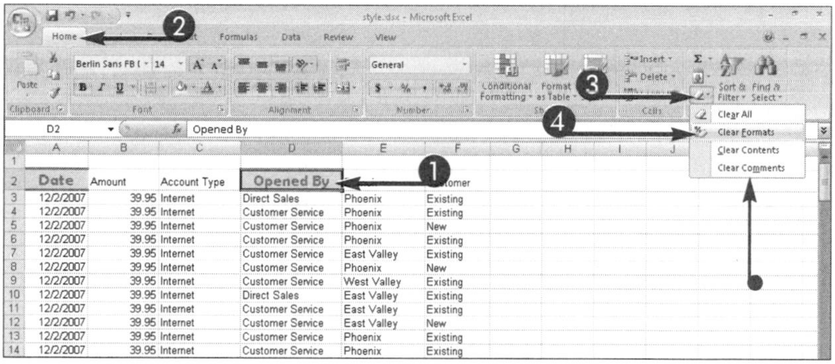

1. Click the cell containing the formatting you want to remove.
2. Click the Home tab.
3. Click the Clear button (🧽).
   - A list appears, displaying the options you can clear.
4. Click an option.

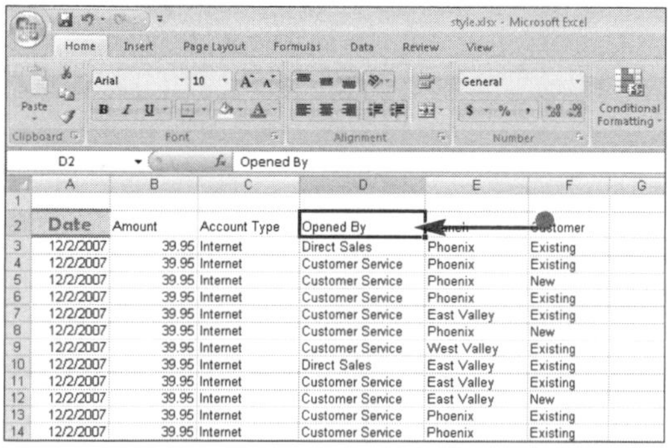

- Excel clears the option you selected.

4 Editing Worksheets

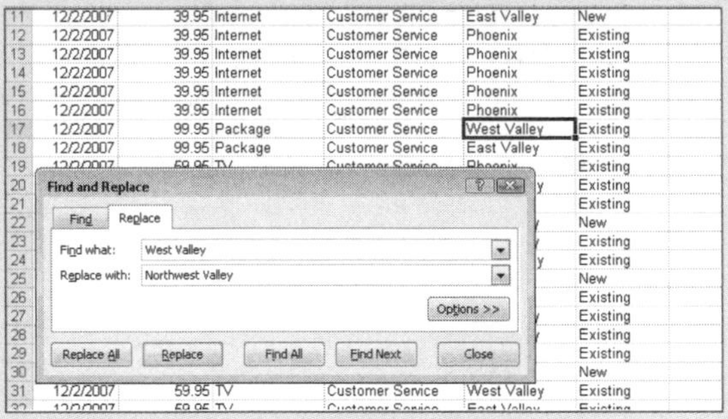

5 Proofreading a Worksheet

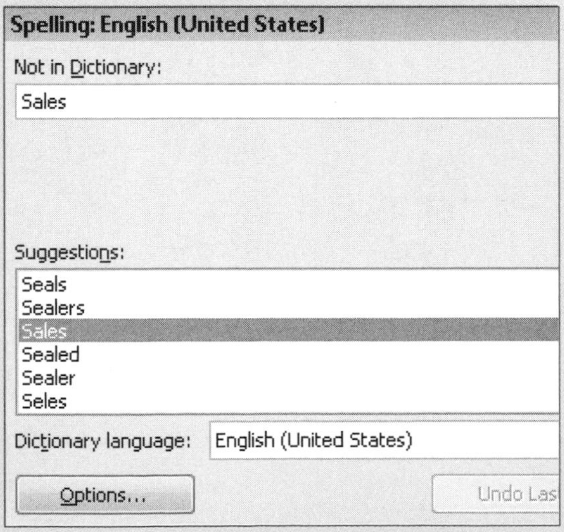

6 Adjusting Worksheets

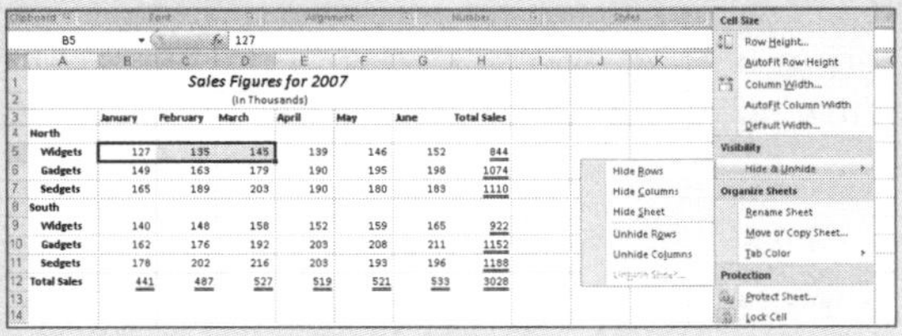

7 Managing Workbook Structure

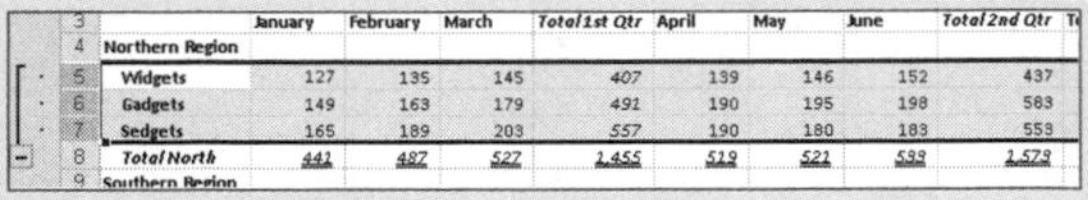

PART II
DESIGNING WORKSHEETS

8 Working with Views

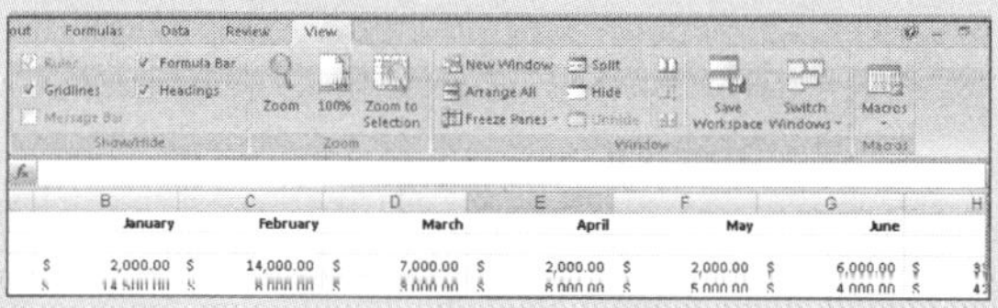

9 Printing Worksheet Information

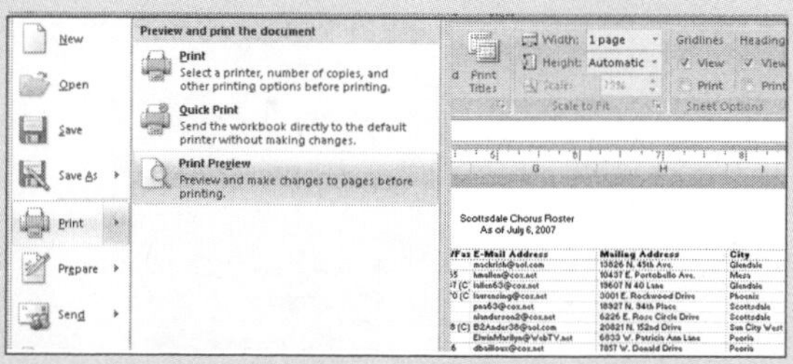

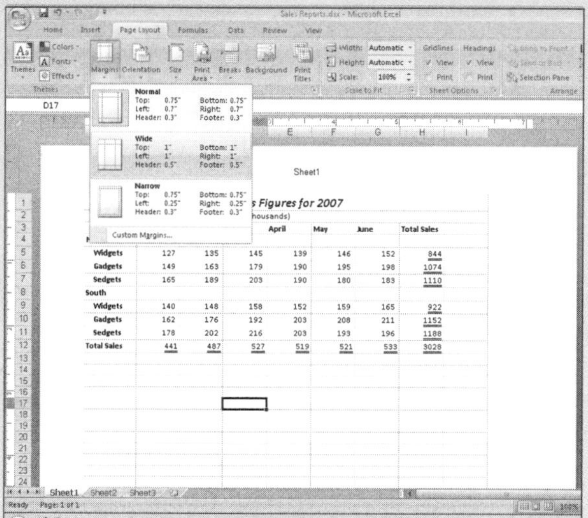

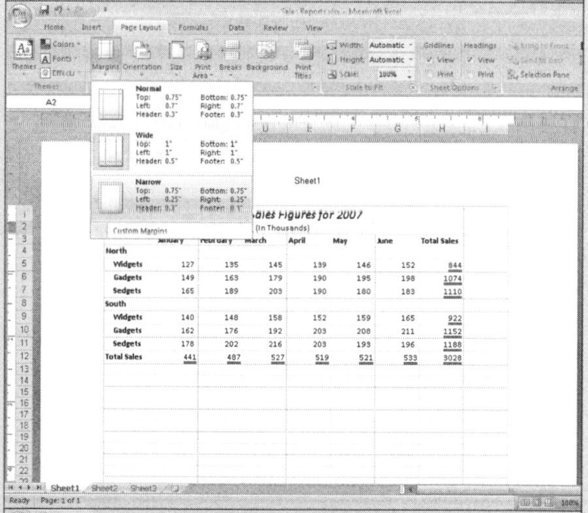

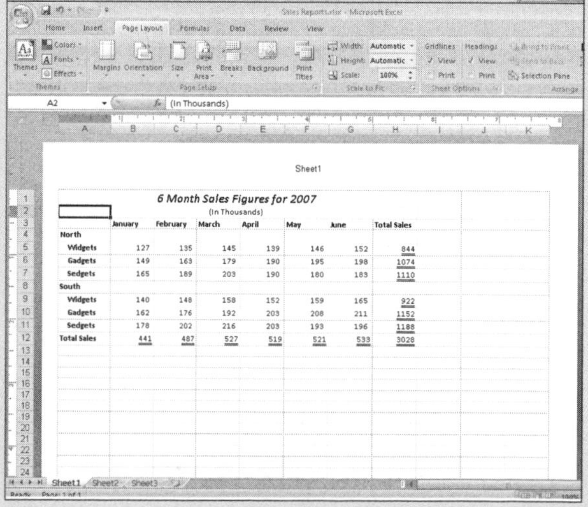

Base a Worksheet on a Template

To save you time and effort, you can create workbooks based on any of dozens of predefined templates. Templates are workbooks that contain predefined information and settings that you can use so that you do not need to create the settings and information yourself. Excel installs some commonly used templates when you install the program. Other templates are available to download from Microsoft's Web site. Chapter 2 describes how to create a new workbook based on templates stored on your computer. This section shows you how to use a template that you download from Microsoft's Web site, also known as Microsoft Online.

You can also create your own templates. Creating a template is particularly useful if you spend a great deal of time setting up and formatting static information, such as row and column headings, so that you can later use the workbook repeatedly to enter information. For example, if you track inventory in Excel and record information each month, you can set up all your part numbers and their locations and format the workbook to enhance its appearance. You can then save the workbook as a template and base each month's inventory entries on your inventory template.

Base a Worksheet on a Template

1. Click .
2. Click New.

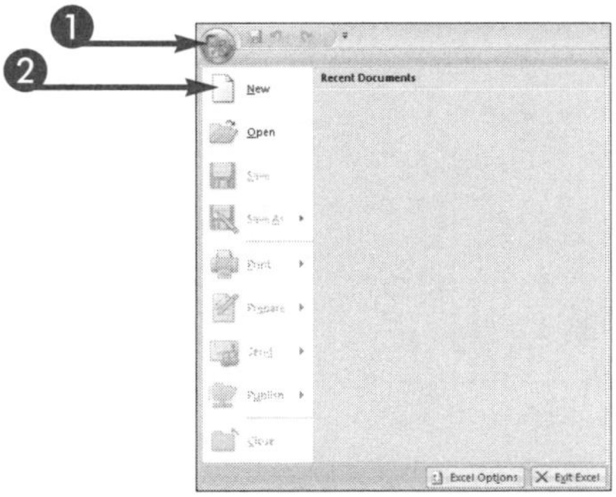

The New Workbook dialog box appears.

3. Click a template category.
4. Click a template in the selected category.
   - A preview of the selected template appears here.
5. Click Download.

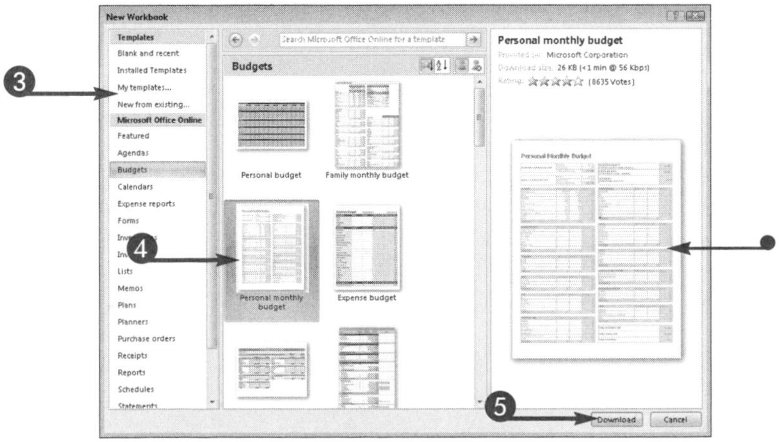

The Microsoft Office Genuine Advantage dialog box appears.

- You can click here to learn more about validation.

6 Click Continue.

If an Internet page appears, click Validate Now.

The status of your copy of Excel is validated to ensure that it is genuine.

A new workbook appears on-screen.

You can edit this workbook the same way you edit any workbook.

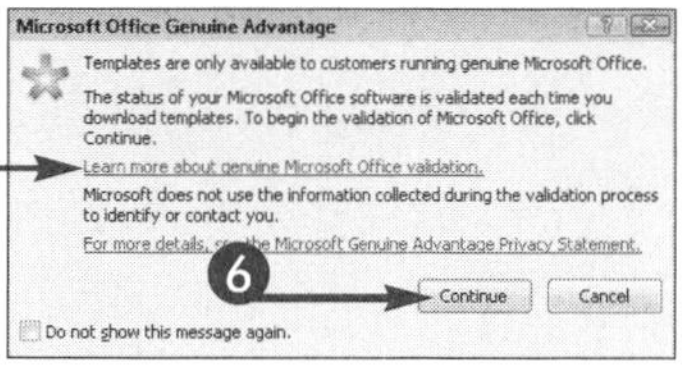

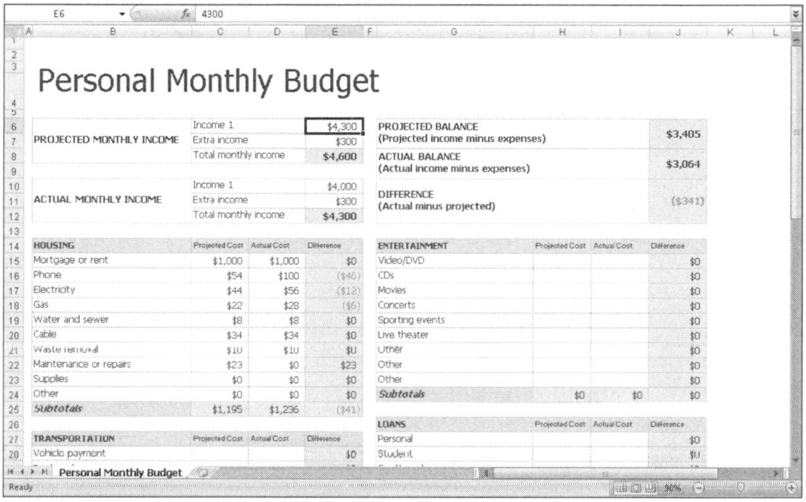

MASTER IT

How do I create my own template?

▼ Open a workbook and set it up the way you want it to appear, entering row and column headings and formatting cells as appropriate. Then click [icon] and click Save As. In the File Name field, type a name for the template. In the Save As dialog box, open the Save as Type drop-down list and choose Excel Template (*.xltx). Windows changes the folder to the default location where Excel stores templates — in Windows Vista, the location is c:\users*username*\AppData\Local\Microsoft\Templates. When you click Save, Excel saves your template.

Do I need to do anything different to base a workbook on a template that I created?

▼ Yes. Follow Steps 1 and 2 in this section. For Step 3, click My Templates. Excel replaces the New Workbook dialog box with the New dialog box, which contains templates that you created. Click the appropriate template and click OK. Excel opens a new workbook based on your template.

What can I do if I do not see a template that meets my needs?

▼ You can search Microsoft Office Online for a template. Follow Steps 1 and 2 in this section. Then, in the Search Microsoft Office Online field that appears above the templates for a particular category, type a description of the template you want and click Start Searching ([icon]). The search results appear below.

Apply a Theme

You can make a positive impression with a workbook that you format using a theme. Themes provide a polished appearance to your workbook by applying a set of fonts, colors, and other predefined formatting details. Themes typically work in Word 2007, Excel 2007, and PowerPoint 2007 so that you can apply a unified look to a collection of files.

Excel applies a theme to any cells in a workbook to which you have applied a style, as described in Chapter 3. If you have not applied styles to any cells in the workbook, you will not see any change in the workbook's appearance when you apply a theme.

Themes that come with Excel appear in the Built-In group in the Themes Gallery. You can download themes from Microsoft Office Online, and any themes that you download appear in the Custom group at the top of the Themes Gallery.

MASTER IT

How do I download a theme?

▼ Click "More Themes on Microsoft Office Online" at the bottom of the Themes Gallery. Excel connects you to the Internet, where you can select a theme. You must go through the Genuine Microsoft Office validation process, after which the theme is downloaded. Each time you are asked to save, you can accept the default name and location.

Apply a Theme

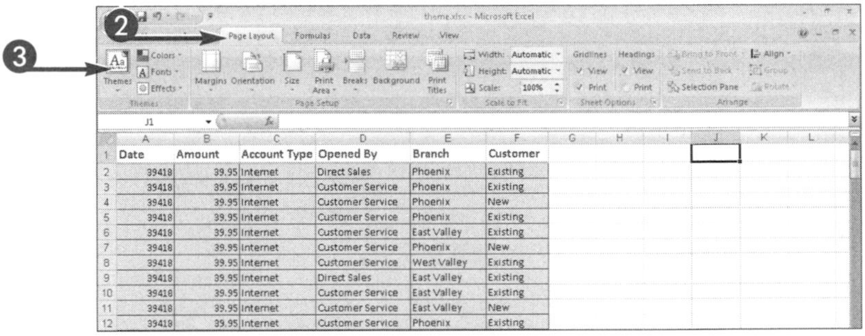

1. Make sure that you have applied styles to the worksheet.

Note: See Chapter 3 for details on applying styles.

2. Click the Page Layout tab.
3. Click Themes.

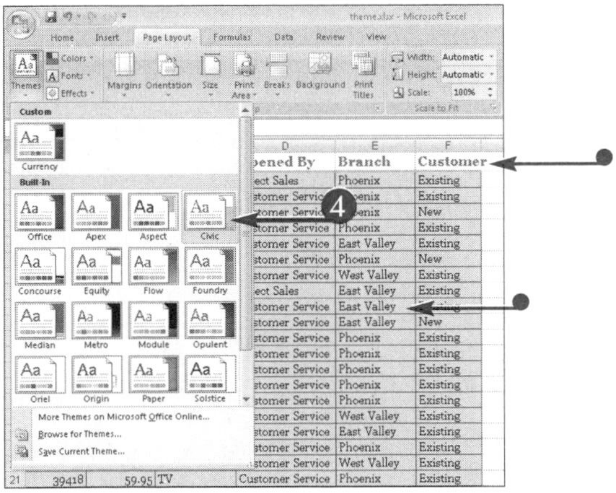

The Themes Gallery appears.

4. Move the mouse pointer over a theme.
   - Styled cells update to match the theme.
5. Click a theme.

   Excel applies the theme to all cells to which you previously applied styles.

Mix and Match Themes

You can mix the fonts and colors of various themes to create the effect you want. If you apply no theme at all, then Excel uses the built-in Office theme by default. To apply a different theme, see the section, "Apply a Theme." You can also mix the colors of one theme with the fonts of another.

You can apply the colors or fonts of any theme to your worksheet if you have previously applied styles to cells in your worksheet. If you have not applied styles, then theme colors and fonts will not affect your worksheet. See Chapter 3 for details on applying styles.

To find the combination you want, take advantage of Excel's Live Preview feature, which enables you to preview the appearance of your workbook in a particular theme font or color. Once you find a combination you like, you can save it.

MASTER IT

How do I save a combination I like as a theme?

▼ Click Themes and then click Save Current Theme at the bottom of the Themes Gallery. The Save Current Theme dialog box appears. Type a name and accept the default location that Excel suggests. Your theme will be available in all workbooks and will appear in the Custom group in the Themes Gallery.

PART II

Mix and Match Themes

1. Click the Page Layout tab.
2. Click Colors to display the Colors Gallery.
   - A border surrounds the currently selected theme color.
3. Move the mouse pointer over a theme color.
   - Styled cells update to match the theme color.
4. Click a color.

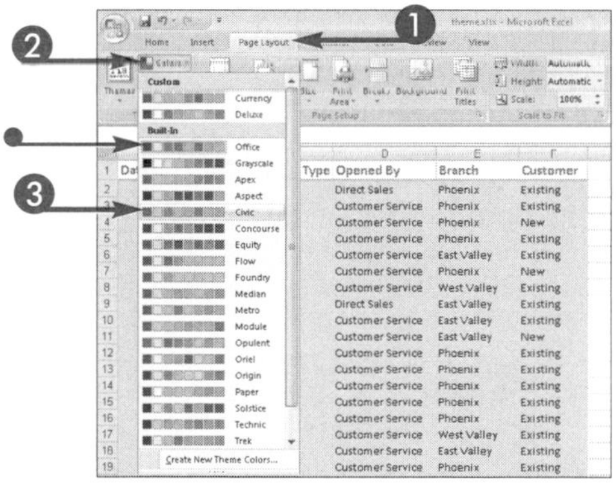

5. Click Fonts to display the Fonts Gallery.
   - A border surrounds the currently selected theme font.
6. Move the mouse pointer over a theme font.
   - Styled cells update to match the theme font.
7. Click a font.

Excel applies the font theme to all cells to which you previously applied styles.

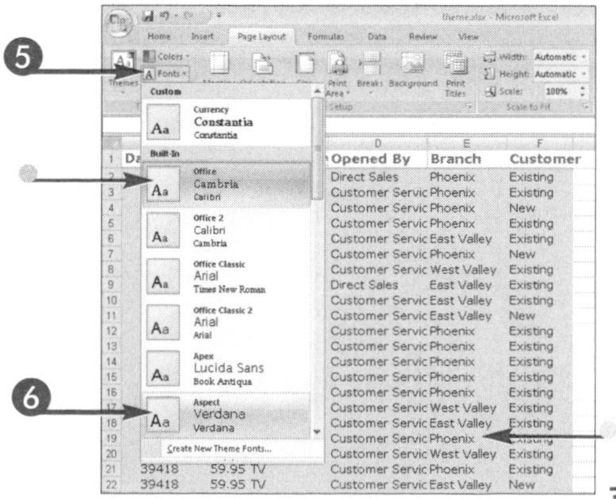

Select Cells

Before you can perform many operations in Excel, you must select the cells that you want to change. For example, if you want to apply styles to cells, you must select the cells before you can apply the styles. To copy or move data, you must select the range of cells you want to copy or move so that Excel knows which cells to copy or move.

When you select cells, Excel highlights them on-screen, giving them a shaded appearance so that you can easily distinguish the selected cells from cells in your worksheet that are not selected.

When you select a group of cells, you select a *range*. To refer to a range, you use a combination of two cell addresses: the address of the cell in the upper-left corner of the range, and the address of the cell in the lower-right corner of the range. When you refer to a range in writing, you separate the two cell addresses using a colon (:). For example, the range C5:D7 includes the cells C5, C6, C7, D5, D6, and D7.

Select Cells

Select a Range

1. Click the first cell you want to select.
2. Drag ✥ down and, if necessary, to the right to select adjacent cells.

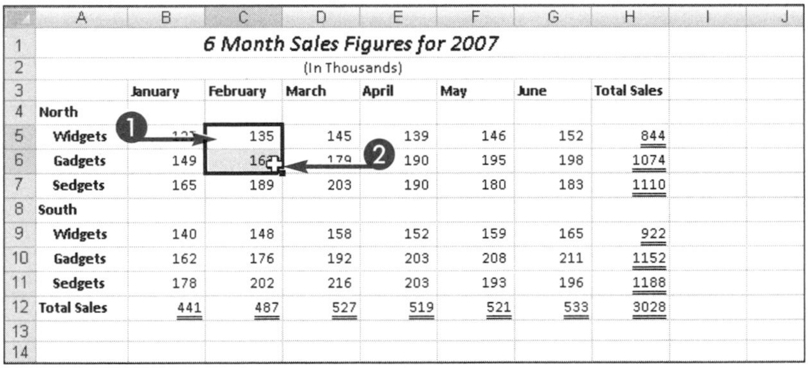

6 Month Sales Figures for 2007

(In Thousands)

	January	February	March	April	May	June	Total Sales
North							
Widgets	[illegible]	135	145	139	146	152	844
Gadgets	149	[illegible]	179	190	195	198	1074
Sedgets	165	189	203	190	180	183	1110
South							
Widgets	140	148	158	152	159	165	922
Gadgets	162	176	192	203	208	211	1152
Sedgets	178	202	216	203	193	196	1188
Total Sales	441	487	527	519	521	533	3028

- Excel selects the cells.

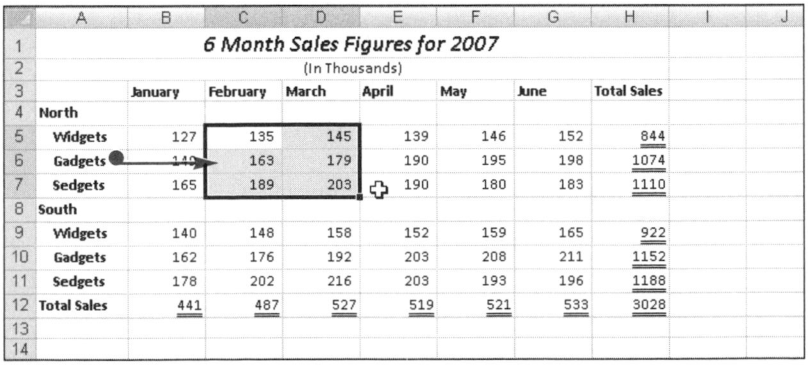

6 Month Sales Figures for 2007

(In Thousands)

	January	February	March	April	May	June	Total Sales
North							
Widgets	127	135	145	139	146	152	844
Gadgets	149	163	179	190	195	198	1074
Sedgets	165	189	203	190	180	183	1110
South							
Widgets	140	148	158	152	159	165	922
Gadgets	162	176	192	203	208	211	1152
Sedgets	178	202	216	203	193	196	1188
Total Sales	441	487	527	519	521	533	3028

Select a Row

1. Move ✥ into the row heading (✥ changes to ➡).
2. Click the number of the row you want to select.
   - Excel selects the row.

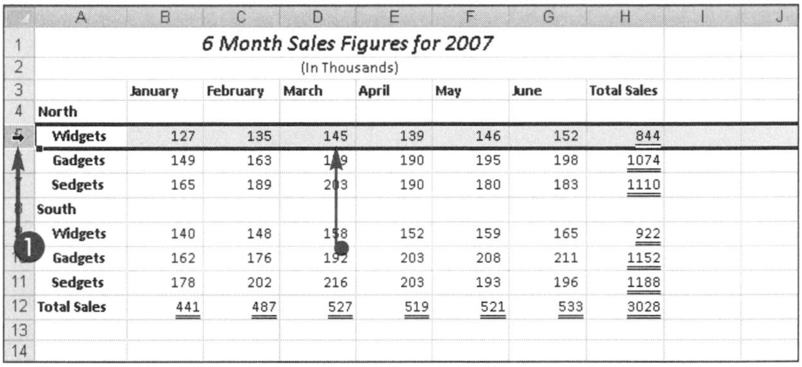

	A	B	C	D	E	F	G	H
1				6 Month Sales Figures for 2007				
2				(In Thousands)				
3		January	February	March	April	May	June	Total Sales
4	North							
5	Widgets	127	135	145	139	146	152	844
6	Gadgets	149	163	179	190	195	198	1074
7	Sedgets	165	189	203	190	180	183	1110
8	South							
9	Widgets	140	148	158	152	159	165	922
10	Gadgets	162	176	192	203	208	211	1152
11	Sedgets	178	202	216	203	193	196	1188
12	Total Sales	441	487	527	519	521	533	3028

Select a Column

1. Move ✥ into the column heading (✥ changes to ⬇).
2. Click the letter of the column you want to select.
   - Excel selects the column

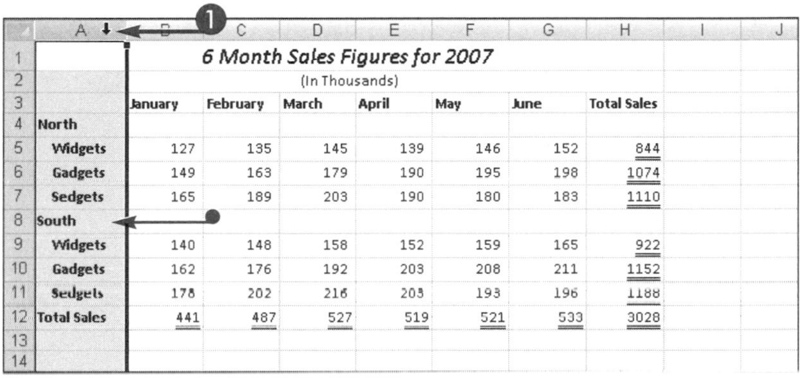

	A	B	C	D	E	F	G	H
1				6 Month Sales Figures for 2007				
2				(In Thousands)				
3		January	February	March	April	May	June	Total Sales
4	North							
5	Widgets	127	135	145	139	146	152	844
6	Gadgets	149	163	179	190	195	198	1074
7	Sedgets	165	189	203	190	180	183	1110
8	South							
9	Widgets	140	148	158	152	159	165	922
10	Gadgets	162	176	192	203	208	211	1152
11	Sedgets	178	202	216	203	193	196	1188
12	Total Sales	441	487	527	519	521	533	3028

MASTER IT

Can I select cells that do not appear side by side in a worksheet?

▼ Yes. For example, suppose that you want to apply the Accounting Double Underlining format to totals that appear below and on the right edge of a set of columns. Click and drag to select the first set of cells. Then, press and hold Ctrl as you click and drag to select the second set of cells. You can continue to select other non-contiguous cells by holding Ctrl as you select them. You can release Ctrl between selections and simply press it again before adding to the current selection.

Can I select more than one row or column at a time?

▼ Yes. You can click and drag in the row number or column letter heading area to select multiple contiguous rows or columns. To select non-contiguous rows or columns, press and hold Ctrl as you click a row number or a column heading.

Can I select a range without dragging?

▼ If the range is contiguous, you can click the first cell and then press and hold Shift as you click the last cell in the range you want to select. Excel selects all cells between the first cell you clicked and the second cell you clicked.

Move or Copy Information

You can reorganize information by moving or copying the information from one set of cells to another. Copying formulas is particularly time-saving. When you move information, Excel deletes the information from the original location and displays it in the new location. Moving information is also called *cutting* information. When you copy information, Excel does not make any changes to the original data, but simply adds a copy of the data in the new location.

You can move or copy information by dragging and dropping or by using tools on the Ribbon. In this section, you see how to drag and drop information in the Step subsection, "Move Data," and you see how to use tools on the Ribbon in the Step subsection, "Copy Data."

When you move or copy information, you first select the information you want to move or copy, and then you select the destination where you want the information to appear. When you select a destination, you can select just the cell that will serve as the upper-left corner to the range where the information will appear. Excel then fills in all of the information using cells adjacent to the upper-left corner cell.

Move or Copy Information

Move Data

1. Select the cells containing the information you want to move.
2. Move the cell pointer to any portion of the outside edge of the selection (✚ changes to ✥).
3. Click and drag the cells to the new location.
   - As you drag, Excel displays an outline of the cells you are moving.

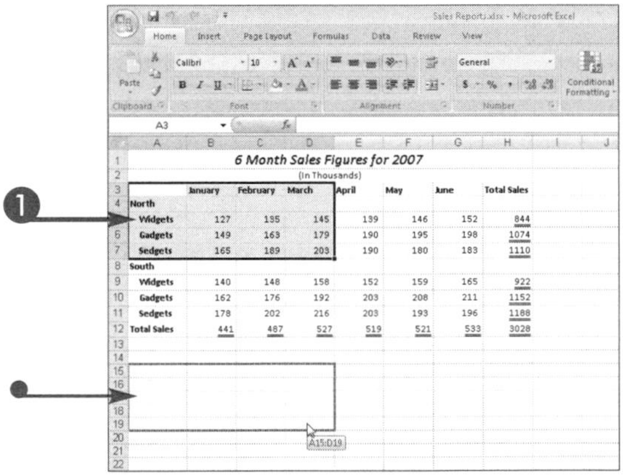

   - When you release the mouse button, the cells appear selected and in the new location.

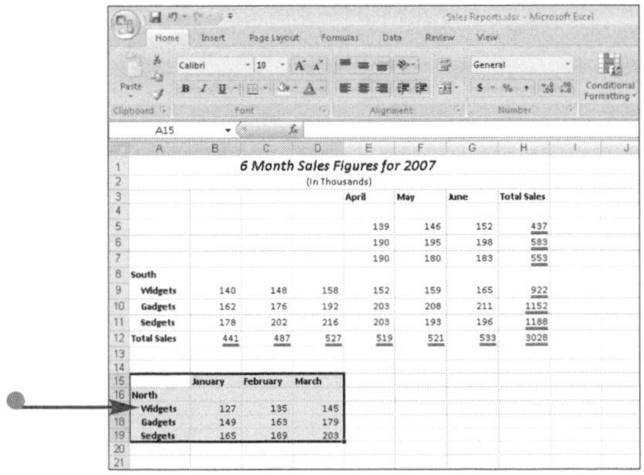

Copy Data

1. Select the cells containing the information you want to copy.
2. Click the Home tab.
3. Click Copy (📋).
   - Excel displays an animated, dotted outline around the selection.
4. Click the cell that you want to use as the upper-left corner of the location where the copy will appear.
5. Click Paste.
   - The selection appears in the new location.

The upper-left corner cell of the copy contains the same information as the upper-left corner of the selection you made in Step 1.

You can copy the selection at another location by repeating Steps 4 and 5.

When you finish copying, press Esc to cancel the animated, dotted outline around the original selection.

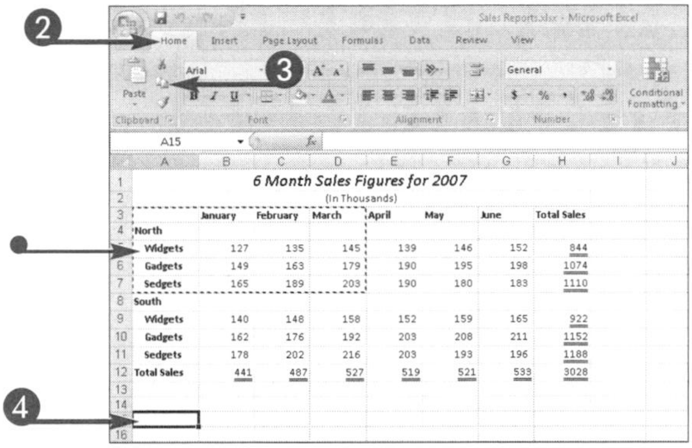

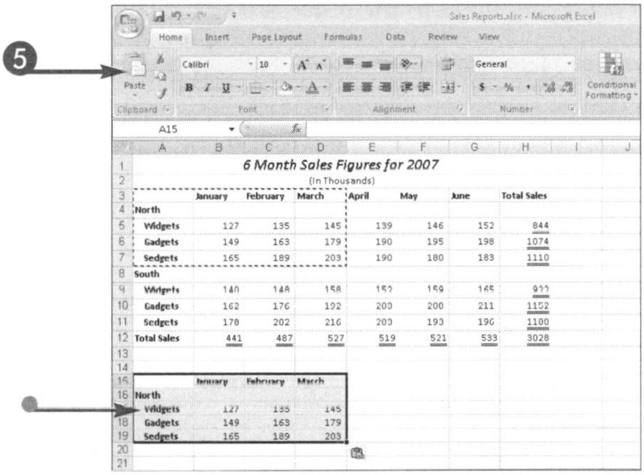

PART II

What happens if I try to move or copy information to a location that already contains information?

▼ Excel displays a warning message that asks if you want to replace the contents of the destination cells. This means that Excel is confirming that you want to overwrite the information in the destination location to which you are copying or pasting. Click OK if you want to overwrite the information; otherwise, click Cancel and select a different destination location.

Can I move without dragging?

▼ Yes. Follow the steps in the subsection, "Copy Data," but, in Step 3, click Cut (✂) instead of 📋. Then complete the rest of the steps. In this case, Excel removes the information from the original location and displays it in the new location.

Can I drag to copy?

▼ Yes. Follow the steps in the subsection, "Move Data," but, in Step 3, press Ctrl while you click and drag. Excel adds a small plus sign to the mouse pointer. Complete the rest of the steps. Excel adds a copy of the selection in the new location.

Find and Replace Information

You can search for information in your worksheet and replace it with other information. For example, suppose that you discover that Part Number 465123 was entered repeatedly as Part Number 465132. You can have Excel search for 465132 and replace it with 465123. Although you can search for just 132, be aware that Excel finds all occurrences of information as you search to replace it, such as in the number 132487. You may therefore not want to replace every occurrence of 132. You can search for it and then skip occurrences that you do not want to replace.

You can search an entire worksheet or you can limit the search to a range of cells that you select before you begin the search. To learn more about selecting cells, see the section, "Select Cells."

To begin a "find and replace" operation, you start by searching for the initial occurrence of the text you want to find and replace. From that point forward, Excel replaces the text if you choose to replace it, and automatically finds the next occurrence of the text.

Find and Replace Information

1. Click the Home tab.
2. Click Find & Select.
3. Click Replace.

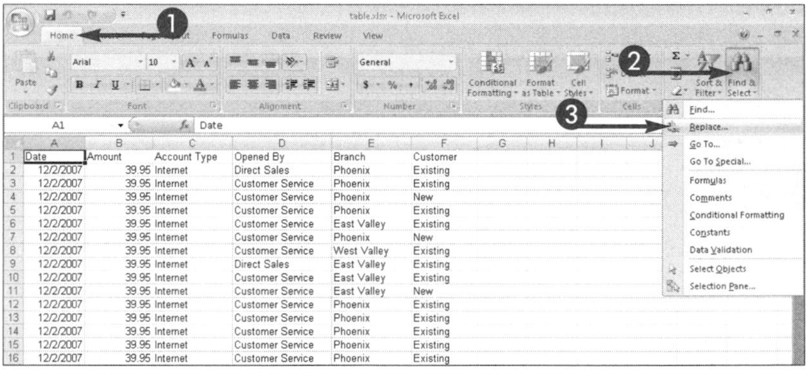

Excel displays the Replace tab of the Find and Replace dialog box.

4. Type the information for which you want to search here.

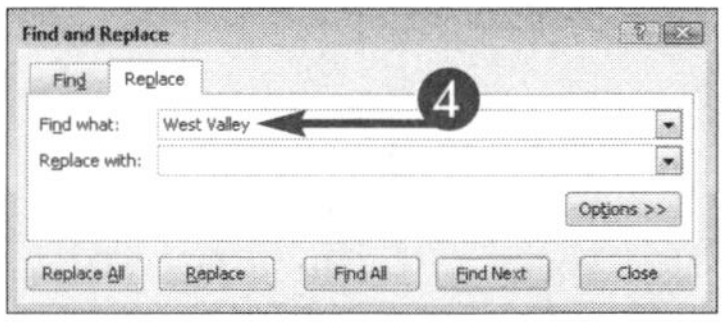

5 Type the information that you want Excel to use to replace the information you typed in Step 4.

6 Click Find Next.

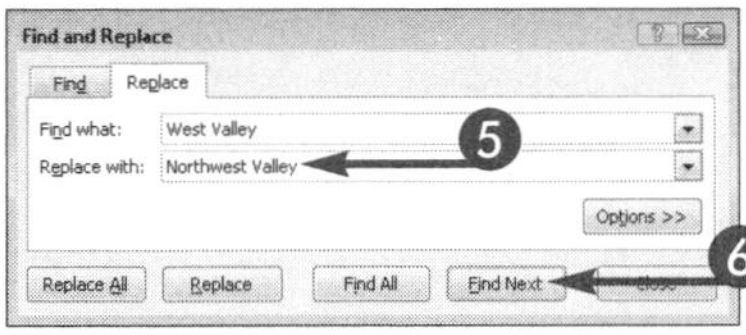

Excel finds the first occurrence of the data.

7 Click Replace.

- Excel replaces the information in the cell.
- Excel finds the next occurrence automatically.

8 Repeat Step 7 until you replace all appropriate occurrences.

Excel displays a message when it cannot find any more occurrences.

9 Click OK and then Close.

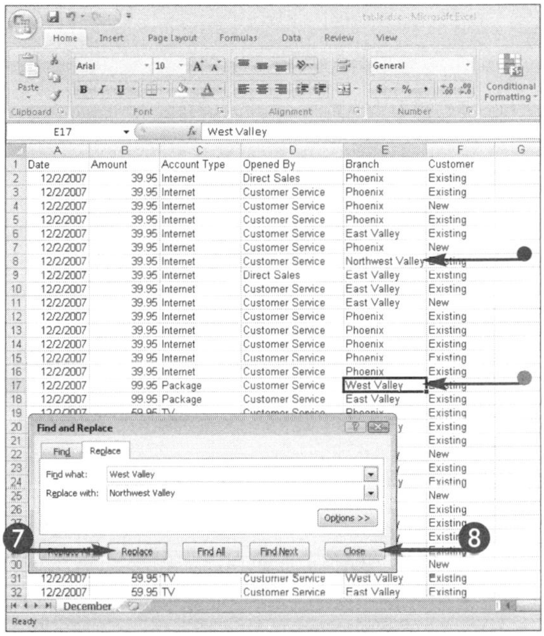

MASTER IT

What happens if I click Options?

▼ Excel expands the Find and Replace dialog box to display additional options that you can set when you search. You can ensure that Excel matches the case of the information for which you search. You can also ensure that Excel matches your search criterion exactly. You can specify where and how Excel searches, and you can add formatting criteria to the search.

What happens if I click Find All?

▼ To see the results, click Options. Excel displays a list of the cells that contain the information for which you searched. The list shows the workbook, worksheet, range name if one exists, cell address, and the value in the cell, which is the value for which you searched.

What if I do not want to replace a particular occurrence?

▼ Click Find Next instead of clicking Replace. Excel skips the occurrence and moves on to the next occurrence.

Can I use Replace All?

▼ Yes, but only if you are sure that you want to change every occurrence of the information you type in Step 4 to the information you type in Step 5.

Check Spelling

You can easily find and correct any spelling mistakes in your worksheet. Excel also checks spelling in charts when they appear in a workbook.

Excel starts to check spelling at the selected cell. You can limit the cells that Excel checks for spelling errors if you select those cells before you begin the spell check. You can also select several worksheets to have Excel check all of them at the same time. See Chapter 7 for details on editing several worksheets simultaneously.

Excel and all other Office programs use a dictionary to determine whether a word is misspelled. If a word that you type in your worksheet does not appear in the dictionary, Excel flags the word as misspelled. When Excel flags a word that it does not recognize, it highlights the cell in the worksheet that contains the word, and attempts to offer alternatives that you can use to correct the misspelling. If the word does not resemble any words in the dictionary, Excel does not suggest alternatives. For example, if your company name is an acronym that does not spell a common word, then Excel flags your company name.

Check Spelling

1. Open the workbook you want to check, and click cell A1.
2. Click the Review tab.
3. Click Spelling.

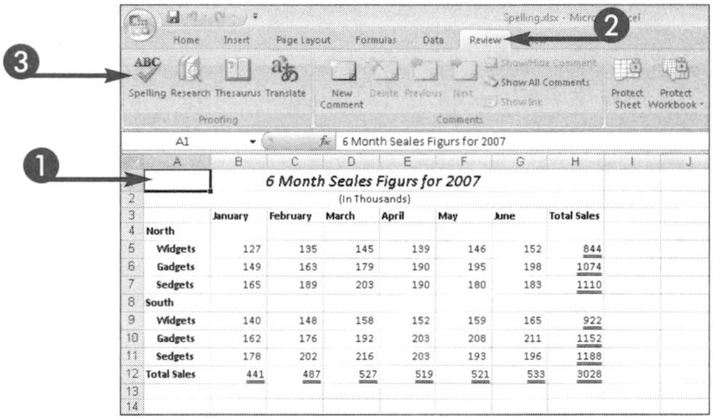

The Spelling dialog box appears and Excel selects the cell containing the unrecognized word.

- The misspelled word appears here.
- Alternatives for the misspelling appear here.
- You can click Ignore Once to continue to check spelling without making a change.
- You can click Ignore All to skip all occurrences of the word.

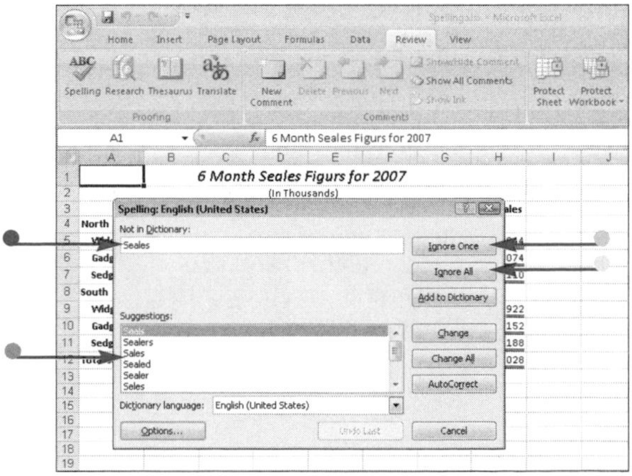

4. Click an alternative suggestion.
5. Click Change to correct the word in the worksheet.
   - If Excel does not suggest an appropriate alternative, you can type the correct spelling here.

   After you identify an action for the first unrecognized word, Excel searches for the next unrecognized word.
6. Continue to change or ignore misspelled words.

   When Excel finds no more unrecognized words, a dialog box appears to tell you that spell checking is complete.
7. Click OK to close the dialog box.

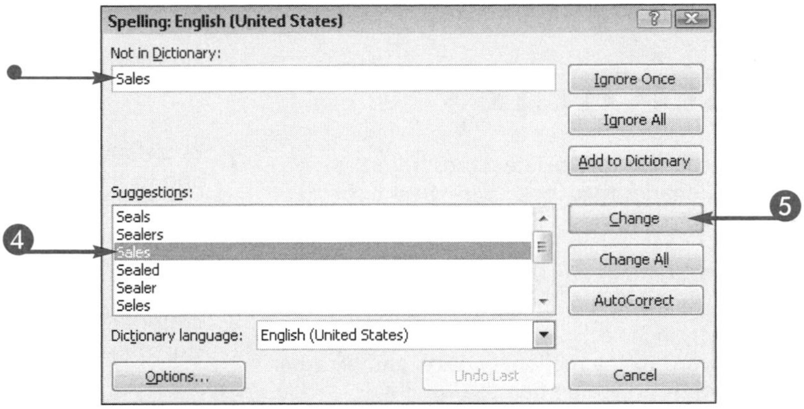

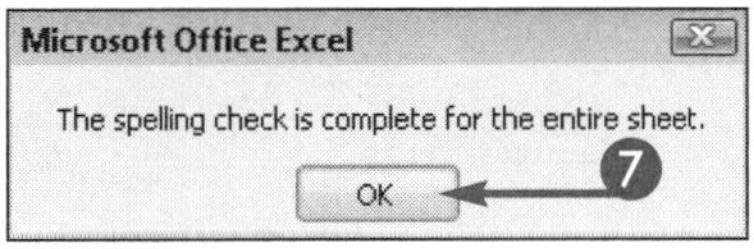

MASTER IT

What can I do if Excel regularly misidentifies a word as misspelled?

▼ You can add the word to the dictionary. This is a particularly useful approach when you use technical terms that Excel does not recognize and flags as misspellings. All Office applications share the same dictionary, and so adding the term in one program prevents other Office applications from flagging it as a misspelling. When the word appears in the Spelling dialog box, click the Add to Dictionary button.

When would I click the AutoCorrect button?

▼ If Excel flags a word that you commonly misspell, you can click the AutoCorrect button. If you do, Excel adds the word to the list of words that Excel automatically corrects when you type instead of waiting until you check spelling. See Chapter 30 for details on working with Excel's AutoCorrect feature.

What happens if I click the Options button?

▼ Excel opens the Excel Options dialog box, which contains the options you can set for proofing your worksheet. You can set options for automatically formatting your worksheets, and that control Excel's behavior when you check spelling. You can also edit the dictionary. For details on setting Spelling options, see Chapter 30.

Edit the Dictionary

You can add and delete words from the dictionaries that Excel uses when it checks spelling without using the Spell Checking feature. (For more details, see the section, "Check Spelling.") Deleting words from the dictionary is particularly useful when you accidentally add a word that is, in fact, incorrectly spelled. If you add a misspelled word to the dictionary, Excel and all other Office programs no longer flag the word as misspelled, which defeats the purpose of spell checking, not only in Excel but in all Office applications.

By default, Office applications separate words that you add to the dictionary from the main dictionary that is installed when you install Office programs. That way, you can easily identify the words that you add, and delete them as needed. To segregate the words that you add, Office applications store these words in a custom dictionary file called CUSTOM.DIC, which is stored in a common location used by all Office applications. You can create other custom dictionaries if you need them, but you may find it easiest to only use one custom dictionary.

Edit the Dictionary

1. Click .
2. Click Excel Options.

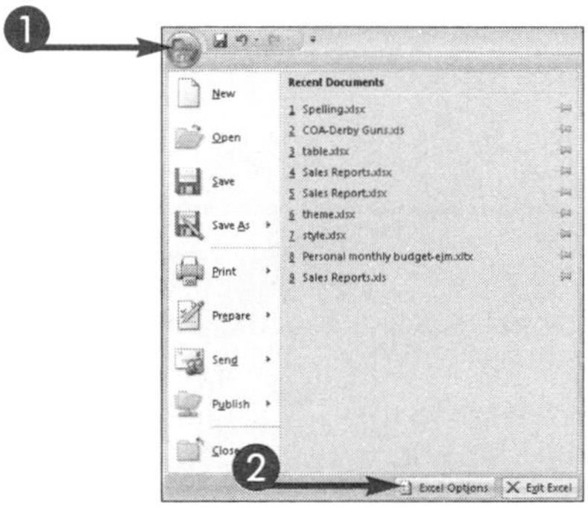

The Excel Options dialog box appears.

3. Click Proofing.
4. Click Custom Dictionaries.

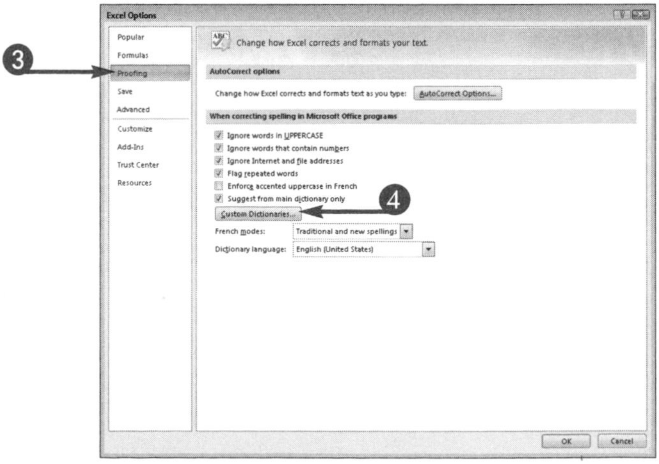

The Custom Dictionaries dialog box appears.

5 Click the dictionary you want to edit (☐ changes to ☑).

6 Click Edit Word List.

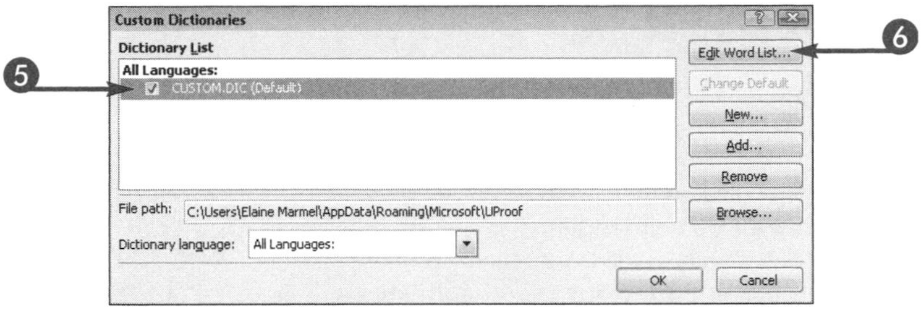

A dialog box appears with the name of the dictionary you selected.

- You can click a word in the list and then click Delete to remove it from the dictionary.
- You can type a word here and click the Add button to add it to the dictionary.

7 Click OK three times to close all of the dialog boxes and return to the worksheet.

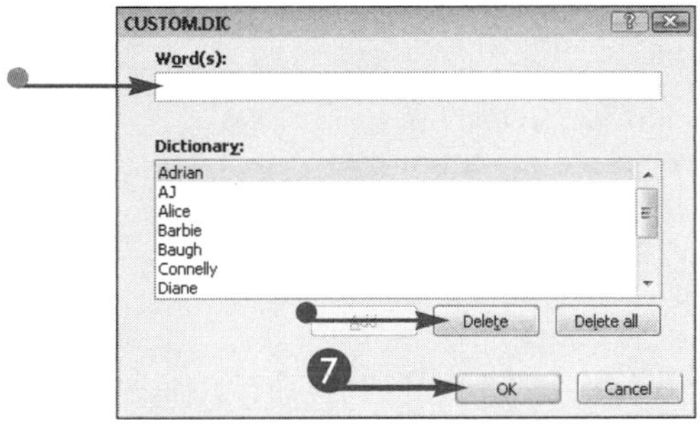

MASTER IT

How can I add a custom dictionary?

▼ Follow Steps 1 to 4 in this section. For Step 5, click the New button. The Create Custom Dictionary dialog box appears. Type a name for your dictionary in the File Name field and click the Save button. The Custom Dictionaries dialog box reappears, and the new dictionary appears in the list of dictionaries.

How do I add words to my custom dictionary instead of to the one that Excel uses by default?

▼ Follow the steps in this section to add words to your custom dictionary using the Custom Dictionaries dialog box. To add words to your custom dictionary during spell checking, set your dictionary as the default. Follow Steps 1 to 5 in this section. Then click the Change Default button, which becomes available once you add more than one dictionary.

Can I edit a word I added to the dictionary that was misspelled?

▼ No. However, to correct a problem, you can delete the word and add its correctly spelled form to the dictionary. Follow Steps 1 to 5 to display the word list for the selected dictionary. Then click the misspelled word and click the Delete button. Click in the Word(s) field, type the word correctly, and click the Add button.

Translate Text

You can translate common words or phrases from your default language to any of a number of languages. You can also take advantage of machine translations and translate an entire worksheet. Machine translation is useful when you open a workbook created in a foreign language and you want to make sure that you are looking at the correct workbook. The machine translation will not be perfect and you should not rely on it for important workbooks, because it may not preserve the full meaning of the text.

You can type the word you want to translate into a cell in your worksheet, select the cell containing the word, or simply type the word into the Research pane. The example in this section shows a translation from English to French.

MASTER IT

What can I do if the language in which I want to work does not appear?

▼ Click Start, click All Programs, click Microsoft Office, click Microsoft Office Tools, and then click Microsoft Office 2007 Language Settings. In the dialog box that appears, click languages in the list on the left and then click Add to include them in the list of enabled languages on the right. If the language is enabled, you may need to install a keyboard layout in Windows; check Windows Help for more information.

Translate Text

1. Click the Review tab.
2. Click Translate.
   - The Research pane appears.

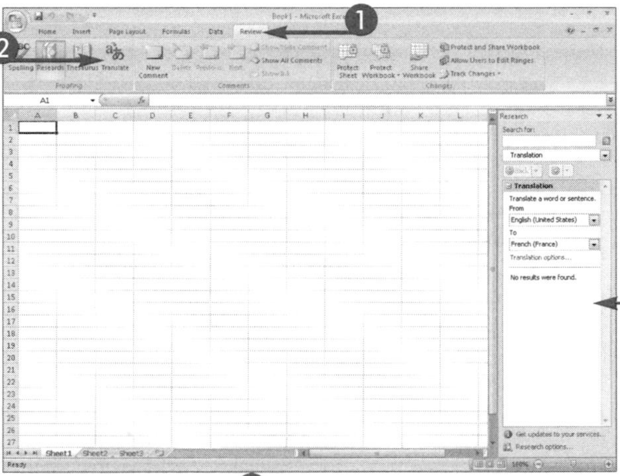

3. Type the word you want to translate.
4. Click ➔.
   - The translation of the word appears here.
   - You can change the languages by clicking the ▾ next to the To and From fields.
5. Click ☒ to close the Research pane when you have finishing translating.

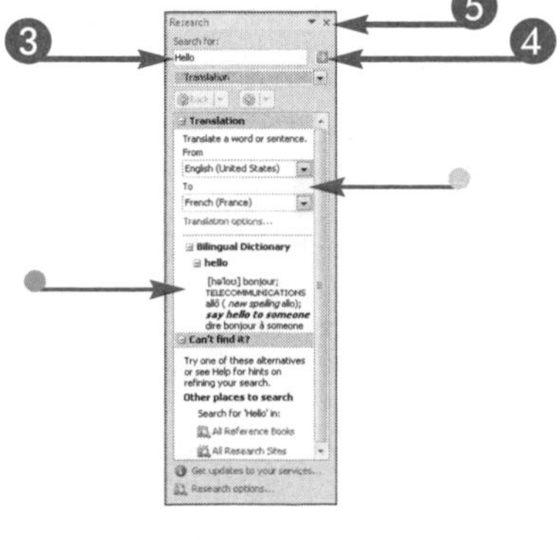

Using the Thesaurus

You can use the thesaurus that comes with Office programs to search for synonyms or antonyms for a word that you specify. Synonyms are words that have a similar meaning to the word you specify. Antonyms are words that mean the opposite of the word you specify.

You can look up a word that appears in your worksheet, or you can work directly in the Research pane that Excel displays when you use the thesaurus. You specify a word and Excel searches for words from all parts of speech with both similar and opposite meanings. You can use the choices that Excel displays in the Research pane to continue searching; once you find the word you want, you can place the word in your worksheet.

MASTER IT

When I click ▾ for a word that the thesaurus displays, what options are available?

▼ Click Insert to place the word in the selected cell in the worksheet. Click Copy to copy the word to the Windows Clipboard. You can then edit a cell and paste the word to an exact location in the text contained in the cell. You can also paste the word into another program. You can click Look Up to have the thesaurus look up the word.

PART II

Using the Thesaurus

1. Click the Review tab.
2. Click Thesaurus.
   - The Research pane appears.

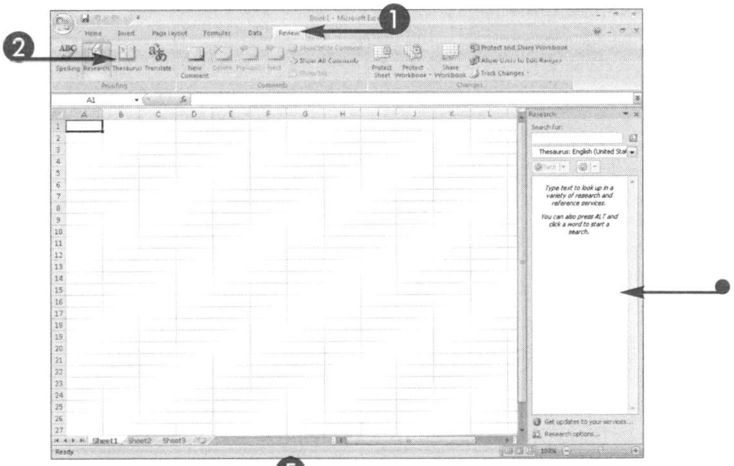

3. Type the word for which you want a synonym or antonym.
4. Click →.
   - Synonyms appear here, and antonyms appear after synonyms.
   - You can move the mouse pointer over any word and click ▾ to display a list of options.
5. Click ✕ to close the Research pane when you finish using the thesaurus.

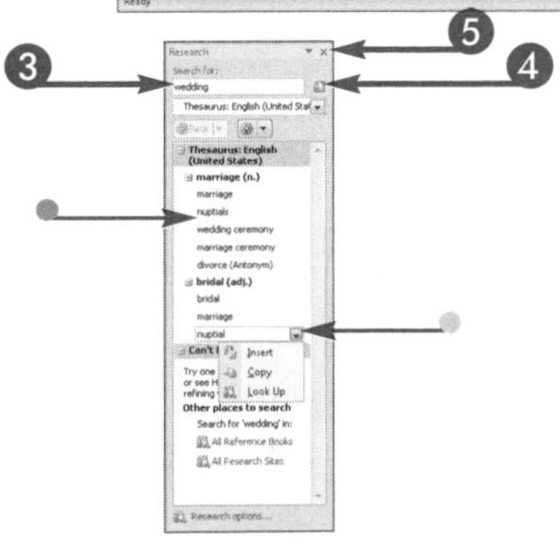

Research Online

You can use connections to online research tools that come with Excel to look up a word in the dictionary or search a variety of sources for information. For example, you can research a topic, or you can use several different sources to obtain essential business news and stock quotes to help you make better business decisions. Excel provides three reference book tools, four research site tools, and two business and financial site tools that you can use for research. The sections "Translate Text" and "Using the Thesaurus" show you how to use two of the three reference book tools.

You can use the Research pane to explore topics. When you search for stock quotes using MSN Money Stock Quotes, the online tool returns the information in the Research pane, as shown in this section. When you use other research tools, you may see links in the Research pane that lead you to pages on the Internet. Typically, if you click a link, your browser opens and displays the targeted page. In some cases, the information found may not be available to you unless you subscribe to the service providing the information.

Research Online

1. Click the Review tab.
2. Click Research.

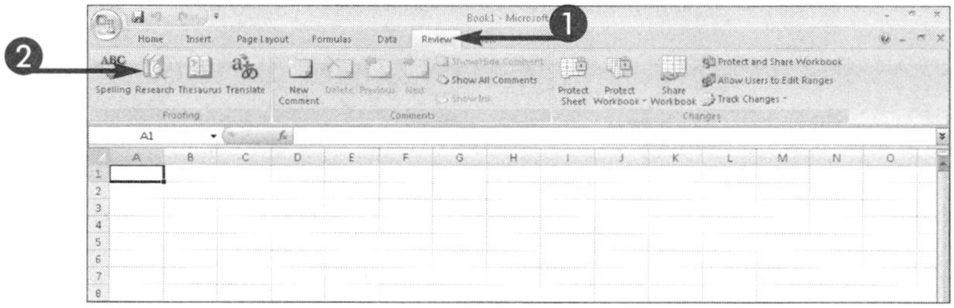

- The Research pane appears on the right side of the Excel window.

You can use this pane to perform various research, such as looking up a word in the thesaurus or translating text. Some research offerings require subscriptions.

Note: *See the sections "Translate Text" and "Using the Thesaurus" for details.*

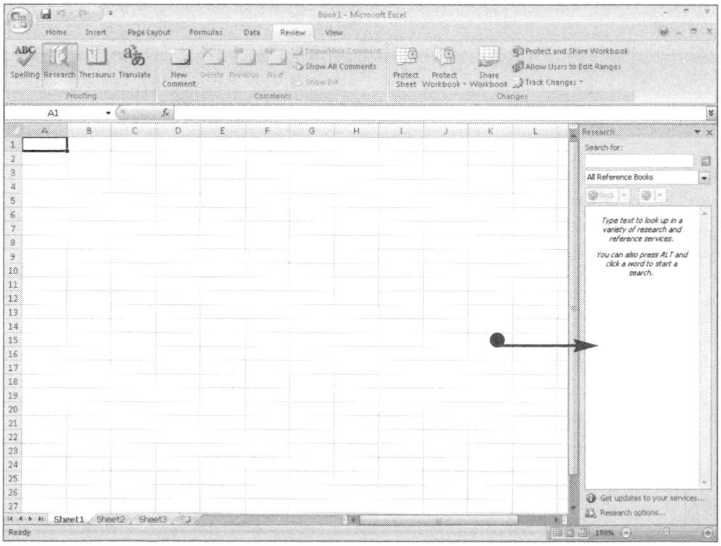

3 Type the word you want to research here.

4 Click ▾ to select a reference book.

- The results appear here.

5 Click ☒ to close the Research pane when you are finished.

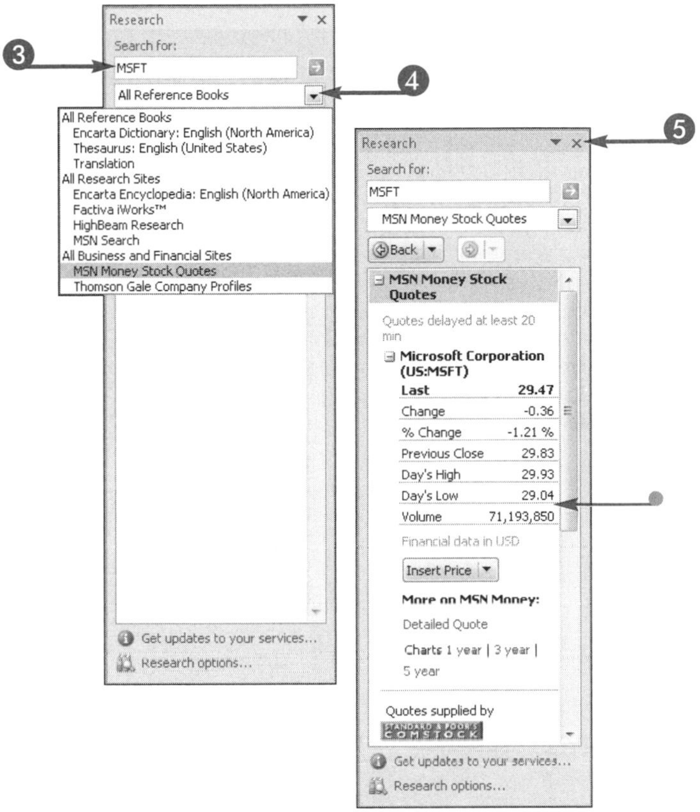

MASTER IT

Can I control the research tools that Excel uses?

▼ Yes. You can choose to activate a variety of services for searching. When you activate a service, you do not purchase a subscription. Click [Office button] and then click Excel Options. In the Excel Options dialog box, click Trust Center and then click the Trust Center Settings button. In the Trust Center dialog box, click Privacy Options and then click the Research Options button. In the Research Options dialog box, click a service to add it to the ones that Excel searches (◎ changes to ☑).

Is there an easy way to determine if the information returned by a tool is free or requires a subscription?

▼ Yes. For services that requirement payment, you see a visual cue. Be aware that all information returned by the reference book tools and MSN Money Stock Quotes is free. Thomson Gale and HighBeam Research provide overview information for free, and more detailed information is available for sale. To easily identify research for which you must pay, look for [icon] near a topic in the Research pane.

Insert and Delete Rows

You can add and delete rows in your worksheet to add or delete information. For example, you may have typed product names in the rows of a worksheet that shows product sales over a period of time, but you did not include the region in which those products were sold. Now you find that you need to add region designations as row titles to segregate sales by region as well as by product. Or, you may need to delete a row because you do not need the information that it contains.

When you add a row, Excel shifts the rows below the new row down and automatically adjusts the row numbers to accommodate the new row. Excel also automatically updates formulas affected by the row you insert. The new row is the same height as the row above it.

Similarly, when you delete a row, Excel removes all the information stored in the row and shifts the rows below the row you deleted upward. Excel also automatically adjusts the row numbers to accommodate the row you deleted and updates formulas affected by the row you deleted.

Insert and Delete Rows

Add a Row

1. Select the row that should appear below the row you are about to add.

Note: *See Chapter 4 for details on selecting a row.*

2. Click the Home tab.
3. Click Insert.

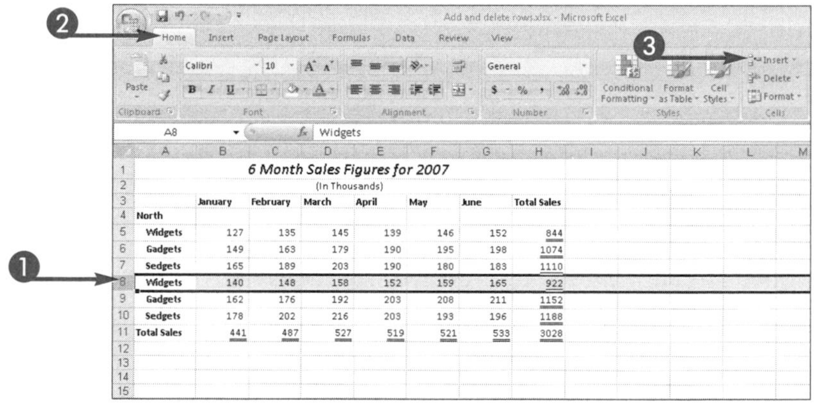

- Excel inserts a new row above the row you originally selected, and shifts all rows below the new row down by one row.

The new row appears selected.

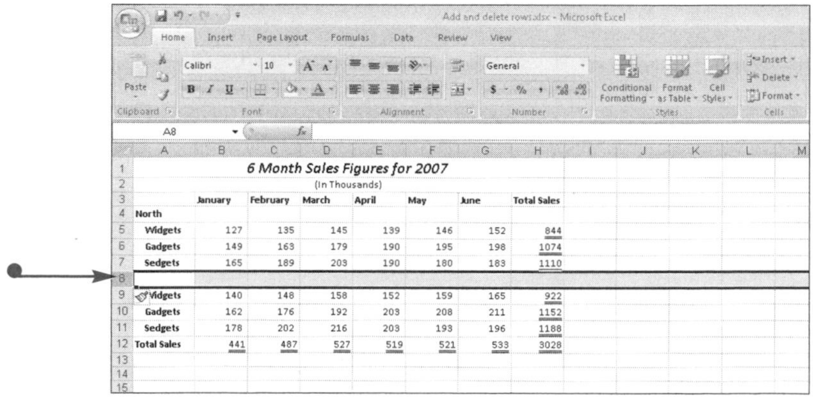

Delete a Row

1. Select the row you want to delete.
2. Click the Home tab.
3. Click Delete.

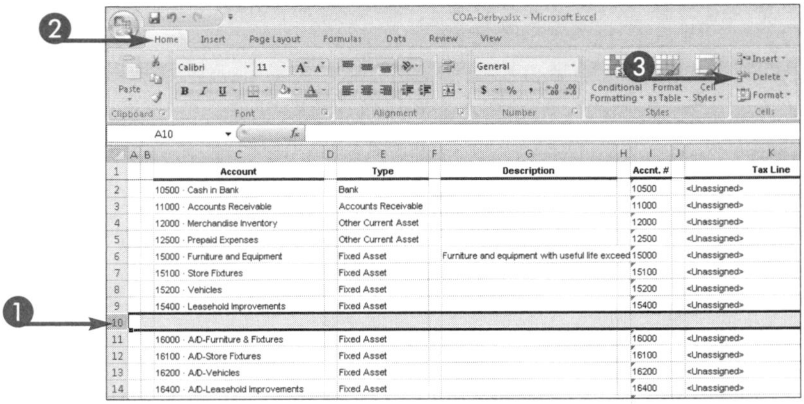

- Excel removes the row and selects the row that moved up to fill the space left by the deleted row.

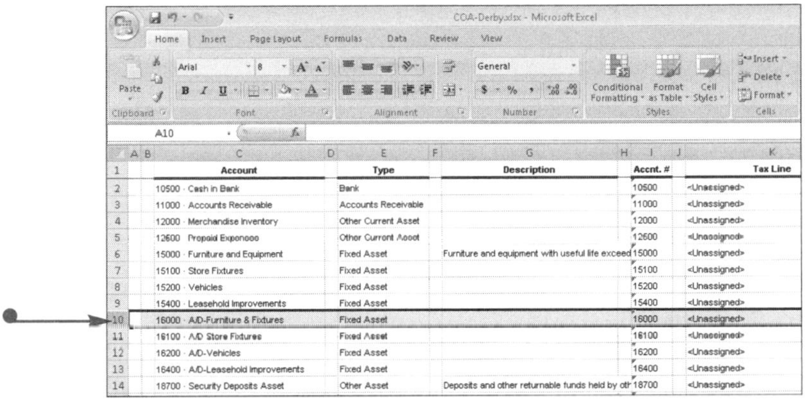

MASTER IT

Can I insert more than one row at a time?

▼ Yes. Excel inserts as many rows at one time as you select. For example, to insert five rows, select five rows, beginning with the first row you want to appear below the new rows. Place the mouse pointer in the row number area over the first row you want to select, and click and drag to select that row and four more. Then, follow Steps 2 and 3 in the subsection, "Add a Row." Excel inserts five rows into your worksheet.

Why does #REF! appear after I delete a row?

▼ If #REF! appears in a cell in your worksheet after you delete a row, the deleted row probably contained a formula that Excel was using to calculate the cell now displaying #REF!. You need to correct the formula in the cell containing #REF!, or you need to undo your action that deleted the row. For basic information on formulas, see Chapter 10.

Why does appear on a button near a row I just inserted?

▼ This button is called a Format Painter Smart Tag. Click it to select formatting for the new row. You can select Format Save As Above, Format Same As Below, or Clear Formatting (◯ changes to ◉).

Insert and Delete Columns

You can add and delete columns in your worksheet to add or delete information. For example, you may originally have typed months in the columns of a worksheet that shows product sales over a period of time, but you started with April and now you want to add March sales to the worksheet. You may also need to delete a column because you do not need the information that it contains.

When you add or delete a column, you start by selecting a column. When you add a column, Excel shifts the columns on the right of the new column over by one column and automatically adjusts the column letters to accommodate the new column. Excel also automatically updates formulas affected by the column you insert. The new column is the same width as the column to its left.

Similarly, when you delete a column, Excel removes all the information stored in the column and shifts the columns on the right of the column that you deleted to the left. Excel also automatically adjusts the column letters to accommodate the column you deleted and updates formulas affected by the column you deleted.

Insert and Delete Columns

Add a Column

1. Select the column that should appear to the left of the column you are about to add.

Note: *See Chapter 4 for details on selecting a column.*

2. Click the Home tab.
3. Click Insert.

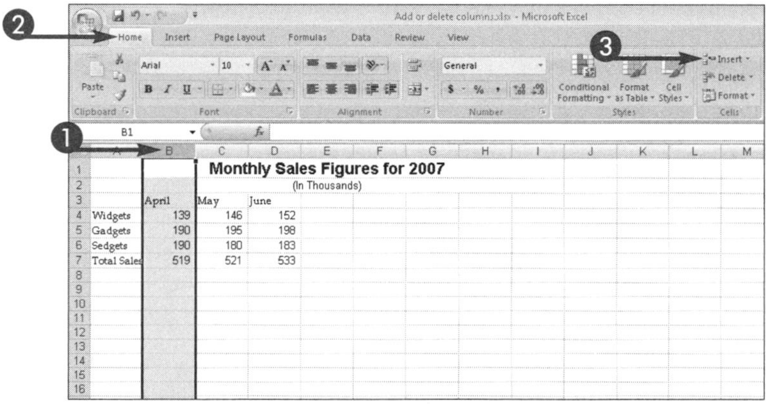

- Excel inserts a new column to the left of the column that you originally selected, and shifts columns on the right of the new column to the right by one column.

The new column appears selected.

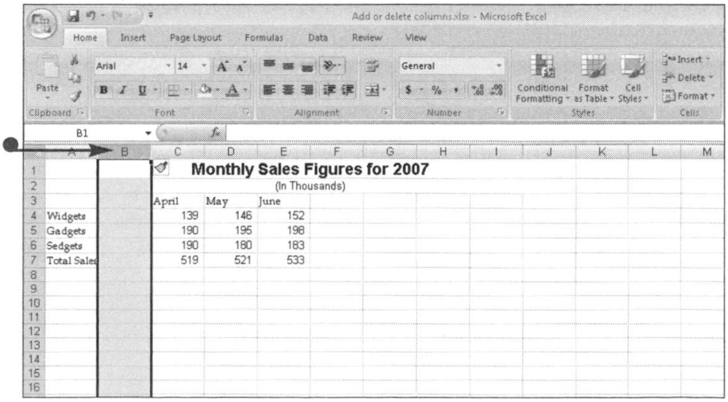

Delete a Column

1. Select the column you want to delete.
2. Click the Home tab.
3. Click Delete.

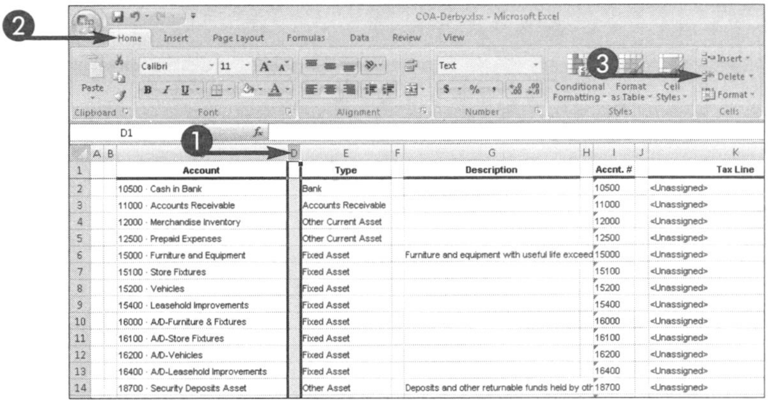

- Excel removes the column and selects the column that moved to the left to fill the space left by the deleted column.

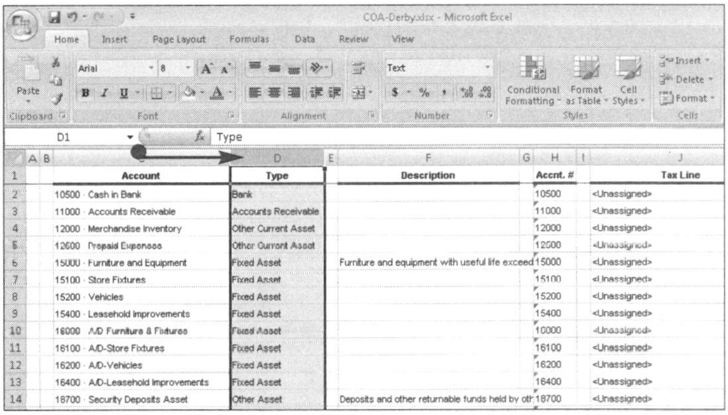

Can I add a group of cells instead of adding an entire column?

▼ Yes. Select the cells that are located where you want the new cells to appear. Excel will move these cells when you insert the new cells. Click the Home tab and then click Insert. To exercise more control over how Excel inserts the cells, click ▾ beside the Insert button instead of clicking the button. Excel displays a dialog box in which you can click an option to indicate whether you want to shift the selected cells down or to the right (○ changes to ◉).

Can I delete more than one column at the same time?

▼ Yes. Move the mouse pointer into the column letter heading area, and click and drag to select all of the adjacent columns that you want to delete. If you want to delete non-contiguous columns, press and hold Ctrl as you click the column heading letters of the columns you want to delete. Then follow Steps 2 and 3 in the subsection, "Delete a Column." Excel deletes the selected columns and shifts to the left columns on the right of the deleted column.

Swap Rows and Columns

You can switch the orientation of the rows and columns of your worksheet. Swapping rows and columns can help you avoid a lot of retyping if you set up a worksheet and then realize that you really want the rows to be columns and the columns to be rows.

When you swap rows and columns, you select the cells containing the information you want to switch. Then, you copy the information and use a special pasting technique that tells Excel to not only paste, but also transpose the orientation of the information as it pastes.

Typically, when you paste the information, you do not paste it into the same location where you originally placed it. Instead, you select a new portion of the worksheet as the destination for the swapped rows and columns. That way, you can easily compare the original data with the newly swapped rows and columns of data. When you select the destination location, you do not need to select all of the cells into which you want Excel to paste the information. Instead, you select the cell that will become the upper-left corner of the new range.

Swap Rows and Columns

1. Select the cells containing the information you want to swap.
2. Click the Home tab.
3. Click .

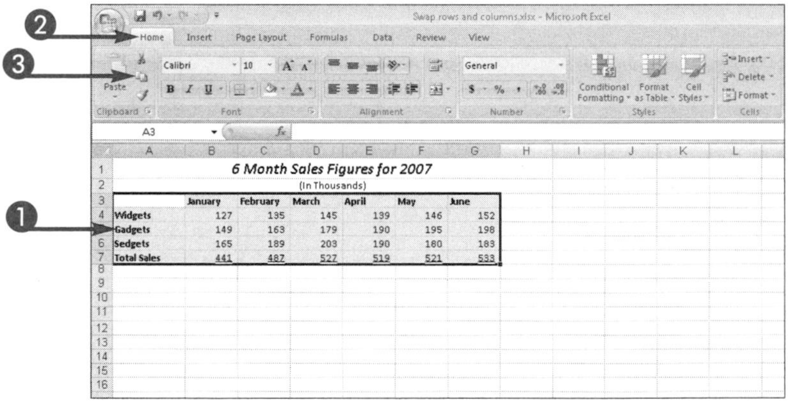

- Excel displays an animated dashed border around the cells you copied.

4. Click the cell that will become the upper-left corner of the swapped rows and columns.

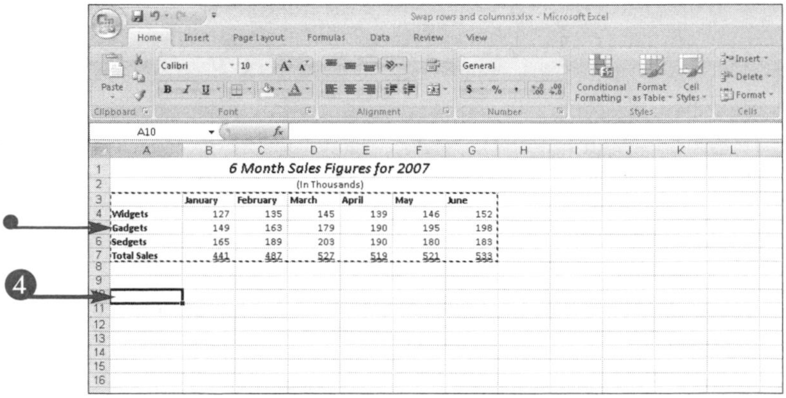

5 Click the bottom of the Paste button to display a drop-down menu.

6 Click Transpose.

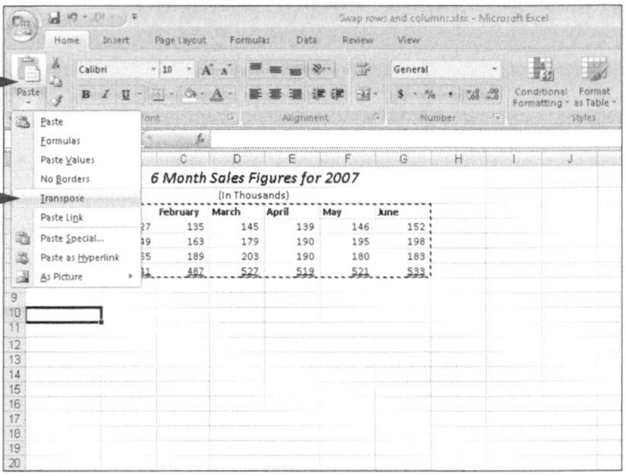

- Excel pastes the information into the selected location, swapping rows and columns. The destination range appears selected.

You can press Esc to eliminate the animated border around the cells you copied.

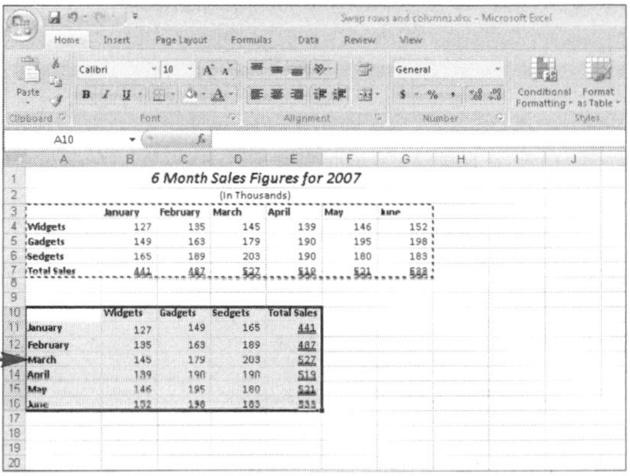

MASTER IT

Why do I need to place the swapped rows and columns in a different location than the original rows and columns?

▼ Most ranges are not square in size; they do not contain the same number of rows and columns. Because Excel is going to switch the rows and columns in the selected range, if you place the swapped version on top of the original version, some extraneous information will appear in some of the rows or columns of the original range, making things very confusing.

Is there a way to place the swapped rows and columns in the location where the original data appears?

▼ Yes. After swapping, clear the formats and the contents of the cells in the original location. For details on clearing the formatting, see Chapter 3. Then cut and paste the swapped rows and columns to the location where the original data appeared. See Chapter 4 for details on moving data.

When I swap columns and rows of a range that contains formulas, what happens?

▼ Excel does not consider cells that contain formulas to be special and therefore also swaps those cells. Excel remembers the formulas and retains them so that they still calculate properly. If formulas appeared originally in a column in your worksheet, they appear in a row after you swap columns and rows.

Adjust Row Height

You may need to adjust the height of a row so that all the information in a cell in that row can be easily seen. For example, if you select a cell, increase the font size, and then type in the cell, some of the text you type may appear cut off on the top. Adjusting the row height improves the appearance of your worksheet and enables you to read all of the text in the cell. You may also want to change the height of rows in a worksheet to add space between the rows to make reading the worksheet easier.

You can use either of two methods to change row height. One method lets you drag to adjust row height and use your eye to determine the appropriate height for the row. The other more precise method lets you use a dialog box to set a precise row height in points, where one point equals approximately 1⁄72 inch. The default row height is 15 points. You can change the height of more than one row simultaneously; just select the rows before you use either method.

Adjust Row Height

Set a Precise Row Height

1. To adjust the height of more than one row, select the rows you want to adjust.

Note: *See Chapter 4 for details on selecting rows.*

2. Click the Home tab.
3. Click Format.
4. Click Row Height.

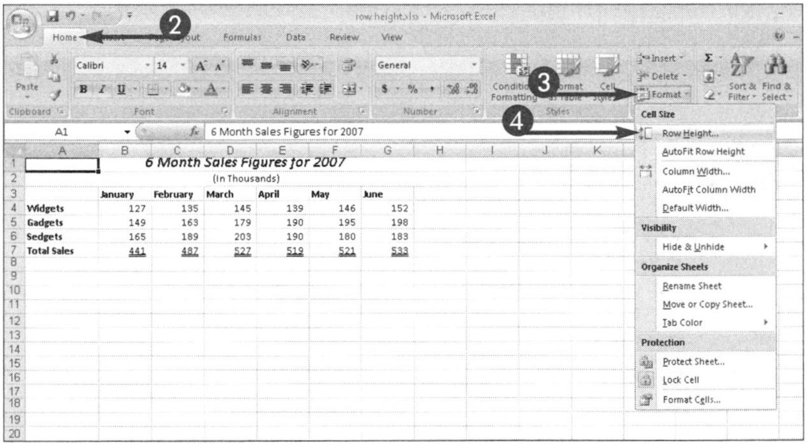

Excel displays the Row Height dialog box.

5. Type the height you want to apply to the row.
6. Click OK.

Excel adjusts the row height.

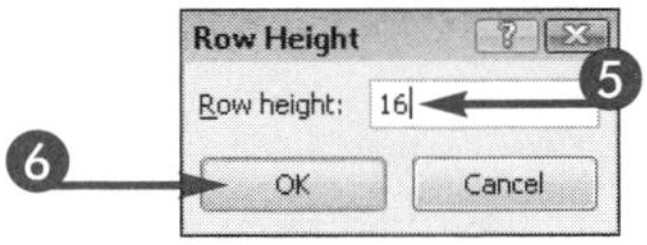

Set Row Height by Dragging

1. Move the mouse pointer into the row number area at the bottom of the row you want to adjust.

   The mouse pointer changes to ‡.

2. Click and drag downward to increase row height, or upward to decrease row height.

   - A dotted line marks the proposed height, and a box displays the measurement of the proposed row height.

3. Release the mouse button.

   - Excel adjusts the height of the row.

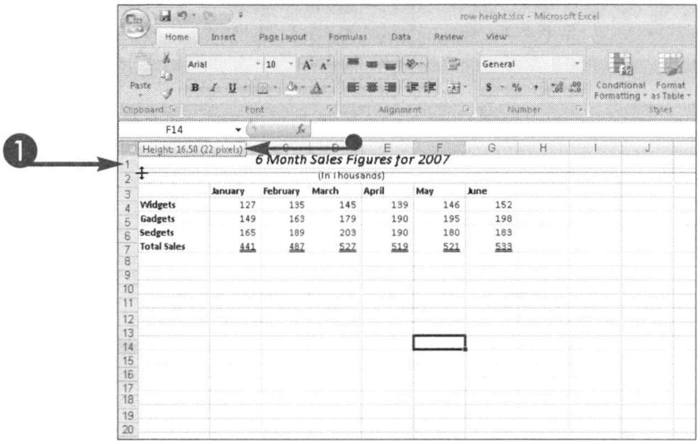

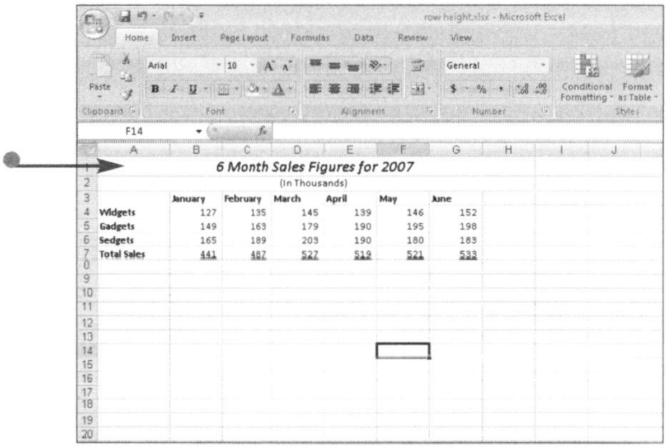

MASTER IT

Can I copy row height from one row to another?

▼ Row height is not a format that Excel copies when it copies formatting. To make one row the same height as another, place the cell pointer in a cell in the row with the height you want to match. Perform Steps 2 to 4 in the subsection, "Set a Precise Row Height," to identify the row height of the model row. Click Cancel and then perform Steps 1 to 6 in the same subsection, typing the height you noted for the model row in Step 5.

What does AutoFit Row Height do?

▼ When you click AutoFit Row Height on the Format drop-down menu, Excel sizes the height of the row so that the tallest entry in the row fits comfortably in the row. Shorter entries in the row may seem to have a lot of height within their cells, but all entries in the row will be legible and easy to read.

Adjust Column Width

You may need to adjust the width of a column so that all the information in a cell in that column can be easily seen. For example, if you type text into cell A1 that is longer than the width of column A, the text appears to spill into cell B1. However, when you type text into cell B1, the text in cell A1 now appears truncated. Adjusting the column width improves the appearance of your worksheet and enables you to read all of the text in cell A1.

You can use either of two methods to change column width. One method lets you drag to adjust column width and use your eye to determine the appropriate width for the column. The other more precise method lets you use a dialog box to set a precise column width in characters. By default, 8.43 characters will fit in a column, and that number is based on using a standard font, which Excel defines as the default text font for worksheets. You can change the width of more than one column simultaneously; just select the columns before you use either method.

Adjust Column Width

Set a Precise Column Width

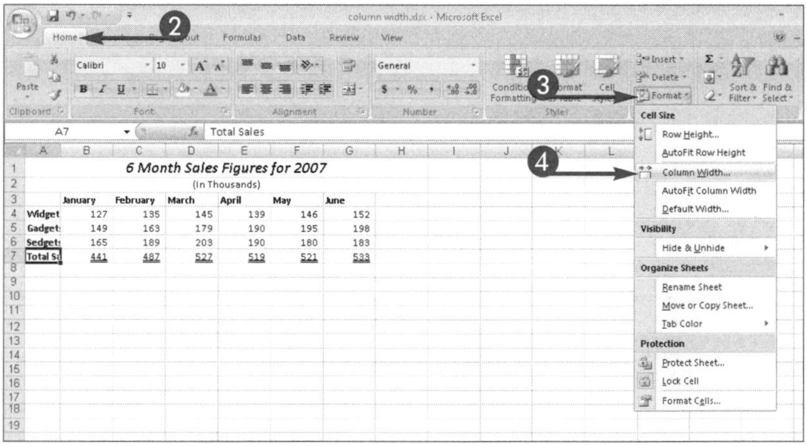

1. To adjust the width of more than one column, select the columns you want to adjust.

Note: *See Chapter 4 for details on selecting columns.*

2. Click the Home tab.
3. Click Format.
4. Click Column Width.

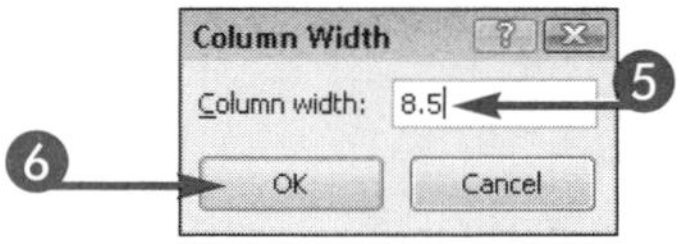

Excel displays the Column Width dialog box.

5. Type the width you want to apply to the column.
6. Click OK.

Excel adjusts the column width.

Set Column Width by Dragging

1. Move the mouse pointer into the column heading area on the right side of the column you want to adjust.

   changes to +.

2. Click and drag to the right to increase column width, or to the left to decrease column width.

   - A dotted line marks the proposed column width, and a pop-up box displays the proposed width.

3. Release the mouse button.

   - Excel adjusts the width of the column.

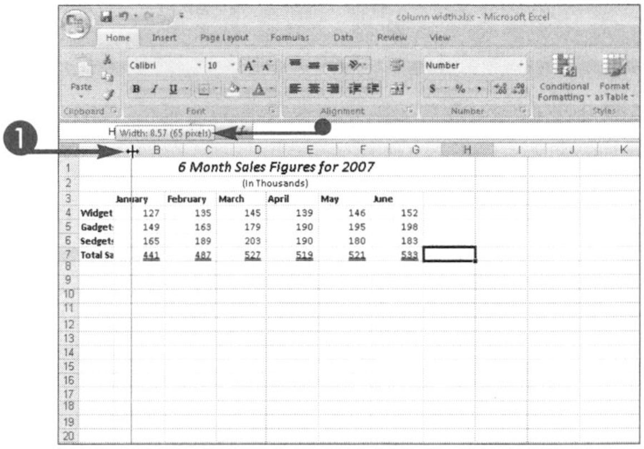

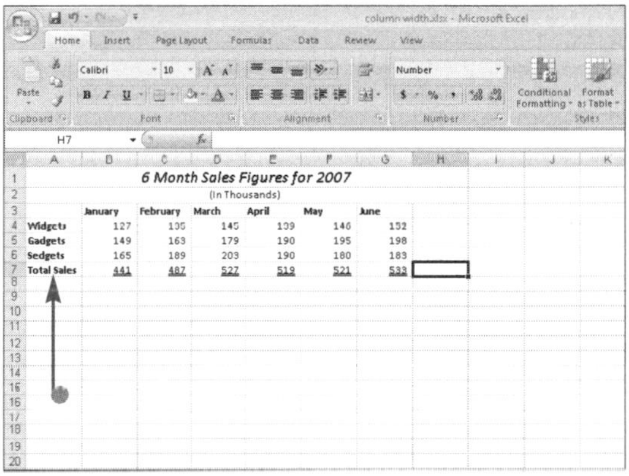

What does a series of pound signs (#) mean?

▼ When you see a series of pound signs in a cell, this means that the cell contains numerical information and the column is not wide enough to display the numbers. To solve this problem, use either of the techniques described in this section to widen the column or have Excel set the width of the column to accommodate the longest entry in the column. Click in the column and then complete Steps 2 and 3 in the subsection, "Set a Precise Column Width." On the Format drop-down menu, click AutoFit Column Width.

Can I change the width of all columns in the worksheet simultaneously?

▼ Yes. Click the button that appears above row 1 and to the left of column A ( ). Excel selects all cells in the worksheet. Then follow the steps in either subsection in this section; Excel will apply your changes to all selected cells.

Can I make Excel automatically size all columns to fit all entries that they contain?

▼ Yes. Click to select all cells in the worksheet. Then move the mouse pointer into the column heading area at the right edge of any column (changes to +). Double-click the column boundary; Excel resizes all selected columns so that they match the width of the longest entry.

Copy Width from One Column to Another

You can copy the width of one column to another column without copying any other elements. Copying the column width can be useful to enhance the appearance of your worksheet. For example, suppose that you resized all of the columns in your worksheet to accommodate the longest entry in a column. Later, after saving and closing the workbook, you reopen it and realize that setting all column widths to accommodate the longest entry in the column has resulted in many different column sizes, and your worksheet is not as readable as you would like. In this situation, you can set the width of one column to a size that you think would be appropriate and then copy that width to other columns in the workbook.

When you copy column widths, you use a special form of copy-and-paste operation. The special form copies only column widths so that you do not need to worry about preserving data in the columns that you resize using the new width. This approach makes it easy to consistently set column widths.

Copy Width from One Column to Another

1. Click a cell in the column that has the width you want to copy.
2. Click the Home tab.
3. Click .

   Excel displays an animated dashed border around the cell you selected.

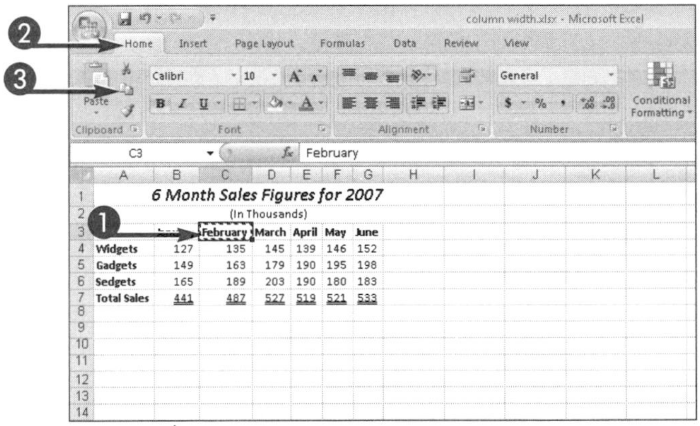

4. Click a cell in the column to which you want to assign the new width.
5. Click the bottom portion of the Paste button.

   Excel displays a drop-down list.

6. Click Paste Special.

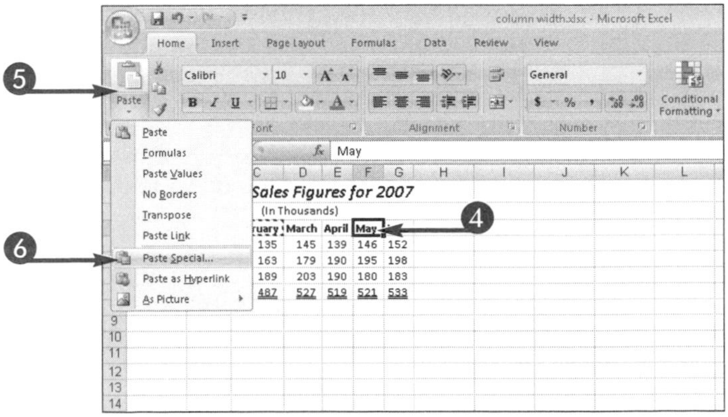

Excel displays the Paste Special dialog box.

7 Click Column Widths (◎ changes to ◉).

8 Click OK.

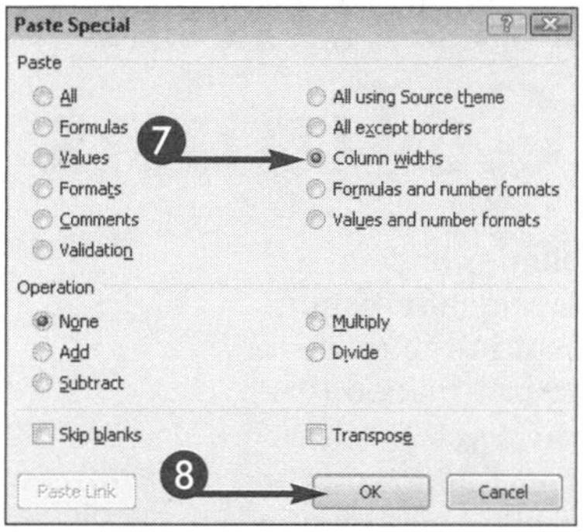

- Excel copies the column width from the column you selected in Step 1 to the column you selected in Step 4.

You can press Esc to cancel the animated dashed border around the cell you selected in Step 1.

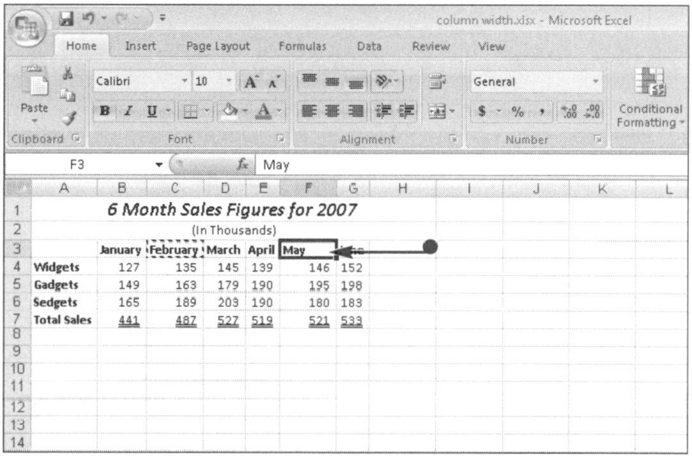

MASTER IT

How can I copy the column width of one column to multiple columns?

▼ Follow Steps 1 to 3. For Step 4, select cells in all of the columns to which you want to copy the column width. If the cells are in columns that are contiguous, you can click and drag to select them, or you can select the first cell and then press and hold Shift and select the last cell. If the cells are in columns that are not contiguous, press and hold Ctrl as you select each cell. Then complete Steps 5 to 8.

Will copying column widths get rid of the pound signs (#) that appear in one column in my worksheet?

▼ Possibly. Pound signs indicate that the cell displaying them contains a number and that the cell's column is not wide enough to display the number. Copying column widths might fix your problem, if you happen to copy the width of a column that is wide enough to accommodate the number in the column that is too narrow. If copying a column width does not solve the problem, then widen the column of the cell displaying the pound signs. See the section, "Adjust Column Width," for details.

Hide and Unhide Rows or Columns

You can hide rows and columns in your worksheet to avoid displaying information that might not be pertinent to the reader or that might be confidential. Hiding information that a reader does not need to see can help you fit the information on fewer printed pages. Hiding rows and columns while you work can also help you focus on particular portions of a worksheet.

Hiding rows or columns does not affect the formulas and functions in your worksheet. Formulas and functions continue to work when you hide them or when you hide cells used by formulas and functions in their calculations. You also do not need to display particular rows or columns to include cells in those rows or columns when you create formulas and functions.

When you hide a row or column, Excel does not display either the information stored in that row or column or the row number or the column letter for the hidden row or column. For example, if you hide column C, Excel displays columns A, B, D, E, and so on, skipping column C.

You can easily redisplay hidden rows and columns at any time.

Hide and Unhide Rows or Columns

Hide Rows or Columns

1. Select a cell in the row or column that you want to hide.

   To hide multiple rows or columns, select cells that span those rows or columns.

2. Click the Home tab.
3. Click Format.
4. Click Hide & Unhide.
5. Click Hide Rows or Hide Columns.

   This example hides columns.

   Excel hides the rows or columns.

   - Hidden row numbers or column letters do not appear in the worksheet.

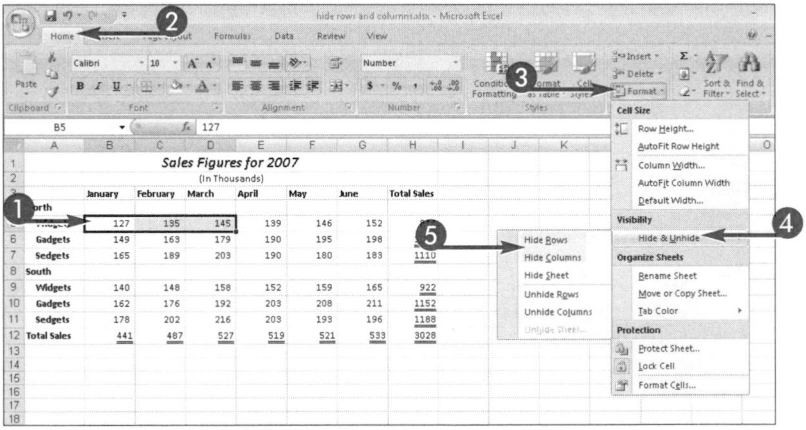

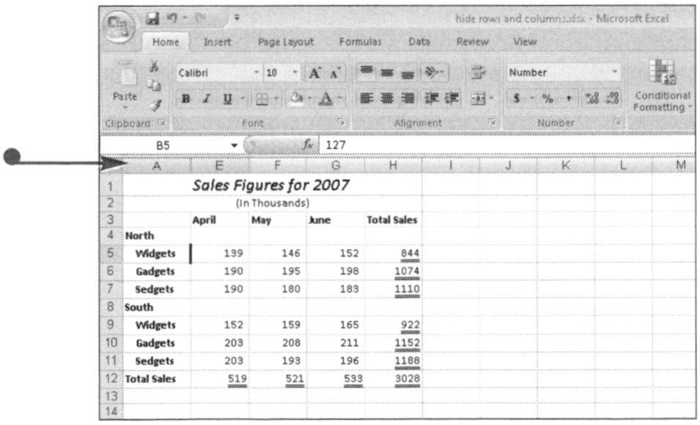

Unhide Rows or Columns

1. Select two cells that span the range of the hidden row or column.
2. Click the Home tab.
3. Click Format.
4. Click Hide & Unhide.
5. Click Unhide Rows or Unhide Columns.

This example unhides columns.

- Excel redisplays the hidden rows or columns and selects the original two cells along with cells from the range that had been hidden.

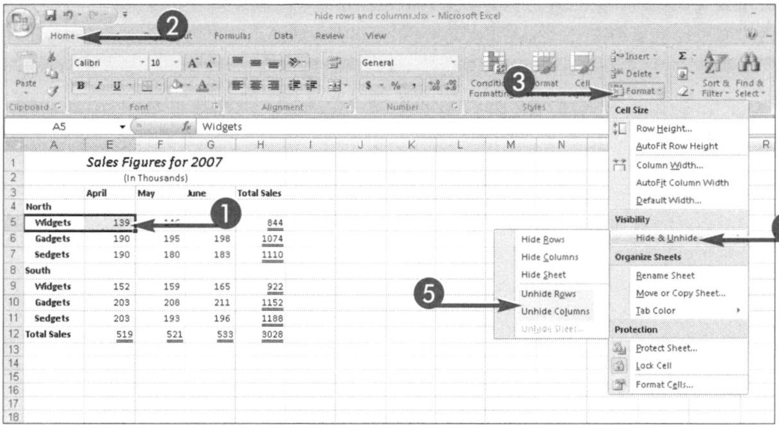

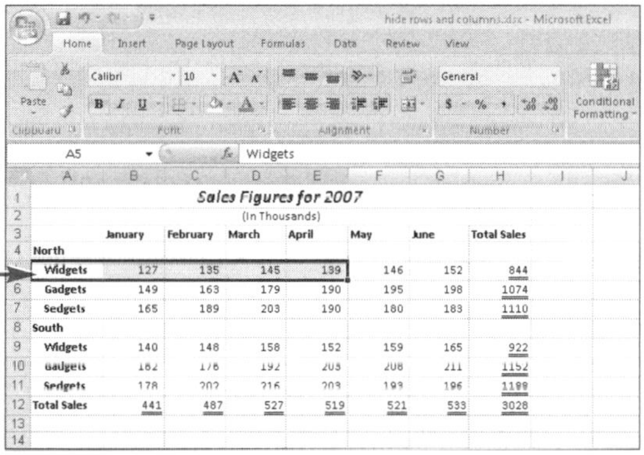

Can I hide row 1 or column A and, if so, how do I redisplay them?

▼ Yes, you can hide row 1 or column A. To redisplay either of them, click the Home tab and then click Find & Select in the Editing group. From the Find & Select menu, click Go To. In the Go To dialog box that appears, type **A1** in the Reference box and click OK. Then, follow Steps 2 to 5 in the subsection, "Unhide Rows or Columns."

Can I hide an entire worksheet in my workbook?

▼ Yes. Click the worksheet's tab to make sure that you are viewing the worksheet. Then, complete Steps 2 to 4 in the subsection, "Hide Rows or Columns." For Step 5, click Hide Sheet. To unhide the sheet, complete Steps 2 to 4 in the subsection, "Unhide Rows or Columns." For Step 5, click Unhide Sheet.

Can I protect information in my workbook by hiding it?

▼ No. Anyone who opens your workbook can unhide the rows or columns that you hide. Remember, because Excel skips the row numbers and column letters of hidden rows and columns, they are easy to identify. To protect information in your workbook, you can assign a password to the workbook. Then, only those who know the password can open the workbook and make changes. For more details, see Chapter 31.

Merge Cells in Columns or Rows

You can merge two or more cells in a worksheet to combine them into one cell. Merging is most commonly used when you want to create a title in a worksheet that stretches across a group of cells. Typically, in this situation, you not only merge cells but you center the text in the resulting merged cell.

You can merge cells in a row or in a column. You can merge and center text within the merged cell simultaneously, as shown in this section, or, once you merge cells, you can use Excel's alignment features to position text that appears within the merged cell. If you merge across rows, you can center the text in the merged cell, or you can align it on the right or left side of the cell. If you merge across columns, you can center the text in the merged cell or you can align it with the top or bottom of the cell.

When you merge cells, you should make sure that no information appears in any of the cells you plan to merge, except for the cell that will be in the upper-left corner of the cells that you select to merge.

Merge Cells in Columns or Rows

Merge Cells Across Columns

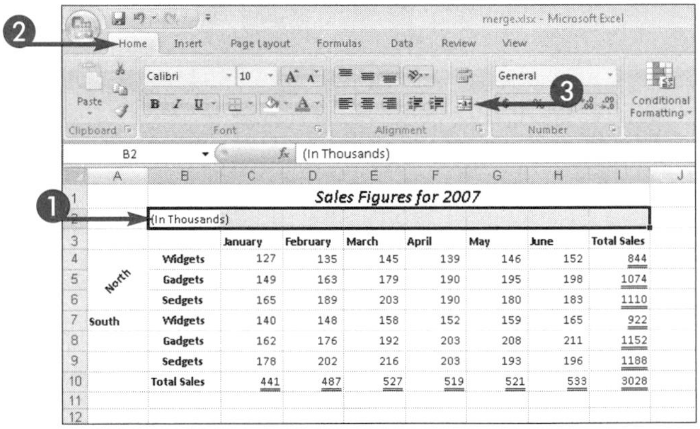

1. Select the cells you want to merge.

Note: *Only the cell serving as the left edge of the selection should contain data.*

2. Click the Home tab.
3. Click Merge & Center (▣).

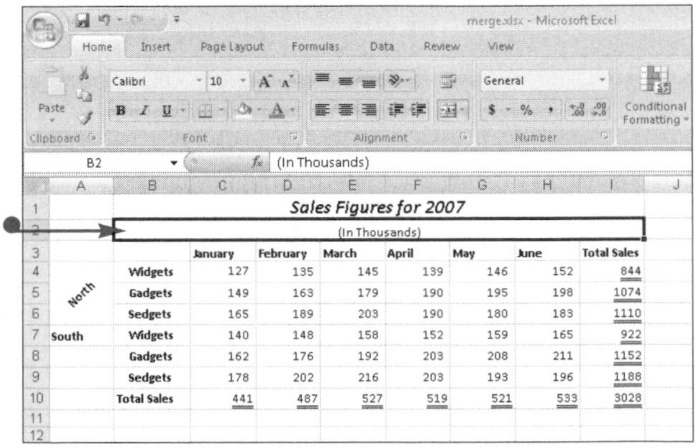

- Excel merges the selected cells into a single cell and centers the text in the cell between the left and right sides of the merged cell.

Merge Cells Across Rows

1. Select the cells you want to merge.

Note: *Only the cell serving as the top edge of the selection should contain data.*

2. Click the Home tab.
3. Click .

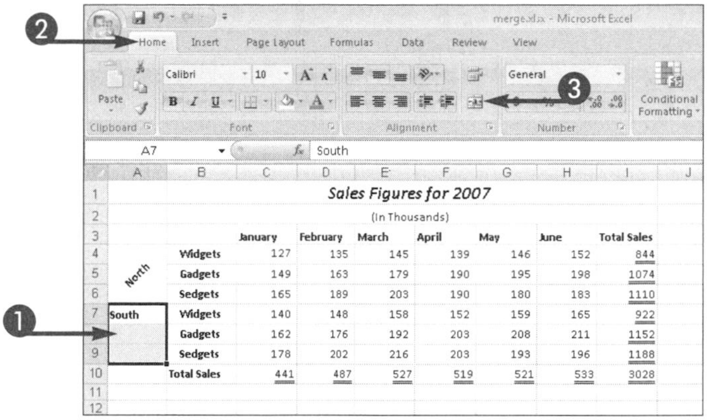

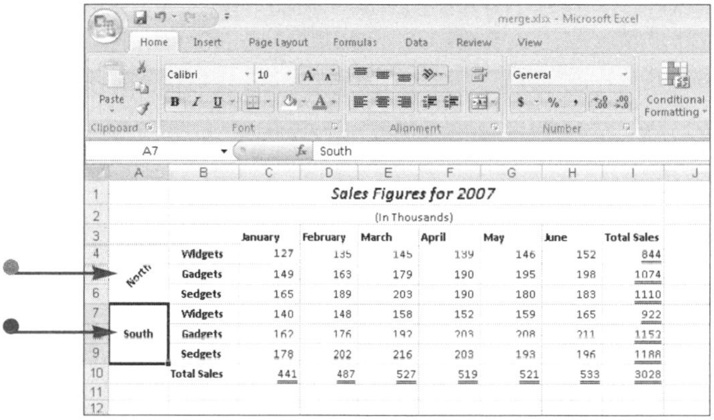

- Excel merges the selected cells into a single cell and centers the text in the cell between the top and bottom of the merged cell.
- You can change the alignment and orientation of text in the merged cell to enhance its appearance.

Note: *See Chapter 3 for details on changing alignment orientation.*

MASTER IT

Can I merge without centering?

▼ Yes. Click beside to view a list of merging choices. If you click either Merge Across or Merge Cells, Excel only merges the selected cells but does not change the alignment already assigned to the cell containing the text. When you click , Excel actually performs two actions. The first combines the selected cells and the second sets the alignment for the merged cell.

What is the difference between the Merge Across command and the Merge Cells command that appear when you click beside ?

▼ When you merge across columns, the two commands perform the exact same function: They both merge without centering. However, when you merge cells across rows, Merge Across does not work. To merge the cells without centering, use the Merge Cells command.

Can I unmerge cells?

▼ Yes. If you are unmerging a single cell, you can select the cell and click to unmerge the cell. However, if you want to unmerge more than one cell simultaneously, do not click because you may lose data. Instead, select the merged cells and click beside . Then click Unmerge Cells.

Set Worksheet Tab Colors

You can assign colors to worksheet tabs to help you identify a worksheet's contents. For example, suppose that your organization has set standards for workbooks that store product sales to help easily evaluate sales for different time periods. In your organization, each workbook that stores product sales numbers should contain four worksheets, with each worksheet storing only one quarter's information. You can color code the worksheet tabs so that, in each workbook, sales for the first quarter always appear on a worksheet that has a red tab. You might assign yellow to the second quarter, green to the third quarter, and blue to the fourth quarter.

To keep your color coding consistent, your organization should decide on a standard that is to be used by everyone who accesses these workbooks. By default, you assign worksheet tab colors on a workbook-by-workbook basis. To automatically assign colors to worksheet tabs for each new workbook, you can create a template that contains worksheets to which you have assigned colors, and then base new workbooks on that template. For details on creating templates, see Chapter 4.

Set Worksheet Tab Colors

Set Tab Color

1. Right-click the tab of a worksheet.
2. Click Tab Color.
3. Select a color.

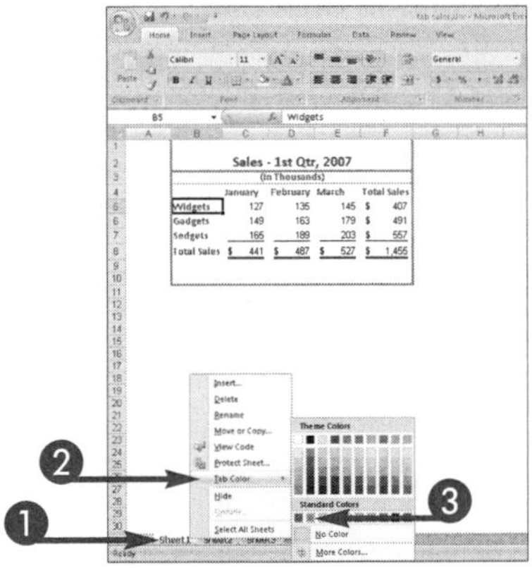

- Excel adds the color to the bottom of the worksheet tab.
- Tab colors are more apparent on worksheets that are not active.

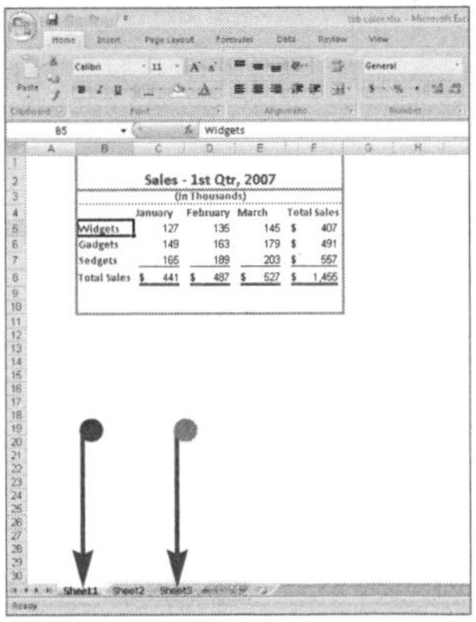

Remove Tab Color

1. Right-click the tab of a worksheet.
2. Click Tab Color.
3. Click No Color.

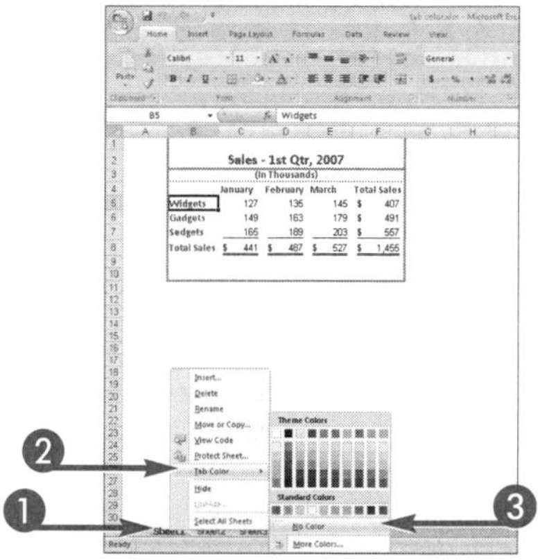

- Excel removes the color from the worksheet tab.

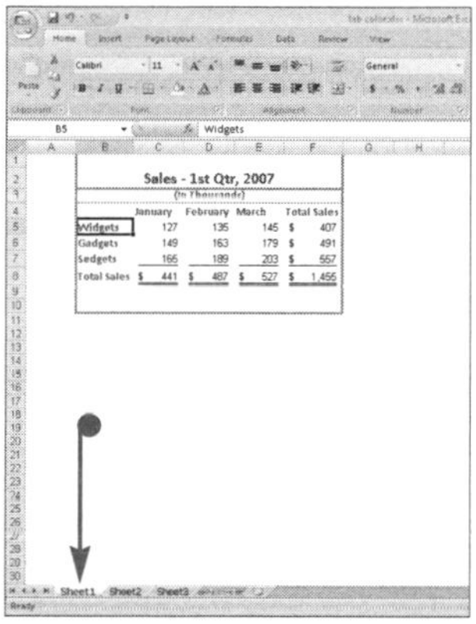

MASTER IT

Does Excel limit the number of colors that I can apply to worksheet tabs?

▼ Not really. In addition to the ten standard colors, you can choose from among ten theme colors, and each theme includes five shades associated with the theme's main color. If none of these colors work for you, you can complete Steps 1 and 2 in the subsection, "Set Tab Color." For Step 3, click More Colors to display the Colors dialog box and set a custom color, based on variations of the standard colors that appear after you complete Steps 1 and 2.

How do I go about setting a custom color?

▼ In the Colors dialog box, you can select from among variations of the standard colors by clicking a color swatch. You can also precisely set a color using one of two models: Using the RGB model, you can specify the relative amounts of red, green, and blue that you want to assign to the color. You can also use the HSL model to set hue, saturation, and luminance levels for a color. As you select colors, a preview shows you the difference between the current choice and your new choice.

Edit Multiple Worksheets Simultaneously

You can simultaneously apply editing changes to more than one worksheet at a time by creating a group of worksheets. For example, this technique is particularly useful when you want to check spelling. You can check a group of worksheets simultaneously instead of checking each worksheet separately.

You can apply other types of editing changes to a group of worksheets, and this type of editing works extremely well if each worksheet is laid out the same way. For example, if your workbook contains four worksheets that each track sales for the same products but for different time periods, you can take advantage of group editing to apply formatting or even to insert formulas. By grouping the worksheets, you do the work once, but Excel applies the work to all worksheets in the group.

If you plan to apply formatting to, or insert formulas into, a group of worksheets, make sure that they are set up identically; otherwise, you risk accidentally overwriting data. If you want to monitor the group editing, you can set up a new window for each worksheet, group the worksheets, and display each worksheet tab in a separate window. See the section, "Arrange Open Worksheets or Workbooks," for details.

Edit Multiple Worksheets Simultaneously

Group Worksheets

1. Press and hold Ctrl as you click the tab for each worksheet you want to select.

   This example selects four worksheets.

   - Excel displays "Group" in the title bar of the workbook.

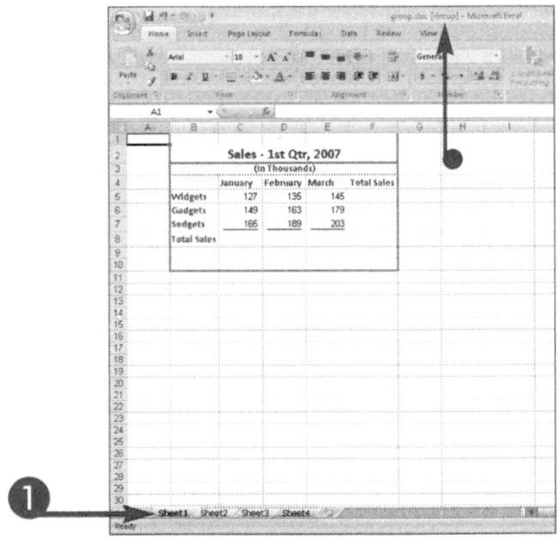

2. Perform an action on Sheet1.

   - This example adds a formula in cell F5 to sum C5, D5, and E5. The formula appears in the Formula Bar, and the result appears in the worksheet.

Note: *See Chapter 10 for details on adding basic formulas.*

3. Click the tab for Sheet2.

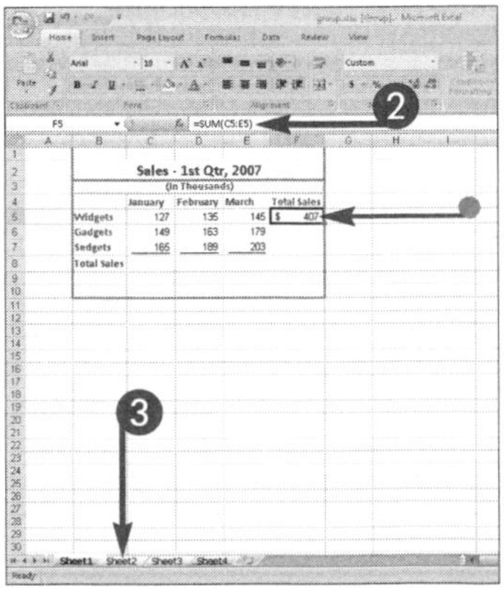

- Sheet2 becomes the active worksheet.
- Excel performs the same action on Sheet2.

You can click the tabs of each of the other worksheets in the group to see that Excel performs the same action on all worksheets in the group.

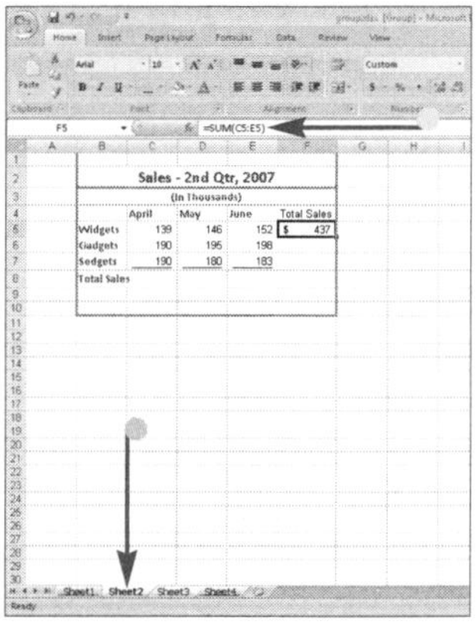

Ungroup Worksheets

1. Right-click the tab of any worksheet.
2. Click Ungroup Sheets.

Excel cancels the group selection, and "Group" disappears from the title bar.

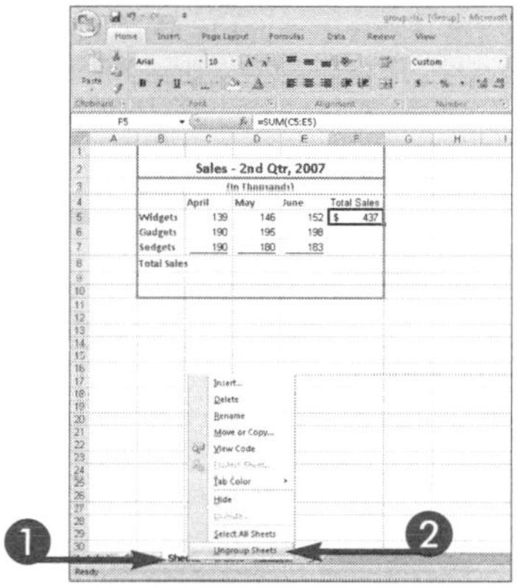

MASTER IT

Can I group worksheets and work on a worksheet other than Sheet1?

▼ Yes. Start by clicking the tab of the worksheet on which you want to work. Then, press and hold Ctrl as you click the other worksheets you want to include in the group. Excel groups the worksheets but displays the first worksheet you clicked as the active worksheet.

Can I add worksheets from the group?

▼ Yes. Perform Step 1 in the subsection "Group worksheets" on the tab of the worksheet you want to add to the group. Any changes you made to the group prior to adding that extra worksheet will not appear on the extra worksheet. Excel will apply future changes to the new group member as well as to the rest of the group.

Is there an easy way to select all worksheets in a workbook?

▼ Yes. Right-click the tab of the worksheet in which you want to edit. Excel makes that worksheet the active worksheet. From the shortcut menu that appears, click Select All Sheets. Excel selects all worksheets in the workbook and displays the worksheet whose tab you right-clicked.

Add or Delete a Worksheet

By default, Excel includes three worksheets in every new, blank workbook that you create, but you can add or delete worksheets in any workbook.

You can add more worksheets if you need to add information to the workbook that you want to separate from information on other worksheets. Using multiple worksheets in a workbook can help you organize information in the workbook. For example, you can store quarterly sales information for products you sell on separate worksheets in the same workbook. You can also store grades for each test you give to a class on separate worksheets.

When you add a worksheet to a workbook, Excel inserts the worksheet in front of the worksheet that you are viewing at the time you add the new worksheet. Excel also displays the new worksheet after you insert it.

You can also delete worksheets that you do not need. For example, if you are tracking prices for a particular stock, you only need one worksheet on which to store the date and the stock's price. You can easily delete the other worksheets in the workbook. After you delete a worksheet, Excel displays the worksheet behind the one you deleted.

Add or Delete a Worksheet

Add a Worksheet

1. Click the tab of the worksheet that you want to appear behind the new worksheet.
2. Click the Home tab.
3. Click ▾ beside the Insert button.
4. Click Insert Sheet.

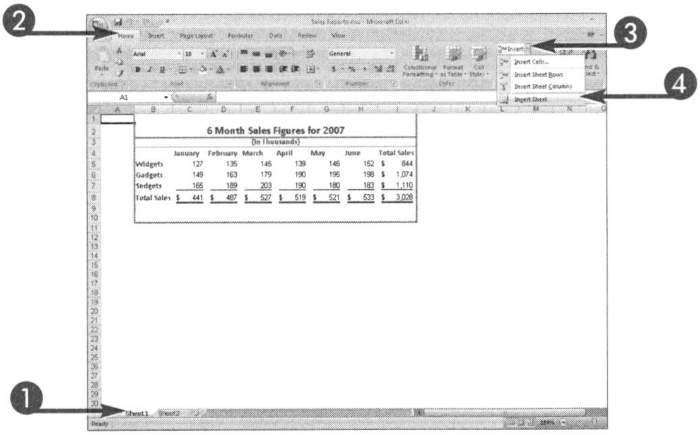

- Excel displays the new worksheet.
- The new worksheet appears in front of the worksheet you selected in Step 1.

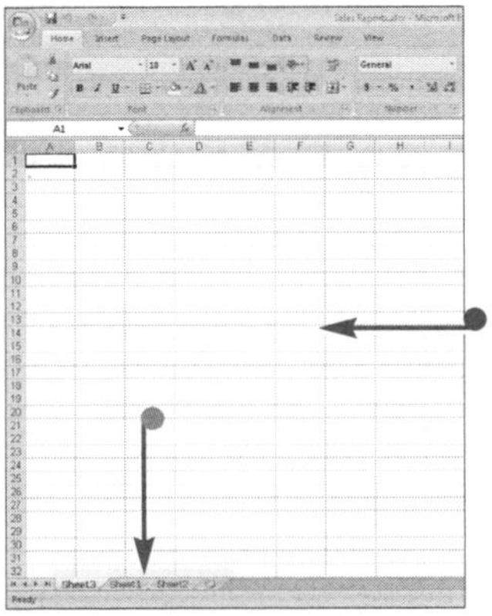

Delete a Worksheet

1. Click the tab of the worksheet you want to delete.
2. Click the Home tab.
3. Click ▾ beside the Delete button.
4. Click Delete Sheet.

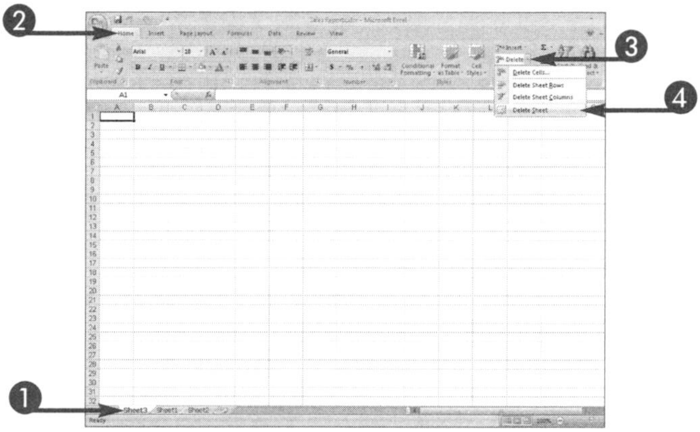

- Excel deletes the worksheet and displays the worksheet behind the deleted worksheet.

Note: *If the sheet contains any data or formatting, Excel warns you before deleting it and you must click the Delete button to delete the sheet.*

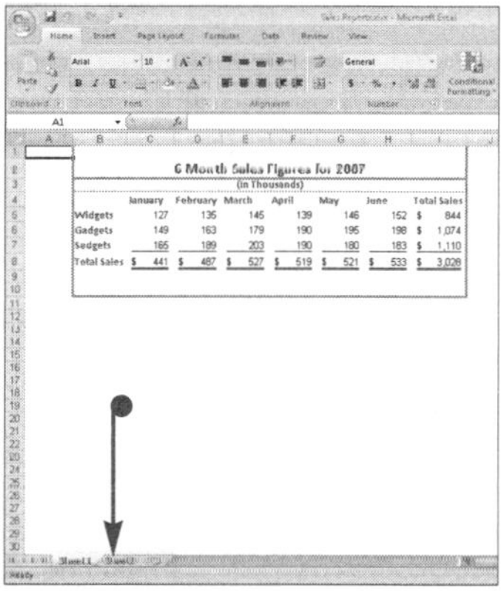

MASTER IT

Is there a way to make Excel insert a new worksheet behind another worksheet?

▼ By default, Excel inserts a new worksheet in front of the active worksheet, and so worksheet placement is a matter of perspective. For example, suppose that you have Sheet1, Sheet2, and Sheet3 in your workbook. To insert a new worksheet behind Sheet1, click Sheet2's tab and then follow the steps in the subsection, "Add a Worksheet." To insert a worksheet behind Sheet3, which is the last worksheet in the workbook, click the Insert Worksheet button (▭) that appears after the last worksheet tab in your workbook. Excel inserts a new worksheet after the last worksheet in the workbook.

When I inserted a new worksheet in front of Sheet2 in my workbook that contained two worksheets, why did Excel place Sheet3 between Sheet1 and Sheet2?

▼ Excel places a new worksheet in the workbook in front of the worksheet that is active when you insert the new worksheet. Excel also consecutively numbers all worksheets that you insert. As a result, when you start with Sheet1 and Sheet2 in your workbook and you select Sheet2 as the active worksheet and follow the steps in the subsection, "Add a Worksheet," Excel places Sheet3 between Sheet1 and Sheet2. However, you can reorder your worksheets. For more information, see the section, "Move or Copy a Worksheet."

Move or Copy a Worksheet

You can move or copy a worksheet to a new location within the same workbook, or to an entirely different workbook. For example, moving a worksheet is helpful if you insert a new worksheet and the worksheet tab names appear out of order. You may also want to move a worksheet that tracks sales for the year to a new workbook so that you can start tracking for a new year.

Copying a worksheet is helpful when you plan to make major editing changes to the worksheet. If you copy the worksheet before you start editing, you can preserve the original worksheet before you make changes. That way, you can easily reinstate the original if the changes you make return unexpected results.

MASTER IT

Is there a way to move a worksheet without using a dialog box?

▼ Yes. You can move a worksheet within the same workbook without using a dialog box. Click and drag the worksheet's tab. As you drag, ✥ changes to ⇱, and ▣ marks the location of the worksheet tab if you release the mouse button.

Move or Copy a Worksheet

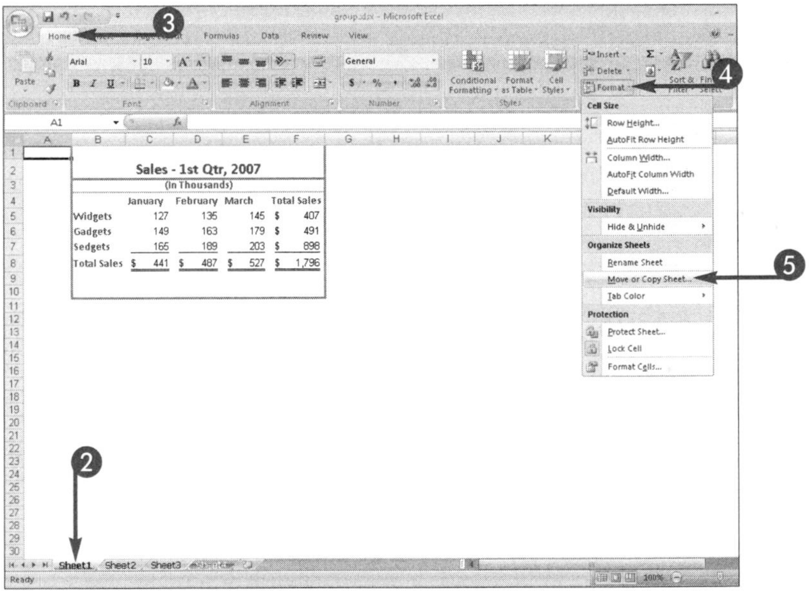

1. If you plan to move a worksheet to a different workbook, open both workbooks and select the one containing the worksheet you want to move.
2. Click the tab of the worksheet you want to move or copy to make it the active worksheet.
3. Click the Home tab.
4. Click Format.
5. Click Move or Copy Sheet.

   The Move or Copy dialog box appears.

   - You can click ▾ to select a workbook for the worksheet.

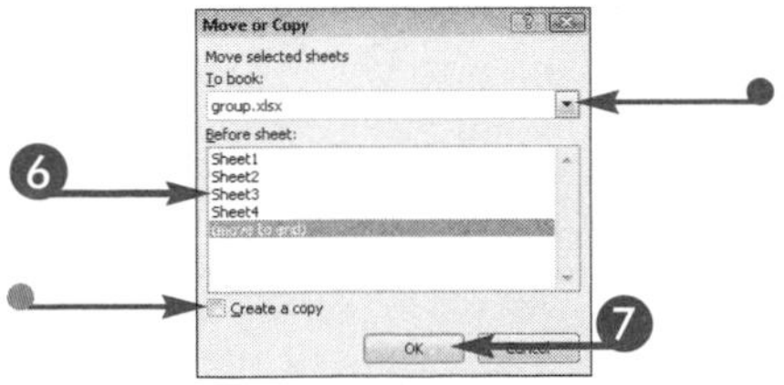

6. Click where you want to place the worksheet that you are moving.

   - You can copy a worksheet by clicking Create a Copy (☐ changes to ☑).

7. Click OK.

Rename a Worksheet

You can rename worksheet tabs from their default names of Sheet1 or Sheet2 to something meaningful that describes the contents of the worksheets. Providing a descriptive name helps you and other users to quickly and easily find worksheets. For example, if your worksheet contains sales data for the first quarter of 2007, you can name the worksheet Qtr1 - 2007. If your worksheet contains test scores for the midterm exam of the first semester of 2007, you can name the worksheet Midterm Exam Scores.

You can supply a name up to 31 characters in length for any worksheet tab. The name can include spaces, but cannot include any of the following characters: / \ [ ] ? : or *. Generally, shorter names work better than longer names for two reasons. First, shorter names take up less space so that you can display and see the complete names of more worksheet tabs. Second, you can use worksheet names in formulas, and so shorter worksheet names make it easier to create a formula that contains a worksheet name. See Chapter 10 for details on creating formulas.

PART II

Rename a Worksheet

1. Click the tab of the worksheet you want to rename.
2. Click the Home tab.
3. Click Format.
4. Click Rename Sheet.

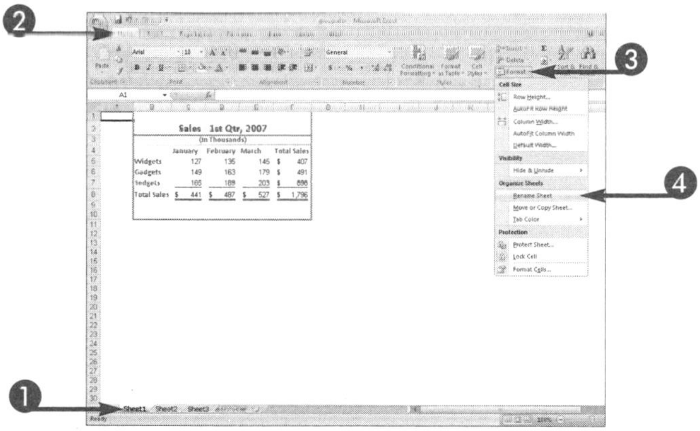

Excel highlights the current name of the worksheet in the worksheet's tab.

5. Type a new name.
6. Press Enter.

Excel saves the new name.

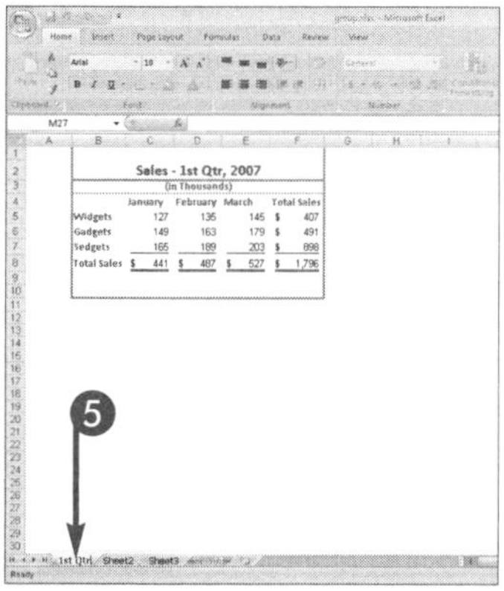

Hide and Unhide a Worksheet

You can hide a worksheet in a workbook to avoid displaying information on-screen that is confidential or that might not be pertinent to the reader. For example, you might want to hide a worksheet that contains sensitive information such as employee salaries or student test grades.

Hiding a worksheet does not affect any formulas and functions in your worksheet. Formulas and functions continue to work when you hide a worksheet that contains them. Formulas and functions also continue to work when you hide a worksheet that contains cells that are being used by formulas and functions in other worksheets. You also do not need to display a particular worksheet to include cells in that worksheet when you create formulas and functions. See Chapter 10 for details on creating basic formulas.

When you hide a worksheet, Excel does not display either the information stored in that worksheet or the worksheet tab of the hidden worksheet. For example, if you hide Sheet2 in a workbook that contains Sheet1, Sheet2, Sheet3, and Sheet4, Excel displays Sheet1, Sheet3, and Sheet4, skipping Sheet2.

You can easily redisplay hidden worksheets at any time.

Hide and Unhide a Worksheet

Hide a Worksheet

1. Click the tab of the worksheet that you want to hide.
2. Click the Home tab.
3. Click Format.
4. Click Hide & Unhide.
5. Click Hide Sheet.

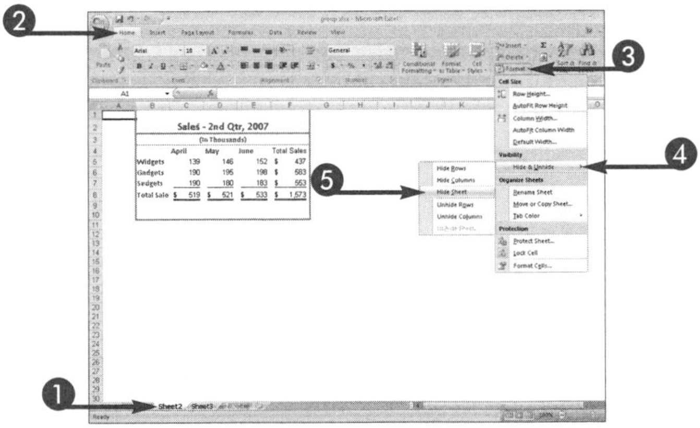

- Excel hides the worksheet.

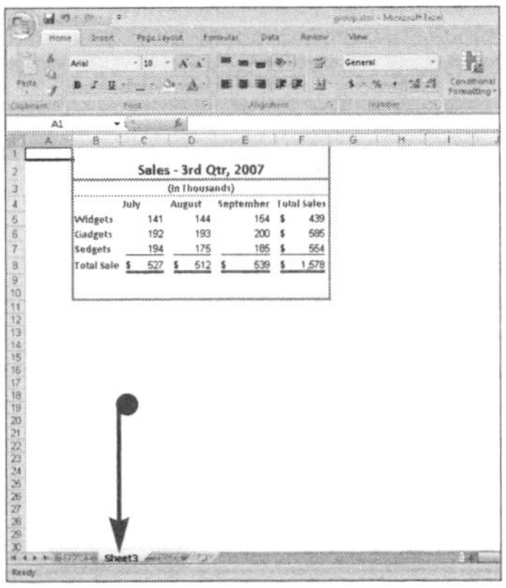

Unhide a Worksheet

1. Click the Home tab.
2. Click Format.
3. Click Hide & Unhide.
4. Click Unhide Sheet.

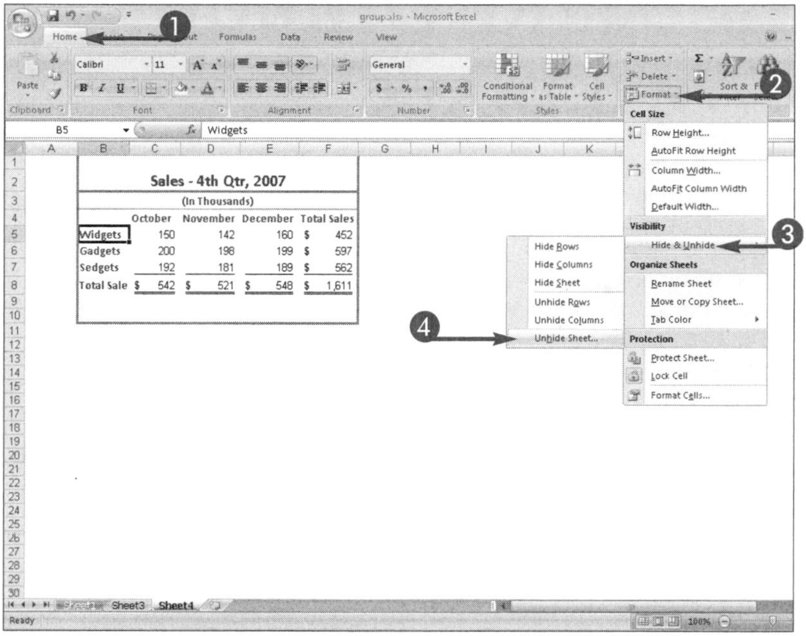

The Unhide dialog box appears.

5. Select the worksheet that you want to unhide.
6. Click OK.

Excel redisplays the worksheet in its original location.

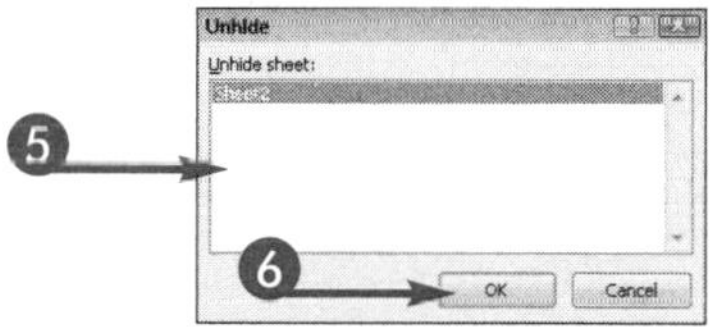

MASTER IT

Can I protect information in my workbook by hiding the worksheet that contains it?

▼ No. Anyone who opens your workbook can unhide the worksheet that you have hidden. If you do not rename the worksheets in your workbook, any reader can also easily deduce that a worksheet seems to be missing and check to see if you hid it. To protect information in your workbook, you can assign a password to the workbook. Then, only those users who know the password can open the workbook and make changes. For more details, see Chapter 31.

Can I unhide a worksheet to a new location?

▼ No. However, after you unhide the worksheet, you can move it to a new location. See the section, "Move or Copy a Worksheet," earlier in this chapter for details on moving or copying a worksheet to a new location in the same workbook or to a new workbook.

Hide and Unhide a Workbook

You can hide entire workbooks that you have open to avoid displaying sensitive information such as employee salaries or student test scores. For example, suppose that you are working on a sensitive workbook and someone unexpectedly enters your office. You can hide the workbook quickly and easily to safeguard the information and, when that person leaves, you can redisplay it.

Hiding a workbook does not affect any information, formulas, or functions in your workbook. Formulas and functions in a workbook continue to work when you hide the workbook. Similarly, formulas and functions in other workbooks that refer to the hidden workbook continue to work. You also do not need to display a particular workbook to include cells in that workbook when you create formulas and functions. See Chapter 10 for details on creating basic formulas.

When you hide a workbook, Excel does not display the workbook in the Windows taskbar or when you try to switch workbooks in Excel. See the section, "Switch to Another Workbook," for details on using Excel commands to view different open workbooks.

You can easily redisplay hidden workbooks at any time.

Hide and Unhide a Workbook

Hide a Workbook

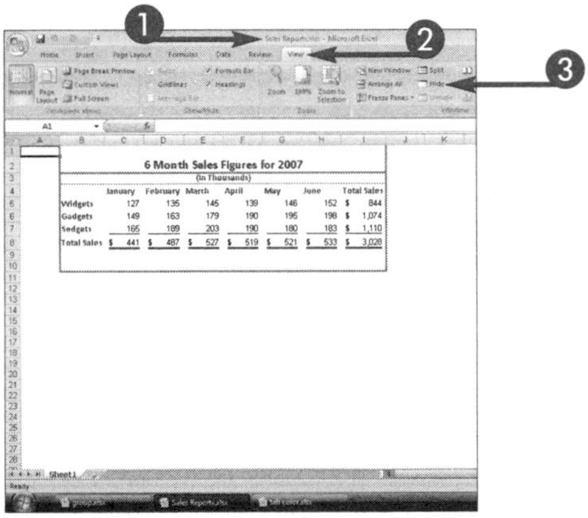

1. Open a workbook that you want to hide.

Note: *You do not need to open other workbooks as you see here. This example shows additional workbooks to help you see the effect of hiding a workbook.*

2. Click the View tab.
3. Click Hide.

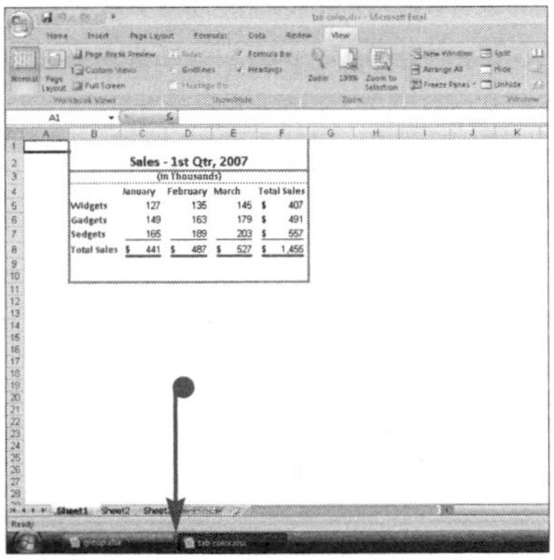

- Excel hides the workbook. No button appears on the Windows taskbar for the workbook.

Unhide a Workbook

1. Click the View tab.
2. Click Unhide.

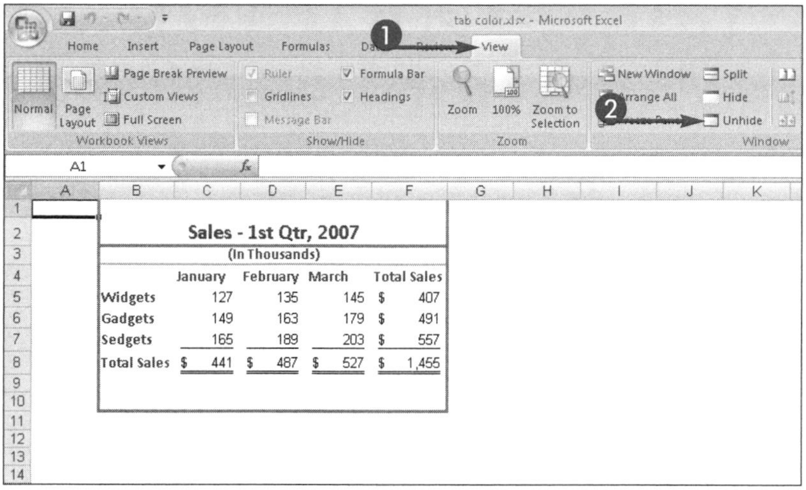

Excel displays the Unhide dialog box.

3. Click a workbook that you want to unhide.
4. Click OK.

Excel redisplays the workbook and makes it the active workbook.

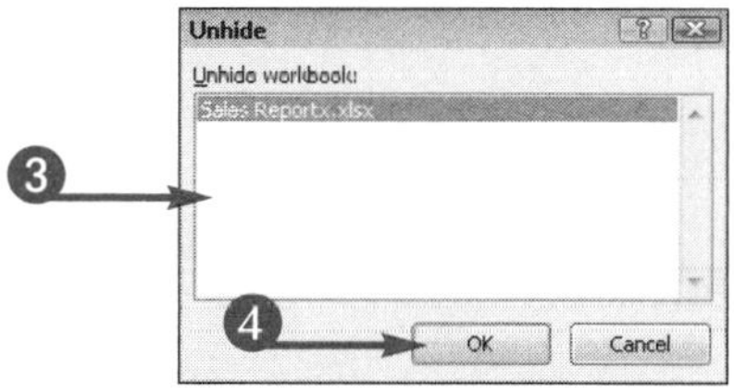

MASTER IT

What happens to a workbook that I hid and that I forget to unhide?

▼ It remains hidden until you attempt to close Excel. At that time, Excel prompts you to save the hidden workbook. Typically, when Excel prompts you, Excel will be open but no workbook will be open, and you should be thinking, "That is odd. Why is Excel prompting me to save a workbook when none is open?" Take advantage of this visual cue and click Cancel at the prompt. Then, follow the steps in the subsection, "Unhide a Workbook," to view the workbook and decide if you want to save the changes.

Is there any visual cue I can use while still working in Excel to determine that hidden workbooks exist?

▼ Yes. If the Unhide button on the View tab is available, you can be certain that hidden workbooks exist. Excel will continue to hide those workbooks until you follow the steps in the subsection, "Unhide Workbooks," to redisplay them or until you close Excel and reopen it. No other action, including arranging all open workbooks so that you can view more than one open workbook simultaneously, will make the workbook reappear. For details on displaying more than one open workbook simultaneously, see the section, "Arrange Open Worksheets or Workbooks."

Arrange Open Worksheets or Workbooks

You can arrange windows on-screen so that you can view the contents of more than one workbook at the same time. This technique can be useful when you need the information stored in one workbook to make updates in another workbook.

Or, suppose that you have several worksheets in the same workbook that you have set up identically because they track similar information. For example, you might have a workbook that tracks product sales, and the workbook may contain four worksheets, one for each quarter of the year. You might decide that you want to group the worksheets to edit them simultaneously. However, you are concerned about accidentally overwriting data. You can monitor the group editing process if you set up a separate window for each worksheet, group the worksheets, and display each worksheet tab in a separate window.

When you display more than one workbook or worksheet on-screen simultaneously, you still work in only one of the windows. The active window is the one that displays the scroll bar, and you can simply click in a window to make it active.

Arrange Open Worksheets or Workbooks

View Multiple Windows

1. Open all of the workbooks that you need, or set up worksheets in separate windows.

Note: *To set up a separate window for each worksheet, see the Tips section on the facing page.*

2. Click the View tab.
3. Click Arrange All.

   The Arrange Windows dialog box appears.

4. Click an option to specify how to arrange the windows (◎ changes to ◉).
5. Click OK.

   Excel arranges the windows as you specified.

   - The active window contains the scroll bar.

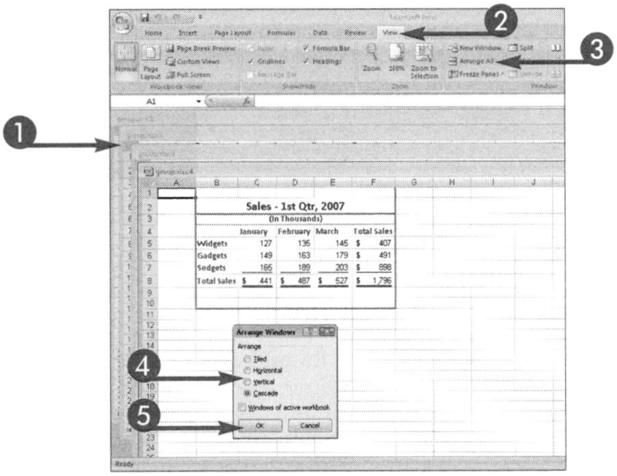

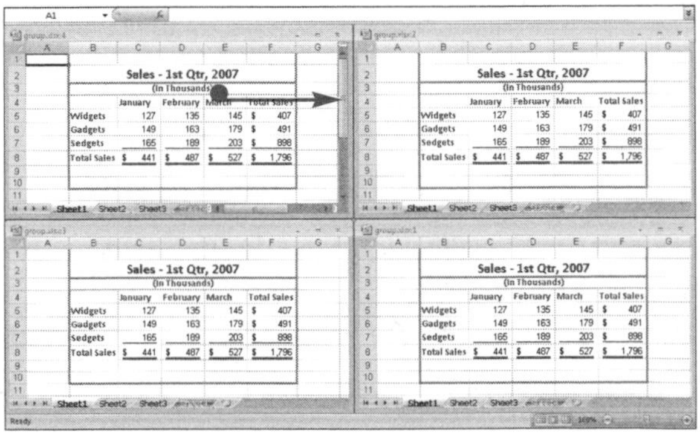

View Only One Window

1. Click anywhere in the window that you want to view exclusively.

   - The scroll bar appears in the window.

   This example selects the window in the upper-right corner of the screen.

2. Click the Windows Maximize button (▢).

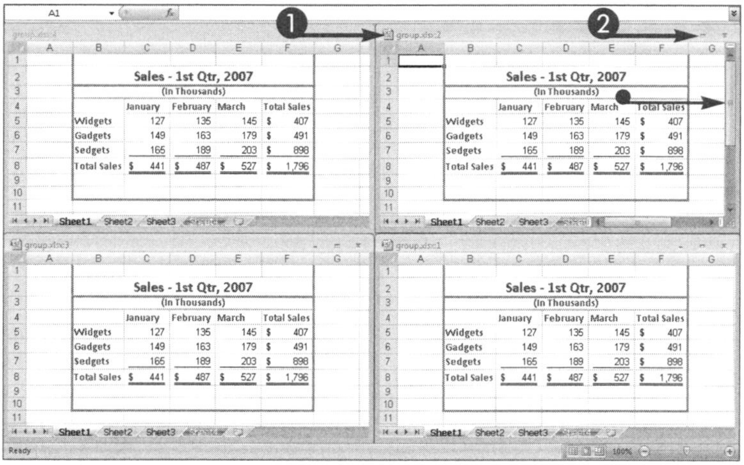

- Excel maximizes the window you selected.

The other windows remain open and you can switch to any of them.

Note: *For details on switching windows, see the section, "Switch to Another Open Workbook."*

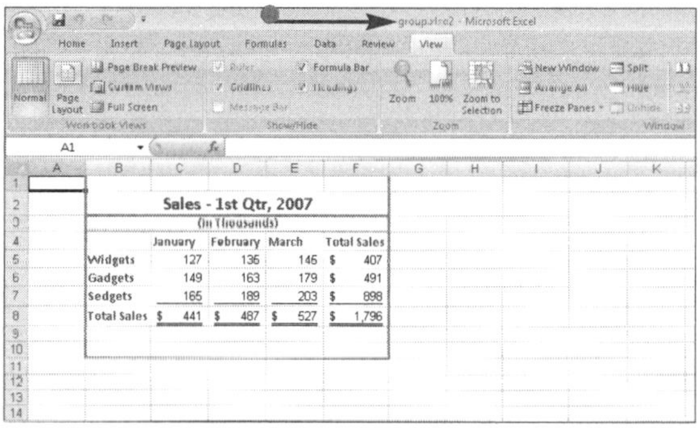

MASTER IT

What do the various arrangement options mean?

▼ You can *tile* windows, which allocates all of your screen space equally to each window. You can *cascade* windows. which stacks the windows so that each window title bar is visible. You can display the windows horizontally, which displays the windows one above the other, or you can display the windows vertically, which displays the windows side by side.

How do I set up a separate window for each worksheet in a workbook?

▼ Open the workbook containing the worksheets that you want to view in separate windows. Then click the View tab and click New Window enough times to create a window for each worksheet in the workbook.

If I arrange worksheets in separate windows, how do I group the worksheets?

▼ After you complete the steps in the subsection, "View Multiple Windows," click in any of the windows to select it. Then follow the steps in the section, "Edit Multiple Worksheets Simultaneously," to group the tabs. Grouping them in one window groups them in all of the windows.

Switch to Another Workbook

You can open multiple workbooks and switch between them as you work using a feature available in Excel. This approach is particularly useful to people who want to view each workbook maximized and do not want to arrange windows as described in the section, "Arrange Open Worksheets or Workbooks."

"Why not use the Windows taskbar to switch between workbooks," you might ask. Well, you can, but many people prefer to avoid using the Windows taskbar to switch between open workbooks. They prefer to use the Windows taskbar to switch only between programs, not documents. As a result, they turn off the option in Excel that allows Excel to display a button on the Windows taskbar for every open workbook. For details on controlling whether Excel displays one button for each workbook on the Windows taskbar, see Chapter 30.

Because Excel contains the feature described in this section that you can use to switch between workbooks, you can work the way you want to work, switching between maximized workbooks without using the Windows taskbar.

Switch to Another Workbook

1. With multiple workbooks open, click the View tab.
2. Click Switch Windows.
   - Excel displays a list of open workbooks.
   - The active workbook displays ☑ beside it.
3. Click the workbook you want to view.
   - Excel displays the workbook you selected.

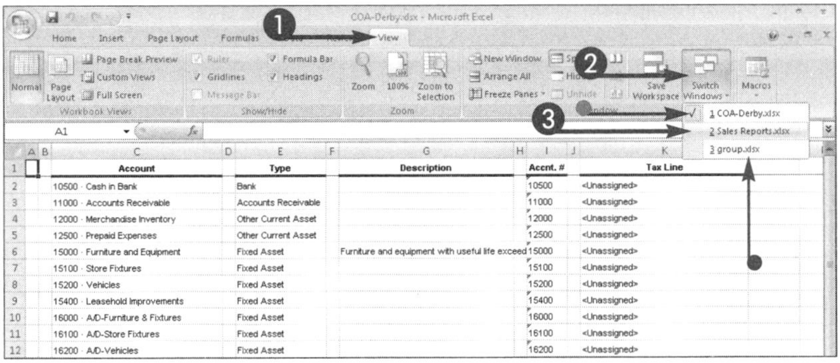

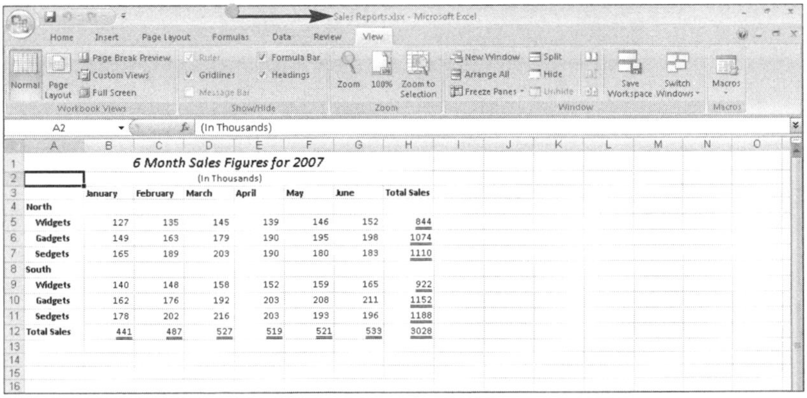

Merge Styles

When you want to copy many styles from one workbook to another, you can merge styles. By default, when you create a new style, Excel makes that style available only in the workbook where you created it. You can make the style available in another workbook if you copy a cell that uses the style into the other workbook, and that method works fine if you only need one style. However, to make many styles in one workbook available in another workbook, you can merge styles.

To merge styles, you need to open the workbook that contains the styles, and the workbook in which you want the styles to appear. Then you can use Excel's Merge Styles feature to copy all of the styles from one workbook to the other.

Merging styles also works well when you have created a style with the same name in two different workbooks but defined the style differently in each workbook. You can merge styles to create a consistent definition for the style in both workbooks. When you merge styles with the same name and different definitions, Excel prompts you to overwrite the existing style with the incoming version.

Merge Styles

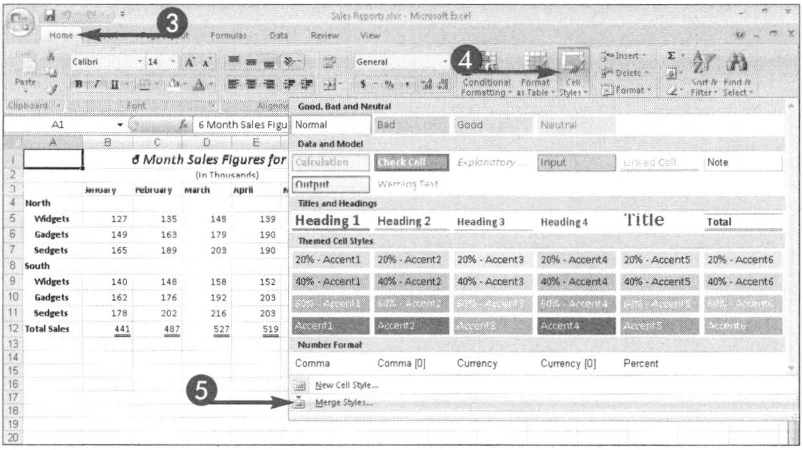

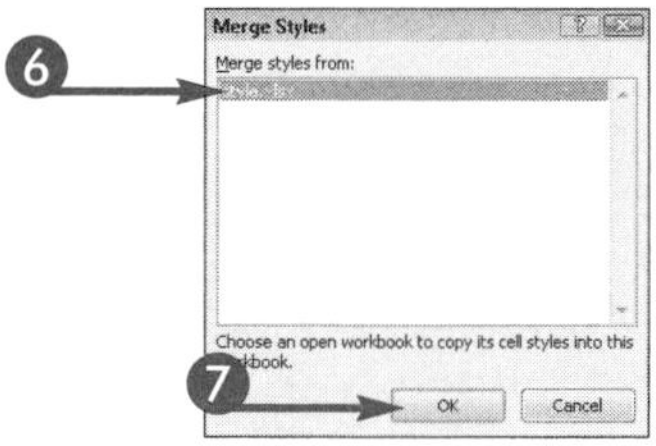

1. Open the workbook containing the styles you want to merge, and the workbook in which you want the styles to appear.
2. Display the workbook into which you want to merge styles.
3. Click the Home tab.
4. Click Cell Styles.
5. Click Merge Styles in the menu that appears.

   The Merge Styles dialog box appears.
6. Click the workbook containing the styles you want to merge.
7. Click OK.

   Excel merges styles into the active workbook.

   You can check the available styles by repeating Steps 3 and 4.

Outline a Worksheet

You can use the Outline feature in Excel to help you focus on particular portions of a worksheet that contains information set up in a hierarchical format. For example, suppose that your worksheet contains sales information for products sold by region over a period of months, with quarterly totals included. You can apply outlining to the workbook so that, in addition to viewing all details, you can view the information in several ways. For example, you can summarize to view quarterly or total sales for each product. You can also summarize to view monthly, quarterly, and total sales by region, or to view only quarterly and total sales by region.

Once you apply an outline to your workbook, Excel displays symbols above the column headings and to the left of the row numbers. You use these symbols to help you control the level of detail that displays as you work with your workbook. These symbols help you quickly hide and unhide rows and columns in your worksheet.

You can create only one outline for each worksheet. If you try to create a second outline on a worksheet, Excel assumes that you want to modify the existing outline.

Outline a Worksheet

Create an Outline

1. Click the Data tab.
2. Click ▾ below Group.
3. Click Auto Outline.

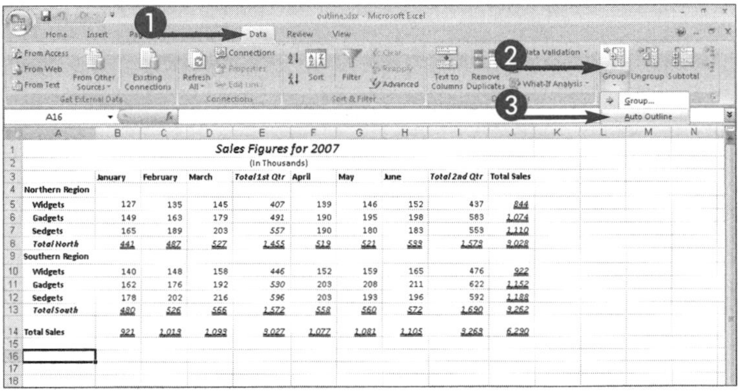

- Excel adds these symbols that represent outline levels of detail.

The example workbook contains three levels of detail that you can view.

- Excel adds these minus signs (⊟) to help you summarize information by columns in the outline.
- Excel adds these ⊟ to help you summarize information by rows in the outline.

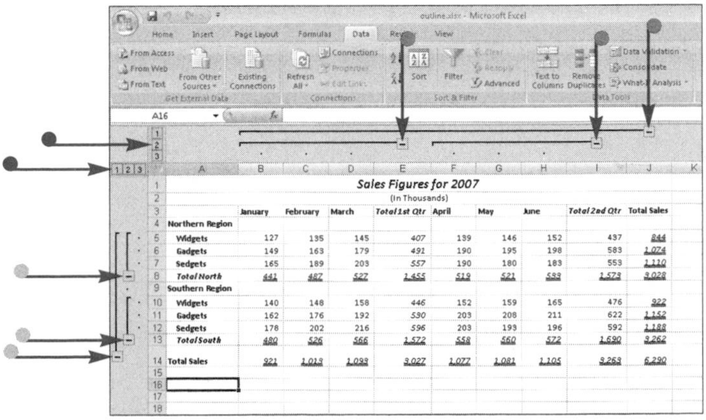

Using the Outline

1. Click [-] ([-] changes to [+]).

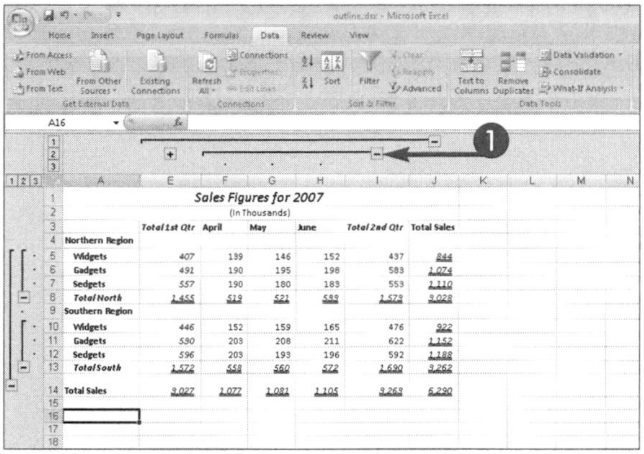

- [-] changes to [+].
- Excel hides details and displays summary data.
- You can click [+] to redisplay details.

In this example, clicking [-] above column headings displays summary data for each product by quarter. Clicking [-] beside row numbers displays summary data by month for the northern and southern districts.

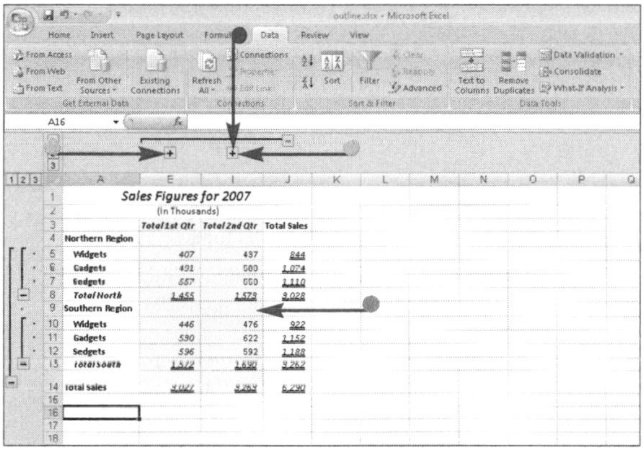

MASTER IT

Why do I not see outline symbols when I follow Steps 1 to 3 on the facing page?

▼ Outline symbols may be turned off in your display options. Click [Office button] and then click Excel Options. On the left side of the Excel Options dialog box, click Advanced. Then scroll down to the Display Options for this Worksheet section, and select Show Outline Symbols If an Outline Is Applied ([ ] changes to [✓]). When you click OK, outline symbols should appear.

What should I do if my summary rows appear above my detail data instead of below it?

▼ Excel may be smart enough to recognize that your summary rows are above your details, and so you may not need to do anything special. However, if Excel does not produce the outline that you expect, see the section, "Manually Create an Outline," to control the information that Excel places in various levels of detail of your workbook.

What do the lines beside [-] mean?

▼ The lines are bars attached to [-] and function the same way that [-] functions. You can click [-] or the bar attached to it to hide details for the associated portion of your workbook. Once you hide details, [+] appears, and you can click [+] or the bar attached to it to display details.

Work with Custom Views of Outline Settings

You can save yourself some time if you create custom views of various outline settings so that you can quickly and easily return to a particular set of outline settings. For example, suppose that your worksheet contains sales information for products sold by region over a period of months, with quarterly totals included. Suppose that you also apply outlining to the workbook so that, in addition to viewing all details, you can view the information in several ways.

In a workbook such as this one, you can view a variety of different summaries of the information. For example, you can summarize to view quarterly sales for each product, and then you can summarize to view total sales for each product. You can also summarize to view monthly sales by region, quarterly sales by region, or total sales by region. Instead of recreating each of these various summaries every time you need them, you can create a custom view for each summary. Then, to display the summary, you simply display the custom view. Excel saves custom views with your workbook, and so they are always available.

Work with Custom Views of Outline Settings

Create a Custom View

1. Set up the worksheet to display the information you want and apply an outline.
2. Click the View tab.
3. Click Custom Views.

   The Custom Views dialog box appears.
4. Click Add.

   The Add View dialog box appears.
5. Type a name for the view you are creating.
   - If you do not want to include print settings and hidden rows, columns, and filter settings, deselect these options (☑ changes to ☐).
6. Click OK and save your workbook.

   Excel saves the view.

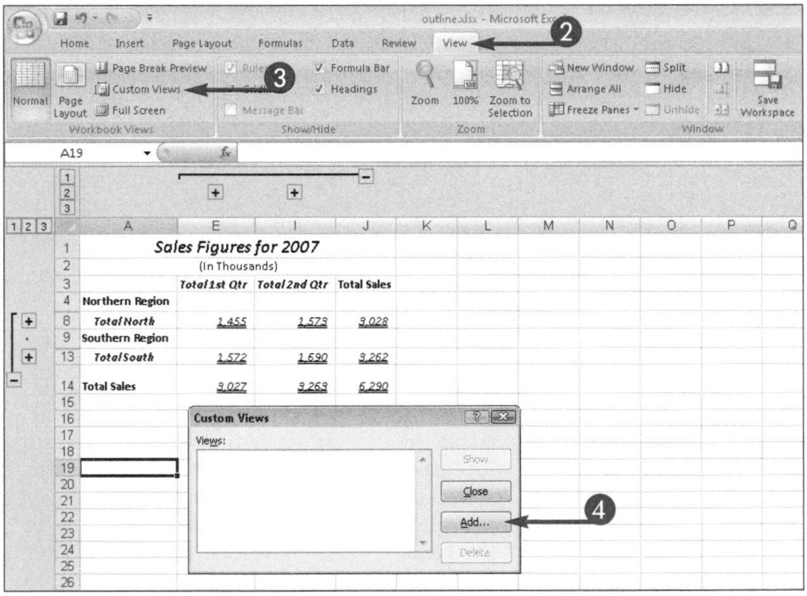

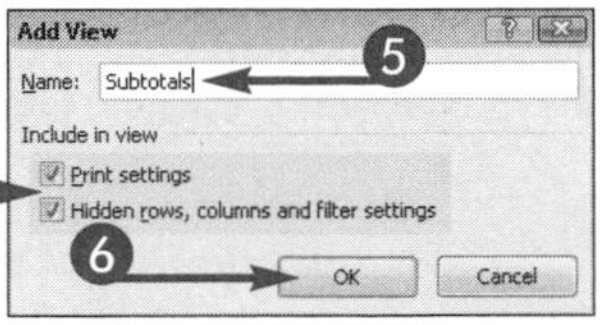

Display a Custom View

1. Open the workbook containing the view you want to use.
2. Click the View tab.
3. Click Custom Views.

   The Custom Views dialog box appears.
4. Click a view to display.
5. Click Show.

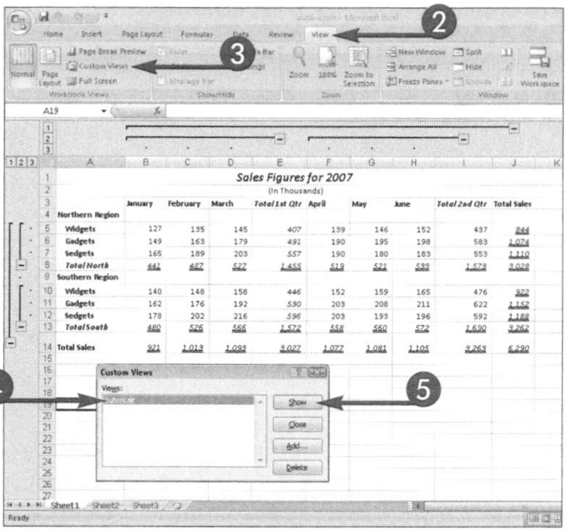

- Excel applies the custom view.

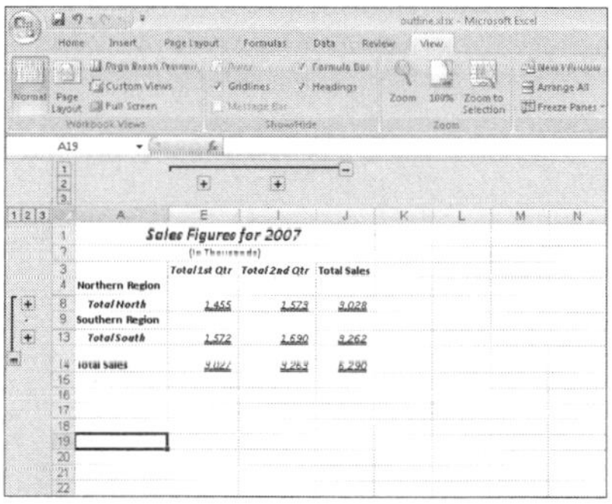

MASTER IT

Why do outline symbols not appear when I display the custom view of an outline that I created?

When you save a custom view, Excel saves the appearance of your data but does not save the fact that you had applied an outline. You probably cleared the outline after you saved the custom view. Interestingly, although Excel does not display the outline symbols, your custom view does display your data summarized the way you set it up using the outline symbols. To redisplay the outline symbols, follow the steps in the section, "Outline a Worksheet."

While I was setting up my outline, why did the Group dialog box appear?

The Group dialog box appears when you select cells while setting up a worksheet to apply an outline. The Group dialog box contains only two options: Rows and Columns. You use this dialog box to outline only the rows or only the columns in your worksheet. When you select an option, Excel applies an outline to either rows or columns, based on your selection. To outline both rows and columns, click Cancel and then make sure that no cells are selected when you create an outline in your worksheet.

Manually Create an Outline

When you apply an outline to a workbook, Excel assumes that summary columns appear at the right of their detail data, and summary rows appear below their detail data, which is the typical way that people lay out workbooks. However, if you organized your data differently, you can override these settings and manually create an outline.

You manually create an outline by selecting the rows and columns that you want to include in each level of detail. You cannot select non-contiguous cells to include in any particular group, so make sure that you do not have any blank rows or columns in your selections and that you have set up your worksheet so that cells containing sets of details appear next to each other. In addition, you typically do not want to include cells in a selection that contains summary totals, because you probably want to hide the details to see just those totals.

If you placed summary rows above their detail data or summary columns to the left of their detail data, Excel may be smart enough to recognize your summary layout. You should therefore try the steps in the section, "Create an Outline," before you manually set up an outline.

Manually Create an Outline

1. Select rows that represent detail for one set of data to summarize.

***Note:** See Chapter 4 to select cells.*

2. Click the Data tab.
3. Click Group.

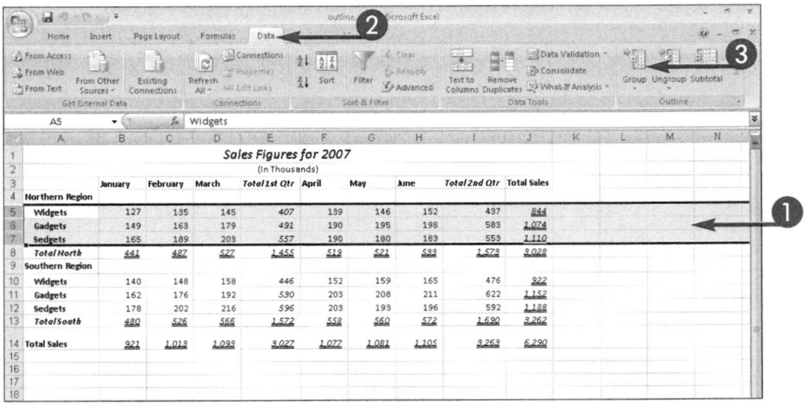

- Excel adds outline symbols to the selected rows.

4. Repeat Steps 1 to 3 for each set of data that you want to be able to summarize.

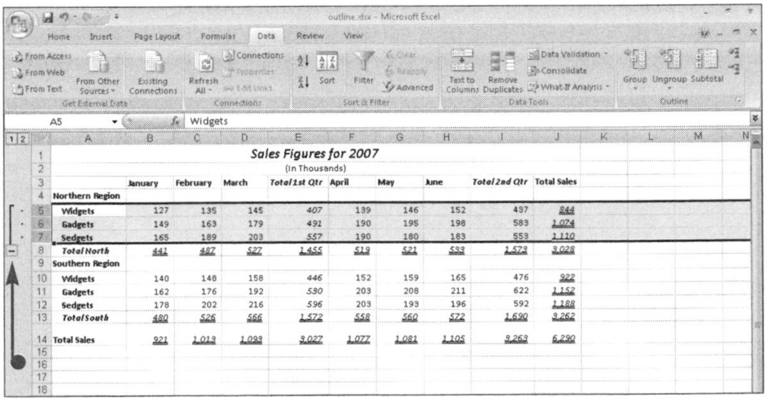

Remove an Outline

If you no longer need to work with your data in outline form, you can remove the outline. When you remove an outline that you previously applied, Excel removes the outline symbols that appear above column headings and to the left of row numbers. In addition, Excel automatically redisplays any columns or rows that you hid using outline symbols to summarize information, displaying all of the detail that you have in your worksheet. As a result, you will not be able to tell that you ever applied an outline to your worksheet.

You cannot undo removing an outline; if you decide that you want the outline back, you must reapply it using the steps in the section, "Create an Outline."

MASTER IT

Because I am not certain that I am finished working with my worksheet's outline, is there a way to temporarily hide outline symbols without removing the outline?

▼ Yes. You can press Ctrl+8 (the number key above the letter keys, not the one on the number pad) to toggle the appearance of outline symbols on and off. The first time you press Ctrl+8, Excel hides the outline symbols. The second time you press Ctrl+8, Excel redisplays the outline symbols.

Remove an Outline

1. Open the workbook containing the outline you want to remove.

Note: *See Chapter 2 to open a workbook.*

2. Click the Data tab.
3. Click under Ungroup.
4. Click Clear Outline.

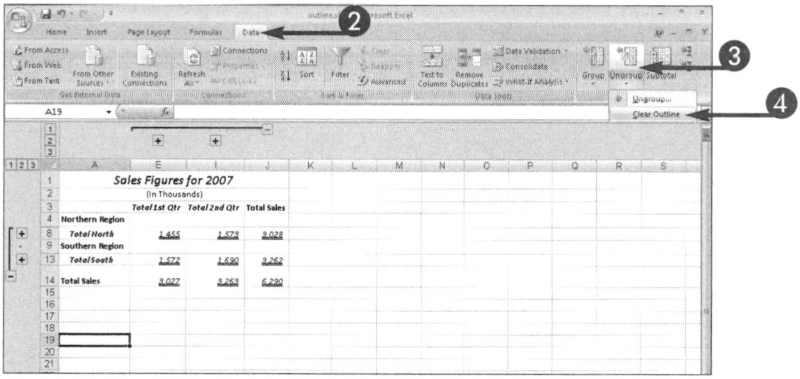

- Excel removes the outline symbols and redisplays all of the detail in your workbook.

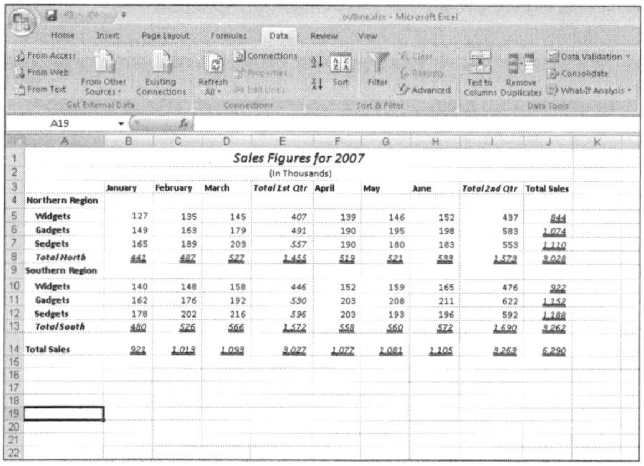

Switch Views

You can switch views of your worksheet to see your worksheet from different perspectives. By default, Normal view is the view that appears when you open a workbook, and most people work in Normal view. Once you print or preview your worksheet, horizontal and vertical page breaks appear as black, dashed lines.

Page Layout view presents the most realistic view of the way your worksheet will appear when you print it. In Page Layout view, you can see and adjust margins, headers, and footers in your worksheet, and each page appears as a page, with no representations for page breaks such as dashed lines. You can work in Page Layout view all of the time, because you have complete access to the Ribbon, Quick Access Toolbar, and Status Bar.

In Page Break Preview, Excel zooms the worksheet so that you can see more of it. Page numbers appear overlaid on each page, and page breaks appear as heavy, blue, dashed lines that you can adjust; see Chapter 9 for details on adjusting page breaks and margins, and adding headers and footers.

In Full Screen view, you can see more of your workbook because Excel hides the Ribbon, the Quick Access Toolbar, and the Status Bar.

Switch Views

1. Open a workbook.

   Excel displays the workbook in Normal view.

   - After you print or preview a worksheet, page breaks appear as black, dashed lines.

2. Click the View tab.
3. Click Page Layout.

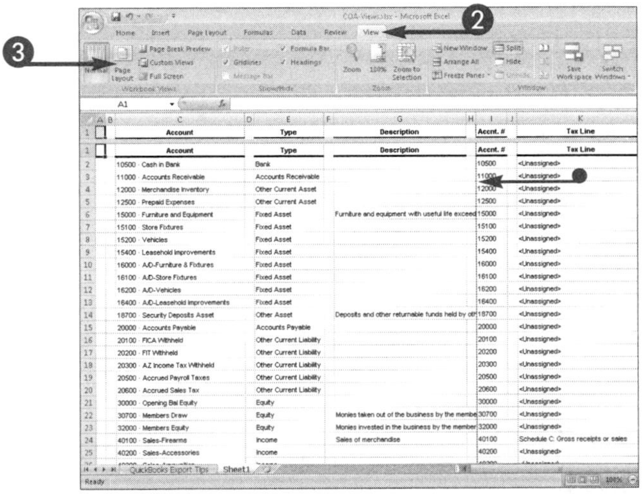

Excel displays the workbook in Page Layout view.

- You can use the rulers to adjust margins.
- You can add header information here.

Note: *See Chapter 9 for details on adjusting margins and adding headers and footers.*

4. Click Page Break Preview.

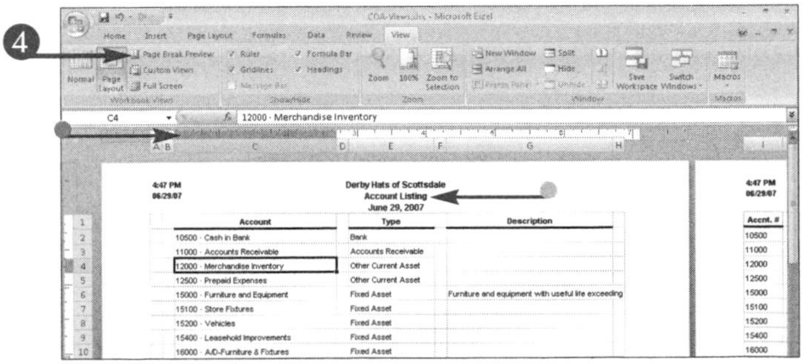

The workbook appears in Page Break Preview and a welcome dialog box appears.

- Excel displays page numbers on each page.
- You can use the dashed blue lines to manage page breaks.

Note: *See Chapter 9 for details on working with page breaks.*

5. Click Full Screen.

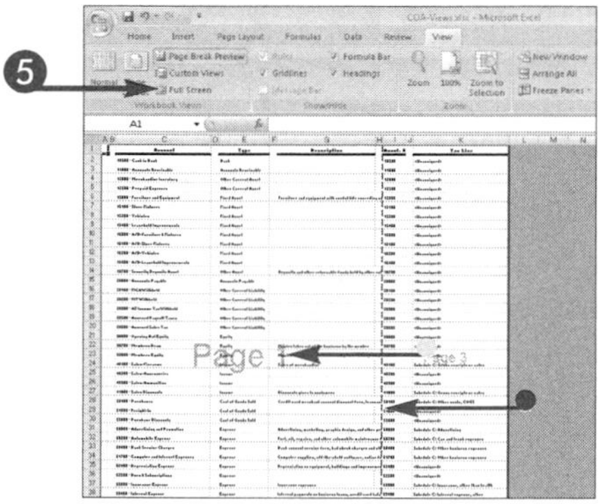

The workbook appears in Full Screen view.

In this view, the Ribbon, Quick Access Toolbar, and Status Bar are hidden, so that you can see more of your workbook on-screen.

You can press Esc to exit Full Screen view and redisplay Excel's tools.

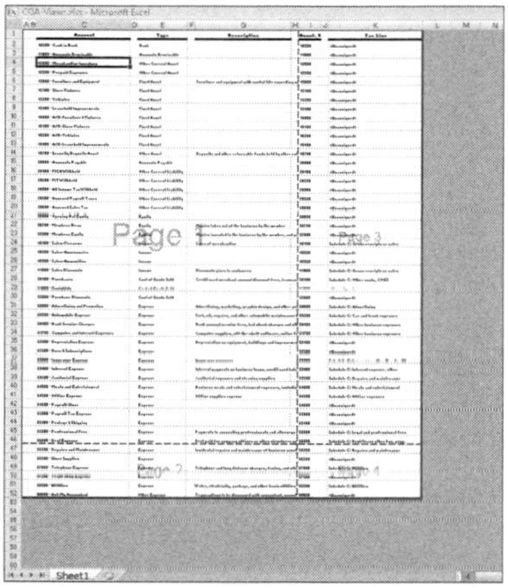

MASTER IT

Is there a quick way to switch views?

▼ Yes, you can use the View buttons in the lower-right corner of the window. Click the Normal button (▦) to display your worksheet in Normal view. Click the Page Layout button (▣) to display your worksheet in Page Layout view. Click the Page Break Preview button (▥) to display your workbook in Page Break Preview. No button exists for Full Screen view, but you can press Alt, followed by W and then E on your keyboard to display the worksheet in Full Screen view.

Is there a way to eliminate margins in Page Layout view so that I can see more of my worksheet?

▼ Yes. Move the mouse pointer to the top or left edge of the worksheet page (↖ changes to ╪). Click the edge; Excel hides margins on all sides of each page. Repeat the process to redisplay the margins.

Can I switch to Full Screen view and have Excel display Page Layout view on-screen instead of Page Break Preview?

▼ Yes. The Full Screen button simply magnifies the current view. When you click the Full Screen button on the View tab, Excel fills the screen with whatever view you are using when you click the Full Screen button.

Zoom In and Zoom Out

You can zoom in and out to increase or decrease the size of what you see on-screen. By default, Excel displays information in your worksheet at 100 percent of its normal size. You can set the zoom percentage to as small as 10 percent or as large as 400 percent. You can set the zoom percentage in an approximate way using the zoom slider, or you can set the zoom percentage precisely using a dialog box.

When you zoom out to a small zoom percentage, you view more of your overall worksheet, and get a better perspective on the layout of the worksheet. Although you can view more of your worksheet, the print size is often too tiny to read.

When you zoom in to a large zoom percentage, you enlarge your worksheet so that you see only a portion of it. Zooming in can be very useful if you find it difficult to read smaller text. By zooming in, you can reduce eye fatigue.

It is important to understand that zooming only affects the view on-screen. Changing the zoom percentage has no effect on the font size in your worksheet or on the way your worksheet prints.

Zoom In and Zoom Out

Zoom by Dragging

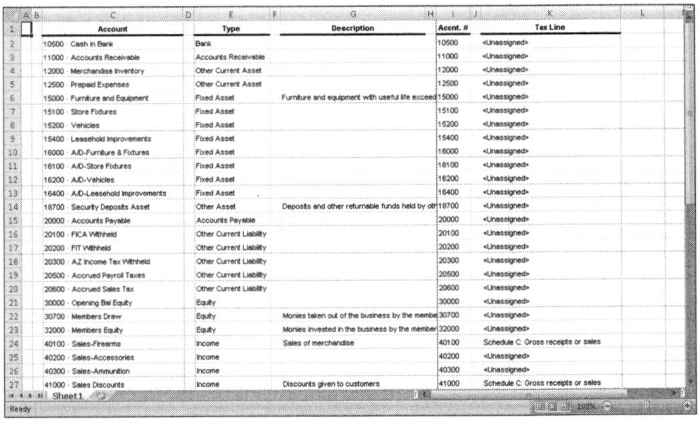

❶ Open a workbook.

Excel displays the workbook at 100 percent of its actual size.

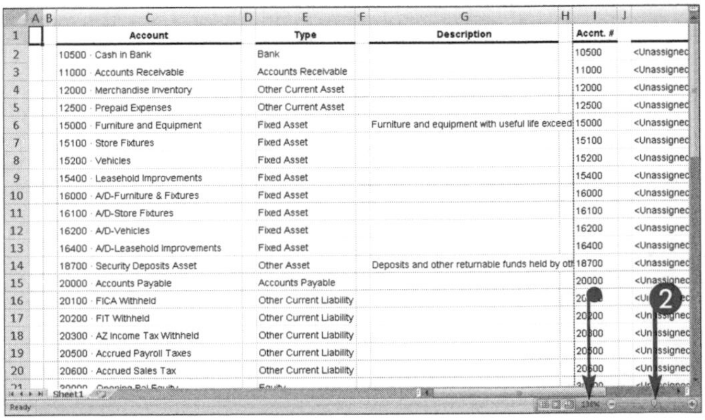

❷ Click and drag the zoom slider to the right.

Excel zooms in, you see less of your worksheet, and the print in your worksheet appears larger.

- The zoom percentage appears here.

3. Click and drag the zoom slider to the left.

   Excel zooms out, you see more of your worksheet, and the print in your worksheet appears smaller.

   - The zoom percentage appears here.

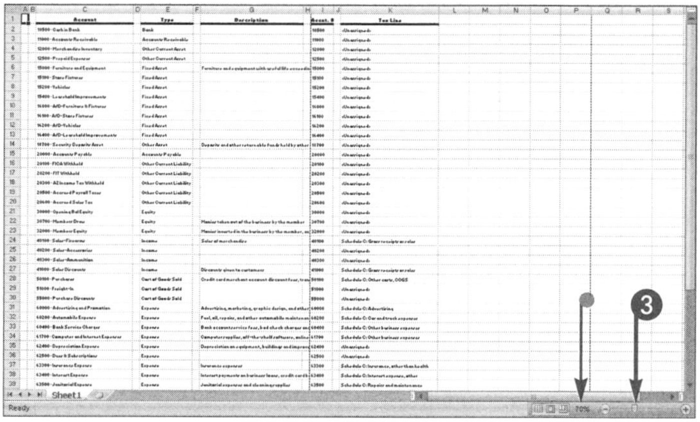

Zoom Precisely

1. Click the View tab.
2. Click Zoom.

   The Zoom dialog box appears.

3. Select a zoom magnification percentage (◎ changes to ◉).

   - You can type an exact zoom percentage here.

4. Click OK.

   Excel zooms to the percentage you specified.

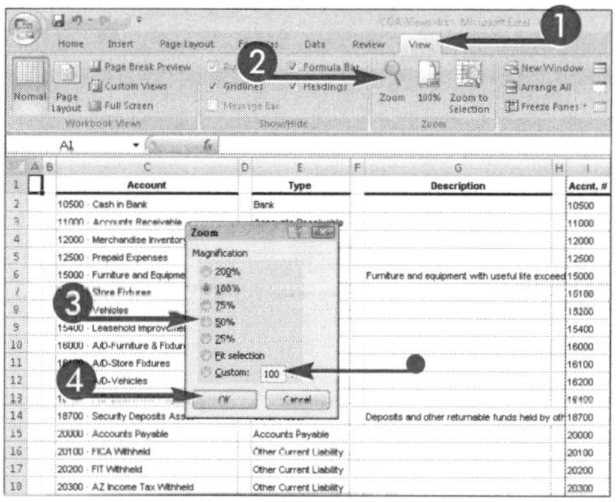

What happens if I click Zoom to Selection on the View tab?

▼ Excel zooms in to the section of your worksheet that contains the cell pointer. This setting is particularly useful to view a range of cells. Select cells before you click Zoom to Selection; Excel magnifies the range you selected. You can quickly and easily zoom to the default 100 percent by clicking the 100% button on the View tab.

Do the plus and minus signs that appear at the ends of the zoom slider serve any purpose?

▼ Yes. Each click of either button zooms using increments of 10 percent. Each time you click the plus sign (⊕), Excel zooms in and makes text larger by 10 percent. Each time you click the minus sign (⊖), Excel zooms out and makes text smaller by 10 percent.

Do I have to be in a particular view to zoom?

▼ You can change the zoom percentage while working in Normal view, Page Layout view, or even Page Break Preview. You cannot change the zoom percentage while working in Full Screen view because the Ribbon and the Zoom controls are hidden.

Create and Use a Custom View

When you change a variety of settings in a worksheet on a regular basis, you can create custom views of your worksheet to save those settings. Then you can use those custom views to quickly and easily return the worksheet to those settings. For example, you might want to create separate custom views to help you focus on various areas of a worksheet. Separate custom views can also be very useful for storing a variety of print settings if you print different areas of your worksheet separately. For details on creating print settings, see Chapter 9.

When you create a custom view, Excel stores the worksheet view — Normal, Page Layout, or Page Break Preview — and the zoom settings. A custom view also stores any cells or ranges that you select, along with the active cell. A custom view also captures window sizes and positions, as well as frozen panes. If you want, you can store print settings and any filter settings in a custom view. A custom view can also store the status of each row or column and whether you have hidden or displayed the row or column.

You cannot create a custom view if your worksheet contains a table; see Chapter 23 for details on tables.

Create and Use a Custom View

Create a Custom View

1. Set up the worksheet to display the information you want to store in the custom view.
   - You can include a range selection, zoom settings, and a view.
2. Click the View tab.
3. Click Custom Views.

   The Custom Views dialog box appears.
4. Click Add.

   The Add View dialog box appears.
5. Type a name for the view you are creating.
   - If you do not want to include print settings and hidden rows, columns, and filter settings, deselect these options (☑ changes to ☐).
6. Click OK and save your workbook.

   Excel saves the view.

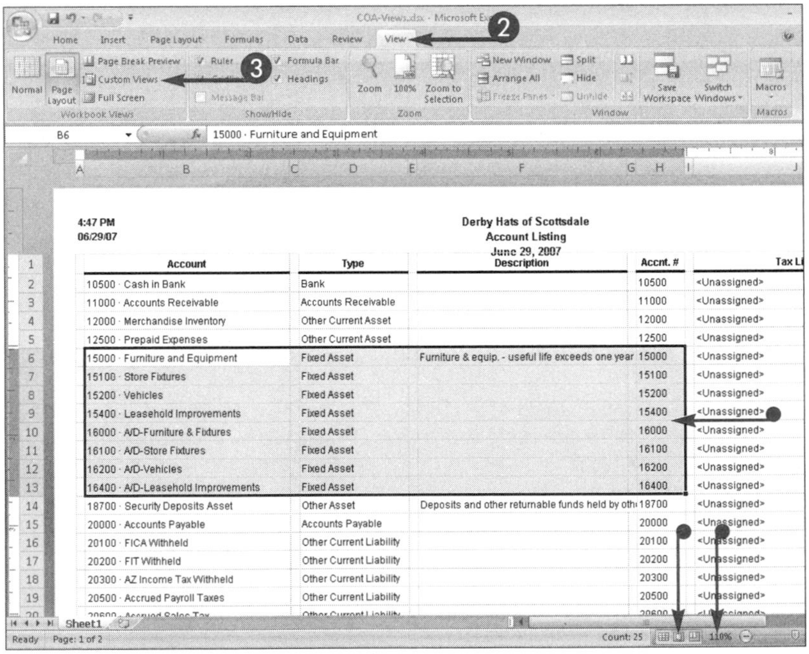

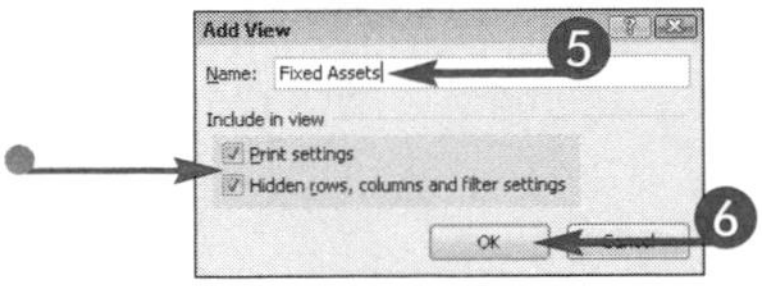

Using a Custom View

1. Open the workbook containing the view you want to use.
   - Excel displays the workbook as you saved it last, including zoom and selections.
2. Click the View tab.
3. Click Custom Views.

   The Custom Views dialog box appears.
4. Click a view to display.
5. Click Show.

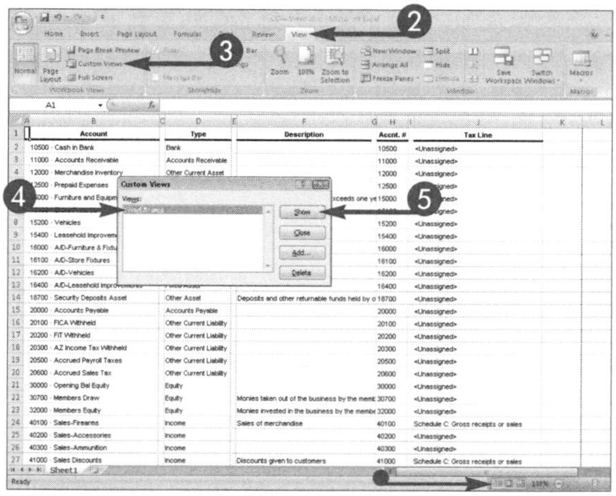

Excel applies the custom view.

- The custom view includes the selected cells.
- The custom view includes your view setting.
- The custom view includes any filters you set.

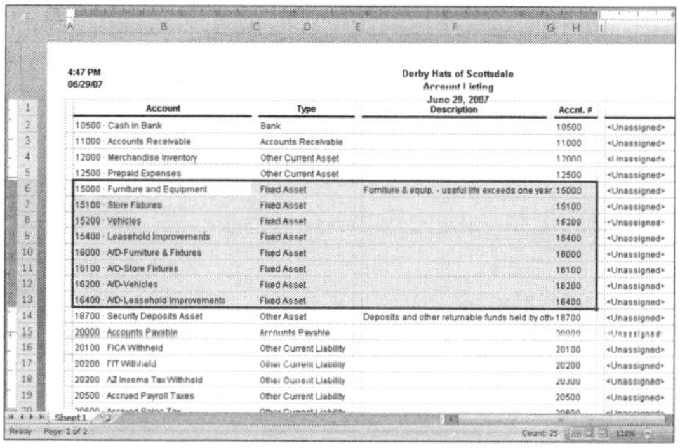

MASTER IT

If I no longer need a custom view, what should I do?

▼ You do not need to do anything, because keeping the custom view in your workbook will not affect anything. However, if you want to get rid of the custom view, you can delete it. Follow Steps 1 to 4 in the subsection, "Using a Custom View." Then click the Delete button.

Can I modify a custom view?

▼ No, but to work around this problem, you can apply an existing custom view and modify your workbook's appearance. Excel permits only one occurrence of any custom view name, and so you must delete the existing custom view. Then you can save the new appearance of your worksheet as a custom view using the name of the deleted custom view.

What are the filter settings that Excel can store in a custom view?

▼ You can set up a worksheet to display only a portion of the information stored in the worksheet. Similar to hiding rows or columns, you can hide information based on criteria that you specify. See Chapter 23 for details on filtering information in a worksheet.

Hide or Display Gridlines

You can hide or display the gridlines of your worksheet on-screen. Gridlines delineate the boundaries of each cell in a worksheet. Displaying gridlines can make the worksheet easier to read, but hiding gridlines can enhance the appearance of the worksheet. For example, you may want to hide gridlines if you are going to project your workbook to a screen for a large group to view. It is also sometimes easier to see the effect of cell borders when you hide gridlines. For details on using cell borders, see Chapter 3.

It is important to understand that hiding or displaying gridlines on-screen has no effect on whether gridlines print when you print your worksheet. To control whether gridlines print, see Chapter 9.

MASTER IT

Can I control the color of the gridlines that Excel displays on-screen?

▼ Yes. Click the Office button and then click Excel Options. On the left side of the Excel Options dialog box, click Advanced and then scroll to the Display Options for this Worksheet section. You can use the Gridline Color drop-down list to set a gridline color.

Hide or Display Gridlines

1. Open a workbook.
   - By default, Excel displays gridlines.
2. Click the View tab.
3. Click Gridlines.

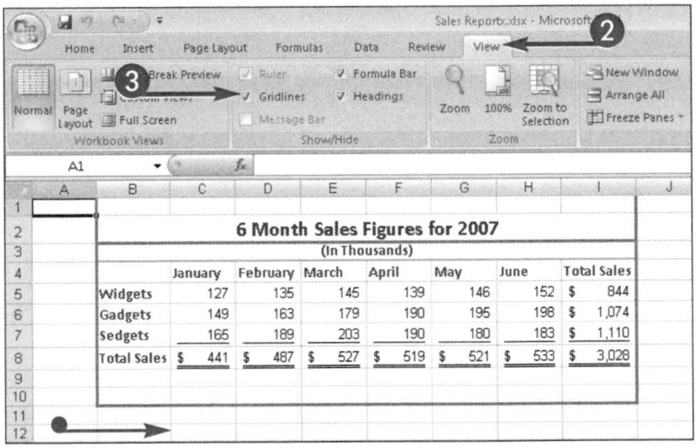

- Excel hides the lines that delineate rows and columns in the worksheet.

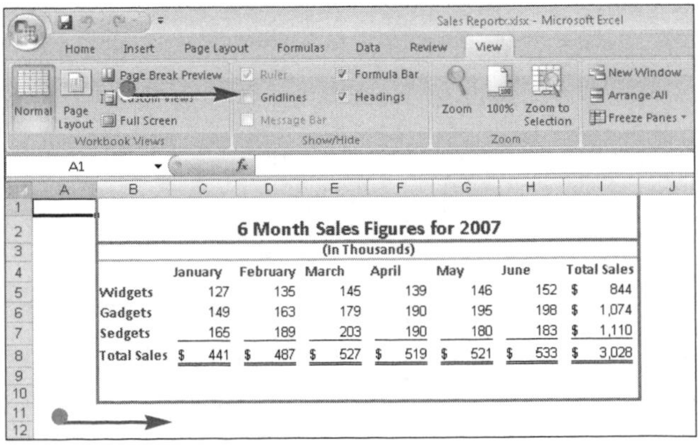

Hide or Display Row Numbers and Column Letters

You can hide or display the row numbers that appear on-screen to the left of each row, and column letters that appear above each column, of your worksheet. You use the row numbers and column letters to identify the address of a cell or a range of cells. Displaying column letters and row numbers is useful as you work on a worksheet, but hiding column letters and row numbers can reduce distractions if, for example, you plan to project your workbook to a screen for a large group to view. To minimize distractions, you can display your worksheet in Full Screen view, or you can hide row numbers, column letters, and the Formula Bar, and minimize the Ribbon. For details on minimizing the Ribbon, see Chapter 30. For details on hiding the Formula Bar, see the section, "Hide or Display the Formula Bar."

It is important to understand that hiding or displaying on-screen row numbers and column letters has no effect on whether row numbers and column letters print when you print your worksheet. By default, Excel does not print row numbers and column letters, but you can change this setting. See Chapter 9 for details.

Hide or Display Row Numbers and Column Letters

1. Open a workbook.
   - By default, Excel displays row numbers and column letters.
2. Click the View tab.
3. Click Headings.

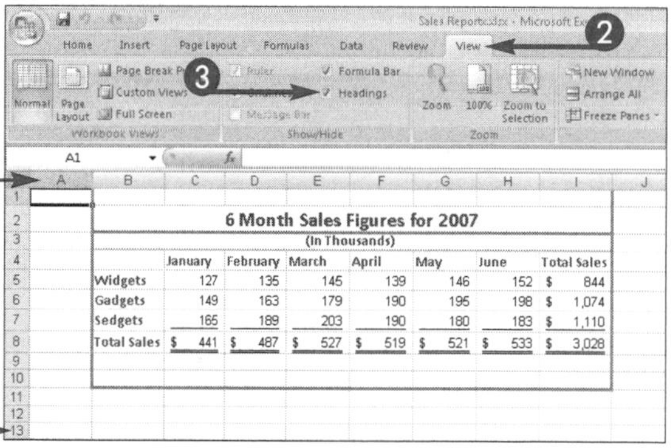

Excel hides the column letters and row numbers in your worksheet.

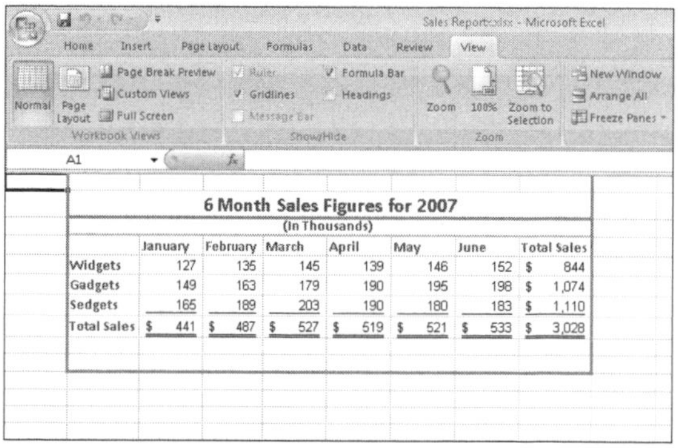

Hide or Display the Formula Bar

You can hide or display the Formula Bar that appears on-screen above the column letters of your worksheet. You use the Formula Bar to identify the address of a cell or a range of cells, as well as to determine the contents of the selected cell. Displaying the Formula Bar is very useful as you work on a worksheet, but hiding the Formula Bar can reduce distractions if, for example, you plan to project your workbook to a screen for a large group to view. To minimize distractions, you can display your worksheet in Full Screen view or you can hide row numbers, column letters, and the Formula Bar, and minimize the Ribbon. For details on minimizing the Ribbon, see Chapter 30. For details on hiding row numbers and column letters, see the section, "Hide or Display Row Numbers and Column Letters."

You cannot print the Formula Bar, and so hiding or displaying it has no effect on printing your worksheet. Although you cannot print the Formula Bar, you can print the contents of cells as they appear in the Formula Bar; see Chapter 18 for details.

Hide or Display the Formula Bar

1. Open a workbook.
   - By default, Excel displays the Formula Bar.
2. Click the View tab.
3. Click Formula Bar.

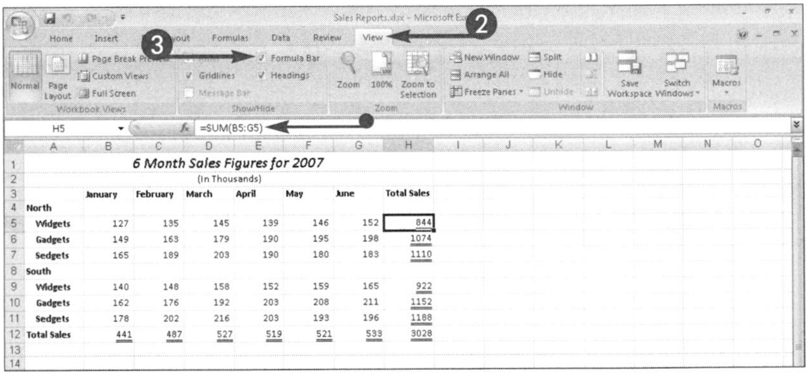

Excel hides the Formula Bar in your worksheet.

- ☑ changes to ☐.

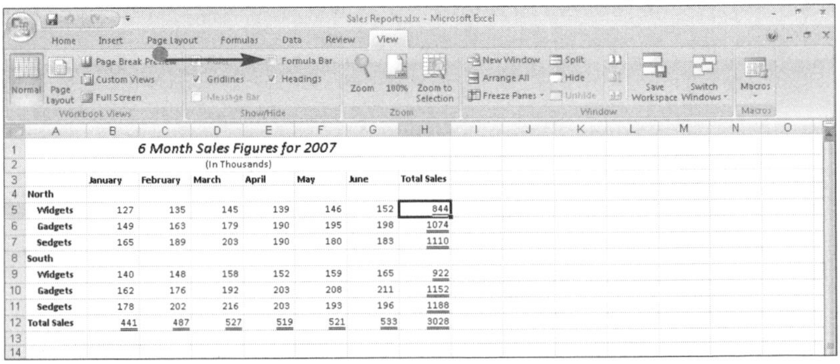

Open a New Window

You can use the New Window feature to view and compare information placed far apart on a worksheet or even stored on different worksheets in the same workbook. When you open a new window for a workbook, the windows scroll independently of each other, and so you can place the cell pointer in one location in one window and in an entirely different location in the other window. However, because you are simply looking at two different views of the same workbook, Excel records any changes you make in both views, regardless of the view you use to make the change.

When you open a new window for a workbook, Excel annotates the title of the workbook in the title bar so that you can identify the window in which you are working, by adding a colon (:) and a sequential number starting with 1. In addition, if you display each workbook as a button in the Windows taskbar, Excel displays two buttons, one for each window, in the Windows taskbar.

When you finish working in multiple windows, you can use the workbook Close button in the upper-right corner to close one window; Excel redisplays the workbook in a single window.

Open a New Window

1. Open a workbook.
   - If you display Windows taskbar buttons for each workbook, a Windows taskbar button appears for the workbook.
2. Click the View tab.
3. Click New Window.

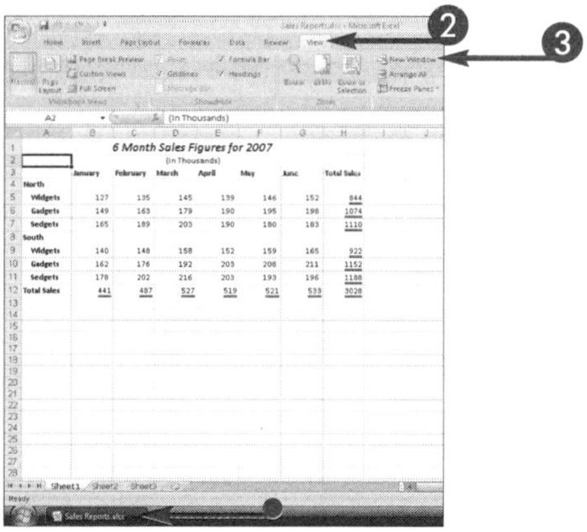

Excel creates a second version of the worksheet you are viewing.

- A colon (:) followed by a 2 appears at the end of the workbook name in the title bar.
- If you display Windows taskbar buttons for each workbook, a Windows taskbar button appears for each window.
- You can click here to close a window and redisplay the workbook in only one window.

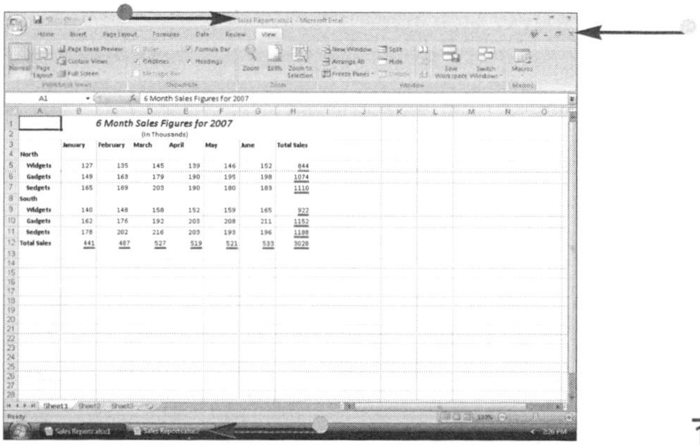

Freeze Column and Row Titles

When you work with a worksheet that contains more information than will fit on one screen, you can freeze one or more rows or columns to keep information in those rows and columns on-screen, regardless of where you place the cell pointer.

Freezing the top row of your worksheet is very useful when it contains headings for columns of information stored on the rows below. For example, your worksheet may contain five or six columns of information that you track about sales that you made to customers, including information such as the date and amount of the sale, the type of product purchased, and who made the sale. As you add new sales to the worksheet, it can be helpful to be able to see the heading for each row.

Freezing the leftmost column of your worksheet is very useful when titles for each row of data appear in the left column and your worksheet contains 12 or 13 columns. For example, the worksheet that you use to track your monthly income and expenses may show your income and expense categories in the leftmost column and one column for each month. As you add new months, it is helpful to see the income and expense categories.

Freeze Column and Row Titles

Freeze the Top Row

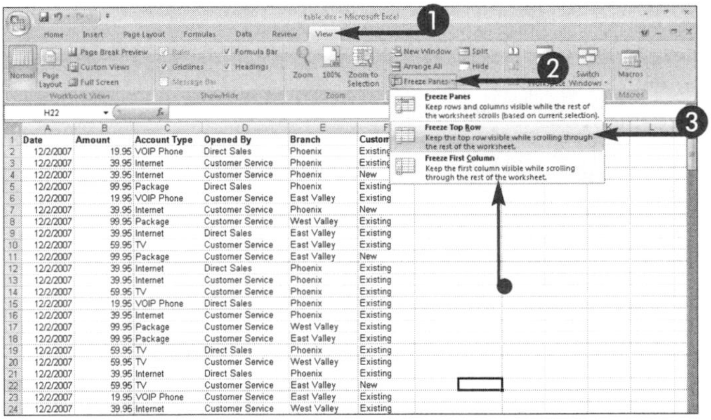

1. Click the View tab.
2. Click Freeze Panes.
   - A drop-down list of options appears.
3. Click Freeze Top Row.

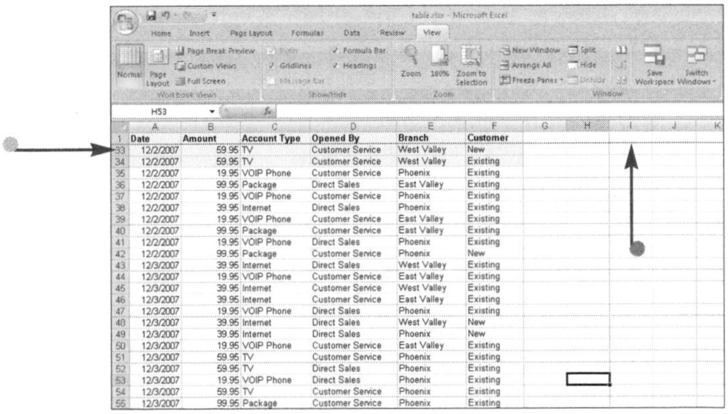

Excel freezes row 1 on-screen.

- A light-gray line indicates that the row is frozen on-screen.

4. Press the Page Down key.
   - Row 1 remains in view, even though row 2 is not in view.

Freeze the First Column

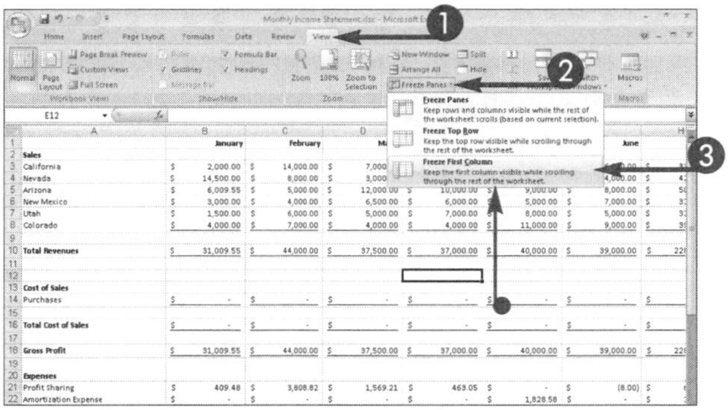

1. Click the View tab.
2. Click Freeze Panes.
   - A drop-down list of options appears.
3. Click Freeze First Column.

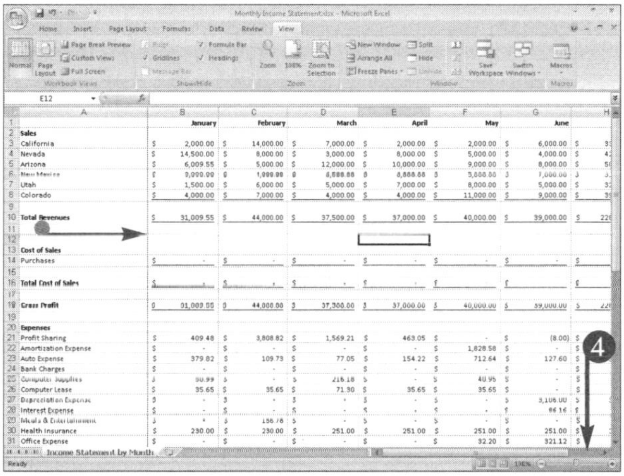

Excel freezes column A on-screen.

- A light-gray line indicates that the column is frozen on-screen.

4. Click a blank area in the horizontal scroll bar on the right side of the scroll box.

MASTER IT

Are there any conditions under which Excel will automatically freeze rows or columns?

▼ Yes. When you define a range as a table, Excel may automatically freeze the top row of the table so that, as you use the Page Down key to move through the table, the column headings remain in view. However, the appearance of this form of freezing is different than what you see when you freeze the top row. When you define a table and use the Page Down key, Excel does not display a light-gray line. Instead, Excel replaces the column letters above the column headings with the actual headings. For details on creating and working with tables, see Chapter 23.

What happens when I try to freeze the first row and then try to freeze the first column?

▼ If you use the steps in the subsection, "Freeze the Top Row," followed by "Freeze the First Column," Excel unfreezes the first row and freezes the first column. The steps in these two subsections are mutually exclusive, and they will not work together to let you freeze both the top row and the first column. However, you can follow the steps in the subsection, "Freeze Rows and Columns," to freeze both the first row and the first column on-screen, as well as to freeze more than one row or column.

continued

Freeze Column and Row Titles *(Continued)*

In many cases, you need to freeze only row 1 or column A to work effectively. However, in some cases, you need to freeze more rows than row 1 or more columns than column A. You may also need to freeze both rows and columns. For example, in your monthly income statement, you may want to view the row titles in the left column that contain your income and expense categories along with the column titles that contain the month designation.

When you want to freeze both rows and columns or more than one row or column, you need to place the cell pointer properly. To freeze multiple rows, you place the cell pointer below the row you want to freeze. To freeze multiple columns, you place the cell pointer to the right of the columns you want to freeze. To freeze both rows and columns, you place the cell pointer below the rows and to the right of the columns you want to freeze.

Freezing rows and columns on-screen does not affect the way your worksheet prints. You can print rows and columns that you need to repeat, but you set that option when you set up your worksheet to print. See Chapter 9 for details.

Freeze Column and Row Titles *(continued)*

Excel displays the next screen of columns.

- Column A remains in view, even though columns B through G are not in view.

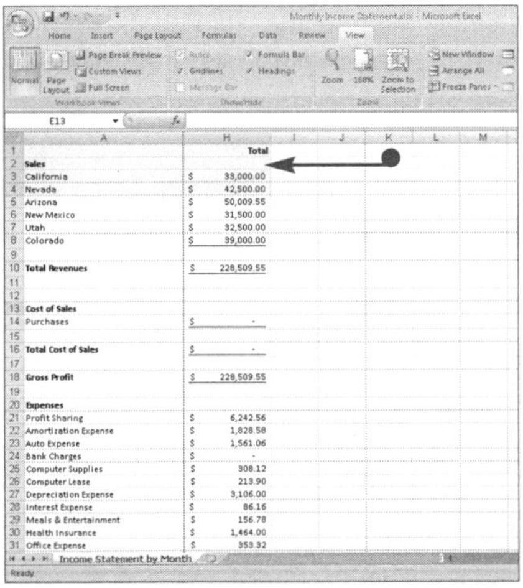

Freeze Rows and Columns

1. Click in the cell located below the row and to the right of the column you want to freeze.
2. Click the View tab.
3. Click Freeze Panes.
   - A drop-down list of options appears.
4. Click Freeze Panes.

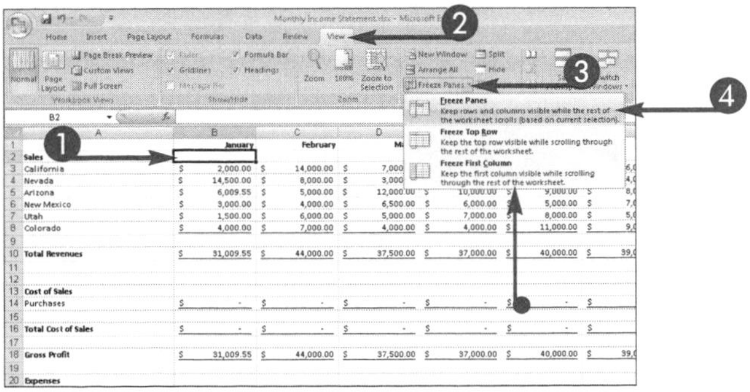

Excel freezes the rows above the cell pointer and the columns to the right of the cell pointer on-screen.

- A light-gray line indicates that the rows and columns are frozen on-screen.

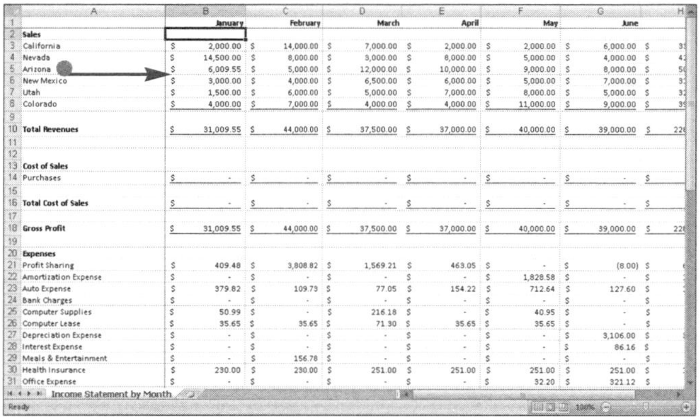

5 Scroll one screen down and to the right.

- The frozen rows and columns remain in view.

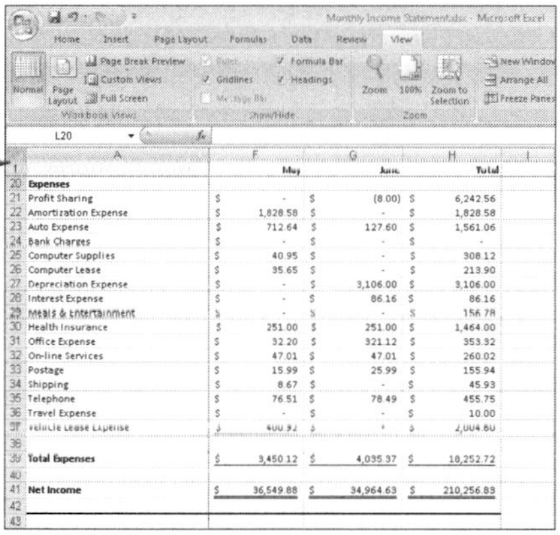

MASTER IT

How do I unfreeze panes?

▼ Click the View tab and then click the Freeze Panes button. From the drop-down menu that appears, click Unfreeze Panes. Excel unfreezes all panes that are frozen. This technique works whether you have frozen only row 1, only column A, or a combination of rows and columns.

Can I freeze more than row 1 and column A simultaneously?

▼ Yes. You can freeze any number of rows and columns. The rows and columns that Excel freezes depend on where you place the cell pointer in Step 1 of the subsection, "Freeze Rows and Columns." For example, if you place the cell pointer in cell C4, Excel freezes columns A and B, along with rows 1 to 3, on-screen at all times.

What happens if I freeze rows and columns and then zoom in on a selection?

▼ The magnification setting that you choose has no effect on the rows and columns that you choose to freeze. Excel zooms in to view the selection, and, at the same time, displays the frozen rows and columns, magnifying both the selection and the frozen rows and columns.

Split a Window

To help you work in different parts of a large worksheet simultaneously, you can split the worksheet window into two horizontal panes, two vertical panes, or even four panes — two horizontal and two vertical.

Each pane has scroll bars so that you can bring different portions of the window into view in different panes. However, the number of scroll bars that you see depends on the number of panes that you create when you split the window. When you create two horizontal panes, one on top of the other, Excel places a scroll bar at the right edge of each pane, but only one scroll bar appears at the bottom of the window. When you create two vertical panes, two scroll bars appear along the bottom of the window, but only one scroll bar appears at the right side of the window. When you create four panes, two scroll bars appear on the right side and two scroll bars appear at the bottom of the window.

Excel synchronizes scrolling when you split the window into panes. For example, when you create two horizontal panes, all horizontal scrolling is synchronized, while you can independently scroll each pane vertically.

Split a Window

Create Two Horizontal Panes

1. Move ✥ into the top of the scroll bar area over the split bar (✥ changes to ↔).
2. Click and drag down to the bottom of the row that should appear last in the top pane.
   - Excel marks the pane position with a gray line.
3. Release the mouse button.

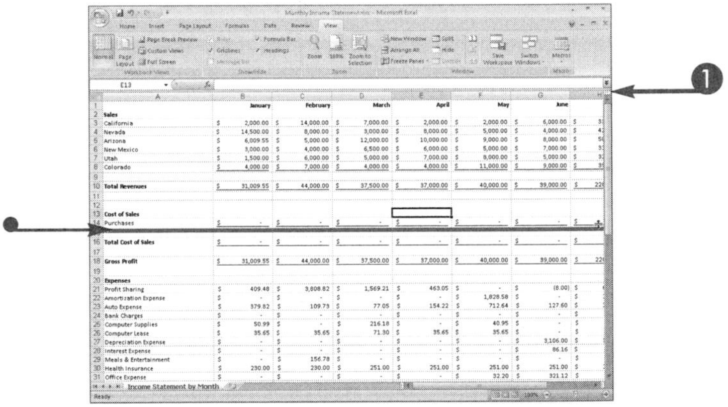

Excel splits the window into two panes.

- You can resize a pane by clicking and dragging the pane border.

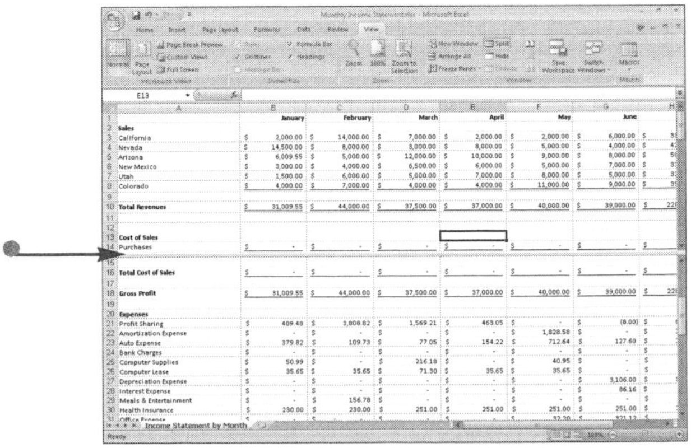

Create a Four-Pane Split

1. Click the cell that should become the upper-left corner of the lower-right pane.
2. Click the View tab.
3. Click Split.

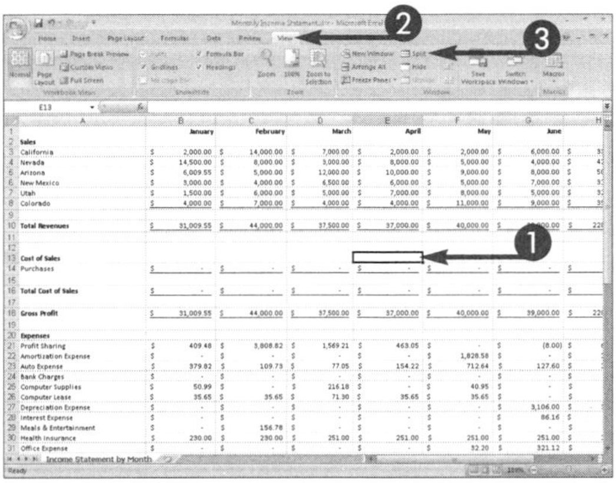

Excel splits the window into four panes.

- This scroll bar controls horizontal scrolling for the two panes on the left.
- This scroll bar controls vertical scrolling for the top two panes.

You can click in any pane to scroll or edit.

You can resize any pane by clicking and dragging its border.

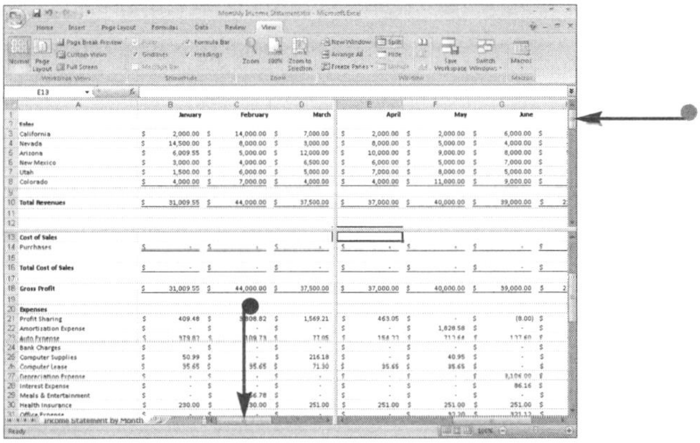

MASTER IT

How do I split the window into two side-by-side panes?

▼ Follow the steps in the subsection, "Create Two Horizontal Panes," but, in Step 1, move the mouse pointer over the split bar that appears in the lower-right corner of the screen at the right edge of the horizontal split bar. Then click and drag left to the left edge of the column that you want to appear as the first column in the right pane.

Is there a quick way to create two panes where one is on top of the other?

▼ Yes. You can place the cell pointer anywhere in column A. Then follow the steps in the subsection, "Create a Four-Pane Split." When you split the screen while the cell pointer is in column A, Excel creates only a two-pane split with the windows placed one on top of the other.

How do I remove the split pane effect?

▼ You can drag the pane border all the way to the right or up, or you can click the View tab and then click Split again. Excel removes any split that exists, whether you split the screen into two side-by-side panes, two panes with one on top of the other, or four panes.

Set Margins

You can control the amount of unprinted area that Excel allots as white space on each side of each printed page by changing the margin settings. By default, Excel sets the top and bottom margins to allow for .75 inch of white space, and the left and right margins to allow for .7 inch of white space. Excel also allows .3-inch margins for the header and footer area.

The margins for the header and footer areas control the distance of the header from the top of the page, and the footer from the bottom of the page. The margins for the header and footer areas should be smaller than the margins for the top and bottom of the page. If the header and footer margins are the same as or bigger than the margins that you set for the top and the bottom of the page, the information in the header or footer area may overlap with the information in your worksheet on the printed page.

Because Page Layout view displays your worksheet as you can expect it to print, you should work in Page Layout view when you adjust margins so that you can see the effects of these adjustments.

Set Margins

Set Wide Margins

1. Click .

   Excel displays the worksheet in Page Layout view.

2. Click the Page Layout tab.
3. Click Margins.
4. Click Wide.

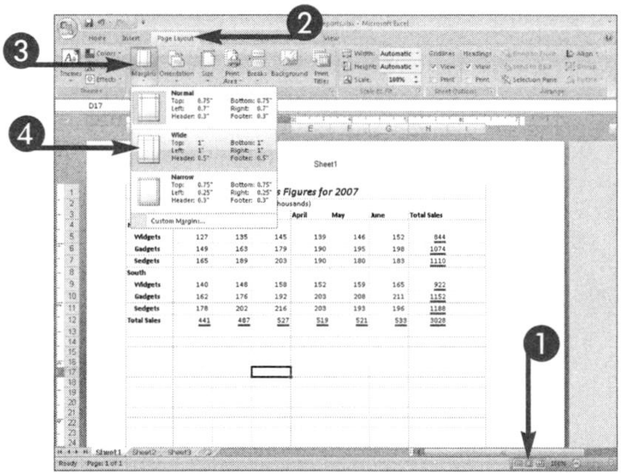

- Excel applies 1-inch margins to all edges of the worksheet.

Set Narrow Margins

1. Click Margins.
2. Click Narrow.

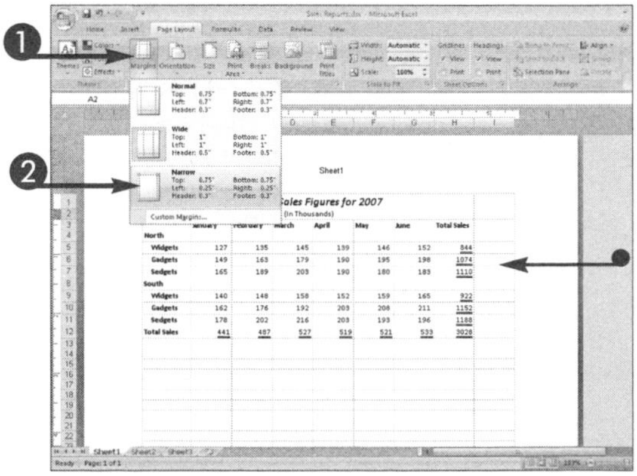

- Excel applies a .75-inch margin to the top and bottom of the page, and a .25-inch margin to the left and right sides of the page.

Set Custom Margins

1. Click the Page Layout tab.
2. In the Page Setup group, click .

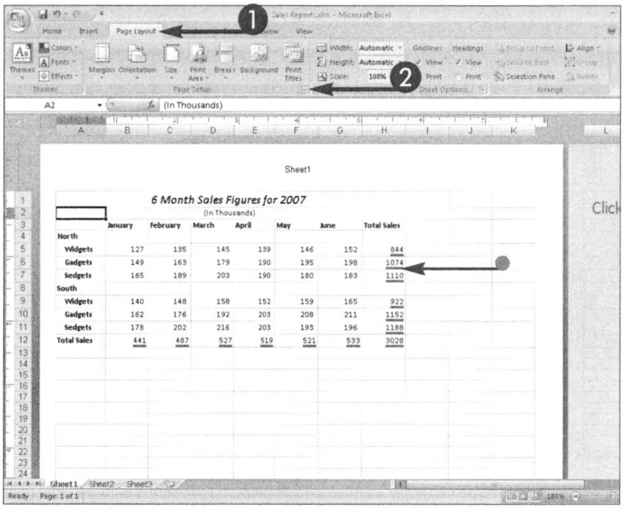

The Page Setup dialog box appears.

3. Click the Margins tab.
   - Use these fields to set left, right, top, and bottom margins.
   - Use these fields to set margins for the header and footer area.
4. Click OK.

Excel saves your settings.

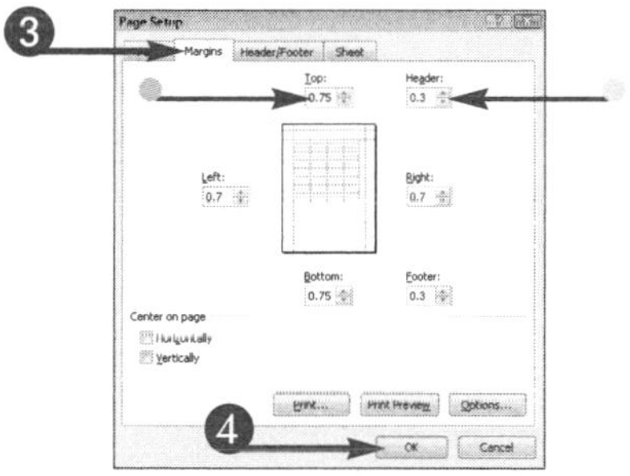

MASTER IT

Can I set different margins for different pages that I print?

▼ Not directly. Excel assigns the same margins to all pages of a worksheet. If you need different margins for different sections that you plan to print, place each section for which you need different margins on separate worksheets. You can then set the margins for each worksheet.

Is there a quick way to set margins?

▼ Yes. You can use the Ruler in Page Layout view and drag to set a margin. Move into the ruler area and position it at either end between the white and the blue portion of the ruler (changes to ↔). Click and drag to the left or right. Dragging the left margin to the left makes the margin narrower. Dragging the right margin to the left makes the margin wider.

Can I control the way Excel positions the information on the page?

▼ Yes. Follow Steps 1 to 3 in the subsection, "Set Custom Margins." In the Center on Page section, click Horizontally to center information between the left and right margins, and click Vertically to center information between the top and bottom margins (changes to).

Add Headers and Footers to a Worksheet

You can add headers and footers to a worksheet to display information at the top and bottom of every printed page. By default, Excel does not supply headers or footers to new workbooks.

When you add headers or footers, you should work in Page Layout view, where you can add the header or footer directly on-screen and see the way it will look when it prints. As you add headers and footers, you can type text directly, or you can add predefined headers and footers that Excel supplies. You can use multiple lines and apply formatting to any header or footer.

When you view the header or footer area, it is not readily apparent that Excel divides each area into three sections represented by boxes. You can use these boxes to print information such as the date, your company name, and the page number. The left box stores information that Excel automatically aligns with the left margin. The center box stores information that Excel automatically centers between the left and right margins. The right box stores information that Excel automatically aligns with the right margin.

Add Headers and Footers to a Worksheet

Add a Header

1. Click ▣.

   Excel displays the worksheet in Page Layout view.

2. Click here.

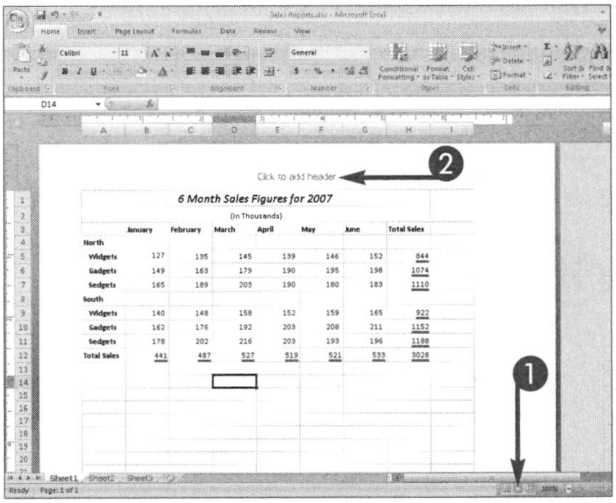

- Excel displays an insertion point in the header.

3. Type a header.

   To include two lines, you can press Enter to start a new line.

4. Click anywhere outside the header to store the header and continue working on the worksheet.

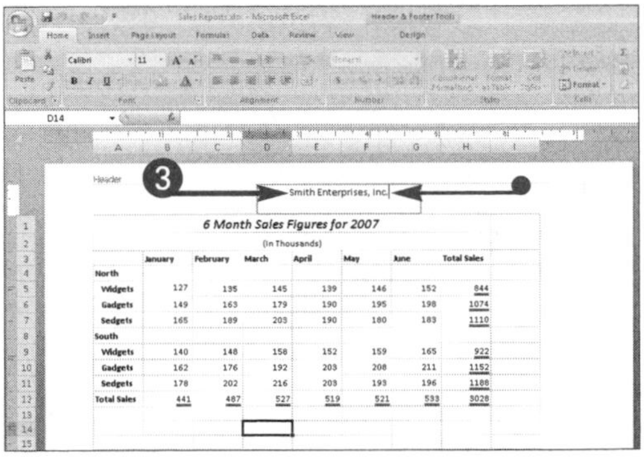

Add a Footer

1. Click [icon].

   Excel displays the worksheet in Page Layout view.

2. Scroll down to view the footer area.

Note: If your worksheet is short, you may need to press Page Down and then scroll up slightly to see the footer area.

3. Click here.

   - Excel displays an insertion point in the footer area.

4. Type a footer.

   To include two lines, you can press Enter to start a new line.

5. Click anywhere outside the footer to store the footer and continue working on the worksheet.

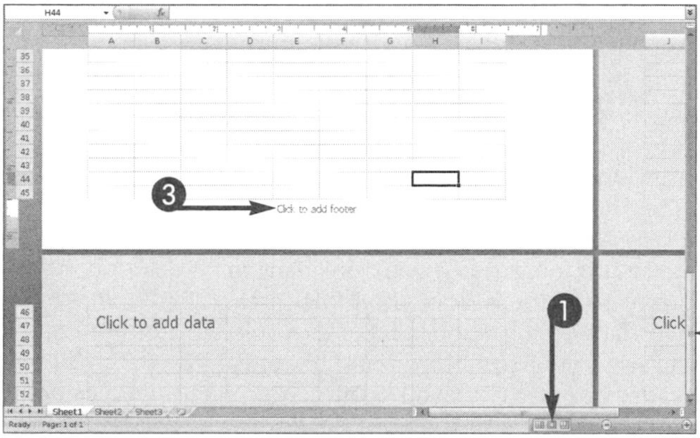

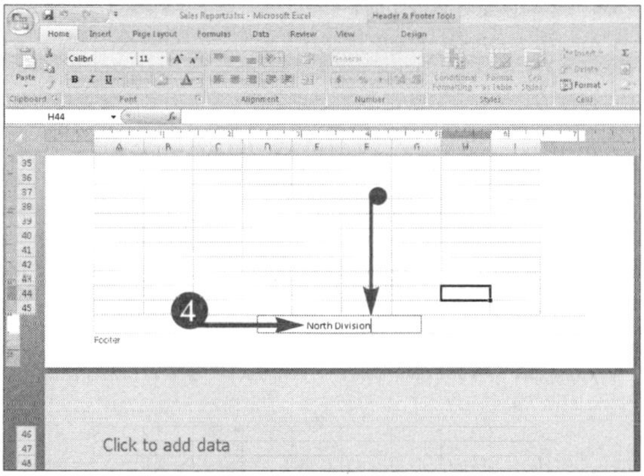

MASTER IT

Must I click in the center box and create a center header before I create a left or right header?

▼ No. Excel displays the prompt, "Click here to add header," only to alert you to the location where you can create a header. As you move [pointer] into the header area, Excel displays a light-blue highlighted background to let you know where each of the three header boxes appear. Click in any box to add a header.

How do I add boldface and italics to the header or footer?

▼ Click the header or footer box that contains the text. Then select the text, click the Home tab, and click the appropriate button in the Font group. You can apply boldface, italics, and underlining to header or footer text. You can also use a different font face, select a different font size, and apply color to the text. You cannot add a border or a fill color.

What kinds of predefined headers and footers can I use?

▼ Excel supplies the same 16 predefined sets of information that you can use in the center box of headers and footers. Excel overwrites any information that you type in the center box with any predefined header or footer you select. View the available choices by clicking in the header or footer area, clicking the Header & Footer Tools Design tab, and then clicking the Header button or the Footer button.

continued

Add Headers and Footers to a Worksheet *(Continued)*

You can set up your own customized headers and footers. You may want to include information that Excel provides in the predefined headers and footers, but you may want to lay out the information in the header and footer area differently than in the way it is supplied. For example, suppose that you want your company name to appear in the center header box and then you want page number information to appear in the right header box. Although you can include page number information using one of Excel's predefined headers, you cannot place it in the right header box. However, you can place it wherever you want by creating a custom header.

When you create a custom header or footer, you supply whatever information you want in each box of the header or footer. You do not need to enter information in all of the boxes; you can use just the ones you want. If you choose to include information such as page numbers or today's date and time, Excel enters codes in the header or footer area to represent the information. When you work outside the header or footer area and when you print the worksheet, Excel displays the results of the code.

Add Headers and Footers to a Worksheet *(continued)*

Customize a Header or Footer

1. Click .

   Excel displays the worksheet in Page Layout view.

2. Click in the header or footer area.

   This example customizes a header.

   - You can click here to add header text aligned with the left margin.
   - You can click here to add header text aligned with the right margin.
   - Excel displays an insertion point in the header.

3. Click here to view the Header & Footer Tools Design context tab.

Note: *This tab becomes available only when you click in the header or footer area.*

4. Type **Page** and press the spacebar.
5. Click Page Number.

   - Excel inserts a code to represent the current page number.

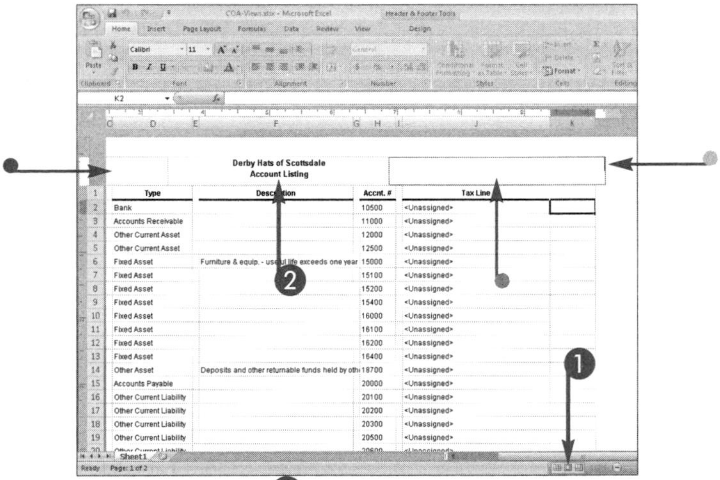

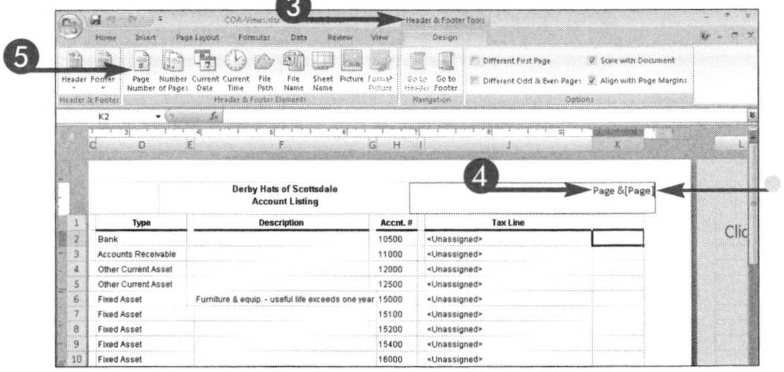

6. Press the spacebar, type **of**, and press the spacebar again.
7. Click Number of Pages.
   - Excel inserts a code to represent the number of pages that will print.
8. Click outside the header or footer area.

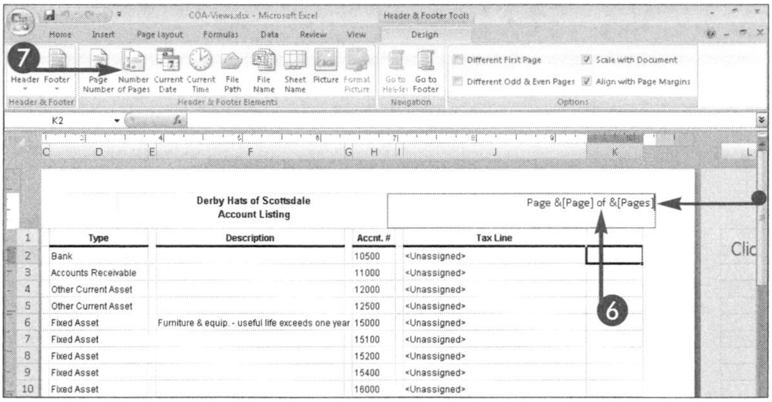

- Excel displays the page number and the number of pages that will print.
- The Header & Footer Tools Design context tab disappears.

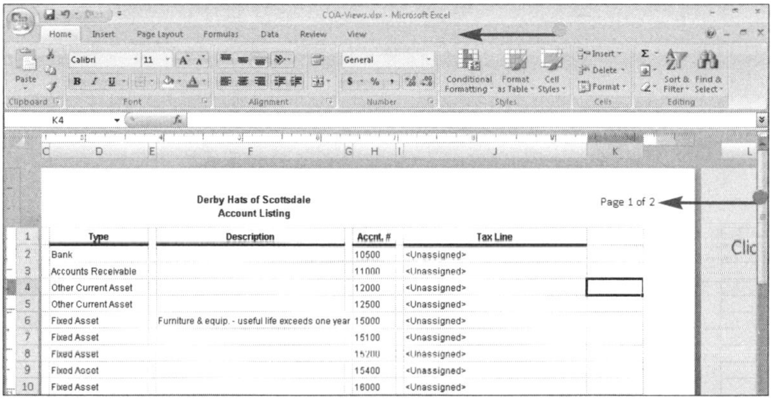

MASTER IT

What do the Different First Page and Different Odd & Even Pages check boxes do?

▼ When you select Different First Page (☐ changes to ☑), Excel enables you to define one header and footer for Page 1 of your worksheet, and then another header and footer that will print on all subsequent pages. When you select Different Odd & Even Pages, Excel enables you to define one header and footer for odd-numbered pages and a different header and footer for even-numbered pages. After selecting either check box, just follow the steps in this section to create the appropriate headers and footers on Page 1 and then on Page 2.

What does the Scale with Document check box do?

▼ By default, Excel selects this check box so that the size of headers and footers will shrink or enlarge if you scale the size of your worksheet for printing. For information on scaling the size of your worksheet, see the section, "Control the Width and Height of Printed Output."

What does the Align with Page Margins check box do?

▼ By default, Excel selects this check box so that text in left headers and footers aligns with the left margin, and right headers and footers align with the right margin. For details on adjusting margins, see the section, "Set Margins."

Select an Area to Print

By default, Excel prints all of the area of a worksheet that you use, but you can print only part of the worksheet if you specify the print area. For example, suppose that you have stored the chart of accounts for your company in an Excel worksheet and you want to print just that portion of the worksheet related to fixed assets. You can identify the accounts that make up your fixed assets as the print area.

To identify the print area, you select it; the area that you choose to print does not need to be contiguous.

You can add to the print area after you set it if you need to print additional cells.

Once you set a print area, Excel remembers that print area. Whenever you print the worksheet, Excel prints that print area and only that area. To print your entire worksheet or to print a different portion of the worksheet, you can clear the print area and then establish a new print area.

You can set the print area from the Ribbon or from the Page Setup dialog box. The example in this section uses the Ribbon.

Select an Area to Print

Set the Print Area

1. Select a range to print.
2. Click the Page Layout tab.
3. Click Print Area.
4. Click Set Print Area.

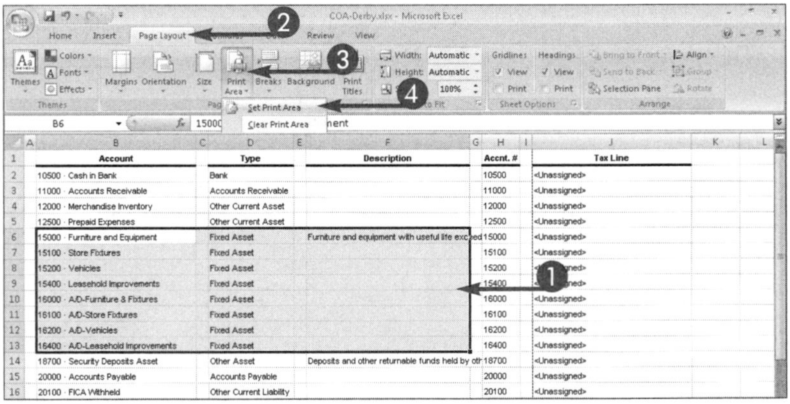

- Excel sets the print area and identifies it by surrounding it with a dashed line.

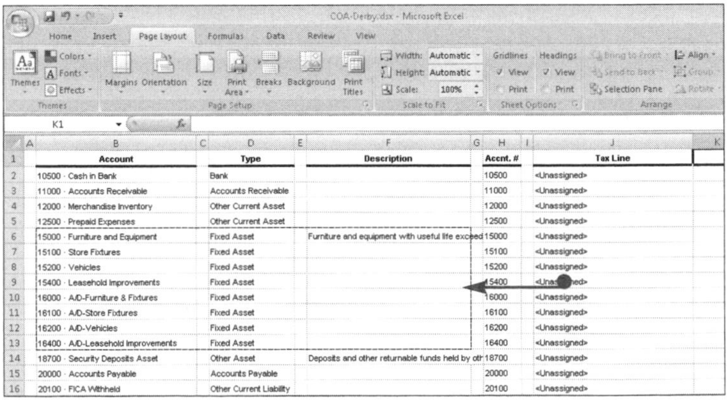

Add to the Print Area

1. Select a range that you did not include in the original print area.
2. Click the Page Layout tab.
3. Click Print Area.
4. Click Add to Print Area.

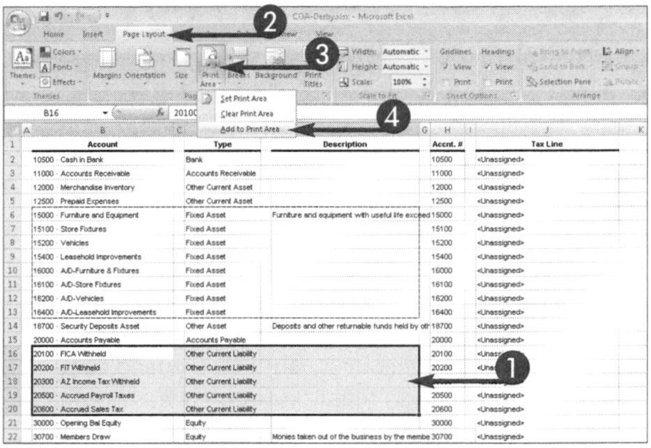

- Excel expands the existing print area to include the new cells that you selected in Step 1.

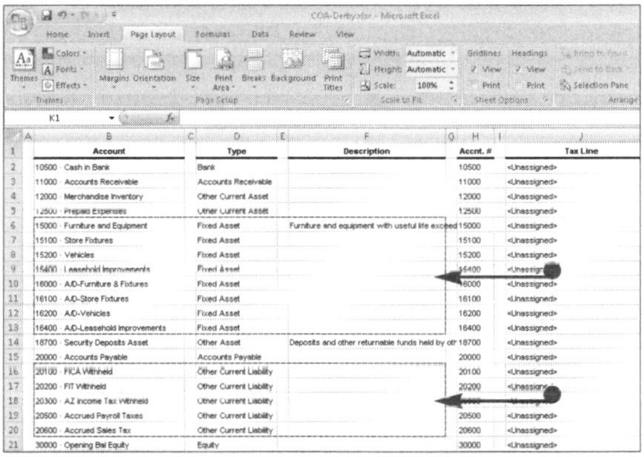

MASTER IT

How do I reset the print area?

▼ Click the Page Layout tab, click Print Area, and then click Clear Print Area. Excel removes the print area that you set, even when the print area includes non-contiguous cells. You can move the print area to a different set of cells without clearing it; just follow the steps in the subsection, "Set the Print Area," and Excel will automatically clear any previously set print area to replace it with the new print area.

When should I use the Page Setup dialog box to set the print area?

▼ The Page Setup dialog box enables you to set a wide variety of options from one location, including margins, headers and footers, and sheet-specific settings. If you have many changes to make to print what you want, then working in the Page Setup dialog box might help you remember to make all of these changes.

Does the print area appear with a dashed outline in other views besides the Normal view?

▼ In Page Layout view, you can identify the print area by the dashed outline. In Page Break Preview, you do not see a dashed outline, but cells in the print area appear in white, and outlined by a heavy blue line. Cells not included in the print area appear gray.

Insert, Adjust, or Remove Page Breaks

By default, Excel fits as much information on a printed page as will fit between the top, bottom, left, and right margins, but you can insert page breaks to force Excel to paginate in different places than the default places. For example, suppose that you want to print the worksheet that contains your chart of accounts, but you want to start new pages as you change major account types. That is, when Excel finishes printing asset accounts, you want liability accounts to start printing on a new page. Also, when Excel finishes printing liability accounts, equity accounts should start printing on a new page. Similarly, Excel should start new pages to begin printing income accounts, cost of sales accounts, and expense accounts. You can insert page breaks to paginate the way you want.

You can insert page breaks from Normal view and Page Layout view. However, you will find it easiest to see the effects of the page breaks that you insert if you work in Page Break Preview to insert, adjust, or remove a horizontal page break, a vertical page break, or both.

Insert, Adjust, or Remove Page Breaks

Insert a Page Break

1. Click ▣ to display the worksheet in Page Break Preview.
2. Click OK to close the Welcome to Page Break Preview dialog box.
   - Blue dashed lines represent page breaks that Excel inserts.

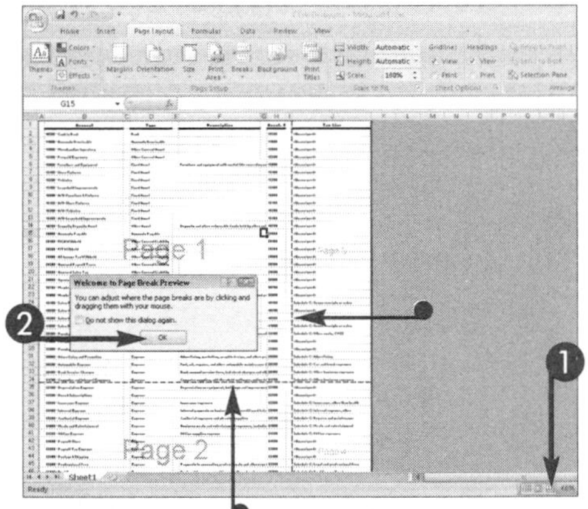

3. Click in the cell at the intersection of the row and column that you want to appear on a new page.
4. Click the Page Layout tab.
5. Click Breaks.
6. Click Insert Page Break.

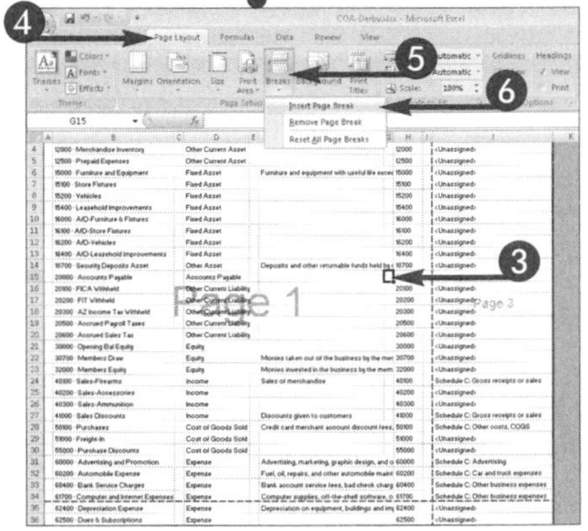

- Excel inserts page breaks above and to the left of the cell you selected in Step 3. Page breaks appear as solid blue lines.

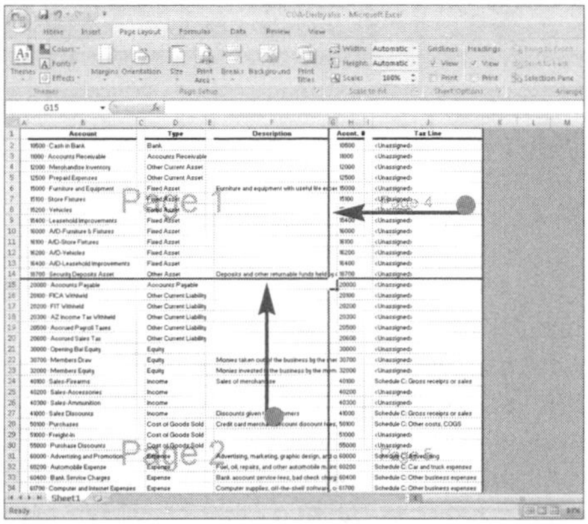

Adjust a Page Break

1. In Page Break Preview, move the mouse pointer over the page break that you want to move (✥ changes to ↔ or ↕).

2. Click and drag the mouse.

   You can drag to the left and up to reduce the number of columns and rows on the page.

   - A line marks the proposed location of the page break. Here, the page break was moved from row 15 to row 28.

3. Release the mouse button to place the page break.

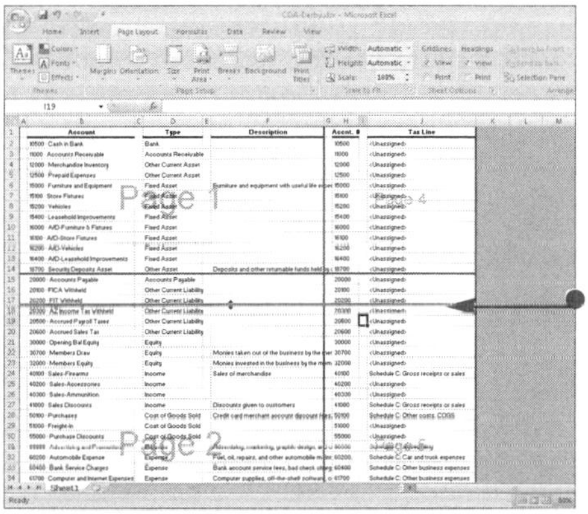

MASTER IT

How can I insert only a horizontal page break or only a vertical page break?

▼ Place the cell pointer in column A of the last row that you want to appear on the page, and then follow the steps in the subsection, "Insert a Page Break." Excel inserts only a horizontal page break. To insert only a vertical page break, place the cell pointer in row 1 of the last column that you want to appear on the page, and then follow the steps in the subsection, "Insert a Page Break." Excel inserts only a vertical page break.

How can I find the location in Page Break Preview to insert the page break when the print is so small?

▼ Zoom to enlarge the print enough so that you can find the location for the page break. You can use the zoom slider or the Zoom dialog box. For details on zooming in, see Chapter 8.

Is there a way to get rid of all page breaks?

▼ You can remove all page breaks that you have inserted, but you cannot remove page breaks that Excel inserts. Click Page Layout and then click Breaks. From the Breaks drop-down menu, click Reset All Page Breaks.

continued

Insert, Adjust, or Remove Page Breaks *(Continued)*

In Normal view, Excel represents page breaks with a dashed line. In Page Layout view, page breaks do not appear, but you can identify where they are by looking at where new pages begin. In Page Break Preview, where page breaks are easiest to identify, a page break that you insert appears as a heavy blue line. Page breaks that Excel inserts, based on how much information will fit between the margins, appear as dashed blue lines.

The location where you place the cell pointer when you insert a page break determines whether Excel inserts only a horizontal page break, only a vertical page break, or both. When you insert a horizontal page break, Excel prints the rows below the page break on a new page. When you insert a vertical page break, Excel prints columns to the right of the page break on a new page.

If you are not happy with the location of a page break that you insert, you can move the page break or you can remove the page break altogether. You cannot make any adjustments to page breaks that Excel inserts, but Excel moves or removes these page breaks to accommodate the ones that you insert.

Insert, Adjust, or Remove Page Breaks *(continued)*

Remove a Page Break

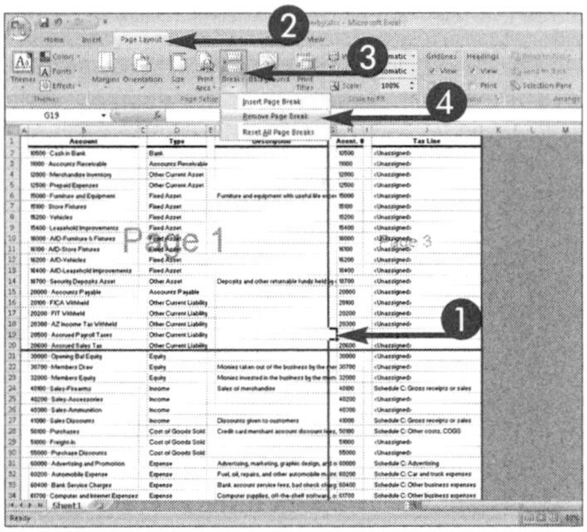

1. In Page Break Preview, click in the row below, or the column to the right of, the page break that you want to remove.

   To move both a horizontal and vertical page break, click the cell in the row below, and in the column to the right of, the page break.

2. Click the Page Layout tab.
3. Click Breaks.
4. Click Remove Page Break.

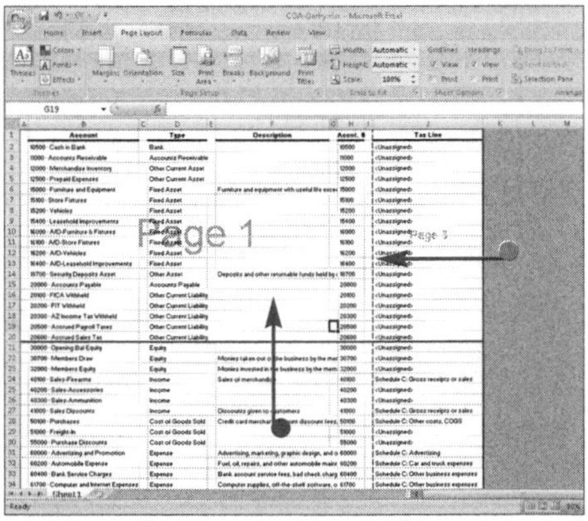

- Excel removes the page break.
- If necessary, Excel inserts its own page break.

Set Page Orientation

When you change the page orientation, you change the way information will print on the page. By default, Excel sets up each worksheet to print in portrait orientation, which prints information onto a letter-sized page of 8 1/2 inches by 11 inches oriented vertically. You can switch to landscape orientation to print the information onto a letter-sized page that is oriented horizontally, effectively rotating 90 degrees to print information at 11 inches by 8 1/2 inches.

Portrait orientation works well when your worksheet does not use many columns. When the columns in your worksheet do not fit a portrait orientation, you can switch to landscape orientation to try to fit all of the columns onto the page when you print.

When you change the orientation, Excel changes it only for the current worksheet. No other worksheets in the workbook are affected.

To help you remember the difference between the orientations, think of paintings, where these orientations got their names. Leonardo da Vinci painted the Mona Lisa *portrait* with the canvas oriented vertically. Georges-Pierre Seurat painted his *landscape*, Sunday Afternoon on the Island of La Grande Jatte, with the canvas oriented horizontally.

Set Page Orientation

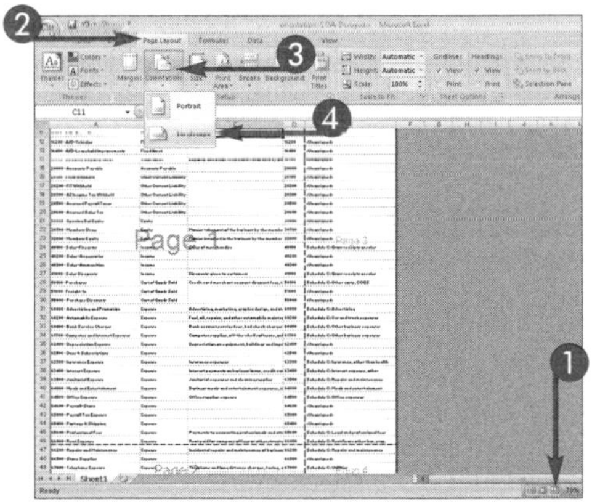

1 Click [icon].

Note: *You can change orientation from any view, but working in Page Break Preview or Page Layout view best demonstrates the effect of switching orientation.*

2 Click the Page Layout tab.

3 Click Orientation.

4 Click Landscape.

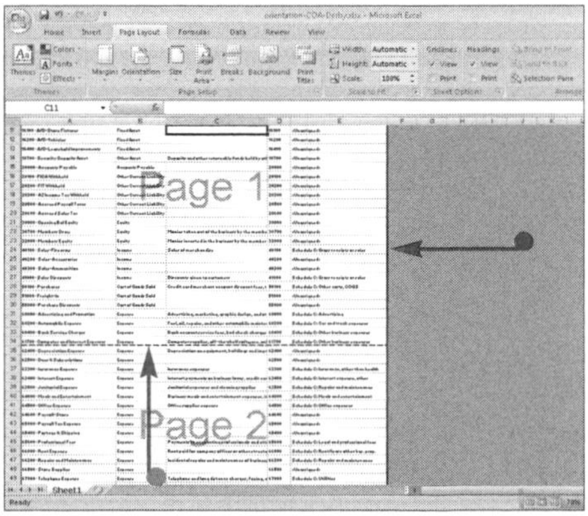

- Excel changes the orientation of the printed page and adjusts vertical page breaks.
- Excel adjusts the horizontal page breaks.

In this example, you could barely see Page 2 in portrait orientation, but in landscape orientation, you can see all of Page 1 and much of Page 2.

Print Row and Column Titles on Each Page

When your printed worksheet is too large to fit on one page, you can use the Print Titles feature to have Excel repeat row and column heading labels on each printed page. This feature makes your worksheet easy to read; if you do not print row and column labels on each page, you might have trouble matching data to its appropriate heading labels.

For example, suppose that your worksheet contains six months of information about the income and expenses for your company. Across the top, your worksheet displays each month's heading, and down the left side, your worksheet displays income and expense categories for your business. Even when you change the orientation of the worksheet, you cannot fit all of the rows and columns on one page. You may not even be able to fit all of the rows and columns on two pages.

To make reading your worksheet easier, you can have Excel repeat, on each printed page, the row containing the month labels and the column containing the income and expense category labels. This allows you to easily match up data with its heading labels without having to read with a ruler or cut and paste printed pages together.

Print Row and Column Titles on Each Page

1. Click .

Note: *You can set titles from any view, but working in Page Layout view best demonstrates the effect of printing titles.*

2. Click the Page Layout tab.
3. Click Print Titles.

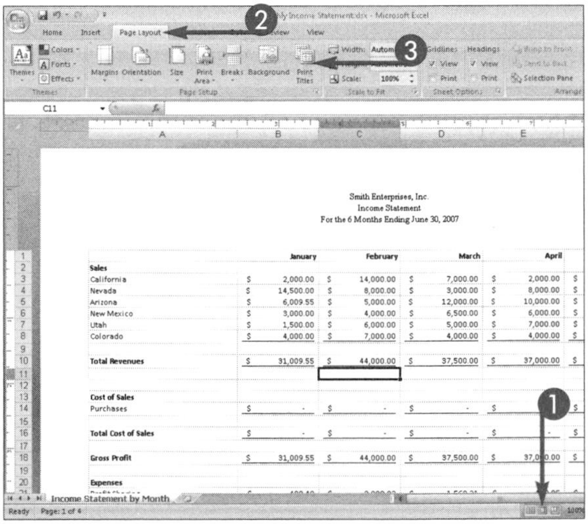

The Sheet tab of the Page Setup dialog box appears.

4. Click .

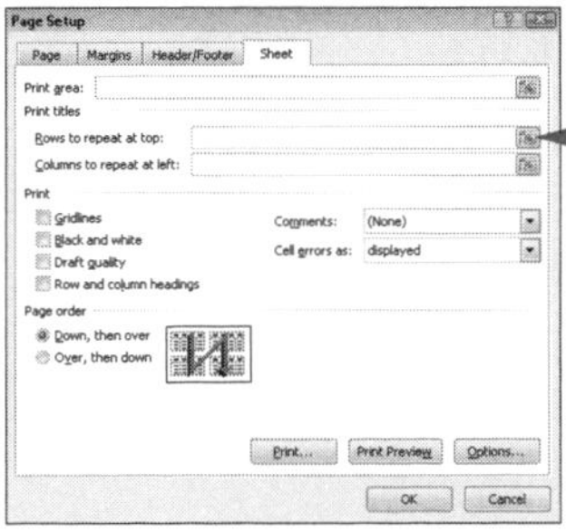

- Excel collapses the Page Setup dialog box so that you can select a row.

5 Click a cell in a row that you want to repeat.

- Excel displays an animated dashed line around the selected row.

6 Click [icon].

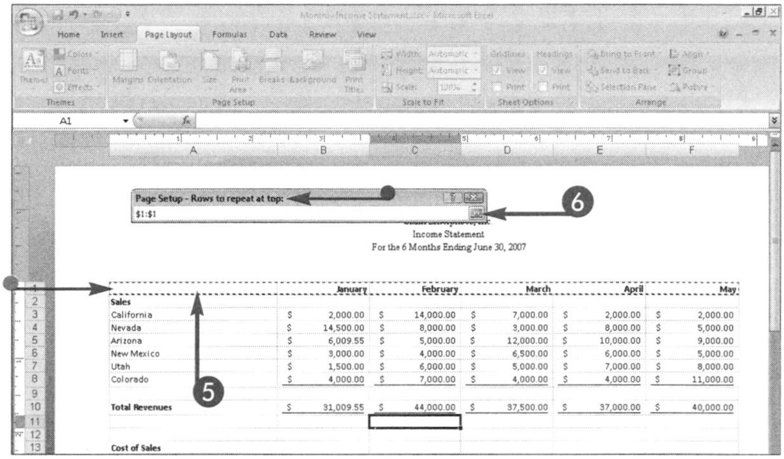

Excel redisplays the Page Setup dialog box.

- The row you selected appears here.
- You can repeat Steps 3 to 5 to establish columns to repeat; in Step 3, click [icon] beside the Columns to Repeat at Left option.

7 Click Print Preview.

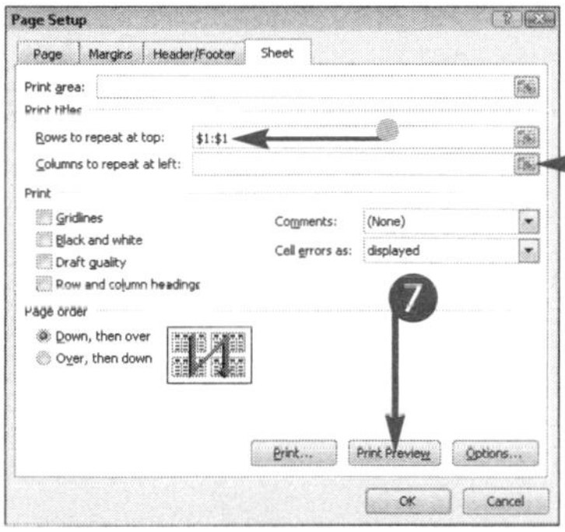

MASTER IT

If I specify a print area, should I include the repeating row and column in the print area?

▼ It does not matter. Excel is smart enough to know that it should print the repeating row or column only once on the page, even if you include the row or column in both the print range and as a repeating row or column.

Can I repeat more than one row or column?

▼ Yes, you can repeat as many rows and columns as you need. When you perform Step 5, click and drag to select cells in more than one row or more than one column; Excel displays an animated border around all the rows or columns you select. When you print, Excel displays all the rows and columns you selected on each printed page.

Can I choose to repeat rows or columns that do not contain labels?

▼ Yes. Excel simply views the rows and columns you select as the rows and columns you want to repeat on each printed page. However, be aware that printing information other than row and column labels might result in a printed worksheet that is difficult to understand, because this feature is intended to help you supply titles for data on every page.

continued

Print Row and Column Titles on Each Page *(Continued)*

You can choose to repeat a row, a column, or both a row and a column to help you to identify what data represents on printed pages where the original heading labels do not appear. When you assign row and column titles and preview or print your worksheet, the titles will appear on all pages. Printing row and column heading labels as titles on each printed page serves much the same purpose as freezing panes on-screen. In each case, you keep the heading labels in sight at all times. However, be aware that the two features are not related and have no effect on each other. Freezing panes does not make Excel print titles, and printing titles does not make Excel freeze panes. For more information on freezing panes, see Chapter 8.

MASTER IT

What is the difference between using the Print Titles feature to repeat a row and printing a header?

▼ Although both features involve printing information on every page, they are otherwise unrelated. A row title prints above your information and within the margins set for the page. A header prints in the top margin area and is not related to specific lines of information in the worksheet.

Print Row and Column Titles on Each Page *(continued)*

- Excel previews how the worksheet will print and displays the first page.

8 Click Next Page.

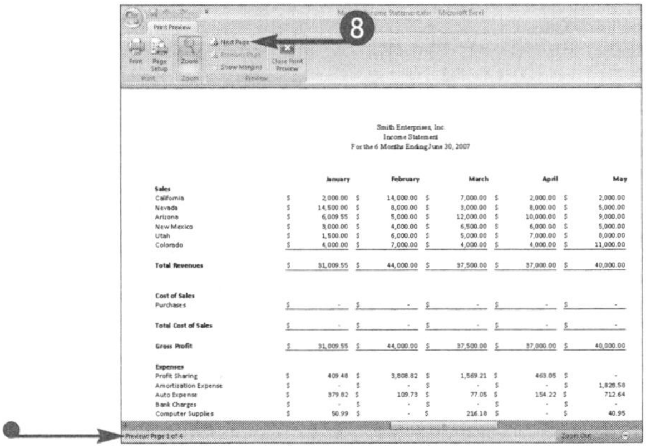

- Excel displays the second page.
- Rows that you chose to repeat appear on the second page as well as the first page.

9 Click Close Print Preview to return to Page Layout view and work on your worksheet.

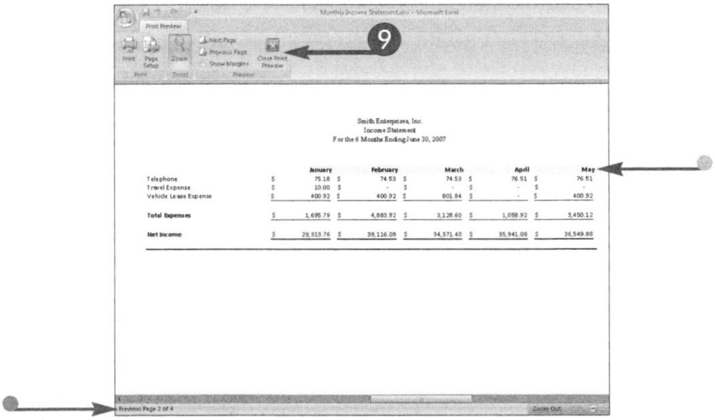

Set Paper Size

By default, the United States version of Excel assumes that you will print your worksheet onto 8 1/2 by 11-inch letter-size paper, but you can change the size of paper to any of a variety of paper sizes. For example, suppose that your worksheet contains six months of information about the income and expenses for your company. Across the top, your worksheet displays each month's heading, and down the left side, your worksheet displays income and expense categories for your business. Even when you change the orientation of the worksheet, you cannot fit all of the rows and columns on one page. You may not even be able to fit all of the rows and columns on two pages. However, it is possible that you can fit all columns of information on one page if you set the orientation of your worksheet to landscape and print your worksheet on 8 1/2 by 14-inch legal-size paper.

Although Excel can print to a variety of paper sizes, keep in mind that your printer may not support all of those paper sizes. Check your printer handbook to determine the paper sizes your printer can use and how to set your printer to use them.

Set Paper Size

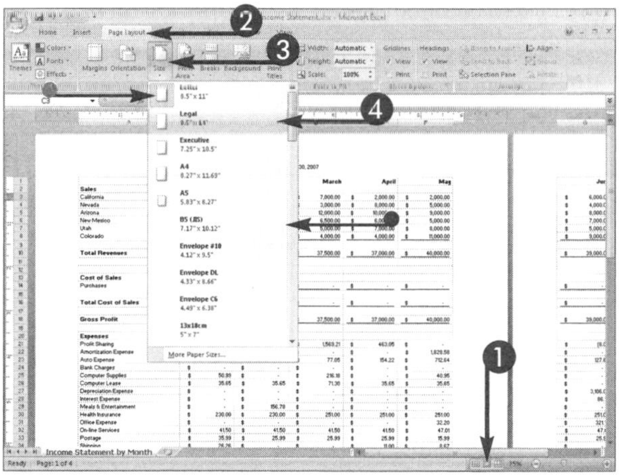

1. Click .

Note: *You can change paper sizes from any view, but Page Layout view best demonstrates the effect of changing paper sizes.*

2. Click the Page Layout tab.
3. Click Size.
   - A drop-down list of paper sizes appears.
   - The current size displays this mark.
4. Select a size.

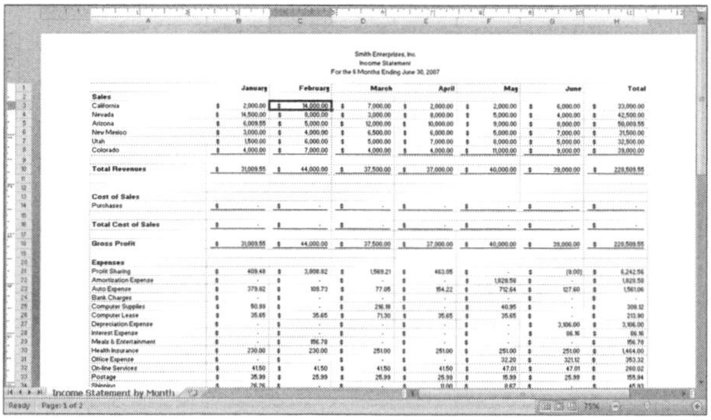

Excel displays the way your worksheet will print using the new paper size.

Control the Width and Height of Printed Output

When changing margins, page orientation, and paper size fail to help you fit your worksheet onto a specific number of printed pages, you can try shrinking the size of the worksheet for printing purposes. This technique works very well when you have only a small amount of information that flows onto extra pages. For example, suppose your worksheet contains 13 columns of address book information for each addressee and your address book contains entries for 100 people. When you print the worksheet onto letter-sized paper in landscape orientation, using narrow margins, the worksheet prints onto six pages. Nine columns of information for each person fit onto three pages, but the last four narrow columns for each addressee print on three extra pages. In this case, you can try scaling the printed worksheet to fit all columns for each addressee onto a single page, reducing the printed pages to three.

When you set scale options in Excel, you can specify the height and width of the printed product using the number of pages you want in each direction. You can also set a scale percentage of less than 100 percent.

Control the Width and Height of Printed Output

1 Click [icon].

Note: *You can set scale options from any view, but Page Layout view best demonstrates the effect of setting scale options.*

Excel displays your worksheet as it will print before scaling.

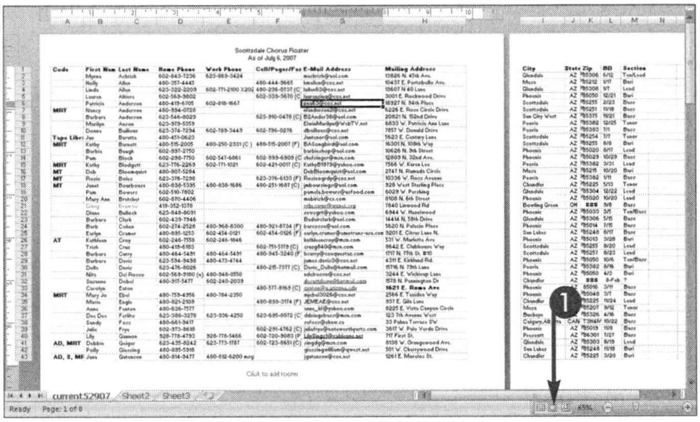

2 Click the Page Layout tab.

- You can set the Scale percentage to less than 100 percent to reduce printed output.
- You can use these options to specify the number of printed pages you want.

This example sets the width of printed output to fit all columns on one page.

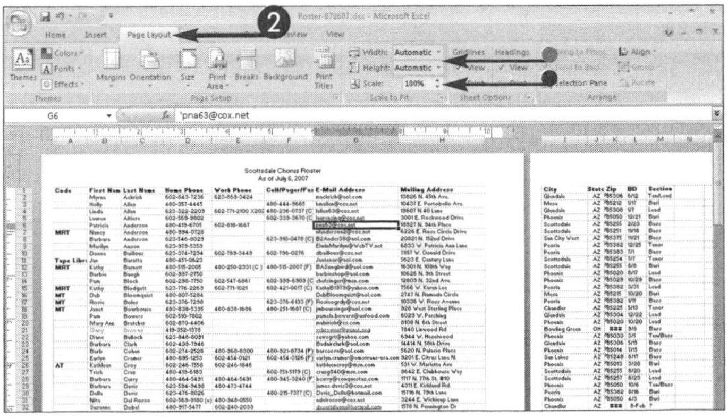

3. Click beside Width.
4. Select the number of pages across for the printed worksheet.

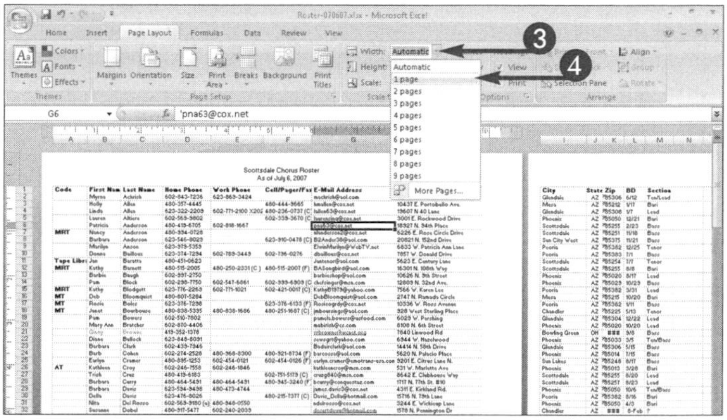

Excel shrinks the worksheet to fit within the scale you set.

- Excel automatically sets the Scale percentage when you change the Width or Height option.

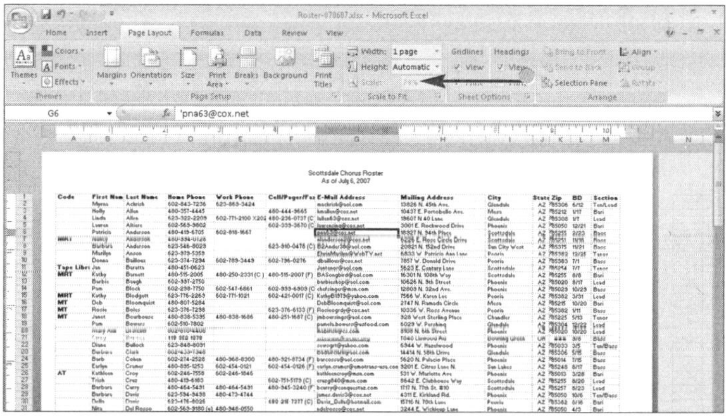

MASTER IT

When I use the steps in this section, am I changing the font size?

▼ In a way, you are changing the font size, but only on the printed page. On-screen, Excel retains the font size settings that you establish for your worksheet, and scaling your worksheet has no effect on these settings. If you print your worksheet scaled to less than 100 percent, scaled to 100 percent, and scaled to larger than 100 percent, the font size on all three printed worksheets will look different. The worksheet scaled to 100 percent will display the actual font size. The font on the other two worksheets will look smaller and larger than the actual font size.

Why did you set only the width for one page and not the height?

▼ Setting the Width option controls the number of columns that print, and setting the Height option controls the number of rows that print on the number of pages you select. When you set only one of the two options, you tell Excel to use however many pages it needs in the direction you left set to Automatic. When you have 100 rows in a worksheet and you set the height to one page, the printed worksheet will be too small to read. If you set the height to seven pages and Excel needs only three pages, then Excel prints the worksheet onto three pages.

Print Gridlines

In some cases, printing gridlines makes the printed worksheet easier to read. Gridlines can be particularly effective when your worksheet contains many rows and columns of data, because gridlines can act like a straightedge and help your eye follow across each printed line on the worksheet. By default, Excel does not print gridlines to delineate cells when you print your worksheet, but you can tell Excel to print gridlines when you print your worksheet.

Printing gridlines and displaying gridlines on-screen are independent activities. You can hide gridlines on-screen and still print them when you print the worksheet. You can also display gridlines on-screen without printing them when you print the worksheet. See Chapter 8 for details on hiding and displaying gridlines on-screen.

MASTER IT

Can I just select the cells and add borders to them to create a gridline effect?

▼ Yes, but that process is actually more difficult than the one shown in this section. In addition, when you use borders to act as gridlines, you see them both on-screen and when you print. Using the technique in this section keeps on-screen gridlines separate from printed gridlines.

Print Gridlines

1. Click the Page Layout tab.
2. Click Print (☑ changes to ◎).

   This example does not display gridlines on-screen.

   The selection has no effect on the appearance of your worksheet on-screen.

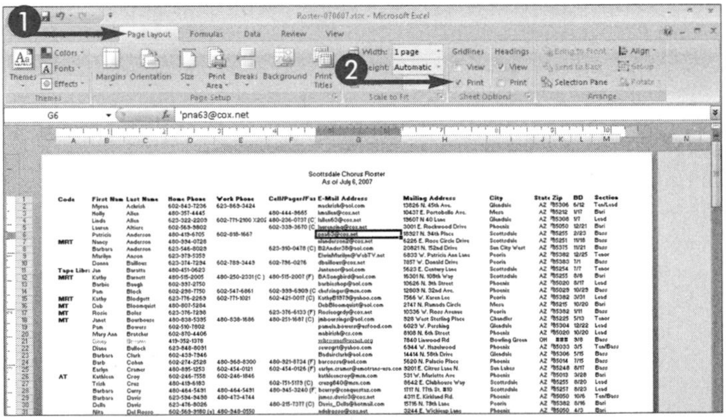

3. Press Ctrl+F2.

   Excel displays the worksheet in Print Preview.

   - Gridlines appear.

Note: Print Preview shows how your worksheet will look printed.

4. Click Close Print Preview to continue working.

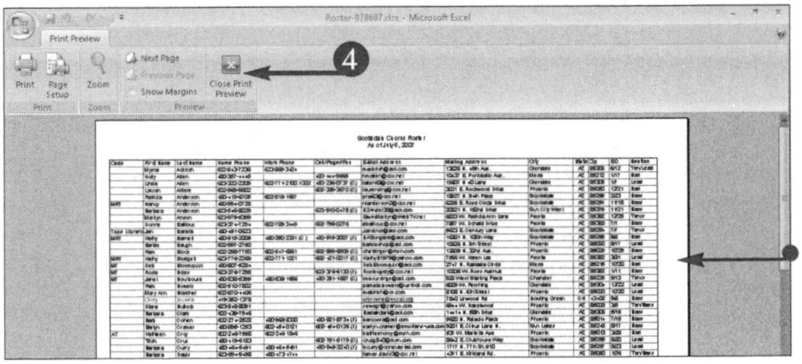

Print Row Numbers and Column Letters

You can print row numbers and column letters when you print your worksheet. Printing row numbers and column letters helps when you are looking at a printed copy of your worksheet and want to identify the cells containing particular pieces of information. In a worksheet that contains information in many rows and columns, printing row and column headings can help you proofread your worksheet. For example, you can print row and column headings and then compare your printed worksheet with the raw data you used when you set up the worksheet. By default, Excel does not print row numbers and column letters, but you can tell Excel to print them when you print your worksheet.

Printing row and column headings and displaying row and column headings on-screen are independent activities. You can hide row and column headings on-screen and still print them when you print the worksheet. You can also display row and column headings on-screen without printing them when you print the worksheet. And, of course, you can both display and print row and column headings on-screen. See Chapter 8 for details on hiding and displaying row and column headings on-screen.

Print Row Numbers and Column Letters

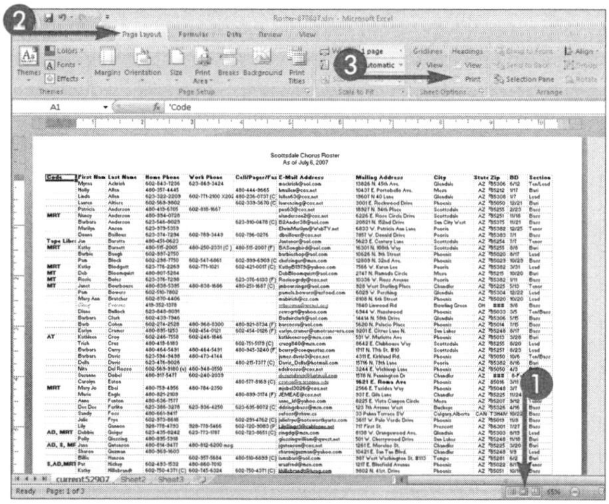

1. Click ▣.

Note: *You can set print options for row and column headings from any view, but Page Layout or Print Preview view best demonstrate the effect of setting these options.*

2. Click the Page Layout tab.

   This example does not display row and column headings on-screen.

3. Click Print (☑ changes to ◎).

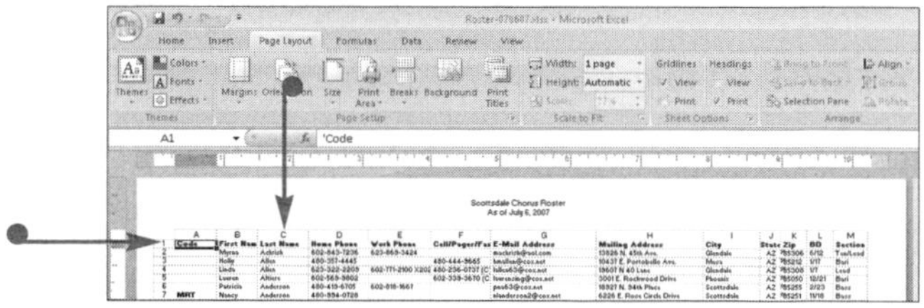

- Excel adds row and column headings to the body of the worksheet that will print when you print the worksheet.

Preview and Print

You can preview and print your worksheet. When you preview your worksheet, Excel displays it exactly as it will print. While Page Layout view gives you a good idea of what your worksheet will look like when you print it, Print Preview is exact. For example, you cannot tell by looking at Page Layout view whether gridlines will print, but you can tell by previewing your worksheet.

While previewing your worksheet, you can identify the page that you are viewing by page number, and you can zoom in to magnify the view.

If you use a black-and-white printer, Print Preview displays your worksheet in black and white. If you use a color printer and have applied color to your worksheet, Print Preview displays the colors.

When you print your worksheet to paper, you can select the printer to use and you can specify whether to print all of your worksheet or only certain page numbers. You can also specify the number of copies to print and choose to print selected cells, the active worksheet, a table if the worksheet contains one, or the entire workbook.

Preview and Print

1. Click .
2. Move your mouse over Print.
3. Click Print Preview.

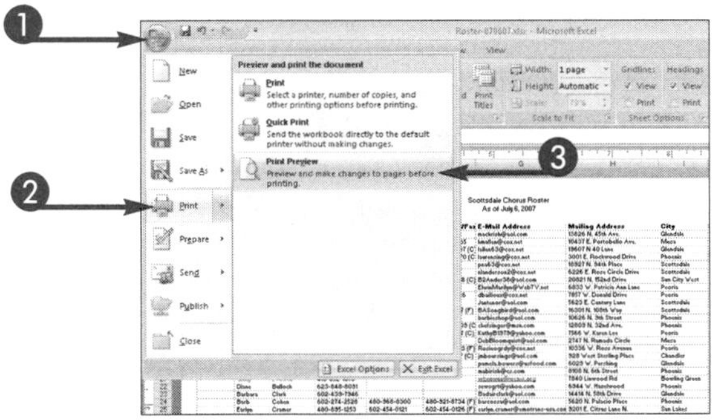

Excel displays the workbook in Print Preview.

- The current page and the total number of pages in the workbook appear.
- You can use these buttons to view subsequent and previous pages.

4. Click Zoom.

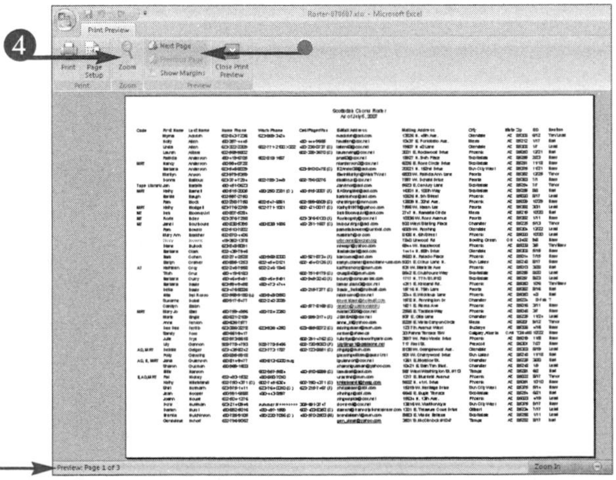

Excel enlarges the view of the worksheet.

- You can click Zoom again to redisplay an entire page.

5 Click Print to display the Print dialog box.

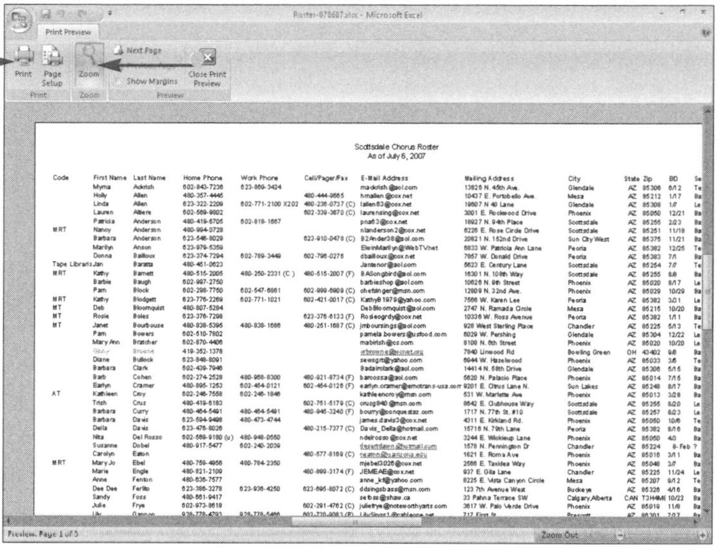

- You can click ▾ to select a different printer.
- You can print the entire worksheet or only selected pages (○ changes to ◉).
- You can print a selection, the active worksheet, or the entire workbook (○ changes to ◉).
- You can specify the number of copies to print.

6 Click OK to print and return to the worksheet.

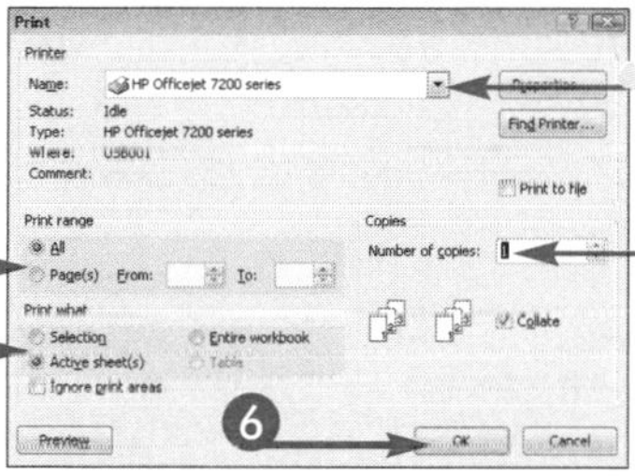

MASTER IT

Why does Excel print only one portion of my worksheet when I choose to print the entire worksheet?

▼ At some point, you have set the print area. You can clear the print area, as described in the section, "Select an Area to Print," or you can select Ignore Print Areas in the Print dialog box (☐ changes to ☑).

Can I print without previewing?

▼ Yes. Click sand then click Print. Excel prints the active worksheet using any settings that you established by following steps in the sections of this chapter. If you did not change any of Excel's default print settings, Excel prints one copy of the entire active worksheet using the currently selected printer.

What does the Show Margins option do?

▼ In Print Preview, you can click Show Margins to display top, bottom, left, and right page margins, as well as header and footer margins and right margins for every column in the worksheet. You can drag the margin markers to change a margin setting. When you drag a column margin marker, you change the width of the column.

10 Performing Basic Math

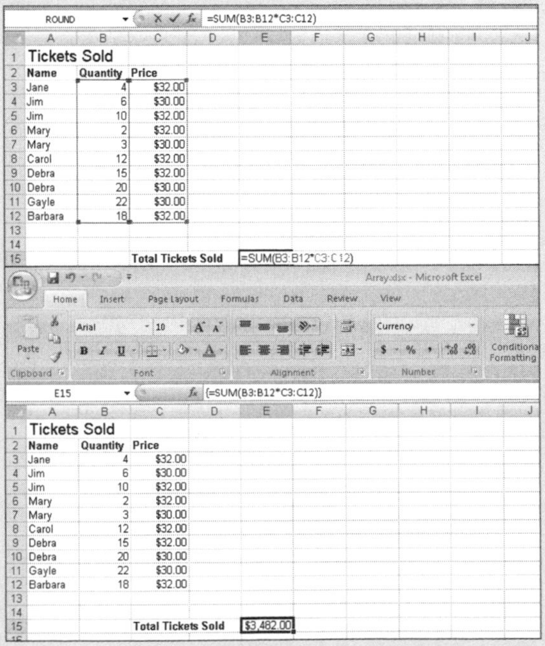

11 Working with Common Formulas

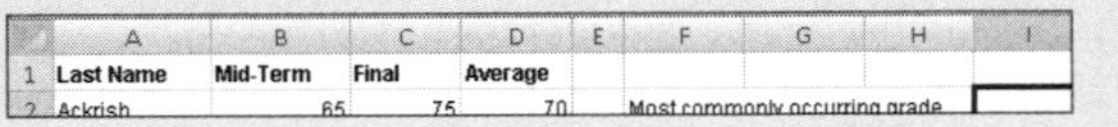

12 Mastering Date and Time Formulas

PART III
CALCULATING DATA

13 Working with Financial Formulas

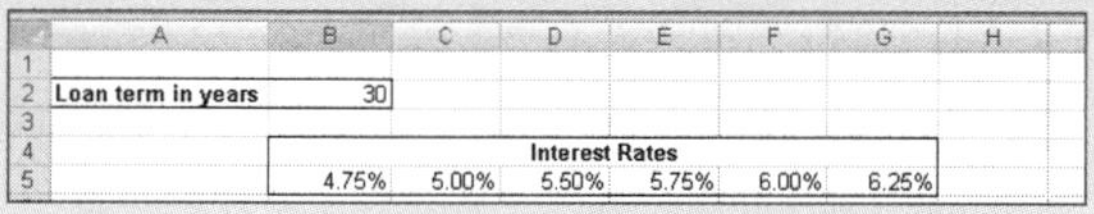

14 Working with Lookup Formulas

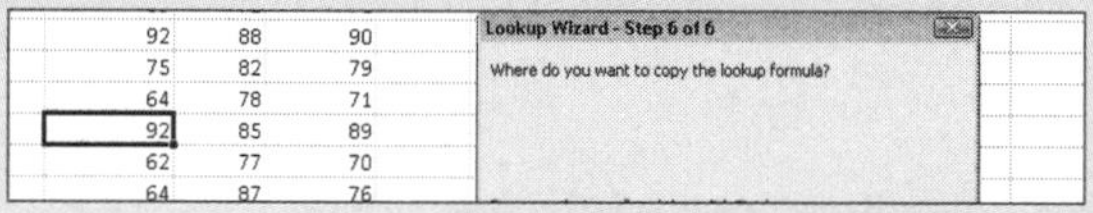

15 Applying Reference, Information, and Text Formulas

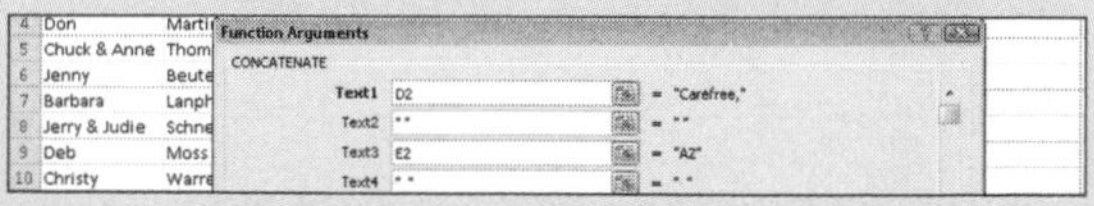

16 Working with Logical and Error Trapping Formulas

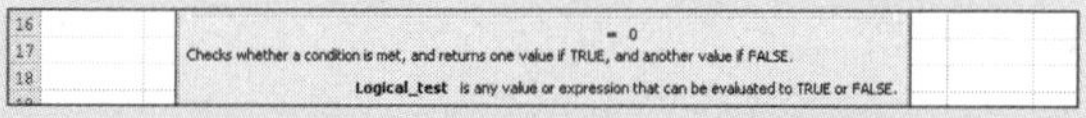

17 Analyzing Tabular Information with Functions

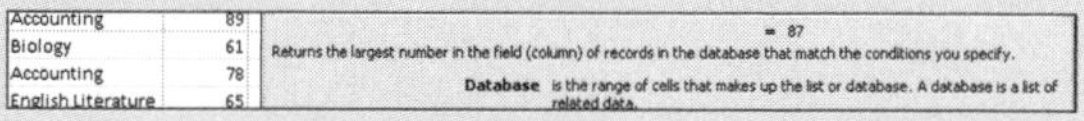

18 Analyzing Formulas and Worksheets

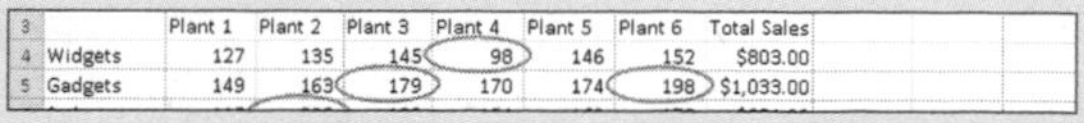

The Basics of Formulas in Excel

You can use Excel to make life much easier when it comes to performing math. Many people consider the math capabilities in Excel to be the heart of the program. Using formulas, you can calculate and analyze data in your worksheet.

You can enter formulas using either of two methods: You can simply type the formula or you can use the mouse and click cells to include in the formula. Later in this chapter, in the sections, "Add Numbers" and "Multiply Numbers," you see examples of using both techniques.

Constants and Cell References

You typically use formulas to perform basic math — add, subtract, multiply, and divide numbers — but you can also calculate percentages and exponents. Every formula begins with an equal sign (=); when you type the equal sign, Excel recognizes that you want to perform a mathematical calculation, and, in many cases, attempts to help you. For example, suppose that you have a worksheet containing the values 1, 2, and 3 in cells A1, A2, and A3. To add those values, you could type the following formula in cell A4:

=1+2+3

Excel displays the result of the formula in cell A4; however, if you select cell A4 and look at the Formula bar, you see the formula that you typed.

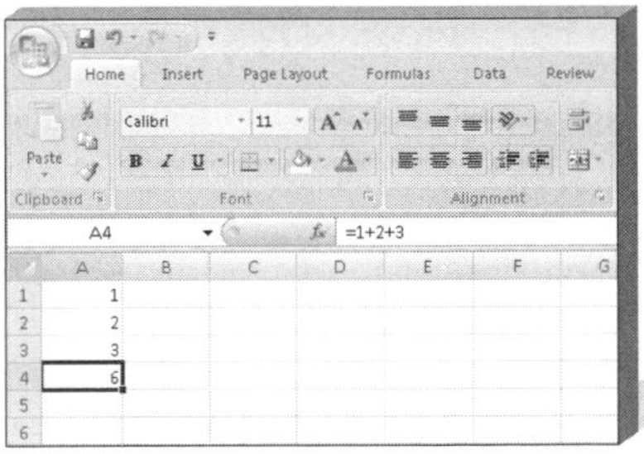

Although you can include raw numbers — *constants* — in your formula, you can also take advantage of Excel's power if you use references to cells containing numbers that you want to include in your formula.

Suppose that you change the formula you type in cell A4 to the following:

=A1+A2+A3

Once again, Excel displays the result, 6, in cell A4. However, if you now change the values in cells A1, A2, and A3, you see Excel automatically update the value displayed in cell A4.

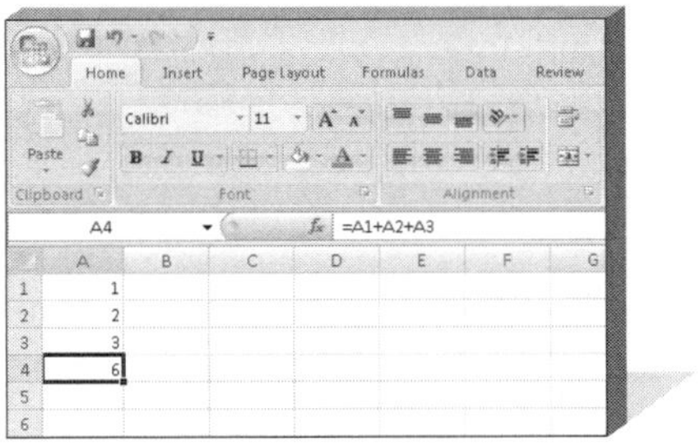

Using cell references while performing math helps you unleash the power of Excel to analyze data because you can change a value in a cell, and Excel automatically updates all formulas in your worksheet that contain a reference to that cell. You can use two different kinds of cell references — absolute and relative. Later in this chapter, in the section, "Absolute and Relative Cell References," you read about the differences between them and the additional power they provide to you.

Formula Operators

In formulas, you can use the following arithmetic operator symbols: addition (+), subtraction (-), multiplication (*), division (/), percent (%), and exponent (^). You can also use the greater than (>), less than (<), equal to (=), greater than or equal to (>=), less than or equal to (<=), and not equal to (<>) symbols to compare values; when you create comparison formulas, Excel returns a value of either TRUE or FALSE.

The Order of Precedence

The order in which you set up a formula controls the result. Excel uses the order of precedence rules that you learned in high school math. In any formula, Excel calculates percentages first and then exponents, followed by multiplication and division. Excel then calculates addition and subtraction, followed by comparison operators. Excel performs the math from left to right, just the way you learned in high school. For example, suppose that your formula reads as follows:

=7+1-3

Excel first adds 7+1 and then subtracts 3 to display a result of 5.

Just like high school math, you can use parentheses ( ) to change the order in which Excel performs calculations, because Excel again follows the rules of precedence and calculates the expression inside the parentheses first. For example, consider the following formula:

=5*1+2

When written in this format, Excel calculates a result of 7 because it multiplies 5 times 1 and then adds 2 to the product. However, suppose you add parentheses so that the formula becomes as follows:

=5*(1+2)

In this case, Excel performs the addition in the parentheses first for a result of 3. Then Excel calculates the product of 5 times 3, returning a result of 15.

Using Functions

Excel uses *functions* to write formulas in an abbreviated way. Chapters 11 to 17 concentrate on the various types of functions you find in Excel, and the following paragraphs provide you with a basic overview of functions.

Each function consists of two parts: the function name and a set of parentheses that contain the *arguments* for the function. Arguments are the values you want Excel to use when making the calculation.

The most common — and probably the most widely used — function is the SUM function. The SUM function is a shortcut for entering a formula that automatically sums entries in a range. In cell A9, you could enter the following formula to sum the values in cells A1 to A8:

=A1+A2+A3+A4+A5+A6+A7+A8

Or, you could enter the SUM function in cell A9:

=SUM(A1:A8)

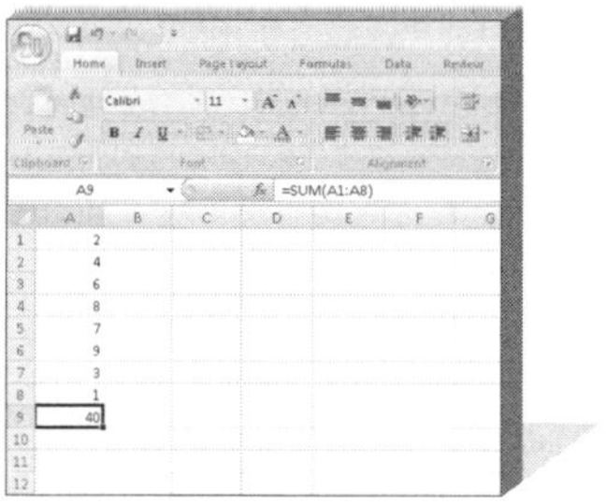

Both the formula and the function return the result of 40 in cell A9, but entering the function is faster and easier, as you see in Chapter 11. Excel recognizes the word "SUM" as the name of the function that adds a contiguous set of values. The range in parentheses, A1:A8, identifies the range of cells containing the values you want Excel to add.

If you are a Lotus 1-2-3 user, you can use an ampersand (@) at the beginning of your function and Excel will recognize it and convert it to an equal sign (=).

PART III

Fill a Range with Information

You can save time and let Excel fill a range with information for you. You can fill a range with a text or number series.

Excel can fill a range with common words that typically follow a sequence. For example, you can type January in cell A1 and use the Fill feature to fill cells beside or below cell A1 with subsequent months to quickly and easily create range labels. Excel uses the word you type in the first cell of the range as the foundation for the series, and builds on that first word. If Excel does not recognize the first word as one that could begin a series, Excel copies the word in the first cell to the rest of the cells in the range.

Excel can fill a range with a series of numbers. You type numbers into the first two cells in the range and Excel uses the contents of these cells to determine the pattern for the series. It then fills subsequent cells in the range accordingly. For example, you can type the numbers 1 and 3 in the first two cells of the range and, when you fill the rest of the range, Excel fills it with odd numbers.

Fill a Range with Information

Fill a Range with Text

1. Type the first word in the series.
2. Click the cell containing the word.
3. Move ✣ over the fill handle in the lower-right corner of the cell (✣ changes to +).
4. Drag + over the cells you want Excel to fill.
   - As you drag, Excel displays each word in the series.
5. Release +.

Excel fills the selected range.

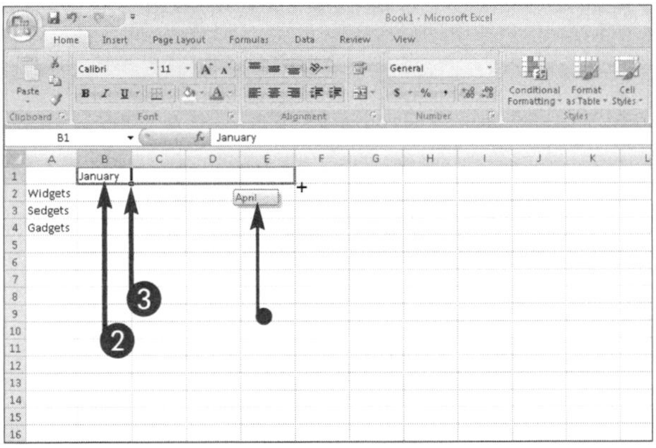

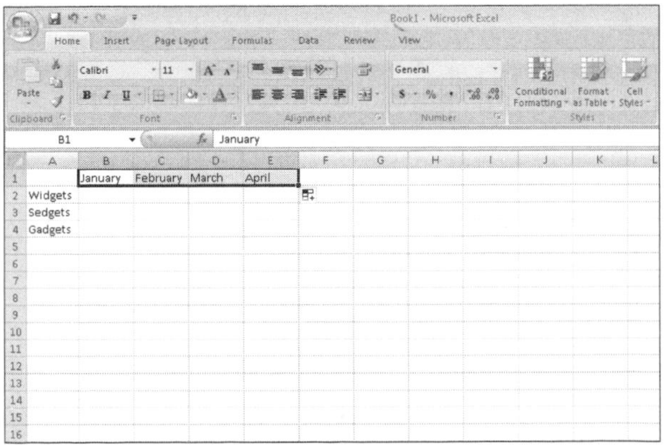

Fill a Range with Numbers

1. Type the first two numbers of the series in two contiguous cells.
2. Select the cells containing the numbers you typed.
3. Move ✥ over the black square in the lower-right corner of the cell (✥ changes to +).
4. Drag + over the cells you want Excel to fill.
   - As you drag, Excel displays each number in the series.
5. Release +.

Excel fills the range using the pattern you established.

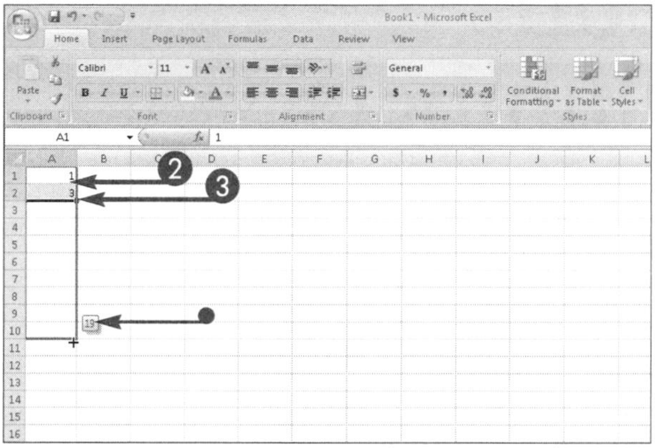

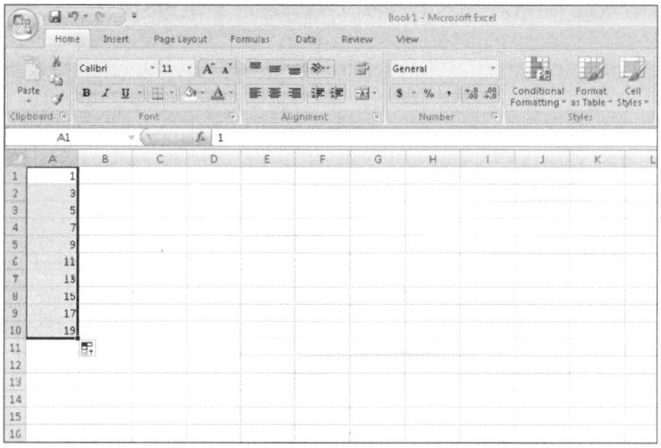

What is that icon that appears after I release the mouse button?

▼ The ⊞ icon is the Auto Fill Options button. You can click it after you fill a series to change Excel's behavior. For example, suppose that you want to copy the information in the first cell to all other cells, without incrementing. After you release the mouse button and Excel fills the range, click ⊞ to display a drop-down list. Click Copy Cells, and Excel changes the information in the cells from incremented information to a copy of the contents of the first cell.

Can I fill a range with a series of dates?

▼ Yes, you can. Type the first date that you want in the range into the first cell of the range, making sure that you use a date format that Excel recognizes. Then, use the steps in either part of this section to drag the fill handle and fill the range; Excel will fill the cells with consecutive dates. If Excel does not fill the range with recognizable dates, change the format of the selected range to either Short Date or Long Date.

Add Numbers

You can use the arithmetic operator plus (+) to create a formula to add numbers in Excel to help you analyze data in your worksheet. When you enter a formula, you always begin by typing an equal sign (=) into an empty cell. Then, you can enter the formula either by typing or by clicking cells with the mouse. If you choose to click cells with the mouse, Excel places small handles around the cell, displays the cell address in a different color in the cell where you intend to store the formula, and displays the cell address in the Formula bar. You press Enter to store a formula in a cell. Excel displays the result of the formula in the cell where you enter it, and the actual formula appears in the Formula bar when you select the cell containing the formula.

You can include constants — numbers — in your formula, or you can include references to cells that contain numbers. The second approach is more powerful, because you can change the value in a cell included in the formula, and Excel automatically updates all cells containing formulas that refer to the cell you changed.

Add Numbers

Add Using Constants

1. Select the cell in which you want to store a formula.
2. Type =.
3. Type a value.
4. Type +.
5. Repeat Steps 3 and 4 until you have typed all of the values in the formula.
6. Press Enter.

- Excel displays the result of the formula in the worksheet.
- The formula appears in the Formula bar when you select the cell containing the formula.

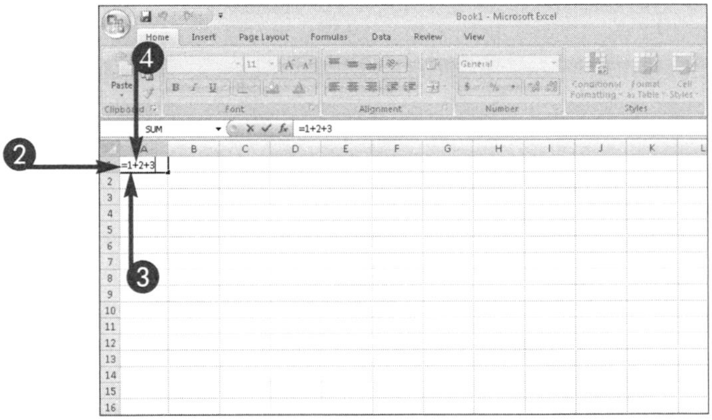

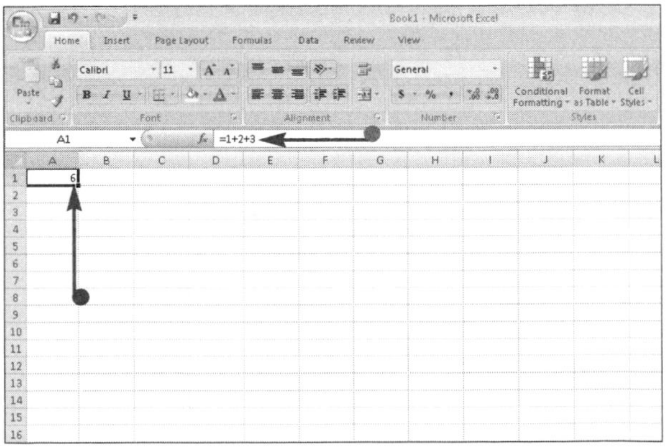

Add Using Cell References

1. Select the cell that will contain the formula.
2. Type =.
3. Click a cell that you want to include in the formula.
4. Type +.
5. Repeat Steps 3 and 4 until you have included all of the necessary cells in the formula.
6. Click ☑ or press Enter.
   - Excel displays the result of the formula in the worksheet.
   - The formula appears in the Formula bar when you select the cell containing the formula.

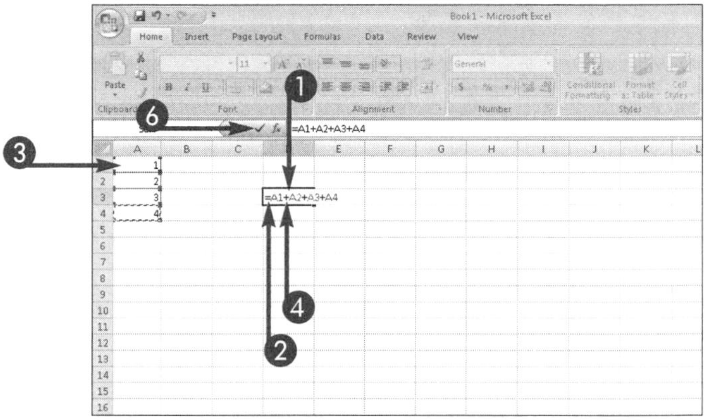

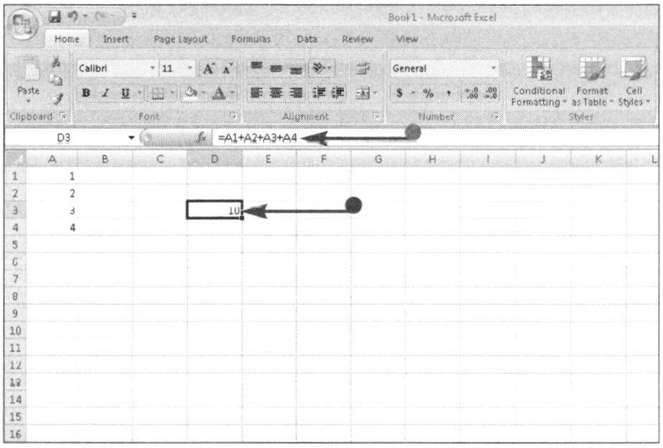

MASTER IT

How do I create a formula that subtracts instead of adds?

▼ You can follow the steps in this section and substitute the minus sign (-) for the plus sign (+) in Step 4. You can also create a formula that includes both subtraction and addition by switching between the plus and minus signs. If your formula results in a negative number, Excel displays the result in the worksheet using the default formatting for the cell containing the formula.

Why did Excel change the cell I clicked to the one below it after I pressed the down-arrow key?

▼ In most circumstances, clicking a cell or using an arrow key has the effect of moving the cell pointer. However, when you create a formula by clicking cells, Excel switches to Point mode. While in Point mode, clicking any cell or using any arrow key on the keyboard has the effect of selecting the cell to include it in the formula.

What do the symbols mean around a cell that I click?

▼ They help identify cells that Excel has included in the formula. The symbols and the box that Excel draws around the cell you click are color-coded and match the color Excel uses for the cell in the formula as you create the formula. The colors are not visible after you click ☑ or press Enter; however, if you edit the cell, the colors in the selected cell and the formula cell reappear.

Multiply Numbers

You can use the asterisk (*) as an arithmetic operator to create a formula to multiply numbers in Excel while analyzing data in your worksheet. When you enter a formula to multiply numbers, you always begin by typing an equal sign (=) into an empty cell. Then, you can enter the formula either by typing or by clicking cells with the mouse; the steps in this section show you how to type a formula, as well as how to enter a formula by clicking cells.

When you store a formula in a cell, Excel displays the result of the formula in the cell where you enter it, and the actual formula appears in the Formula bar when you select the cell containing the formula.

You can include constants — numbers — in your formula, or you can include references to cells that contain numbers. The second approach is more powerful, because you can change the value in a cell included in the formula, and Excel automatically updates all cells containing formulas that refer to the cell you changed.

Multiply Numbers

Multiply Using Constants

1. Select the cell in which you want to store a formula.
2. Type =.
3. Type a value.
4. Type *.
5. Repeat Steps 3 and 4 until you have typed all of the values in the formula.
6. Press Enter.

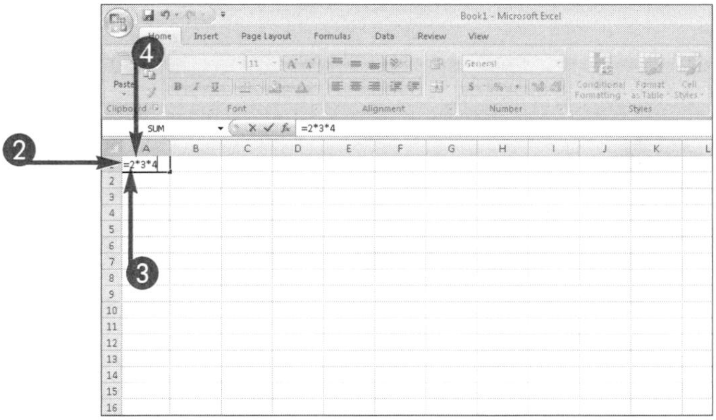

- Excel displays the result of the formula in the worksheet.
- The formula appears in the Formula bar when you select the cell containing the formula.

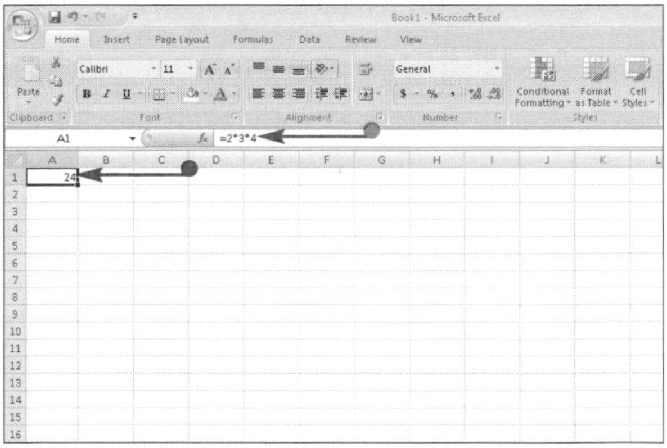

Multiply Using Cell References

1. Select the cell that will contain the formula.
2. Type =.
3. Click a cell that you want to include in the formula.
4. Type *.
5. Repeat Steps 3 and 4 until you have included all of the necessary cells in the formula.
6. Click ☑ or press Enter.
   - Excel displays the result of the formula in the worksheet.
   - The formula appears in the Formula bar when you select the cell containing the formula.

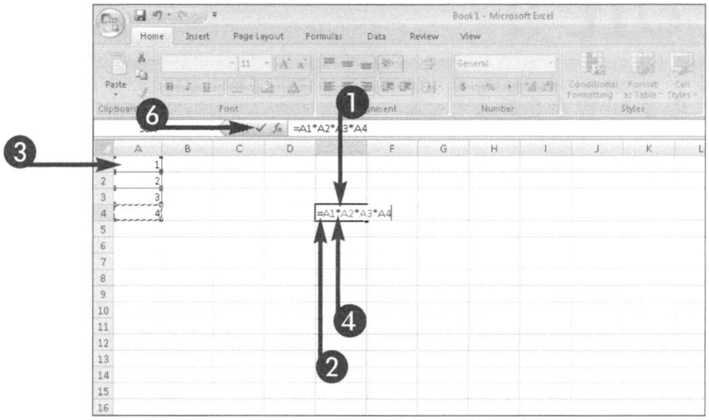

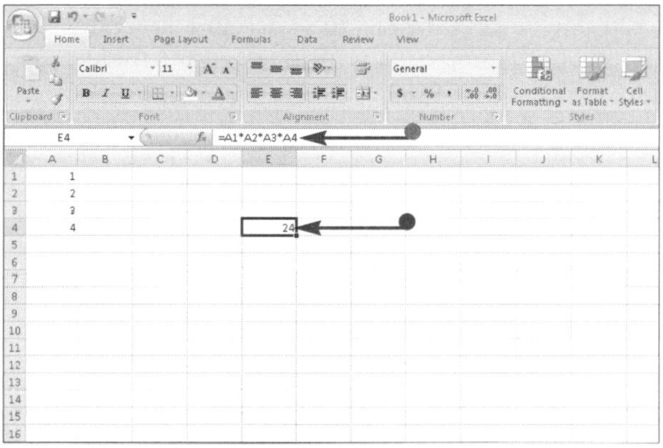

MASTER IT

How do I create a formula that divides instead of multiplies?

▼ You can follow the steps in this section and substitute the forward slash (/) as the division sign for the asterisk (*) in Step 4. You can also create a formula that includes both multiplication and division by switching between the asterisk and forward slash. If your formula results in a negative number or a fraction, Excel displays the result in the worksheet using the default formatting for the cell containing the formula.

Why do I see #DIV/0! in the cell where I created my formula?

▼ In your formula, you divided by zero, which is a mathematical impossibility. The error you see is Excel's way of telling you that the formula includes a forward slash followed by a zero or a reference to a cell with a zero value. To eliminate the error, double-check your formula and remove the portion of it that contains the reference to zero. See the section, "Edit a Formula," for help in changing the formula.

When I use the pointing technique to create a formula, can I point to a cell in another worksheet?

▼ Yes. Use the steps in the subsection, "Multiply Using Cell References," to create your formula. To include the cell in a different worksheet, simply click the appropriate worksheet tab and then click the cell containing the value that you want to include in the formula. If you have additional values to include in the formula, type an operator and click the next cell. Otherwise, press Enter.

Edit a Formula

You can change a formula by editing it. You can edit a formula in the worksheet or in the Formula bar.

When you edit a cell, Excel switches to Edit mode and you need to position the insertion point at the correct location to make changes. The method you choose to switch to Edit mode determines the location of the insertion point immediately after switching to Edit mode. If you choose to edit the cell in the worksheet and you double-click the cell to switch to Edit mode, the insertion point appears somewhere in the middle of the cell. However, if you switch to Edit mode by pressing F2 on a standard keyboard layout, the insertion point appears at the end of the cell.

If you choose to edit the cell in the Formula bar, you can select the location for the insertion point at the same time that you switch to Edit mode.

While you edit a cell, Excel outlines each cell referred to by the formula in a separate color and uses the same colors to display the cell addresses in the cell you are editing — the one containing the formula.

Edit a Formula

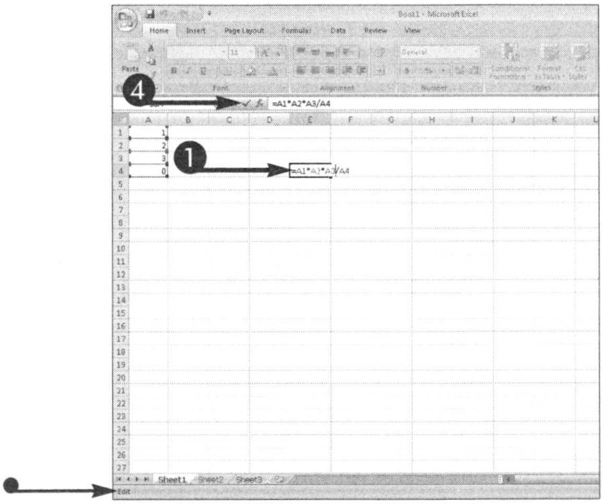

1. In the worksheet, double-click the cell containing the formula you want to change.

Note: *You can select the cell in the worksheet and click in the Formula bar or press F2.*

- Excel switches to Edit mode.

2. Use the arrow keys to position the insertion point where you need to edit.
3. Make the changes you want.
4. Click ☑ or press Enter.

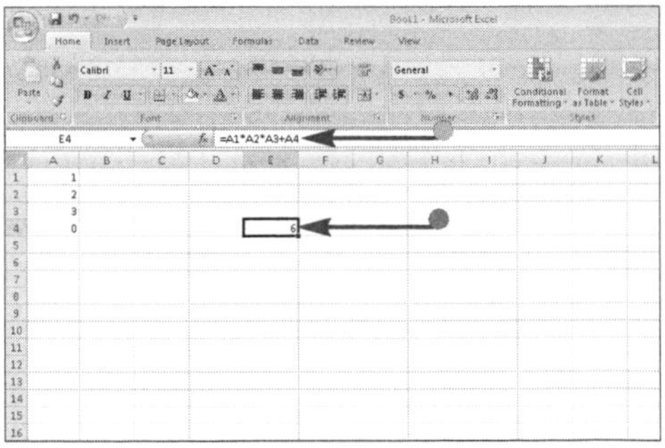

- Excel displays the result of the formula in the worksheet.
- The formula appears in the Formula bar when you select the cell containing the formula.

Quickly Calculate Common Values

You can quickly determine certain common values without creating formulas. For example, you can determine the sum, average, count, numerical count, minimum, or maximum value in a selection without creating a formula. Excel can display these common values for a selection in the Status bar. The Sum value is, of course, the total of a group of numbers, and the Average value is the average of the group. The Count value displays the number of cells that contain information. The Numerical Count value displays the number of cells that contain numbers, but not text. The Minimum and Maximum values display the smallest and largest number in a group, respectively.

MASTER IT

Why do I see some of the common values but not all of them?

▼ You can control which of these common values appear on the Status bar. Right-click anywhere on the Status bar to display the Customize Status Bar menu. In the second group from the bottom, you see the common values that you can display. A check mark beside a common value indicates that Excel is currently displaying that value on the Status bar. Click a common value that has no check mark beside it to display it.

Quickly Calculate Common Values

1. Type information into a range of cells.

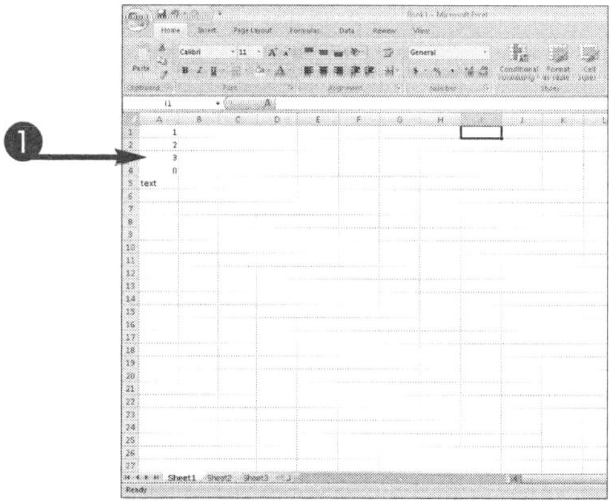

2. Select the range.
   - Excel displays common values for the selected range in the Status bar.

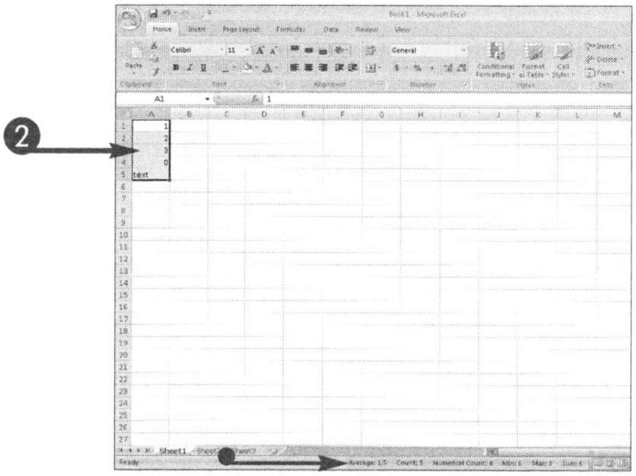

Absolute and Relative Cell References

When you create formulas that refer to cell addresses instead of constants — as most formulas should — you can use one of three types of cell reference: relative, absolute, or mixed. The format of the cell reference comes into play when you start copying formulas, which is one of the most common operations you perform in Excel.

Relative Cell References

When you use a relative cell reference in a formula and then copy the formula from one cell to another, Excel adjusts the cell references in the formula to refer to the cells at the new location of the formula. For example, suppose that you create a formula using relative cell references in cell B8 that adds cells B5 to B7. The formula in B8 would be as follows:

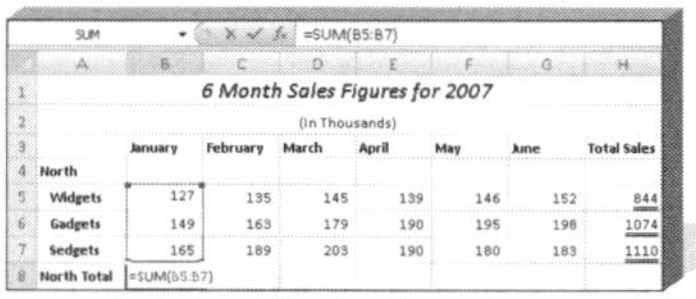

=SUM(B5:B7)

Then, suppose that you copy that formula to cell C8. In column C, Excel adjusts the formula to add the numbers in column C instead of those in column B, producing the following formula in cell C8:

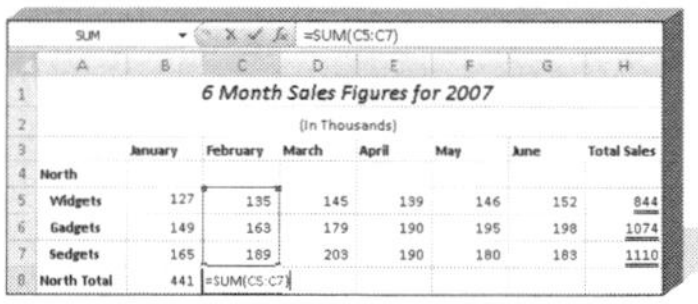

=SUM(C5:C7)

If Excel had not adjusted the formula, the sum in cell C8 would have appeared to be the same as the sum in cell B8.

Creating a relative cell reference is not difficult; you simply type the column letter and row number in the formula.

Absolute Cell References

When you use an absolute cell reference in a formula and copy the formula, Excel does not change the cell reference. Absolute cell references are useful in situations such as when a formula must always refer to the value in a particular cell. For example, suppose that your worksheet shows sales by product over time and you want to show each product's percentage of total sales. Total sales for each product appear in cells H5 to H7, with total sales for all products appearing in cell H8. You want to place your formulas that calculate each product's percentage of total sales in cells I5 to I7, with 100 percent of sales appearing in cell I8. The formula in cell I5 should be H5/H8; the formula in cell I6 should be H6/H8; and the formula in cell I7 should be H7/H8. To display 100 percent in cell I8, the formula should be H8/H8.

In each formula, the divisor value is always H8 — the cell that contains total sales. If you want to create the formula in cell I5 and copy it to cells I6 to I8, you need to use an absolute cell reference in the divisor portion of the formula. To create an absolute cell reference, you simply include a dollar sign ($) before both the column letter and the row number in the formula. As a result, the formula in cell I5 should read as follows:

=H5/$H$8

If you use the pointing method to create your formula, you can press F4 on your keyboard to change a cell reference to an absolute cell reference in the formula. When you press F4, Excel inserts the dollar signs for you automatically. Note that some new keyboards allow you to press a key to assign alternate functions to the function keys, and pressing F4 may not work if you are using non-standard functions for your keyboard's function keys.

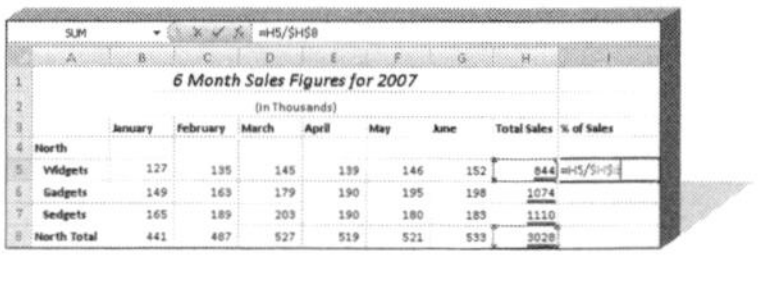

When you copy this formula, Excel adjusts the portion of the formula that contains a relative cell reference, but leaves the portion that contains the absolute cell reference unchanged. As a result, the portion of the formula that refers to the cell containing total sales continues to refer to the cell that contains the total sales for all regions — in this example, cell H8. Copying the formula to cell I6 produces the following formula:

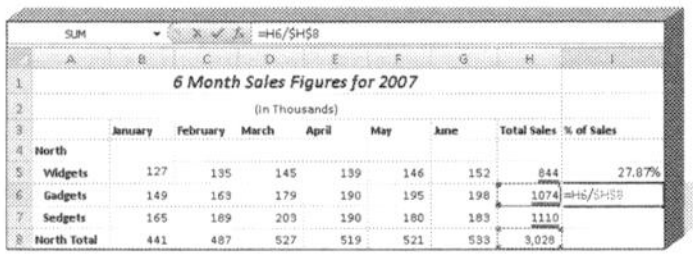

=H6/$H$8

If you create a formula containing relative cell references and then discover you needed to include an absolute cell reference, you can click the cell and press F2 to edit it. You can then place the insertion point anywhere in the cell reference that you need to change to an absolute cell reference and press F4 or type the dollar signs needed.

Mixed Cell References

Situations will arise where you need to use a mixed cell reference in a formula. A mixed cell reference in a formula contains both a relative and an absolute cell reference. You might also say that a mixed reference contains one changing cell reference and one unchanging cell reference. For example, in a mixed cell reference, the row number might be relative (and change), while the column letter must be absolute (and remain unchanged). The column letter might also be relative while the row number must be absolute. You find an example of using mixed cell references in the section in Chapter 13 that describes using Excel's PMT function to create a table of loan payments for mortgage amounts at varying rates of interest.

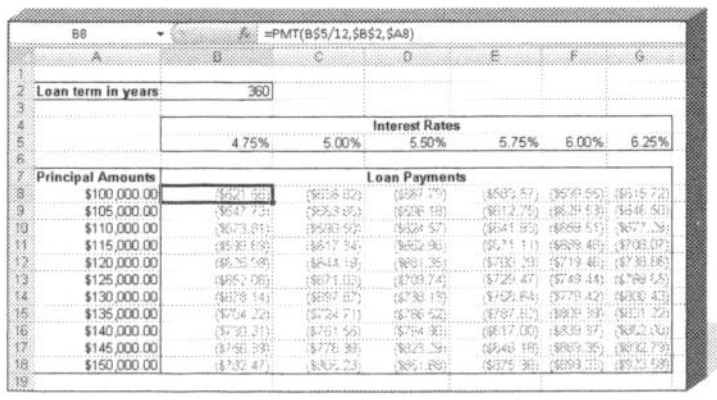

When you create the formula that calculates the loan payment, you want to be able to copy the formula across each row to see the payment for a given amount of principal at differing rates. In addition, you want to be able to copy the formula down each column to see the payment for one interest rate at varying principal amounts.

To create the portion of the formula that calculates the payment amount for various interest rates and a single principal amount, you need to keep the row constant but vary the column when you refer to the interest rate. In the PMT function, the first argument listed controls the interest rate, and, if you look at the Formula bar, you see that the mixed reference for the first argument contains a dollar sign before the row number but not the column letter. When you copy this formula across each row, Excel changes the column letter for the first argument but not the row number.

To create the portion of the formula that calculates the payment amount for one interest rate and several principal amounts, you need to keep the column constant and vary the row number when you refer to the principal amount. In the PMT function, the last argument listed controls the principal amount. Again, if you look at the Formula bar, you see that the mixed reference for the last argument contains a dollar sign before the column letter but not the row number. When you copy this formula down each column, Excel changes the row number for the last argument but not the column letter.

Although you can create a mixed cell reference as you create a formula, in most cases, you will realize after you create the formula that you need a mixed cell reference. You can edit the formula and position the insertion point anywhere in the cell reference you need to mix. You then you can type the dollar sign or press F4 repeatedly until the dollar sign appears in the proper place.

Copy a Formula

To save time, you can copy a formula from one cell to another instead of typing the same formula into several cells. For example, if your worksheet shows sales by month for several products, you can create the formula that totals sales in a given month for all products, and then save time by copying the formula to create total sales for the other months.

Excel's behavior when you copy a formula depends on whether the formula contains relative cell references or absolute cell references. Absolute cell references contain dollar signs ($) before the column letter and row number.

If the formula contains relative cell references, Excel adjusts the formula as it copies. For example, when you copy the formula that sums cells in column B to column C, Excel adjusts the copy of the formula to sum cells in column C.

If the formula contains an absolute cell reference, Excel does not adjust the absolute cell reference when you copy the formula. For example, when you copy a formula that contains the absolute cell reference $H$8 from cell I5 to cell I6, you see $H$8 in both cells.

Copy a Formula

Copy Relative Cell References

1. Click the cell containing the formula you want to copy.
   - In the Formula bar, the formula appears with a relative cell reference.
2. Click the Home tab.
3. Click [copy icon].

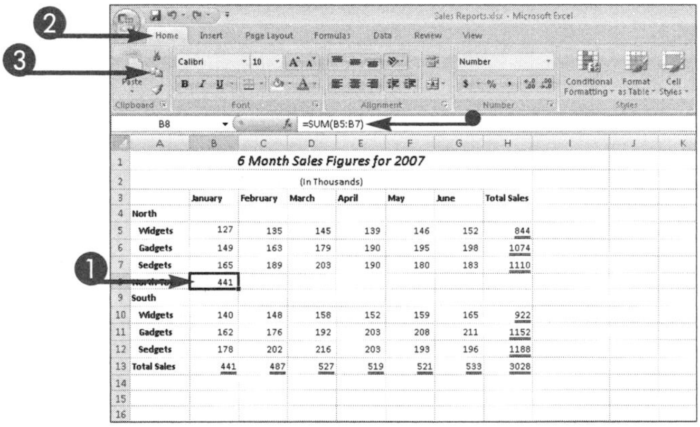

4. Select the cells where you want the formula to appear.
5. Click Paste.
   - Excel copies the formula to the selected cells.
   - The adjusted formula appears in the selected cells.

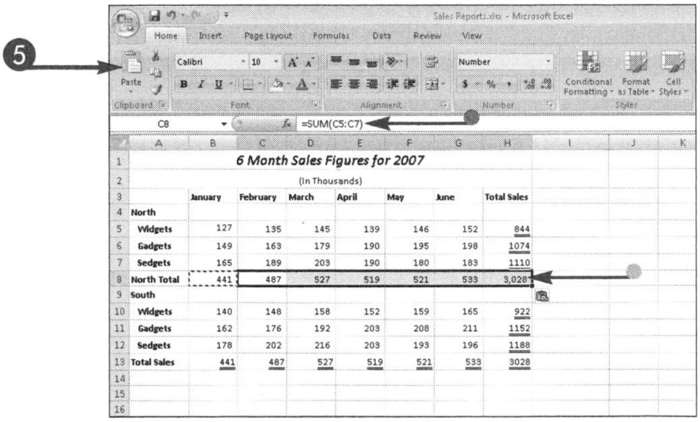

Copy Absolute Cell References

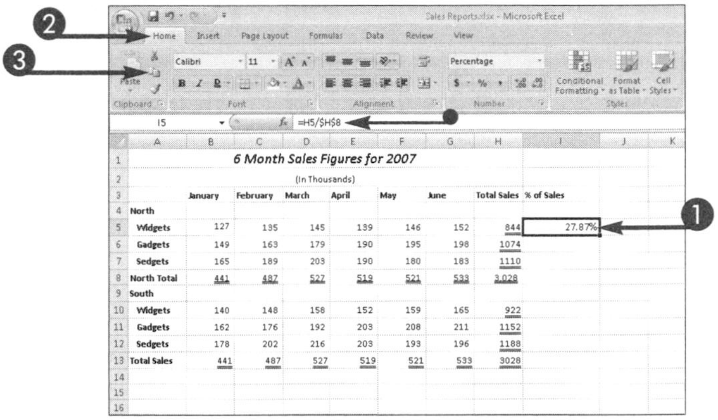

1. Click the cell containing the formula you want to copy.
   - In the Formula bar, the formula appears with an absolute cell reference.
2. Click the Home tab.
3. Click .

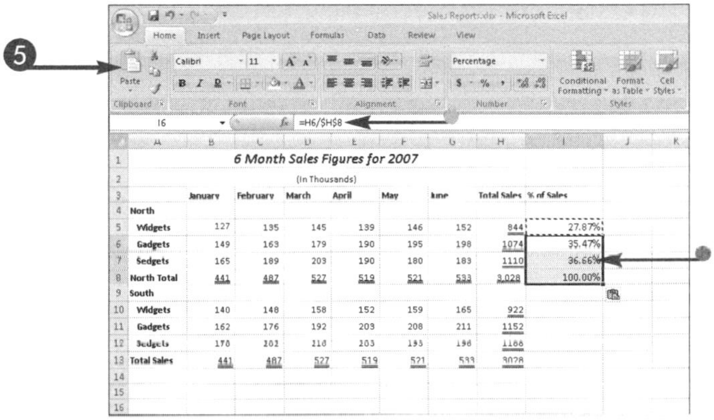

4. Select the cells where you want the formula to appear.
5. Click Paste.
   - Excel copies the formula to the selected cells.
   - The formula in the selected cells adjusts only relative cell references; absolute cell references remain unchanged.

Can you give me an example of when I might use an absolute cell reference?

▼ One of the most common reasons to use an absolute cell reference involves calculating a percentage. For example, you may want to calculate the percentage of total sales represented by each product you sell. When you create the formula, you divide each product's sales by total sales. The cell containing the total sales value does not change in the formula. So, to copy the formula without changing the cell containing the total sales value, you use an absolute cell reference in the formula for the cell containing total sales.

Can I create an absolute cell reference without typing the dollar sign?

▼ Yes. If you create the formula by clicking cells, you can press F4 on a keyboard using standard function keys after clicking the cell and Excel will insert the dollar signs. If you press F2 on a keyboard using standard function keys to edit the formula, you can change the relative cell reference to absolute by positioning the insertion point anywhere in the cell reference and pressing F4 on a keyboard using standard function keys.

Is there another way to copy a formula?

▼ Yes. If you are copying the formula to adjacent cells, you can use the Fill handle. Select the cell containing the formula and then drag the Fill handle — the small black square in the lower-right corner of the cell — either across or down.

Change a Formula to a Value

You can convert a formula to the value it produces. Suppose that you create a formula in cell D9 that uses cells C5 and C6 and some constants. Suppose that you also want to use the calculated value in cell D9 in another formula in cell F12. To ensure that the calculated value in cell D9 does not change — perhaps because you change the value in cells C5 or C6 — you can convert the formula in cell D9 to a value. That way, you can use the calculated value in cell D9 with no danger of the value changing because of some other change you make in your worksheet.

You change a formula to a value by copying the formula and then using one of the Paste options to paste the value produced by the formula instead of pasting the formula. You can overwrite the formula by pasting the value into the cell containing the formula. You can also retain the formula in the original cell and paste its value into a different cell by simply selecting a different cell before you paste.

Change a Formula to a Value

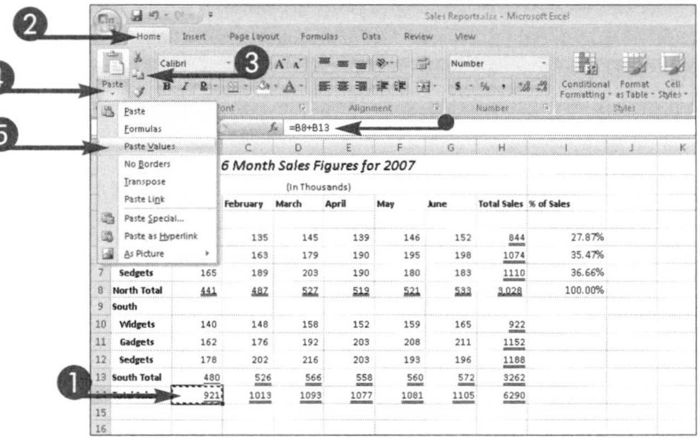

1. Select a cell containing the formula.
   - The formula appears in the Formula bar.
2. Click the Home tab.
3. Click [copy icon].
4. Click the bottom of the Paste button to display the Paste menu.
5. Click Paste Values.

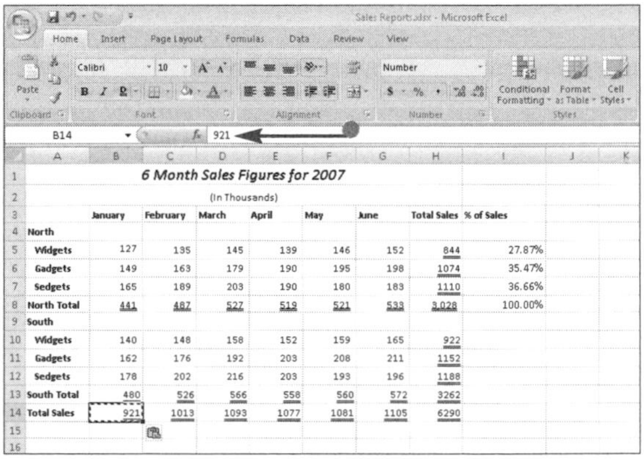

- Excel converts the formula to a value.

Add Data in One Range to Another

You can add data in one range to data in another range. Suppose that you track monthly sales for three products, and you set up your worksheet so that you can track quarterly sales. To do that, you enter sales information for the three products into a worksheet for the first quarter of the year in cells A3 to D7. Then, for the second quarter, you enter sales information for the same products into cells A11 to D15.

Now suppose that you would like to see the six-month totals for all three products. You could reorganize your worksheet and create new formulas or edit existing formulas. However, you do not need to do all that work. Instead, you can leave your worksheet structured as you originally set it up and simply select a new location to store the totals of the two ranges. Then, you can add the ranges together and store the totals in the new location.

To add the ranges together to create six-month total sales for the products, you use a special version of the Copy-and-Paste operation.

Add Data in One Range to Another

1. Select a set of cells to add.
2. Click [Copy icon].

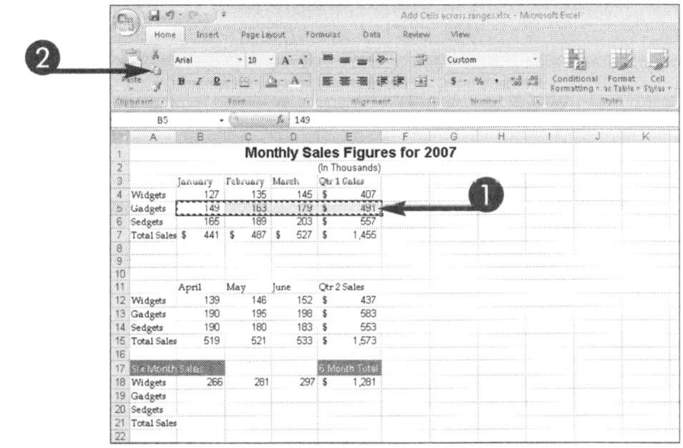

3. Select the first cell in the range where the total will appear.
4. Click Paste.

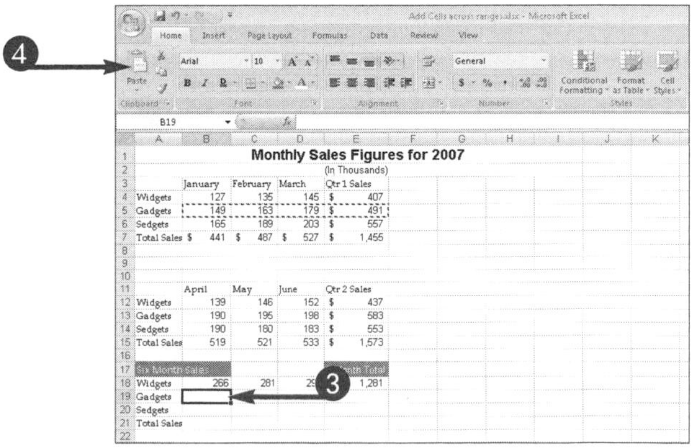

continued

Add Data in One Range to Another *(Continued)*

When you use the Paste Special dialog box, you are not limited to adding ranges. You can also subtract, multiply, and divide ranges. Using the options at the top of the Paste Special dialog box, you can copy information and then perform the following types of pasting operations:

Option	***Purpose***
All	Paste the contents, formats, and data validation of a copied cell or range.
Formulas	Paste only values and formulas without formatting.
Values	Paste values and formula results — but not formulas — with no formatting. See the section, "Change a Formula to a Value," for details on using this option.
Formats	Paste only the formatting but not the contents of a copied cell or range.
Comments	Paste comments attached to, but not the contents of, a copied cell or range.
Validation	Paste the validation criteria of a copied cell or range so that you can apply the same validation criteria to two cells or ranges. See Chapter 18 for information on using validation criteria.
All Using Source Theme	Paste all information, but use the formatting of the cell or range you copied. This option is important only if you are copying and pasting between two workbooks that use different document themes.
All Except Borders	Paste all information except the border information of the cell or range you copied.
Column Widths	Paste only column width information from the copied cell or range.
Formulas And Number Formats	Paste values, formulas, and number formats but no other formatting from the copied cell or range.
Values and Number Formats	Paste all constants, values that result from formulas, and number formats but no formulas from a copied cell or range.

Add Data in One Range to Another *(continued)*

Excel copies the information.

5. Select the next set of cells to add.
6. Click .

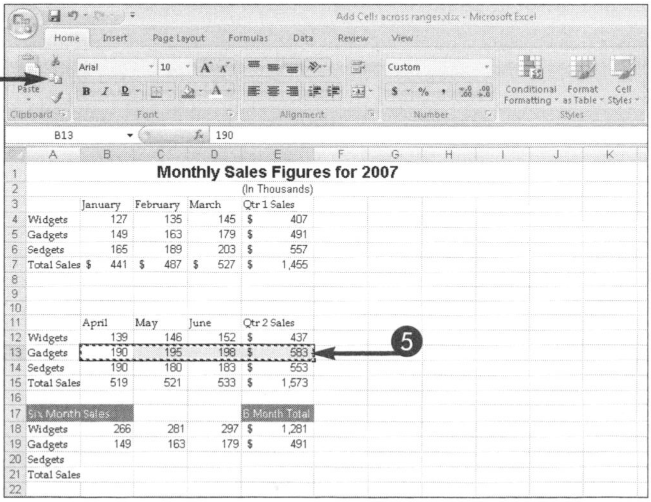

7. Select the same cell you selected in Step 3.
8. Click the bottom of the Paste button.
9. Click Paste Special.

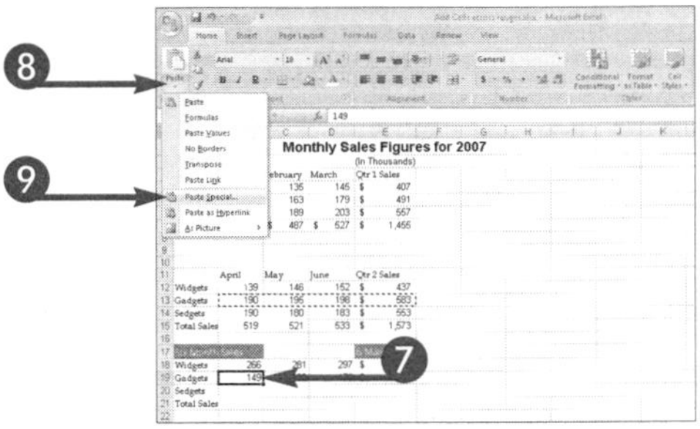

The Paste Special dialog box appears.

10. Click Add (◯ changes to ◉).
11. Click OK.

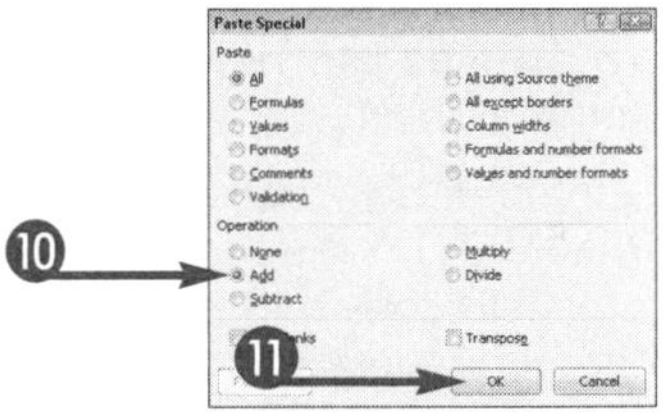

- Excel adds the first range you copied to the second range you copied.

You can press Esc to cancel copying.

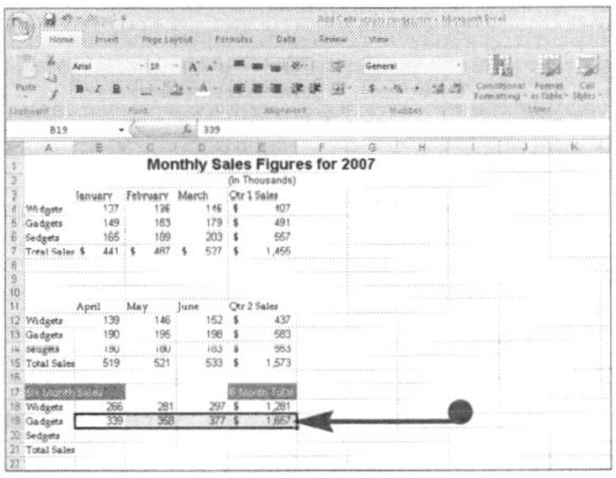

MASTER IT

In the Paste Special dialog box, what does the Transpose option do?

▼ Using this option helps you flip columns and rows when you paste. As a result, what appears as columns in the range you copy becomes rows in the range where you paste, and what appears as rows in the range you copy becomes columns in the range where you paste. Excel also adjusts any formulas that you copy to maintain their integrity.

In the Paste Special dialog box, what does the Skip Blanks option do?

▼ This option helps you avoid overwriting information in the cells where you are pasting. If the range you copy contains blank cells, selecting this option prevents Excel from copying those blank cells and overwriting cells that contain information in the range where you paste the information.

When I add two ranges, how does Excel treat relative, absolute, and mixed cell references?

▼ Excel honors all cell references when you add, subtract, multiply, or divide two ranges. Formulas continue to work as you would expect.

Add Data in One Worksheet to Another

You can add data stored in one worksheet to data stored in another worksheet. For example, suppose that you create a workbook to store sales information by month about the products you sell. You decide in advance to store each quarter of the year's sales information on a separate worksheet so that you can view any quarter's data by selecting that worksheet in the workbook.

Suppose that you decide that you want a summary worksheet that adds up the totals from the four quarters. You could copy and paste the information from the four worksheets into a fifth worksheet and then spend considerable time editing the worksheet to obtain the totals. You could also use formulas on the fifth worksheet to create totals for the sales data in the four worksheets.

When you add cells on different worksheets, you must include the name of the worksheet tab when you refer to the cell. Excel expects you to separate the worksheet name from the cell address by using an exclamation point (!). For example, the name of cell B3 on Sheet 4 would be as follows:

Sheet4!B3

You will find it easiest to specify cells to add across worksheets by clicking the cells you want to add.

Add Data in One Worksheet to Another

1. In the workbook containing the worksheets with the data you want to add, display the sheet where you want the totals to appear.
2. Click the cell where the first total should appear.
3. Type =.

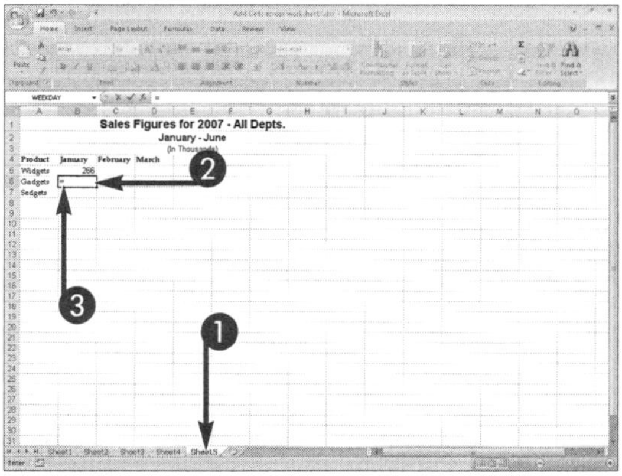

4. Click the first sheet containing data you want to total.
5. Click the cell containing the data you want to add.
   - The formula begins to appear in the Formula bar.

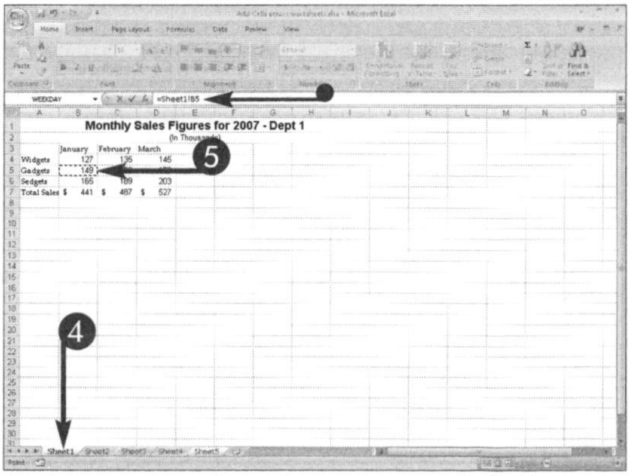

6 Press +.

- The mathematical operator appears in the Formula bar.

7 Click the next sheet containing data you want to total.

8 Click the cell containing the data you want to add.

9 Repeat Steps 6 to 8 until you have selected all the cells containing data you want to add.

10 To complete the formula, click ☑ or press Enter.

- The result of the calculation appears in the cell you selected in Step 2.
- The formula appears in the Formula bar.

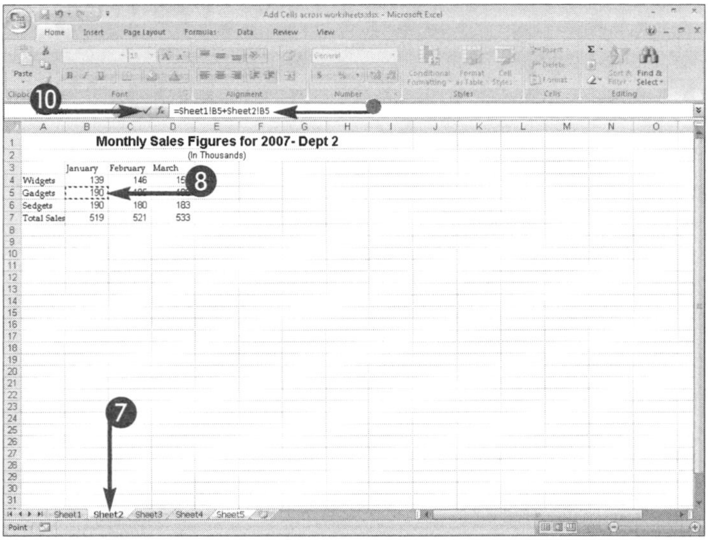

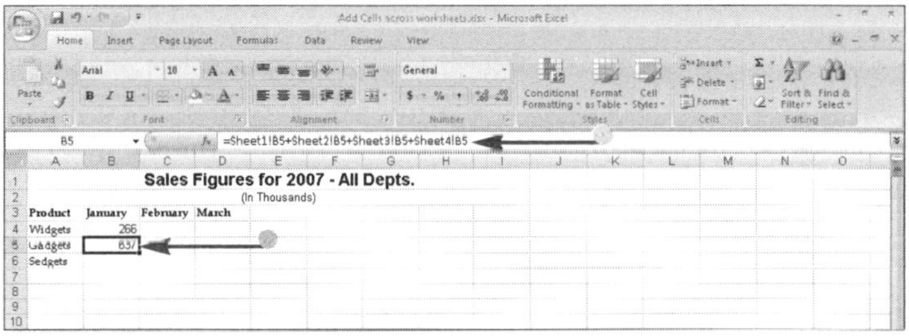

MASTER IT

Am I limited to using only relative cell references in a formula that contains both worksheet names and cell addresses?

▼ No, you can use absolute cell references, relative cell references, or mixed cell references in the formula. You can create an absolute or mixed cell reference as you create the formula. You can also follow the steps in this section to create the formula and then edit it, place the insertion point in the cell address for which you want to create an absolute or mixed reference, and then press F4 repeatedly until the cell reference appears as you want.

What happens if I copy formulas that contain both worksheet names and cell addresses?

▼ Excel copies the formulas the same way it copies any formula, honoring any relative cell references, absolute cell references, or mixed cell references. In fact, you can create the formula that adds cells across worksheets only once and propagate the formula by copying.

Can I subtract cells across worksheets?

▼ You can add, subtract, multiply, or divide cells across worksheets. In Step 6, substitute the appropriate mathematical operator for the operation you want to perform: - for subtraction, * for multiplication, or / for division.

Using Cell Names and Range Names

To more easily find information or use cell ranges in a formula, you can assign a name to a range that helps you understand the purpose of the range. Suppose that your worksheet contains sales information for widgets for the months of January to June in cells B5 to G5. You can name the range "widgets" or "widget_sales" and then create a formula that adds the sales for widgets instead of adding cells B5 to G5.

When you create a range name, Excel tries to suggest a name using a label near the selected range. Each name can be no more than 255 characters and must be unique. The first character must be a letter, an underscore (_), or a backslash (\). You cannot use spaces in a range name; instead, substitute the underscore or the dash. You cannot name a range using cell references such as A1 or $F$6, nor can you name a range using either the uppercase or lowercase forms of the letters C and R. You can use uppercase and lowercase letters in a range name, but Excel ignores case. For example, if you try to use the range names Sales and SALES in the same worksheet, Excel prompts you for a unique name for the second range name.

Using Cell Names and Range Names

Assign a Name

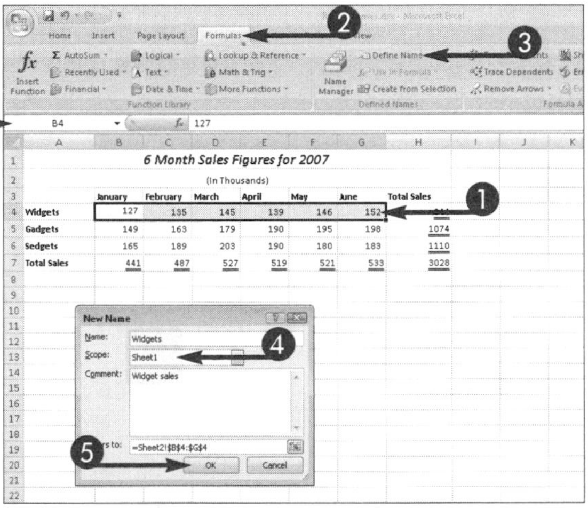

1. Select the range to which you want to assign a name.
   - Excel displays the name of the leftmost cell in the selection here.
2. Click the Formulas tab.
3. Click Define Name.

The New Name dialog box appears.

4. If necessary, type a name in the Name box or add a comment.
5. Click OK.

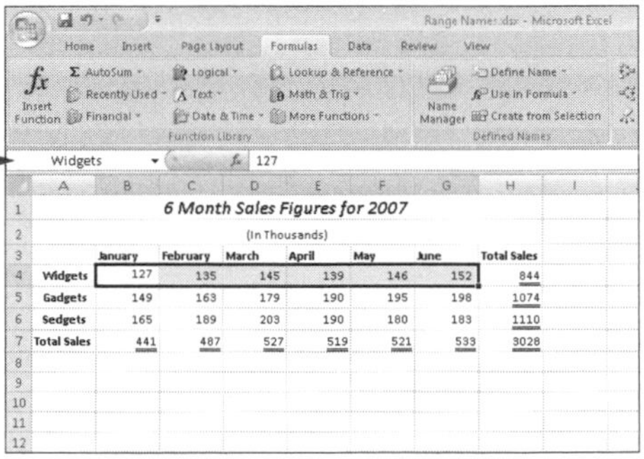

- Excel displays the name of the selected range here instead of the first cell in the selected range.

Go to a Named Range

1. Click here.
2. Click the name of the range you want Excel to select.
   - Excel selects the cells in the named range.

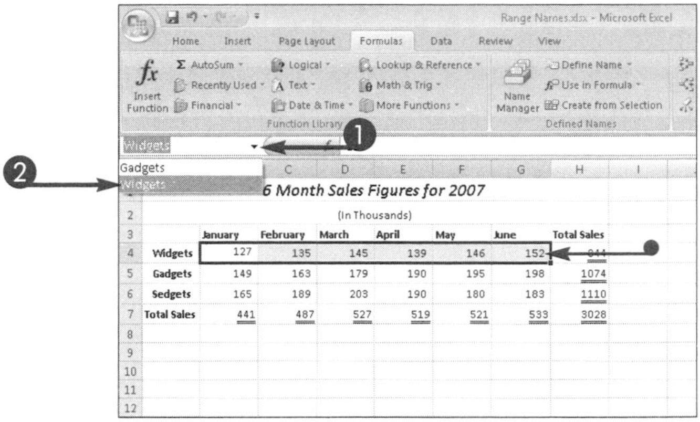

Use a Name in a Formula

1. Select the cell where you want the formula to appear.
2. Create the formula using the range name instead of the cell range.

Note: *If you use a function and include a range you named as an argument, Excel suggests the range name instead of the cell references.*

In the Formula bar, Excel displays the named range instead of cell references.

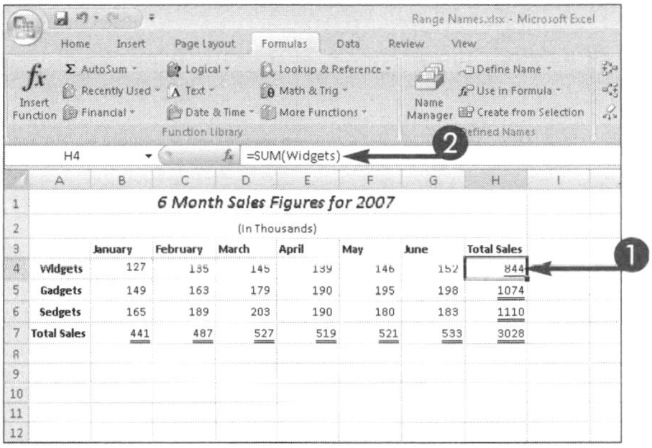

MASTER IT

What is the purpose of the Scope box?

▼ The scope identifies where Excel will recognize the name. If you select the scope of Workbook, Excel recognizes the name on any sheet in your workbook. You can also limit the use of the name to a particular worksheet by selecting that worksheet in the Scope box; in this case, Excel recognizes the name only in the worksheet you select. Names must be unique within their scope.

Can I define a name without using a dialog box?

▼ Yes, you can define a name for your entire workbook without using a dialog box. Select the range you want to name and click in the Name box to the left of the Formula bar where Excel displays the cell address of the leftmost cell in the selected range. Type the name you want to assign to the range and press Enter.

Can I assign names only to ranges?

▼ No, you can also assign names to constants or formulas. Click the Formulas tab and then click Define Name to display the New Name dialog box. In the Refers To box, type = and then type either the constant or the formula you want to name. Click OK. You can now refer to the constant or formula by name.

Edit and Delete Cell or Range Names

You can make changes to a cell or range name or its definition, or you can add a comment to remind you of the cell or range name's purpose; comments appear in the Name Manager window. You can also delete a cell or range name. To edit or delete a cell or range name, you work in the Name Manager window.

When you edit a cell or range name, you can change its name, the cells to which it refers, or its comment, but you cannot change its scope. To redefine the scope of a cell or range name, you must delete the cell or range name and recreate it. You can read about deleting cell or range names in this chapter; to recreate a cell or range name, use the steps in the section, "Using Cell Names and Range Names."

When you delete a cell or range name, you delete only the name you assigned to the cell or range. You do not delete the contents of the cell or range or any formatting you may have applied to the range. However, you may create errors on your worksheet in formulas that refer to the range name you deleted.

Edit and Delete Cell or Range Names

Edit a Name

1. Click the Formulas tab.
2. Click Name Manager.

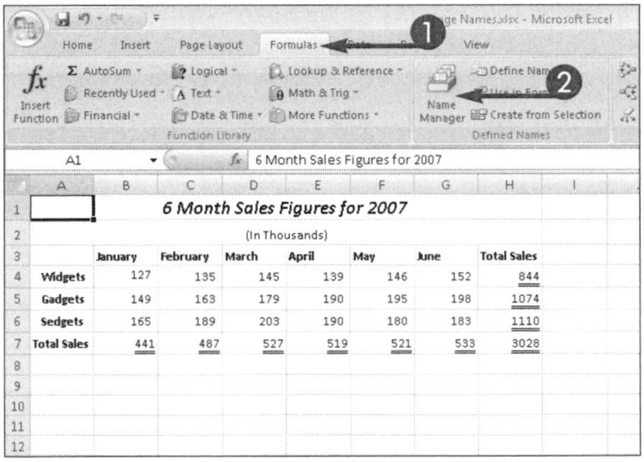

The Name Manager dialog box appears.

3. Click a name.
4. Click Edit.

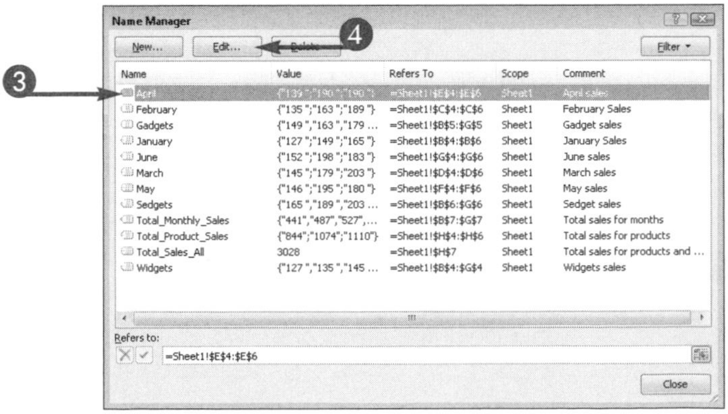

The Edit Name dialog box appears.

- You can change the name.
- You can add a comment.
- You can change this information to redefine the range.

5 Click OK.

Excel redisplays the Name Manager window.

You can click Close or edit other names.

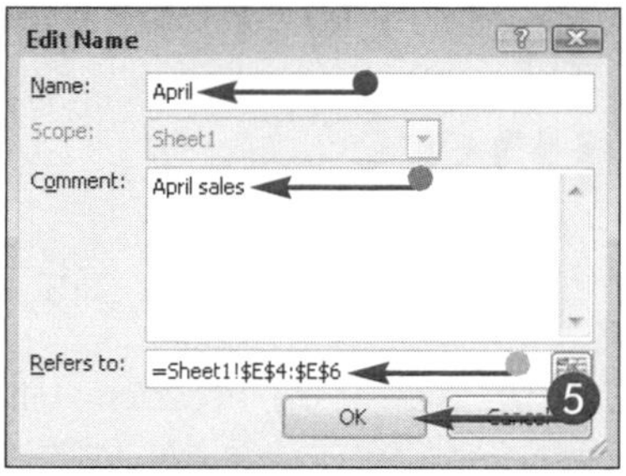

Delete a Name

1 Perform Steps 1 to 3 in the subsection, "Edit a Name."

2 Click Delete.

Excel prompts you to confirm that you want to delete the selected name.

3 Click OK to delete the name.

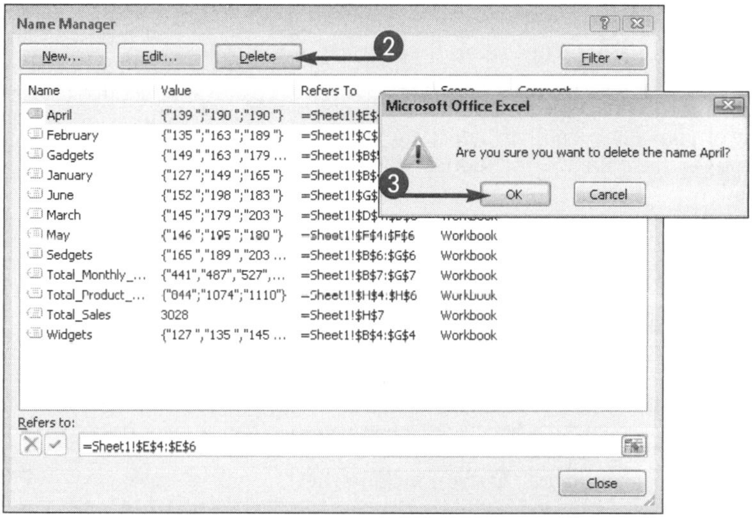

MASTER IT

What happens if I click the Filter button in the Name Manager window?

▼ A list appears that enables you to limit the information that appears in the window. You can limit the names to those with a scope of worksheet or those with a scope of workbook. You can display only names with errors or names without errors. You can also display names that you define or table names. For details on table names, see Chapter 23.

How can I identify errors on my worksheet that were created by deleting a range name?

▼ Excel displays the #NAME error in any cell that uses a range name that you deleted. When you delete a range name that is used in a formula, the formula becomes invalid. To resolve the problem, either click [undo icon] to restore the range name, or edit the formula and supply the cell address in place of the name.

What does the Value column in the Name Manager window show?

▼ In the Value column, you see the values that appear in the cells defined in the range. If a cell in the range contains a formula, you see the result of the formula rather than the formula in the Value column. The formula appears in the Refers To column.

Create Range Names from Headings

Instead of creating range names one at a time, you can let Excel create range names using row and column labels in your worksheet.

When you let Excel create range names using labels, you select the range of data for which you want to create range names, including the labels. You can create range names from labels that appear in the row above your data, the row below your data, the column to the left of your data, and the column to the right of your data. You can select any or all of these options to describe the location of the labels in the selection.

If your workbook contains any duplicate labels, Excel creates a label for the first occurrence of the label and then, when trying to create a label for the next occurrence, Excel asks if you want to overwrite the label. To avoid this problem, make sure that your row and column labels are unique.

When you create range names from row and column labels, Excel automatically creates range names with scopes that extend to your entire workbook. You cannot use this technique to create range names for a single worksheet in the workbook.

Create Range Names from Headings

Create Range Names

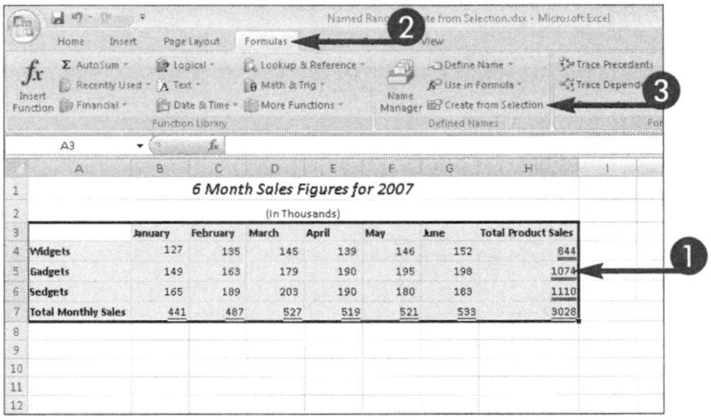

1. Select the range for which you want to create names, making sure that you include the labels.
2. Click the Formulas tab.
3. Click Create from Selection.

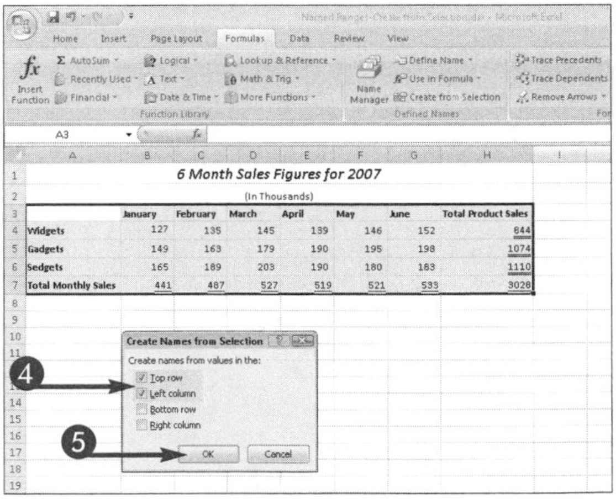

The Create Names from Selection dialog box appears.

4. Click the options that describe the location of the labels you want to use to create range names (☐ changes to ☑).
5. Click OK.

Excel creates the labels.

Note: *If the workbook contains any duplicate labels, a message appears about overwriting a label.*

View Range Names You Created

1. Click the Formulas tab.
2. Click Name Manager.

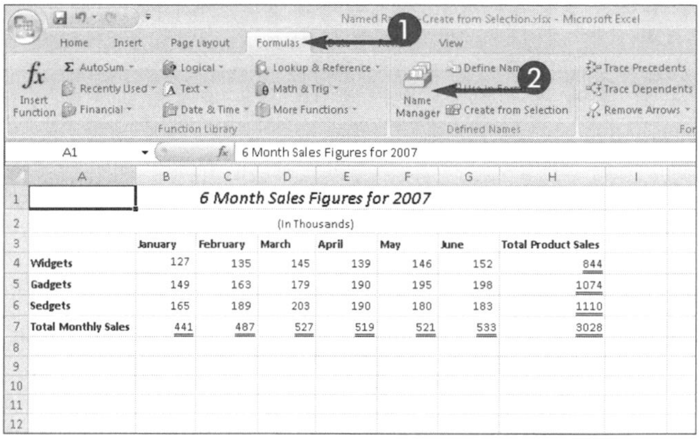

The Name Manager window appears.

Excel displays the range names you created from labels.

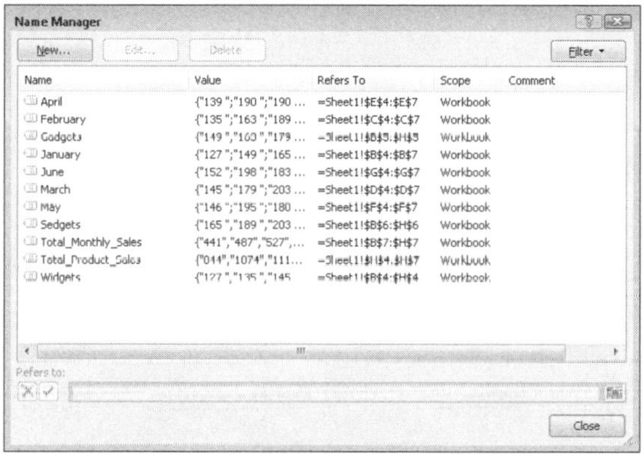

How do I know which options to click in the Create Names from Selection dialog box?

▼ You click the options that describe the rows that contain labels in your selection. Excel assigns the labels as the range name. In the example in this section, labels appear in the row above the data and in the column to the left of the data. If no labels appeared in the column to the left of the data, then it would be appropriate to select only the Top Row option so that Excel could create range names for the columns below the labels.

Can I have Excel automatically create one label to identify all of the rows and columns that I select?

▼ Yes. Type the label you want Excel to associate with the entire range of selected rows and columns in the cell in the upper-left corner of the selected rows and columns; this cell is often blank. In the examples in this section, the cell is A3. When you automatically create labels from row and column headings, Excel assigns the entire selected range to the label in the upper-left corner of the selected range.

Apply Names to Existing Formulas

After you create range names, if you have existing formulas in your worksheet or workbook, you can update those formulas to use the named ranges instead of the cell addresses. Be aware that, although you create range names in a worksheet or workbook, Excel does not automatically apply those range names to cells that contain formulas that refer to named ranges. You need to apply the range names to update existing formulas.

You can use the Apply Names dialog box to use range names instead of cell addresses in formulas that refer to named ranges. In the Apply Names dialog box, you have a variety of options to set. In most cases, you want to leave the default options set as Excel displays them. For example, by default, Excel ignores relative, absolute, and mixed cell references when it replaces cell addresses with named ranges. You can change this default behavior to force Excel to replace only those cell references that use the same type of references as are used in your names. However, Excel automatically creates range names using absolute cell addresses, and, if you change Excel's default behavior, Excel cannot apply range names to cells containing relative cell references.

Apply Names to Existing Formulas

1. Create range names using the steps in the sections, "Using Cell Names and Range Names" or "Create Range Names from Headings."
2. Click the Formulas tab.
3. Click beside Define Name.
4. Click Apply Names.

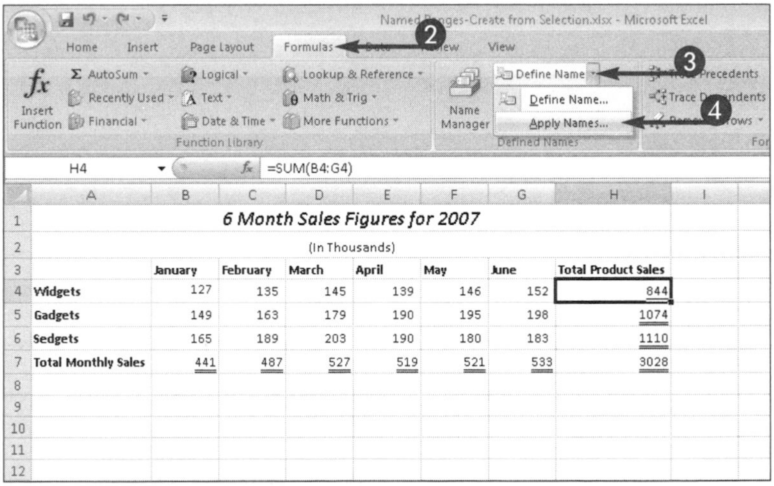

The Apply Names dialog box appears.

- You can click here (✓ changes to ☐) to force Excel to use the relative, absolute, and mixed cell references you established in formulas.
- You can click here (✓ changes to ☐) to avoid using the row and column labels in formulas.

Note: *In most cases, you should leave these options selected.*

5. Click Options.

The Apply Names dialog box expands.

- Click here (☑ changes to ☐) to force Excel to display column and row names in a formula when the formula appears in the same row or column as the name.
- Click here (◯ changes to ◉) to display row names before column names when you display both names.
- Click here ◯ changes to ◉) to display column names before row names when you display both names.

6 Click OK.

7 Click a cell containing a formula that refers to a named range.

- The Formula bar displays range names instead of cell addresses.

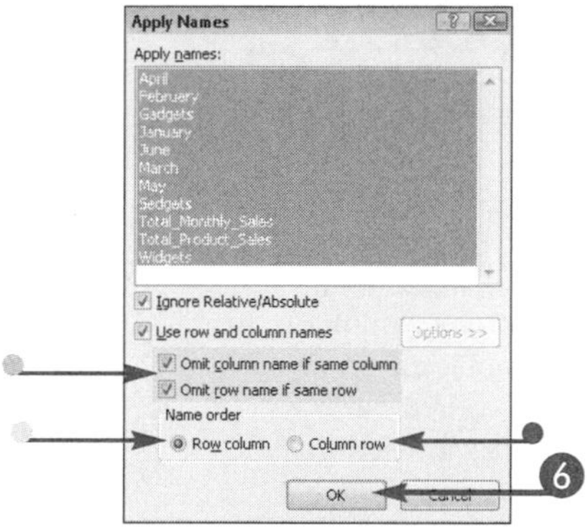

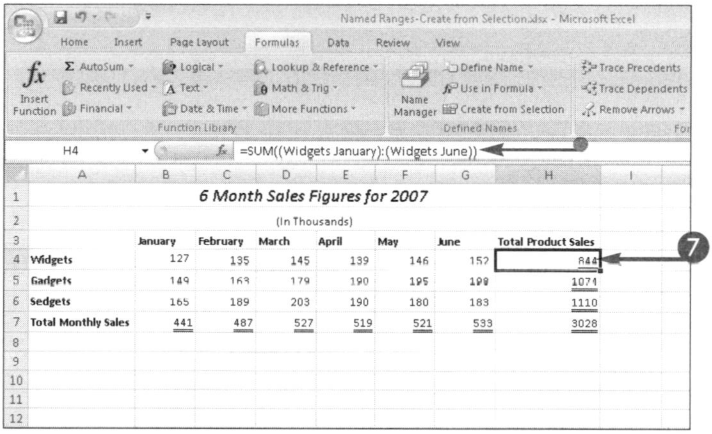

PART III

MASTER IT

Is there a way that I can print the list of cell or range names?

▼ Yes. Select an empty area in your workbook, press F3 or click the Formulas tab, click Use in Formula, and click Paste Names to display the Paste Name window. Then click the Paste List button; Excel pastes each name and its corresponding cell address. You can print the list by selecting it, clicking [icon], and then clicking Print. In the Print dialog box that appears, click the Selection option in the Print What section.

Why do I see a message that Microsoft Office Excel cannot find any references to replace?

▼ You have either already applied all existing names, or you have changed some of the options in the Apply Names dialog box from their defaults. If you have already applied all existing names, you do not need to do anything else. If you changed defaults in the Apply Names dialog box, reset them to their original options and try again.

What does the Use in Formula button do?

▼ The Use in Formula button appears below the Define Name button; after you define names, they appear in a list on the Use in Formula button, making it easy for you to include a range name in a formula. In the cell where you are creating the formula and at the appropriate position in the formula, click the Use in Formula button to display the list and then select the range name from the list.

Understanding Arrays

Although programmers often use arrays, you should not let that scare you. In Excel, an array is a group of items. You can think of an array as a range. You can create formulas called *array formulas* that operate on arrays, and you can also create *array constants*, such as the ones in the figure that you can use — like you use constants — in formulas or array formulas. The array constants in the figure include numbers, but array constants can also include text or logical values. If you include text in an array constant, you must enclose the text in pairs of quotation marks ("").

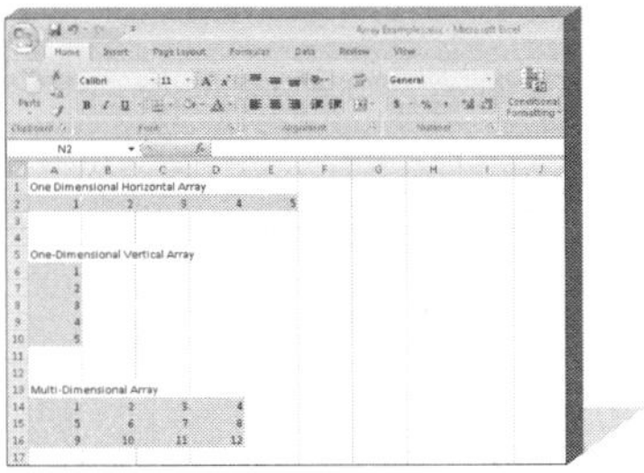

In Excel, arrays can be one-dimensional and horizontal in appearance, in which case the array appears in a row. Arrays can be one-dimensional and vertical in appearance, in which case the array appears in a column. Finally, arrays can also be multi-dimensional, in which case the array appears in a range.

You can use arrays to do many different things; for example, you can count characters in a range, sum the three (or any number) largest values in a range, count the number of errors in a range, determine whether a particular entry appears in a range, or compute an average for a range that includes zeros and exclude the zero values, just to name a few.

Array Formulas

You can also create formulas that use arrays, and these array formulas can save you time and ensure consistency and accuracy. For example, suppose that you have a formula that multiplies values in a row, and you need this formula to appear in ten rows. You can create the formula and then copy it down the column to place it in the ten rows. You can also create an array formula. The original formula you create in cell D3 might look like this:

=B3*C3

You then need to copy it to the other cells in column D.

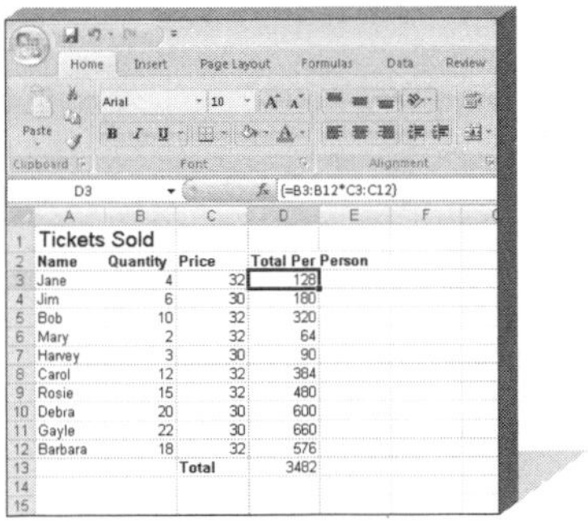

However, you can create one array formula that applies to all of the cells in column D. The array formula would look like this:

=B3:B12*C3:C12

When you enter an array formula, Excel encloses the formula in curly brackets ({}). You must also press Ctrl+Shift+Enter to create an array formula; you cannot simply press Enter when you finish typing. In addition, the array formula appears in all of the cells in the array — in this example, in cells D3 to D12 — without you copying it into all of the cells. Excel enters the array formula in all cells that you specify at the time you create the array formula.

You gain the following advantages by using an array formula:

- You can ensure that you make the same calculation for all cells included in the array range by using an array formula.
- When you change an array formula, Excel updates all of the cells containing the array formula.
- Because array formulas are not widely understood, novices with whom you share your workbook will be less likely to tamper with your calculations.

Using array formulas also has some disadvantages:

- Excel prevents you from inserting a new row or column into the array range.
- If you add rows or columns at the bottom or side of an array range, you need to update the array formula to include the new data.

Arrays and Excel Functions

You can use Excel functions with array formulas. Array formulas that include functions can help you perform multiple calculations simultaneously. For example, in the preceding example, you had to calculate the Total Per Person so that you could create the total quantity sold value that appears in cell D13. However, you can use a function in an array formula that enables you to make the calculation for the total quantity sold without creating the intermediary formulas that appeared in column D.

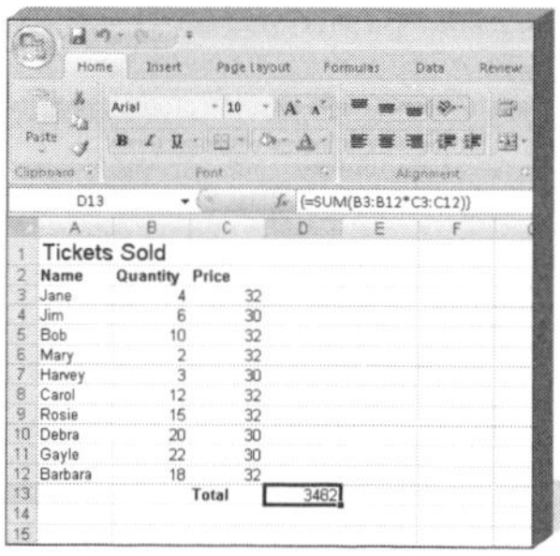

By entering the following array formula that includes a function, you tell Excel to multiply the values in cells B3 to B12 by the values in cells C3 to C12, and then sum the results, as follows:

=SUM(B3:B12*C3:C12).

Again, when you enter the formula, Excel encloses it in curly brackets ({}) to indicate that the formula is an array formula.

Entering Array Constants in a Worksheet

You can easily create an array constant. Suppose that you want to enter the values 1 to 12 in cells B1 to B12. Select the cells in which the array values will appear and type the following:

={1;2;3;4;5;6;7;8;9;10;11;12}

Then press Ctrl+Shift+Enter; Excel enters the values into cells B1 to 12.

If you want to enter the same array constant into Row 1, select cells A1 to L1 and enter the same formula, but separate the values with a comma (,) instead of a semicolon (;).

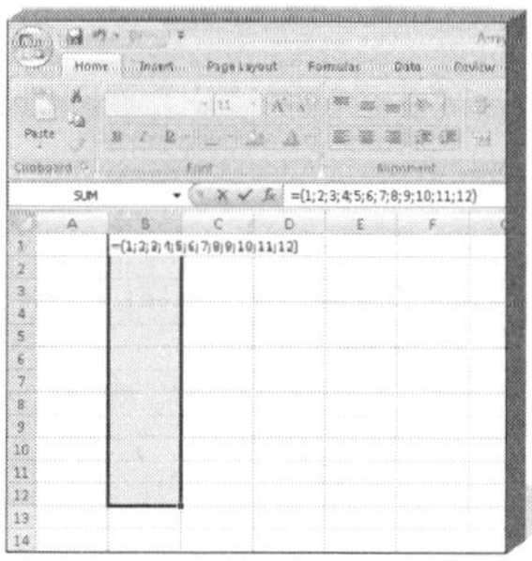

To enter the same array constant as a multi-dimensional array that spans four columns and three rows, select a range such as cells D1 to G3 and enter the formula in the following way:

={1,2,3,4;5,6,7,8;9,10,11,12}

Note that you separate values that appear in the same row with commas and values that appear in different rows with semicolons.

One final thing to remember: you must always select the number of cells into which you want to place array values before you start typing the formula, and you must select as many cells as you need. If you select too few cells, Excel does not display all of your array values. If you select too many cells, Excel displays #N/A in the cells for which no array values exist.

Create an Array Formula

You can create an array formula to perform the same operation on multiple cells simultaneously. Using an array formula eliminates the need to create a formula and then copy and paste it in adjacent cells. For example, suppose that your worksheet lists a series of quantities and individual prices, and you want to know the product of the quantity times the price for each item in the list. You could create a formula that multiplies the quantity times the price and then copy it to the appropriate cells. However, using arrays, you could create one array formula that Excel automatically enters into all of the cells, thereby calculating the values you need for all of the listed items.

When you enter an array formula, you select all of the cells into which you want Excel to enter the formula. The size of your selection must match the size of ranges you will use in the calculation. For example, suppose that you plan to use two columns of data that contain ten values each in the array formula. In the location where you place the array formula, you must select ten cells in a columnar fashion.

You must press Ctrl+Shift+Enter to store an array formula.

Create an Array Formula

1. Set up your worksheet to include the information you need to make your calculation.

   This example calculates Total Per Person for tickets sold at various prices.

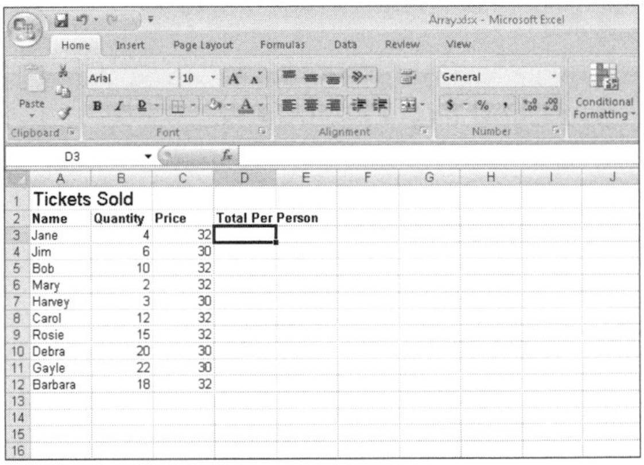

2. Select the cells in which the array formula should appear.

Note: *Select the number of cells in which Excel will display values. If you select too few cells, Excel does not display all of the values. If you select too many cells, Excel displays #N/A in the cells for which no values exist.*

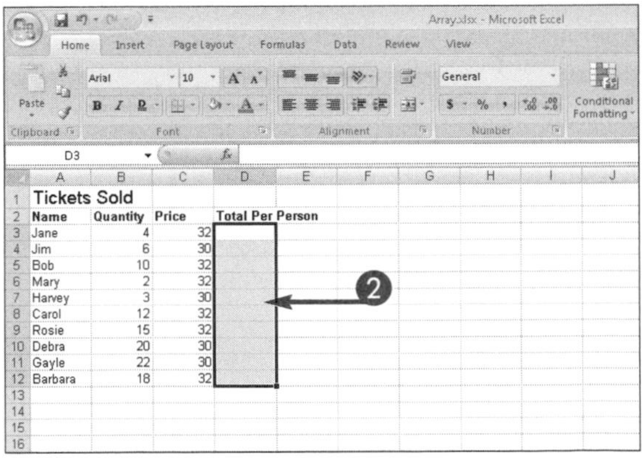

3 Type **=B3:B12*C3:C12**.

Note: *Instead of typing cell addresses, you can use the mouse to select the cells you want to include.*

- As you type, the formula appears in the Formula bar and the first selected cell.

4 Press Ctrl+Shift+Enter.

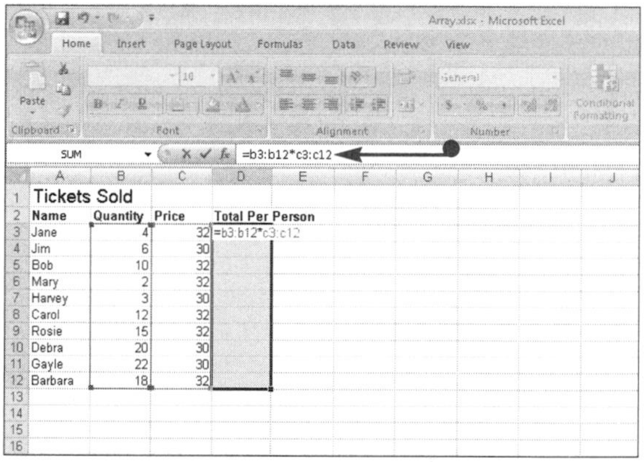

- The result of the formula appears in each of the cells you selected in Step 2.
- Excel displays the formula you entered in the Formula bar. The same formula appears in each of the cells you selected in Step 2.
- Excel adds curly brackets ({}) that you did not type to the beginning and the end of the formula.

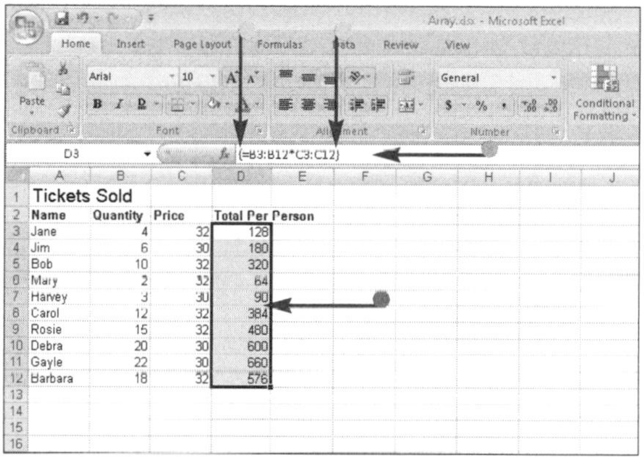

MASTER IT

Can I change an array formula?

▼ Yes. Select all of the cells that contain the array formula. Then press F2 or click in the Formula bar and make the changes you want. Be sure to press Ctrl+Shift+Enter to complete the editing process. You can use this technique to add rows of data to an array calculation. Insert the information at the top or bottom of the current list of values. Then edit the formula to expand the array formula.

Is there a faster way to select an array?

▼ Yes. Click any cell that is part of the array formula. Then press F5 to display the Go To dialog box. In the Go To dialog box, click the Special button to display the Go To Special dialog box. Click the Current Array option and click OK. Excel selects the entire array.

Why did Excel calculate only the first value in the range after I entered the array formula?

▼ You might have selected only the first cell of the range that you wanted Excel to calculate. In this case, Excel creates the array formula in only one cell. You might also have selected all of the cells that you wanted Excel to calculate and then pressed Enter instead of pressing Ctrl+Shift+Enter.

Using the SUM Function in an Array Formula

You can use any of Excel's built-in functions in an array formula. For example, you can calculate the total dollar amount of tickets sold for all salespeople at all prices without calculating each individual salesperson's sales or the individual sales at a given ticket price. You can also calculate the maximum or minimum change between two sets of numbers, or you can count the number of characters in a range. The list is virtually endless, and so the example in this section shows you how to use the SUM function to simultaneously multiply two sets of values and then sum their products without calculating the individual products first. You can read more about the SUM function in Chapter 11.

As you read in the section, "The Basics of Formulas in Excel," earlier in this chapter, every Excel function uses arguments, which are the cell references or constants that you want Excel to use when making the calculation. When you use a function in an array formula, the arguments you use must contain the same number of values. That is, if the function requires two arguments and you use B2:B45 for the first argument, the second argument should include at least 43 cells in another column.

Using the SUM Function in an Array Formula

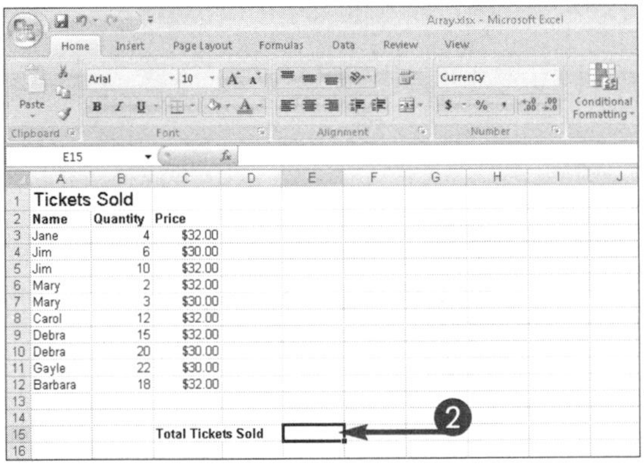

1. Set up your worksheet to include the information you need to make your calculation.

   This example calculates total dollars for tickets sold, regardless of who sold them or the ticket price.

2. Click the cell in which you want the array formula to appear.

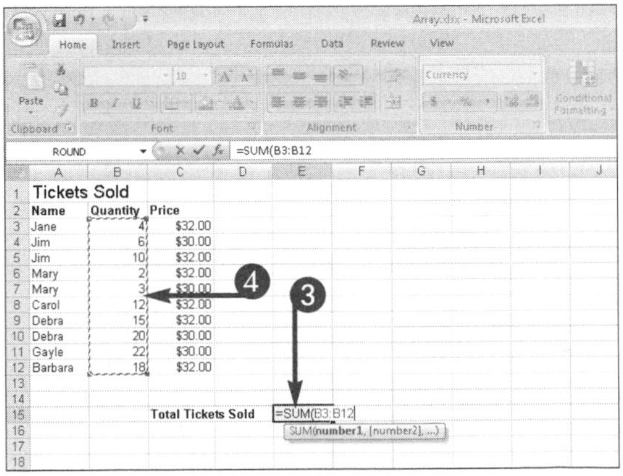

3. Type **=SUM(**.
4. Select the cells that make up the first part of the argument for the function.

   This examples uses cells B3 to B12.

5 Type *.

6 Select the cells that make up the second part of the argument for the function.

This example uses cells C3 to C12.

7 Type).

8 Press Ctrl+Shift+Enter.

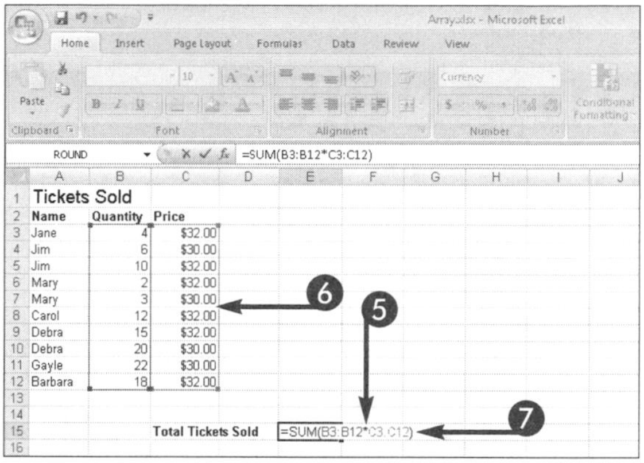

- The result of the formula appears in the cell you selected in Step 2.
- Excel displays the formula you entered in the Formula bar.
- Excel adds curly brackets ({}) that you did not type to the beginning and the end of the formula.

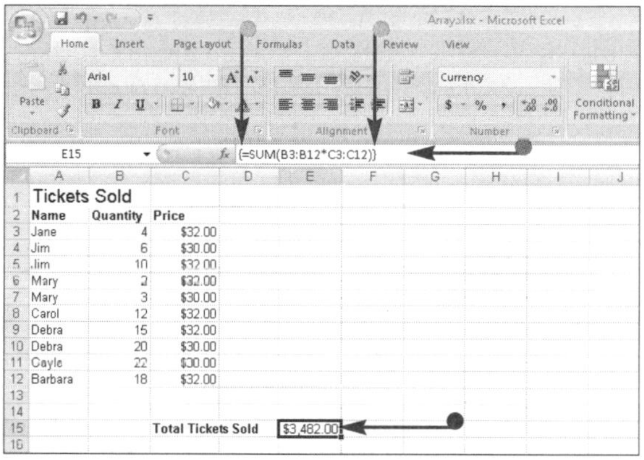

MASTER IT

Can I convert an array formula to a regular value?

▼ Yes. Select the cell containing the array formula and click [icon]. Then, without selecting another cell, click the bottom of the Paste button to display a list of choices. Click Paste Values; Excel converts the array formula to the value it previously calculated. You can click [icon] to redisplay the array formula.

Can I convert an existing list of information into an array formula at a different location in the worksheet?

▼ Yes. Suppose that your list appears in cells B2 to B10. Select as many blank cells as you have list items. Make sure that you select the same shape; that is, if your items appear in a column, select blank cells in a column, such as cells D2 to D10. Type = and then select the constants. Press Ctrl+Shift+Enter; in cells D2 to D10, Excel enters the array formula {=B2:B10}.

Can I convert an array formula that contains cell references into an array constant without cell references?

▼ Yes. Suppose that you want the array constant to appear at the same location as the array formula. Select the cells that contain the array formula and press F2 to edit the formula. Then press F9; Excel converts all cell references to the values displayed in those cells. Press Ctrl+Shift+Enter to store the array constant.

Sum Numbers

You can use the SUM function, probably the most commonly used function, to quickly add a group of numbers. This function is used so often by so many people that Excel displays two buttons for it on the Ribbon — one on the Home tab and one on the Formulas tab. Although the one on the Home tab is called the SUM button and the one on the Formulas tab is called the AutoSum button, they both work the same way.

The SUM function uses the format =SUM(*arguments*). Arguments are parameters (such as a range containing values) that Excel needs to make a calculation. The SUM function requires and typically uses only one argument — the range to add — but you can add several ranges with one SUM function. As you enter the function, Excel guesses which cells you want to add and outlines the selection with an animated, dashed border. If necessary, you can select different cells to include as the argument using the mouse or the keyboard.

You can type the function or you can enter it using one of the buttons on the Ribbon. If you type the function, you can type it in lowercase or uppercase letters.

Sum Numbers

1. Click the cell in which you want to store the function.
2. Click the Home tab.
3. Click the Sum button (Σ).

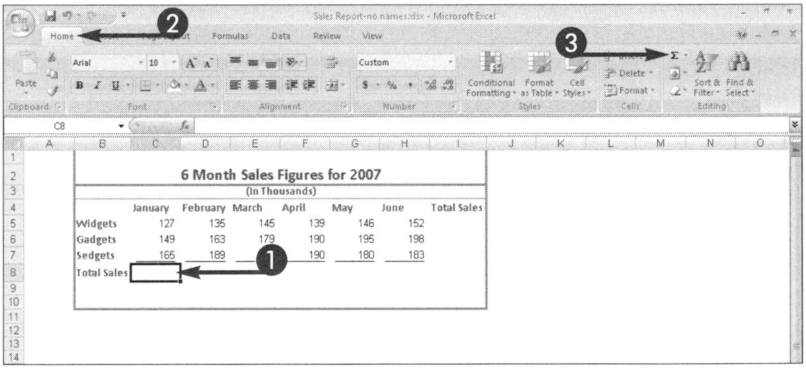

- Excel begins the function.
- Excel guesses which cells you want to add.
- You see information here that describes the syntax of the formula. The bold portion shows you where you are in the process of building the formula.

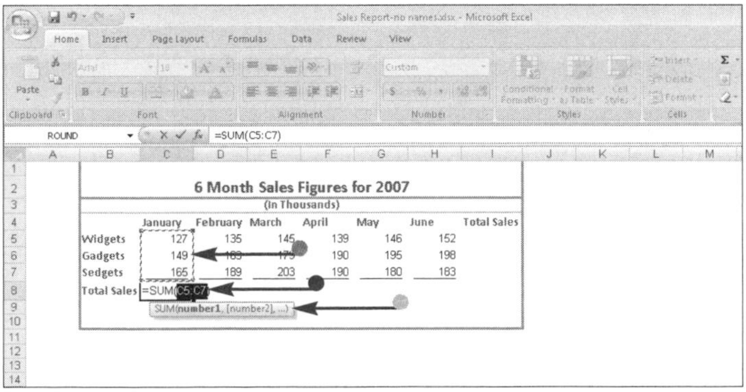

❹ If Excel guesses correctly, press Enter.

Note: *If Excel guesses incorrectly, select the cells with the mouse or with the keyboard and then press Enter. See Chapter 4 for details on selecting cells.*

- Excel displays the result of the formula in the cell you clicked in Step 1.

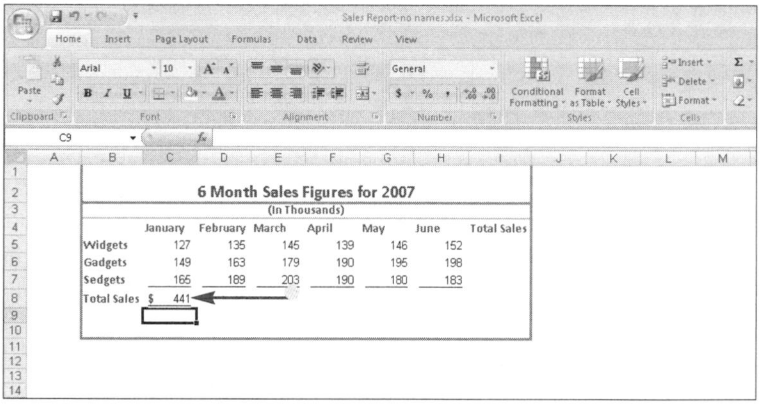

❺ Click the cell you selected in Step 1.

- Excel displays the function in the Formula bar.

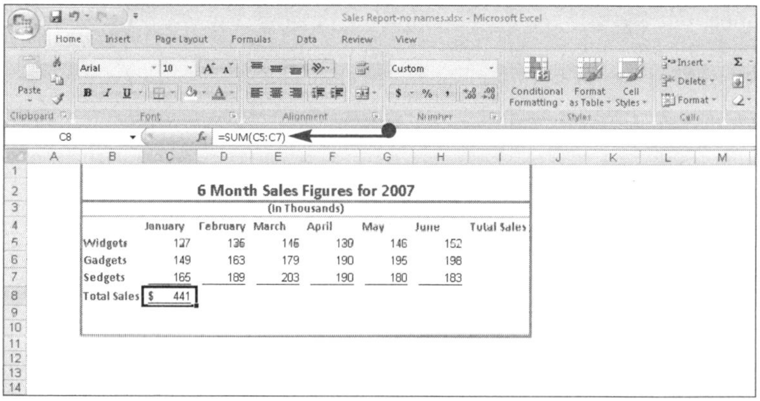

MASTER IT

Can I use the SUM function to add values in non-contiguous cells?

▼ Yes. Complete Steps 1 to 3. If Excel correctly guesses the first range you want to include in the sum, reselect that range. Then, type a comma (,) and select the next range you want to include in the sum. Repeat this process of selecting ranges and separating them with commas until you have selected all of the ranges you want to include in the sum. Each range you select is an argument, and you can include up to 255 ranges in the sum. When you have selected all of the arguments, press Enter. A SUM function that includes non-contiguous ranges might look like =SUM(B2:B4,M6) or =SUM(D7,C5,G6).

Why do I see pound signs (#) in a cell that contains a SUM function?

▼ Excel displays pound signs in cells — not just cells containing formulas or functions — when the column is not wide enough to display the contents of the cell, including the cell's formatting. For example, you may be able to see three-digit values that you entered in some cells in column C, but in others, Excel displays pound signs. If this occurs, then you probably applied different formatting to the cells displaying the pound signs than the formatting you applied to the cells containing the values you can see. Widen the column to correct the problem; see Chapter 6 for details.

Calculate a Running Balance

You can create a formula to calculate a running balance. You can use a running balance in many situations. For example, you can use a running balance formula to keep track of your checkbook balance or to keep track of inventory levels based on inventory received and sold. Attorneys can use a running balance to keep track of funds deposited and withdrawn by clients.

You use the SUM function to keep track of a running balance, but the formula uses multiple arguments. The formula for a running balance must account for the previous balance (or the opening balance), additions to the balance, and subtractions from the balance. So, in a formula that uses the SUM function to track a running balance, you typically see three arguments.

You can use a variation of the running balance formula to calculate a running total. You can use a running total formula to calculate additions but not withdrawals. For example, you could use a running balance to keep track of the balance in a savings account into which you make deposits throughout the year without withdrawing money, in order to save for a specific item.

Calculate a Running Balance

1. Set up the worksheet so that you have columns for the date, deposits you make, the numbers of the checks that you write, the amounts of the checks, and a column to hold your running balance.

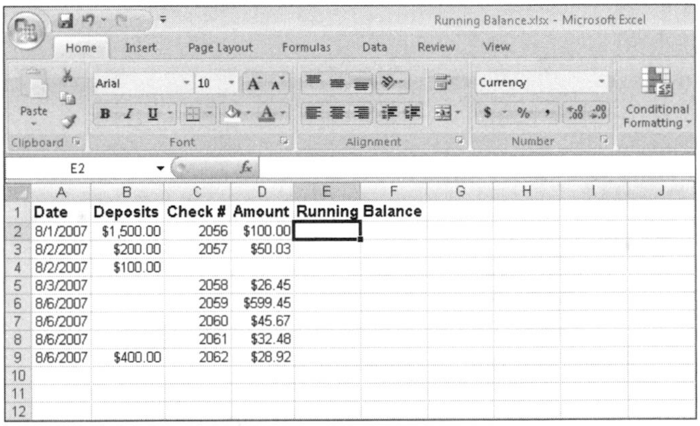

2. Click the cell where the running balance will appear.
3. Type **=B2-D2**.

Note: *This formula establishes the opening balance by subtracting checks from deposits.*

4. Press Enter or click ✓.

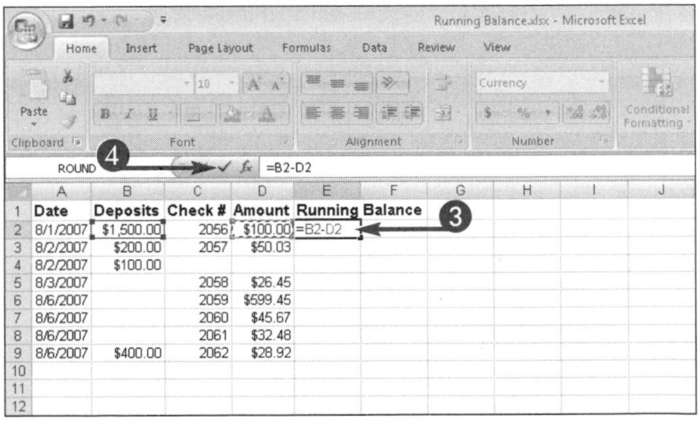

- Excel makes the calculation and displays the result in the cell you selected in Step 2.

5 In the cell below the one you selected in Step 2, type **=SUM(E2,B3,-D3)**.

Note: *This formula enters the sum of deposits you made and the running balance number and subtracts the checks you wrote.*

6 Press Enter or click ☑.

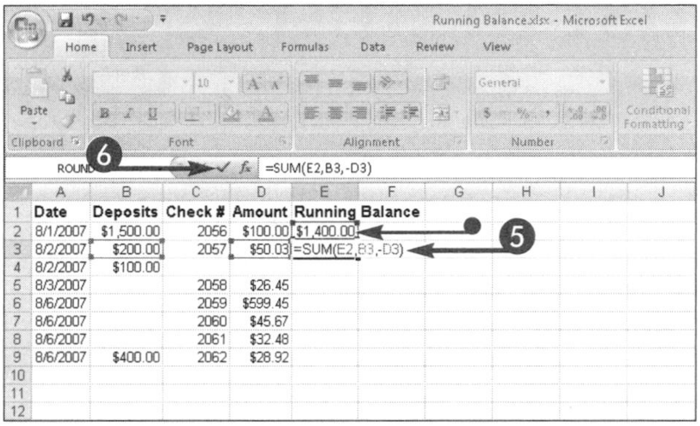

7 Click the cell containing the formula you entered in Step 5.

- Excel displays the formula in the Formula bar.

8 Drag the Fill handle down.

- Excel copies the formula down the column.

Each time you enter a deposit or check, Excel updates the running balance.

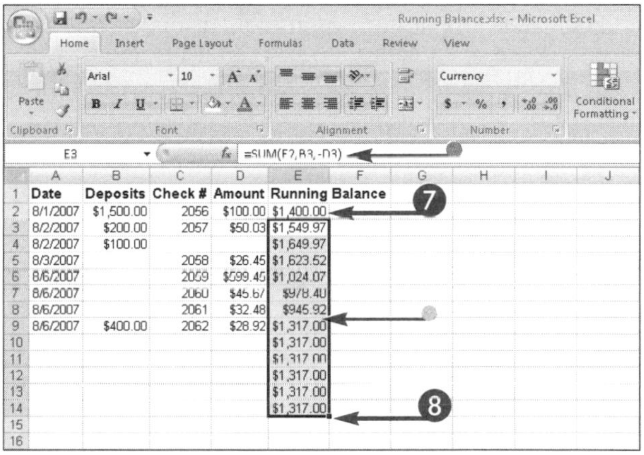

MASTER IT

Why do I need a special formula to establish the opening balance?

▼ Actually, you do not need to use the formula shown in Step 3 to establish the opening balance. You can use the formula shown in Step 5 to establish the opening balance, because Excel ignores cells containing text when calculating a SUM function. However, using the formula shown in Step 3 clarifies that the purpose of the formula is to establish an opening balance. If you prefer to use one formula, substitute the formula in Step 5 for the one shown in Step 3.

How do I create a formula for a running total?

▼ The running total formula closely resembles the formula for a running balance. However, in the formula for a running total, you only add values; you do not subtract any values. The number of arguments for a SUM function that calculates a running total depends on the number of different values you need to add. For example, if you want to track savings account deposits, you can set up a worksheet that contains columns for the deposit date, the amount deposited, and the running total. In Row 1 of columns A and B, type dates and deposits. In cell C2, type the formula **=SUM(B$2:B2)**. Then copy the formula down column C.

Install and Use the Conditional Sum Wizard

Excel comes with several very powerful tools that are not installed by default but are available as add-ins. Throughout this book, you will find tasks that use some of these tools. For example, to easily calculate a conditional sum, you can use the Conditional Sum Wizard.

You install all of the add-in tools using the same technique. You should not need your Office 2007 disc when you install any of the add-in tools. Think of this process as more of an activation than an installation.

You can calculate a conditional sum to sum only certain cells in a range. When you calculate a conditional sum, you establish criteria for Excel to use when selecting cells to include in the calculation of the sum.

You can use the SUMIF function to calculate a conditional sum if you have only one criterion to specify. If you want to specify multiple criteria for Excel to use to select cells to include in the range that you sum, you can use the SUMIFS function. Or, you can simplify the process by using the Conditional Sum Wizard.

Install and Use the Conditional Sum Wizard

Install the Wizard

1. Click .
2. Click Excel Options.

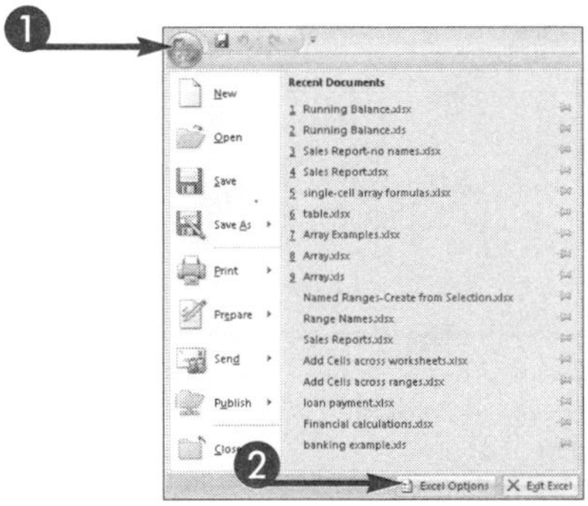

The Excel Options dialog box appears.

3. Click Add-Ins.
   - The Conditional Sum Wizard appears here in the list.
4. Click Go.

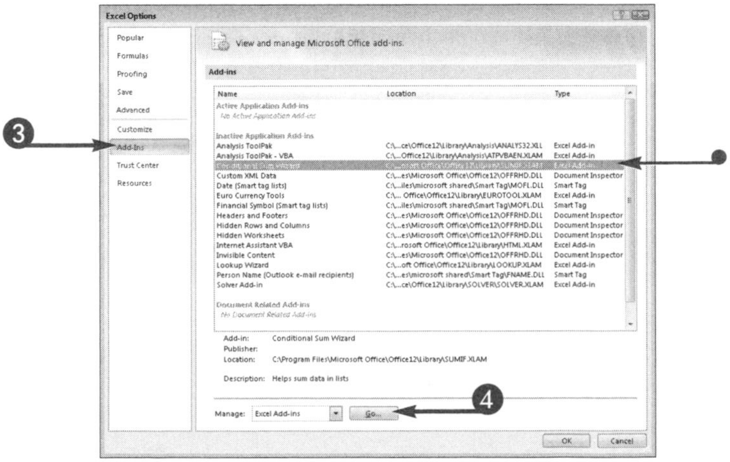

The Add-Ins dialog box appears.

5. Click Conditional Sum Wizard (☐ changes to ☑).

6. Click OK.

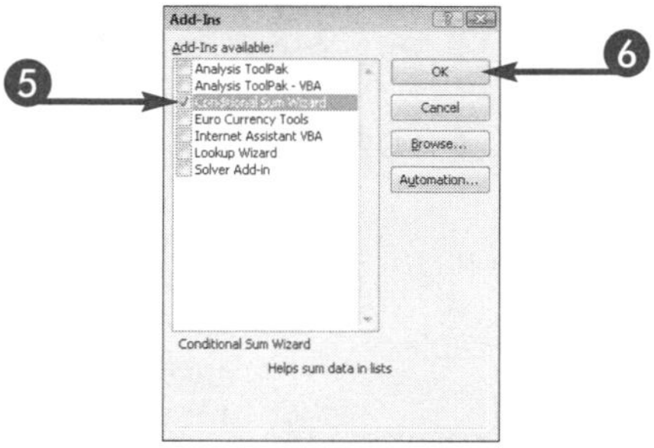

Note: *You may see a message box asking you to confirm the installation; click Yes.*

Excel installs the Conditional Sum Wizard.

7. Click the Formulas tab.

- The Conditional Sum Wizard appears in the Solutions group at the end of the Formulas tab.

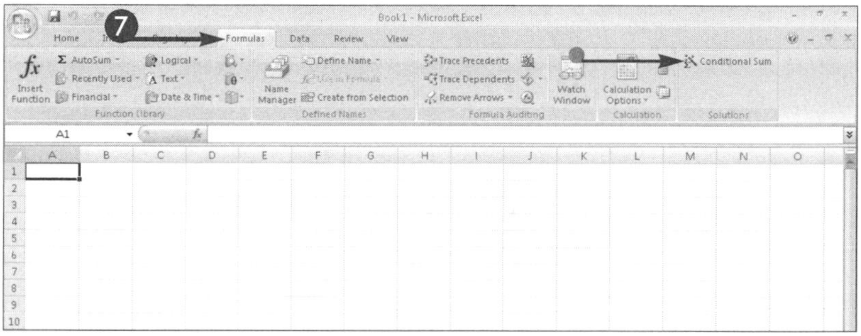

PART III

MASTER IT

When would I use the SUMIF function instead of the Conditional Sum Wizard?

▼ SUMIF is perfect for calculating a simple conditional sum that depends on only one criterion. For example, suppose that your worksheet contains bakery sales by item; the range includes A1:D50, and, in column A, you list the item sold, in column B, you list the quantity sold, the selling price in column C , and in column D, you list the total sale price. You want to know how many chocolate chip cookies the bakery sold, and the first chocolate chip cookie entry appears in cell A2. You can use this SUMIF function: =SUMIF(A1:A50,A2,B1:B50)

Can I uninstall the Conditional Sum Wizard?

▼ Yes. Repeat Steps 1 to 3. The Conditional Sum Wizard appears in the list of installed add-ins. Click Go, and, in the Add-Ins dialog box, click the Conditional Sum Wizard (☑ changes to ☐). Click OK. The Conditional Sum Wizard no longer appears in the Solutions group on the Formulas tab.

Can I install other add-ins when I install the Conditional Sum Wizard?

▼ Yes, you can. In the Add-Ins dialog box, click each add-in that you want to install (☐ changes to ☑) and click OK. Each of the add-ins that you install appears either in the Solutions group on the Formulas tab or in the Analysis group on the Data tab.

continued

Install and Use the Conditional Sum Wizard *(Continued)*

Suppose that you manage sales for the local cable company that has three offices in your area. You track sales of different types of cable services sold by all of the branch offices in a single Excel workbook. In your workbook, you track the date a service was sold, the amount and type of the service, who sold the service — your customer service department or a direct marketer — the branch office that sold the service, and whether the service was sold to a new customer or an existing customer.

Using the Conditional Sum Wizard, you can make a variety of different calculations. For example, you can calculate the total dollars sold for a particular type of cable service by a particular branch office. Or, you can calculate the total dollars sold for all cable services by customer service representatives to new customers. Or, you can calculate the total dollars sold for a particular type of cable service by a particular branch to new customers on a particular date. You can also calculate the same value for existing customers so that you can compare the dollars generated by new business and the dollars generated by existing customers on a given date.

Install and Use the Conditional Sum Wizard *(continued)*

Use the Conditional Sum Wizard

1. Click the cell where the formula should appear.
2. Click the Formulas tab.
3. Click here to start the Conditional Sum Wizard.
4. Select the range you want Excel to evaluate when calculating the sum.
   - Excel displays the selected range here.
5. Click Next.
6. Select a column in the range to sum.
7. Click ▾ to select the column containing the criterion you want to set, a comparison operator, and the criterion.
8. Click Add Condition.
9. Repeat Steps 6 and 7 for each criterion you want to set.
10. Click Next.

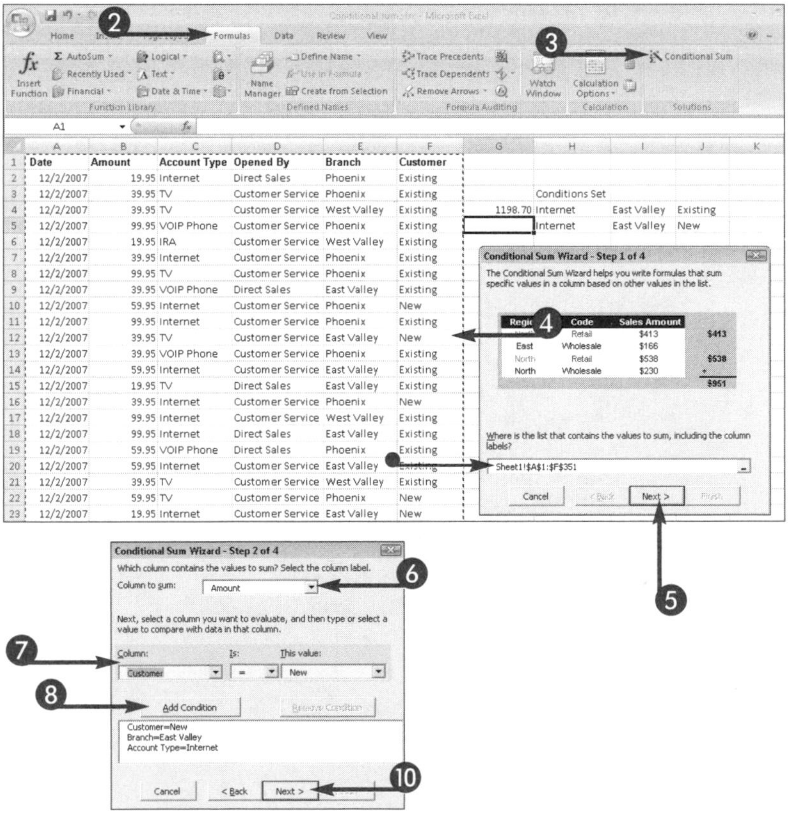

⓫ Click an option to specify how Excel should enter the formula in your worksheet (◯ changes to ◉).

Note: *This example enters both the formula and the criteria.*

⓬ Click Next.

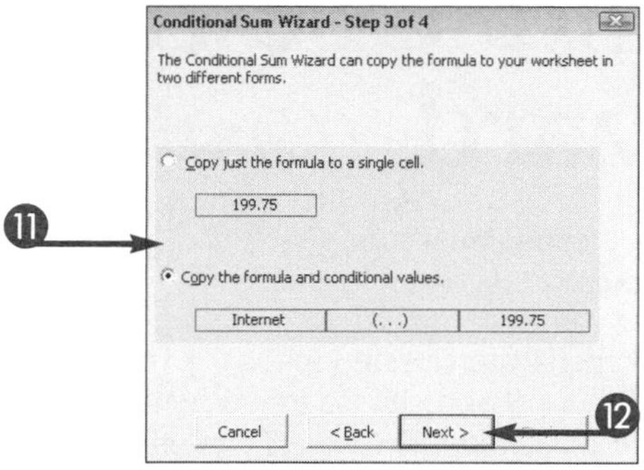

⓭ Click the cell where the value of the first criterion should appear.

- You can click here to collapse the wizard dialog box and click a cell.
- The cell you select appears here.

⓮ Click Next.

Note: *Excel displays the same dialog box for each criterion you set up in Steps 6 and 7.*

⓯ Repeat Steps 13 and 14 for each criterion.

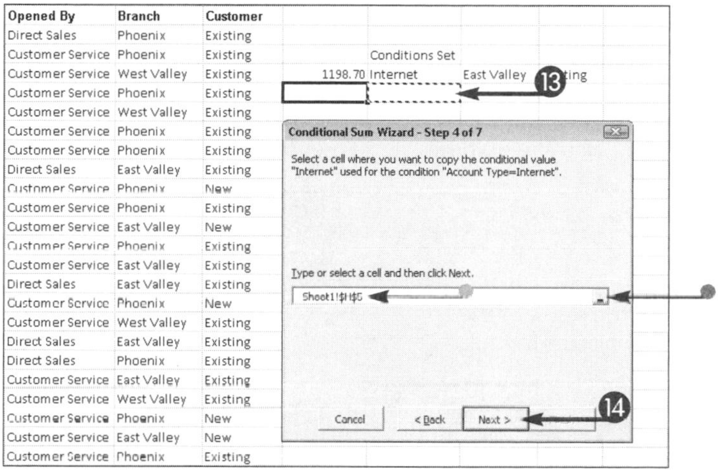

MASTER IT

What happens if I include the values of the criteria as well as the calculation, and then later decide that I do not want the criteria?

▼ If you delete the criteria values, Excel removes the result of the calculation from your worksheet. If you click the cell containing the calculation, you still see the formula in the Formula bar, but Excel no longer calculates it. The wizard ties the criteria values to the calculation, and so, to remove the criteria, you must recalculate the value. In the third dialog box of the wizard, click the Just Copy The Formula To A Single Cell option (◯ changes to ◉). Excel will not prompt you for locations for the criteria values.

Is the Conditional Sum Wizard limited to adding values?

▼ No, you can set the column to add as a non-numeric column, and Excel will count the occurrences of the criteria you set and display the number of times that the criteria occur. For example, you can set the Column To Sum option to Branch in the example, and then set criteria such as Account Type = Internet, Branch = West Valley, Date = 12/2/2007, and Customer = New. In this case, Excel counts the number of new customers that ordered Internet service through the East Valley office on December 2, 2007.

continued

Install and Use the Conditional Sum Wizard *(Continued)*

When you calculate a conditional sum, Excel offers you the choice of just entering the calculation in your worksheet or entering both the calculation and the criteria you selected for the calculation into your worksheet. If you choose to enter the criteria as well as the calculation, Excel prompts you individually for cells in which to store each criterion as well as the result of the calculation. You can place the information anywhere you want in the worksheet.

When you specify locations for the criteria and the results of the calculation, you can collapse the Conditional Sum Wizard dialog boxes or you can simply click a cell in your worksheet without collapsing any of the dialog boxes.

The formula that Excel uses to calculate a conditional sum is actually a combination of the SUM function and the IF function, demonstrating that you can combine functions to make a calculation in Excel. You can read more about the SUM function in the section, "Sum Numbers," earlier in this chapter. You can read more about the IF function in Chapter 16.

Install and Use the Conditional Sum Wizard *(continued)*

16 Click the cell in which you want to store the result of the conditional sum formula.

- You can click here to collapse the wizard dialog box and click a cell.
- The cell you select appears here.

17 Click Finish.

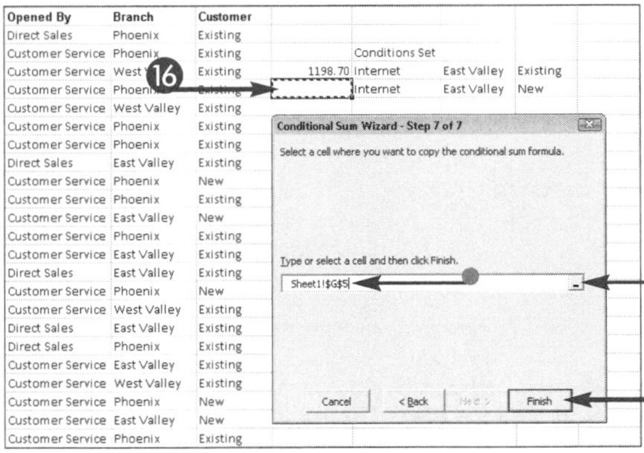

- Excel displays the conditional sum in your worksheet.
- The formula Excel creates to display the conditional sum is a combination of the SUM function and the IF function.

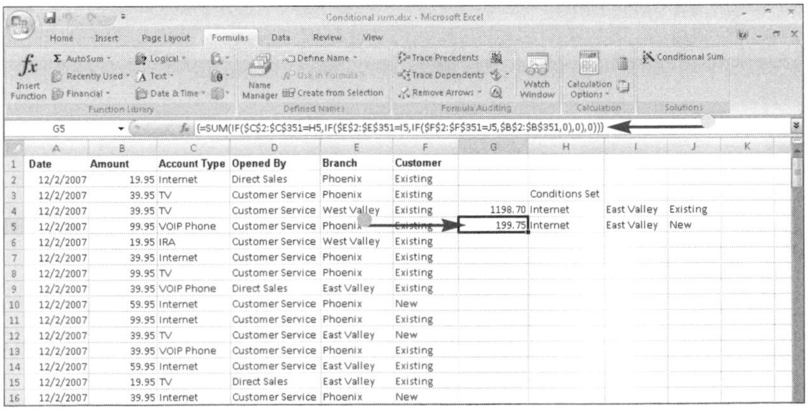

Calculate a Percentage

You can easily calculate a percentage in Excel. As you may recall from high school math, a percentage identifies the portion of the total represented by one value. For example, if you sell three products, you may want to calculate each product's percentage of total sales.

When you calculate a percentage, you typically start with a fraction. You divide the top number in the fraction, called the *numerator*, by the bottom number in the fraction, called the *denominator*, to obtain a decimal value. You then multiply the decimal value by 100 to obtain the percentage value.

When you calculate each product's percentage of total sales, you use the individual product's sales as the numerator and the total sales for all products as the denominator. Excel makes the process a bit easier; although you still divide the product's individual sales by the total sales for all products, instead of multiplying by 100, you apply the Percentage format. Excel then displays the decimal value as if you had multiplied it by 100.

You should make the reference to the denominator an absolute cell reference so that you can accurately copy the formula to other cells.

Calculate a Percentage

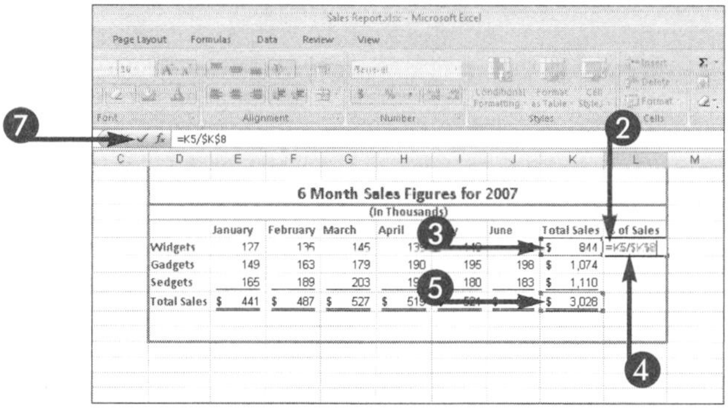

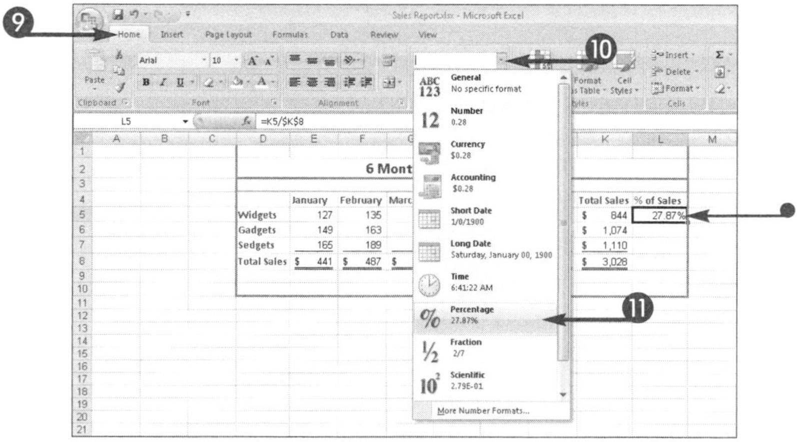

1. Click the cell in which you want to store the formula.
2. Type =.
3. Click the cell containing the value that should serve as the numerator of the equation.
4. Type /.
5. Click the cell containing the value that should serve as the denominator of the equation.
6. Press F4 to convert the cell reference to an absolute reference.
7. Press Enter or click ☑.
8. Click the cell containing the formula.
9. Click the Home tab.
10. Click here to display available number formats.
11. Click Percentage.
    - Excel converts the decimal to a percentage.

Calculate an Average

You can calculate the average value in a range using the AVERAGE function. For example, if you have collected sales data for a product over several months, then you can use the AVERAGE function to calculate the average for sales during the time period. This function works very much like the SUM function, discussed earlier in this chapter in the section, "Sum Numbers." The AVERAGE function requires only one argument — the range that you want Excel to consider when calculating the average. If you want, you can supply up to 255 additional arguments.

The AVERAGE function computes the arithmetic mean of a range by adding the values in the range and then dividing by the number of values that were added. Instead of using the simple AVERAGE function to calculate the average of the range C6 to H6, you could obtain the same results using this formula:

=SUM(C6:H6)/COUNT(C4:C8).

The COUNT function is a statistical function with several variations in Excel; you can read about one of these variations in the section, "Count the Number of Cells Containing Information," later in this chapter.

Calculate an Average

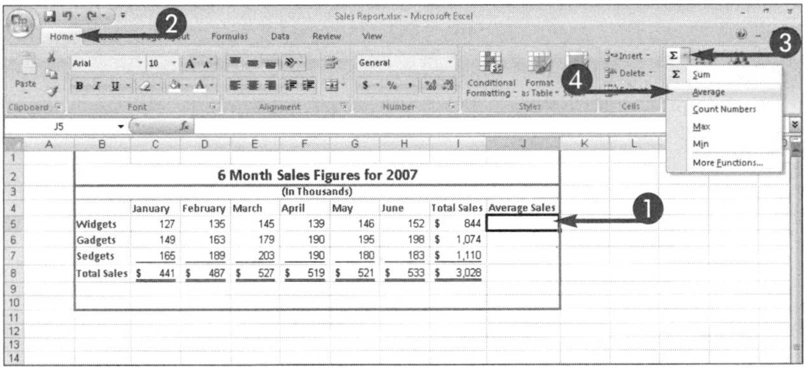

1. Click the cell in which you want to store the formula.
2. Click the Home tab.
3. Click here.
4. Click Average.

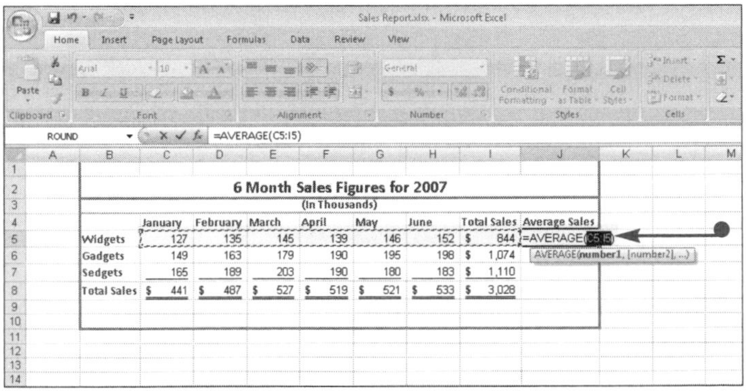

- Excel displays the formula and includes a suggested range for the argument.

5 If Excel guesses correctly, click ☑.

If Excel guesses incorrectly, you can select the correct range to average and then click ☑.

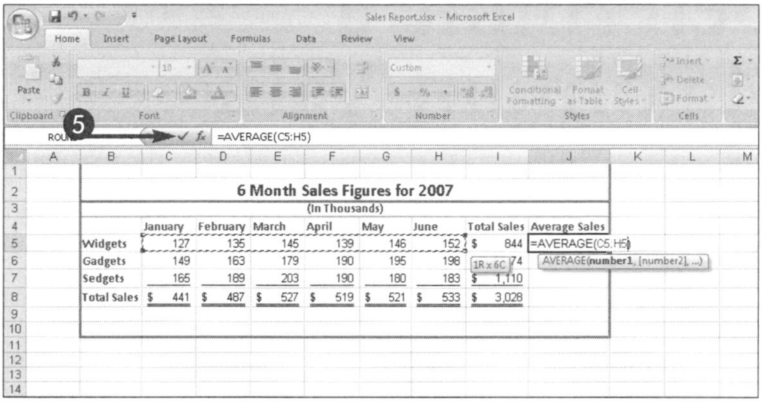

- The average for the selected range appears in the cell you selected in Step 1.
- Excel displays the formula in the Formula bar.

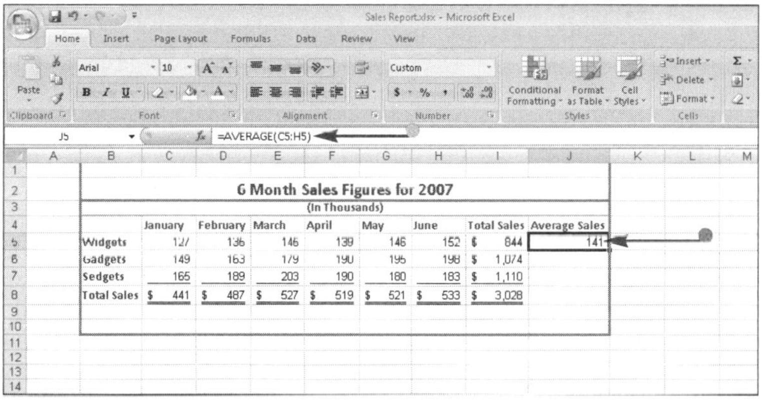

MASTER IT

I decided to try typing the function. When I did, why did Excel suggest some functions that seemed to match my typing?

▼ You experienced Excel's Formula Autocomplete feature. Whenever you type an equal sign (=) followed by some letters, Excel tries to help you select a function. You can press the down-arrow key to highlight the function you want to use and then press the Tab key to select the function. Excel enters the function name and an opening parenthesis. You can then continue typing the formula by entering its arguments and typing the closing parenthesis.

When typing the AVERAGE function, I noticed the AVERAGEIF function; what does this function do?

▼ Like its cousin, the SUMIF function, the AVERAGEIF function calculates a conditional average that depends on only one criterion. For example, suppose that your worksheet contains bakery sales by item. The data appears in the range A1:D50, and you list the item sold in column A, the quantity sold in column B, the selling price in column C, and the total sale price in column D. You want to know the average number of sales for chocolate chip cookies. If the first chocolate chip cookie entry appears in cell A2, you can use this AVERAGEIF function: =AVERAGEIF(A1:A50,A2,B1:B50)

Determine a Maximum Value

You can calculate the maximum value in a range using the MAX function. For example, suppose that you have collected sales data for a product over several months. You can use the MAX function to determine the highest sales that occurred in the time period for which you have collected data. Or, suppose that you have collected data about home prices in a particular neighborhood. You can identify the most expensive home using the MAX function. Or, suppose that you teach a class at the local junior college. You can use the MAX function to find the highest test score for each test that you give to your students.

The MAX function works very much like the SUM function (discussed earlier in this chapter in the section, "Sum Numbers") and the AVERAGE function (discussed in the preceding section, "Calculate an Average"). The MAX function requires only one argument — the range you want Excel to consider when determining the largest value in the range. If you want, you can supply up to 255 additional arguments.

Determine a Maximum Value

1. Click the cell in which you want to store the formula.
2. Click the Home tab.
3. Click here.
4. Click Max.

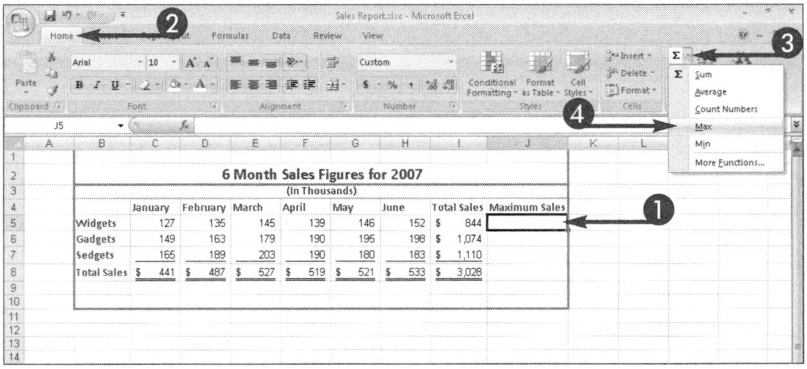

- Excel displays the formula and includes a suggested range for the argument.

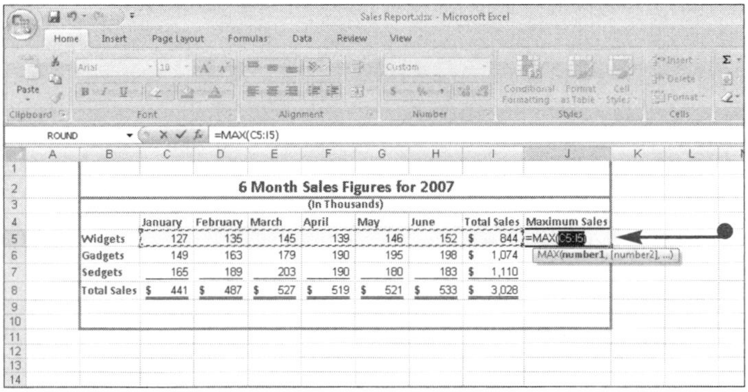

5 If Excel guesses correctly, click ✓.

If Excel guesses incorrectly, you can select the correct range to average and then click ✓.

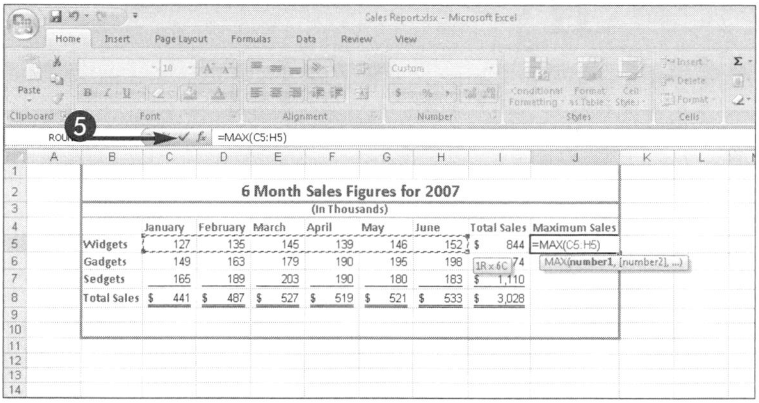

- The maximum value for the selected range appears in the cell you selected in Step 1.
- Excel displays the formula in the Formula bar.

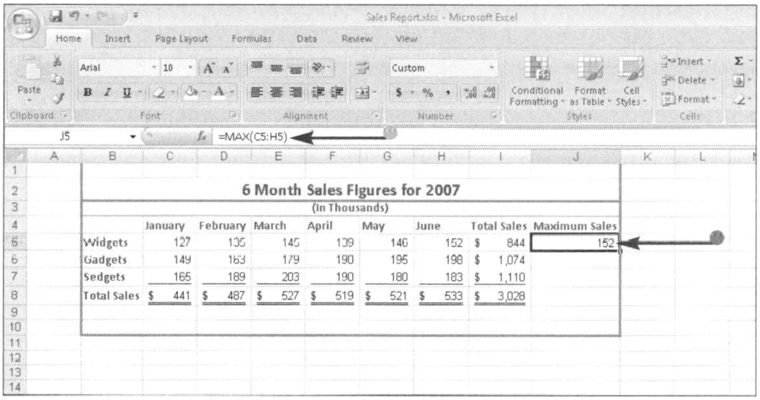

MASTER IT

How would I specify more than one argument for the MAX function?

▼ After you select the range that you want to use for the first argument, type a comma (,). Then select the next cell or range that you want to include as an argument for the function. Continue this process, separating arguments with commas, until you have selected all of the cells that you want to include as arguments. Then click ✓ or press Enter.

The maximum value that Excel returned for the selected range seems high to me; what did I do wrong?

▼ Review the range you selected for Excel to evaluate and make sure that it does not include a "totals" value. In the example in this section, Total Sales appears in column I. Including column I in the range that Excel uses to determine the maximum value artificially inflates the values in the range.

Is there a way to use the MAX function to find the second-biggest value in a range?

▼ No, but you can use the LARGE function, which uses two arguments. The first argument identifies the range you want to evaluate, and the second argument identifies the hierarchical order of the value you want to identify. Suppose your values appear in the range D1:D25. You can use the following formula to find the second-largest value in the list: =LARGE(D1:D25,2).

Identify a Minimum Value

You can calculate the minimum value in a range using the MIN function. If you have collected house prices for a particular neighborhood, the MIN function is the tool to use to find the least expensive house in the neighborhood. Or, if you have collected sales data for a product over several months, you can use the MIN function to identify the lowest sales that occurred in the time period for which you have collected data. Or, you can use the MIN function to find the lowest test score for each test you give to the class that you teach at the local junior college.

The MIN function works very much like the SUM function (discussed earlier in this chapter in the section, "Sum Numbers"), the AVERAGE function (discussed earlier in the section, "Calculate an Average"), and the MAX function (discussed in the preceding section, "Determine a Maximum Value"). The MIN function requires only one argument — the range you want Excel to consider when determining the largest value in the range. If you want, you can supply up to 255 additional arguments.

Identify a Minimum Value

1. Click the cell in which you want to store the formula.
2. Click the Home tab.
3. Click here.
4. Click Min.

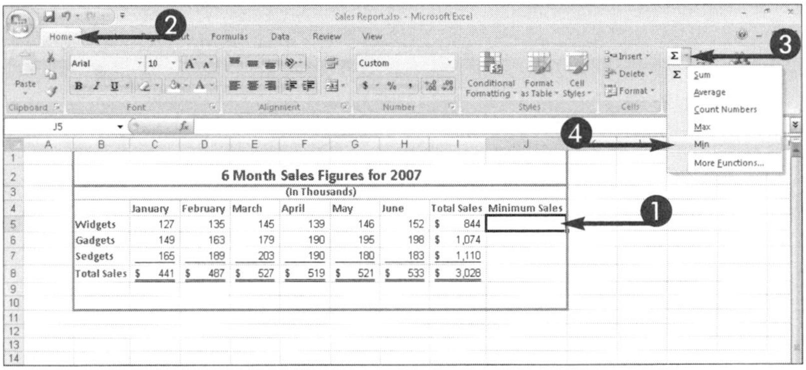

- Excel displays the formula and includes a suggested range for the argument.

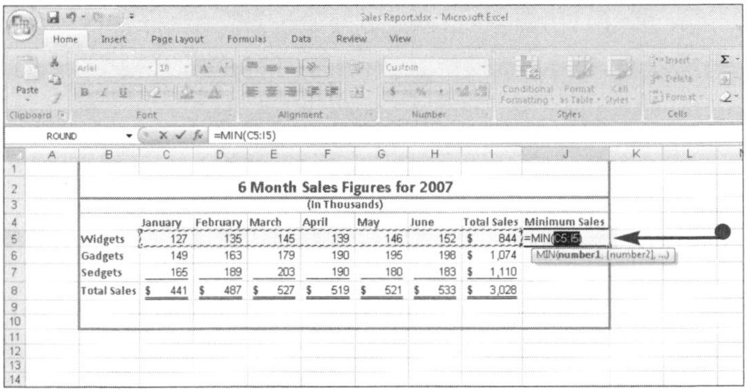

5 If Excel guesses correctly, click ☑.

If Excel guesses incorrectly, you can select the correct range to average and then click ☑.

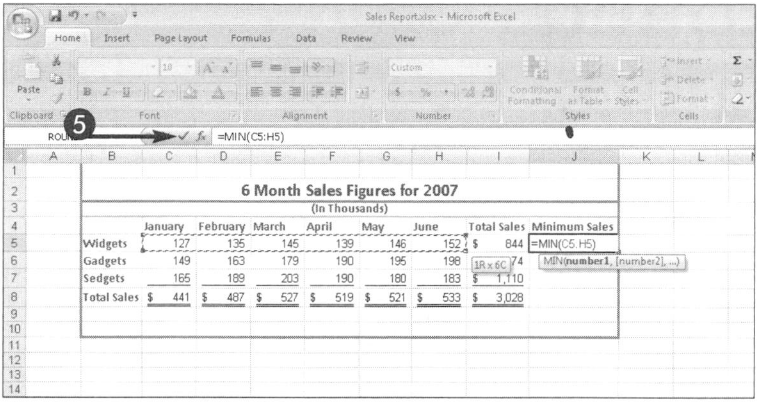

- The minimum value for the selected range appears in the cell you selected in Step 1.
- Excel displays the formula in the Formula bar.

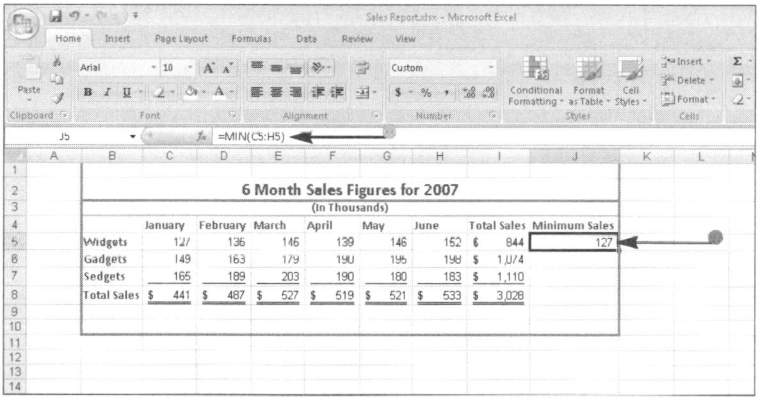

MASTER IT

Can I find the five smallest values in a list using the MIN function?

▼ You can use the MIN function to find the smallest value and then create four formulas using the SMALL function to identify the next four smallest values. The SMALL function uses two arguments: the range you want to evaluate and the hierarchical order for the value you want to find. If your values appear in the range D1:D25, you can use the following formula to find the second-smallest value in the list: =SMALL(D1:D25,2). To find the third-smallest value, use the formula, =SMALL(D1:D25,3). The formulas, =SMALL(D1:D25,4) and =SMALL(D1:D25,5) return the fourth- and fifth-smallest values, respectively.

Can I use the SMALL function instead of the MIN function to find the minimum value in a range?

▼ Yes, you can. Set up the SMALL function to identify the range you want to evaluate and use "1" as the hierarchical order number. For example, if the range of numbers you want Excel to evaluate appears in the range D1:D10, use the following formula to find the minimum value: =SMALL(D1:D10,1). The formulas, =MIN(D1:D10) and =SMALL(D1:D10,1), are equivalent formulas. Both formulas return the smallest value in the range D1:D10 and you can use them interchangeably.

Round Values

You can use the ROUND function to round the fractional portion of a value up or down to as many digits as you specify. Also, while you can format the number to display only two digits — and Excel properly rounds the displayed value — when you use the value in a calculation, Excel uses the original number stored in the cell, which can affect the results of the calculation.

However, you can change the way Excel stores the number by using the ROUND function, and, because Excel uses the values stored in the cell for calculations, rounding can affect your calculations.

The ROUND function takes two arguments: the number or the cell containing the number to round, and the number of digits to which you want to round the number. The ROUND function rounds up or down, depending on the number being rounded. If the number being rounded is between 0 and 4, Excel rounds down. If the number being rounded is between 5 and 9, Excel rounds up.

There are also two variations of the ROUND function that you can use to control the direction in which Excel rounds: ROUNDUP and ROUNDDOWN.

Round Values

1. Click the cell in which you want to store the function.
2. Click the Formulas tab.
3. Click Insert Function.

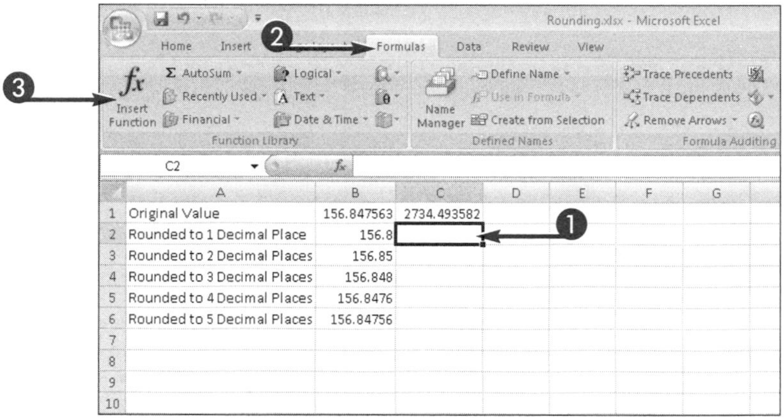

The Insert Function dialog box appears.

4. Type a description here of the function you want to use, such as **round** or **rounding**.
5. Click Go.

   Excel lists suggested functions here.

6. Click ROUND.
   - A description of the selected function appears here.
7. Click OK.

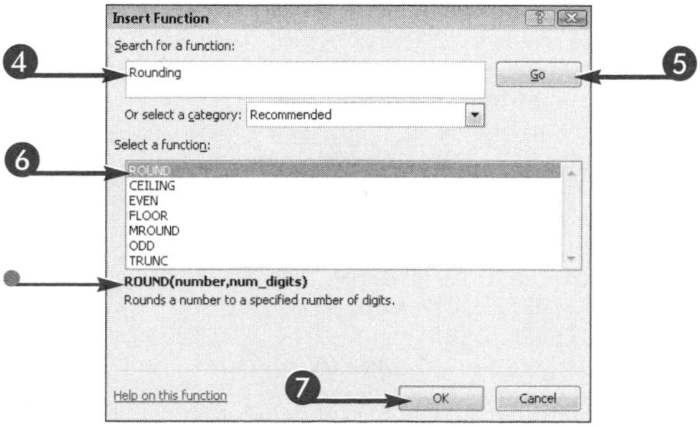

The Function Arguments dialog box appears.

8 Click here.

9 Click the cell in the worksheet containing the number you want to round.

10 Click here and type the number of digits you want to display.

- The result you can expect appears here.

11 Click OK.

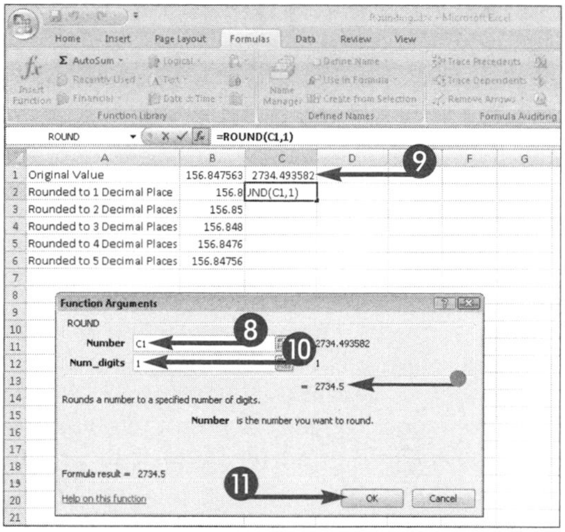

- Excel displays the result of the formula in the cell you selected in Step 1.
- The formula appears in the Formula bar.

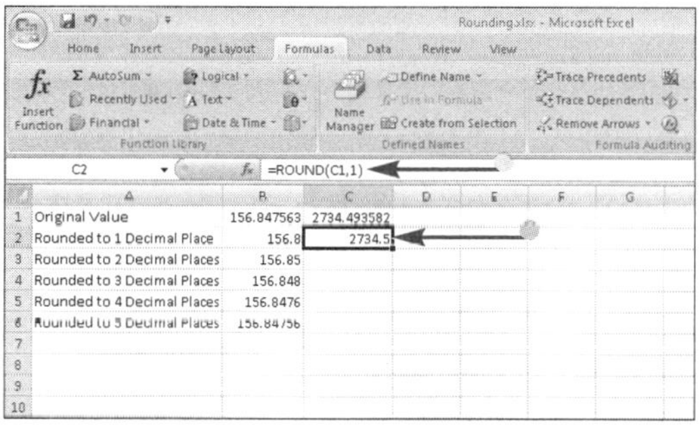

MASTER IT

What happens if I type a negative number for Num_digits?

▼ If you type **-1**, Excel rounds the digit closest to the decimal point up or down to the nearest value of ten. If you type **-2**, Excel rounds the first two digits to the left of the decimal to the nearest value of 100. Consider the value 2734.49. If you set the ROUND function argument to -1, Excel returns 2730. If you type **-2**, Excel returns 2700. If you change the value to 2755.49 and round the value with an argument of -1, Excel returns 2760. If you use an argument of -2 on this number, Excel returns 2800.

Can I round the value to the left of the decimal point?

▼ When you round the portion of the number to the left of the decimal point, Excel automatically eliminates all of the values to the right of the decimal point. Follow the steps in this section. In Step 10, type **0** to round the digit immediately to the left of the decimal.

How do I use the ROUNDUP and ROUNDDOWN functions?

▼ Both functions take the same arguments as the ROUND function. In Step 4, type **round up** or **round down** to find the correct functions. The ROUNDUP function always rounds the value up, and the ROUNDDOWN function always rounds the value down, regardless of the number's value.

Count the Number of Cells Containing Information

You can count the number of cells that contain values or dates in any range you specify using one of several counting functions available in Excel. Suppose that your worksheet contains names of students and their associated test scores. You may want to count the number of students in the worksheet to make sure that you entered all of their names. Or, you may want to count the number of test scores in the range. Or, you may want to count the number of blank cells in the range to identify missing test scores.

The COUNT function does not count cells in the range that contain text. If the range A1:A10 contains the numbers 1 to 10, the COUNT function returns the value 10. However, if cell A3 contains a word such as "Widgets," the COUNT function returns the value 9 for the range A1:A10.

To count all of the cells in a given range, including cells that contain text, you can use the COUNTA function, as shown in this section. The COUNTA function counts all non-blank cells in the range you specify.

You can also count blank cells only, and you can count cells based on conditions that you specify.

Count the Number of Cells Containing Information

1. Click the cell in which you want to store the function.
2. Click the Formulas tab.
3. Click Insert Function.

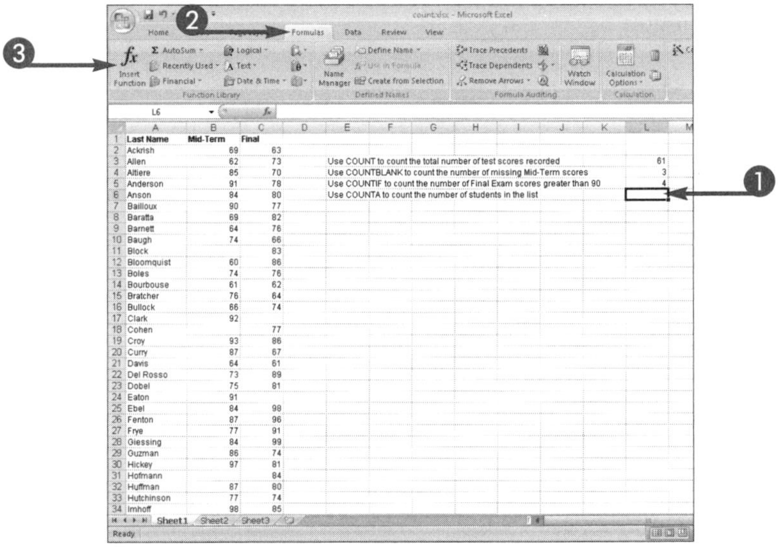

The Insert Function dialog box appears.

4. Type a description here of the function you want to use, such as **count** or **counting**.
5. Click Go.
   - Excel lists suggested functions here.
6. Click COUNTA.
   - A description of the selected function appears here.
7. Click OK.

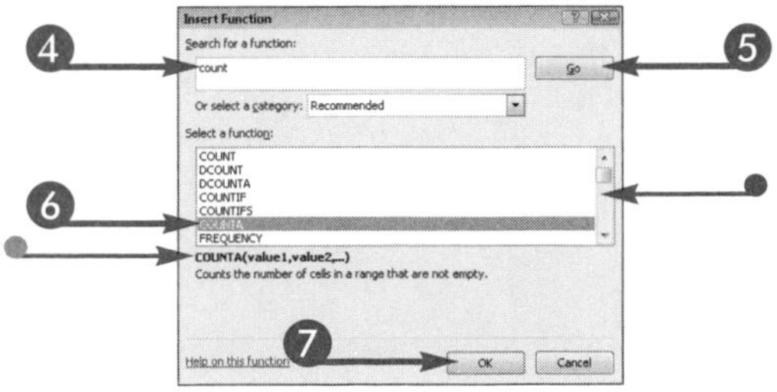

The Function Arguments dialog box appears.

8. Click here.
9. Select the range in the worksheet that you want to count.
   - The result you can expect appears here.
10. Click OK.

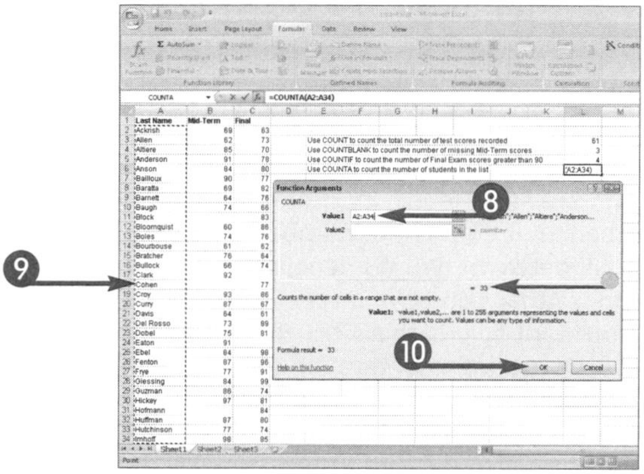

- Excel displays the result of the formula in the cell you selected in Step 1.
- The formula appears in the Formula bar.

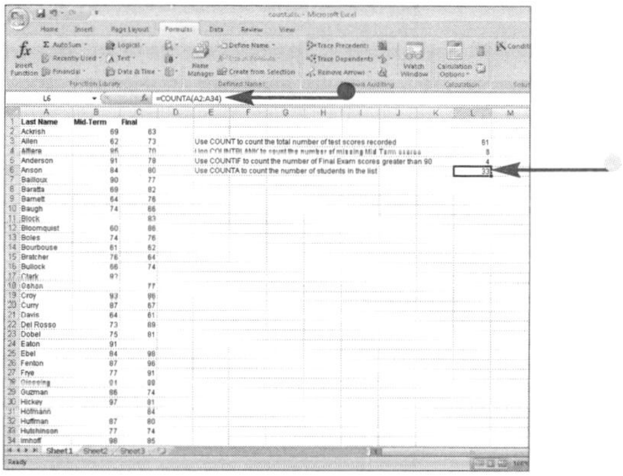

MASTER IT

How do I use the COUNT function?

▼ When you want to count numeric values only in a range, you use the COUNT function the same way that you use the COUNTA function. Follow the steps in this section. In the example, if you select B1:B34 as the range to count, Excel returns 30, excluding B1, B11, B18, and B31 because they contain text or are blank. You use the COUNTBLANK function in exactly the same way.

How do I use the COUNTIF function?

▼ The COUNTIF function lets you set conditions when Excel counts. You select a range for Excel to count and then type criteria or select a cell containing criteria. In the example, the range is C1:C34 and the criteria is >=90. Excel adds quotation marks around the criteria, so that the formula reads =COUNTIF(C1:C34,">=90").

Can I use the COUNTIF function and specify multiple criteria?

▼ No, you can use the COUNTIFS function, which is new to Excel 2007. You set the criteria range twice — once for each set of criteria. To count all of the test scores between 70 and 79, set the first range to C1:C34. Then, in the first criteria box, type **>=70**. Select C1:C34 for the second range and in the second criteria box, type **<=79**. Excel enters the formula =COUNTIFS(C1:C34,">=70",C1:C34,"<=79") and returns the value 10.

Create a Frequency Distribution

You can create a frequency distribution of numbers that counts the number of values that fall between two numeric intervals. For example, suppose that you have a set of numeric test scores, and you want to create a frequency distribution of the grades to determine the number of students who scored less than or equal to 60, the number of students who scored between 61 and 70, the number of students who scored between 71 and 80, the number of students who scored between 81 and 90, and the number of students who scored between 91 and 100, so that you can assign letter grades.

You can create five COUNTIFS formulas, as described in the section, "Count the Number of Cells Containing Information," or you can use the Histogram tool in the Analysis ToolPak. See the section, "Calculate a Conditional Sum," for instructions on installing the Analysis ToolPak.

When you use the Histogram tool, you identify the range containing your data, the bin range (which identifies the intervals into which you want to group the numbers), and an output range, where Excel will display the results.

Using the Histogram tool, you can create both a frequency distribution list and a corresponding chart.

Create a Frequency Distribution

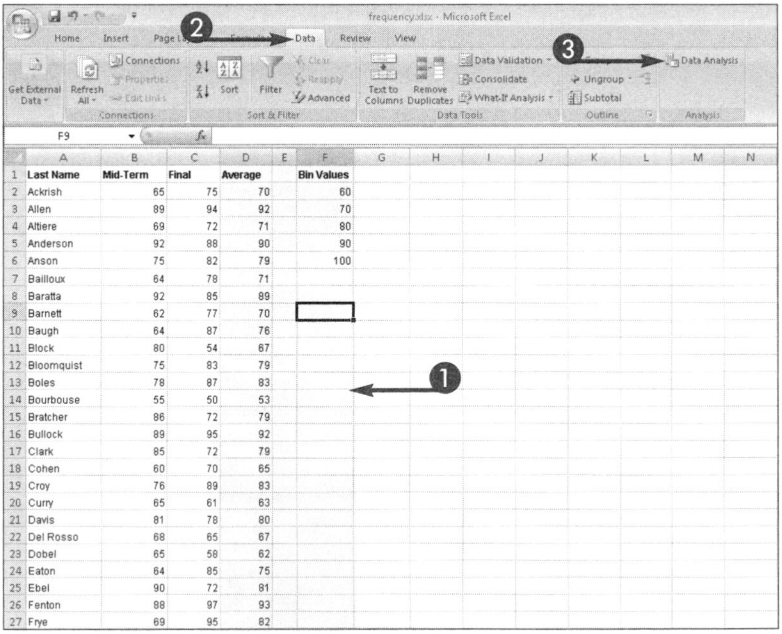

1. Set up your worksheet with the values that you want to evaluate and a bin range that identifies the highest number in each interval that you want Excel to evaluate.
2. Click the Data tab.
3. Click Data Analysis.

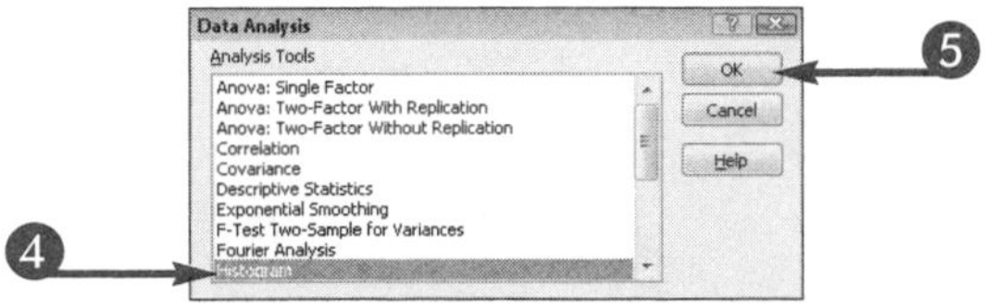

The Data Analysis dialog box appears.

4. Click Histogram.
5. Click OK.

The Histogram dialog box appears.

6 Click here and then select the input range in the worksheet.

7 Click here and then select the bin range in the worksheet.

8 Click here and then select the starting cell in the worksheet for the output range.

- You can also click here to produce a chart (☐ changes to ☑).

9 Click OK.

- Excel displays the Frequency Distribution table here.
- If you chose to include the chart, the Histogram appears.

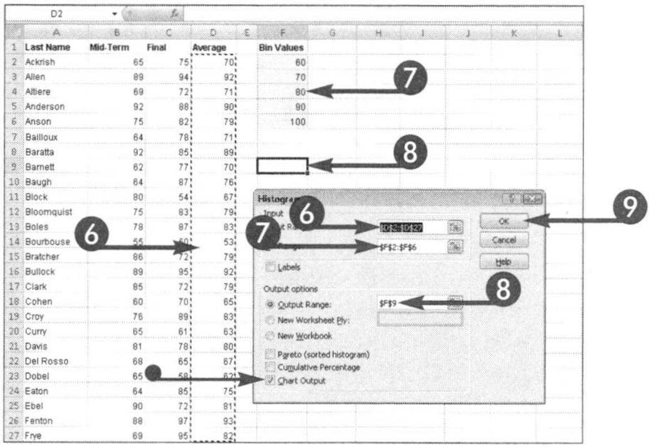

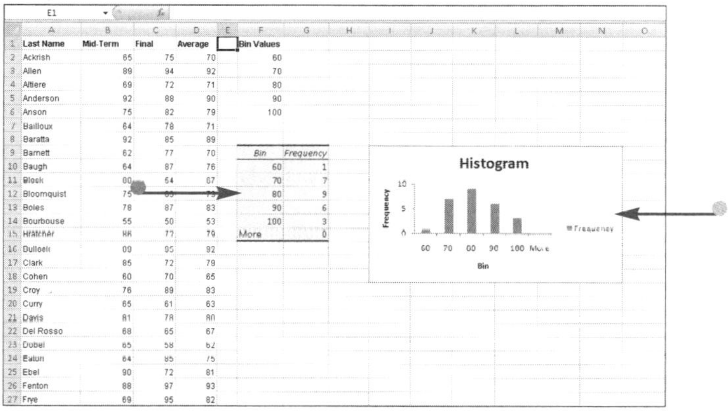

MASTER IT

Is there a function that I can use to create a frequency distribution if I must share my workbook with someone who uses Excel 2003?

▼ Yes, you can use an array formula. Set up your bin range to display two columns that represent the lowest grade and the highest grade in each range. Suppose that you enter the lowest values in cells F2 to F6 and the highest values in cells G2 to G6, and the input range is D2:D27. The array formula that you type in H2 would be as follows: **{=SUM(($D$2:$D$27>=F2)*($D$2:$D$27<=G2))}**. Remember that you do not type the curly braces ({}), but press Ctrl+Shift+Enter to enter the array formula.

If I adjust the numbers in the input range, will the frequency distribution automatically update?

▼ Not if you use the Histogram tool as described in this section. If you need to make changes to the data that you use to create the frequency distribution, you can rerun the Histogram tool, or you can set up formulas that use the new COUNTIFS function as described in the section, "Count the Number of Cells Containing Information," earlier in this chapter.

When should I click the Label option in the Histogram dialog box?

▼ Select this check box to generate labels in the frequency distribution table *only if* the first row or column of your bin range contains labels.

Find the Most Frequently Occurring Value in a Range

You can calculate the mode value of a list of values using Excel's MODE function. The mode value is the most frequently occurring value in the list. For example, suppose that your worksheet contains test scores for students. You may have set up a frequency distribution as described in the section, "Create a Frequency Distribution," to identify the number of scores that fell within a particular range. Now, you want to know what score occurred most often in the list.

Along with the mode value, you may want to calculate two other common statistical values when evaluating the scores: the mean value — also called the average value — and the median value. The mean value is calculated by adding all of the values in the list and dividing by the number of values that you added. The median value is the value that appears at the middle of a list of values. The mean, median, and mode values may or may not be the same.

The MODE function evaluates only cells that contain values and ignores cells containing text. The function takes only one argument: the range that you want Excel to evaluate.

Find the Most Frequently Occurring Value in a Range

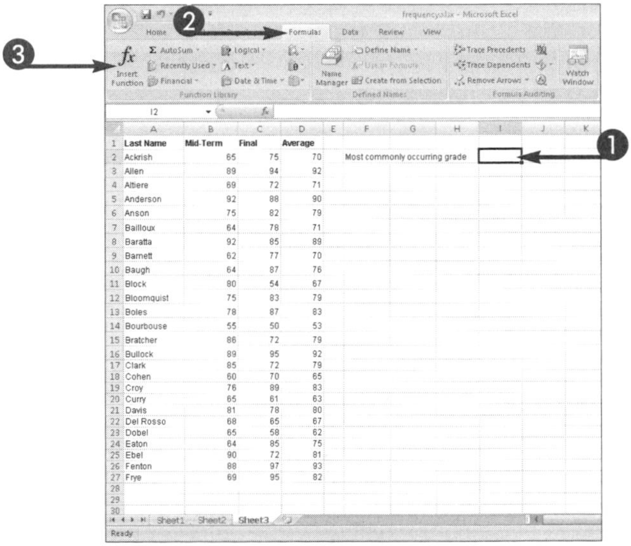

1. Click the cell in which you want to store the function.
2. Click the Formulas tab.
3. Click Insert Function.

The Insert Function dialog box appears.

4. Type a description here of the function you want to use.

   This example uses the description, "most commonly occurring value."
5. Click Go.

   Excel lists suggested functions here.
6. Click MODE.
   - A description of the selected function appears here.
7. Click OK.

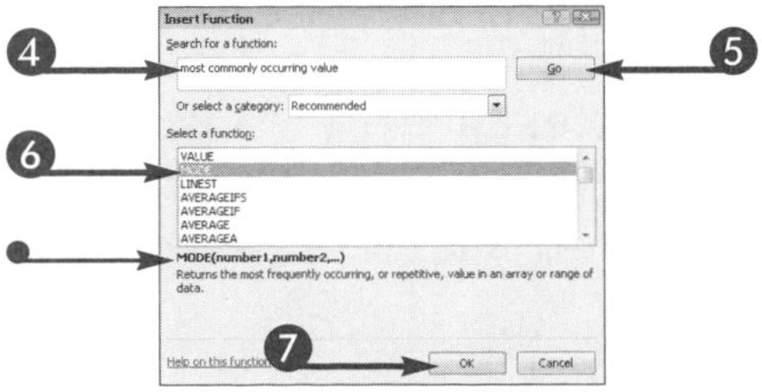

The Function Arguments dialog box appears.

8 Click here.

9 Select the range in the worksheet that you want to count.

- The result that you can expect appears here.

10 Click OK.

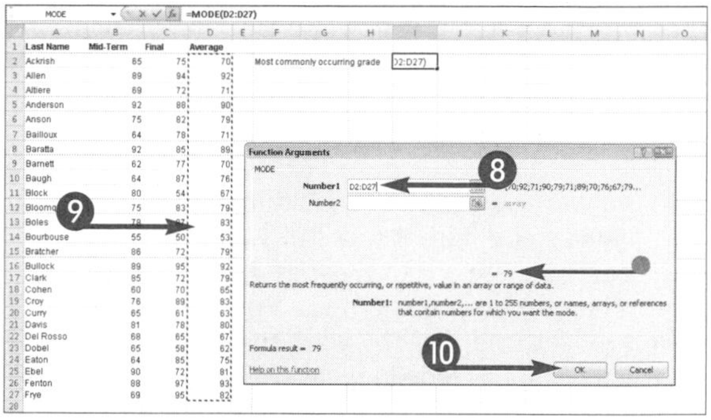

- Excel displays the result of the formula in the cell you selected in Step 1.
- The formula appears in the Formula bar.

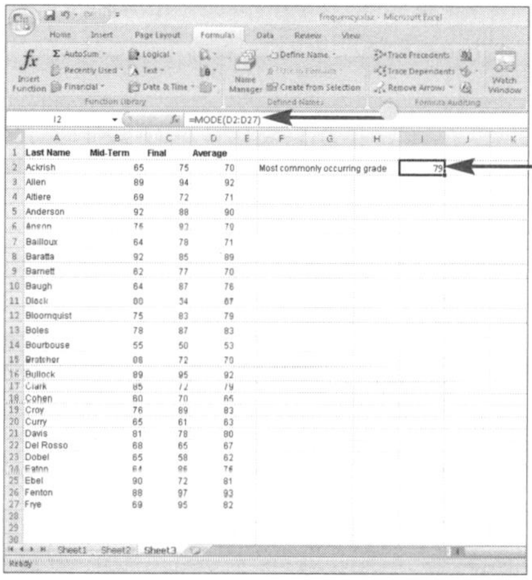

PART III

MASTER IT

How do I calculate the mean value?

▼ You can use the AVERAGE function to calculate the mean value. This function works very much like the MODE function, typically taking only one argument. See the section, "Calculate an Average," for more information.

How do I calculate the median value?

▼ You can use the MEDIAN function. Follow the steps in this section, substituting a description of **middle** in Step 4. Select the range of values for which you want to determine the midpoint value, and complete the rest of the steps in this section.

Can I count the number of times the mode value occurs in the range?

▼ Yes. Use the COUNTIF function combined with the MODE function. Suppose that the range of values that you want to evaluate appears in the range D2:D27. Use the following formula to calculate how often the mode value appears in the list: =COUNTIF (D2:D27,MODE(D2:D27)).

Calculate a Subtotal

You can use the SUBTOTAL function to create a variety of different types of subtotals to help you evaluate a list of values. For example, suppose that you keep track of sales of different types of cable services sold daily by your customer service departments in three locations, as well as services sold by telemarketers. In addition, you track the type of service purchased, the type of customer — new or existing — who purchased the service, and the date of the purchase.

To display a meaningful subtotal, you first sort the information in the order by which you want subtotals to appear. For example, if you want to display subtotals by date, you must sort the information by date. If you want the subtotals to appear by customer service branch location, you must sort the information by customer service branch location.

You are not limited to simply subtotaling sums of numbers such as sales dollars. For example, you can use the SUBTOTAL function to count the number of sales made on a given date. The function can also help you to calculate the largest sale made on a given date or the number of sales made to new customers.

Calculate a Subtotal

Sort the Information

1. Click any cell in the range you want to sort.
2. Click the Home tab.
3. Click Sort & Filter.
4. From the drop-down list that appears, click Custom Sort.

   Excel selects the entire range and the Sort dialog box appears.

5. Click here and select the column by which you want to sort the range.
   - You can click here to sort by other cell characteristics.
   - You can click here to change the sort order.
6. Click OK.

   Excel sorts the range.

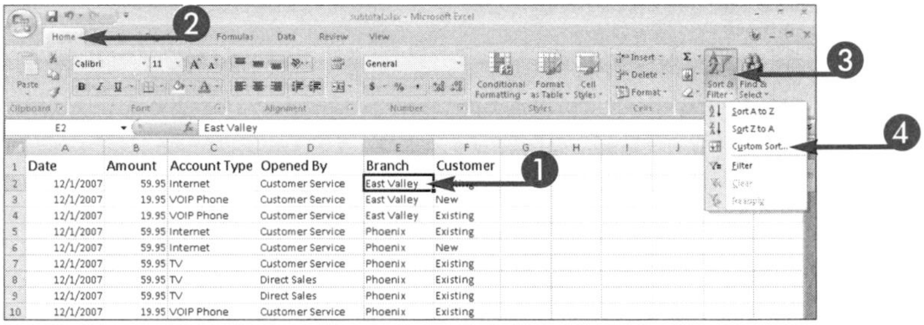

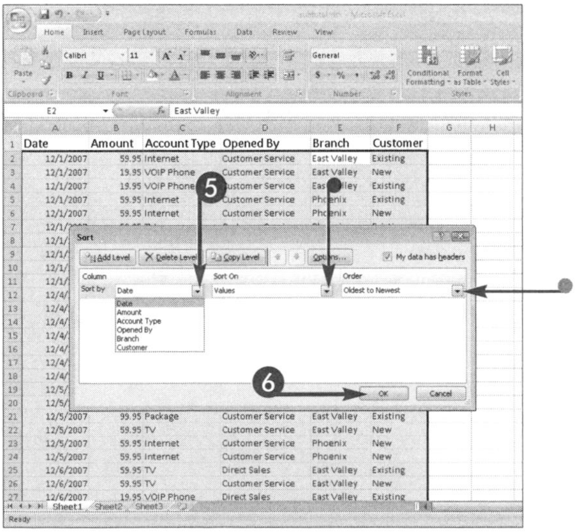

Calculate a Subtotal

1. Click the Data tab.
2. Click Subtotal.

   The Subtotal dialog box appears.

3. Click here to select the field by which you want to subtotal.
4. Click here to define the type of subtotal.
5. Click here to select the fields you want to subtotal (☐ changes to ☑).
6. Click OK.

   - Excel displays subtotals below the field that you selected in Step 5 each time the value in the field that you selected in Step 3 changes.

7. Click any subtotal.

   - The formula appears in the Formula bar.

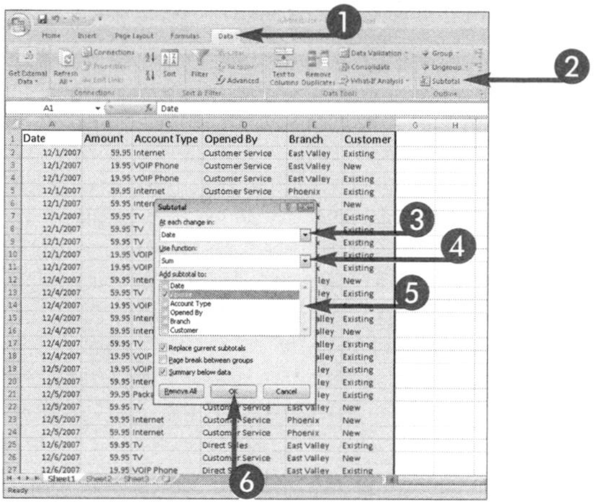

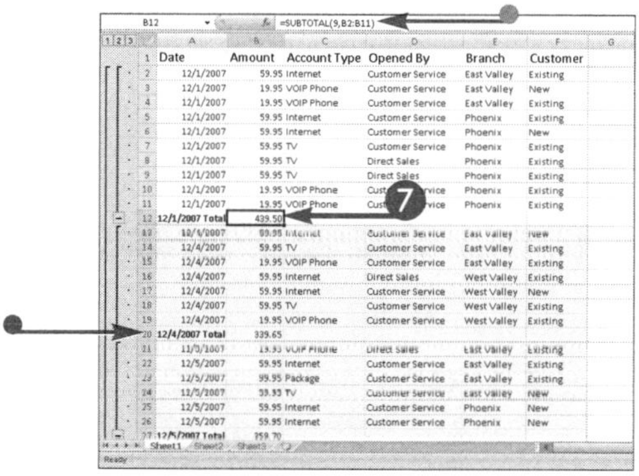

PART III

MASTER IT

In the formula, what is the purpose of the first argument, listed as "9"?

▼ The first argument of the SUBTOTAL function determines the function that Excel uses to subtotal, as follows:

1	AVERAGE
2	COUNT
3	COUNTA
4	MAX
5	MIN
6	PRODUCT
7	STDEV
8	STDEVP
9	SUM
10	VAR
11	VARP

Can I calculate different types of subtotals for the same data?

▼ Yes. For example, suppose that you want to calculate the total amount sold on each date, as well as the number of services sold by each branch on each date. Follow the steps in the subsection, "Calculate a Subtotal," to calculate the first subtotal. Then, repeat the steps, selecting Branch in Step 3, Count in Step 4, and Account Type in Step 5. Then, before you click OK in Step 6, click Replace Current Subtotals (☑ changes to ☐). When you click OK in Step 6, Excel adds another subtotal line to the list.

Calculate Elapsed Days between Dates

You can easily calculate the number of days that have elapsed between two dates. Suppose that you need to know the number of days a certain item was on sale during the year to monitor sales during promotional periods. You can enter the start and end dates of each promotion, let Excel calculate the number of days for each promotional period, and then sum the promotional days.

When you enter the starting and ending dates into a worksheet, use a format that Excel recognizes as a date format. The default date format that Excel recognizes and assigns to dates that you enter is the short date format, which is set up in the Windows Regional and Language Options dialog box. When your Regional and Language options use United States settings, Excel also recognizes the following entry formats as dates: 8-26-07, 8-26-2007, 8/26/07, 8/26/2007, 8-26/07, August 26, 2007, 26-Aug-2007, 2007/8/26, Aug 26, August 26, 8/26, and 8-26.

Because Excel stores dates that it recognizes as numbers, you can perform various mathematical calculations on dates. See the section, "View the Serial Number for a Date or Time," for details on how Excel views dates as numbers.

Calculate Elapsed Days between Dates

1. Type the starting dates in one column.
2. Type the ending dates in another column.

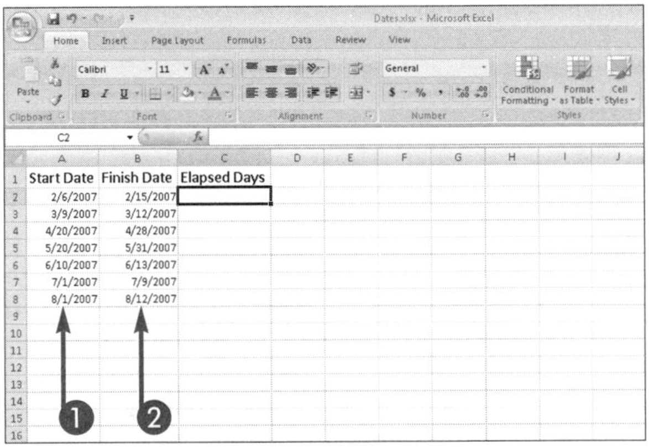

3. Click the cell in which you want to store the calculation.
4. Type =.
5. Click the cell containing the ending date.

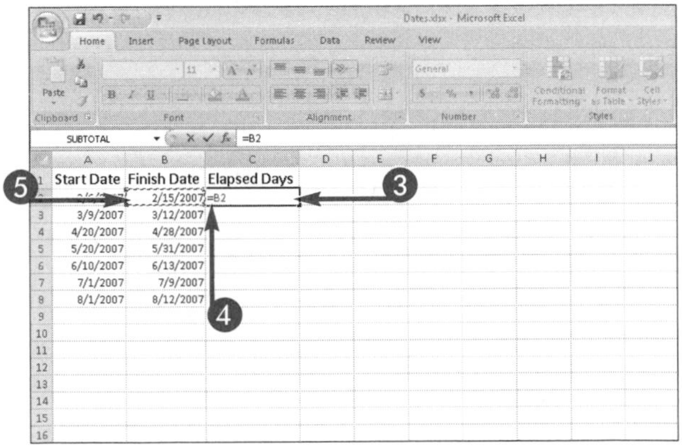

6 Type -.

7 Click the cell containing the starting date.

8 Click ☑.

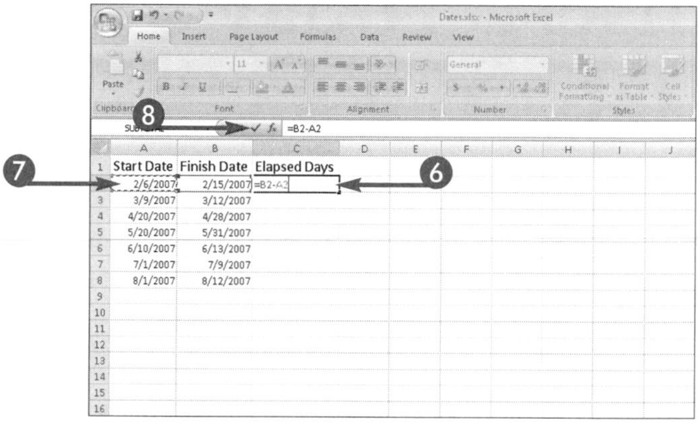

- Excel displays the number of days that elapsed between the ending date and the starting date.
- The formula appears here.

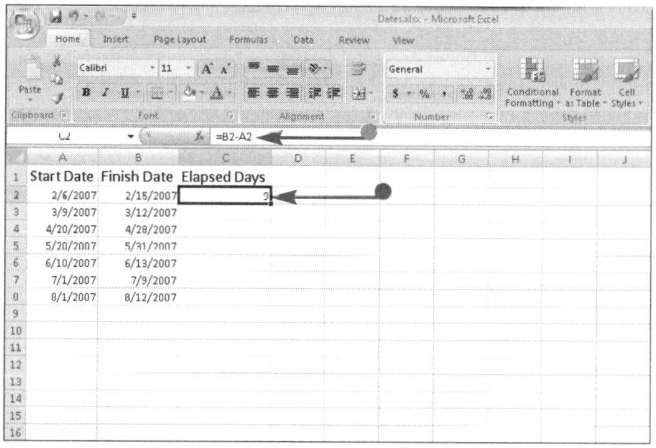

MASTER IT

How can I calculate the number of workdays and exclude weekends from my calculation?

▼ You can use the NETWORKDAYS function. This function requires two arguments: the start date and the end date. If you want, you can provide a range that contains dates of holidays that should also be excluded. If your start date appears in cell A2, your end date appears in cell B2, and your holidays appear in the range G2:G11, use the following formula: =NETWORKDAYS(A2,B2, G2:G11).

The timeframe between my dates is much longer. Can I display the value in months?

▼ Yes. Follow the steps in this section to create the formula with some changes. In Step 4, type =(. In Step 7, click the cell containing the starting date, and type). Before performing Step 8, type **/12**. Enclosing the subtraction in parentheses ensures that Excel performs the calculations in the proper order and calculates the subtraction before dividing by the number of months.

Why do I see a date in the year 1900 instead of the number of elapsed days?

▼ The cell in which you stored the formula is formatted as a date. Click the Home tab. In the Number group, click ▾ and select General to display the value of the elapsed days.

I typed "August 26 2007" in a formula. Why does Excel not recognize it as a date?

▼ You omitted the comma after 26. As a result, Excel does not recognize the date and treats it as text.

Insert Today's Date in a Cell

You can quickly and easily enter today's date in any cell using the TODAY function. Suppose that you have a worksheet that you update regularly, and then distribute printed copies of it to others. By placing today's date in a cell, you date the worksheet so that anyone viewing it knows the date for which the information they are viewing is valid.

When you use the TODAY function, Excel stores a non-static date in your worksheet that updates each time you open the workbook. For example, if today is August 26, 2007, the cell containing the TODAY function displays August 26, 2007. However, if you reopen the workbook on August 31, 2007, the cell containing the TODAY function will read August 31, 2007. If you do not want the date to update each time you open the workbook, you can convert the date to a static value.

In addition to the TODAY function, you can use either of two related functions: the NOW function and the DATE function. For details on the NOW function, see the section, "View the Serial Number for a Date or Time." For details on the DATE function, see the section, "Calculate an Excel Date Number."

Insert Today's Date in a Cell

1. Click the cell in which you want to store the function.
2. Click the Formulas tab.
3. Click Insert Function.

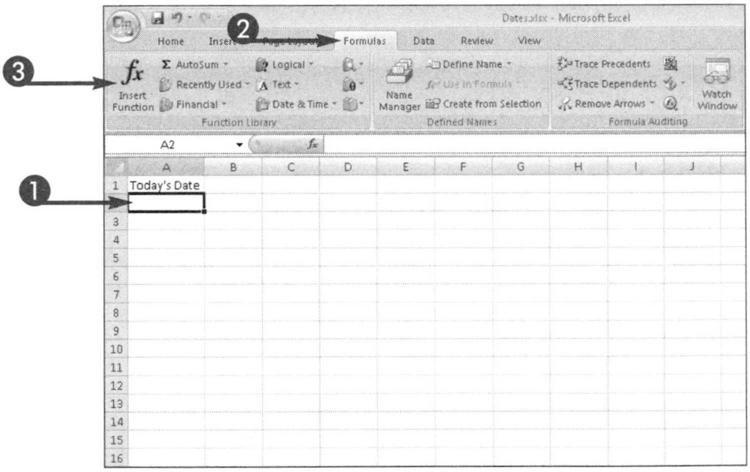

The Insert Function dialog box appears.

4. Type a description here for the function you want to use.

   This examples uses today's date.
5. Click Go.
6. Click TODAY.
   - A description of the selected function appears here.
7. Click OK.

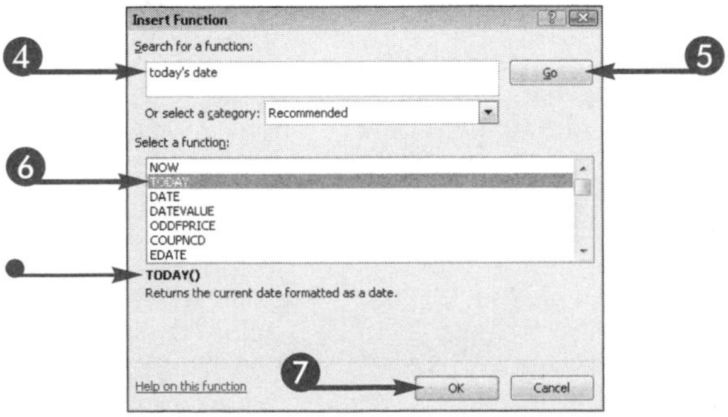

The Function Arguments dialog box appears.

- The dialog box explains that the function takes no arguments.

8 Click OK.

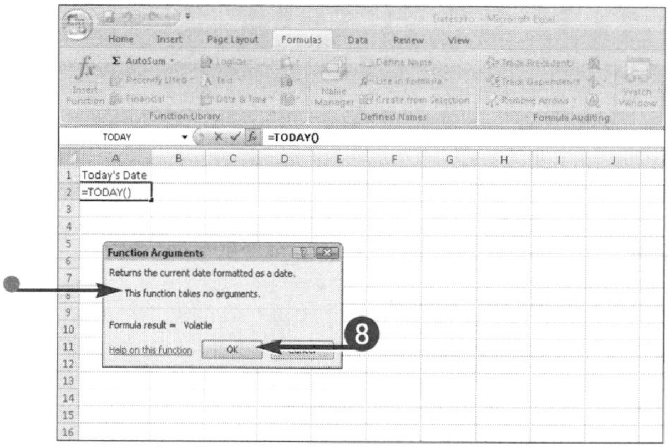

- Excel displays the result of the formula in the cell you selected in Step 1.
- The formula appears in the Formula bar.

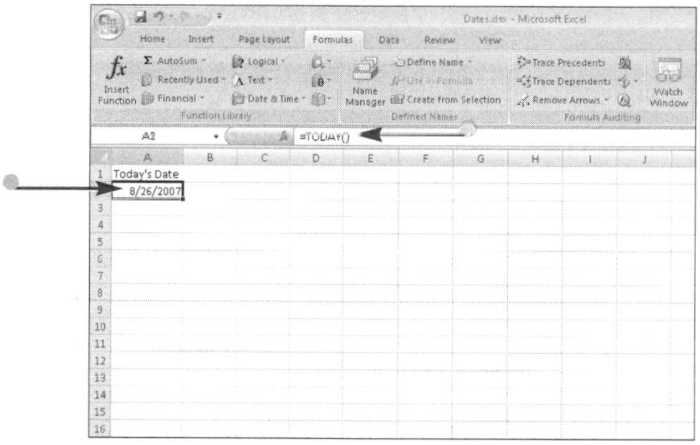

MASTER IT

If I do not want the date to change each time I open the workbook, how should I set up the TODAY function?

▼ Instead of using the TODAY function and following the steps in this section, click the cell in which you want to display the date as a static value. Then press Ctrl+; and press Enter, or click ✓. Excel enters today's date as a static value that does not update when you reopen the workbook tomorrow.

How does the NOW function differ from the TODAY function?

▼ When you use the NOW function, Excel enters both today's date and the current time in hours and minutes. When you use the TODAY function, Excel enters only today's date. If you use the NOW function, you can watch Excel update the time portion of the function by periodically pressing the F9 key.

What does the DATE function do?

▼ The DATE function helps you enter a specific year, month, and date in a your worksheet. You can avoid using the DATE function by typing the specific date using a date format that Excel recognizes; see the section, "Calculate Elapsed Days between Dates," for a list of date formats that Excel recognizes when your Regional and Language options use United States settings.

Work with Times

You can use times in calculations. For example, you can determine the amount of rainfall that occurred between two different times. You can enter a time in any cell by typing the time in a format that Excel recognizes. The default time format that Excel recognizes appears in the Windows Regional and Language Options dialog box. When your Regional and Language options use United States settings, Excel also recognizes the following entry formats as time: 8:10:35 PM, 8:10:35 pm, 8:10 PM, 8:10 pm, 8:10, and 20:10. When you do not enter "AM" or "PM," you can control the time that Excel enters by using the 24-hour clock; for example, 20:10 equals 8:10 PM.

You can also enter a time using the TIME function, as described in this section. The TIME function takes three arguments — one for the hour, one for the minute, and one for the second. When you use the TIME function, Excel enters a static time in the worksheet as a serial number that Excel recognizes and displays as a time, automatically assigning a custom format to the cell. To learn more about the serial numbers that Excel uses for dates and times, see the section, "View the Serial Number for a Date or Time."

Work with Times

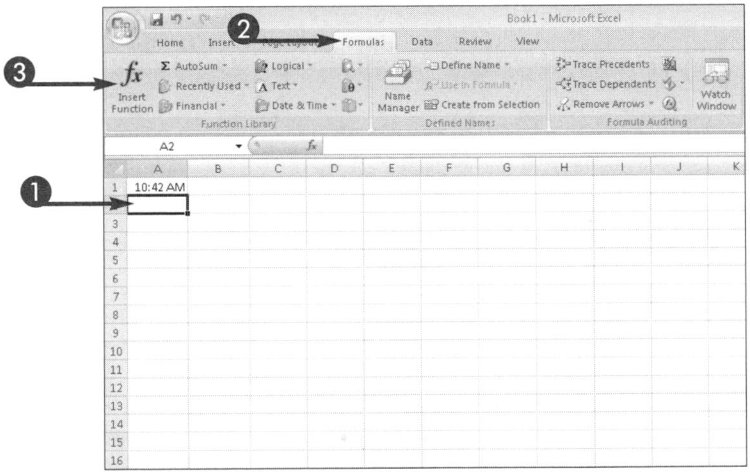

1. Click the cell in which you want to store the function.
2. Click the Formulas tab.
3. Click Insert Function.

The Insert Function dialog box appears.

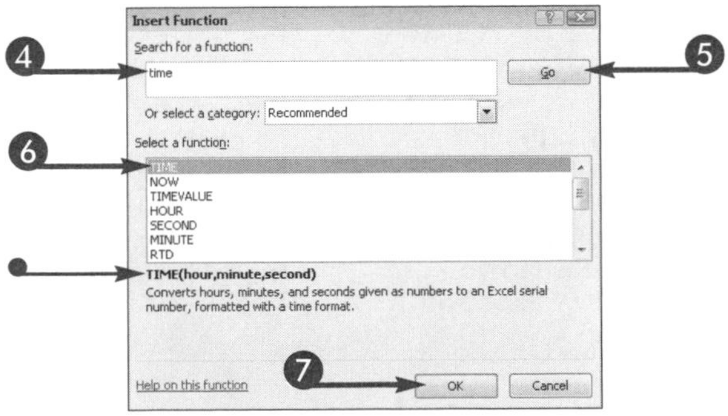

4. Type a description here for the function that you want to use.

   This example uses time.
5. Click Go.
6. Click TIME.
   - A description of the selected function appears here.
7. Click OK.

The Function Arguments dialog box appears.

8 Click here and type a number for hours.

Note: Use the 24-hour clock to enter a PM time.

9 Click here and type a number for minutes.

10 Click here and type a number for seconds.

Note: You can select cells for any of these values.

11 Click OK.

- Excel displays the result of the formula in the cell you selected in Step 1.
- The formula appears in the Formula bar.

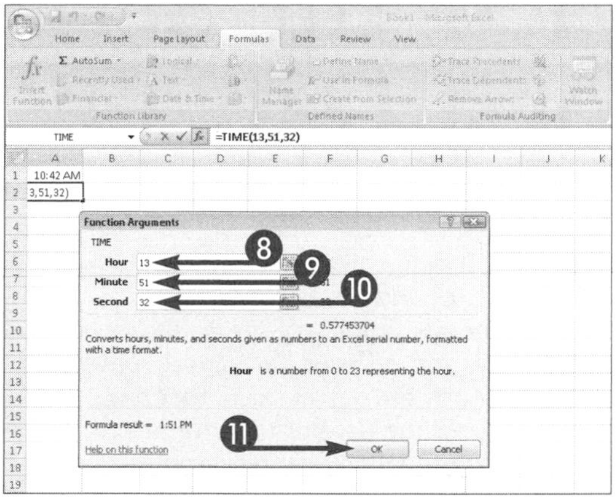

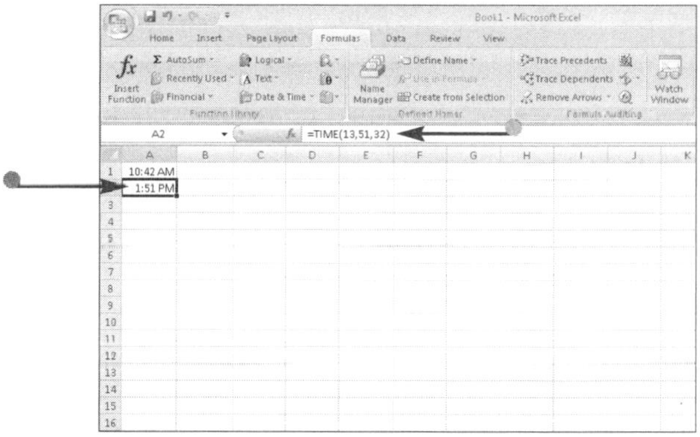

MASTER IT

How can I convert a time stored as a text string to a time stored as a number?

▼ Use the TIMEVALUE function, which takes only one argument — a string that represents the time. Type the time, separating hours, minutes, and seconds using a colon, or select a cell that contains a time stored as text. After you create the function, format the cell using a time format. Click the Home tab, click ▾ in the Number group, and select Time.

How do I calculate the difference between two times?

▼ Type the times into cells, such as A1 and A2, without using the TIME function. If the later time appears in cell A2, then use the formula, =(A2-A1)*24, and format the cell as General. Remember to use the 24-hour clock to enter times later than 12:00 PM, and subtract the later time from the earlier time; calculating a negative time results in pound signs (#) appearing in the formula cell.

What is the decimal value that appears in the Function Arguments dialog box?

▼ The decimal value is the serial number Excel calculates that corresponds to the time you enter. See the section, "View the Serial Number for a Date or Time," for details on serial numbers.

Are there limits to the numbers I can use in the TIME function?

▼ For hours, the value must be between 0 and 23. For minutes and seconds, the value must be between 0 and 59.

View the Serial Number for a Date or Time

You can eliminate the confusion that sometimes arises when working with date and time functions in Excel if you understand how Excel treats dates and times. Excel does not handle dates and times as simple entries. In the background, without any action on your part, Excel converts to a serial number any entry you make that remotely resembles one of the date or time formats that Excel recognizes. The *serial number* represents the number of days that have elapsed since the imaginary date January 0, 1900. January 1, 1900 is serial number 1, January 2, 1900 is serial number 2, December 31, 1900 is serial number 366, and so on.

Excel also applies the serial number concept to times; the serial number for a time is represented by a decimal value and represents the number of hours, minutes, and seconds that have elapsed since midnight, which is 0.00000000. For example, 1:00 AM is serial number .0416666667, noon is .500000000, and so on.

If you import date or time entries or you enter a date or time as a text entry, you need to convert the entries to serial numbers in order to use them in calculations.

View the Serial Number for a Date or Time

View a Date Serial Number

1. Type a date into a cell.

   If you used a recognizable format, Excel displays the date as a date.

2. Click the cell containing the date.
3. Click the Home tab.
4. Click ▾.
5. Select General.

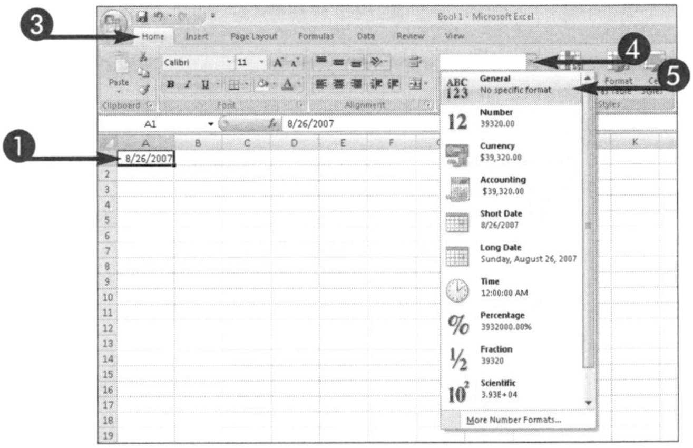

Excel displays the date as a serial number in both the worksheet and the Formula bar.

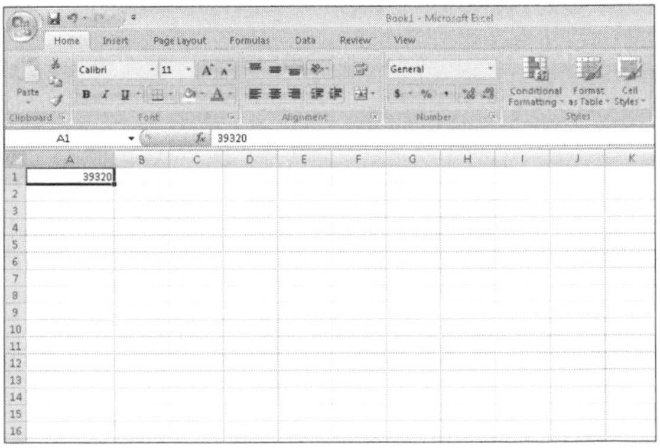

Convert the Current Date and Time to a Serial Number

1. Type **=NOW()** into a cell and click ✓.
   - Excel displays the current date and time.
2. Click the Home tab.
3. Click the Copy button.
4. Click another cell.
5. Click the down arrow on the Paste button.
6. Click Paste Values.
   - Excel pastes the serial number for the date and time in the cell you selected in Step 4.

Note: *The portion of the serial number to the left of the decimal represents the date, and the portion to the right of the decimal represents the time.*

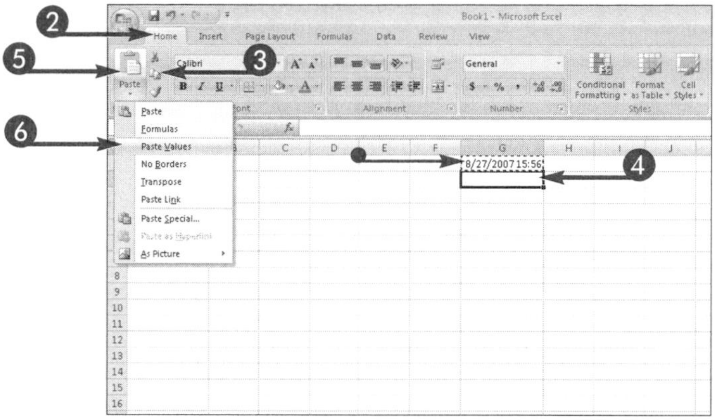

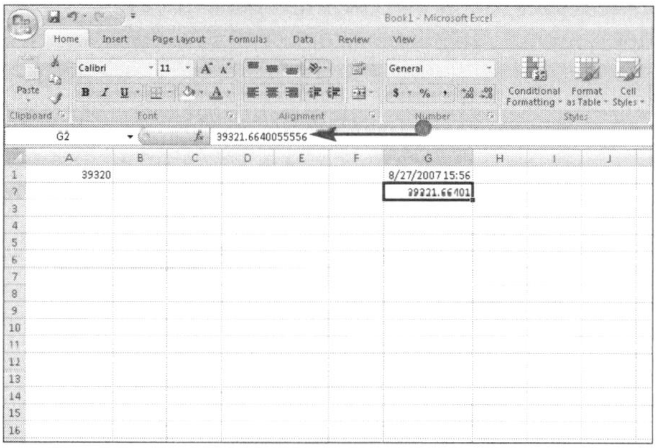

MASTER IT

Are the date and time that Excel enters when I use the NOW function static or changing?

▼ They are changing; they will update each time you recalculate the workbook by entering a formula or function, pressing F9, or closing and reopening the workbook. You can convert them to static values. Select the cell and press Ctrl+; to convert the date portion. Then, press the spacebar and press Ctrl+Shift+; to convert the time portion.

Can I directly enter a static date and a time in the same cell?

▼ You can enter a combination of a recognizable date format followed by a recognizable time format. For example, if you use U.S. settings in the Regional and Language Options dialog box, and you type **08/27/07** followed by a space and then type **16:09:00** and press Enter, Excel displays "08/27/2007 16:09" in the worksheet. In the Formula bar, you see the following: "08/27/2007 4:09:00 PM".

Why do I need to know about serial numbers?

▼ If your use of dates and times is minimal and you do not use them in calculations, you probably do not need to know about serial numbers. However, if you use dates or times in calculations, then understanding serial numbers can help you achieve the proper results, because Excel actually uses serial numbers in date and time calculations.

Calculate a Serial Date Number

You can use the DATE function to create a date. This function is particularly useful if you have imported date information into Excel and the different parts of each date appear in separate columns. For example, the month may appear in one column, the date in a second column, and the year in a third column. You can use the DATE function to create a fourth column that combines the values in the original three columns into entries that contain the complete date; Excel can then recognize these entries as dates and can use them properly in calculations.

The DATE function takes three arguments: the month, the day, and the year. You can type these values, or you can click cells in the worksheet that contain the values.

The DAY, MONTH, and YEAR functions are related to the DATE function; you can use them to identify the number of a day, month, or year of a date that you have displayed as a serial number. Each function takes only one argument: a serial number between 1 and 31 for the DAY function, a serial number between 1 and 12 for the MONTH function, and a serial number between 1900 and 9999 for the YEAR function.

Calculate a Serial Date Number

1. Click the cell in which you want to store the function.
2. Click the Formulas tab.
3. Click Insert Function.

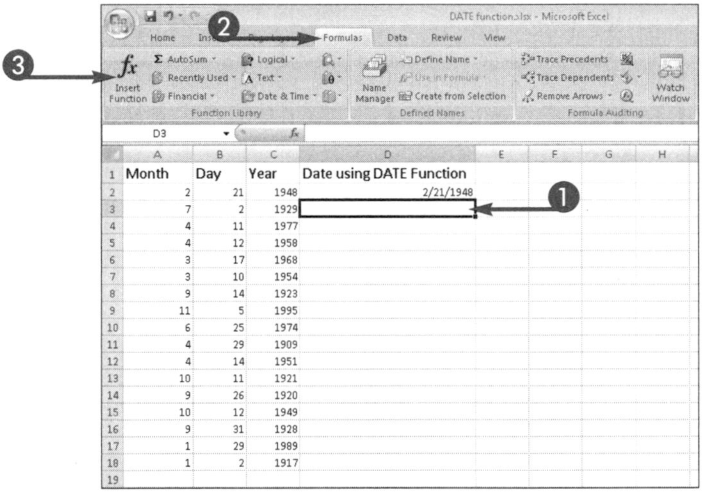

The Insert Function dialog box appears.

4. Type a description here of the function you want to use.

   This example uses date.
5. Click Go.
6. Click DATE.
   - A description of the selected function appears here.
7. Click OK.

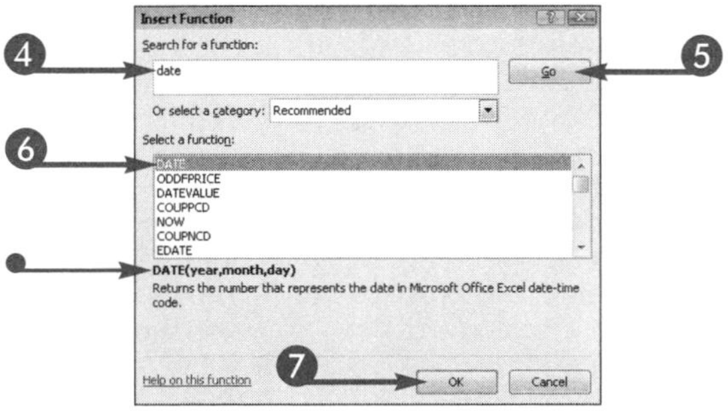

The Function Arguments dialog box appears.

8. Click here and type the cell address that contains a year value.
9. Click here and type the cell address that contains a month value.
10. Click here and type the cell address that contains a day value.
11. Click OK.

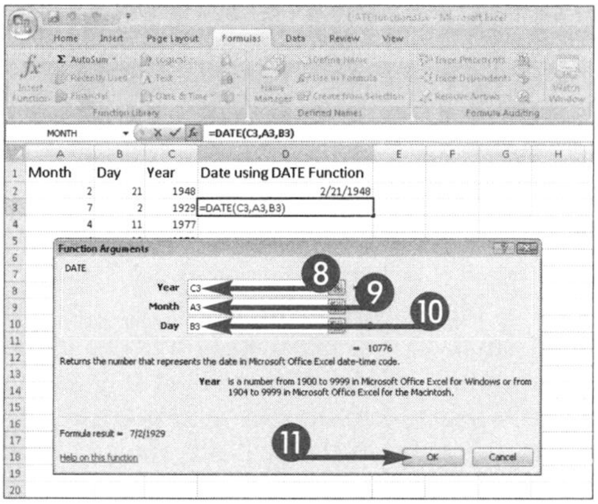

- Excel displays the result of the formula in the cell you selected in Step 1.
- The formula appears in the Formula bar.

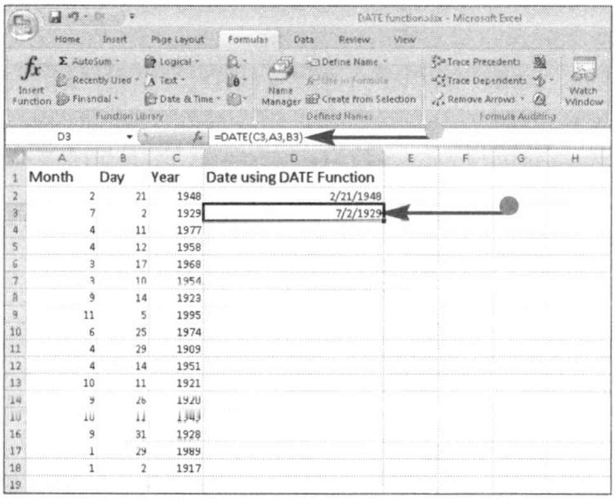

MASTER IT

How do I use the DAY, MONTH, or YEAR functions?

▼ Each function requires only one argument — a number or a cell containing a number. Each function is most often used to determine the day, month, or year of a date, expressed as a serial number. For example, if you type **July 2, 2008** in cell A1 and apply the General format, Excel returns the serial number 39631 — the number of days that have elapsed since January 1, 1900. If you then use the DAY function with cell A1 as the argument, Excel returns 2 — the second day of July. If you use the MONTH function, Excel returns 7, and if you use the YEAR function, Excel returns 2008.

When I used the YEAR function with an argument of 2008, why did Excel return 1905?

▼ The YEAR function converts a serial number to a year. 2008 was not a year when you used it as an argument; it was a serial number representing the 2,008th day since January 1, 1900. When you remember that the YEAR function displays only the year portion of the serial date, you will find that many serial numbers serving as arguments to the YEAR function return identical values. For example, if you supply any of the serial numbers between 1828 and 2192 to the YEAR function, Excel displays 1905 for all of them.

Convert a Text Date to a Date Value

You can use the DATEVALUE function to convert a date formatted as a text string to a date that Excel can use in calculations. This function is particularly useful if you have imported date information into Excel and the dates came into Excel formatted as text entries. That is, the date entry appears in a cell formatted as text, or an apostrophe precedes the entry in the cell; the apostrophe signals Excel that whatever follows should be treated as text, even if Excel would have ordinarily formatted the entry differently. You can use the DATEVALUE function to convert these date-like text entries into valid date entries; Excel can then handle them properly in calculations.

The DATEVALUE function takes only one argument: the text entry that you want Excel to treat as a date. You can either type the argument or you can point to a cell that contains the date formatted as a text entry. When you use the DATEVALUE function, Excel displays the serial number for the date, but you can change the appearance of the serial number to a date format.

Convert a Text Date to a Date Value

1. Click the cell in which you want to store the function.
2. Click the Formulas tab.
3. Click Insert Function.

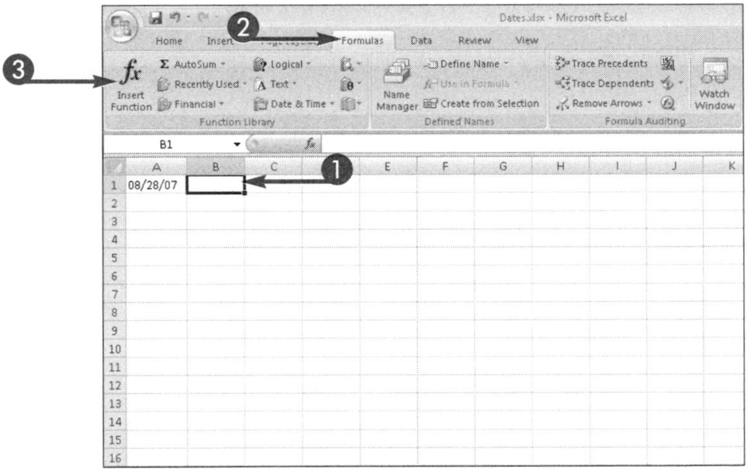

The Insert Function dialog box appears.

4. Type a description here of the function you want to use.

   This example uses date.

5. Click Go.
6. Click DATEVALUE.
   - A description of the selected function appears here.
7. Click OK.

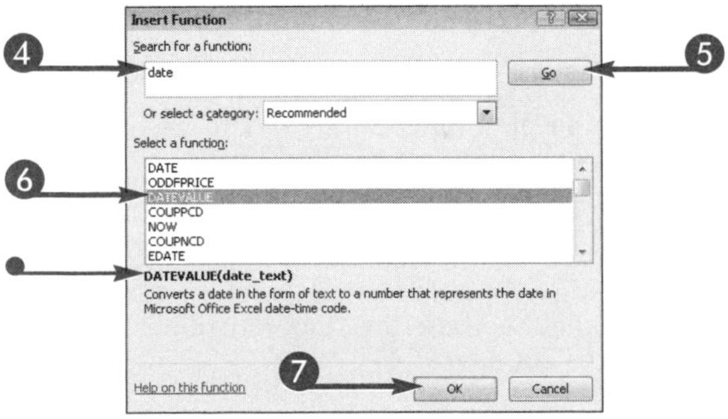

The Function Arguments dialog box appears.

8. Click here.
9. Click the cell in the worksheet containing a date formatted as text.
   - Excel displays the anticipated result here.
10. Click OK.

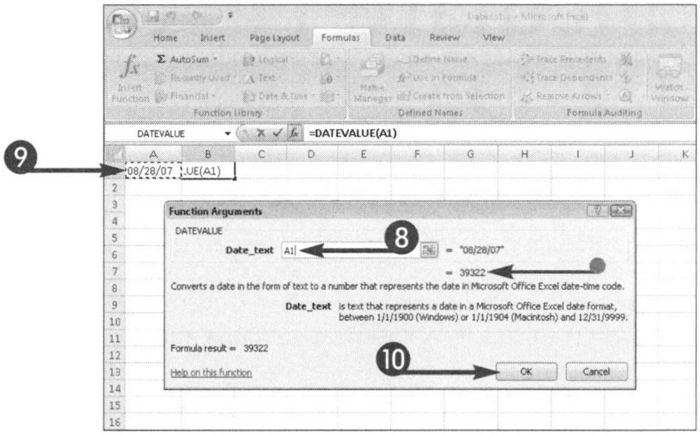

- Excel displays the result of the formula in the cell you selected in Step 1.
- The formula appears in the Formula bar.

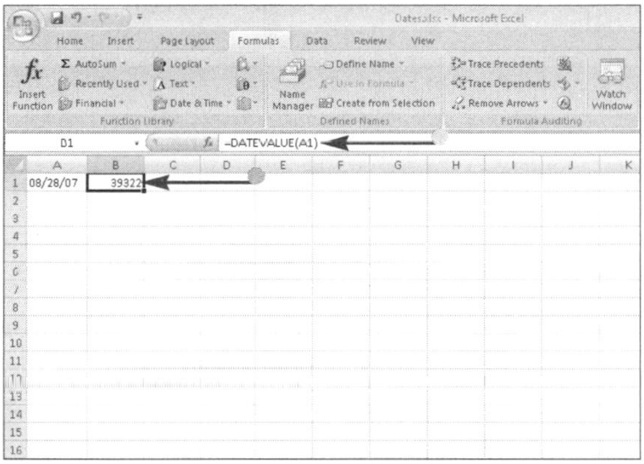

PART III

MASTER IT

How do I change a serial number to make it look like a date?

▼ Click the Home tab and then click ▾ in the Number group. From the drop-down list that appears, select Short Date or Long Date. Short Date returns the format 8/27/2007, and Long Date returns the format Tuesday, August 28, 2007 if you use US settings in the Regional and Language Options dialog box.

Why does Excel return a #VALUE! error when I use the DATEVALUE function?

▼ You probably supplied a cell containing a value as an argument; it may have been a value, a value formatted as a date, or even a value formatted as text. The DATEVALUE function requires a number that is formatted as text and looks like a recognizable date for its argument.

How did you manage to get the date format 08/28/07 to appear in this example?

▼ By formatting the cell as text. When you format a cell as text, you essentially tell Excel to leave your entry exactly as you typed it. You can create a date-like entry like this one either by formatting the cell as text or by preceding the entry with an apostrophe when you type it. If you choose to format the cell as text, you must apply the formatting before you type the entry.

Calculate Part of a Date

You can use the WEEKDAY function to determine the day of the week on which a particular date fell or will fall. You can make the determination for dates that you enter into your worksheet, or you can use it in combination with the DATE function to specify a date that you have not stored in your worksheet.

The WEEKDAY function converts a serial number to a value that represents the day of the week. Excel lets you define three different ways to associate numbers with the days of the week: By default, Excel assigns 1 to Sunday, 2 to Monday, 3 to Tuesday, and so on, assigning 7 to Saturday. If you prefer, you can assign 1 to Monday, 2 to Tuesday, and so on, with 7 being assigned to Sunday. Or, you can use the numbers 0 to 6 instead of 1 to 7, and assign 0 to Monday, 1 to Tuesday, and so on, with 6 being assigned to Sunday.

The WEEKDAY function requires one argument: the serial number that you want to convert. You can type the serial number as the argument, or you can point to a cell that contains the serial number.

Calculate Part of a Date

Using an Excel Serial Number

1. Click the cell in which you want to store the function.
2. Click the Formulas tab.
3. Click Insert Function.

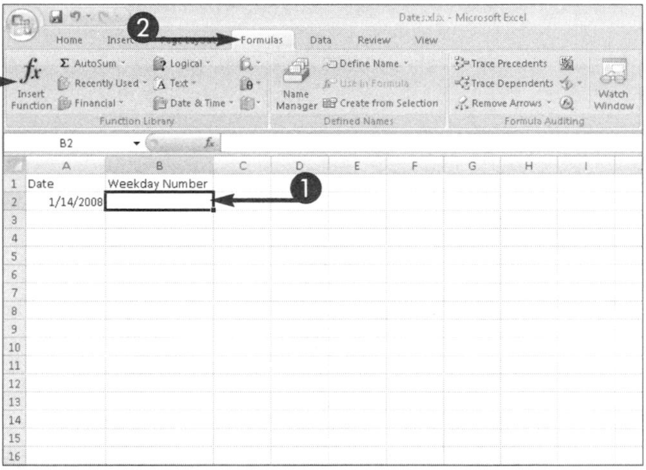

The Insert Function dialog box appears.

4. Type a description here of the function you want to use.

   This example uses week day.

5. Click Go.
6. Click WEEKDAY.
   - A description of the selected function appears here.
7. Click OK.

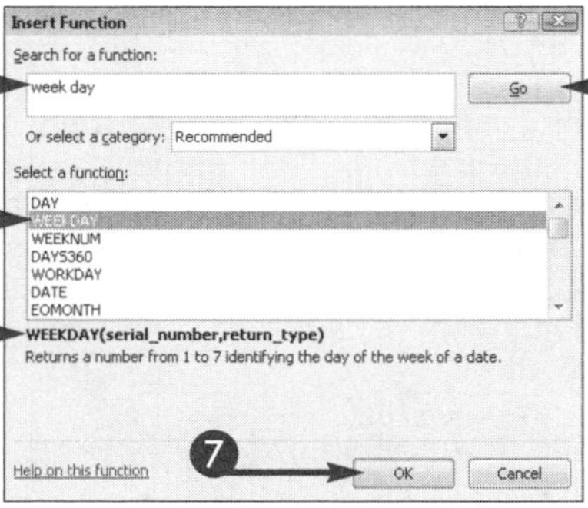

The Function Arguments dialog box appears.

8. Click here.
9. Click the cell in the worksheet containing a date.
   - Excel displays the anticipated result here.
10. Click OK.

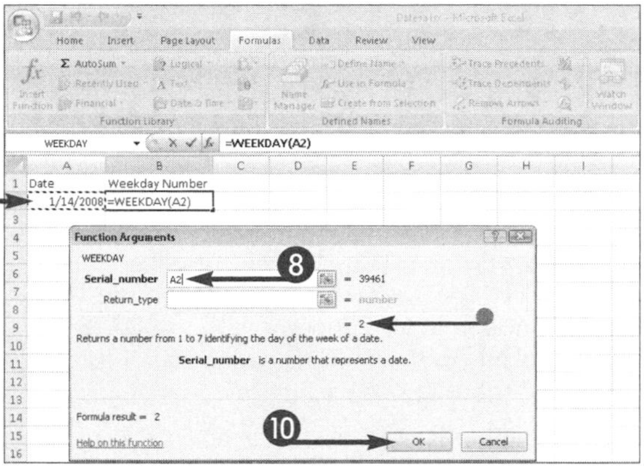

- Excel displays the result of the formula in the cell you selected in Step 1.

Note: *In this example, January 14, 2008 is a Monday.*

- The formula appears in the Formula bar.

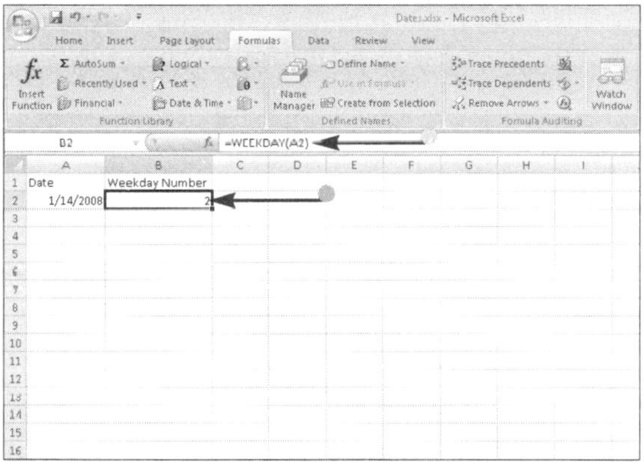

PART III

MASTER IT

Why does Excel sometimes return the weekday number, and other times an error?

▼ The WEEKDAY function can be particular. Sometimes, it is smart enough to recognize a date formatted as text as a date, and sometimes it does not recognize the date. When the WEEKDAY function does not recognize an entry as a date, it returns an error because it is trying to convert a serial number. For best results, always format your date entries as dates.

Why does Excel say that January 14, 2008 is a Sunday?

▼ When you set up the WEEKDAY function, you probably specified a return value of 2. In this case, Excel assigns 1 to Monday, not Sunday. As a result, when Excel returns a value of 1 under these circumstances, the result actually refers to Monday and is the equivalent of specifying no return value and seeing a result of 2.

When would I specify a return value other than 1?

▼ Specifying a return value argument for the WEEKDAY function is a matter of personal preference and possibly convenience. Some people feel that the first day of the week is Monday, not Sunday. Others feel that the first day of the week is Monday and that it should be numbered as 0. If you need to share your workbook with someone who shares these sentiments, specify a return value argument.

continued

Calculate Part of a Date *(Continued)*

Suppose that you want to know the day of the week for a date that you do not have stored in your worksheet. Do you need to enter the date to use the WEEKDAY function? No. You can use the WEEKDAY function in conjunction with the DATE function. You set up the DATE function to act as the argument for the WEEKDAY function.

The DATE function is used in the section, "Calculate a Serial Date Number." To briefly review, the DATE function requires three arguments: the month, the day, and the year. The DATE function then converts the information you supply in the arguments to a serial number. In this section, you use the DATE function as the argument for the WEEKDAY function to determine the day of the week for a date not stored in your worksheet.

When you specify the arguments for the DATE function, you must use a serial number between 1 and 31 for the DAY argument, a serial number between 1 and 12 for the MONTH argument, and a serial number between 1900 and 9999 for the YEAR argument.

Calculate Part of a Date *(continued)*

Using a Calendar Date

1. Click the cell in which you want to store the function.
2. Type **=WEEKDAY(DATE(**

Note: *As you type, Excel suggests functions that match your typing. You can use the down arrow if necessary to point at one, and press Tab to select it. Excel fills in opening parentheses as appropriate.*

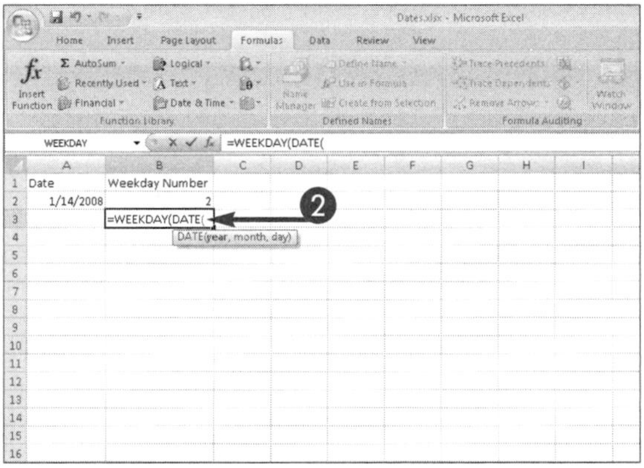

3. Type a number for the year.
4. Type a comma (,).
5. Type a number for the month, followed by a comma.
6. Type a number for the day.

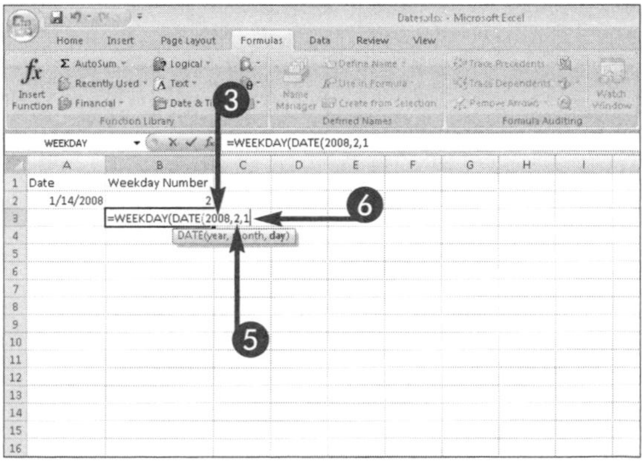

7 Type)).

8 Click ☑ or press Enter.

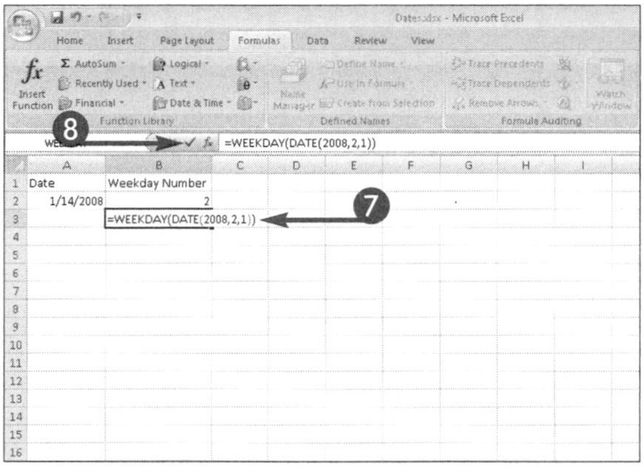

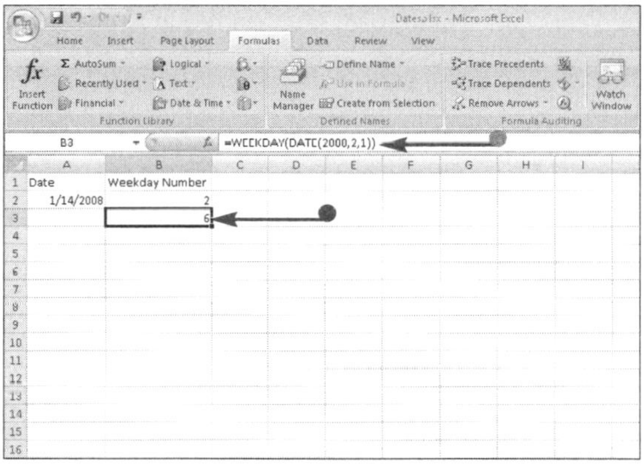

- Excel displays the result of the formula in the cell you selected in Step 1.
- The formula appears in the Formula bar.

In this example, Excel returns 6, indicating that February 1, 2008 is a Friday.

MASTER IT

Why does Excel return 7 when I type 08 for the year, 02 for the month, and 01 for the day?

▼ You typed a two-digit year. Excel typically interprets two-digit years as occurring between 1900 and 1999. To ensure that Excel uses the correct year, use all four digits of the year. Select the cell containing the function and press F2 to edit it. Change 08 to **2008** and press ☑; Excel updates the result of the formula to 6.

What happens if I use negative numbers as arguments for the DATE function?

▼ You cannot use a negative number for the year argument, but you can for the month and the day argument. Excel subtracts negative values for the Month argument from the year value. For example, if your DATE function reads =DATE(2008,-2,1), Excel returns 10/1/2007 — the first day of the month that occurs two months before 2008 begins.

What happens if I use an argument greater than 12 for a month in the DATE function?

▼ Excel adds the months to the year value. For example, if your DATE function reads =DATE(2007,14,1), Excel returns February 1, 2008. You can do the same thing with day arguments greater than 31. For example, if your DATE function reads =DATE(2008,1,32), Excel returns February 2, 2008.

Determine the Week of the Year

You can use the WEEKNUM function to determine the week of the year in which a particular date fell or will fall. You can make the determination for dates you enter into your worksheet, or you can use the WEEKNUM function in combination with the DATE function to specify a date that you have not stored in your worksheet.

The WEEKNUM function converts a serial number to a value between 1 and 53 that represents the week of the year. The WEEKNUM function requires one argument: the serial number that you want to convert. You can type the serial number as the argument, or you can point to a cell that contains the serial number. Excel considers the week containing January 1 to be the first week of the year. However, European standards dictate that the first week of the year is the one with four or more days falling in the new year. If you use a European setting in your Regional and Language Options dialog box, the WEEKNUM function returns week numbers that are not correct for years in which the first week of January has three days or less.

Determine the Week of the Year

1. Click the cell in which you want to store the function.
2. Click the Formulas tab.
3. Click Insert Function.

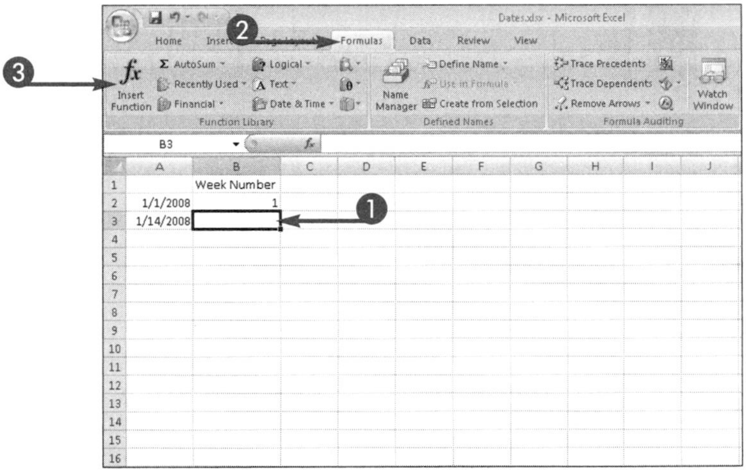

The Insert Function dialog box appears.

4. Type a description here of the function you want to use.

   This example uses week number.
5. Click Go.
6. Click WEEKNUM.
   - A description of the selected function appears here.
7. Click OK.

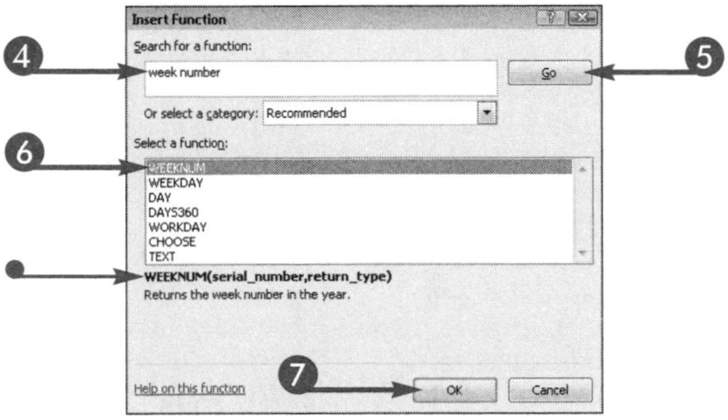

The Function Arguments dialog box appears.

8. Click here.
9. Click the cell in the worksheet containing a date.
   - Excel displays the anticipated result here.
10. Click OK.

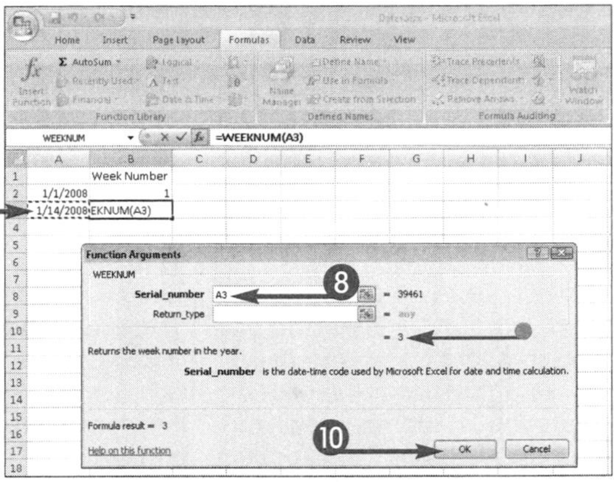

- Excel displays the result of the formula in the cell you selected in Step 1.

Note: *In this example, January 14, 2008 occurs in the third week of 2008.*

- The formula appears in the Formula bar.

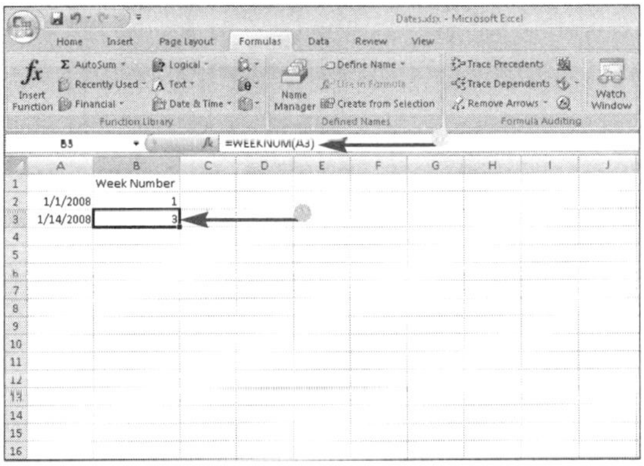

MASTER IT

How does the Return Type argument of the WEEKNUM function work?

▼ Excel uses a numbering system to define the day on which a week begins, and you can choose between two numbering systems. By default, Excel assumes that weeks begin on Sunday, and so it assigns 1 to Sunday, 2 to Monday, 3 to Tuesday, and so on, assigning 7 to Saturday. If you prefer, you can set up weeks to begin on Monday and assign 1 to Monday, 2 to Tuesday, and so on, with 7 being assigned to Sunday.

Why does the WEEKNUM function return an error?

▼ Because the WEEKNUM function operates on serial numbers, it is important that the argument for the function be a serial number. You may get unexpected results if you use the function with a date that is not formatted as a date. For best results, format the cell containing the function's argument as a date.

Can I use the WEEKNUM function without entering a date in my worksheet to use as the argument?

▼ Yes, you can use the WEEKNUM function in conjunction with the DATE function. For example, if you want to know the week number for the date August 28, 2007, type the following function into a cell: =**WEEKNUM(DATE (2007,8,28))**. Excel returns 35.

Calculate a Due Date

You can use the WORKDAY function to calculate a due date based on working days. The WORKDAY function counts the number of days between two dates, excluding Saturdays and Sundays. Suppose that you are placing an order online and the shipper promises to deliver the item within ten working days from the date of your order. Or your boss tells you to submit a report in 20 working days. You can use the WORKDAY function to determine what date actually falls 14 days from your order date, or 20 working days from the date your boss gave you an assignment.

The WORKDAY function requires two arguments: the starting date expressed as a serial number or formatted as a date, and the number of working days. You can also specify a range in your worksheet that contains holidays for which you want Excel to account when calculating a due date based on working days. For example, a shipper may not be working on Labor Day or Christmas, and so, to calculate the expected arrival date, you want to exclude those holidays. Excel excludes the dates in the holiday range, along with Saturdays and Sundays, when calculating the due date.

Calculate a Due Date

1. Click the cell in which you want to store the function.
2. Click the Formulas tab.
3. Click Insert Function.

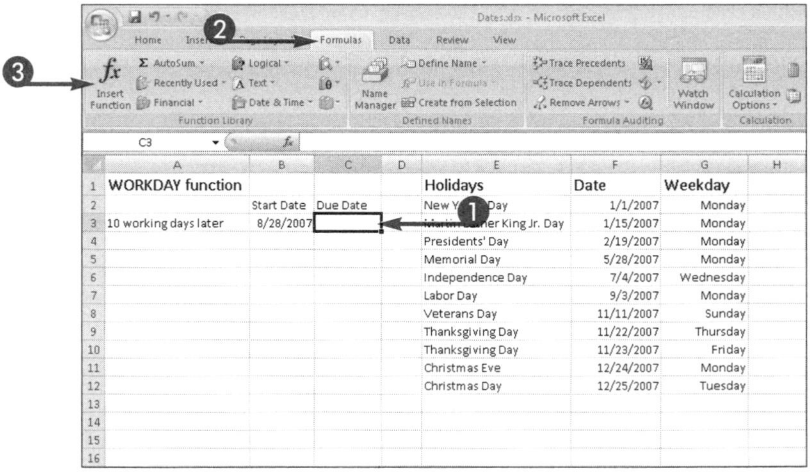

The Insert Function dialog box appears.

4. Type a description here of the function you want to use.

   This example uses working days.

5. Click Go.
6. Click WORKDAY.
   - A description of the selected function appears here.
7. Click OK.

   The Function Arguments dialog box appears.

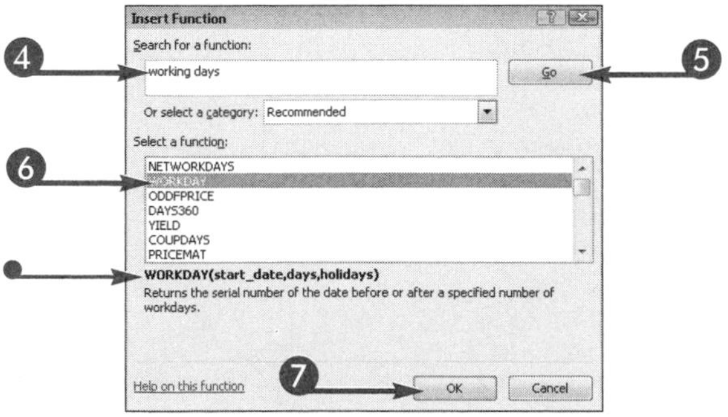

8. Click here and type the cell address that contains the start date.
9. Click here and type the number of working days.
10. Click here and type a range in the worksheet that contains holidays.
11. Click OK.

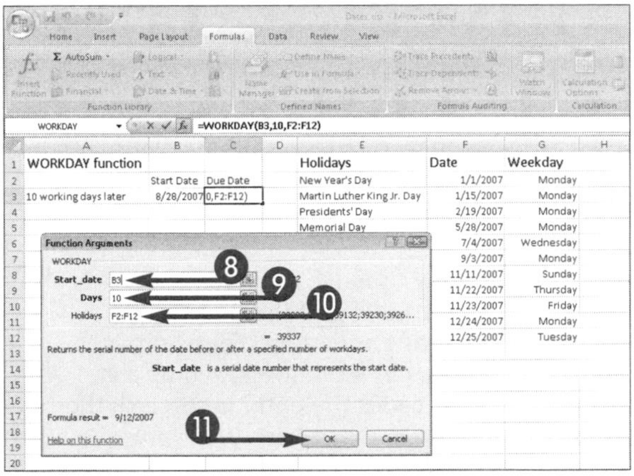

Excel displays the result of the formula in the cell you selected in Step 1 as a serial number.

12. Click the Home tab.
13. Click ▾ and select Short Date.
    - Excel displays the value as a date.
    - The formula appears in the Formula bar.

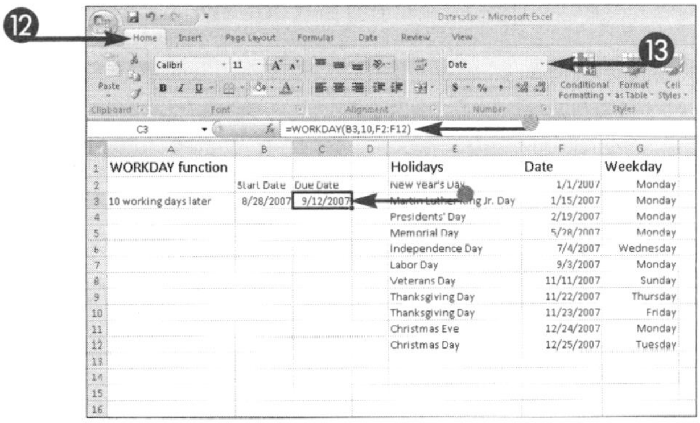

Can I calculate the number of working days between two dates?

▼ Yes, by using the NETWORKDAYS function. This function uses two required arguments — the starting date and the ending date — and you can also specify a range containing holidays to exclude in the calculation. For example, you may store 8/28/2007 as the starting date in cell B4, 9/12/2007 as the ending date in cell C4, and the range containing holidays that include Labor Day in cells F2 to F12. In this case, you would use this formula to calculate the number of working days between the two dates: =NETWORKDAYS (B4,C4,F2:F12). Excel returns 11, the total number of working days between the two dates.

Can I use a negative number for the Days argument in the WORKDAY function?

▼ Yes. Using a negative number for the Days argument tells Excel to calculate a date prior to the date you specify as the start date. If you use the negative number -6 for the Days argument in the WORKDAY function, Excel calculates a date six days earlier than the date you specify for the start date argument. For example, suppose that you store 9/4/2007 in cell C5, and holidays in cells F2 to F12. Excel returns 8/24/2007 if you enter the following function: =WORKDAY(C5,-6,F2:F12).

Convert a Text Time to a Time Value

You can use the TIMEVALUE function to convert a time formatted as a text string to a time that Excel can use in calculations. This function is particularly useful if you have imported time information into Excel and the times came into Excel formatted as text entries. For example, the time entry appears in a cell formatted as text, or an apostrophe precedes the entry in the cell; the apostrophe signals Excel that whatever follows should be treated as text, even if Excel would have ordinarily formatted the entry differently. You can use the TIMEVALUE function to convert these time-like text entries into valid time entries that Excel can then use properly in calculations.

The TIMEVALUE function takes only one argument: the text entry that you want Excel to treat as a time value. You can either type the argument or you can point to a cell that contains the date formatted as a text entry. When you use the TIMEVALUE function, Excel displays the serial number for the time, but you can change the appearance of the serial number to a time format.

Convert a Text Time to a Time Value

1. Click the cell in which you want to store the function.
2. Click the Formulas tab.
3. Click Insert Function.

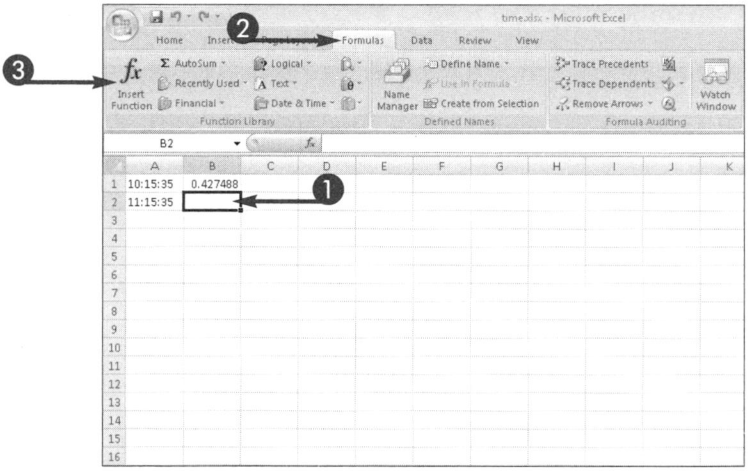

The Insert Function dialog box appears.

4. Type a description here of the function you want to use.

   This example uses time.

5. Click Go.
6. Click TIMEVALUE.
   - A description of the selected function appears here.
7. Click OK.

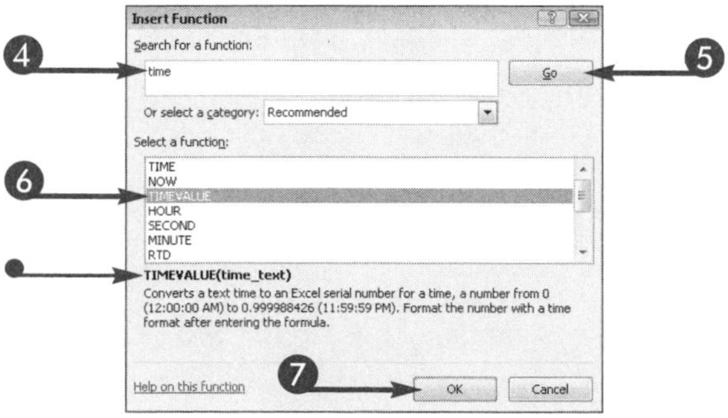

The Function Arguments dialog box appears.

8 Click here.

9 Click the cell containing the text entry you want to convert.

- The expected result appears here.

10 Click OK.

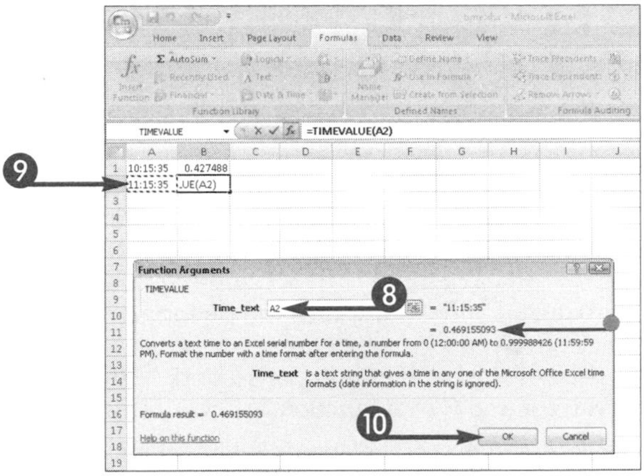

- Excel displays the result of the formula in the cell you selected in Step 1 as a serial number.
- The formula appears in the Formula bar.

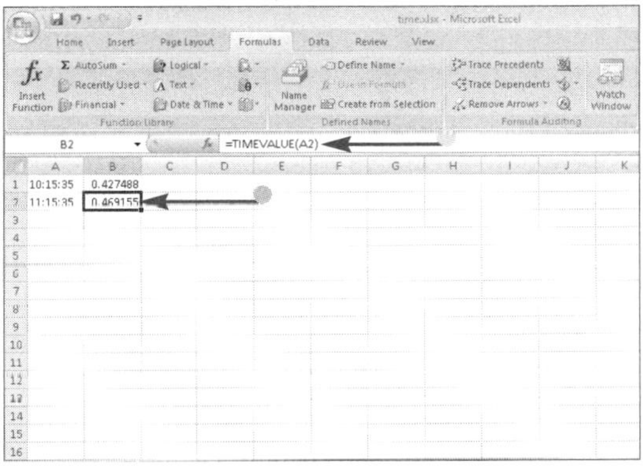

PART III

How do I display the results of the formula as a time instead of a serial number?

▼ Click the cell containing the TIMEVALUE formula. Then click the Home tab and click in the Number group. From the drop-down list that appears, select Time. Excel displays the value in the default time format that appears in the Regional and Language Options dialog box.

What would happen if I formatted cell B2 in your example as a time?

▼ Excel would display the same value that you see in cell A2, but you would also see the AM parameter and the value would be right-justified in the cell, unlike the contents of cell A2, which are left-justified. The right-justification and the AM parameter are visual clues that Excel is treating the contents of the cell as a time value and not a text entry.

Is there a logical reason for the serial number that Excel displays for the time value?

▼ Yes. All time values are expressed as decimal values between 0 and 0.99999. A time value of 0 represents 12:00:00 AM, a time value of .99998 represents 11:59:58 PM, and a time value of .5 represents 12:00:00 PM. Other decimal values represent various hours of the day.

Convert a Time Value into Hours, Minutes, or Seconds

You can use the HOUR, MINUTE, or SECOND functions to determine the hour, minute, or second value of a serial number in your worksheet. The serial number can be expressed as a decimal between 0 and .99999 or it can be formatted as a time. Depending on the function you choose to use, Excel returns the hour, minute, or second; in this example, you use the HOUR function.

These functions can be particularly useful if you have imported time information into Excel, where the times came into Excel as single entries representing the time and you need to work with only a portion of each time entry. You can use the HOUR, MINUTE, or SECOND function to convert these entries into separate hour, minute, or second entries to use in calculations.

The HOUR function takes only one argument: the value from which you want to determine the hour. You can either type the argument or you can point to a cell that contains the value. When you use the HOUR function, Excel displays the hour in 24-hour clock format.

Convert a Time Value into Hours, Minutes, or Seconds

1. Click the cell in which you want to store the function.
2. Click the Formulas tab.
3. Click Insert Function.

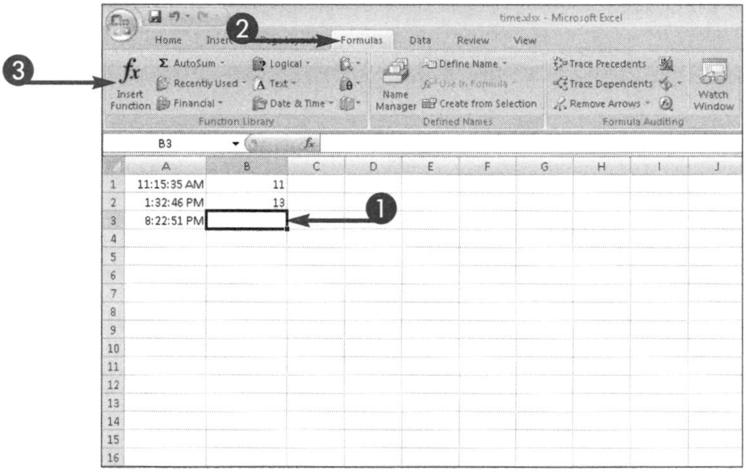

The Insert Function dialog box appears.

4. Type a description here of the function you want to use.

   This example uses hours.
5. Click Go.
6. Click HOUR.
   - A description of the selected function appears here.
7. Click OK.

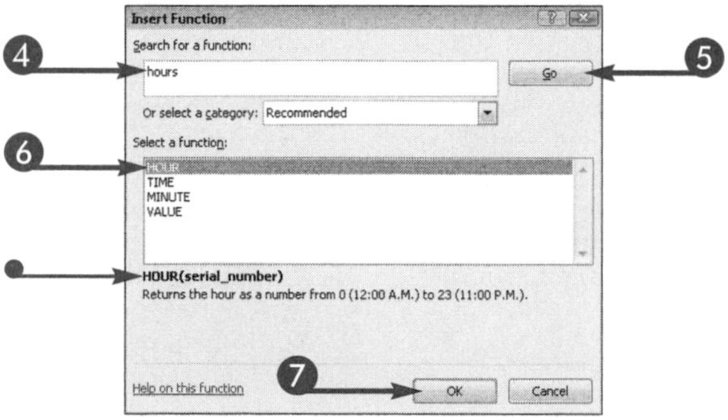

The Function Arguments dialog box appears.

8 Click here.

9 Click the cell containing the text entry you want to convert.

- The expected result appears here.

10 Click OK.

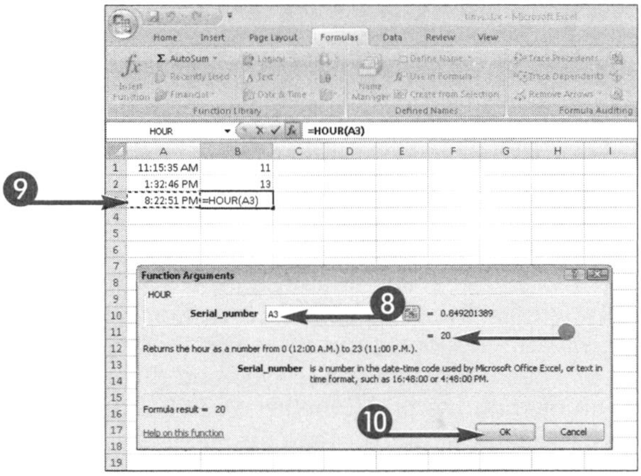

- Excel displays the result of the formula in the cell you selected in Step 1 as a serial number.
- The formula appears in the Formula bar.

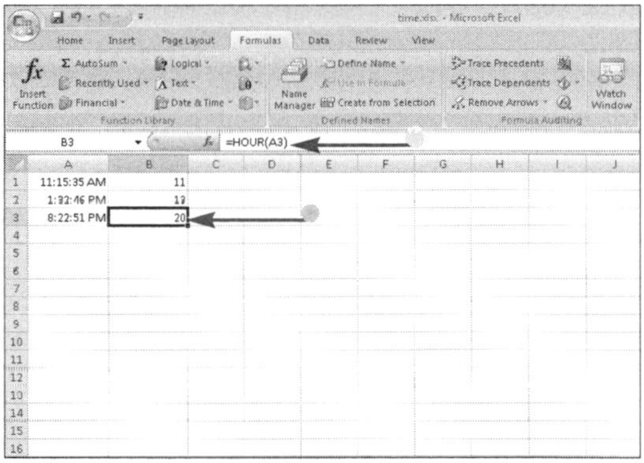

PART III

MASTER IT

How do I use the MINUTE or SECOND functions?

▼ Like the HOUR function, each function requires only one argument — a number or a cell containing a number. Although you can use either function to determine the minute or second associated with a serial number, you rarely know the serial number. As a result you are more likely to use these functions in conjunction with the HOUR function to divide a time into its hour, minute, and second components.

Why does Excel return 12:00 AM for both 39648 in cell A1 and 42587 when I format them as a time?

▼ Both numbers that you typed are whole numbers, not decimal values. If you examine the Formula bar, you will see that Excel evaluated their dates as July 19, 2008 and August 5, 2016, respectively. Because no decimal values appeared with either number, Excel assumed zero for the time portion of the values and set the time for both values to midnight.

What should I do if the data I import contains both a date and a time in a single entry?

▼ When the Regional and Language Options dialog box uses U.S. settings, Excel recognizes combination date and time values as valid date entries, and you can use the HOUR, MINUTE, or SECOND functions to extract those values from the entries. If Excel does not recognize the values as dates, see the section, "Convert a Text Time to a Time Value."

Calculate the Present Value of an Investment

You can use the PV function in Excel to help you determine the present value of an investment. Suppose that you win a prize and you are offered $5,000 today or equal payments of $100 per month for five years at an interest rate of eight percent compounded annually; which should you choose? The PV function can tell you and the organization offering the prize whether $5,000 today is less than, equal to, or greater than the value of $100 per month for five years at an interest rate of eight percent compounded annually. You can use the PV function to calculate the value of an annuity or to determine how much you will pay overall if you make a series of loan payments.

The PV function requires three arguments: the interest rate, the number of payment periods, and the payment amount. Make sure you express values in similar timeframes and base them on the frequency with which interest is compounded. If interest is compounded monthly, you must express all values in the function in a monthly timeframe. By default, Excel assumes that payments occur at the end of the period.

Calculate the Present Value of an Investment

1. Set up your worksheet so that the cash flow amount, the interest rate, and the number of payment periods appear in separate cells.

Note: *Express all amounts using the same timeframe.*

2. Click the cell in which you want to store the function.
3. Click the Formulas tab.
4. Click Insert Function.

   The Insert Function dialog box appears.

5. Type a description here of the function you want to use.

   This example uses present value.

6. Click Go.
7. Click PV.
   - A description of the selected function appears here.
8. Click OK.

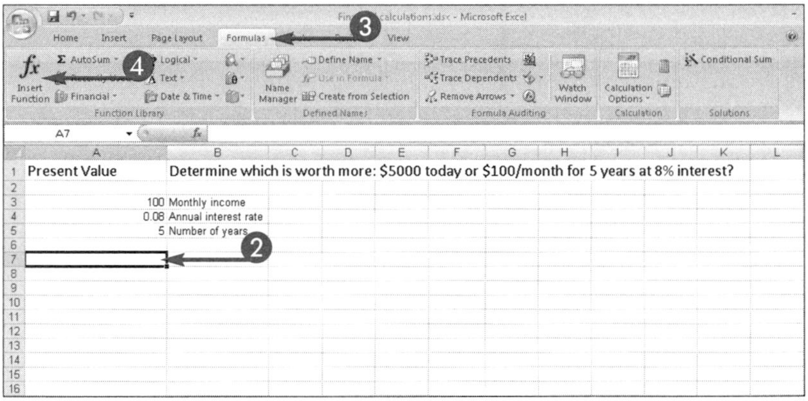

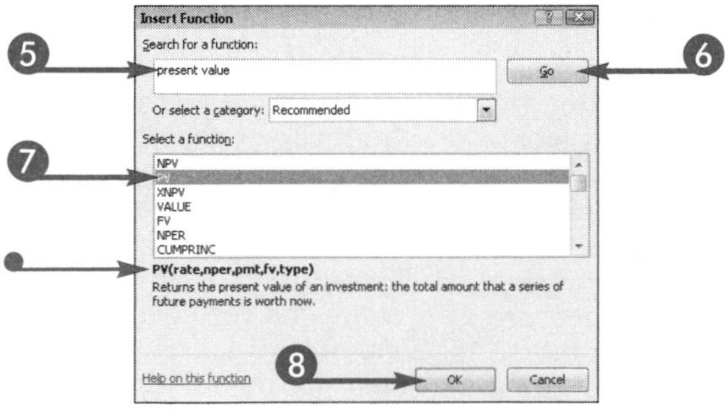

The Function Arguments dialog box appears.

9 Click here and click the cell containing the annual interest rate.

10 Type **/12**.

11 Click here and click the cell containing the number of payments.

12 Type ***12**.

13 Click here and click the cell containing the amount per period.

14 Click OK.

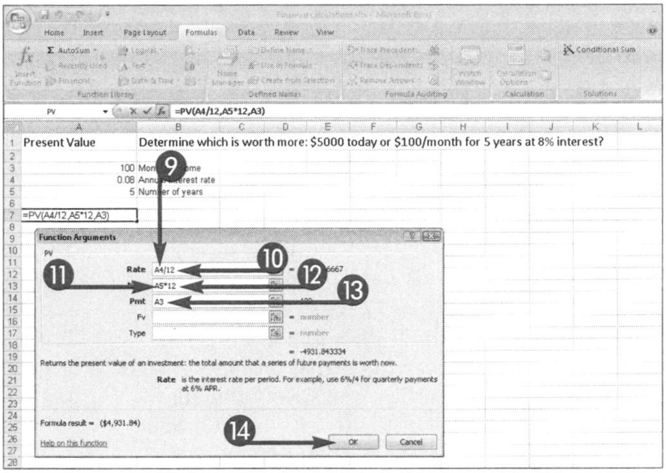

- Excel displays the result of the formula in the cell you selected in Step 2 as a serial number.
- The formula appears in the Formula bar.

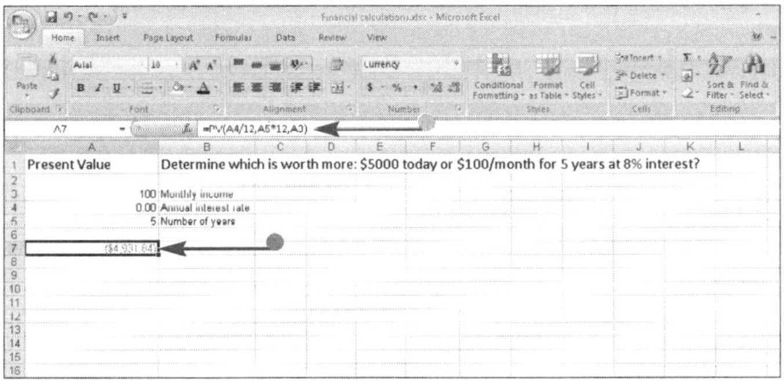

MASTER IT

Why do I need to perform Step 10?

▼ To accurately calculate the present value, the arguments should all be expressed in the same timeframe unit as the frequency with which interest is compounded. In the example, interest is compounded monthly but appears as an annual rate. To compensate for monthly compounding, you must divide the annual interest rate by 12 to determine the monthly interest rate, and multiply the number of periods by 12 to determine the total number of months for which you receive payments. If you express all of the variables in the worksheet using the frequency of interest compounding, you can skip Steps 10 and 12.

Why is the amount negative?

▼ Remember, the PV function can be used to determine the value of an annuity, which is an investment in which you make periodic payments to receive a lump sum at the end of the payment period. So, by default, Excel displays the amount as a negative number to imply that the person performing the calculation would be paying out the money. In the example, the issuer of the prize is paying out the money, and so the end result is negative. If you want to see the amount as a positive number — that is, you want to think of the calculation as one where you receive money — enter the payment amount as a negative number.

Calculate the Net Present Value of an Investment

You can use the NPV function in Excel to help you determine the present value of an investment with unequal cash flows. *Net present value* compares the value of a dollar today to the value of that same dollar in the future, taking into account the investment's rate of return and the cash flows generated from the investment. Suppose that you are considering an investment that requires you to initially invest $1,000. Over five years, you annually receive unequal payments of $200, $400, $600, $800, and $1,000 at an interest rate of eight percent. You can use the NPV function to calculate the investment's net present value. If the net present value is positive, you will make money on the investment, but if the net present value is negative, you will lose money.

The NPV function requires a minimum of two arguments: the interest rate and at least two values representing outgoing or incoming cash flows. You can specify an initial investment amount if the initial investment amount occurs at the end of the first period. Make sure you use values with similar timeframes and base them on the frequency with which interest is compounded.

Calculate the Net Present Value of an Investment

1. Set up your worksheet so that the cash flow amounts and the interest rate appear in separate cells.

Note: *Express the amounts using the same timeframe.*

2. Click the cell in which you want to store the function.
3. Click the Formulas tab.
4. Click Insert Function.

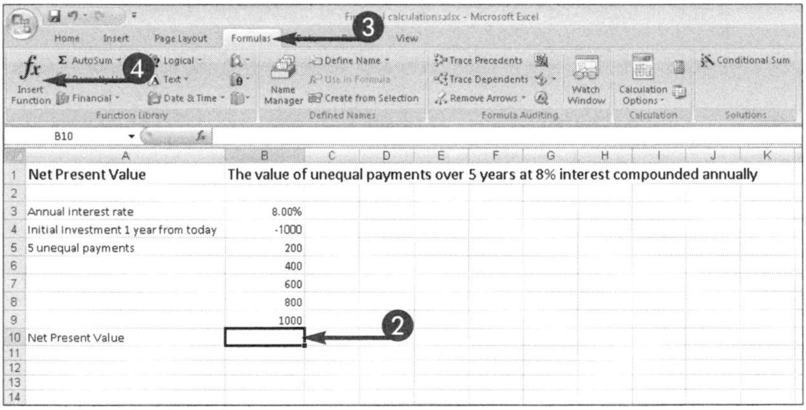

The Insert Function dialog box appears.

5. Type a description here of the function you want to use.

This example uses net present value.

6. Click Go.
7. Click NPV.

- A description of the selected function appears here.

8. Click OK.

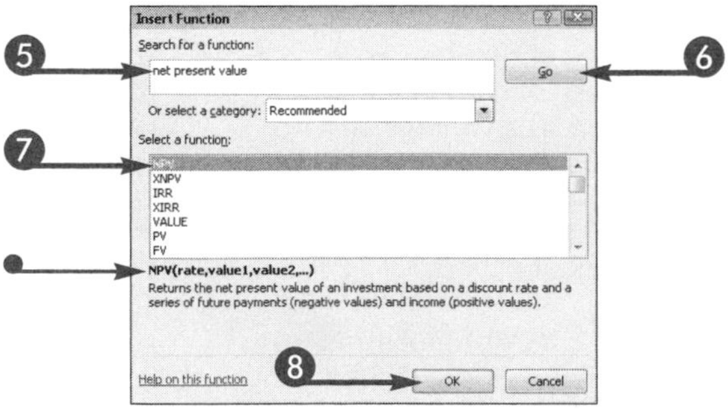

The Function Arguments dialog box appears.

9 Click here and click the cell containing the annual interest rate.

The cell address appears in the Rate field.

10 Click here and select the cells containing the amounts per period.

The range appears in the Value1 field.

11 Click OK.

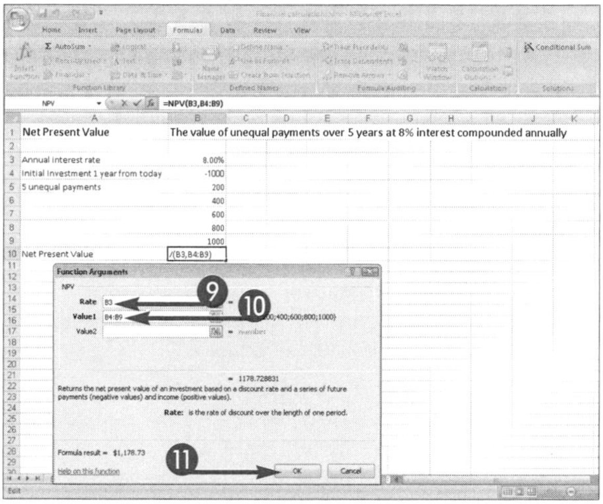

- Excel displays the result of the formula in the cell you selected in Step 2 as a serial number.
- The formula appears in the Formula bar.

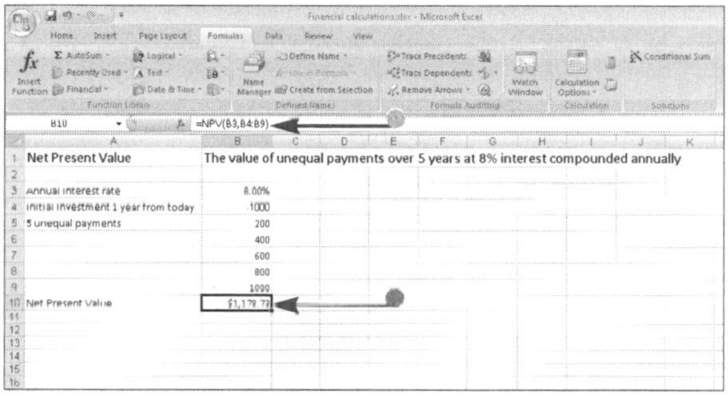

MASTER IT

What should I do if my initial investment occurs at the beginning of the first period?

▼ Do not include it in the NPV function as an argument; instead, add it to the NPV value to obtain an accurate net present value. Suppose that you record the interest rate in cell B3, the unequal payment amounts in the range B5:B9, and the initial investment value (being made at the end of the first period) in cell B4. In this case, you can use the following formula: =NPV(B3,B5:B9)+B4.

What am I doing wrong if Excel keeps returning a value of $0 for the net present value?

▼ In all likelihood, you have set up the order of the arguments incorrectly. The first argument must be the rate of return. Then, if appropriate, you can include an original investment amount, followed by the values for each of the cash flows you expect to receive.

What if the expected cash flows occur irregularly?

▼ Use the XNPV function. Suppose that you initially invest $1,000 at 5 percent on January 1, 2008, and you receive $2,000, $3,000, $2,500, and $3,500 on March 1, October 1, March 1, 2009, and October 1, 2009, respectively. If your worksheet stores the interest rate in cell A2, the dollars in the range A3:A6, and the dates in the range B3:B6, your XNPV function would look like this: =XNPV(.05,A2:A6,B2:B6).

Calculate the Future Value of an Investment

You can calculate the future value of an investment using the FV function. For example, suppose that you want to know what your retirement account will be worth after investing $2,000 at the beginning of each year for 20 years if you earn seven percent on the investment. The FV function can give you the answer.

The FV function requires three arguments: the interest rate, the number of payment periods, and the payment amount. You can also specify a Present Value argument, which is the value of the transaction in the present, and the Type argument, which indicates when payments occur — at the beginning or the end of the period. By default, Excel assumes that payments occur at the end of the period.

When you set up your worksheet, you must place the interest rate, the number of periods, and the payment amount in separate cells. Make sure that you express the amounts using the same timeframe, and base them on the frequency with which interest is compounded. For example, if interest is compounded annually, you express the number of payments, the payment amount, and the interest rate as annual values.

Calculate the Future Value of an Investment

1. Set up your worksheet so that the cash flow amount, the interest rate, and the number of payment periods appear in separate cells.

Note: *Express all amounts using the same timeframe.*

2. Click the cell in which you want to store the function.
3. Click the Formulas tab.
4. Click Insert Function.

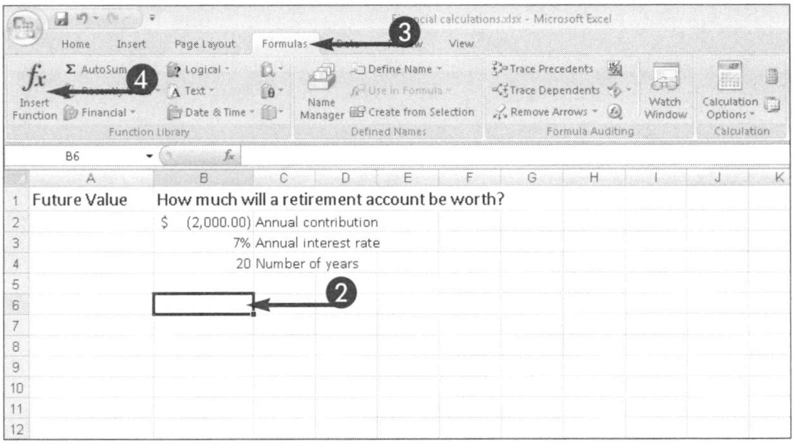

The Insert Function dialog box appears.

5. Type a description here of the function you want to use.

   This example uses future value.

6. Click Go.
7. Click FV.
   - A description of the selected function appears here.
8. Click OK.

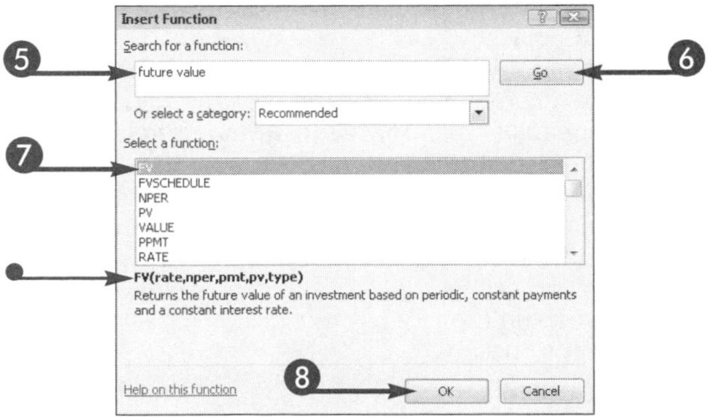

The Function Arguments dialog box appears.

9. Click here and click the cell containing the interest rate.

   The cell address appears in the Rate field.

10. Click here and click the cell containing the number of periods.

    The cell address appears in the Nper field.

11. Click here and click the cell containing the amount per period.

    The cell address appears in the Pmt field.

12. Click OK.

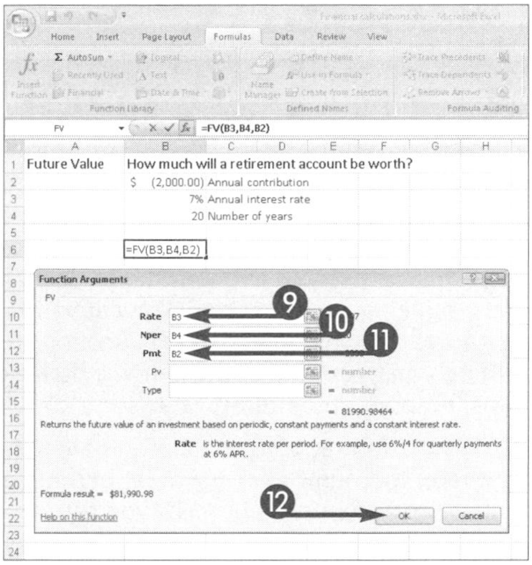

- Excel displays the result of the formula in the cell you selected in Step 2 as a serial number.
- The formula appears in the Formula bar.

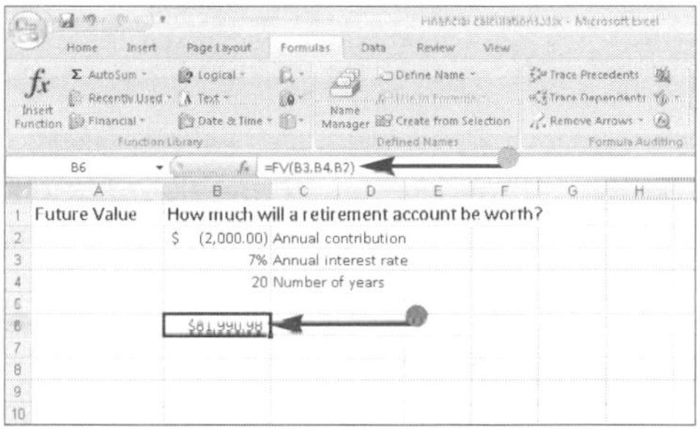

MASTER IT

Why did you format the annual contribution as a negative amount?

▼ The negative amount identifies an amount you pay out as opposed to an amount you receive. The example assumes that you place $2,000 in your retirement account at the beginning of each year, and so you are paying out money. If you express the annual contribution as a positive number, the resulting future value appears negative.

What effect does omitting the optional arguments for the FV function have on the result?

▼ If you omit the PV argument, Excel assumes that the Present Value argument is zero. If you omit the Type argument or include it and set it to zero, Excel assumes that you make payments at the end of each period. If you include the argument and set it to one, Excel assumes you make payments at the beginning of each period.

When would I include a PV amount?

▼ Suppose that you have previously saved $10,000 in your retirement account and you decide now that you will put away $2,000 each year for 20 years. To calculate the value of your retirement account, you would include the $10,000 you already have as a negative number in cell B5, and the formula would look like this: =FV(B3,B4,B2,B5).

Calculate a Loan Payment

You can calculate the amount you can expect to pay each period for a loan using the PMT function. Suppose that you are thinking about buying a house and you are considering several different principal amounts to borrow at various interest rates. You can use the PMT function to determine what your loan payment will be for each principal amount and interest rate.

The PMT function requires three arguments: the interest rate, the number of payment periods, and the principal loan amount. Optionally, you can also specify a Future Value argument, which is the principal amount of the loan after making the last payment, and the Type argument, which indicates when payments occur — at the beginning or the end of the period. By default, Excel assumes that payments occur at the end of the period.

When you set up your worksheet, you must place the interest rate, the number of periods, and the payment amount in separate cells. To accurately calculate the loan payment, the timeframe for the interest rate and the number of periods should be the same. The calculation should be based on the frequency with which interest is compounded.

Calculate a Loan Payment

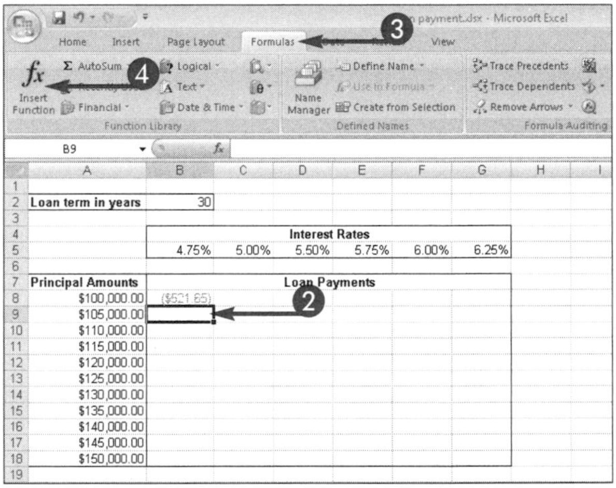

1. Set up your worksheet so that the principal amounts, the interest rates, and the number of payment periods appear in separate cells.
2. Click the cell in which you want to store the function.
3. Click the Formulas tab.
4. Click Insert Function.

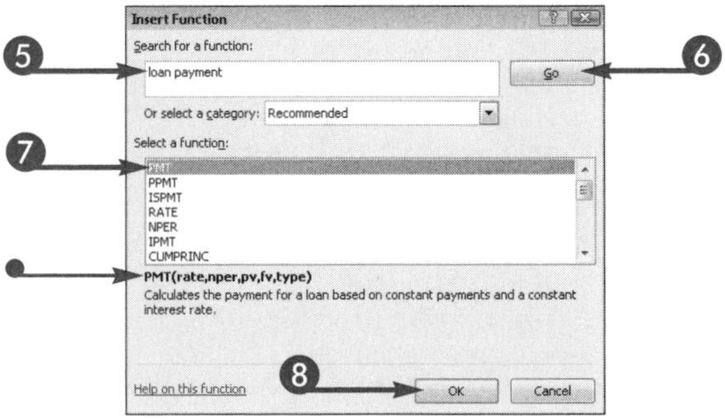

The Insert Function dialog box appears.

5. Type a description here of the function you want to use.

This example uses loan payment.

6. Click Go.
7. Click PMT.
   - A description of the selected function appears here.
8. Click OK.

The Function Arguments dialog box appears.

9. Click here and click the cell containing the annual interest rate.

   The cell address appears in the Rate field.

10. Type **/12**.

11. Click here and click the cell containing the number of payments.

    The cell address appears in the Nper field.

12. Type ***12**.

13. Click here and click the cell containing the amount per period.

    The cell address appears in the PV field.

14. Click OK.

- Excel displays the result of the formula in the cell you selected in Step 2 as a serial number.
- The formula appears in the Formula bar.

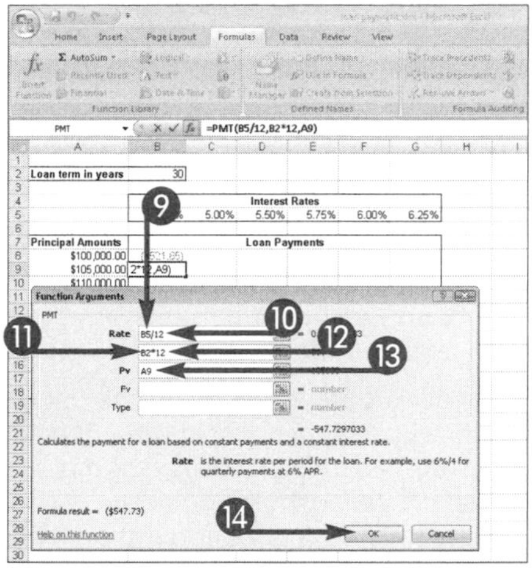

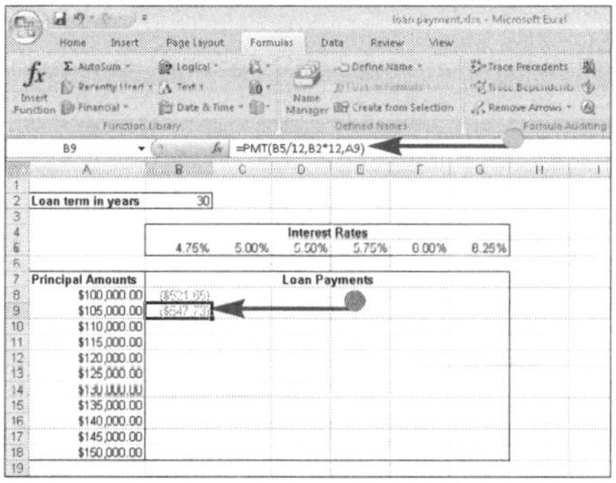

MASTER IT

Is there a way to set up the formula so that I can copy it?

▼ Yes, you can use absolute cell references, as appropriate. Suppose that you set up your worksheet with the loan term in cell B2, interest rates in the range B5:G5, and varying principal amounts in the range A8:A18. You want to be able to copy the formula across each row, calculating the loan payment for a single principal amount at varying interest rates. You also want to be able to copy the formula down each column, calculating payments for a single interest rate and varying principal amounts. Use this formula in cell B8 and copy it to the range B8:G18: =PMT(B$5/12$B$2,$A8).

When would I specify a future value in the function?

▼ You would specify a future value in the function if you expect the balance of the loan to be greater than zero. By default, if you omit the parameter, Excel calculates the function assuming that you will pay off the loan in its entirety and its future value will be zero.

When would I specify a parameter for the Type argument?

▼ If you omit the Type parameter or set it to zero, Excel assumes that payments occur at the end of each period. If you set the parameter to one, Excel assumes that payments occur at the beginning of each period.

Depreciate Assets

You can depreciate an asset to allocate a value to it at a particular point in the asset's life. Depreciation takes into consideration both the asset's original cost and its useful life.

You can depreciate assets over time using one of five Excel functions, and the function you choose depends on the method of depreciation you want to apply, as described in the table. Choosing a depreciation method is something you should discuss with your accountant; it is not simply a matter of personal preference. This section shows the Straight Line method.

Depreciation Methods

Depreciation Method	*Description*
Straight Line	Depreciates the asset by the same amount each year of the asset's life. The formula is Asset Cost – Salvage Value / Number of Periods.
Declining Balance	Depreciates the asset by the same rate each year, which results in a different depreciation amount each year.
Double-Declining Balance	Accelerates depreciation by doubling the Straight Line depreciation rate and then applying it to the declining balance of the asset's cost.
Sum Of The Year's Digits	Accelerates depreciation more than the Straight Line method, allocating a large depreciation amount in the earlier years of an asset's life.
Variable-Declining Balance	Calculates depreciation for any period in the asset's life that you specify using the Double-Declining Balance method or any method you specify.

Depreciate Assets

1. Set up your worksheet so that the original cost, the salvage value, and the asset life appear in separate cells.
2. Click the cell in which you want to store the function.
3. Click the Formulas tab.
4. Click Insert Function.

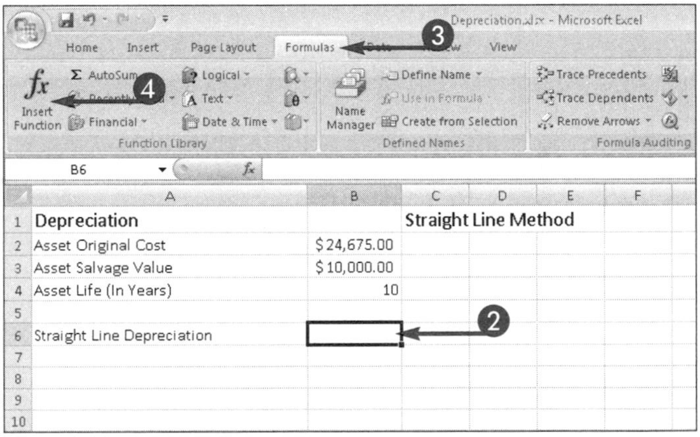

The Insert Function dialog box appears.

5. Type a description here of the function you want to use.

   This example uses straight line depreciation.
6. Click Go.
7. Click SLN.
   - A description of the selected function appears here.
8. Click OK.

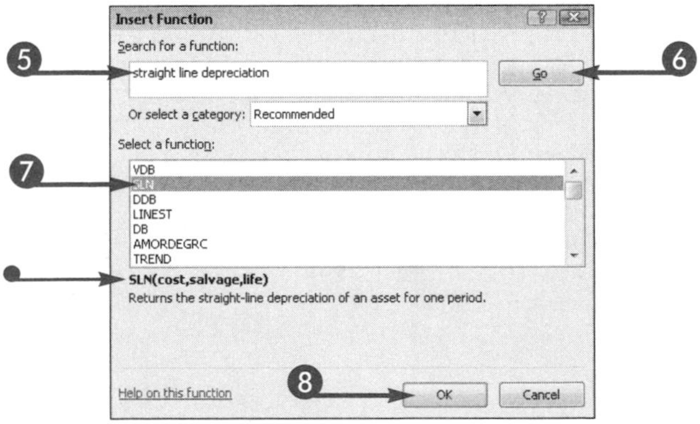

The Function Arguments dialog box appears.

9. Click here and click the cell containing the original cost.

   The cell address appears in the Cost field.

10. Click here and click the cell containing the salvage value.

    The cell address appears in the Salvage field.

11. Click here and click the cell containing the asset life.

    The cell address appears in the Life field.

12. Click OK.

    - Excel displays the result of the formula in the cell you selected in Step 2 as a serial number.
    - The formula appears in the Formula bar.

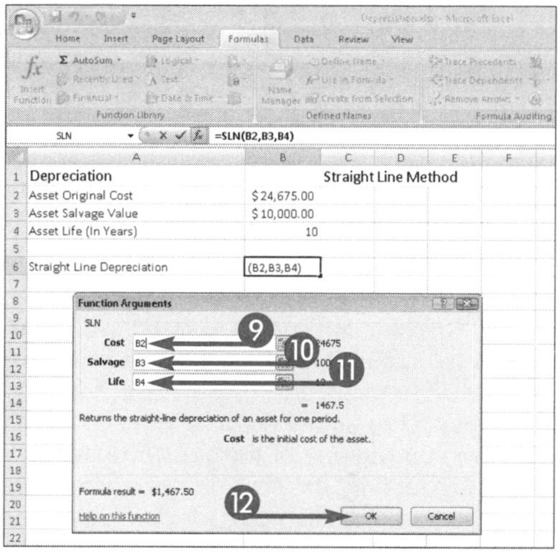

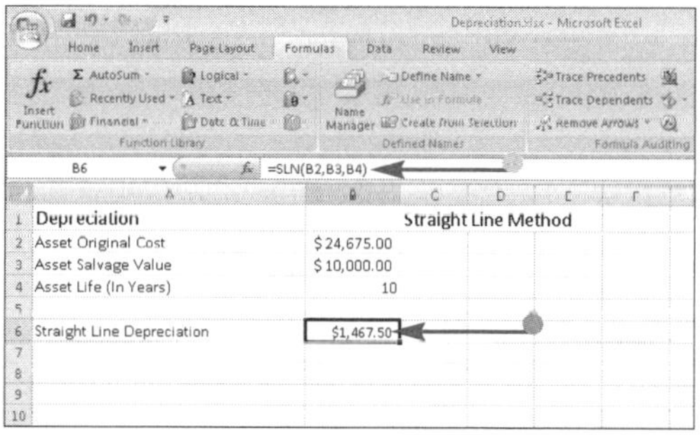

PART III

MASTER IT

Can you show me how to use the function that calculates declining balance depreciation?

▼ Suppose you set up your worksheet with the original cost in cell A1, the salvage value in cell A2, and the asset life of ten years in cell A3, and you placed the values 1 to 10 in the range A6:A15. To calculate the first year's depreciation, use the following formula in cell B6: =DB($A$1, $A$2,$A$3,A6). The absolute cell references enable you to copy the formula to the range B7:B16. You can also include, as the last argument, a month argument that represents the number of months during the first year that you used the asset. If you omit the argument, Excel assumes that you used the asset for 12 months.

Can you show me how to use the function that calculates Double-Declining Balance depreciation?

▼ Suppose you once again set up your worksheet with the original cost in cell A1, the salvage value in cell A2, and the asset life of ten years in cell A3, and you placed the values 1 to 10 in the range A6:A15. To calculate the first year's depreciation, use the following formula in cell C6: =DDB($A$1,$A$2,$A$3,A6). The absolute cell references enable you to copy the formula to the range C7:C16. You can also include, as the last argument, a factor argument that represents the rate at which the balance declines. If you omit the argument, Excel assumes a rate of two, which doubles the declining balance rate.

Look up a Single Value in a Column

You can use the VLOOKUP function to find a value in one column of a range of related values. In the range, information on any given row provides all the information about that row.

The VLOOKUP function vertically searches the leftmost column of the range to find a value you specify. When the VLOOKUP function finds the value in the leftmost column, it searches across the row for one of the values in that row; you use one of the VLOOKUP function's arguments to identify the column containing the value you want to find. For example, suppose that you have stored daily rainfall values in your worksheet for each day of the year. You can set up a VLOOKUP function to quickly search the column containing the day numbers and find the rainfall value that corresponds to any of the 365 days that you specify.

The VLOOKUP function takes three arguments: First, you identify the cell containing the value for which you want to search. Second, you identify the range containing all of the data that Excel should search. Third, you identify the column containing the information that you want Excel to display.

Look up a Single Value in a Column

1. In your worksheet, list the values that Excel should search in columns.

Note: If necessary, set up a cell to contain the value for which Excel should search.

2. Click the cell in which you want to store the function.
3. Click the Formulas tab.
4. Click Insert Function.

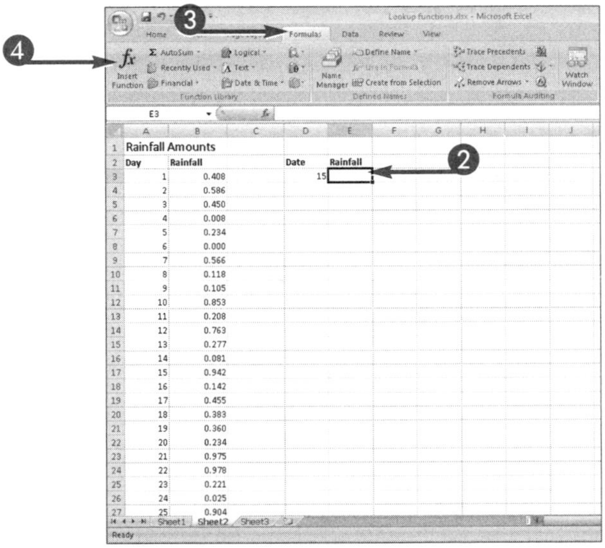

The Insert Function dialog box appears.

5. Type a description here of the function you want to use.

   This example uses vertical lookup.

6. Click Go.
7. Click VLOOKUP.

   - A description of the selected function appears here.

8. Click OK.

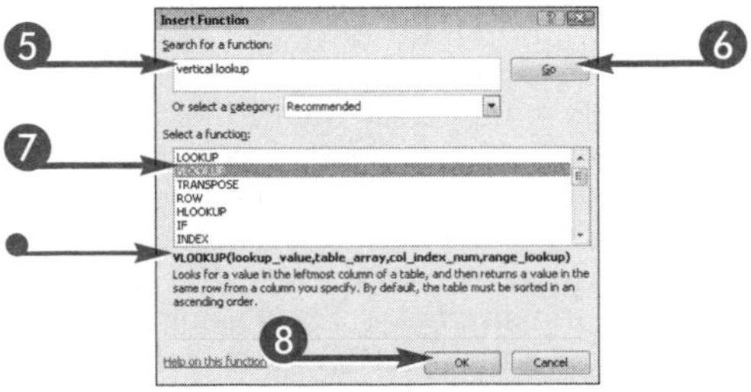

The Function Arguments dialog box appears.

9. Click here and click the cell containing the search value.

   The selected cell's address appears in the Lookup_value field.

10. Click here and select the range containing all of the values.

    The selected range appears in the Table_array field.

11. Type the number of the column containing the value you want to find.

Note: *The leftmost column is 1.*

12. Click OK.

- Excel displays the result of the formula in the cell you selected in Step 2 as a serial number.
- The formula appears in the Formula bar.

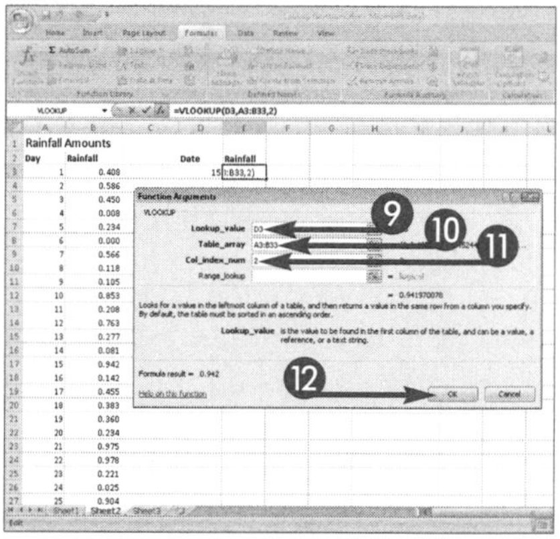

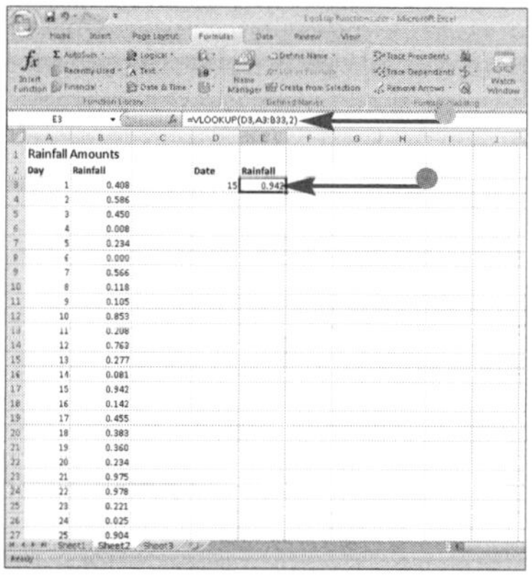

MASTER IT

What does the Range_lookup argument do?

▼ You can use this argument to tell Excel whether to return an exact match or an approximate match to the Lookup_value you specify in Step 9. If you omit the argument or set the argument to TRUE, Excel finds an approximate match. If you set the argument to FALSE, Excel finds only exact matches. In this example, the syntax for the function that includes a Range_lookup argument would be as follows: =VLOOKUP(D3, A3:B33,2,FALSE).

Can I use the VLOOKUP function with text instead of values?

▼ Yes, you can. You can search for a text string by typing the text that you want to find in the Lookup_value field. You can also have Excel return text stored in a cell. However, you cannot use the Range_lookup argument to specify whether Excel should find an exact match or an approximate match.

Are there any restrictions concerning the range that I select in Step 10?

▼ Yes. The leftmost range must contain the text or value for which Excel will search. If the leftmost column contains values, each value must be unique, and the entries must be sorted from lowest to highest. If the leftmost column contains text entries, each entry must be unique, and the entries must be sorted alphabetically.

Look up a Single Value in a Row

You can use the HLOOKUP function to find a value in one row of a range of related values. In the range, information in any given column provides all of that particular type of information.

The HLOOKUP function horizontally searches the top row of the range to find a value that you specify. When the HLOOKUP function finds the value in the top row, it searches down that column for one of the values in the column; you use one of the arguments of the HLOOKUP function to identify the row containing the value you want to find. For example, suppose that you have stored students' numeric grades in a worksheet and you would like to translate numeric grades to the letters A, B, C, D, and F. You can use the HLOOKUP function to quickly find the letter grade corresponding to a number grade.

The HLOOKUP function takes three arguments: First, you identify the cell containing the value for which you want to search. Second, you identify the range containing the data that Excel should search. Third, you identify the row containing the information you want Excel to display.

Look up a Single Value in a Row

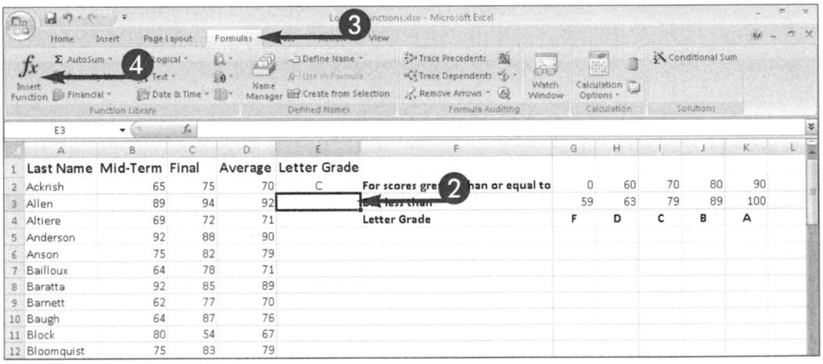

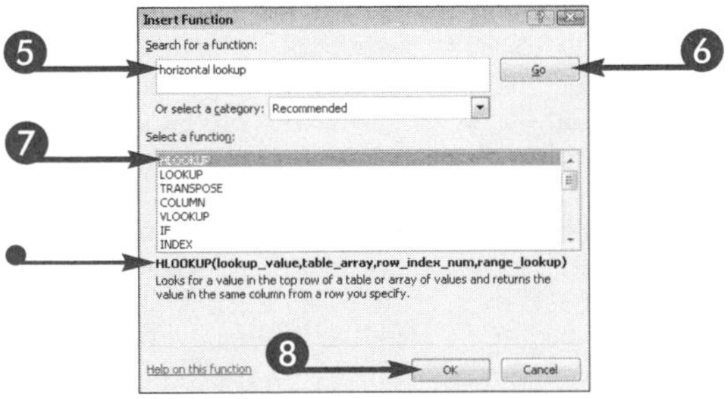

1. In your worksheet, list in rows the values that Excel should search.

   Note: *Be sure to sort the information based on the first row.*

2. Click the cell in which you want to store the function.
3. Click the Formulas tab.
4. Click Insert Function.

   The Insert Function dialog box appears.

5. Type a description here of the function you want to use.

   This example uses horizontal lookup.

6. Click Go.
7. Click HLOOKUP.
   - A description of the selected function appears here.
8. Click OK.

The Function Arguments dialog box appears.

9 Click here and click the cell containing the search value.

The selected cell address appears in the Lookup_value field.

10 Click here and select the range containing all of the values you want to search.

The selected range appears in the Table_array field.

11 Type the number of the row containing the value you want to find.

Note: *The top row is 1.*

12 Click OK.

- Excel displays the result of the formula in the cell you selected in Step 2 as a serial number.
- The formula appears in the Formula bar.

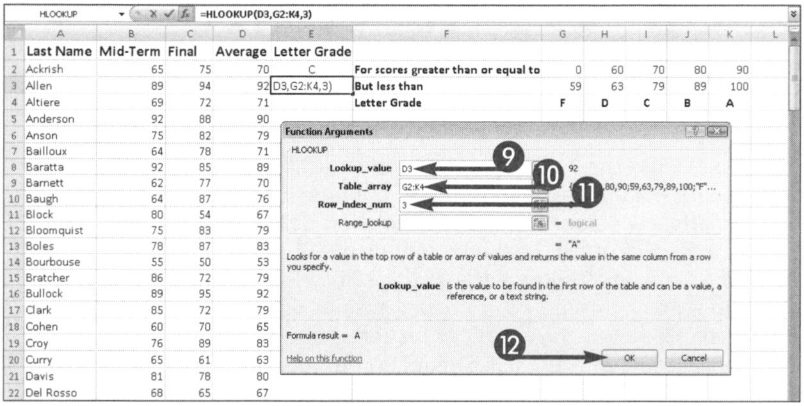

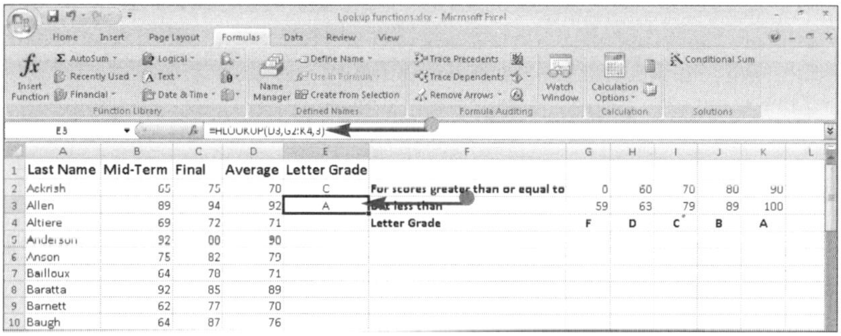

PART III

MASTER IT

Why did Excel return a #NAME! error for an HLOOKUP function that I set up?

▼ You need to remember that the order of the information in the range that you search is important. The information in the table must appear from lowest to highest, or, if you are searching text, the text entries must appear alphabetically. In addition, the entries in the top row of the table must be unique. Otherwise, Excel returns an error.

Can I use a cell reference instead of an HLOOKUP function?

▼ Yes, you can. However, using a cell reference does not account for changes that you make to the value that you would have used for the Lookup_value argument. If you make a change to that cell, Excel does not update the cell containing the cell reference — the one in which you would have stored an HLOOKUP function.

I saw the LOOKUP function in the Insert Function dialog box; how does it work?

▼ The LOOKUP function works on a single row or single column range where the values are sorted in ascending or alphabetical order. You supply a search value, a single row or column range to search, and a single row or column range where Excel can store the values it finds. The two single row or column ranges must be the same size.

Look Up a Value in a Table

You can use the MATCH function to find the row or column position number in a range for a particular value. The MATCH function does not return a value; instead, it returns the relative position of a value in a range. Because the MATCH function does not return an actual value, it is not often used by itself. However, the MATCH function is often used in conjunction with the INDEX function to return the value at a particular position in a range.

Used in combination, these two functions can help you perform a two-way lookup. That is, you can search down columns and across rows of a range and return the value in a single cell within that range.

The MATCH function requires two arguments, and you can specify an optional third argument. You must define the cell containing the value for which you want to search and the range to search. When searching a column, you specify only the column you want to search. When searching a row, you specify only the row you want to search.

You can set the Match-type argument to one of three values: 1, 0, or -1. If you omit this argument, Excel sets the value to 1.

Look Up a Value in a Table

Determine the Position of a Value

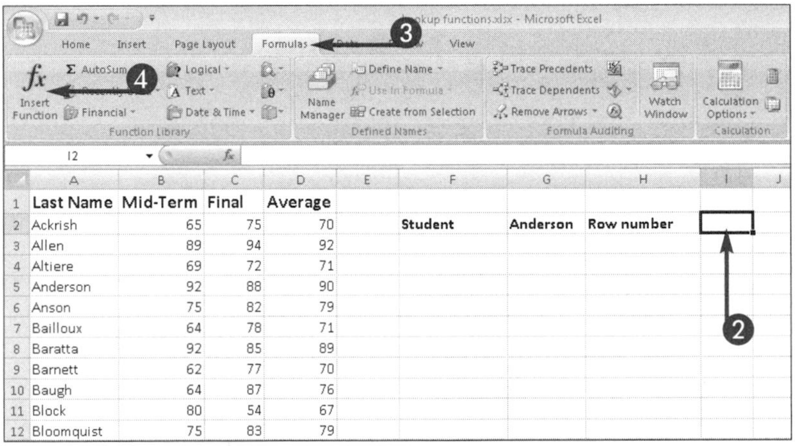

1. In your worksheet, list the values that Excel should search in rows.
2. Click the cell in which you want to store the function.
3. Click the Formulas tab.
4. Click Insert Function.

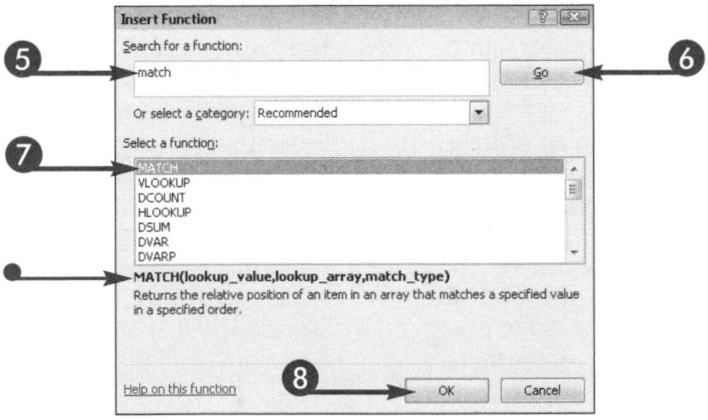

The Insert Function dialog box appears.

5. Type a description here of the function you want to use.

   This example uses match.

6. Click Go.
7. Click MATCH.
   - A description of the selected function appears here.
8. Click OK.

The Function Arguments dialog box appears.

9. Click here and click the cell containing the search value.

   The selected cell's address appears in the Lookup_value field.

10. Click here and select the range containing the values to search.

    The selected range appears in the Lookup_array field.

11. Type the value for the Match_type argument.

    This example uses 0.

12. Click OK.

- Excel displays the result of the formula in the cell you selected in Step 2 as a serial number.
- The formula appears in the Formula bar.

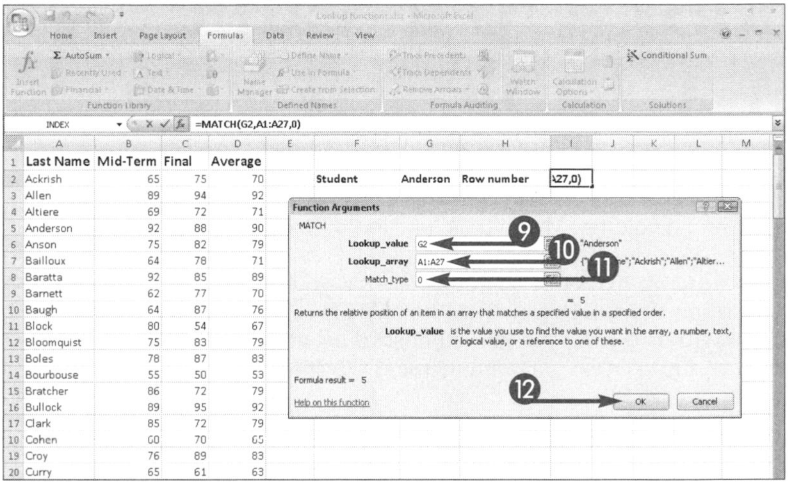

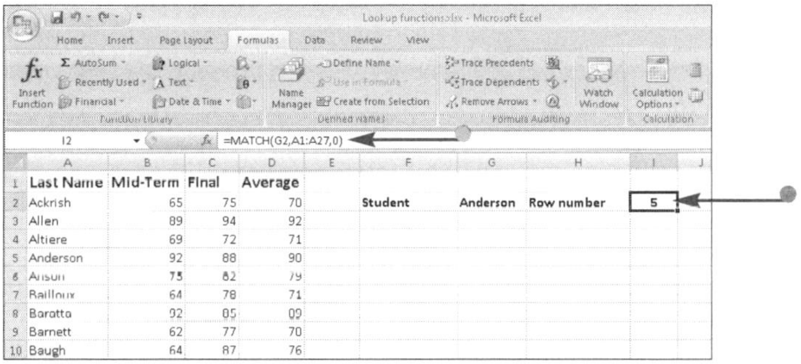

MASTER IT

What happens when I omit the Match_type argument or set it to 1?

▼ When you omit the Match_type argument or set it to 1, Excel finds and returns the location of the largest value that is less than or equal to the lookup value — the first argument of the MATCH function. To use this setting, you must sort the values in the range in descending or reverse alphabetical order.

What happens when I set the Match_type argument to 0?

▼ When you set the Match_type argument to 0, Excel searches for and returns the location of the first value that exactly equals the lookup value. If you use this setting, the order of the values in the range that you search do not matter; they do not need to be in ascending or descending order.

What happens when I set the Match_type argument to -1?

▼ When you set the Match_type argument to -1, Excel searches for and returns the location of the smallest value in the range that is greater than or equal to the Lookup Value argument. To use this setting, you must sort the values in the range in descending or reverse alphabetical order.

continued

Look Up a Value in a Table *(Continued)*

You can use the INDEX function to return a value that appears at the intersection of a row and a column. The INDEX function differs from the MATCH function because the INDEX function returns the value that appears in the cell that you identify using the INDEX function; the MATCH function returns the relative row number or column number of the cell that you identify using the MATCH function.

While you can simply specify the row number and column number as you set up the INDEX function, the power of the INDEX function comes from using it in conjunction with the MATCH function. Because the MATCH function returns row numbers and column numbers, you can use the results of the MATCH function as arguments of the INDEX function.

The INDEX function requires three arguments: you must identify the range you want to search, the row number of the range, and the column number of the range. In addition, Excel offers two ways of using the INDEX function: You can use it in its array format or in its reference format. The example in this section shows the array format.

Look Up a Value in a Table *(continued)*

Return the Value

1. Click the cell in which you want to store the function.
2. Click the Formulas tab.
3. Click Insert Function to display the Insert Function dialog box.
4. Type a description here of the function you want to use.

   This example uses index.
5. Click Go.
6. Click INDEX.
7. Click OK.

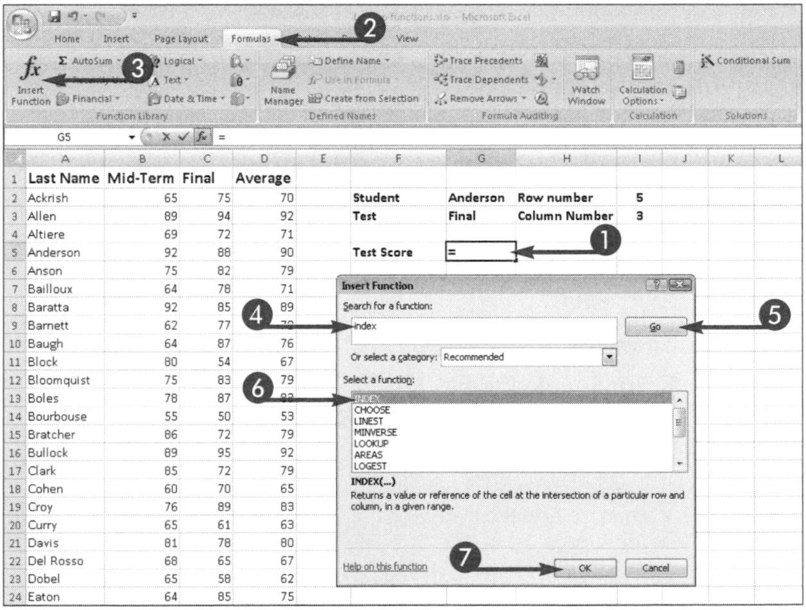

The Select Arguments dialog box appears.

8. Click here.
9. Click OK.

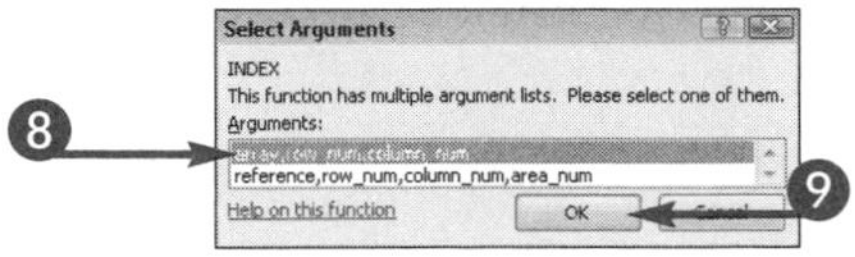

The Function Arguments dialog box appears.

⑩ Click here and select the range containing all of the values to search.

The selected range appears in the Array field.

⑪ Click here and click the cell containing the row number.

The cell address appears in the Row_num field.

⑫ Click here and click the cell containing the column number.

The cell address appears in the Column_num field.

⑬ Click OK.

- Excel displays the result of the formula in the cell you selected in Step 1 as a serial number.
- The formula appears in the Formula bar.

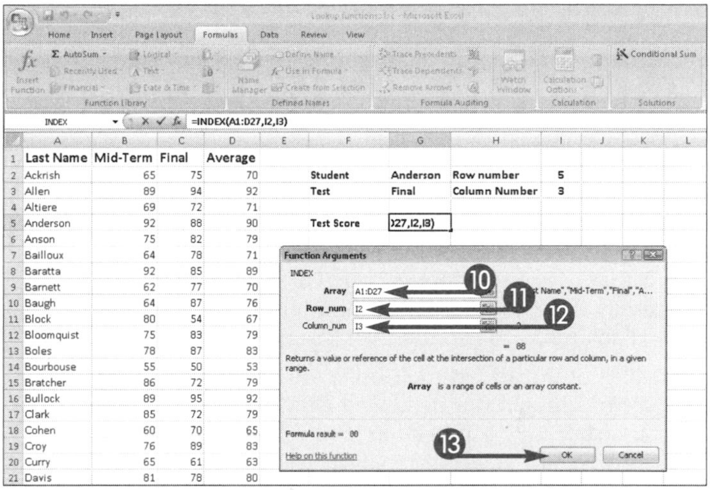

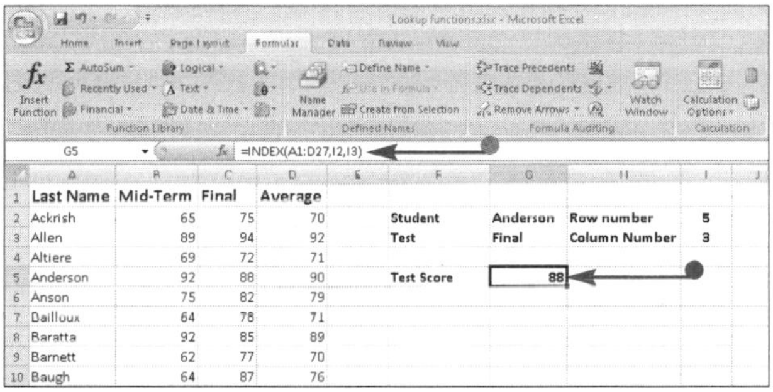

PART III

MASTER IT

How do I use the Reference, row_num, column_num, area_num argument in the Select Arguments dialog box for the INDEX function?

▼ Using this version of specifying arguments, you can select more than one range to search. You can specify multiple ranges, placing the ranges in parentheses separate from other arguments, and then use the Area_num argument to identify which of the ranges you want Excel to search. The formula, =INDEX((A1:B6,C1:D7),3,2,1), would return the value in cell B3, the cell located at the third row, second column, in the first range.

What formula did you use to set up the MATCH function for the column number?

▼ The lookup value appears in cell G3, and the Lookup_array range is A1:D1. The formula is =MATCH(G3,A1:D1,0), and the Match_type argument is set to zero to return the location of the first value in the range that equals the lookup value.

Can I combine the INDEX and MATCH functions to display a value in a cell located at a specific intersection?

▼ Yes, you can. Using the worksheet in this example, the formula would be as follows: =INDEX(A1:D27,MATCH(G2,A1:A27,0),MATCH(G3,A1:D1,0)). Instead of trying to set up this complicated formula, you might want to consider using the Lookup Wizard, as described in the next section.

Using the Lookup Wizard

Excel comes with several very powerful tools that you can use for a variety of calculations; these tools are not installed by default, but are available as add-ins. Throughout this book, you will find tasks that use some of these tools. For example, to easily identify the value in a cell at the intersection of a row and a column, you can use the Lookup Wizard.

You install all of the add-in tools using the same technique. You should not need your Office 2007 disc when you install any of the add-in tools. Think of this process as more like activating than installing a tool.

You can have Excel return the value that appears at the intersection of a row and a column in a range that you specify. You can use a combination of the INDEX and MATCH functions by manually typing the function, but the syntax of the combined functions is complex; correctly typing the combined functions can be complicated. You may find it easier to use the Lookup Wizard, which creates the combined functions for you by asking you a series of questions.

Using the Lookup Wizard

Install the Lookup Wizard

1. Click the Formulas tab.
   - The Lookup Wizard does not appear in the Solutions group.
2. Click [Office button].
3. Click Excel Options.

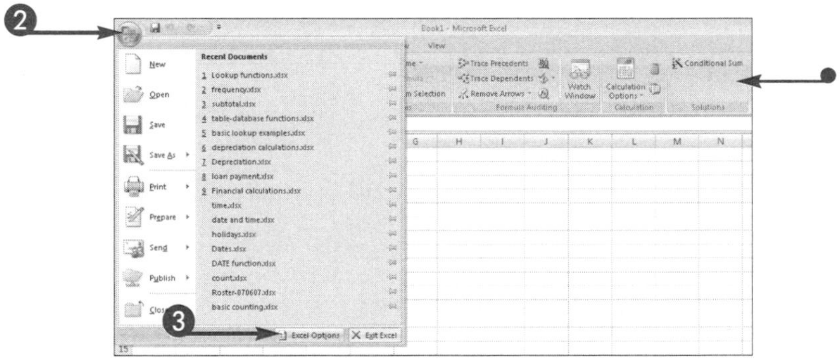

The Excel Options dialog box appears.

4. Click Add-Ins.
   - Currently installed add-ins appear here.
   - Add-ins not yet installed appear here.
5. Click here and choose Excel Add-ins.
6. Click Go.

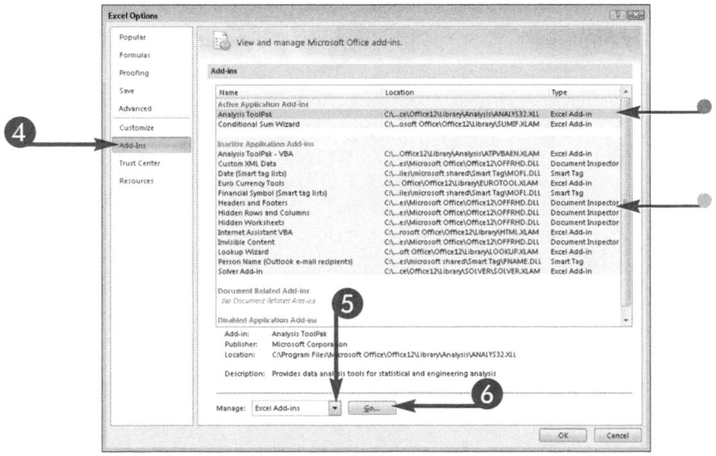

The Add-Ins dialog box appears.

7 Click here to select the Lookup Wizard (☐ changes to ☑).

8 Click OK.

Excel adds the Lookup Wizard to the Solutions group on the Formulas tab.

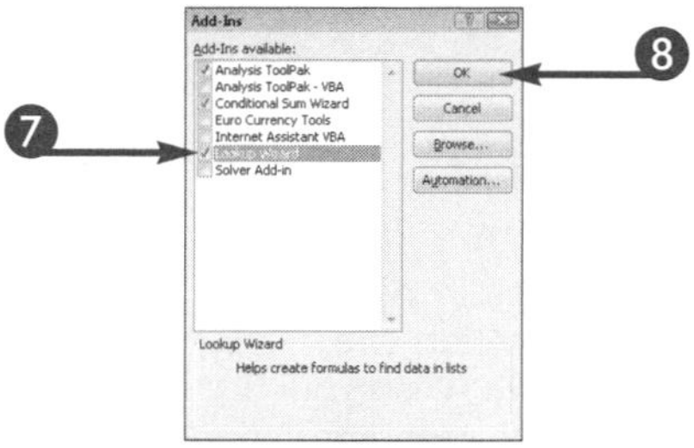

Using the Lookup Wizard

1 Click in the range you want to search.

2 Click Lookup to start the Lookup Wizard.

- Excel proposes a range to search.

3 If necessary, select a different range.

4 Click Next.

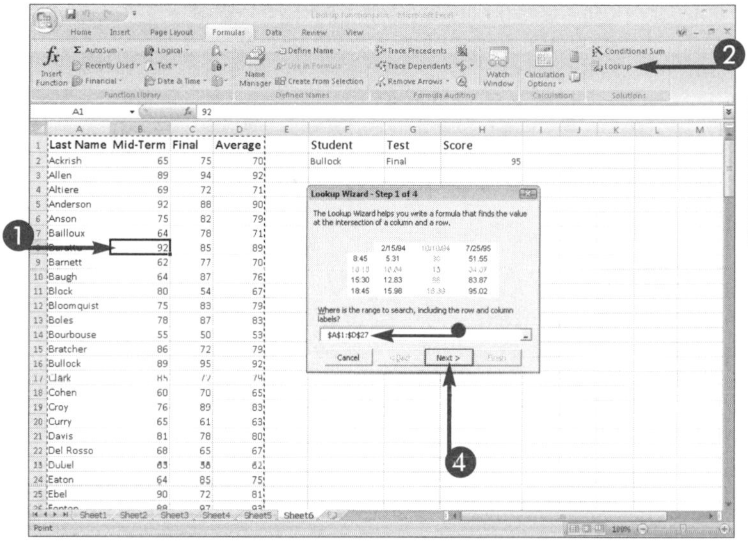

When would I use the MATCH and INDEX functions instead of the Lookup Wizard?

▼ The approach you take to find the values you want is really a matter of personal preference. The Lookup Wizard creates a function that combines the MATCH and INDEX functions for you automatically. If you are really comfortable with Excel's functions and prefer to create the combination functions yourself, or, if you do not want to use a wizard, you can enter the functions without using the Lookup Wizard. See the section, "Look Up a Value in a Table," for details on creating the combined functions without using the Lookup Wizard.

Can I uninstall the Lookup Wizard?

▼ Yes. Repeat Steps 2 to 4 in the subsection, "Install the Lookup Wizard." The Lookup Wizard appears in the list of installed add-ins. Click Go, and, in the Add-Ins dialog box, click the Lookup Wizard (☑ changes to ☐). Click OK and then click the Formulas tab. The Lookup Wizard no longer appears in the Solutions group.

Can I install other add-ins at the same time that I install the Lookup Wizard?

▼ Yes, you can. In the Add-Ins dialog box, click each add-in that you want to install (☐ changes to ☑) and click OK. Each of the add-ins that you install appears either in the Solutions group on the Formulas tab or in the Analysis group on the Data tab.

continued

Using the Lookup Wizard *(Continued)*

The Lookup Wizard can help you easily display a value that appears at the intersection of a row and a column in a range, even when your worksheet contains dozens of rows and columns. For example, suppose that you are a teacher and you have a worksheet that contains test score information as well as grades for class projects. The worksheet contains information for several tests and several projects for all of the students in the class. In your worksheet, you list the students in column A, and the various scores in subsequent columns. Using the Lookup Wizard, you can easily pull out any variation of test or project scores for any given student. You identify the range containing the scores, the column containing the score you want to see, and the row containing the student's name, and Excel does the rest.

Or, suppose that you maintain a worksheet that contains parts that your company manufactures and the scheduled manufacturing dates for each part. Using the Lookup Wizard, you can quickly and easily identify the scheduled manufacturing date for any part.

Using the Lookup Wizard (continued)

The Lookup Wizard - Step 2 of 4 dialog box appears.

5 Click here to select the column containing the value you want to find.

6 Click here to select the row containing the value you want to find.

7 Click Next.

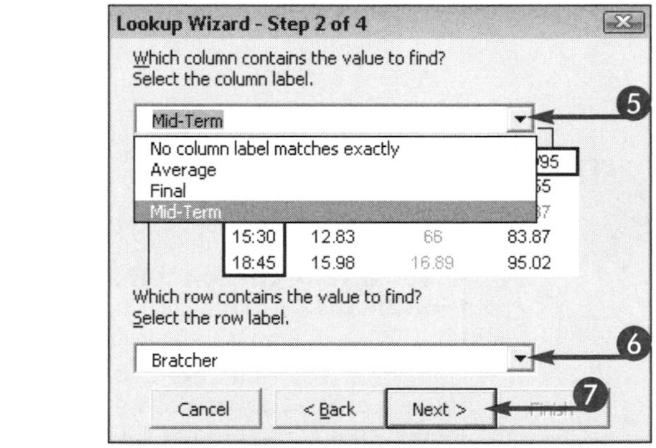

The Lookup Wizard - Step 3 of 4 dialog box appears.

8 Click an option to copy the formula into the workbook (○ changes to ◉).

Note: *This example copies the formula and the lookup parameters.*

9 Click Next.

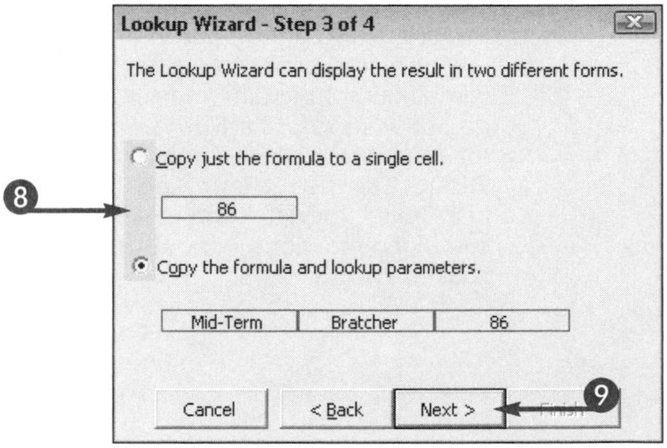

The Lookup Wizard - Step 4 of 6 dialog box appears.

- You can use this dialog box to select a cell to hold one of the labels that describe the value.

⑩ Click here.

Excel collapses the dialog box so that you can click in the worksheet.

⑪ Click the cell where you want the label to appear.

- Excel enters the address of the cell you selected.

⑫ Click .

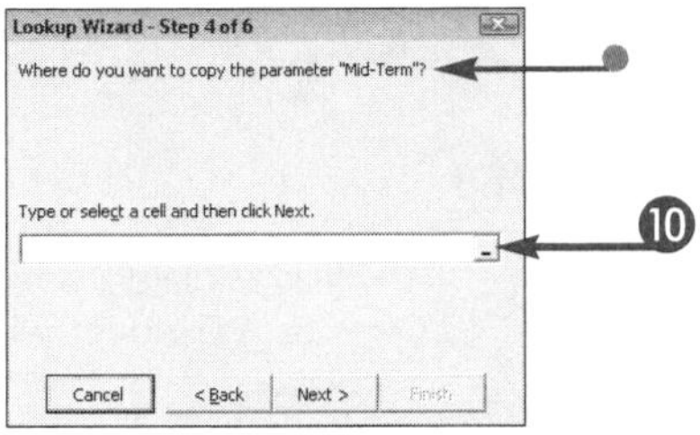

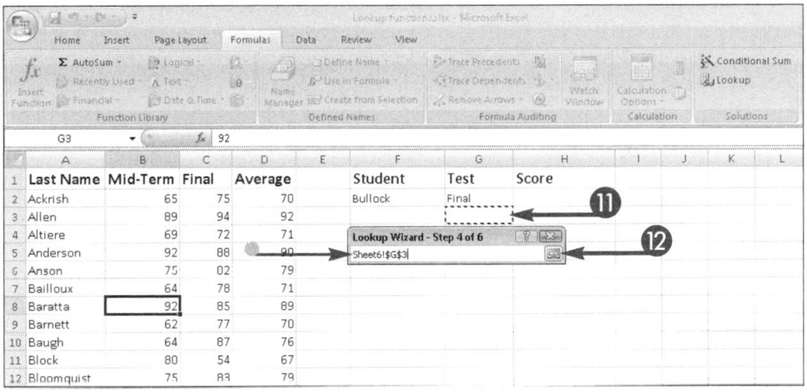

MASTER IT

What happens if I choose the Copy Just the Formula to a Single Cell option?

▼ Excel does not display the Lookup Wizard - Step 4 of 6 dialog box or the Lookup Wizard - Step 5 of 6 dialog box, and so you can skip Steps 10 to 15. The dialog box labeled Lookup Wizard - Step 6 of 6 appears when you perform Step 9, but uses the name Lookup Wizard - Step 4 of 4. You can collapse the dialog box as described in Steps 10 to 12, or you can click a cell in the worksheet to select it. When you click the Finish button in Step 17, Excel enters the formula in the cell you selected, but no labels appear near the cell.

What happens if I include the labels as well as the calculation, and then I later decide that I do not want the labels?

▼ If you delete the labels, Excel displays an #N/A error in the cell containing the combined MATCH and INDEX functions. If you click the cell containing the calculation, you still see the formula in the Formula bar, but Excel can no longer calculate it correctly. The wizard ties the labels to the calculation, and so, to remove the labels, you must rerun the wizard. In the third dialog box of the wizard, click the Copy Just The Formula To A Single Cell option (○ changes to ◉).

continued

Using the Lookup Wizard *(Continued)*

When you use the Lookup Wizard to identify the value in a cell at the intersection of a specific row and column, Excel offers you the choice of either entering just the calculation in your worksheet, or entering both the calculation and the criteria you selected for the calculation into your worksheet. If you choose to enter the criteria as well as the calculation, Excel prompts you individually for cells in which to store each criterion, as well as the result of the calculation. You can place the information anywhere you want in the worksheet.

When you specify locations for the criteria and the results of the calculation, you can collapse the Lookup Wizard dialog boxes, or you can simply click a cell in your worksheet without collapsing any of the dialog boxes.

Once you complete the Lookup Wizard dialog boxes, Excel enters a formula that combines the INDEX and MATCH functions. You can read more about using these functions individually and together in the section, "Look Up a Value in a Table." The Lookup Wizard produces the same results as manually combining these functions; however, the technique provided by the Lookup Wizard is easier than typing the functions.

Using the Lookup Wizard *(continued)*

Excel redisplays the Lookup Wizard - Step 4 of 6 dialog box with the address of the cell you selected.

13 Click Next.

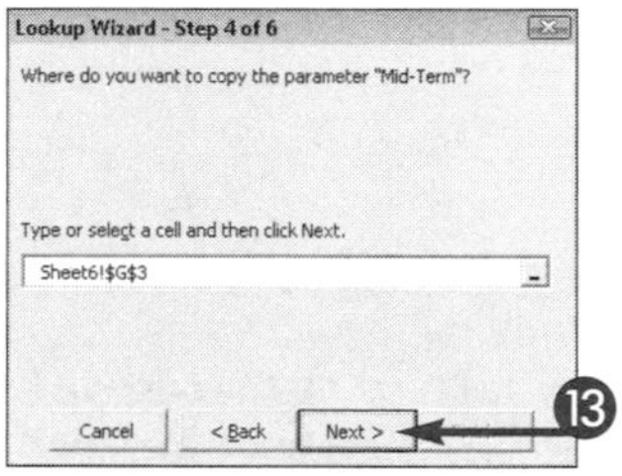

The Lookup Wizard - Step 5 of 6 dialog box appears.

14 Repeat Steps 10 to 12 to select a cell to hold one of the labels that describe the value.

15 Click Next.

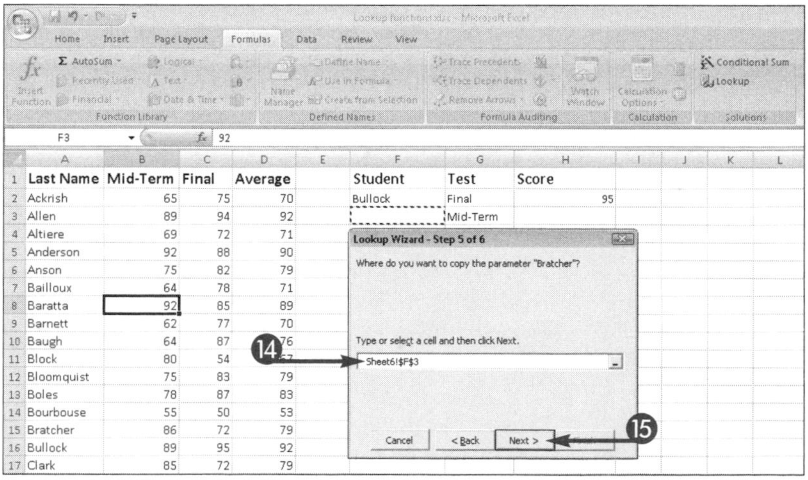

The Lookup Wizard - Step 6 of 6 dialog box appears.

16. Repeat Steps 10 to 12 to select a cell to hold one of the labels that describe the value.
17. Click Finish.

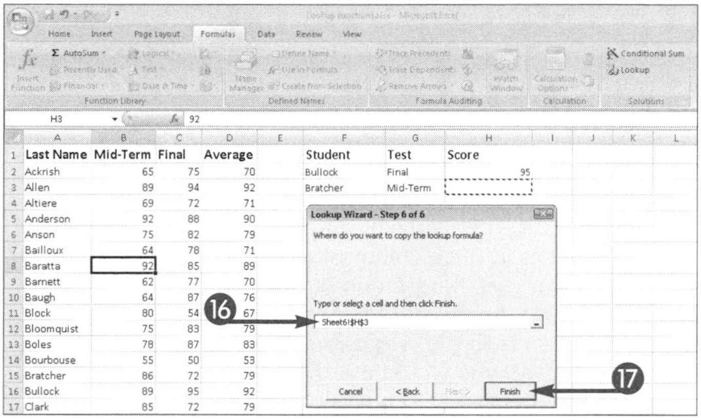

Excel redisplays your worksheet.

18. Click the cell containing the formula.

- The result of the formula appears in the worksheet.
- The formula appears in the Formula bar.

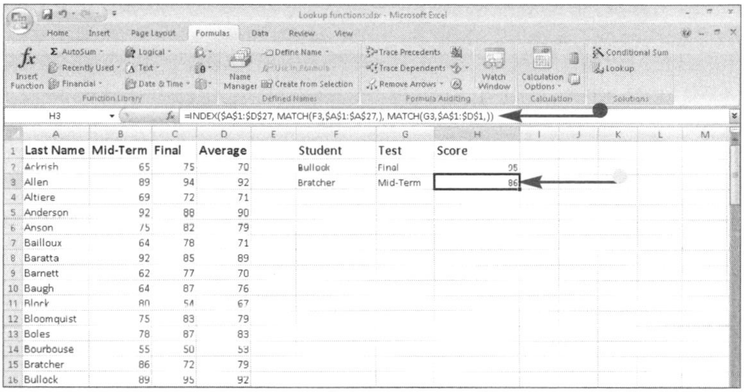

PART III

MASTER IT

Why do the values in my columns appear instead of the labels when I use the Lookup Wizard?

▼ When you specified the range that contains the information you want Excel to search in the Lookup Wizard - Step 2 of 4 dialog box, you did not include the labels that probably appear in the first row of your range. If you rerun the wizard and include the labels in your selection, you will not see values in the columns in the Lookup Wizard - Step 2 of 4 dialog box. Instead, you will see labels. The same principle applies to any row headings that you may have; be sure to include them in the range to search.

When I use the Lookup Wizard, must the range I search contain numbers?

▼ No. The range can contain numbers or text. The Lookup Wizard returns whatever you have stored in the cell it identifies as the intersection of the row and column that you identify when you use the wizard. For example, if the cell contains "Monday," then the Lookup Wizard displays "Monday" in the cell you specify.

What happens if the cell for which I search is blank?

▼ Excel returns zero as the result of the Lookup Wizard. The function that appears in the Formula bar appears in the same format as the function you see as the result of the Lookup Wizard; if you type text or a value into the blank cell, Excel updates the results of the Lookup Wizard.

Choose a Value from a List

You can use the CHOOSE function to look up the information in a list and substitute other information for it. For example, suppose that your worksheet lists dates in three columns for the month, the day, and the year. Month numbers appear in the column containing the months, and you would like to change the numbers to the words representing month names. In this case, you would use the CHOOSE function.

To use the CHOOSE function, set up a separate list in your worksheet that provides the possible results for Excel to return. The Index_num argument of the CHOOSE function must be a number or a cell containing a number between 1 and 254; this argument identifies the cell you want to convert. Other arguments, value1 through value254, identify the cells containing the possible substitutions. The order of the value arguments determines which result Excel displays. Excel considers the value1 argument as the first item in the list, and subsequent value arguments increment sequentially. Excel compares the Index_num argument that you set to its corresponding position in the list of value arguments, and returns the appropriate substitution. For example, if the Index_num argument is 4, then Excel returns the contents of the cell listed as the value4 argument.

Choose a Value from a List

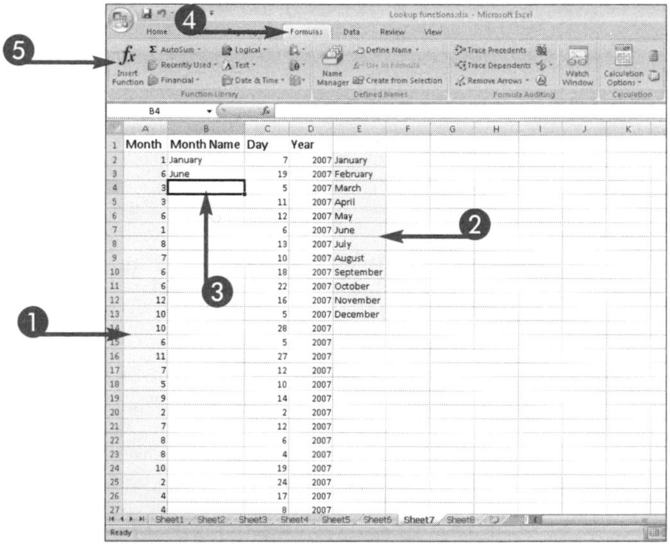

1. In your worksheet, list the values that Excel should change.
2. List the cells containing the information you want to use as substitutions.
3. Click the cell in which you want to store the function.
4. Click the Formulas tab.
5. Click Insert Function.

The Insert Function dialog box appears.

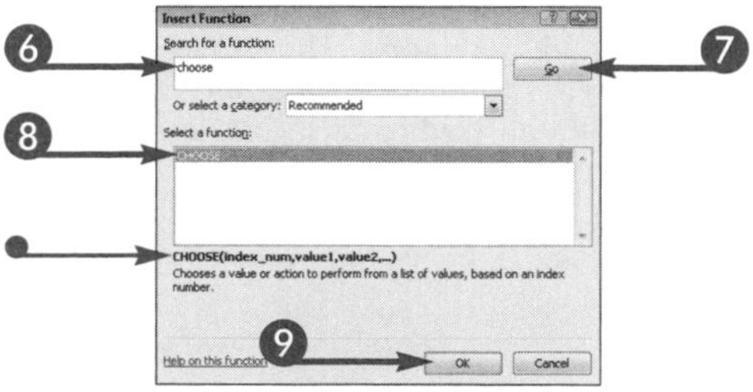

6. Type a description here of the function you want to use.

   This example uses choose.

7. Click Go.
8. Click CHOOSE.
   - A description of the selected function appears here.
9. Click OK.

The Function Arguments dialog box appears.

10. Click here and click the cell you want Excel to change.

11. Click here and click the cell containing the first possible substitute.

    The selected cell's address appears in the Index_num field.

12. Repeat Step 11, clicking the cell containing each subsequent possible substitute.

    The selected cell's address appears in the Value1 field.

13. Click OK.

- Excel displays the result of the formula in the cell you selected in Step 3.
- The formula appears in the Formula bar.

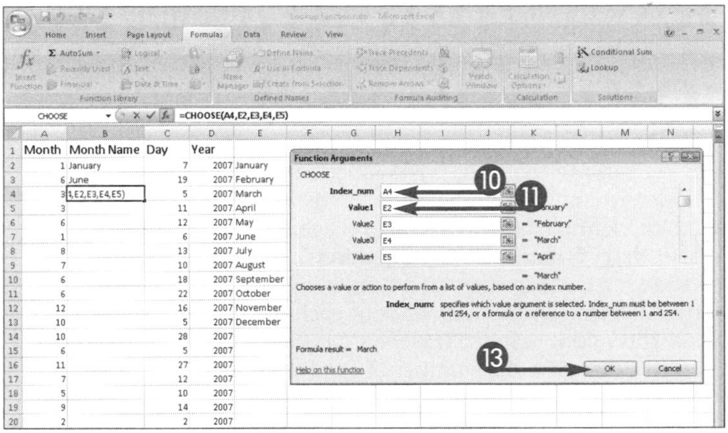

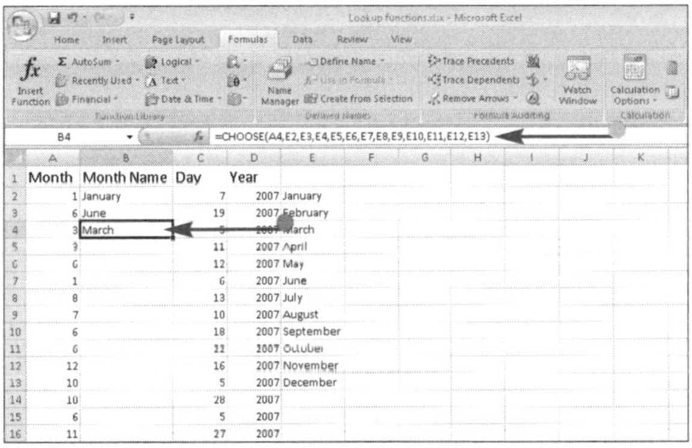

MASTER IT

Why did I get a #VALUE! error as the result of my CHOOSE function?

▼ You probably selected a range of values for the value1 argument instead of selecting individual cells. The CHOOSE function chooses a value from the list of values specified as arguments. If you specify the range A1:A4 as an argument for the CHOOSE function, Excel reads the range as the value1 argument, not the value1, value2, value3, and value4 arguments. To specify the arguments correctly, you must list them individually, separated by commas. For example, instead of =CHOOSE(2,A1:A4), you should use =CHOOSE(2,A1,A2,A3,A4). Click each cell to select it. The order in which you select the cells determines which one Excel substitutes, based on the Index_num argument value.

Is there an easy way to copy the function down a column?

▼ Yes. Edit the function by selecting the cell in which it appears and pressing F2. Change all of the cell references *except the first one* — the Index_num argument — to an absolute cell reference. To do this, place the insertion point in a cell reference and press F4 to insert the dollar signs that signify an absolute cell reference. In the example, the function would look like this: =CHOOSE(A4,$E$2,$E$3,$E$4,$E$5, $E$6,$E$7,$E$8,$E$9, $E$10,$E$11, $E$12,$E$13). When you copy this formula down the column, Excel adjusts only the first argument, which represents the cell you want to change. The rest of the arguments continue to point at the same range.

Determine the Number of Columns in a Selection

You can use the COLUMNS function to determine the number of columns in a range. For example, suppose that you keep a worksheet that contains name and address information for the members of a club, along with other miscellaneous information about each club member. You might want to use the COLUMNS function to determine the number of columns in your worksheet that contain membership information.

The COLUMNS function can also be very useful if you assigned a name to a range and you want to determine the number of columns in the named range; the COLUMNS function makes it very easy to determine this information.

You also might want to use the number of columns in a range as part of a calculation, and you can use the result of the COLUMNS function to return that number. That is, you can nest the COLUMNS function in another function to perform a calculation. For example, you can use the result of the COLUMNS function as the Index_num argument of the CHOOSE function. See Chapter 14 for details on the CHOOSE function.

The COLUMNS function takes only one argument: the range for which you want to determine the number of columns.

Determine the Number of Columns in a Selection

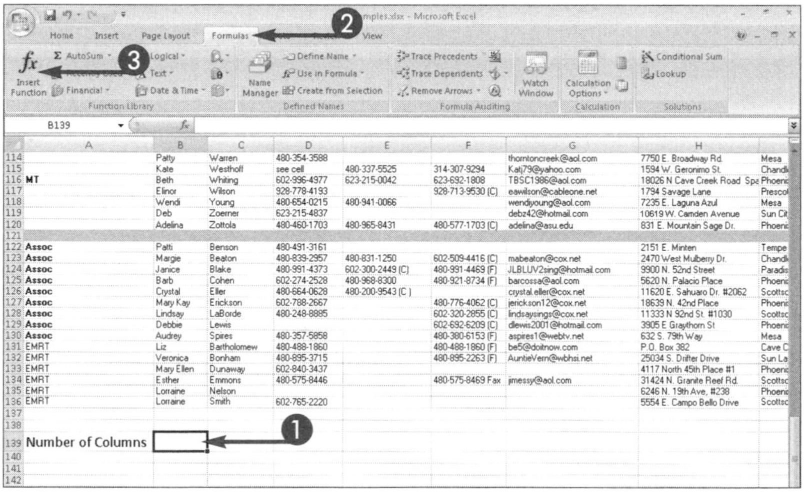

1. Click the cell in which you want to store the function.
2. Click the Formulas tab.
3. Click Insert Function.

The Insert Function dialog box appears.

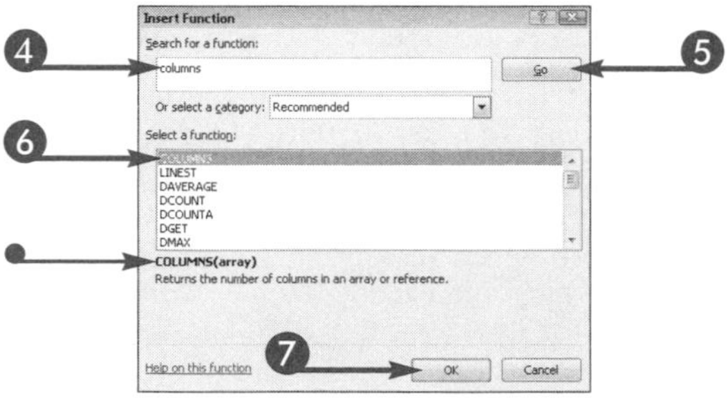

4. Type a description here of the function you want to use.

   This example uses columns.
5. Click Go.
6. Click COLUMNS.
   - A description of the selected function appears here.
7. Click OK.

The Function Arguments dialog box appears.

8 Type a range name or select a range in the worksheet.

9 Click OK.

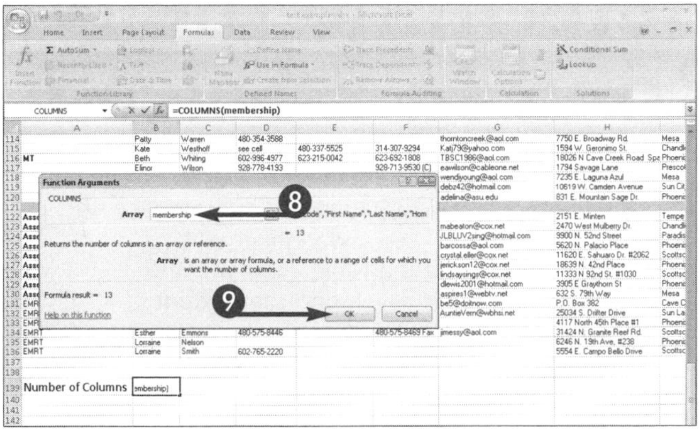

- Excel displays the result of the formula in the cell you selected in Step 1.
- The formula appears in the Formula bar.

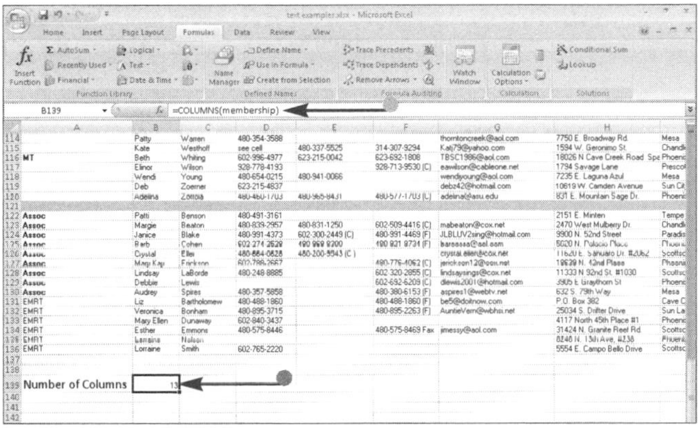

In Step 4, I accidentally typed "column" instead of "columns" and found the COLUMN function; how does it differ from the COLUMNS function?

▼ While the COLUMNS function returns the number of columns in a range or an array, the COLUMN function returns the number of a specified column. Column A is considered 1, and each successive column is sequentially numbered. If you use the formula =COLUMN(H136), Excel returns 8 because H is the eighth column. If you use a range as the argument, Excel considers only the first value in the range, and so the formula =COLUMN(H136:L153) also returns 8. However, if you use an array as the argument, Excel returns an array as the result of the formula.

Can I use the COLUMNS function with an array as the argument?

▼ Yes. Simply select the array as the argument of the COLUMNS function; Excel returns the number of columns in the array range. For example, suppose that you selected the range A1:C2 and typed the following formula: **={1,2,3;4,5,6}**. Excel fills the range A1:C1 with the numbers 1, 2, and 3, and the range A2:C2 with the numbers 4, 5, and 6. If you select any cell in the range, you see the array formula. If, in cell D4, you type **=COLUMNS(A1:C2)**, Excel returns 3, the number of columns in the array range, as the result.

Determine the Number of Rows in a Selection

You can use the ROWS function to determine the number of rows in a range. For example, suppose that you keep a worksheet that contains sales information for a cable company; the worksheet tracks sales each day, listing the amount of the sale, the type of cable product sold, who made the sale, the branch office from which the sale was generated, and whether the sale was made to a new or an existing customer. You might want to use the ROWS function to determine the number of sales made in a given timeframe. For example, you might want to know the number of sales on a given day, in a given week, or for an entire month.

The ROWS function can also be very useful if you assigned a name to a range and you want to determine the number of rows in the named range; the ROWS function makes it very easy to determine this information. You can also use the ROWS function as the argument for another function.

The ROWS function takes only one argument: the range for which you want to determine the number of columns.

Determine the Number of Rows in a Selection

1. Click the cell in which you want to store the function.
2. Click the Formulas tab.
3. Click Insert Function.

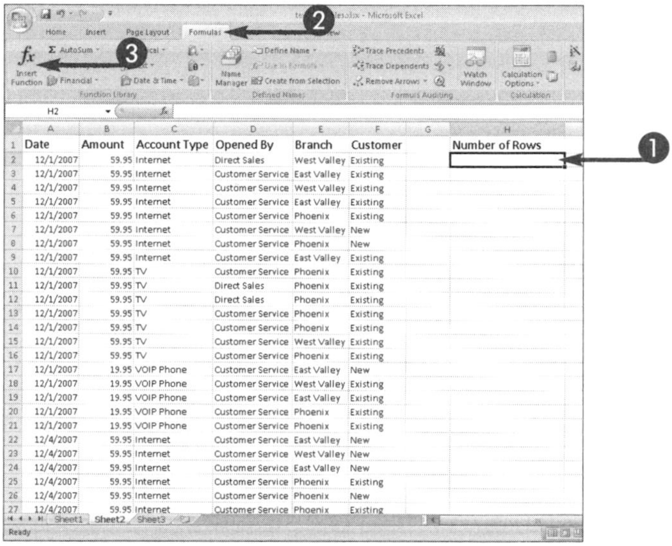

The Insert Function dialog box appears.

4. Type a description here of the function you want to use.

   This example uses rows.

5. Click Go.
6. Click ROWS.

   - A description of the selected function appears here.

7. Click OK.

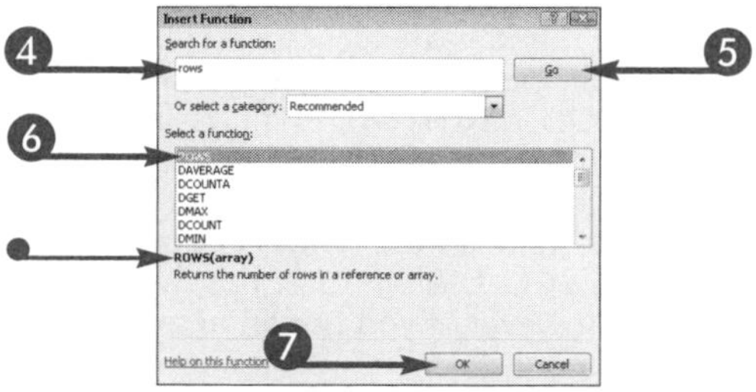

The Function Arguments dialog box appears.

8. Type a range name or select a range in the worksheet.
9. Click OK.

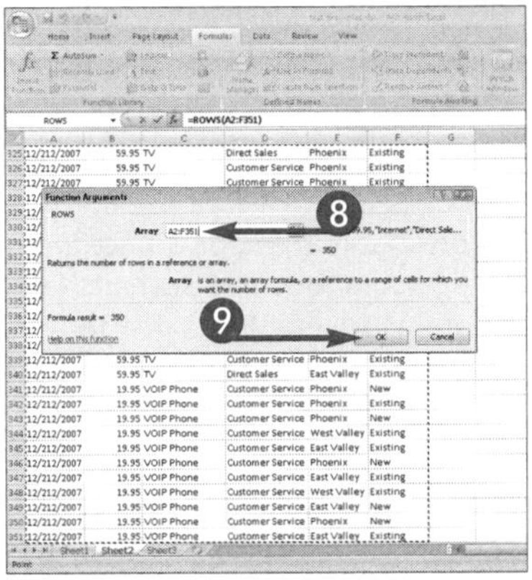

- Excel displays the result of the formula in the cell you selected in Step 1.
- The formula appears in the Formula bar.

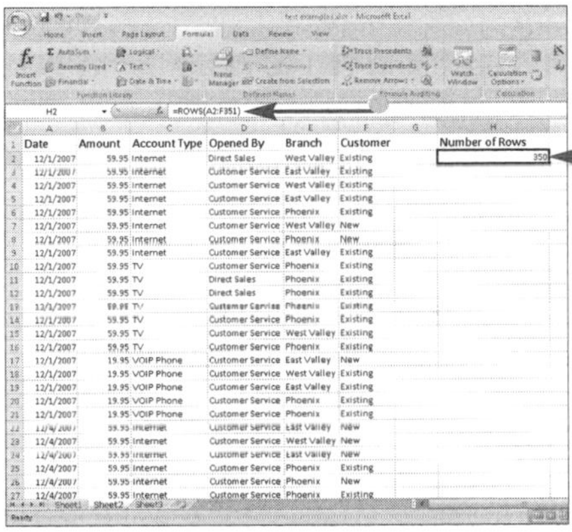

MASTER IT

In Step 4, I accidentally typed "row" instead of "rows" and found the ROW function; how does it differ from the ROWS function?

▼ While the ROWS function returns the number of rows in a range or an array, the ROW function returns the number of a specified row. Row 1 is considered 1, and each successive row is sequentially numbered. If you use the formula =ROW(H136), Excel returns 136. If you use a range as the argument, Excel considers only the first value in the range, and so the formula =ROW(H136:L153) also returns 136. However, if you use an array as the argument, Excel returns an array as the result of the formula.

Can I use the ROWS function in conjunction with another function?

▼ Yes. For example, you can use the result of the ROWS function as the Index_num argument of the CHOOSE function to specify the number in a list of substitutes that Excel should use when making a substitution. See Chapter 14 for details on the CHOOSE function.

Can I combine the COLUMNS and ROWS functions to find the total number of cells in a range?

▼ Yes. Suppose that you store sales information in the range A2:F351. You can use the following formula to determine the number of cells in the range: =COLUMNS(A2:F351) *ROWS(A2:F351). Excel returns 2100 because the COLUMNS function returns 6 and the ROWS function returns 350.

Change Text Case

Although you ordinarily think of doing mathematical calculations in a spreadsheet, Excel also contains several functions that you can use to perform operations on text entries, known as *string* operations.

You often need to use text functions when you work with data that you import into Excel from other programs. For example, suppose that you purchase a mailing list for your direct mail business. You intend to send letters to everyone on the list to advertise your products and services, and you want to use the mail merge feature in your word processor to create the letters. When you open the file containing the mailing list, you discover that all of the names appear in all uppercase letters. You need to change the way the information appears before you can use it in a mail merge operation.

You can import the file into Excel and use the PROPER function to change the appearance of the text in the mailing list. The PROPER function capitalizes the first letter of each word and changes all other letters to lowercase. The PROPER function also capitalizes any letter that appears in the text argument that is preceded by any character other than a letter.

Change Text Case

Use Proper Case

1. Click the cell in which you want to store the function.
2. Click the Formulas tab.
3. Click Insert Function.

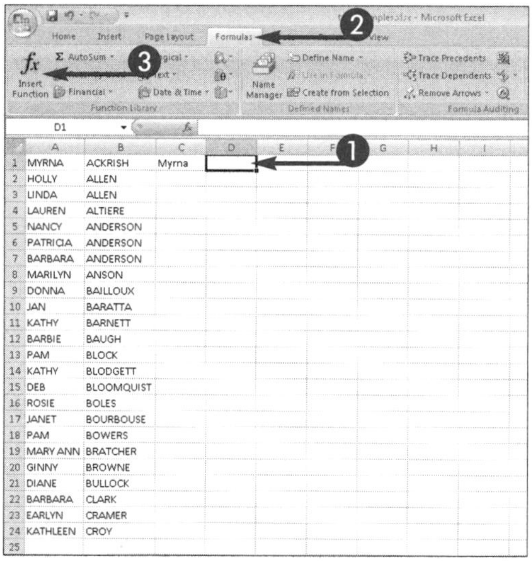

The Insert Function dialog box appears.

4. Type a description here of the function you want to use.

   This example uses proper.

5. Click Go.
6. Click PROPER.
   - A description of the selected function appears here.
7. Click OK.

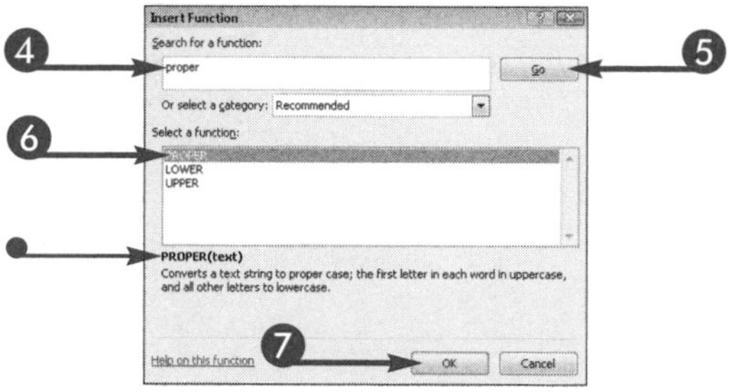

The Function Arguments dialog box appears.

8. Click the cell you want to use as the argument.
   - Anticipated results appear here.
9. Click OK.

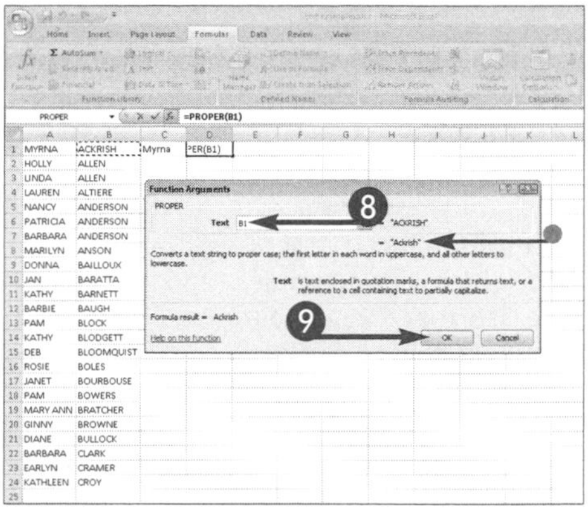

- Excel displays the result of the formula in the cell you selected in Step 1.
- The formula appears in the Formula bar.

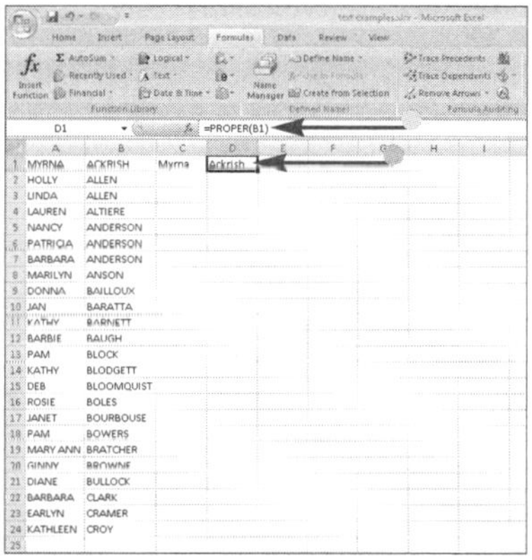

MASTER IT

What does the PROPER function do when I have more than one word in a cell?

▼ The PROPER function capitalizes the first letter of each word in the cell. For example, suppose that cell A1 contains "sales for products in june." If you type the function, **=PROPER(A1)**, in cell B1, then Excel capitalizes each word in cell B1, displaying "Sales For Products In June."

What does the PROPER function do when I have multiple words in a cell and some of the words contain numbers?

▼ The PROPER function capitalizes the first letter of each word, as well as any letter that appears after any character that is not a letter. For example, suppose that cell A1 contains "sales for product 1h32b." If you type the function, =**PROPER(A1)**, in cell B1, then Excel displays "Sales For Product 1H32B" in cell B1.

To enter the formula in adjacent cells, must I go through the steps to enter the formula again?

▼ No, you can copy the formula to the adjacent cells using either the Fill handle or by clicking the Copy button on the Home tab, selecting the cells to which you want to copy the formula, and then clicking the Paste button. When Excel copies the formula, it adjusts the formula because the argument is stored in the original cell as a relative cell reference.

continued

Change Text Case *(Continued)*

You can use the UPPER function to change text in a cell so that it all appears in uppercase letters. For example, suppose that your boss has decided that the part numbers for inventory parts that you use in your worksheet must all appear in uppercase. However, you find it difficult to remember to switch between upper- and lowercase as you move from cell to cell in your worksheet. In fact, you find it easiest to type everything in lowercase letters. You can use the UPPER function to convert the contents of any cell so that all letters in the cell appear in uppercase.

The UPPER function takes only one argument: the text you want to display in uppercase. You can type the text as the argument, or you can supply a cell address containing the text that you want to display in all uppercase letters. When you use the UPPER function, Excel changes all letters in the argument so that they appear in uppercase. If you supply an argument that contains multiple words, Excel displays all of the words in the argument in uppercase letters.

Change Text Case *(continued)*

Use Uppercase Letters

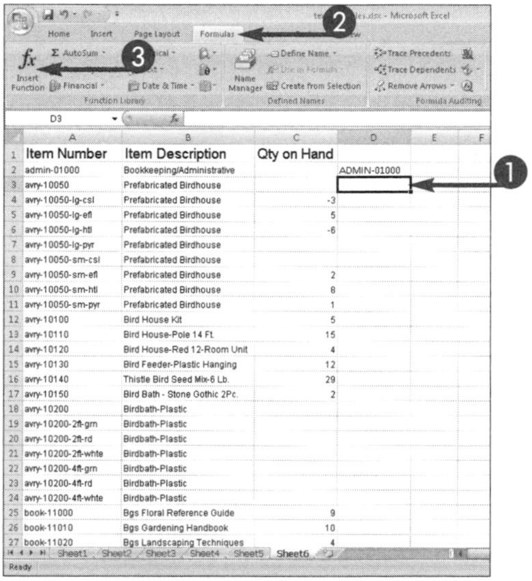

1. Click the cell in which you want to store the function.
2. Click the Formulas tab.
3. Click Insert Function.

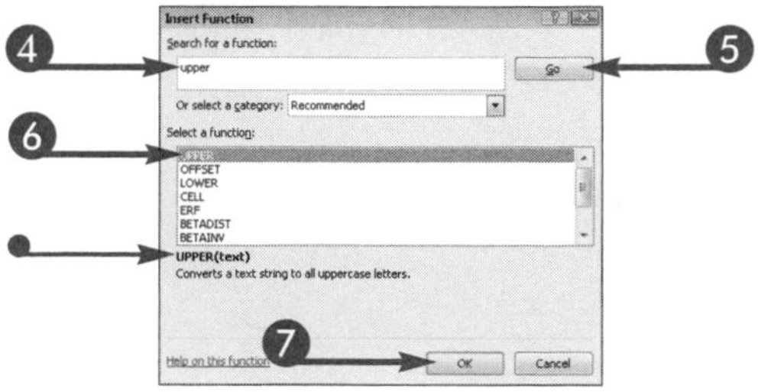

The Insert Function dialog box appears.

4. Type a description here of the function you want to use.

   This example uses upper.

5. Click Go.
6. Click UPPER.
   - A description of the selected function appears here.
7. Click OK.

The Function Arguments dialog box appears.

8. Click the cell that you want to use as the argument.
   - Anticipated results appear here.
9. Click OK.

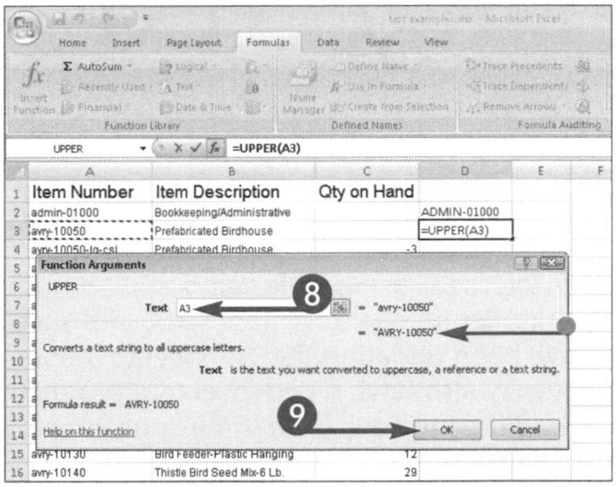

- Excel displays the result of the formula in the cell you selected in Step 1.
- The formula appears in the Formula bar.

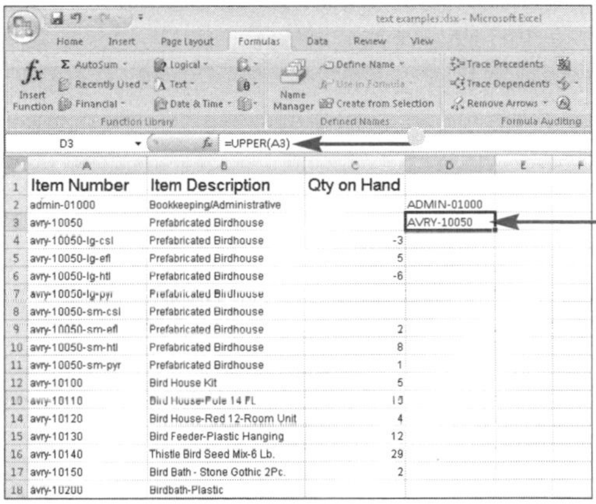

How do I get the results of the UPPER function to replace the information that I want to convert to uppercase letters?

▼ First, copy the formula down the column. Select the cells containing the formula, click the Home tab, and click . Then, click under Paste and click Paste Values. Excel converts the formulas to values. Finally, select the column you just converted to values, click , click the first cell you want to replace, and click Paste.

How does the UPPER function handle numbers mixed in with letters?

▼ The UPPER function ignores numbers and operates only on letters. Numbers remain in the text string in their original location. The UPPER function operates only on the text around them, changing the text so that all letters appear in uppercase. If some letters already appear as uppercase letters, Excel does not change them.

If you typed everything in lowercase letters, how did you get Column B to appear with uppercase and lowercase letters?

▼ Using the PROPER function, the contents of Column B can be changed from all lowercase letters to proper case, as shown in this example. Follow the steps in the subsection, "Use Proper Case," to make this change.

continued

Change Text Case *(Continued)*

You can use the LOWER function to convert text in your worksheet so that it all appears in lowercase. For example, suppose that you keep a worksheet of inventory item sales, and several people have been updating the worksheet. Various individuals may also have typed inventory product numbers in different ways so that the appearance of the product numbers is inconsistent. Your vendor uses all lowercase letters when referring to the part numbers, and so you want to change all of the part numbers so that they appear in lowercase. If you do not want to enforce case rules on those entering the information, then you can use the LOWER function.

The LOWER function takes only one argument: the text you want to display in lowercase. You can type the text as the argument, or you can supply a cell address containing the text that you want to display in all lowercase letters. When you use the LOWER function, Excel changes all letters in the argument so that they appear in lowercase. If you supply an argument that contains multiple words, Excel displays all of the words in the argument in lowercase letters.

Change Text Case *(continued)*

Use Lowercase Letters

1. Click the cell in which you want to store the function.
2. Click the Formulas tab.
3. Click Insert Function.

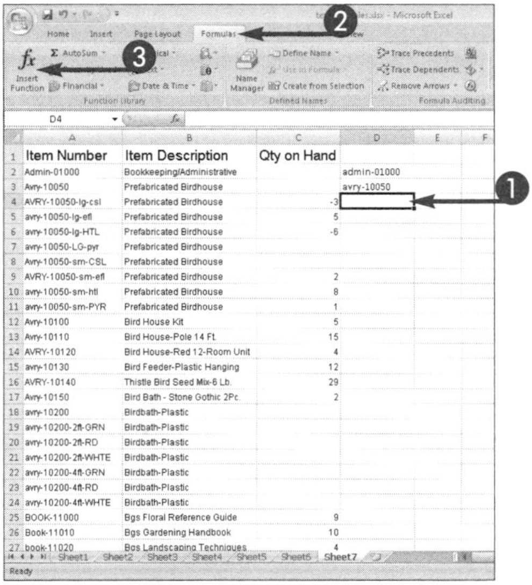

The Insert Function dialog box appears.

4. Type a description here of the function you want to use.

   This example uses lowercase.

5. Click Go.
6. Click LOWER.
   - A description of the selected function appears here.
7. Click OK.

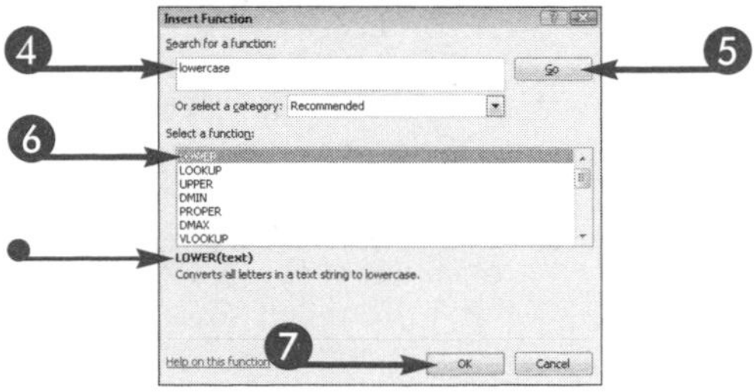

The Function Arguments dialog box appears.

8. Click the cell you want to use as the argument.
   - Anticipated results appear here.
9. Click OK.

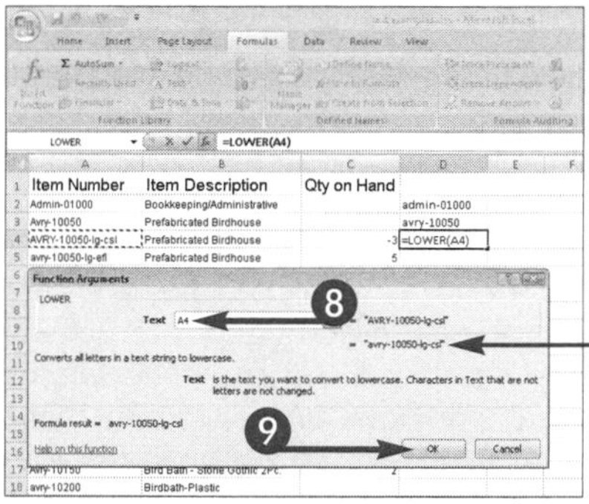

- Excel displays the result of the formula in the cell you selected in Step 1.
- The formula appears in the Formula bar.

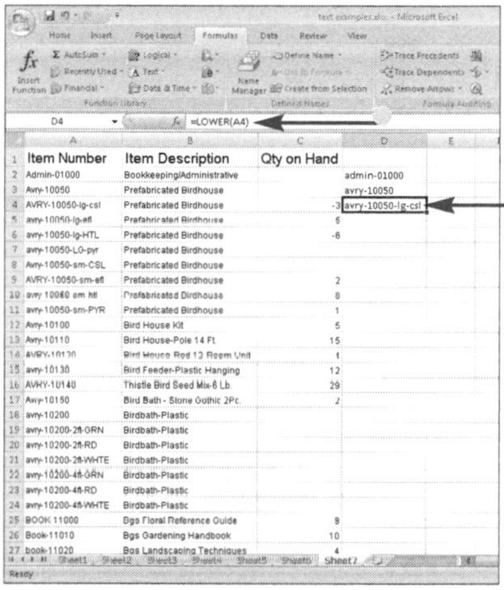

MASTER IT

How does the LOWER function handle numbers?

▼ Like the UPPER function, the LOWER function ignores numbers and operates only on letters. Numbers remain in the text string in their original location. The LOWER function operates only on the text around them, changing the text so that all letters appear in lowercase. If some letters already appear as lowercase letters, Excel does not change them.

Can you give me another example of when I might use the LOWER function?

▼ Suppose that you imported information into Excel that appears in a mixture of proper case, uppercase, and lowercase. You may also need to combine information that appears in several cells to use in sentences. You can use the LOWER function to change all of the text to lowercase and reduce the amount of editing that you need to do. For more information on combining text, see the section, "Join Text."

How does the LOWER function handle punctuation?

▼ It ignores punctuation. For example, suppose that cell A1 contains two sentences, such as, "This is text. I want it all in lowercase letters." If you type **=LOWER(A1)** in cell B1, then Excel displays the following in cell B1: "this is text. i want it all in lowercase letters."

continued

Change Text Case *(Continued)*

Although Excel does not contain a function that creates sentence case, you can use a combination of functions to generate sentence case for a cell. For example, suppose that you receive a workbook from someone that contains directions for using the workbook in cell A1, and the directions appear in all uppercase letters because the file was generated by a program other than Excel. You can change the appearance of the text in cell A1 using a combination of the LOWER, UPPER, LEFT, RIGHT, and LEN functions.

Initially, you convert all of the text in cell A1 to lowercase. Next, you use the UPPER, LEFT, RIGHT, and LEN functions to make the first letter in the cell appear in uppercase, identifying the letter using the LEFT function. Then, you combine the newly uppercase letter with the rest of the string using the RIGHT and LEN functions together. You use the LEN function to determine how many characters appear in the cell, and the RIGHT function to operate on all of those characters except for the first character.

You cannot use the Insert Function Wizard to create this kind of combination function.

Change Text Case *(continued)*

Apply Sentence Case

1. Click the cell in which you want to store the LOWER function.
2. Type =**LOWER(**.
3. Click the cell containing the string you want to convert to lowercase.
4. Type) and click ☑.

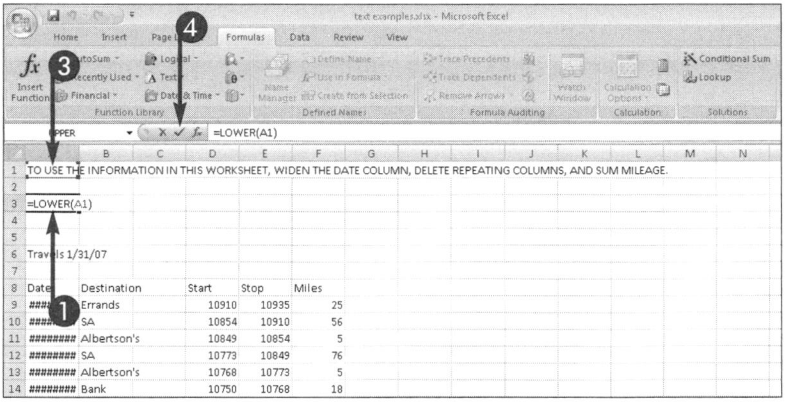

- The phrase appears in lowercase letters in the cell you selected in Step 1.

5. Click another cell in which to store the sentence case function combination.
6. Type =**UPPER(LEFT(**
7. Click the cell you selected in Step 1.

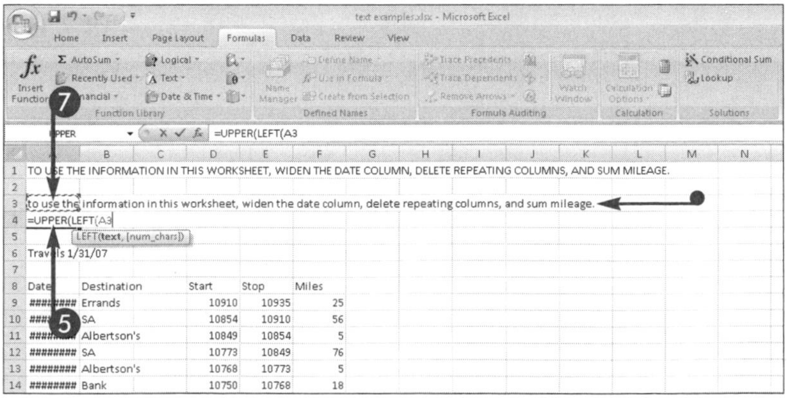

8 Type **,1))&RIGHT(**

9 Click the cell you selected in Step 1.

10 Type **,LEN(**

11 Click the cell you selected in Step 1.

12 Type **)-1)**

13 Click ☑.

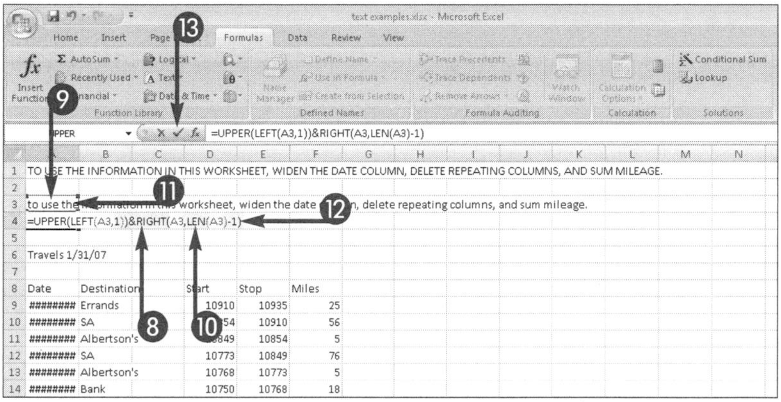

- Excel displays the result of the formula in the cell you selected in Step 1.
- The formula appears in the Formula bar.

Note: *You can replace the information in the original cell with the information you generated by converting the function to a value and then copying it. See the section, "Change Text to Values," for details.*

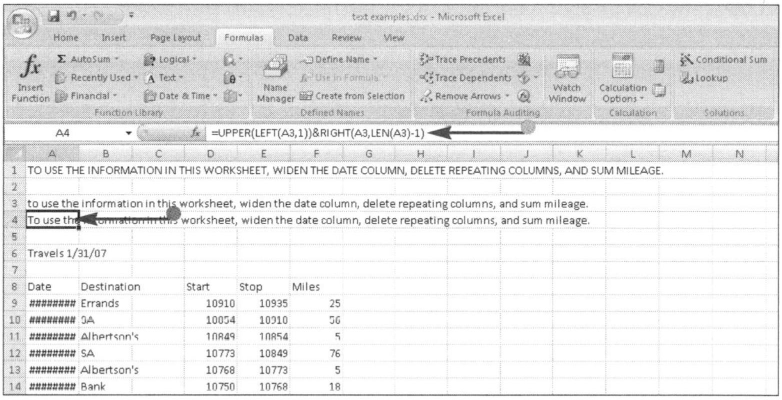

MASTER IT

What does the LEFT function do?

▼ Using the LEFT function, you can tell Excel to work with a specified number of characters on the left side of a string of characters. The function takes two arguments: the cell containing the string, and the number of characters at the left side of the string that you want Excel to use. If you enter a number equal to or larger than the number of characters in the string, Excel works with the entire string.

What does the RIGHT function do?

▼ The RIGHT function works like the LEFT function, only from the right side of a string. Using the RIGHT function, you can tell Excel to work with a specified number of characters on the right side of a string of characters. The function takes two arguments: the cell containing the string, and the number of characters at the right side of the string that you want Excel to use.

What does the LEN function do?

▼ You can use the LEN function to determine the number of characters in a string. The function takes only one argument: the cell containing the string whose length you want to find. As shown in this example, the LEN function is often used in conjunction with the LEFT and RIGHT functions.

Join Text

You can join text stored in several cells so that the text appears in a single cell. For example, suppose that you receive a file that contains name and address information. In the workbook you receive, the city, state, and Zip code appear in separate cells. For your purposes, things would work better if they all appeared in one cell, in the format where a comma and a space follow the city name and two spaces separate the state from the Zip code. You can use the CONCATENATE function to join the text in the three cells into a single cell.

The CONCATENATE function actually requires as many arguments as you have text to join, up to 255 arguments. This example shows how to assign five arguments to the CONCATENATE function. Three of the arguments are cells containing city, state, and Zip code information. The other two arguments add space between the city and state, and between the state and the Zip code.

You may want to convert the function to a value when you finish so that you can copy and paste the cells wherever you need them. See the section, "Change Text to Values," for details.

Join Text

1. Click the cell in which you want to store the function.
2. Click the Formulas tab.
3. Click Insert Function.

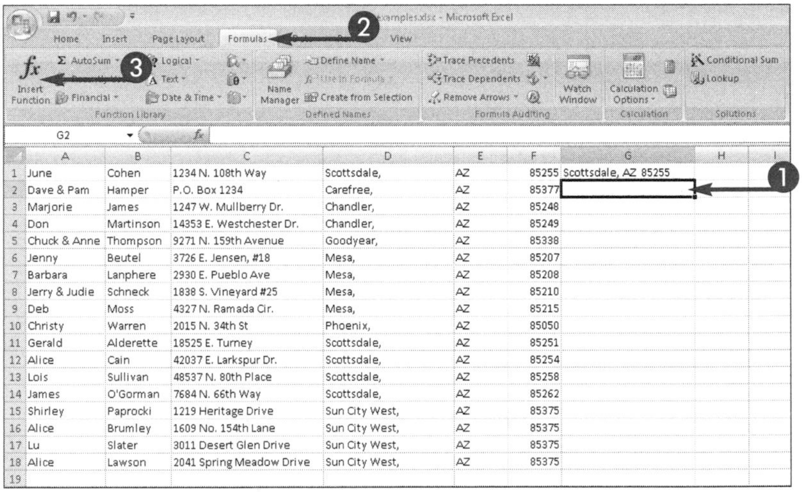

The Insert Function dialog box appears.

4. Type a description here of the function you want to use.

   This example uses join.

5. Click Go.
6. Click CONCATENATE.
   - A description of the selected function appears here.
7. Click OK.

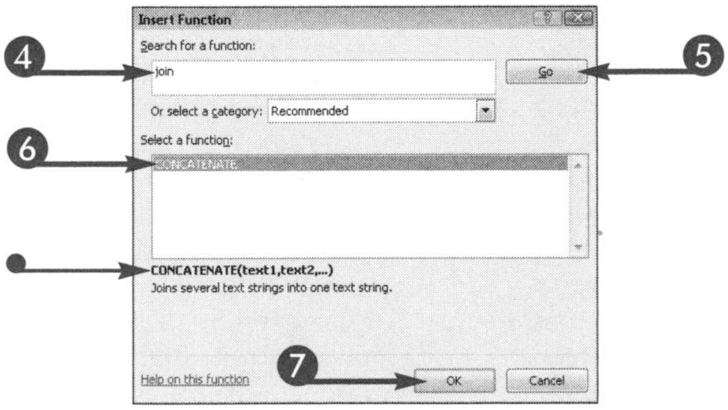

The Function Arguments dialog box appears.

8. Click here and click the cell representing the first argument.
9. Click here and type a space.
10. Repeat Steps 8 and 9 to include all information.

Note: Specify arguments in the order in which you want the joined text to appear.

11. Click OK.

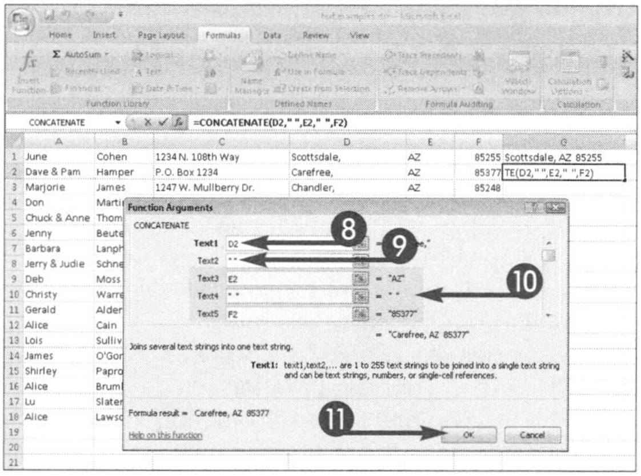

- Excel displays the result of the formula — the joined text — in the cell you selected in Step 1.
- The formula appears in the Formula bar.

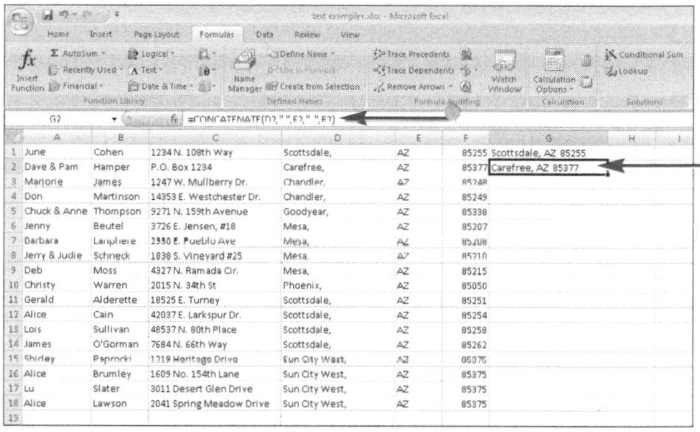

MASTER IT

Is there a way to join text without using a function?

▼ Yes. Excel automatically views the ampersand (&) as a concatenation operator, and you can use it to join cells. Suppose that you want to join the city, state, and Zip code shown in cells D3, E3, and F3, respectively, in the example. If you type **=D3&" "&E3&" "&F3** in cell G3, Excel displays "Chandler, AZ 85248" in cell G3. Type quotation marks around any text strings, such as spaces, that you want to include but have not stored in cells. In this example, one space appears between the first set of quotation marks, and two spaces appear between the second set of quotation marks.

Why did you perform Step 9?

▼ The CONCATENATE function simply joins information that you type into the Insert Function Wizard, or information that appears in cells. In most cases, you need space when you join two or more cells. You must explicitly include space when you use the CONCATENATE function. In the example, if no spaces were included, Excel would have returned "Carefree,AZ85377" as if it were all one word. You include spaces as arguments to the function wherever you want Excel to insert spaces in the end result. The same principle is true if you use the ampersand operator to join text. You must include spaces, enclosed in quotation marks, at appropriate places in the string.

Split Up Text

You can split text stored in one cell so that it appears in multiple cells. For example, suppose that the person responsible for show ticket sales in your organization stored the names and addresses of those who purchased tickets in a workbook, typing the city, state, and Zip code in a single cell. As the keeper of your organization's address list, your job is to combine the information in the ticket sales workbook with the mailing list workbook that you keep. However, in your workbook, you have separated the city, state, and Zip code into three columns. You need to separate the data that you receive in the workbook so that you can copy and paste it into the mailing list workbook that you maintain.

Using the Text to Columns feature in Excel, you can split up the text in the ticket sales workbook. When you use this feature, you describe the characters that separate your data in the cell. If a character, such as a comma, a semicolon, or a tab, separates each portion of the information in the cell, then your data is most likely delimited. If the information in the cell is separated by spaces, then your data is most likely fixed width.

Split Up Text

1. Click a cell in your worksheet that contains information that you want to split into separate cells.
2. Click the Data tab.
3. Click Text to Columns.

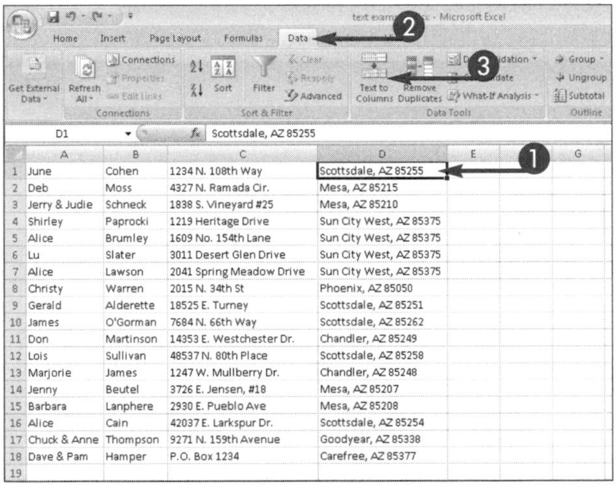

The Convert Text to Columns Wizard - Step 1 of 3 dialog box appears.

4. Click an option to describe how your data is separated in the cell (◎ changes to ◉).

Note: *If you want to control where cell breaks appear, choose Fixed Width. This example uses Fixed Width.*

5. Click Next.

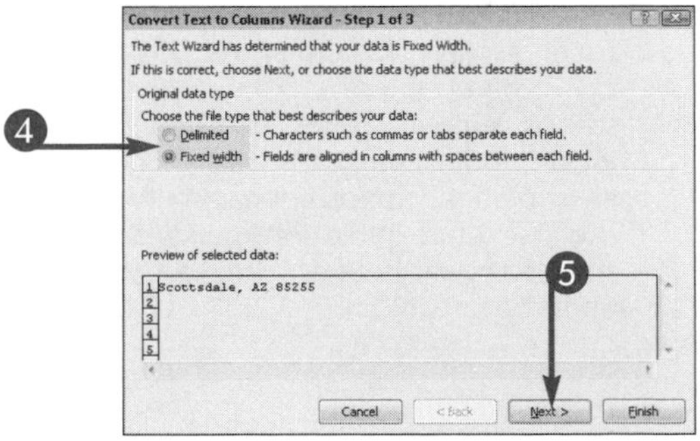

The Convert Text to Columns Wizard - Step 2 of 3 dialog box appears.

- You can click to add, double-click to delete, or a drag to move a break line.

This example demonstrates moving a line break.

6 Click Next.

The Convert Text to Columns Wizard - Step 3 of 3 dialog box appears, where you can set a column format for each new column.

7 Click Finish.

- Excel splits the data in the cell that you selected in Step 1 into multiple cells.

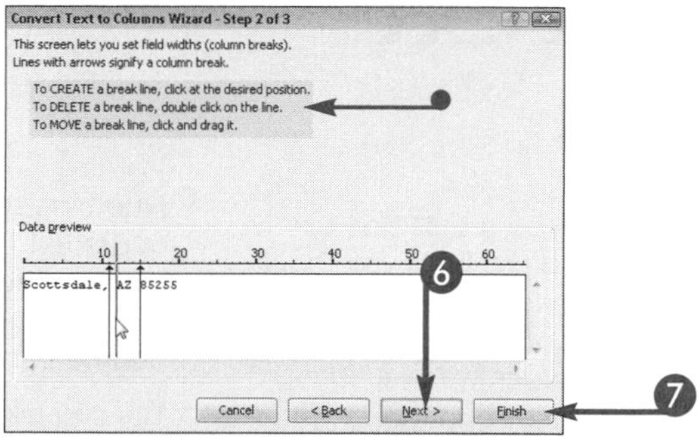

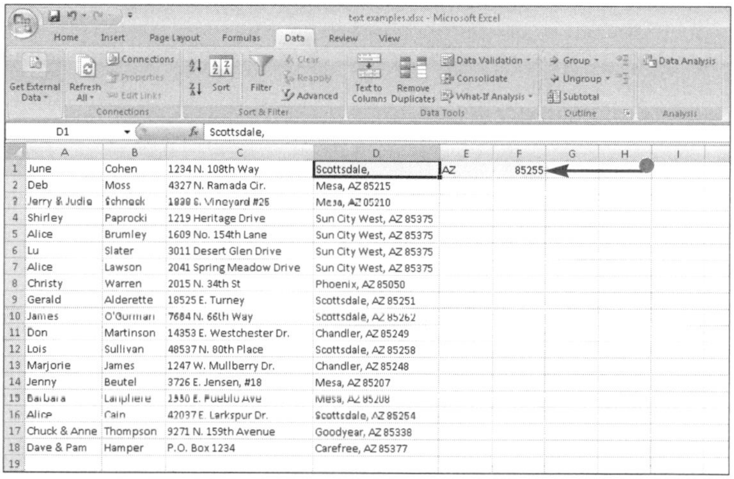

MASTER IT

Can I split multiple cells simultaneously?

▼ If the cells contain text that is unequal in length, then it is difficult to split cells simultaneously. However, if several of the cells contain the same text, you can select those cells and then perform the steps in this section. You may find it easier to sort the data so that all cells containing the same data appear grouped together. Click anywhere in the data, click the Data tab, and click Sort. In the Sort dialog box that appears, select the column by which you want to sort from the Sort By list and click OK.

What happens if I choose Delimited in Step 4?

▼ In the dialog box that appears, you click check boxes (☐ changes to ☑) to identify the characters that delimit your data — tab, semicolon, comma, space, or other — and you specify the character. You cannot control where line breaks appear using the Delimited option.

What kinds of formats can I assign to the new columns?

▼ You can assign a General format, a Text format, or a Date format. You can also eliminate a portion of the data entirely by clicking the column representation containing that portion of the data and clicking the Do Not Import Column (Skip) option (◯ changes to ◉).

Change Text to Values

You can convert numbers stored as text to values. Suppose that you receive a workbook that contains information that was generated by exporting information from another program. Numbers often appear as text values in Excel. If you select a number in such a workbook and look at the Formula bar, you will notice that an apostrophe (') appears to the left of the number. In addition, the number appears left-aligned in the cell. The apostrophe is a universal symbol to Excel that the contents of the cell are text.

Numbers stored as text display a green triangle in the upper-left corner of the cell. Also, if you select the cell, a Smart Tag button appears. You can use the Smart Tag button to decide how you want Excel to handle numbers that are stored as text.

You can use these values stored as text in formulas, and Excel returns correct mathematical results. However, if anyone else uses your workbook, the left-alignment of these numbers may confuse them. The green triangles can also become very annoying to see.

Change Text to Values

- Numbers preceded by apostrophes (') appear left-aligned, and a green triangle appears in the upper-left corner of the cell.

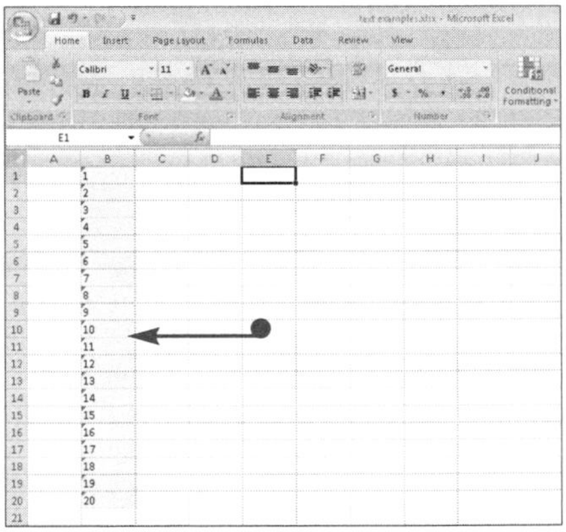

1. Select a cell containing a triangle in the upper-left corner.

- An apostrophe precedes the number in the Formula bar.
- A Smart Tag button (⟐) appears.

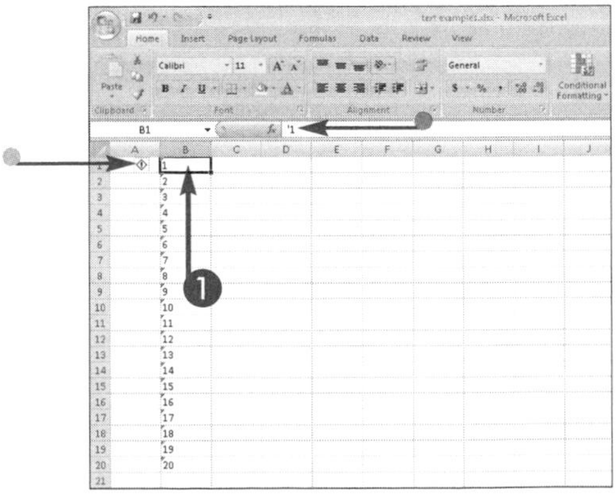

2 Click ◈.

Excel displays a list of options. The first item on the list describes the reason why ◈ appears.

3 Click Convert to Number.

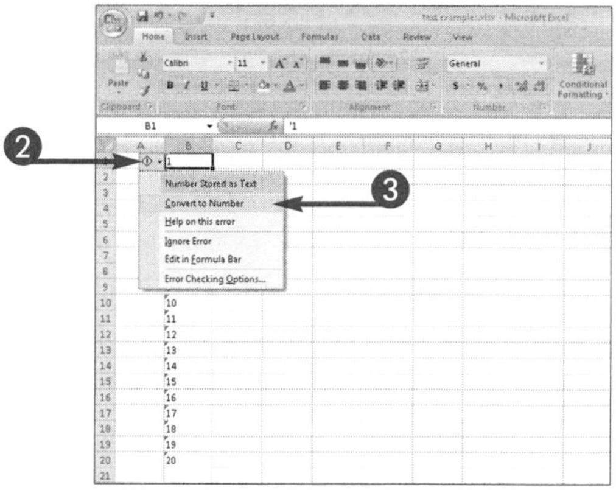

- Excel removes the apostrophe from the cell.
- Excel right-aligns the number in the cell.

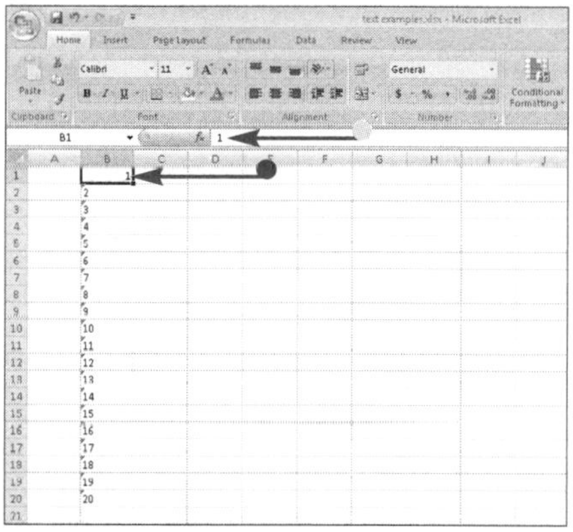

MASTER IT

Can I use a number formatted as text in a formula?

▼ In most cases, yes, you can. Excel assumes that you do not want the number to be treated as text and gives you the correct answer to the formula that you set up. However, in case anyone else uses your worksheet, you should format the numbers as numbers to avoid confusion.

Can I convert more than one cell at a time?

▼ Yes, you can. Select all of the cells that you want to convert and ◈ still appears. Then, follow the steps in this section. Excel converts all of the cells that you select to numbers stored as numbers, removing the apostrophe that precedes each number and right-aligning the numbers in their cells.

What should I do to get rid of the green triangles if I want to treat the numbers as text?

▼ Select the cells, click ◈, and choose Ignore Error. Excel removes the green triangle and ◈ from the cell, but the apostrophe remains in the cell if you view the Formula bar, and the cell contents remain left-aligned. Interestingly, Excel returns correct mathematical results if you use the contents of the cell in a formula.

Combine Text and Values

You can combine text and values in a cell, treating the value as a value, not as text that you type. Suppose that your worksheet contains a total for sales in cell B6 that may not be final, and you want to use the value stored in cell B6 in another cell, where you also include text. For example, cell B6 may display $500,000 and you may want to store a phrase such as, "Total profit is $500,000" in cell E11. If the value in cell B6 changes, you want Excel to automatically update the value in cell E11. If you simply type the phrase in cell E11, Excel does not automatically update the value in cell E11 if cell B6 changes. However, Excel does update the value in cell E11 if you store a formula in cell E11 instead of a text phrase.

The formula that you use concatenates text and also uses the TEXT function. The TEXT function takes two arguments: The first argument is a value or a cell containing a value. The second argument describes the way you want Excel to format the value. You use a combination of pound signs (#), commas (,), zeros (0), and, if appropriate, dollar signs ($) to describe the way you want Excel to format the number.

Combine Text and Values

1. Click the cell in the worksheet where you want to display text combined with a value.

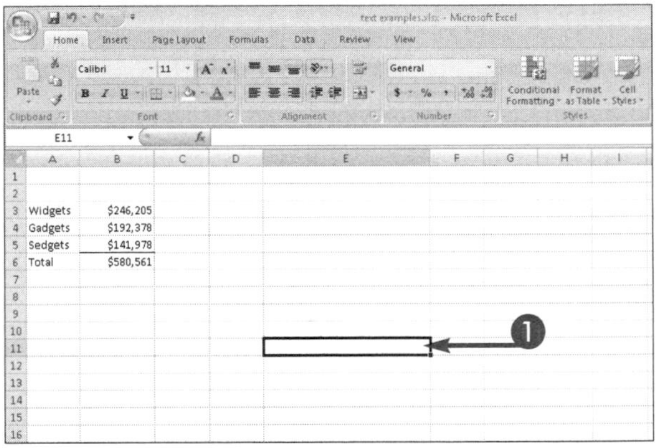

2. Type =" and then type the text phrase.

   This example uses ="Total gross profit is ".
   A space appears after the last word in the text phrase.

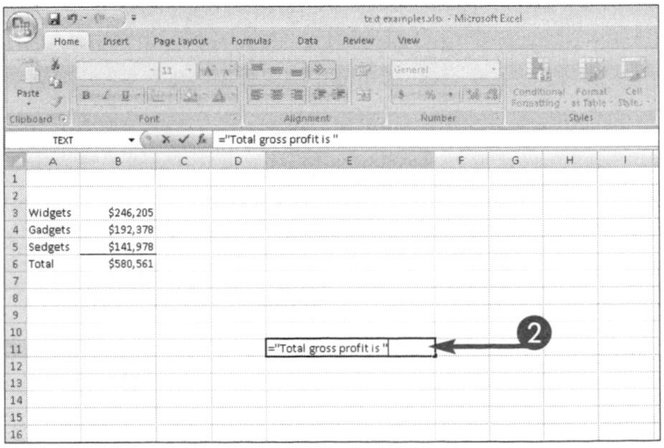

3 Type **&TEXT(**.

4 Click the cell containing the value you want to include in the phrase.

5 Type **,"$#,##0")**.

6 Click ☑.

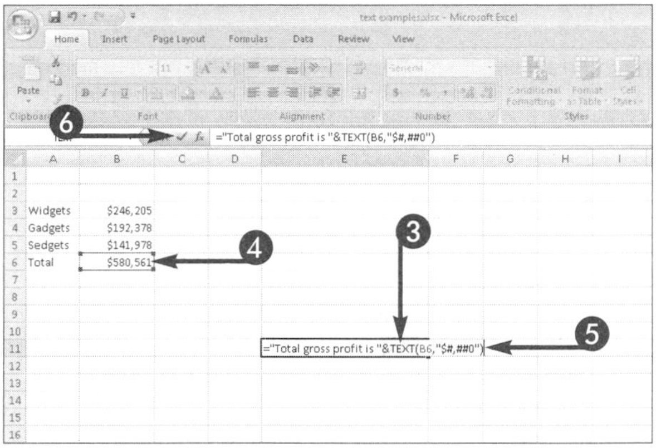

- Excel displays the result of the formula in the cell you selected in Step 1.
- The formula appears in the Formula bar.

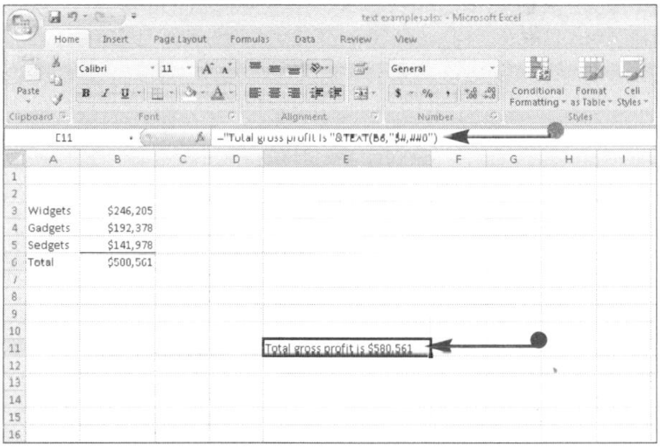

MASTER IT

What does the TEXT function do?

▼ The TEXT function converts a value to text in a format that you specify using two arguments: the value you want to convert, and the format string you want Excel to use to display the value. You can use any number format found in the Category box on the Number tab of the Format Cells dialog box, or you can create your own format.

What do the pound signs (#) in the number format represent?

▼ Pound signs (#) are digit placeholders. When you use a pound sign as part of a number format, Excel displays only significant digits for each place in the number where you use a pound sign. Excel does not display insignificant zeros.

What does the 0 in the number format represent?

▼ Zeros (0) are also digit placeholders. However, when you use a zero as part of a number format, Excel displays both significant digits and insignificant digits for each place in the number where you use a zero, if a number has fewer digits than there are zeros.

Remove Spaces from Imported Data

Often, data that you import into Excel arrives with spaces padding the front or the back of the data; you can use the TRIM function to eliminate those spaces. Suppose that you import an address list and find that all of the first names are preceded by a single space, and all of the last names have three extra spaces at the end of the name. In addition, all of the street addresses contain varying numbers of extra blank spaces mixed in the address at different locations, with no two street addresses containing the same amount of extra spaces in the same location. You can use the TRIM function to clean up your list.

The TRIM function can eliminate leading spaces that appear in front of text in a cell, or trailing spaces that appear after text in a cell. The TRIM function is also smart enough to remove excess spaces that appear within a text string, replacing any sequence of two or more spaces with a single space. If the phrase you want to trim contains the requisite single space between words, the TRIM function does not delete that space.

The TRIM function takes only one argument: the cell containing the text and excess spaces.

Remove Spaces from Imported Data

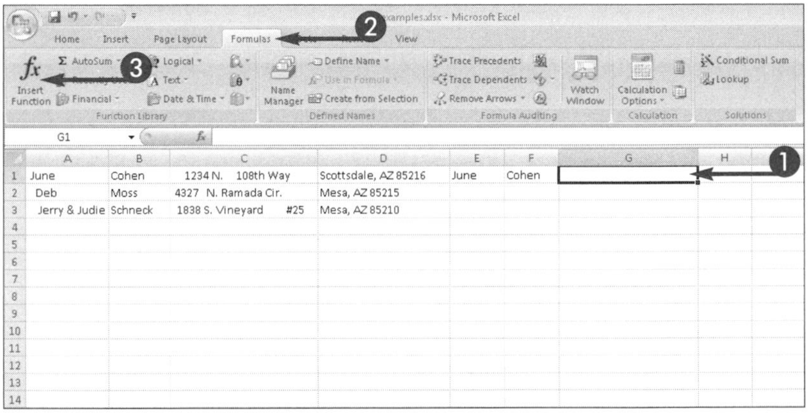

1. Click the cell in which you want to store the function.
2. Click the Formulas tab.
3. Click Insert Function.

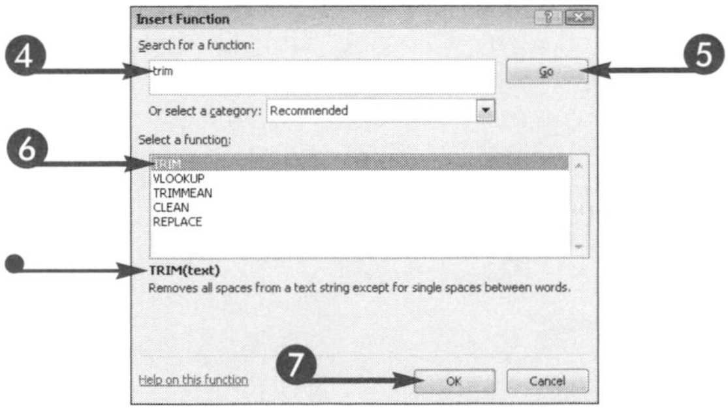

The Insert Function dialog box appears.

4. Type a description here of the function you want to use.

   This example uses trim.
5. Click Go.
6. Click TRIM.
7. Click OK.

The Function Arguments dialog box appears.

8 Click the cell containing the text you want to trim.

- Anticipated results appear here.

9 Click OK.

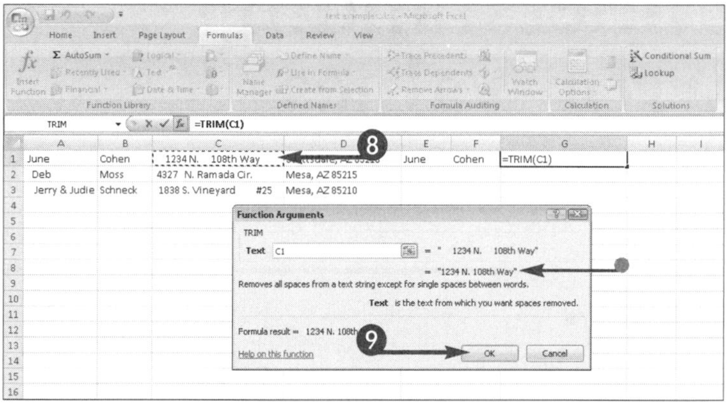

- Excel displays the result of the formula in the cell you selected in Step 1.
- The formula appears in the Formula bar.

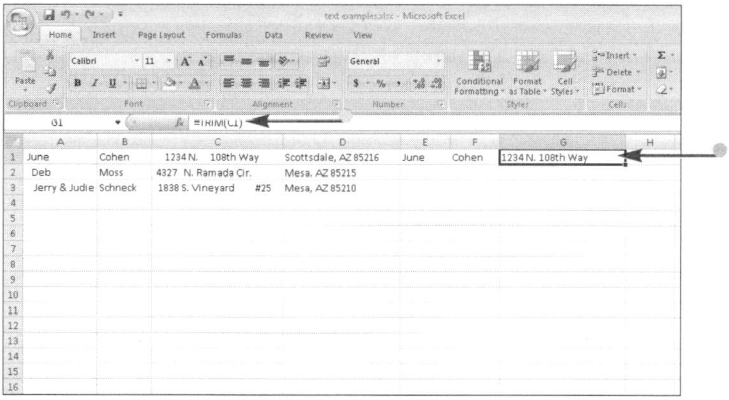

MASTER IT

Will the TRIM function work if the data contains unprintable characters?

▼ No, but you can use the CLEAN function. The CLEAN function removes all non-printing characters from a text string. The CLEAN function takes only one argument: the text you want to clean, or the cell address containing the text you want to clean.

How can I determine that extra blank spaces are stored at the end of a text string?

▼ Spaces at the end can be difficult to find. Click the cell and then press F2 to edit the contents of the cell. In the Formula bar, the insertion point appears at the end of the contents of the cell. If the insertion point does not appear immediately after the last typed character, the cell contains trailing spaces.

Can I copy the TRIM formula?

▼ Yes, you can. Copying the formula makes it easy to remove extra spaces from a worksheet. After you create new cells without excess spaces, convert them to values so that you can delete the original cells. Select the new cells, click the Home tab, and click [icon]. Then, click [icon] under Paste and click Paste Values. Excel replaces the TRIM function with the results of the TRIM function.

Understanding Error Values

When Excel cannot properly calculate a formula you enter, it returns one of seven possible errors. Tracking down these errors and correcting them can be tricky unless you understand what causes an error to appear.

#DIV/0! Errors

The #DIV/0! error appears in your worksheet when you attempt to divide a value by zero. Dividing by zero is not a valid mathematical operation. Excel also returns this error if you attempt to divide by a blank cell, because Excel treats a blank cell as if it contains the value zero. As a result, you commonly see this error when you set up a formula for data that you have not yet entered. In the figure, the worksheet cell displays the #DIV/0 error, and the Formula bar displays the formula that caused the error.

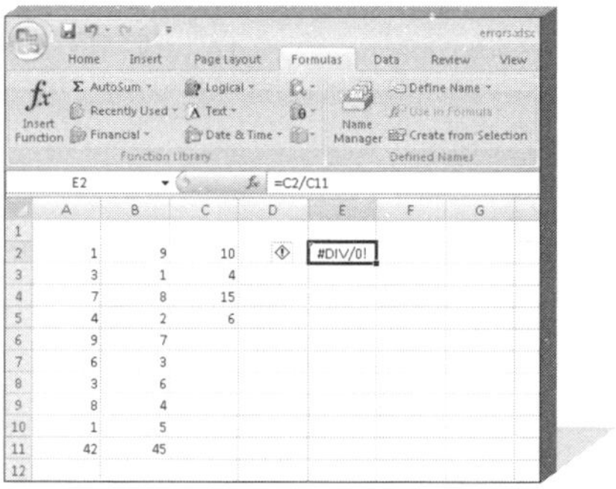

#N/A Errors

Excel displays the #N/A error when Excel needs a value in a formula that is not available. For example, Excel displays #N/A if you omit a required argument from a function, such as the range that you want Excel to search in the VLOOKUP or HLOOKUP functions. In the figure, the worksheet cell displays the #N/A error and the Formula bar displays the formula that caused the error. For details on the VLOOKUP or HLOOKUP functions, see Chapter 14.

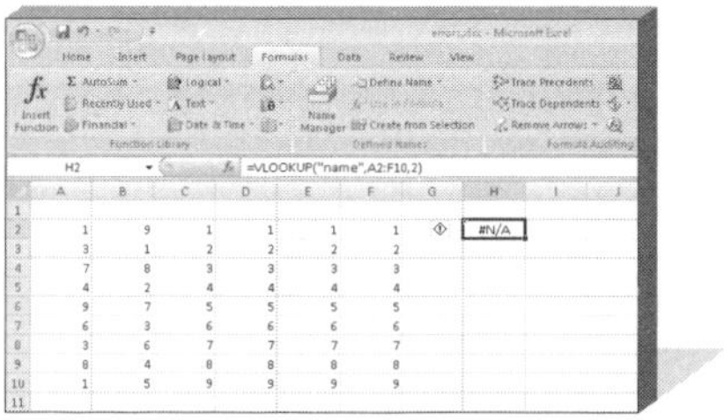

When you need to enter a value that you do not yet have in a cell, you can manually enter **#N/A** — or the corresponding #N/A function — in the cell to create a placeholder reminder for yourself.

#NAME? Errors

The #NAME? error appears when your worksheet contains a problem associated with a named cell or range. You see this error if you use a name that you have not yet defined in a formula or function. This error also appears if you misspell a cell or range name, or if you enter a formula in a cell that uses a named range and then you delete the range name; Excel displays #NAME? in the cell because the range name is no longer available and Excel does not convert the named range back to cell references. In the figure, the worksheet cell displays the #NAME? error, and the Formula bar displays the formula that caused the error.

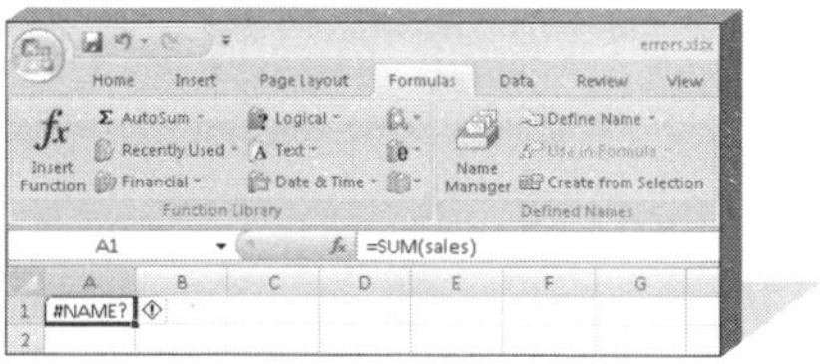

Excel also displays the #NAME? error if you use a worksheet function that is available only in an add-in that you have not installed.

#NULL! Errors

Excel displays the #NULL! error when a formula attempts to use the intersection of two ranges that do not intersect. Excel uses the Space character to indicate the intersection of two ranges, and so you may accidentally introduce this error if you type a space to separate arguments when you mean to type a comma. In the figure, the worksheet cell displays the #NULL! error, and the Formula bar displays the formula that caused the error.

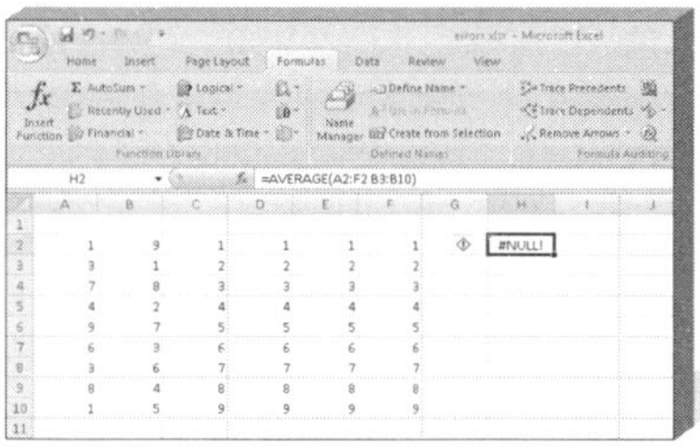

However, if you replace the space between the two ranges in the formula shown in the figure, Excel returns a valid value for the function, because it now reads as follows:

=AVERAGE(A2:F2,B3:B10)

#NUM! Errors

Excel displays a #NUM! error when you enter a formula and use an illogical argument. For example, you cannot calculate the square root of a negative number, and so, if you enter the formula =SQRT(-16), Excel returns a #NUM! error. In the figure, the worksheet cell displays the #NUM! error, and the Formula bar displays the formula that caused the error.

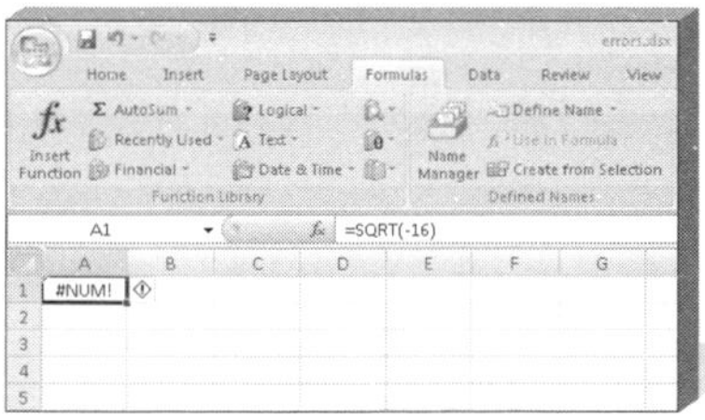

#REF! Errors

The #REF! error appears whenever cell references become invalid, which can occur in a variety of ways. For example, you may delete a cell that is used in some formulas. Or, you may cut the contents of a cell and then paste it into a cell to which a formula refers. Or, you may copy a formula to a location that invalidates a cell reference in the formula. In each of these cases, Excel displays an #REF! error. Suppose that you type a value in cell A1. Then, in cell B2, you type a formula that references cell A1. If you copy the formula in cell B2 to cell B1, the formula is no longer valid, because it attempts to refer to a non-existent cell above cell A1, as shown in the figure.

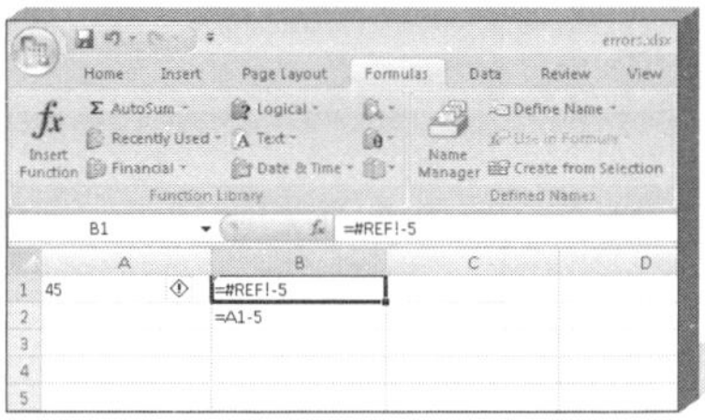

#VALUE! Errors

Excel displays the #VALUE! error under several different conditions. For example, you see a #VALUE! error if you attempt to add text and numbers, as shown in the figure.

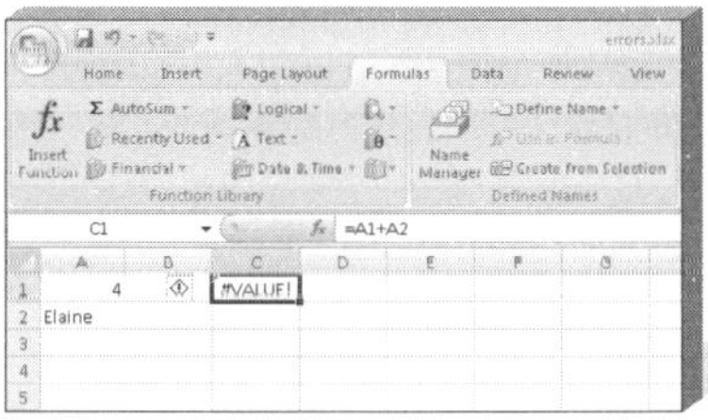

Excel also displays the #VALUE! error if you attempt to use a range for a function's argument when you should have used a single value. For example, the lookup_value argument of the VLOOKUP and HLOOKUP functions must be a value or a single cell containing a value. If you supply a range, Excel returns the #VALUE! error.

The #VALUE! error also appears if you attempt to enter an array formula and forget to press Ctrl+Shift+Enter. For more information on array formulas, see Chapter 10.

Logical Functions

Excel contains a few logical functions that you can use to test for conditions. Some logical functions, such as the IF function, let you specify the action Excel should take if the condition is true, and the action that Excel should take if the condition is false. Other logical functions, like the AND function, simply return values of TRUE or FALSE. Some of the logical functions actually help you to test for error conditions to help you catch errors before they happen. In the rest of this chapter, you explore some of the more commonly used logical functions available in Excel.

Make a Decision

When you want to make a simple decision, you can use the IF function. For example, suppose that your worksheet contains daily rainfall values for one month and the average rainfall value for the month. You can use an IF function to classify each daily value as above or below the average rainfall.

The IF function requires three arguments: the logical test, the value to enter if the test is true, and the value to enter if the test is false. The values for the results of the logical test can be numbers or text; if you type text in the Function Arguments dialog box, Excel automatically inserts quotation marks around the text.

You can nest IF functions by specifying another IF function for either the true value or the false value. For example, you could create a nested IF function that classifies rainfall values into categories of High, Average, or Low. Be aware that this use of the IF function can quickly become complicated, and works well only when you are setting up three or four comparisons. The other functions described in this chapter provide alternative solutions to nesting IF functions.

Make a Decision

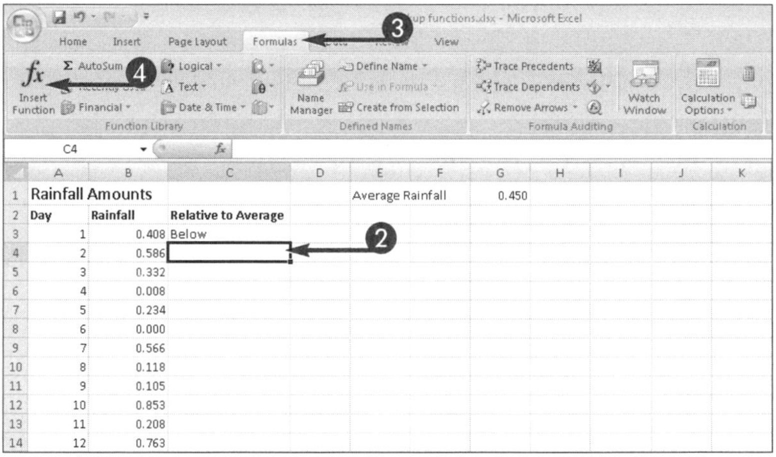

1. In your worksheet, list the values Excel should compare, and a value to which Excel should compare all other values.
2. Click the cell in which you want to store the function.
3. Click the Formulas tab.
4. Click Insert Function.

The Insert Function dialog box appears.

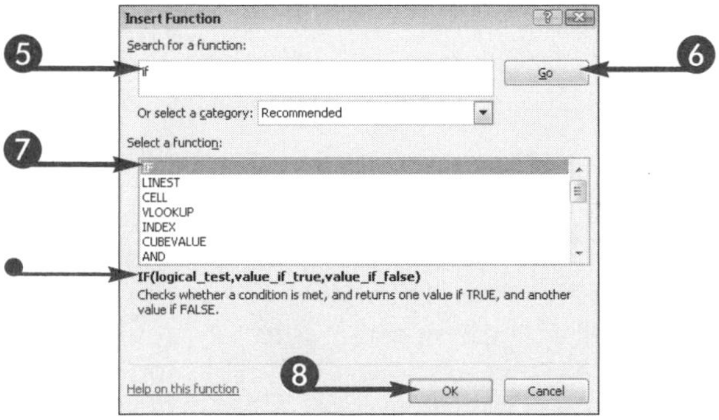

5. Type a description here of the function you want to use.

   This example uses if.
6. Click Go.
7. Click IF.
   - A description of the selected function appears here.
8. Click OK.

The Function Arguments dialog box appears.

9 Click here and type the logical test.

Note: *A logical test must evaluate to true or false, as described in the concept.*

10 Type the value to display if the logical test is true.

11 Click here and type the value to display if the logical test is false.

Note: *If you type text, Excel supplies the quotation marks.*

12 Click OK.

- Excel displays the result of the formula in the cell you selected in Step 2.
- The formula appears in the Formula bar.

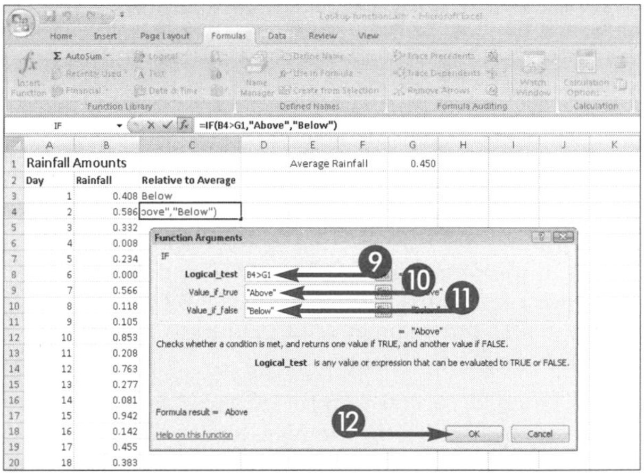

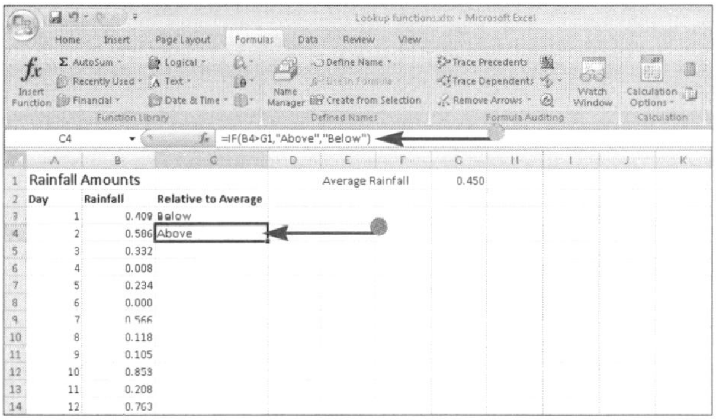

MASTER IT

What would a nested IF function look like that classifies rainfall in the example as High, Average, or Low?

▼ This nested IF function would actually evaluate two conditions instead of one. Using the worksheet set up in the example, use the following formula in any cell in C3:C33: =IF(B5>G1,"Above", IF(B5<G1,"Below","Average")). In this function, "Above" is the value Excel returns if the statement B5>G1 is true. If the statement is false, then Excel evaluates the nested IF function IF(B5<G1) and returns a value of "Below" if that statement is true. If that statement is false, Excel returns a value of "Average."

Can I set up the IF function to return no value at all?

▼ Yes. Suppose that you want Excel to return no value at all if the result of the test is true. For the value that is the true argument, type a pair of quotation marks with nothing between them. The quotation marks serve as a placeholder and, if Excel evaluates the logical expression as true, Excel displays nothing in the worksheet; the formula still appears in the Formula bar. You can also use the pair of quotation marks for the value that is the false argument.

Test for True or False

You can use the AND function to test for a series of conditions and determine whether all of them are true. For example, suppose that you need to monitor the value in cell D2 to determine whether it is greater than the value in cell B2 and less than or equal to the value in cell C2. In this situation, you can use the AND function.

The AND function can take up to 255 arguments. Typically the arguments for the AND function are comparisons that use the mathematical operators =, >, <, >=, <=, or <>. The AND function tests each argument to determine whether it is true. If all of the arguments are true, the cell containing the AND function displays TRUE. If *any* of the arguments is not true, the cell containing the AND function displays FALSE.

The AND function does not identify for you the arguments that did not test as true. You need to trace the arguments of the AND function to identify the ones that are true and the ones that are false. You can use Excel's features to trace precedents and dependents to help you identify the cells to which the arguments refer. See Chapter 18 for details on tracing precedents and dependents.

Test for True or False

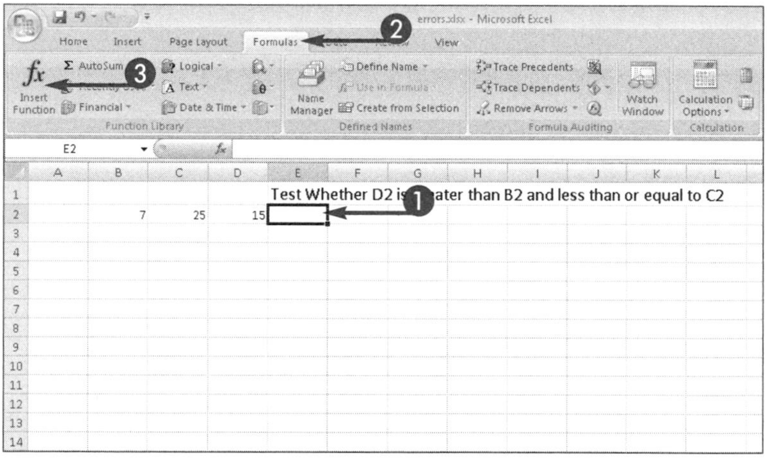

1. Click the cell in which you want to store the function.
2. Click the Formulas tab.
3. Click Insert Function.

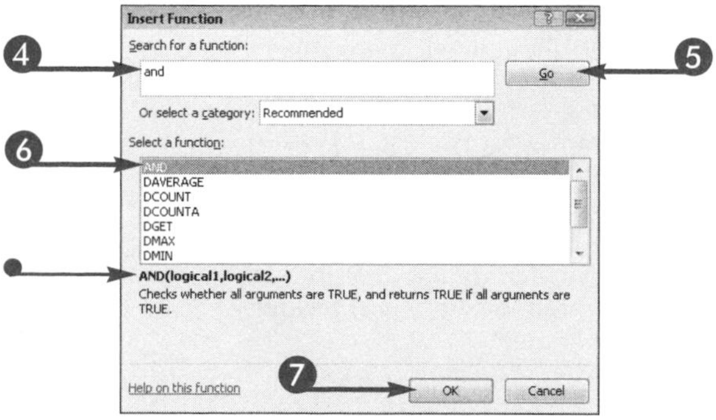

The Insert Function dialog box appears.

4. Type a description here of the function you want to use.

   This example uses and.

5. Click Go.
6. Click AND.
   - A description of the selected function appears here.
7. Click OK.

The Function Arguments dialog box appears.

8. Click a cell, type a comparison operator, and type a comparison value.
9. Click here.
10. Repeat Steps 8 and 9 for each test you want the AND function to perform.
11. Click OK.

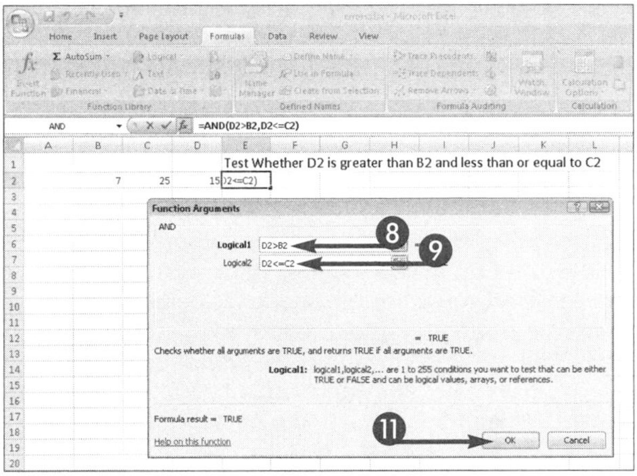

- Excel displays the result of the formula in the cell you selected in Step 1.
- The formula appears in the Formula bar.

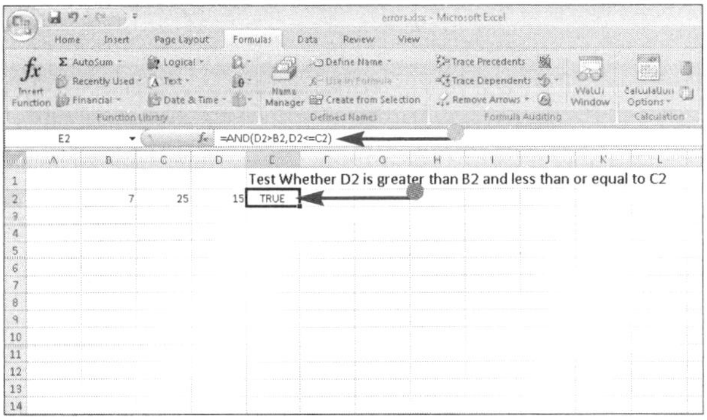

Is there a way to test whether only some of the conditions are true?

▼ Yes. You can use the OR function. The OR function operates the same way that the AND function operates, taking up to 255 logical arguments that typically contain comparisons that use the mathematical operators =, >, <, >=, <=, or <>. The OR function also returns a value of TRUE or FALSE. However, in the case of the OR function, Excel displays TRUE if *any* of the conditions is true, and Excel displays FALSE if all of the arguments that you specify fail to pass the tests you set up.

Is there a way to test whether a condition is false?

▼ Yes. You can use the NOT function. The NOT function operates the same way that the AND and OR functions operate, but it takes only one logical argument, which typically contains a comparison that uses the mathematical operators =, >, <, >=, <=, or <>. The NOT function also returns a value of TRUE or FALSE. However, in the case of the NOT function, Excel displays TRUE if the argument does not pass the test you set up, and Excel displays FALSE if the argument you specify passes the test you set up.

Avoid Displaying Errors

You can use the IF function to avoid displaying errors that you know will occur when you enter a formula. For example, suppose that you want to set up a worksheet to track sales figures for the year and you want to include formulas that calculate the percent of total sales for each plant you operate. You also want to set up the worksheet now, before you have all of the information to fill in the worksheet. When you calculate the percent of total sales, you divide each plant's sales by total sales. Because you do not presently know total sales, the formula you enter makes Excel divide by zero, and your worksheet contains a series of #DIV/0! errors.

If you know that you are introducing these errors, you can avoid them by using the IF function to give Excel an alternative value to enter instead of the error. You are using the IF function in this section because you know the cell containing the grand total for sales will contain a formula that sums to zero. The formula shown in this section does not hide other error values, such as #REF! or #NAME?.

Avoid Displaying Errors

- Cell J4 displays #DIV/0! because it attempts to divide cell I4, which contains zero, by cell I9, which also contains zero.

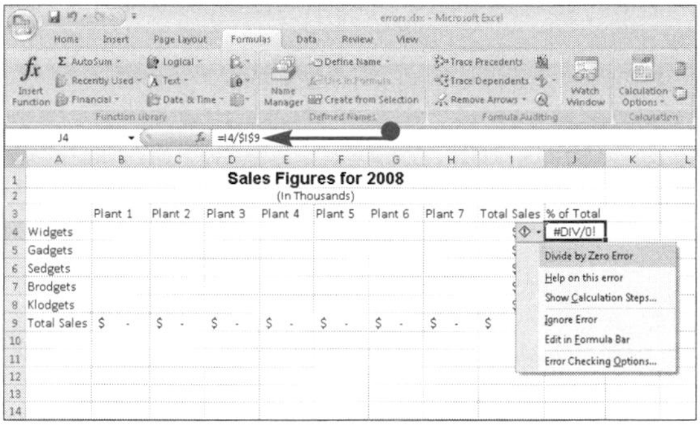

1. Click the cell in which you want to store the function.
2. Click the Formulas tab.
3. Click Insert Function to display the Insert Function dialog box.
4. Type a description here of the function you want to use.

   This example uses if.
5. Click Go.
6. Click IF.
7. Click OK.

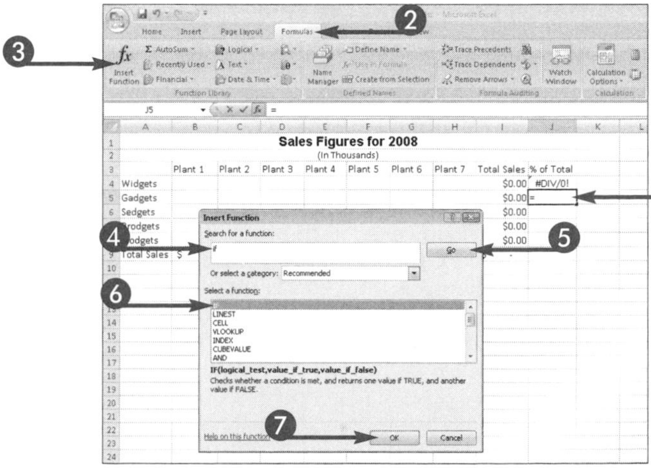

The Function Arguments dialog box appears.

8 Click a cell, type a comparison operator, and type a comparison value.

9 Type the value Excel should return if the argument specified in Step 8 is true.

10 Type the value Excel should return if the argument specified in Step 8 is false.

11 Click OK.

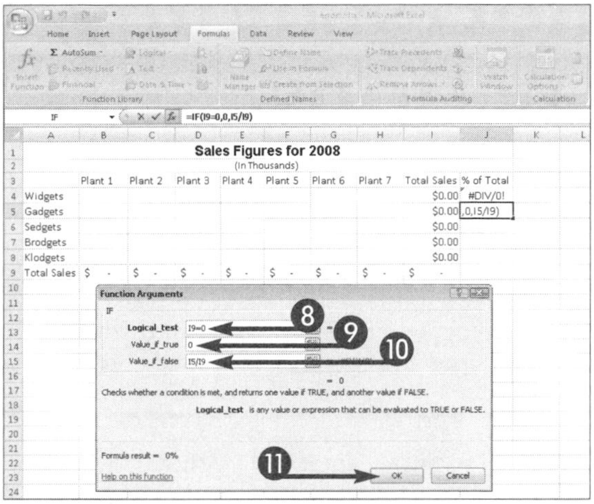

- Excel displays the result of the formula in the cell you selected in Step 1.
- The formula appears in the Formula bar.

Instead of displaying the #DIV/0! error, the IF function makes Excel display 0.

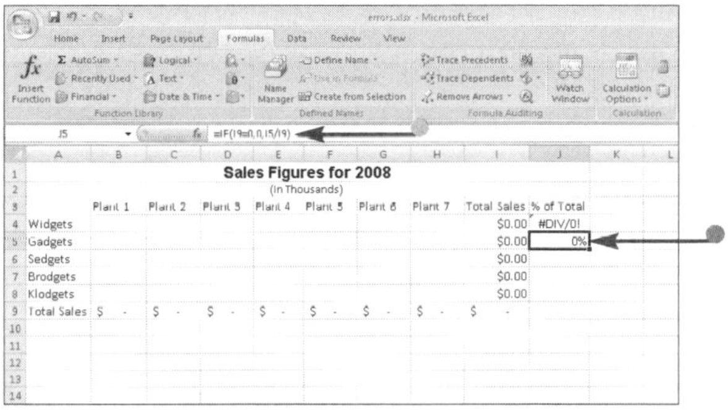

Is there a way that I can make Excel not display the #REF! or #NAME? errors?

▼ Yes. To stop Excel from displaying all errors, including the #N/A error, you can add the ISERROR function to the IF function. The ISERROR function requires one argument — a value — and returns TRUE if the cell you specify as the argument contains any type of error. To use the ISERROR function in this example, the formula in the % of Total column would be =IF(ISERROR(I9),0, IF(I9=0,0,I5/I9)). To be able to copy this formula across or down, use an absolute cell reference for the cell containing total dollars. In this example, I9 would be $I$9.

Is there a way that I can make Excel not display any errors except the #N/A error?

▼ Yes. To stop Excel from displaying all errors except the #N/A error, add the ISERR function to the IF function. The ISERR function works just like the ISERROR function, and requires one argument — a value. The ISERR function returns TRUE if the cell you specify as the argument contains any type of error except #N/A. To use the ISERR function in this example, the formula in the % of Total column would be =IF(ISERR(I9),0,IF(I9=0,0,I5/I9)). The ISERROR function is new to Excel 2007; for compatibility with prior versions of Excel, use the ISERR function.

Understanding Database Functions

Do not let the word *database* frighten you. A database is nothing more than a collection of related information. The telephone book is a simple database that contains name, address, and telephone number information for many people. In database terminology, each person's entry in the book is considered a *record* and each record is made up of fields. In the telephone book analogy, the person's first name is a field, the person's last name is another field, the street address is another field, and so on. When you set up a database, you can decide which fields you want to include. For example, you can store the city, state, and Zip code as one field or as three separate fields. The choice is yours.

You can set up a simple database in an Excel worksheet. Each row can contain a record and each column can display the fields. You need to make sure that all of the information you want Excel to consider as part of the database appears in contiguous rows and columns. The first row of your database should contain the labels that describe each field. In the figure, the database contains 24 records — the number of rows you see excluding the first row — and seven fields named First Name, Last Name, Phone, Address, City, State, and Zip. There is nothing special about this information other than the way you organize it.

	A	B	C	D	E	F	G	H
1	First Nєme	Last Name	Phone	Address	City	State	Zip	
2	Myrna	Andrews	602-843-7249	3826 N. 45th Ave.	Glendale	AZ	85306	
3	Holly	Anton	480-357-4462	437 E. Portobello Ave.	Mesa	AZ	85212	
4	Linda	Atkinson	623-322-2271	9607 N 40 Lane	Glendale	AZ	85308	
5	Lauren	Autry	602-569-9884	3098 E. Rockwood Drive	Phoenix	AZ	85050	
6	Nancy	Barman	480-994-0742	226 E. Rose Circle Drive	Scottsdale	AZ	85251	
7	Patricia	Barrett	480-419-6792	8927 N. 94th Place	Scottsdale	AZ	85255	
8	Barbara	Bellamy	623-546-8006	821 N. 152nd Drive	Sun City West	AZ	85375	
9	Marilyn	Bird	623-979-5304	833 W. Patricia Ann Lane	Peoria	AZ	85382	
10	Donna	Blackburn	623-374-7216	57 W. Donald Drive	Peoria	AZ	85383	
11	Jan	Broadus	480-451-0698	623 E. Century Lane	Scottsdale	AZ	85254	
12	Kathy	Cartisano	480-515-2045	301 N. 108th Way	Scottsdale	AZ	85255	
13	Barbie	Cason	602-997-2762	626 N. 9th Street	Phoenix	AZ	85020	
14	Pam	Chittester	602-298-7784	2809 N. 32nd Ave.	Phoenix	AZ	85029	
15	Kathy	Churchill	623-776-2201	566 W. Karen Lee	Peoria	AZ	85382	
16	Deb	Clark	480-807-5225	747 N. Ramada Circle	Mesa	AZ	85215	
17	Rosie	Connelly	623-376-7271	336 W. Ross Avenue	Peoria	AZ	85382	
18	Janet	Connelly	480-838-5354	9928 West Sterling Place	Chandler	AZ	85225	
19	Pam	Connelly	602-510-7874	8929 W. Pershing	Glendale	AZ	85304	
20	Mary Ann	Crosby	602-870-4421	108 N. 6th Street	Phoenix	AZ	85020	
21	Ginny	Crugnale	419-352-1323	840 Linwood Rd	Bowling Green	OH	43402	
22	Diane	DeMello	623-848-8048	944 W. Hazelwood	Phoenix	AZ	85033	
23	Barbara	Dosal	602-439-7913	4414 N. 58th Drive	Glendale	AZ	85306	
24	Earlyn	Dula	480-895-1275	201 E. Citrus Lane N.	Sun Lakes	AZ	85248	
25	Kathleen	Everly	602-246-7512	9531 W. Marlette Ave	Phoenix	AZ	85013	

Once you have entered database information into an Excel database, you can use a series of database functions in Excel to perform a variety of tasks. You can quickly and easily count, sum, or average records in the database range. For example, in a database that contains names and addresses, you can count the number of records with a particular Zip code. In this chapter, you explore many of the tasks you can perform with information that you set up in Excel as a database.

All of the database functions work only on numbers stored as numbers, and operate in the same basic way: They perform a calculation on a field that you identify for the records that meet criteria you set. All database functions use three arguments:

- The *database range* argument identifies the rows and columns that Excel should consider as the database. The database range argument always includes the top row — the one that contains the field names.
- The *field* argument identifies the field you want the function to consider when it performs its tasks.
- The *criteria* argument is a range that includes the name of the field in the database that Excel should search, and the actual information for which you want Excel to search. The easiest way to handle criteria is to set up a range that is separate from the database range, and to copy all of the field names to that range. Then, you can type the specific piece of information you want Excel to use as a criterion in the cell below the field name. When you set up the criteria range in any function argument, you select both the field name and the cell containing the piece of information.

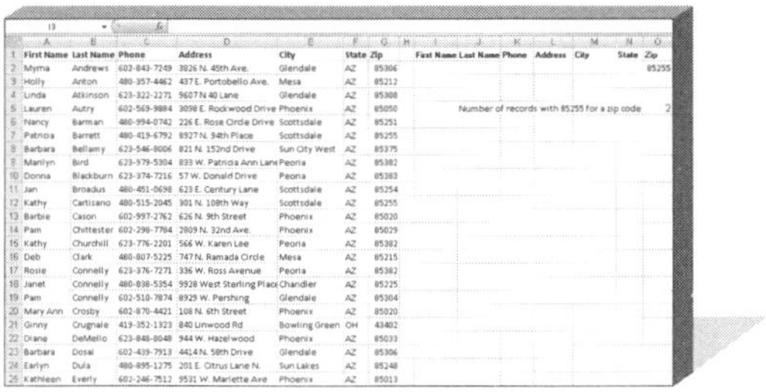

You can set up multiple criteria when using various database functions. The physical placement of the criteria in the criteria range determines how Excel handles multiple criteria. If you place one or more criteria on the same line in the criteria range, Excel returns only those records that meet all of the criteria. This is called an AND criterion. If you place one or more criteria on separate lines in the criteria range, Excel returns records that meet *any* of the criteria. This is called an OR criterion. You can also combine an AND criterion with an OR criterion.

When you specify criteria, you can use mathematical operators to compare information. For example, you can search for records with Zip codes that are greater than or equal to 25468. You can use the following mathematical operators to make comparisons while using Excel database functions: < for less than, > for greater than, <= for less than or equal to, and >= for greater than or equal to.

It is very important to understand that Excel handles simple databases well, but it was never intended to handle large databases, like a city telephone book, or complex databases, like relational databases. In a *relational database*, you set up several tables that contain information and you relate the tables — hence the name *relational* — using some common piece of information that you store in all of the tables. For example, in a human resources database, you might find several tables that store employee information: a table containing each employee's name and address, a table containing hiring information, a table containing review information, and a table containing work history that describes the job performed and the department in which it is performed. The list of possible tables could go on, but you get the idea. The common piece of information stored in each table might be an ID number assigned to each employee. Complex database software can use that common piece of information to search all of the tables and pull information about a particular employee from any or all of the tables. If your needs are complex, you should not try to use Excel for database needs. Instead, consider using Access.

Sum Records That Meet a Single Criterion

Excel contains two different functions that you can use to sum records that meet a single criterion that you establish: the database function DSUM or the SUMIF function.

Suppose that you keep a worksheet containing sales information for a cable company; the worksheet tracks sales each day, listing the amount of the sale, the type of cable product sold, who made the sale, the branch office from which the sale was generated, and whether the sale was made to a new or an existing customer. You can use the DSUM function to calculate the sum of sales made by a particular branch office.

The DSUM function takes three arguments: the range containing the database information, the field containing the information you want to sum, and the criteria range, which should include the labels from the database range and a value you want Excel to use as the criterion when calculating the sum. In this example, Excel sums sales made by the Phoenix branch.

You can, but are not required to, name the ranges that you intend to use as the arguments of the function; for example, you might name the range containing the database information "database" and the range containing the criteria "criteria."

Sum Records That Meet a Single Criterion

Use the DSUM Function

1. Type the criterion you want Excel to use in the row below the criteria range labels under the column in which the criterion appears.
2. Click the cell in which you want to store the function.
3. Click the Formulas tab.
4. Click Insert Function.

   The Insert Function dialog box appears.
5. Type a description of the function you want to use.

   This example uses database sum.
6. Click Go.
7. Click DSUM.
   - A description of the selected function appears here.
8. Click OK.

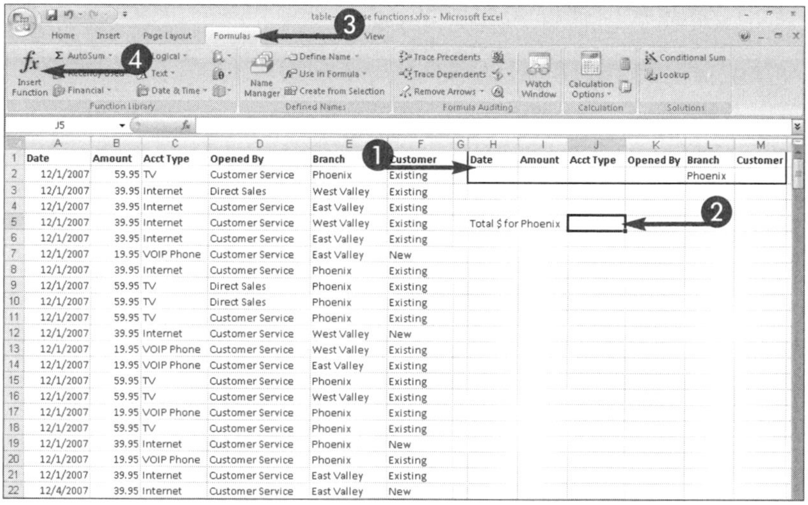

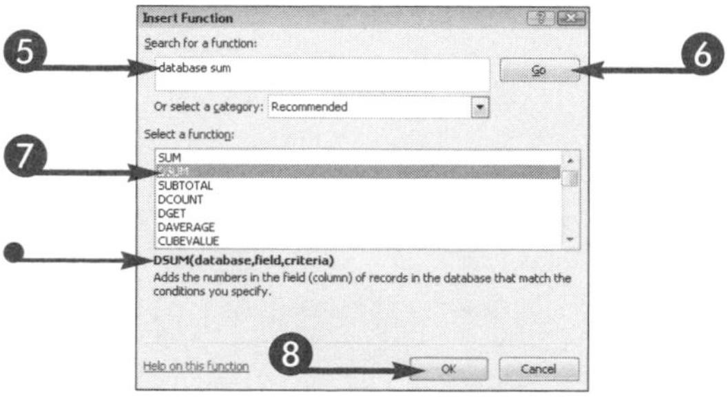

The Function Arguments dialog box appears.

9. Type a range name or select the range for the database in the worksheet.
10. Select the field label Excel should sum.

    The label's cell address appears in the Field field.

11. Select the criteria range, including labels.

    The select range appears in the Criteria field.

12. Click OK.

- Excel displays the result of the formula in the cell you selected in Step 2.
- The formula appears in the Formula bar.

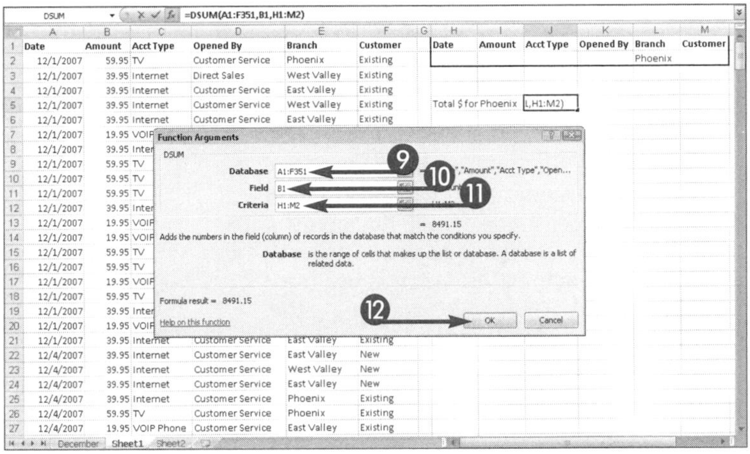

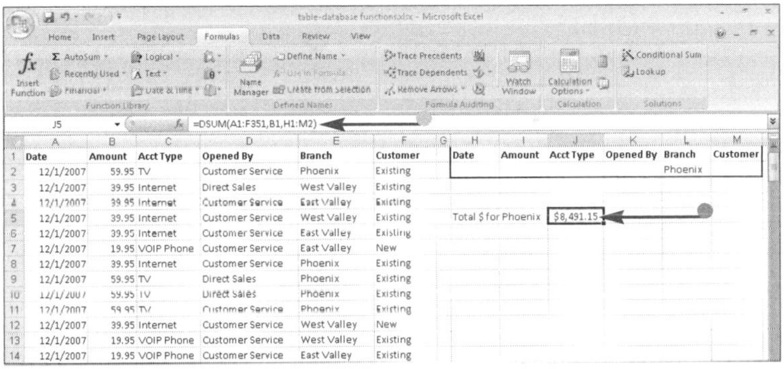

MASTER IT

Is there an easier way to select the database and criteria ranges?

▼ If you plan to calculate several database functions, you will find it useful to assign range names to both the range that serves as the database range argument and the range that serves as the criteria range argument. To create a range name, click the Formulas tab and then click Define Name to display the New Name dialog box. In the Name box, type the name you want to assign. Do not change the Scope setting and, in the Refers To box, select the range to which you want to assign the name. Click OK; Excel names the range you selected.

Can I use the DSUM function to add up values that are greater than an amount I specify?

▼ Yes. You set up the function the same way as shown in this section, but you set up the criterion in the criteria range differently. The example shows "Phoenix" in cell L2, under the Branch label. Suppose that you want to add up values greater than or equal to 39.95 in the Amount column. In the criteria range, delete "Phoenix" from cell L2 and, in cell I2, under the Amount label, type **=">=39.95"**. Be sure to include the quotation marks and the leading equal sign.

continued

Sum Records That Meet a Single Criterion *(Continued)*

You can use the SUMIF function to calculate the sum of values that match a criterion you specify. Because the SUMIF function is not a database function, you do not need to set up a criteria range to use the function. Instead, you use the arguments of the SUMIF function to identify the information you want Excel to sum.

The SUMIF function requires two arguments: the range you want to sum and a criterion value or comparison operation. For example, you can sum all of the values in a column of numbers that are less than a value you specify.

You can also specify a third argument, as shown in the example in this section. When you use three arguments, the first argument identifies the range that contains the criterion for which you want to calculate a sum. The second argument identifies the criterion value, and the third argument identifies the range containing the values you want Excel to sum. In this example, Excel sums sales, stored in column B, made by the Phoenix branch. Branch names appear in column E, and the criterion is Phoenix.

Sum Records That Meet a Single Criterion *(continued)*

Use the SUMIF Function

1. Click the cell in which you want to store the function.
2. Click the Formulas tab.
3. Click Insert Function.

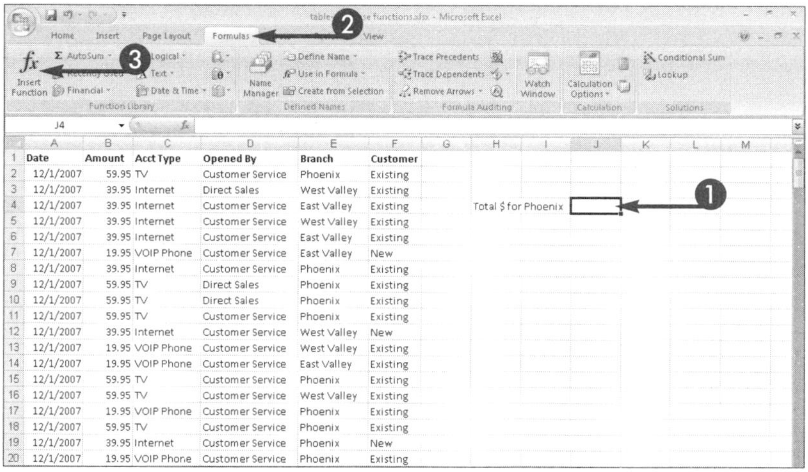

The Insert Function dialog box appears.

4. Type a description here of the function you want to use.

   This example uses sum.

5. Click Go.
6. Click SUMIF.
   - A description of the selected function appears here.
7. Click OK.

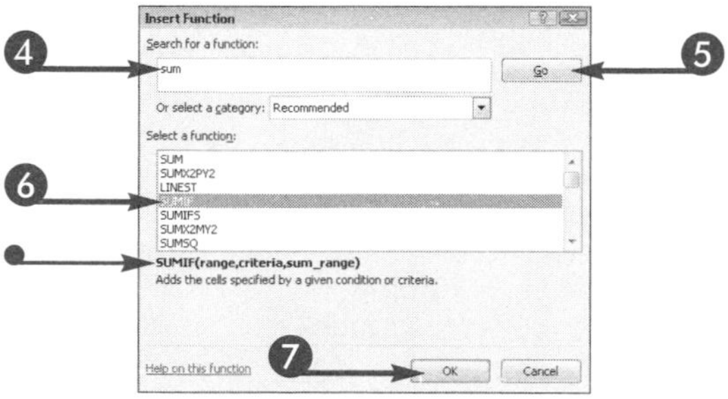

The Function Arguments dialog box appears.

8. Select the range containing the criterion you want to sum.

   The selected range appears in the Range field.

9. Click any cell containing the criterion.

   The cell address appears in the Criteria field.

10. Select the column containing the values to sum.

    The selected range appears in the Sum_range field.

11. Click OK.

    - Excel displays the result of the formula in the cell you selected in Step 1.
    - The formula appears in the Formula bar.

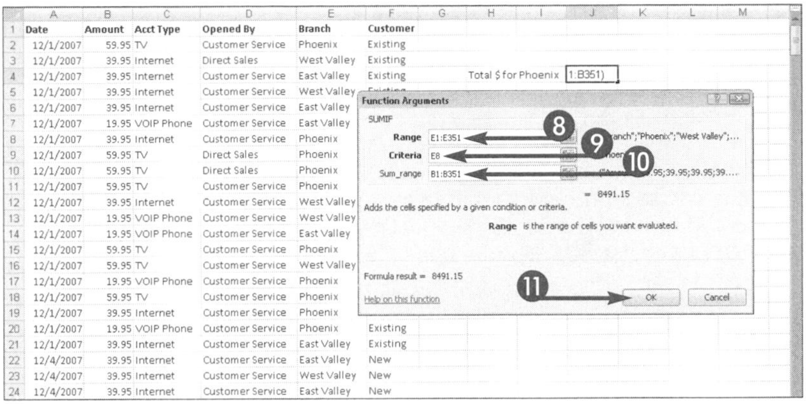

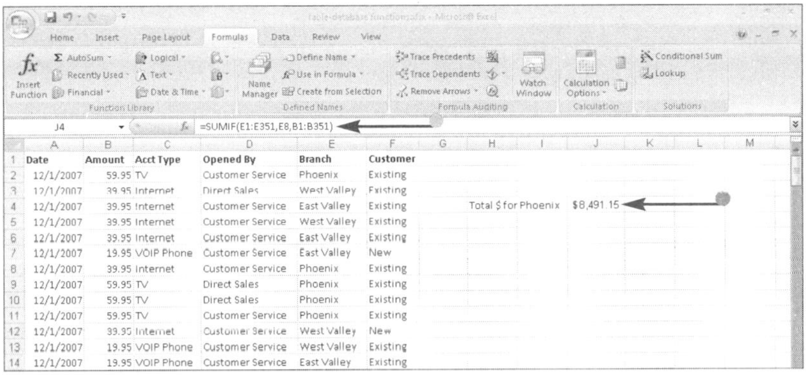

MASTER IT

Can I add values that are greater than a value I specify?

▼ Yes. In Step 8, select the range containing the values you want to sum. In Step 9, instead of selecting a cell in the worksheet, type a comparison operation. In the example, you can type **>59.95** to sum all sales greater than $59.95. You can omit the Sum_range argument specified in Step 10. The SUMIF function for the example would be =SUMIF(B1:B351,">59.95"). Using this function, Excel reads through B1:B351, sums all occurrences of values greater than $59.95, and ignores all other values.

When I omit the Sum_range argument, what does Excel do?

▼ Excel evaluates the SUMIF function using only the range that you specify in Step 8 and the criterion you set in Step 9. You use the Sum_range argument when you want to set one range to specify where the criteria appear in the worksheet, and another range for Excel to sum, based on the specific criterion you set. You omit the argument when the criterion appears in the range you want to sum. Typically, you omit the argument when you want to sum values by comparing them to other values.

Sum Records That Meet Multiple Criteria

Excel contains two different functions that you can use to sum records that meet multiple criteria that you establish: the database function DSUM or the SUMIFS function.

Suppose that you keep a worksheet containing sales information for a cable company; the worksheet tracks sales each day, listing the amount of the sale, the type of cable product sold, who made the sale, the branch office from which the sale was generated, and whether the sale was made to a new or an existing customer. You can use the DSUM function to calculate the sum of sales made by a particular branch office to new customers.

The DSUM function takes three arguments: the range containing the database information, the field containing the information you want to sum, and the criteria range, which should include the labels from the database range and the values you want Excel to use as the criteria when calculating the sum. In this example, Excel sums sales made to new customers by the Phoenix branch.

Using the DSUM function, you can set up the criteria so that Excel sums records that match any or all of the criteria. The example in this section sums records that meet all specified criteria.

Sum Records That Meet Multiple Criteria

Use the DSUM Function

1. Type the criteria you want Excel to use in the row below the criteria range labels under the columns in which the criteria appear.
2. Click the cell in which you want to store the function.
3. Click the Formulas tab.
4. Click Insert Function.

   The Insert Function dialog box appears.

5. Type a description here of the function you want to use.

   This example uses database sum.

6. Click Go.
7. Click DSUM.
   - A description of the selected function appears here.
8. Click OK.

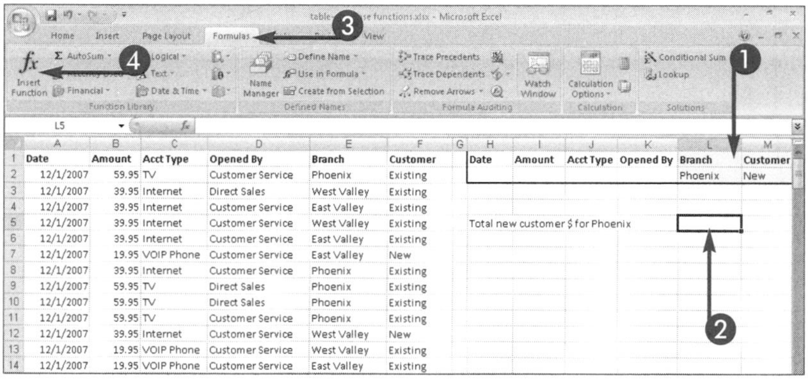

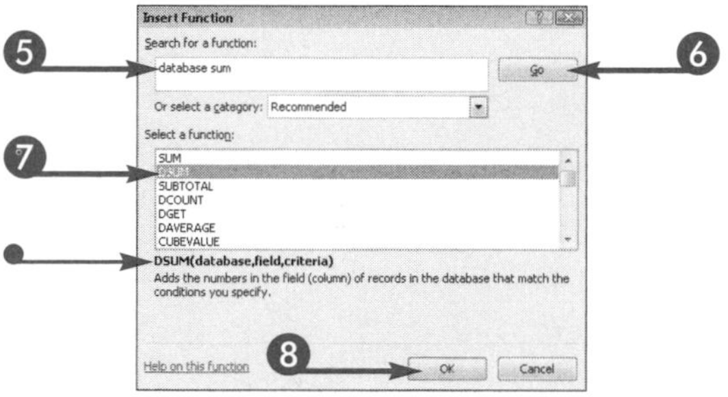

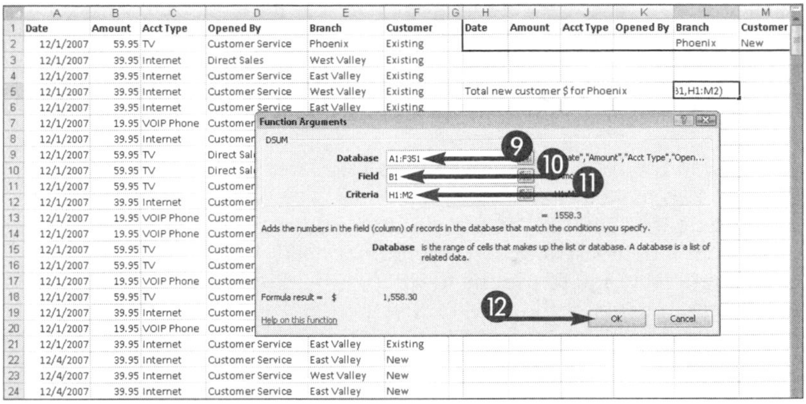

The Function Arguments dialog box appears.

9. Type a range name or select the range for the database in the worksheet.
10. Click here and select the field label Excel should sum.

    The cell address appears in the Field field.

11. Click here and select the criteria range, including labels.

    The selected range appears in the Criteria field.

12. Click OK.
    - Excel displays the result of the formula in the cell you selected in Step 2.
    - The formula appears in the Formula bar.

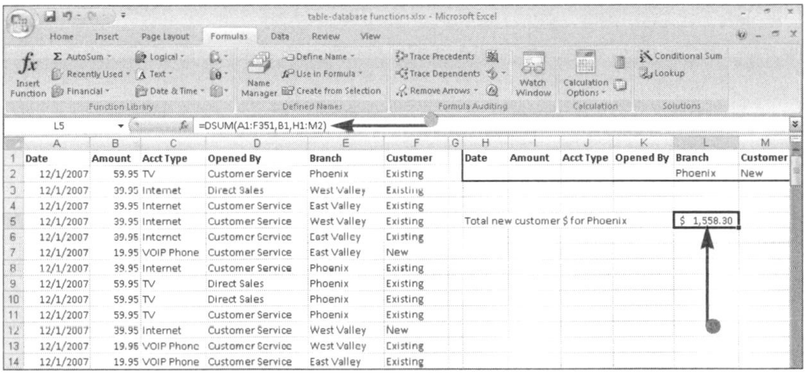

Master It

What did you do to make Excel find records that meet all of the criteria you specified?

▼ When you place the criteria on the same row in the criteria range, Excel assumes that you want to include only records that match all of the criteria you specify. This approach creates an AND condition for the criteria; Excel includes records that meet the first criterion *and* records that meet the second criterion *and* records that meet the third criterion, and so on. When you use an AND condition approach for setting criteria, you can set as many criteria as you have fields in your database.

Can I set up criteria so that Excel sums records that meet any of the criteria I specify?

▼ Yes. You can create an OR condition for the criteria so that Excel sums records that meet the first criterion *or* the second criterion *or* the third criterion, and so on. To create an OR condition, place each criterion on a separate row in the criteria range. When you use an OR condition approach, you can set far more criteria than the number of fields in the database because you can establish multiple criteria for any field. In the example, you can sum sales to new customers by the Phoenix branch or the East Valley branch.

continued

Sum Records That Meet Multiple Criteria *(Continued)*

You can use the SUMIFS function to calculate the sum of values that match up to 127 criteria that you specify. Because the SUMIFS function is not a database function, you do not need to set up a criteria range to use the function. Instead, you use the arguments of the SUMIFS function to identify the information you want Excel to sum.

The SUMIFS function takes a minimum of three arguments: The first argument identifies the range from which Excel should calculate the sum; the second argument identifies the range containing the first criterion; and the third argument works in conjunction with the second argument to identify the criterion. You can specify up to 126 additional pairs of arguments that specify a range containing another criterion and the corresponding criterion. Each criterion range that you specify must be the same size and shape as the range you specify as the first argument of the SUMIFS function.

The SUMIFS function sums cells in the first range that you specify, only if the cells meet all of the criteria that you specify in the subsequent arguments.

Sum Records That Meet Multiple Criteria *(continued)*

Use the SUMIFS Function

1. Click the cell in which you want to store the function.
2. Click the Formulas tab.
3. Click Insert Function.

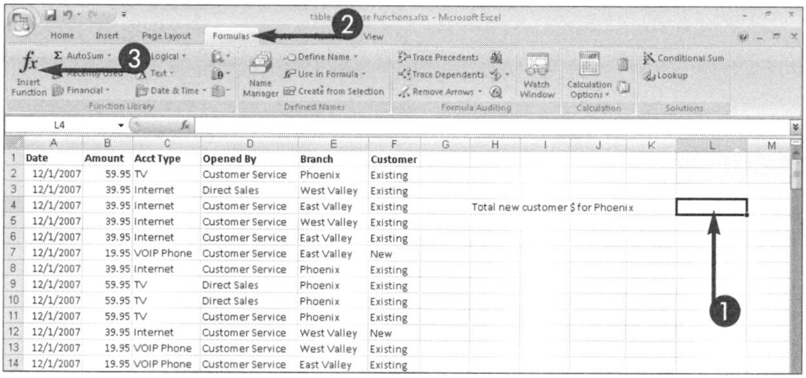

The Insert Function dialog box appears.

4. Type a description here of the function you want to use.

   This example uses sum.

5. Click Go.
6. Click SUMIFS.

   - A description of the selected function appears here.

7. Click OK.

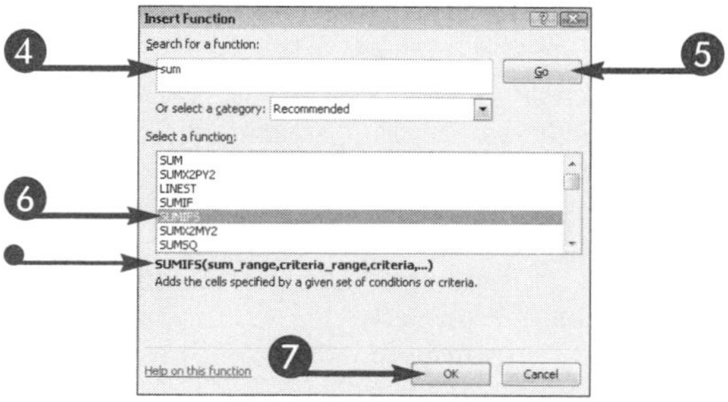

The Function Arguments dialog box appears.

8. Select the range containing the values you want to sum.

   The selected range appears in the Sum_range field.

9. Select the range containing the criterion.

   The selected range appears in the Criteria_range1 field.

10. Click any cell containing the criterion.

    The cell address appears in the Criteria1 field.

11. Repeat Steps 8 and 9 for each criterion you want to establish.

12. Click OK.

    - Excel displays the result of the formula in the cell you selected in Step 1.
    - The formula appears in the Formula bar.

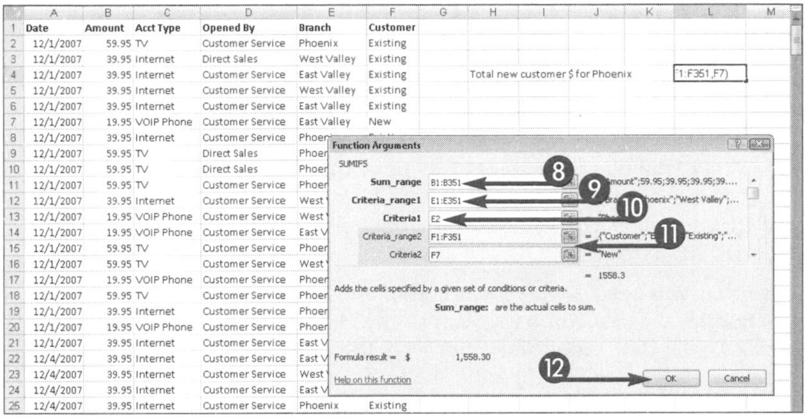

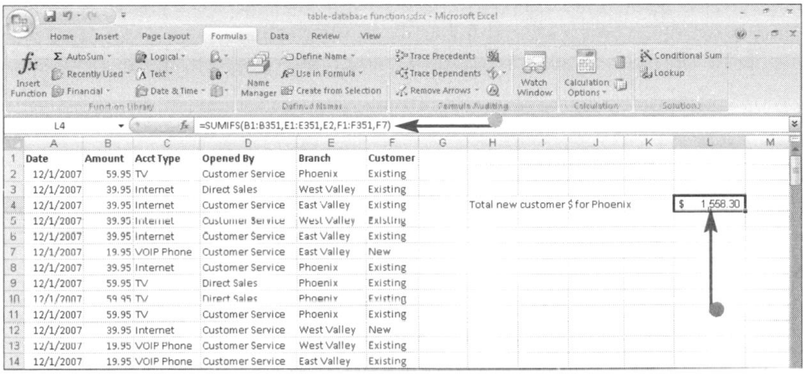

PART III

MASTER IT

Why did I get a #VALUE! error from the SUMIFS function I set up?

In all likelihood, you specified a range for the first argument that is not the same size as the criteria range. It is also possible that all of the ranges you set up for both the first argument and the subsequent criteria range arguments are different-sized ranges. Every range you specify for the SUMIFS function must be equal in size. For example, if you specify A1:A20 for the first argument and you want to use values in columns E and G for criteria, you must select ranges containing 20 rows in both columns; otherwise, Excel returns an error for the function.

Can I use mathematical comparisons to sum with the SUMIFS function?

Yes, you can set up criteria that contain any of the mathematical operators =, <, >, <=, and >= and then include a value for comparison. However, the ranges you specify for each argument must contain numbers. Consequently, to set up a function that uses mathematical comparisons using the example in this section, you would need to use column B for all of the ranges you specify. For example, you could have Excel sum all of the values that are less than $39.95 and greater than or equal to $19.95; the function would be: =SUMIFS(B1:B351, B1:B351,"<39.95", B1:B351,">=19.95").

Count Records That Meet a Single Criterion

Excel contains two different functions that you can use to sum records that meet a single criterion that you establish: the database function DCOUNT or the COUNTIF function.

Suppose that you keep a worksheet containing sales information for a cable company, and the worksheet tracks sales each day, listing the amount of the sale, the type of cable product sold, who made the sale, the branch office from which the sale was generated, and whether the sale was made to a new or an existing customer. You can use the DCOUNT function to count the number of sales made by a particular branch office.

The DCOUNT function takes three arguments: the range containing the database information, the field containing the information you want to count, and the criteria range. The field containing the information you want to count must be a field of numeric data, because database functions only work with numeric data. The example in this section demonstrates counting values that represent dollar sales. The criteria range should include the labels from the database range and a value you want Excel to use as the criterion when counting. In this example, Excel counts the number of accounts opened by the East Valley branch.

Count Records That Meet a Single Criterion

Use the DCOUNT Function

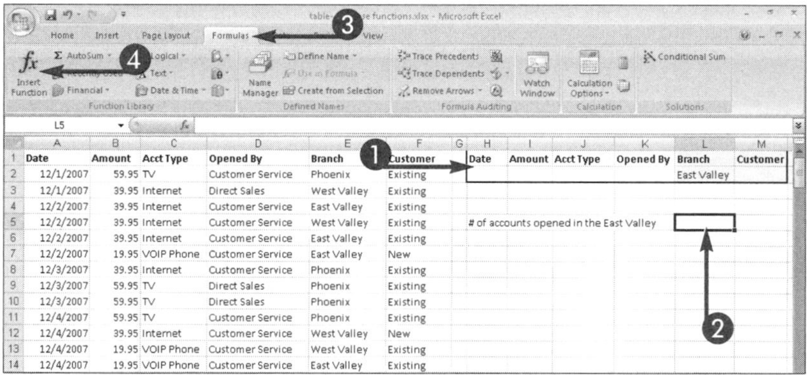

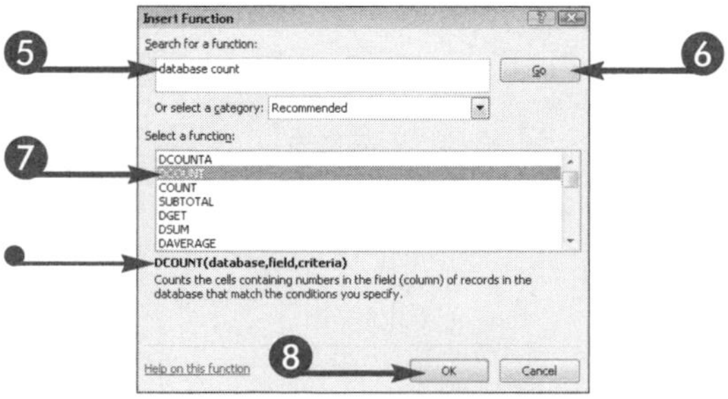

1. Type the criterion you want Excel to use in the row below the criteria range labels under the column in which the criterion appears.
2. Click the cell in which you want to store the function.
3. Click the Formulas tab.
4. Click Insert Function.

   The Insert Function dialog box appears.
5. Type a description here of the function you want to use.

   This example uses database count.
6. Click Go.
7. Click DCOUNT.
   - A description of the selected function appears here.
8. Click OK.

The Function Arguments dialog box appears.

9. Type a range name or select the range for the database in the worksheet.
10. Select the field label Excel should count.

    The label's cell address appears in the Field field.

11. Select the criteria range, including labels.

    The selected range appears in the Criteria field.

12. Click OK.

- Excel displays the result of the formula in the cell you selected in Step 2.
- The formula appears in the Formula bar.

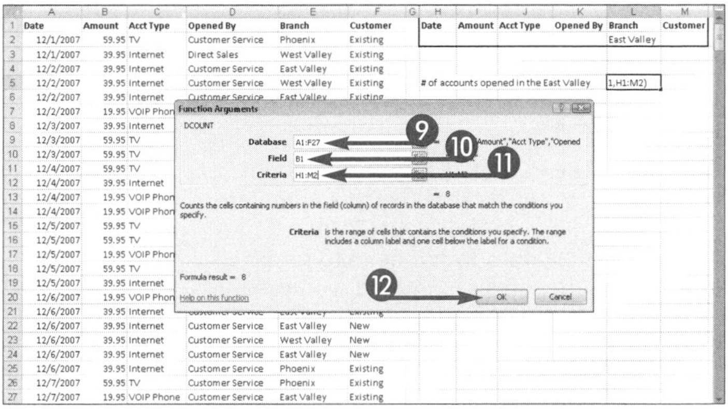

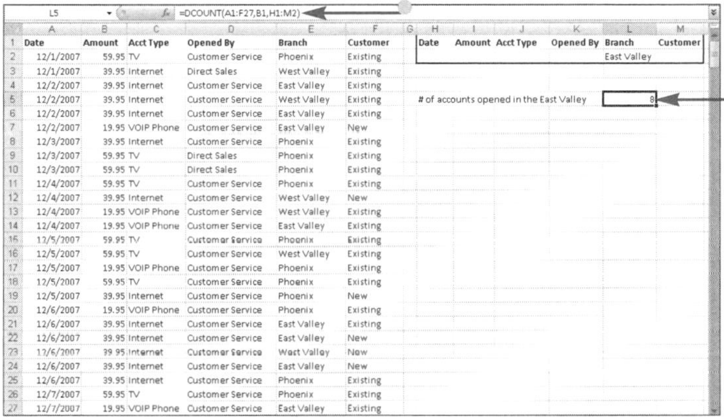

MASTER IT

Why do you select cell B1 in the example for Step 10 instead of selecting cell E1, if you are counting sales made by a particular branch?

▼ Database functions in general cannot operate on fields containing text entries. Consequently, in the example, you cannot use the data in columns C, D, E, or F for the second argument of the DCOUNT function. The function in the example tells Excel to count the number of cells in column B that contain values and also to display "East Valley" — the criterion established in the criteria range — on the same row. If you examine the figures closely, you will find eight rows that contain "East Valley" in column E.

For the criteria range, must I include all of the labels in the database range?

▼ No. You need to include only the label and the row below it in the criteria range for the criterion you want to set. In this example, you could have set the criteria range to L1:L2. To perform a lot of database calculations, set up a criteria range that contains all of the labels in the database range and create a range name for it. Then, enter the criterion under the appropriate label for each calculation. To retain a calculation but make another calculation, convert the first calculation to a value by clicking the Home tab, clicking , clicking under Paste, and then clicking Paste Values.

continued

Count Records That Meet a Single Criterion *(Continued)*

You can use the COUNTIF function to count the number of entries that match a criterion you specify. Because the COUNTIF function is not a database function, you do not need to set up a criteria range to use the function. Instead, you use the arguments of the COUNTIF function to identify the information you want Excel to count.

The COUNTIF function requires two arguments: the range you want to count and a criterion value. Unlike the DCOUNT database function, you do not need to count a range that contains numbers; you can count a range that contains text. In the example in this section, you count the number of accounts opened by the East Valley branch of a cable company.

If the range you want to count contains numbers, you can use a comparison operation for the criterion value; for example, you can count all the entries in a column of numbers that are greater than or equal to a value you specify. In the example worksheet in this section, you might want to count the $59.95 accounts that are opened.

Count Records That Meet a Single Criterion *(continued)*

Use the COUNTIF Function

1. Click the cell in which you want to store the function.
2. Click the Formulas tab.
3. Click Insert Function.

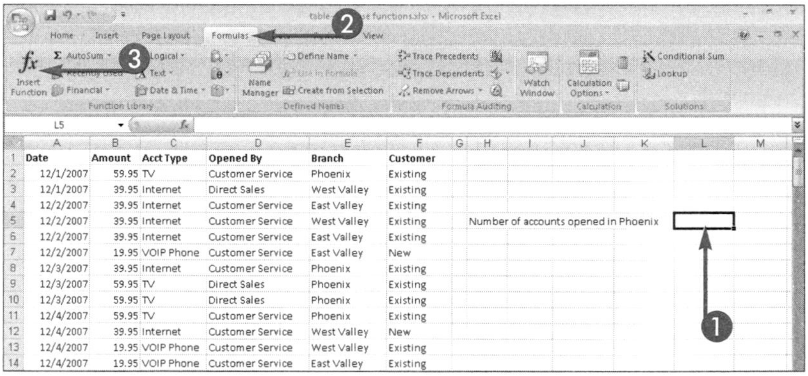

The Insert Function dialog box appears.

4. Type a description here of the function you want to use.

   This example uses count.

5. Click Go.
6. Click COUNTIF.
   - A description of the selected function appears here.
7. Click OK.

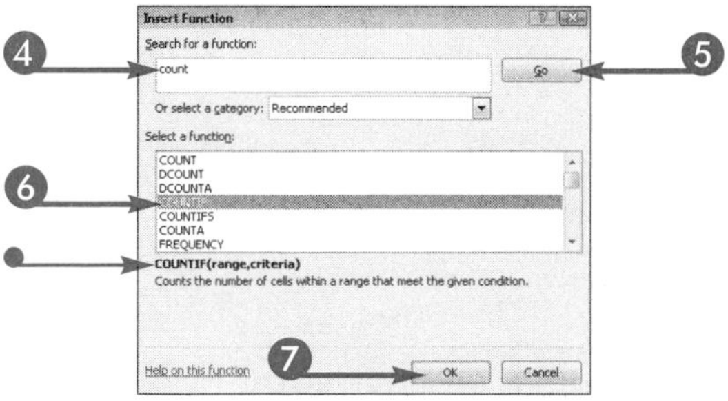

The Function Arguments dialog box appears.

8. Select the range containing the criterion you want to count.

   The selected range appears in the Range field.

9. Click any cell containing the criterion.

   The clicked cell's address appears in the Criteria field.

10. Click OK.

    - Excel displays the result of the formula in the cell you selected in Step 1.
    - The formula appears in the Formula bar.

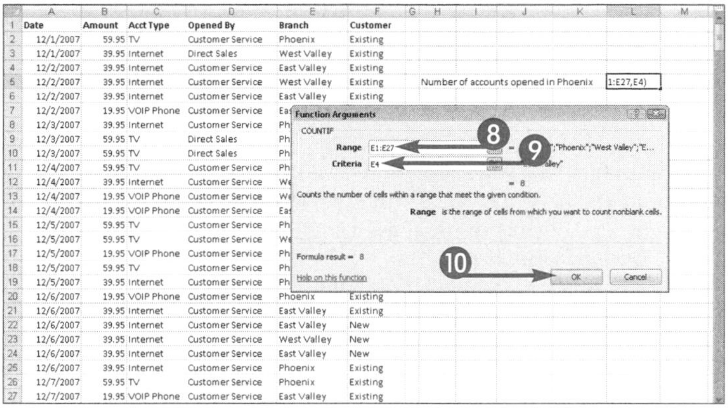

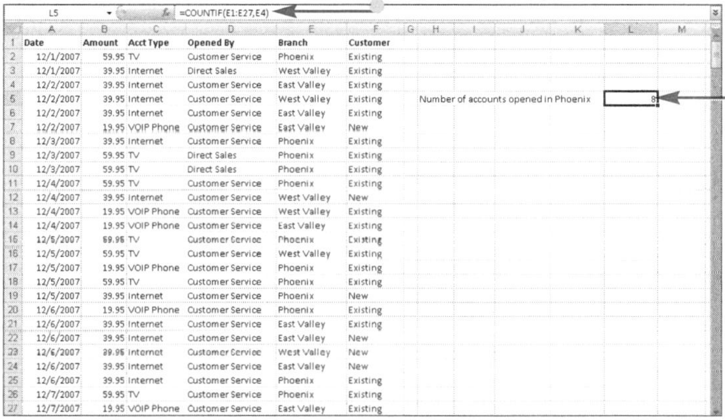

PART III

MASTER IT

If I were to use the example worksheet to count the number of $59.95 accounts that are opened, what would the function look like?

▼ Using the COUNTIF function, the formula would be COUNTIF(B1:B27,"=59.95"). You can follow the steps in this section to create this function. However, in Step 9, do not select a cell. Instead, type the mathematical comparison. You do not need to enter the quotation marks around the criterion value when you complete the step; Excel automatically supplies them.

Is there a way to use COUNTIF to determine the number of cells that do not contain text?

▼ Yes. You can use wildcard characters with the COUNTIF function, using the asterisk as part of the function. Suppose that the range of data containing cells you want to count is A1:A10. The function you would use to count the number of cells in this range that do not contain text would look like this: =COUNTIF(A1:A10,"<>"&"*").

Can I use the COUNTIF function to determine the number of cells in one range that contain two different values?

▼ Yes. You can add the results of two COUNTIF functions. Suppose that, using the example worksheet, you want to know the number of accounts opened by both the East Valley and West Valley branches. Your function would look like this: =COUNTIF (E1:E27,E4)+COUNTIF(E1:E27,E5).

Can I include blank cells in the range I want to count?

▼ Yes, but the COUNTIF function ignores them.

Count Records That Meet Multiple Criteria

Excel contains two functions that you can use to count records that meet multiple criteria that you establish: the database function DCOUNT or the COUNTIFS function.

Suppose that you keep a worksheet containing sales information for a cable company; the worksheet tracks sales each day, listing the amount of the sale, the type of cable product sold, who made the sale, the branch office from which the sale was generated, and whether the sale was made to a new or an existing customer. In this example, Excel counts sales made from the East Valley branch on December 6, 2007.

The DCOUNT function takes three arguments: the range containing the database information, the field containing the information you want to count, and the criteria range. The field containing the information you want to count must be a field of numeric data, because database functions only work with numeric data. The example in this section demonstrates counting values that represent dollar sales. The criteria range should include the labels from the database range and values you want Excel to use as criteria when counting.

Count Records That Meet Multiple Criteria

Use the DCOUNT Function

1. Type the criteria you want Excel to use in the row below the criteria range labels under the columns in which the criteria appear.
2. Click the cell in which you want to store the function.
3. Click the Formulas tab.
4. Click Insert Function.

   The Insert Function dialog box appears.
5. Type a description here of the function you want to use.

   This example uses database count.
6. Click Go.
7. Click DCOUNT.
   - A description of the selected function appears here.
8. Click OK.

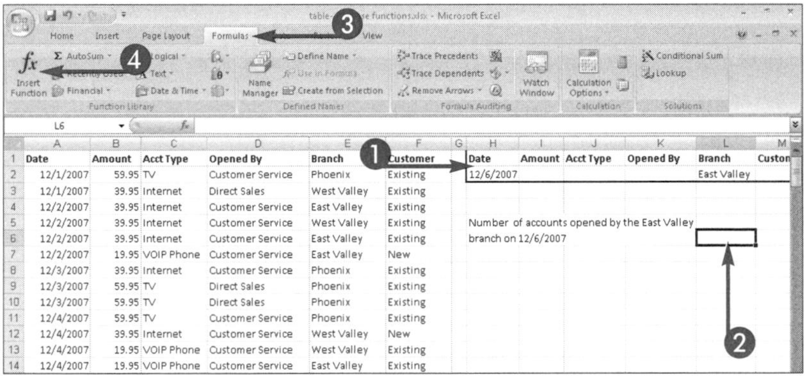

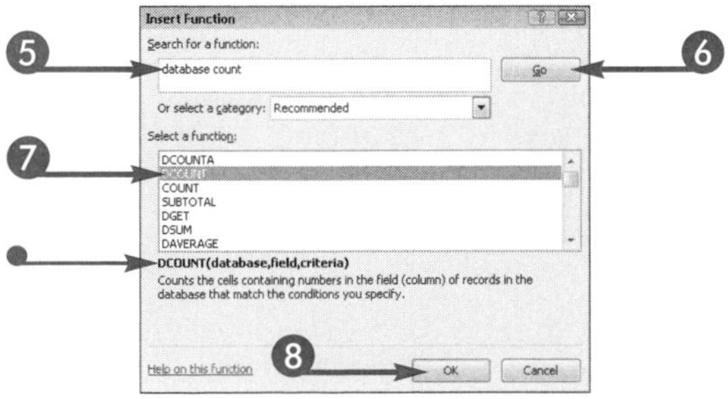

The Function Arguments dialog box appears.

9 Type a range name or select the range for the database in the worksheet.

10 Select the field label Excel should count.

The label's cell address appears in the Field field.

11 Select the criteria range, including labels.

The selected range appears in the Criteria field.

12 Click OK.

- Excel displays the result of the formula in the cell you selected in Step 2.
- The formula appears in the Formula bar.

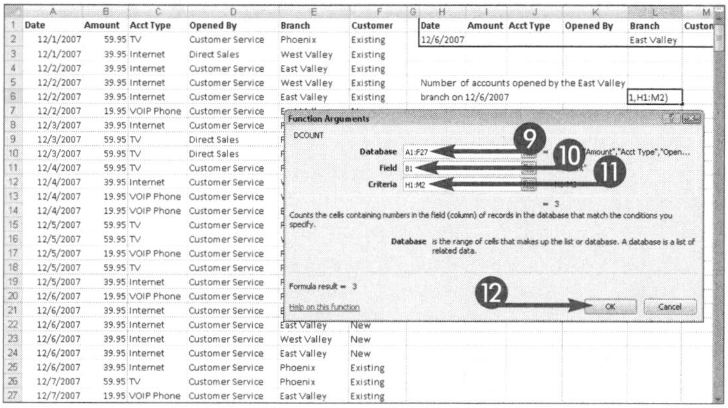

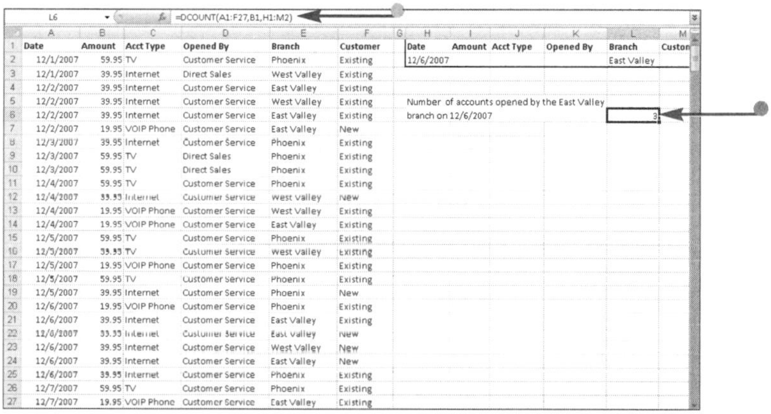

PART III

MASTER IT

Can I use the DCOUNT function to count several different things and keep the results of all of the things that I count?

▼ Yes, you can. You must first convert the function's result to a value before you make changes to the criteria range. Set up the DCOUNT function to calculate the first count. Then, convert the result to a value by clicking the Home tab, clicking , clicking below Paste, and then clicking Paste Values. Now that the value is no longer the result of a formula, you can change the criteria in the criteria range without affecting the first calculation. Convert the result of each count to a value before you set up the next count.

Can I use the DCOUNT function to count sales made by the East Valley branch or sales made on 12/6/2007?

▼ Yes, you can create an OR condition for the criteria. The example uses an AND condition, which returns the value when all conditions are met. An OR condition returns a value based on meeting any of the specified criteria. To count the records that meet the condition of occuring on 12/6/2007 or being generated at the East Valley branch, place the two criteria on separate rows below the appropriate criteria range heading. Then, expand the criteria range; in the example, it is H1:M2. To create the OR condition, you would make the range H1:M3.

continued

Count Records That Meet Multiple Criteria *(Continued)*

You can use the COUNTIFS function to count cells that match up to 127 criteria that you specify. Because the COUNTIFS function is not a database function, you do not need to set up a criteria range to use the function. Instead, you use the arguments of the COUNTIFS function to identify the information you want Excel to count.

The COUNTIFS function takes a minimum of two arguments, but, to use multiple criteria, you must specify at least four arguments. The arguments work in pairs. The first argument of each pair identifies the range Excel should search while counting; this range contains a criterion that Excel will use when counting. The second argument of the pair identifies the criterion in the first argument's range that Excel should use while counting. You can establish up to 127 pairs of arguments. The COUNTIFS function counts cells in the first range you specify only if the cells meet all of the criteria you specify in all of the arguments.

Each criterion range that you specify — the first argument of each pair of arguments — must be equal in size and shape.

Count Records That Meet Multiple Criteria *(continued)*

Use the COUNTIFS Function

1. Click the cell in which you want to store the function.
2. Click the Formulas tab.
3. Click Insert Function.

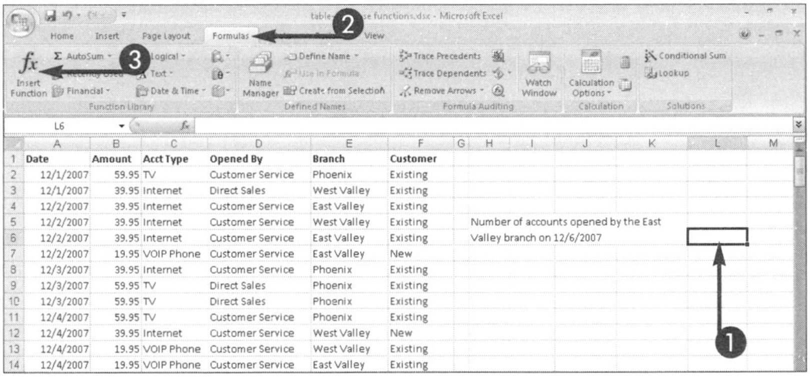

The Insert Function dialog box appears.

4. Type a description here of the function you want to use.

   This example uses count.

5. Click Go.
6. Click COUNTIFS.
   - A description of the selected function appears here.
7. Click OK.

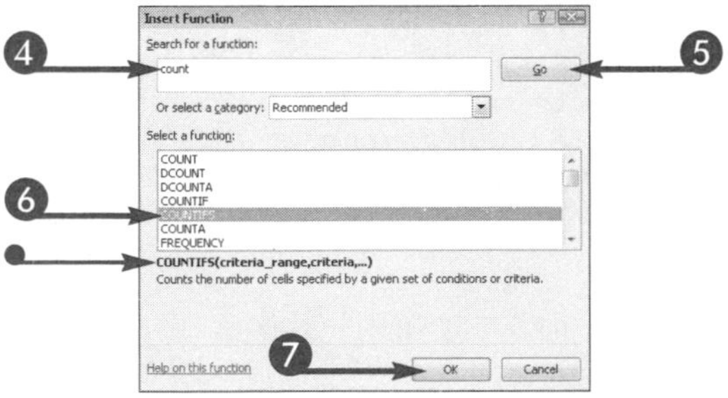

The Function Arguments dialog box appears.

8. Select the range containing the entries you want to count.
9. Click in the Criteria1 field and then click any cell in the range you selected in Step 8 that contains the criterion.
10. Repeat Steps 8 and 9 for each criterion you want to establish.
11. Click OK.

- Excel displays the result of the formula in the cell you selected in Step 1.
- The formula appears in the Formula bar.

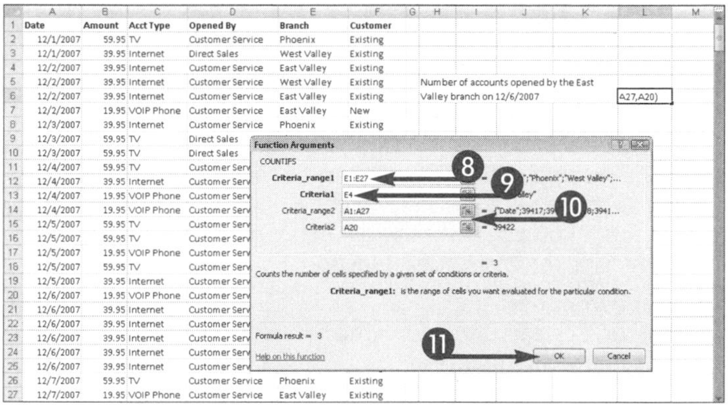

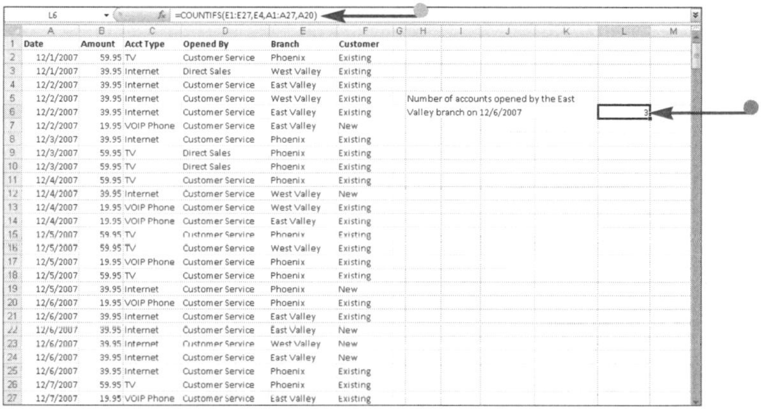

MASTER IT

I used a COUNTIFS function and sent my workbook to an Excel 2003 user, who told me the function did not work. What is going on?

▼ The COUNTIFS function is new to Excel 2007 and is not available to users of earlier versions of Excel. To create a function that works in earlier versions of Excel, you need to combine two COUNTIF functions. Using the example worksheet, the function would look like this: =COUNTIF (E1:E27,E4)-COUNTIF(A1:A27,A20). In the example, because the entries in column A are dates, Excel may return a value for this function that is formatted as a date. If you set the format to General, Excel returns the same answer to this function as it returned to the COUNTIFS function.

How can I use the COUNTIFS function to create an OR condition when counting values?

▼ You cannot use the COUNTIFS function to create an OR condition. By design, the COUNTIFS function returns values based on all conditions you set being true. If you want to use an OR condition for counting, use the database function DCOUNT, described in the first part of this section, and place the criteria you specify on separate rows.

Can I include blank cells in the range I evaluate using the COUNTIFS function?

▼ Yes, you can, but Excel ignores the cells and does not include them in the count.

Average Records That Meet a Single Criterion

Excel contains two different functions that you can use to average records that meet a single criterion that you establish: the database function DAVERAGE or the AVERAGEIF function.

Suppose that your worksheet tracks classes taken by students and the grades each student earned in each class. A student's name might appear several times in the worksheet because the student may have taken several different classes. Further suppose that you want to know the average grade earned by all students for a particular class. You can use the DAVERAGE function to calculate this average.

The DAVERAGE function takes three arguments: the range containing the database information, the field containing the values you want to average, and the criteria range. The field containing the values you want to average must be a field of numeric data, because database functions only work with numeric data. The example in this section demonstrates averaging numeric grades for students. The criteria range should include the labels from the database range and a criterion you want Excel to use when calculating the average. The example in this section uses one of the class names as the criterion.

Average Records That Meet a Single Criterion

Use the DAVERAGE Function

1. Type the criterion you want Excel to use in the row below the criteria range labels under the column in which the criterion appears.
2. Click the cell in which you want to store the function.
3. Click the Formulas tab.
4. Click Insert Function.

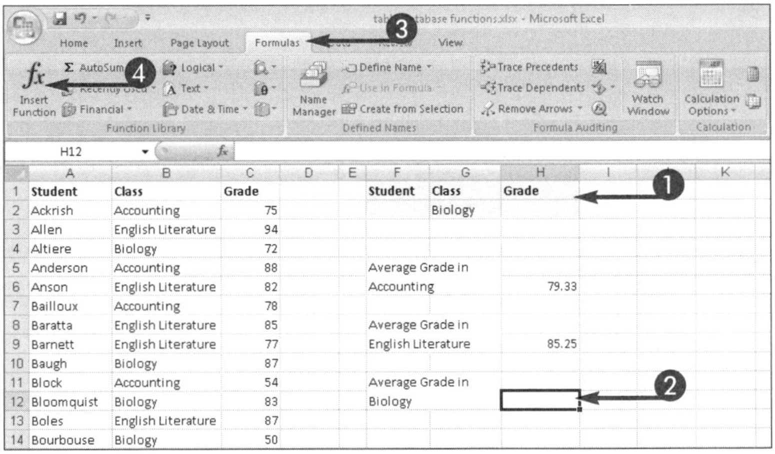

The Insert Function dialog box appears.

5. Type a description here of the function you want to use.

   This example uses database average.

6. Click Go.
7. Click DAVERAGE.
   - A description of the selected function appears here.
8. Click OK.

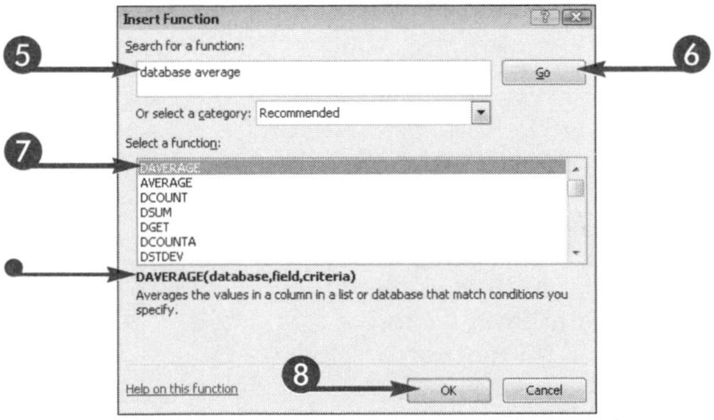

The Function Arguments dialog box appears.

9. Type a range name or select the range for the database in the worksheet.
10. Select the field label Excel should sum.

    The label's cell address appears in the Field field.

11. Select the criteria range, including labels.

    The range appears in the Criteria field.

12. Click OK.

- Excel displays the result of the formula in the cell you selected in Step 2.
- The formula appears in the Formula bar.

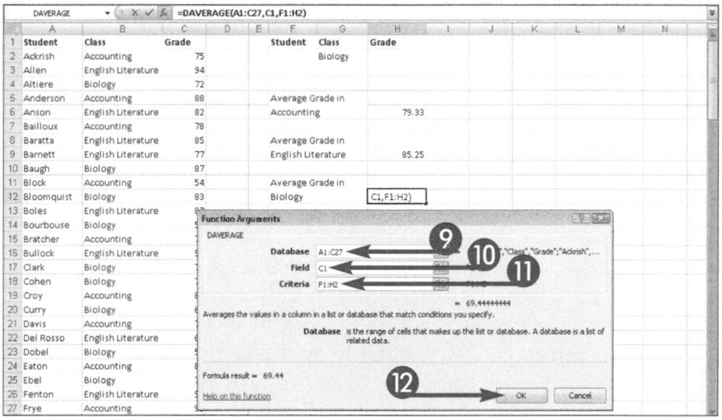

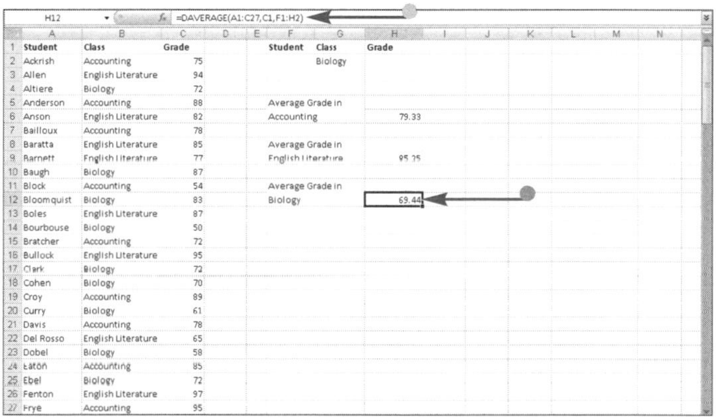

Master It

Why does my DAVERAGE function return a #DIV/0! error?

▼ In all likelihood, you misspelled the criterion that appears in the second row of the criteria range. Or, you might have misspelled a range name you assigned to the database range or the criteria range. Or, instead of selecting a field as the second argument, you might have typed the field name and misspelled it. Look for spelling errors in your DAVERAGE function and correct them; Excel should then properly calculate the average.

Must I place the criteria range beside the database range?

▼ You can place the criteria range anywhere you want in the worksheet, but placing it below the database range is not advisable. If the criteria range appears below the database range, adding new records to the database range can be difficult; you may even accidentally overwrite the criteria range. Placing the criteria range beside the database range simply makes it easier to add records to the database range.

I manually checked the result of DAVERAGE by pulling out the values and using the AVERAGE function. Why is Excel returning the wrong value for the DAVERAGE function?

▼ You may have accidentally specified the database range or the criteria range inaccurately. Using the example worksheet, suppose that you set the criteria range to be F1:H3 instead of F1:H2. Excel would return a different value for the DAVERAGE function than the one shown in this section because Excel would include blank criteria when evaluating.

continued

Average Records That Meet a Single Criterion *(Continued)*

You can use the AVERAGEIF function to calculate the average of values that match a criterion you specify. Because the AVERAGEIF function is not a database function, you do not need to set up a criteria range to use the function. Instead, you use the arguments of the AVERAGEIF function to identify the information you want Excel to average.

The AVERAGEIF function requires three arguments: The first argument is the range that contains the criterion value that you want Excel to use to calculate the average. The second argument is the criterion value. The third argument is the range containing the values that Excel should use to calculate the average. The third argument must contain numbers, but the other two arguments can contain text. The first and third arguments must be equal in length. In this example, Excel averages grades earned in a biology class. The possible criteria appear in column B. The criterion for biology appears in several different cells in column B, but the example uses cell B4. The numeric grades that Excel uses to calculate the average appear in column C.

Average Records That Meet a Single Criterion *(continued)*

Use the AVERAGEIF Function

1. Click the cell in which you want to store the function.
2. Click the Formulas tab.
3. Click Insert Function.

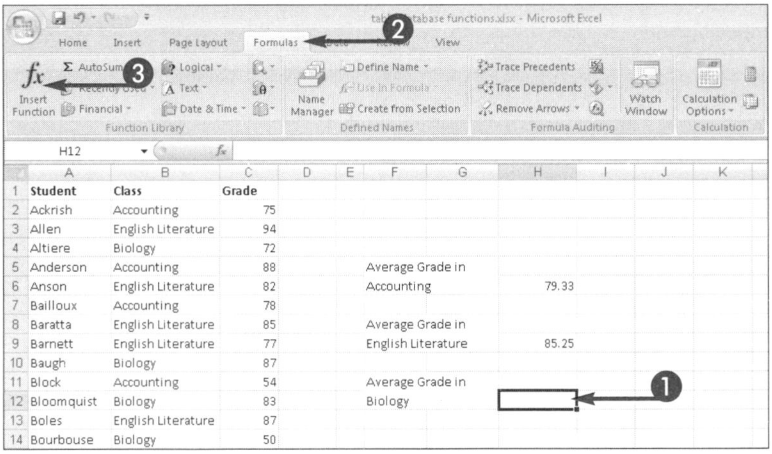

The Insert Function dialog box appears.

4. Type a description here of the function you want to use.

   This example uses average.

5. Click Go.
6. Click AVERAGEIF.
   - A description of the selected function appears here.
7. Click OK.

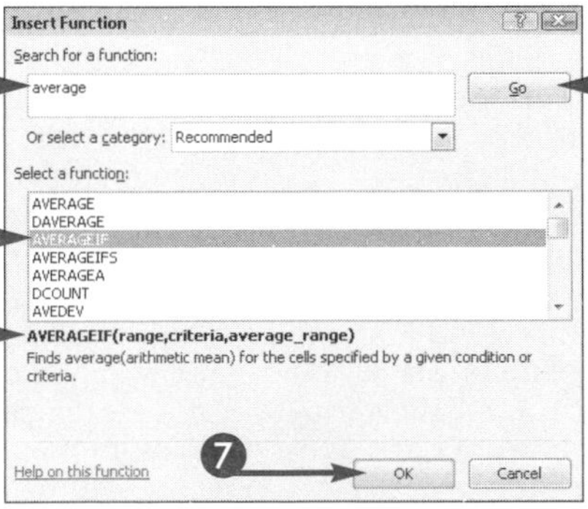

The Function Arguments dialog box appears.

8 Select the range containing the criterion you want to average.

9 Click any cell in the range selected in Step 8 that contains the criterion.

10 Select the cells containing the values to average.

11 Click OK.

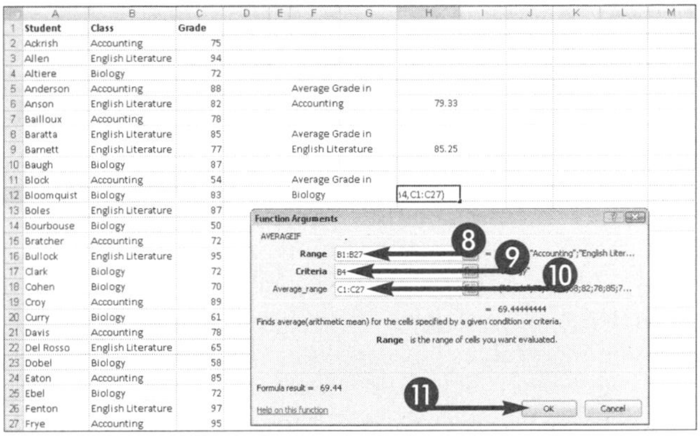

- Excel displays the result of the formula in the cell you selected in Step 1.
- The formula appears in the Formula bar.

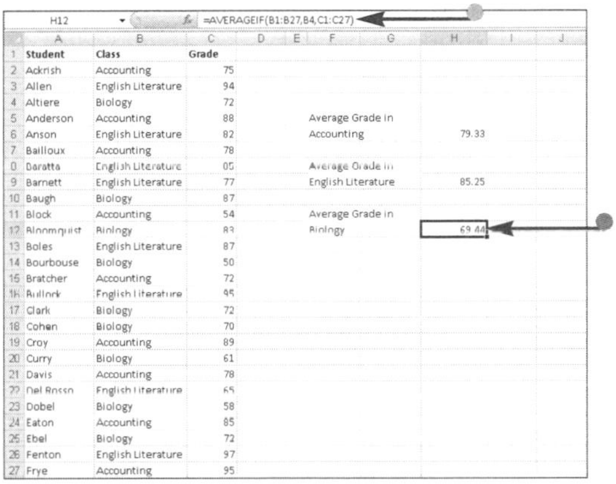

MASTER IT

The number Excel calculates consists of many digits; how can I get Excel to display the value using fewer digits?

▼ You can use a number format to specify the number of digits to display. Applying a number format does not affect the value Excel stores in the cell for use in other calculations. Select the cell containing the result of the formula and click the Home tab. Click ▾ in the Number group to select the Number format; by default, this format displays digits to the right of the decimal point. Click the increase decimal button to increase the number of digits Excel displays to the right of the decimal point, or click the decrease decimal button to decrease the number of digits Excel displays to the right of the decimal point.

Is there a way that I can both round and change the value Excel stores to use in other calculations?

▼ Yes, you can use the ROUND function in conjunction with the AVERAGEIF function. The ROUND function takes two arguments: the value to round and the number of digits to which you want to round the number. To round the results of the AVERAGEIF function to display only one decimal place using the example worksheet, use the following function: =ROUND(AVERAGEIF(B1:B27,B4,C1:C27),1). You can edit the cell containing the AVERAGEIF function and type **ROUND(** immediately after the equal sign at the beginning of the function. Then, at the end of the function, type **,1)**.

Average Records That Meet Multiple Criteria

Excel contains two different functions that you can use to average records that meet a single criterion that you establish: the database function DAVERAGE or the AVERAGEIFS function.

Suppose that your worksheet contains daily sales information for a cable company, listing the amount of the sale, the type of cable product sold, who made the sale, the branch office from which the sale was generated, and whether the sale was made to a new or an existing customer. You can use the DAVERAGE function to find the average sales made by a particular branch office on a particular date to new customers.

The DAVERAGE function takes three arguments: the range containing the database information, the field containing the values to average, and the criteria range. The field containing the values to average must contain numbers. The criteria range should include the labels from the database range and criteria you want Excel to use when calculating the average. You can set up the criteria using an AND condition to average records that match all of the criteria, or an OR condition to average records that match any of the criteria. The example in this section uses an AND condition.

Average Records That Meet Multiple Criteria

Use the DAVERAGE Function

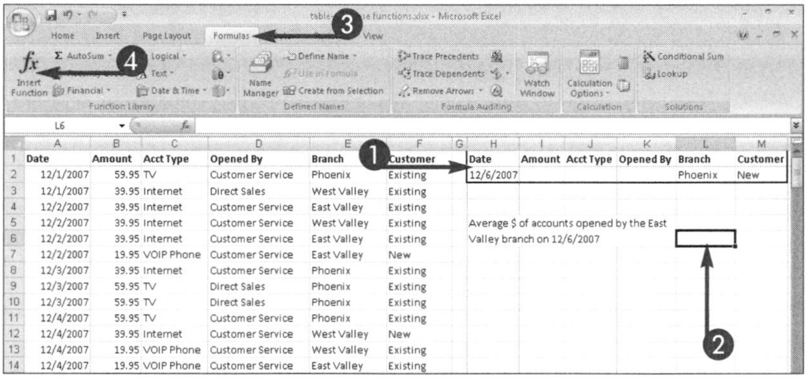

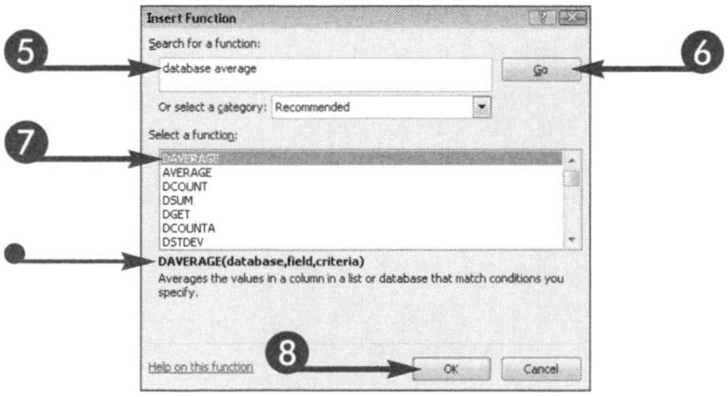

1. Type the criteria you want Excel to use below the criteria range labels under the column in which the criterion appears.
2. Click the cell in which you want to store the function.
3. Click the Formulas tab.
4. Click Insert Function.

   The Insert Function dialog box appears.
5. Type a description here of the function you want to use.

   This example uses database average.
6. Click Go.
7. Click DAVERAGE.
   - A description of the selected function appears here.
8. Click OK.

The Function Arguments dialog box appears.

9 Type a range name or select the range for the database in the worksheet.

The selected cell or range appears in the Database field.

10 Select the field label Excel should sum.

11 Select the criteria range, including labels.

12 Click OK.

- Excel displays the result of the formula in the cell you selected in Step 2.
- The formula appears in the Formula bar.

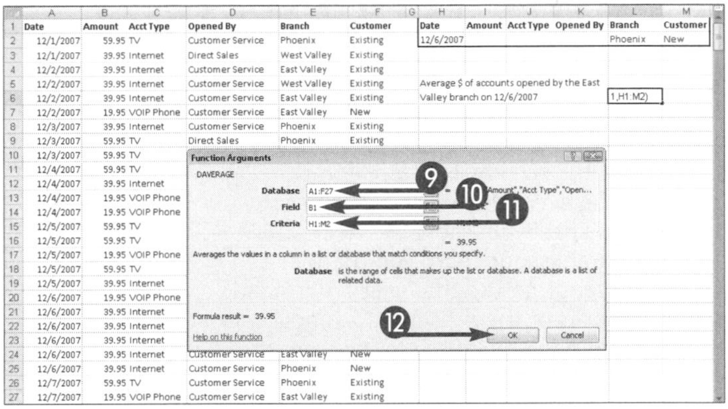

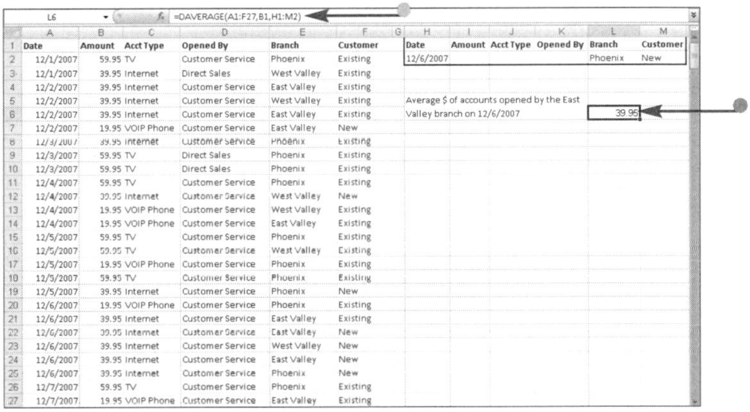

MASTER IT

How does Excel know the difference between an AND condition and an OR condition?

▼ Excel uses the way in which you place criteria in the criteria range to determine the condition. If you place all of your criteria on a single line in the criteria range and you specify the criteria range to include no more than two lines, then Excel treats the criteria as an AND condition. If you place criteria on separate lines in the criteria range and expand the criteria range, Excel treats criteria as an OR condition. Be careful not to include more rows in the criteria range than you set conditions; Excel includes blank rows in the calculation.

How many criteria can I establish?

▼ Using an AND condition, you can set one criterion for each field in the criteria range. Using an OR condition, you can set as many criteria as you want on separate lines. For example, using the example worksheet, you can set a combination of conditions and calculate the average dollar amount for accounts opened on December 6, 2007 by the East Valley and Phoenix branches combined. The function you use would not change, but the criteria range would expand to include H1:M3. Cells H2 and H3 would contain the date 12/6/2007. Cell L2 would contain East Valley, and cell L3 would contain Phoenix. Using the values in the sample worksheet, Excel would return $35.95 as the average value.

continued

Average Records That Meet Multiple Criteria *(Continued)*

You can use the AVERAGEIFS function to calculate the average of values that match criteria you specify. Because the AVERAGEIFS function is not a database function, you do not need to set up a criteria range to use the function. Instead, you use the arguments of the AVERAGEIFS function to identify the information you want Excel to average.

The AVERAGEIFS function requires a minimum of three arguments, and two of them — the criteria range and the criterion — work in pairs. To calculate the average using more than one criterion, you specify additional criteria ranges and criteria values.

The first argument you specify is the range containing the values that Excel should average. All subsequent arguments work in pairs. The second argument is a range that contains one of the criteria values that Excel should use to calculate the average. The third argument is a criterion value. The first argument must contain numbers, but the other two arguments can contain text. The range you average and each subsequent criteria range must be equal in length.

In this example, Excel averages the dollar value of accounts opened by one cable company branch on a particular date.

Average Records That Meet Multiple Criteria *(continued)*

Use the AVERAGEIFS Function

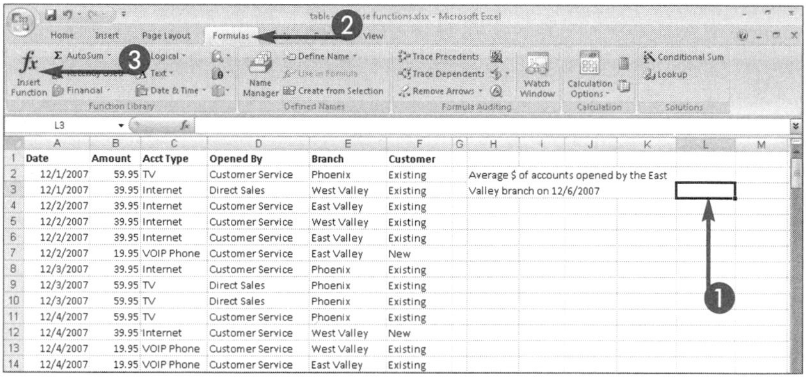

1. Click the cell in which you want to store the function.
2. Click the Formulas tab.
3. Click Insert Function.

The Insert Function dialog box appears.

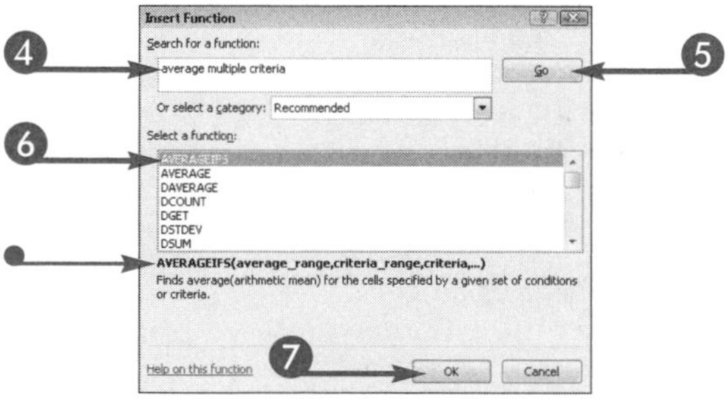

4. Type a description here of the function you want to use.

   This example uses average multiple criteria.
5. Click Go.
6. Click AVERAGEIFS.
   - A description of the selected function appears here.
7. Click OK.

The Function Arguments dialog box appears.

8. Select the range containing the values to average.
9. Click here and select the range containing the first criterion you want to average.
10. Click any cell in the range selected in Step 8 that contains the criterion.
11. Repeat Steps 9 and 10 for each criterion you want to establish.
12. Click OK.
    - Excel displays the result of the formula in the cell you selected in Step 1.
    - The formula appears in the Formula bar.

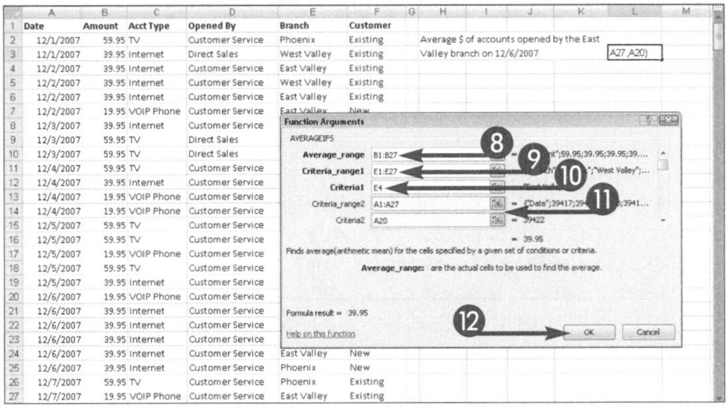

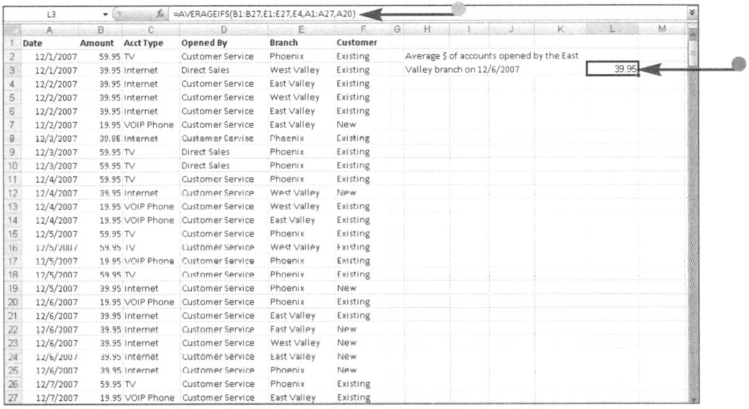

PART III

MASTER IT

Why does my AVERAGEIFS function return a #DIV/0! error?

▼ It is possible that no cells in the criteria ranges meet the criteria you specify. If you know cells meet the criteria, then, in all likelihood, the range you selected for Excel to average does not contain numbers. If the range you want Excel to average contains numbers formatted as text, select all of the cells that you want to convert. Click [◈] and then click Convert to Number.

I manually checked the result of AVERAGEIFS by adding the values and dividing by the number of values. Why is Excel returning the wrong value for the AVERAGEIFS function?

▼ If the criteria range contains empty cells, Excel treats them as zero instead of ignoring them. Try the function again, making sure that all cells in all criteria ranges contain entries.

How does AVERAGEIFS behave if only some criteria I specify are true?

▼ AVERAGEIFS operates using an AND condition. Therefore, AVERAGEIFS includes values in the range you specify for the first argument — the range containing the values to average — only if all criteria you specify in subsequent arguments are true.

Find the Smallest Record That Meets Criteria

You can use the DMIN function to find the smallest value in a database range that meets criteria you specify. Suppose that your worksheet tracks classes taken by students, and the grades each student earned in each class. The student's name might appear several times in the worksheet because the student may have taken several different classes. Further suppose that you want to know the average grade earned by all students for a particular class. You can use the DMIN function to determine the lowest grade earned by all students in a particular class.

The DMIN function takes three arguments: the range containing the database information, the field containing the values you want Excel to use to find a minimum, and the criteria range. The field Excel uses to calculate the smallest value must contain numeric values, because database functions only work with numeric data. The criteria range should include the labels from the database range and criteria you want Excel to use when calculating the smallest value. The example in this section uses one of the class names as the criterion.

Find the Smallest Record That Meets Criteria

1. Type the criterion you want Excel to use below the criteria range labels under the column in which the criterion appears.
2. Click the cell in which you want to store the function.
3. Click the Formulas tab.
4. Click Insert Function.

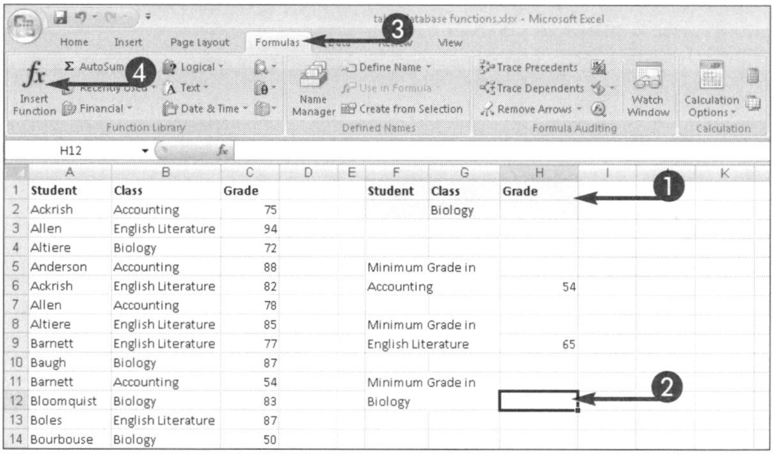

The Insert Function dialog box appears.

5. Type a description of the function you want to use.

   This example uses minimum.

6. Click Go.
7. Click DMIN.

   - A description of the selected function appears here.

8. Click OK.

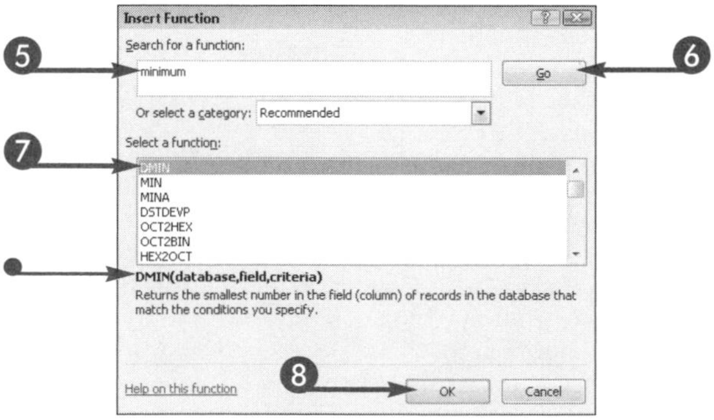

The Function Arguments dialog box appears.

9. Type a range name or select the range for the database in the worksheet.

10. Select the field label for which Excel should calculate a minimum.

    The label's cell address appears in the Field field.

11. Select the criteria range, including labels.

    The selected range appears in the Criteria field.

12. Click OK.

    - Excel displays the result of the formula in the cell you selected in Step 2.
    - The formula appears in the Formula bar.

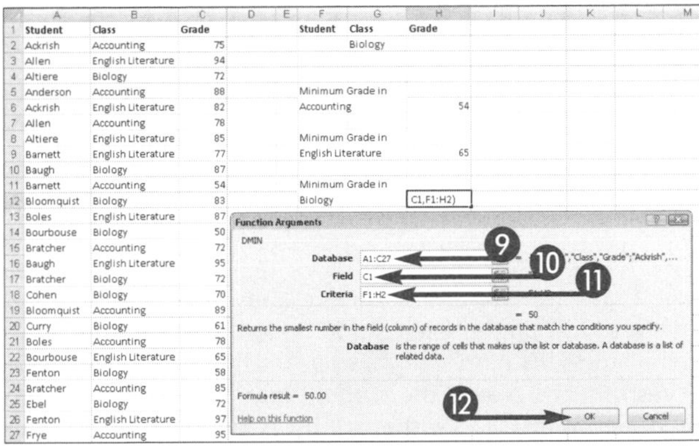

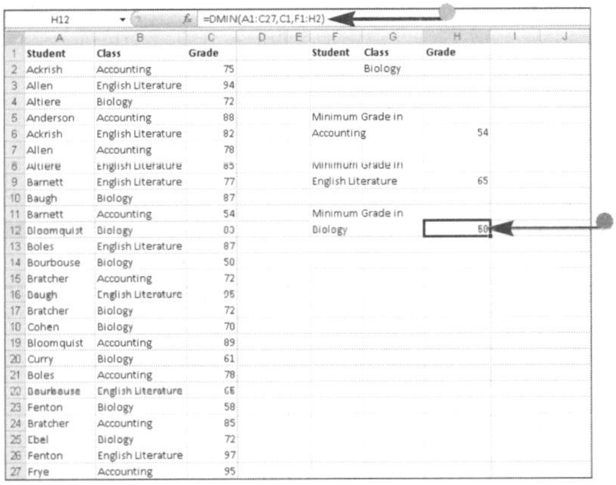

Master It

Can I set more than one criterion and still calculate a minimum?

Yes. To calculate a minimum that meets all of the criteria you specify, enter all of the criteria on the same row just below the criteria range labels. In this case, all of the criteria must be true or Excel returns zero as the minimum. To calculate a minimum that meets any of the criteria you specify, enter the criteria values on separate rows below the criteria range labels, and expand the criteria range to include the labels and all of the rows on which you enter criteria. In this case, Excel returns the lower of the values, based on the criteria you set.

How did you get the worksheet to display three different minimum values? When I change the criteria range, Excel changes the calculated value.

You can approach this situation in two different ways: you can set up multiple criteria ranges, each is displaying different criteria, or you can convert the result of the function to a value before you change the criterion in the criteria range. To convert the function to a value as shown in the example, click the Home tab and click [Paste icon]. Then, click [▼] under Paste and click Paste Values. You can now change the criterion without affecting the previously calculated value.

Find the Largest Record That Meets Criteria

You can use the DMAX function to find the largest value in a database range that meets criteria you specify.

Suppose that your worksheet tracks classes taken by students and the grades each student earned in each class. The student's name might appear several times in the worksheet because the student may have taken several different classes. Further suppose that you want to know the highest grade earned by all students for a particular class. You can use the DMAX function to determine this grade.

The DMAX function takes three arguments: the range containing the database information, the field containing the values you want Excel to use to find the largest value, and the criteria range. The field Excel uses to calculate the largest value must contain numeric values, because database functions only work with numeric data. The criteria range should include the labels from the database range and criteria you want Excel to use when calculating the maximum value. The example in this section uses one of the class names as the criterion.

Find the Largest Record That Meets Criteria

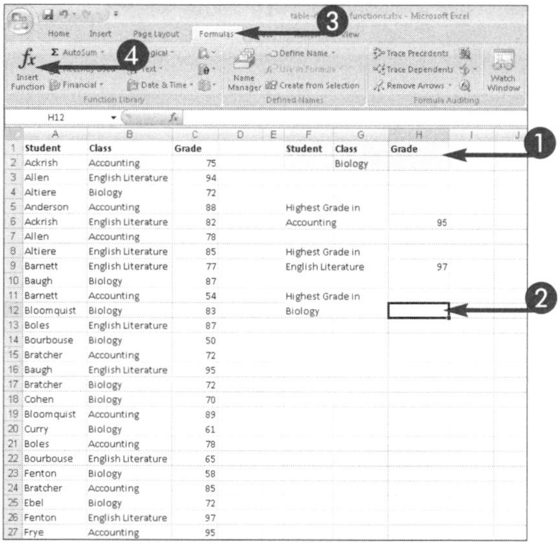

1. Type the criterion you want Excel to use below the criteria range labels under the column in which the criterion appears.
2. Click the cell in which you want to store the function.
3. Click the Formulas tab.
4. Click Insert Function.

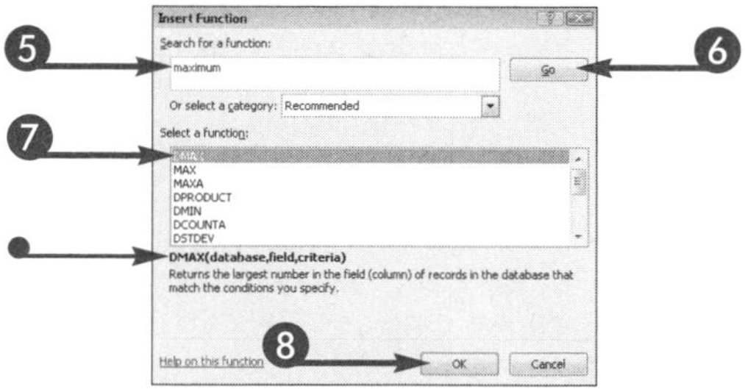

The Insert Function dialog box appears.

5. Type a description here of the function you want to use.

   This example uses maximum.
6. Click Go.
7. Click DMAX.
   - A description of the selected function appears here.
8. Click OK.

The Function Arguments dialog box appears.

9. Type a range name or select the range for the database in the worksheet.

10. Select the field label for which Excel should calculate a maximum.

    The label's cell address appears in the Field field.

11. Select the criteria range, including labels.

    The range appears in the Criteria field.

12. Click OK.

    - Excel displays the result of the formula in the cell you selected in Step 2.
    - The formula appears in the Formula bar.

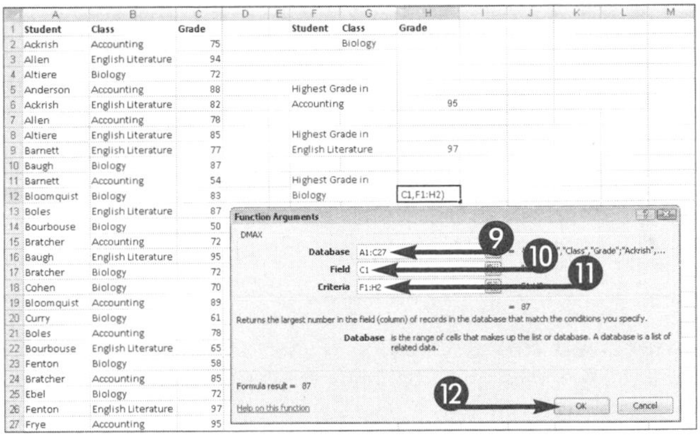

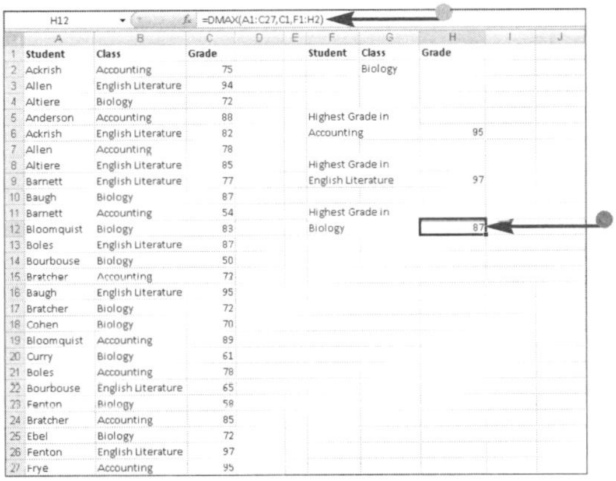

MASTER IT

Can I use the DMAX function to find the largest value in an Access table?

▼ Yes, you can, but the Access table information must appear in Excel. You can simply copy the Access table and paste it into Excel if you do not intend to change any information. However, if you want to be able to update the Access table information while working in Excel, you must connect Excel and Access. See Chapter 32 for details. Once the Access table information appears in Excel, follow the steps in this section to create the function by identifying a database range, a criteria range, and a range containing values from which Excel should find the largest.

Are there any rules to follow concerning where I place the criteria range?

▼ The only rule associated with the criteria range is that it must contain a label that appears in the first row that exactly matches the label in the database range. In addition, the criteria range must contain at least one row below the label. There are a few additional guidelines. For example, make sure that the criteria range does not extend into the database range. To add to a database range, you usually add rows. While Excel does not restrict you from placing the criteria range below the database range, placing the criteria range beside the database range allows for growth.

Understanding Excel Errors

Chapter 16 describes the functions you can use to trap errors that Excel returns. However, you can accidentally create errors that may not be apparent. This chapter describes errors that can occur and techniques you can use to find errors.

Mismatched Parentheses

Every left parenthesis must have a corresponding right parenthesis. If you try to enter a formula and you do not match all parentheses, Excel usually displays a message telling you that your formula is missing a parenthesis, and you typically need to correct the error to store the formula. However, under some circumstances, Excel corrects the error for you. For example, if you type

=SUM(C1:C10

and press Enter, forgetting the final parenthesis, Excel adds the parenthesis for you and stores the formula.

In other cases, Excel attempts to guess where the parenthesis should appear and offers a potential correction. But be careful, because Excel does not always guess correctly. For example, if you type

=AVERAGE(SUM(A1:A5,SUM(B1:B5))

Excel volunteers to correct the formula by adding another parenthesis at the end of the formula. That may be the formula you want, or you may actually want

=AVERAGE(SUM(A1:A5),SUM(B1:B5))

Take advantage of the color coding Excel uses when you edit a cell containing a formula. The color coding can help you identify matching sets of parentheses and decide on correct placement.

Cells Filled with Pound Signs

Pound signs (#) filling a cell can mean that the cell is not wide enough to display the value stored in the cell. Widen the cell or change the type of number format assigned to the cell to see if the problem disappears.

If the problem remains, the cell probably contains a formula that returns an invalid date or time. Excel does not support dates prior to 1900 or negative time values. If you enter -1 or a formula that returns a negative number into a cell and format the cell as a date or time, Excel fills the cell with pound signs.

Cells Containing Spaces

Some Excel users think that they can erase the contents of a cell by selecting the cell, pressing the spacebar, and pressing Enter. It is true that the cell then appears to be blank. In reality, though, it contains a single space — it is not empty.

In some circumstances, placing a blank space into a cell may not matter. However, if you include that cell in a COUNTA function, Excel includes the cell in the count — which probably was not what you intended. As a habit, you should not erase cells by storing a blank space. Instead, you should click the Home tab and click to erase the contents of a cell.

Similarly, text entries that contain extra spaces can cause formulas that compare cells containing text entries to return seemingly inaccurate results. Typically, you find extra spaces in text entries that you import into Excel. When you import values, Excel strips away extra trailing spaces, but when you import text, Excel does not strip away trailing spaces. And, because spaces are not visible, you often cannot tell that a text entry in a cell contains trailing spaces unless you edit the cell. Select it and press F2. If you discover extra trailing spaces and they are causing formulas that compare text strings to return inaccurate results, consider using the TRIM function to remove the trailing spaces. See Chapter 15 for more details.

Absolute and Relative Cell References

Using a relative cell reference when you should have used an absolute cell reference can introduce mistakes in a worksheet. When you copy a formula containing a relative cell reference, Excel automatically adjusts the cell reference to refer to the corresponding location. For example, if you copy

=SUM(A1:A5)

from cell A6 to cell B6, Excel stores the following formula in cell B6:

=SUM(B1:B5)

However, that might not be what you want. For example, when you calculate percentages, you want to use an absolute cell reference. Suppose that you want to calculate January's sales, which are stored in cell B2, as a percentage of total sales, which are stored in cell B14, and then to copy the formula to calculate the percentage of sales for the rest of the months between February and June. If you store the following formula to calculate January's percentage in cell C2

=B2/B14

and then copy it, Excel stores the following formula to calculate February's percentage of sales:

=B3/B15

In reality, the formula should be

=B3/B14

At best, the cell by which you try to divide is empty and Excel displays a #DIV/0! error. At worst, the cell contains a value and Excel returns a properly calculated but completely wrong percentage. See Chapter 10 for details on properly using absolute and relative cell references.

Operator Precedence Problems

You can accidentally introduce a calculation error by misplacing or omitting parentheses. Excel follows the straightforward rules you learned in high school math class to determine the order in which to calculate a formula. Suppose that cells A1, A2, and A3 contain the numbers 1, 2, and 3, respectively. The following two formulas return different results, and the parentheses determine the results:

=A1+(A2*A3)

=(A1+A2)*A3

See Chapter 10 for details on the order of precedence rules that Excel follows.

Cells Do Not Add Properly

Sometimes, Excel appears to add a series of numbers incorrectly. In the figure, 1/3 is entered into cells A1 to A3 and formatted using a General format. You would expect, based on what you see, that the sum in cell A4 would be .999999. However, Excel calculates the sum correctly because it uses the actual values stored in cells A1 to A3 rather than the numbers that Excel displays.

In a similar way, lack of precision can make a calculation appear inaccurate. Excel can store numbers with 15-digit accuracy; Excel stores numbers with more digits as an approximation. For example, the formula

=(4.1-4.2)+1

returns a result of .9. However, if you format the cell to display 15 decimal places, Excel returns 0.899999999999999.

To handle either of the situations just described, you can use the ROUND function. See Chapter 11 for more information.

Circular References

Circular references occur when a formula refers to itself. That is, you store a formula in cell A5 that includes a reference to cell A5. Excel might display a warning if it discovers a circular reference, but you can check for circular references on your own; the section, "Check for Formula Errors," shows you how to find circular references.

Using Data Validation to Control Data Entry

You can use Excel's Data Validation feature to control data entry. Read more about this feature in the section, "Control Data Entry."

Display and Print Formulas in Cells

You can display formulas in the worksheet as well as the Formula bar and then print the worksheet while it displays formulas. When tracking down an error or when familiarizing yourself with an unfamiliar worksheet, it is helpful to view the formulas in the cells where you stored them. When you display formulas, Excel shows formulas in cells that contain formulas, and values or text in cells that do not contain formulas. This approach helps you view information in context. Seeing the formulas in the location where you store them can trigger an idea that might help you understand why something is not working as you expected it to work.

You can print the worksheet after you display formulas in the cells where you have stored them, but printing is most effective if you print row and column headings along with the information in your worksheet. That way, you can study the worksheet on paper as if it were on-screen. By displaying row and column headings, you can easily identify where each formula is located without looking at the workbook on-screen. Because displaying formulas requires more column width for each cell, you might want to print using landscape orientation.

Display and Print Formulas in Cells

1. While viewing the worksheet containing the formulas you want to display and print, click the Formulas tab.
2. Click the Show Formulas button (▦).

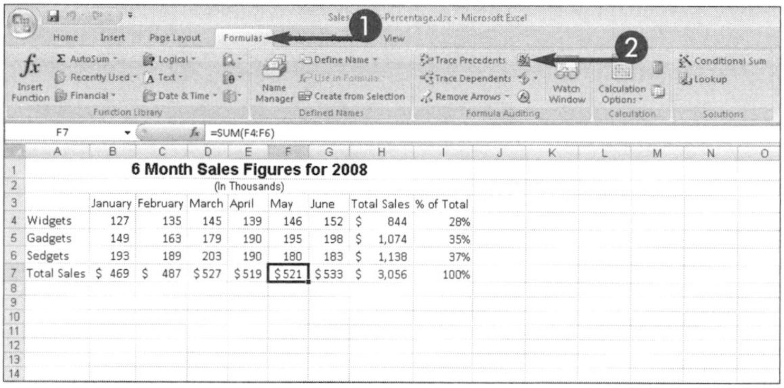

- Excel displays formulas in the worksheet as well as in the Formula bar.

3. Click the Page Layout tab.

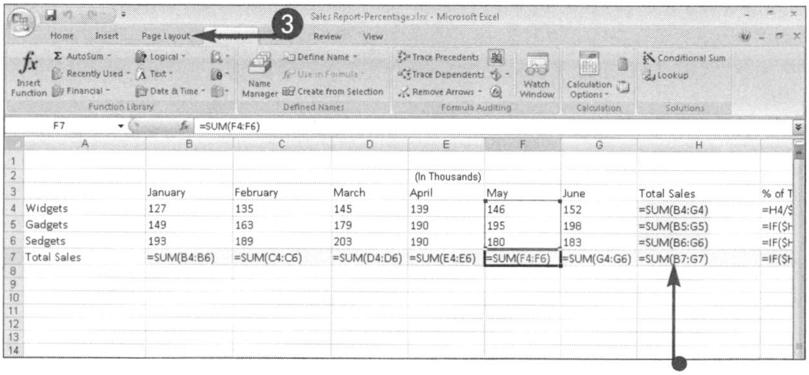

4. Click Print (changes to).
5. Click Orientation.
6. Click Landscape.
7. Click .

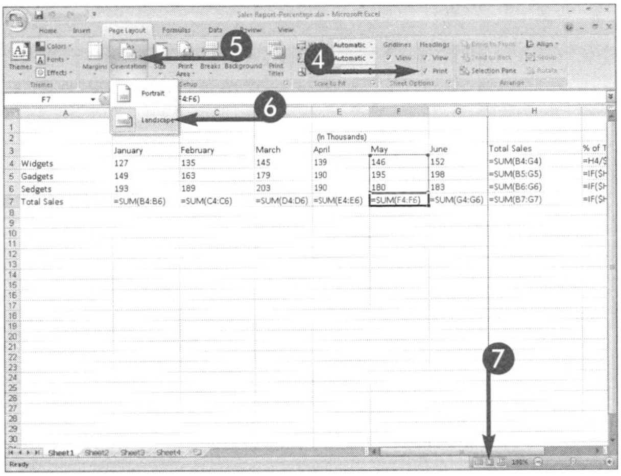

Excel displays the worksheet in Page Layout view, where the worksheet appears the same way it will print.

- Formulas appear in cells containing formulas.
- These column headings will print.
- These row headings will print.

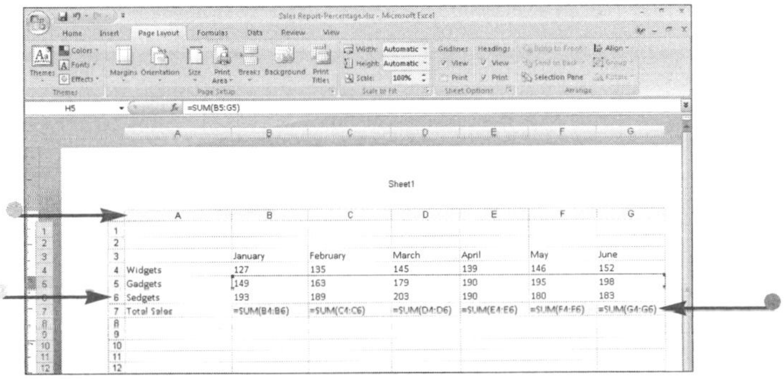

MASTER IT

How do I print the worksheet?

▼ Click and point at Print. On the menu that appears, you can click Print to display the Print dialog box, where you can specify printing options such as the printer to which you want to print and the number of copies you want to print. You can also click Quick Print to send the worksheet to the default printer and print a single copy of the worksheet.

Do I need to click to display the worksheet in Page Layout view before printing?

▼ No. Displaying the worksheet in Page Layout view gives you a good idea of the way the worksheet will appear when you print it. If you view the worksheet in Page Layout view before printing, you may identify other settings you want to change before printing in order to save paper and ink.

How do I stop displaying formulas in cells that contain formulas?

▼ Follow Steps 1 and 2. You can click (a toggle button) to display formulas, and click it again to stop displaying formulas.

Do row and column headings print only once, or will they continue to print each time I print the worksheet?

▼ Row and column headings will continue to print unless you repeat Steps 3 and 4.

Identify Cells Containing Formulas

Using the Go To Special dialog box, you can have Excel highlight cells that contain formulas. The highlighting is temporary; Excel removes it as soon as you move the insertion point.

You can limit the cells that Excel highlights to specific types of formulas. For example, you can have Excel highlight only those cells that contain text formulas. You can also have Excel highlight only those cells that contain number formats. When you turn on formula cell highlighting, Excel automatically highlights cells that meet the criteria you specify, and selects the first cell in the worksheet that contains a formula meeting the criteria. Excel defines the first cell in the worksheet, based on the cell's row and column position. The cell that Excel selects has the lowest row number and the earliest alphabetical column letter of all cells containing formulas.

Highlighting cells that contain formulas can also help you identify one common error — the formula that has been accidentally replaced with a value. Suppose that you change the contents of a cell and expect the change to cause updating elsewhere, but no updating occurs. In this situation, a cell that you thought contained a formula may actually contain a value.

Identify Cells Containing Formulas

1. Click the Home tab.
2. Click Find & Select.

   Excel displays a drop-down menu.
3. Click Go To Special.

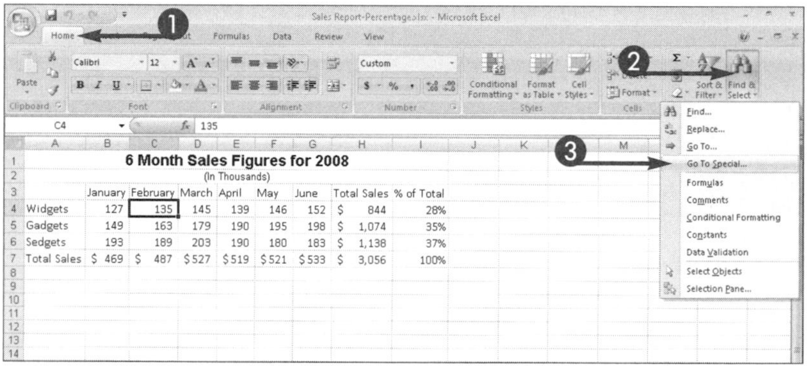

The Go To Special dialog box appears.

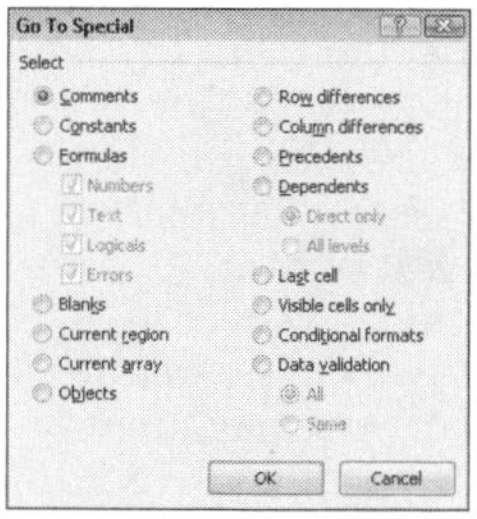

4 Click Formulas (◎ changes to ◉).

5 Click OK.

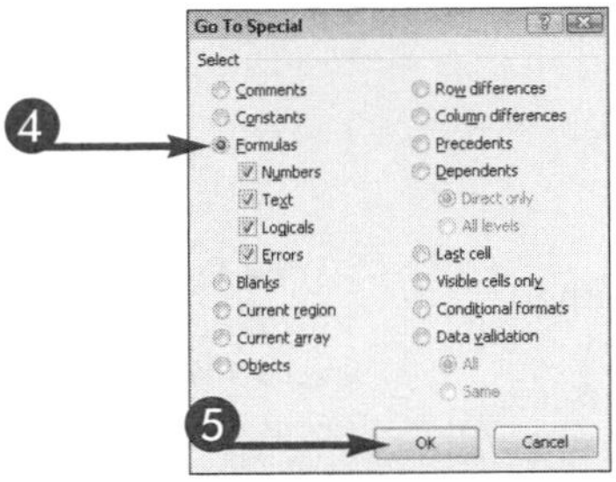

Excel highlights cells in the worksheet that match the criteria you set in the Go To Special dialog box.

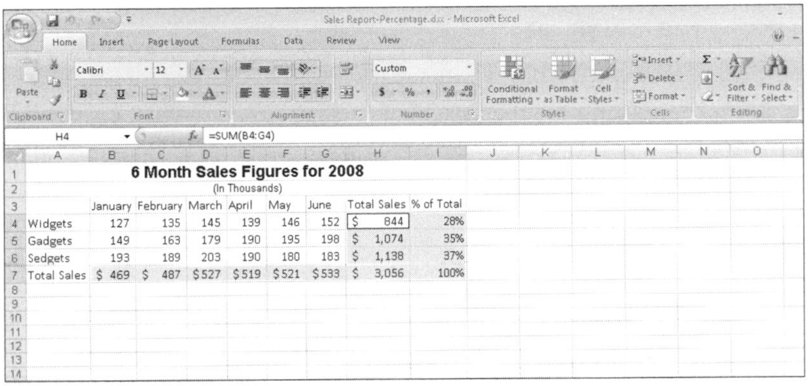

MASTER IT

How does highlighting help me find a cell that should have contained a formula but does not?

▼ Typically, you set up a worksheet so that cells containing formulas appear close to each other. In the example worksheet, row 7 and columns H and I contain formulas. It would probably catch your attention if, for some reason, a cell in row 7 or in columns H or I did not appear highlighted.

Can I limit the cells that Excel considers for highlighting?

▼ Yes, you can select a range of cells before beginning the steps in this section. In this case, Excel searches only the selected cells and highlights only those cells within the selected range that meet the criteria you set in the Go To Special dialog box.

What happens if I select Dependents in the Go To Special dialog box?

▼ Before you select this option in the Go To Special dialog box, make sure that you select a cell containing a formula. Then, when you select Dependents in the Go to Special dialog box, Excel highlights the cells that depend on the formula contained in the selected cell.

Evaluate Formulas

You can use the Evaluate Formula feature to have Excel guide you through the steps required to arrive at the result of a formula. You can think of the Evaluate Formula feature as a way to watch Excel calculate in slow motion. This feature is a good way to help you understand a complex formula. For example, suppose that someone sends you a worksheet that contains a nested IF function. If you select the cell and use the Evaluate Formula feature, you can see exactly how Excel arrives at the result it displays in the cell.

As the Evaluate Formula feature works through a formula, it underlines the portion it is currently evaluating and then displays the result of the evaluation in italics. You can always identify an evaluated portion of a formula because it appears in italics, and you can always identify the portion that Excel will evaluate next because it appears underlined.

By watching the calculations Excel makes using the Evaluate Formula feature, you may also discover why a particular formula is returning a result that you did not expect.

Evaluate Formulas

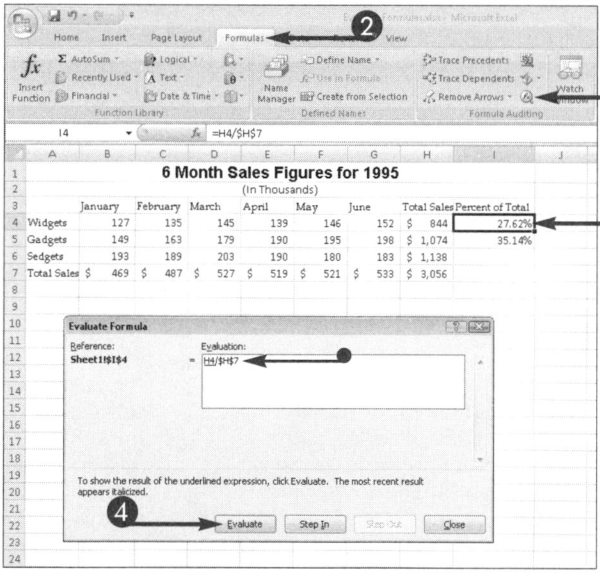

1. Click the cell containing the formula you want to evaluate.
2. Click the Formulas tab.
3. Click the Evaluate Formula button ( ).

   The Evaluate Formula window opens.

   - Excel underlines the first cell reference in the formula that it will evaluate.
4. Click Evaluate.

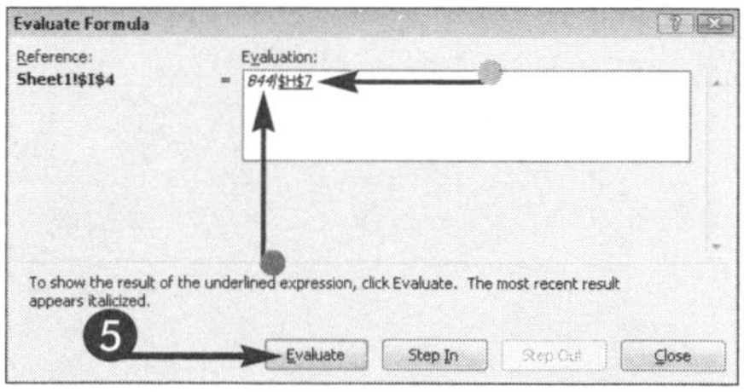

- Excel changes the cell reference to the value stored in the cell and displays the value in italics.
- Excel underlines the next portion of the formula it will evaluate.

5. Click Evaluate.

- Excel changes the cell reference to the value stored in the cell and displays the value in italics.

6 Click Evaluate.

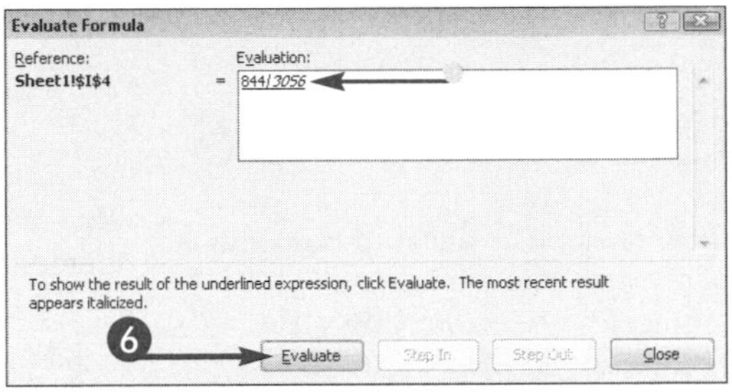

- Excel displays the results of the calculation.
- Click Close to close the Evaluate Formula window.

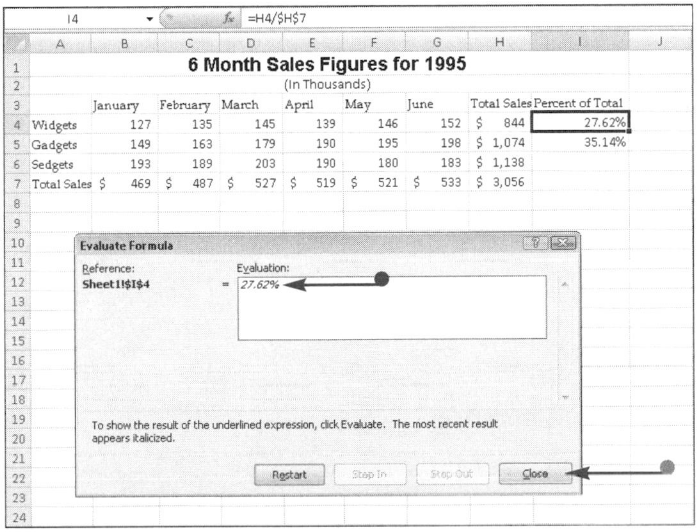

PART III

MASTER IT

What does the Step In button do?

▼ When you click the Step In button, Excel selects the cell that was underlined in the Evaluate Formula dialog box, and a second box appears below the Evaluation field. In the second field, Excel displays the contents of the newly selected cell. If the newly selected cell contains a formula, Excel displays that formula and gives you the opportunity to evaluate it. You can click the Step Out button to return to evaluating the original formula.

How many times do I need to click the Evaluate button?

▼ You click the Evaluate button as many times as needed to let Excel completely evaluate the formula. The actual number of times you click Evaluate depends on the length and complexity of the formula you are evaluating. For example, to evaluate a formula that contains an IF function, you may need to click Evaluate eight or nine times.

How can the Evaluate Formula feature help me discover why a formula returns an unexpected result?

▼ Formulas like IF functions or nested formulas can be difficult to understand because of the intermediate steps required to perform the calculation. The Evaluate Formula feature shows you each step in the formula as it happens. By slowing down the process and showing you the order of calculation, you may understand why a formula returns unexpected results.

Check for Formula Errors

You can use tools available in Excel to help you find and resolve errors in a worksheet. Although many errors are obvious because Excel displays an error message in the cell, such as #REF!, #VALUE!, and #NAME?, other errors are not as obvious. For example, cells containing formulas that omit adjacent cells are not always errors. As a result, Excel does not display an error in the cell. Instead, you see a Smart Tag indicator in the cell. Also, cells containing circular references do not display any visual characteristic that would alert you to a circular reference. Circular references are formulas that contain references to the cell in which the formula is stored.

Excel's Error Checking feature can help you find circular references. Once you identify a circular reference, you can decide if the formula is valid and, if not, you can correct it. In addition, for cells containing errors such as #DIV/0! and #VALUE!, you can use the Error Checking feature to visually identify the cells involved in the error, which often helps you correct the error. You can also use any Smart Tags in your worksheet to help you correct possible errors.

Check for Formula Errors

Find Circular References

1. Click the Formulas tab.
2. Click ▾ beside the Error Checking button (⚠).
3. Click Circular References.
4. Click the cell reference that Excel displays.

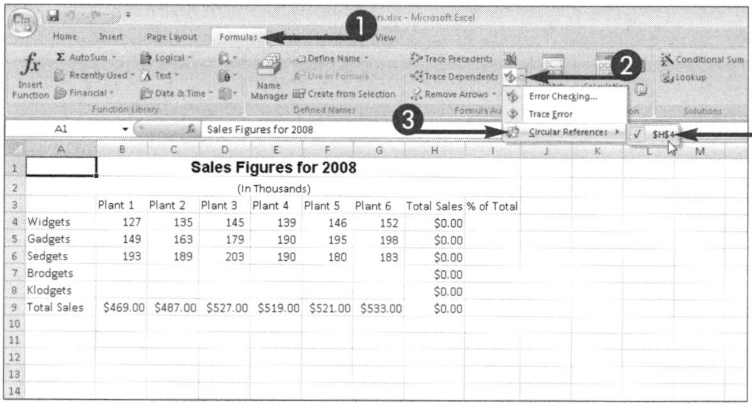

- Excel selects the cell in the worksheet.
- The formula appears in the Formula bar.

Note: The formula refers to itself.

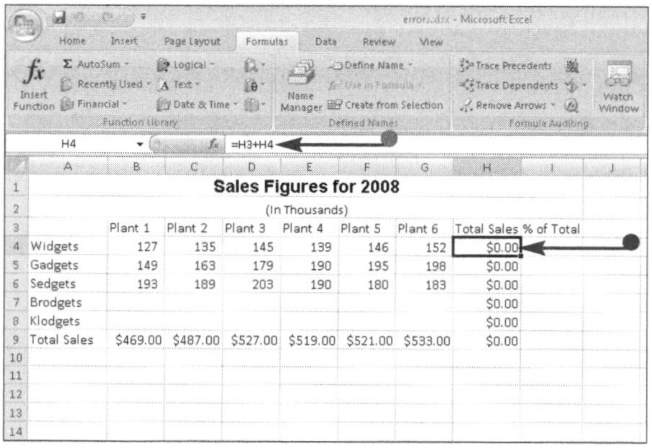

Trace the Source of an Error

1. Select a cell containing an error.
2. Click the Formulas tab.
3. Click beside .
4. Click Trace Error.

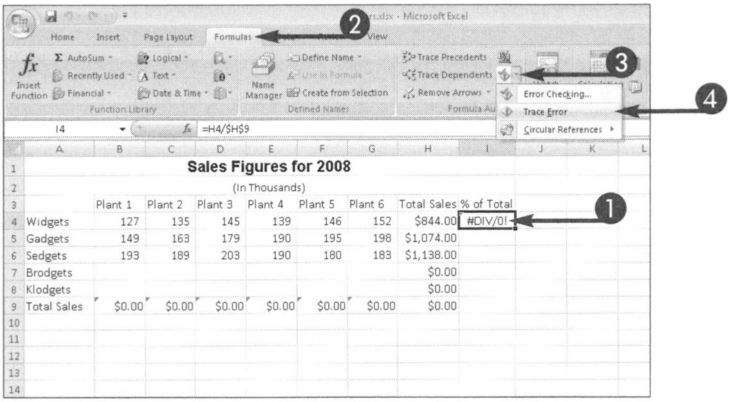

- Excel adds lines that visually connect the cell containing the error and any cells referenced by the cell containing the error.

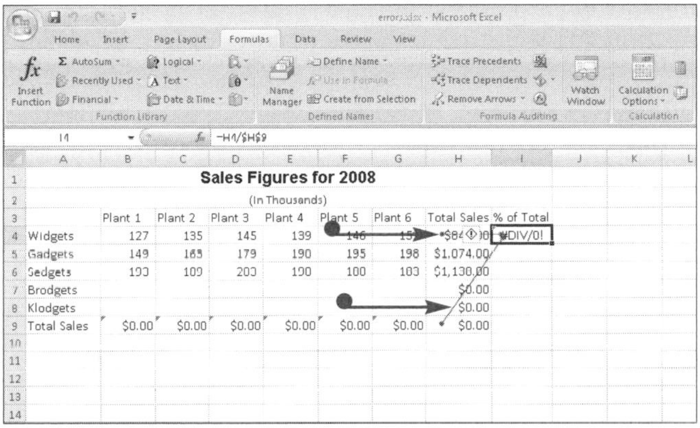

MASTER IT

Can I have Excel guide me through finding all of the errors in my worksheet?

▼ Yes. You can use the Error Checking window to find and correct errors other than circular references in the same way that a spell-checker checks for and corrects spelling errors. Click the Formulas tab, click beside , and click Error Checking. Excel displays the Error Checking window.

What does a Smart Tag indicator look like, and how do I use it to correct a problem?

▼ Cells containing Smart Tag indicators display a small, green triangle in the upper-left corner. When you select the cell, appears. Click ; Excel describes the problem it found and offers choices to correct the problem, including the option to ignore the error, which makes the green triangle disappear.

When I finish correcting the error, how do I get rid of the tracing lines?

▼ If you click the Formulas tab and then click Remove Arrows in the Formula Auditing group, Excel removes the error-tracing arrows.

I tried to follow the steps in the subsection, "Find Circular References," but the command was not available. What did I do wrong?

▼ Nothing. Your worksheet contains no circular references.

Trace Cell Relationships

You can use two of Excel's Formula Auditing tools, the Trace Precedents and Trace Dependents tools, to help you trace the relationships between cells. These tools come in handy even if your worksheet does not contain errors. They provide visual cues that help you determine cell relationships. Using these visual cues may help you to understand the relationships in an unfamiliar worksheet. You may also be able to determine why a particular formula is not producing the result you expect. For example, the visual cues provided by tracing precedents and dependents may show you that a formula is using incorrect cells or omitting cells. You may also want to check dependents for a formula before you delete it, because deleting the formula could have a ripple effect throughout your workbook.

By tracing precedents, you can identify the cells that contribute to a formula's result. You can trace precedents only for cells containing formulas. By tracing dependents, you can identify the cells containing formulas that use a particular cell. Unlike tracing precedents, you can trace dependents for a cell that does not contain a formula, as well as a cell that does contain a formula.

Trace Cell Relationships

Trace Precedents

1. Select a cell that contains a formula.
2. Click the Formulas tab.
3. Click Trace Precedents.

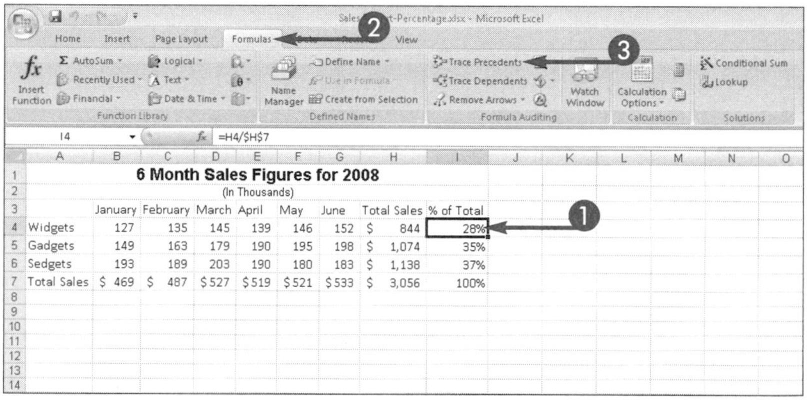

- Excel adds lines to the worksheet that point toward the cell you selected in Step 1. The lines come from the cells that contribute to the formula's calculation.

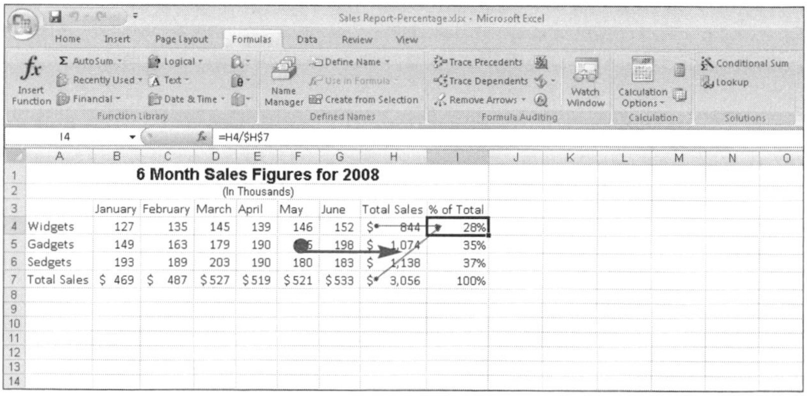

Trace Dependents

❶ Select a cell.

Note: *The cell does not need to contain a formula.*

❷ Click the Formulas tab.

❸ Click Trace Dependents.

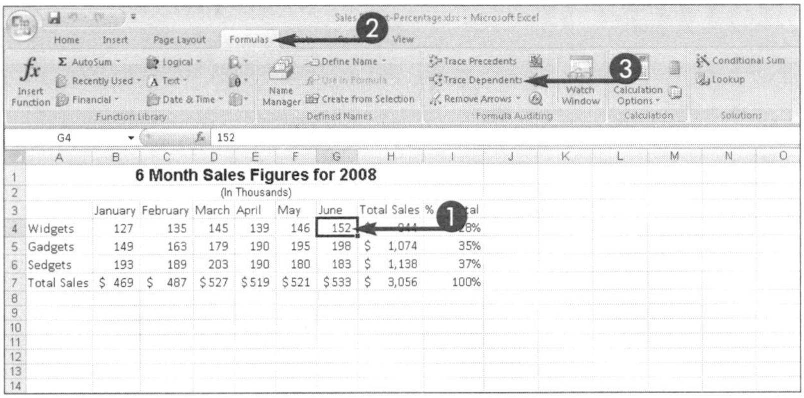

- Excel adds lines to the worksheet that point away from the cell you selected in Step 1. The lines point to the cells containing formulas that use the cell you selected in Step 1 in their calculations.

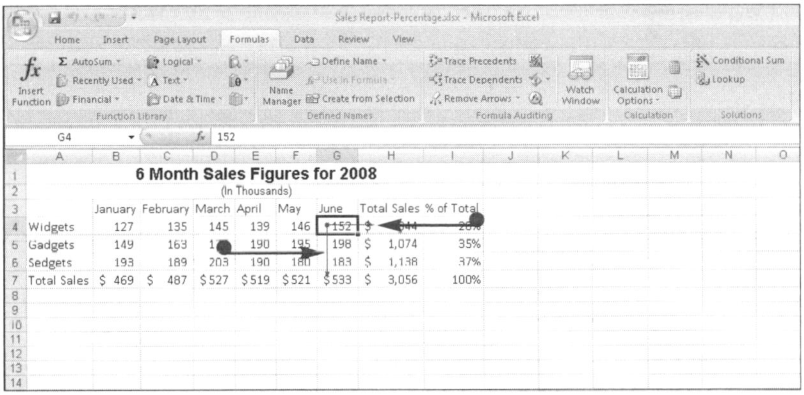

What happens if I click the Trace Precedents or Trace Dependents buttons more than once?

▼ Excel adds another generation of precedent arrows or dependent arrows to your worksheet. That is, using the example worksheet, the precedents for cell I4 are cells H4 and H7. If you click the Trace Precedents button again, Excel adds arrows to identify the precedents for cell H4 — the range B4:G4 — and the precedents for cell H7 — the range B7:G7.

How do I remove the lines when I do not want to view dependents or precedents anymore?

▼ Click the Remove Arrows button to remove all lines. If you have traced both dependents and precedents, you can remove only precedents or only dependents by clicking ▾ beside the Remove Arrows button. From the menu that Excel displays, select the type of lines you want to remove. Each click removes the last generation of precedent or dependent arrows you added.

What happens if I click the Watch Window button in the formula auditing group?

▼ Excel opens the Watch Window, which you can use to monitor the value in a selected cell. The Watch Window is useful when your worksheet is large. You can add a cell to it and leave the window open as you scroll around the worksheet to make changes. Even if the cell disappears from view, the Watch Window shows you what effect your changes have on the cell.

Control Data Entry

You can use the Data Validation feature in Excel to control data entry and therefore avoid errors. The Data Validation feature is particularly useful if you build a worksheet for other users and you want to ensure that the information that they enter is appropriate. For example, your worksheet may require that the users enter numbers that fall between two values. If you use the Data Validation feature, you can ensure that Excel does not accept text entries in those cells, nor will Excel accept values that fall outside the range you specify.

When you use the Data Validation feature, you set up a criterion for a cell or a range that describes the kind of data the user can enter. You can think of this criterion as a rule associated with data entry. The rule dictates the kind of information Excel will allow the user to enter into the cell.

You can also set up an error alert that appears if the user enters information that is not valid for the cell. The alert appears in the form of a message that you define; for example, you can tell the user in the message what information is valid to enter into the cell.

Control Data Entry

Set Up Validation Criteria

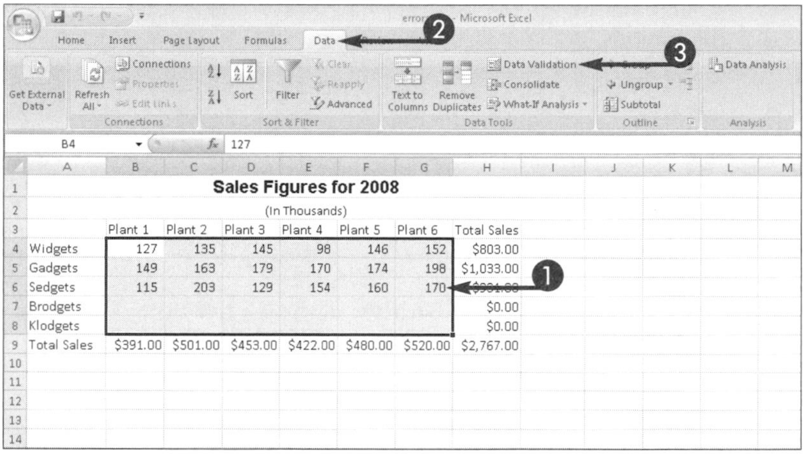

1. Select the cells to which the data validation criterion should apply.
2. Click the Data tab.
3. Click Data Validation.

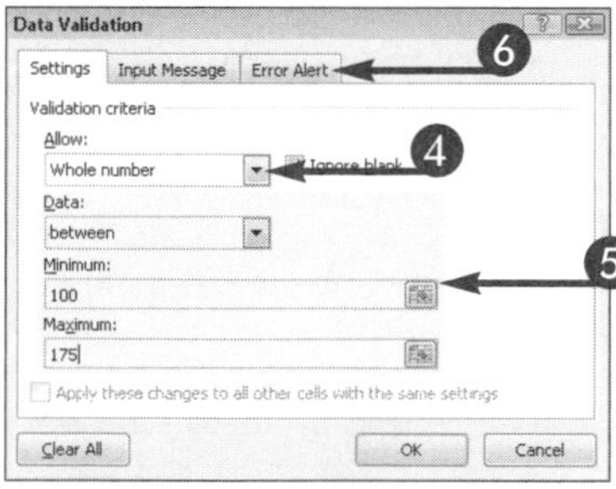

The Data Validation dialog box appears.

4. Click here and select a criterion.

   Excel displays options; the options that appear depend on your choice in Step 4.

5. Use these options to define the criterion.
6. Click the Error Alert tab.

7. Click here to select an action when a user enters invalid data.
8. Click here and type a message to display to the user.
9. Click here and type a message title.
10. Click OK.

Excel saves the criterion and error alert information.

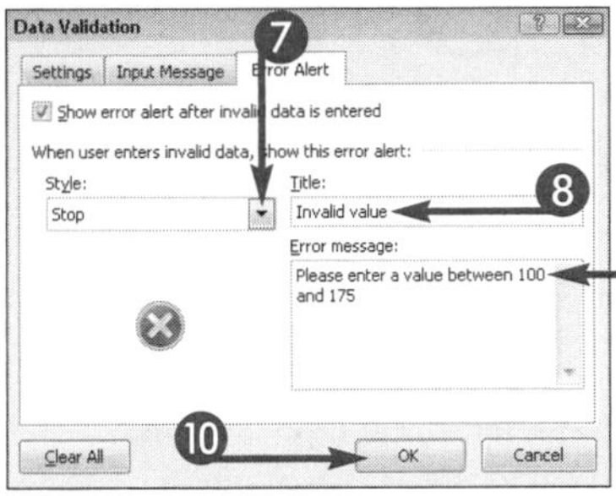

Test Data Validation

1. Select a cell in the data validation range.
2. Type an invalid value.
   - Excel displays the error alert you set up.

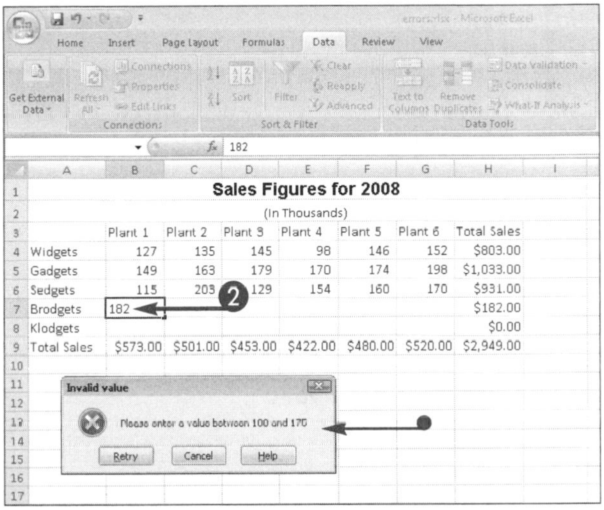

PART III

MASTER IT

When would I use the Input Message tab?

▼ You use the Input Message tab to set up a message that appears when the user clicks the cell. The message appears in the form of a tip and does not interfere with data entry. For example, you can use the input message to describe the kind of data the user should enter into the cell to help the user avoid entering information that is unacceptable.

What happens if the user clicks the Retry button when an alert message appears?

▼ Excel dismisses the message and selects the value that was previously typed in the cell. When the user types, the previous entry attempt is automatically replaced with the new entry. When the user presses Enter or clicks ☑, Excel reevalutes the entry. If it is valid, Excel enters it into the cell. If it is not valid, the alert message appears again.

What kinds of Error Alert styles are available?

▼ You can choose from three styles: Stop, Warning, and Information. If you use the Stop style, Excel does not accept information that does not match the established rules. If you select either Warning or Information, the user can enter invalid information, but Excel displays the message you set up to alert the user that the information is not valid. The difference between the Warning and Information styles is in the user's perception.

continued

Control Data Entry *(Continued)*

You can permit a user to enter information that does not conform to the data validation rule you have established for a cell or range, and then let Excel show you the invalid data after the fact.

This approach works well when you do not want to display messages to the user during data entry. For example, you may want the user to enter sales values into a range. Later, when you review the worksheet, you may want to set up criteria that will help you identify cells that contain values outside a range you deem acceptable for sales. You can use Data Validation circles to highlight the cells that do not meet your standard.

You set up the data validation rules as described earlier in this section, but you do not set up either an input message or an error alert. You can set up the validation rules before or after data entry. To the person entering information, nothing seems unusual and they see no messages as they work. When you are ready, you display Data Validation circles.

Control Data Entry *(continued)*

Circle Cells Containing Invalid Data

1. Click the Data tab.
2. Click ▾ beside Data Validation.
3. Click Circle Invalid Data.

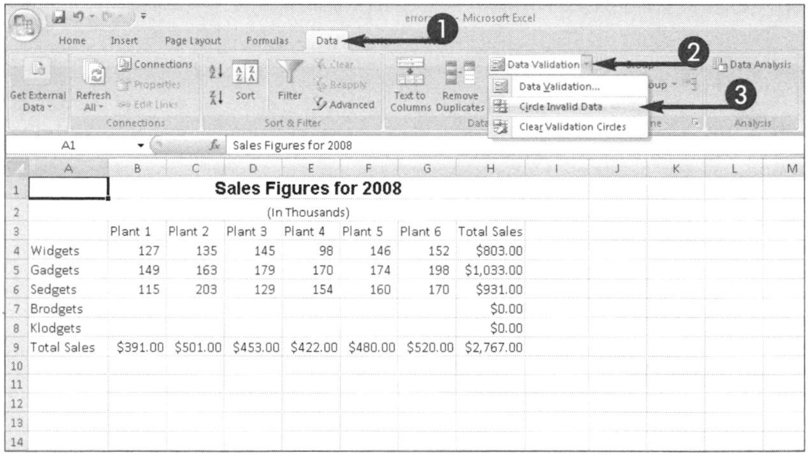

Excel circles values on the worksheet that do not conform to the Data Validation criterion.

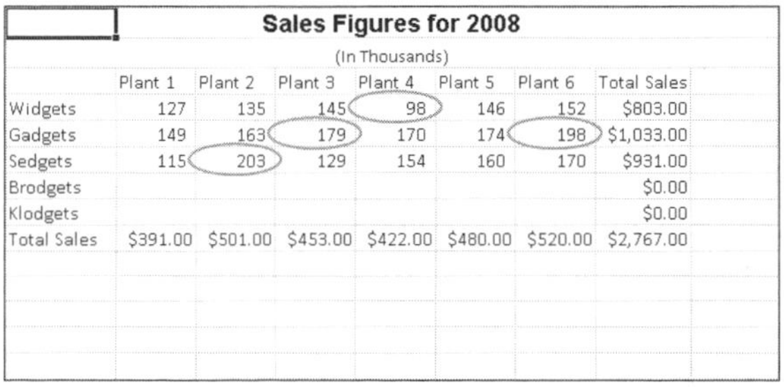

Remove the Circles

1. Click the Data tab.
2. Click ▾ beside Data Validation.
3. Click Clear Validation Circles.

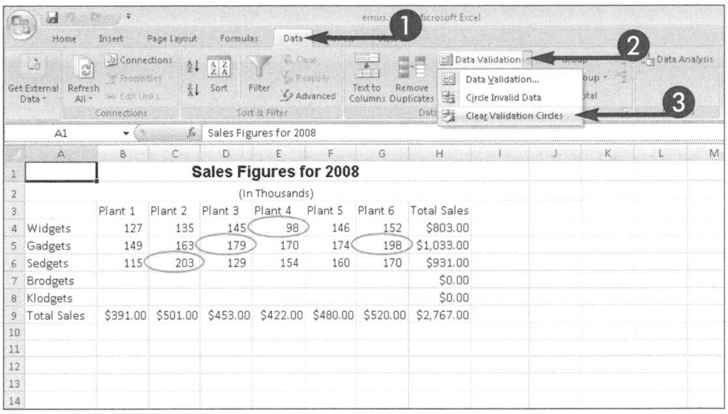

- Excel removes the Data Validation circles but remembers the criterion.

If you repeat Steps 1 and 2, Excel redisplays cells that contain invalid values.

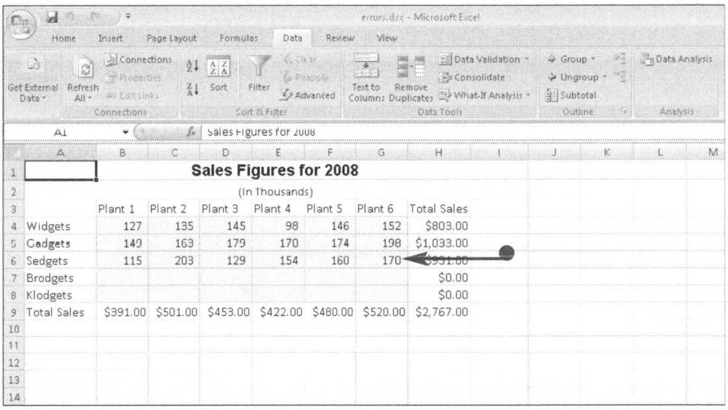

MASTER IT

How do I avoid setting up an error alert?

▼ To avoid setting up an error alert, follow the steps in the subsection, "Set Up Validation Criteria," but instead of performing Steps 7 to 9, click Show Error Alert After Invalid Data Is Entered (☑ changes to ☐) and click OK. Excel then permits the user to enter invalid information but tracks the invalid entries.

Can I identify cells for which Data Validation rules have been established?

▼ Yes. Click the Home tab and click Find & Select. From the drop-down list, click Go To Special. In the Go To Special dialog box that appears, click Data Validation (○ change to ◉). Then click All or Same (○ change to ◉) and click OK. If you click All, Excel selects all cells for which Data Validation rules exist. If you click Same, Excel selects all cells with Data Validation rules that match the selected cell.

What kinds of criteria can I set up?

▼ You can set up criteria based on any value, whole numbers, decimals, dates, times, text length, or data that appear in a list. You can also select Custom and set up a formula for Excel to use to determine whether information entered is valid. For example, you can allow only text entries in a range or cell, such as cell A1 by entering the formula =ISTEXT(A1).

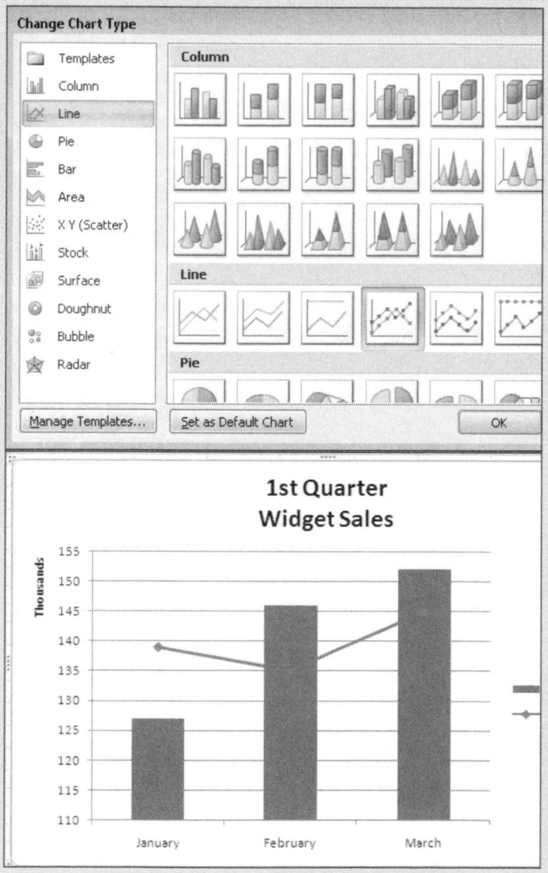

Change Chart Type
Templates
Column
Line
Pie
Bar
Area
X Y (Scatter)
Stock
Surface
Doughnut
Bubble
Radar
Manage Templates...
Set as Default Chart
OK
1st Quarter
Widget Sales
Thousands
155
150
145
140
135
130
125
120
115
110
January
February
March

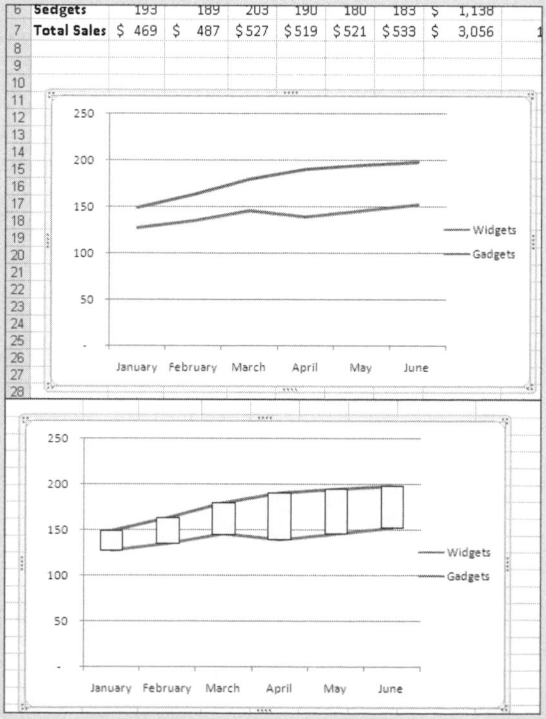

7 Total Sales $ 469 $ 487 $ 527 $ 519 $ 521 $ 533 $ 3,056
250
200
150
100
50
January
February
March
April
May
June
Widgets
Gadgets

PART IV

MASTERING EXCEL CHARTS

21 Formatting Charts

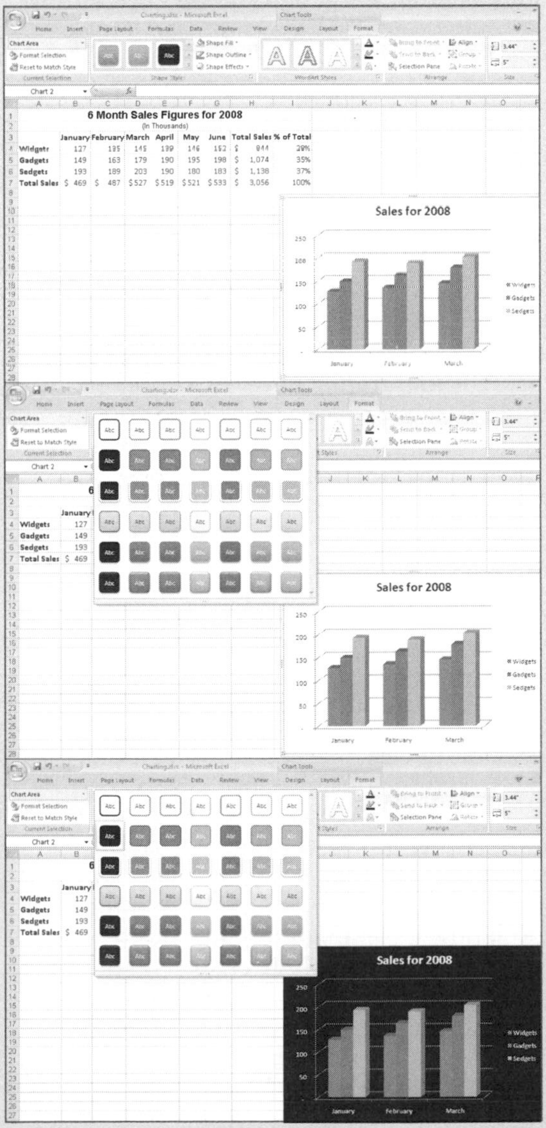

22 Working with Graphic Elements

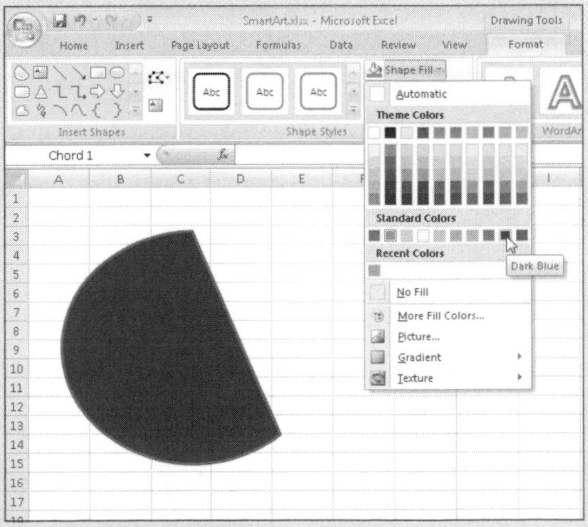

Understanding Charts

You can use Excel's charting features to create charts that depict the numbers in your Excel worksheet. When you create a chart, you can embed it in the same worksheet where the numbers appear. When you embed a chart, you can print it alongside your data.

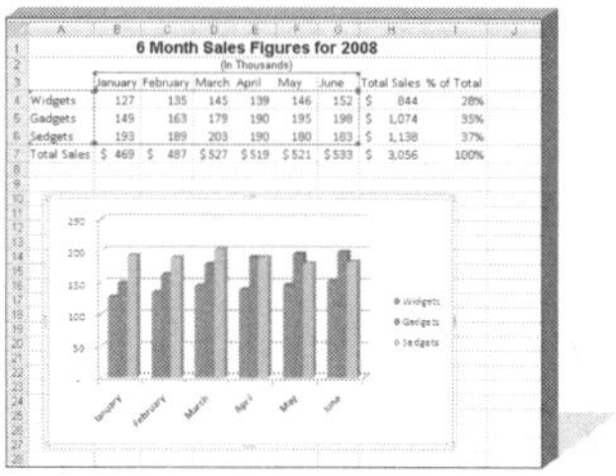

If you prefer, you can place the chart in its own sheet, where the chart fills the entire sheet. When you want to print a chart on a page of its own, or you have many charts to create, it is best to place each chart in its own sheet.

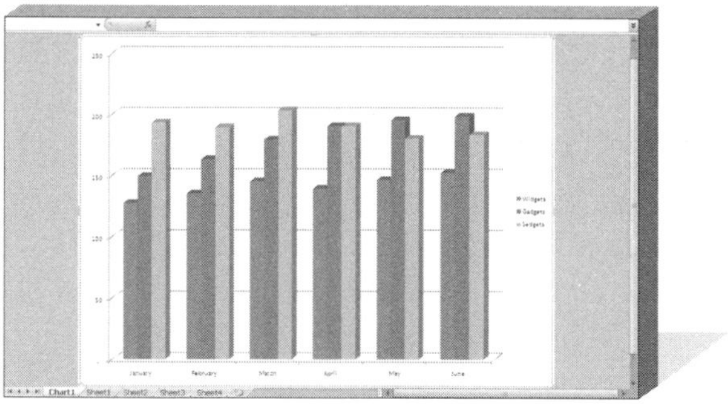

You can always move an embedded chart to its own chart sheet, or move a chart on a chart sheet to a worksheet.

Each chart that you create is based on data stored in an Excel worksheet. If you make changes to the data used in a chart, Excel automatically adjusts the chart to reflect the changes, so your chart is always up to date. Unless you select cells before creating a chart, Excel guesses at the data you want to include in the chart, but you can easily modify Excel's selection to include whatever information you want.

When you work with charts, Excel adds tabs to the Ribbon under the heading Chart Tools. Within the Chart Tools heading, Excel displays three tabs: the Design tab, the Layout tab, and the Format tab. Chart tools are available only when you select an embedded chart or a chart on a chart sheet.

You can create a variety of charts in Excel to help you convey the message you intend. Among the more common types of charts you can create are the column, line, pie, bar, area, and scatter charts. You use column and bar charts to compare values from different categories of data. Line charts show changes over time and are most useful when you want to emphasize trends. Pie charts show the relationship of one component of data to the overall total. Area charts show trends as well as the contribution of each data value to the total.

Also available but not as widely used are specialized surface, doughnut, bubble, radar, and stock charts used in scientific and financial studies.

In addition to selecting a chart type, Excel makes it easy to produce an elegant-looking chart by applying built-in chart layouts and styles. Chart layouts help you position various chart elements; for example, some chart layouts place a title above the chart, others place it below the chart, and still others eliminate the title altogether. Chart styles help you apply color schemes to chart elements in a consistent manner.

Understanding the Chart Window

Each chart you create is made up of different chart elements that help convey the meaning of the chart. You can customize each chart element, as described in the tasks throughout Part IV of this book.

A Chart Area
The chart area includes all of the chart elements that appear inside the boundary that surrounds the chart on a chart sheet, or in the chart window of an embedded chart.

B Chart Title
The chart title displays the name of the chart so that the reader knows the subject of the chart. The chart title can appear above or below the chart, or you can choose not to display a chart title.

C Data Series
A data series is a set of data values. This example contains three data series: one for Widgets, one for Gadgets, and one for Sedgets. Each of the data series contains six data values, one for each month shown on the chart. Typically, one data series represents a single row or column in your data.

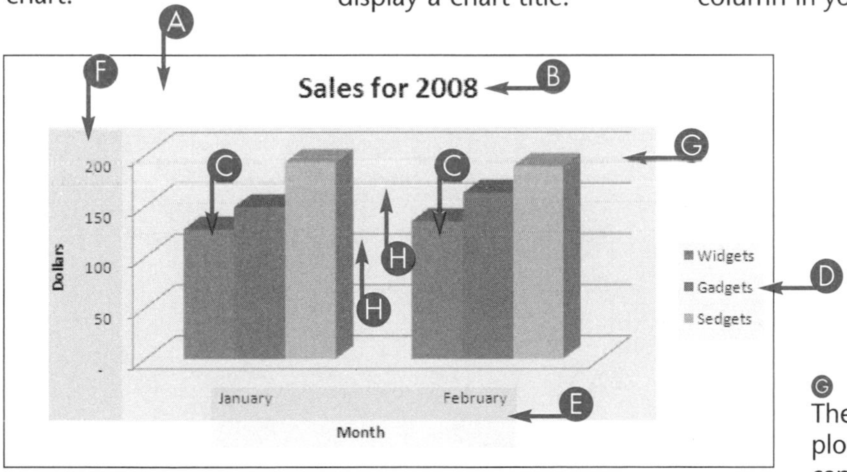

D Legend
The legend helps the reader identify what each data series represents. Your chart does not need to include a legend, but excluding the legend can make the chart more difficult to understand.

G Plot Area
The chart data appears in the plot area of a chart. As you can see in this example, you can apply a different color to the plot area.

E Category Axis
The category axis runs horizontally along the bottom of the chart. On the category axis, Excel displays the labels that correspond to each data point. In this example, the categories correspond to months. Below the category axis, Excel displays the title for the category axis, which is Month in this example. Not all charts contain a category axis; for example, you will not find any axes on a pie chart.

F Value Axis
The value axis runs vertically along the side of the chart and displays values by which you can measure the data series. This example shows only one value axis, but some charts contain two value axes — one on the left side of the chart and one on the right side. Still other charts, like the pie chart, do not contain any value axes.

H Gridlines
Gridlines help the reader assess the value of each data point in a data series. Although the example shows only horizontal gridlines, you can set both horizontal and vertical gridlines. You can also display both major and minor gridlines; the example shows major gridlines, with minor gridlines appearing between the major gridline marks.

Create a Column Chart

You can create a chart using worksheet information to present numeric data visually. Charted information is often easier to understand than the numbers behind the chart. To create a chart, you organize the information in your worksheet into rows and columns, using labels to identify the information in each row and column.

Suppose that you want to create a column chart to plot sales over several months for three products. In this situation, the numbers for each product appear on separate rows and represent a data series. In a column chart, each data series appears as a column. The months of the sales appear on the category axis. When you create this chart, you do not include any totals that you may have calculated in the worksheet because totals would not make sense in the context of showing sales for three products over several months.

As you create a chart, you choose the type of chart; Excel provides several possible variations for each chart type. You can also select a chart layout and a chart style. A chart layout controls whether and where to show chart elements such as the title and the legend. A chart style controls the colors of various portions of the chart.

Create a Column Chart

1. Select the cells you want to chart.

Note: *If you do not select cells, Excel takes its best guess about the data you want to chart.*

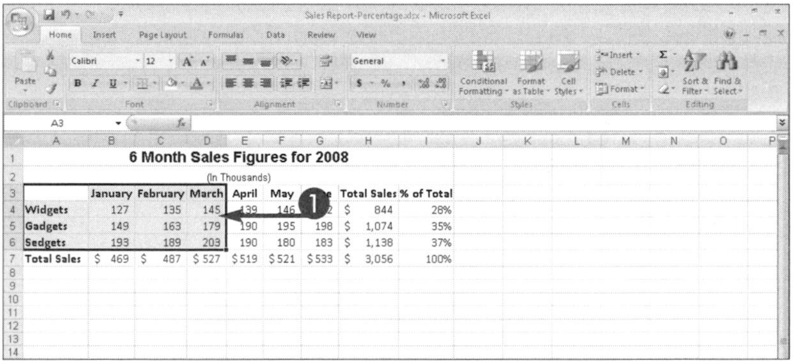

2. Click the Insert tab.
3. Click a chart type.
   - Excel displays samples of the variations available for the chart type.
4. Click a chart type.

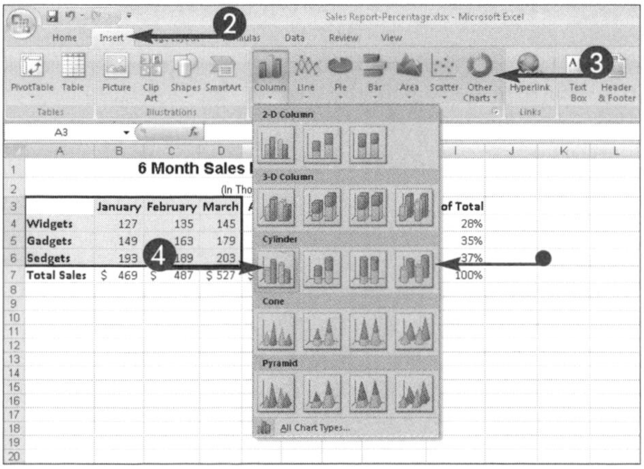

- Excel creates a chart using the data selected in Step 1 and the chart type selected in Step 3.
- Chart Tool tabs appear on the Ribbon

5 Click here to select a chart layout.

Each chart layout contains different elements. You can click each layout to apply it and see the differences.

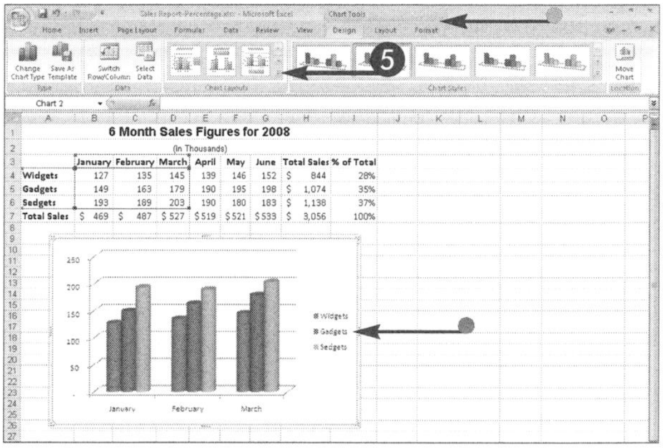

- Excel applies the layout to the chart.

6 Click anywhere outside the chart to continue working in the worksheet.

- When you do this, Excel no longer displays the tabs associated with Chart Tools.

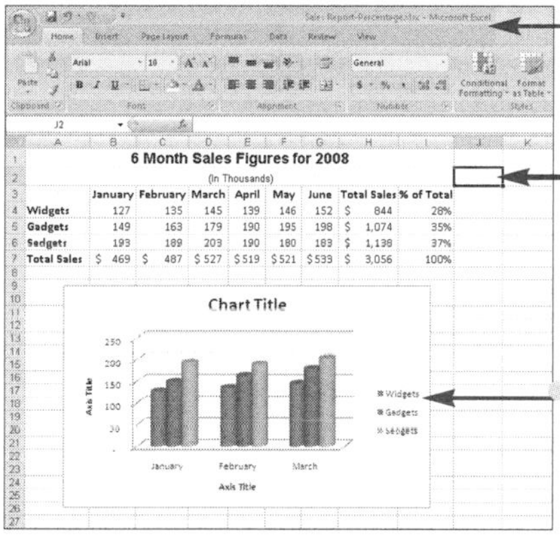

MASTER IT

I forgot to select data and Excel created a blank chart. What happened?

▼ If you place the cell pointer outside of the range of data you expect to use for your chart, Excel does not know what data to use to create the chart. As a result, Excel creates a blank chart. If you try the same experiment again and place the cell pointer on any cell containing data that you want to use in your chart, Excel guesses which data to include and displays something other than a blank chart. You can also place the cell pointer in a blank cell within the range where data appears, and Excel displays something other than a blank chart.

If a chart layout is optional, under what circumstances would I choose one?

▼ Chart layouts are simply a predefined set of chart elements positioned in various locations. For example, if you know that you want a chart title, legend, and labels for each axis, choosing a chart layout with those elements can help you set up your chart faster than if you add those elements to the chart individually. Even if the layout does not place the elements exactly where you want them, you can move the elements. If the layout you choose contains more elements than you want, you can delete the extra elements.

Create a Pie Chart

You can use a pie chart to help you focus on relative proportions in relation to totals. Each pie slice represents a percentage of the total of 100 percent. For example, suppose your worksheet contains sales information for three products over several months, and you want to examine the sales of one product over those months to see if any particular month shows significantly higher sales than other months. If sales for one particular month exceed all other months, you can then start researching what your company did differently during that month to increase sales.

A pie chart contains only one data series. The example uses one product's sales as the data series, and the pie slices each represent sales for a particular month. As a result, to ensure that your pie chart makes sense, make sure that you select information for only one data series — that is, several data points related to only one element.

A pie chart does not display either a value axis or a category axis, but Excel uses the numbers you select to represent the information Excel needs for the value axis. Excel sometimes does not identify the pie slices; instead, Excel assigns numbers to the slices that you can change.

Create a Pie Chart

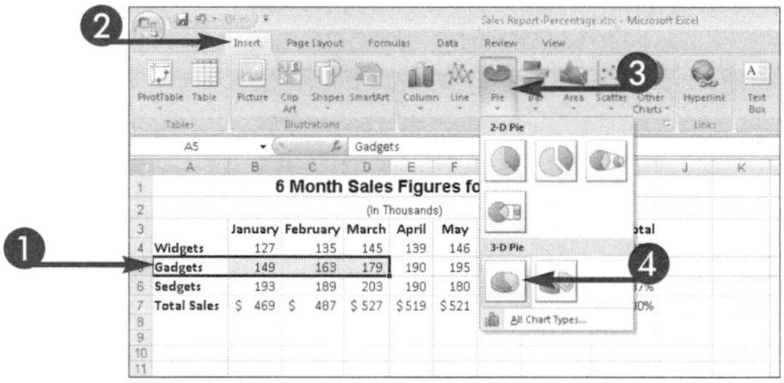

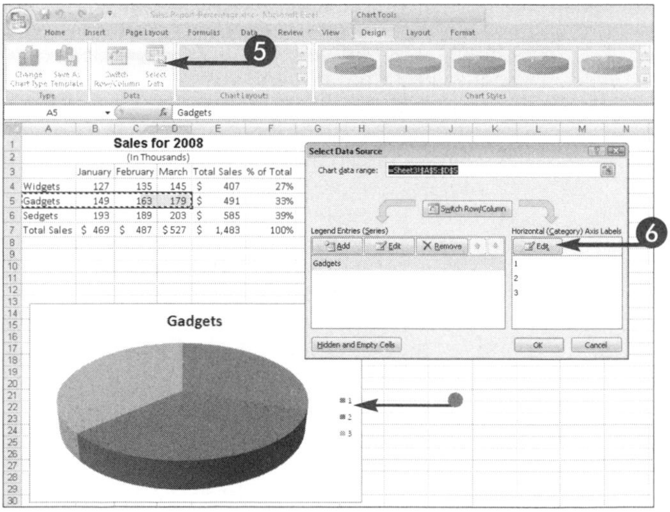

1. Select the cells you want to chart.

Note: *If you do not select cells, Excel guesses which data you want to chart.*

2. Click the Insert tab.
3. Click Pie.
   - Excel displays samples of the variations available for the pie chart type.
4. Click a variation.
   - Excel creates a pie chart using the data selected in Step 1 and the chart type selected in Step 3.
5. Click Select Data.

   The Select Data Source dialog box appears.
6. Click Edit.

Excel displays the Axis Labels dialog box.

7. Drag to select the labels that identify each pie slice.
8. Click OK.

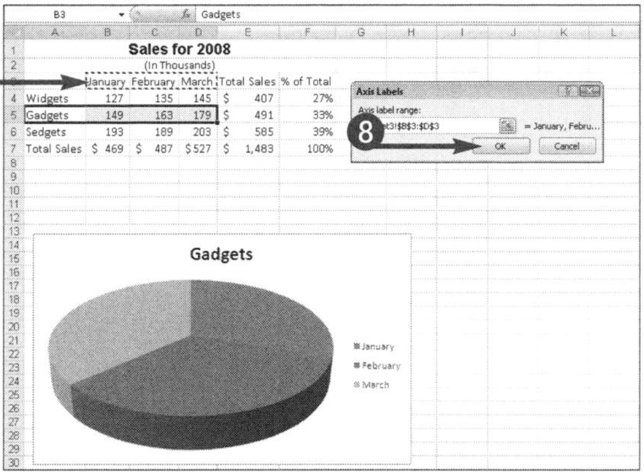

Excel redisplays the Select Data Source dialog box.

- New labels appear for the category axis.
- New labels appear for the pie slices.

9. Click OK to close the Select Data Source dialog box.

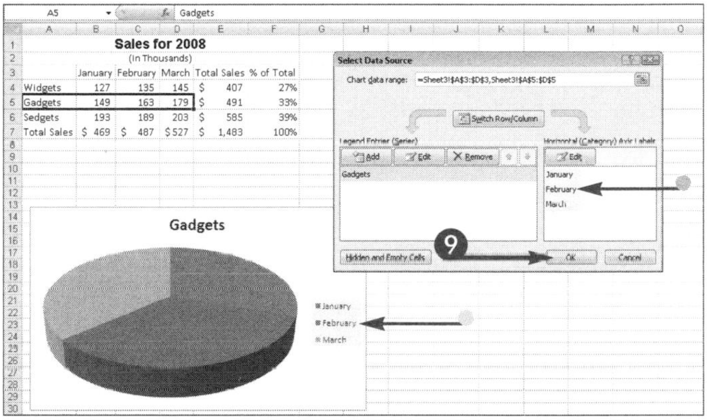

MASTER IT

Using the example worksheet, how would I select data if I wanted to view each product's contribution to February sales?

▼ Select cells C3 to C6 and follow Steps 2 to 4 to create the chart. Excel may display numbers instead of each product's name. Follow Steps 5 to 9 to complete the chart, and, in Step 7, select the labels in the worksheet that represent the product names you are charting. Excel replaces the numbers with product names after you complete the steps.

What happens to the pie chart if I change a data value in the range I used to create the chart?

▼ Excel recalculates each pie slice's relative percentage of the total and updates the chart automatically. Excel must adjust all of the pie slices because each pie slice represents a percentage of 100 percent, rather than a specific number. If any slice's value increases, the other slices must decrease to compensate and retain 100 percent as the total.

What happens if I click the Hidden and Empty Cells button in the Select Data Source dialog box?

▼ Excel displays the Hidden and Empty Cell Settings dialog box, which you can use to specify how Excel should handle empty cells in the range you choose to chart. You can show empty cells as gaps in the chart or as zero values. You can also decide whether to show data in hidden rows and columns.

Change the Chart Type

After you create a chart, you can switch to a different chart type. The chart type you choose should be the one that best explains your information. Excel contains a wide variety of chart types from which to choose, the most common of which are the column, line, pie, bar, area, and scatter charts.

Column charts display vertical bars and help you show changes to information over time or compare information such as sales for several products. Bar charts also help you compare information, but the bars run horizontally instead of vertically; because the bars run horizontally, long category labels may be easier to read on a bar chart. Line charts show changes over time and are useful to identify trends. Pie charts show the relationship of one data series to the overall total. Area charts show trends as well as the contribution of each data value to the total. Scatter charts are often used to show the relationship between two variables such as sales calls and sales made.

You can switch chart types effectively as long as the data you chart can be displayed. For example, you cannot create an effective pie chart for more than one data series.

Change the Chart Type

1. Click anywhere in the chart area to select the chart.
   - Excel displays this border around the chart.
   - The tabs associated with Chart Tools appear.

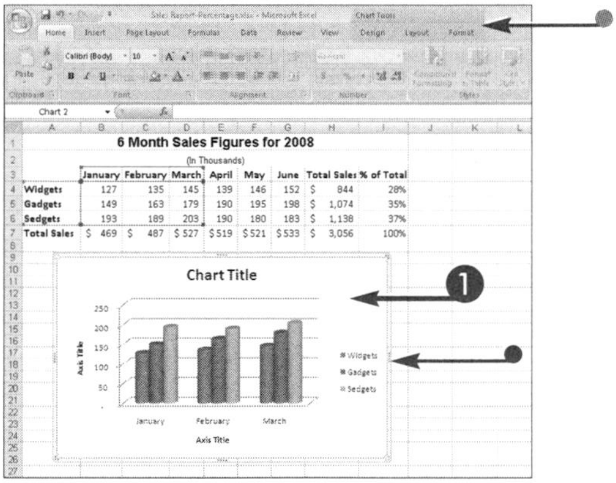

2. Click the Design tab.
3. Click Change Chart Type.

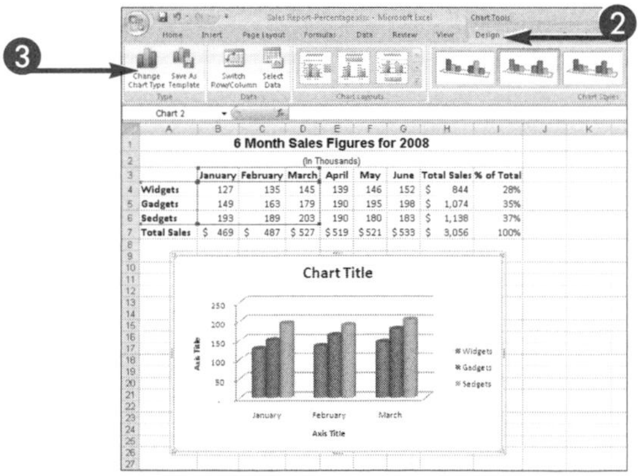

The Change Chart Type dialog box appears.

4 Select a different chart type.

5 Select a variation for the new chart type.

6 Click OK.

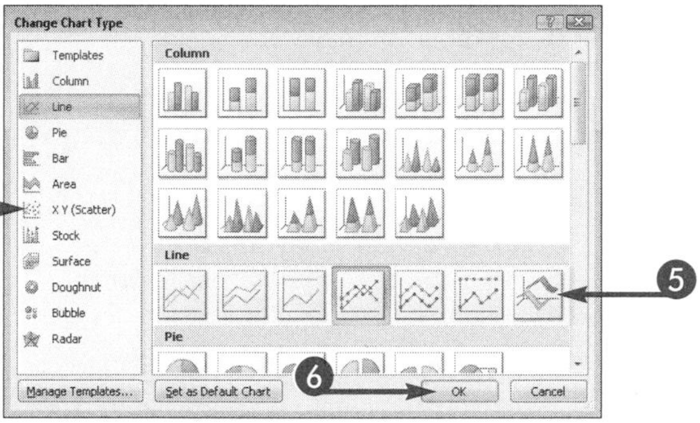

Excel applies the new chart type to your chart.

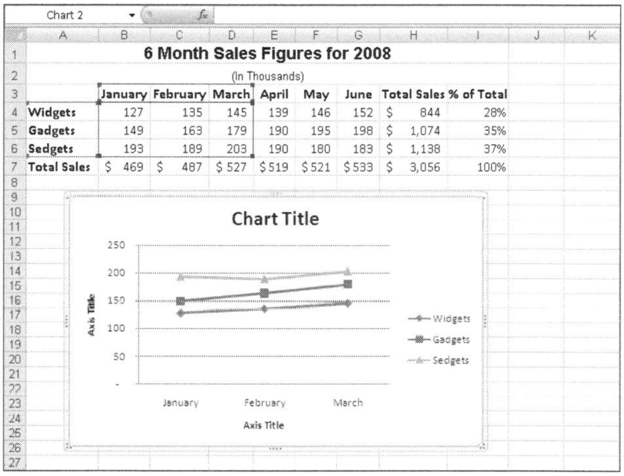

MASTER IT

When would I use a doughnut chart?

▼ You can use a doughnut chart instead of a pie chart. Both charts show the relationship of parts to a whole, but you can display more than one data series in a doughnut chart. A doughnut chart has a hole in the middle (hence the name) and displays each data series as concentric rings wrapped around each other. Using the example worksheet, you could create a doughnut chart that shows sales for each product as separate data series, wrapping the products around each other. Each data series would contain three parts representing the months of the sales.

When would I use a stock chart?

▼ Although plotting stock information such as high, low, open, and close amounts for prices and volume are the primary uses for a stock chart, you can use a stock chart for other reasons. For example, you can use a stock chart to plot high, low, and average temperatures for various days. A stock chart that shows stock price information typically shows prices on the value axis and dates on the category axis. A stock chart that includes trade volume as well as stock price information typically uses two value axes — one for the volume and one for the stock price.

Select a Chart Layout

By applying a chart layout, you can save a lot of time and effort. Chart layouts are predefined sets of chart elements that you can apply as a group to a chart. Although you do not need to apply a chart layout, using a chart layout helps you quickly apply many of the chart elements you want to display. If you select a chart layout that contains more elements than you want, you can easily delete the extra elements. If a chart element does not appear in the position you prefer, you can move it. Chapter 20 describes many ways to delete and reposition chart elements and add chart elements if necessary.

Excel has different chart layouts for each chart type, and so the available layouts depend on the type of chart you create. Using chart layouts, you can add axis titles, reposition the chart legend, remove gridlines, add a chart title, and add a data table to the chart. A data table appears below the chart in the chart window and displays the data points used to build the chart.

Select a Chart Layout

1. Click anywhere in the chart area to select the chart.
   - Excel displays this border around the chart.
   - The tabs associated with Chart Tools appear.
2. Click the Design tab.
3. Click here to display a drop-down gallery of available layouts, and select one.

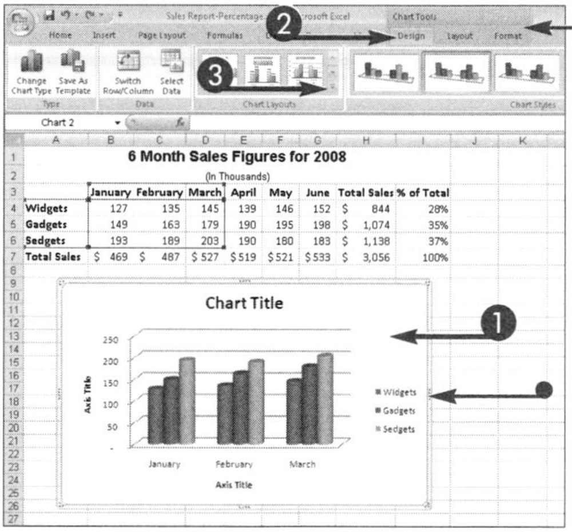

Excel applies the layout, adding, moving, and removing elements such as the chart title and gridlines.

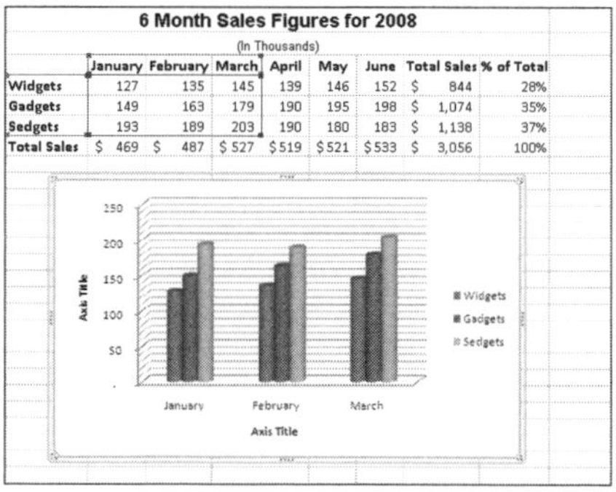

Change the Chart Style

You can apply a chart style to your chart to quickly and easily change the colors of various chart elements. For example, some chart styles apply different shades of the same color to the bars on a column or bar chart, or to the slices of a pie chart. Other chart styles use entirely different, unrelated colors for each set of bars on the column or bar chart, or the slices of the pie chart. The color schemes available using chart styles can vary from chart type to chart type. If a particular chart type includes a floor, and side and back walls — as the column and bar chart types do — then Excel provides chart styles that help you assign different colors to the floor, side wall, and back wall.

Some chart styles apply a white or transparent background to the plot area, while other chart styles set the background of the plot area to black, providing dramatic contrast. Some chart styles provide thin outlines around each data series or pie slice.

Chart styles are optional; you do not need to apply them, but they can help you create an effective, dramatic-looking chart very quickly and easily.

Change the Chart Style

1. Click anywhere in the chart area to select the chart.
   - Excel displays this border around the chart.
   - The tabs associated with Chart Tools appear.
2. Click the Design tab.
3. Click here to display a drop-down gallery of available styles, and select one.

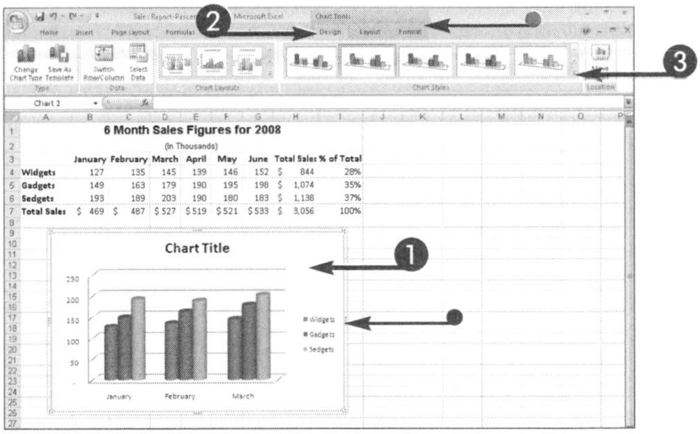

Excel applies the layout, adding, moving, and removing elements such as the chart title and gridlines.

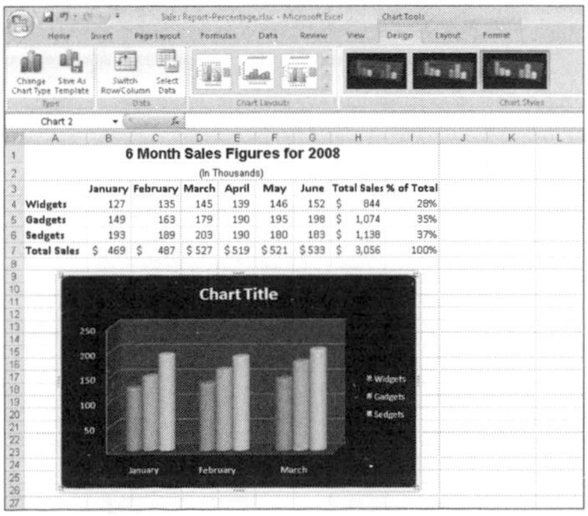

Move a Chart to a Separate Sheet

You can place a chart on a separate sheet in your workbook. Nothing else appears on a chart sheet except the chart. By default, Excel creates embedded charts that appear on the same worksheet as the data you use to create them, but you can move a chart to its own sheet in the workbook.

Placing the chart on a separate chart sheet makes it easier to print the chart on a page by itself. If you plan to create many charts from a particular set of data, you may want to consider using chart sheets instead of embedded charts. First, placing many embedded charts on the worksheet containing your data can clutter up your worksheet and make it difficult to read. In addition, finding a particular chart is not easy on a worksheet that contains many charts. However, if you use chart sheets, you can easily find a particular chart because you can rename chart sheet tabs to describe the chart. You can even organize the chart sheet tabs alphabetically or in some numerical sequence to make finding a particular chart quick and easy.

Move a Chart to a Separate Sheet

❶ Click anywhere in the chart area to select the chart.

- Excel displays this border around the chart.
- The tabs associated with Chart Tools appear.

❷ Click the Design tab.

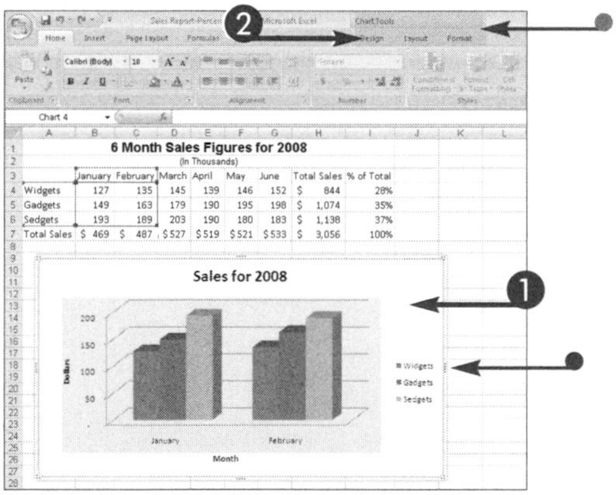

The charting tools on the Design tab appear.

❸ Click Move Chart.

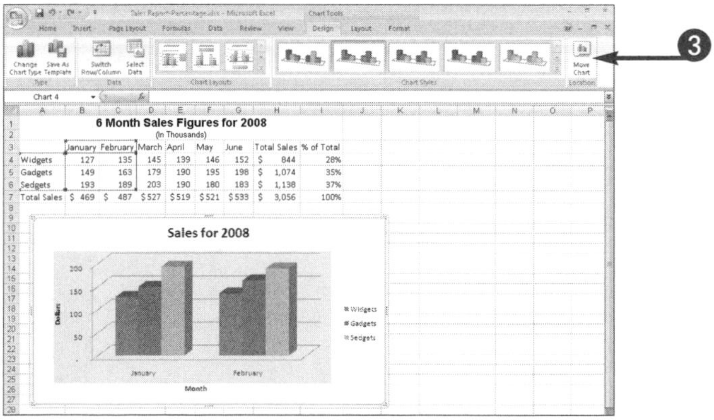

The Move Chart dialog box appears.

4 Click New Sheet (◎ changes to ◉).

5 Click OK.

Excel displays the chart in a new sheet in the workbook.

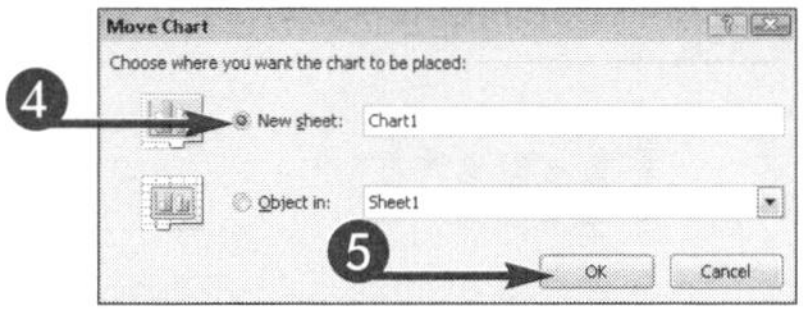

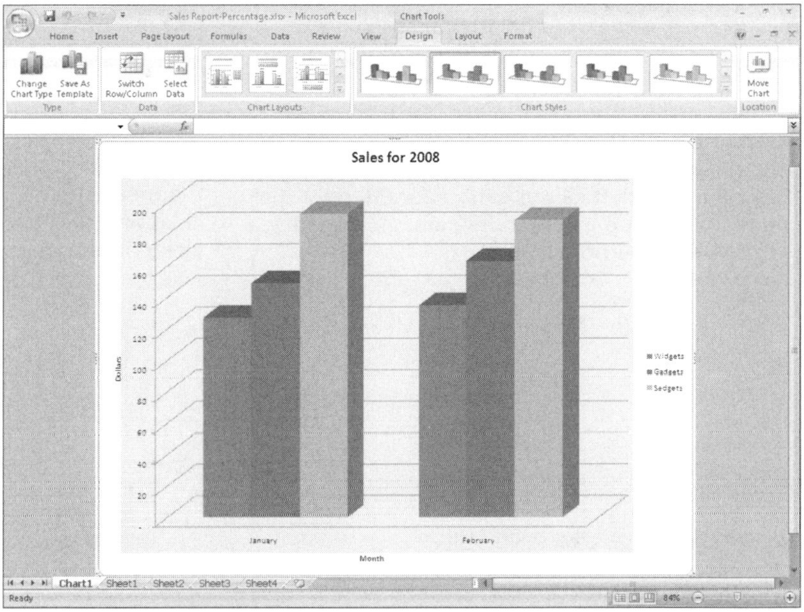

MASTER IT

How do I rename a chart sheet?

▼ You can supply a new name for the chart in the Move Chart dialog box. After you complete Step 4, click in the field beside the New Sheet option and type a name. If you have already moved the chart to a chart sheet, right-click the chart sheet's tab and choose Rename. Excel highlights the chart sheet name; simply type a new name to replace the existing name, and press Enter.

I cannot see the entire chart on the chart sheet without scrolling. Is there a way to fix that?

▼ Yes. You can adjust the zoom factor. Click the chart to select it. In the lower-right corner of the screen, click ⊖ to reduce the size of the chart. The first click reduces the chart size to the nearest whole number. Each successive click reduces the chart size by 10 percent.

Can I convert a chart located on a chart sheet to an embedded chart?

▼ Yes, you can. Follow the steps in this section. In Step 4, click the Object In option (◎ changes to ◉). In the field beside the Object In option, click ▾ to select the worksheet onto which you want to place the chart. When you click OK, Excel moves the chart to the selected worksheet and deletes the chart sheet.

Reposition an Embedded Chart

You can reposition a chart that Excel embeds in a worksheet to a different place in the worksheet. When Excel embeds the chart, it places the chart somewhere near the data used to create the chart, but not necessarily where you want the chart to appear. For example, Excel may cover up worksheet data with the chart, or Excel may place the chart in a location that causes extra pages to print that you do not need. You can reposition an embedded chart to suit your purposes.

When you want to print both the chart and the worksheet data used to create the chart on the same page, you can leave the chart embedded in a worksheet instead of placing the chart on a separate chart sheet. However, you are not limited to the location Excel selects for the embedded chart.

To move a chart, you select it. Then, when you move the mouse pointer over the outside portion of the chart area without pointing at any specific chart element, the mouse pointer changes, alerting you that you can move the chart.

Reposition an Embedded Chart

1. Click anywhere on the chart to select it.
   - Excel displays this border around the chart.
   - The tabs associated with Chart Tools appear.
   - Excel indicates here that you selected the chart.

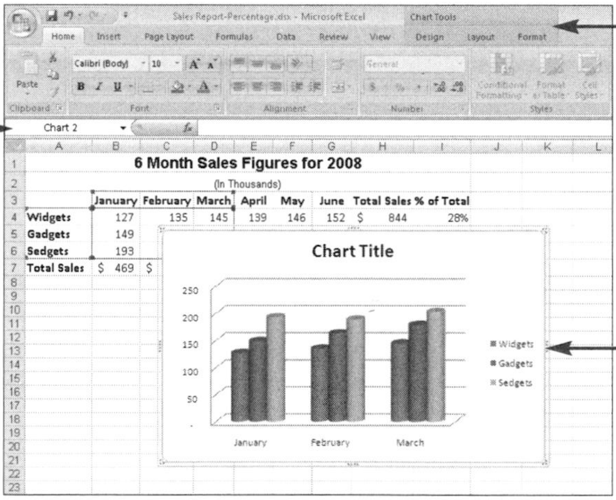

2. Move the mouse pointer inside the chart area (✥ changes to ✥).

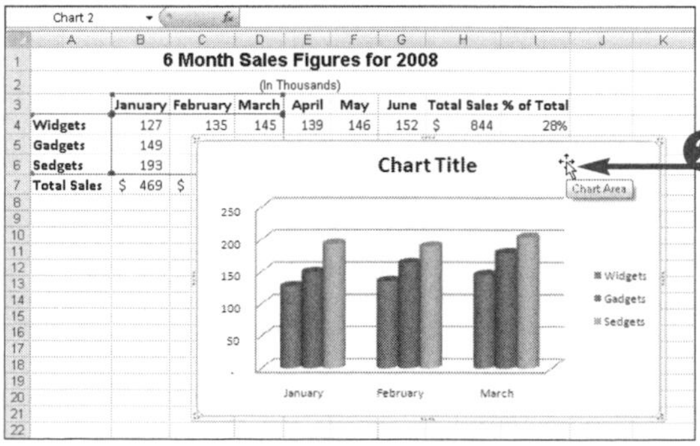

3 Drag the chart to its new location.

- As you drag, Excel displays an outline of the chart so that you know where the chart will appear.

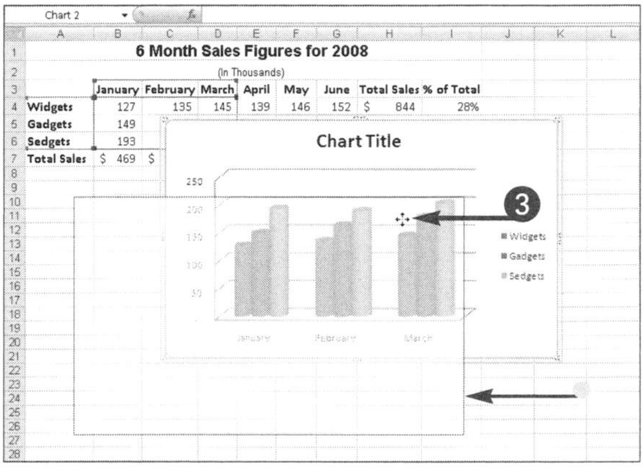

Excel displays the chart in the new location.

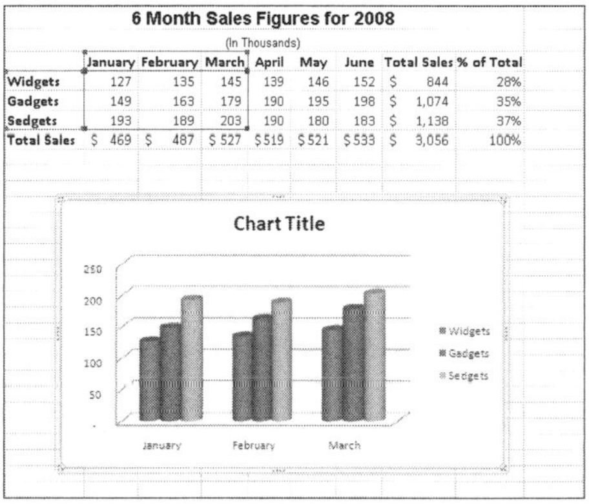

MASTER IT

Can I move an embedded chart to a different worksheet without placing it in a chart sheet?

▼ Yes. You can cut and paste the chart. Select the chart in the worksheet where you created it. Then, right-click and click Cut. Click the tab of the worksheet on which you want the chart to appear. In that worksheet, right-click a cell near where you want the upper-left corner of the chart to appear, and click Paste.

Can I move part of a chart?

▼ Yes, you can drag any element of a chart to a new location in the chart. For example, you can drag the chart title to a different position in the chart window. You can also drag the slices of a pie chart. For example, you might want to pull out a pie slice to call special attention to it. When you click any chart element, round circles appear around the element. You can then drag the element to reposition it.

If I move an embedded chart to a different worksheet and change the chart's data on the original worksheet, what happens?

▼ Excel retains the link between the chart and the data in the cells that you used to create it. As a result, if you make a change to the data, even though the chart appears on a different worksheet, Excel updates the chart.

Resize an Embedded Chart

You can change the size of a chart that Excel embeds in a worksheet. When Excel embeds a chart, it creates the chart at a default size that may be too small or too large to suit your purposes. You can adjust the size of the chart window. When you adjust the size of the chart window, all of the chart elements in the window grow or shrink in relation to the changes that you make.

When you resize an embedded chart, you must first select it. In the border that Excel displays around the chart window, dots appear at particular locations. In the four corners of the window, Excel displays three dots in the border. In the middle of the top, bottom, left, and right sides of the border, Excel displays four dots. You use these dots to resize the chart window. The shape of the mouse pointer changes when you move it over any of these sets of dots; the mouse pointer becomes a pair of arrows. Excel displays this mouse pointer shape to let you know when you can resize the chart.

Resize an Embedded Chart

1. Click anywhere on the chart to select it.
   - Excel displays this border around the chart.
   - Excel indicates that you selected the chart.

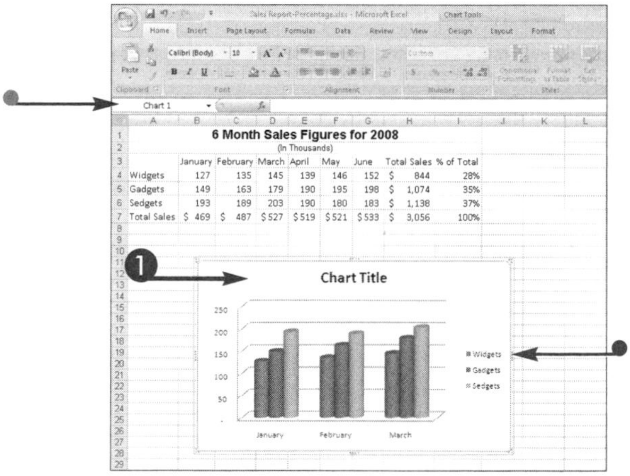

2. Move the mouse pointer over any set of dots in the border of the chart (✥ changes to ⤢, ⇕, or ⇔).

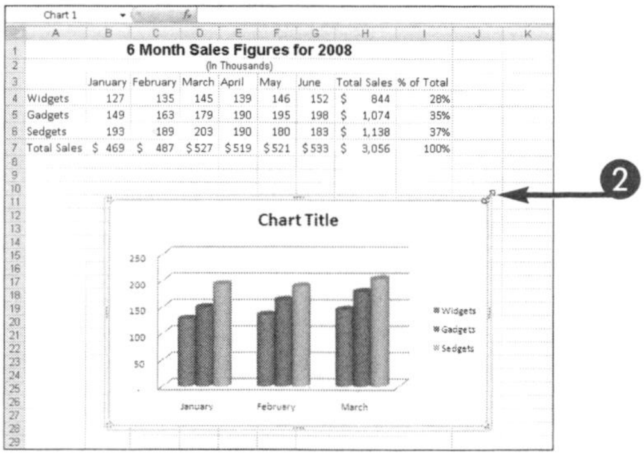

3 Drag the edge of the chart outward to increase its size, and inward to reduce its size (⤢, ⇕, or ⇔ changes to +).

- As you drag, Excel displays an outline of the chart, depicting its new size.

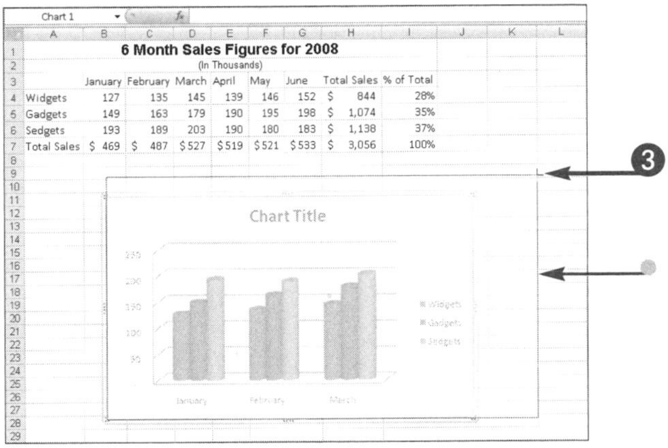

Excel displays the newly sized chart.

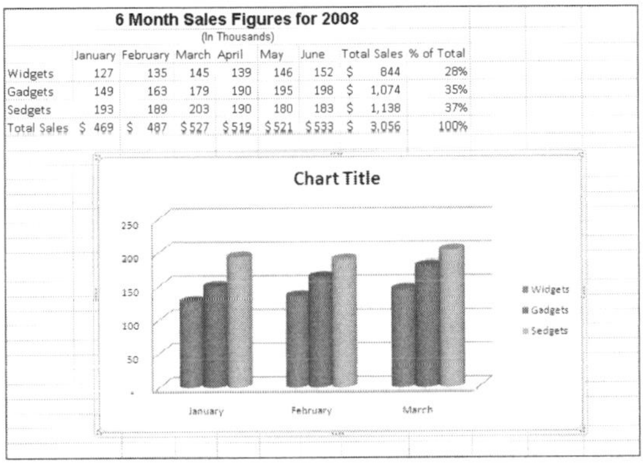

MASTER IT

What must I do differently to see ⇔ or ⇕?

▼ To see ⇔, move the mouse pointer over the four dots that appear on the left or right side of the chart border. Resizing either side of the chart border makes the chart wider or narrower. To see ⇕, move the mouse pointer over the four dots that appear on the top or bottom of the chart border. Resizing the top or bottom of the chart border makes the chart taller or shorter.

Why did you place the mouse pointer over a corner of the chart to resize it?

▼ When you drag a corner of a chart to resize it, you can resize both the height and the width of the chart simultaneously. You can make the same adjustment by dragging a side and either the top or bottom of the chart, but you must drag twice to make this adjustment.

Can I resize a chart in a chart sheet?

▼ No. By default, a chart in a chart sheet takes up the entire sheet, and so the chart sheet determines the size of the chart. You can zoom in or out while viewing the chart in a chart sheet, but zooming does not affect the size of the chart. When you print the chart, it prints at the same size, whether you view it at 150 percent or 75 percent.

Change the Data Included in the Chart

You can change the data that Excel includes in a chart after you create the chart. For example, suppose that you initially decide to include six months worth of sales data for three products on a single column chart. After you create the chart, you realize that the chart includes too much information and therefore is difficult to read. You do not need to delete the chart and start again; instead, you can modify the chart to eliminate some data, and Excel updates the chart to reflect the new data selection. Conversely, if you discover after creating a chart that you need to add data, you can modify the chart to include the extra data without starting from the beginning.

You use the Select Data Source dialog box to change the data that you include in a chart. From this dialog box, you can use the Legend Entries (Series) section of the dialog box to add, change, or remove data series. You can also reorder the data series on the chart. In the Horizontal (Category) Axis Labels section of the Select Data Source dialog box, you can change the labels that appear on the category axis.

Change the Data Included in the Chart

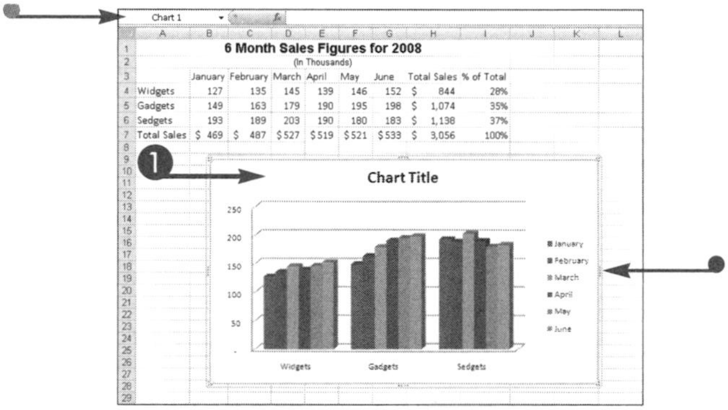

1. Click anywhere on the chart to select it.
   - Excel displays this border around the chart.
   - Excel indicates here that you selected the chart.

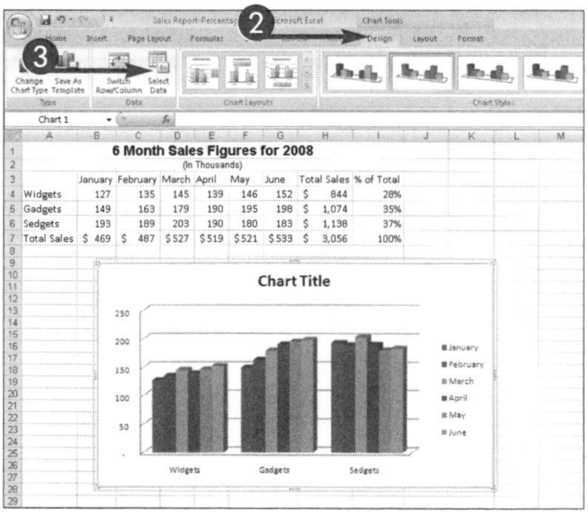

2. Click the Design tab.
3. Click Select Data.

The Select Data Source dialog box appears.

- Excel highlights the data currently included in the chart.

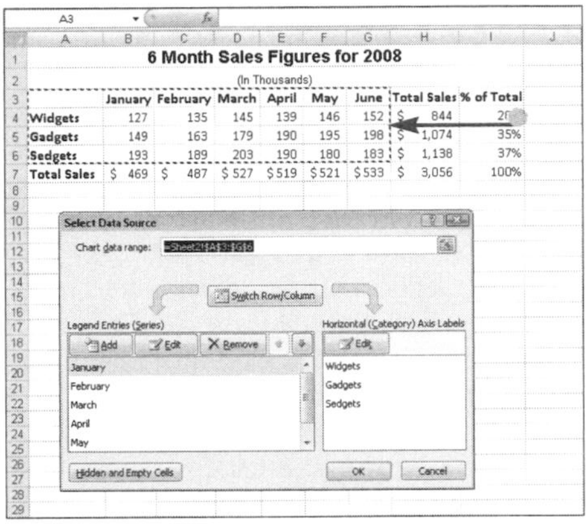

4 In the worksheet, select a different range of data to include in the chart.

- Excel collapses the Data Source dialog box as you select the range.

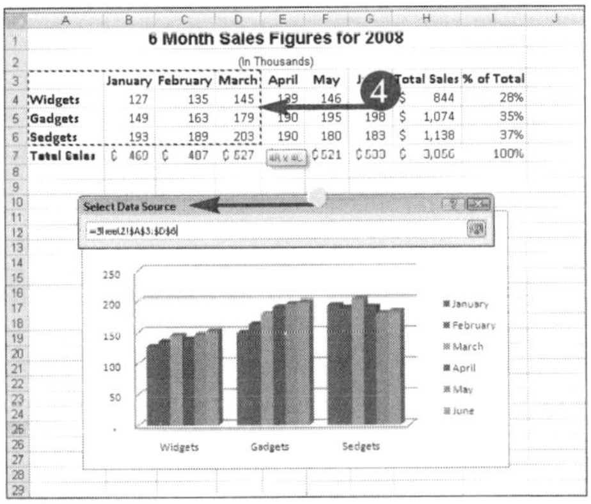

PART IV

MASTER IT

Can I change the order of the data on the chart without editing the data in the worksheet?

▼ Yes. You can use the Select Data Source dialog box to change the order of the legend entries. Click an entry in the Legend Entries (Series) section of the Select Data Source dialog box and then click the Up Arrow button (▲) or the Down Arrow button (▼). Excel reorders the placement in the legend, and in a column or bar chart, it reorganizes the bars.

What should I do if I simply want to delete a particular range from the chart?

▼ If the range appears in the Legend Entries (Series) section of the Select Data Source dialog box, click the range and then click the Remove button. If the entry appears in the Horizontal (Category) Axis Labels section of the Select Data Source dialog box, follow the steps in this section to select a different range to include in the chart.

What can I do when I click the Edit button in the Legend Entries (Series) section of the Select Data Source dialog box?

▼ If you click one of the series in that section of the dialog box, Excel displays the Edit Series dialog box. Using this dialog box, you can change the title for the data series by selecting a different cell or typing a label. You can also change the cells that make up the data series.

continued

Change the Data Included in the Chart *(Continued)*

If the data you want to remove appears in the Legend Entries (Series) section of the Select Data Source dialog box, you can use controls in the dialog box to remove the data from the chart. If the data you want to remove appears in the Horizontal (Category) Axis Labels section of the Select Data Source dialog box, you can use the steps in this section to adjust the data included in the chart. The same is true if you want to add data to the chart; the placement of the data determines the technique you use.

MASTER IT

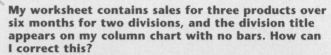

My worksheet contains sales for three products over six months for two divisions, and the division title appears on my column chart with no bars. How can I correct this?

▼ In the range you selected to chart, you included a title for which you have no data. If the spare title appears in the Legend Entries (Series) section of the Select Data Source dialog box, click it and click the Remove button. If the spare title appears in the Horizontal (Category) Axis Labels section of the dialog box, reselect the data for the chart using the steps in this section and do not select the titles for which you have no data.

Change the Data Included in the Chart *(continued)*

The Select Data Source dialog box reappears with updated information.

5 Click OK.

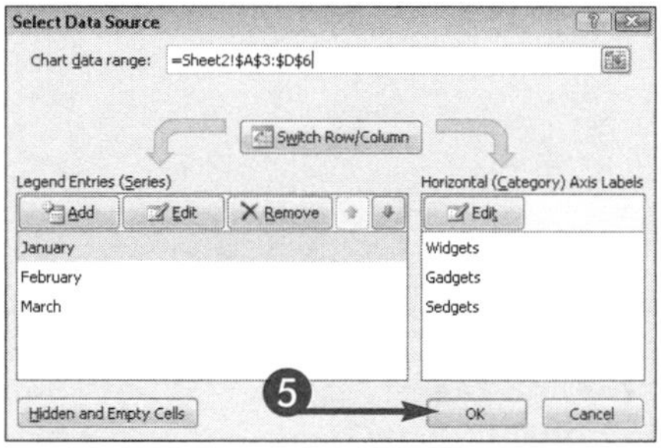

Excel displays the revised chart.

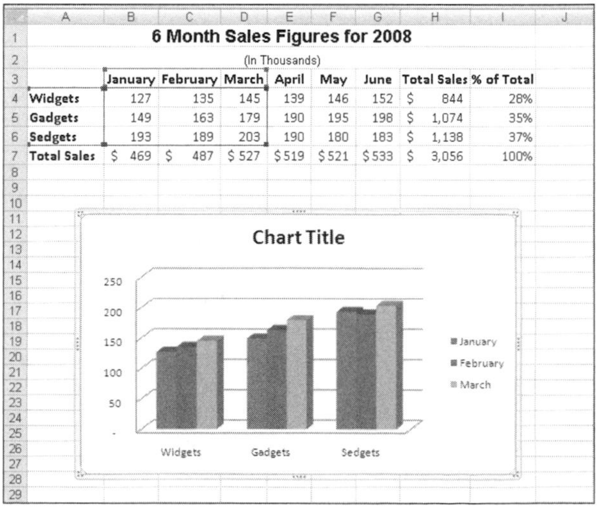

Switch Rows and Columns on the Chart

You can swap the data that appears on a chart. Suppose that you want to include six months worth of sales data for three products on a single column chart. You can set up the chart to display the product names along the category axis, where each bar on the chart represents a month. After you create the chart, you may find that the chart is difficult to read with so many bars. However, if you reorganize the chart to show the months along the category axis, each data point displays only three bars and the chart is much easier to read.

MASTER IT

How can I swap the information that appears on the chart and edit some of the axis titles?

▼ You can follow the steps in this section to swap the data and then click the Select Data button to open the Select Data Source dialog box to make the title changes. Or, from the Select Data Source dialog box, you can click the Switch Row/Column button to swap the data and also edit the titles. See the section, "Change the Data Included in the Chart," for details on changing the axis titles.

PART IV

Switch Rows and Columns on the Chart

❶ Click anywhere on the chart to select it.

- Excel displays this border around the chart.
- Excel indicates that you have selected the chart.

❷ Click the Design tab.

❸ Click Switch Row/Column.

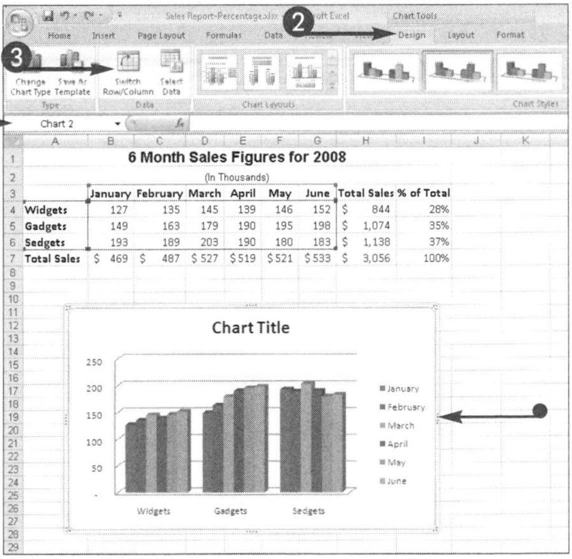

Excel swaps the rows and columns on the chart.

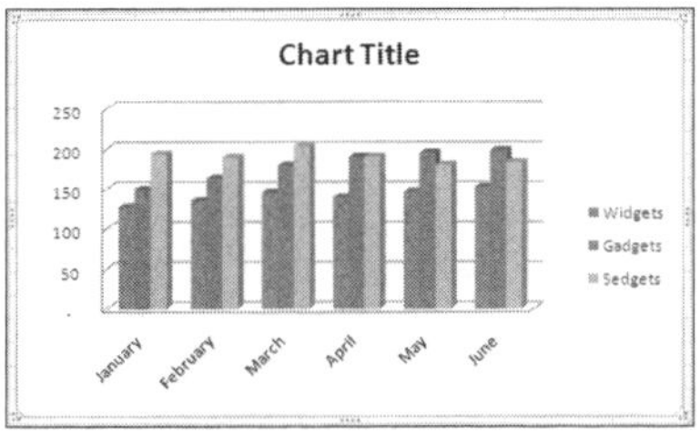

Create a Combination Chart

You may find that a combination of two different types of charts best expresses the information you want to convey. Suppose that you track projected and actual sales for a product. You can show the two data series on the same chart, but presenting them both as lines or columns will not distinguish them. You can create a combination chart to show the two series using two different chart types; for example, you can create a combination chart that shows one series as a line and another as a column.

A combination chart can also be useful when you plot two data series with widely varying values. For example, if you plot sales and profit, the profit amount is typically a much smaller amount than the sales amount. In this case, you can use a combination chart to clearly distinguish the types of data series, as well as to set up a second vertical axis for the varying values.

You can combine variations of 2-D chart types on one chart, but you cannot combine 3-D charts, nor can you combine a bubble chart with any other chart type. You also cannot combine a 2-D chart type with a 3-D chart type.

Create a Combination Chart

1. Click the chart to select it.
   - The tabs associated with Chart Tools appear.

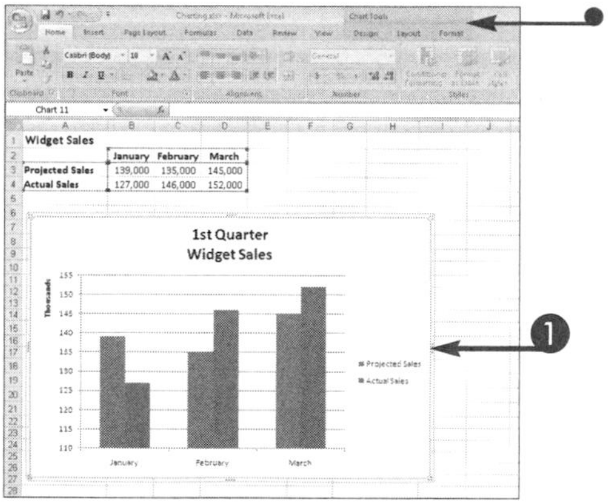

2. Click the Design tab.
3. Click the data series you want to display as a different chart type.
   - Excel displays handles like these around all of the selected data series.
4. Click Change Chart Type.

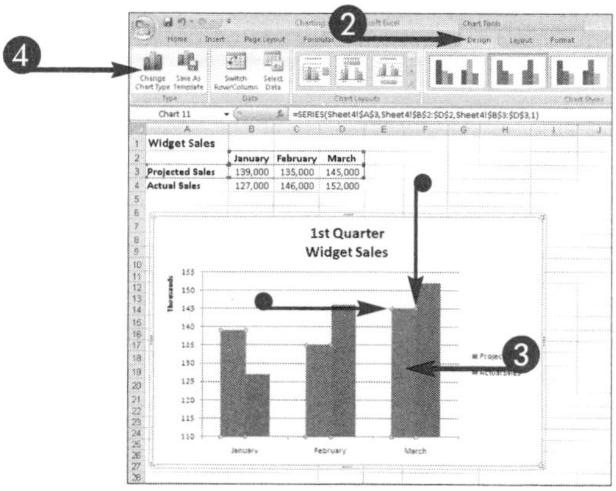

The Change Chart Type dialog box appears.

5 Click the type of chart you want to use for the selected data series.

6 Select a variation of the chart type.

7 Click OK.

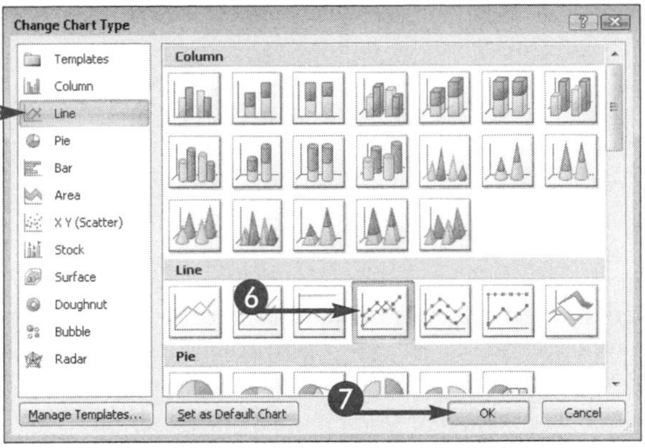

Excel displays the two data series using different chart types.

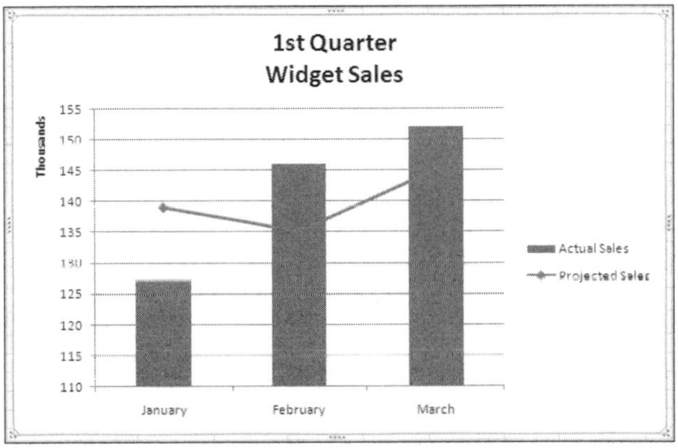

MASTER IT

How do I set up a second vertical axis on a combination chart?

▼ Select the chart and click the Layout tab. Click the data series you want to display using a different chart type and click the Format Selection button. Excel displays the Format Data Series dialog box. On the Series Options tab, select Secondary Axis (◎ changes to ◉). Then, click Close and continue with Steps 2 to 7 in this section. Excel creates a chart displaying two chart types and two vertical axes.

I tried to change the chart type for one data series, but Excel changes the entire chart. What did I do wrong?

▼ You did not select the data series that you wanted to display using a different chart type before you opened the Change Chart Type dialog box. Make sure that you click the data series and that handles — small circles — appear around all edges of each data series marker on the chart. Then, complete Steps 4 to 7 in this section.

Can I display more than two chart types on a single chart?

▼ Yes, you can; you can assign a different chart type to each data series that you plot on the chart. However, be aware that using many different chart types on a single chart can cloud your message instead of conveying it. Too many chart types can be a distraction.

Create a Chart Template

You can make many enhancements to charts, and if you make the same enhancements over and over, you might want to create a chart template to save time. A chart template stores all of the enhancements that you make to a chart so that you can quickly and easily apply them again to charts you create in the future.

For example, suppose that you create a combination chart containing two data series that displays one data series as a column and one as a line. You then add a chart title, a legend, and a vertical axis title, and you apply borders to the chart and set border styles, including beveling the chart edge.

Further suppose that you need to create a series of charts for a presentation and you want to apply the same enhancements to all of the charts. If you create a chart template, you can apply all of the enhancements only once — to the chart that you save as a template. Then, you can create all of the other charts by basing them on the template; Excel automatically applies the enhancements stored in the template to each chart.

Create a Chart Template

Save a Chart Template

1. Set up a chart so that it contains all of the enhancements you want to use on future charts.
2. Click the chart to select it.
   - The tabs associated with Chart Tools appear.
3. Click the Design tab.
4. Click Save As Template.

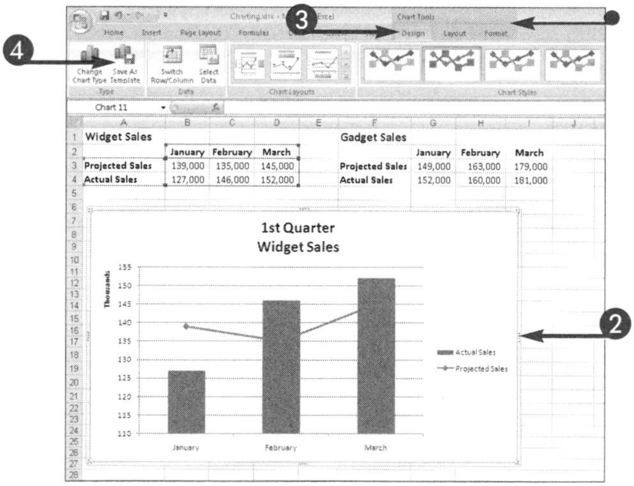

The Save Chart Template dialog box appears.

5. Type a name for the template here.
6. Click Save.

Excel saves the template.

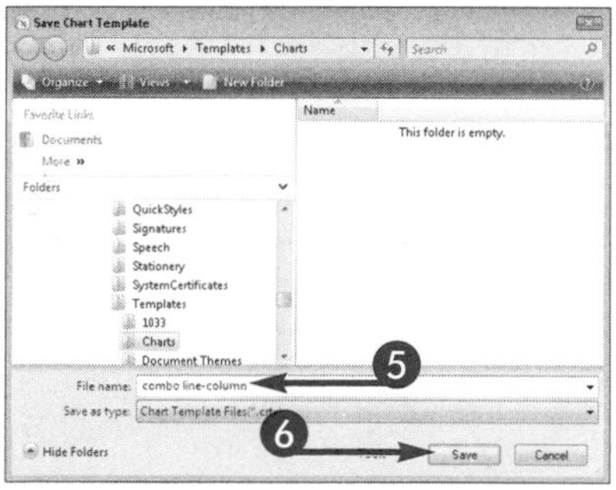

Use a Chart Template

1. Select the data you want to chart.
2. Click Insert.
3. Click Other Charts.
4. Click All Chart Types.

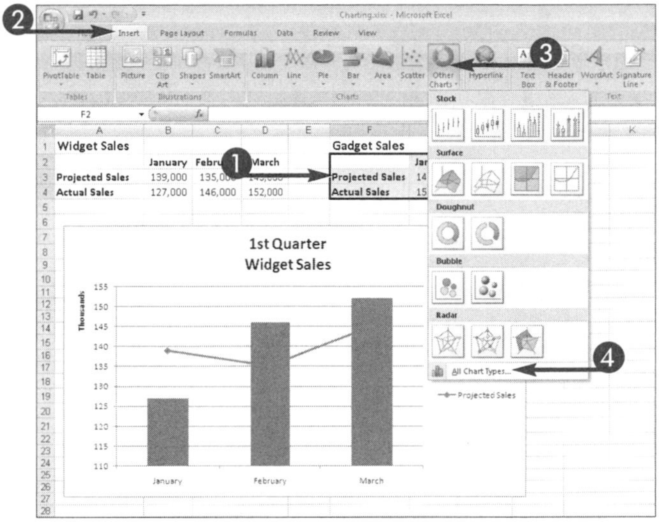

The Insert Chart dialog box appears.

5. Click Templates.
6. Select a template to use.
7. Click OK.

Excel creates a new chart using the data selected in Step 1 and the template selected in Step 6.

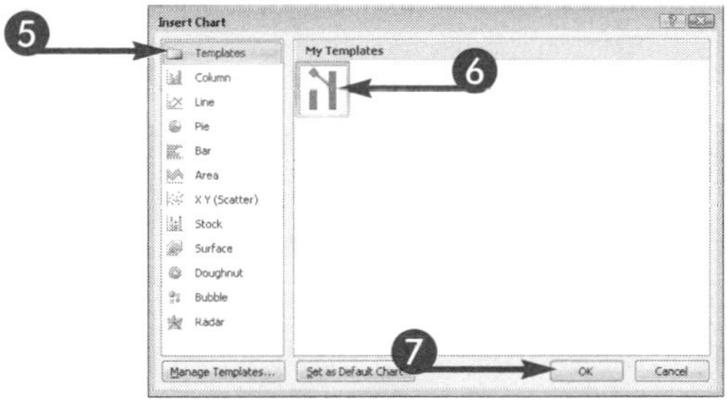

PART IV

MASTER IT

What happens if I try to chart more than two data series using a combination chart template that I created using only two data series?

▼ Suppose that you made the first data series a line chart and the second data series a column chart. If you plot three data series using the template, Excel plots the first of your data series as a line and the remaining data series as columns.

Can I delete or rename a chart template?

▼ Yes. Click a chart to select it and then click the Design tab and the Change Chart Type button. In the Change Chart Type dialog box, click the Management Templates button. Excel displays a window that shows the chart templates you saved. Click one and press Delete to delete it. When you finish, click [X] to close the window.

Can I select data in a different worksheet or workbook and use my chart template?

▼ Yes. Your chart template is available to you from any Excel workbook. You can use any chart template that you create to chart data contained on any worksheet you open.

Can I identify the template name before I select it?

▼ Yes. Hover the mouse over the template in the Insert Chart dialog box.

Add a Chart Title

You can add a title to any chart you create. A good chart title helps the reader focus on the information you want to convey in the chart.

Some chart layouts automatically provide a chart title, but you can add a chart title to any layout that does not automatically include one. When you add a chart title or select a layout that includes a chart title, Excel supplies generic text to represent the chart title. You can change this generic text to help your reader identify the purpose of the chart.

You can also change the position of the chart title within the chart window, even if your chart is not embedded in your worksheet but appears on its own chart sheet. When you reposition a chart title, you drag it to a new location. You will find it easiest to not select the element before you reposition it; instead, you can select and reposition in one step.

You can also delete a chart title if you do not want one to appear on your chart.

Add a Chart Title

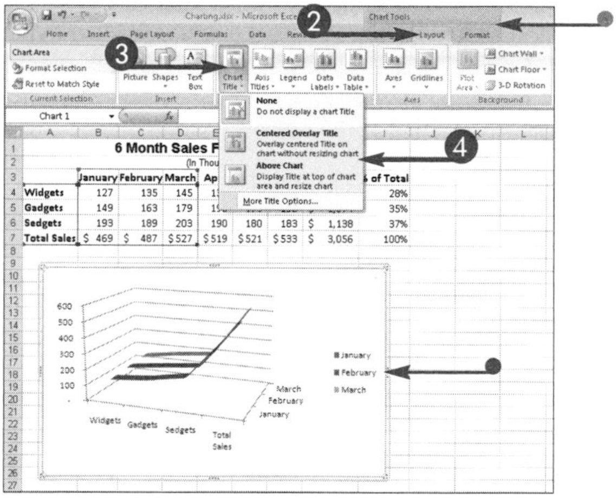

1. Click anywhere in the chart area to select the chart.
   - Excel displays this border around the chart.
   - The tabs associated with Chart Tools appear.
2. Click the Layout tab.
3. Click Chart Title to display chart title options.
4. Click a chart title option.

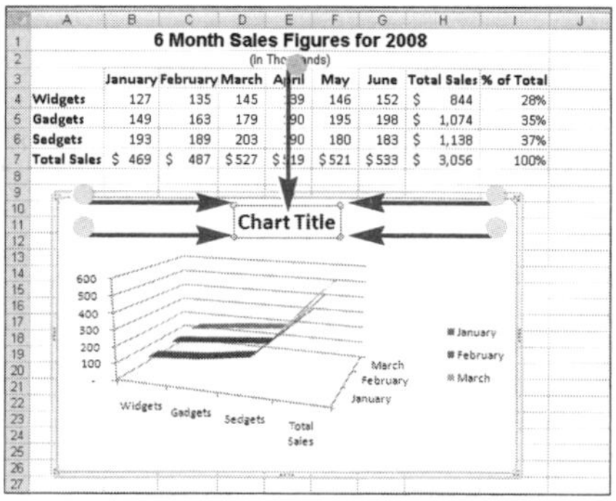

- Excel adds a generic title to the chart and selects it.
- These handles indicate that the chart element is selected.

5. Click in the box containing the chart title.
   - Excel displays an insertion point in the box.
6. Delete any title text you do not need, and type any text you want.
7. Click outside the title chart element.

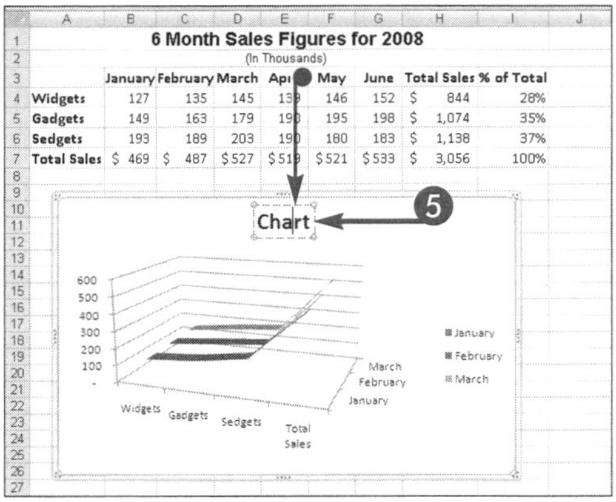

- Excel displays the title on your chart.

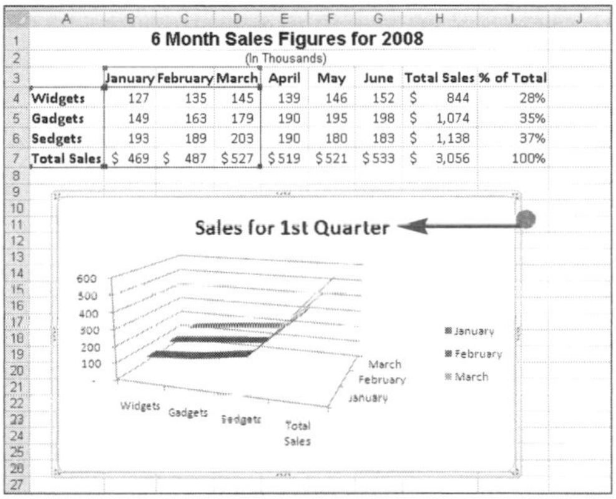

MASTER IT

What is the difference between the Centered Overlay Title option and the Above Chart option?

▼ If you choose Above Chart, Excel adds the title to the chart and resizes and repositions the chart information to accommodate the chart title in the chart area window. If you choose Centered Overlay Title, Excel floats the title on the chart and does not resize or reposition chart information. Using this option, it is possible that the title will appear on top of chart information. You can manually resize the chart window to solve this problem.

Can I place the title in a different location in the chart window?

▼ Yes. Click a white space in the chart window but do not click the chart title element. Then, move the mouse pointer over the chart title element and make sure that you see the tool tip, "Chart Title" (pointer changes to move pointer). Click and drag the title to the new location.

Can I select a cell containing the title text I want Excel to use?

▼ No, but you can add freeform text to your chart by adding a text box. Click the Layout tab and then click Text Box. Move the mouse pointer into the chart where you want the upper-left corner of the box to appear. Then, drag down and to the right.

Format the Chart Title

You can add a variety of formatting to a chart title to improve its appearance or call attention to it. You can fill the space occupied by the chart title with a background color that is solid or a gradient of colors. You can also add a picture or texture fill to the background area of the chart title element.

You can add a border to the chart title element. When you add a border, you add a line that delineates the space occupied by the chart title; the line can be solid or made up of any of several varieties of dashes. You can control the width of the line and the way the line wraps around the corners of the chart title element's space. You can also add a shadow to the chart title element or select a 3-D format.

In addition to controlling the border and space within the chart title element, you can control the way Excel displays the chart title text within the element's space. For example, you can align the chart title text with the top, middle, or bottom of the box, and you can center the text vertically within any of these alignments.

Format the Chart Title

Display the Format Chart Title Dialog Box

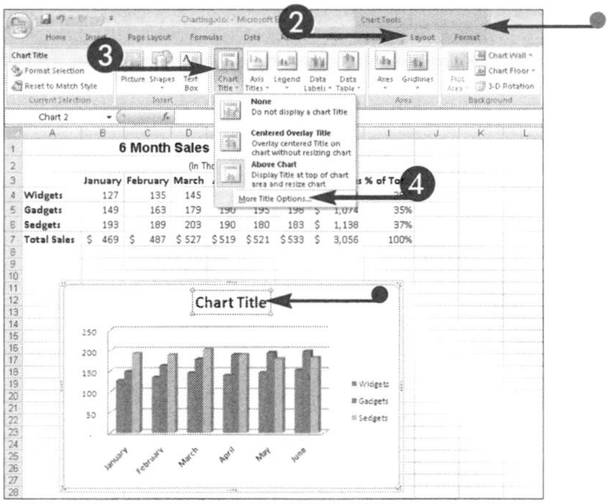

1. Click the chart title to select it.
   - Excel places handles around the title.
   - The tabs associated with Chart Tools appear.
2. Click the Layout tab.
3. Click Chart Title to display chart title options.
4. Click More Title Options.

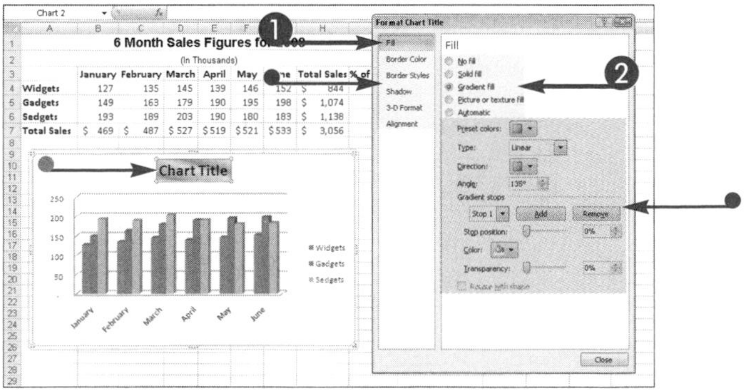

The Format Chart Title dialog box appears.

- You can add these formats to the chart title.

Add a Fill

1. Click Fill.
2. Click a type of fill.
   - These options change, depending on the type of fill you select.
3. Select options for the fill.
   - Excel displays the results on the chart.

Add a Border Color

1. Click Border Color.
2. Click a line style.

Note: *Click Solid Line to select a line color and transparency.*

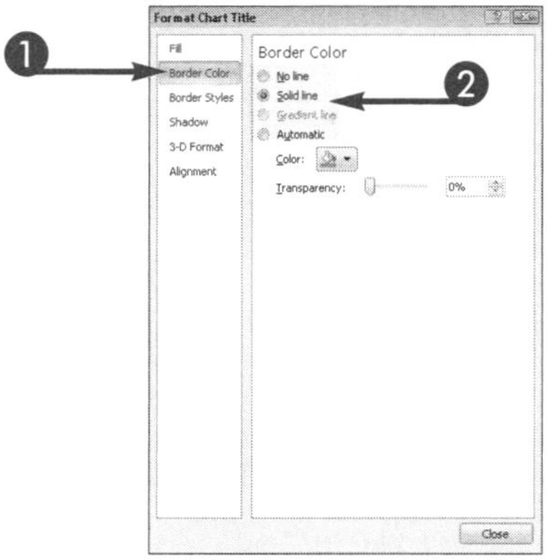

3. Click here to display a color palette and select a color.
   - Using Live Preview, Excel displays your choices.
4. Click Close to save your selections.

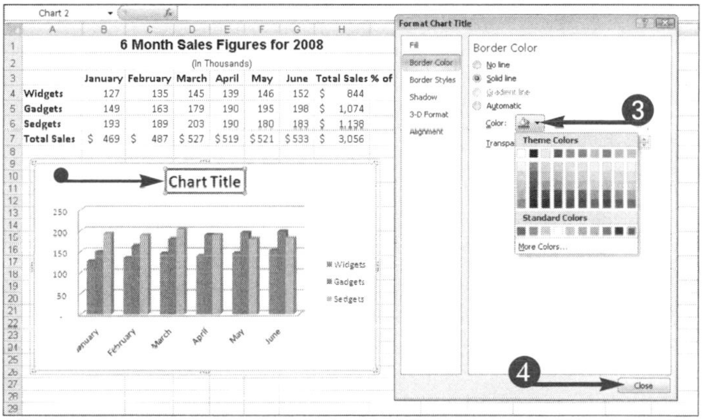

MASTER IT

Can I make the border line thicker?

▼ Yes. Click Border Styles on the left side of the Format Chart Title dialog box and then select a width. The example uses a width of two points. You can also set the line style to a single line or select from a variety of compound line types that combine two or three lines, some of different thicknesses. You can also select a solid line or one of several dashed variations.

How do I align the chart title text?

▼ Follow Steps 1 to 4 in the subsection "Display the Format Chart Title Dialog Box." Then, click Alignment in the list on the left. You can select a vertical alignment for the text, as well as set the text direction. The default text direction is horizontal, but you can rotate text to any angle or display text stacked from top to bottom, which works well if you position the chart title down one side of the chart.

How do I get rid of a border line?

▼ Select the border line that you want to hide. In the Format Chart Title dialog box, click Border Color. On the right side of the dialog box, select the No Line option (○ changes to ◉).

How do I set a 3-D format?

▼ Follow Steps 1 to 4 in the subsection, "Display the Format Chart Title Dialog Box." Then, click 3-D Format in the list on the left. Select a bevel style, and set the appropriate width and height.

Display the Horizontal Axis Title

You can add a title to the horizontal axis of a chart. A good axis title helps the reader understand the information you want to convey in the chart.

Some chart layouts automatically provide a horizontal axis title, but you can add a horizontal axis title to any layout that does not automatically include one. When you add a horizontal axis title or select a layout that includes a horizontal axis title, Excel supplies generic text to represent the title. You can change this generic text to help your reader identify the purpose of the horizontal axis on the chart.

You can also change the position of the horizontal axis title within the chart window, even if your chart is not embedded in your worksheet but appears on its own chart sheet. When you reposition a horizontal axis title, you drag it to a new location. You will find it easiest to not select the element before you reposition it; instead, you can select and reposition it in one step.

You can also delete a horizontal axis title if you do not want it to appear on your chart.

Display the Horizontal Axis Title

1. Click anywhere in the chart area to select the chart.
   - The tabs associated with Chart Tools appear.
2. Click the Layout tab.
3. Click Axis Titles to display title options.
4. Click Primary Horizontal Axis Title.
5. Click Title Below Axis.

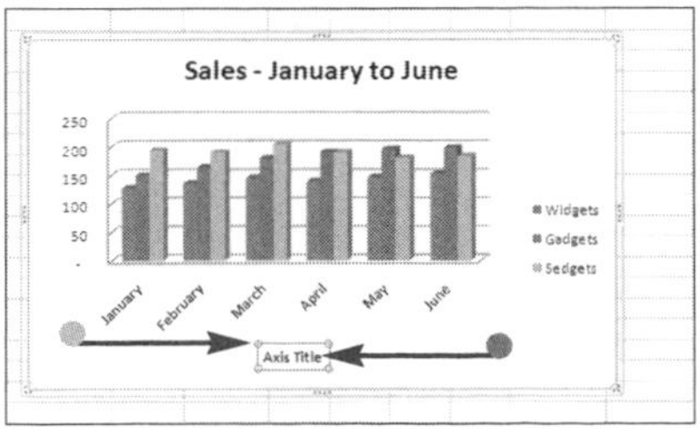

- Excel adds a generic axis title and selects it.
- These handles indicate that the chart element is selected.

Round handles at each corner of the chart element indicate that it is selected.

6. Click in the box containing the axis title.
   - Excel displays an insertion point in the box.
7. Delete any text you do not need, and type any text you want.
8. Click outside the axis title element.

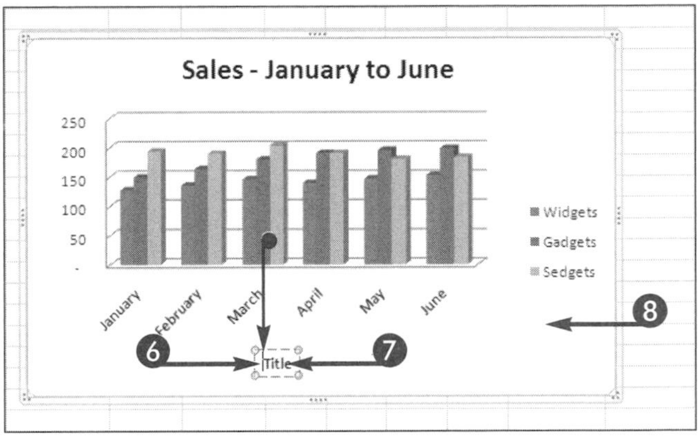

- Excel displays the axis title on your chart.

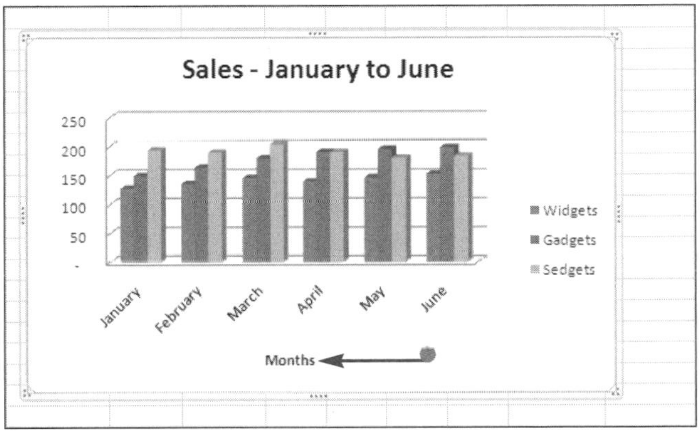

Can I place the title in a different location in the chart window?

▼ Yes, but you should leave it near the horizontal axis. Click a white space in the chart window, but do not click the horizontal axis title element. Then, move the mouse pointer over the horizontal axis title element and make sure that you see the tool tip, "Horizontal (Category) Axis Title" (pointer changes to move pointer). Click and drag the title to the new location.

Can I make the horizontal axis title font larger?

▼ Yes. Click the horizontal axis title chart element to select it. Then, click the Home tab and click ▾ beside font size. Select a different font size from the list. You can also change the font using the same technique, but clicking ▾ beside the font name.

Can I select a cell containing the axis title text I want Excel to use?

▼ No. You must change the generic title text, "Axis Title." Ignore Steps 1 to 5. Click the horizontal axis title element to select it, and then complete Steps 6 to 7.

How do I delete a horizontal axis title?

▼ Follow Steps 1 to 4, and, in Step 5, select None. You can also select the horizontal axis title and press Delete.

Format the Horizontal Axis Title

You can add a variety of formatting to the horizontal axis title to improve its appearance or call attention to it. You can fill the space occupied by the title with a background color that is solid or a gradient of colors.

You can add a border to the horizontal axis title element. When you add a border, you add a line that delineates the space occupied by the horizontal axis title; the line can be solid or made up of any of several varieties of dashes. You can control the width of the line and the way the line wraps around the corners of the horizontal axis title element's space. You can also add a shadow to the horizontal axis title element or select a 3-D format.

In addition to controlling the border and space within the horizontal axis title element, you can control the way Excel displays the horizontal axis title text within the element's space. For example, you can align the text with the top, middle, or bottom of the horizontal axis title box and you can center the text vertically within any of these alignments.

Format the Horizontal Axis Title

Display the Format Axis Title Dialog Box

1. Click the axis title to select it.
   - The tabs associated with Chart Tools appear.
2. Click the Layout tab.
3. Click Axis Titles.
4. Click Primary Horizontal Axis Title.
5. Click More Primary Horizontal Axis Title Options.

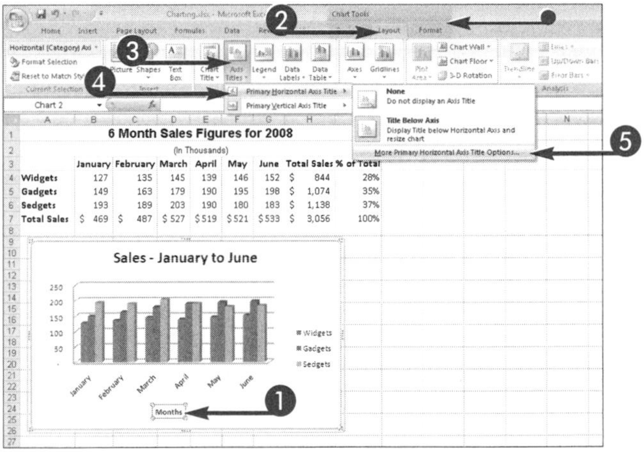

The Format Axis Title dialog box appears.

- You can add these formats to the axis title.

Add a Border Color

1. Click Border Color.
2. Click Solid Line. (◯ changes to ◉).
3. Click here to select a color from the color palette.

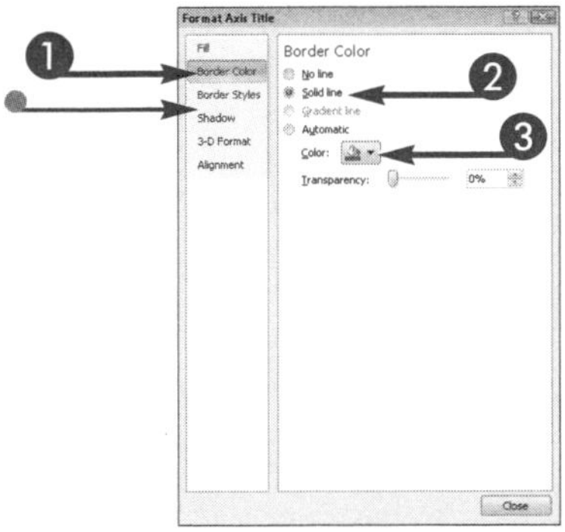

Set a Border Style

1. Click Border Styles.
2. Select a line width.
3. Click here and select a compound type.

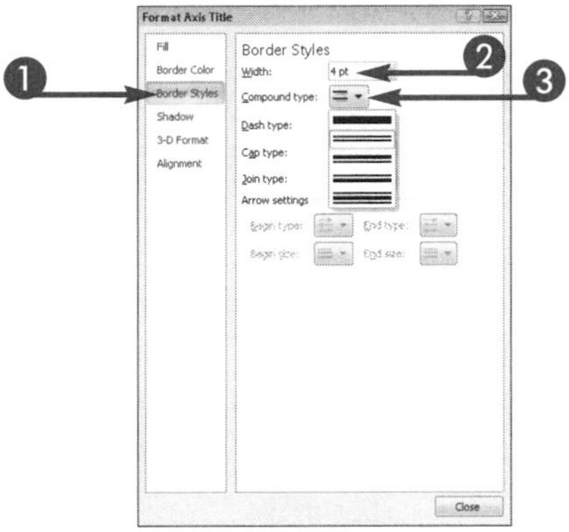

4. Click here and select a dash type.
   - Using Live Preview, Excel displays your choices.
5. Click Close to save your selections.

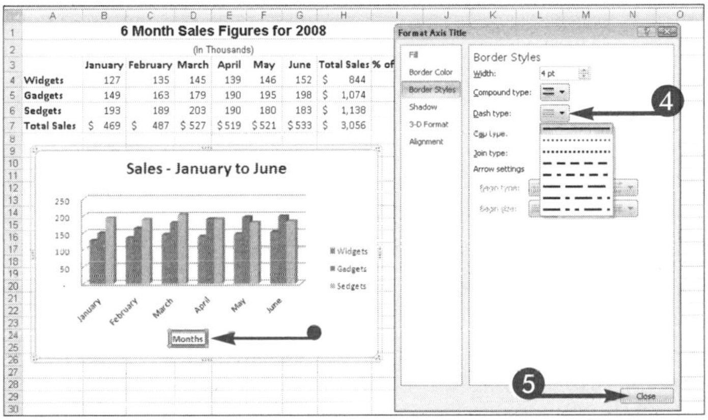

PART IV

MASTER IT

Under Border Color options, what does the Transparency option do?

▼ The Transparency option is most effective when you initially select a dark color. You can use the Transparency option to lighten the effect you select. If you apply a fill color, you can also set the Transparency option to lighten the fill effect, making the title easier to read.

What options are available when I click Fill?

▼ You can apply a solid fill, a gradient fill, or a texture fill to the background area of the horizontal axis title. If you choose to apply a solid or gradient fill, you select a color and a transparency; for the gradient fill, you can also set features such as the type, direction, and angle of the gradient.

Can I set a border style without selecting a border color?

▼ Yes. On the Border Color tab, you must select Solid Line for the options on the Border Styles tab to become available.

Under Border Styles, what does the Cap Type option control?

▼ The Cap Type option controls the appearance of the border as it goes around a corner. You can set the cap type to Square, Round, or Flat.

Display the Vertical Axis Title

You can add a title to the vertical axis of a chart. A good axis title helps the reader understand the information you want to convey in the chart.

Some chart layouts automatically provide a vertical axis title, but you can add a vertical axis title to any layout that does not automatically include one. When you add a vertical axis title or select a layout that includes a vertical axis title, Excel supplies generic text to represent the title. You can change this generic text to help your reader identify the purpose of the vertical axis on the chart.

You can also change the position of the vertical axis title within the chart window, even if your chart is not embedded in your worksheet but appears on its own chart sheet. When you reposition a vertical axis title, you drag it to a new location. You will find it easiest to not select the element before you reposition it; instead, you can select and reposition it in one step.

You can also delete a vertical axis title if you do not want it to appear on your chart.

Display the Vertical Axis Title

1. Click anywhere in the chart area to select the chart.
   - The tabs associated with Chart Tools appear.
2. Click the Layout tab.
3. Click Axis Titles to display title options.
4. Click Primary Vertical Axis Title.
5. Click Vertical Title.

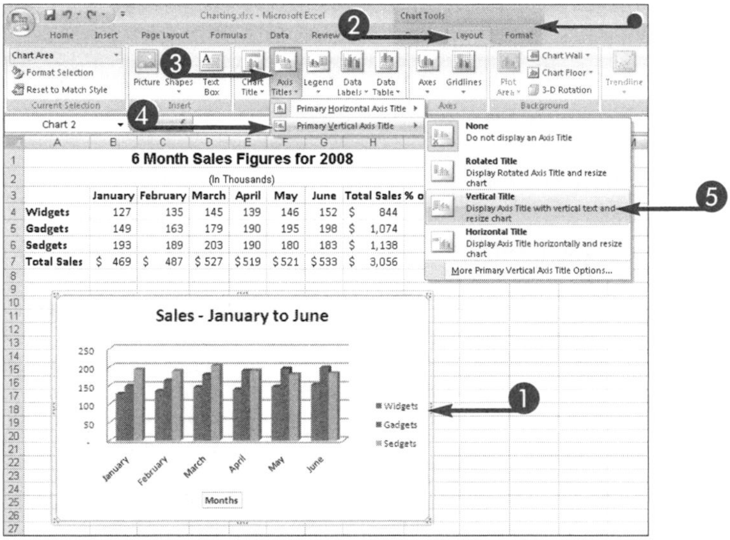

- Excel adds a generic vertical axis title and selects it.

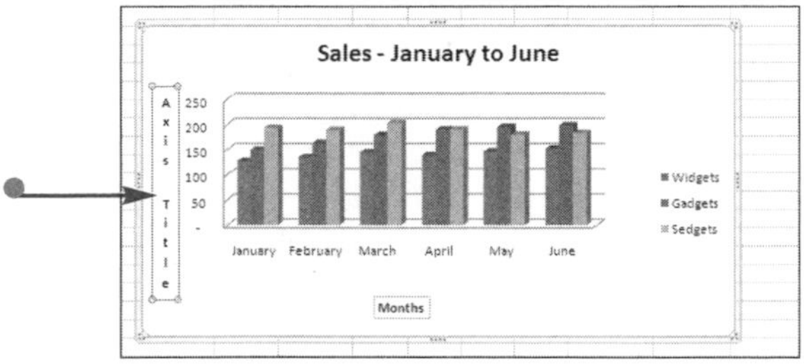

6 Click in the box containing the axis title.

- Excel displays an insertion point in the box.

7 Delete any text you do not need, and type any text you want.

8 Click outside the axis title element.

- Excel displays the axis title on your chart.

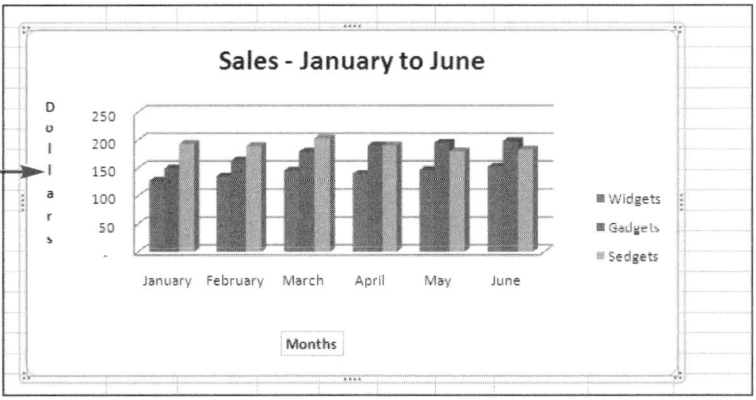

MASTER IT

The vertical axis title is too close to the vertical axis scale. Can I move it?

▼ Yes, but you should leave it near the vertical axis. Click a white space in the chart window but do not click the vertical axis title element. Then, move the mouse pointer over the vertical axis title element and make sure that you see the tool tip, "Vertical (Category) Axis Title" (pointer changes to move pointer). Click and drag the title to the new location.

I like the position of the vertical axis title, but the chart is too far over to the left. How can I separate them?

▼ You can move the plot area instead of moving the vertical axis. Click a white space in the chart window to avoid selecting any chart elements. Then, move the mouse pointer to the bottom of the chart window between the horizontal axis title and the labels on the horizontal axis. When you see the tool tip, "Plot Area," click and drag (pointer changes to move pointer).

What happens when I select the Rotated Title option in Step 5?

▼ Excel adds a vertical axis title that contains text that appears rotated 90 degrees counter-clockwise.

How do I delete a vertical axis title?

▼ Follow Steps 1 to 4, and, in Step 5, select None. You can also select the vertical axis title and press Delete.

Format the Vertical Axis

You can add a variety of formatting to the vertical axis title to improve its appearance or call attention to it. You can fill the space occupied by the title with a solid background color, a gradient of colors, or a texture.

You can also add a border to the vertical axis title element. When you add a border, you add a line that delineates the space occupied by the vertical axis title; the line can be a solid or made up of any of several varieties of dashes. You can control width of the line and the way the line wraps around the corners of the vertical axis title element's space. You can also add a shadow to the vertical axis title element or select a 3-D format.

In addition to controlling the border and space within the vertical axis title element, you can control the way Excel displays the vertical axis title text within the element's space. For example, you can align the text with the top, middle, or bottom of the vertical axis title box, and you can center the text vertically within any of these alignments.

Format the Vertical Axis

Display the Format Axis Title Dialog Box

1. Click the axis title to select it.
   - The tabs associated with Chart Tools appear.
2. Click the Layout tab.
3. Click Axis Titles.
4. Click Primary Vertical Axis Title.
5. Click More Primary Vertical Axis Title Options.

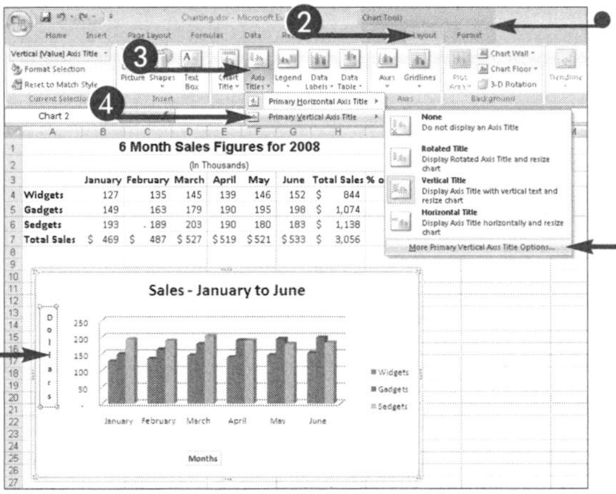

The Format Axis Title dialog box appears.

- You can add these formats to the axis title.

Add a Solid Fill

1. Click Fill.
2. Click Solid Fill.
3. Click here to display a color palette and select a color.
   - Using Live Preview, Excel displays your choices.

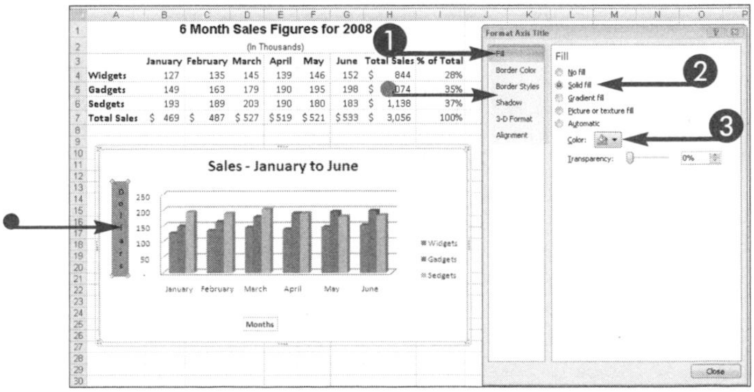

Add a Shadow

1. Click Shadow.
2. Click Presets.
   - Excel displays a gallery of shadow choices.
3. Select a preset shadow.

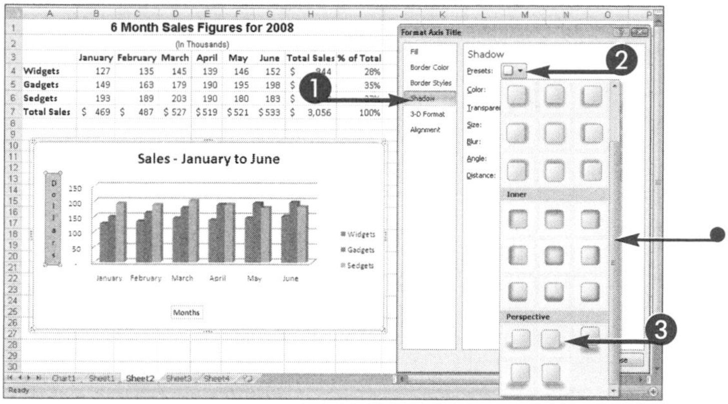

- Excel displays the preset you selected.
- You can use these options to control the appearance of the shadow.

4. Click Close to save your selections.

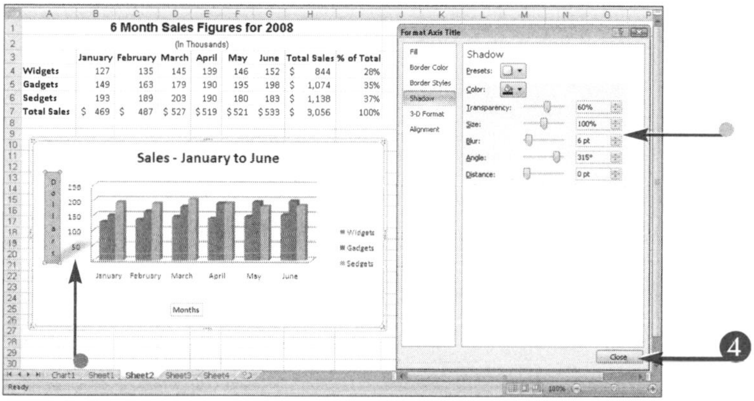

MASTER IT

What does the Blur option do to the shadow?

▼ The Blur option controls how distinct or fuzzy the edges of the shadow appear. A blur of zero points results in a shadow with completely distinct edges. The higher the point value you set for the blur, the fuzzier the edges of the shadow become. Typically, you want the blur to be at least six points.

What does the Distance option control on a shadow?

▼ The Distance option controls how far away from the chart element the shadow appears. If you set the distance to zero points, the shadow appears to be attached to the chart element. However, if you set the distance to six points, the shadow appears to be slightly disconnected from the chart element.

When setting a shadow, what does the Transparency option do?

▼ You can use the Transparency option to control how dark the shadow appears. The lower the Transparency number, the darker the shadow appears.

Can I set the shadow size to a value larger than 100 percent?

▼ Yes. Excel displays a larger shadow on the chart element. If you select a large enough percentage, the shadow may disappear off the chart.

Reposition or Hide the Chart Legend

You can move the chart legend to a new location, or you can hide it altogether. The chart legend displays color coding that helps you identify the various data series that appear on the chart so that you know which numbers apply to each data series. The legend makes reading and understanding the chart much easier. On a column or bar chart, the color coding of the legend helps you determine which color bar represents each data series. On a pie chart, the color coding of the legend helps you identify each piece of the pie.

Most of the chart layouts you apply contain a legend automatically. You can move the legend to a different location on the chart or, if you feel the legend is distracting or extraneous, you can hide the legend. If you hide the legend and later change your mind, you can add the legend back to the chart. Conversely, if you choose a chart layout that does not contain a legend, you can add a legend to the chart. You can also increase the space allotted to the legend on the chart.

Reposition or Hide the Chart Legend

Reposition the Legend

1. Click the chart to select it.
   - The tabs associated with Chart Tools appear.
2. Click the Layout tab.
3. Click Legend.
4. Click a legend position.

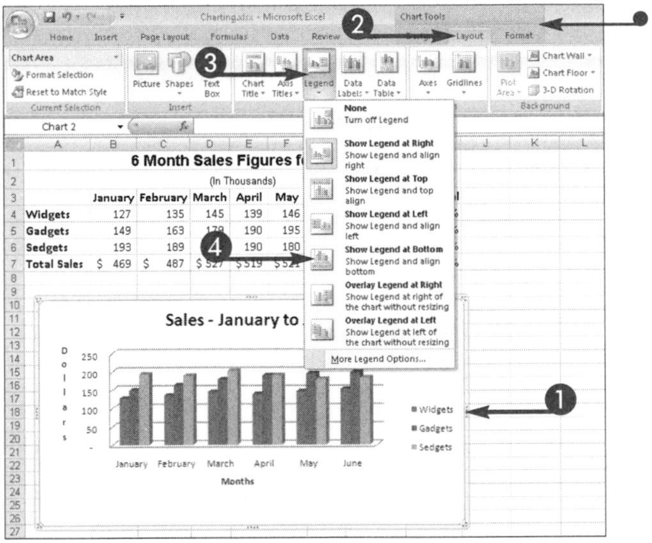

- The legend appears in its new location.

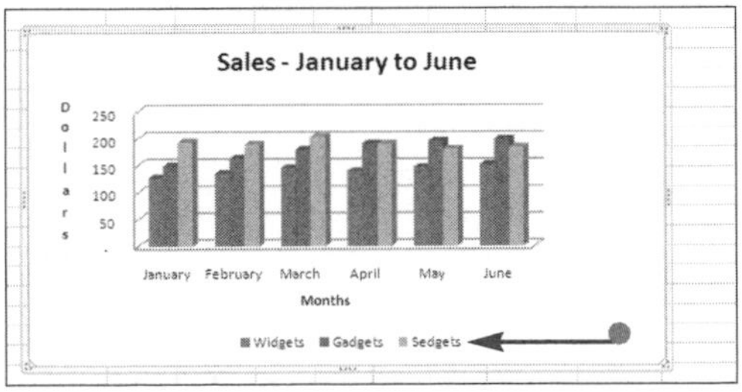

Hide the Legend

1. Click the chart to select it.
   - The tabs associated with Chart Tools appear.
2. Click the Layout tab.
3. Click Legend.
4. Click None.

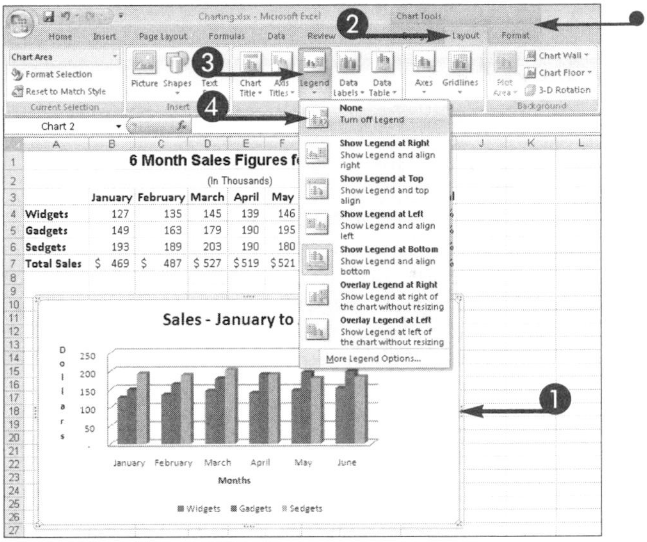

The legend does not appear on the chart.

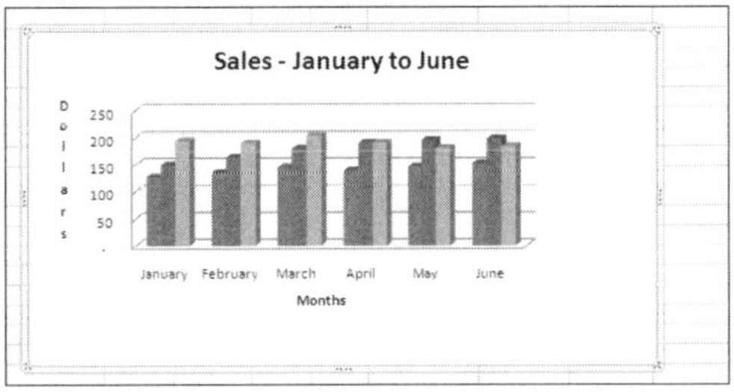

MASTER IT

What happens if I click More Legend Options?

▼ The Format Legend dialog box appears. From this dialog box, you can select a legend position, as well as set fill, border color, border styles, and shadow options for the legend. For example, you can display a solid line around the legend border and select a color for the line. Using Border Styles options, you can select a line width and type.

How do I change the space allotted to the legend?

▼ Click the legend to select it. Then, move the mouse pointer over any of the eight handles that surround the legend (✥ changes to ⇔, ⇕, or ⤢). Drag the handle outward to increase the space allotted to the legend. Drag the handle inward to decrease the legend's space.

Why would I want to hide the legend?

▼ You might want to hide the legend if you choose to display data labels that identify the data series. In this case, the legend would then contain extraneous information and become a distraction rather than a useful and helpful part of the chart. For more information on data labels, see the section, "Show Data Labels."

Show Data Labels

You can use data labels to add information to the chart that might not otherwise appear. By default, when you display data labels, Excel displays the value associated with each data series. However, you can change the information that is displayed by the data label. For example, you can display the data series name as a data label; when you display the data series name, you typically do not need a chart legend, and so you can hide the legend. For details on hiding the legend, see the section, "Reposition or Hide the Chart Legend." On a pie chart, you can display each pie slice's percentage of the whole pie. You can also display more than one data series label simultaneously. For example, on a pie chart, you could display both the percentage and the category name for each slice.

By default, Excel does not display data labels when you initially create your chart because adding data labels can often make a chart appear crowded; in some cases, you might not be able to read the information on the chart because of the data labels. Data labels are generally not helpful on charts containing multiple data series.

Show Data Labels

Display Data Labels

1. Click the chart to select it.
   - The tabs associated with Chart Tools appear.
2. Click the Layout tab.
3. Click Data Labels.
4. Click a position for the data labels.

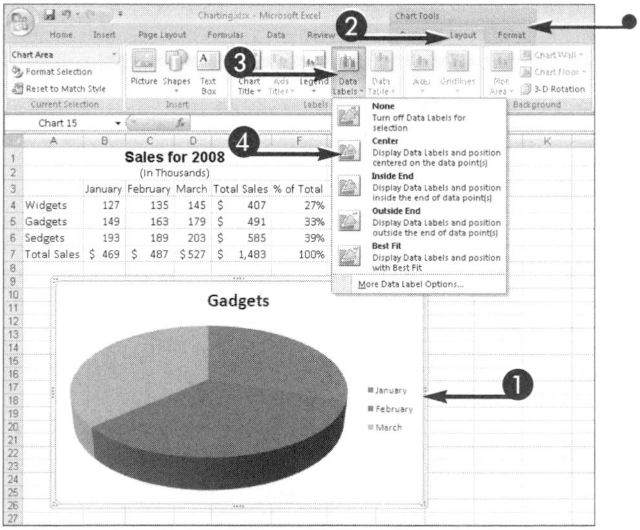

- Excel displays data labels on the chart.

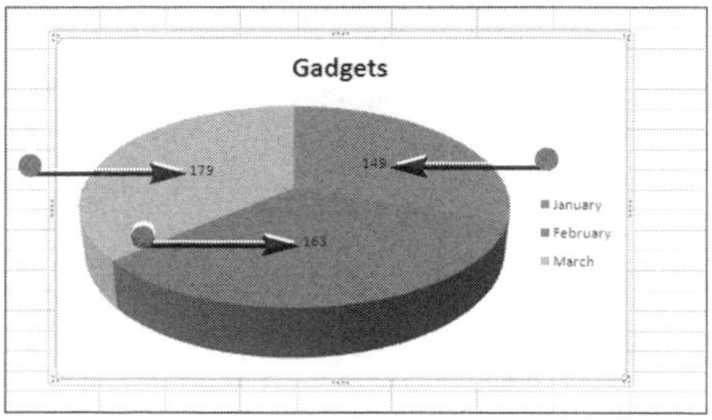

Setting Data Label Options

1. Click the chart to select it.
   - The tabs associated with Chart Tools appear.
2. Click the Layout tab.
3. Click Data Labels.
4. Click More Data Label Options.

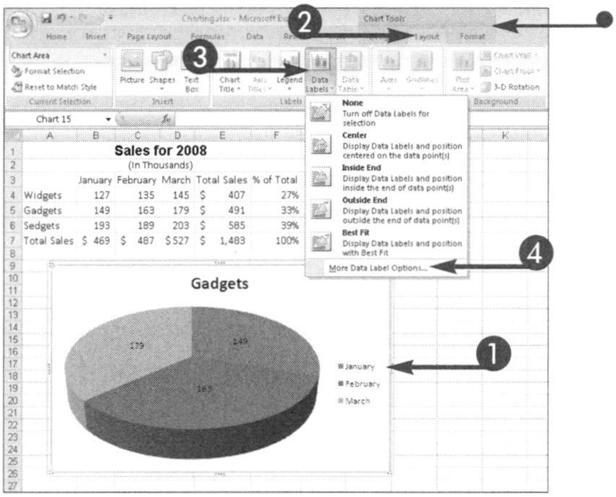

The Format Data Labels dialog box appears.

- You can click these options to select the data to display.
- You can click these options to position the data labels.
- Using Live Preview, Excel displays the result of your choices.

5. Click Close.

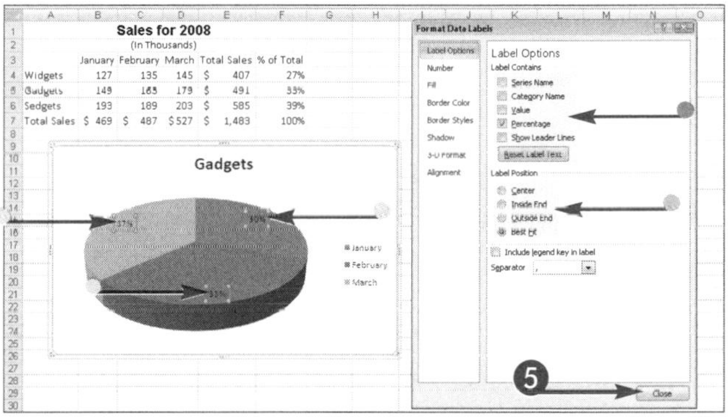

MASTER IT

How do I hide data labels?

▼ Repeat the steps in the subsection, "Display Data Labels," and, in Step 4, click None. Excel hides the data labels. If your data labels contain series information and you also hide the legend, you might want to redisplay it so that readers can more easily understand the chart.

My column chart contains bars for sales of three products over six months, and the data labels overlap. Is there anything I can do?

▼ Data labels do not usually work well when your chart presents a lot of information. Try placing the chart in a chart sheet, where Excel allocates more space to it. If the data labels still are legible, consider using a data table instead of data labels; see the section, "Show the Data Table."

Excel only seems to format the data labels for the first series on my column chart. How do I format data labels for the second series?

▼ When your chart contains only one data series — like pie charts do — you do not need to worry about selecting a data series to format. However, when your chart contains more than one data series, you need to select the data series you want to format by clicking it in the chart.

Show the Data Table

As part of most charts, you can display a table that contains the data points used in the chart. The data table is useful if you want to present both the chart and its underlying data to the reader without printing the raw data in the worksheet. Displaying the data table can be particularly useful if you place your chart in a chart sheet, because you can then print both the chart and the data it uses on a single page.

One of the data table options enables you to include legend information in the data table. When you choose this format for the data table, you do not need a chart legend, and so you can hide it. For details on hiding the legend, see the section, "Reposition or Hide the Chart Legend."

Data tables are not available on pie charts because you can easily display data values on pie slices using data labels; for details, see the section, "Show Data Labels."

You can control the appearance of the lines in a data table by formatting the data table. By default, the table shows horizontal, vertical, and outside lines, but you can choose which lines to display.

Show the Data Table

Display the Data Table

1. Click the chart to select it.
   - The tabs associated with Chart Tools appear.
2. Click the Layout tab.
3. Click Data Table.
4. Click a data table style.

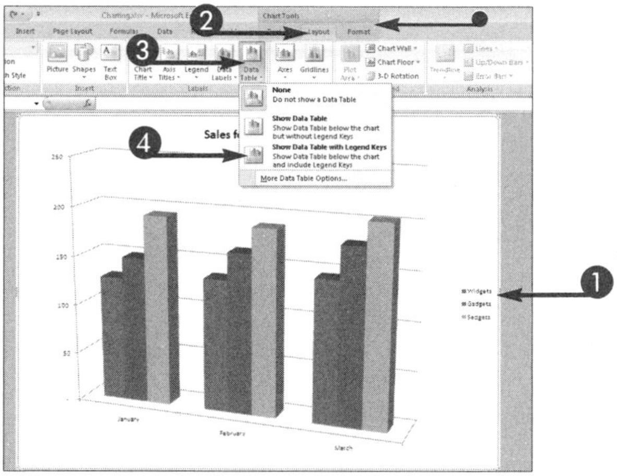

- Excel displays the data table at the bottom of the chart.

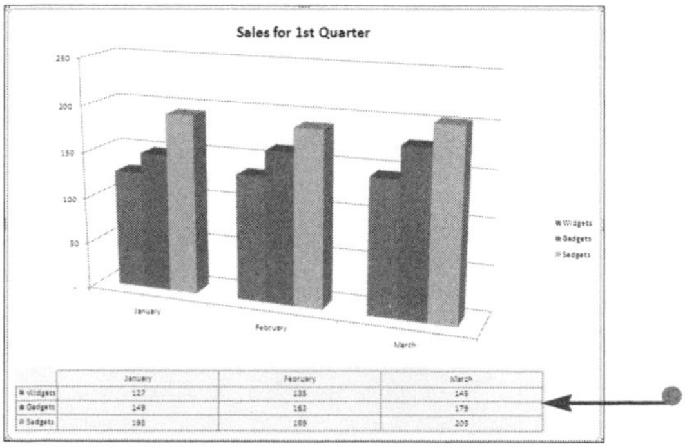

Format the Data Table

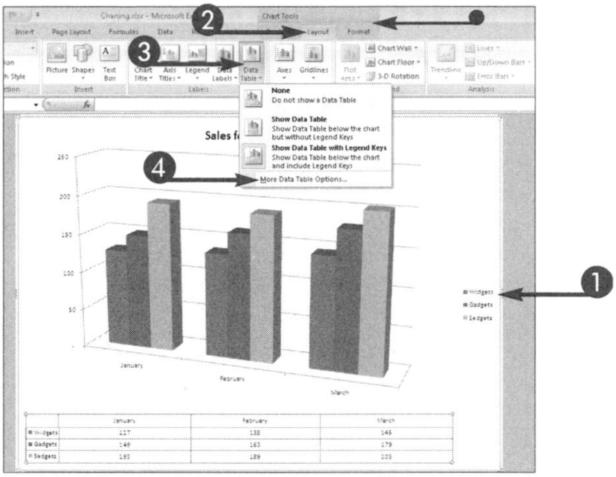

1. Click the chart to select it.
   - The tabs associated with Chart Tools appear.
2. Click the Layout tab.
3. Click Data Table.
4. Click More Data Table Options.

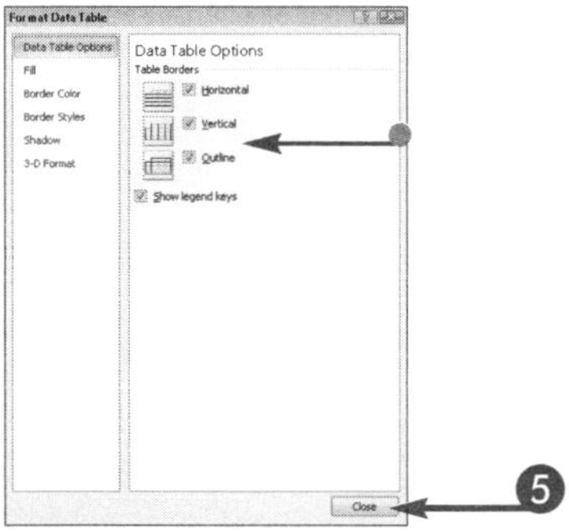

- You can click these options to select the lines to display in the table.

Using Live Preview, Excel displays the result of your choices.

5. Click Close.

MASTER IT

What is the difference between the two formats for the data table?

▼ One option displays just the data table without any legend information. The other — the one used in this example — also adds legend colors to the data table. When you choose the second format, you really do not need to display a legend. Hiding the legend in this case makes the chart less complicated. See the section, "Reposition or Hide the Chart Legend," for details on hiding the legend.

How do I remove a data table if I decide that I do not want to include it?

▼ Follow Steps 1 to 3 in the subsection, "Display the Data Table." In Step 4, choose None. Excel removes the data table and enlarges other chart information to redistribute the chart proportionately within the chart window.

Can I fill the table cells in the data table with a background color?

▼ When you fill the data table, Excel fills just the area where the data points appear, and so it does not appear that you are filling the background of the table cells. However, if you fill the plot area, Excel displays a background color for the plot area, including the data table.

Format the Plot Area

You can format the plot area, which is the background area behind a chart, to improve its appearance or call attention to it. For example, you can fill the plot area with a solid color, a gradient color that changes over the background area, or a texture.

You can also display a border line around the plot area. When you add a border to the plot area, you add a line that delineates the space occupied by the plot area. The line can be solid or made up of several varieties of dashes. You can control the color and width of the line and the way the line wraps around the corners of the plot area element's space.

Some formatting settings are available only if you select other formatting options. For example, if you set a fill color for the plot area or display a border line around the plot area, you can also set a shadow for the plot area and control several shadow factors, including its size and angle. If you set a fill color, you can also select 3-D formatting options that apply a bevel of your choice to the edge of the plot area.

Format the Plot Area

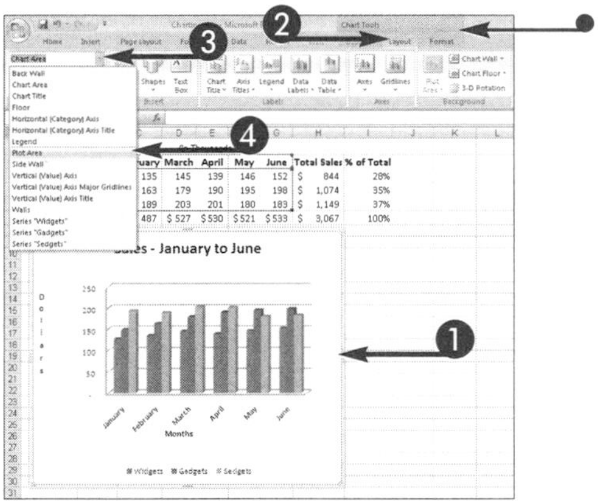

1. Click the chart to select it.
   - The tabs associated with Chart Tools appear.
2. Click the Layout tab.
3. Click ▾.
4. Click Plot Area.

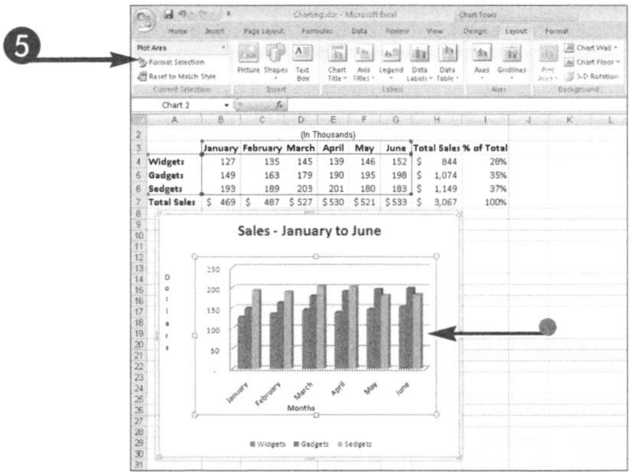

- Excel selects the plot area.

5. Click Format Selection.

The Format Plot Area dialog box appears.

6 Click a type of formatting.

Note: *This section applies a fill.*

7 Click options for the formatting type.

8 Click Close.

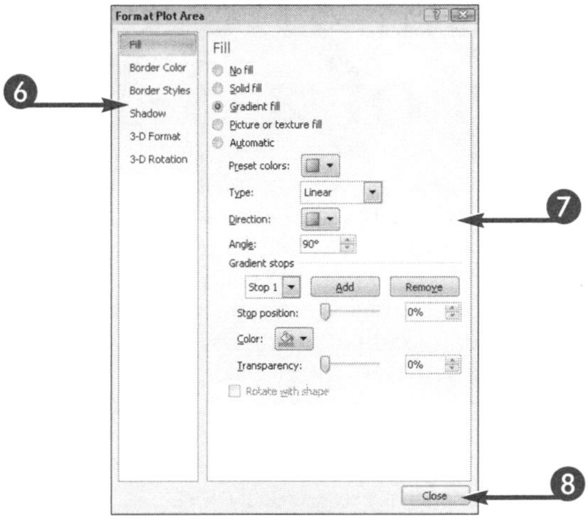

- Excel applies the formatting you selected to the plot area.

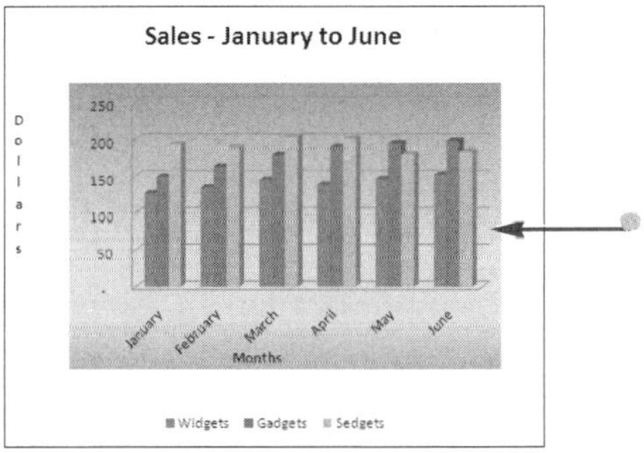

MASTER IT

Can I change the size of the plot area?

▼ Yes. Select the plot area using Steps 1 to 4 in this section. Then move the mouse pointer over one of the eight handles that identify the plot area (✣ changes to ⇔, ⇕, or ⤢). Drag away from the chart center to enlarge the plot area, or toward the chart center to reduce the plot area.

Can I change the location of the plot area?

▼ Yes. Select the plot area using Steps 1 to 4 in this section. Then move the mouse pointer over the edge of the plot area until you see the Plot Area screen tip. Click and drag the plot area to a new location. You can resize and move a chart's plot area to make room for additional information, such as a shape, on the chart. See Chapter 22 for information on shapes.

Is there an easy way to remove plot area formatting?

▼ Yes. Select the plot area using Steps 1 to 4 in this section. Then, click the Reset to Match Style button, which appears just below the list you use in Step 3. Excel removes any formatting you applied to the plot area.

Format the Chart Walls of a 3-D Chart

You can format the walls of most 3-D charts to improve the chart's appearance or to call attention to the walls. Walls are not available on all 3-D charts; you will not find walls on pie charts, but you will find them on line, column, and bar charts. Line, column, and bar charts have two walls — a back wall and a side wall. Chart walls appear behind or to the side of the lines or bars on the chart, and delineate the area in which you see gridlines. When you format the chart walls, Excel formats both the side wall and the back wall simultaneously.

You can fill the chart wall area with a solid color, a gradient color that changes over the background area, or a texture.

You can also display a border line around the chart walls. When you add a border to the chart walls, you add a line that delineates the space occupied by the chart walls. The line can be solid, and you can control the color and width of the line.

You can also control the rotational appearance of the chart by changing the chart scale settings, as shown in this example.

Format the Chart Walls of a 3-D Chart

1. Click the chart to select it.
   - The tabs associated with Chart Tools appear.
2. Click the Layout tab.
3. Click ▾.
4. Click Walls.

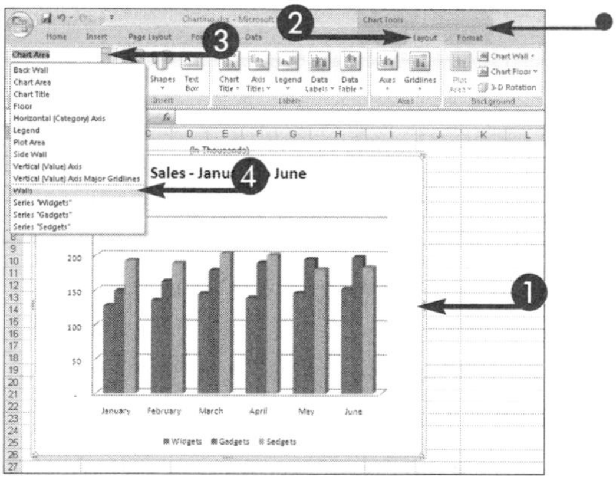

- Excel selects the chart walls.

5. Click Chart Wall.
6. Click More Walls Options.

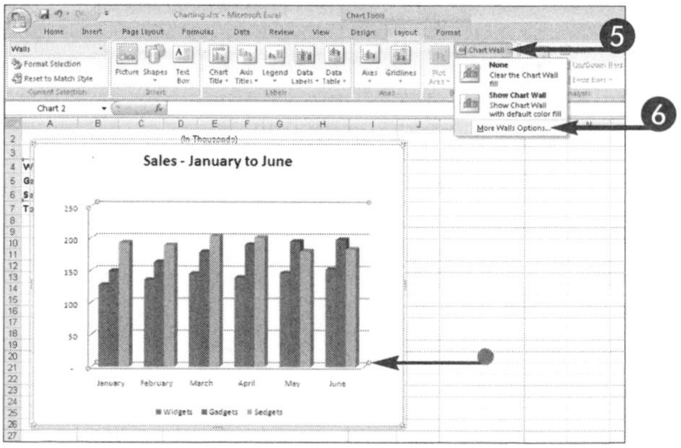

The Format Walls dialog box appears.

7 Click a type of formatting.

Note: *This section changes 3-D Rotation settings.*

8 Click Right Angle Axes (☑ changes to ☐).

9 Click Close.

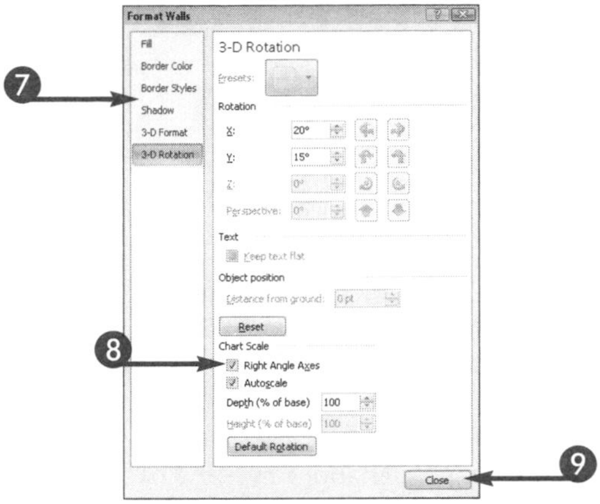

Excel applies the formatting you selected to the chart walls.

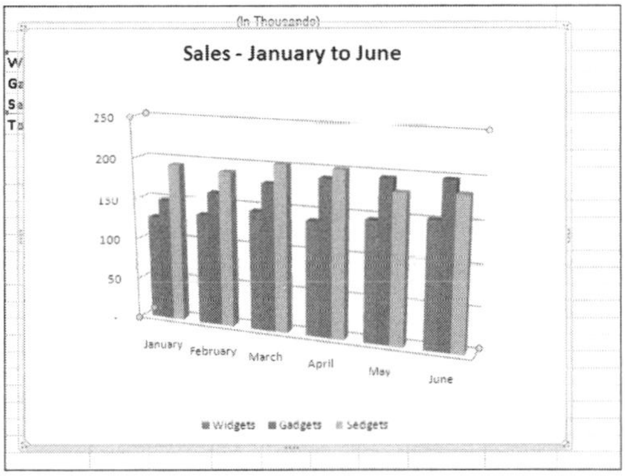

MASTER IT

Can I format only one chart wall?

▼ Yes. Suppose that you want to add a fill to the side wall only. Select Side Wall from the list shown in Step 3. Then, click the Format Selection button that appears below the list of chart elements on the Layout tab. Excel displays the Format Wall dialog box. Any settings you make in this dialog box affect only the selected wall.

Can I remove formatting that I applied to both walls from only one wall?

▼ Yes. Suppose that, after applying a fill to both walls, you decide that you want the fill only on the side wall. Select Back Wall from the list shown in Step 3. Click the Format Selection button below the list of chart elements. Under Fill options, select No Fill (○ changes to ◉). Excel removes the fill from the back wall but retains the fill on the side wall.

What happens when I click None on the list that appears when I click Chart Wall?

▼ Excel removes any formatting you applied to both the side wall and the back wall of the chart.

When I click Chart Wall, what does the Show Chart Wall command that appears on the menu do?

▼ When you click Show Chart Wall, Excel displays the chart wall using the default color, which is usually white.

Format the Chart Floor of a 3-D Chart

You can format the floor of most 3-D charts to improve the chart's appearance or to call attention to the floor. A chart floor is not available on all 3-D charts; you will not find a chart floor on a pie chart, but you will find a chart floor on a line, column, or bar chart. The chart floor appears under the lines or bars on the chart.

You can fill the chart floor area with a solid color, a gradient color that changes over the background area, or a texture.

You can also display a border line around the chart floor. When you add a border to the chart floor, you add a line that delineates the space occupied by the chart floor. The line can be solid and you can control the color and width of the line.

You can control the appearance of the floor's surface by applying a special effect. You can also control the translucency of the chart floor.

You can control the depth of the chart floor by changing the chart scale settings, as shown in this example.

Format the Chart Floor of a 3-D Chart

1. Click the chart to select it.
   - The tabs associated with Chart Tools appear.
2. Click the Layout tab.
3. Click ▾.
4. Click Floor.

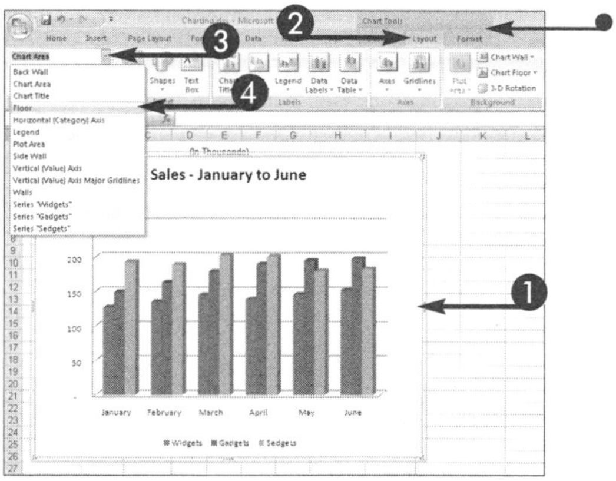

- Excel selects the chart floor.

5. Click Chart Floor.
6. Click More Floor Options.

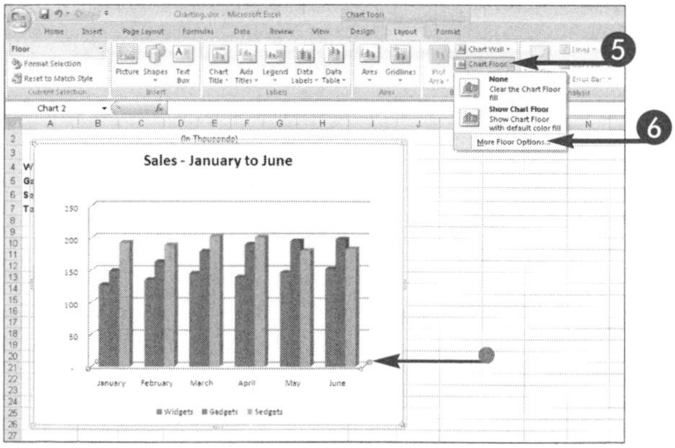

The Format Floor dialog box appears.

7 Click a type of formatting.

Note: *This section changes the depth of the floor, a 3-D Rotation setting.*

8 Type a number between 0 and 2000.

9 Click Close.

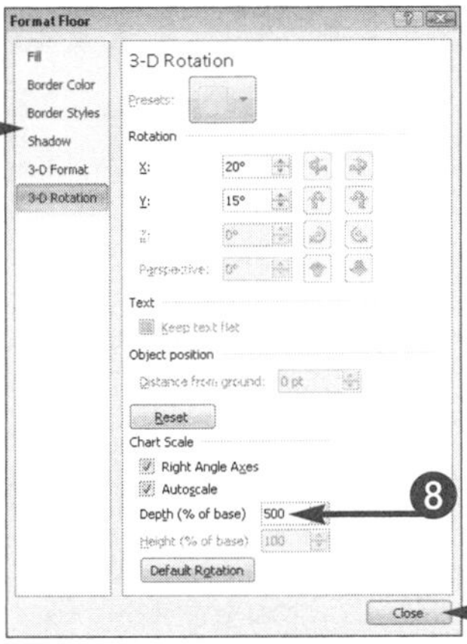

Excel changes the depth of the chart floor.

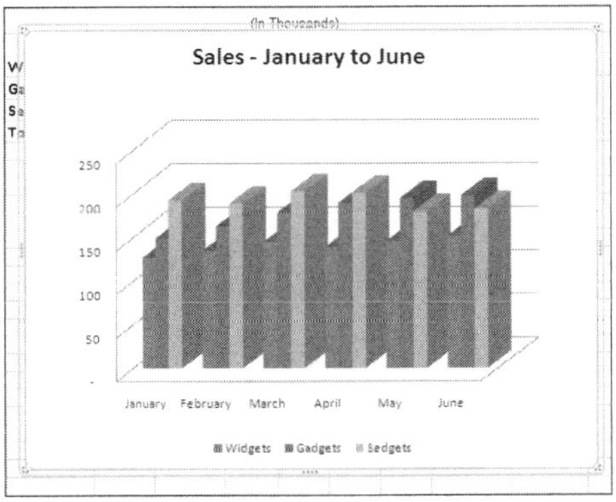

MASTER IT

Is there a faster way to select the chart floor?

▼ Yes. You can click anywhere in the chart window to select the chart and display the Chart Tools tabs. Then, click the Layout tab and perform Steps 5 and 6. Excel displays the Format Floor dialog box and simultaneously selects the chart floor. This technique works even if you accidentally select a different chart element when you select the chart to display the Chart Tools tabs.

What does the Presets button do?

▼ Excel provides some built-in rotation or perspective effects and displays them when you click the Presets button. However, these built-in preset options are not available for charts; you can apply these preset rotation and perspective options to shapes. See Chapter 22 for information on shapes.

Can I fill in the color of the floor?

▼ Yes. Complete Steps 1 to 6 in this section. For Step 7, select Fill. For Step 8, select Solid Fill, Gradient Fill, or Picture or Texture Fill (◯ changes to ◉). Depending on the option you select, you can now provide additional information about colors or select a texture or image file to display on the chart floor.

PART IV

Change the Rotation of a 3-D Chart

You can change the rotation of any 3-D chart to add visual interest to the chart. Changing the rotation of a 3-D chart can increase or decrease the sense of depth the viewer perceives when viewing the chart.

When you change the rotation of a chart, you can adjust the X axis, the Y axis, and, if your chart contains one, the Z axis. Changing the X-axis value turns the chart sideways. Increasing the value for the X axis turns the chart clockwise; decreasing the X-axis value turns the chart counter-clockwise.

Changing the Y-axis and Z-axis values flips the chart from top to bottom. Increasing the Y-axis and Z-axis values rotates the chart forward, and decreasing these values rotates the chart backwards.

You can also adjust the perspective of a 3-D chart. Adjusting the perspective of a chart is similar to adjusting the field of vision while using a camera. When you set the perspective of your chart to its highest value, your chart looks like you are viewing it through a wide-angle camera lens.

The example in this section adjusts the rotation of a pie chart.

Change the Rotation of a 3-D Chart

1. Click the chart to select it.
   - The tabs associated with Chart Tools appear.
2. Click the Layout tab.
3. Click 3-D Rotation.

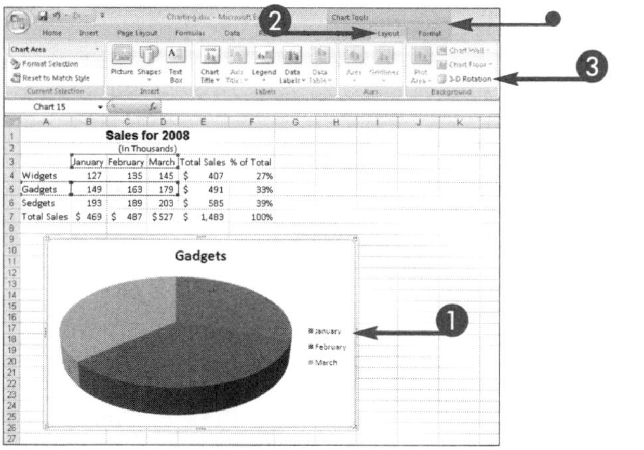

The Format Chart Area dialog box appears, showing 3-D Rotation options.

4. Type a value between 0 and 359.1.

Note: *The pie rotates clockwise as the numbers get larger.*

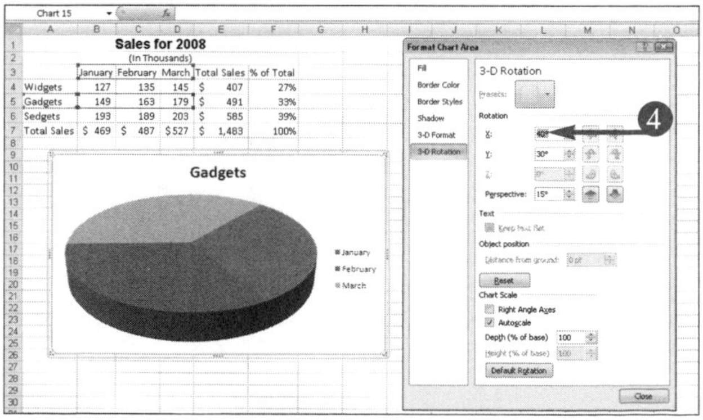

❺ Type a value between 0 and 90.

Note: *The pie rotates down as the numbers get larger.*

❻ Click Close.

Excel displays the new rotation settings.

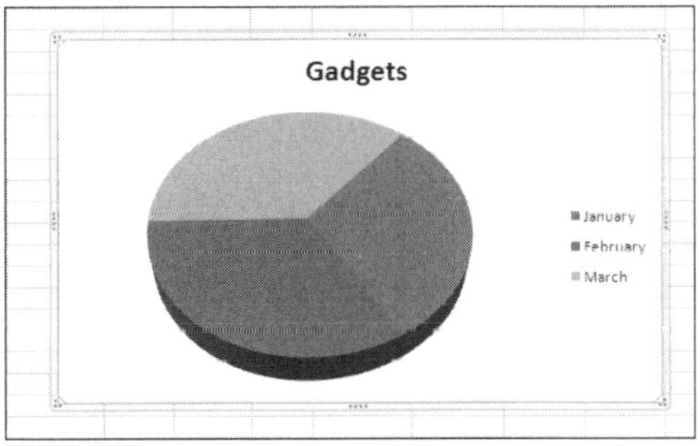

PART IV

MASTER IT

What happens if I deselect the Right Angle Axes option?

▼ If you are working with a pie chart, this check box has no effect. If you are working with a bar or column chart and you deselect this option, Excel no longer displays the axes at right angles. You enter a value between 0 and 2000 in the Depth (% of base) field to control the depth of the axes, regardless of whether you display the axes at right angles.

What does the Autoscale option control?

▼ While the Autoscale check box is selected, you can control only the depth of the chart. If you click the Autoscale option (☑ changes to ☐), you can control both the depth and the height of your chart. You can enter a value between 0 and 2000 for the chart's depth, and a value between 5 and 500 for the chart's height.

In my 3-D column chart, the data series in front is blocking the data series in back. How can I fix this?

▼ Rotation is not the answer in this case. You need to change the order of the data series. Click the Design tab and, in the Data group, click the Select Data button. In the Select Data Source dialog box that appears, click one of the elements on the left side of the dialog box and use ▲ or ▼ to change its position.

Set Axis Options

Using Axis options, you can control the appearance of the axes on a chart. Pie and doughnut charts have no axes, and so this section does not apply to those types of charts. All 2-D charts have at least two axes and might have three or four axes if you use secondary vertical and horizontal axes. Three-dimensional charts have at least two axes and, if the chart truly measures three sets of values, a 3-D chart has three axes.

When you format axes, the options available depend on whether you select a vertical or a horizontal axis.

For example, by default, Excel sets the minimum and maximum values and the intervals between them on the vertical axis using the chart's data, but you can override the values and set your own. On the horizontal axis, you can adjust the interval between labels to make Excel skip some labels.

You can also add major and minor tick marks to any axis to help the reader line up the axis values. When you add tick marks, you can control their placement; you can display the tick marks inside the axis, outside the axis, or across the axis.

Set Axis Options

1. Click the chart to select it.
   - The tabs associated with Chart Tools appear.
2. Click the Layout tab.
3. Click ▾.
4. Click Horizontal (Category) Axis.

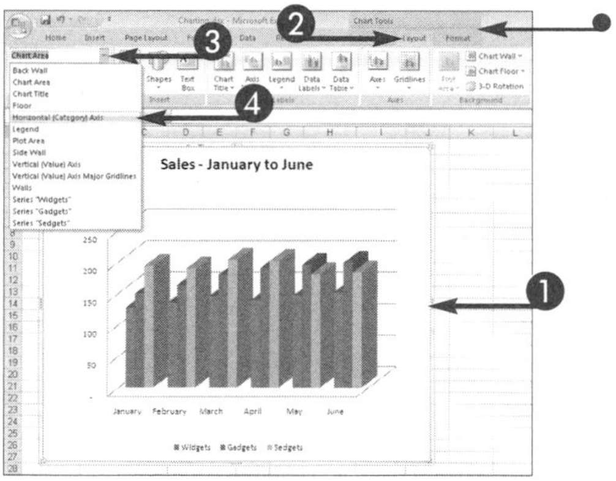

5. Click Format Selection.

   The Format Axis dialog box appears.
6. Click a type of formatting.

Note: *This section adjusts axis options.*

7. Click here to select a type of major tick marks.
   - Excel adds major tick marks to the horizontal axis.

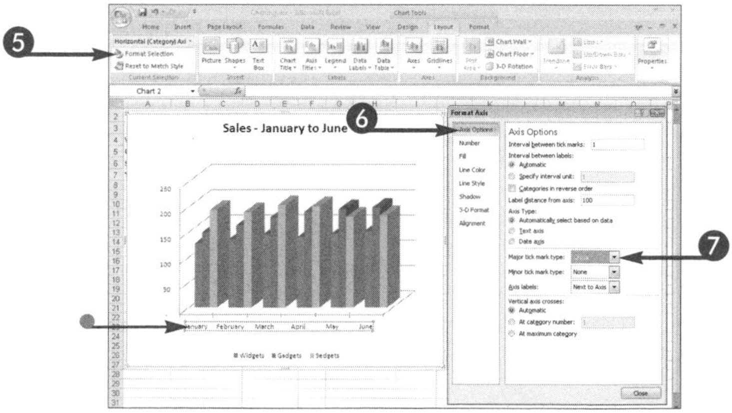

8. Click ▾.
9. Click Vertical (Value) Axis.

   Excel selects the vertical axis and changes the Axis options available in the Format Axis dialog box.

10. Click here to select a type of major tick marks.

    You can use the other Axis options to change the appearance of the vertical axis.

11. Click Close.

- Excel includes major tick marks on the horizontal axis.
- Excel includes major tick marks on the vertical axis.

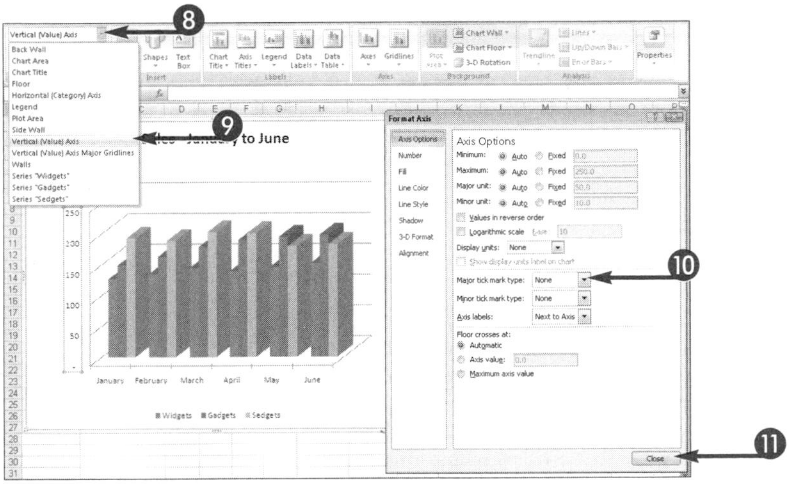

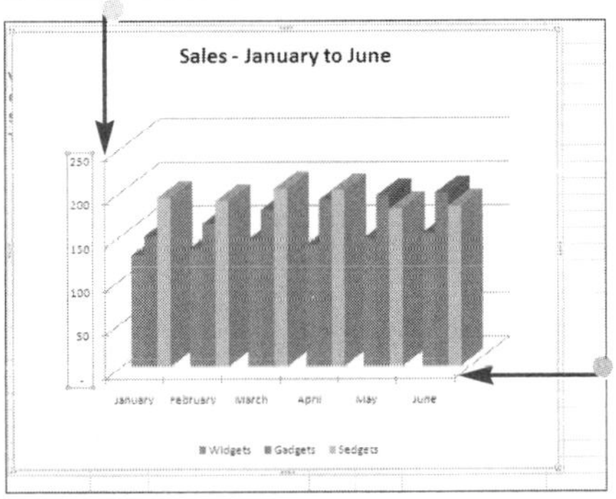

MASTER IT

What do the Axis Type options for a horizontal axis do?

▼ By default, Excel sets up the horizontal axis based on the data you select for your chart. Excel automatically recognizes dates and times if you include them in your chart and sets up intervals of equal duration for the dates or times. You can override this behavior using the Axis Type options. You can force Excel to create a text- or date-based category axis.

My vertical axis uses large numbers. Can I display smaller numbers but not lose the meaning of my chart?

▼ Yes. Select the vertical axis and click Format Selection to display the Format Axis dialog box. Click ▾ beside Display Units and select an appropriate value. For example, if you select Hundreds, Excel adjusts the chart by dividing the vertical axis numbers by 100 and then displaying the word Hundreds beside the axis.

When would I adjust the scale of the vertical axis?

▼ Adjusting the scale of the vertical axis can have a dramatic visual effect and possibly make the chart unintentionally present a false picture of the data. Suppose that your data ranges from 7,400 to 9,600 over several months. If you use values on the vertical scale of 0 to 10,000, the changes over time seem minor. However, if you use values of 7,000 to 10,000, the changes seem much more dramatic.

Change Horizontal and Vertical Gridlines

You can add or remove both horizontal and vertical gridlines on a chart. Gridlines help the person reading the chart match up information on the axes with bars or lines in the chart. Essentially, gridlines can make reading the chart easier.

Gridlines are not a requirement, but, by default, Excel includes horizontal gridlines on most charts. Gridlines are an extension of the marks on each axis that correspond to axis labels. Horizontal gridlines help the reader line up the values on the vertical axis with the data points in the chart to determine the numerical value of the data points. Sometimes, horizontal gridlines alone are sufficient, but some charts — typically XY charts — can benefit if they display vertical gridlines as well as horizontal gridlines. Gridlines are not available for pie charts or doughnut charts.

When you display gridlines, you can choose to display major gridlines, minor gridlines, or both. Major gridlines correspond to each value listed on the vertical axis or each item listed on the horizontal axis. Minor gridlines appear between major gridlines and help further clarify amounts as they relate to data points on the chart.

Change Horizontal and Vertical Gridlines

Change Horizontal Gridlines

1. Click the chart to select it.
   - The tabs associated with Chart Tools appear.
2. Click the Layout tab.
3. Click Gridlines.
4. Click Primary Horizontal Gridlines.
5. Click the type of gridlines to display.

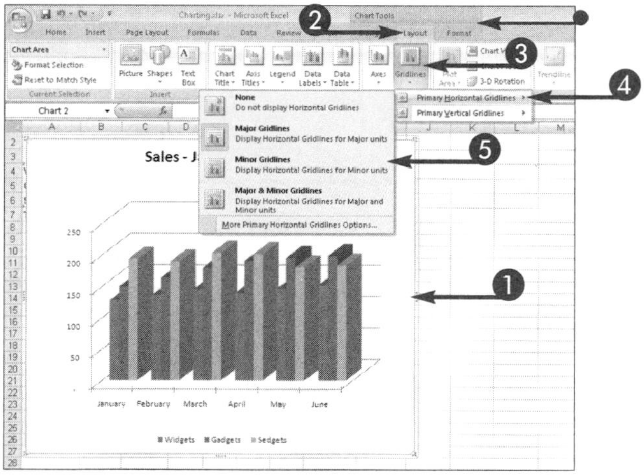

Excel displays the type of horizontal gridlines you selected.

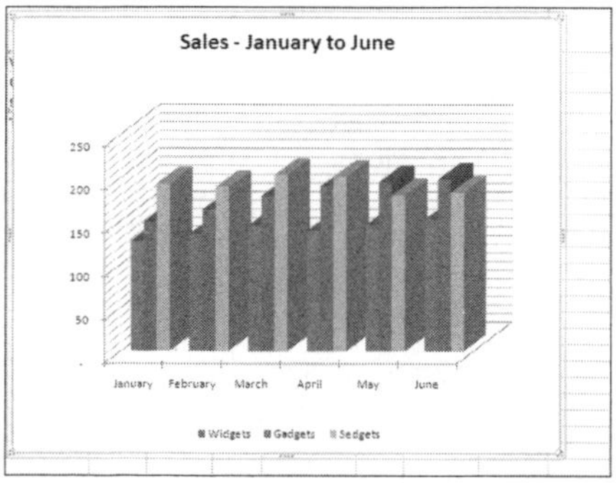

Change Vertical Gridlines

1. Click the chart to select it.
   - The tabs associated with Chart Tools appear.
2. Click the Layout tab.
3. Click Gridlines.
4. Click Primary Vertical Gridlines.
5. Select the type of gridlines to display.

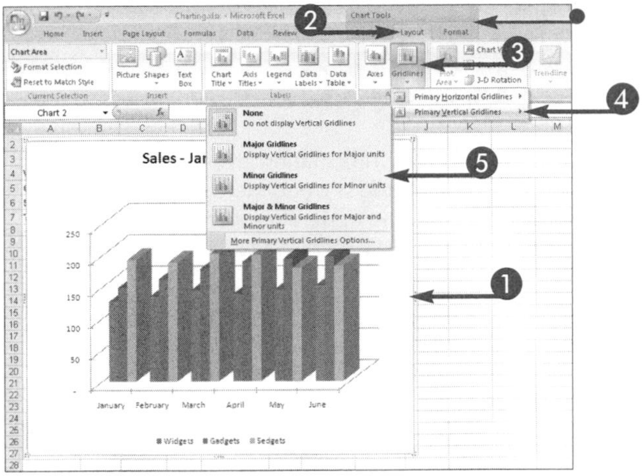

Excel displays the type of vertical gridlines you selected.

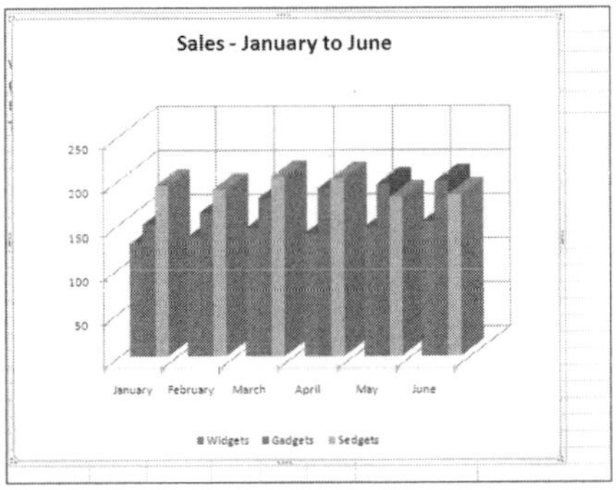

MASTER IT

How do I know when to use gridlines?

▼ Using gridlines is a matter of personal preference. If you believe that adding gridlines will help a reader understand the information on your chart, use gridlines. However, be careful, because adding gridlines can interfere with a reader's understanding by making a chart that contains many data points look cluttered.

Can I change the color of gridlines?

▼ Yes. Click a gridline to select all of the gridlines. Then, click the Layout tab. On the Ribbon, click Gridlines and then click Primary Horizontal Gridlines or Primary Vertical Gridlines, as appropriate. Click the last command on the menu to display the Format Gridlines dialog box. Click Line Color on the left and then click either Solid Line or Gradient Line (◯ changes to ◉) and select a color.

Can I change the style of gridlines?

▼ Yes. Click a gridline to select all of the gridlines. Then, click the Layout tab. On the Ribbon, click Gridlines and then click Primary Horizontal Gridlines or Primary Vertical Gridlines, as appropriate. Click the last command on the menu to display the Format Gridlines dialog box. Click Line Style on the left. You can change the gridline's width and dash type.

Add a Trendline

When you chart information over time, you may want to add a trendline to the chart to point out the general movement of the chart's data. A trendline may help the reader predict future data.

Trendlines are available only for charts that can show trends, such as 2-D line, column, or bar charts. Trendlines are not available for pie, radar, surface, doughnut, 2-D stacked, or 3-D charts.

Suppose that your XY chart plots points based on height and weight combinations. Presumably, your data show that, as height increases, weight also increases. You can add a trendline to help show the relationship between height and weight.

Trendlines can be used in regression analysis to predict future values based on existing data points. You can add six different types of trendlines to a chart: exponential, linear, logarithmic, polynomial, power, and moving average. The information you chart determines the type of trendline that you should use.

When you add a trendline, Excel calculates its R-squared value, which is a number between 0 and 1 that identifies how closely the estimated values for the trendline correspond to your data points. When the R-squared value is at or near 1, the trendline is most reliable.

Add a Trendline

Add a Trendline

1. Click the chart to select it.
   - The tabs associated with Chart Tools appear.
2. Click the Layout tab.
3. Click Trendline.
4. Click the type of trendline to display.

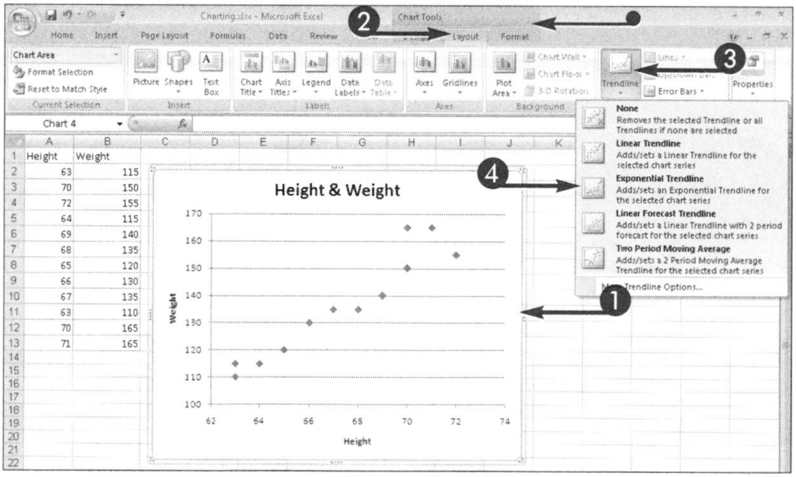

- Excel adds a trendline to the chart.

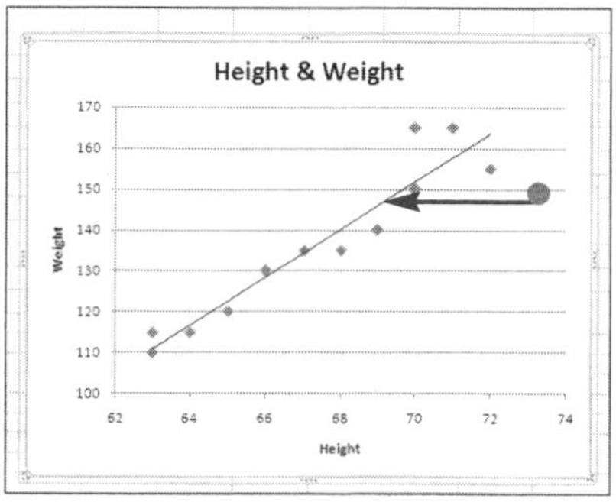

Format a Trendline

1. Click the trendline to select it.
   - The tabs associated with Chart Tools appear.
2. Click the Layout tab.
3. Click Trendline.
4. Click More Trendline Options.

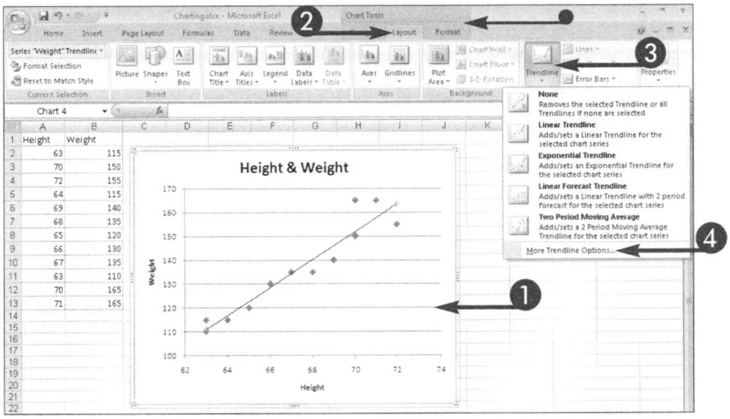

The Format Trendline dialog box appears.

- The type of trendline you selected appears here.
- The options available depend on the type of trendline you select.

5. Set options as appropriate.
6. Click Close to save your settings.

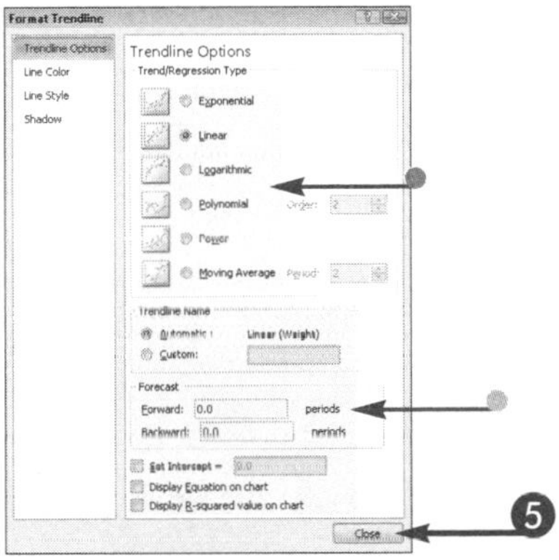

PART IV

MASTER IT

How do I select a trendline type?

▼ The data you chart drives the decision. The linear trendline is a straight line, while the exponential, logarithmic, polynomial, and power trendlines are all curved lines, and the moving average trendline smooths out widely varied data points. The trendline you choose should match your data; watch the R-squared values to help assess the reliability of the trendline.

How can I determine the R-squared value?

▼ You can display it on the chart. In the Format Trendline dialog box, click Display R-squared Value On Chart.

What does the Set Intercept option do?

▼ This option is available for exponential, linear, or polynomial trendlines. You can use the Set Intercept option to identify the point on the vertical axis where you want the trendline to cross the axis.

What does Display Equation On Chart do?

▼ To produce each type of trendline, Excel uses a different equation. Select this option to display the equation Excel uses to calculate and display the type of trendline you select.

How do I remove a trendline?

▼ Click the trendline to select it. Click the Layout tab, and then click Trendline. From the drop-down menu, click None.

Add Line Markers on a Chart

You can add lines to a chart to make reading the chart easier. The types of lines you can add to a chart depend on the type of chart you set up. In general, you cannot add lines to pie or doughnut charts or to 3-D column or bar charts. You can add lines to 2-D stacked bar or column charts, and 2-D or 3-D area or line charts. To add some types of lines, the chart must contain at least two data series.

You can use series lines on 2-D stacked bar or column charts. Series lines connect the various series on the chart and help the reader's eyes to focus on the trends of one particular data series on a stacked chart.

Drop lines are available on 2-D or 3-D area or line charts. You use drop lines to connect the data point with the horizontal axis, helping the reader to line up data points with the horizontal axis.

High-low lines are available on 2-D line charts with multiple data series, and appear by default on stock charts. High-low lines connect the highest and lowest values in each data series.

Add Line Markers on a Chart

Add Series Lines

1. Click the chart to select it.
   - The tabs associated with Chart Tools appear.
2. Click the Layout tab.
3. Click Lines.
4. Click Series Lines.

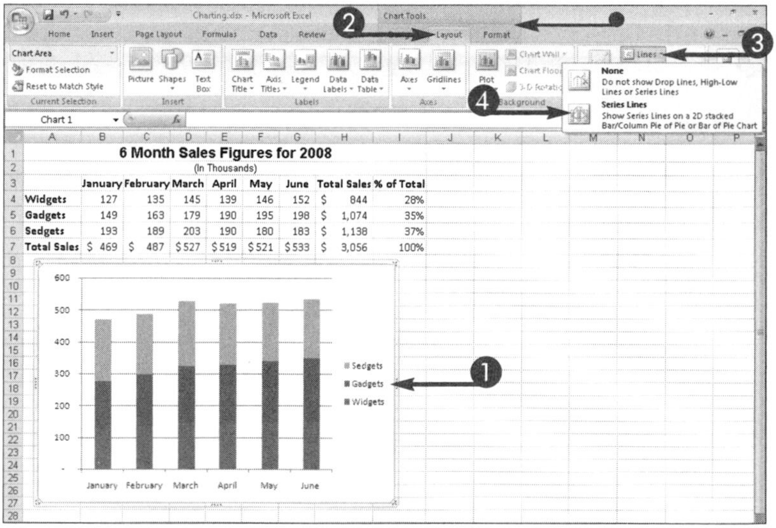

- Excel adds lines that connect the data series.

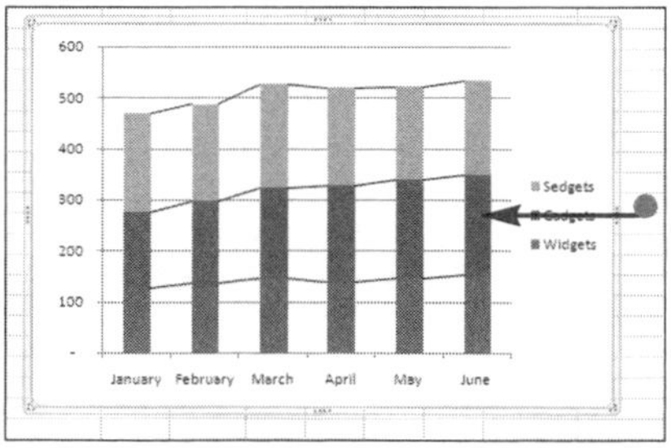

Add Drop or High-Low Lines

1. Click the chart to select it.
   - The tabs associated with Chart Tools appear.
2. Click the Layout tab.
3. Click Lines.
4. Click the type of lines you want to add.

Note: *This example adds drop lines.*

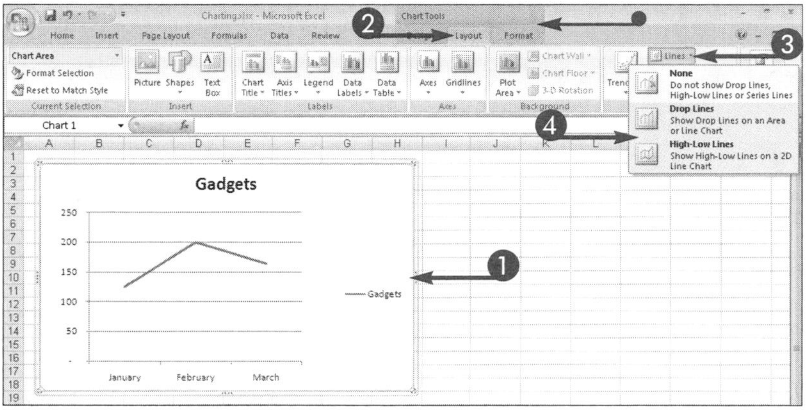

- Excel adds lines to the chart.

Note: *Drop lines extend from each data point to the horizontal axis, while high-low lines connect the highest and lowest values in each data series.*

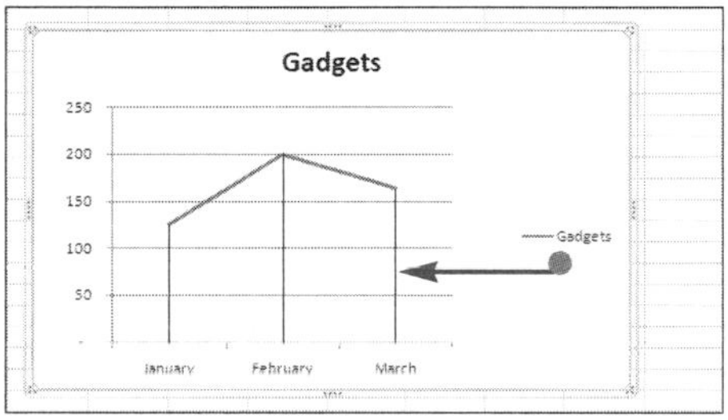

MASTER IT

How do I remove lines if I change my mind?

▼ Click the chart to select it. The tabs associated with Chart Tools appear. Click the Layout tab and then click Lines. From the drop-down menu that appears, click None. Excel removes the lines from the chart. If you decide immediately after adding lines that you want to remove them, click [undo].

Can I format lines?

▼ Yes, you can. Click any line on the chart to select all of the lines. Then, click the Layout tab and click Format Selection. The Format dialog box appears for that specific line type. You can control the color and thickness of the line as well as whether it is solid, dotted, or dashed. You can also can add a shadow to the line.

I tried to add high-low lines to a line chart, but nothing happened. Why?

▼ You probably tried to add high-low lines to a line chart containing only one data series. To display high-low lines, your chart must contain at least two data series, because high-low lines connect the highest and lows data points in each data series.

Add Bars to Charts

You can add bars to charts to help clarify chart information. You can add up/down bars to charts to help the reader identify the difference between data points in the first data series and the last data series. By default, up/down bars appear on stock charts, such as the Open-High-Low-Close chart and the Volume-Open-High-Low-Close chart. Up/down bars are available only on 2-D line charts with multiple data series.

You can also add error bars to a 2-D line, area, bar, column, XY, or bubble chart with single or multiple data series. Error bars help identify a degree of uncertainty — potential error — in the data points. You can specify the error amount using a standard error, a percentage, a standard deviation, a fixed value, or a custom amount. If you display error bars with a standard error or a standard deviation, Excel uses pre-established formulas to calculate and display the error bars. If you display error bars with a percentage, a fixed value, or a custom amount, you can define the error amount. You can also format the appearance of error bars.

Add Bars to Charts

Add Up/Down Bars

1. Click the chart to select it.
   - The tabs associated with Chart Tools appear.
2. Click the Layout tab.
3. Click Up/Down Bars.
4. Click Up/Down Bars.

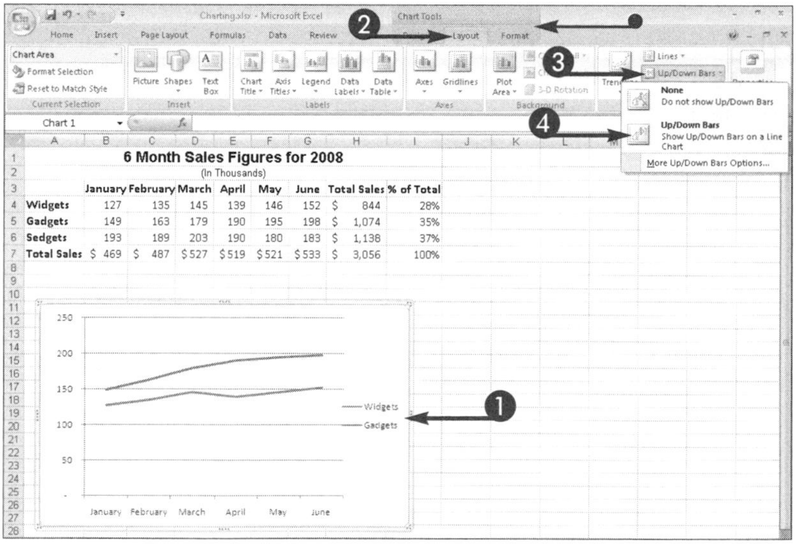

- Excel adds up/down bars that connect the data series.

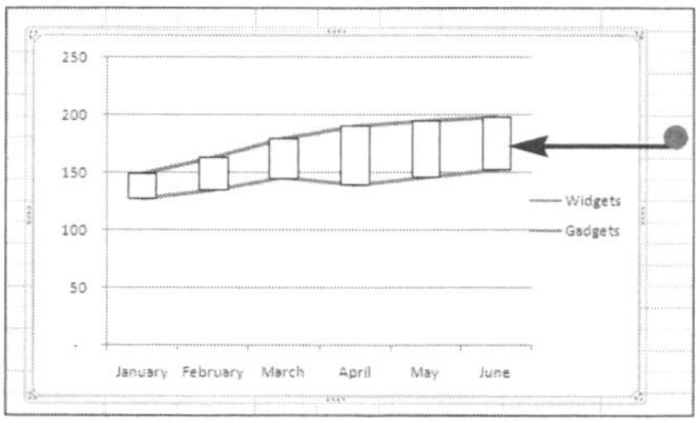

Add Error Bars

1. Click the chart to select it.
   - The tabs associated with Chart Tools appear.
2. Click the Layout tab.
3. Click Error Bars.
4. Click the type of error bars you want to add.

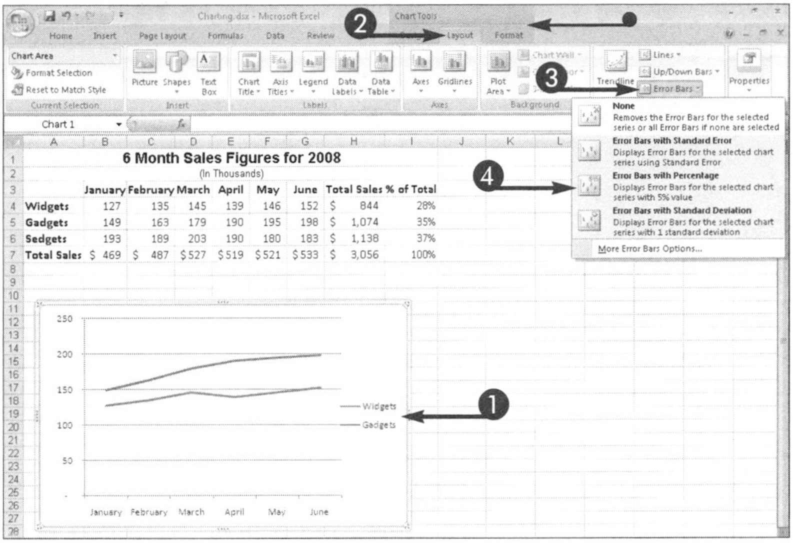

- Excel adds error bars to the data series.

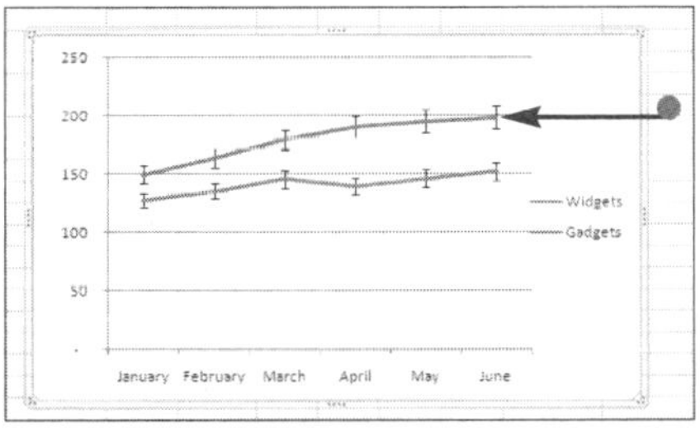

PART IV

MASTER IT

What is the default percentage Excel uses when I select Error Bars with Percentage, and how do I change it?

▼ Excel uses 5 percent. You can change the percentage by clicking any error bar to select the error bars. Then, on the Layout tab, click Error Bars and click More Error Bars Options. In the Format Error Bars dialog box that appears, beside the Percentage option that is already selected, change the value.

Can I format up/down bars?

▼ Yes. You can fill them with a color or a texture, and you can assign a border color. You can determine the thickness of the border line and whether it appears as a solid line, a dashed line, or a dotted line. You can also add a shadow and a bevel to an up/down bar. Click an up/down bar to select all of them. Then, on the Layout tab, click Up/Down Bars and click More Up/Down Bars Options.

Can I control the appearance of error bars?

▼ Yes. You can control whether error bars appear above, below, or in both directions on data points. You can also control whether caps — small perpendicular lines — appear on the ends of error bars. You can control the line color, width, and style of error bars from the Format Error Bars dialog box. Click an error bar to select it. Then, on the Layout tab, click Error Bars and click More Error Bars Options.

Set Chart Element Shape Styles

You can format the shape of any chart element using shape styles. Shape styles are combinations of different formatting options that you can apply to the chart area of any chart or to any individual element of your chart, including the data series. Shape styles apply predefined combinations of border edges, line styles, solid and gradient fills, and 3-D perspectives to the selected chart element. Using shape styles, you can quickly and easily create a professional-looking chart.

As you work with shape styles, Excel 2007's Live Preview feature helps you try different combinations of shape styles and colors until you find one that you feel effectively conveys your message. When you open the Shape Styles Gallery and move your mouse over a shape style, Excel displays the effect that applying the shape style will have on your chart if you select the style.

If you apply a shape style to the chart area of your chart and then change the chart type, Excel applies the shape style to the new chart type. That way, your chart retains formatting that you apply, even if you change the chart type.

Set Chart Element Shape Styles

1. Click the chart or chart element to which you want to apply a shape style.

Note: This example applies the shape style to the chart area.

- The tabs associated with Chart Tools appear.

2. Click the Format tab.
3. Click here.

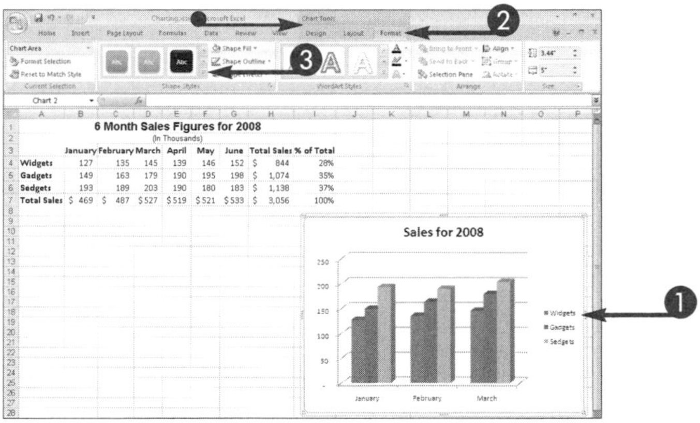

- Excel displays the shape styles that are available to you.

4. Move your mouse pointer over a shape style, but do not click.
   - The Live Preview feature temporarily applies the shape style to the chart element you selected in Step 1 so that you can preview its effect.
5. Click a shape style.

Excel applies the shape style to the selected element.

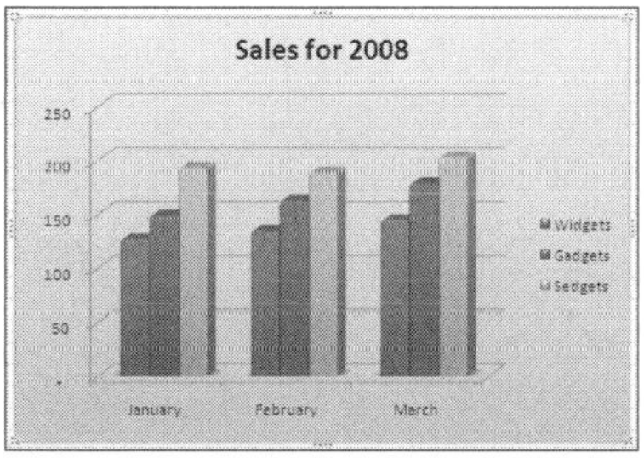

MASTER IT

After I select a shape style, what do I do if I want to remove it?

▼ If you decide to remove the shape style immediately or shortly after you apply it, you can click [undo] to remove it. If you do not click [undo] immediately after applying the shape style, Excel undoes all actions you have taken since applying the shape style, starting from the last action. If you have done a lot of work to your chart that you do not want to undo, select the element to which you applied the shape style, click the Format tab under Chart Tools, and then click Reset to Match Selection to return the selected chart element to its default appearance.

Does Excel fill the plot area and the chart area when you select the chart?

▼ Sometimes, typically for 3-D chart types, Excel does fill both the plot area and the chart area. For 2-D line charts, Excel often fills only the chart area and not the plot area, but you can fill the plot area by selecting it and applying the same shape style to it.

Does the Live Preview feature work on all charts?

▼ No. Live Preview is not available when you try to apply a shape style to a chart stored in its own chart sheet. Live Preview does work on embedded charts.

Set Fill Colors for Chart Element Shapes

You can apply a shape fill color or texture to any chart element you select. Shape fill colors and textures override any other colors you may have applied to a chart element, including those colors associated with shape styles. You can apply a shape fill color or texture to the chart area of any chart or to any individual element of your chart, including the data series. When you apply a shape fill, you can apply a solid color or choose from a variety of gradient fill colors or textures. Using shape fill colors and textures, you can quickly and easily create a professional-looking chart.

As you work with shape fill colors and textures, the Excel 2007 Live Preview feature helps you try different combinations of shape fill colors or textures until you find one that you feel effectively conveys your message. When you open the Shape Fill Gallery and move your mouse over a shape fill color or texture, Excel displays the effects that applying the shape fill will have on your chart if you select the shape fill.

Set Fill Colors for Chart Element Shapes

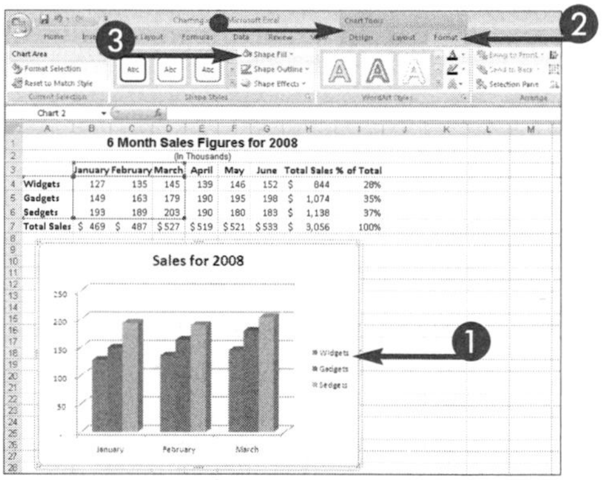

1. Click the chart or chart element to which you want to apply a shape fill.

Note: This example applies a shape fill texture to the chart area.

- The tabs associated with Chart Tools appear.

2. Click the Format tab.
3. Click Shape Fill.

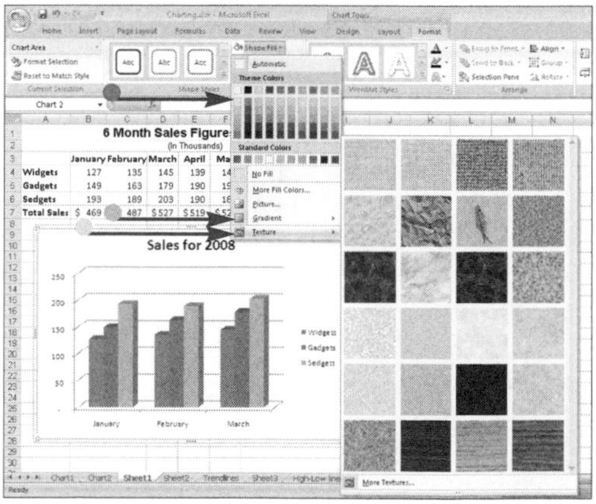

- Excel displays the shape fill colors that are available to you.
- To see fill color gradients, you can click here.
- To see fill textures, you can click here.

4 Move your mouse pointer over a shape fill, but do not click.

- The Live Preview feature temporarily applies the shape fill to the chart element you selected in Step 1 so that you can preview its effect.

5 Click a shape fill.

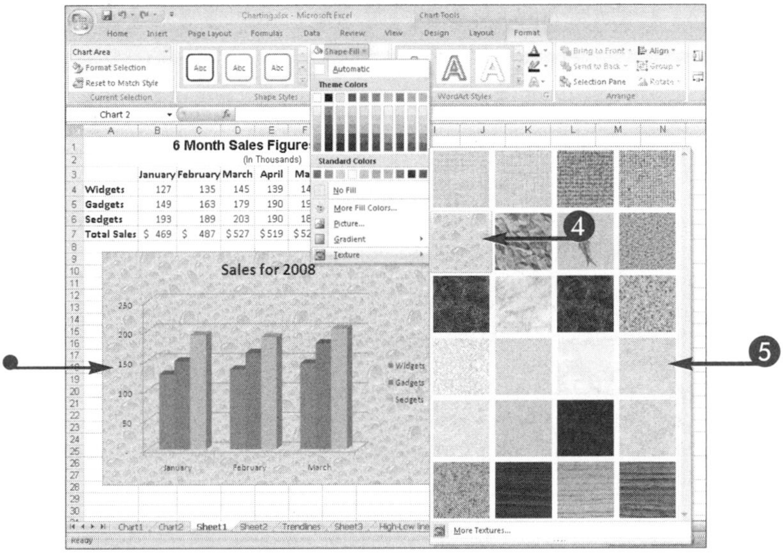

Excel applies the shape fill to the selected element.

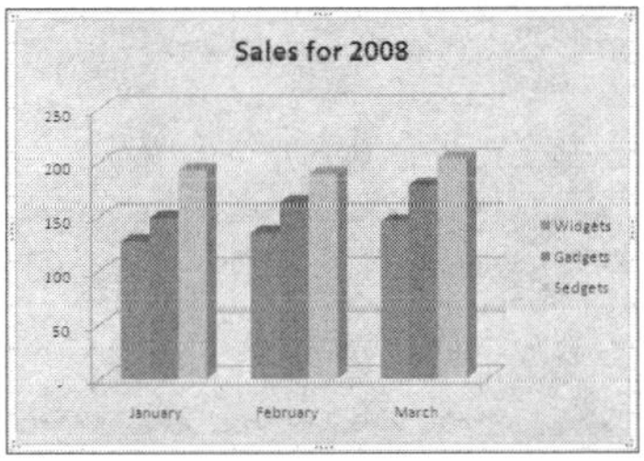

PART IV

MASTER IT

If I want to change the colors of all of the data series, can I change them all simultaneously?

▼ No. You cannot select all of the data series at the same time, and further, it would not make sense to select them and change their colors simultaneously because you would make all data series the same color. You must select them separately and change their colors.

Can I apply a shape style and a shape fill?

▼ In a way, yes. By applying both a fill color and a shape style, you effectively change the color of the shape style. If the shape style includes a border, applying a shape fill has no effect on the border. The order in which you apply them determines whether the shape style or the shape fill takes precedence. The last format you apply is the one Excel displays.

What happens if I apply a gradient fill?

▼ Excel applies the gradient based on the fill color applied to the chart element. So, for a gradient fill to appear, you must first apply a fill color, by either applying a shape style or by completing the steps in this section twice — once to apply a fill color from the theme colors that appear after you complete Step 3, and once more to apply the gradient.

Set the Shape Outline for a Chart Element

You can apply a shape outline to any chart element you select. When you apply a shape outline to a chart element, you can select a color and a weight for the outline, and you can define the appearance of the line Excel uses for the outline. Any shape outline you apply overrides any other outline characteristics you may have applied to a chart element, including those associated with shape styles. You can apply a shape outline to the chart area of any chart or to any individual element of your chart, including the data series. Using shape outlines can help delineate various chart elements, helping you to quickly and easily create a professional-looking chart.

As you work with shape outlines, the Excel 2007 Live Preview feature helps you try different combinations of shape outline colors until you find one that you feel effectively conveys your message. When you open the Shape Outline Gallery and move your mouse over a shape outline color, Excel displays the effects that applying the shape outline color will have on your chart if you select the shape outline. Live Preview does not display the various line types and weights; you must select those to view their effects.

Set the Shape Outline for a Chart Element

Outline a Chart Element

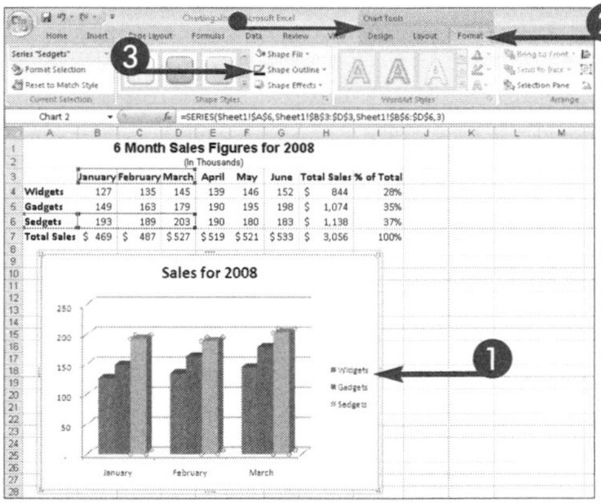

1. Click the chart or chart element to which you want to apply a shape outline.

Note: *This example applies a shape outline to one data series.*

- The tabs associated with Chart Tools appear.

2. Click the Format tab.
3. Click Shape Outline.

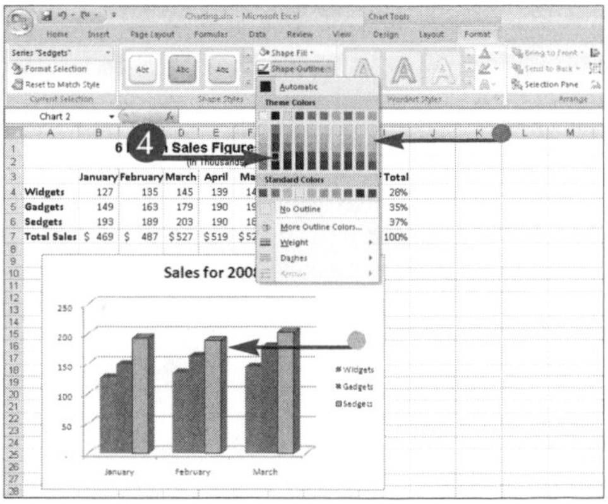

- Excel displays the shape outline colors that are available to you.

Note: *You can point the mouse at a color to preview the selected chart element outlined in that color.*

4. Click a color.

- Excel applies the outline color to the selected chart element.

Set the Outline Weight

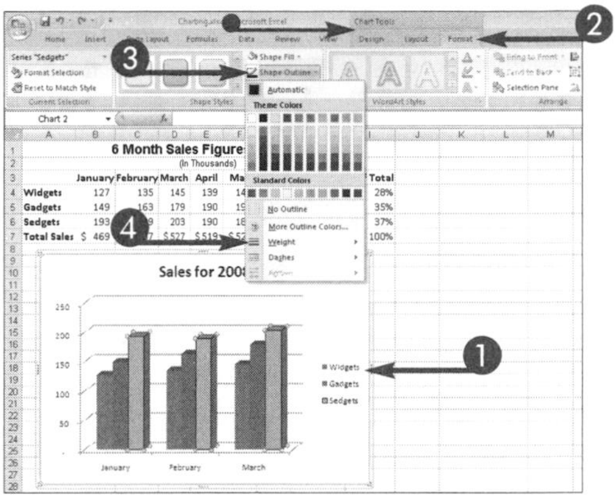

❶ Click a chart element with an outline.

Note: *This example applies the outline weight to one data series.*

- The tabs associated with Chart Tools appear.

❷ Click the Format tab.

❸ Click Shape Outline.

❹ Click Weight.

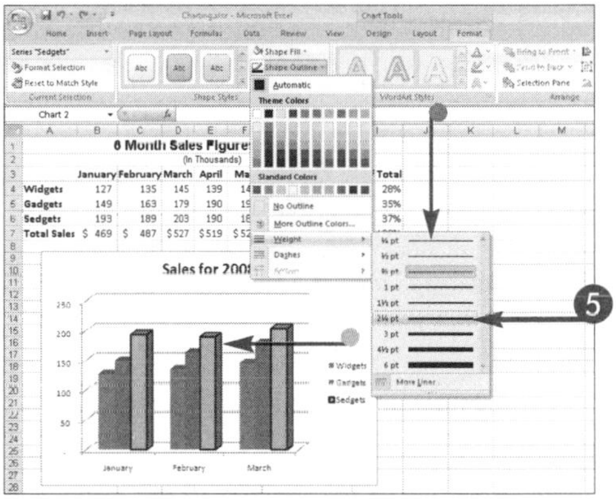

- Excel displays the line weights that are available for the chart element outline.

Note: *You can point the mouse at a line weight to preview how the selected chart element will appear using that line weight.*

❺ Click a line weight.

- Excel applies the shape fill to the selected element.

MASTER IT

Can I control the appearance of the outline?

▼ Depending on the chart element, yes. Click the chart shape containing the outline and then click the Format tab under Chart Tools. Click Shape Outline and click Dashes. Excel displays a variety of different types of dashed and dotted lines that you can use to outline the selected shape.

For what chart elements can I control the appearance of the outline?

▼ You can control the appearance of the chart area outline, the legend outline, the outlines of the vertical and horizontal axis titles, and the chart title. You cannot control the appearance of the outline for a data series, the vertical and horizontal axes, or the plot area.

Can I apply the same outline to all data series simultaneously?

▼ No, because you cannot select all data series simultaneously. Select each data series and apply an outline using the steps in this section. To apply the same outline to other data series, select those data series and follow the steps again.

Set Shape Effects for Chart Elements

You can apply a shape effect to a chart or selected chart elements. When used well, chart effects add artistic interest to your chart. You typically add shape effects to the entire chart rather than individual chart elements, but you can add some shape effects to some elements.

You can add a shadow or a bevel to a chart, or you can apply a 3-D rotation effect to turn the chart in varying directions.

You can add a glow to the chart, which adds a fuzzy color to the edge of the chart; glows are available in preset pastel colors, but you can select any color for a glow. You can also determine the size of the glow effect that Excel applies to your chart.

You can add a soft edge to your chart; a soft edge fades the outside edge of the chart so that the edge appears transparent. For example, when you apply a soft edge to an embedded chart, the gridlines from cells appear as if they are inside the chart. When you apply a soft edge to a chart, you can determine the size of the soft edge that Excel applies.

Set Shape Effects for Chart Elements

Apply a Glow

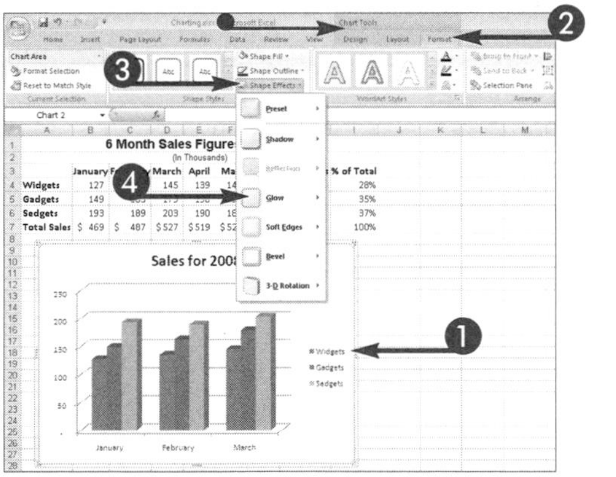

1. Click the chart or chart element to which you want to apply a shape outline.

Note: This example applies a glow to the chart.

- The tabs associated with Chart Tools appear.

2. Click the Format tab.
3. Click Shape Effects.
4. Click Glow.

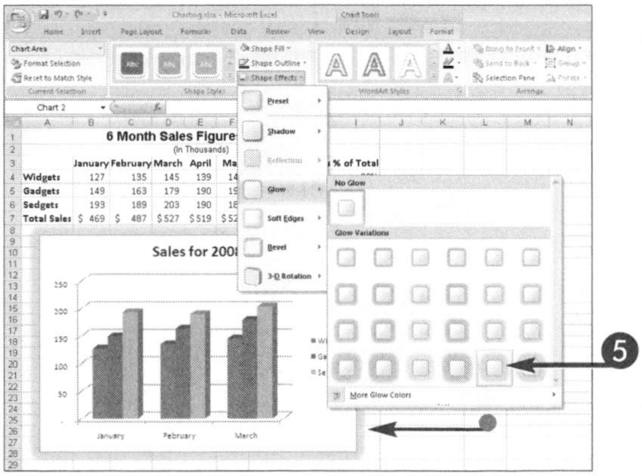

Excel displays the glow options that are available to you.

Note: You can point the mouse at a glow to preview the selected chart element outlined in that color.

5. Click a glow.

- Excel applies the glow to the selected chart element.

Apply a Soft Edge

1. Click the chart or chart element to which you want to apply a soft edge.

Note: *This example applies a soft edge to the chart.*

- The tabs associated with Chart Tools appear.

2. Click the Format tab.
3. Click Shape Effects.
4. Click Soft Edge.

Excel displays the soft edge options that are available to you.

Note: *You can point the mouse at a soft edge to preview the selected chart element using that soft edge.*

5. Click a soft edge.

- Excel applies the soft edge to the selected chart element.

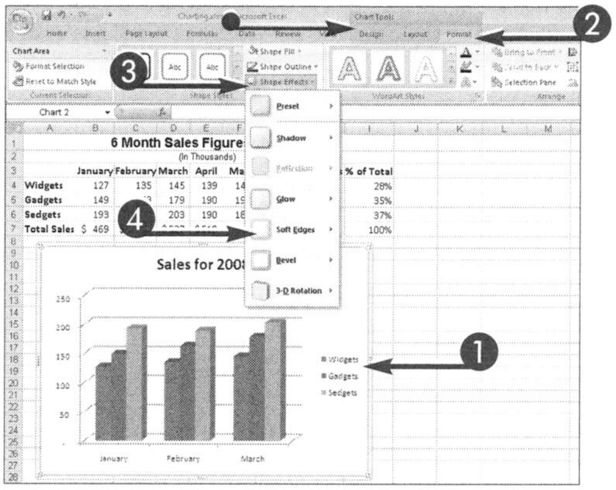

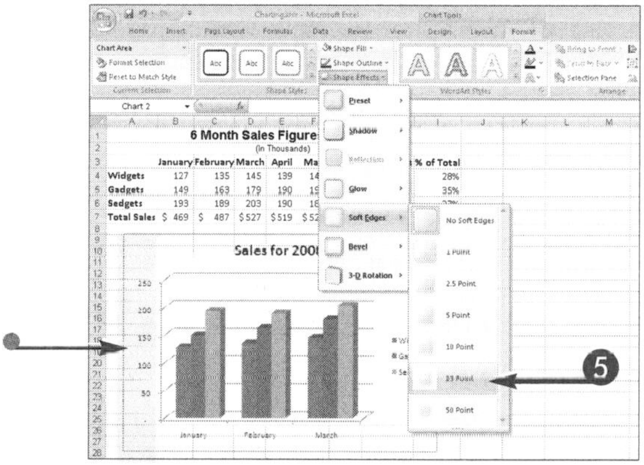

MASTER IT

To which parts of a chart can I apply shape effects?

▼ Most shape effects are available only for the entire chart. You can apply any preset except for a reflection to the chart. Reflections are not available for any chart elements. Glows and soft edges are not available for data series, chart walls, the chart floor, and the plot area. You also cannot apply a bevel to the plot area. And, although some shape effects appear to be available for other chart elements, applying them seems to have no effect.

What is a Preset shape effect?

▼ A Preset shape effect is a predefined combination of bevels, shadows, and 3-D rotations. Using a preset saves time because you can apply all three shape effects simultaneously. To apply a Preset shape effect, select the chart and then click the Format tab under Chart Tools. Click Shape Effects and click Preset. Excel displays the 12 available Preset shape effects. Click one to apply it.

Can I apply a shape effect to a chart in a chart sheet?

▼ Yes, but, because most of the shape effects apply to the actual chart, you may not be able to see the shape effect on a chart stored in a chart sheet. For example, you can apply a shadow to a chart stored in a chart sheet, but you will not see any change. If you move the chart sheet to a worksheet, you can see the effect.

Copy Chart Formatting

You can copy chart formatting from one chart to another. Suppose that you need to create two charts and you want to apply the same formatting to both charts. If you expend a great deal of effort setting up the first chart, you can save a lot of time if you copy the formatting from the first chart to the second chart instead of reapplying the same formatting to the second chart.

To copy chart formatting, you create the first chart and apply all of the formatting, design, and layout elements that you want to the chart, using the techniques described in this chapter and in Chapters 19 and 20. Then, you create the second chart, but do not format it. You can create the second chart in the same worksheet, a different worksheet, a chart sheet, or a different workbook. Then, you use the technique described in this section to copy the elements of the first chart to the second chart.

If you have several charts to create that should use the same chart design, layout, and formatting elements, you can create a chart template, which may be faster for you than copying chart formatting. See Chapter 19 for details on creating a chart template.

Copy Chart Formatting

1. Create a chart that contains all of the design, layout, and formatting elements you want to copy.

Note: *This example copies into the same worksheet.*

2. Create a second chart.
3. Click the first chart to select it.
4. Click the Home tab.
5. Click [copy icon].

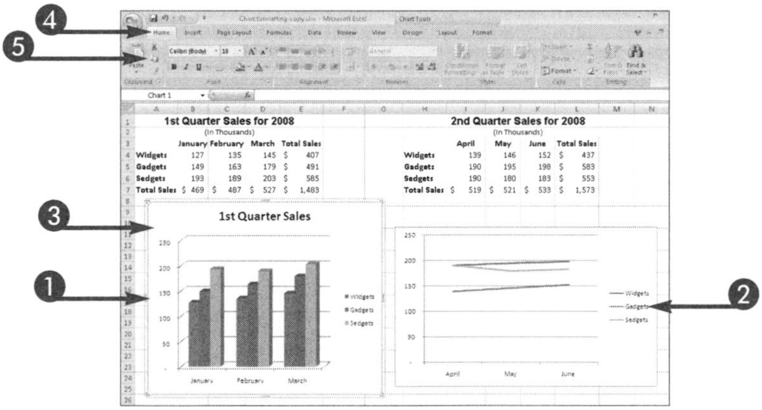

6. Click the other chart to select it.
7. Click [▾] below Paste.
8. Click Paste Special.

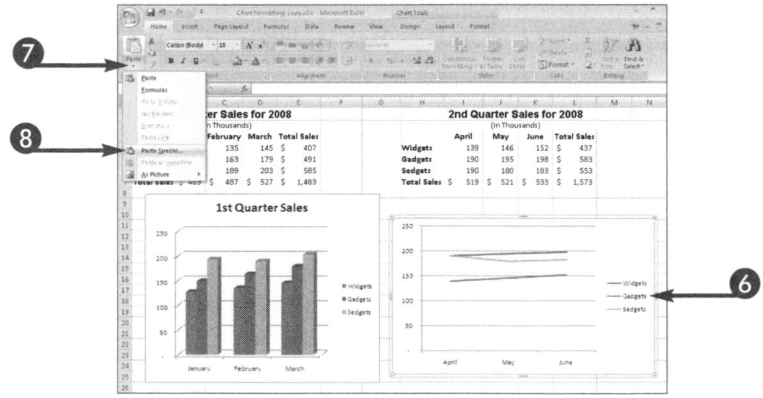

The Paste Special dialog box appears.

9 Click Formats (◎ changes to ◉).

10 Click OK.

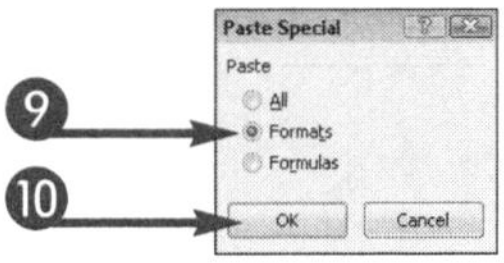

- Excel applies all of the design, layout, and formatting elements of the first chart to the second chart.
- The second chart retains its data series.

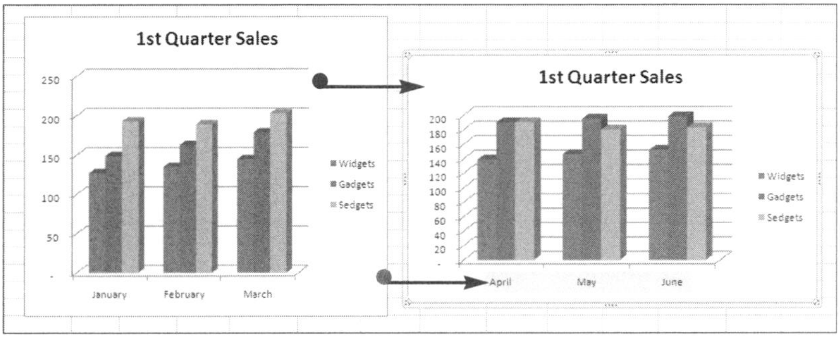

MASTER IT

What is the difference between copying formatting and creating a chart template?

▼ When you create a chart template, you save a model that contains all of the chart design, layout, and formatting elements that you want to use. When you create a new chart, you can select your chart template as the chart type. When you copy formatting, you must first create a model and, although you can save the model in the worksheet, you cannot base another chart on it. Instead, you need to open the workbook containing the chart to copy its design, layout, and formatting to another chart.

Can I simply copy and paste the first chart without creating the second chart?

▼ Yes, but the copy-and-paste operation works a little differently and, after you finish the operation, you need to change the data used in the chart. This is because Excel copies the actual chart, including the data series, instead of copying just the chart design, layout, and formatting. Copy the first chart as described in this section. Then, to paste an exact copy, click an empty cell, press and hold Ctrl, and click Paste (do not click ▾ below Paste). The Paste Special dialog box does not appear; instead, a duplicate appears of the chart that you copied. To change the data series, see Chapter 19.

PART IV

Understanding Graphic Elements

Excel contains graphic elements that you can use to help convey your meaning and enhance the appearance of a worksheet or a chart. You can create graphic elements from the Shapes Gallery or with the SmartArt, Text Box, and WordArt buttons on the Insert tab of the Ribbon. You can also import graphics created by others using the Picture and Clip Art buttons, and insert symbols such as the symbol for *pi*, the copyright symbol (©), and the trademark symbol (™).

Shapes include predefined lines, rectangles, block arrows, mathematical symbols, flowchart symbols, stars and banners, and callout markings, along with a variety of basic objects such as triangles, slanted rectangles, and hearts.

SmartArt graphics are predefined layouts that you can use to describe relationships. For example, you can use a SmartArt graphic to create a company organization chart or a flow chart that describes a process.

Text boxes allow you to annotate a worksheet or chart with information that is not stored in a worksheet cell or chart element. You might, for example, use a text box to add a comment to a chart that points out some distinguishing information shown on the chart.

Using WordArt, you can insert decorative text that is stretched, shadowed, rotated, or skewed on a worksheet or in a chart. You can also insert decorative text that has been predefined to fit into a particular shape.

Pictures are photographs stored in digital form. Clip Art refers to pre-drawn images that you can use to help you illustrate a point.

All graphic elements are discrete elements in the worksheet that you can select, and you select graphics so that you can operate on them in some way, such as reshaping, resizing, or moving them. Although there are many different types of graphic objects, you operate on all of them using the same basic techniques.

To select a graphic element, you simply click it, and white sizing handles, circular and square, appear around the perimeter of the graphic. If the graphic can be rotated, a green circular rotation handle also appears at the top of the graphic, connected to a sizing handle. On some drawn elements (especially 3-D ones), yellow diamond-shaped handles also appear at the places where you can manipulate some part of the element's shape.

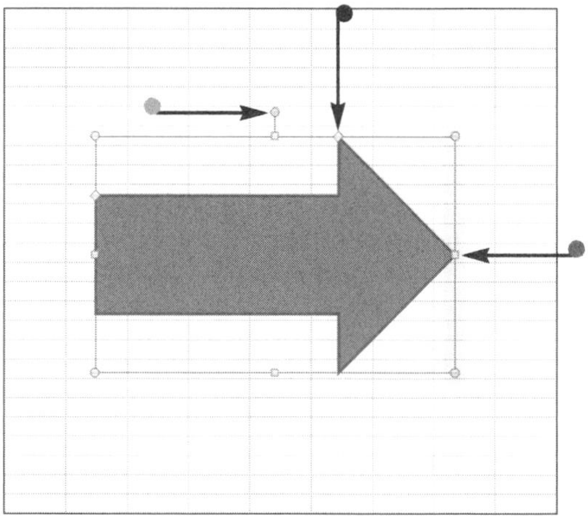

You can select more than one graphic element at the same time in the worksheet by pressing and holding the Shift key or Ctrl key as you click each element. When you select more than one element, any changes you make to one element affect all of the selected elements.

Excel stores each graphic you add to a worksheet on different invisible layers that reside on top of the worksheet and over the worksheet data in the cells below. If you move a graphic element over a cell that contains an entry, the graphic hides the data beneath it. And, if you position one graphic element on top of another graphic element, the graphic element on top covers up the graphic element below.

Excel makes it easy to move the graphic elements on the same worksheet to other layers using the Selection and Visibility task pane, which appears on the right side of the program window. Graphic elements appear ordered in the list; elements appearing at the top of the list obscure elements below if they overlap. See the section, "Position Graphic Elements," for details.

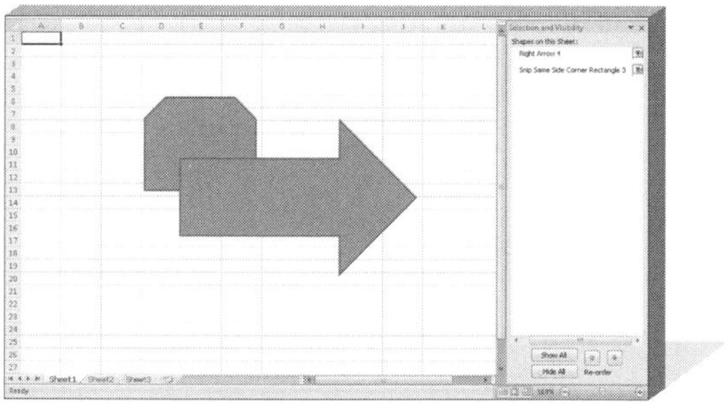

When you are dealing with two graphic elements, one on top of the other, Excel enables you to align them in a variety of ways. And, when you need to work with more than one graphic element at the same time to move, resize, or rotate them, you can make it a lot simpler by grouping these elements. When you select more than one individual graphic element, Excel displays handles around each individual element.

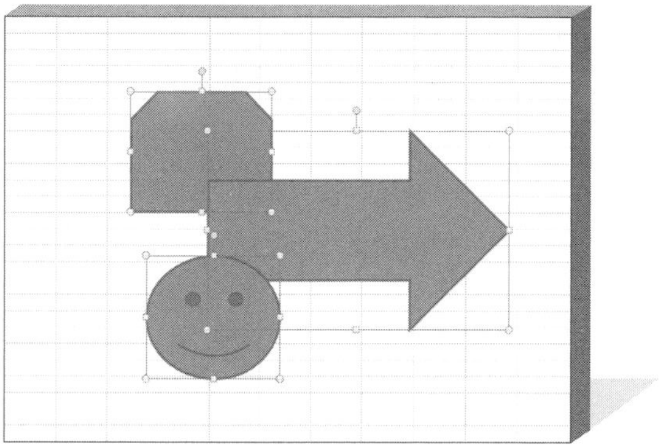

When you group graphic elements, Excel treats them as a single graphic element, so that you can move, size, or rotate all of them simultaneously. When you select a grouped graphic element, Excel displays handles around the group rather than around each individual element.

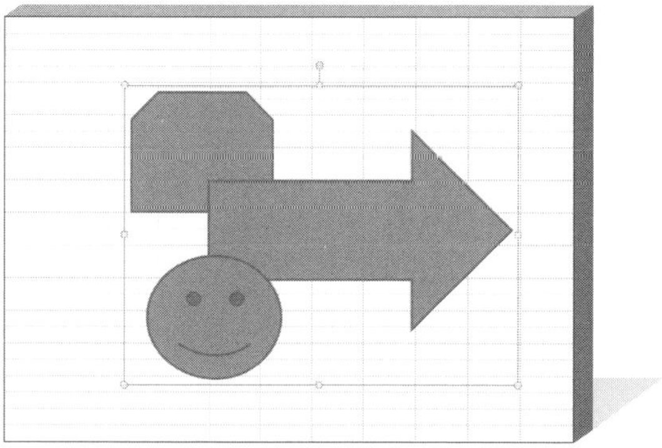

If you no longer want to work with the graphic elements as a group, you can reverse the action to separate them into independent elements once again. For details on aligning and grouping graphic elements, see the section, "Align Graphic Elements."

Include a Shape in a Worksheet

You can include a pre-defined shape in a worksheet or on a chart. Adding a shape is a fast and easy way to increase interest or to draw attention to some pertinent details of the worksheet or chart. For example, you might want to add an arrow to a chart to point at an important data series element on the chart. Or, you might want to add an arrow that points in two directions in a worksheet to demonstrate a connection between the information contained in two cells that you want the reader to notice.

Excel organizes shapes into different categories, including Lines, Rectangles, Basic Shapes, Block Arrows, Equation Shapes, Flowchart, Stars and Banners, and Callouts. Most of the categories are self-explanatory, but the Basic Shapes category contains unusual shapes such as moons, clouds, and cylinders.

When you add a shape to a worksheet, Excel lets you specify the location and size of the shape as you create it. You can later move and resize the shape or, if you later decide you do not need the shape, you can delete it.

Include a Shape in a Worksheet

1. Click the Insert tab.
2. Click Shapes.

   The gallery of available shapes appears.
3. Click a shape.

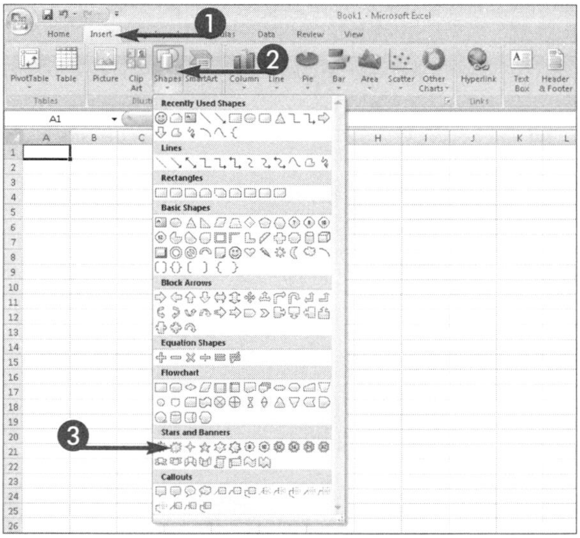

- The mouse pointer changes to +.

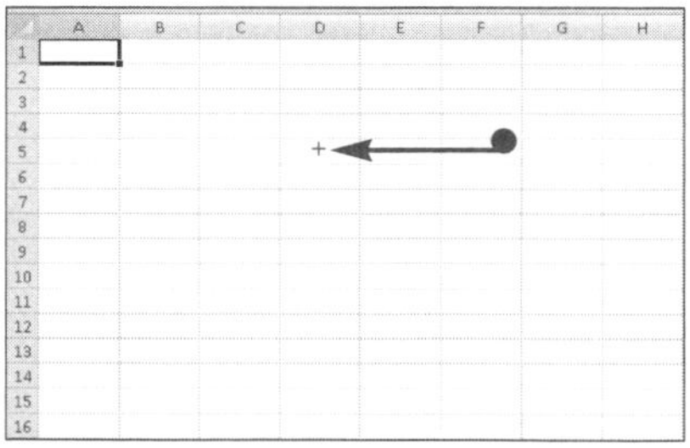

4. Position the mouse pointer at the location where the upper-left corner of the shape should appear.
5. Drag down and to the right.
   - The shape begins to appear.

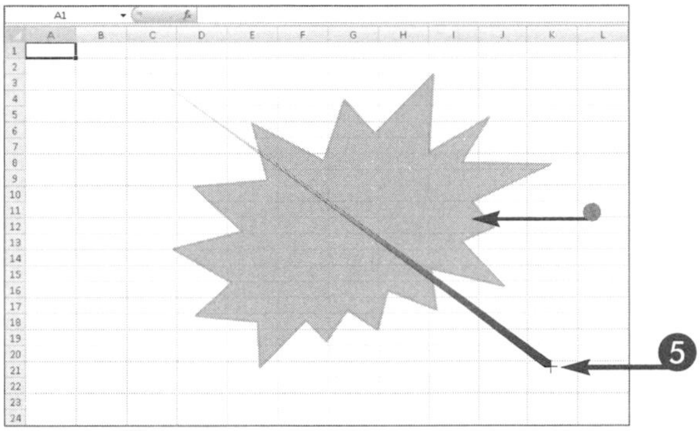

6. Release the mouse button when the shape is the size you want.
   - When you release the mouse button, Excel displays the shape.
   - Handles like these indicate that the shape is selected.
   - The Format tab under Drawing Tools becomes available. You can use these tools to modify the shape.

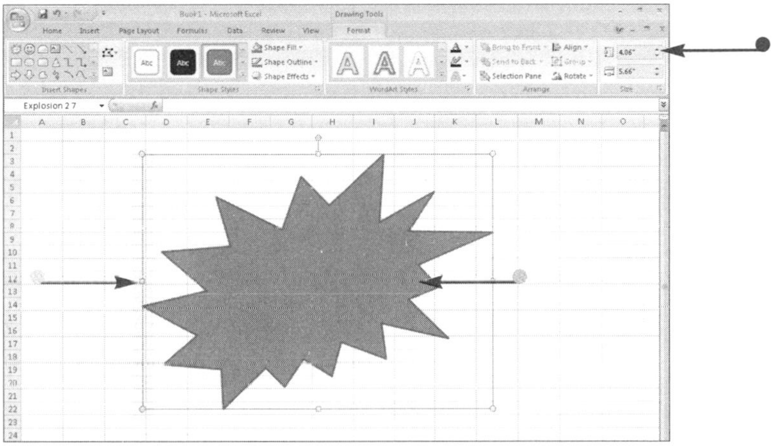

MASTER IT

Can I control the proportions of the shape as I draw it?

▼ Yes, you can. Complete Steps 1 to 3. Then press and hold the Shift key and complete Steps 4 to 6. After Step 6, release the Shift key. As long as you press and hold the Shift key while you draw, Excel does not permit the shape to become out of proportion.

Can I force a shape to fall within row or column borders?

▼ Yes, you can. Complete Steps 1 to 3. Then press and hold the Alt key and complete Steps 4 to 6. After Step 6, release the Alt key. As long as you press and hold the Alt key while you draw, Excel ensures that the shape fits within the gridlines shown for rows or columns. Note that you are not forcing the shape to appear within a single cell.

How can I insert text in a shape?

▼ For some shapes, you can click the shape and start typing. For other shapes, you need to add a text box to the shape to include text inside the shape. Excel displays the text box on top of the shape with a background of white surrounded by a thin outline. To make the text box transparent, apply the same fill color to the shape and the text box and remove the text box's outline, as described in the section, "Insert a Text Box."

Insert a Text Box

You can add a text box to a worksheet or chart to include additional information. For example, you can use a text box to add text to a shape.

Text boxes are useful for labeling shapes or adding comments to a worksheet or chart, to describe specific items in the worksheet or chart. When you draw a text box, Excel wraps any text you type in the box so that it automatically fits between the left and right sides of the box. If you draw a text box that is not long enough to accommodate the text, you need to resize the text box; otherwise, the text appears to spill outside the bottom boundary of the box. You can also insert a default-sized text box that expands to the right as you type, without wrapping text.

After you create a text box, you can move or resize it; for details, see the section, "Move or Resize a Graphic Element." If you decide that you no longer need a text box, you can delete it. When you delete a text box, Excel deletes the box and any text you entered in the box.

Insert a Text Box

1. Click the Insert tab.
2. Click Text Box.

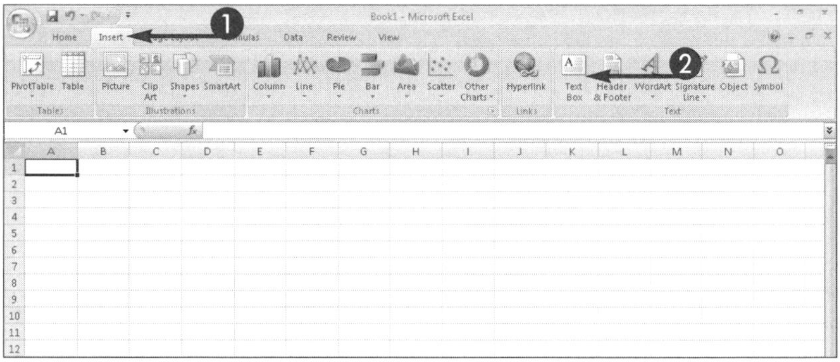

- The Text Box mouse pointer (↓) appears.

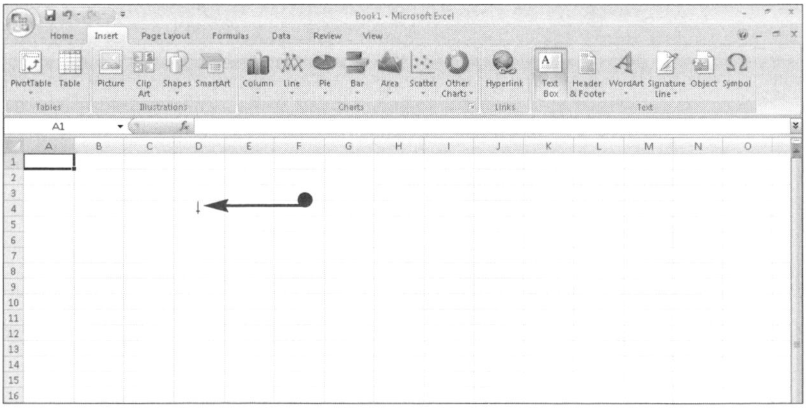

3. Position the mouse pointer at the location where the upper-left corner of the text box should appear.

4. Drag down and to the right.

   - The ↓ changes to +, and the text box begins to appear.

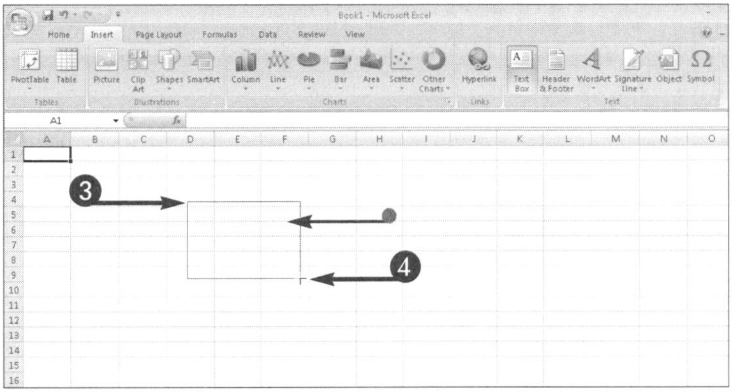

5. Release the mouse button when the text box is the size you want.

   - Excel displays the text box with an insertion point blinking inside.
   - Handles like these indicate that the text box is selected.
   - The Format tab under Drawing Tools becomes available. You can use these tools to modify the text box.

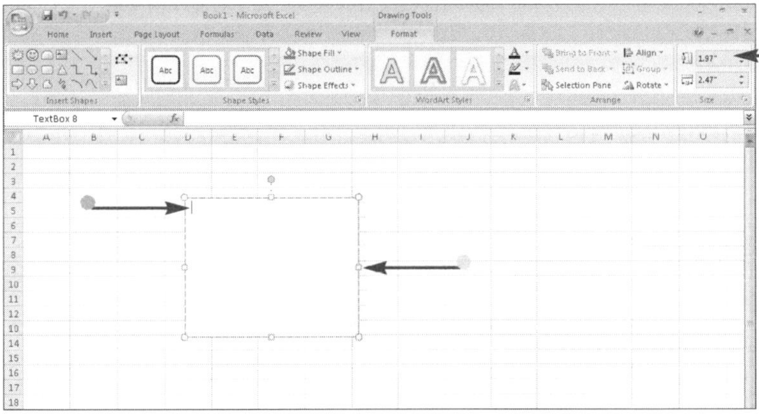

PART IV

MASTER IT

How do I remove the outline that appears around a text box?

▼ To remove the outline that appears around a text box, click the text box to select it; Excel displays white circular and square sizing handles around the text box. Click the Format tab under Drawing Tools and then click Shape Outline. Click No Outline from the drop-down list that appears.

How do I create a default-sized text box, and can I make it wrap text?

▼ To create a default-sized text box, complete the steps in this section but, in Step 4, do not drag. Instead, click. As you type in this box, it expands to the right. Type all of your text and then resize the text box to make the text wrap into the space you designate by the box's size.

How do I delete a text box if I do not want to use it any longer?

▼ Click the outside border of the text box; Excel displays sizing handles and, if rotation and sizing are available for the graphic, those handles also appear. The mouse pointer changes to ✣ when you move it over the text box border. Press the Delete key, and Excel removes the text box from your worksheet or chart.

Work with SmartArt

You can add a SmartArt graphic to your worksheet to provide a visual depiction of information or ideas. Like charts, SmartArt graphics provide a visual way to help a reader understand a point. Unlike charts, SmartArt graphics are not based on numeric data. Instead, they are pre-designed visual representations that can be used in a variety of situations. For example, you can create an organization chart or a process flow chart using different SmartArt graphics.

SmartArt graphics are available for the following categories: List, Process, Cycle, Hierarchy, Relationship, Matrix, and Pyramid. Most of the items available in the List category work best with non-sequential list information. You can use Process graphics to depict information that follows steps and Cycle graphics to depict information or events that flow in a circular fashion. Hierarchy graphics are often used to produce organizational charts, and Relationship graphics can show both hierarchical relationships and other types of relationships, such as converging ideas. Matrix graphics help show the relationship of quadrants to a whole, and Pyramid graphics show proportional relationships.

As you add text to SmartArt graphic shapes, Excel automatically adjusts the font size to fit the shape.

Work with SmartArt

Add SmartArt

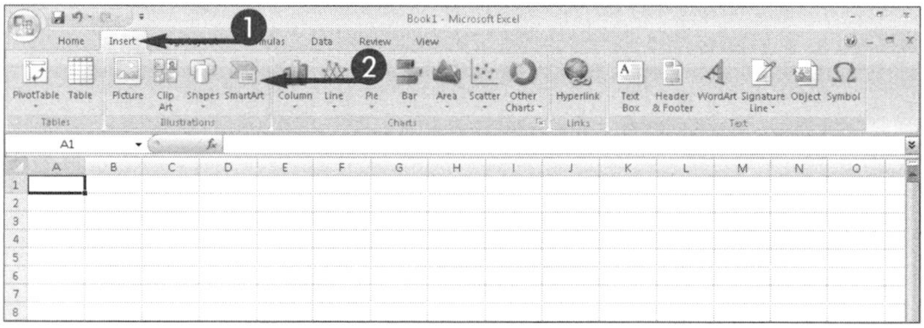

1. Click the Insert tab.
2. Click SmartArt.

The Choose a SmartArt Graphic dialog box appears.

- You can click a SmartArt Graphic category here.

3. Click a SmartArt Graphic shape.
4. Click OK.

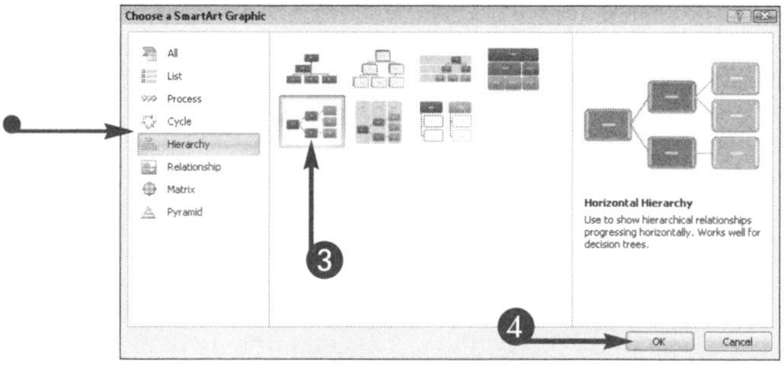

- The SmartArt graphic appears in your workbook.

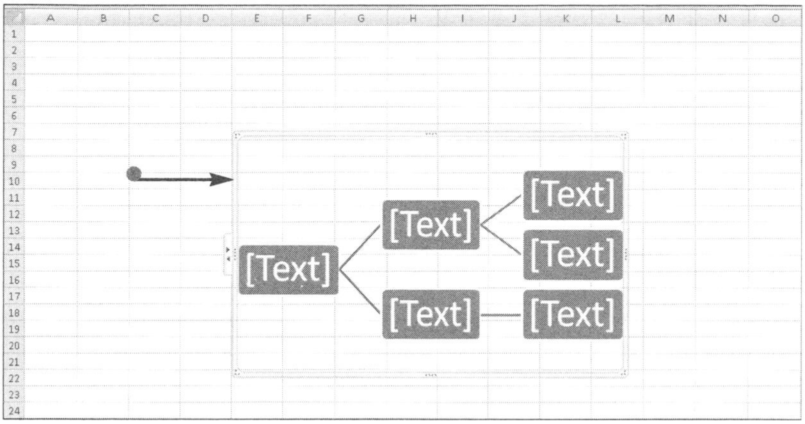

5. Click any box to select it.
   - An insertion point appears in the box.
6. Type the text you want in the box.
7. Click anywhere outside the box to store the text.
8. Repeat Steps 5 to 7 for each box in the SmartArt graphic.

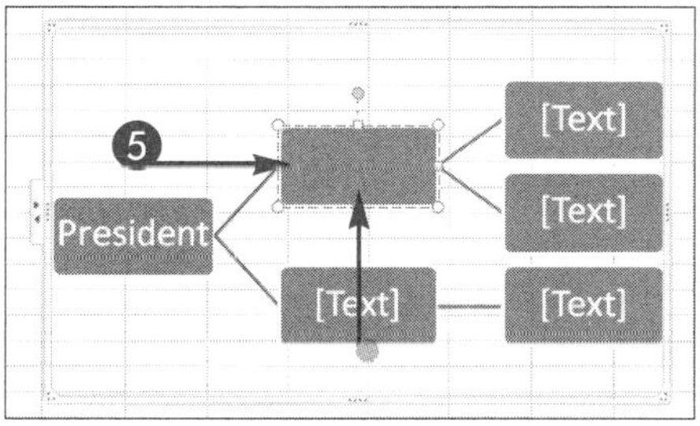

MASTER IT

Is there another way to enter text into the SmartArt graphic's shape?

▼ Yes, you can use the Text pane, a separate window that appears when you click Text pane on the Design tab under SmartArt Tools. Each shape in the graphic is represented in the Text pane as a bullet in outline format. Click a bullet and type; Excel displays the text in both the Text pane and the SmartArt graphic. Click the Text pane button again to hide the Text pane.

Can I type more than one line of text in a box?

▼ Yes, you can. If you simply type continuously, Excel automatically wraps the text you type to fit within the boundaries of the box, resizing the font as needed. If you want new text to appear on a new line, simply press Enter to start the new line and continue typing.

Can I make any changes to the layout of the SmartArt graphic?

▼ Yes, you can. After you insert the graphic, click it to select it and then click the Design tab under SmartArt Tools. At the left side of the Ribbon, buttons appear that control the layout; the buttons that are available depend on the SmartArt graphic. For example, you may be able to flip the graphic's layout from right to left, add bullets, or promote and demote shapes.

continued

Work with SmartArt *(Continued)*

Excel includes a default number of shapes in each SmartArt graphic, and the number of shapes you see depends on the SmartArt graphic you select. However, regardless of the number of shapes that appear, you can add or delete shapes as needed.

When you add a shape to a SmartArt graphic, Excel automatically adjusts the size of the other shapes in the SmartArt graphic to make the new shape proportionate to the other shapes in the graphic. If necessary, you can enlarge the entire SmartArt graphic; see the section, "Move or Resize a Graphic Element," for more details on resizing.

Excel adds a new shape to a SmartArt graphic in relation to another shape that is already part of the graphic. As a result, when adding a shape, you need to select an existing shape in the graphic that will eventually appear above, below, before, or after the new shape you add.

MASTER IT

How do I delete a shape?

- Click the outside border of the shape within the SmartArt graphic to select it; round and square white handles appear around the selected shape. Press the Delete key. Excel deletes the shape and adjusts the size of the remaining shapes to fill the SmartArt graphic boundary.

Work with SmartArt *(continued)*

Add Shapes

1. Click a shape that appears near the location where you want to add a shape.
2. Click the bottom of the Add Shape button.

   Excel displays a drop-down menu of shape placement choices.
3. Click the choice that describes where you want to position the new shape in the SmartArt graphic.

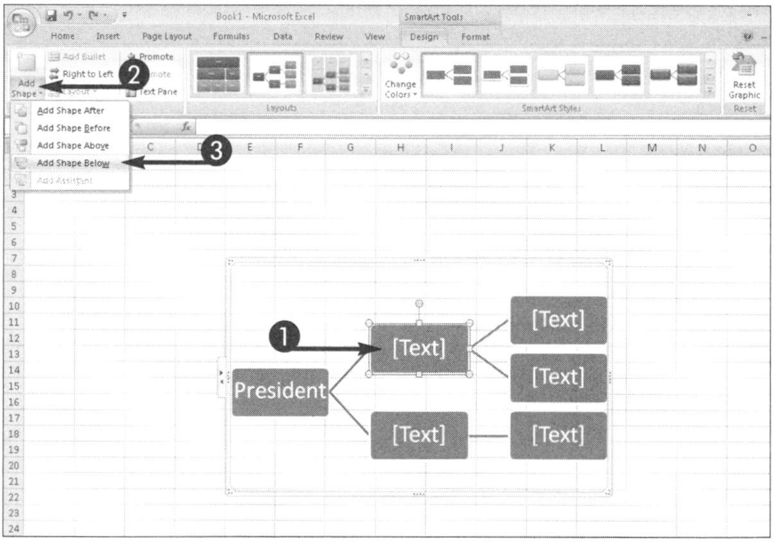

- Excel adds a shape to the SmartArt graphic.

Note: *To add text to the new shape, right-click it and choose Edit Text or use the Text pane.*

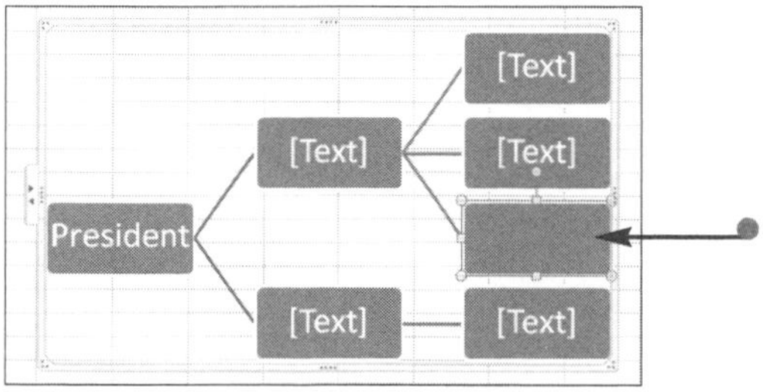

Apply a SmartArt Style

You can apply a SmartArt style to make dramatic changes to the appearance of the SmartArt graphic you inserted in your worksheet. For example, you can change the outline style that surrounds shapes within the SmartArt graphic. You can also apply a variety of effects such as bevels, shadows, and 3-D rotations to the SmartArt graphic. SmartArt styles are collections of predefined formatting options that combine outline styles for individual shapes within the graphic, and effects such as shadows, bevels, or 3-D rotations. Some SmartArt styles also include subtle color changes to the background of a SmartArt graphic.

As a result, when you apply a SmartArt style, you save a lot of time because you actually apply several different formats simultaneously.

When you apply a SmartArt style, you do not affect any of the information in the SmartArt graphic; you only affect the appearance of the information. For example, SmartArt styles do not rearrange any of the shapes in the SmartArt graphic element. You only rearrange the shapes if you change the layout of the graphic. For details on changing the organization of a SmartArt graphic, see the section, "Apply a SmartArt Layout."

Apply a SmartArt Style

1. Click the SmartArt graphic to select it.
   - This border appears around the graphic.
   - SmartArt Tools appear on the Ribbon.
2. Click the Design tab.
3. Click here.

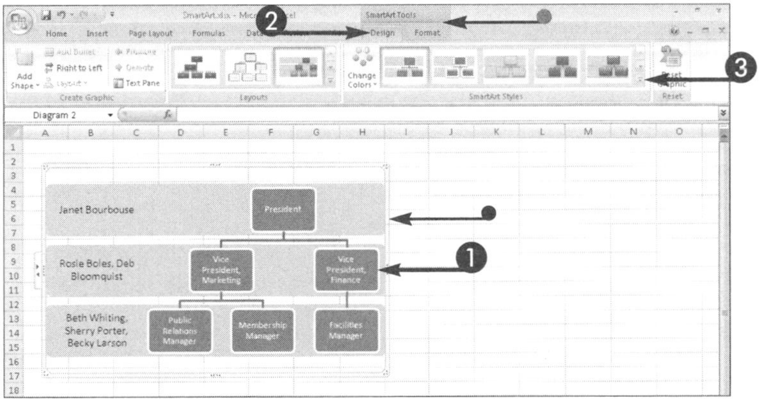

The SmartArt Styles Gallery appears.

4. Point at a style.
   - Live Preview displays the graphic using the style.
5. Click a style to apply it.

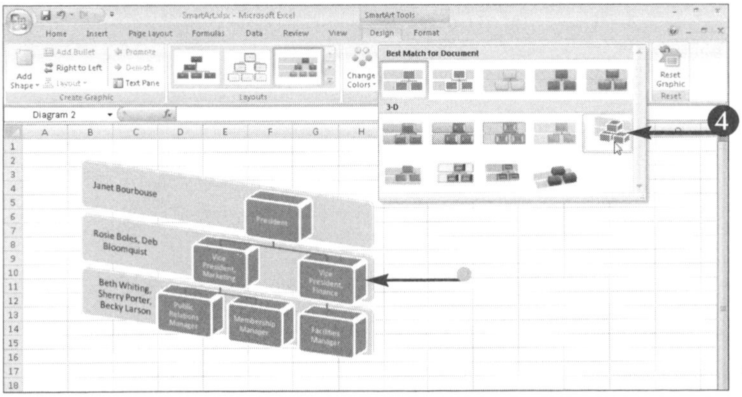

Apply a SmartArt Layout

You can change the appearance of a SmartArt graphic by applying a different layout. When you first create a SmartArt graphic, you select a layout from the Choose a SmartArt Graphic dialog box. If you decide that you do not like the layout you originally selected, you do not need to delete your SmartArt graphic and recreate it. Instead, you can change the layout.

By default, the layouts Excel displays in the Layout Gallery are associated with the type of SmartArt graphic that you originally inserted. However, you are not restricted to switching between the layouts that are available in the original group.

Be aware that switching layouts can cause some information in your SmartArt graphic to become extraneous. For example, when you switch from a labeled hierarchy to a non-labeled hierarchy, Excel stores the label information in shape boxes as part of the hierarchy, which probably is not what you intended.

MASTER IT

How can I switch to a layout in a different layout group?

▼ Follow Steps 1 to 3. When the Layout Gallery appears, click More Layouts at the bottom of the gallery. Excel displays the Choose a SmartArt Graphic dialog box.

Apply a SmartArt Layout

1. Click the SmartArt graphic to select it.
   - This border appears around the graphic.
   - SmartArt Tools appear on the Ribbon.
2. Click the Design tab.
3. Click .

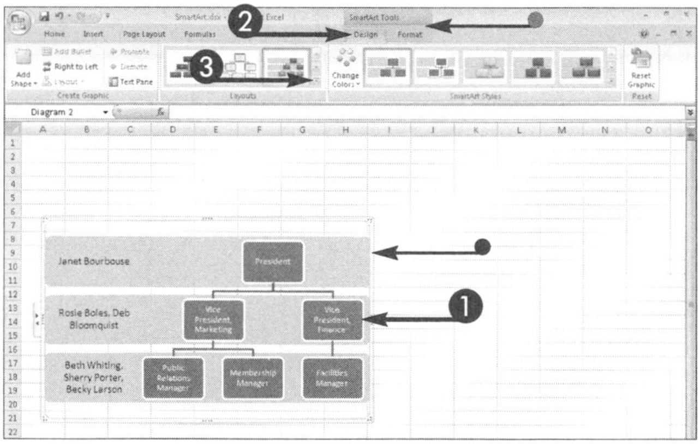

The SmartArt Layout Gallery appears.

4. Point at a layout.
   - Live Preview displays a preview of the graphic using the layout.
5. Click a layout to apply it.

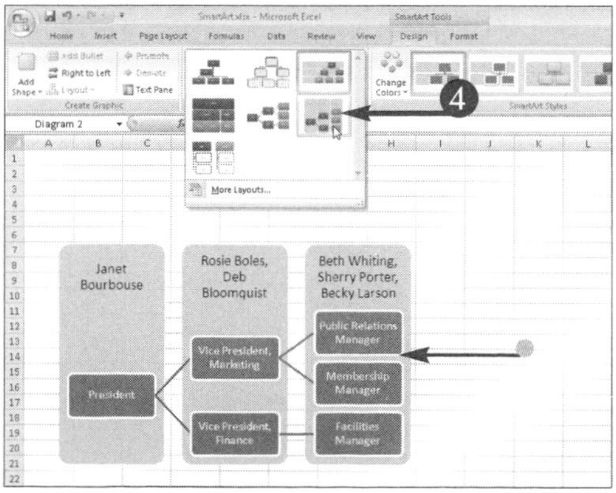

Change the Color of a SmartArt Graphic

You can change the colors of the shapes in a SmartArt graphic element. When you add a SmartArt graphic to a worksheet, Excel uses default colors for the graphic, but you can change the colors. You can select from eight different color palettes: Primary Theme Colors, Colorful, and Accents 1 to 6. The Colorful palette enables you to apply different colors to various shapes in the diagram, while the other palettes enable you to apply shades of whichever color you choose to the various shapes in the diagram.

Changing the colors does not affect the organization of a SmartArt graphic, nor does it affect any style you might have applied. In addition, changing colors does not affect other individual attributes that you might have applied, such as a shadow, a bevel, or a 3-D rotation.

MASTER IT

How can I make my SmartArt graphic look like the example in the Choose a SmartArt Graphic dialog box?

▼ You need to apply a color and a style. Complete Steps 1 to 3. For Step 4, click Colorful — Accent Colors in the Colorful group. Then, from the SmartArt Styles Gallery, select the Cartoon 3-D style. For details on selecting a style, see the section, "Apply a SmartArt Style."

Change the Color of a SmartArt Graphic

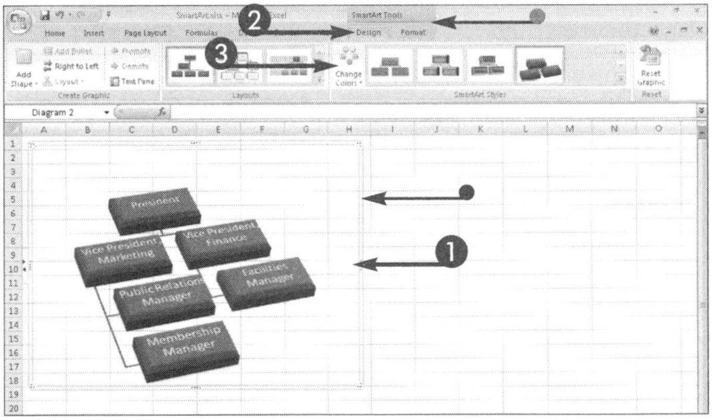

1. Click the SmartArt graphic to select it.
   - This border appears around the graphic.
   - SmartArt Tools appear on the Ribbon.
2. Click the Design tab.
3. Click Change Colors.

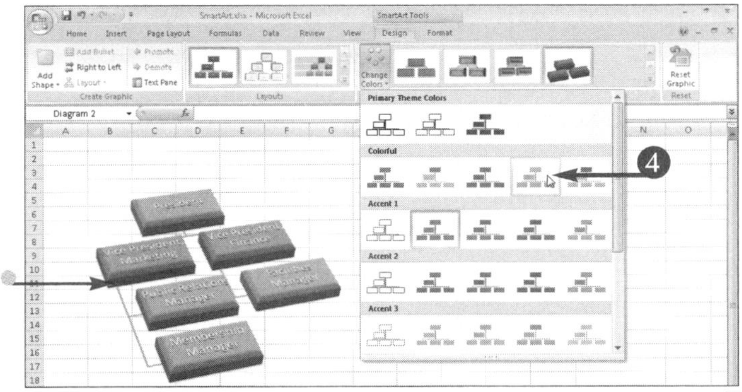

The SmartArt Colors Gallery appears.

4. Point at a color scheme.
   - Live Preview displays the graphic using the color scheme.
5. Click a color scheme to apply it.

Add WordArt to a Worksheet

You can use WordArt to create artistic graphic effects in text. These graphics can help enhance the appearance of a title or draw attention to an important point in your worksheet or on a chart or other graphic element.

WordArt text effects go beyond simply changing the font, font size, and color of text. Using WordArt, you can skew, rotate, and stretch text, add shadows to text, and make text appear three-dimensional.

When you add a WordArt text effect, Excel adds the Format tab under Drawing Tools to the Ribbon; you can change the appearance of the WordArt text effect by applying a Shape style or a different WordArt style, or you can add or change fill colors, outline effects, shadows, reflections, glows, soft edges, bevels, or 3-D rotation.

You can move and resize a WordArt text effect using the same techniques you use to move or resize any graphic element; see the section, "Move or Resize a Graphic Element," for more details.

You do not need to worry if you make a spelling mistake in a WordArt text effect, as the Excel spelling checker will find the mistake.

Add WordArt to a Worksheet

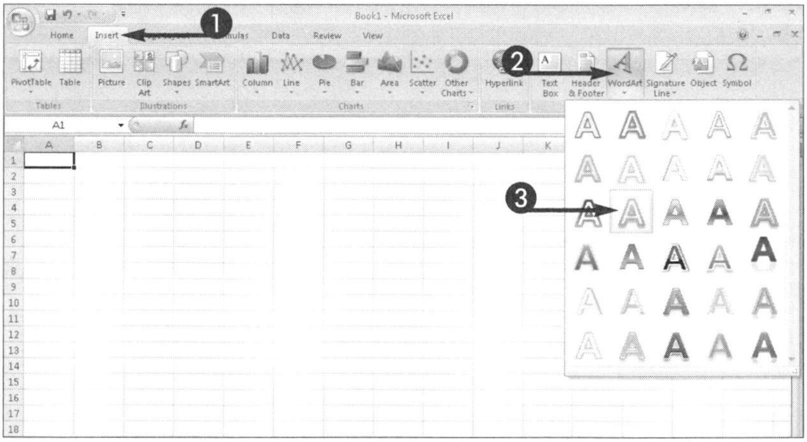

1. Click the Insert tab.
2. Click WordArt.

   The WordArt Styles Gallery appears.
3. Click a WordArt style.

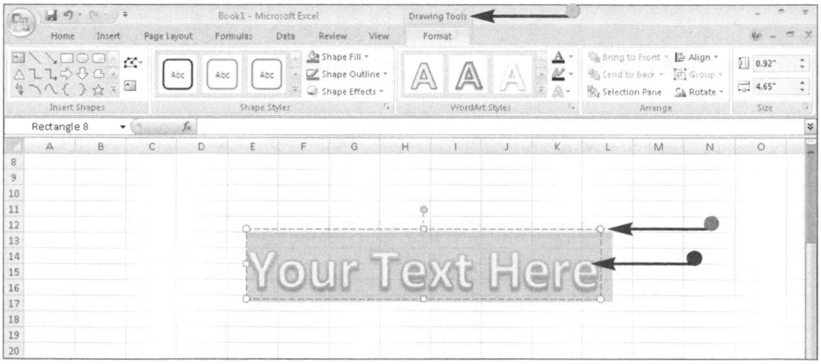

- Excel adds the WordArt effect to the worksheet.
- Handles like these appear around the selected WordArt effect.
- Drawing Tools appear on the Ribbon.

Note: *"Your Text Here" is selected so that you can automatically replace it when you type.*

4 Type the text you want to display in WordArt.

- As you type, an insertion point marks your location.

5 When you finish typing, click outside the WordArt effect.

Excel displays your WordArt effect.

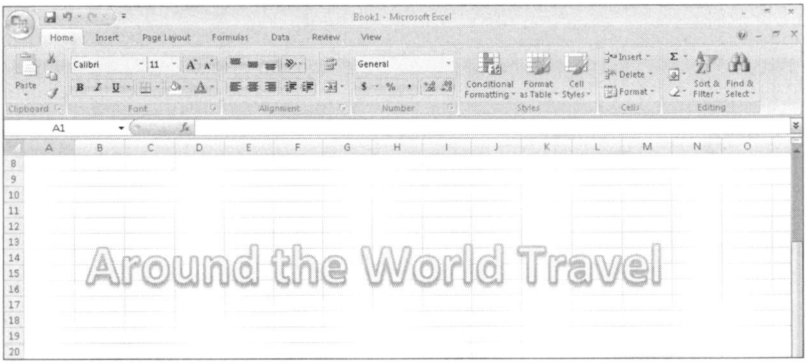

MASTER IT

How do I apply WordArt to charts and other graphic elements?

▼ You can apply WordArt to any graphic element that includes text. For example, you can apply WordArt to a chart or a shape that includes a text box, but you cannot apply WordArt to a picture. Select the graphic element. Then click the Format tab for that particular type of graphic element and apply a WordArt style.

How do I change to a different WordArt style?

▼ Click anywhere in the WordArt effect. When you see the insertion point, click anywhere on the outer boundary of the effect to select the entire effect. On the Format tab under Drawing Tools, in the WordArt Styles section, click the More button (▾) to display the WordArt Styles Gallery and select a new style.

Why do I need to click the outer boundary of a WordArt effect when I want to change the style?

▼ If you click inside the WordArt effect and then change the style, Excel applies the effect only to the word containing the insertion point. However, by clicking the border of the effect, you select the entire effect, and so the style change applies to the entire effect.

Insert a Symbol

In some worksheets, you may need to use special typographical symbols not found on your keyboard, such as the trademark or copyright symbols. You can use the Symbol window in Excel to insert these special characters into your worksheet. You can also determine a symbol's Unicode characters from the Symbol window. *Unicode* is a character-encoding standard that uses more than one byte to represent each character. This approach enables almost all of the world's written languages to be represented by a single character set. If you know the Unicode characters that produce a particular letter or symbol, you can enter the letter or symbol without using the Symbol window.

The symbols and characters available in the Symbol window depend on the font you select; not all symbols and characters are available in all font sets. You can select a font while working in the Symbol window to find and insert different symbols and characters. The Symbol font set includes arrows and bullets as well as Greek letters and scientific symbols. You can, for example, insert fractions or π, the symbol for *pi*.

Symbols that you insert are graphic images; you cannot use them in calculations, even if they represent numbers.

Insert a Symbol

1. Click the cell in which you want to store the symbol.
2. Click the Insert tab.
3. Click Symbol.

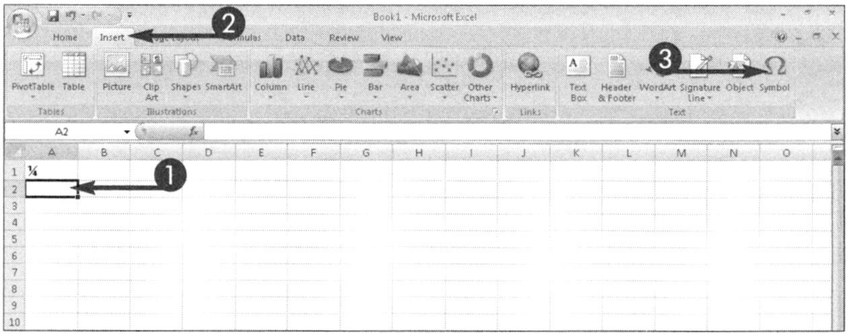

The Symbol window appears.

4. Click here to select a font.

- You can select subsets for some fonts; the available subsets depend on the font.
- Recently used symbols appear here.

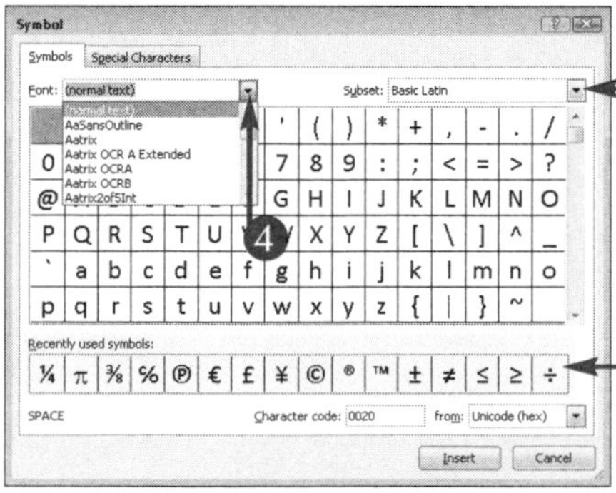

The characters that are available for the selected font appear in the window.

5. Click the character you want to insert.
   - The character's Unicode character code appears here.
6. Click Insert.

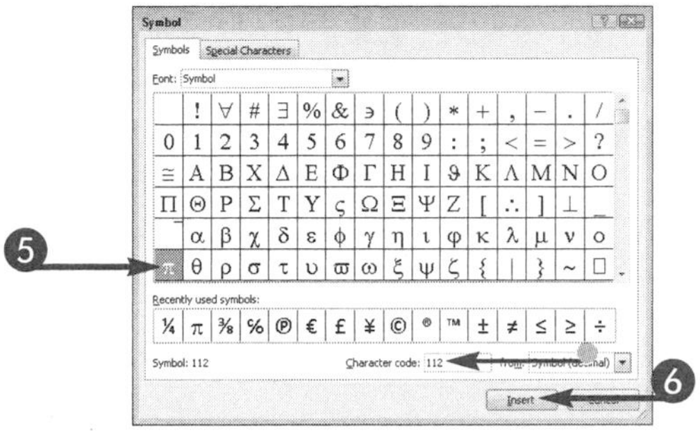

- The character appears in the cell you selected in Step 1.
- The Symbol window remains open.
- You can repeat these steps to enter additional symbols, or you can click Close.

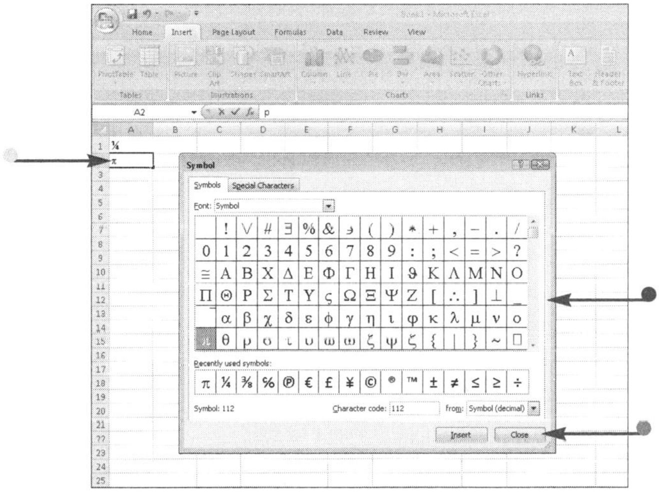

MASTER IT

What appears on the Special Characters tab of the Symbol window?

▼ The Special Characters tab contains a list of commonly used special characters along with their names. For example, on this tab, you find the em dash (—), the en dash (–), the ellipsis (...), and the nonbreaking space character ( ). Many of these special characters are difficult to find in the font sets on the Symbols tab, and so listing them on the Special Characters tab by name makes them easy to find and insert. You insert one of these characters by selecting it and clicking Insert. Using the Special Characters tab is no different than finding the character on the Symbols tab and inserting it from there.

Why would I want to insert a symbol using its Unicode characters?

▼ If you use a symbol frequently, you may find inserting it using its Unicode characters faster than opening the Insert window and finding the character to insert it.

How do I insert a symbol using its Unicode characters?

▼ Press the Num Lock key to enable the numbers on the number pad. Click the cell in which you want to enter the symbol and then click the Home tab. From the Font list, select the font set that contains the symbol. Press and hold the Alt key and, using the numeric keypad, type the symbol's Unicode value. Release the Alt key, and Excel inserts the symbol.

Add a Picture to a Worksheet

You can add pictures such as digital photos or scanned images to an Excel worksheet. Like other graphic elements, pictures can add interest to a worksheet or help convey an idea. You can add pictures stored in their own graphics files using the steps in this section. You can also add pictures that are created in a graphics program but that are either not stored in their own file or stored in a file format that Excel does not support.

When you add a picture to a worksheet, Excel adds the Format tab under Picture Tools to the Ribbon. You can change the appearance of the picture by applying a Picture Style or changing the picture's shape. You can also add a border to the picture in a color of your choice, and you can control the weight and style of the border line. You can add picture effects such as shadows, reflections, glows, soft edges, bevels, or 3-D rotation. In addition, you can change the brightness or contrast of the picture, and recolor the picture.

If you want to move or resize a picture, see the section, "Move or Resize a Graphic Element," for more details.

Add a Picture to a Worksheet

1. Click the cell where you want Excel to anchor the upper-left corner of the picture.

2. Click the Insert tab.
3. Click Picture.

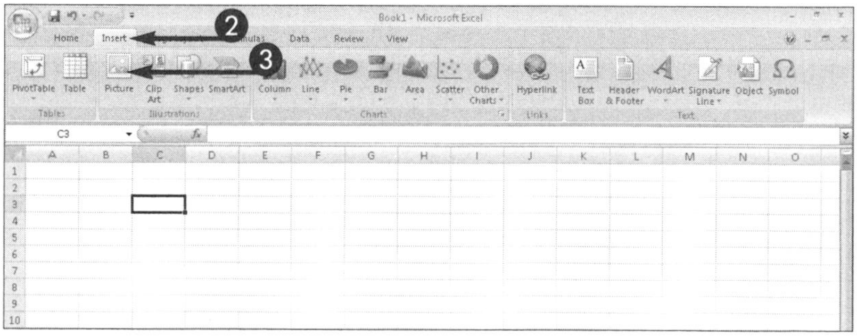

The Insert Picture dialog box appears.

4. Navigate to the folder containing the picture you want to insert in your worksheet.
5. Click the picture.
6. Click Insert.

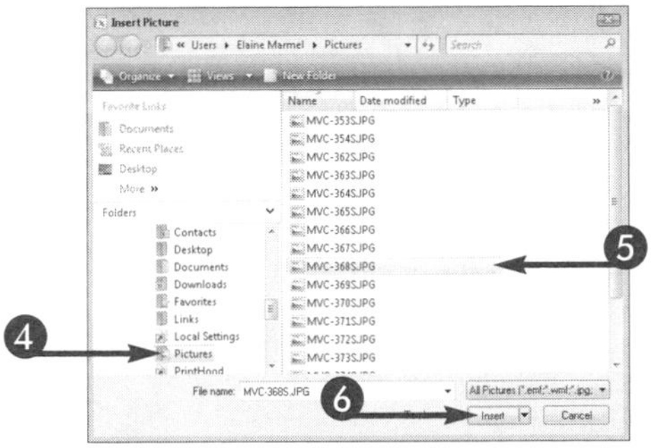

- The picture appears in the worksheet; its upper-left corner appears in the cell you selected in Step 1.
- Round and square white handles surround the picture.
- Picture Tools appear on the Ribbon.

PART IV

MASTER IT

How can I add a picture that was created in another program?

▼ If Excel does not support the file type of the picture, you can add it using the Windows Clipboard. While viewing the picture on-screen, select it, click Edit, and click Copy. If you cannot select the picture, press the PrintScreen key. Switch to Excel, select the cell where you want to anchor the upper-left corner of the picture, click the Home tab, and click Paste.

How do I delete a picture?

▼ Click anywhere on the picture to select it; round and square white handles appear around the selected picture. Press the Delete key or click the Home tab and click ☐. From the menu that appears, click Clear All.

Can I make a picture appear as a background wallpaper on a worksheet?

▼ Yes, you can. Click the Page Layout tab and, in the Page Setup group, click Background. In the Sheet Background dialog box that appears, navigate to and click the image that you want to display as a wallpaper on the worksheet. Click Open; Excel repeats the image over the entire worksheet. To remove the image, click the Page Layout tab and, in the Page Setup group, click Delete Background.

Insert Clip Art in a Worksheet

You can add a Clip Art image to a worksheet. Like other graphic elements, Clip Art images can add interest to a worksheet or chart or they can help convey an idea. Before you can use Clip Art, the Clip Art Gallery must be installed. If it is not installed, Excel displays a message that prompts you to install it; simply follow the on-screen prompts.

When you add a Clip Art image to a worksheet, Excel displays the Format tab under Picture Tools on the Ribbon; you can change the appearance of the picture by applying a Picture Style or changing the Clip Art image's shape. You can also add a border to the Clip Art image in a color of your choice, and you can control the weight and style of the border line. You can add effects such as shadows, reflections, glows, soft edges, bevels, or 3-D rotation. In addition, you can change the brightness or contrast of the Clip Art image, as well as recolor the Clip Art image.

If you want to move or resize a Clip Art image, see the section, "Move or Resize a Graphic Element," for more details.

Insert Clip Art in a Worksheet

1. Click the cell where you want Excel to anchor the upper-left corner of the Clip Art image.
2. Click the Insert tab.
3. Click Clip Art.
   - The Clip Art pane appears.

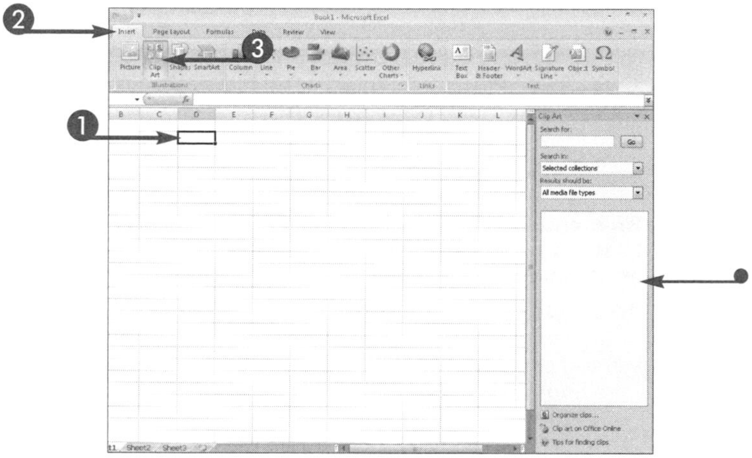

4. Click here and type a term that describes the type of Clip Art you want.
5. Click Go.

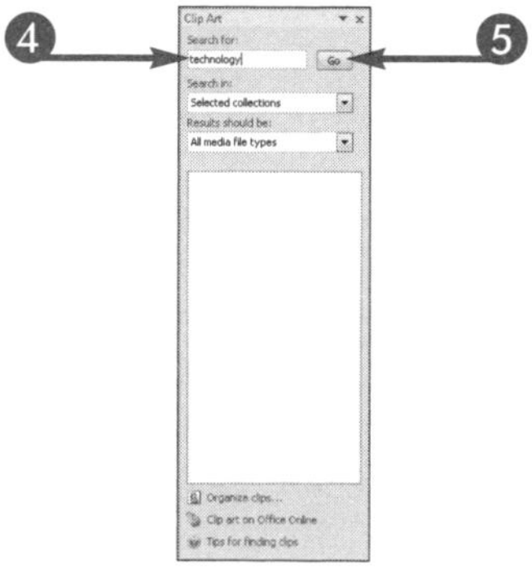

- Clip Art images that match your search term appear in the Clip Art pane.

6. Click an image.

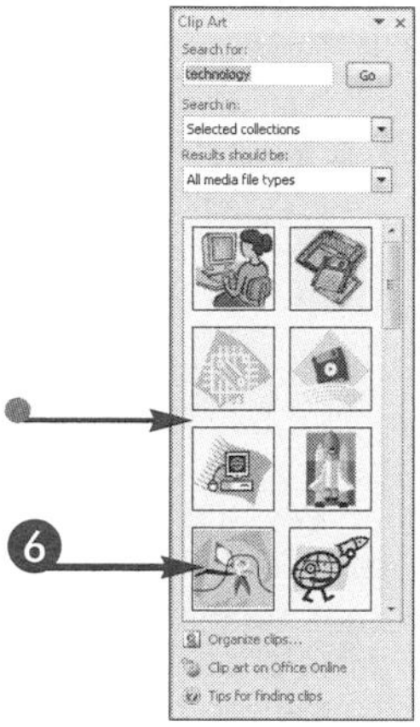

- The Clip Art image appears in the worksheet; its upper-left corner appears in the cell you selected in Step 1.
- Round and square white handles surround the image.
- Picture Tools appear on the Ribbon.

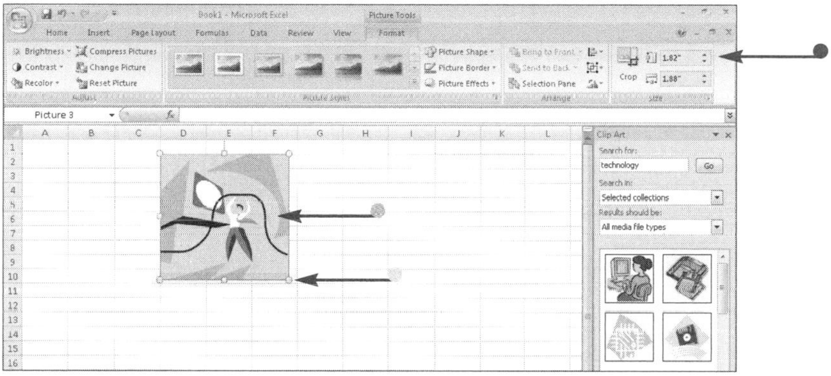

MASTER IT

What happens if I click ▾ beside the Search In option?

▼ The Search In list box, located in the Clip Art pane, controls where Excel looks for images to match the search term you supply in Step 4. By default, Excel searches My Collections, Office Collections, and, if they are available, Shared Collections. My Collections are collections of Clip Art that you create yourself. Office Collections come with Office 2007 products. Shared Collections reside on your network. The Web Collections option is also available but not selected by default; you can use it to search the Microsoft Office Online collection for Clip Art.

What does the "All media file types" option mean?

▼ The Results Should Be list box, located in the Clip Art pane, controls the type of media files that any search will return. This option, selected by default, looks for Clip Art, photographs, movies, and sounds during any search. You can click ▾ and remove any of these file types from the search.

How do I delete a Clip Art image?

▼ Click anywhere on the Clip Art image to select it; round and square white handles appear around the selected image. Press the Delete key or click the Home tab and click the Clear button. From the menu that appears, click Clear All.

Move or Resize a Graphic Element

You can move or resize a graphic element to make it work more effectively in your worksheet or on your chart. You move or resize all graphics using the same techniques, regardless of whether you are working with a shape, a SmartArt graphic, a text box, WordArt, a picture, or a Clip Art image. Symbols are the exception — you treat them like cell entries. To move symbols, you cut and paste them, and to resize them, you change the font size.

You can move a graphic to another location in a worksheet or to a different position on a chart. You cannot move a graphic that you placed on a chart outside the chart boundaries.

To resize a graphic, you can use the white circular and square handles that appear around the perimeter of the graphic when you select it. You can use the square handles that appear at the top and bottom to change the height of the graphic, and you can change the graphic's width using the square handles on each side of the graphic. You can use the round handles to change the graphic element's height and width simultaneously.

Move or Resize a Graphic Element

Move an Element

1. Click the graphic element to select it.
   - Handles appear around the graphic element.
2. Place the mouse pointer over an outside edge of the graphic element (✥ changes to ✥).

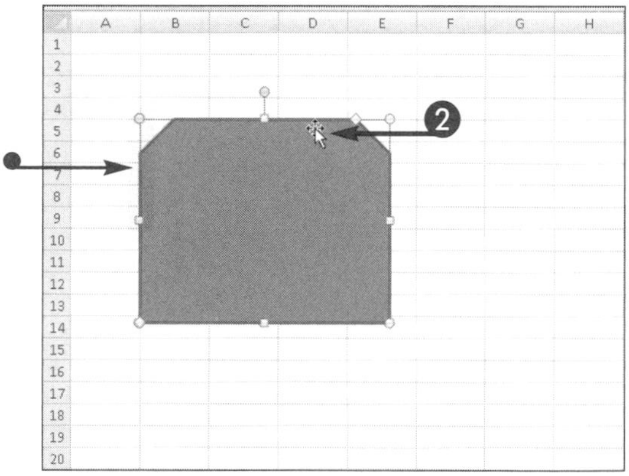

3. Drag the graphic element to a new location, releasing the mouse button when the graphic element appears where you want it.
   - As you drag, a lighter version of the graphic shows you its current position.

   The graphic element appears in the new location.

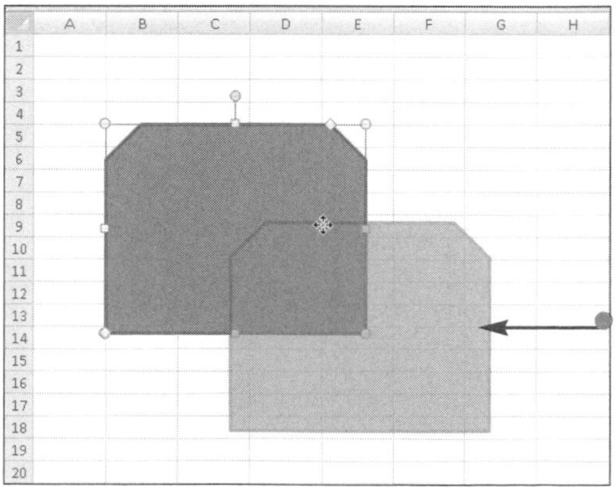

Resize an Element

1. Click the graphic element to select it.
   - Handles appear around the graphic element.
2. Place the mouse pointer over a handle (✥ changes to ⇔, ⇕, or ⤢).

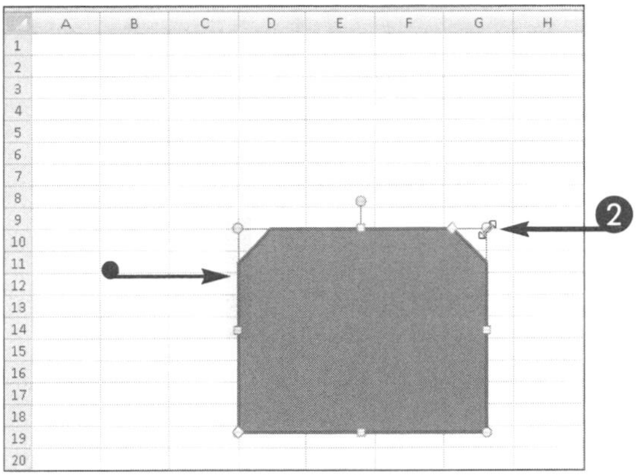

3. Click and drag the handle (⇔, ⇕, or ⤢ changes to +)

Note: *Drag out to increase the size or drag in to decrease the size.*

- As you drag, a lighter version of the graphic shows you its current size.

When you release the mouse button, Excel resizes the graphic element.

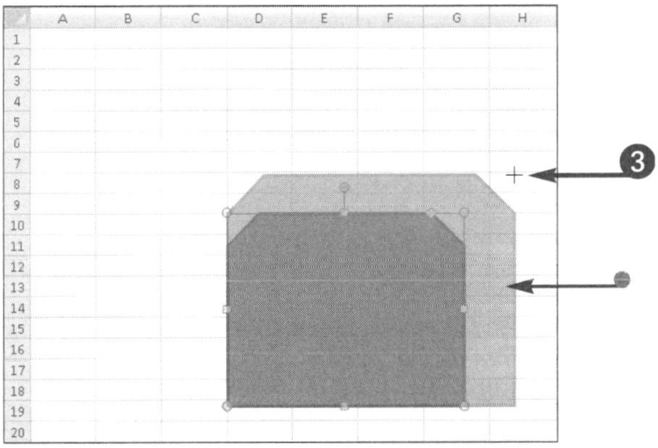

PART IV

MASTER IT

Can I resize without dragging?

▼ Yes, you can use the Size fields that appear at the right edge of the Format tab under Drawing Tools, Picture Tools, or SmartArt Tools; the name of the Tools tab depends on the type of graphic you select. Click the graphic to select it and click the Format tab. At the right edge of the Ribbon, change either the height or width, and Excel automatically adjusts the other parameter.

When I resize by dragging, can I retain the relationship of the shape's height and width?

▼ Yes, you can. Follow the steps in the subsection, "Resize an Element," but in Step 3, press and hold the Shift key as you drag the handle. Excel makes both sides of the graphic element larger or smaller in the same proportion.

Can I move or resize several graphic elements simultaneously?

▼ Yes. Select all of the graphic elements by clicking the first one and then holding down the Ctrl key as you click each of the other graphic elements. When you move the elements, Excel moves them all in the same direction by the same amount. When you resize the elements, Excel resizes them all by the same amount.

Change the Shape of a Graphic Element

You can change the shape of a picture, text box, Clip Art image, or an individual shape in a SmartArt graphic element. For a shape, you can switch to a different shape or, if the shape includes a shaping handle, you can modify the silhouette of the shape.

To change the shape of a graphic element, you select it. Then, you use the Format tab under Drawing Tools, Picture Tools, or SmartArt Tools on the Ribbon, depending on the type of graphic element you selected, to apply a different shape to the graphic element. For pictures and Clip Art, you use the Picture Shape button, and for SmartArt shapes, you use the Change Shape button. This example demonstrates changing the shape of a text box.

MASTER IT

How can I change the silhouette of a shape?

▼ Click the shape to select it. White round and square sizing handles appear around the shape. If Excel permits you to modify the silhouette of the shape, small yellow diamonds also appear. Drag one of these yellow diamonds either toward or away from the center of the graphic element; Excel modifies the silhouette of the graphic element.

Change the Shape of a Graphic Element

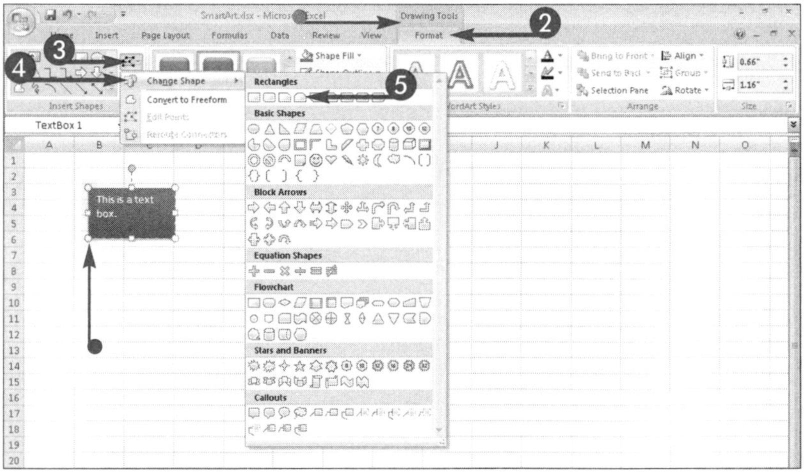

1. Click the graphic element to select it.
   - Handles appear around the graphic element.
   - Tools appear for the graphic element on the Ribbon.
2. Click the Format tab.
3. Click the Edit Shape button (⋯).
4. Click Change Shape to display the Shape Gallery.
5. Click a shape.

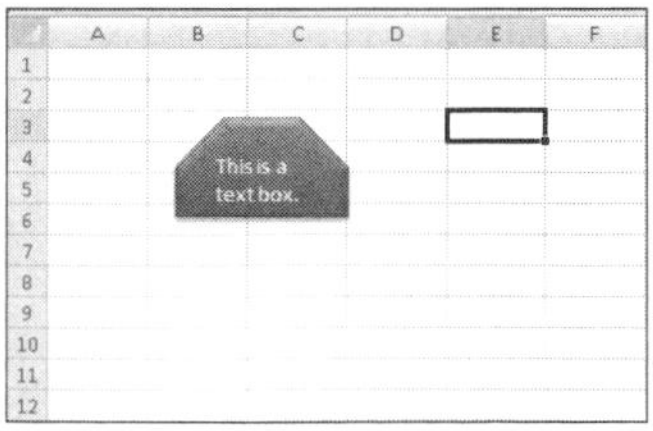

Excel applies the new shape to the graphic element.

Modify a Graphic Element Border

You can change the border of a shape, picture, text box, Clip Art image, or an individual shape in a SmartArt graphic element. Suppose, for example, that you want to include text inside a shape. You add a text box to the shape and type your text and then decide that you want the text to appear as if it were part of the shape and not in a separate text box. You can change the fill color of the text box to match the fill color of the graphic, but a light-gray line still delineates the outline of the text box. You can remove the text box's outline to make the text box indistinguishable from the background of the shape.

To change the border of a graphic element, you first select it. Then you use the Format tab under Drawing Tools, Picture Tools, or SmartArt Tools on the Ribbon, depending on the type of graphic element you selected, to change or remove the border of the graphic element. For pictures and Clip Art, you use the Picture Border button, and for shapes, text boxes, and SmartArt shapes, you use the Shape Outline button. This section demonstrates removing the border of a text box.

PART IV

Modify a Graphic Element Border

1. Click the graphic element to select it.
   - Handles appear around the graphic element.
   - Tools appear for the graphic element on the Ribbon.
2. Click the Format tab.
3. Click Shape Outline.
   - You can click here to change the appearance of the border.
4. Click No Outline.
   - Excel removes the outline, making the text box appear invisible inside the shape.

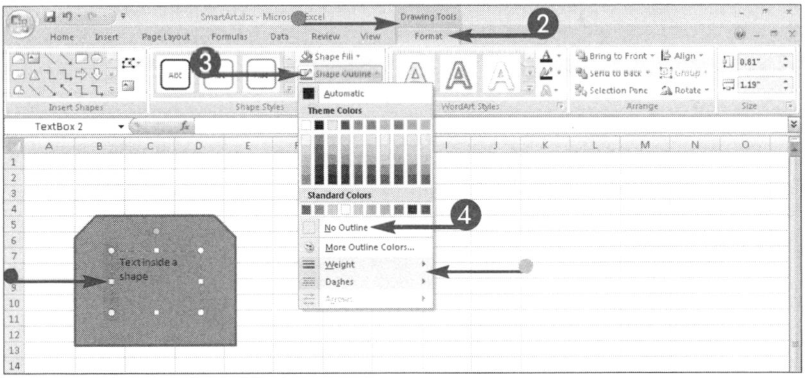

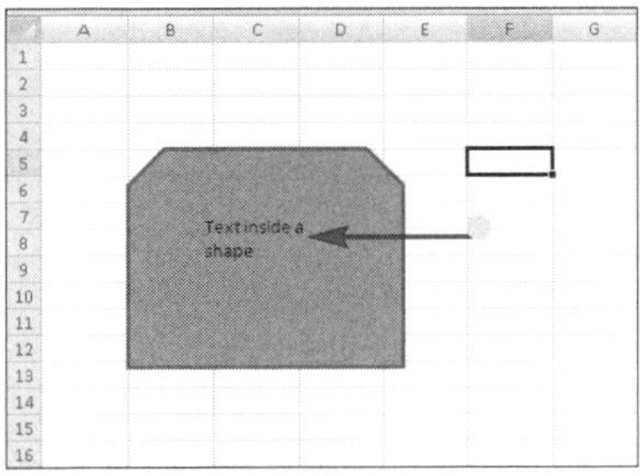

Add an Effect to a Graphic Element

To increase the interest and attractiveness of a graphic element, you can add effects such as bevels, shadows, reflections, glows, soft edges, and 3-D rotations.

Bevels are decorative edges that you can add to a graphic element. Shadows appear behind a graphic element and give it depth. Reflections appear at the bottom of a graphic element and look like soft, faded mirror images. Glows add colorful, fuzzy edges to a graphic element. Soft edges add degrees of transparency around the edges of a graphic element. Three-dimensional effects provide dimension and rotate a graphic element.

You can also add preset effects, which are predefined combinations of bevels, shadows, reflections, glows, soft edges, and 3-D rotations.

Most effects are available for all types of graphic elements. You may find that some effects are not available for the outer border of a SmartArt graphic element, but you can apply most effects to the shapes that make up the SmartArt graphic.

MASTER IT

Is there a way that I can add predefined combinations of effects, borders, and fills?

▼ Yes, you can use styles. Styles are collections of predefined formatting options that combine outlines, graphic element shapes, fills, and effects such as shadows, bevels, or 3-D rotations.

Add an Effect to a Graphic Element

1. Click the graphic element to select it.
   - Handles appear around the graphic element.
   - Tools appear for the graphic element on the Ribbon.
2. Click the Format tab.
3. Click Picture Effects or Shape Effects, depending on the type of graphic selected.

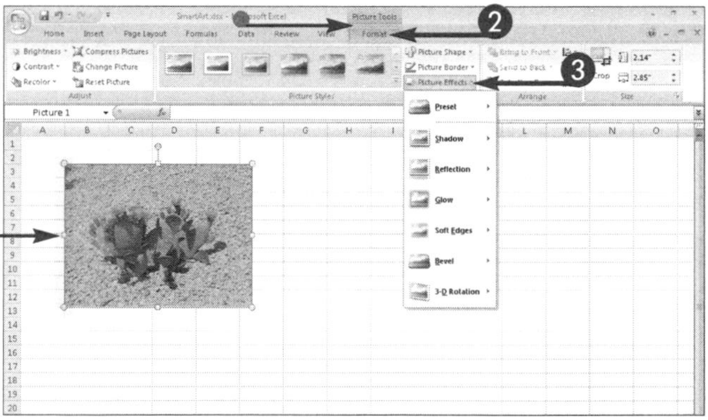

4. Click a type of effect.

   The gallery appears for that effect.
5. Point at an effect.
   - Live Preview displays the graphic using the effect.
6. Click an effect to apply it.

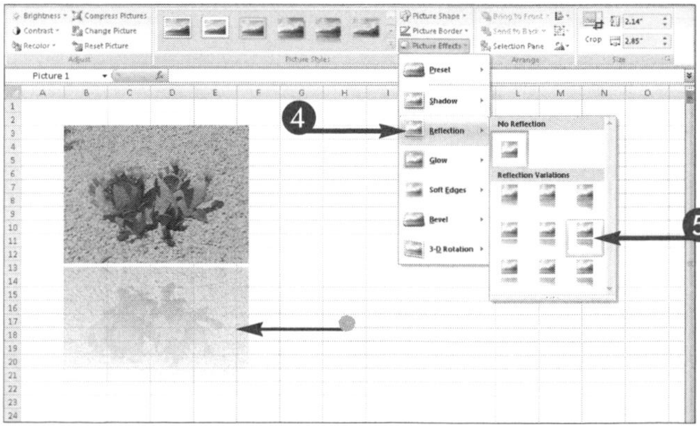

Change the Brightness of a Graphic Element

You can change the brightness of a Clip Art image or a picture graphic element by adding or removing light from the image. The Brightness option in Excel controls the relative lightness or darkness of the overall image. Changing brightness is particularly effective when you work with a digital photo that was taken with either not enough light or too much light. For example, the photo may have been taken indoors and the camera's flash may not have been used, resulting in a dark photo. Or, the photo may have been taken outdoors on a sunny day and the photographer may have accidentally included a flash in the picture, creating an overly bright photo.

You can easily increase or decrease the brightness of a Clip Art image or a digital photo in ten-degree increments using the options that appear on the Brightness drop-down list. For more control over the level of light in the image, you can display the Picture Corrections Options dialog box, where you can control brightness using slider controls or by typing an exact brightness amount.

Change the Brightness of a Graphic Element

1. Click the picture or Clip Art image to select it.
   - Handles appear around the graphic element.
   - Picture Tools appear on the Ribbon.
2. Click the Format tab.
3. Click Brightness.

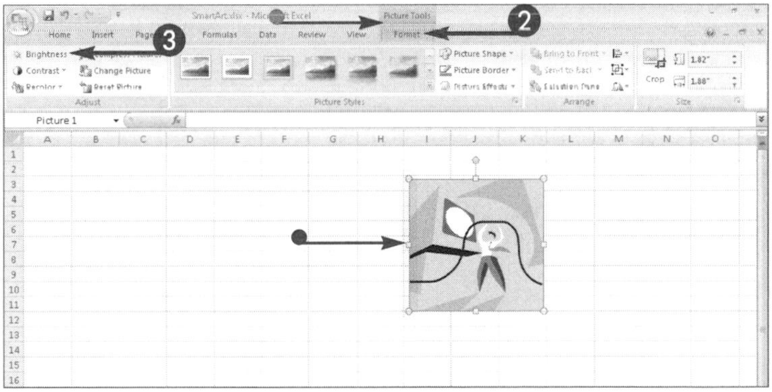

The Brightness Gallery appears.

4. Point at an option in the Brightness Gallery.
   - Live Preview displays the Clip Art image or picture using the brightness level you selected.
5. Click a brightness level to apply it.

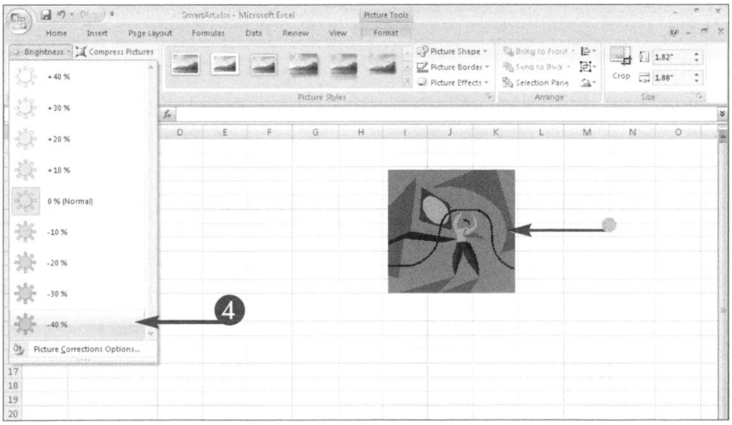

Change the Contrast of a Graphic Element

You can change the contrast of a Clip Art image or a picture graphic element. The Contrast option in Excel adjusts the difference between the lightest and darkest parts of the image.

To better understand contrast, consider photography. In black-and-white photography, contrast is considered high, normal, or low. In a high-contrast image, you see primarily white and black with few or no middle gray tones, such as a computer in a black box set against a light background. In a low-contrast scene, highlights and shadows have very little difference in densities, and all colors or tones within the scene are very similar in appearance, such as a computer in a light gray box against a light background. Most scenes have normal contrast, but some elements within the scene may appear very light or white, while some may appear very dark or black, and many elements may appear as various tones of gray.

Colors with opposite characteristics, such as red and green, contrast strongly when placed together. Cold colors such as blue almost always contrast with warm colors such as red; cold colors tend to retreat, while warm colors advance. Light colors contrast against dark ones, and a bold color offsets a weak color.

Change the Contrast of a Graphic Element

1. Click the picture or Clip Art image to select it.
   - Handles appear around the graphic element.
   - Picture Tools appear on the Ribbon.
2. Click the Format tab.
3. Click Contrast.

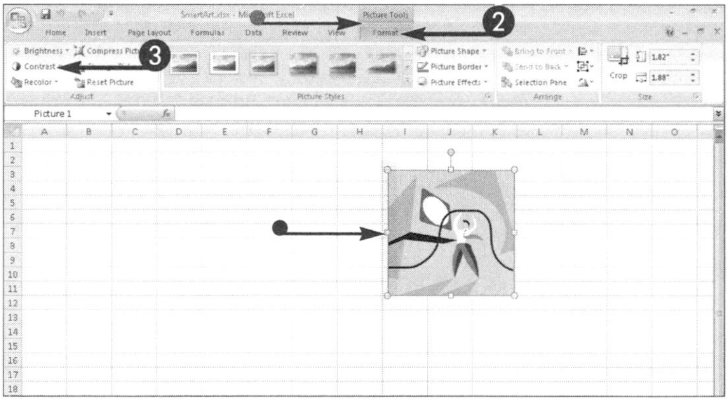

The Contrast Gallery appears.

4. Point at an option in the Contrast Gallery.
   - Live Preview displays the Clip Art image or picture using the contrast level you selected.
5. Click a contrast level to apply it.

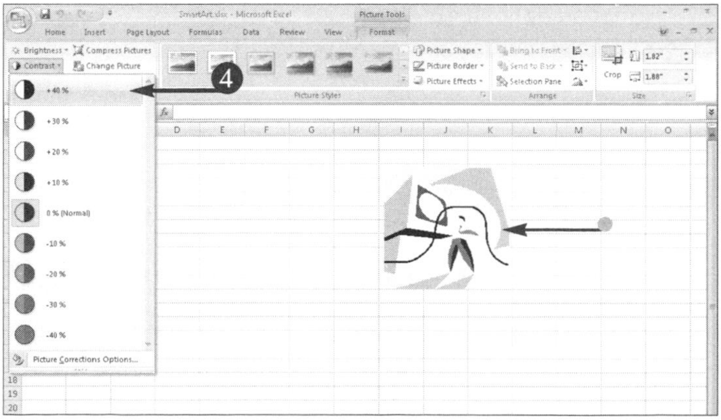

Recolor a Graphic Element

You can recolor a digital picture or a Clip Art image, or you can change the fill color of a shape, text box, WordArt, or SmartArt graphic element. When you recolor a digital picture or a Clip Art image, you apply a color cast to the image; using recoloring, you can make a color image appear in grayscale or even black and white.

When you change the fill color of a shape, text box, WordArt, or SmartArt graphic element, you change the background color of the element. This example describes how to change the fill color. If you are trying to change the color of the text of your WordArt element, you need to change its style. See the section, "Add WordArt to a Worksheet," for details.

MASTER IT

How do I recolor a digital picture or Clip Art image?

▼ Click the picture or Clip Art image to select it. Handles appear around the graphic element, and Picture Tools appear on the Ribbon. Click the Format tab and click Recolor. The Recolor Gallery appears. Point at an option in the Recolor Gallery, and Live Preview displays the Clip Art image or picture using the Recolor option. Click a contrast level to apply it.

Recolor a Graphic Element

1. Click a shape, text box, WordArt graphic, or SmartArt shape to select it.
   - Handles appear around the graphic element.
   - Drawing Tools appear on the Ribbon.
2. Click the Format tab.
3. Click Shape Fill.

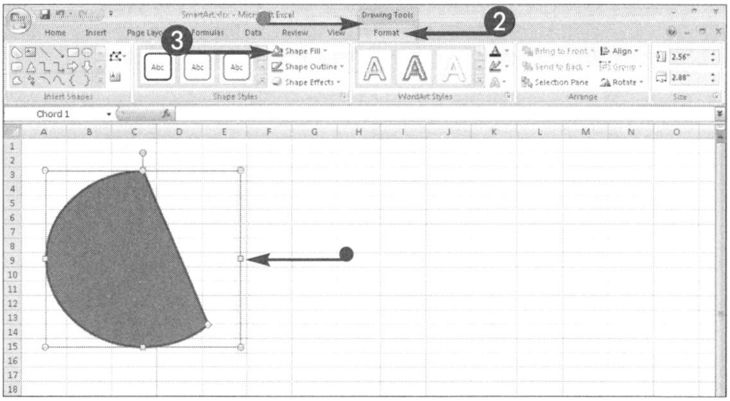

The Shape Fill Gallery appears.

4. Point at a color in the gallery.
   - Live Preview displays the selected graphic element using the color you selected.
5. Click a color to apply it.

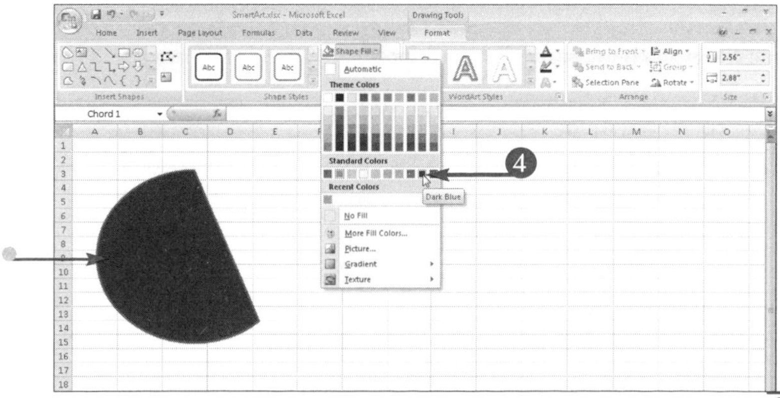

Compress Graphic Elements

You might want to optimize graphic elements in a workbook before you save the workbook. You optimize graphic elements by compressing them, which can make the file size of the workbook containing them somewhat smaller than if you leave the images uncompressed.

To be able to compress a graphic image, you must insert it using one of the buttons on the Insert tab of the Ribbon in the Illustrations group. You can compress only the selected picture or all pictures in the workbook. When compressing, you can reduce the resolution of a picture or reduce the color format of the image. If you reduce the color format, Excel makes the color take up fewer bits per pixel, with no loss of quality. This example reduces a color format.

You cannot optimize vector graphics, which are pictures that contain a drawing format that uses lines or squares, and that use file extensions such as .wmf, .emf, and .eps. You can optimize high-resolution digital photographs with file extensions of .jpeg or .jpg, .bmp, .gif, .tiff, and .png. You can compress Clip Art images from the Clip Art Gallery if they are photographs.

Compress Graphic Elements

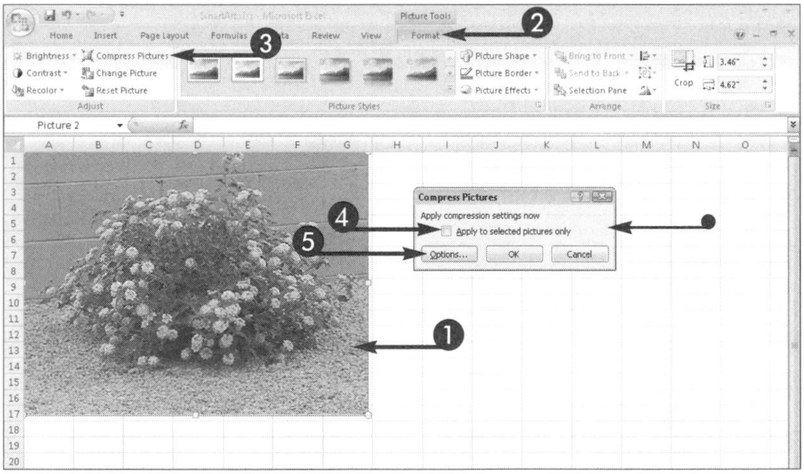

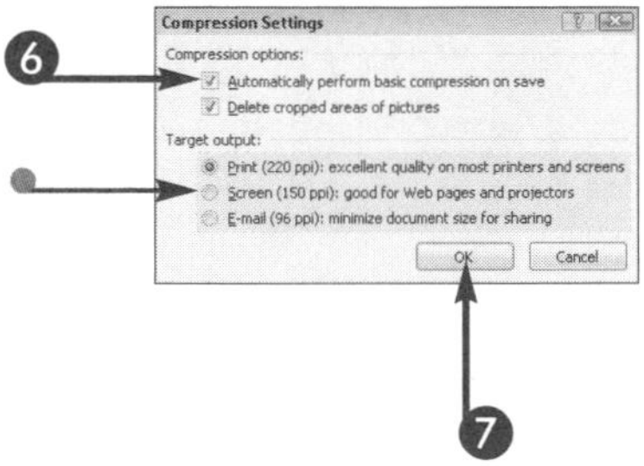

1. Click the picture to select it.
2. Click the Format tab under Picture Tools.
3. Click Compress Pictures.
   - The Compress Pictures dialog box appears.
4. Click here (☐ changes to ☑) to compress only the selected picture.
5. Click Options.

   The Compression Settings dialog box appears.
6. Make sure that you select this option (☐ changes to ☑).
   - You can click these options to reduce resolution.
7. Click OK to save the compression settings.
8. Click OK in the Compress Pictures dialog box.

   Excel compresses pictures when you save the workbook.

Crop a Graphic Element

You can crop a graphic element to reduce its size, eliminate extraneous information, or focus the reader's attention on a particular portion of the graphic element. When you crop a graphic element, you remove a portion of the graphic. You can crop digital pictures and Clip Art images, but you cannot crop shapes, text boxes, WordArt, Smart Art graphics, or shapes within SmartArt graphics.

When you crop an image, you can set options that tell Excel to discard the cropped portions of the image when you save the workbook. For details on setting these options, see the section, "Compress Graphic Elements."

If you change your mind about the cropped appearance of your picture, you can reset the picture from the Format tab under Picture Tools on the Ribbon. You can also use cropping to add a margin around a picture; this technique is called *outcropping*.

MASTER IT

If I cannot crop a shape, text box, WordArt image, or SmartArt graphic, is there another way to change their size?

▼ Yes, you can resize them using the techniques described in the section, "Move or Resize a Graphic Element."

Crop a Graphic Element

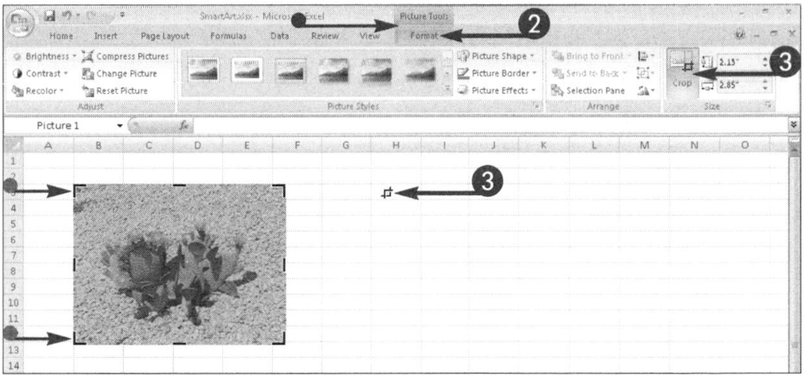

1. Click the picture to select it.

   Handles appear around the graphic element.

   - Picture Tools appear on the Ribbon.

2. Click the Format tab.
3. Click Crop (changes to).

   - Cropping handles appear around the picture.

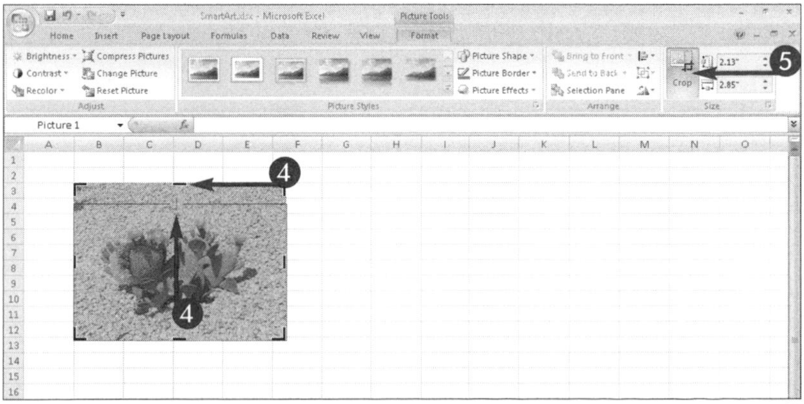

4. Drag a cropping handle.

Note: *Drag in to crop and out to outcrop.*

When you release the mouse button, Excel crops the picture.

5. Click Crop to deactivate the Crop feature.

Position Graphic Elements

Because Excel stores graphic elements in different layers on a worksheet, you might accidentally obscure one graphic element with another, or you might obscure worksheet data with a graphic element. You can reposition graphic elements within the worksheet.

Excel stores each graphic that you add to a worksheet on different invisible layers that reside on top of the worksheet and over the worksheet data in the cells below. If you move a graphic element over a cell that contains information, the graphic hides the data beneath it. If you position one graphic element on top of another graphic element, depending on the layers associated with each graphic element, the graphic element on top might cover up the graphic element below.

Excel makes it easy to move the graphic elements on the same worksheet to other layers using the Selection and Visibility task pane. The Selection and Visibility task pane lists graphic elements, and the order in which the graphic elements appear determines which will obscure other elements if the graphic elements overlap. The graphic elements appear in order; that is, the graphic element at the top of the list obscures elements below it in the list if they overlap.

Position Graphic Elements

1. Click a graphic element to select it.
   - Handles appear around the graphic element.
   - Picture Tools, Drawing Tools, or SmartArt Tools appear on the Ribbon, depending on the type of graphic you select.
2. Click the Format tab.
3. Click Selection Pane.

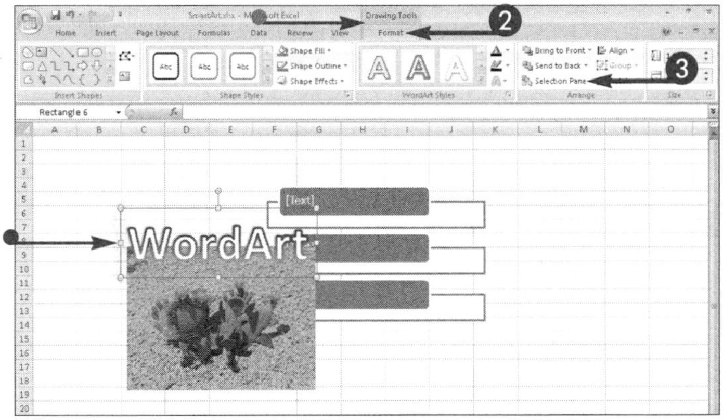

Excel displays the Selection and Visibility task pane, listing each graphic element.

Note: *The element at the top of the list obscures elements listed below it if they overlap.*

4. Click an element in the list to select it.
5. Click Send to Back.

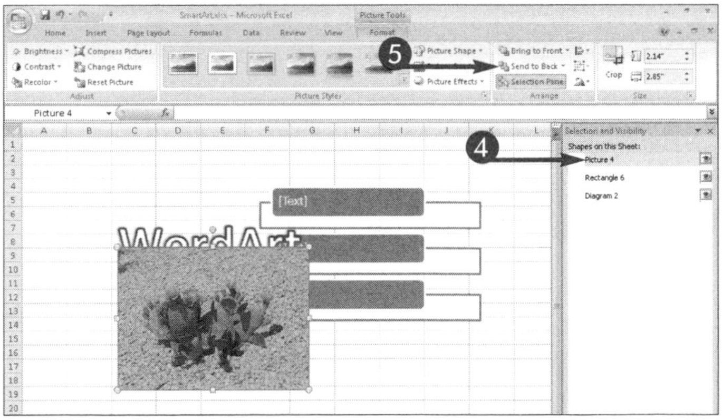

- Excel repositions the graphic element at the bottom of the list.
- Excel repositions the graphic element on the worksheet under the other graphic elements.

6 Click Bring to Front.

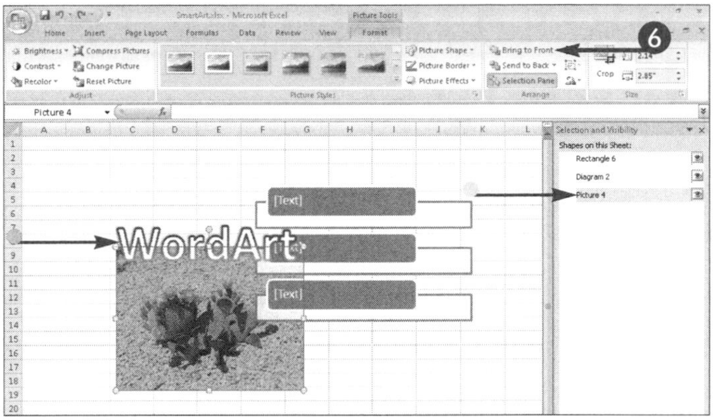

- Excel repositions the graphic element at the top of the list.
- Excel repositions the graphic element on the worksheet on top of the other graphic elements.

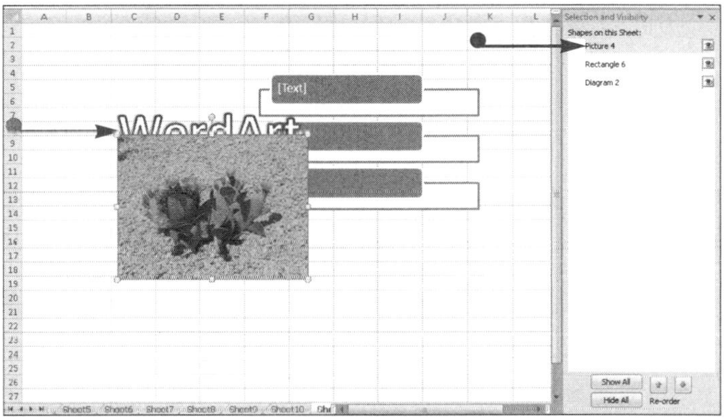

MASTER IT

What does the eye icon mean that appears beside each graphic in the Selection and Visibility task pane?

▼ The eye icon indicates whether a graphic is visible in the worksheet. You can click the eye icon to hide a graphic so that it is not visible on the worksheet. When you click the eye icon, the graphic disappears from view in the worksheet, and the eye icon becomes a blank square in the Selection and Visibility task pane.

Can I move a graphic to a position other than the top or bottom layers of the worksheet?

▼ Yes. In the Selection and Visibility task pane, select the graphic you want to move. Then use the Reorder arrows, and at the bottom of the pane, to move the graphic up or down in the list.

What kinds of graphic elements appear in the Selection and Visibility task pane?

▼ All types of graphic elements appear, including charts, shapes, text boxes, WordArt, SmartArt, Clip Art, pictures, and embedded objects.

When I select a SmartArt graphic element, how can I display the Selection and Visibility task pane?

▼ On the Format tab, click Arrange and then click Selection Pane.

Align Graphic Elements

You can align two or more graphic elements in a worksheet. You can align their left edges, their right edges, their vertical centers, their tops, their horizontal middles, or their bottoms. If you are aligning three or more graphic elements, you can also align them so that you equally distribute the distance between them either horizontally or vertically.

Depending on the alignment option that you select, objects move straight up, down, left, or right, and they might cover another object on the worksheet; you can either move the other object or undo the alignment. When you align objects by their middles or centers, no object necessarily remains stationary, and all of the objects might move.

You can also group objects so that they function as one object, and you can align grouped objects with other objects.

MASTER IT

How do I group graphic elements?

▼ Select the graphic elements you want to group by holding the Ctrl key as you click the outer boundary of each graphic element. Then click the Format tab under Drawing Objects or Picture Tools. In the Arrange group, click the Group button. From the drop-down list that appears, click Group.

Align Graphic Elements

1. Click a graphic element to select it.
2. Press and hold Ctrl and repeat Step 1.
3. Repeat Steps 1 and 2 for each graphic element you want to align.
   - Picture Tools or Drawing Tools appear here.
4. Click the Format tab.
5. Click the Align button.
6. Click an alignment option.

   Excel aligns the graphic elements.

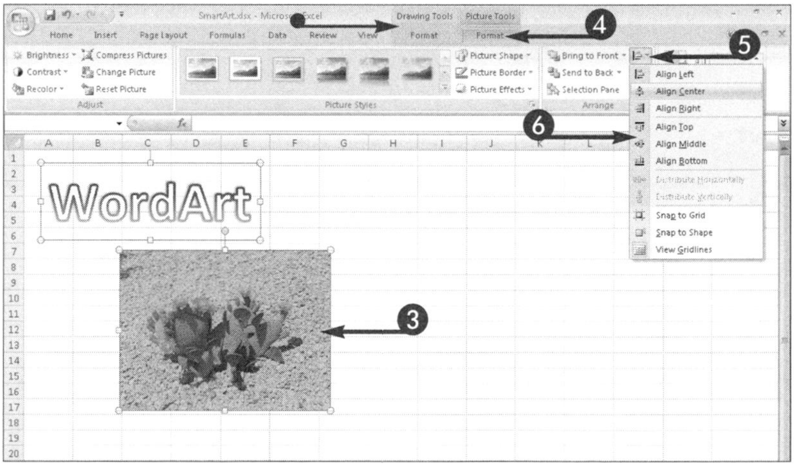

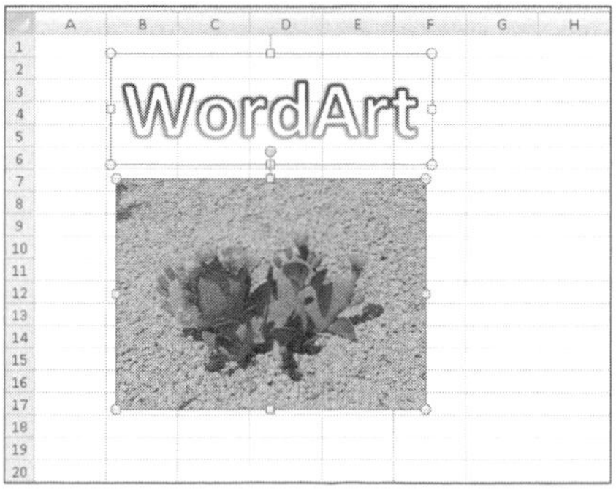

Rotate Graphic Elements

You can rotate a shape, text box, WordArt graphic element, Clip Art image, or picture. Rotating can add interest to your graphic element. You can drag to rotate to an angle that pleases your eye, or you can quickly rotate by 90 degrees either left or right using the Rotate command on the Ribbon. You can also display a graphic element upside down by flipping it vertically, or you can flip it horizontally to display a mirror image of the graphic element. To flip a graphic element, you can use commands on the Rotate menu.

If you want to rotate a graphic element using precise angles or you want to change its size and simultaneously rotate it, you can use the Size and Properties dialog box. You open this dialog box using the last command on the Rotate menu.

MASTER IT

How do I rotate a graphic element 90 degrees to the left?

▼ You can use the Rotate button on the Ribbon. Click the graphic element to select it. Picture Tools or Drawing Tools appear on the Ribbon, depending on the type of graphic you select. Click the Format tab and then click the Rotate button in the Arrange group. From the drop-down menu, click Rotate Left 90°.

Rotate Graphic Elements

1. Click a graphic element to select it.
   - Handles appear around the graphic element.
   - Picture Tools or Drawing Tools appear on the Ribbon, depending on the type of graphic you select.
2. Move the mouse pointer over the round green circle at the top of the graphic element (✥ changes to ↻).
3. Drag the mouse in the direction you want to rotate (↻ changes to ⟳).
   - Live preview shows the rotation in progress.
4. Release the mouse pointer when the graphic element has rotated to the degree you want.

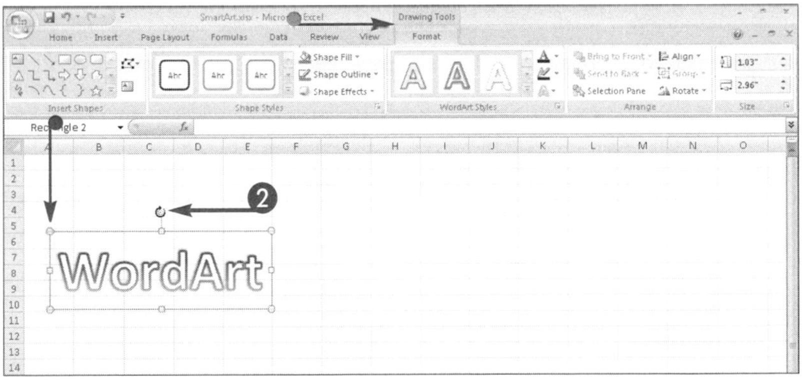

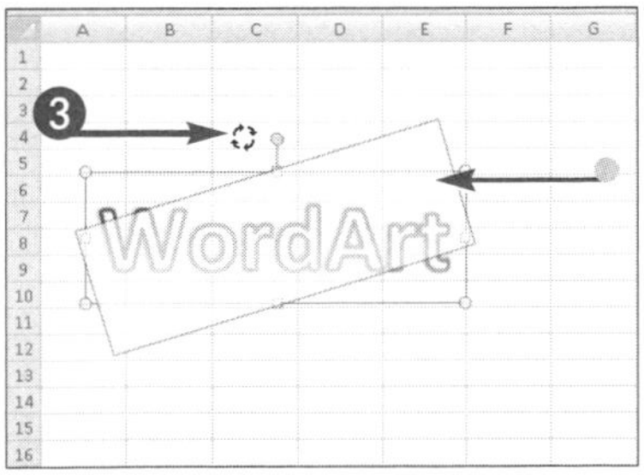

23 Working with Tables

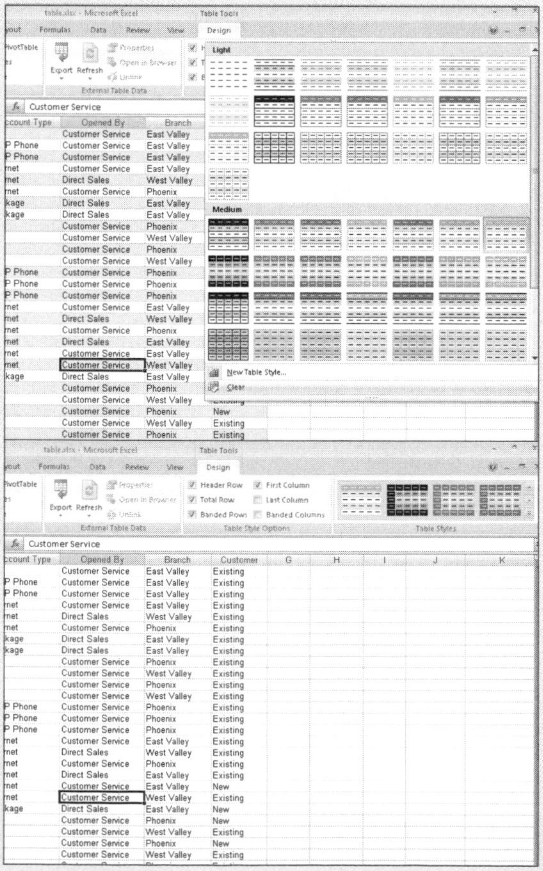

24 Summarizing Data with PivotTables and PivotCharts

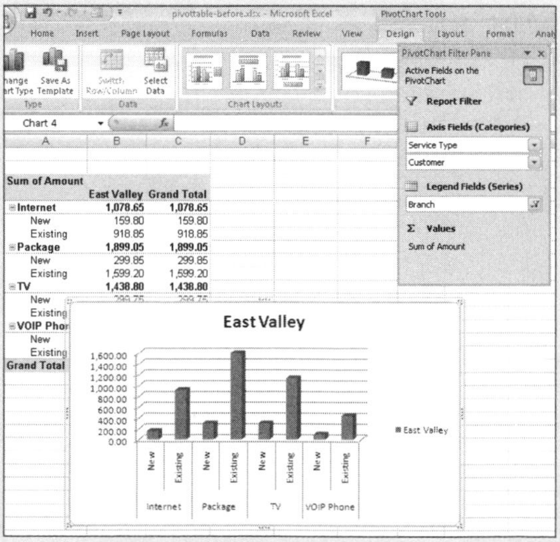

PART V
ANALYZING DATA

25 Visually Analyzing Data

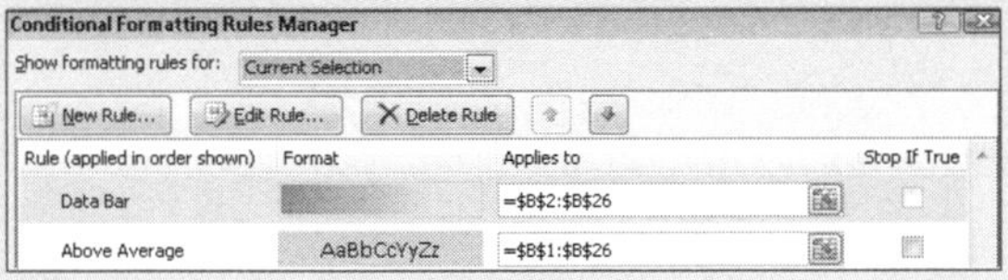

26 Linking and Consolidating Worksheets

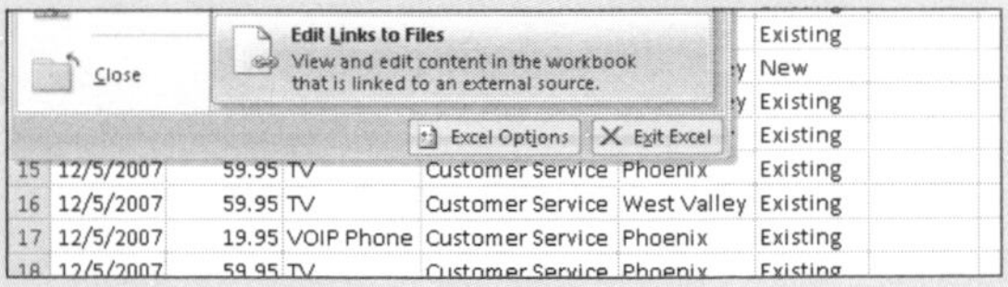

27 Performing What-If Analysis

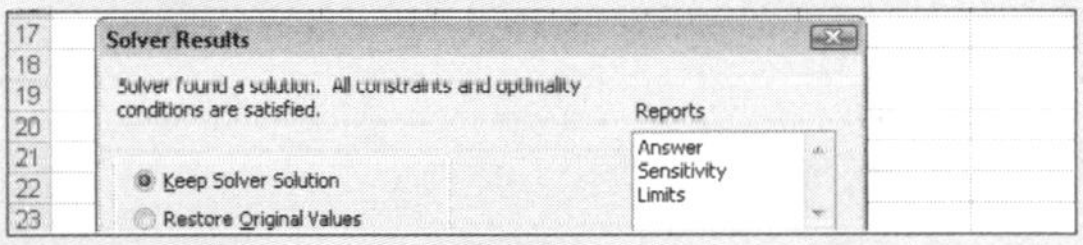

28 Performing Advanced Statistical Analysis

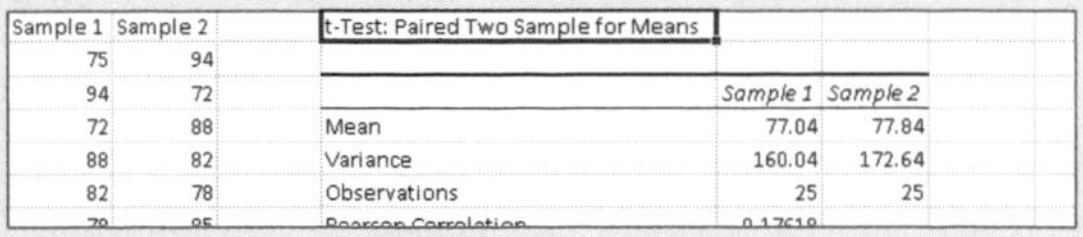

Create a Table

You can create a table from any rectangular range of related data in a worksheet. Each row in a table contains information about a single entity or event, and each column contains a specific piece of information. The first row can, but does not need to, contain labels that describe each column's information.

When you create a table, Excel identifies the information in the range as a table and simultaneously formats the table and adds AutoFilter arrows to each column. You can also easily add a summary row to a table that summarizes data in some way. When you press the Tab key with the cell pointer in a table, the cell pointer stays in the table, moving right to the next cell and to the next table row when you tab from the last column. When you scroll down a table so that the header row disappears, Excel replaces the column letters with the labels that appear in the header row. When you create a formula that references table cells, you can refer to the table by name or by using the column labels. Any formulas that you enter in a column are automatically propagated to all other cells in the column.

Create a Table

1. Set up a range in a worksheet that contains similar information for each row.
2. Click anywhere in the range.

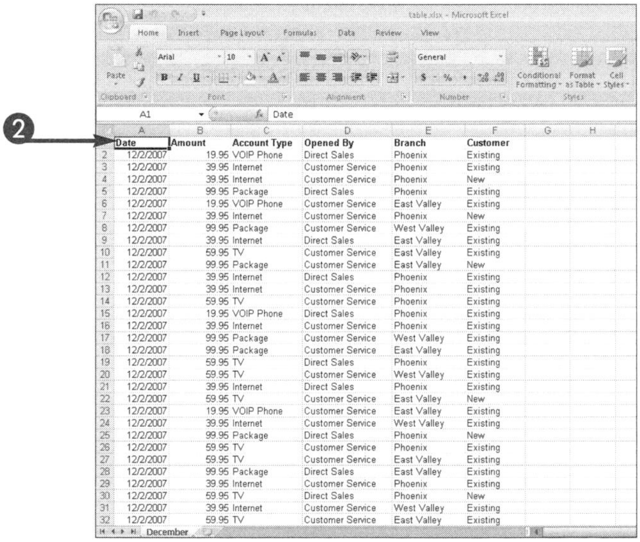

3. Click the Insert tab.
4. Click Table.

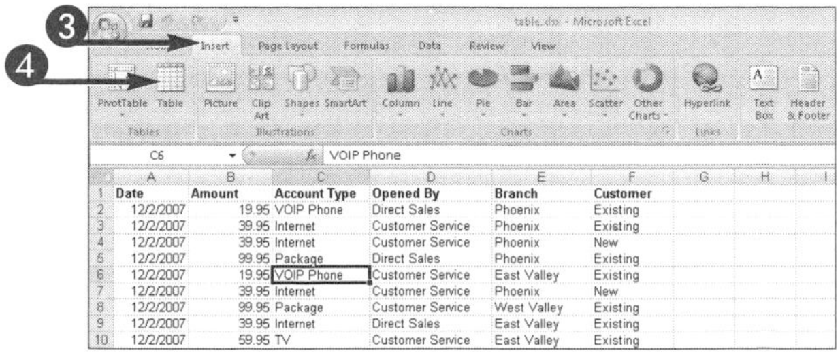

The Create Table dialog box appears, displaying a suggested range for the table.

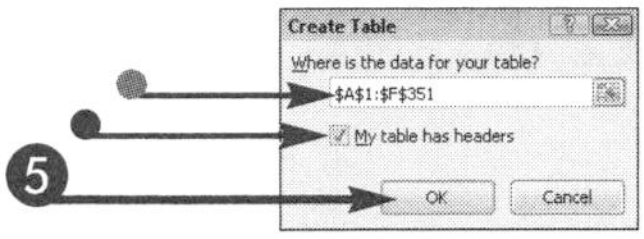

- You can click here (☑ changes to ☐) if labels for each column do *not* appear in Row 1.
- You can drag in the worksheet to select a new range that defines the table boundaries.

5 Click OK.

Excel creates a table and applies a table style to it.

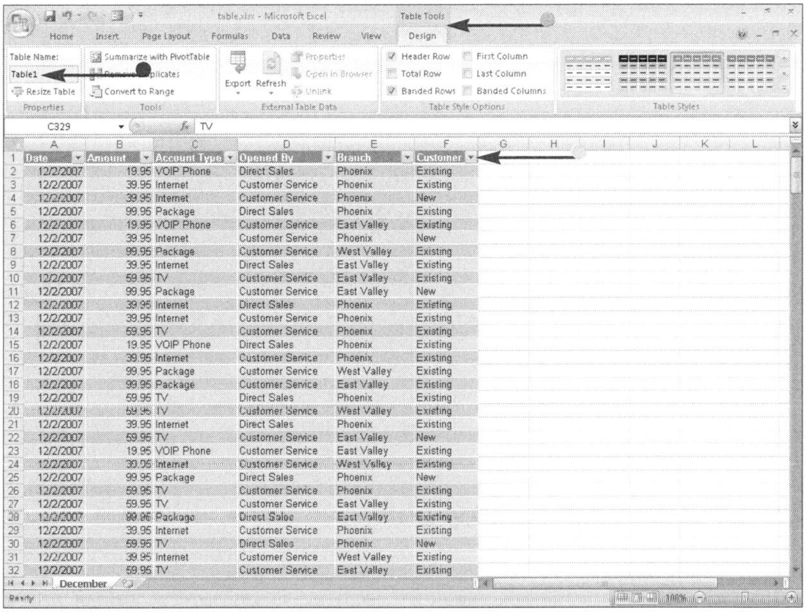

- Table Tools appear on the Ribbon.
- A ▾ appears in each column title.
- Excel assigns the table a generic name.

MASTER IT

Can I change the table's name?

▼ Yes, you can. Click the Design tab under Table Tools. Then, in the Properties group, click in the Table Name field and delete the generic name. Type a new name and click anywhere outside the Table Name field. When you click outside the Table Name field, Excel assigns the new name to the table.

What happens if my range does not contain labels in the first row?

▼ Assuming that you deselected the My Table Has Headers option, as described in Step 5, Excel inserts a row at the top of the range and provides generic labels for each column (Column1, Column2, Column3, and so on). A ▾ appears beside each generic column title.

When should I use a table and when should I use a database range?

▼ The two are similar in the way they allow you to organize information, and you can perform all of the same functions in a database that you can in a table. However, displaying most of the common information, such as the largest value, or selecting records that match a criterion are easier in a table than in a database.

PART V

Change the Size of a Table

After you create a table, you can easily increase its size by adding rows or columns to the table. You can automatically add columns to the right edge of a table, and you can automatically add rows to the bottom of a table unless you have added a row containing totals to the bottom of the table, as described in the section, "Work with the Total Row." You can also add rows or columns within the table instead of adding them to the edges of the table.

You can decrease the size of a table by eliminating rows or columns from the table. When you delete rows or columns from a table, Excel eliminates the information that appears in the rows or columns without affecting cells outside the table. Suppose that cell C40 contains information and is not part of the table you defined that covers the range A1:F25. If you delete column C from the table, then Excel retains the information in cell C40.

You can also move a table to a different location in the same worksheet or to a different worksheet.

Change the Size of a Table

Increase Table Size

1. Click a cell in a column or row that is adjacent to the table.
2. Type an entry.

Note: *What you type is not relevant.*

3. Press Enter or click ✓.

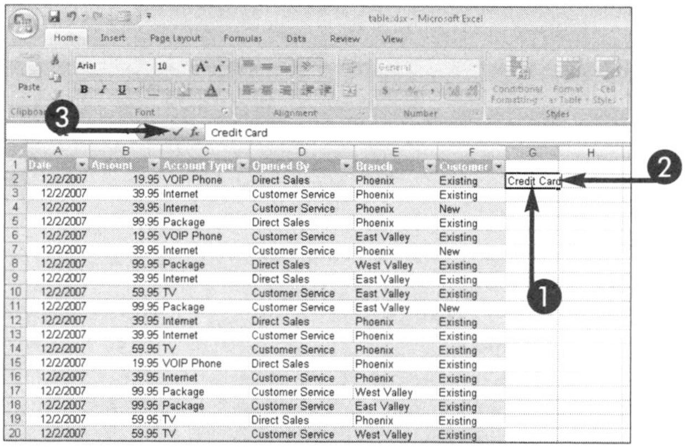

- Excel stores the entry in the cell and expands the table to include a new row or column.

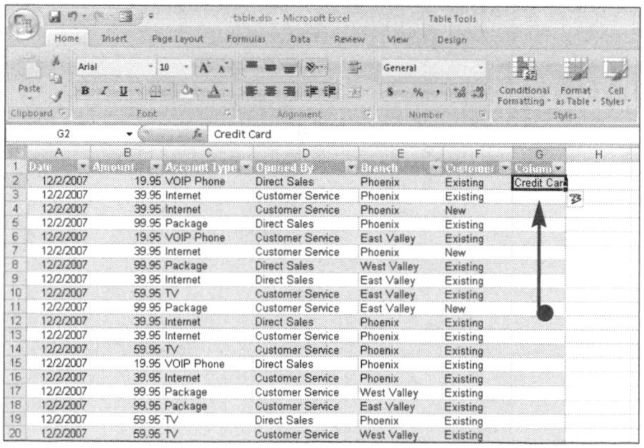

Reduce Table Size

1. Right-click any cell in the row or column you want to remove from the table.
2. From the menu that appears, click Delete.
3. Click Table Columns or Table Rows.

Note: *This example removes a column.*

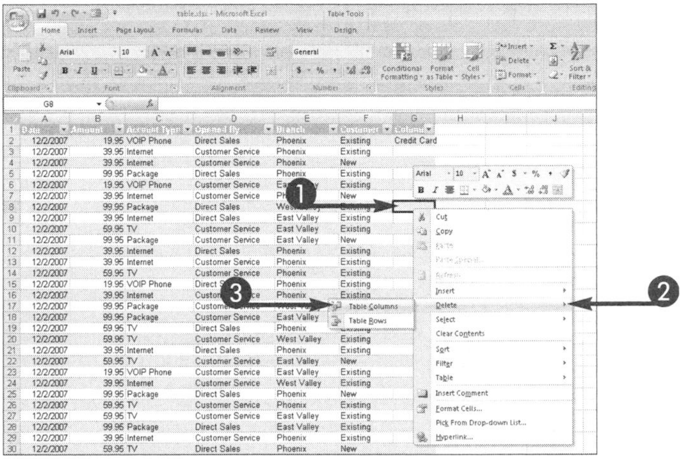

- Excel removes the column from the table and any information it contained.

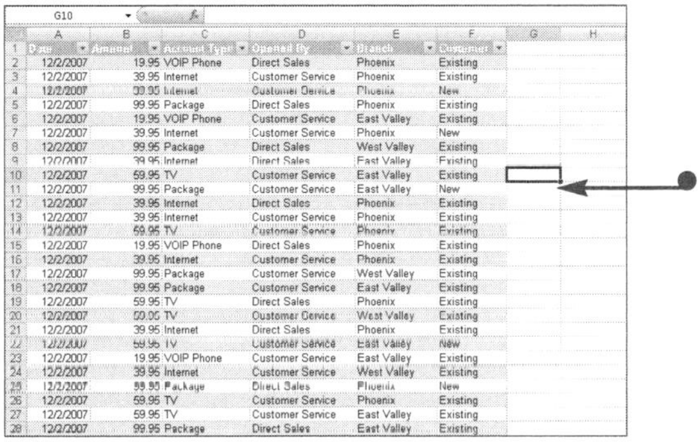

MASTER IT

How do I move a table to another location?

▼ To move a table within the same worksheet, click in the table and place ✚ on the outside border of the table (✚ changes to ✥). Drag the table to the new location. To move the table to a new worksheet, select the table, click ✂ on the Home tab, select the cell representing the upper-left corner of the table on new worksheet, and click Paste on the Home tab.

How do I select a table?

▼ Move ✚ to the upper-left corner of the label cell in the upper-left corner of the table (✚ changes to ↘). Then click. You can also select table rows or columns by moving ✚ into the column heading area or to the left side of the entry in the left column of the table (✚ changes to ↓ or →). Click to select the table row or column.

How do I add a row or column in the middle of the table?

▼ Right-click a cell that appears to the right of the column or below the row that you want to add. When Excel displays a shortcut menu, click Insert. Click Table Columns to the Left to insert a column to the left of the selected cell. Click Table Rows Above to add a row above the selected cell.

Use a Data Entry Form

You can manage the data in a table by working directly in the table, or you can use a form to manage the data in the table. In fact, you can use a form to manage data in a range that you have not formatted as a table, as long as Excel can recognize your data as a table. Excel can recognize your data as a table if you make sure that you include a row of column labels at the top of the range. Many people prefer to use a data entry form to work with table data because, using a data entry form, you can enter new data, edit existing data, and find data.

To display a form that you can use to manage data, you use a command that does not appear on the Ribbon by default. However, you can add the command to the Quick Access toolbar by customizing it. When you finish customizing the Quick Access toolbar, a new button appears on it that you can use to display a data entry form for your table or range.

Use a Data Entry Form

Display the Form Button

1. Click ▾.
2. Click More Commands.

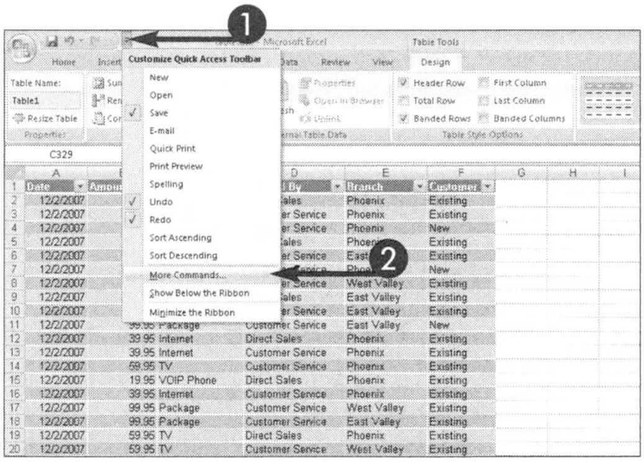

The Customize page of the Excel Options dialog box appears.

3. Click ▾.
4. Click Commands Not in the Ribbon.
5. From this list, click Form.
6. Click Add.
   - The Form command appears here.
7. Click OK.

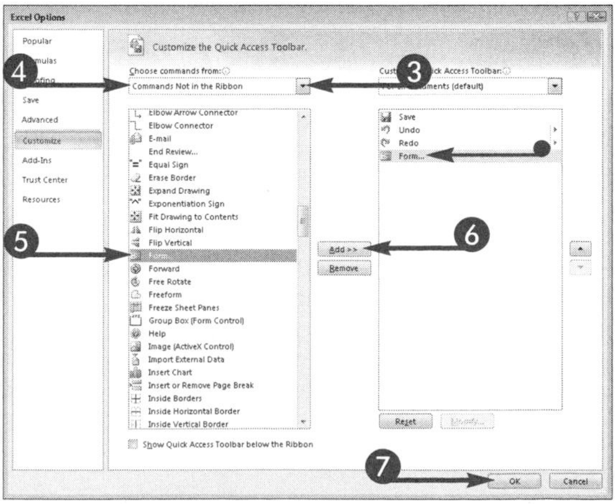

Enter Data

8 Click the Form button ( ).

- The data entry dialog box opens, displaying the information on the row containing the cell pointer.

9 Click New.

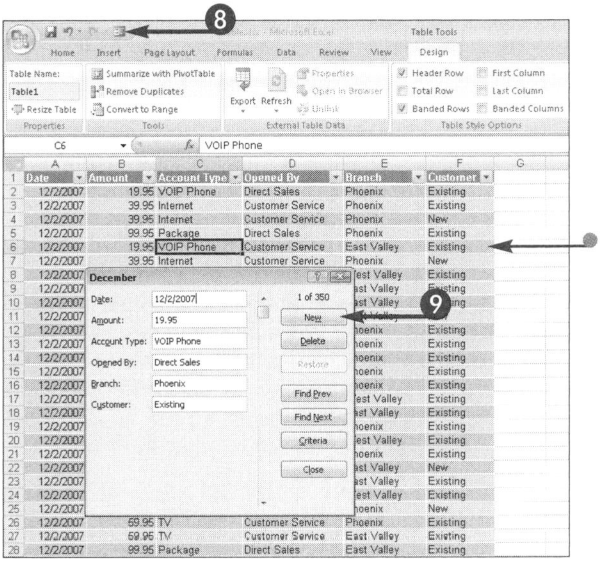

A blank form appears.

10 Fill in the form.

11 Click New to save the information and start entering new information.

12 Repeat Steps 9 to 11 for each new row of information you want to add to the table.

Excel adds the new information to the table.

13 Click Close when you are done.

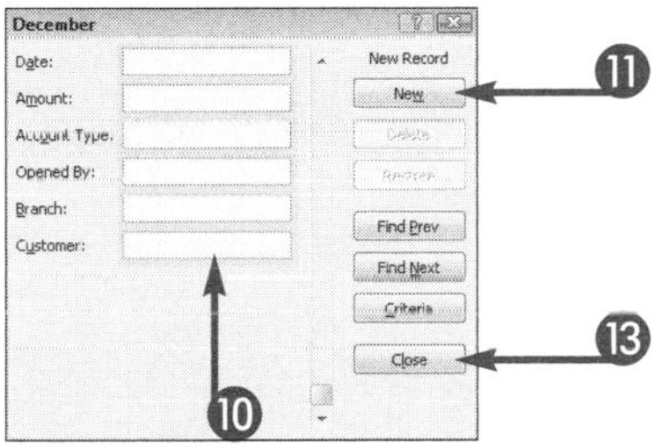

MASTER IT

Can I control the placement of the Form button on the Quick Access Toolbar?

▼ Yes, you can control the placement of all of the buttons on the Quick Access Toolbar. Complete Steps 1 and 2 in the subsection, "Display the Form Button." In the right-hand column, click the Form button. By default, it appears at the bottom of the list. Click and to move the button up or down in the list, which results in the button moving left or right on the Quick Access Toolbar.

When I add new data, where does Excel put it?

▼ If the data in your table is not sorted, Excel places the new information in the first row of the table, just below the column headings. If your data is sorted, Excel places the new information in the table in the row where it would appear based on the sort.

When I add new data, must I fill in all of the fields listed on the form?

▼ No. From a technology standpoint, none of the fields on the form are required and Excel does not force you to fill in all of the fields. However, if you do not fill in all of the fields, some of the entries in your table will be incomplete.

continued

Use a Data Entry Form *(Continued)*

In addition to adding new entries, you can use the form to search for entries as well as to edit or delete existing entries. When you search for entries, you establish search criteria using the form. The more criteria you enter on the form, the more you narrow the search. Excel searches initially from the top of the table and displays the entry that matches your query. You can determine which entry you are viewing by looking in the upper-right corner of the Form window, where Excel displays the entry's record number. Remember that the record number does not correspond to the row number and, in fact, will be one less than the row number because Excel does not count the first row of the table, which contains the labels, as an entry. If more than one record matches your search criteria, you can click buttons to view the next or previous entries.

Once you find a record, you can examine the entry in the Form window or in the table behind the Form window. You can also make changes to the entry in the Form window or in the table, and you can use the Form window to delete a record.

Use a Data Entry Form *(continued)*

Search for an Entry

❶ Click ▤.

❷ Click Criteria.

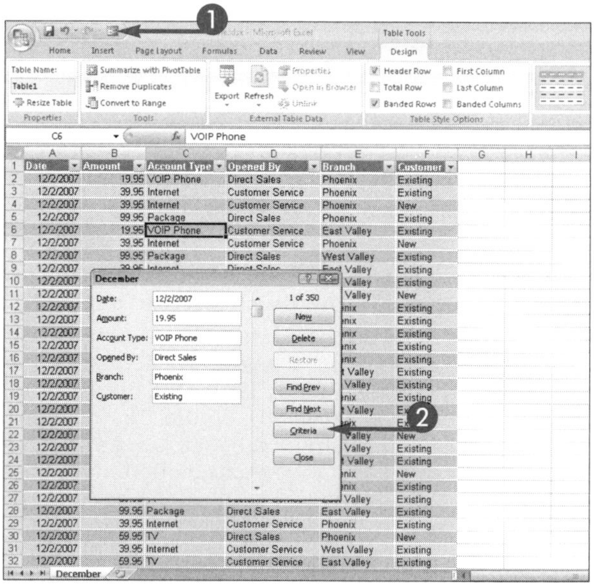

A blank form appears.

❸ Type your criteria.

❹ Click Find Next or Find Prev.

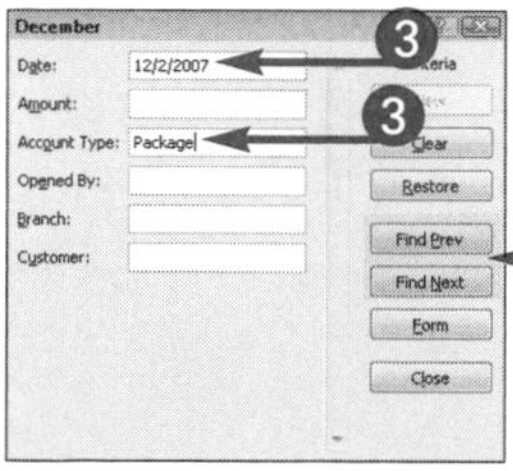

- Excel finds a record that matches the criteria.

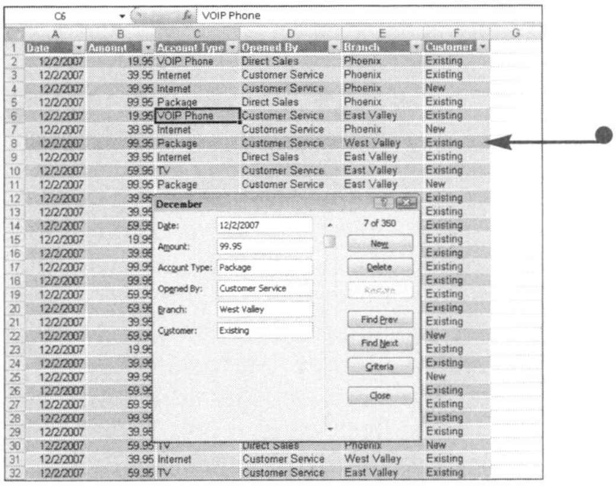

Edit an Entry

1. Modify the record as needed.

Note: *This example changes the Opened By field from Customer Service to Direct Sales.*

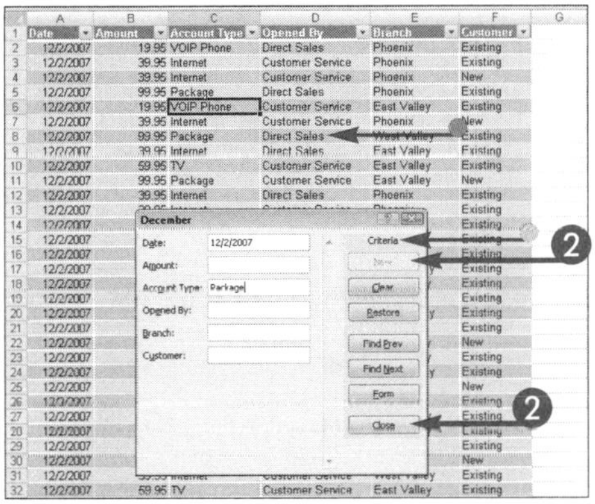

2. Click New, Criteria, or Close.
   - Excel saves the record.
   - If you click Criteria, the button disappears from the form, but the mode appears on the form.

How do I delete an entry using the Form window?

▼ Complete Steps 1 to 4 in the subsection, "Search for an Entry," to find and display the entry you want to delete. While viewing the entry in the Form window, click the Delete button. If you change your mind about deleting the record, close the Form window and click ↶.

Can I use the Restore button to retrieve an entry I deleted?

▼ No, you cannot. You must close the Form window and click ↶. You can use the Restore button to remove any typing while setting criteria or editing an entry, but the Restore button only works if you click it before you save the entry. Once you save the entry, you must close the Form window and click ↶ to undo changes.

What does the Clear button do?

▼ The Clear button removes criteria that you specify in the Form window so that you can change the criteria and search for a different entry. If you mis-type while specifying criteria and Excel does not find any entries that match the criteria, Excel might display the first entry in the table or the last entry you viewed. Close the Form window and reopen it to specify new criteria.

Create a Drop-Down List for Data Entry

You can control the information entered into a table by providing a list of valid entries for each column in the table. That way, when a user wants to add entries to a table, the user can open the list and select the appropriate choice from the list. Using this technique ensures that the information stored in the table remains consistent. Consistency is important when you later want to find a particular entry in a table. If the entries are made inconsistently, you will have a harder time finding the entry. Even a simple spelling mistake can stop you from finding an entry. For example, if you search for "Internet" and the entry you are trying to find contains a misspelling of "Internet," Excel cannot find the entry. However, if you provide a list of entries from which to select, misspellings and inconsistently entered information are no longer an issue.

Before you establish a list of valid entries, you need to list the valid entries in a range outside your table. Then you can identify them as the valid entries when you set up the drop-down list for each column of your table.

Create a Drop-Down List for Data Entry

1. Outside the table in your worksheet, create ranges that contain valid entries for each column of the table.
2. Select the cells in the first column for which you want to establish a list of valid entries.

Note: Do not select the column label.

3. Click the Data tab.
4. Click Data Validation.

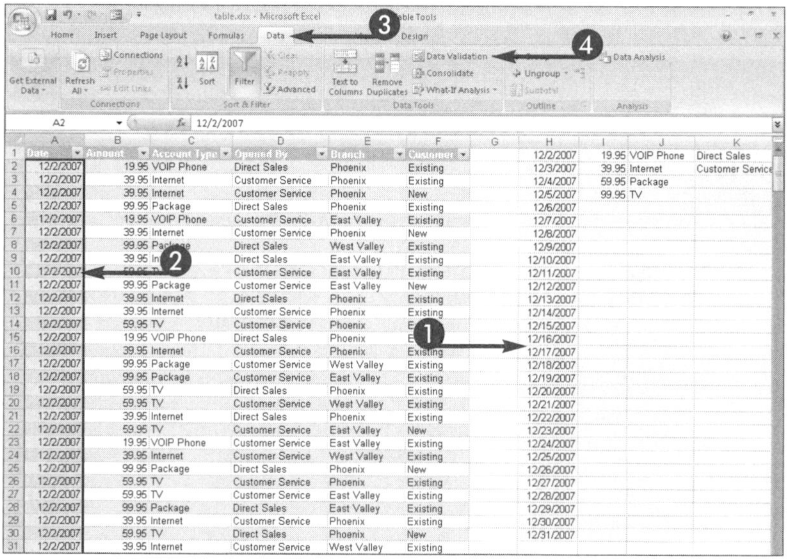

The Data Validation dialog box appears.

5. Click ▾.
6. Click List.
7. Click ▦.

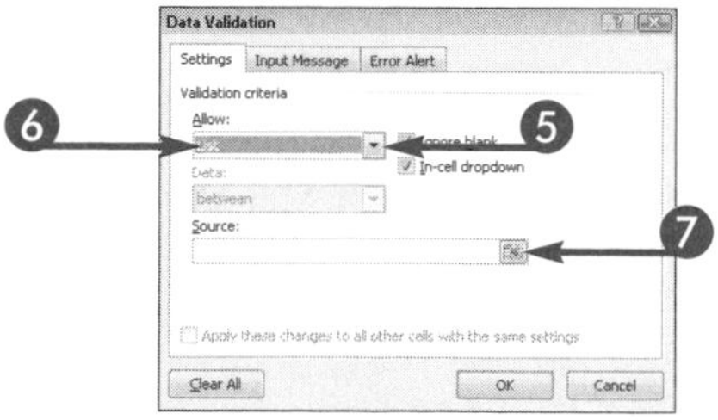

Excel collapses the Data Validation dialog box.

8. Drag to select the range containing the valid entries for the selected column.

9. Click .

Excel redisplays the Data Validation dialog box.

10. Click OK.

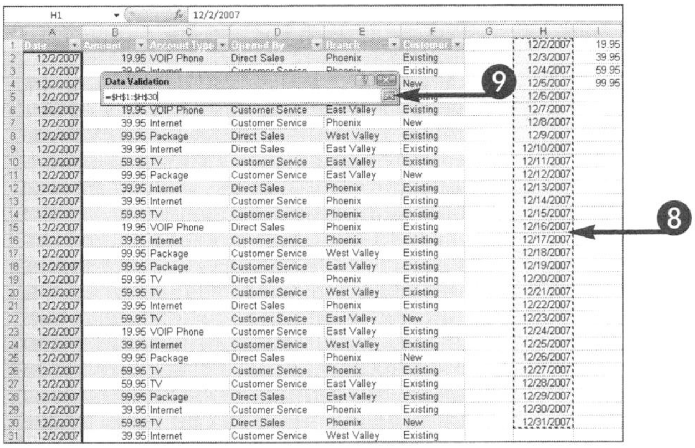

Excel establishes the valid list entries for each cell you selected in Step 2.

11. Click outside the selected range to cancel the selection.

12. Click any cell in the range you selected in Step 2.

Excel displays beside the cell.

13. Click .

- Excel displays the valid entries for the cell.

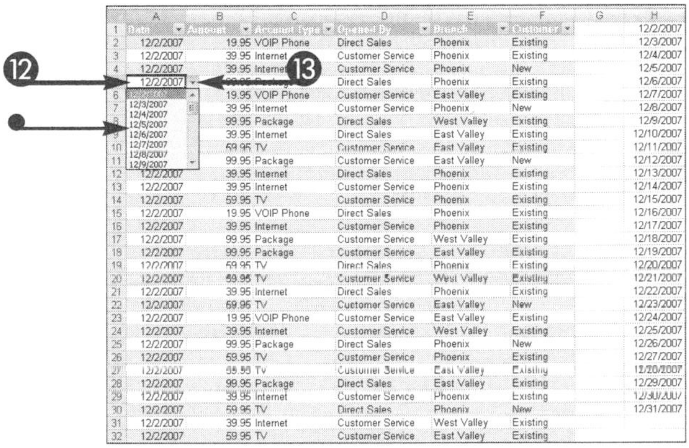

MASTER IT

Does it matter where I put the list of valid entries?

▼ Yes. The list should be on the same worksheet as your table. If you place the list on a separate worksheet, then you need to create a named range for the list. Do not perform Steps 7 to 9; instead, type the name of the range in the Source field in the Data Validation dialog box.

Is there another way to establish a list of valid entries?

▼ If your list is short, you can skip Step 1 and Steps 7 to 9, and type the entries directly in the Source field in the Data Validation dialog box. Separate the entries using the list separator specified in the Regional Settings dialog box — use a comma if you use United States regional settings.

Can a user type information into the cell if I set up a list of valid entries?

▼ Yes. The user does not need to select a value from the list, as long as the user enters a valid value. If the user enters an invalid value, an error dialog box appears, explaining that only valid values can be entered in the cell. The user can then click the Cancel button and open the list to identify the valid values.

PART V

Filter or Sort Table Information

When you create a table, Excel automatically adds AutoFilter arrows to each column; you can use these arrows to quickly and easily filter and sort the information in the table in a variety of ways.

When you filter a table, you display only those rows that meet conditions you specify, and you specify those conditions by making selections from the AutoFilter lists. Suppose that your worksheet contains a table that tracks daily sales by a cable service provider, and your table shows the date of purchase, the amount, the type of account, whether the sale was made by Customer Service or by telemarketers, the branch office responsible for the sale, and whether the sale was made to a new or existing customer. You can filter the table to display, for example, only those sales made to new customers by a particular branch office.

You can also use the AutoFilter arrows to sort information in a variety of ways. Excel recognizes the type of data stored in table columns and offers you sorting choices that are appropriate for the type of data. For example, in a column containing numbers you can sort from smallest to largest, while in a column containing text you can sort alphabetically.

Filter or Sort Table Information

Filter a Table

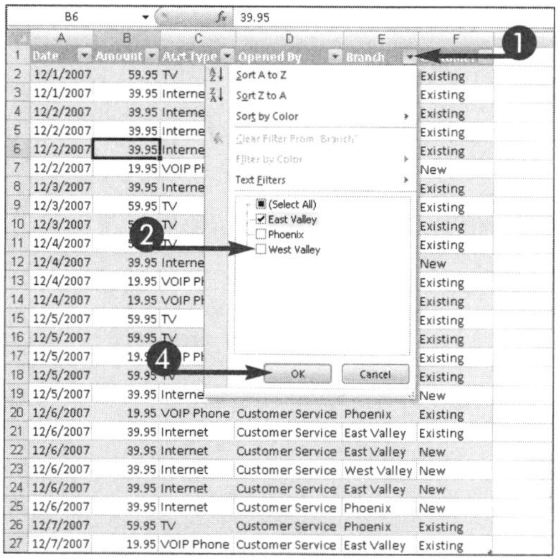

1. Click ▾ next to the column heading you want to use for filtering.

   Excel displays a list of possible filters.

2. Click a filter choice (☐ changes to ☑).
3. Repeat Step 2 until you have selected all of the filters you want to use.
4. Click OK.

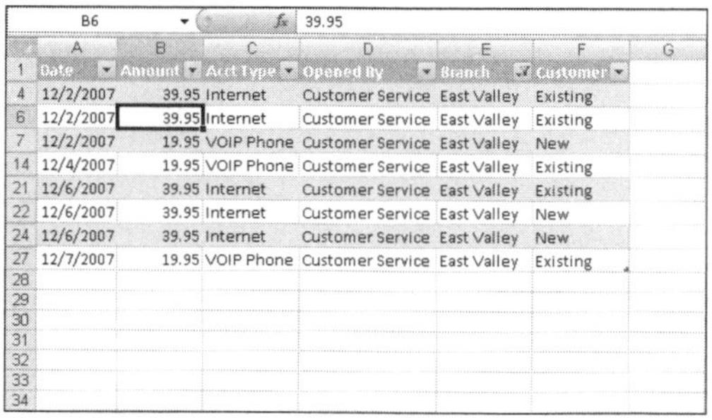

Excel removes data meeting the criteria you selected in Step 2 from view.

Sort a Table

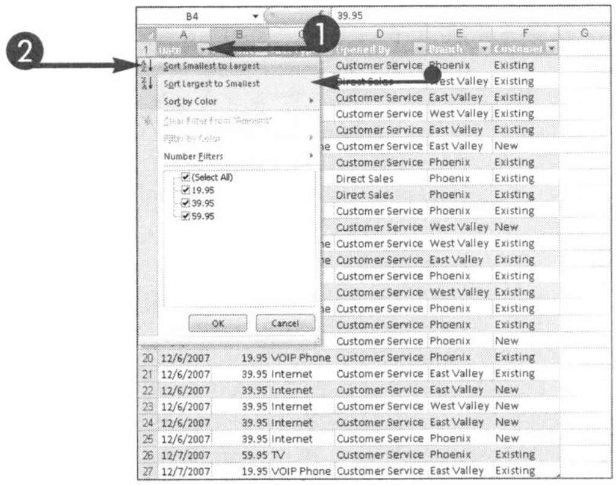

1. Click ▾ next to the column heading you want to use for filtering.
   - Excel displays a list of possible sort orders.
2. Click a sort order.

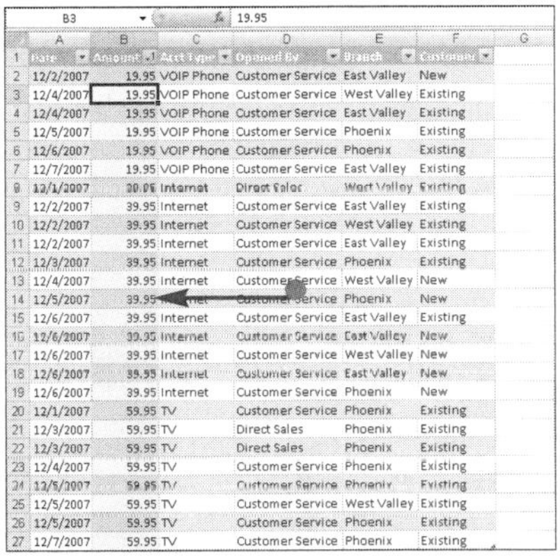

- Excel reorders the information based on your choice in Step 2.

MASTER IT

How does the Sort by Color option work?

▼ If you apply font colors, cell colors, or both to some cells in the table, you can then sort the table information by the colors you assigned. You can manually assign colors or you can assign colors using Conditional Formatting; see Chapter 25 for details on using Conditional Formatting.

What happens if I click Number Filters?

▼ Excel recognizes the kind of data stored in each column of a table and offers you additional filtering choices based on the data type. Number filters include choices such as Equals, Greater Than, Between, and Top 10. For example, if your table contains sales data by sales person, then choosing Top 10 displays the entries for the top ten salespeople in the table.

I do not see the Autofilter ▾. What should I do?

▼ Click the Data tab and then click the Filter button. This button toggles on and off the appearance of the AutoFilter ▾ in a table.

How do I remove filtering so that I can see all of the table data?

▼ Click each AutoFilter ▾, and then click Clear Filter From or click Select All (☐ changes to ☑).

Change the Table Style

You can apply a table style to your chart to change the colors in your table. Table styles are combinations of colors, and the Excel Table Styles Gallery organizes the available color combinations into three categories: Light, Medium, and Dark. While the three categories remain, you can change the color combinations that are available in each category if you change the document theme in the workbook from the Page Layout tab. For details on working with themes, see Chapter 4.

You can select a table style from the Table Styles Gallery or, if you cannot find a table style that suits your needs, you can create your own table style using the New Table Quick Style dialog box.

Table styles do not override any formatting you may have applied to the cells in the table before you converted the range to a table. If you find that you cannot apply a table style, you can remove the manually applied formatting.

MASTER IT

How do I remove manually applied formatting?

▼ To remove background fill colors, click the Home tab, and then click ▾ beside [icon] and click No Fill. To remove font colors, repeat this process using the Font Color button on the Ribbon, which appears immediately beside [icon].

Change the Table Style

1. Click anywhere in the table.
   - Table Tools appear on the Ribbon.
2. Click the Design tab.
3. Click ▾.

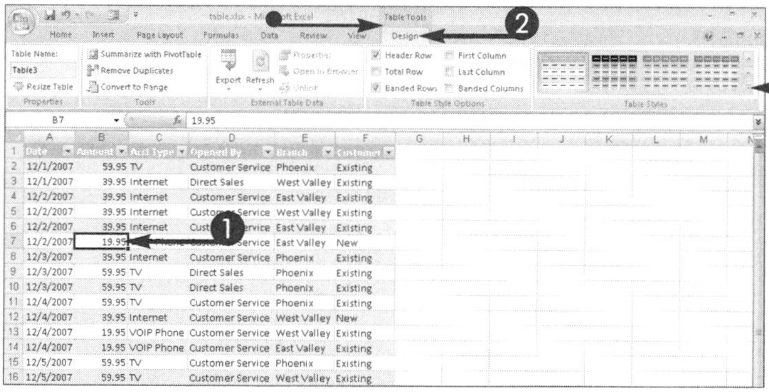

The Table Styles Gallery appears.

4. Point at a style.
   - Live Preview displays the table using the style.
5. Click a style to apply it.

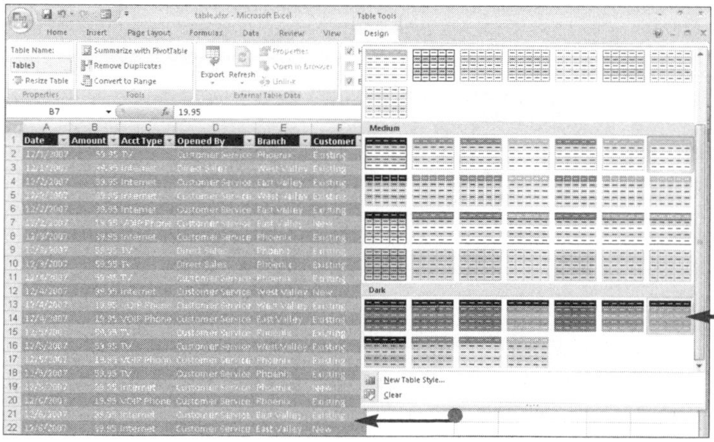

Apply Special Formatting

You can apply special formatting to the first column, the last column, or both the first and last columns of the table. When you apply special formatting to the first or last column, Excel applies boldface to the words or numbers that appear in those columns, making them stand out to draw the reader's attention to them. If the table style uses black type, then the special formatting makes the black type in the specified column bolder. Similarly, if the table style uses white type, then the special formatting makes the white type in the specified column bolder.

You would apply special formatting to the first column, the last column, or both first and last columns for a number of reasons. You might apply special formatting to the last column, for example, if it contains totals for values in the columns to the left of it. You might apply special formatting to the first column if the information in that column drives the information in the table; for example, if the table contains the grades of students for a variety of tests and the student names appear in the first column, you might apply special formatting to the first column.

Apply Special Formatting

1. Click anywhere in the table.
   - Table Tools appear on the Ribbon.
2. Click the Design tab.
3. Click First Column or Last Column (☐ changes to ☑, or ☑ changes to ☐).

Note: *This example applies special formatting to the first column.*

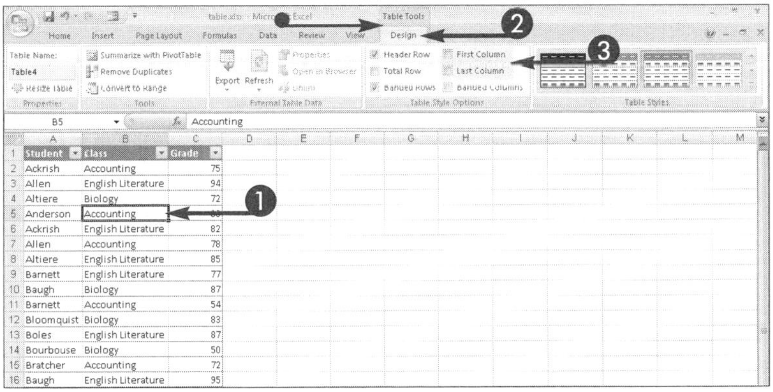

- Excel adds the formatting to your table.

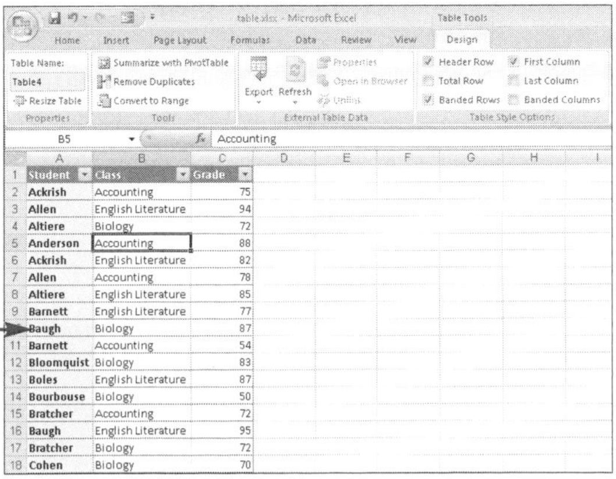

Display or Hide Banding

You can add row and column banding to a table to improve its appearance and its readability. The effect of row banding depends on the style originally applied to the table.

In many cases, row banding displays the rows of a table in an alternating pattern using two shades of the same color. In other cases, row banding results in Excel applying color to the gridlines that separate the rows.

Some table styles automatically include row banding, while other table styles do not, and you can add or remove row banding to or from any table, regardless of the style applied to the table.

Table styles do not automatically include column banding. Column banding can display the columns of a table in an alternating pattern using two shades of the same color. Column banding can also add color to the gridlines that separate the columns.

You can add column banding to any table, and you can display both row and column banding simultaneously. You might find that your table becomes more difficult to read when you apply banding to both rows and columns, unless the banding effect simply colors the gridlines that separate rows and columns.

Display or Hide Banding

Display Column Bands

1. Click anywhere in the table.
   - Table Tools appear on the Ribbon.
2. Click the Design tab.
3. Click Banded Columns (☐ changes to ☑).

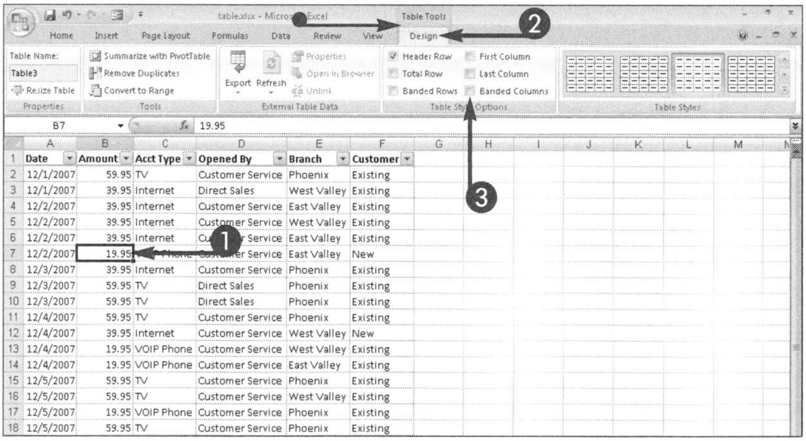

- Excel adds banding to the columns of your table.
- In this example, Excel applies shading to alternate columns.

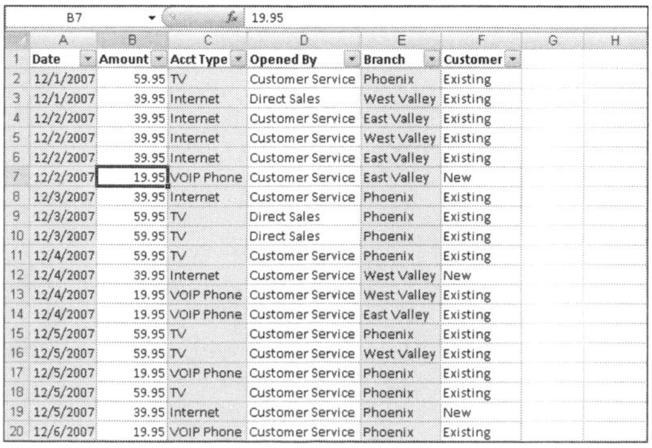

Display Row Bands

1. Click anywhere in the table.
   - Table Tools appear on the Ribbon.
2. Click the Design tab.
3. Click Banded Rows (☑ changes to ☐).

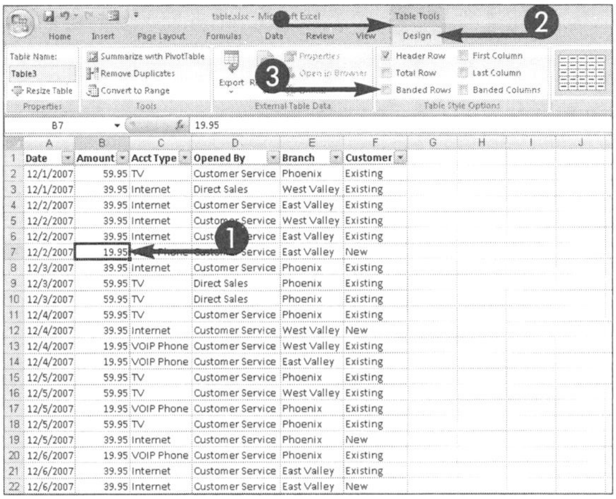

Excel adds banding to the rows of your table.

In this example, Excel applies shading to alternate rows.

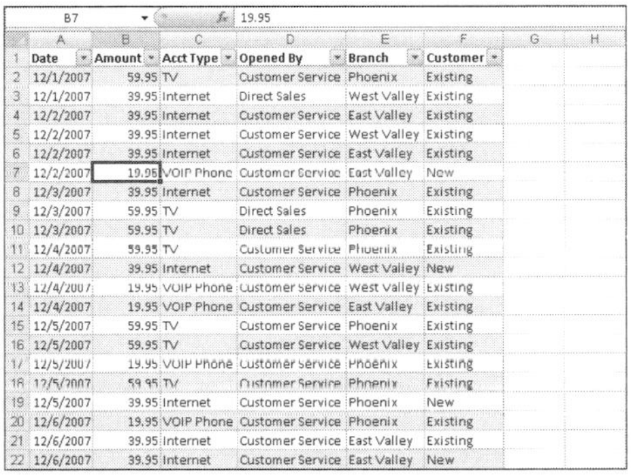

PART V

MASTER IT

I followed the steps and nothing happened. What did I do wrong?

▼ You probably did not do anything wrong, and Excel probably did add banding. Follow the steps to remove banding and then repeat the process. However, before you begin, look carefully at the gridlines in your table. Then examine them again after you add banding. Based on your table style, Excel probably added color to the gridlines instead of adding shading to alternating rows or columns.

If I remove banding and then switch to a different table style, does Excel automatically add banding?

▼ No. Each of the table styles has a redefined method for applying banding — either by using shading on alternating rows or columns or by adding color to gridlines. However, if you remove banding, Excel applies the next table style you select without its banding attributes. You can view them by adding banding to the new style.

How do I remove row or column bands?

▼ Adding or removing banding to rows or columns is a toggle operation; performing the steps once adds banding, and repeating them removes banding. To remove banding, repeat the steps in either subsection, Display Column Bands or Display Row Bands. When you perform Step 3, ☑ changes to ☐ and Excel removes the banding from your table.

Hide or Display the Header Row

You can hide or display the header row in a table. Excel displays the header row by default. As you scroll down in a table, the header row disappears, but Excel replaces the column letters with the labels stored in the header row.

At times, you might find it appropriate not to display the column titles that appear in the first row of the table. For example, if your table did not contain a header row when you created it, Excel displays generic headings in the first row of the table. If you are not working with filtering or sorting the table, you might find these generic titles distracting, and so you may prefer to view column letters as you scroll through the table.

When you hide the header row, Excel removes the AutoFilter arrow and any filters you applied. In addition, although you can refer to the header row in formulas even if you hide the header row, references to a hidden header row return zero values. When you redisplay the header row, formulas calculate properly. When you hide the header row, Excel adjusts all other worksheet references, and formulas might return unexpected results.

Hide or Display the Header Row

1. Click anywhere in the table.
   - Table Tools appear on the Ribbon.
2. Click the Design tab.
3. Click Header Row (☑ changes to ☐).

Note: *This example hides the header row.*

- Excel hides the header row in your table.

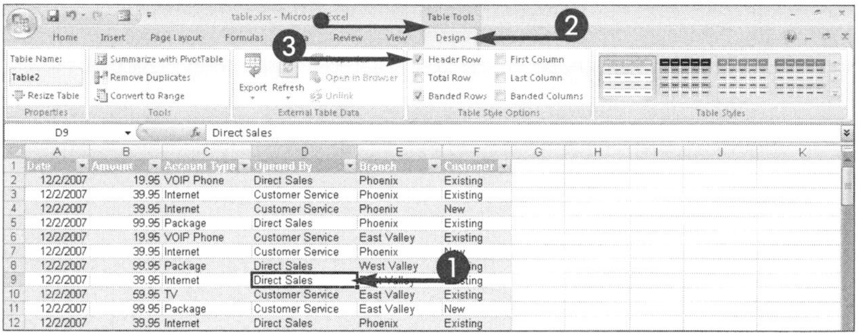

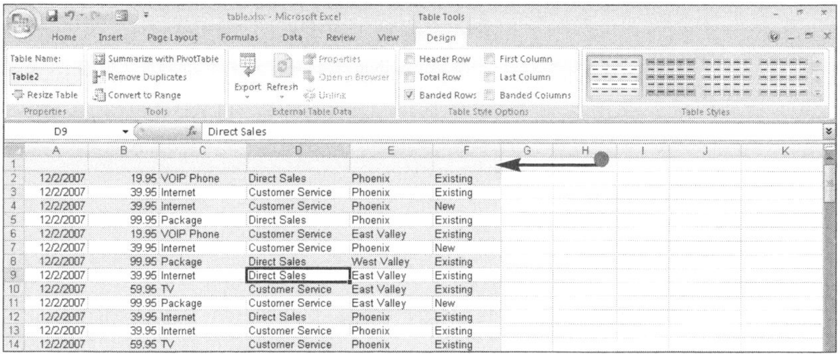

Work with the Total Row

You can add a total row to your table. The total row contains formulas that summarize the information in the table columns in various ways. Excel does not add a total row to the table by default.

When you add a total row to a table, , Excel displays a total in the last column of that row. If the last column of the table contains numbers, Excel will most likely include a formula that sums the numbers in the last column. If the last row contains text, Excel will most likely include a formula that counts the number of non-blank entries in the last table column.

In the total row, Excel makes available the most widely used summarizing formulas, and so you can easily change the formula. For example, you can use the Average formula to calculate the average of the numbers in the column, or you can use the Count Numbers formula to calculate the number of cells containing numbers in the column. You can use the Max formula to determine the maximum value in the column and the Min formula to determine the minimum value in the column.

Work with the Total Row

Add a Total Row

1. Click anywhere in the table.
   - Table Tools appear on the Ribbon.
2. Click the Design tab.
3. Click Total Row (☐ changes to ☑).

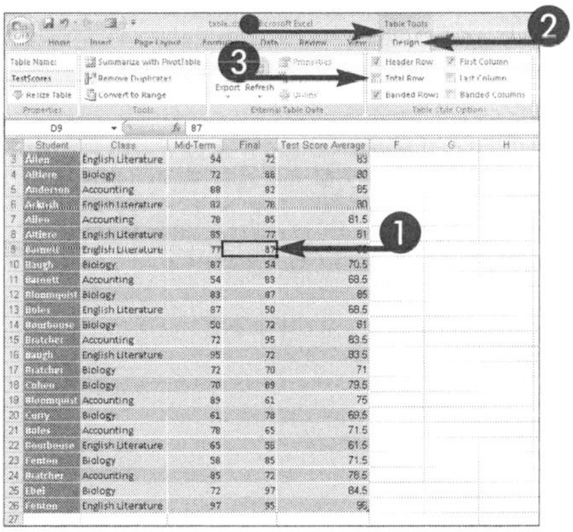

- Excel adds a total row to the bottom of your table.

In this example, the total row inserts the average test score for all students.

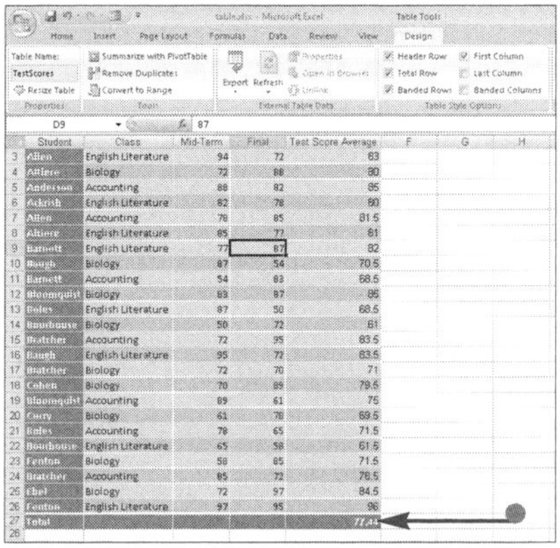

continued

Work with the Total Row *(Continued)*

When you add a total row to a table, you also find available two other commonly used summarizing formulas. You can use the StdDev formula to display the standard deviation of the values in the last column, and you can use the Var formula to display the statistical variance of the numbers in the last column.

You are not limited to using the common summarizing formulas; you can also insert any of the other functions available in Excel.

By default, the total row displays a formula in the last column of the table only, but you can display formulas in any and all of the cells in the total row, as appropriate for your table. You will find that the same formulas as the ones in the last cell of the total row are available to you in any cell along the total row.

The formulas you create using the total row do not use cell references; instead, they use references that refer to the table name and the labels in the first row of the table. When you create a table, Excel automatically creates a named range for the table; you can view it in the Name Manager window.

Work with the Total Row *(continued)*

Change the Formula

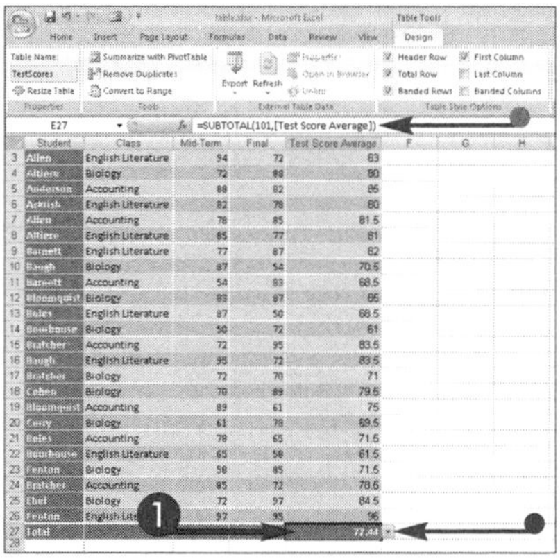

❶ Click the cell in the total row that contains a formula.

- Excel displays ▾ beside the cell.
- The formula in the cell appears here.

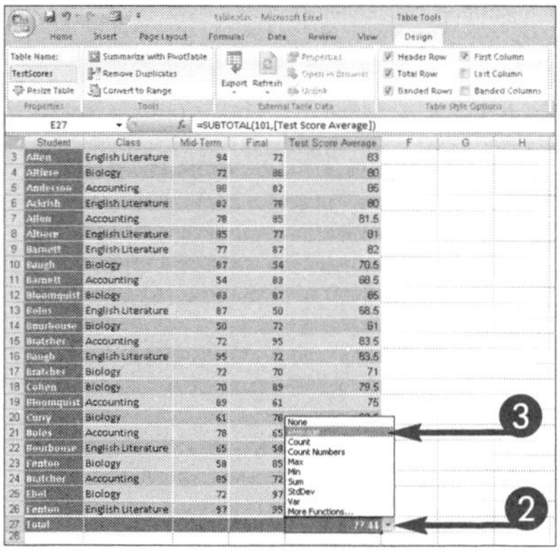

❷ Click ▾.

Excel displays the formulas from which you can choose.

❸ Click a formula to select it.

Add Other Formulas to the Total Row

1. Click the cell in the total row to which you want to add a formula.

   Excel displays ▾ beside the cell.

2. Click ▾.

   Excel displays the formulas from which you can select.

3. Select a formula.

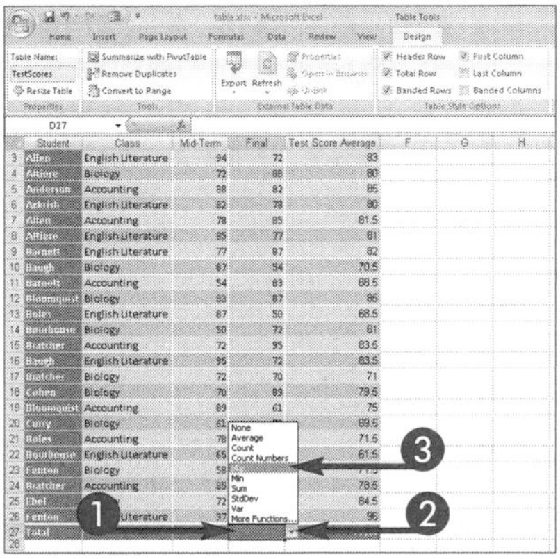

- Excel displays the result of the formula here.
- The formula appears here.

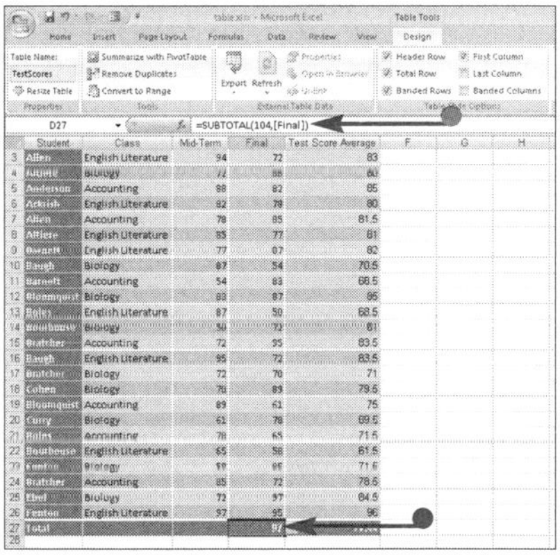

MASTER IT

Can I create a formula outside the table that refers to the total row?

▼ Yes, you can, and the formula returns proper results as long as you display the total row. However, if you hide the total row, the formula that refers to it returns an error. The error continues to appear as long as the total row is hidden; if you redisplay the row, Excel can recalculate the formula and once again return a proper result.

Can I add a total column as the last column of my table?

▼ Yes, but using a different technique. To add a total column, place the cell pointer in the first column outside your table, on any row below the label row. Then create your formula. When you press Enter or click ✓ in the Formula Bar, Excel expands the table to include the appropriate number of rows in the column and creates the formula in every cell in the column that is part of the table.

What do the numbers in the formulas, such as 101 and 104, mean?

▼ When you add a total row, you actually use the SUBTOTAL function. As its first argument, you identify the function — such as Average or Sum — that you want to use in the subtotal, using a number between 1 and 11. In the total row of a table, the values that represent the type of function to use range from 101 to 111.

Filter to Hide Duplicates

If you have a table that contains duplicate entries, you might want to hide the duplicates. You can filter the table to hide the rows containing duplicate entries, or you can have Excel copy unique entries to another location in your worksheet.

Suppose, for example, that you provided sales records to a data entry person to enter into your worksheet, and the data entry person accidentally recorded the entries for some sales twice and for other sales three times. In this case, you have several duplicate entries in your table that should not be there. To continue working with your table, you can hide the duplicate entries. When you are ready, you can delete the duplicates; see the section, "Remove Duplicates from a Table," for details on eliminating the duplicate entries.

When you filter your table to hide duplicates, you identify the range that Excel should evaluate when looking for duplicate entries. You also decide whether to simply hide the duplicate entries in the table or display the unique entries in another location in your worksheet. If you choose to display unique entries in another location, you identify the range where you want the unique entries to appear.

Filter to Hide Duplicates

1. Click any cell in the table.
2. Click the Data tab.
3. Click Advanced.

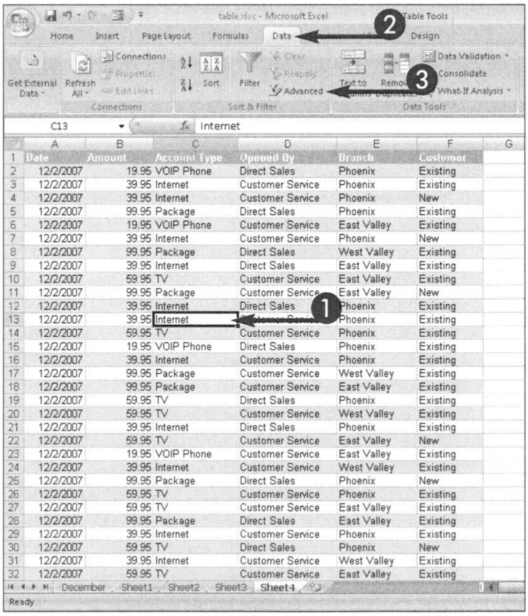

The Advanced Filter dialog box appears.

- Excel suggests the range to assign to the table.

4. Click here to hide duplicates in the table.

5 Click Unique records only (☐ changes to ☑).

6 Click OK.

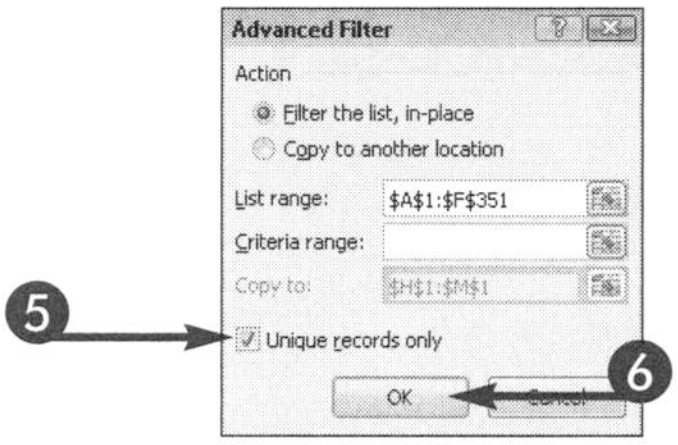

- Excel hides the rows in the table that contain duplicate entries.

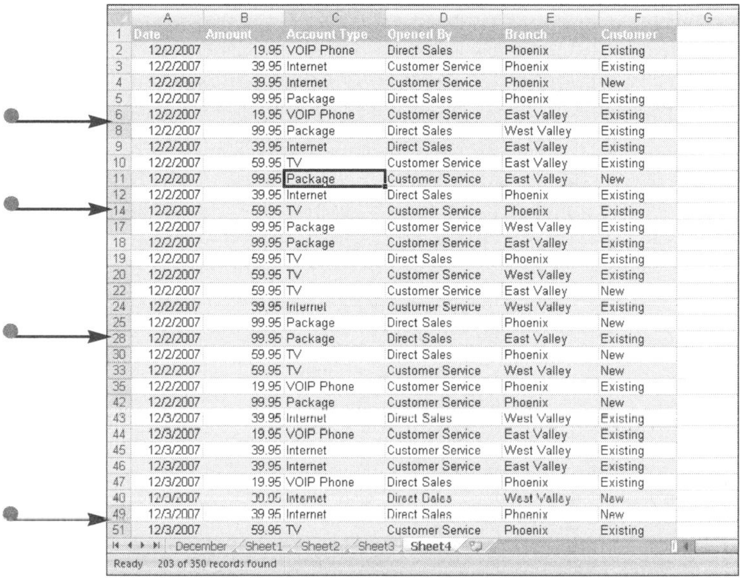

MASTER IT

How do I copy unique entries to a new location?

▼ Complete Steps 1 to 3. Then, in Step 4, click Copy To Another Location. Excel makes the Copy To field available. You can click ▦ or you can simply click the cell in the worksheet that you want to use as the upper-left corner of the range of unique entries. Complete Steps 5 and 6, and Excel copies unique entries to the new location you indicated.

What do I do with the Criteria Range field?

▼ You can filter using criteria in the same way that you calculate database functions using a criteria range. For filtering, the criteria range must be at least three rows, the first row must contain the labels shown in the table, and you must leave one blank row between the criteria range and the table. For details on using a criteria range, see Chapter 17.

How do I view the duplicate entries again?

▼ Click anywhere in the table. Then click the Data tab and, in the Sort & Filter group, click Clear. Excel removes any filters you have applied to the table and redisplays all the entries in the table, both unique and duplicate.

Remove Duplicates from a Table

If you have a table that contains duplicate entries, you can remove the duplicates. Suppose, for example, that you provided sales records to a data entry person to enter into a table in your worksheet, and the data entry person got distracted and accidentally recorded some entries multiple times; upon reviewing your table, you have found entries for some sales twice and for other sales three times. In this case, you have several duplicate entries in your table that should not be there. You can hide the duplicate entries by filtering, as described in the section, "Filter to Hide Duplicates," or you can remove the duplicate entries.

When you remove duplicate entries from a table, you identify the columns in the table that Excel should evaluate when looking for duplicate entries. Excel classifies entries as duplicate if the values match in the columns that you select. Therefore, the more columns you include, the stricter you make the requirements for identifying duplicates.

Removing duplicates from a table is a relatively permanent action. That is, you can retrieve the duplicates only if you undo the action or close the workbook without saving.

Remove Duplicates from a Table

1. Click anywhere in the table.
   - Table Tools appear on the Ribbon.
2. Click the Design tab.
3. Click Remove Duplicates.

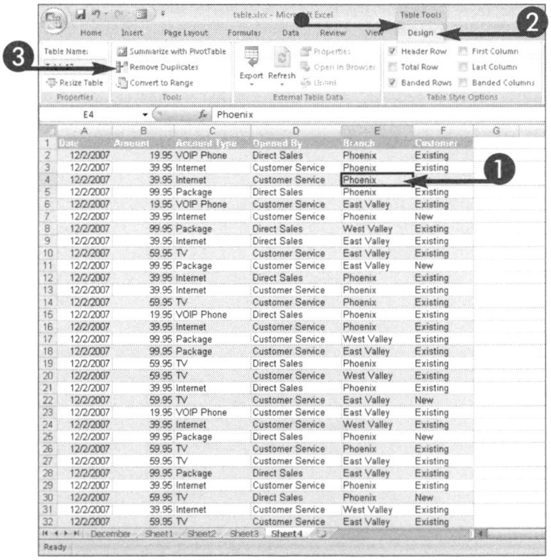

Excel displays the Remove Duplicates dialog box.

- By default, Excel selects all columns to match when evaluating for duplicate entries.

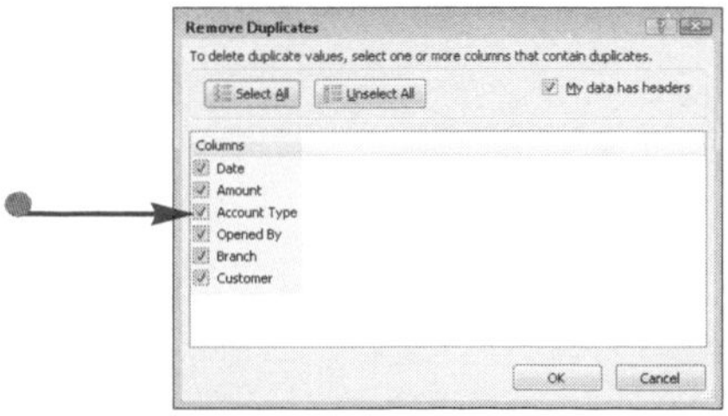

4 Click to remove a column from consideration when classifying entries as duplicates (☑ changes to ☐).

5 Repeat Step 4 as many times as needed.

6 Click OK.

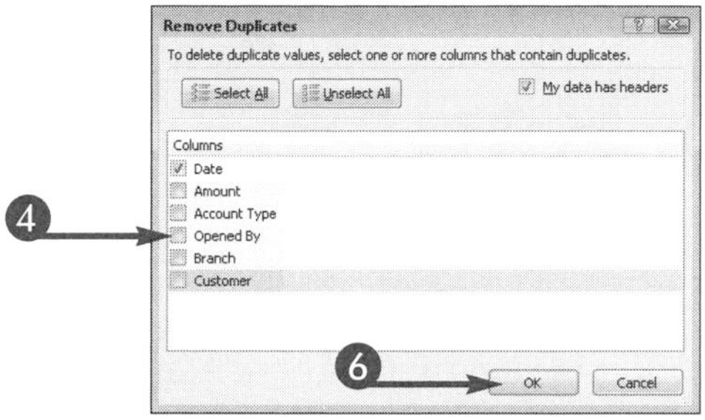

Excel removes the duplicate entries and displays a message telling you how many entries were removed and how many remain.

7 Click OK.

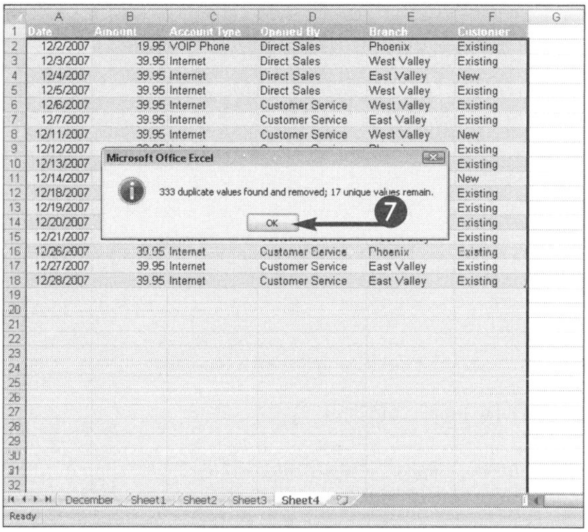

MASTER IT

Is there a way to make sure I can get back the entries Excel removes from the table?

▼ Yes. Before you remove duplicates, copy the table to a new worksheet. That way, you keep the original table and a new version that excludes duplicates. To copy the table, click an outer boundary of the table to select it. Then right-click and, from the shortcut menu that appears, click Copy. Switch to another worksheet, right-click the cell that should serve as the upper-left corner of the table, and click Paste in the shortcut menu. Now that you have safeguarded the information in the original table, complete the steps in this section to remove duplicates from the original worksheet.

How do I decide which columns to leave checked?

▼ If you leave one column checked, Excel compares the values in that column for each entry. If the values in that column match for two entries, Excel considers one of the entries a duplicate. If you leave two columns checked, Excel compares the values in both columns for each entry; if the values in both columns match, Excel considers one of the entries a duplicate. If you leave all of columns in your table checked, Excel classifies an entry as a duplicate only if all of the values in the entry match another entry in the table. You set stricter requirements for duplicate classification by including more columns.

Convert a Table to a Range

You can convert a table back to a range if you no longer need the tools associated with tables. When you convert a table back to a range, Excel leaves the formatting applied from the table style in place on the range. Special formatting applied to the first or last column remains, and if you had included a total row in the table, it remains. However, Excel no longer treats the range like a table. The table name disappears from the Name Manager window, and Table Tools are no longer available. Labels remain in the first row, but if you scroll down the table, Excel no longer replaces column letters with the labels in the first row. You can no longer expand the table size by typing in blank cells immediately adjacent to the table boundaries.

On the other hand, suppose that you really want to retain the use of Table Tools in general, but you do not want your table to be formatted using the colorful table styles that Excel applies to a table by default. In this case, you can simply clear the table formatting instead of converting the table back to a range.

Convert a Table to a Range

Clear Table Formatting

1. Click anywhere in the table.
   - Table Tools appear on the Ribbon.
2. Click the Design tab.
3. Click ▾ in the Table Styles group to display the Table Styles Gallery.
4. Click Clear.

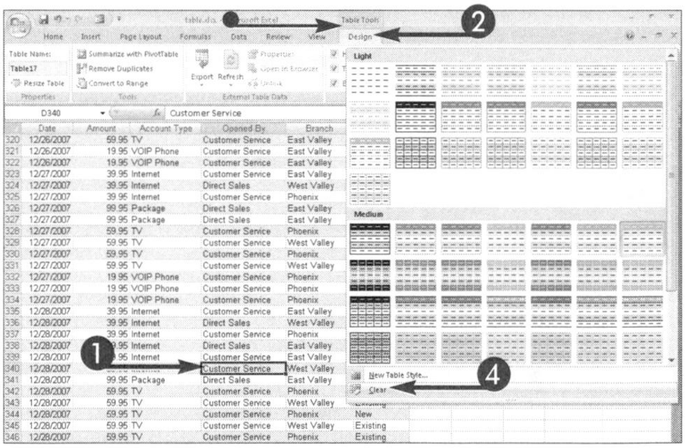

- Excel removes the visual formatting from the table.
- The table remains a table, and Table Tools are still available.

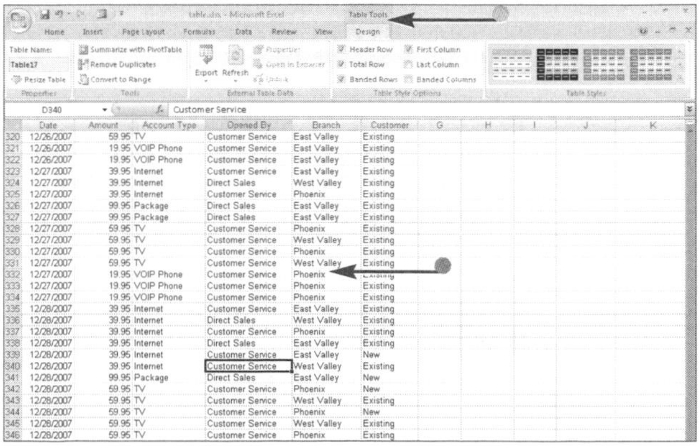

Convert to a Range

1. Click anywhere in the table.
   - Table Tools appear on the Ribbon.
2. Click the Design tab.
3. Click Convert to Range.

   A message appears, asking you to confirm the action.
4. Click Yes.

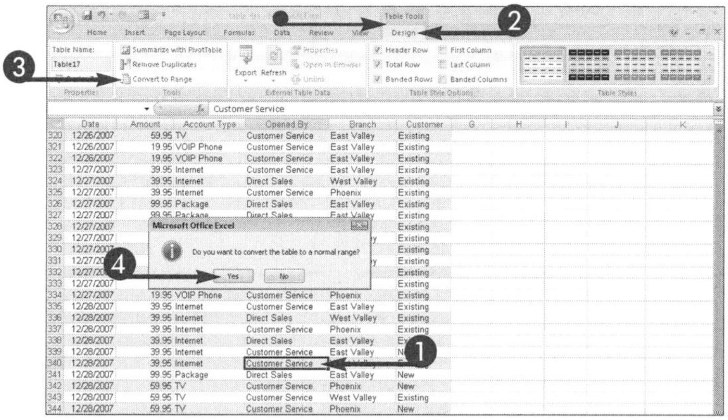

Excel converts the table to a range.

- The table formatting remains.
- Table Tools are no longer available.

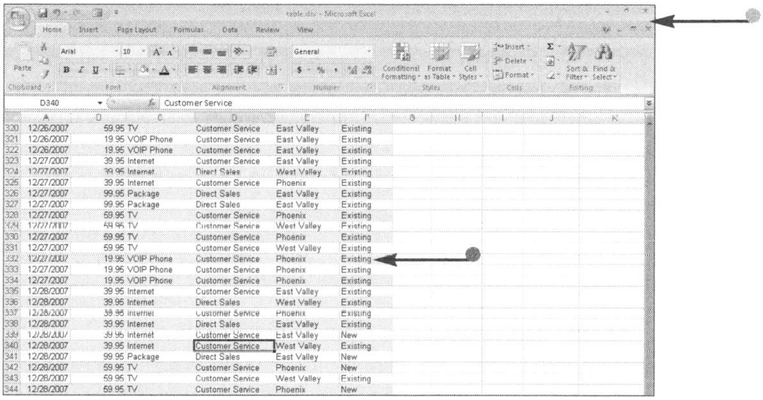

MASTER IT

If I remove table formatting, can I still make the first or last column appear in boldface type?

▼ Yes, but not by clicking the First Column or Last Column options on the Ribbon. Instead, you must think of the table as a range, even though it is still a table, and apply range formatting. Select the first or last column in the table by clicking their column letters. Then click the Home tab and, in the Font group, click B. Excel makes the type in the selected column appear in boldface. To remove the boldface appearance, repeat this process.

Is there a way that I can display my table using black and white and apply row banding that is a shade of gray?

▼ Yes. You do not want to clear table formatting. Make sure that you have selected the Office theme by clicking the Page Layout tab and then, from the Themes Gallery, click Office. Next, click anywhere in the table and then click the Design tab under Table Tools. In the Table Styles Gallery, select Table Style Light 1, which should be the second choice in the Light category of table styles. Finally, make sure that the Banded Rows option is selected in the Table Style Options group.

Understanding PivotTables

A PivotTable provides an easy way to summarize information stored in a range, a table, or an external data source. Using a PivotTable helps you present endless rows and columns of numbers in a variety of meaningful ways.

Suppose your worksheet contains sales information by day for various types of sales made by a cable service provider. The worksheet tracks the date of the sale, the amount, the type of service, whether the sale was made by Customer Service or direct marketing, the branch that made the sale, and the type of customer — new or existing — who made the purchase. Just viewing the worksheet in its native form would not help you analyze any of the information.

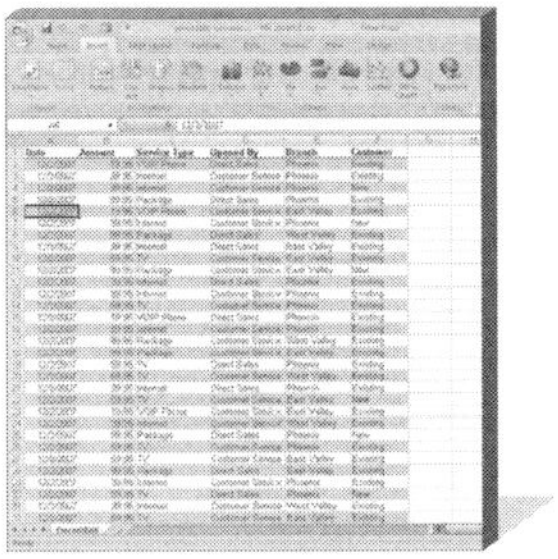

For example, viewing it in its native form, you could not determine total sales for the month for any individual type of service. Nor could you determine which branch made the most sales. Nor could you identify which branch sold the most of any particular type of cable service. There are a lot of questions you cannot answer by simply viewing the data in its native form.

You could spend time sorting and filtering the data and setting up a series of formulas that would answer most of your questions, but using a PivotTable is a much quicker and easier way to find the answers. Creating a PivotTable takes only a few seconds, does not require any formulas, and displays the information in an attractive format that Excel refers to as a PivotTable report. When you create a PivotTable, Excel automatically displays the PivotTable Field List, which you use to modify the PivotTable.

The term *pivot* means "to rotate." In the case of a PivotTable, you rotate your data to examine it from a variety of perspectives. The PivotTable helps you easily move fields around, nest fields within each other, and group information in many different ways. As a result, a PivotTable is really not static; it changes as you pivot the fields in the table. You can also add information to the underlying range you use to create a PivotTable and then update the PivotTable to include that information.

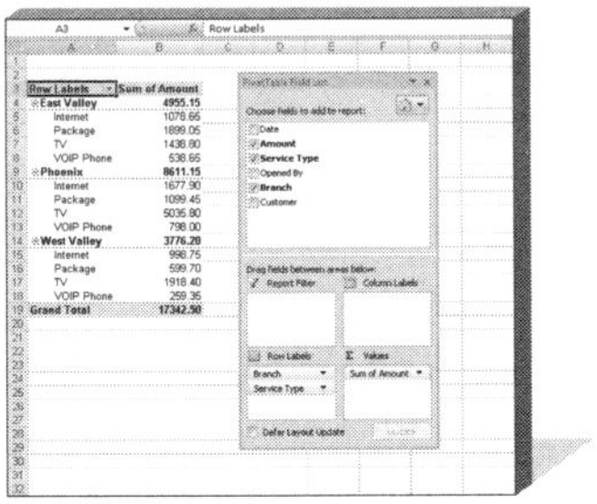

In a PivotTable, Excel automatically summarizes the data by calculating a sum, but you can use a variety of summarizing statistical functions. This makes PivotTables useful not only to summarize numeric data but also to summarize text data, such as identifying the number of people who reside in a certain Zip code.

You can sort and filter information in a PivotTable, and you can group information in a variety of ways. You can also format a PivotTable by adjusting the PivotTable's layout, applying styles, hiding and displaying row and column headers, and adding and removing row and column banding.

You can add or remove blank rows, hide or display subtotals, hide or display grand totals, and include calculated fields in a PivotTable. You can also use the data in a PivotTable to create a PivotChart — a chart based on the PivotTable information — that you can use to help you further analyze the data.

When you work with PivotTables, you should be familiar with some terms, in order to make working with them much easier.

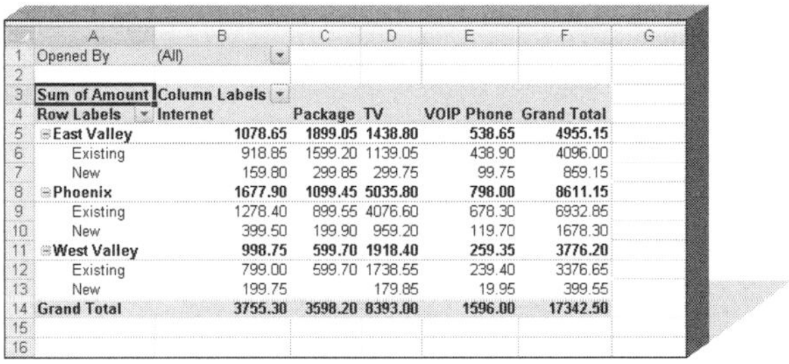

	A	B	C	D	E	F	G
1	Opened By	(All)					
2							
3	Sum of Amount	Column Labels					
4	Row Labels	Internet	Package	TV	VOIP Phone	Grand Total	
5	East Valley	1078.65	1899.05	1438.80	538.65	4955.15	
6	Existing	918.85	1599.20	1139.05	438.90	4096.00	
7	New	159.80	299.85	299.75	99.75	859.15	
8	Phoenix	1677.90	1099.45	5035.80	798.00	8611.15	
9	Existing	1278.40	899.55	4076.60	678.30	6932.85	
10	New	399.50	199.90	959.20	119.70	1678.30	
11	West Valley	998.75	599.70	1918.40	259.35	3776.20	
12	Existing	799.00	599.70	1738.55	239.40	3376.65	
13	New	199.75		179.85	19.95	399.55	
14	Grand Total	3755.30	3598.20	8393.00	1596.00	17342.50	
15							
16							

An *item* is an element that appears as a row or column header. In the figure, Internet, Package, TV, and VOIP (voice-over-Internet-protocol) Phone are items in the Service Type field. The Branch field has three items: East Valley, Phoenix, and West Valley.

Column labels refer to fields that have a column orientation in the PivotTable, each occupying a column. In the figure, Service Type represents a column field that contains four nested columns: Internet, Package, TV, and VOIP Phone.

Grand totals appear below the rows in a PivotTable or to the right of the columns in a PivotTable, and display totals for all of the rows or columns in the PivotTable. You can choose to display grand totals for rows, columns, both, or neither. The PivotTable in the figure shows grand totals for both rows and columns.

A *group* is a collection of items treated as a single item. You can group items manually or automatically (grouping dates into months, for example). The PivotTable in the figure does not have any defined groups.

Refresh refers to the action you take to recalculate the PivotTable after making changes to the source data.

Row labels refer to fields that have a row orientation in the PivotTable, each occupying a row. In the figure, Branch represents a row field. You can also have nested row fields. In the figure, New and Existing are nested rows under each branch name.

Source data are the data used to create a PivotTable. Source data can reside in a worksheet as a range, a table, or an external database.

Subtotals display subtotal amounts for rows or columns in a PivotTable. The PivotTable in the figure displays subtotals for each branch.

A *report filter* is a field that has a page orientation in the PivotTable. You can display only one item (or all items) in a report filter at one time. In the figure, Opened By represents a table filter that enables you to display services sold by either Customer Service or Direct Sales.

The *Values area* refers to an area of the PivotTable Field List that displays the cells in the PivotTable that contain the summary data, and the way in which those cells are summarized in the PivotTable.

Create a PivotTable Using Numeric Data

You can create a PivotTable using numeric data stored as a list in a range, a table, or an external data source. A PivotTable summarizes list information to help you analyze it in meaningful ways.

Suppose that you work for a cable service provider, keeping a worksheet that tracks sales information by day, including the date of the sale, the amount, the type of service, whether the sale was made by Customer Service or Direct Sales, the branch that made the sale, and the type of customer — new or existing — who made the purchase. Using this information, you can answer questions such as the following:

What were the total sales for VOIP phone service during the month?

Which branch — the East Valley, Phoenix, or the West Valley — sold the most during the month?

Which branch made the most Internet cable service sales during the month?

Who bought the most packaged cable services during the month — new or existing customers?

Just viewing the worksheet in its native form would not help you analyze any of the information. However, creating a PivotTable can help you quickly and easily answer all of those questions.

Create a PivotTable Using Numeric Data

1. Click inside the range or table of information you want to use to create a PivotTable.
2. Click the Insert tab.
3. Click PivotTable.

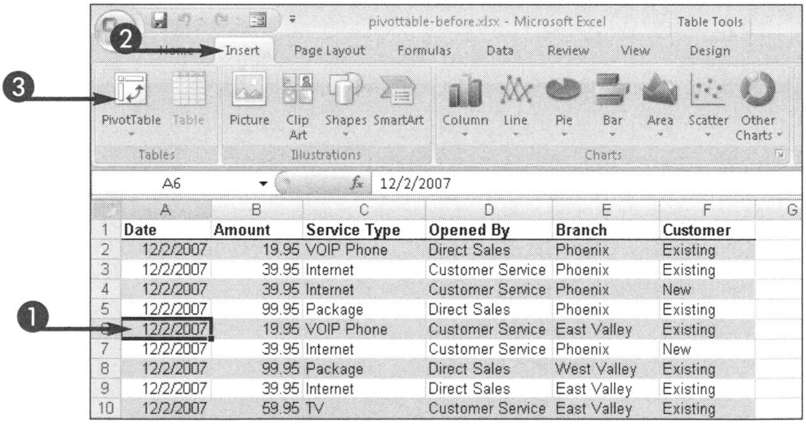

Excel displays the Create PivotTable dialog box.

- Excel guesses at the table or range you want to use to create the PivotTable.

4. If necessary, select a different range.
5. Click an option to place the PivotTable report (◎ changes to ◉).

   This example places the PivotTable on a separate worksheet.

6. Click OK.

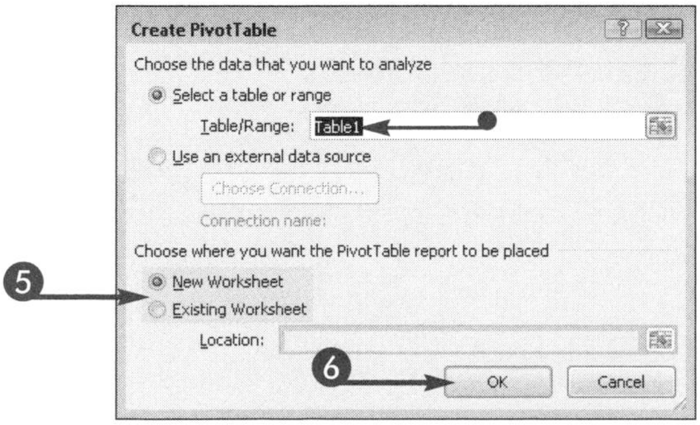

- Excel displays a PivotTable skeleton.
- PivotTable Tools appear on the Ribbon.
- The PivotTable Field List appears on the right side of the window.

7 Click fields to add them to the report (☐ changes to ☑).

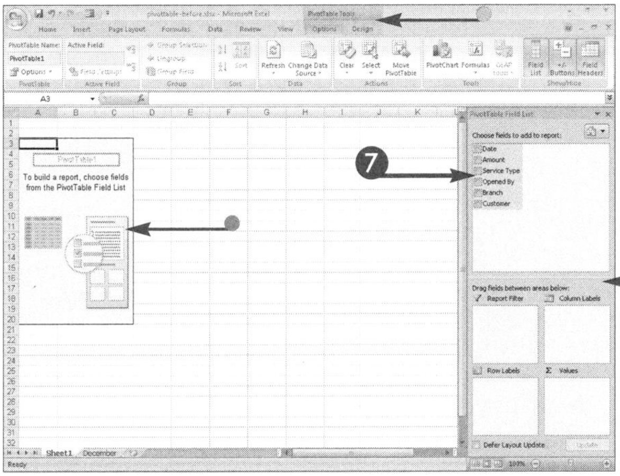

Excel displays the PivotTable report.

- Each field added to the report appears in one of the four areas in the Areas section of the PivotTable Field List.

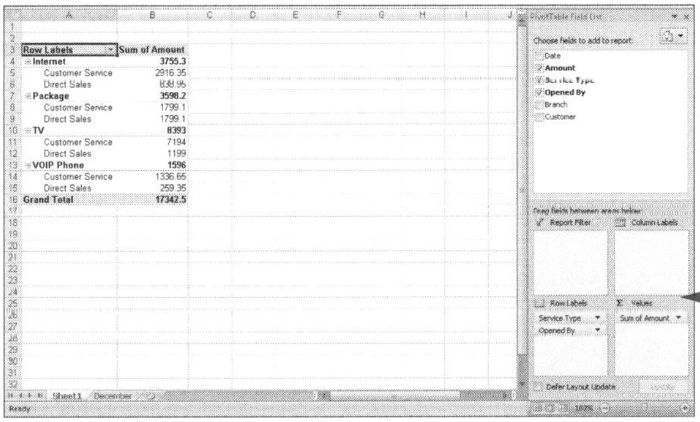

PART V

MASTER IT

How do I use an external data source as the foundation for my PivotTable?

▼ In the Create PivotTable dialog box, click Use An External Data Source (◯ changes to ◉). Then click the Choose Connection button to display the Existing Connections dialog box, where you can click the name of the connection. See Chapter 32 for more information on sharing data.

I placed my PivotTable on the same worksheet as the source data, and now I realize that it should be on a separate worksheet. What should I do?

▼ You can move the PivotTable, but not by cutting and pasting. Click in the PivotTable to display the PivotTable Tools on the Ribbon. Then click the Options tab and, in the Actions group, click Move PivotTable. The Move PivotTable dialog box appears. Choose to place the PivotTable on a new worksheet.

What does the Clear button in the Actions group on the Ribbon do?

▼ You can use this button to clear filters you may have applied. You can also use this button to remove all of the fields from the PivotTable. This can be useful if you decide you simply want to start again; clicking the Clear button is faster than removing the check marks from all of the fields. See the section, "Filter a PivotTable," for details on filtering.

Pivot Elements in a PivotTable

You can control the appearance of a PivotTable report using the Areas section of the PivotTable Field List. By default, when you add a field to the report using the Fields section of the PivotTable Field List, Excel adds non-numeric fields to the Row Labels area and numeric fields to the Values area. If your data contains any Online Analytical Processing (OLAP) date and time hierarchy fields, Excel adds them to the Column Labels area.

Excel automatically nests fields if more than one field appears in any given area. Excel also nests the fields in the order in which they appear in the area.

However, you are not limited to the default placement. You can reorder fields within an area or you can move fields between the areas to adjust the appearance of the report and the way in which information is summarized. You move fields into the Row Labels area or the Column Labels area to display information in rows or columns, respectively. You move a field into the Values area to summarize information using that field, and you move a field into the Report Filter area so that you can filter the entire report by that field.

Pivot Elements in a PivotTable

1. Create a PivotTable and add fields to it.

Note: *For more information, see the section, "Create a PivotTable Using Numeric Data."*

- Excel places numeric fields in the Values area.
- Excel places non-numeric fields in the Row Labels area.

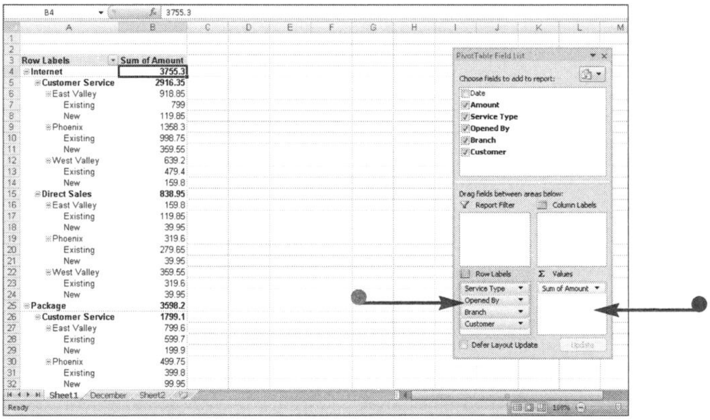

2. Drag a field from the Row Labels area to the Report Filter area.

- Excel reorganizes the report and adds the report filter.

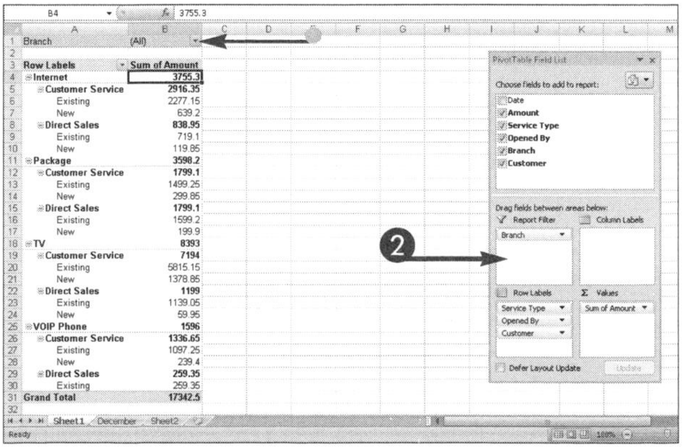

3 Drag a field from the Row Labels area to the Column Labels area.

- Excel reorganizes the report and adds the columns.

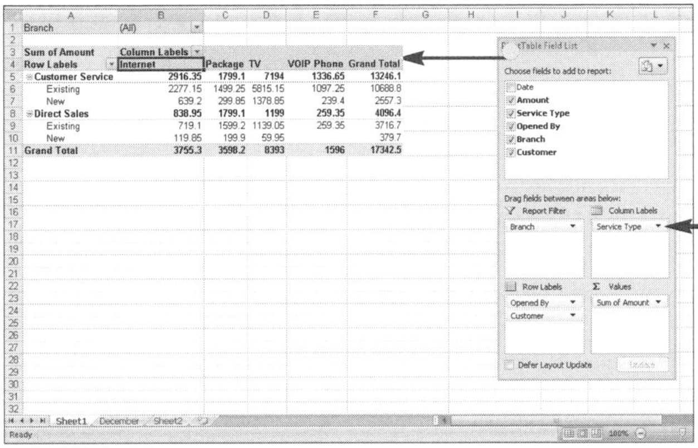

4 In any area, drag a field up to reposition it in the table.

Note: *This example reorders the rows in the report.*

- Excel reorganizes the report and changes the order of the rows.

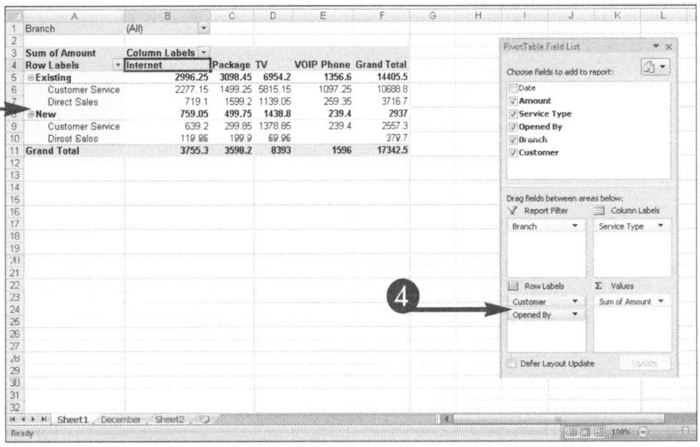

MASTER IT

I noticed that the numbers in the PivotTable display using two decimal places. How did you do that?

▼ Click any value in the PivotTable. Then click the Options tab under PivotTable Tools. In the Active Field group, click Field Settings. In the Value Field Settings dialog box that appears, click the Number Format button. In the Format Cells dialog box that appears, select a format to apply to numbers; the example uses the Number format.

How does the PivotTable Field List work?

▼ The top portion of the list is the Fields section and the bottom portion is the Areas section. The field list displays the column names of the source data, and you use the Fields section to add and remove fields from the PivotTable. You use the Areas section to determine the placement of fields on the report. See the section, "Pivot Elements in a PivotTable," for details on using the Areas section.

Can I drag fields from the PivotTable Field List directly onto the PivotTable?

▼ Not by default, but you can enable a setting that allows you to drag and drop fields onto the PivotTable. Right-click anywhere in the PivotTable and, on the shortcut menu that appears, click PivotTable Options. In the PivotTable Options dialog box that appears, click the Display tab. Then click Classic PivotTable Layout (☐ changes to ☑). Click OK to save the setting.

Change PivotTable Display Options

You can change the appearance of the PivotTable field headers and you can control the appearance of the Field List.

By default, PivotTable field headers appear as "Row Labels" and "Column Labels," and you can use the drop-down lists that these field headers provide to filter the information that appears in the table. If you want, you can change the generic labels to more meaningful labels that describe the rows and columns of your PivotTable by typing in new labels. You can also hide the field headers.

The PivotTable Field List is also quite versatile. It appears by default when you select a cell in the PivotTable, but you can hide it from view. You can also make it float on-screen or dock it along the right side — its default location — or the left side of the screen. You can reorganize its layout to display only the Fields section or only the Areas section, and you can control the position of the sections when you display both sections or when you display only one section.

Change PivotTable Display Options

Show or Hide Field Headers

1. Click in the PivotTable.
   - PivotTable Tools appear on the Ribbon.
   - Field headers appear by default.
2. Click the Options tab.
3. Click Field Headers.

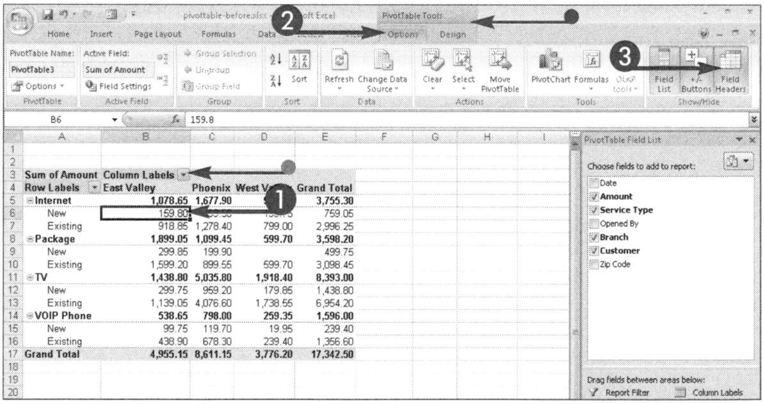

- Excel hides the field headers.
- You can redisplay them by clicking Field Headers again.

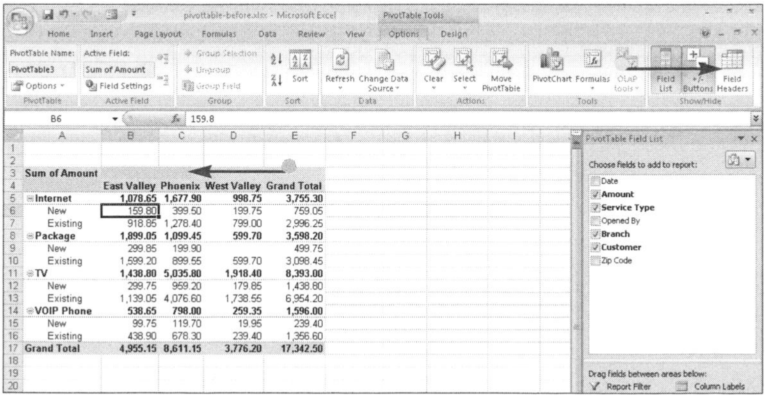

Show or Hide the PivotTable Field List

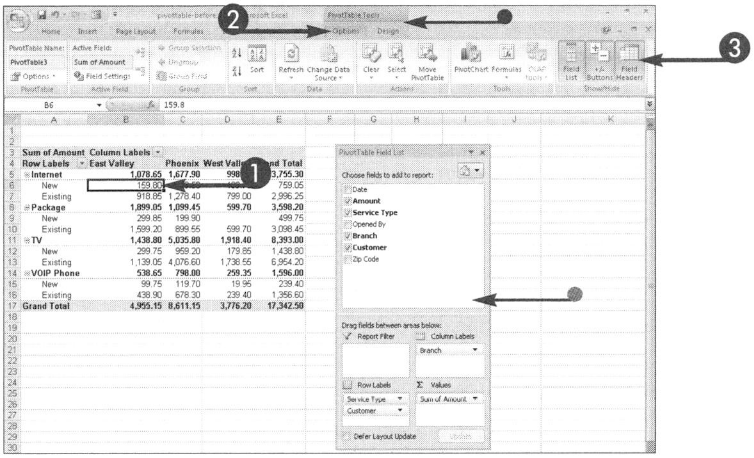

1. Click in the PivotTable.
   - PivotTable Tools appear on the Ribbon.
   - The PivotTable Field List appears.
2. Click the Options tab.
3. Click Field List.

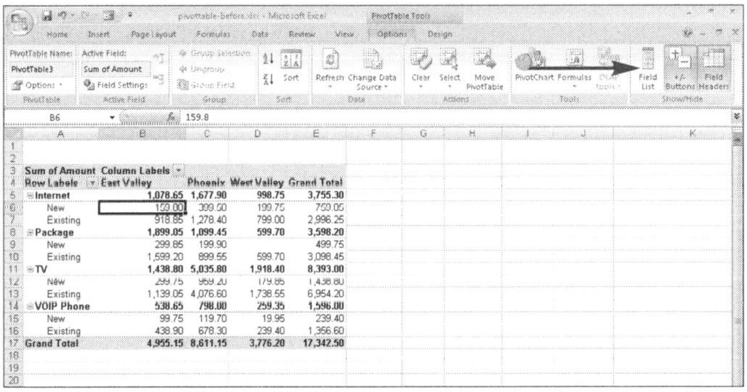

Excel no longer displays the PivotTable Field List.

- You can redisplay the PivotTable Field List by clicking Field List again.

MASTER IT

How do you get the PivotTable Field List to float on the screen?

▼ Drag the title bar of the PivotTable Field List to undock it; as you drag, changes to . Redock it by dragging to the right or left edge of the Excel window until it appears to fall off the screen. While it is undocked, you can resize the outer border of the list.

What does the button in the upper-right corner of the PivotTable Field List do?

▼ You can use that button to organize the appearance of the two sections of the PivotTable Field List. The default appearance is stacked, but you can display both sections side-by-side, or you can display just the Fields section or just the Areas section. If you display only the Areas section, you can control the layout of the four panels.

What does the Defer Layout Update option do?

▼ Excel automatically updates a PivotTable each time you make a change using the PivotTable Field List. If, however, your PivotTable works with a lot of data, you may want to switch to manual updating to improve performance. Click the Defer Layout Update check box (changes to) to use manual updating. Click the Update button to update the PivotTable to reflect layout changes.

Create a PivotTable with Non-Numeric Data

Although most PivotTables are created from numeric data, numeric data is not necessary to create a PivotTable. You can create a PivotTable using non-numeric data stored in a range, a table, or an external data source. A PivotTable that summarizes non-numeric list information counts information instead of summing it.

Suppose that you have generated a mailing list that contains name, address, city, state, and Zip code information for 75 people. None of this information is numeric, Zip code notwithstanding, but you can use the information to create a PivotTable that counts information rather than summing it. For example, using this information, you might want to know how many addresses appear in each Zip code, or you might want a count of the number of Zip codes associated with a particular city. Just viewing the worksheet in its native form would not help you analyze any of the information. You could set up functions to answer your questions, but doing so would be more work than creating a PivotTable. A PivotTable can help you quickly and easily answer all of those questions.

Create a PivotTable with Non-Numeric Data

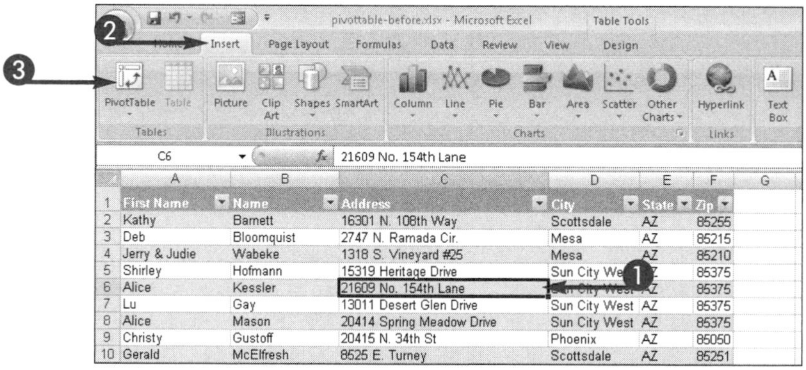

1. Click inside the range or table of information you want to use to create a PivotTable.
2. Click the Insert tab.
3. Click PivotTable.

Excel displays the Create PivotTable dialog box.

- Excel guesses at the table or range you want to use to create the PivotTable.

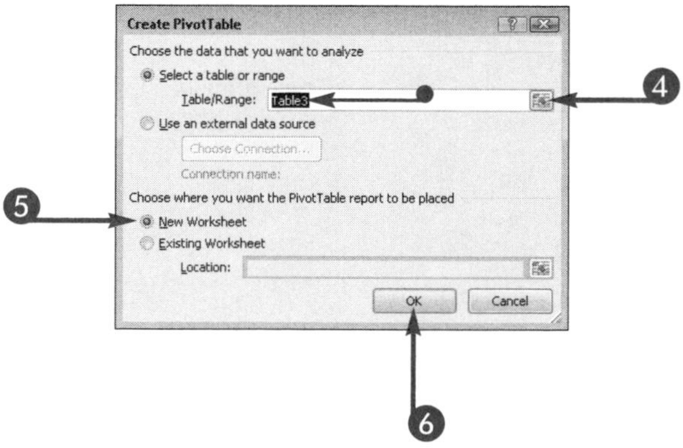

4. If necessary, select a different range.
5. Click an option to place the PivotTable report (◎ changes to ◉).

   This example places the PivotTable on a separate worksheet.

6. Click OK.

- Excel displays a PivotTable skeleton.
- PivotTable Tools appear on the Ribbon.
- The PivotTable Field List appears on the right side of the window.

7 Click fields to add them to the report (☐ changes to ☑).

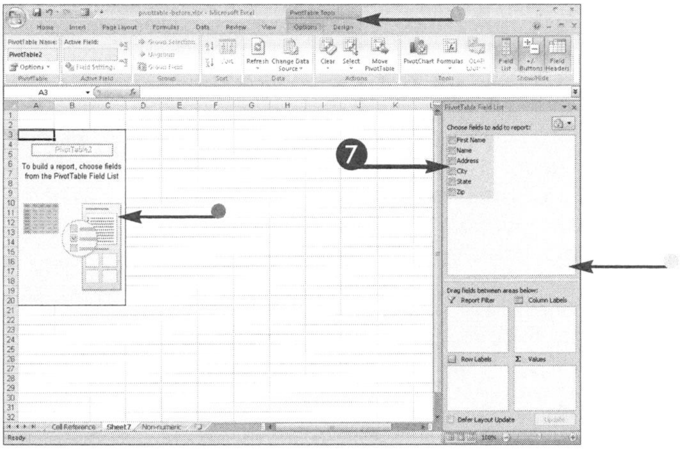

Excel displays the PivotTable report.

- Each field added to the report appears in one of the four areas in the Areas section of the PivotTable Field List.

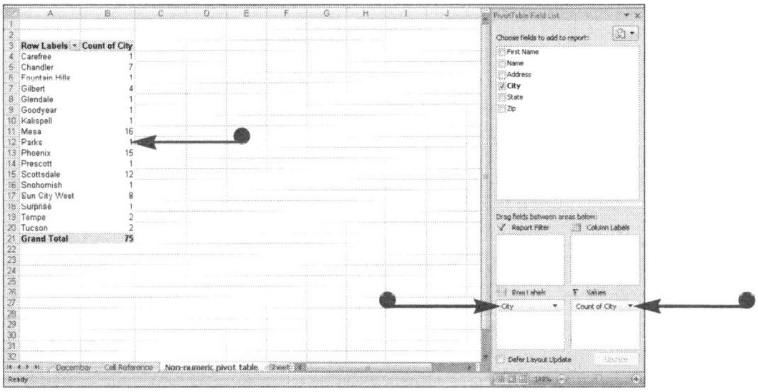

Why did Excel sum the Zip code field when I added it to the Values area?

▼ Although the Zip code field is not a number that we use in mathematical equations, it is technically a number. Even if you format the field in the underlying data source using a general format, Excel still treats it as a number and automatically tries to sum the field's values. You can easily change the formula by right-clicking any Zip code in the PivotTable and clicking Summarize Data By. From the shortcut menu that appears, click Count, and Excel updates both the PivotTable and the label that appears in the Values area.

How did you get the City field to appear in both the Row Labels area and the Values area?

▼ You can add two instances of the same field to the PivotTable if one of the instances appears in the Values area. To add two instances of a field to the PivotTable, click the field in the Field section, and Excel adds the field to the Row Labels area. You can move the field to the Column Labels area or the Report Filter area as necessary. Next, drag the same field from the Fields section to the Values area. Excel adds another instance of the field to the PivotTable.

Filter a PivotTable

You can filter a PivotTable report by any field that appears in the Report Filter, Column Labels, or Row Labels area in the PivotTable Field List. To best understand filters, suppose that you create a PivotTable from a worksheet that tracks sales information for a cable service provider by day, including the date of the sale, the amount, the type of service, whether the sale was made by Customer Service or Direct Sales, the branch that made the sale, and the type of customer — new or existing — who made the purchase.

When you filter the PivotTable report using the Report Filter field, you essentially look at a page of information at a time. If you place the Branch field in the Report Filter area of the PivotTable Field List, you can view all of the sales information for all branches or for one selected branch.

If you place the Service Type in the Row Labels area, you can view all or any combination of the types of services you offer simultaneously.

If you place the Customer in the Column Labels area, you can view sales for new customers, existing customers, or both.

Filter a PivotTable

1 Set up a PivotTable so that you have at least one field in each of the areas in the PivotTable Field List.

- Excel displays ▾ beside each field that you can use to filter the report.

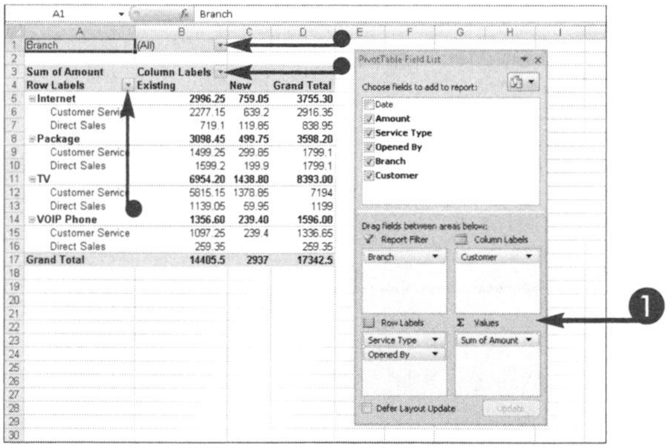

2 In the PivotTable, click ▾ beside the field listed in the Report Filter area.

3 Click one item in the list.

4 Click OK.

Excel updates the PivotTable to display information for only the item you selected.

- The ▾ changes to the filter icon.

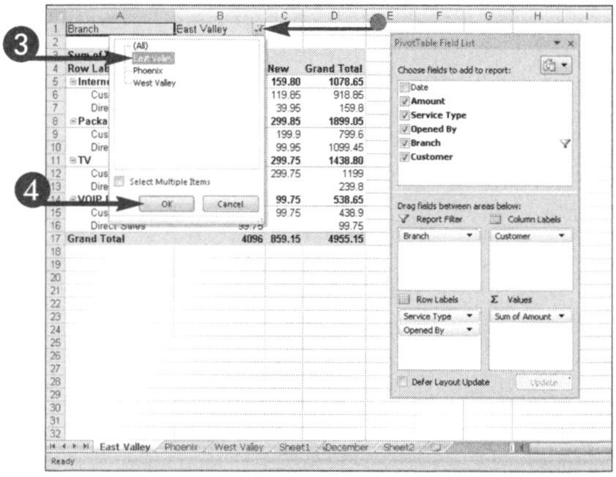

5. In the PivotTable, click ▾ next to Column Labels.
6. Click (Select All) (☑ changes to ☐).
7. Click only one item in the list (☐ changes to ☑).

   This example uses the Existing option.
8. Click OK.

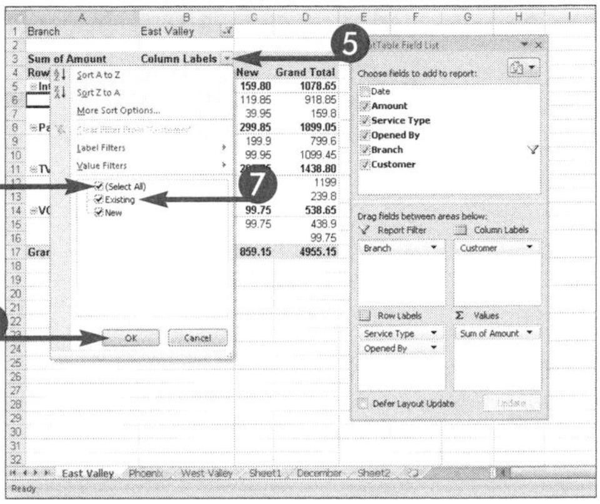

- Excel updates the PivotTable to display information for only the item you selected.
- The ▾ changes to [filter icon ▾].

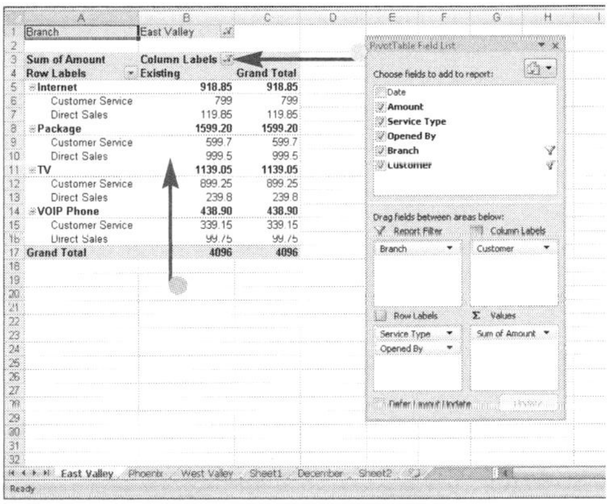

MASTER IT

How do I select multiple items for the Report Filter?

▼ Follow Steps 1 and 2. In the list box that appears, click Select Multiple Items (☐ changes to ☑); Excel adds check boxes to each of the items in the list. Click All (☑ changes to ☐) and then click the items you want to use as your filter (☐ changes to ☑).

What does the icon beside the Branch and Customer fields in the PivotTable Field List mean?

▼ The AutoFilter icon ([filter icon]) indicates that the fields have filters applied. If you move [pointer] over [filter icon], Excel displays a drop-down list button (▾). Click the button to view and change the filter. The ▾ is also available when you do not see [filter icon] beside a field in the PivotTable Field List, and you can use it to set the filter instead of clicking ▾ in the PivotTable.

How do I filter rows?

▼ Follow Steps 4 to 7, but click ▾ beside Row Labels in Step 4.

How do I remove filters?

▼ Click [filter icon ▾] on any filtered field. From the list that appears, click (All) or (Select All). Depending on the filter list you open, ☐ changes to ☑. Click OK, and Excel removes the filter and redisplays all of the available information.

Sort Information in a PivotTable

You can sort Row and Column field information in a PivotTable. By default, Excel sorts PivotTable information alphabetically from A to Z.

When you sort a PivotTable by a Row or Column field, you reorder the summary values in the table based on criteria you establish. You can sort any row or column in the traditional way — alphabetically from A to Z, numerically from smallest to largest, or from earliest to latest date. You can also sort in reverse alphabetical, numeric, or date order. You can set up custom sorts; for example, you can sort by the amounts in the PivotTable.

To identify the field by which to sort, you position the cell pointer. If you place the cell pointer on a value in the table, Excel sorts the data in the column containing the cell pointer in the order you specify, maintaining the information across each row. For example, the information for December 12 does not change, but its position in the PivotTable does change. If you place the cell pointer in the Row Labels row, Excel changes the order of the columns in the table to reflect your selected sort order.

Sort Information in a PivotTable

Traditional Sorting

1. Click in the Row Labels row or anywhere in the column you want to sort.
2. Click the Options tab under PivotTable Tools.
3. Click here to sort from A to Z or from earliest to latest.
4. Click here to sort from Z to A or from latest to earliest.

   This example sorts from Z to A or from latest to earliest.

- Excel re-sorts the PivotTable.

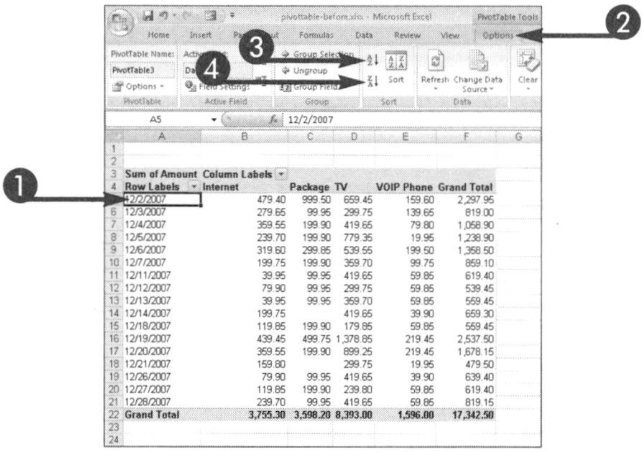

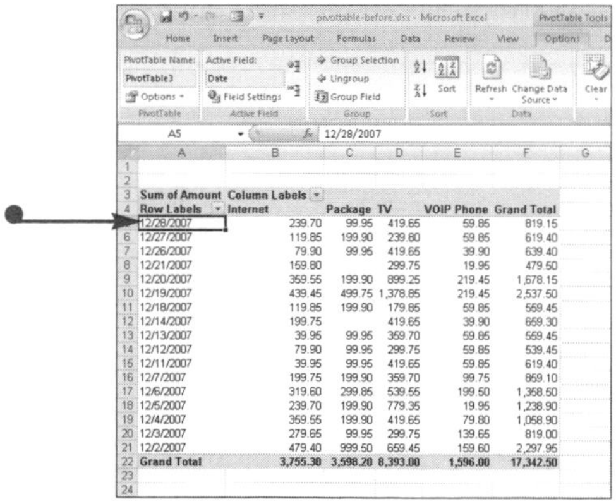

Custom Sorting

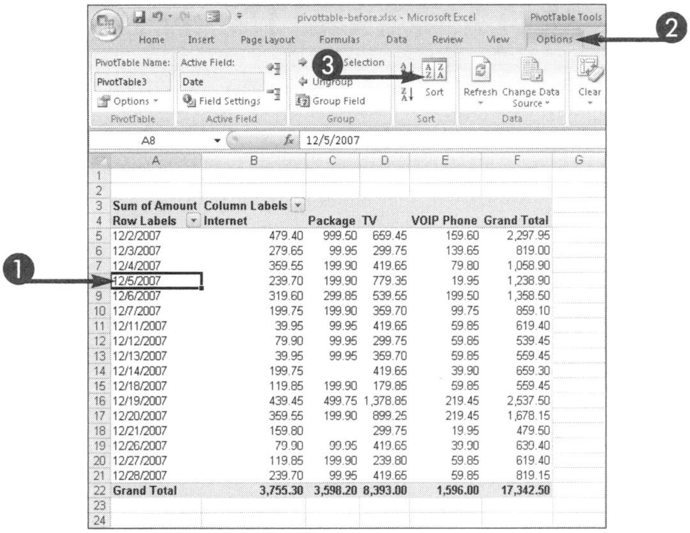

1. Select a field by which to sort.
2. Click the Options tab under PivotTable Tools.
3. Click Sort.

The Sort dialog box appears.

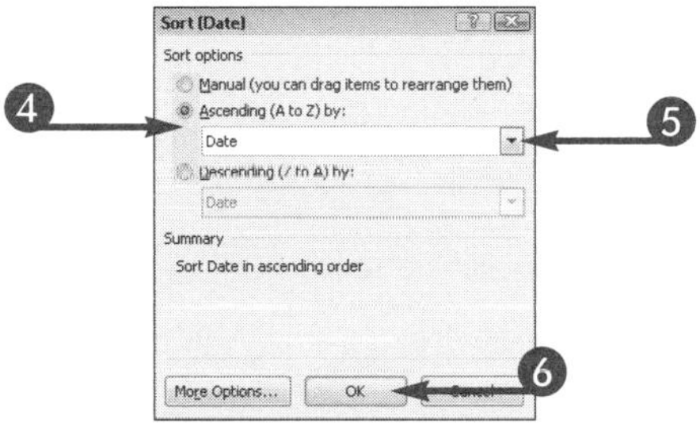

4. Click a sort option (◎ changes to ◉).
5. Click ▾ to sort by the currently selected field or a different field.
6. Click OK.

Excel reorders the data in the PivotTable.

MASTER IT

I clicked a value in the table and clicked Sort, and this displayed the Sort By Value dialog box. How do I use this dialog box?

▼ In this dialog box, you can identify whether to sort values from smallest to largest or largest to smallest. You can also specify a sort direction — top to bottom or left to right. If you sort top to bottom, Excel sorts the table data in the order you selected using the values in the column you selected when you opened the dialog box. If you sort left to right, Excel reorders the table columns in the order you selected using the values in the row you selected when you opened the dialog box.

What does the Manual sort option do?

▼ When you select Manual, you are not limited to sorting based on a particular method such as alphabetically from A to Z or based on a particular field. Instead, you can drag row or column labels within the rows or columns to reorder information the way you want it to appear.

If I do not like the sort I selected, how can I undo it?

▼ Click [Undo] or, to resort the table in its default order, follow the steps in the subsection, "Traditional Sorting."

Group Items in a PivotTable

You can group information in a PivotTable to display summary information in even more ways. Suppose that your worksheet contains state names such as Arizona, California, Nevada, Florida, Georgia, and Alabama. You could create two groups: one for the Southwestern Region and one for the Southeastern Region. If your worksheet contains sales information for a cable service provider like the one used throughout this chapter, you could create a group for Internet, TV, and VOIP phone service so that you can compare combined sales of these individual items with sales of packages that contain all three items.

You can also group dates in special ways. Suppose that the table of data on which your PivotTable is based contains lines of information for individual dates. By default, the PivotTable summarizes the information by date, but you can group those dates by weeks, months, quarters, or years. You can also group time-related data by seconds, minutes, or hours, as well as by days, weeks, months, quarters, or years.

You can group information stored in contiguous or noncontiguous rows or columns; when you group information stored in noncontiguous rows or columns, Excel reorders the rows or columns in the PivotTable.

Group Items in a PivotTable

Group Dates by Weeks

1. Set up the PivotTable so that it displays a row for each date you want to group.
2. Click the label of a date.
3. Click the Options tab under PivotTable Tools.
4. Click Group Selection.

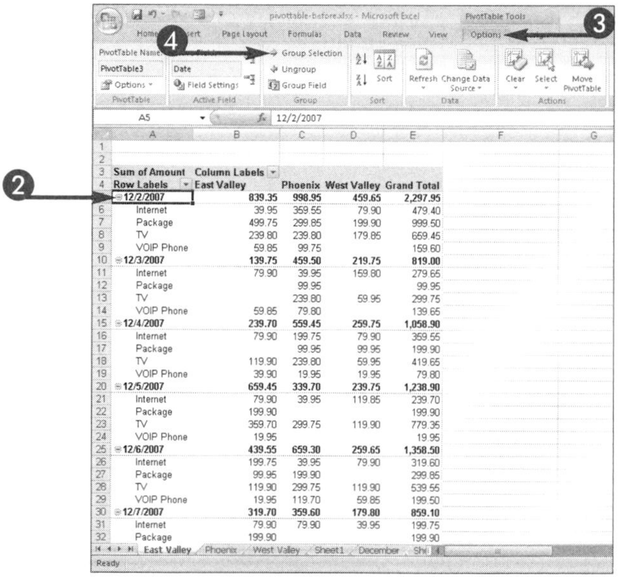

The Grouping dialog box appears.

5. Confirm the starting and ending dates.
6. Click Days to select it as a grouping method.

Note: *You can click more than one grouping method.*

7. Click Months to remove it from the selection.
8. Type **7** here.
9. Click OK.

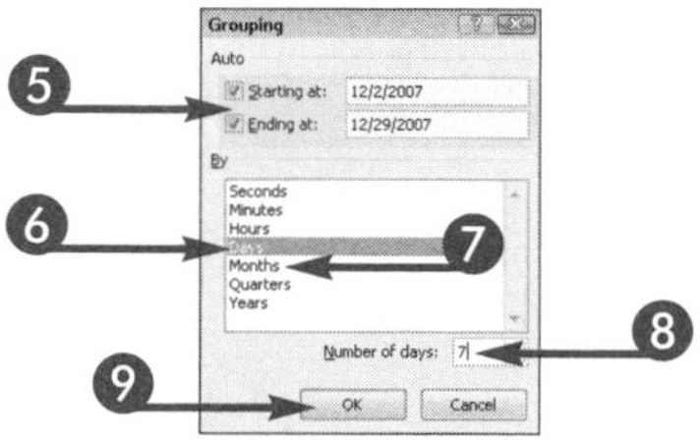

Excel groups the information by week.

- If you click ⊟ beside a group label, ⊟ changes to ⊞ and Excel hides the rows below the group.

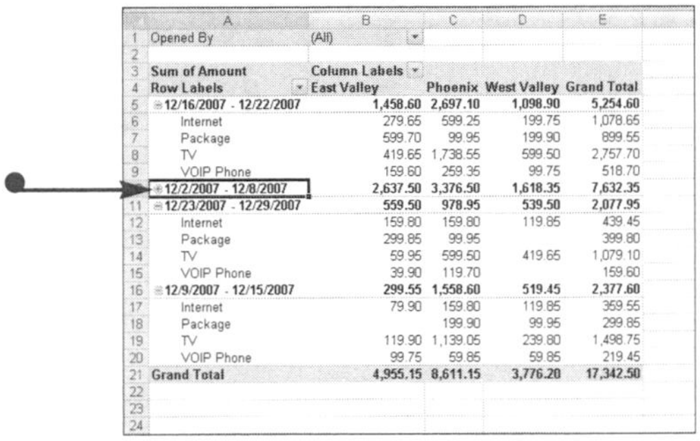

Remove a Group

1. Click the label of a group name.
2. Click the Options tab under PivotTable Tools.
3. Click Ungroup.

Excel removes the group.

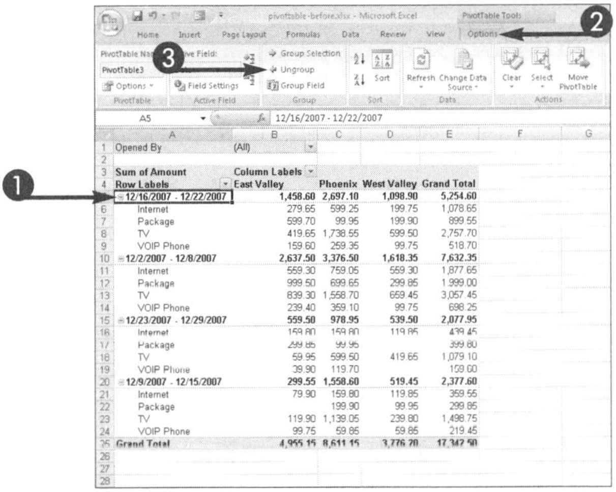

What do I do differently if I want to group something other than a date?

▼ First, select multiple row or column labels. To select multiple rows or columns, press and hold Ctrl as you click each label. If the rows or columns you click are not contiguous, Excel reorders the rows or columns in the PivotTable to make them contiguous when you create the group. To create the group, complete Steps 3 and 4. A Grouping dialog box does not appear; instead, Excel simply creates the group and names it Group1. A ⊟ appears beside Group1, and if you click it, ⊟ changes to ⊞ and Excel hides the details of the group, and instead displays totals for the group.

What happens if I click the Group Field button?

▼ The Grouping dialog box shown in this section appears. The Group Field button is available when you group dates, times, or numeric values. When you group numeric values, you specify the interval by which to group the information. For example, if your PivotTable contains ages, you could create age groups that span five years.

Are there any grouping limitations?

▼ Yes. You cannot add a calculated item to a grouped field. If you want to do this, you must first ungroup the items, add the calculated item, and then regroup the items. Also, you cannot group items for OLAP source data that does not support the CREATE SESSION CUBE statement.

Apply a Style to the PivotTable

You can apply a built-in style to a PivotTable to quickly and easily change the colors of various parts of the PivotTable. Each PivotTable style stores a combination of font, border, and fill color settings for the elements that make up the PivotTable.

Some PivotTable styles apply one shade of a color to the column headings and total row, and another shade to the rows that designate groups in the PivotTable. Other PivotTable styles apply one color shading to the column headings and total row, a second color shading to rows that designate groups, and a third shade to the rows in each group in the PivotTable. These two types of styles can most effectively call attention to groups in a PivotTable.

Still other PivotTable styles color the row gridlines in the color scheme of the style instead of hiding the gridlines, like the PivotTables shown so far in this chapter. And some PivotTable styles apply the same shade of color to the column headings and the leftmost column of the PivotTable, and then use a second shade for the rest of the PivotTable.

Apply a Style to the PivotTable

1. Click in the PivotTable.
   - PivotTable Tools appear on the Ribbon.
2. Click the Design tab.
3. Click ▾.

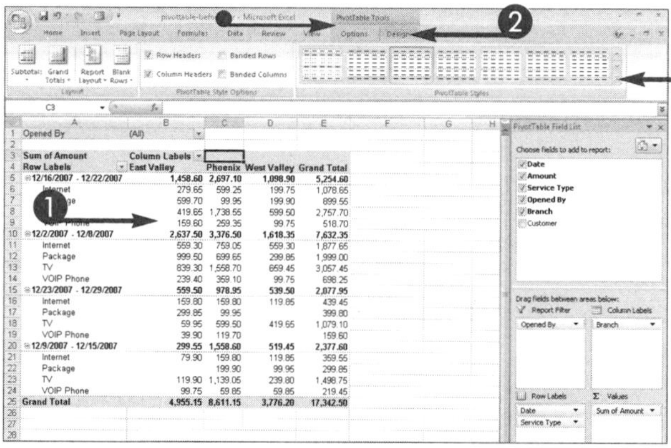

The PivotTable Styles Gallery appears.

4. Move your mouse pointer over a style, but do not click.

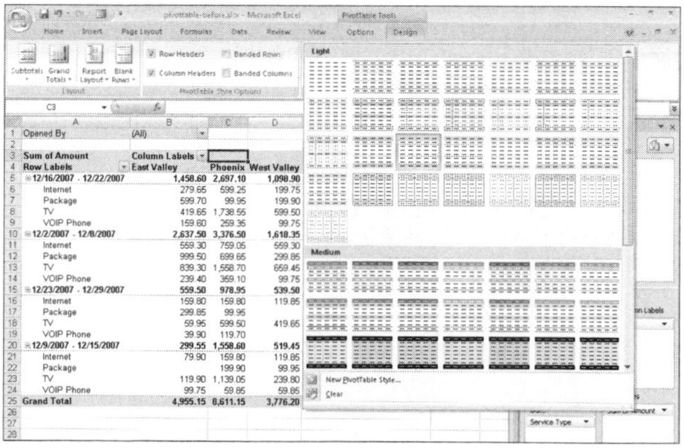

- Excel's Live Preview feature temporarily applies the style to the PivotTable so that you can see its effect.

5. Click a style.

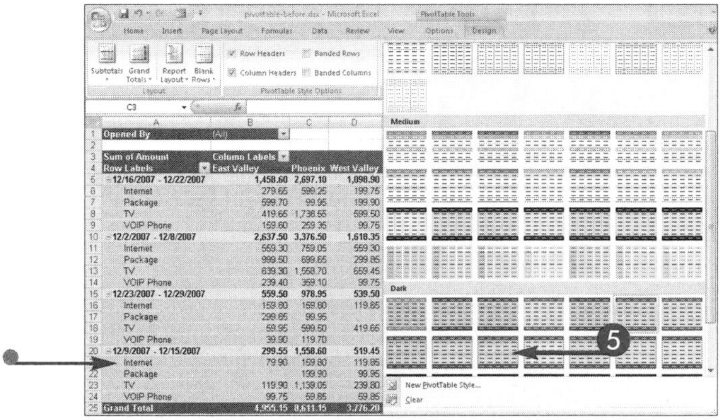

- Excel applies the style to the PivotTable.

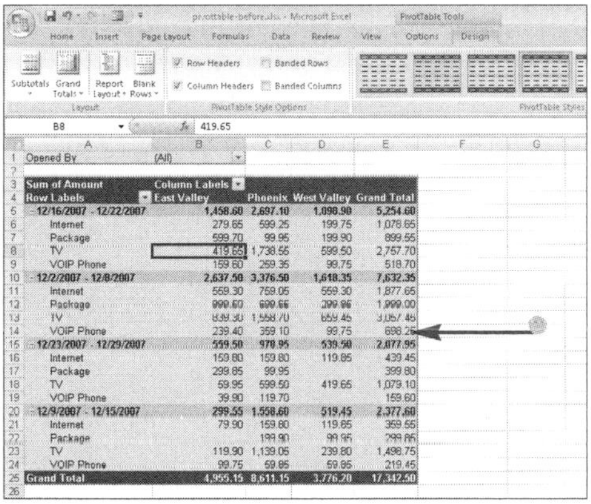

MASTER IT

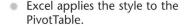

After I select a PivotTable style, what do I do if I want to remove it?

▼ If you decide to remove the PivotTable style immediately or shortly after you apply it, you can click [Undo] to undo the application of the style. If you do not click [Undo] immediately after applying the style, Excel undoes all actions you have taken since applying the style, starting from the last action. If you have done a lot of work that you do not want to undo, you can follow the steps in this section to apply a different style. You can also click Clear at the bottom of the PivotTable Style Gallery; Excel removes all color from the PivotTable.

How do I create a new PivotTable style?

▼ Follow Steps 1 to 3. At the bottom of the PivotTable Style Gallery, click New PivotTable Style. Excel displays the New PivotTable Quick Style dialog box. Each element that you can format appears in the Table Element list. Click an element and then click the Format button. The Format Cells dialog box appears, displaying three tabs: the Font tab, the Border tab, and the Fill tab. Using these tabs, you can set font characteristics, border styles and colors, and a fill color for the selected element. After you save the new style, it appears in the Custom section of the PivotTable Style Gallery.

Set PivotTable Style Options

You can control whether Excel applies a style's defined coloring to the column headers and row headers, and you can add or remove row and column banding.

By default, most PivotTable styles apply special coloring and font effects to the column headers and the row headers. Some styles apply boldface to the column and row headers, while other styles apply boldface and color shading to the column and row headers. Some styles apply the same color to both the column and row headers, but use a darker shade for the column headers. Other styles apply black or dark gray to the column headers and then apply two shades of the same color to the row headers and the PivotTable contents. You can remove column and row header style effects.

You can also apply banding to rows and columns. The net effect of applying banding depends on the style applied to the table. In some cases, adding row and column banding displays the rows and columns of the PivotTable in an alternating pattern using white and another color. In other cases, adding row and column banding results in Excel applying color to the gridlines that separate the rows.

Set PivotTable Style Options

Adjust Row and Column Headers

❶ Click in the PivotTable.

- PivotTable Tools appear on the Ribbon.

❷ Click the Design tab.

- By default, Excel applies style options to column headers.
- By default, Excel applies style options to row headers.

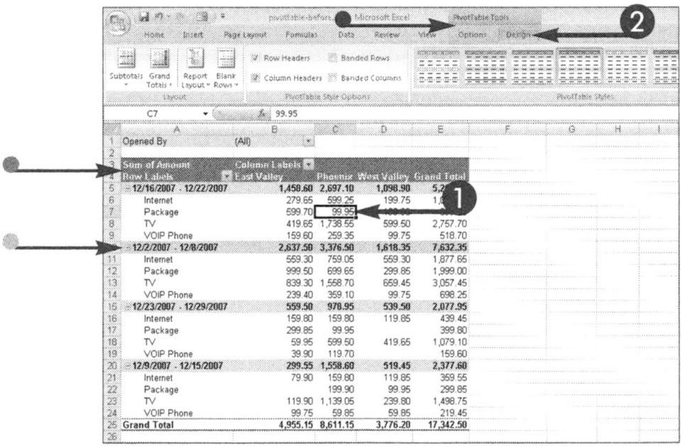

❸ Click Row Headers and click Column Headers (☑ changes to ☐).

- Excel removes style options from column headers.
- Excel removes style options from row headers.

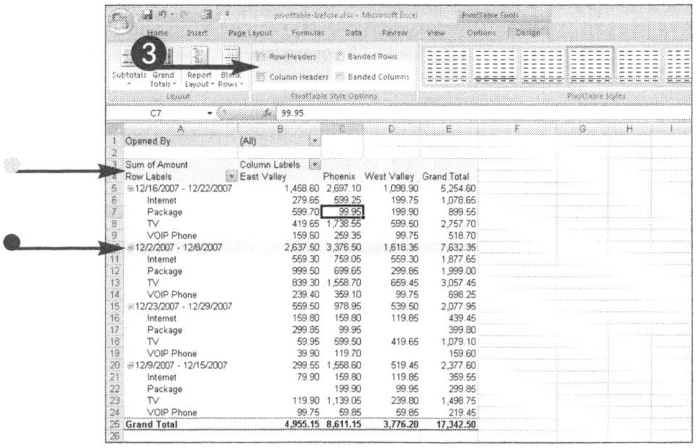

Display Row and Column Banding

1. Click in the PivotTable.
   - PivotTable Tools appear on the Ribbon.
2. Click the Design tab.
   - By default, Excel does not display row or column banding.

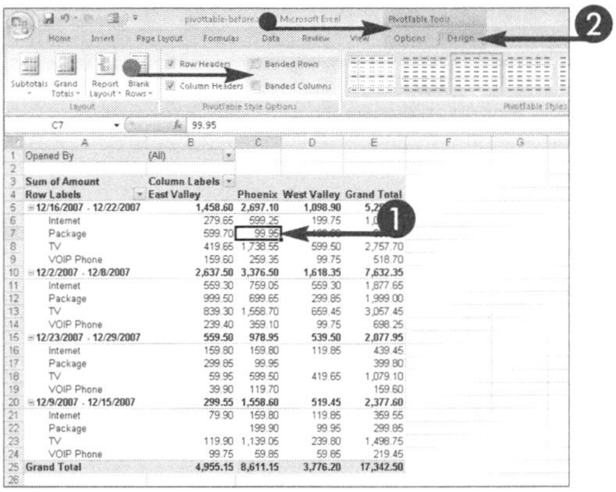

3. Click Banded Rows and click Banded Columns (☑ changes to ☐).
   - Excel adds row banding.
   - Excel adds column banding.

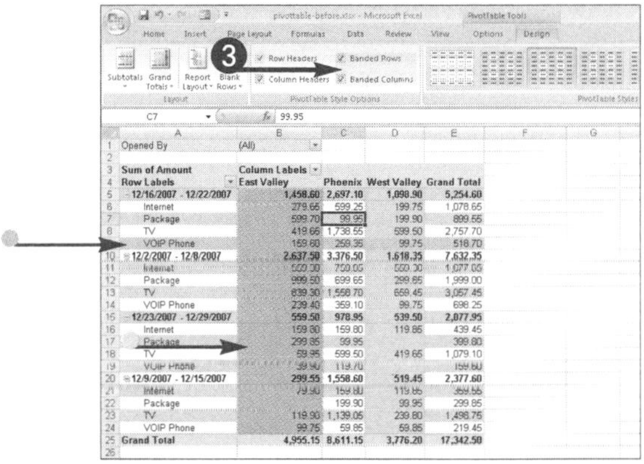

If I remove row headers and column headers, and then switch to a different PivotTable style, does Excel automatically add row headers and column headers?

▼ No. Excel applies the state of the Row Headers and Column Headers check boxes to each style you apply. As long as the check boxes are selected, Excel includes the formatting stored in each style for Row Headers and Column Headers as you change the PivotTable's style. Similarly, as long as the check boxes are not selected, Excel excludes the font and color options stored with any style you select. Excel behaves the same way when you select or deselect the Banded Rows and Banded Columns check boxes.

I followed the steps to apply banded rows and columns, and nothing happened. What did I do wrong?

▼ You probably did not do anything wrong, and Excel probably did add banding. Click Banded Rows and click Banded Columns to remove banding (☐ changes to ☑), and then repeat the process. However, before you begin, look carefully at the gridlines in your table. Then examine them again after you add banding. Based on your PivotTable style, Excel probably added color to the gridlines instead of adding shading to alternating rows or columns, and so the banding is not as noticeable as banding of alternating shades.

Add or Remove Blank Rows

You can add or remove blank rows to or from a PivotTable to improve readability. To insert blank rows, you must include at least two fields in the Row Labels area. When you insert blank rows, Excel displays them in the PivotTable in each set of rows after the last occurrence of the last item that appears in the Row Labels area.

Suppose that your worksheet contains sales information by day for various types of sales made by a cable service provider, and tracks the date of the sale, the amount, the type of service, whether the sale was made by Customer Service or Direct Sales, the branch that made the sale, and the type of customer — new or existing — who made the purchase.

Further suppose that you set up your PivotTable to display the type of service as columns in the table and you include the branch, who made the sale, and the type of customer — existing or new — in the Row Labels area in that order. When you add blank rows, Excel inserts the blanks after the last listing of New in each group.

The appearance of blank rows is most noticeable when you hide the item detail.

Add or Remove Blank Rows

Add Blank Rows

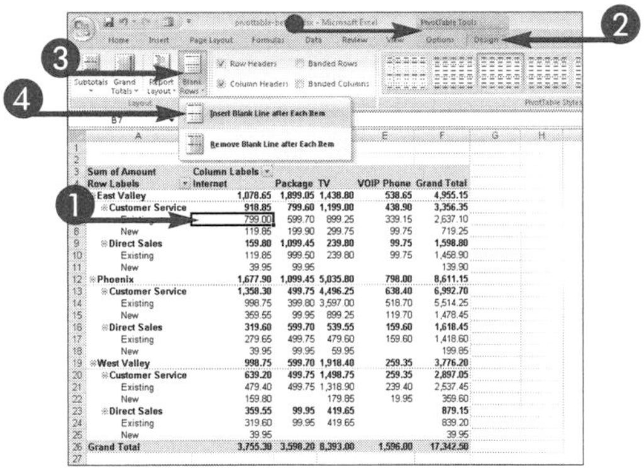

1. Click in the PivotTable.
   - PivotTable Tools appear on the Ribbon.
2. Click the Design tab.
3. Click Blank Rows.
4. Click Insert Blank Line after Each Item.

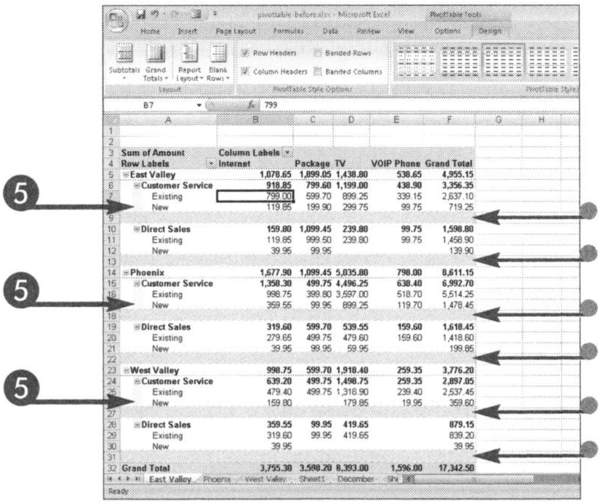

- Excel inserts blank lines after the last occurrence of the last item listed in the Row Labels area.

5. Click each ⊟ in the PivotTable for the second-to-the-last field listed in the Row Labels area.

Note: *In this example, click each ⊟ beside Customer Service and Direct Sales.*

- Blank lines become more obvious.

Note: *If you click each ⊟ for each field listed in the Row Labels section, blank lines become even more obvious.*

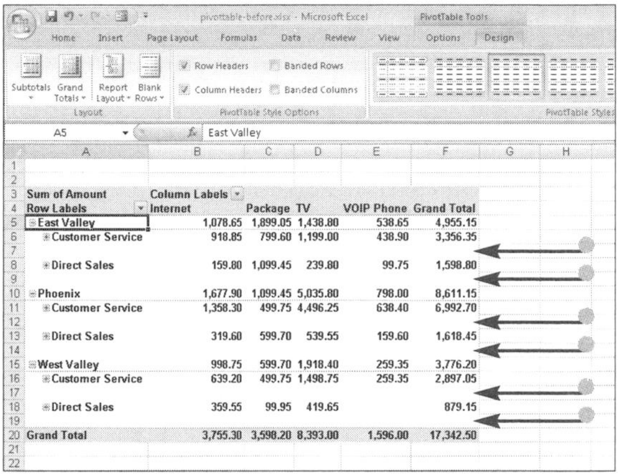

Remove Blank Rows

1. Click in the PivotTable.
   - PivotTable Tools appear on the Ribbon.
2. Click the Design tab.
3. Click Blank Rows.
4. Click Remove Blank Line after Each Item.

   Excel removes the blank lines.

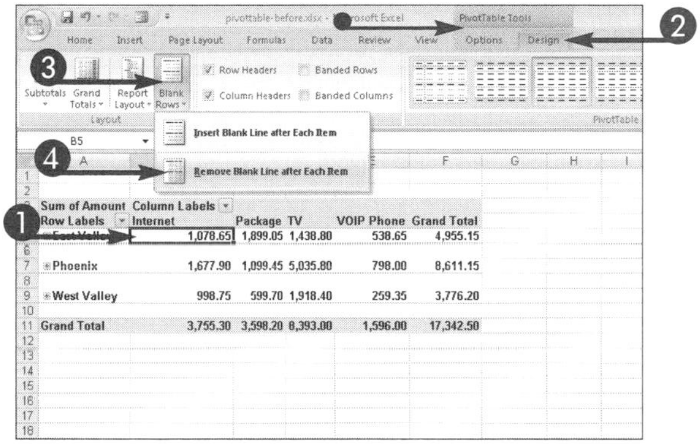

MASTER IT

I inserted blank rows, but nothing happened. What did I do wrong?

▼ You probably included only one field in the Row Labels area of the PivotTable Field List. Because Excel inserts the blank rows after the last item listed in the PivotTable in each section of rows, you must include at least two fields in the Row Labels area. The blank rows are intended to separate the last item in a section of rows from the next row label that begins a section of rows. If you include only one field in the Row Labels area, your PivotTable contains only one section of rows and Excel cannot insert any blank rows.

Is there an easier way to hide and display details than clicking ⊟ and ⊞?

▼ Yes. Excel calls hiding or displaying details *collapsing* or *expanding* a field. To collapse a field, right-click any label for the field in the PivotTable and click Expand/Collapse. From the shortcut menu, click Collapse Entire Field. To expand a field, right-click any listing of the field and click Expand/Collapse. From the shortcut menu that appears, click Expand Entire Field. Buttons to expand or collapse an entire field also appear on the Options menu in the Active Field group. To expand or collapse only the selected label, click one of the choices that includes the field name on the bottom of the shortcut menu.

Adjust the PivotTable Layout

You can change the layout of a PivotTable to display the data in three possible formats. In the Compact Form, Excel displays each row label and item label on a separate line, indenting new lines by two characters as new row sections occur to show the nested relationship of the information. You can use this format to minimize scrolling.

In the Outline Form, Excel retains the vertical spacing you see in the Compact Form, starting each row label and item label in a new line, but Excel indents each label significantly so that columns do not overlap. This layout makes the nested relationships very distinct. In this layout, Excel also does not display the phrases "Row Labels" and "Column Labels." Instead, field labels appear.

In the Tabular Form, Excel retains the horizontal spacing you see in the Outline Form, but changes the vertical spacing from both the Compact Form and the Outline Form. In the Tabular Form, instead of displaying each row label on a separate line, Excel displays row label entries on the same line for each row grouping.

Adjust the PivotTable Layout

1. Click in the PivotTable.
   - PivotTable Tools appear on the Ribbon.
2. Click the Design tab.
3. Click Report Layout.
4. Click Show in Outline Form.

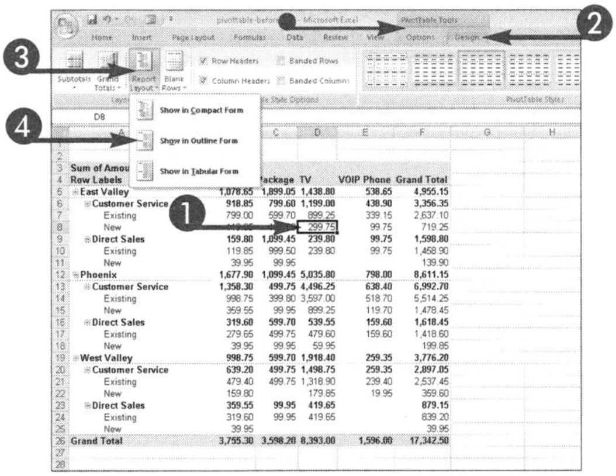

- Excel displays the PivotTable in Outline Form.

Each row label and item label appears on a separate line, but each label is indented significantly so that columns do not overlap.

5. Click Report Layout.
6. Click Show in Tabular Form.

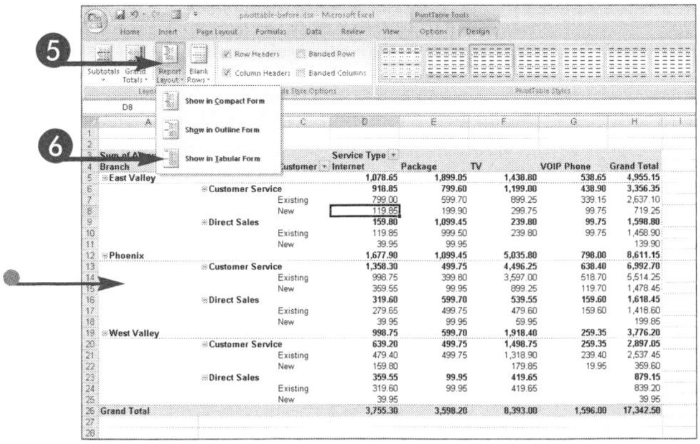

- Excel displays the PivotTable in Tabular Form.

Each row label and item label begins on the same line.

7 Click Report Layout.

8 Click Show in Compact Form.

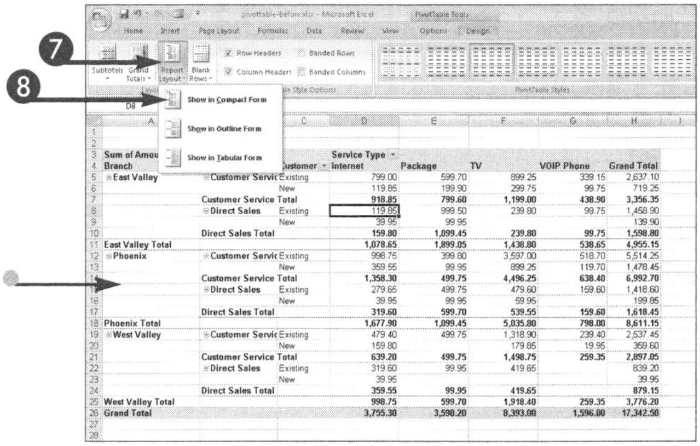

Excel displays the PivotTable in Compact Form.

The Compact Form is the default view for a PivotTable.

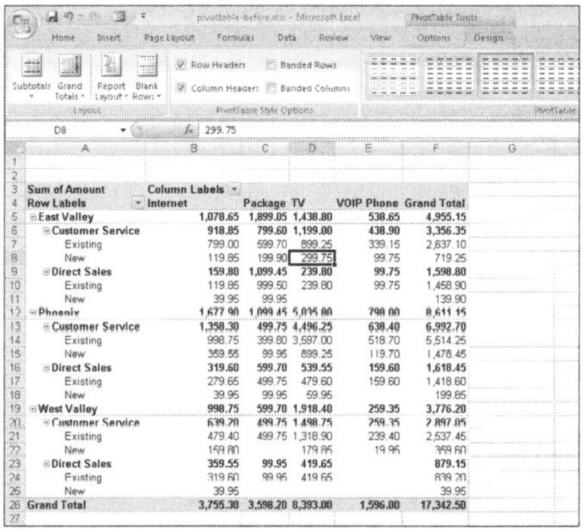

MASTER IT

Is there a way to merge cells in a PivotTable?

▼ Yes, you can merge cells containing labels. When you merge label cells, Excel centers the column labels horizontally and vertically within their cells. You may not notice vertical centering unless you change the row height of the label cells. Click the PivotTable and then click the Options tab. In the PivotTable group, click Options. In the PivotTable Options dialog box, on the Layout & Format tab, click Merge and Center Cells with Labels (☐ changes to ☑). To unmerge cells, click Merge and Center Cells with Labels (☑ changes to ☐). When unmerged, labels appear left- and bottom-justified in their cells.

Can I apply manual formatting to the layout of my choice?

▼ Yes. You can apply any of the formatting available in the Format Cells dialog box. To display this dialog box, select the cell or range in the PivotTable you want to format. Then right-click and, from the shortcut menu that appears, click Format Cells. Keep in mind that you cannot use the Merge Cells check box under the Alignment tab of the Format Cells dialog box in a PivotTable.

Can I apply Conditional Formatting to a PivotTable?

▼ Yes. You can conditionally format a PivotTable report. For details on applying Conditional Formatting, see Chapter 25.

Hide or Display Subtotals

You can hide or show subtotals for each row label group in a PivotTable and, if you display subtotals, you can control where they appear. By default, Excel displays subtotals at the top of each group in the Compact Form and the Outline Form layouts, and at the bottom of each group in the Tabular Form layout. In addition, Excel includes subtotals in all PivotTable styles.

If you display subtotals at the bottom of each group, Excel adds a subtotal row below the details of the group that includes a label for the group as well as the group subtotal. When you display subtotals at the top of each group, Excel displays subtotals on the row where the group label appears, above the details for the group. When you hide subtotals, you may not notice any change in the row organization in the Compact Form and the Outline Form; Excel simply does not display the subtotal value. When you hide subtotals and use the Tabular Form, Excel removes the rows that display subtotals, and so removing subtotals from the Tabular Form layout shortens the PivotTable report.

Hide or Display Subtotals

Hide Subtotals

1. Click in the PivotTable.
   - PivotTable Tools appear on the Ribbon.
   - Excel displays subtotals by default.
2. Click the Design tab.
3. Click Subtotals.
4. Click Do Not Show Subtotals.

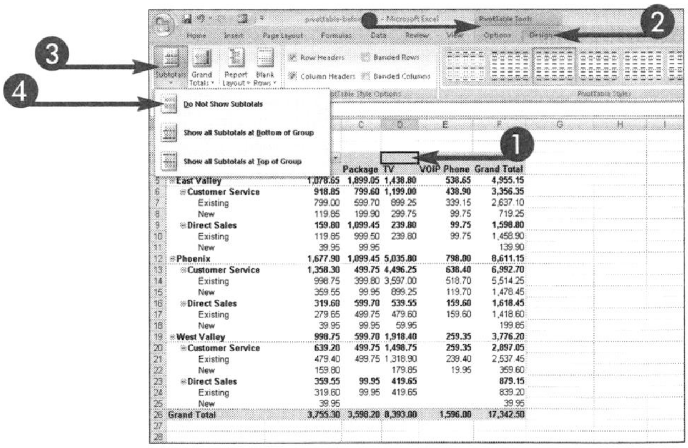

- Excel removes the subtotals from the PivotTable.

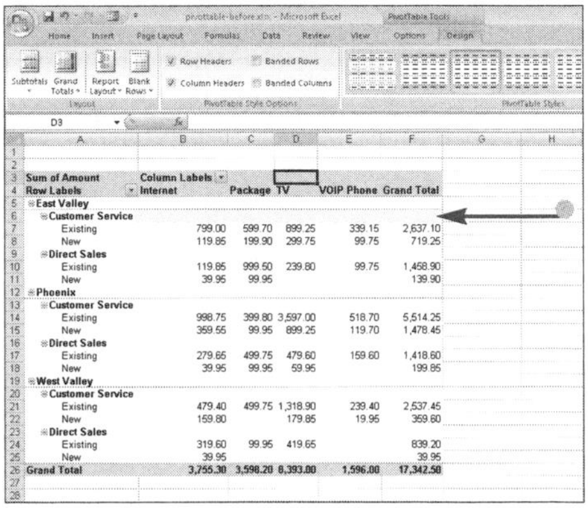

Display Subtotals

1. Click in the PivotTable.
   - PivotTable Tools appear on the Ribbon.
2. Click the Design tab.
3. Click Subtotals.
4. Click Show All Subtotals at Bottom of Group or click Show All Subtotals at Top of Group.

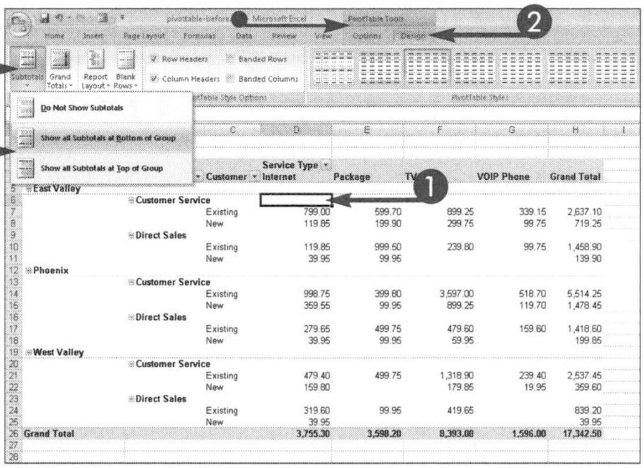

- Excel displays subtotals on the PivotTable.

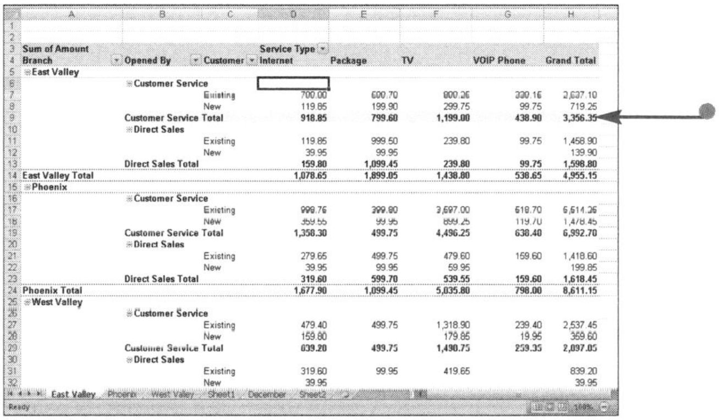

MASTER IT

Is there a way to see the rows from my original table that make up a particular subtotal?

▼ Yes, you can see the details behind any value in the PivotTable. Right-click the subtotal for which you want to see the background information. From the shortcut menu that appears, click Show Details. Excel adds a worksheet to your workbook and displays the new worksheet. It contains only those lines from your original table that make up the subtotal you selected.

Can I change the type of subtotal — for example, can I count instead of sum?

▼ Yes, but, to ensure that your subtotals make sense, consider also changing the values displayed in the PivotTable. To leave the PivotTable data unchanged and change only the subtotal, right-click the subtotal label you want to change and click Field Settings. Click Custom (◯ changes to ◉) in the Field Settings dialog box. Then click Count in the list below and click OK.

If I change the report layout while hiding subtotals, does Excel automatically redisplay the subtotals?

▼ No. Excel remembers the setting for subtotals, regardless of the layout or style you apply to the PivotTable. To view subtotals after hiding them, you must redisplay them. Follow the steps in the subsection, "Display Subtotals."

Hide or Display Row and Column Grand Totals

You can hide or show row and column grand totals in a PivotTable and, if you display totals, you can control the combination of totals that appears. By default, Excel displays totals for both rows and columns, but you can choose to display grand totals for rows only, for columns only, or for neither.

When you display grand totals for both rows and columns, Excel includes a grand total column at the right edge of the PivotTable and a grand total row at the bottom of the table. When you display grand totals for rows only, Excel displays a grand total column at the right edge of the PivotTable that contains a total for each row in the table. When you display grand totals for columns only, Excel displays a grand total row at the bottom edge of the PivotTable that contains a total for each column in the table.

The report layout you use does not affect the appearance of grand totals, and displaying grand totals does not affect the appearance of subtotals. For more information on subtotaling in a PivotTable, see the section, "Hide or Display Subtotals."

Hide or Display Row and Column Grand Totals

1. Click in the PivotTable.
   - PivotTable Tools appear on the Ribbon.
   - Excel displays grand totals by default.
2. Click the Design tab.
3. Click Grand Totals.
4. Click On for Rows Only.

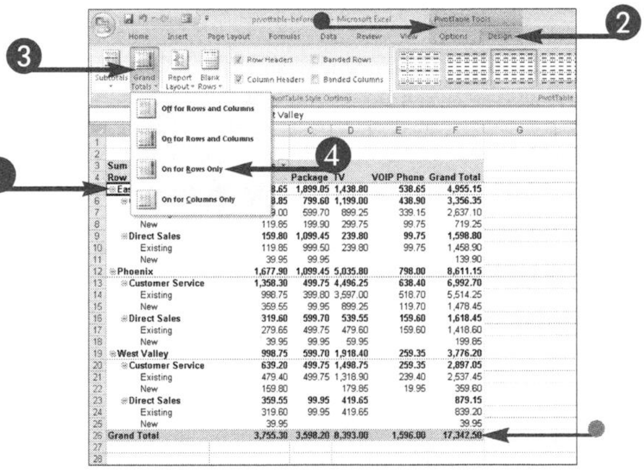

- Excel displays grand totals for rows.

5. Click Grand Totals.
6. Click On for Columns Only.

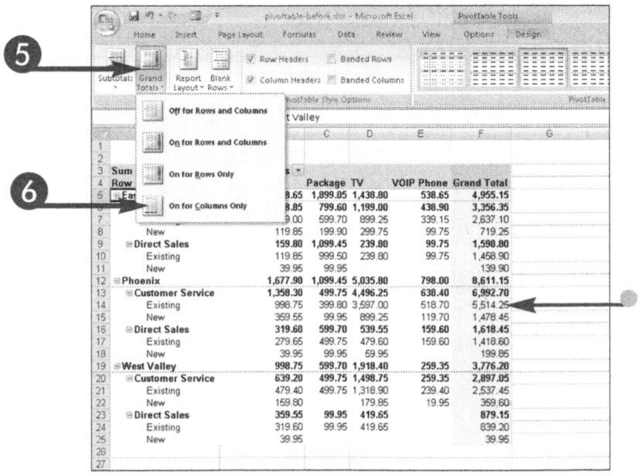

- Excel displays grand totals for columns.

7. Click Grand Totals.
8. Click Off for Rows and Columns.

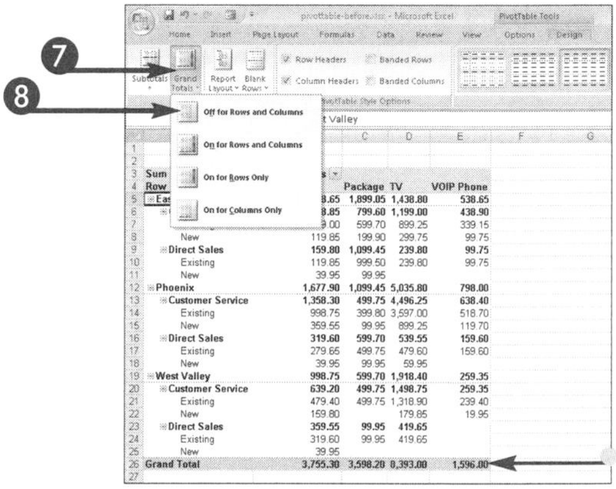

- Excel does not display grand totals.

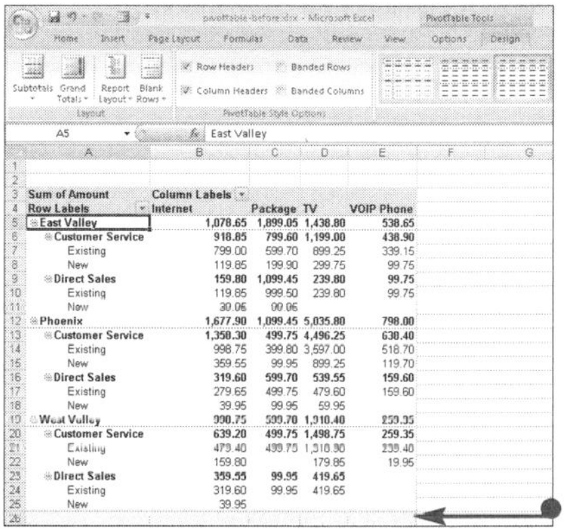

MASTER IT

Is there a way to set Excel's default behavior for displaying or hiding grand totals?

▼ Yes. Click a cell in the PivotTable and then click the Options tab under PivotTable Tools. In the PivotTable group, click Options and then click the Totals & Filters tab. Two check boxes appear in the Grand Totals section. Click Show Grand Totals for Rows (☑ changes to ☐) to hide grand totals for rows on all PivotTables. Click Show Grand Totals for Columns (☑ changes to ☐) to hide grand totals for columns on all PivotTables.

How does Excel handle filtered items in grand totals?

▼ By default, Excel includes filtered items in grand totals, but you can change the behavior to exclude filtered items from grand totals. Click a cell in the PivotTable to display PivotTable Tools on the Ribbon. Then click the Options tab. In the PivotTable group, click the Options button to display the PivotTable Options dialog box, and then click the Totals & Filters tab. Click the Allow Multiple Filters Per Field option (☑ changes to ☐) to exclude filtered items from all PivotTables, and then click OK.

Change Values in a PivotTable

By default, Excel sums values in a PivotTable, but you can summarize PivotTable data using a variety of common functions. When you change the way Excel summarizes the information in your PivotTable, Excel changes the data that appears in the table, as well as the subtotals and the totals.

In addition, you can summarize your data in some interesting and more unusual ways. You can select a field to act as the base field and then display the data in the PivotTable as the difference from the value of the base field, a percentage of the value of the base field, or a percentage difference from the value of the base field. You can also use the initial value in the base field as a starting point and display subsequent values as a running total. And, you can display the data in each row or column as a percentage of the total for the row or column. You can also display data as a percentage of the grand total of all data. You can calculate a value using this formula:

((Value in Cell) x (Grand Total of Grand Totals))/((Grand Rows Total) x (Grand Columns Total)).

Change Values in a PivotTable

1. Click in the PivotTable.

   The PivotTable Field List appears.

   - If you do not see the PivotTable Field List, click the Options tab under PivotTable Tools and click Field List.

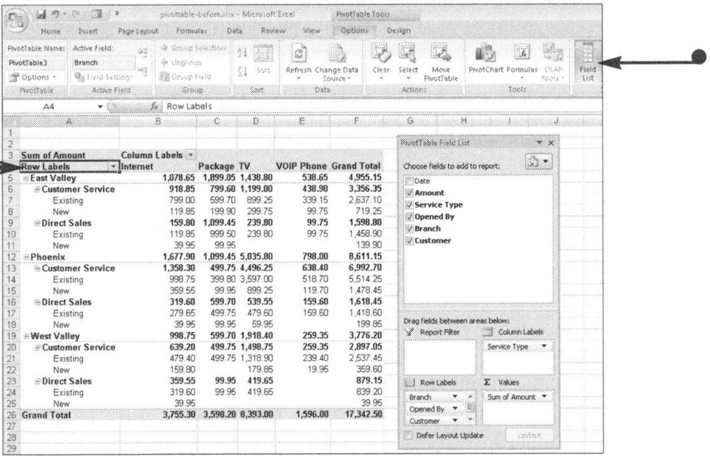

2. Click ▾ in the field in the Values area that you want to change.
3. Click Value Field Settings.

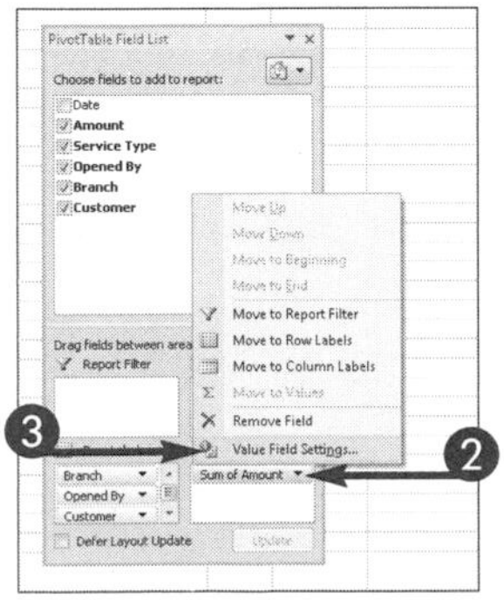

The Value Field Settings dialog box appears.

4 Click the function you want to use to summarize values.

5 Click OK.

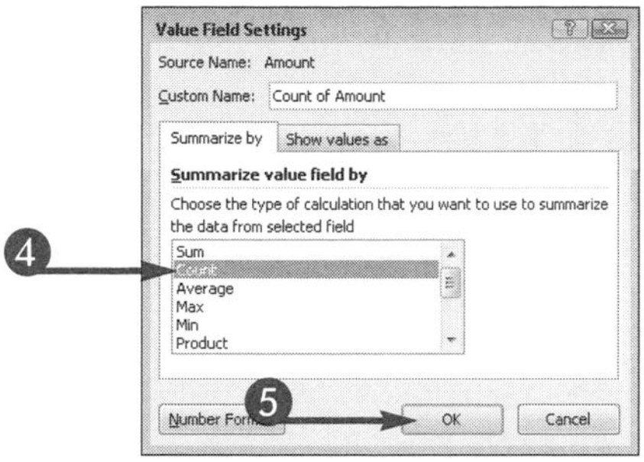

- Excel changes the name of the field in the Values area.
- Excel changes the PivotTable to summarize information using the function you selected in Step 4.

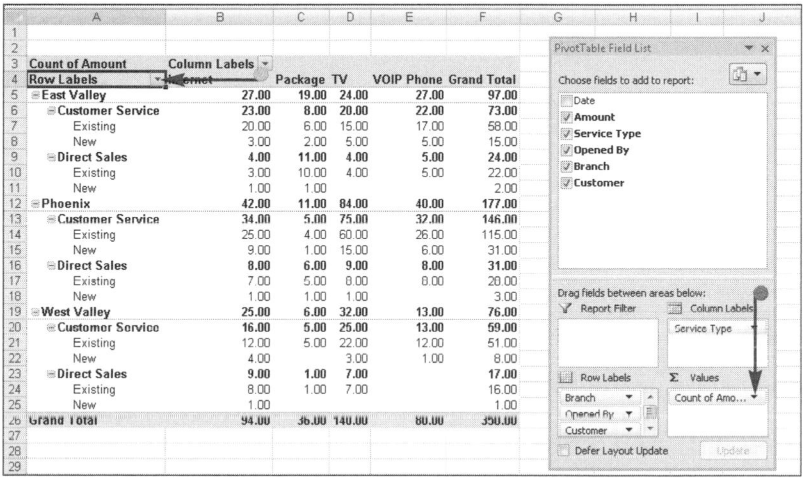

MASTER IT

Can I both sum and count information in the same PivotTable?

▼ Yes. Drag the field on which you want to summarize into the Values area — you may have two occurrences of the same field. Then complete Steps 2 to 5. Excel displays two sets of values — in this case, a sum and a count — in the PivotTable.

How can I summarize my data to display a percentage of the total?

▼ Complete Steps 1 to 3 to display the Value Field Settings dialog box. Click the Show Values As tab. Click ▾ to open the Show Values As list and click % of Total. Click OK, and Excel changes all of the values in the PivotTable to the percentage they represent of the total.

How can I summarize my data to display it as a difference from a value I select?

▼ Complete Steps 1 to 3. In the Value Field Settings dialog box, click the Show Values As tab. Click ▾ and click Difference From. In the Base Field list, select the field, and in the Base Item list, select the value you want to assign to the base field. Click OK, and Excel changes all of the values in the PivotTable.

Change Data in the PivotTable

You can make changes to a PivotTable's source data and then update the PivotTable to reflect the changes. You can change the information stored in the source range or table, and the structure of the source range or table — to add or remove rows or columns — and update the PivotTable to reflect the changes.

Suppose that your worksheet contains sales information by day for various types of sales made by a cable service provider. The worksheet tracks the date of the sale, the amount, the type of service, whether the sale was made by Customer Service or Direct Sales, the branch that made the sale, and the type of customer — new or existing — who made the purchase.

Further suppose that you have created a PivotTable based on this source data, and now management tells you about a price error for one of the services; for a month all of the information was recorded at an old price point instead of a new price point that was effective at the beginning of the month. You can update the source table and then have Excel update the PivotTable to reflect the change.

Change Data in the PivotTable

Change Data in the Source Table

1. Click in the PivotTable.
   - PivotTable Tools appear on the Ribbon.
2. Take note of the values displayed.
3. Click the worksheet containing the source information.

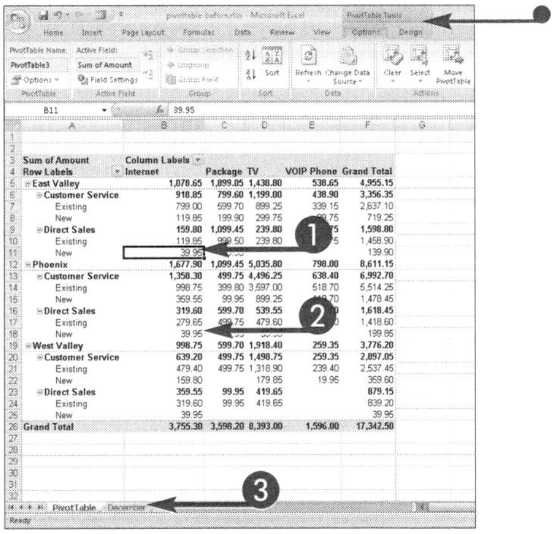

4. Make a change to the source data.

Note: *This example changes Internet service pricing from $39.95 to $34.95.*

5. Click the tab of the worksheet containing the PivotTable.

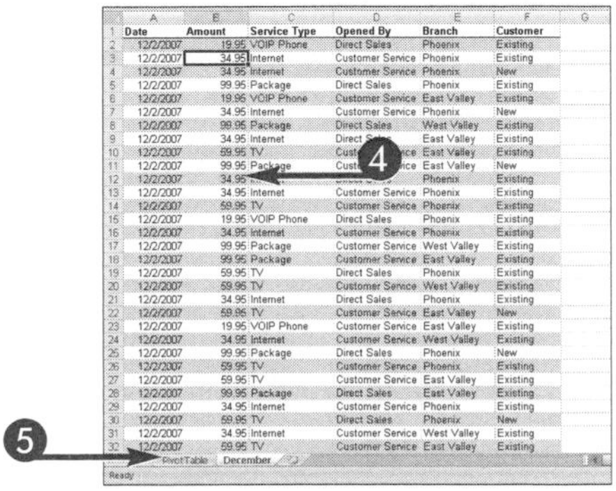

6 Click the Options tab.

7 Click Refresh.

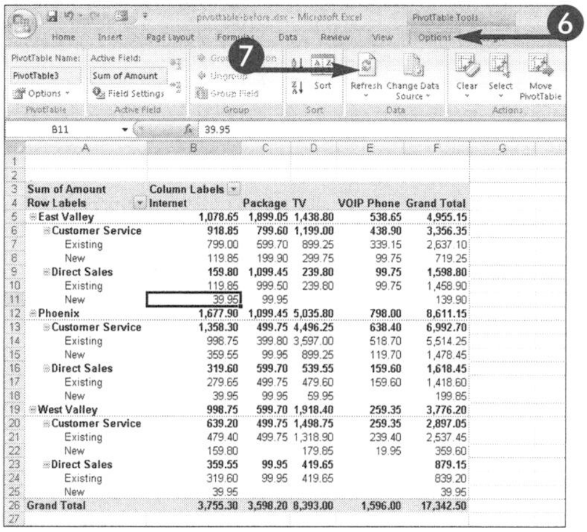

Sum of Amount	Column Labels				
Row Labels	Internet	Package	TV	VOIP Phone	Grand Total
East Valley	1,078.65	1,899.05	1,438.80	538.65	4,955.15
Customer Service	918.85	799.60	1,199.00	438.90	3,356.35
Existing	799.00	599.70	899.25	339.15	2,637.10
New	119.85	199.90	299.75	99.75	719.25
Direct Sales	159.80	1,099.45	239.80	99.75	1,598.80
Existing	119.85	999.50	239.80	99.75	1,458.90
New	39.95	99.95			139.90
Phoenix	1,677.90	1,099.45	5,035.80	798.00	8,611.15
Customer Service	1,358.30	499.75	4,496.25	638.40	6,992.70
Existing	998.75	399.80	3,597.00	518.70	5,514.25
New	359.55	99.95	899.25	119.70	1,478.45
Direct Sales	319.60	599.70	539.55	159.60	1,618.45
Existing	279.65	499.75	479.60	159.60	1,418.60
New	39.95	99.95	59.95		199.85
West Valley	998.75	599.70	1,918.40	259.35	3,776.20
Customer Service	639.20	499.75	1,498.75	259.35	2,897.05
Existing	479.40	499.75	1,318.90	239.40	2,537.45
New	159.80		179.85	19.95	359.60
Direct Sales	359.55	99.95	419.65		879.15
Existing	319.60	99.95	419.65		839.20
New	39.95				39.95
Grand Total	3,755.30	3,598.20	8,393.00	1,596.00	17,342.50

Excel updates the PivotTable to reflect the changes in the source data.

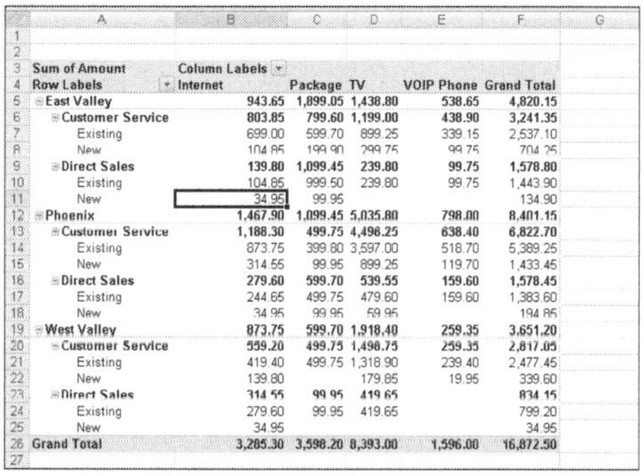

Sum of Amount	Column Labels				
Row Labels	Internet	Package	TV	VOIP Phone	Grand Total
East Valley	943.65	1,899.05	1,438.80	538.65	4,820.15
Customer Service	803.85	799.60	1,199.00	438.90	3,241.35
Existing	699.00	599.70	899.25	339.15	2,537.10
New	104.85	199.90	299.75	99.75	704.25
Direct Sales	139.80	1,099.45	239.80	99.75	1,578.80
Existing	104.85	999.50	239.80	99.75	1,443.90
New	34.95	99.95			134.90
Phoenix	1,467.90	1,099.45	5,035.80	798.00	8,401.15
Customer Service	1,188.30	499.75	4,496.25	638.40	6,822.70
Existing	873.75	399.80	3,597.00	518.70	5,389.25
New	314.55	99.95	899.25	119.70	1,433.45
Direct Sales	279.60	599.70	539.55	159.60	1,578.45
Existing	244.65	499.75	479.60	159.60	1,383.60
New	34.95	99.95	59.95		194.85
West Valley	873.75	599.70	1,918.40	259.35	3,651.20
Customer Service	559.20	499.75	1,498.75	259.35	2,817.05
Existing	419.40	499.75	1,318.90	239.40	2,477.45
New	139.80		179.85	19.95	339.60
Direct Sales	314.55	99.95	419.65		834.15
Existing	279.60	99.95	419.65		799.20
New	34.95				34.95
Grand Total	3,285.30	3,598.20	8,393.00	1,596.00	16,872.50

MASTER IT

How did you change all of the $39.95 values in the source worksheet to $34.95?

▼ You do not need to change each value individually. On the Home tab, click Find & Select. From the menu that appears, click Replace. In the Find and Replace dialog box, type the information you want to change in the Find What field, and the information to use as the replacement in the Replace With field. Then click Replace All. Excel displays the number of replacements it makes. Click Close to close the Find and Replace dialog box. If you are dissatisfied with the results, click [undo] to undo the action. Excel changes all of the replaced values back to their original values.

What should I do if I only need to change a field title and not the values in the source range or table?

▼ Make the change in the source range or table worksheet. Then switch to the worksheet containing the PivotTable, click Options, and click Refresh. Excel displays the newly titled field in the field list, and the former title for the field disappears. However, the newly titled field does not appear in the PivotTable, even if the field under its former name did appear. Click the field in the Fields section to add it to the PivotTable and then move it to the appropriate area. See the section, "Pivot Elements in a PivotTable," for details.

continued

Change Data in the PivotTable *(Continued)*

You can add fields to a PivotTable if you need to add columns to the source range or table. For example, suppose that management decides to track the customer's Zip code for each sale to get a better idea of the geographic areas that are contributing to sales. The Zip code field is added to the source table that contains daily sales, and now you need to incorporate the Zip code field into the PivotTable. Or, suppose that management decides to change the title of a field in the source range or table, from "Opened By" to "Sold By," to better describe the purpose of the field. You can incorporate this change in the PivotTable.

To make these kinds of structural changes appear in a PivotTable, you update the underlying source range or table and then use the information it contains to update the PivotTable. The technique that you use to make the PivotTable reflect changes to the source information does not change whether your PivotTable is based on a source range or a source table.

Change Data in the PivotTable *(continued)*

Change the Structure of the Source Table

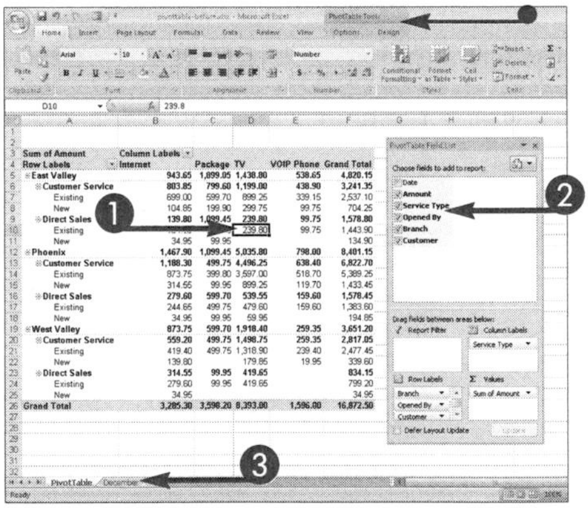

1. Click in the PivotTable.
   - PivotTable Tools appear on the Ribbon.

   The PivotTable Field List appears.

Note: *If you do not see the PivotTable Field List, click the Options tab under PivotTable Tools and click Field List.*

2. Take note of the available fields.
3. Click the tab of the worksheet containing the source information.

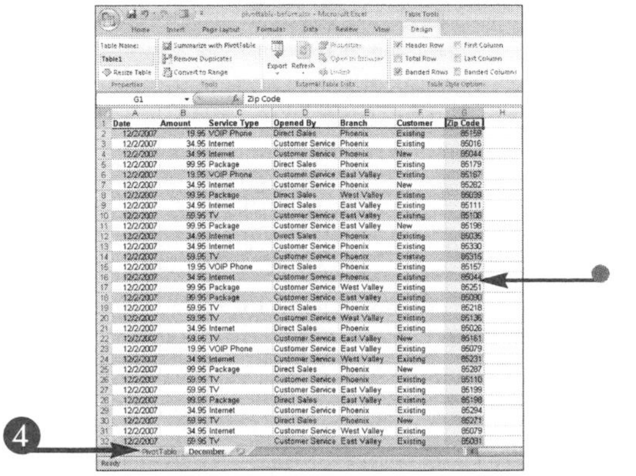

   - A field of data appears that is not available to the PivotTable.

Note: *If the source range is a table and the new field is not part of the table, add the new field to the table.*

4. Click the worksheet containing the PivotTable.

5. Click the Options tab under PivotTable Tools.
6. Click Refresh.

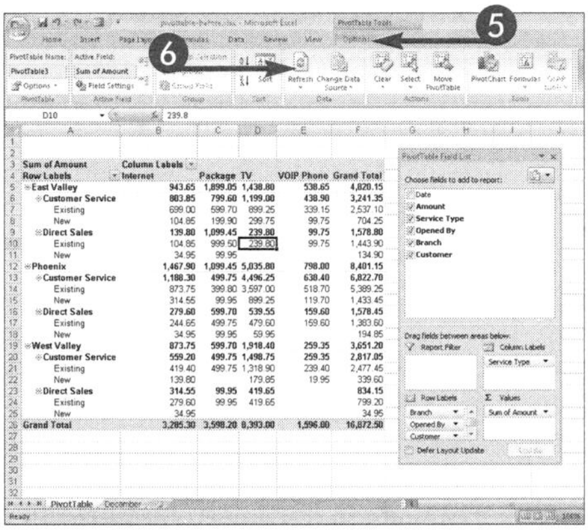

- Excel adds the new field to the PivotTable Field List.

You can add the field to the PivotTable by clicking it in the Fields section (☐ changes to ☑).

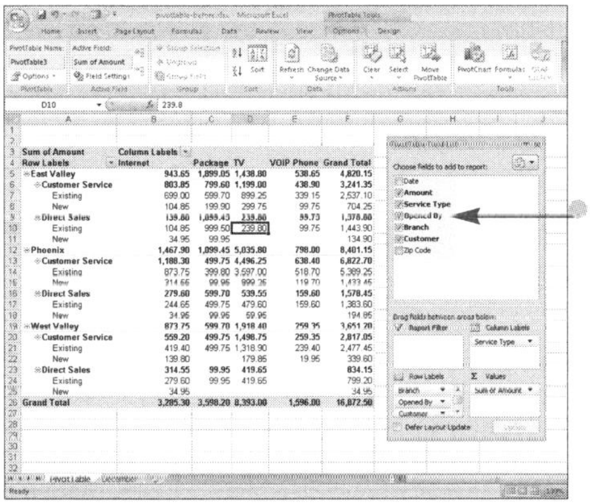

How do I add a column to the table that provides the source data for my PivotTable?

▼ To add a column to the PivotTable source table, click in the source table and click the Design tab under Table Tools. Then click Resize Table in the Properties group. In the Resize Table dialog box that appears, make sure that the table range includes all of the columns you ultimately want to be available for your PivotTable, and click OK.

How do I add a new field to the PivotTable if the source data is in a range that is not defined as a table?

▼ Assuming that you have already added the new field to the range, switch to and click in the PivotTable and click the Options tab. Click the Change Data Source button and select the source range for the PivotTable, including the new field. Excel lets you switch to a different worksheet to set the range.

What should I do to my PivotTable if I delete rows or columns from the source range or table?

▼ You use the same procedure whether you delete rows or columns. Delete the information from the source range or table by selecting it and clicking the Home tab. Then click ▾ beside the Delete button and click Delete Cells, Delete Sheet Rows, or Delete Table Rows. Then click in the PivotTable and, from the Options tab, click Refresh.

Add a Calculated Item to a PivotTable

You can add calculated items to your PivotTable. A calculated item uses the choices of a field to calculate a value that does not appear in the source range or table. For example, suppose that your worksheet is tracking sales information for a cable provider who sells Internet service, TV service, VOIP telephone service, and a package that combines all three types of services. You might want to create a calculated item to add sales of the Internet-based services. You could set up a formula in the source range or table to make the calculation, and then include the field from the source range or table in the PivotTable, but adding a calculated item to your PivotTable would probably be faster and easier.

When you create a calculated item, you start by clicking a label in the PivotTable that represents one of the choices of the field for which you want to create a calculated item. You then use the Insert Calculated Item dialog box to create a formula. This example creates a calculated item for the Service Type field.

Add a Calculated Item to a PivotTable

1. Click a row or column label.
   - PivotTable Tools appear on the Ribbon.
2. Click the Options tab.
3. Click Formulas.
4. Click Calculated Item.

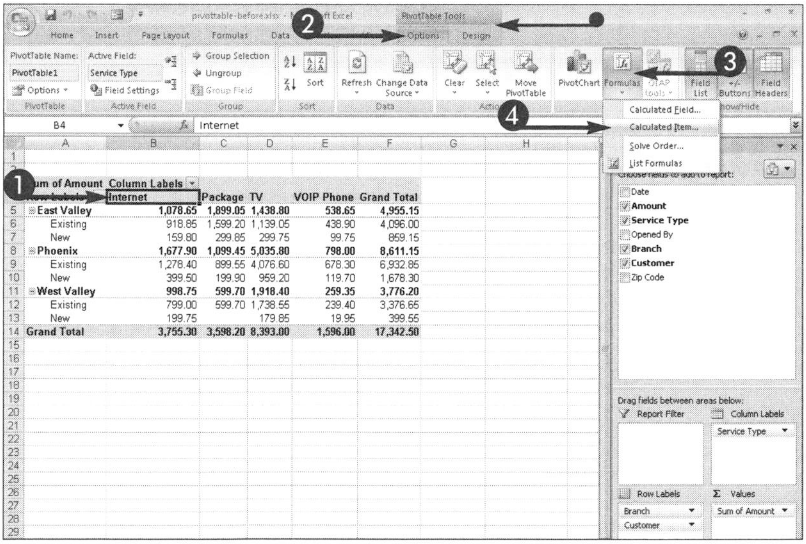

The Insert Calculated Item dialog box appears.

5. Type a name for the calculated item here.
6. Press Tab and type =.

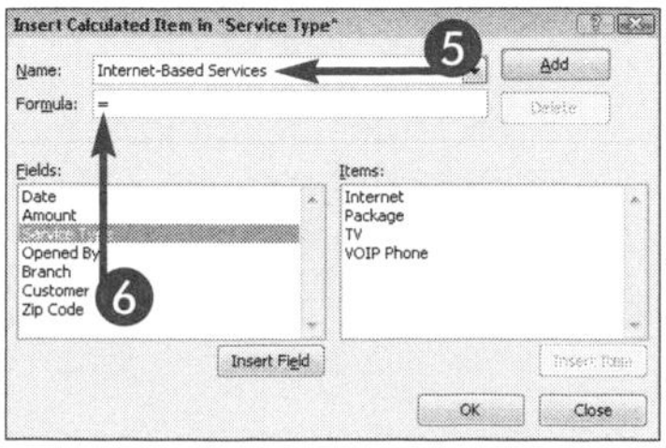

7. Click an item.
8. Click Insert Item.
9. Type a mathematical operator.
10. Repeat Steps 7 and 8 until the formula is complete.
11. Click Add.
12. Click OK.

- Excel adds the calculated item to the PivotTable.

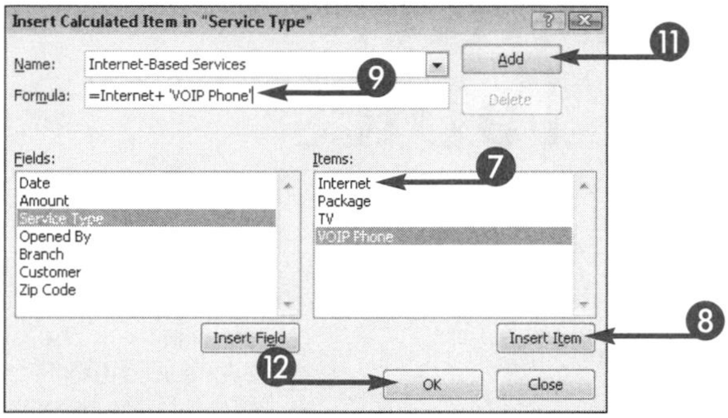

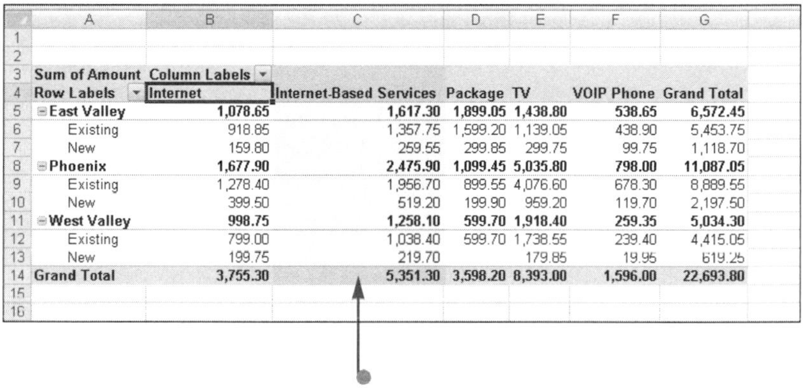

Sum of Amount	Column Labels					
Row Labels	Internet	Internet-Based Services	Package	TV	VOIP Phone	Grand Total
East Valley	1,078.65	1,617.30	1,899.05	1,438.80	538.65	6,572.45
Existing	918.85	1,357.75	1,599.20	1,139.05	438.90	5,453.75
New	159.80	259.55	299.85	299.75	99.75	1,118.70
Phoenix	1,677.90	2,475.90	1,099.45	5,035.80	798.00	11,087.05
Existing	1,278.40	1,956.70	899.55	4,076.60	678.30	8,889.55
New	399.50	519.20	199.90	959.20	119.70	2,197.50
West Valley	998.75	1,258.10	599.70	1,918.40	259.35	5,034.30
Existing	799.00	1,038.40	599.70	1,738.55	239.40	4,415.05
New	199.75	219.70		179.85	19.95	619.25
Grand Total	3,755.30	5,351.30	3,598.20	8,393.00	1,596.00	22,693.80

MASTER IT

What happens if I do not select the correct label in Step 1?

▼ The title of the Insert Calculated Item dialog box displays the label of the field you selected instead of the label you should have selected. You can, however, select the correct field. Before you perform Step 7, click the correct field in the Fields list. The title of the dialog box does not change, but you can proceed to complete Steps 7 to 12 and create the calculated field.

I noticed the Calculated Field option when creating a calculated item. What is the difference?

▼ A calculated field is a new field in a PivotTable that you create using other fields in the PivotTable. For example, you could use a calculated field to calculate a sales commission. You use essentially the same procedure to create a calculated field as you use to create a calculated item.

In the example, why does VOIP Phone appear in single quotation marks?

▼ Whenever the item name consists of more than one word, Excel places it in single quotation marks to identify the beginning and end of the item name.

Are there any restrictions concerning creating a calculated item?

▼ Yes. You cannot create calculated items in PivotTables that are connected to an OLAP data source.

Cell References and PivotTables

You can create a formula outside a PivotTable that refers to data in the PivotTable, and you can create the formula using the same techniques you use to create any formula. However, if you create the formula using the pointing method, Excel automatically substitutes the typical formula with a much more complicated formula that uses the GETPIVOTDATA function, and this conversion works in your favor.

Suppose that you have created a PivotTable from a worksheet that contains sales information by day for various cable products made by three branch offices of a cable service provider, including the type of customer — new or existing — who purchased the service. Now, you want to create a formula outside the PivotTable that calculates each branch's percentage of total sales. If the branch sales appear in the range B4:B6 and the total sales appear in cell B7, the formula for the first branch's percentage of sales would typically be B4/B7. As you see in this example, when you use the pointing technique to create the formula, Excel automatically converts it to a complicated formula that uses the GETPIVOTDATA function.

Cell References and PivotTables

1. Set up a PivotTable.
2. Outside the PivotTable, set up labels for the formulas you want to add.
3. Click in the cell where you want to create a formula that references the PivotTable.

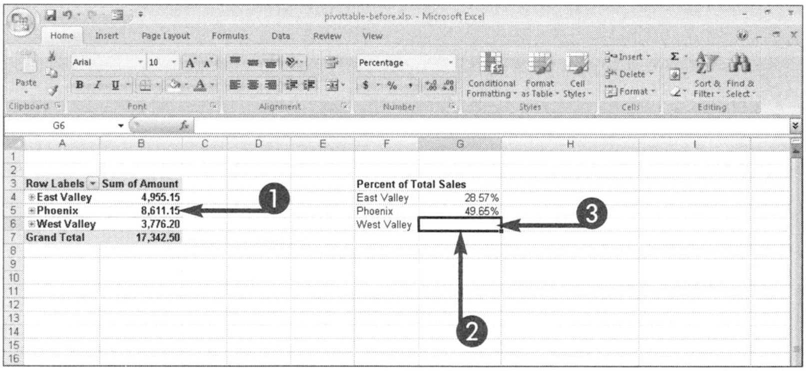

4. Type =.
5. Click cell B4.
   - Excel automatically inserts the GETPIVOTDATA function.

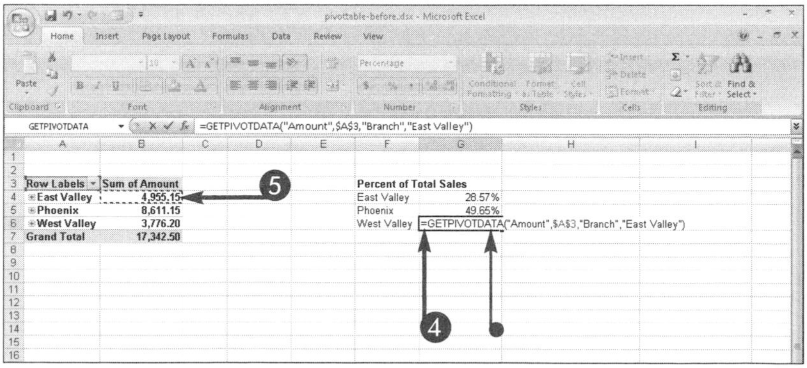

6 Type /.

7 Click cell B7.

- Excel automatically inserts another GETPIVOTDATA function.

8 Press Enter or click ☑.

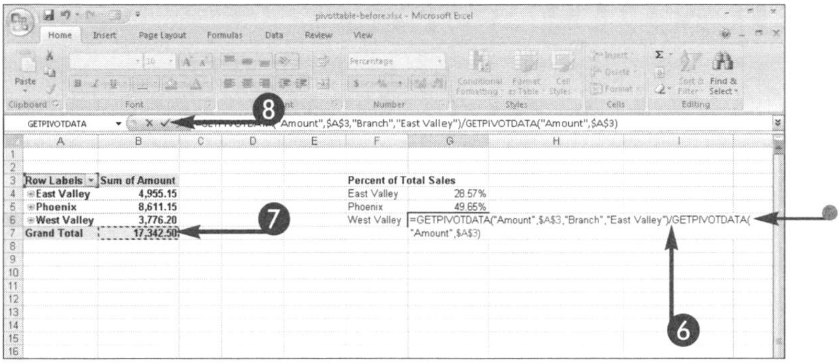

Excel stores the formula.

9 Click in the PivotTable and add a field.

- Although the cells you clicked in Steps 5 and 7 are now cells D5 and D8, the formula you entered still returns accurate results.

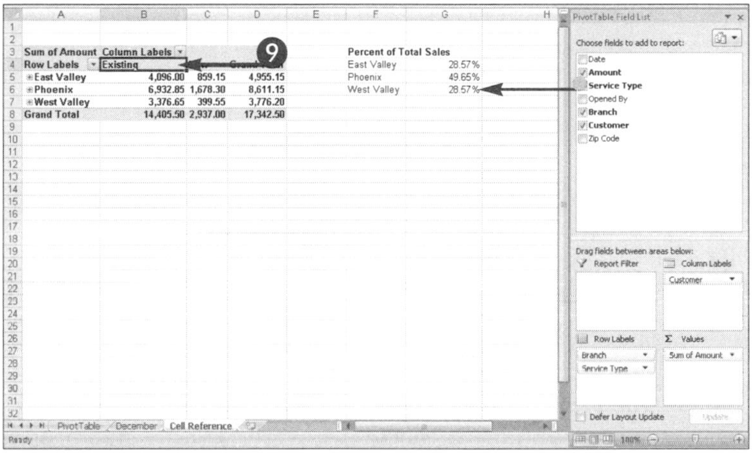

MASTER IT

Why does Excel convert the formula?

▼ Excel makes this conversion for you so that, as you make changes to the PivotTable, the formula continues to reference the cells you intended to reference. If you use simple cell references and then change the appearance of the PivotTable, the formula returns an error.

Is there a technique to enter the formula that does not result in Excel converting it to the GETPIVOTDATA function?

▼ Yes. If you type the formula instead of clicking cells as you enter the formula, Excel does not convert the formula to the GETPIVOTDATA function. In addition, as you make adjustments to the PivotTable, the formula you entered becomes inaccurate.

I tried this and Excel did not convert my formula to a GETPIVOTDATA function. Why not?

▼ The PivotTable must be set up to generate PivotTable data. By default, Excel sets up all PivotTables to generate the data, but you may have accidentally turned off the feature. Click in the PivotTable, click the Options tab, and in the PivotTable group, click ▾ beside the Options button. Click Generate GetPivotData to display ☑ beside it.

Working with a PivotChart

You can use your PivotTable to create a chart that presents the data graphically. Charted information is often easier to understand than the numbers behind the chart.

During the process of creating a PivotChart, you choose the type of chart; Excel provides several possible variations for each chart type. After you create the chart, you can select a chart layout and a chart style. A chart layout controls whether and where to show chart elements such as the title and the legend. A chart style controls the colors of various portions of the chart. See Chapter 19 for details on charts.

If you create a PivotChart from your PivotTable data and then make changes to the PivotTable data, Excel automatically updates the PivotChart to reflect your changes. In addition, when you change the pivot organization of your PivotTable, Excel automatically updates the PivotChart to reflect the reorganization. And, if you filter your PivotTable, Excel reflects the filter dynamically in the PivotChart. You can also set a filter while viewing the PivotChart, and Excel applies the filter to the PivotTable.

Working with a PivotChart

Create a PivotChart

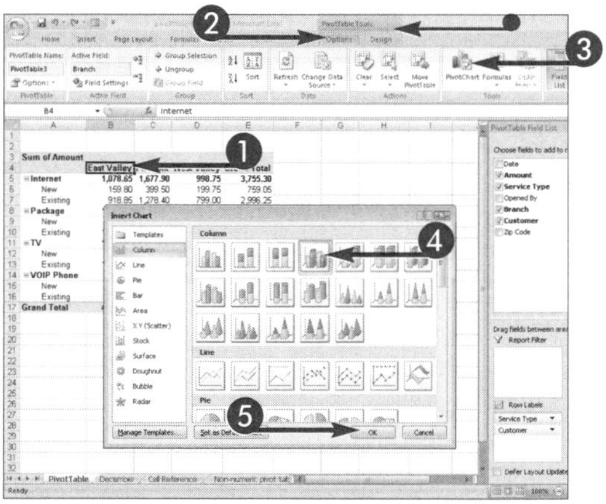

1. Click in the PivotTable.
   - PivotTable Tools appear on the Ribbon.
2. Click the Options tab.
3. Click PivotChart.

   Excel displays the Insert Chart dialog box.
4. Click a chart type.
5. Click OK.

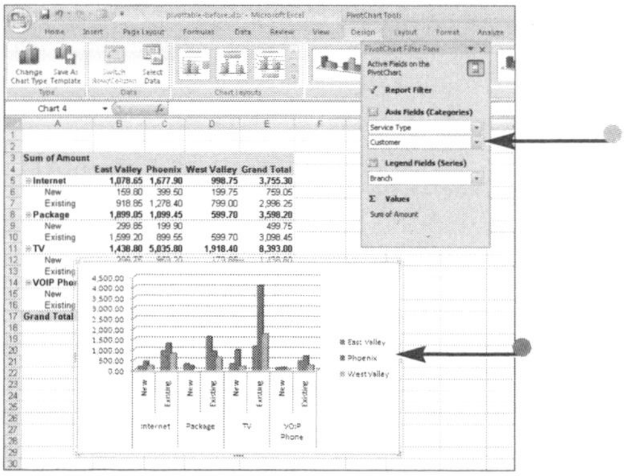

- Excel displays a PivotChart.
- The PivotChart Filter Pane appears as long the PivotChart is selected.

Filter the PivotChart

1. Click ▾ beside any of the fields shown in the PivotChart Filter Pane.
2. Click (Select All) (☑ changes to ☐).
3. Click an item that you want to display.
4. Repeat Step 3 as needed.
5. Click OK.

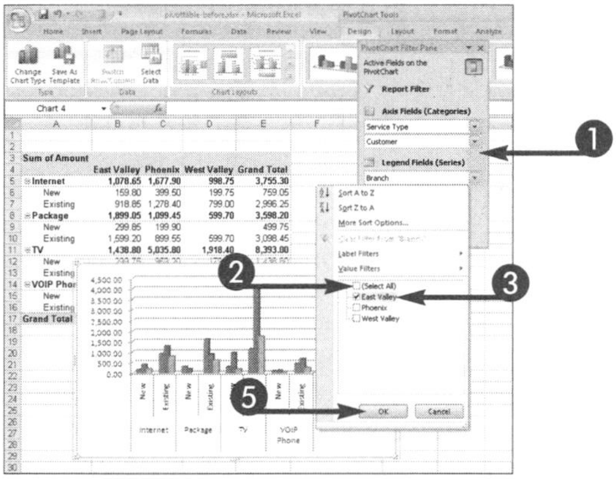

- Excel updates the PivotChart.
- Excel updates the PivotTable.

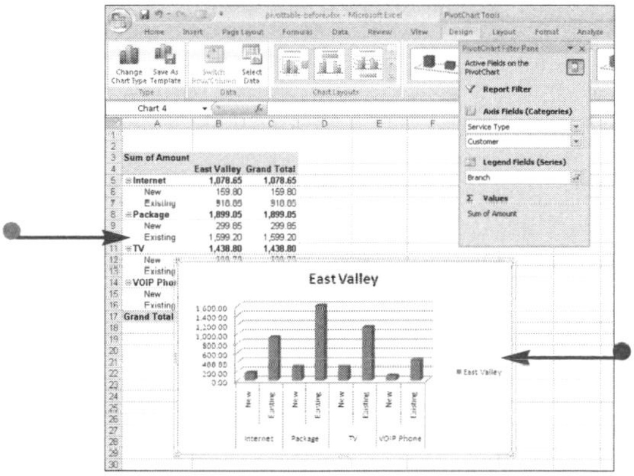

MASTER IT

What happens if I create a PivotChart and then delete the PivotTable?

▼ Although you must create a PivotChart from a PivotTable, you do not need to retain the PivotTable to retain the PivotChart. If you delete the PivotTable, Excel retains the PivotChart and converts the chart's series formulas to data stored in arrays.

Is there a way to create a PivotChart that appears in a chart sheet instead of on the same worksheet as the PivotTable?

▼ You cannot specify the location of the PivotChart as you create it, but, after you create it, you can move it. When you click a PivotChart, PivotChart Tools appear on the Ribbon. Click the Design tab and then click the Move Chart button. Excel then displays the Move Chart dialog box.

Can I create more than one PivotChart from the same PivotTable?

▼ Yes, you can. You can also format each chart individually, applying different design, layout, and format characteristics to each chart. However, if you make changes to the underlying data, all PivotTables update to show the same information. For example, if you pivot the table, all of the charts pivot to reflect the change.

Highlight Cells That Are Greater Than a Specified Value

You can use *Conditional Formatting* to highlight cells in a range that are greater than a value you specify. When you use Conditional Formatting, you set criteria for information in a range and Excel identifies the cells in the range that meet the criteria. You can also highlight values that are less than a value you specify, or equal to a value you specify. For example, if your worksheet contains test scores, then you can highlight all of the scores that are higher than a value you specify.

When you highlight cells that are greater than, less than, or equal to a value you specify, Excel compares the contents of the cells in the range you identify to a value you specify. You can also identify the types of formatting you want to apply. You can apply light-red fill with dark-red text, yellow fill with dark-yellow text, green fill with dark-green text, light-red fill, red text, or a red border. If none of those suit you, you can define your own custom format, which can include a combination of font styles and effects, number formats, border styles and colors, and fill patterns and colors.

Highlight Cells That Are Greater Than a Specified Value

1. Select the range of cells you want Excel to consider for Conditional Formatting.
2. Click the Home tab.
3. Click Conditional Formatting.

   A menu of choices appears.

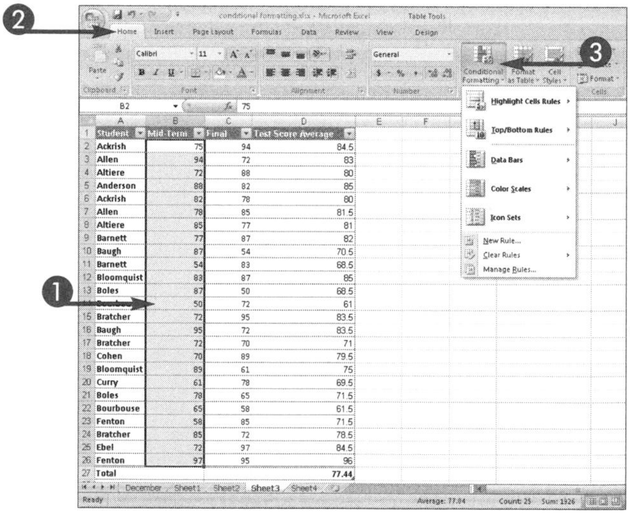

4. Click Highlight Cells Rules.
5. Click Greater Than.

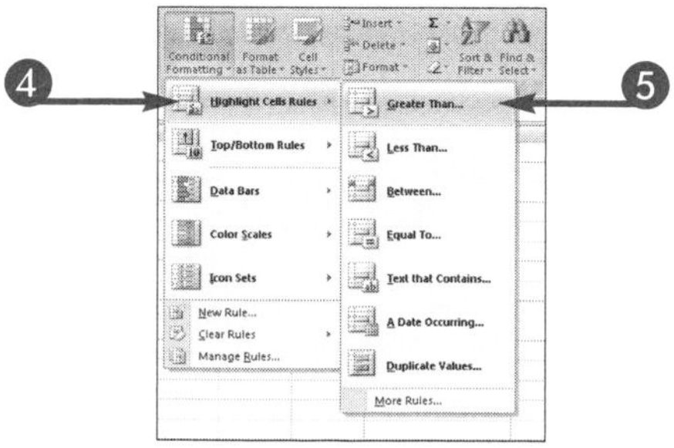

The Great Than dialog box appears.

6 Type a value or click a cell in the selected range to identify the value you want Excel to use when comparing.

7 Click ▾ to display the ways you can format cells that meet the condition, and click a choice.

8 Click OK.

- Excel applies the highlighting to the cells that match the criterion you specified.

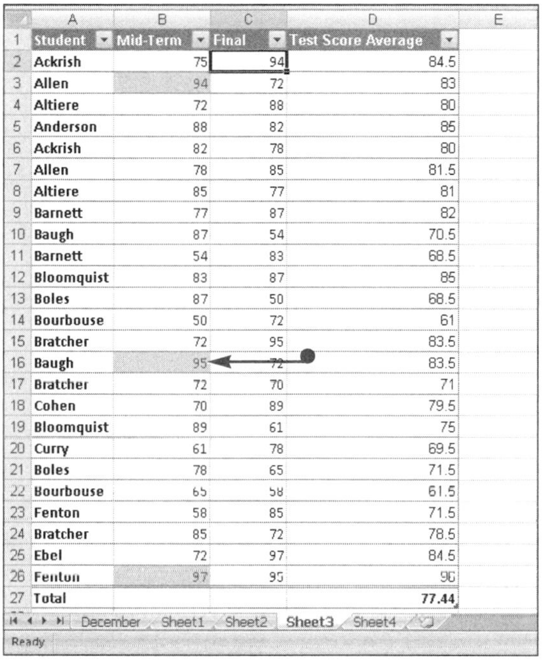

	A	B	C	D	E
1	Student	Mid-Term	Final	Test Score Average	
2	Ackrish	75	94	84.5	
3	Allen	94	72	83	
4	Altiere	72	88	80	
5	Anderson	88	82	85	
6	Ackrish	82	78	80	
7	Allen	78	85	81.5	
8	Altiere	85	77	81	
9	Barnett	77	87	82	
10	Baugh	87	54	70.5	
11	Barnett	54	83	68.5	
12	Bloomquist	83	87	85	
13	Boles	87	50	68.5	
14	Bourbouse	50	72	61	
15	Bratcher	72	95	83.5	
16	Baugh	95	72	83.5	
17	Bratcher	72	70	71	
18	Cohen	70	89	79.5	
19	Bloomquist	89	61	75	
20	Curry	61	78	69.5	
21	Boles	78	65	71.5	
22	Bourbouse	65	58	61.5	
23	Fenton	58	85	71.5	
24	Bratcher	85	72	78.5	
25	Ebel	72	97	84.5	
26	Fenton	97	95	96	
27	Total			77.44	

MASTER IT

Can I highlight cells greater than a value in a regular table or a PivotTable?

▼ Yes. You do not need to work with regular ranges; you can work with tables and PivotTables. However, to make Conditional Formatting results more apparent, make sure that you apply a fairly simple table or PivotTable style that does not hamper or obstruct your seeing the effects of Conditional Formatting. Select the cells in the table or PivotTable that you want Excel to evaluate. Even though the example in this section used a column, the range that you select can also be a row. Then, follow the steps in this section.

How do I highlight cells that are less than a value?

▼ You follow the steps in this section to highlight cells that are less than a value that you specify, or equal to a value that you specify with one exception. In Step 5, click Less Than or click Equal To. A dialog box the same as the Greater Than dialog box appears, using a different title. You identify your comparison value and select a highlight you want to apply, as described in this section.

Can I highlight cells that are not equal to a particular value?

▼ Yes. You create your own Conditional Formatting rule for this kind of formatting. See the section, "Create a New Conditional Formatting Rule," for details.

Identify the Top Ten Items in a List

Using Conditional Formatting, you can create your own "top ten" list and highlight the cells in a range that contain the ten highest values. When you create a list of top items, you identify the range that you want Excel to evaluate and the number of top values you want to identify. Excel examines the cells in the range and applies the highlighting of your choice to cells that meet the criteria.

Suppose, for example, that your worksheet contains test scores for students in a class, and you want to highlight the top ten scores. When you identify the top ten scores, Excel highlights them but does not rank them in order from lowest to highest or highest to lowest.

You identify the types of formatting you want to apply. You can apply light-red fill with dark-red text, yellow fill with dark-yellow text, green fill with dark-green text, light-red fill, red text, or a red border. If none of those suit you, you can define your own custom format, which can include a combination of font styles and effects, number formats, border styles and colors, and fill patterns and colors.

Identify the Top Ten Items in a List

1. Select the range of cells you want Excel to consider for Conditional Formatting.
2. Click the Home tab.
3. Click Conditional Formatting.

   A menu of choices appears.

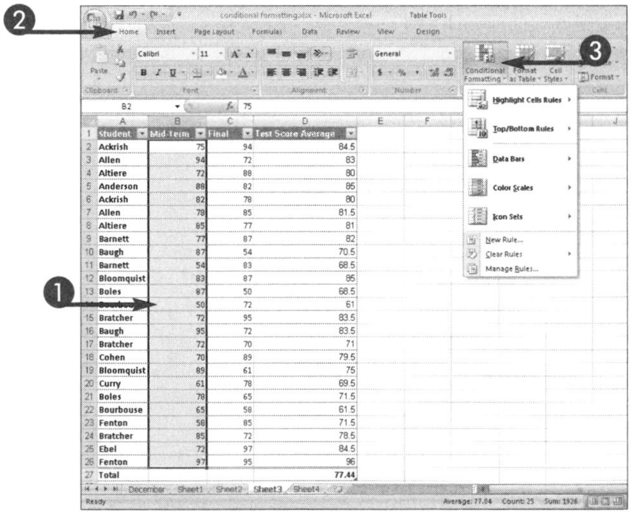

4. Click Top/Bottom Rules.
5. Click Top 10 Items.

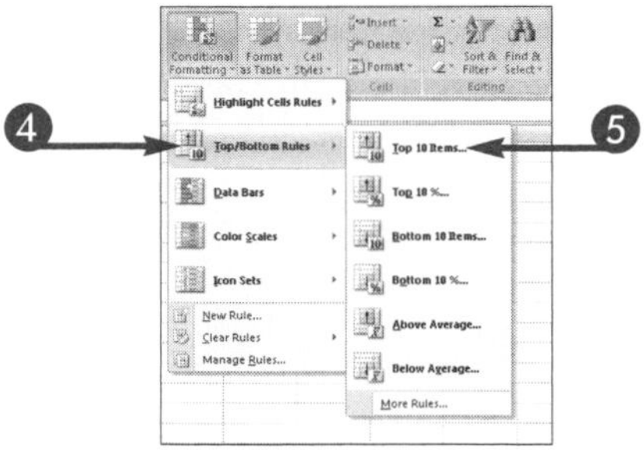

The Top 10 Items dialog box appears.

6 Type a value to identify the number of items you want Excel to highlight.

7 Click ▾ to display the ways you can format cells that meet the condition, and click a choice.

8 Click OK.

- Excel applies the highlighting to the cells that match the criterion you specified.

Note: *Excel may highlight more than ten items. Suppose that the first nine values were higher than 91, and the next value of 90 appears in two cells. Excel highlights eleven values in the top ten list.*

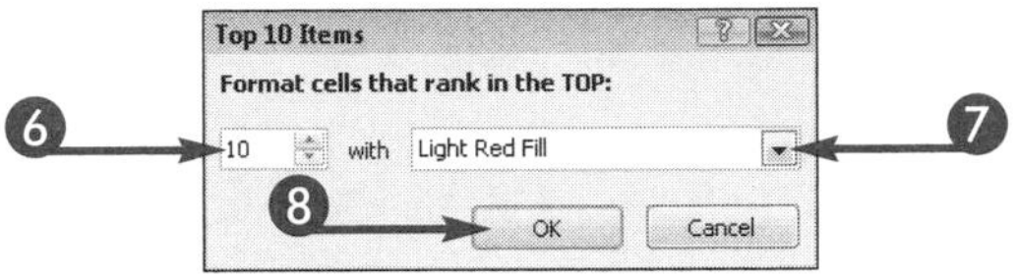

	A	B	C	D	E
1	Student	Mid-Term	Final	Test Score Average	
2	Ackrish	75	94	84.5	
3	Allen	94	72	83	
4	Altiere	72	88	80	
5	Anderson	88	82	85	
6	Ackrish	82	78	80	
7	Allen	78	85	81.5	
8	Altiere	85	77	81	
9	Barnett	77	87	82	
10	Baugh	87	54	70.5	
11	Barnett	54	83	68.5	
12	Bloomquist	83	87	85	
13	Boles	87	50	68.5	
14	Bourbouse	50	72	61	
15	Bratcher	72	95	83.5	
16	Baugh	95	72	83.5	
17	Bratcher	72	70	71	
18	Cohen	70	89	79.5	
19	Bloomquist	89	61	75	
20	Curry	61	78	69.5	
21	Boles	78	65	71.5	
22	Bourbouse	65	58	61.5	
23	Fenton	58	85	71.5	
24	Bratcher	85	72	78.5	
25	Ebel	72	97	84.5	
26	Fenton	97	95	96	
27	Total			77.44	

December | Sheet1 | Sheet2 | Sheet3 | Sheet4

Ready

PART V

MASTER IT

Can I highlight the ten lowest values?

▼ Yes. Follow the steps in this section, but in Step 5, click Bottom 10 Items. Again, you do not need to highlight exactly ten items; you can choose to highlight more or less than ten items. You can also select the type of highlighting you want to apply, as described in Step 7.

Can I highlight both the top ten items and the bottom ten items in the list at the same time?

▼ Yes. In fact, you can apply any number of Conditional Formatting rules to a specified range. However, you probably need to create a legend to identify the formatting you apply. Excel does not contain a built-in feature to create a legend, but you can apply the formatting manually to the legend cell.

How can I create a legend for Conditional Formatting in this example?

▼ Suppose that you apply a green fill to the top five items and a red fill to the bottom five items in the range B2:B26. In cell F2, type **Top 5** and, in cell F3, type **Bottom 5**. Then, select cell F2, click the fill button, and apply the same green that appears in the range B2:B25. Select cell F3, click the fill button, and apply the same red that appears in the range B2:B25.

Highlight the Bottom Five Percent of a List

As described in the section, "Identify the Top Ten Items in a List," you can highlight the top items in a list based on raw values; you can also use Conditional Formatting to have Excel highlight the bottom or top items in a list, based on percentage ranking. The items that make up the bottom five percent of a list might not be the same as the bottom five items.

When you create a list of items based on percentage values, you identify the range that you want Excel to evaluate and the percentage value you want Excel to use while evaluating. You also identify the types of formatting you want to apply. Excel examines the cells in the range and applies the highlighting of your choice to the values that fall into the bottom percentage range that you specify.

Suppose, for example, that your worksheet contains test scores for students in a class. You can highlight the scores that fall into the bottom five percent of all scores. When you identify the bottom five percent of the scores, Excel highlights them but does not rank them in order from lowest to highest or highest to lowest.

Highlight the Bottom Five Percent of a List

1. Select the range of cells you want Excel to consider for Conditional Formatting.
2. Click the Home tab.
3. Click Conditional Formatting.

   A menu of choices appears.

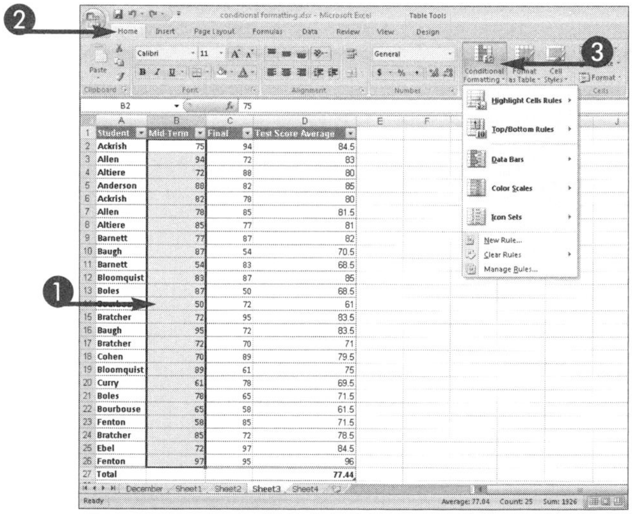

4. Click Top/Bottom Rules.
5. Click Bottom 10%.

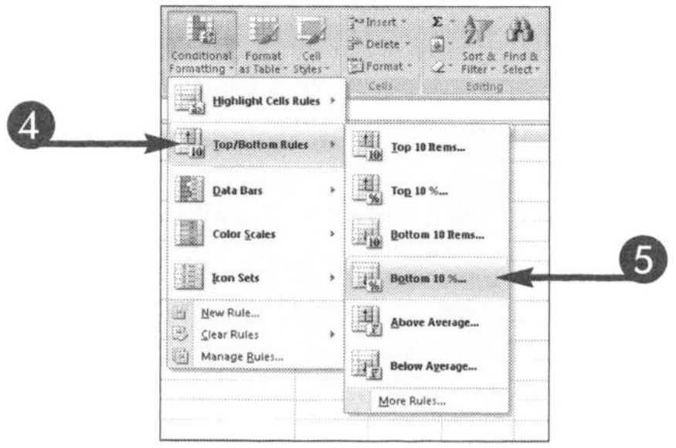

The Bottom 10% dialog box appears.

6 Type **5** to identify the percentage ranking for cells that you want Excel to highlight.

7 Click ▾ to display the ways you can format cells that meet the condition, and click a choice.

8 Click OK.

- Excel applies the highlighting to the cells that match the criterion you specified.

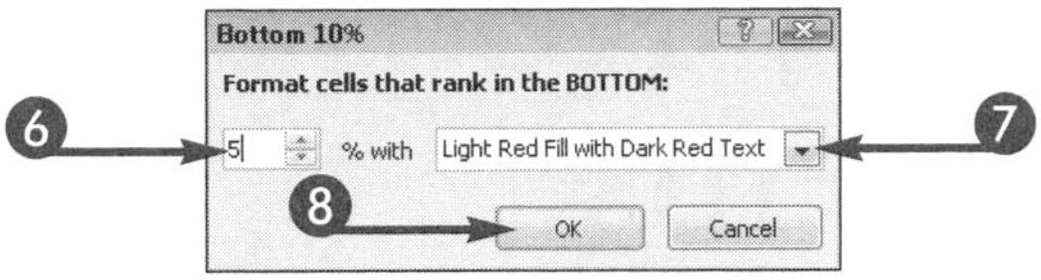

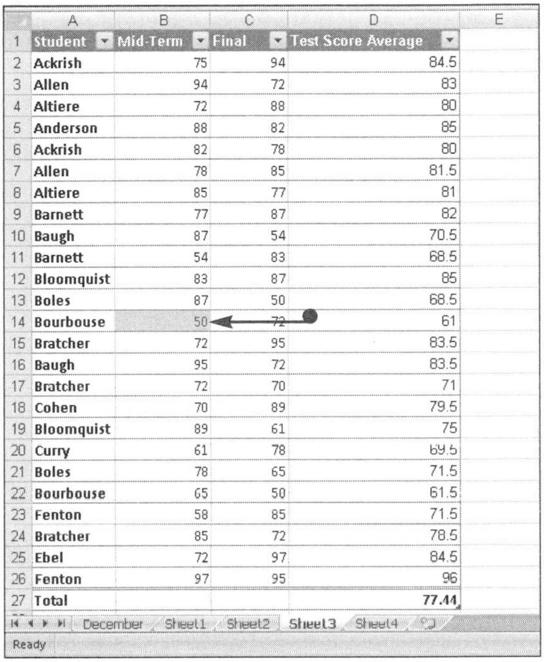

	A	B	C	D	E
1	Student	Mid-Term	Final	Test Score Average	
2	Ackrish	75	94	84.5	
3	Allen	94	72	83	
4	Altiere	72	88	80	
5	Anderson	88	82	85	
6	Ackrish	82	78	80	
7	Allen	78	85	81.5	
8	Altiere	85	77	81	
9	Barnett	77	87	82	
10	Baugh	87	54	70.5	
11	Barnett	54	83	68.5	
12	Bloomquist	83	87	85	
13	Boles	87	50	68.5	
14	Bourbouse	50	72	61	
15	Bratcher	72	95	83.5	
16	Baugh	95	72	83.5	
17	Bratcher	72	70	71	
18	Cohen	70	89	79.5	
19	Bloomquist	89	61	75	
20	Curry	61	78	69.5	
21	Boles	78	65	71.5	
22	Bourbouse	65	50	61.5	
23	Fenton	58	85	71.5	
24	Bratcher	85	72	78.5	
25	Ebel	72	97	84.5	
26	Fenton	97	95	96	
27	Total			77.44	

MASTER IT

What kind of formatting can I apply to cells that fall in the bottom five percent of the list?

▼ You can apply light-red fill with dark-red text, yellow fill with dark-yellow text, green fill with dark-green text, light-red fill, red text, or a red border. You can also define your own custom format, which can include a combination of font styles and effects, number formats, border styles and colors, and fill patterns and colors.

If I apply more than one Conditional Format and they conflict, what happens?

▼ If formats conflict, Excel applies only the format that you applied last. For example, using the list in the example, if you apply red fill to the bottom five percent of items and green fill to the bottom five items in that order, Excel applies green fill to cells B11, B14, B20, B22, and B23, changing the red fill applied to cell B14 to green.

Can I copy Conditional Formatting to another range?

▼ Yes, you can. Select the range that contains the Conditional Formatting and click . Then select the range to which you want to copy the formatting and click ▾ below the Paste button. From the list that appears, click Paste Special. In the Paste Special dialog box, click Formats and click OK.

Identify Above-Average List Items

You can use Conditional Formatting to highlight the items in a list that exceed or fall below the average of the values in the list. Suppose, for example, that your worksheet contains test scores for students in a class. You can highlight the scores that exceed the average score achieved on a test.

When you highlight values that are higher than the average value of a list, you identify the range that you want Excel to evaluate and the formatting you want Excel to apply to values in the list that are larger than the average value of the list. Excel examines the cells in the range, comparing them to the average value for the range, and applies the highlighting of your choice to the values that exceed the average value in the list.

You can apply light-red fill with dark-red text, yellow fill with dark-yellow text, green fill with dark-green text, light-red fill, red text, or a red border. If none of those suit you, you can define your own custom format, which can include a combination of font styles and effects, number formats, border styles and colors, and fill patterns and colors.

Identify Above-Average List Items

1. Select the range of cells you want Excel to consider for Conditional Formatting.
   - The range's average appears here.
2. Click the Home tab.
3. Click Conditional Formatting.

   A menu of choices appears.

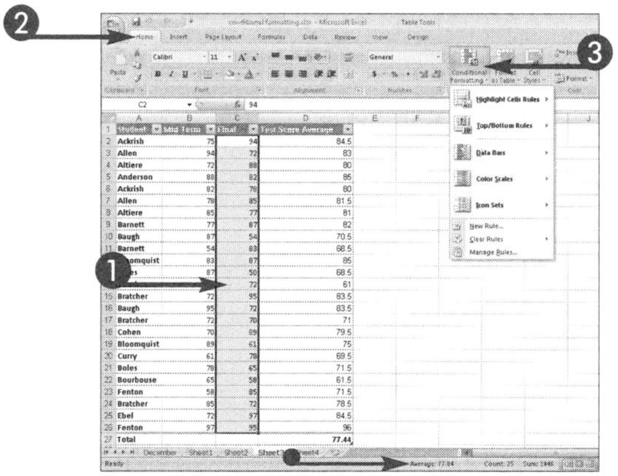

4. Click Top/Bottom Rules.
5. Click Above Average.

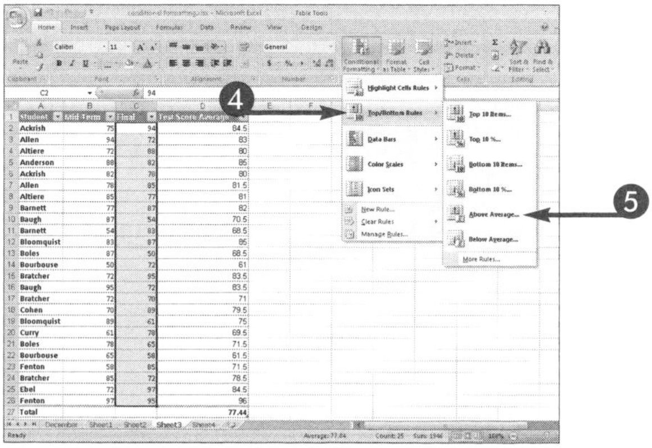

The Above Average dialog box appears.

6 Click ▾ to display the ways you can format cells that meet the condition, and click a choice.

7 Click OK.

- Excel applies the highlighting to the cells that match the criterion you specified.

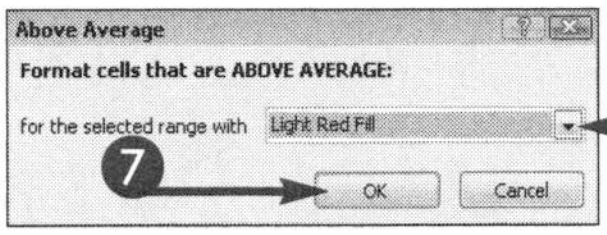

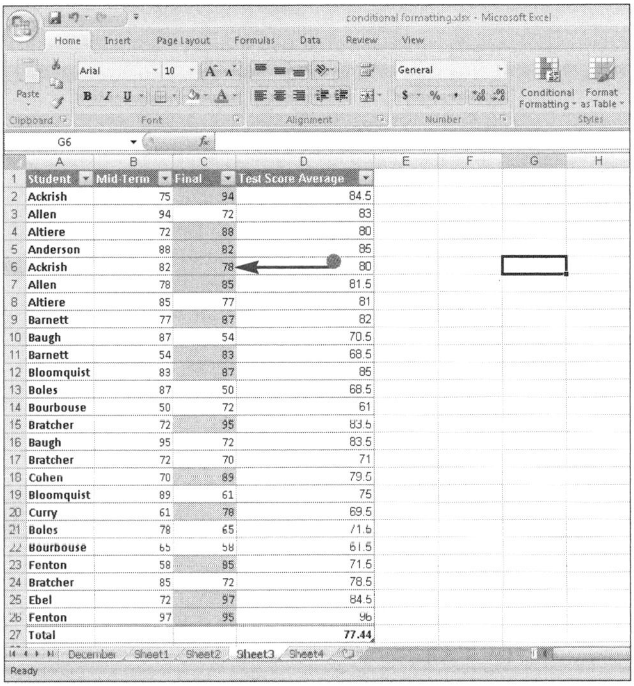

MASTER IT

I do not see the range's average. How can I make it appear?

▼ While you do not need the average to appear to apply Conditional Formatting to values that exceed the average, displaying the average can be useful. First, make sure that you have selected the range. Then, right-click the Status Bar where the average should appear. A menu appears; click Average to place ☑ beside it. Excel then displays the average in the Status Bar.

How does Excel know what formatting I apply to a selected range?

▼ Each time you apply a form of Conditional Formatting, Excel creates a Conditional Formatting rule. You can view these rules and change the way they affect the Conditional Formatting in your worksheet in the Conditional Formatting Rules Manager window, which is discussed in the section, "Manage Conditional Formatting Rules," later in this chapter.

How can I highlight the values in the list that are below the list's average?

▼ You can highlight both the above-average and the below-average values at the same time, but be sure that you use different formatting for each. To apply formatting to values that fall below the average, complete Steps 1 to 7, but, in Step 5, click Below Average.

Highlight Values Falling Between Two Numbers

You can use Conditional Formatting to highlight values in a list that fall between two numbers. Suppose, for example, that your worksheet contains test scores for students in a class. You can highlight the scores that fall between 70 and 80.

When you highlight values in a list that fall between two values, you identify the range that you want Excel to evaluate and the two values you want Excel to use while evaluating. You also specify the formatting you want Excel to apply to values in the list that fall between the two values you specify. Excel examines the cells in the range, comparing them to the two values you supply, and it applies the highlighting of your choice to the values that fall between the two numbers you provide.

You can apply light-red fill with dark-red text, yellow fill with dark-yellow text, green fill with dark-green text, light-red fill, red text, or a red border. If none of those suit you, you can define your own custom format, which can include a combination of font styles and effects, number formats, border styles and colors, and fill patterns and colors.

Highlight Values Falling Between Two Numbers

1. Select the range of cells you want Excel to consider for Conditional Formatting.
2. Click the Home tab.
3. Click Conditional Formatting.

   A menu of choices appears.

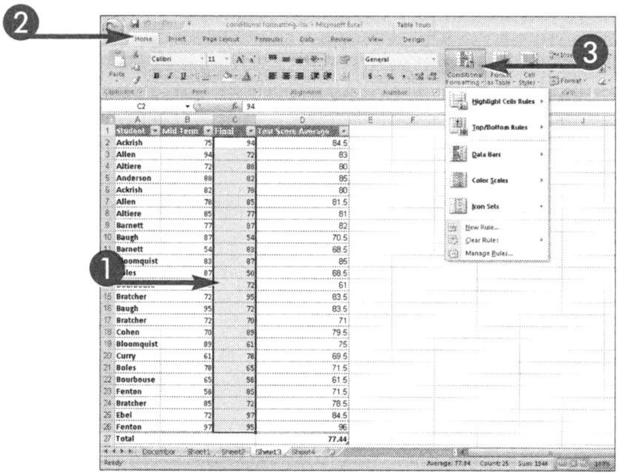

4. Click Highlight Cells Rules.
5. Click Between.

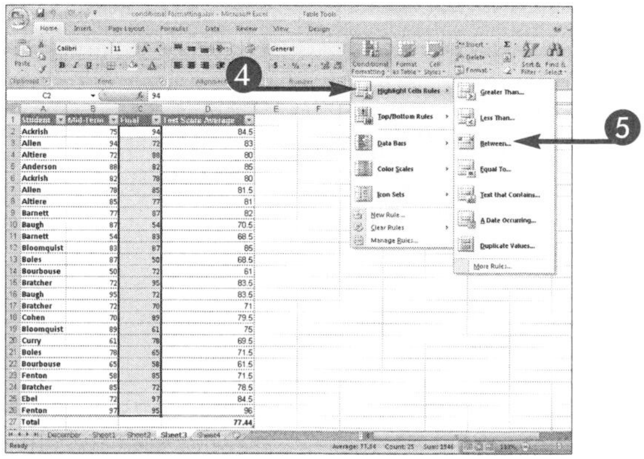

The Between dialog box appears.

6. Type the lower value here.
7. Type the higher value here.
8. Click ▾ to display the ways you can format cells that meet the condition, and click a choice.
9. Click OK.

- Excel applies the highlighting to the cells that match the criterion you specified.

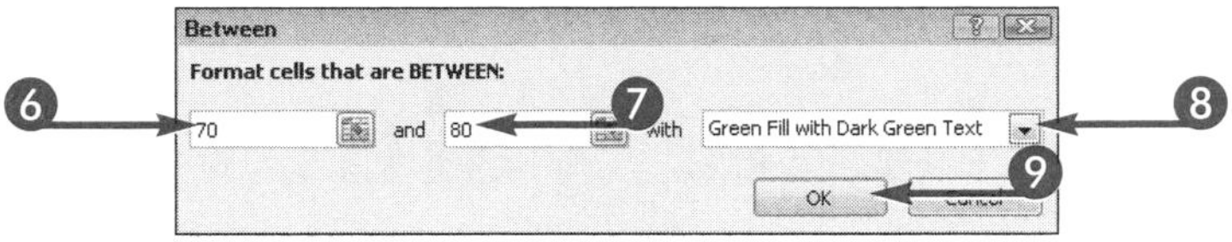

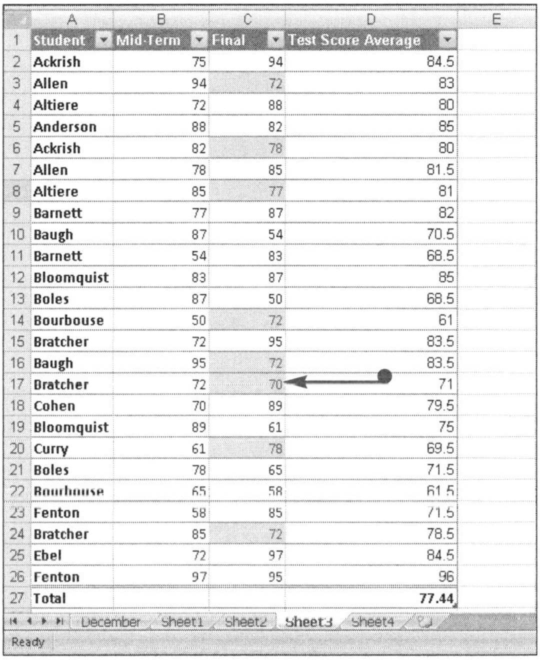

	A	B	C	D	E
1	Student	Mid-Term	Final	Test Score Average	
2	Ackrish	75	94	84.5	
3	Allen	94	72	83	
4	Altiere	72	88	80	
5	Anderson	88	82	85	
6	Ackrish	82	78	80	
7	Allen	78	85	81.5	
8	Altiere	85	77	81	
9	Barnett	77	87	82	
10	Baugh	87	54	70.5	
11	Barnett	54	83	68.5	
12	Bloomquist	83	87	85	
13	Boles	87	50	68.5	
14	Bourbouse	50	72	61	
15	Bratcher	72	95	83.5	
16	Baugh	95	72	83.5	
17	Bratcher	72	70	71	
18	Cohen	70	89	79.5	
19	Bloomquist	89	61	75	
20	Curry	61	78	69.5	
21	Boles	78	65	71.5	
22	Bourbouse	65	58	61.5	
23	Fenton	58	85	71.5	
24	Bratcher	85	72	78.5	
25	Ebel	72	97	84.5	
26	Fenton	97	95	96	
27	Total			77.44	

MASTER IT

Can I apply Conditional Formatting to an empty range?

▼ Yes, you can establish Conditional Formatting rules for a range before you enter any information into the range; however, you do not see any effect until you enter information into the range. The formatting you set up stays with the cells you select when you create the rules. If you select the range D1:D7 and then insert a column to the left of column D, the formatting rules move to the range E1:E7.

Can I select a range of cells in the worksheet to use for the values in Steps 6 and 7?

▼ No, you cannot use a range in Steps 6 or 7. You can click a cell in the worksheet that contains a single value you want to use in the comparison, but you cannot compare a range of cells to one or two other ranges of cells.

What happens if I move or copy a range to which I have applied Conditional Formatting?

▼ Excel moves or copies the Conditional Formatting along with the cell contents when you move or copy the range. As a result, in the new location, you see not only the cells' values but also the Conditional Formatting applied to them. If you enter new values in a range that used to hold conditionally formatted cells, Excel does not apply Conditional Formatting to the new data.

Highlight Duplicate Values

You can use Conditional Formatting to highlight duplicate values in a range. Often, duplicate values within a range are not acceptable, and you can use Conditional Formatting to identify any duplicate values in a range. You may also just be curious to identify data points that repeat in a list. Suppose, for example, that your worksheet contains test scores for students in a class. You can identify the scores that more than one student received.

When you highlight duplicate values, Excel highlights all values that appear more than once in the range that you specify. You identify the range that you want Excel to evaluate and you specify the formatting you want Excel to apply to the values in the list that appear more than once.

You can apply light-red fill with dark-red text, yellow fill with dark-yellow text, green fill with dark-green text, light-red fill, red text, or a red border. If none of those suit you, you can define your own custom format, which can include a combination of font styles and effects, number formats, border styles and colors, and fill patterns and colors.

Highlight Duplicate Values

1. Select the range of cells you want Excel to consider for Conditional Formatting.
2. Click the Home tab.
3. Click Conditional Formatting.

   A menu of choices appears.

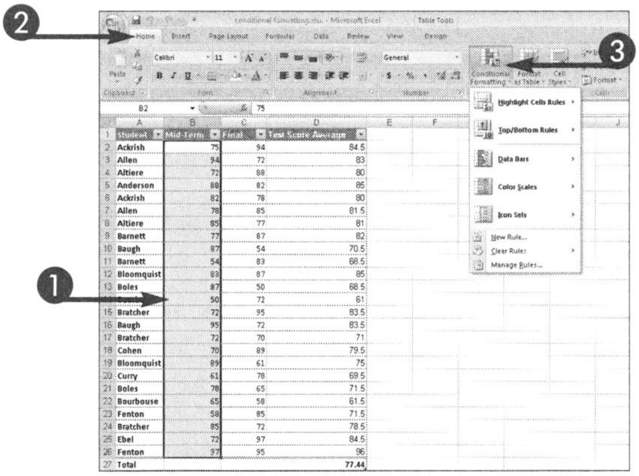

4. Click Highlight Cells Rules.
5. Click Duplicate Values.

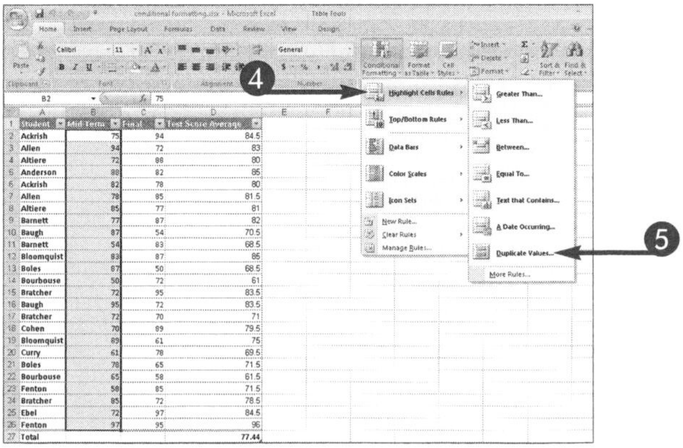

The Duplicate Values dialog box appears.

6 Click ▾ to display the ways you can format cells that meet the condition, and click a choice.

7 Click OK.

- Excel applies the highlighting to the cells that match the criterion you specified.

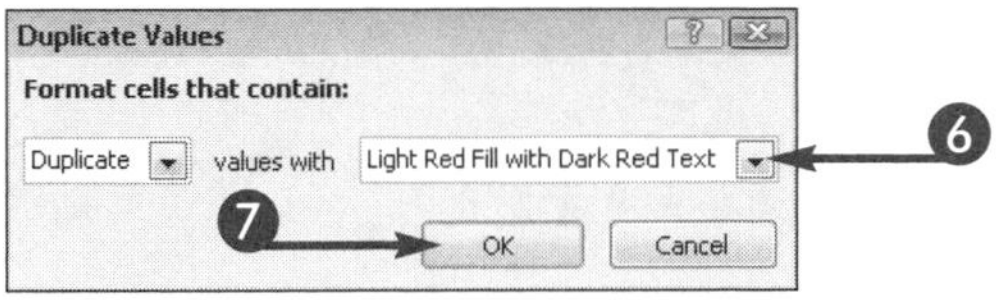

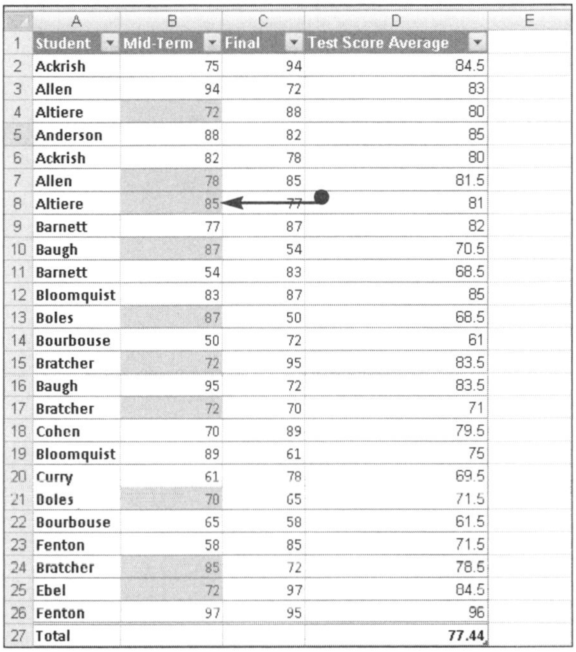

	A	B	C	D	E
1	Student	Mid-Term	Final	Test Score Average	
2	Ackrish	75	94	84.5	
3	Allen	94	72	83	
4	Altiere	72	88	80	
5	Anderson	88	82	85	
6	Ackrish	82	78	80	
7	Allen	78	85	81.5	
8	Altiere	85	77	81	
9	Barnett	77	87	82	
10	Baugh	87	54	70.5	
11	Barnett	54	83	68.5	
12	Bloomquist	83	87	85	
13	Boles	87	50	68.5	
14	Bourbouse	50	72	61	
15	Bratcher	72	95	83.5	
16	Baugh	95	72	83.5	
17	Bratcher	72	70	71	
18	Cohen	70	89	79.5	
19	Bloomquist	89	61	75	
20	Curry	61	78	69.5	
21	Doles	70	65	71.5	
22	Bourbouse	65	58	61.5	
23	Fenton	58	85	71.5	
24	Bratcher	85	72	78.5	
25	Ebel	72	97	84.5	
26	Fenton	97	95	96	
27	Total			77.44	

MASTER IT

Can I highlight unique values in a range instead of highlighting duplicate values?

▼ Yes, you can. Complete Steps 1 to 6. Before you complete Step 7, click the leftmost ▾ in the Duplicate Values dialog box and click Unique. Then click OK; Excel highlights unique values in the range you selected in Step 1 instead of highlighting values that appear more than once in the range.

Can I highlight both duplicate values and unique values in the same range?

▼ Yes, but make sure that you apply different formatting; otherwise, all values in the range will have Conditional Formatting, but you will not be able to distinguish the purpose of the Conditional Formatting. To apply both types of formatting, follow the steps twice, selecting Duplicate in the leftmost drop-down list of the Duplicate Values dialog box the first time, and Unique the second time.

Are there any restrictions to formatting duplicate values in PivotTables?

▼ Yes, there is one restriction. By their very nature, PivotTables summarize entries in a table or range that may contain many duplicate entries. You cannot apply Conditional Formatting to identify unique or duplicate values to any fields in the Values area of a PivotTable, but you can apply the Conditional Formatting to the table or range used to create the PivotTable.

Highlight Cells Containing Specific Text

You can use Conditional Formatting to highlight cells in a range that contain specific text. Suppose that your worksheet contains sales information by day for various types of sales made by a cable service provider. You can highlight all sales of a particular type of service.

When you highlight cells in a range that contain specific text, you identify the range that you want Excel to evaluate, the text you want Excel to use when evaluating, and the formatting you want Excel to apply to values in the range that contain the specified text. Excel examines the cells in the range and applies the highlighting of your choice to the cells that contain the specified text.

You can apply light-red fill with dark-red text, yellow fill with dark-yellow text, green fill with dark-green text, light-red fill, red text, or a red border. If none of those suit you, you can define your own custom format, which can include a combination of font styles and effects, number formats, border styles and colors, and fill patterns and colors.

Highlight Cells Containing Specific Text

1. Select the range of cells you want Excel to consider for Conditional Formatting.
2. Click the Home tab.
3. Click Conditional Formatting.

   A menu of choices appears.

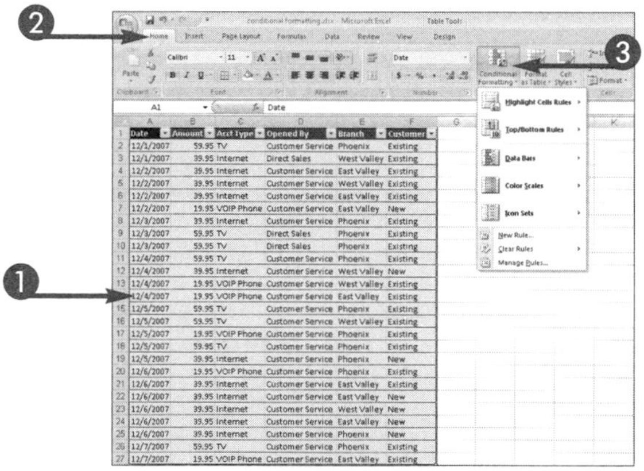

4. Click Highlight Cells Rules.
5. Click Text that Contains.

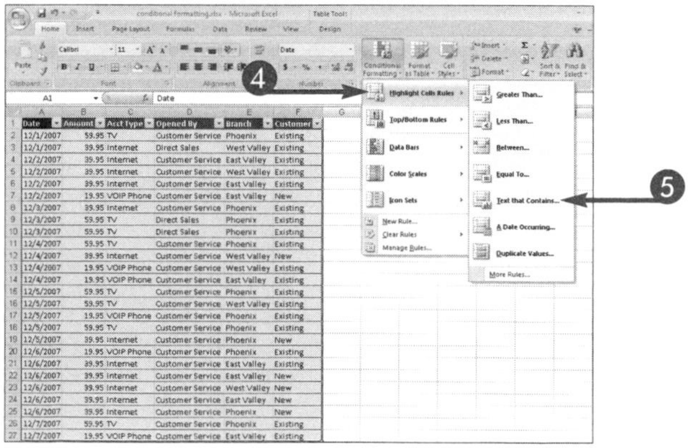

The Text That Contains dialog box appears.

6 Type the text you want Excel to highlight.

7 Click ▾ to display the ways you can format cells that meet the condition, and click a choice.

8 Click OK.

- Excel applies the highlighting to the cells that match the criterion you specified.

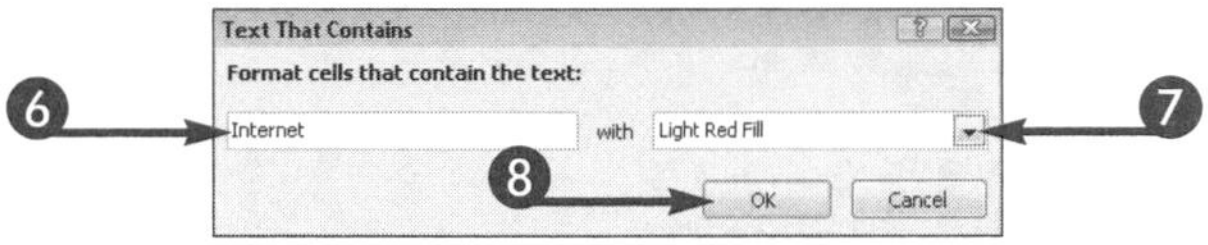

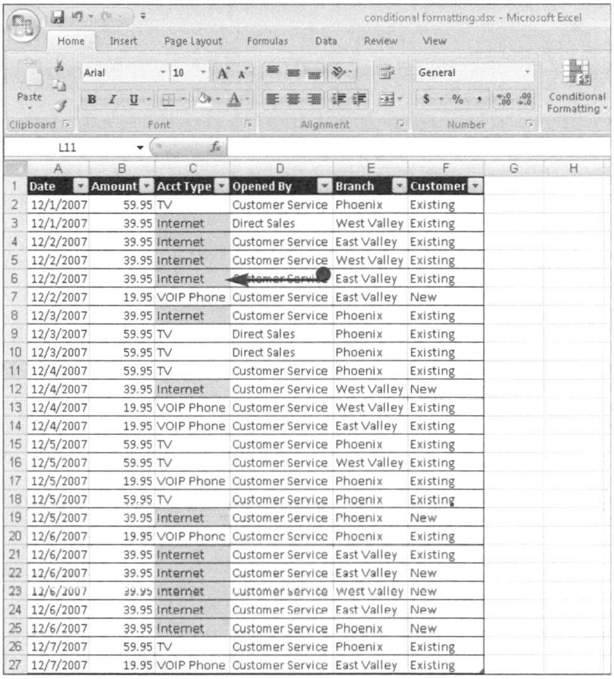

	Date	Amount	Acct Type	Opened By	Branch	Customer
2	12/1/2007	59.95	TV	Customer Service	Phoenix	Existing
3	12/1/2007	39.95	Internet	Direct Sales	West Valley	Existing
4	12/2/2007	39.95	Internet	Customer Service	East Valley	Existing
5	12/2/2007	39.95	Internet	Customer Service	West Valley	Existing
6	12/2/2007	39.95	Internet	Customer Service	East Valley	Existing
7	12/2/2007	19.95	VOIP Phone	Customer Service	East Valley	New
8	12/3/2007	39.95	Internet	Customer Service	Phoenix	Existing
9	12/3/2007	59.95	TV	Direct Sales	Phoenix	Existing
10	12/3/2007	59.95	TV	Direct Sales	Phoenix	Existing
11	12/4/2007	59.95	TV	Customer Service	Phoenix	Existing
12	12/4/2007	39.95	Internet	Customer Service	West Valley	New
13	12/4/2007	19.95	VOIP Phone	Customer Service	West Valley	Existing
14	12/4/2007	19.95	VOIP Phone	Customer Service	East Valley	Existing
15	12/5/2007	59.95	TV	Customer Service	Phoenix	Existing
16	12/5/2007	59.95	TV	Customer Service	West Valley	Existing
17	12/5/2007	19.95	VOIP Phone	Customer Service	Phoenix	Existing
18	12/5/2007	59.95	TV	Customer Service	Phoenix	Existing
19	12/5/2007	39.95	Internet	Customer Service	Phoenix	New
20	12/6/2007	19.95	VOIP Phone	Customer Service	Phoenix	Existing
21	12/6/2007	39.95	Internet	Customer Service	East Valley	Existing
22	12/6/2007	39.95	Internet	Customer Service	East Valley	New
23	12/6/2007	39.95	Internet	Customer Service	West Valley	New
24	12/6/2007	39.95	Internet	Customer Service	East Valley	New
25	12/6/2007	39.95	Internet	Customer Service	Phoenix	New
26	12/7/2007	59.95	TV	Customer Service	Phoenix	Existing
27	12/7/2007	19.95	VOIP Phone	Customer Service	East Valley	Existing

MASTER IT

In Step 6, can I specify a number instead of text?

▼ Yes, this feature is not actually limited to text. You can use it to highlight a number that you specify. If the range you select in Step 1 contains numbers, Excel searches the range and highlights the cells containing the number you supply in Step 6.

Can I select a cell that contains the text I want Excel to use when evaluating for Conditional Formatting?

▼ No, you must type the entry into the field in the Text That Contains dialog box. However, Excel suggests the text that appears in the first cell you include in the selection you specify in Step 1. If that text entry is the one you want to highlight, you only need to select the type of Conditional Formatting.

When I use Conditional Formatting to highlight text, must the text match cell contents exactly?

▼ No. You can type a portion of the text, number, or date that you want Excel to use when selecting cells to format. If any cell in the range contains a portion of the text, number, or date that you specify, Excel applies the formatting to the entire cell.

Highlight Cells Containing a Date

You can use Conditional Formatting to highlight cells in a range that contain a date. Suppose that today is December 5, 2007, and your worksheet contains sales information by day for sales made by a cable service provider. You can highlight the date of all sales made, for example, yesterday.

To highlight cells in a range that contain date information, you need to identify the range that you want Excel to evaluate. You then select a relative date from a list, such as tomorrow, last week, or last month. Finally, you identify the formatting you want Excel to apply to cells in the range that contain the specified date. Excel examines the cells in the range and applies the highlighting of your choice to the cells that match the date you selected.

You can apply light-red fill with dark-red text, yellow fill with dark-yellow text, green fill with dark-green text, light-red fill, red text, or a red border. If none of those suit you, you can define your own custom format, which can include a combination of font styles and effects, number formats, border styles and colors, and fill patterns and colors.

Highlight Cells Containing a Date

1. Select the range of cells you want Excel to consider for Conditional Formatting.
2. Click the Home tab.
3. Click Conditional Formatting.

   A menu of choices appears.

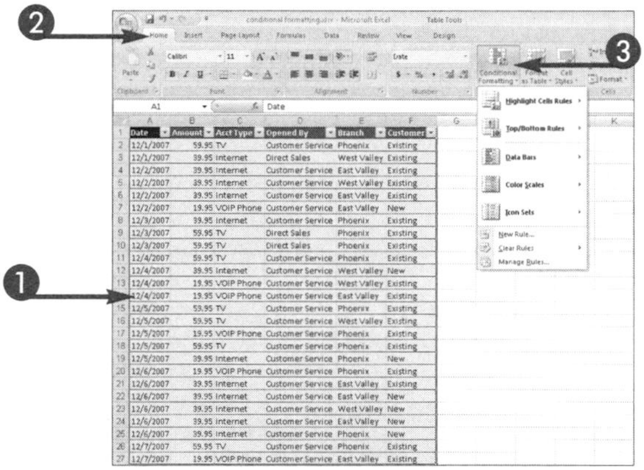

4. Click Highlight Cells Rules.
5. Click A Date Occurring.

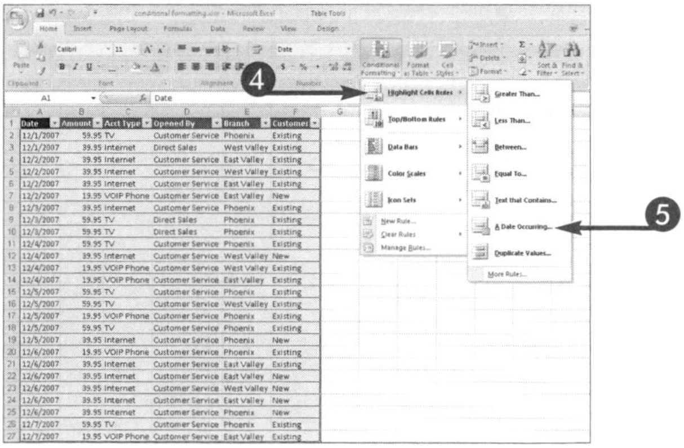

The A Date Occurring dialog box appears.

6 Click ▾ to select the date you want Excel to match.

7 Click ▾ to display the ways you can format cells that meet the condition, and click a choice.

8 Click OK.

- Excel applies the highlighting to the cells that match the criterion you specified.

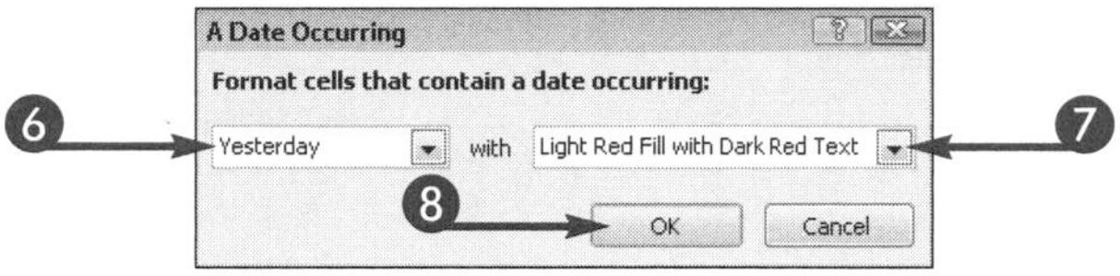

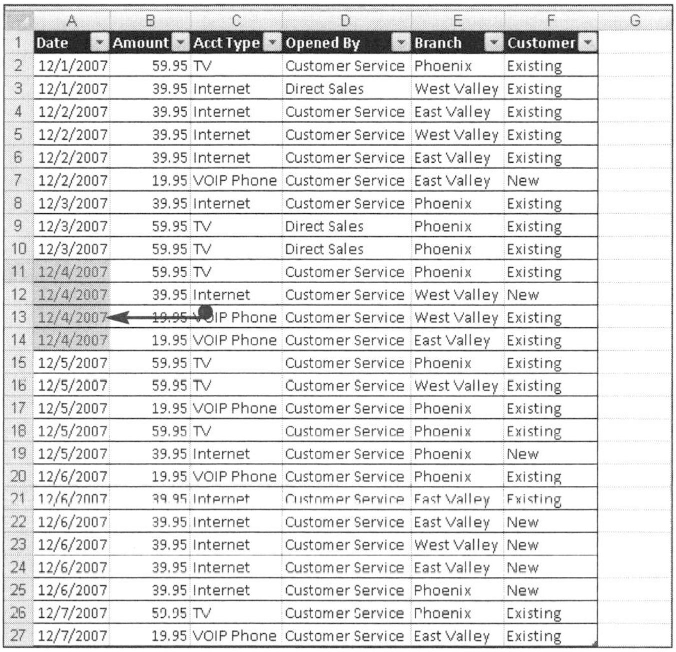

	A	B	C	D	E	F	G
1	Date	Amount	Acct Type	Opened By	Branch	Customer	
2	12/1/2007	59.95	TV	Customer Service	Phoenix	Existing	
3	12/1/2007	39.95	Internet	Direct Sales	West Valley	Existing	
4	12/2/2007	39.95	Internet	Customer Service	East Valley	Existing	
5	12/2/2007	39.95	Internet	Customer Service	West Valley	Existing	
6	12/2/2007	39.95	Internet	Customer Service	East Valley	Existing	
7	12/2/2007	19.95	VOIP Phone	Customer Service	East Valley	New	
8	12/3/2007	39.95	Internet	Customer Service	Phoenix	Existing	
9	12/3/2007	59.95	TV	Direct Sales	Phoenix	Existing	
10	12/3/2007	59.95	TV	Direct Sales	Phoenix	Existing	
11	12/4/2007	59.95	TV	Customer Service	Phoenix	Existing	
12	12/4/2007	39.95	Internet	Customer Service	West Valley	New	
13	12/4/2007	19.95	VOIP Phone	Customer Service	West Valley	Existing	
14	12/4/2007	19.95	VOIP Phone	Customer Service	East Valley	Existing	
15	12/5/2007	59.95	TV	Customer Service	Phoenix	Existing	
16	12/5/2007	59.95	TV	Customer Service	West Valley	Existing	
17	12/5/2007	19.95	VOIP Phone	Customer Service	Phoenix	Existing	
18	12/5/2007	59.95	TV	Customer Service	Phoenix	Existing	
19	12/5/2007	39.95	Internet	Customer Service	Phoenix	New	
20	12/6/2007	19.95	VOIP Phone	Customer Service	Phoenix	Existing	
21	12/6/2007	39.95	Internet	Customer Service	East Valley	Existing	
22	12/6/2007	39.95	Internet	Customer Service	East Valley	New	
23	12/6/2007	39.95	Internet	Customer Service	West Valley	New	
24	12/6/2007	39.95	Internet	Customer Service	East Valley	New	
25	12/6/2007	39.95	Internet	Customer Service	Phoenix	New	
26	12/7/2007	59.95	TV	Customer Service	Phoenix	Existing	
27	12/7/2007	19.95	VOIP Phone	Customer Service	East Valley	Existing	

MASTER IT

What date choices are available to me?

▼ The date choices are relative dates rather than specific dates. You can highlight cells containing dates for yesterday, today, tomorrow, in the last seven days, last week, this week, next week, last month, this month, or next month. Because the dates are relative, as days pass, the cells that Excel highlights change.

Can I have Excel apply Conditional Formatting to cells containing a particular date?

▼ Yes. Select the range containing the cells to evaluate and click the Home tab, click Conditional Formatting, click Highlight Cells Rules, and then click Equal To. In the Equal To dialog box that appears, type the date you want Excel to highlight and then click ▾ to select the type of formatting to apply. Click OK, and Excel highlights the date you specified.

Can I have Excel apply Conditional Formatting to cells containing dates between a range of dates?

▼ Yes. Select the range containing the cells to evaluate and click the Home tab, click Conditional Formatting, click Highlight Cells Rules, and then click Between. In the Between dialog box that appears, type or select cells containing the earliest date and the latest date you want Excel to highlight. Then click ▾ to select the type of formatting to apply. Click OK, and Excel highlights the date you specified.

Add Data Bars to Represent Data Values

Using Conditional Formatting, you can display data bars in cells in a selected range. Data bars provide you with visual cues that help you quickly compare cell values in a range.

When you add data bars to cells in a range, Excel adds a horizontal bar of gradient color to each cell in the selected range. The length of the data bar in any cell is based on the value in the cell in relation to the values of all the cells in the selected range, and the differences in bar length become more apparent when you increase the column width. Cells containing higher values in the selected range display longer data bars than cells containing lower values in the range.

When you apply Conditional Formatting using data bars, Excel assigns a data bar to every cell in the range you select, even if the value in the cell is zero. Excel assigns a data bar length equal to ten percent of the cell's width to the smallest value in the range.

You can select the color of the data bars from blue, green, red, orange, light blue, or purple.

Add Data Bars to Represent Data Values

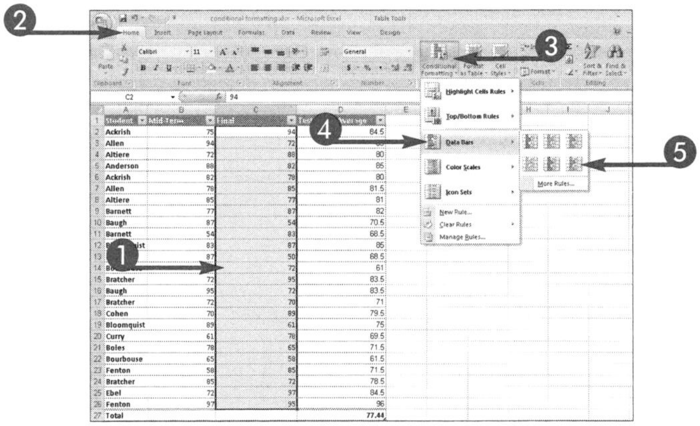

1. Select the range of cells you want Excel to consider for Conditional Formatting.
2. Click the Home tab.
3. Click Conditional Formatting.
4. Click Data Bars.
5. Click a color choice for the data bars.

Note: *As you point at each color choice, Live Preview displays the choice.*

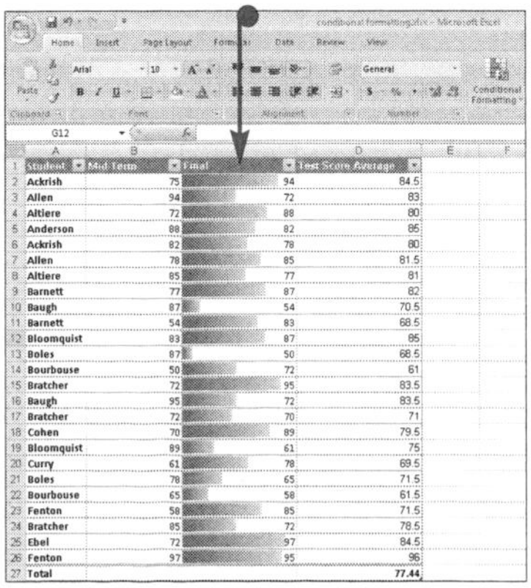

- Excel applies the data bars to the cells.

Apply Color Scales to Data

Using Conditional Formatting, you can apply a color scale background to cells in a selected range to provide you with visual cues to quickly compare cell values in a range.

When you add color scale backgrounds to cells in a range, Excel adds a shade of color to all cells in the selected range, even if the value in a cell is zero. The value in the cell, in relation to the values in all cells in the selected range, determines the shade Excel assigns to the cell. Excel offers eight possible color scales that you can apply to a selected range. Four of the color scales use combinations of two colors, and the other four color scales use combinations of three colors. The colors Excel applies use a gradient, and so, if you use a two-color combination scale, Excel applies many more colors than just two.

From the two-color combination color scales, you can apply yellow-red, red-yellow, green-yellow, or yellow-green combinations. From the three-color combination color scales, you can apply green-yellow-red, red-yellow-green, blue-yellow-red, or red-yellow-blue combinations. Excel applies the first color to higher values in the selected range and the last color to lower values in the selected range.

Apply Color Scales to Data

1. Select the range of cells you want Excel to consider for Conditional Formatting.
2. Click the Home tab.
3. Click Conditional Formatting.
4. Click Color Scales.
5. Click a color scale choice.

Note: As you point at each color choice, Live Preview displays the choice.

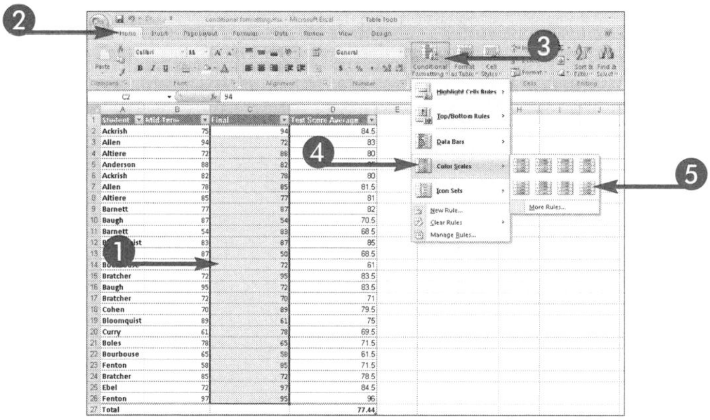

- Excel applies the color scale to the cells.

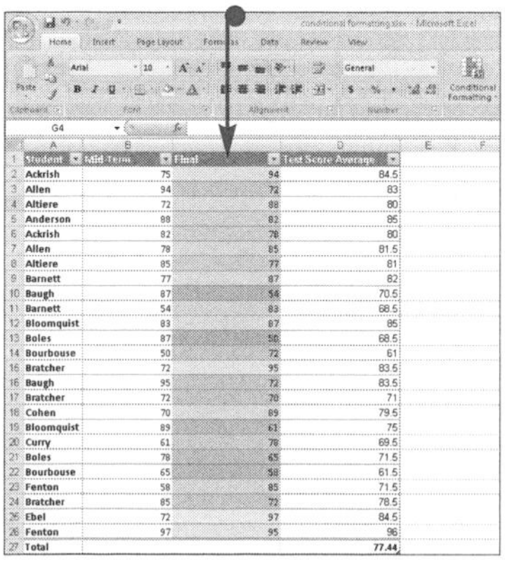

Use Icon Sets to Highlight Values in a List

Using Conditional Formatting, you can add icon sets to cells in a selected range to help you quickly compare cell values in the range. When you add icon sets to cells in a range, Excel displays an icon in all cells in the selected range. The value in the cell, in relation to the values in all cells in the selected range, determines the icon Excel displays in the cell.

Icons are available in sets; you can assign a three-icon set, a four-icon set, or a five-icon set. Excel assigns the symbols in each icon set using percentages of the selected range. When you use a three-icon set, Excel divides the values in the selected range into three evenly divided percentage groups; that is, each icon in a three-icon set is associated with the top, middle, or bottom 33 percent of the possible values. For a four-icon set, Excel divides the values in the selected range into four evenly divided percentage groups, and for a five-icon set, Excel divides the values in the selected range into five evenly divided percentage groups. You can also set your own percentage groups. See the section, "Manage Conditional Formatting Rules," for details.

Use Icon Sets to Highlight Values in a List

1. Select the range of cells you want Excel to consider for Conditional Formatting.
2. Click the Home tab.
3. Click Conditional Formatting.
4. Click Icon Sets.
5. Click an icon set choice.

Note: *As you point at each choice, Live Preview displays the choice.*

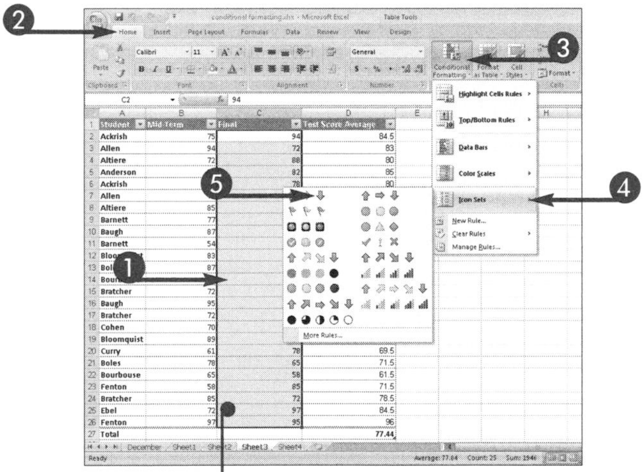

- Excel applies the icon set to the cells.

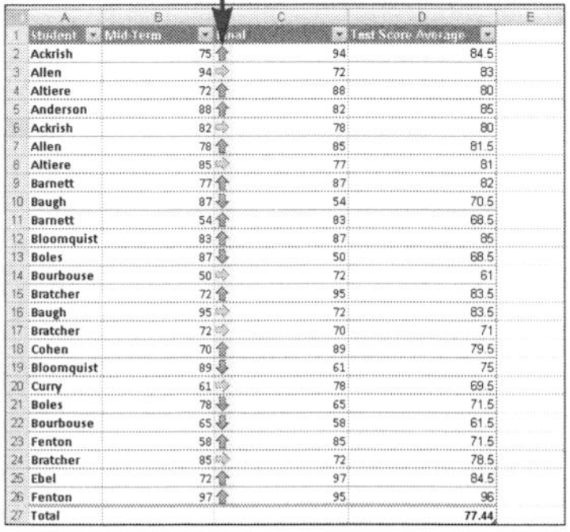

Clear Conditional Formats

You can apply as many Conditional Formats as you want to any worksheet or given range. However, at some point, you may decide that you want to remove all Conditional Formats because you do not need them anymore; they have served their purpose and now you want to eliminate them. You can easily clear all Conditional Formats from your worksheet. You can also clear Conditional Formatting from a particular range instead of clearing all Conditional Formatting from your worksheet.

To clear Conditional Formatting from your entire worksheet, you do not need to select any cells. However, to clear Conditional Formatting from a particular range, you start by selecting that range.

When you clear Conditional Formatting, you do not remove any data from the worksheet or the selected range. You also do not remove any other formatting that you may have applied to the worksheet or selected range. Instead, you eliminate Conditional Formatting rules. Excel creates a rule each time you apply any Conditional Format. When you eliminate a Conditional Formatting rule, Excel no longer displays the Conditional Formatting associated with that rule on the worksheet or in the selected range.

Clear Conditional Formats

❶ Select the range of cells from which you want Excel to remove Conditional Formatting.

Note: *Skip Step 1 to remove all Conditional Formatting.*

❷ Click the Home tab.

❸ Click Conditional Formatting.

❹ Click Clear Rules.

❺ Click a choice.

Note: *This example clears rules from a range.*

Excel removes the Conditional Formatting from the selected cells, worksheet, or table.

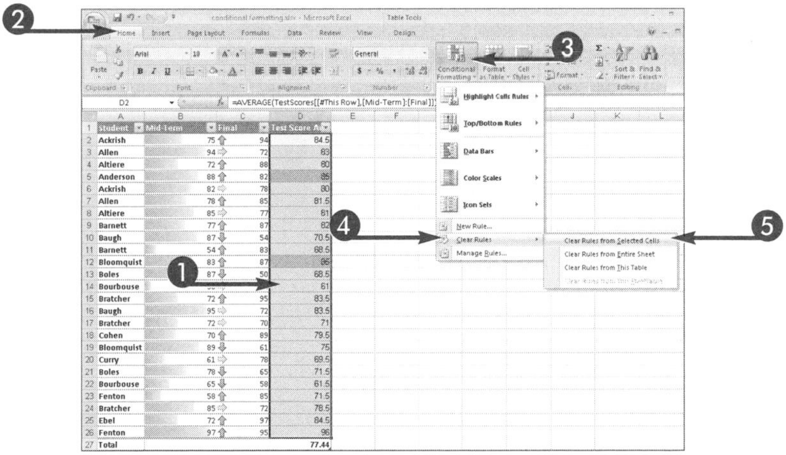

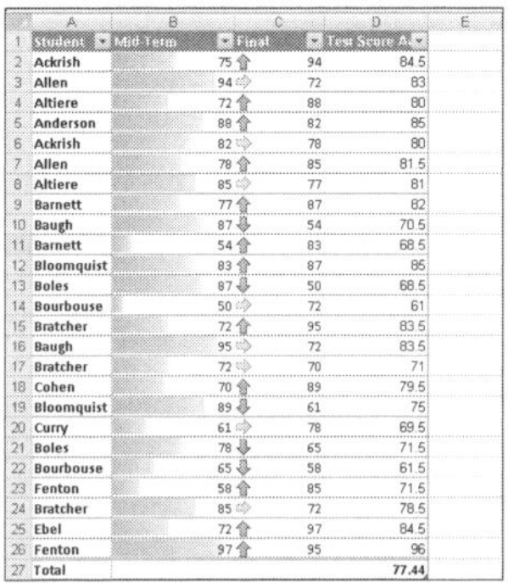

Manage Conditional Formatting Rules

Each time you add Conditional Formatting to a range, Excel creates a rule that describes the behavior of the Conditional Formatting. By default, Excel applies Conditional Formatting rules in the order that you create them, but you can change the order. You can also modify rules, create new rules, and delete rules.

Suppose that you have added three Conditional Formatting rules to one range. The first rule you added applies data bars to the range. The second rule identifies values that are above average compared to the other values in the range. And the third rule identifies duplicate values in the range. Further suppose that you decide that you want only one of the three Conditional Formatting rules to apply to each of the values in the range; Excel should identify above-average values, then duplicate values from those that are not above average, and finally display data bars in all remaining cells.

Using the Conditional Formatting Rules Manager, you can reorder and set up the rules so that Excel applies only one of the three formats to each cell in the range.

Manage Conditional Formatting Rules

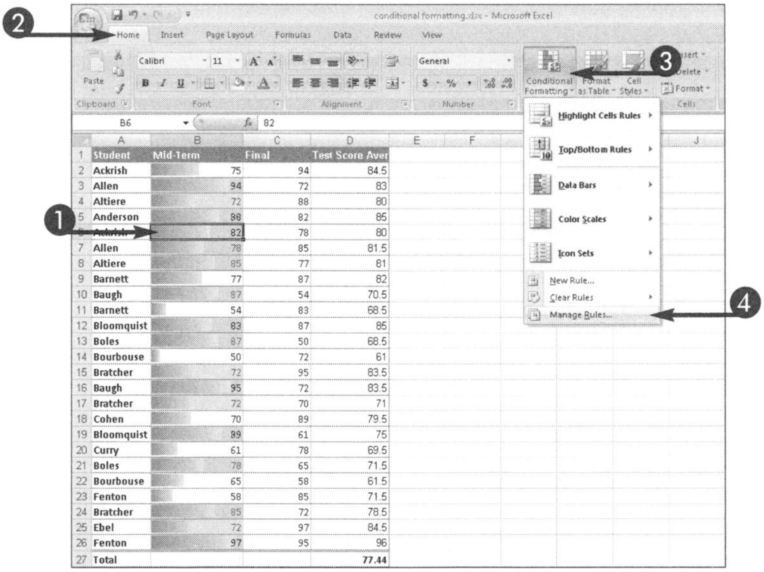

1. Click any cell that contains Conditional Formatting.
2. Click the Home tab.
3. Click Conditional Formatting.
4. Click Manage Rules.

The Conditional Formatting Rules Manager dialog box appears.

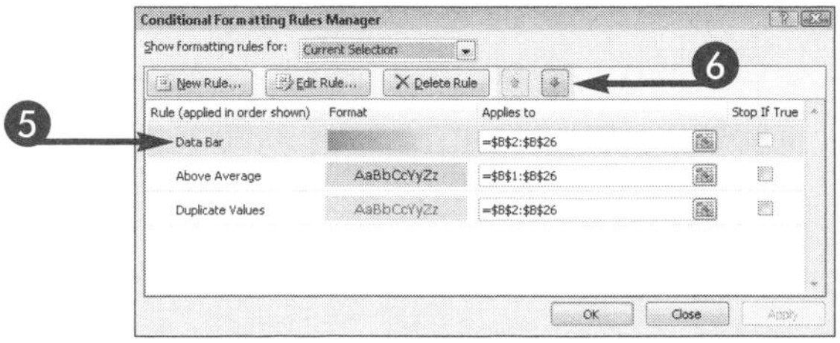

5. Click a rule that you want to reorder.
6. Click or to change the rule's position in the list.

Note: *Excel applies rules in the order they appear in the list.*

7. Click here for each rule (☐ changes to ☑).

Note: *If a rule is true for a cell, Excel stops applying the rules. If the rule is not true, Excel continues to the next rule in the list.*

8. Click OK.

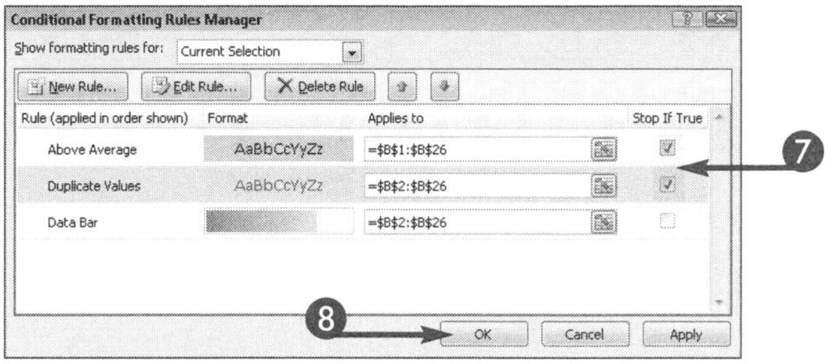

Excel changes the Conditional Formatting that is applied to the range.

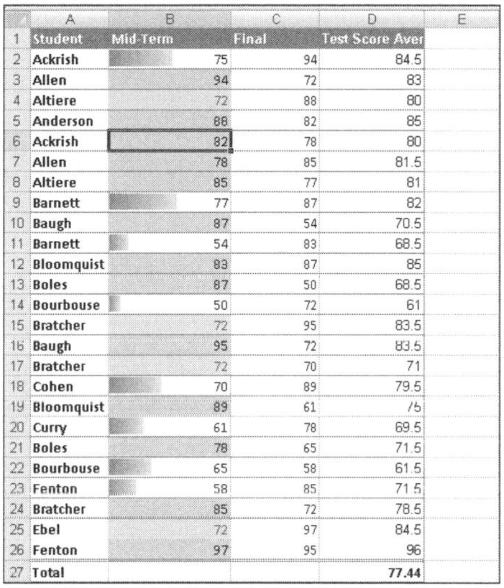

	A	B	C	D	E
1	Student	Mid-Term	Final	Test Score Aver	
2	Ackrish	75	94	84.5	
3	Allen	94	72	83	
4	Altiere	72	88	80	
5	Anderson	88	82	85	
6	Ackrish	82	78	80	
7	Allen	78	85	81.5	
8	Altiere	85	77	81	
9	Barnett	77	87	82	
10	Baugh	87	54	70.5	
11	Barnett	54	83	68.5	
12	Bloomquist	83	87	85	
13	Boles	87	50	68.5	
14	Bourbouse	50	72	61	
15	Bratcher	72	95	83.5	
16	Baugh	95	72	83.5	
17	Bratcher	72	70	71	
18	Cohen	70	89	79.5	
19	Bloomquist	89	61	75	
20	Curry	61	78	69.5	
21	Boles	78	65	71.5	
22	Bourbouse	65	58	61.5	
23	Fenton	58	85	71.5	
24	Bratcher	85	72	78.5	
25	Ebel	72	97	84.5	
26	Fenton	97	95	96	
27	Total			77.44	

MASTER IT

Using the Conditional Formatting Rules Manager, can I change the percentages associated with icon sets?

▼ Yes, you can. Apply icon sets as described in the section, "Use Icon Sets to Highlight Values in a List." Then, click any cell that contains an icon and complete Steps 1 to 4 in this section. Click the rule in the Conditional Formatting Rules Manager dialog box and click Edit Rule. The Edit Formatting Rule dialog box appears. At the bottom, the values for each group appear as percentages. You can type a new value and you can change the type of value from a percentage to a number, a percentile, or a formula. You can also enclose the icon in a circle and hide the values.

What happens if I click the Delete Rule button in the Conditional Formatting Rules Manager dialog box?

▼ You can use the Delete Rule button to delete a specific Conditional Formatting rule. Select the rule and then click Delete Rule. Excel deletes the rule so that the Conditional Formatting no longer appears. Excel retains the contents of the affected cells as well as any other formatting you applied.

Create a New Conditional Formatting Rule

Excel offers a large variety of predefined Conditional Formatting rules, as described throughout this chapter. However, in situations where you cannot find a rule that suits your needs, you can create your own rule.

You can create Conditional Formatting rules that are similar to the predefined rules; for example, you can create a rule that highlights the top five percent of the values in a list. You can also create a rule based on a formula, as shown in this example. When you create a Conditional Formatting rule based on a formula, you identify the range to which it applies, the formula you want Excel to use when determining whether to apply formatting, and the formatting you want Excel to apply. The formula you use in the Conditional Formatting rule evaluates to "true" or "false"; when the formula evaluates to true, Excel applies the formatting.

For example, suppose that you would like to apply Conditional Formatting so that a total appears only if all cells referenced by the SUM function contain numbers. The example in this section hides the sum by applying a white font color to it; the Conditional Formatting displays the sum when the conditions are met.

Create a New Conditional Formatting Rule

1. Set up your worksheet.
   - In this example, a sum is stored in cell B6, and the font color of cell B6 is white.
2. Select the cells to which the new rule should apply.
3. Click the Home tab.
4. Click Conditional Formatting.
5. Click New Rule.

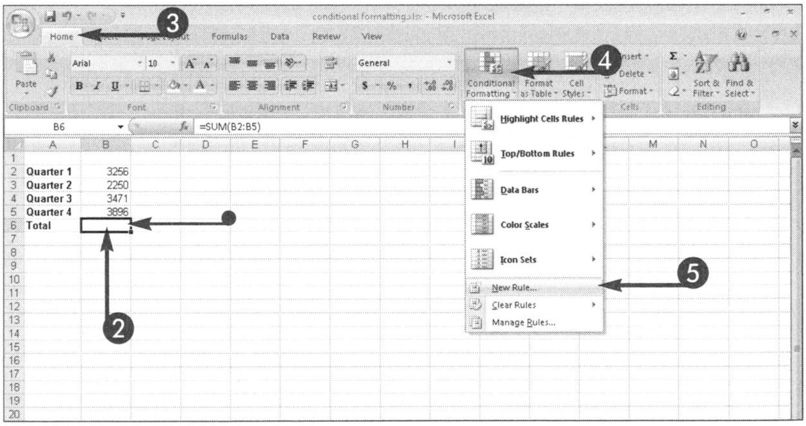

The New Formatting Rule dialog box appears.

6. Click here to create a formula.
7. Type a formula here that evaluates to true or false.
8. Click Format.

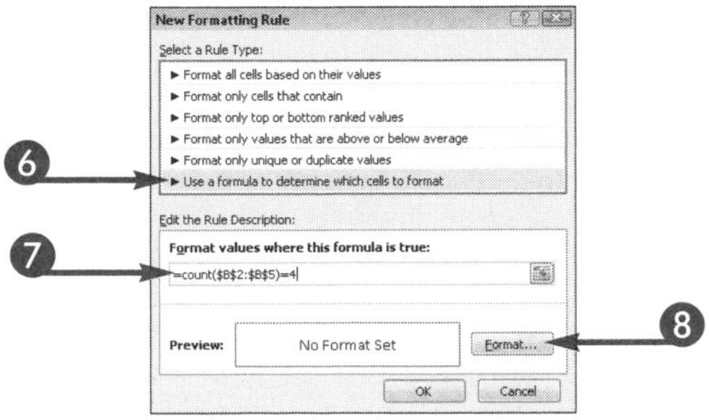

The Format Cells dialog box appears.

9 Click the tabs and select the formatting you want to apply if the conditions are true.

- This example applies a blue fill color.

10 Click OK twice.

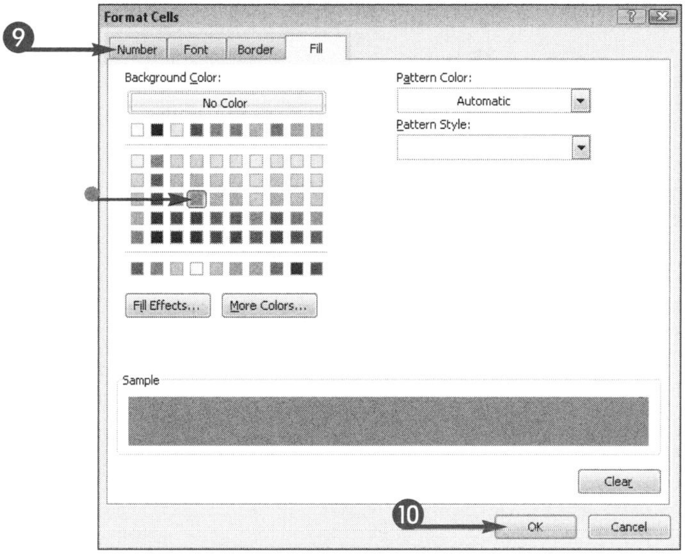

Excel closes the Format Cells dialog box and the New Formatting Rule dialog box.

- Excel applies the formatting if the conditions are true.

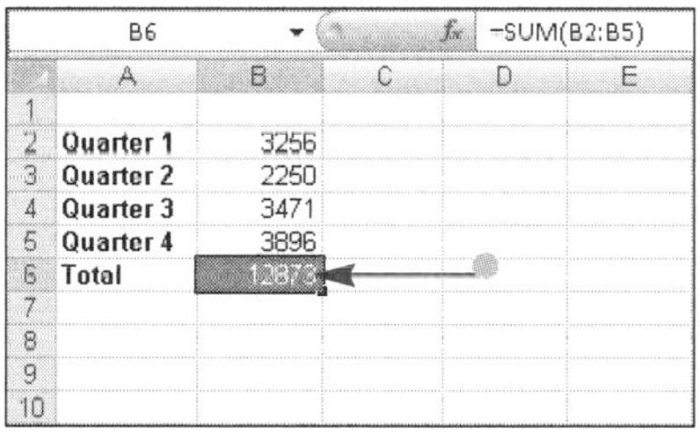

MASTER IT

Can I create a rule that formats cells if they do not contain a particular value?

▼ Yes. Complete Steps 1 to 5. In Step 6, select Format Only Cells That Contain from the list at the top. In the Edit The Rule Description section, click the second ▾ and change Between to Not Equal. In the third field, type a value. Then complete Steps 8 to 10.

Can I create a rule that formats cells if the values in them do not fall between two values?

▼ Yes. Complete Steps 1 to 5. In Step 6, select Format Only Cells That Contain from the list at the top. In the Edit The Rule Description section, click the second ▾ and change Between to Not Between. In the third and fourth fields, type values. Then complete Steps 8 to 10.

Can I change the cells to which a rule applies after I create the rule?

▼ Yes. Click a cell formatted by the rule. Then click the Home tab and click Conditional Formatting. Click Manage Rules to display the Conditional Formatting Rules Manager dialog box. Click the rule and click in the Applies To field. Then click the cells in the worksheet to which the rule should apply. Click the Apply button to see the change, and click OK to save the change.

Link Worksheets by Pointing

You can link the information stored in one workbook to another workbook to ensure that you have up-to-date information at all times. Suppose that your company keeps daily sales records in a workbook that is updated each day by another employee. Your job is to summarize the daily sales information so that you can then produce a variety of charts that show sales trends over time. You need the daily sales information to do your job.

Yes, you could open the other employee's workbook and copy the information into your own workbook. However, if you create a workbook that contains link formulas — also called external reference formulas — to the daily sales workbook, your workbook will always contain the latest data.

When you link workbooks, the one containing the link formulas is called the *dependent* workbook. The workbook containing the information is called the *source* workbook. You can create external reference formulas using several different techniques. The example in this section demonstrates how to use cells in the source workbook as the reference in a formula stored in the dependent workbook.

Link Worksheets by Pointing

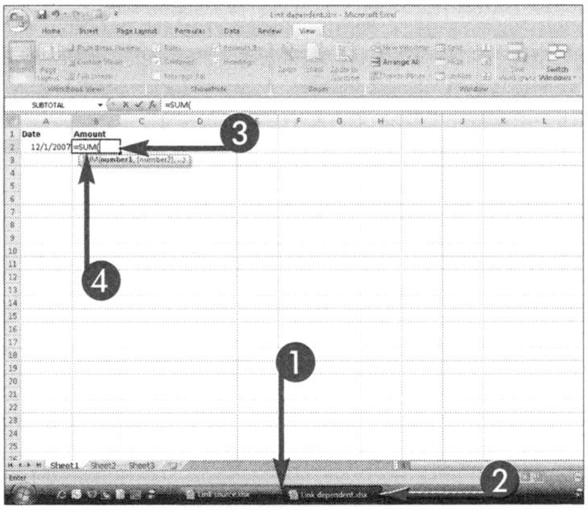

1. Open the source workbook and the dependent workbook.
2. Display the dependent workbook.
3. Click the cell that should contain the link formula.
4. Type the formula up to the point where you need to refer to a cell in the source workbook.

Note: *To learn more about working with common formulas, see Chapter 11.*

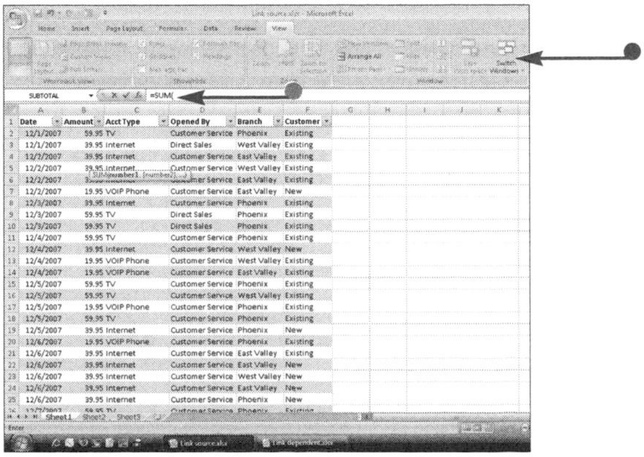

5. Switch to the source workbook.
   - You can click the taskbar button for the workbook, or you can click the View tab and then click Switch Windows on the Ribbon.
   - The Formula Bar shows that entry of a formula is in progress.

6 Click the cell or range you need for the formula.

7 Press Enter or click ☑.

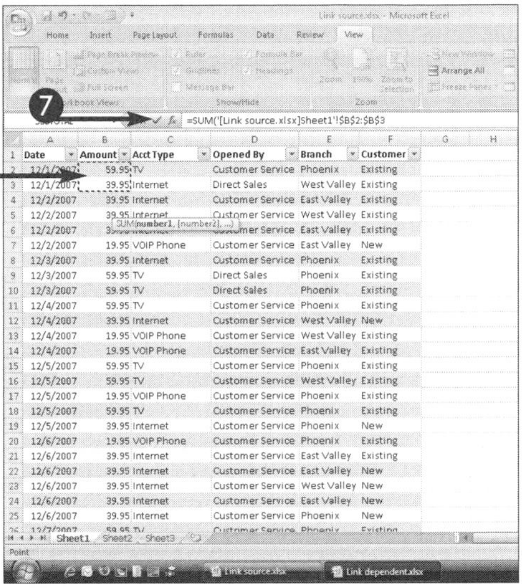

Excel switches back to the dependent workbook.

- In the cell you selected in Step 3, Excel displays the result of the formula.
- The formula, including the external reference, appears in the Formula Bar.

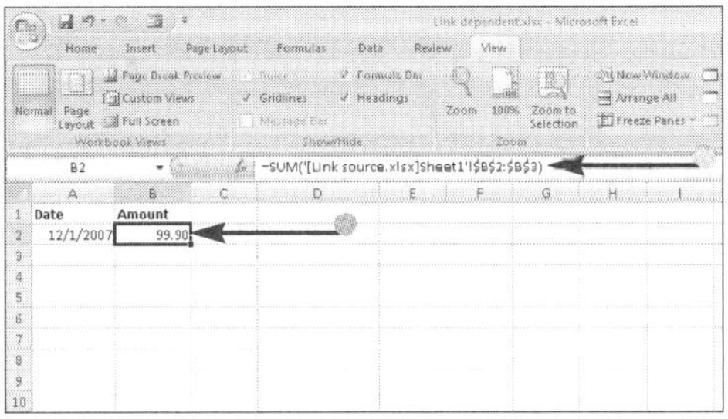

MASTER IT

Can you explain the syntax of the external reference?

▼ Because the reference is external, it includes the workbook name and the worksheet within the workbook in addition to the actual cell address. Excel encloses the workbook name in square bracket ([]) and then lists the worksheet name. Excel separates the worksheet name from the cell reference with an exclamation point (!). If either the workbook name or the worksheet name includes a space, Excel encloses both of them in single quotation marks ('). If the source workbook is located on a network, the reference also includes a drive letter and pathname.

Can I type an external reference in a link formula?

▼ Yes, you can. And if you do type the external reference, you do not need to open the source workbook to create the link formula. However, because the references are long, you run the risk of introducing typographical errors in the link formula.

How does Excel update a workbook that contains an external reference?

▼ When you open the workbook, Excel updates the links using the source workbook. If the source workbook becomes unavailable — perhaps because someone moved it to another location — you can update the links manually. See the section, "Update Links," for details.

Paste Links

In addition to referring to an external range by pointing, you can link a dependent worksheet to a source worksheet using the Paste Link command. The Paste Link command is a special form of the Paste command that creates a link when you copy data.

Creating links by copying and pasting is particularly useful when you need to copy a large amount of information from a workbook that changes regularly to another workbook. Suppose that your company keeps daily sales records in a workbook that is updated each day by another employee, and you need the daily sales information to do your job. You can create a linked copy of the information in the other employee's workbook. That way, each time the other employee updates the source workbook, Excel automatically updates your dependent workbook, and your workbook always contains the latest data.

This section presents an example of creating a link formula that simply displays the contents of a source workbook cell in the dependent workbook; the link is created by copying and pasting information.

Paste Links

1. Open the source workbook and the dependent workbook.
2. Display the source workbook.
3. Select the cell or range for which you want to create links.
4. Click .

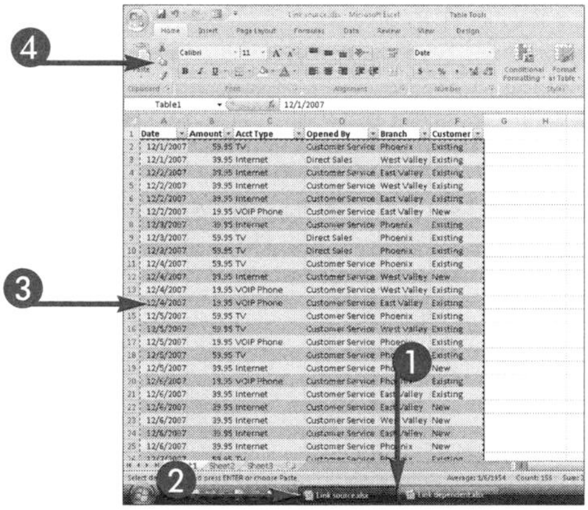

5. Switch to the dependent workbook.
   - You can click the taskbar button for the workbook, or you can click the View tab and then click Switch Windows on the Ribbon.
6. Click the cell that should contain the first link formula.

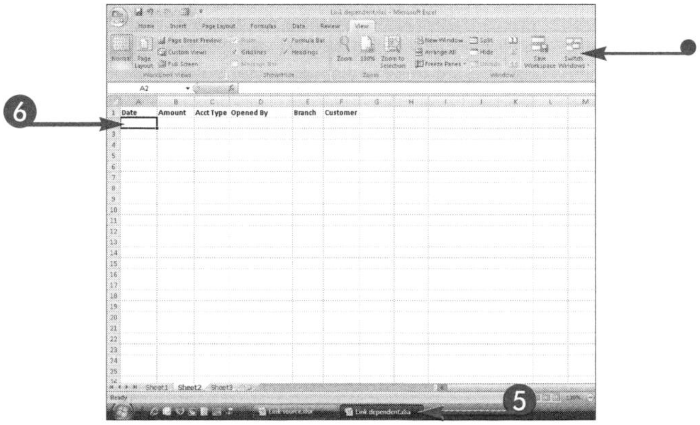

7 Click the Home tab.

8 Click ▾ under the Paste button.

9 From the drop-down menu, click Paste Link.

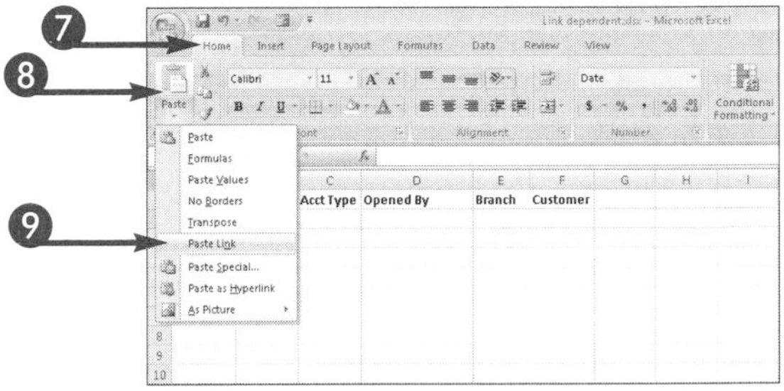

Excel copies the range from the source workbook to the dependent workbook.

- Each cell in the dependent workbook contains a formula that links it to the source workbook.

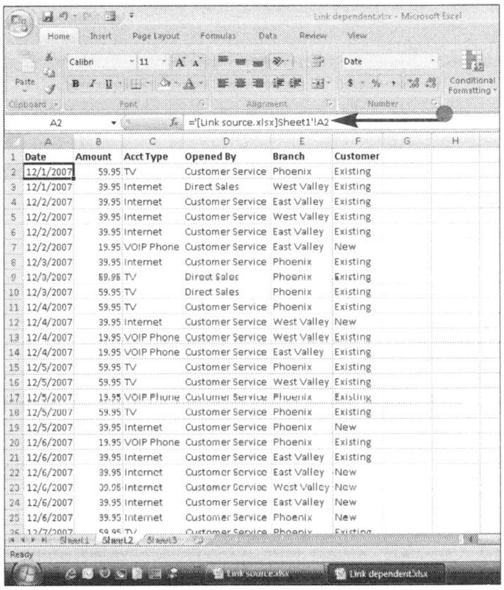

MASTER IT

Can I type a formula that just displays the contents of one cell in another?

▼ Yes. The formula is nothing more than an equal sign (=) followed by the address of the cell containing the information you want to display. If the cell resides in another workbook, the format for the external link formula would be =[*WorkbookName*]*Sheet name*!*CellAddress*. When you use the Paste Link command as shown in this section, Excel produces this formula.

I tried to use the Paste Link command and it is not available. What am I doing wrong?

▼ You are probably trying to copy information into a range formatted as a table. While you can copy information *from* a table into a range, you cannot copy information from a range into a table or copy information from a table into a table. To use the Paste Link command, the range in the dependent workbook must be a range and not a table.

What happens if I insert a row in the source workbook?

▼ If you open the dependent workbook and change the structure of the source workbook, Excel properly adjusts the external references in the dependent workbook. However, if you do not open the dependent workbook, the references are not updated. If you want to work independently in the two workbooks, establish named ranges in the source workbook that you use in the link formulas.

Update Links

You can make Excel update links in a dependent workbook. If you open both the dependent workbook and the source workbook, Excel automatically updates links. However, suppose that you have been working in the dependent workbook for a while and you want to ensure that it contains the latest information. That is, you want to update the dependent workbook with any changes that may have been made to the source workbook. You do not need to close the dependent workbook and reopen it; you can use the Edit Links dialog box.

By default, Excel sets a workbook containing links to use the Automatic Update of Links option and then disables automatic updating. As a result, when you open both the dependent workbook and the source workbook, Excel updates links. However, if you open only the dependent workbook, a security warning appears just below the Ribbon, telling you that automatic updating of links has been disabled.

You do not need to open the source workbook to update the links in the dependent workbook. You can update the links in the dependent workbook if you temporarily enable automatic updating of links.

Update Links

Update Links Manually

1. Display the dependent workbook.
2. Click .
3. Click Prepare.
4. Click at the bottom of the Prepare menu.

Note: *In the figure is not visible, but its counterpart appears at the top of the menu.*

5. Click Edit Links to Files.

The Edit Links dialog box appears.

6. Click the appropriate source file.
7. Click Update Values.

Excel updates the links in the dependent workbook.

8. Click Close.

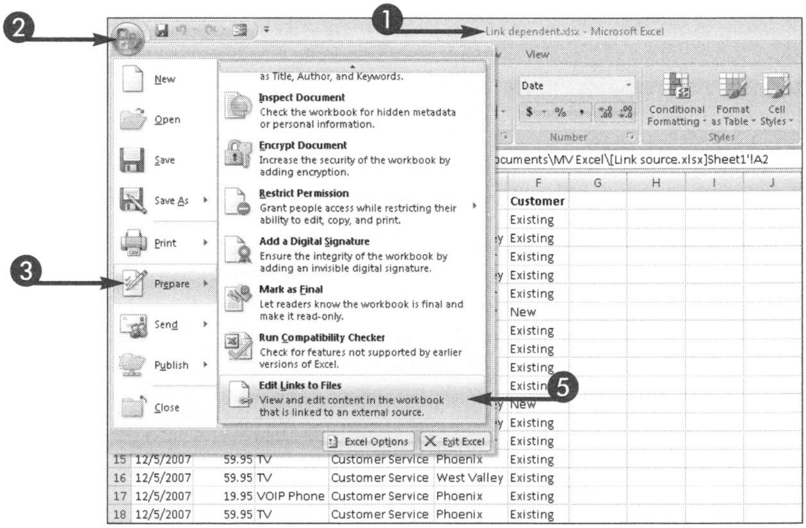

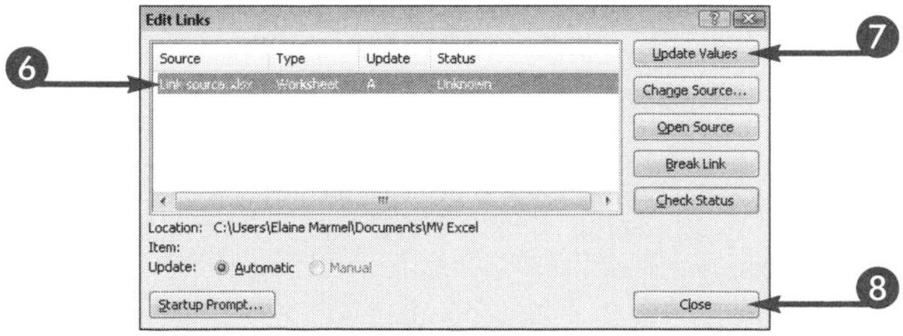

Update When the Source File Is Closed

1. Open the dependent workbook but not the source workbook.
   - A security warning appears.
2. Click Options.

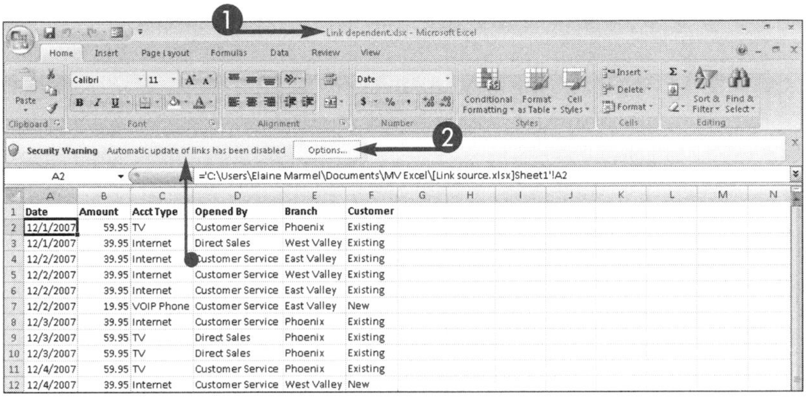

The Microsoft Office Security Options dialog box appears.

3. Click Enable this content (◎ changes to ◉).
4. Click OK.

Excel updates the dependent workbook.

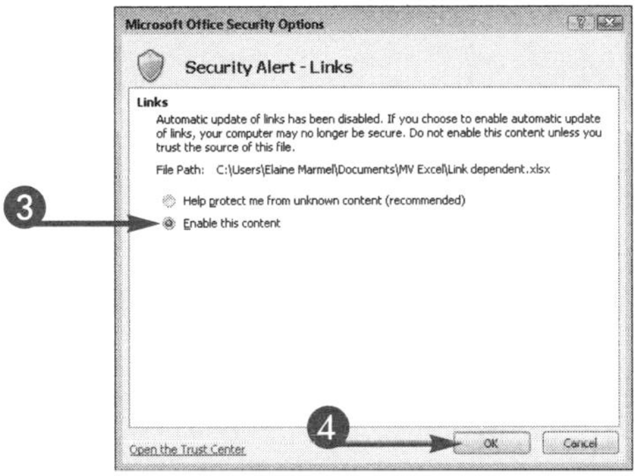

MASTER IT

Why do I see the security warning every time I open the dependent workbook without opening the source workbook?

▼ Although you follow the steps in the subsection, "Update When the Source File is Closed," Excel allows automatic updating only for the current session while the dependent workbook is open. Once you close the workbook, Excel disables automatic updating again and the security warning reappears the next time you open the dependent workbook.

How can I permanently enable automatic updating?

▼ Follow Steps 1 and 2 in the subsection, "Update When the Source File is Closed." In the Microsoft Office Security Options dialog box, click the Open the Trust Center link in the lower-left corner. In the Trust Center dialog box that appears, click External Content and then click Enable Automatic Update for All Workbook Links (not recommended) (◎changes to ◉).

Why is enabling automatic updating not recommended?

▼ When you enable automatic updating, you take a risk because you permanently enable automatic updating for all workbooks containing links, not just for the current workbook. It is possible that a source workbook can become infected with a virus and, if you allow automatic updating, the dependent workbook can also become infected just by opening it.

Switch the Link Source

You can switch to a different source workbook if necessary. For example, you may find that the source workbook now resides in a different location than when you established the link, or the name of the source workbook may have changed. It is also possible that an entirely new workbook has been created and you want to use it as the link source. In any case, the link formulas in the dependent workbook will not function properly. You do not need to recreate all of the links to accommodate the new location of the source workbook or its new name; you can fix the link formulas by updating the name of the source workbook.

Switching to a different source workbook is not difficult. You use the same procedure to change the source workbook whether the original source workbook is now located in a different folder, or the name of the source workbook is no longer what it was when you created link formulas in the dependent workbook. To switch to a different source workbook, you use the Edit Links dialog box.

Switch the Link Source

1. Open the dependent workbook.
2. Click [Office button].
3. Click Prepare.
4. Click [▾] at the bottom of the Prepare menu.

Note: *In the figure [▾] is not visible, but its counterpart appears at the top of the menu.*

5. Click Edit Links to Files.

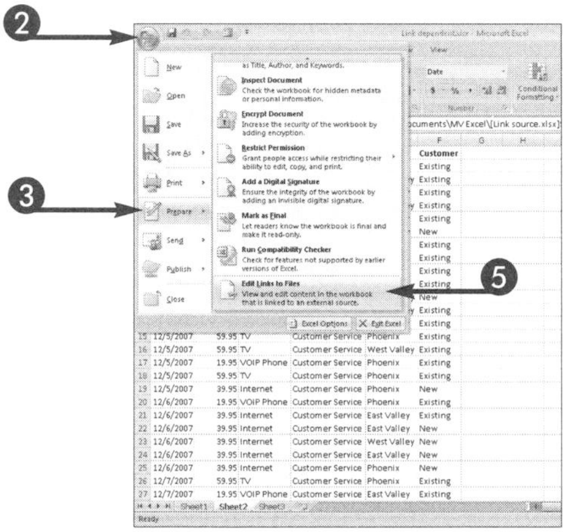

The Edit Links dialog box appears.

6. Click the appropriate source file.
7. Click Change Source.

   The Change Source dialog box appears.

8. Navigate to the location of the source workbook.
9. Click OK.

   Excel redisplays the Edit Links dialog box, showing the new source file.

10. Click Close.

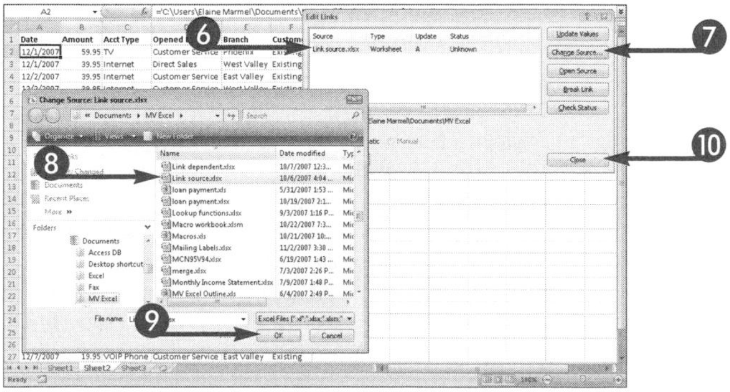

Disable Links

If you decide that you no longer need the external references to the source workbook that are stored in the dependent workbook, you can disable the links. When you disable links, Excel converts the external reference to a value. Suppose, for example, that the source workbook is named source.xlsx and, in the dependent workbook in cell G11, you have a link to the range C3:C12 on Sheet1 in the source workbook. In this case, your link formula would read:

=SUM([source.xlsx]Sheet1!$C$3:$C$12)

Further suppose that the sum of the range C3:C12 on Sheet1 of source.xlsx is 26. If you break the link between the two workbooks, cell G11 would now read:

26

Be aware that if you break links between a source workbook and a dependent workbook, you cannot undo the operation. The only way to recover is to immediately close the dependent workbook without saving. If you are unsure about whether you really want to disable links, save the dependent workbook using a new name; the newly named file is a backup. Then, complete the steps in this section and, if you do not like the results, you can delete the original dependent workbook and work in the backup workbook.

Disable Links

1. Display the dependent workbook.
2. Click .
3. Click Prepare.
4. Click at the bottom of the Prepare menu.

Note: *In the figure is not visible, but its counterpart appears at the top of the menu.*

5. Click Edit Links to Files.

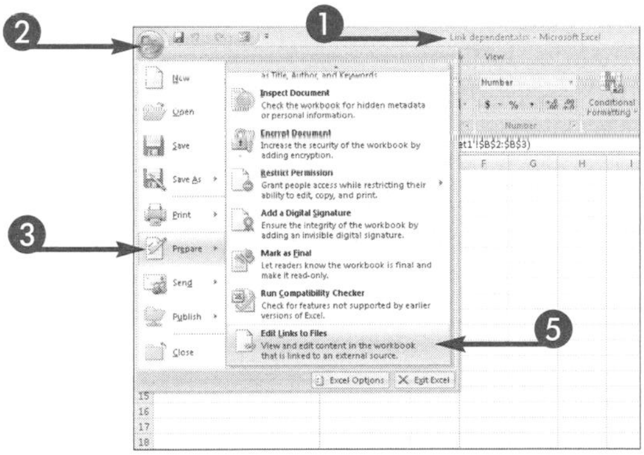

The Edit Links dialog box appears.

6. Click the appropriate source file.
7. Click Break Link.

   Excel warns you that breaking links cannot be undone.

8. Click Break Links.

   Excel breaks the selected link and converts link formulas to values.

9. Click Close.

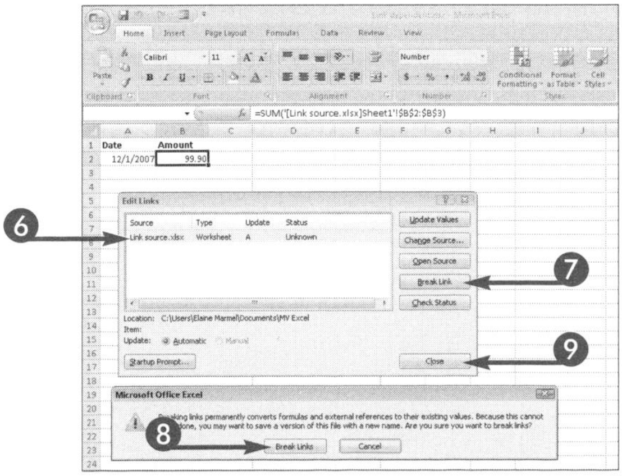

PART V

Consolidate Data by Position

You can combine information from multiple worksheets onto a single worksheet by consolidating. Suppose that you receive workbooks containing product sales information from several different divisions in your company, and your job is to combine the information to produce overall product sales figures and charts.

You can easily consolidate information if the workbooks or worksheets are laid out exactly the same way or very similarly, based on the information's relative position in the workbook. If your worksheets are laid out very differently, you can try consolidating using labels; for more information, see the section, "Consolidate Data Using Labels."

Typically, when you consolidate information, you want to add corresponding information in each worksheet. However, Excel does not limit you to summing.

You can consolidate worksheets in the same workbook by inserting a new worksheet; see Chapter 7 for more details. You can also simply start a new workbook; you typically start a new workbook when consolidating several workbooks. The other workbooks do not need to be open, but opening them makes consolidation easier. This example consolidates data on separate sheets in the same workbook. The destination range appears on the new worksheet and contains the consolidated data.

Consolidate Data by Position

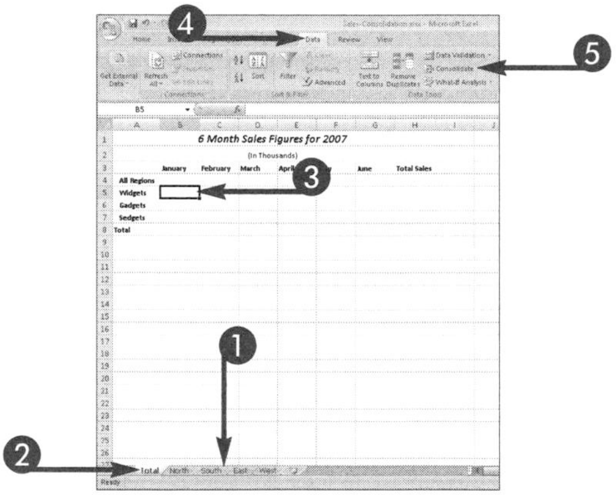

1. Open the workbook containing the data you want to consolidate.
2. Insert a new worksheet or open a new workbook.
3. Click the cell that will be the upper-left corner of the destination range.
4. Click the Data tab.
5. Click Consolidate.

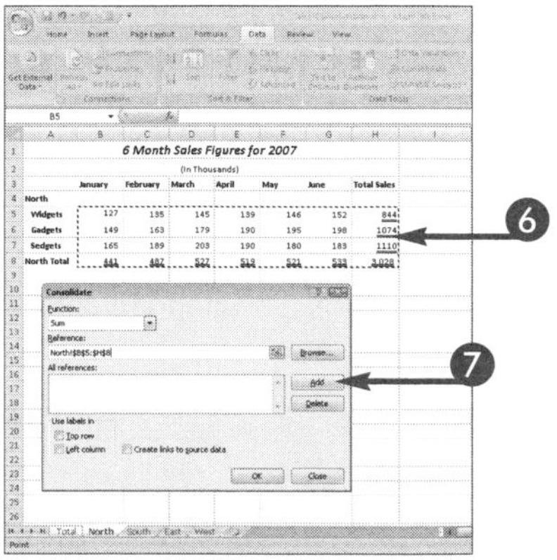

The Consolidate dialog box appears.

6. Select the first range you want to consolidate.

Note: *You can click any worksheet or workbook with the Consolidate dialog box open.*

7. Click Add.
8. Repeat Steps 6 and 7 for each range you want to consolidate.

- The ranges you add appear here.

Note: *Excel assumes you want to consolidate the same range in each worksheet you display.*

9 Click OK.

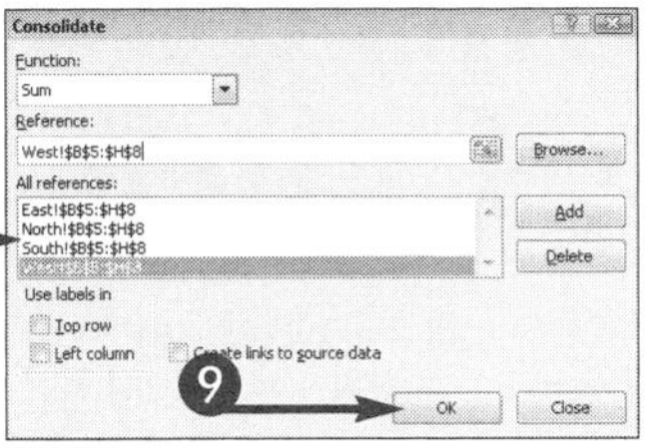

- Excel redisplays the worksheet you displayed in Step 2.
- Excel fills in the sum of the numbers you selected in each worksheet.

Note: *Excel fills in values, not formulas.*

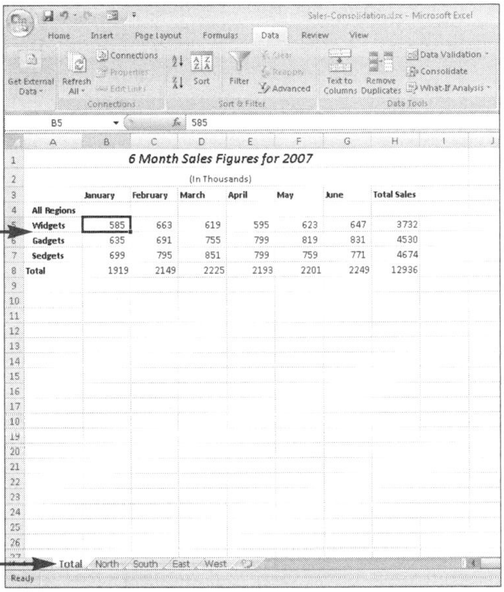

MASTER IT

Can Excel consolidate text as well as numbers?

▼ No. Consolidation is designed to perform some sort of mathematical calculation. If you try to include text when selecting data to consolidate, Excel accepts the reference but does not display the contents of any cells that contain text in the destination range. Instead, those cells are blank in the destination range.

I expect the source data range to grow. Is there a way to create the destination range to accommodate growth?

▼ Yes. Instead of selecting a range that contains the data you want to consolidate, select entire columns that include the data you want to consolidate. Then, as the data in the source range grows, the consolidation will accommodate it.

Can Excel create formulas instead of entering values when consolidating?

▼ Yes. Excel can create link formulas that you can then update if the data in one of the worksheets you include in the consolidation changes. In the Consolidate dialog box, click Create Links To Source Data (☐ changes to ☑). The destination range serves as the dependent worksheet, and the data you identify to consolidate serves as the source workbook or workbooks.

PART V

Consolidate Data Using Labels

You can combine information from multiple worksheets onto a single worksheet by consolidating. Suppose that you receive workbooks containing product sales information from several different divisions in your company, and your job is to combine the information to produce overall product sales figures and charts. If the information you want to consolidate is not laid out the same way in each worksheet, you might be able to consolidate using labels to identify similar data. This form of consolidation does not produce as clean a result as consolidating by the relative position of information — as described in the section, "Consolidate Data By Position" — but it does enable you to consolidate workbooks that are not laid out exactly the same way.

You place consolidated information on a blank worksheet. If you want to consolidate worksheets in the same workbook, you need to insert a new worksheet as described in Chapter 7. You can also start a new workbook; you typically start a new workbook when consolidating several workbooks. Although you do not need to open the workbooks to consolidate them, opening them makes consolidation easier. This example consolidates data on separate sheets in the same workbook. The destination range on the new worksheet contains the consolidated data and should be blank when you start.

Consolidate Data Using Labels

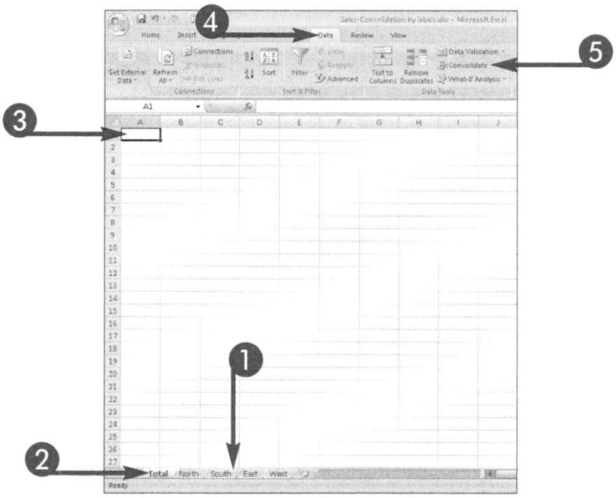

1. Open the workbook containing the data you want to consolidate.
2. Insert a new worksheet or open a new workbook.
3. Click the cell that will be the upper-left corner of the destination range.
4. Click the Data tab.
5. Click Consolidate.

The Consolidate dialog box appears.

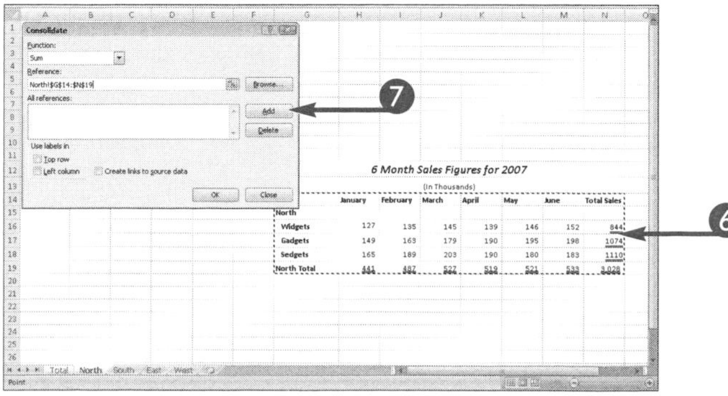

6. Select the first range you want to consolidate, including row or column labels.

Note: *You can click any worksheet or workbook with the Consolidate dialog box open.*

7. Click Add.
8. Repeat Steps 6 and 7 for each range you want to consolidate.

- The ranges you add appear here.

9. Click one or both of these check boxes to identify the labels Excel should use to match the data (☐ changes to ☑).

   - You can click here to create link formulas for consolidated values (◎ changes to ◉).

10. Click OK.

   - Excel redisplays the worksheet you displayed in Step 2.
   - Excel takes its best guess at filling in the sum of the numbers you selected in each worksheet.
   - Any information that was not identical in the ranges you consolidated appears separately in the destination range.

Note: *Excel fills in values or formulas in the destination range.*

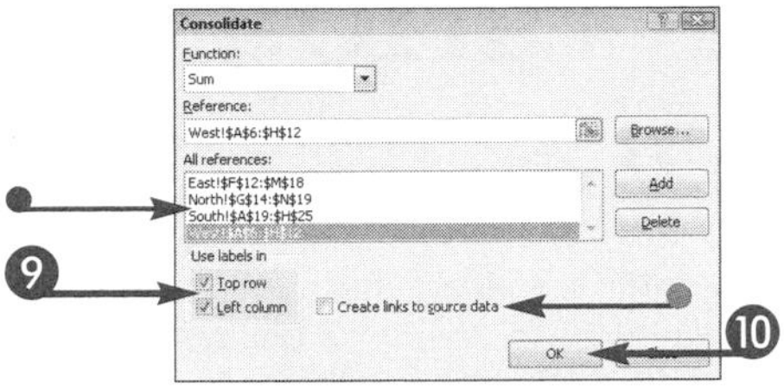

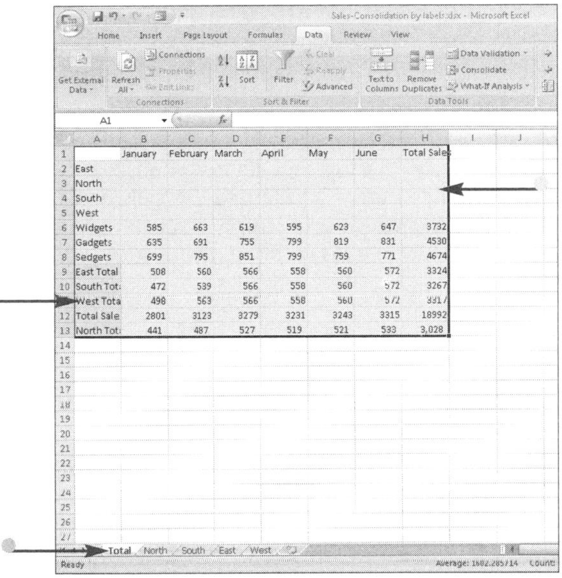

Can I perform other calculations when consolidating besides summing?

▼ Yes. You can use any of these statistical functions: AVERAGE, COUNT, COUNTA, MAX, MIN, PRODUCT, STDEV, STDEVP, VAR, or VARP. To select a calculation other than SUM, click ▾ under Function in the Consolidate dialog box and click a calculation in the list that appears. For details on the purpose of these functions, see Appendix A and Chapters 10 to 17.

Why is the destination range a single cell?

▼ If you select a single cell for the destination range, Excel expands the destination range to accommodate as much consolidated information as necessary. If you select a row, Excel expands the destination range downward. If you select a column, Excel expands the destination range to the right. If you select a range, Excel does *not* expand the destination range.

Can I make multiple consolidations in a worksheet?

▼ Not exactly. You can create one consolidation per worksheet, but you can add or remove source areas and then redo a consolidation. If you consolidate without creating links to the source data, removing all of the source areas from a consolidation does not affect the consolidation. To remove source areas — and effectively clear a consolidation — reopen the Consolidate dialog box, select each reference, and click Delete.

Create Various Scenarios

Using the Scenario Manager, you can explore different possible outcomes for a given set of data. Creating different possible outcomes is often referred to as creating a *what-if* model. That is, by modifying certain data, you answer the question, "What would happen if I made this change?"

When you work with scenarios, you use a worksheet that contains some values that do not change and others than do change. You identify the cells that contain changing values and supply a scenario name. Then you supply variables for the changing cells.

Suppose, for example, that you want to evaluate a potential mortgage payment, given several different down payments and interest rates. You can create as many scenarios as you want using different down payment and interest rate percentages, naming each scenario so that you can identify it. You can then display the information you store for each case at any time for analysis.

You may also want to create "Best Case," "Worst Case," and "Most Likely Case" scenarios so that you can switch between and analyze the impact of each case should it occur.

Create Various Scenarios

1. Select the non-changing cells of your model.
2. Click the Data tab.
3. Click What-If Analysis.
4. Click Scenario Manager to display the Scenario Manager dialog box.
5. Click Add.

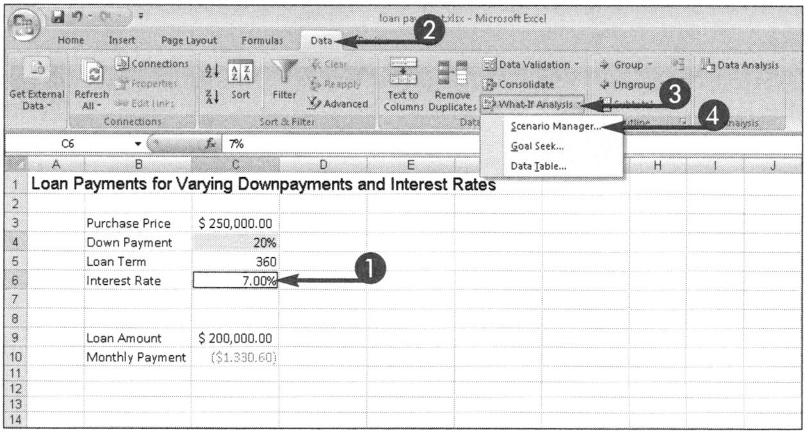

The Add Scenario dialog box appears.

6. Type a scenario name here.
7. Verify that the addresses are correct for the changing cells.
8. Click OK.

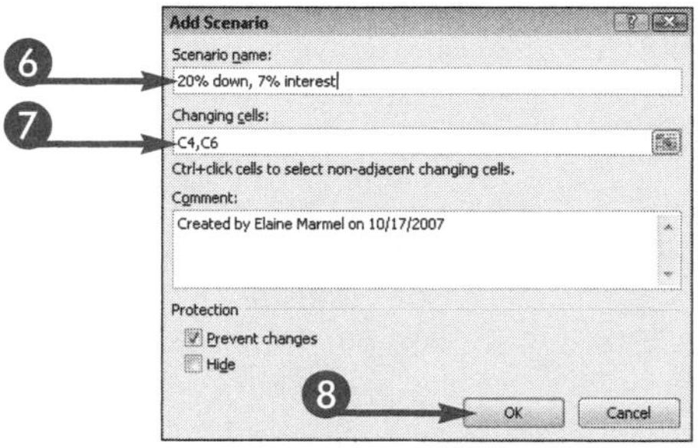

The Scenario Values dialog box appears.

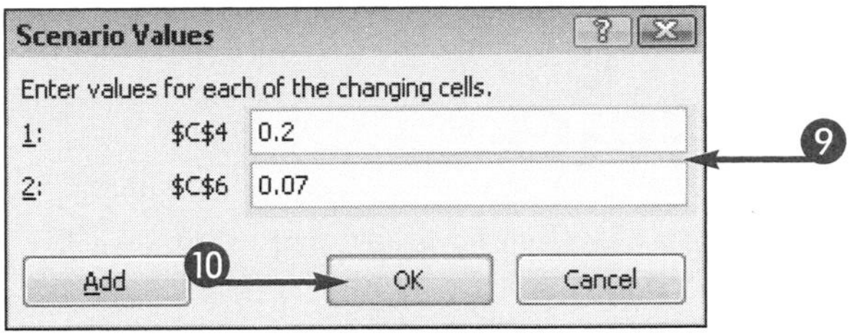

9 Type values for each changing cell.

Note: *If the cells selected in Step 1 contain values, Excel suggests those values.*

You can click Add to create another scenario, and Excel redisplays the Add Scenario dialog box; complete Steps 5 to 10 for each scenario.

10 Click OK when you finish creating scenarios.

The Scenario Manager dialog box reappears.

- Defined scenarios appear here.

11 Click Close.

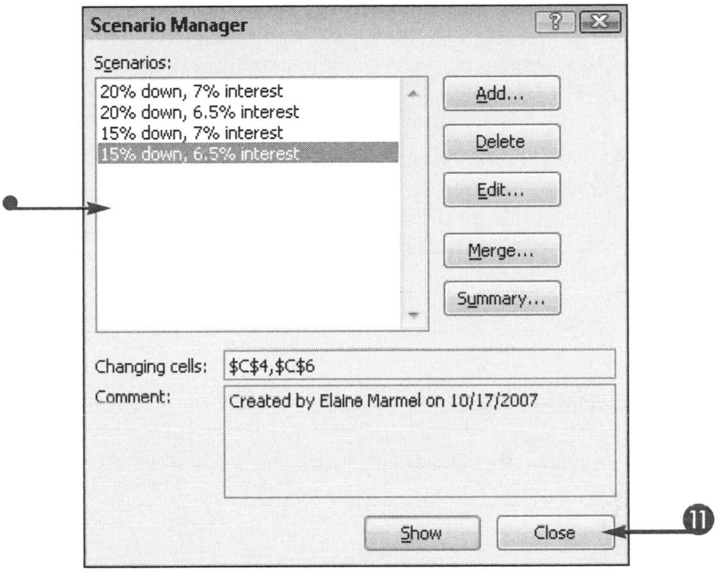

MASTER IT

Can I make changes to a scenario after I create it?

▼ Yes. Complete Steps 1 to 4. Click the scenario you want to change and then click Edit. The Edit Scenario dialog box appears. In this dialog box, you can change the scenario name or the addresses of the changing cells. Click OK and Excel displays the Scenario Values dialog box. Using this dialog box, you can enter new values for the scenario. Click OK to redisplay the Scenario Manager dialog box.

If I no longer need a scenario, how do I delete it?

▼ Complete Steps 1 to 4. Click the scenario you want to change and then click Delete. Be aware that you cannot undo this action. If you delete a scenario and then decide you need it, you can either close the workbook without saving or you must recreate the scenario using the steps in this section.

What do the Protection options in the Add Scenario dialog box do?

▼ These options are in effect only when you choose the Scenario option while protecting the worksheet. If you protect a scenario, nobody can modify it unless they know the password. If you hide a scenario, it does not appear in the Scenario Manager dialog box. See Chapter 31 for details on protecting a worksheet.

Display a Scenario

You can display a scenario at any time using the Scenario Manager dialog box. When you use the Scenario Manager to display a scenario, Excel updates the changing cells you defined to display the values stored in the scenario you select. You can switch between scenarios as often as you want to review the information each scenario provides.

You can display any scenario you see in the Scenario Manager dialog box; by default, Excel displays scenarios that are available in the worksheet. Scenarios created on other worksheets in the same workbook are available only when you display the other worksheets. It is also possible that scenarios may be hidden if the worksheet was protected.

When you close your workbook, Excel prompts you to save the workbook, even if you close the workbook displaying the same scenario that appeared when you opened the workbook. Each time you display a different scenario, Excel treats the worksheet as if you had manually changed the values in the changing cell. Because all of your scenarios are saved with the worksheet, you can safely save the workbook displaying any scenario.

Display a Scenario

1. Display the Scenario Manager dialog box.

Note: *To display the Scenario Manager dialog box, complete steps 1 to 4 in the section, "Create Various Scenarios."*

- Defined scenarios appear here.

2. Click a scenario.
3. Click Show.

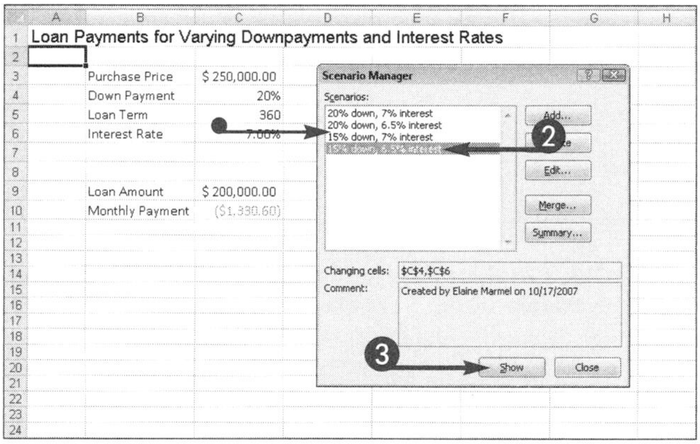

- The results of the scenario appear in the worksheet.

4. Repeat steps 2 and 3 for each scenario you want to view.
5. Click Close when you are done.

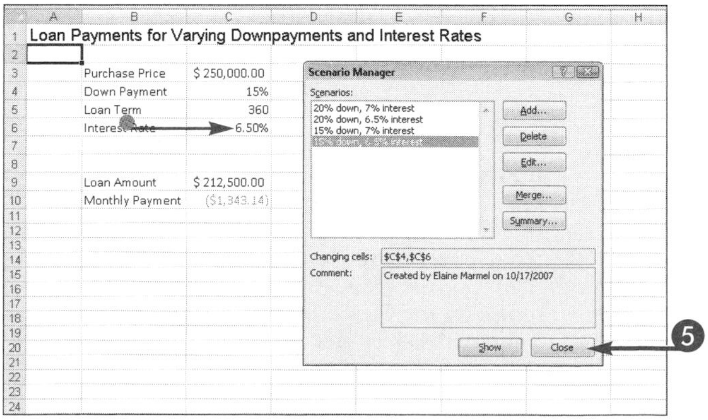

Switch Scenarios Quickly

If you switch scenarios often, you may find it more convenient to use the Scenario button than to open the Scenario Manager dialog box. When you click the Scenario button on the Quick Access Toolbar, Excel displays a list of scenarios that are available in the worksheet; you simply click a scenario to display it.

As you switch worksheets, the scenarios that display when you click the Scenario button change, based on the scenarios available in the worksheet you are currently viewing.

The Scenario button is not available on any of the tabs of the Ribbon. To use the Scenario button, you must customize the Quick Access Toolbar by adding the Scenario button. You can add any button to the Quick Access Toolbar, including buttons that do not appear on the Ribbon; Excel does not restrict you to adding only buttons that appear on the Ribbon.

When you customize the Quick Access Toolbar, the buttons you can add are organized in groups in the Excel Options dialog box. When you find the group that contains the button you want to add, you can locate the button in that group.

Switch Scenarios Quickly

1. Click ▾.
2. From the menu that appears, click More Commands to display the Excel Options dialog box.
3. Click ▾ and click Commands Not in the Ribbon.
4. Scroll down the list and click Scenario.
5. Click Add.
6. Click OK.

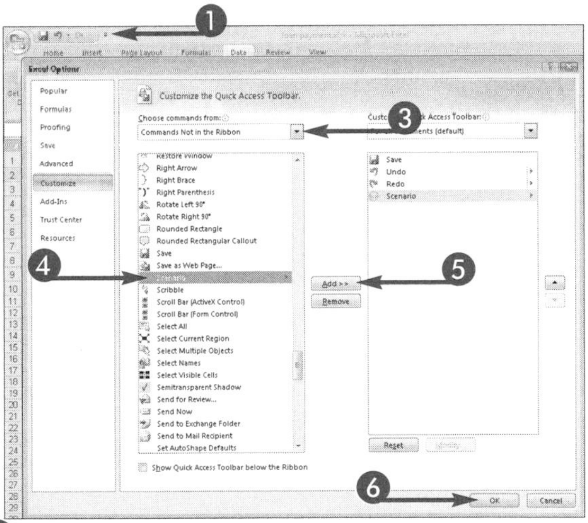

The Scenario button (▭▾) appears on the Quick Access Toolbar.

7. Click ▭▾.

Available scenarios appear.

- This ☑ identifies the currently displayed scenario.

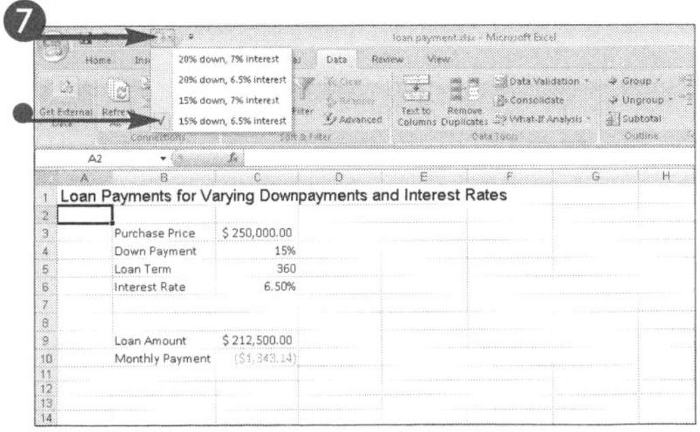

Merge Scenarios

On occasion, you may want to merge scenarios created in one workbook with scenarios created in another workbook. For example, if you work in a workgroup situation, it is entirely possible that different departments may be using the same model and have created different scenarios on separate sheets in the same workbook, or even in different workbooks. Suppose, for example, that the marketing department set up scenarios using one set of values for the changing cells, while the finance department copied the model information to a new worksheet and then set up their own scenarios on the new worksheet using an entirely different set of values for the changing cells. In the meantime, the operations department copied the model information into an entirely different workbook and then set up scenarios using *their* own set of values for the changing cells. You can easily merge the scenarios together onto one worksheet in one workbook so that you can switch between all of the available models.

If you are merging scenarios across workbooks, be sure that you open all of the workbooks involved before you start the process described in this section. This example merges scenarios from different sheets in the same workbook.

Merge Scenarios

1. Open the workbooks that contain the scenarios you want to merge.
2. Select the worksheet where all of the scenarios should ultimately be available.
3. Click the Data tab.
4. Click What-If Analysis.
5. Click Scenario Manager.

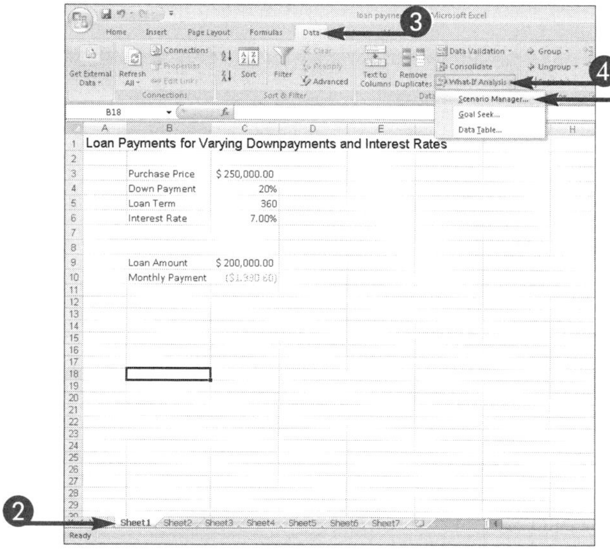

The Scenario Manager dialog box appears.

6. Click Merge.

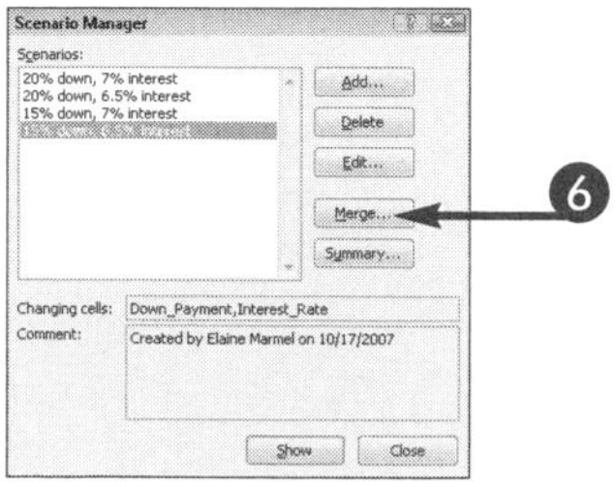

The Merge Scenarios dialog box appears.

7 Click a worksheet.

8 Click OK to merge scenarios from the selected worksheet to the active worksheet displayed in the workbook.

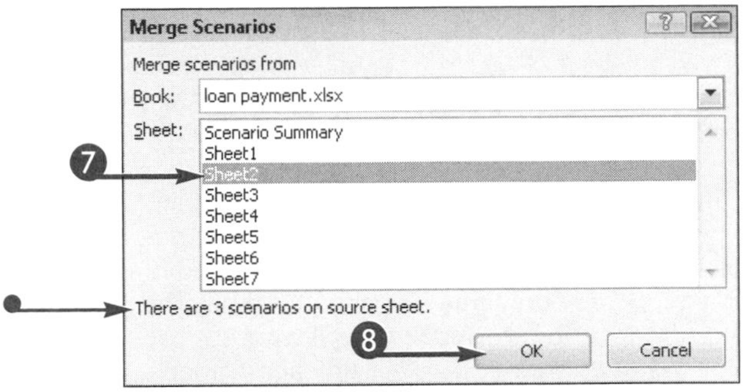

The Scenario Manager dialog box reappears.

- The scenarios you merged appear here, along with scenarios originally stored in the active worksheet.

9 Repeat Steps 6 to 8 for each worksheet containing scenarios you want to merge.

10 Click Close.

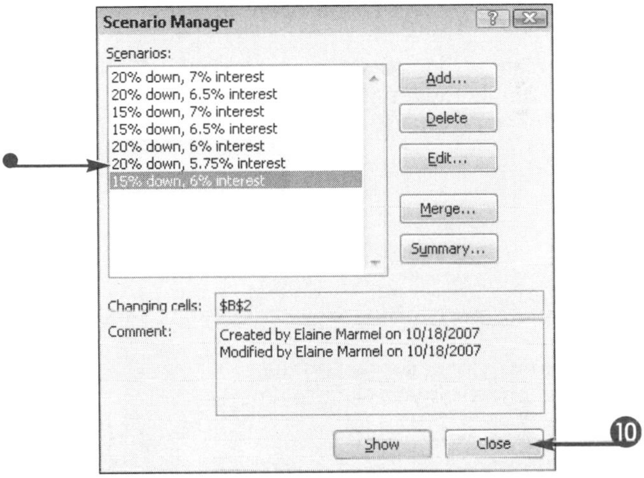

MASTER IT

My scenarios ended up in the wrong workbook. What did I do wrong and how do I fix it?

▼ You selected the wrong worksheet in Step 2. Before you begin the merge process, you should be looking at the worksheet in which you want all scenarios available. To correct the problem, open all of the workbooks containing scenarios that you want to merge. Then select the worksheet in the workbook where you want all scenarios to be available when you finish. When that worksheet is the active worksheet, perform Steps 3 to 10, remembering to select the workbook containing the scenarios you want to merge before completing Step 7.

Should I do anything differently if I am merging scenarios from another workbook?

▼ Yes. Before you complete Step 7, click ▾ beside the Book field and select the workbook containing the scenarios you want to merge. Excel then displays the names of the worksheets in that workbook. You can then complete Steps 7 to 10 to select scenarios from those worksheets and merge them into the active worksheet and workbook.

Create a Scenario Report

Creating scenarios is an effective way to help you consider a variety of possible outcomes. However, by design, the Scenario Manager enables you to view only one scenario at a time. There are circumstances under which you will want to compare scenarios. Rather than set up each scenario and then print the worksheet, you can create a scenario summary report.

When you create a scenario summary report, Excel asks you to identify the result cells — those cells that are affected in your scenario by the changing cells.

Excel then displays a report that shows you the cell addresses for the changing cells and the result cells. In the first column of the report, you see the current values on the worksheet for the changing cells and the result cells. The other columns in the report present information for each scenario; in each column, you see the values you established for the changing cells and the values for the result cells.

To make the scenario report more meaningful, you can assign range names to each changing cell and each result cell.

Create a Scenario Report

1. Click the worksheet containing the scenarios on which you want to report.
2. Click the Data tab.
3. Click What-If Analysis.
4. Click Scenario Manager.

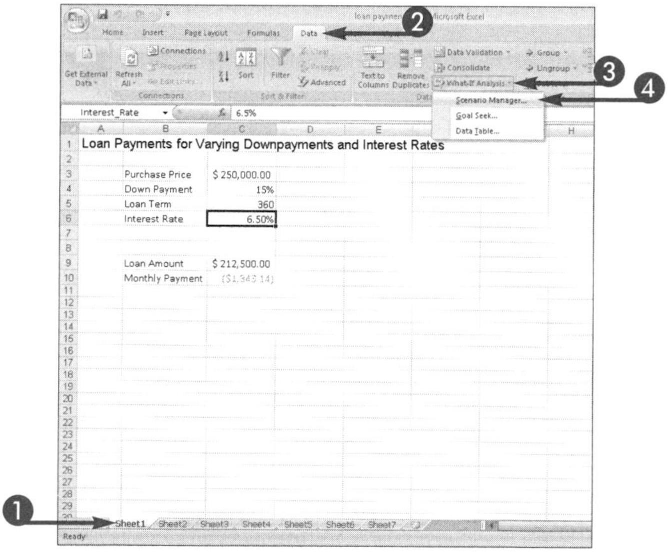

The Scenario Manager dialog box appears.

- Available scenarios appear here.

5. Click Summary.

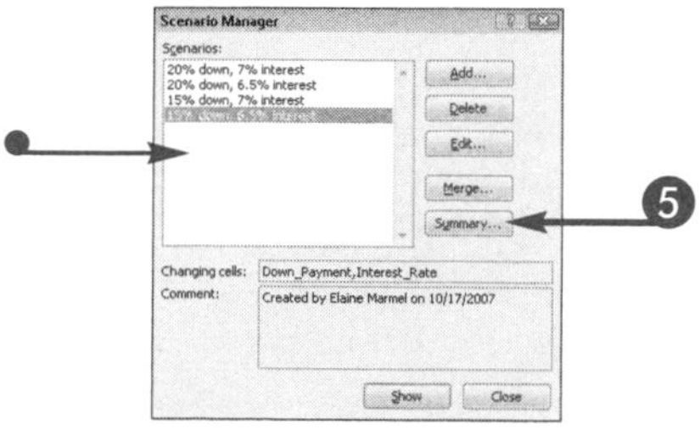

The Scenario Summary dialog box appears.

6. Double-check the addresses of the result cells; if they are incorrect, select the correct cells in the worksheet.

7. Click OK.

- Excel creates a Scenario Summary worksheet for the report.
- This column shows the values for the changing and results cells at the time you created the report.
- Stored scenario titles appear here.
- Stored scenario values appear highlighted in gray.

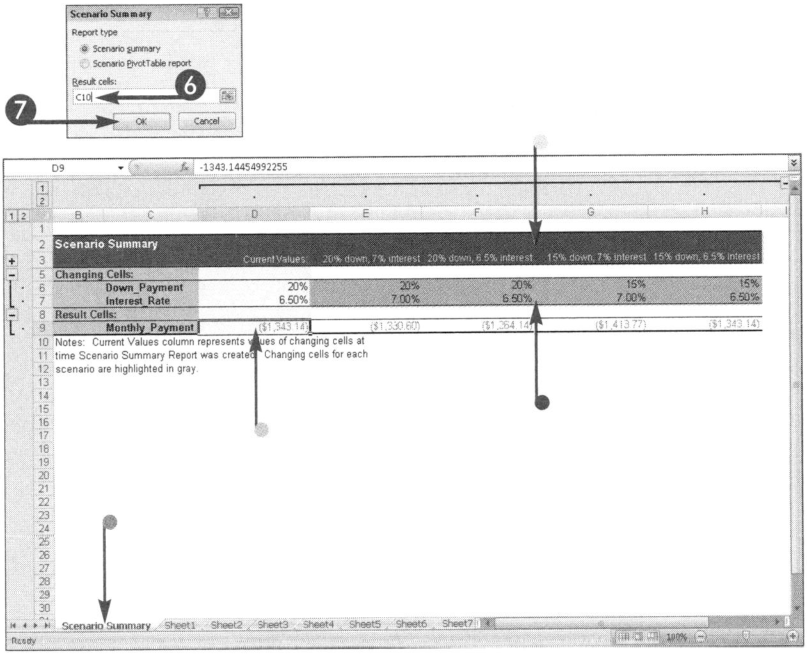

How do I assign range names?

▼ If you assigned labels to the various cells, you can easily assign the label name as a range name. Click the cell to which you want to assign a name — not the label cell, but the cell containing the value. Click the Formulas tab and then click Define Name. The New Name dialog box appears, suggesting the label you assigned to the value in the Name field. You can change the name or, if you like the label, click OK. Repeat this process for each cell to which you want to assign a range name. Although nothing seems to happen, Excel stores the range names and displays them on the scenario summary report.

Can I change the values that appear in the Current Values column?

▼ The report is not dynamic, and so although you can change the values of the changing cells, Excel does not automatically update the result cells. You can manually change the value in the result cells, or you can switch back to the sheet containing the scenarios, select a different scenario, and follow the steps in this section to create another scenario summary report.

If I do not assign range names, what changes on the report?

▼ In the first column of the report, the cell addresses of the changing cells and the result cells appear instead of the range names shown in this example.

Create a Scenario PivotTable

For simple cases, where you look at only one or possibly two result cells, creating a scenario summary report is usually sufficient to help you compare a variety of possible outcomes. However, if your scenarios are more complex and include several input and result cells, you may find a scenario PivotTable to be more useful when comparing scenarios. By its very nature, a PivotTable provides great flexibility, allowing you to rearrange the data to view it in a variety of different ways. Looking at the scenario results in different ways may point out information you might otherwise have missed. For details on working with PivotTables and even producing charts from PivotTable information, see Chapter 24.

When you create a scenario PivotTable report, Excel asks you to identify the result cells — those cells that are affected in your scenario by the changing cells. Excel then displays a PivotTable report that shows you one arrangement of the changing and result cells, using the cell addresses for the cells. To make the scenario PivotTable report more meaningful, you can assign range names to each changing cell and each result cell.

Create a Scenario PivotTable

1. Click the worksheet containing the scenarios on which you want to report.
2. Click the Data tab.
3. Click What-If Analysis.
4. Click Scenario Manager.

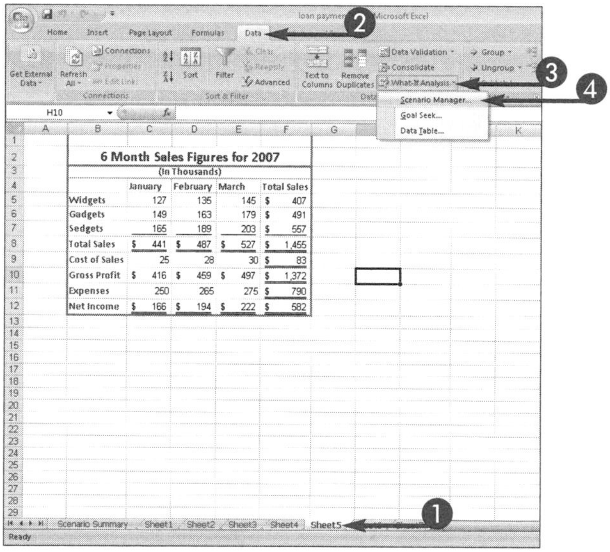

The Scenario Manager dialog box appears.

- Available scenarios appear here.

5. Click Summary.

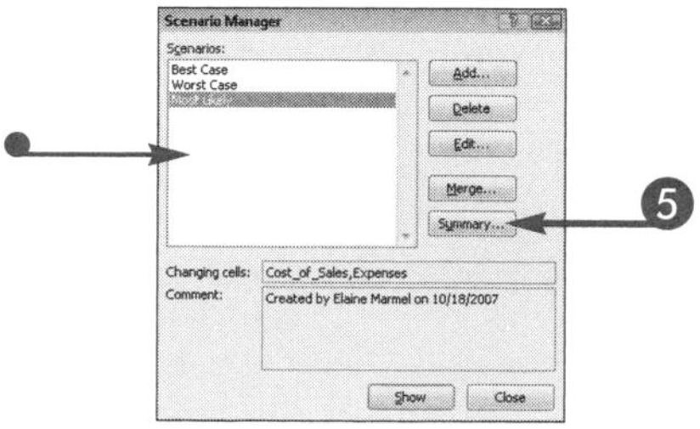

The Scenario Summary dialog box appears.

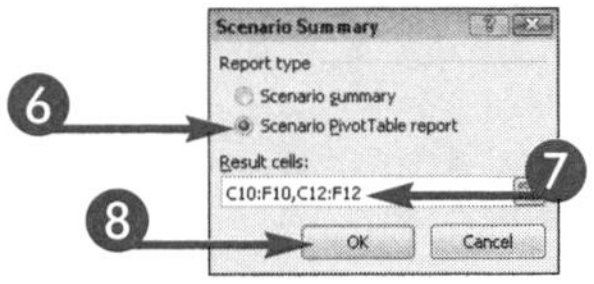

6 Click Scenario PivotTable Report (◎ changes to ◉).

7 Verify that the addresses of the result cells are correct; if they are incorrect, select the correct cells in the worksheet.

8 Click OK.

- Excel creates a Scenario PivotTable worksheet.
- You can change the information displayed in the PivotTable using the PivotTable Field List. For details on working with PivotTables, see Chapter 24.

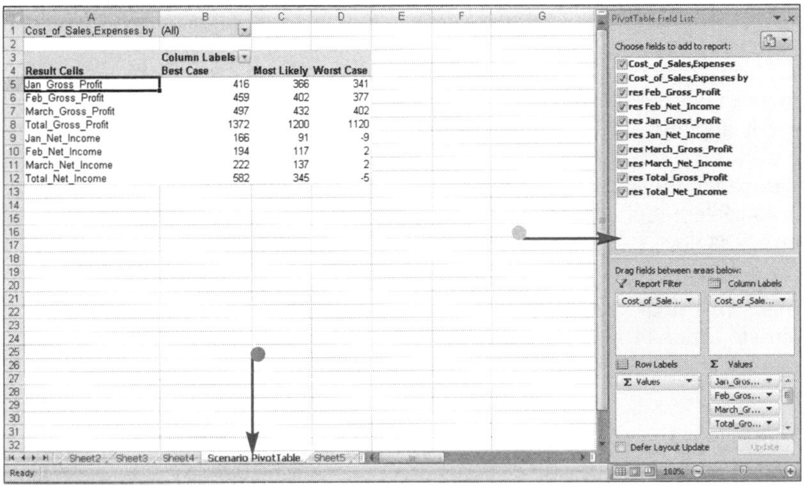

MASTER IT

Can I create a name for more than a single cell?

▼ Yes, you can. Select all of the cells you want to define by a single name. Then click the Formulas tab and click Define Name. The New Name dialog box appears. In the Name field, type a name for the selected cells; use an underscore character (_) to represent a space. Then click OK.

How do I select more than one set of cells for the result cells?

▼ Select the first set of cells. Then press and hold the Ctrl key as you select the second set of cells. Repeat this process of holding the Ctrl key as you select cells for each set of cells you want to include. Excel defines each range in the usual way, separating the first and last cell addresses with a colon (:). Excel separates each range with a comma (,).

Is there a limit on the number of changing cells I can define?

▼ Yes. You can define no more than 32 changing cells. If you attempt to define more than 32 cells, Excel displays an error message.

Is there anything special I need to do to keep the results of a Scenario PivotTable report?

▼ Yes. You need to save the workbook. If you close the workbook without saving, Excel does not save the Scenario PivotTable report.

Create a Data Table to Summarize Loan Possibilities

You can create a data table to help you analyze the effects of changing one input variable on other variables in a calculation. For example, when you take out a loan, the amount of the loan payment depends on the amount you borrow, the interest rate on the loan, and the length of time you have to repay the loan. When you vary any one of these four elements, the other three elements will change.

Suppose that you want to know how much your loan payment will be at several different interest rates. You can create a one-input data table in Excel that calculates your payment at varying interest rates while holding the loan amount and term constant.

To use a data table, you must first set up the worksheet so that it contains the formula you need to calculate. Then, in a separate area, you create a skeleton for the data table. You set up the input values that Excel should use in the calculation as a column, and establish cell references to the values you want calculated as a row across the top of the data table area. The cell in the upper-left corner of the data table remains blank.

Create a Data Table to Summarize Loan Possibilities

Understanding the Setup

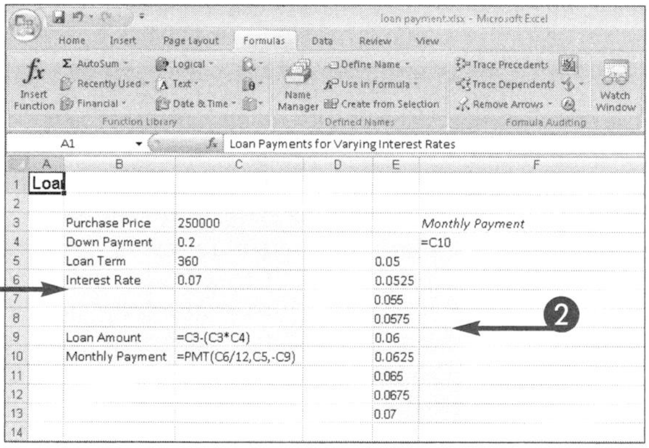

1. Set up the values in the worksheet needed to make a single calculation.

2. Set up an area for the data table.

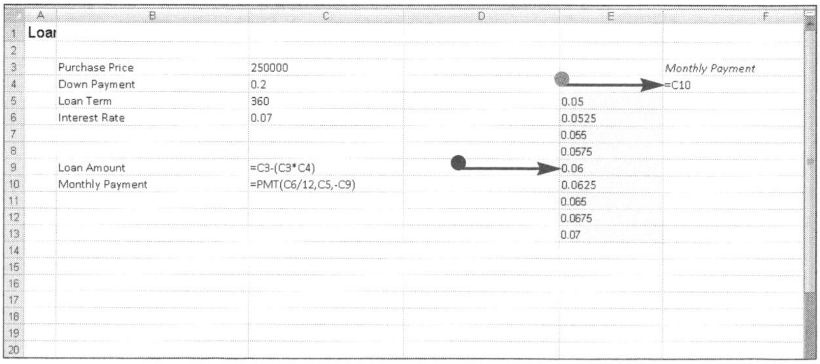

- Input values appear in a column.
- Formulas or references to formula cells appear in a row.

In this example, the data table's formula row is F. The formula in cell F4 refers to the formula stored in cell C10.

Create a Data Table

1. Select the data table range.
2. Click the Data tab.
3. Click What-If Analysis and select Data Table from the drop-down menu.

   The Data Table dialog box appears.
4. Click .
5. Click the worksheet cell that represents the input values.
6. Click OK.

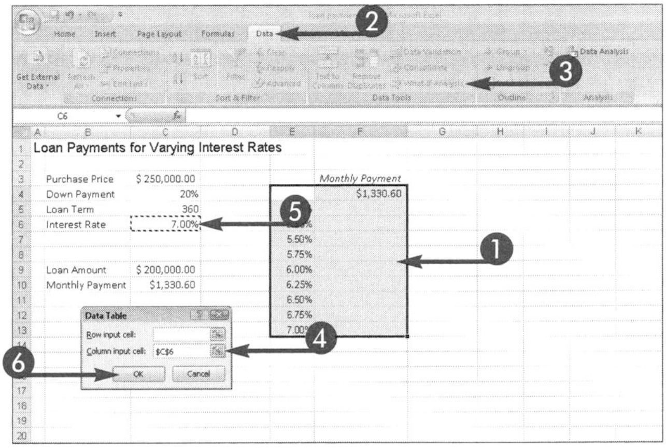

Excel fills in the data table with calculated values.

- The calculated values appear here.
- The array formula appears in the Formula Bar.

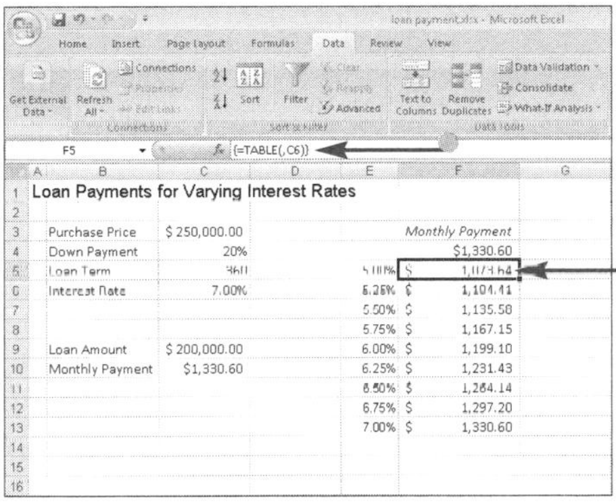

MASTER IT

How do I decide whether to use the Row Input Cell field or Column Input Cell field in Step 4?

▼ You can place input values in a column of the data table, as shown in this example, or in a row; the formulas or references to formula cells appear in the data table's other dimension. The location of the input values determines the field you use; use the Column Input Cell field when the input values appear in a column.

Is there a way to hide the calculated values that appear in the references to cells containing formulas?

▼ Yes. You can select the cells in the data table that contain references to formulas in the worksheet and change the font color to match the background of the cells. If you click the cell, the Formula Bar still displays the formula, but its result will not be visible in the cell.

Instead of the loan payment amounts, my data table just repeats the Monthly Payment label. What did I do wrong?

▼ You included the label when you selected the data table in Step 1 of the subsection, "Create a Data Table." Select only the row containing formulas and the column containing input values.

Create a Data Table to Model Sales Projections

You can create a data table to help you analyze the effects of changing two input variables on other variables in a calculation. For example, when you calculate projected sales, you usually use last year's sales as a starting point, and then you estimate the projected growth rate of sales as well as the projected ratio of expenses to sales. You can vary both the projected growth rate of sales and the projected ratio of expenses to sales to calculate a series of possible projected sales.

When you want to change two variables, you create a two-input data table in Excel. You first set up the worksheet so that it contains the formula you need to calculate. Then, in a separate area, you create a skeleton for the data table. You set up one set of input values in the leftmost column of the data table area, and the other set of input values as the top row of the data table area. In the cell in the upper-left corner of the data table, you create a formula that references the cell in the worksheet that calculates projected sales.

Create a Data Table to Model Sales Projections

Understanding the Setup

1. Set up the values in the worksheet needed to make a single calculation.

Note: *This example calculates projected sales by typing the formula* ***=B2+(B2*B3)-(B2*B4)***.

2. Set up an area for the data table.

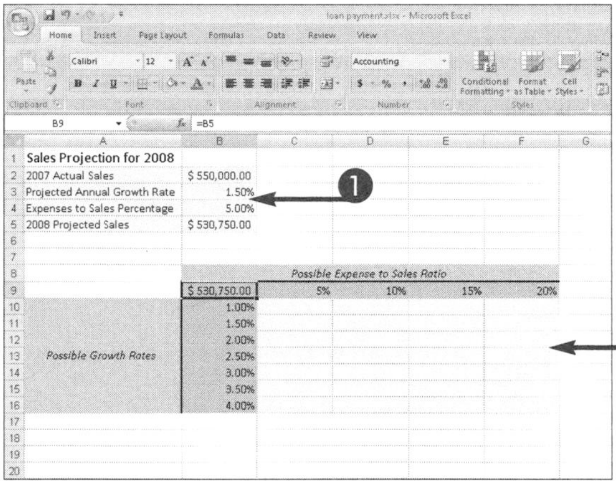

- In this example, input values for the first variable appear in a column.
- In this example, input values for the second variable appear in a row.
- In this example, the formula or reference to a formula cell appears here.
- In this example, the data table's formula cell is B9. The formula in cell B9 refers to the formula stored in cell B5.

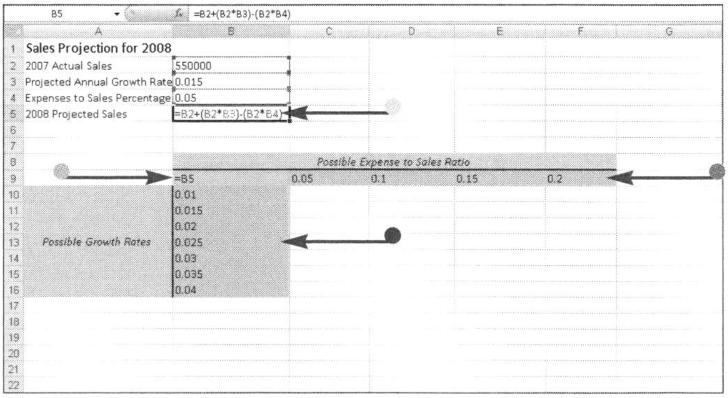

Create a Data Table

1. Select the data table range.
2. Click the Data tab.
3. Click What-If Analysis and select Data Table from the drop-down menu.
4. Click here and click the worksheet cell that represents the row of input values.
5. Click here and click the worksheet cell that represents the column of input values.
6. Click OK.

Excel fills in the data table with calculated values.

- The calculated values appear here.
- The array formula appears in the Formula Bar.

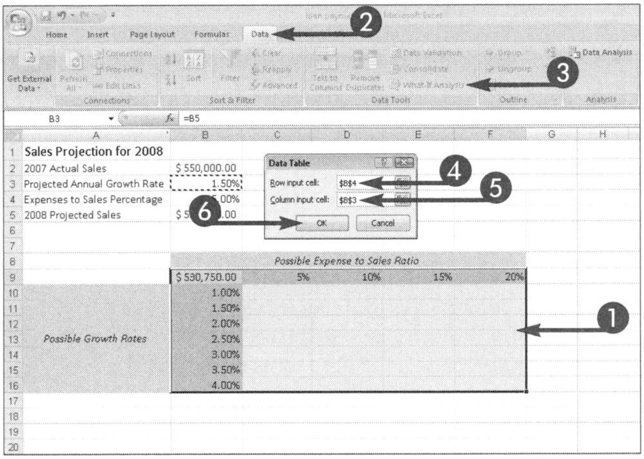

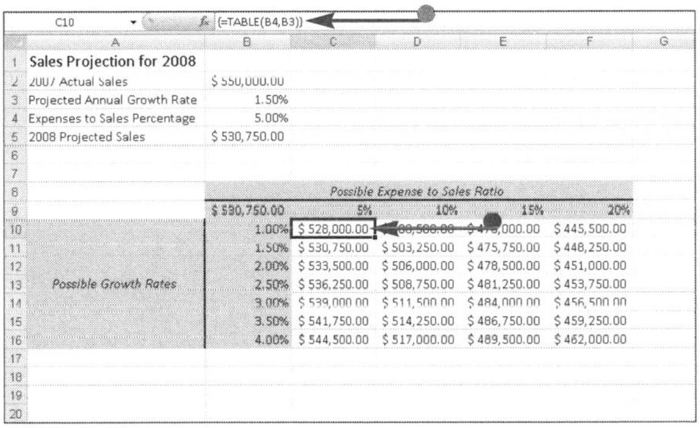

MASTER IT

What is an array formula?

▼ An array formula is a single formula that produces results in multiple cells. This example demonstrates using an Excel feature that generates an array formula, but you can create your own array formulas using special techniques. To learn more about working with arrays, see Chapter 10.

I want to delete the results and start again, but I see an error message telling me that I cannot change part of a data table. What should I do?

▼ The error message actually means that you cannot delete a single cell of an array formula. Instead, you need to select all of the cells that contain output in the data table before you press the Delete key.

If I want to change one or more of the input variables, do I need to redo the entire table?

▼ No, you do not. You can change any or all of the input variables in the top row of the table or in the left column of the table, and Excel automatically updates the table to reflect the change to the input variable or variables.

Seek a Goal

You can use the Goal Seek command to identify the number you need to fill in a formula to achieve a particular result. Suppose that you are buying a house and you know the price of the house and the interest rate you can get on your loan. You are concerned about the monthly payment; you want to be able to make the payment without falling short on cash each month. As a result, you want to know how much you need to put down to make the monthly mortgage payment be the amount you want to pay.

Using the Goal Seek command, Excel identifies the value to enter in a single input cell to produce the desired result in a formula cell. You set up your worksheet to contain the formula that calculates the value you want to know, and you enter the values you know in other cells in the worksheet. Then you use the Goal Seek command to fill in blanks in a sentence. For the mortgage payment example, the sentence you complete is: "Set the payment amount to $800 by changing the down payment amount."

Seek a Goal

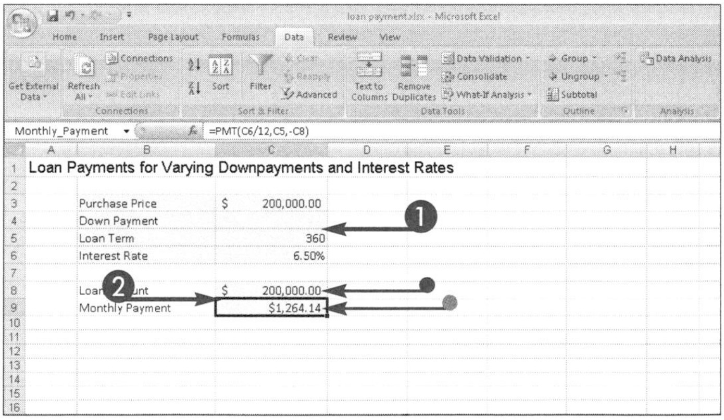

1. Enter the known values needed to make a single calculation.
2. Enter the formulas needed to calculate a solution.
   - This example formula deducts the down payment from the purchase price.
   - This example formula calculates a monthly mortgage payment by typing the formula **=PMT(C6/12,C5,-C8)**.

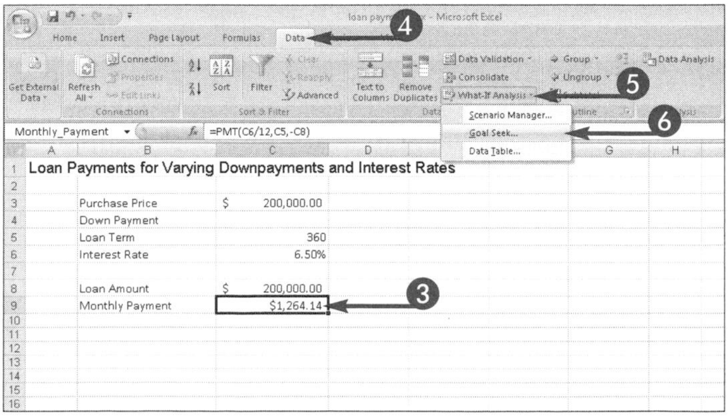

3. Select the cell containing the formula you want to solve.
4. Click the Data tab.
5. Click What-If Analysis.
6. Click Goal Seek.

The Goal Seek dialog box appears.

7. Make sure the cell selected in Step 3 appears here.
8. Type the result you want the formula to display.
9. Click here and select the cell in the worksheet that Excel should change to achieve your desired result.
10. Click OK.

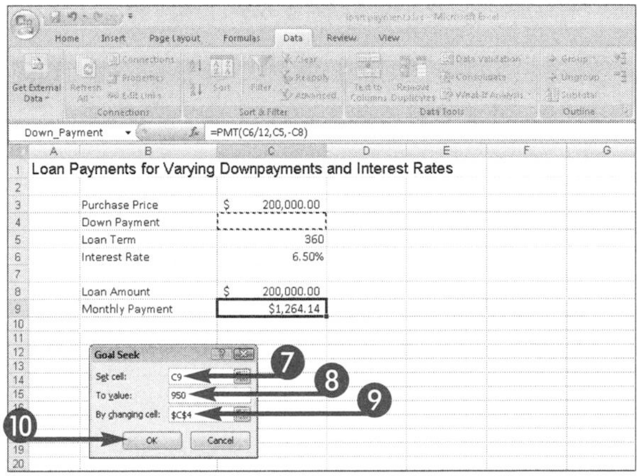

The Goal Seek Status dialog box appears, telling you the outcome.

- Excel adjusts the cell you selected in Step 9 to achieve the goal you specified in Step 6.
- The formula now shows the value you specified in Step 9.

11. Click OK to save the result.

Note: *Click Cancel to redisplay the original values.*

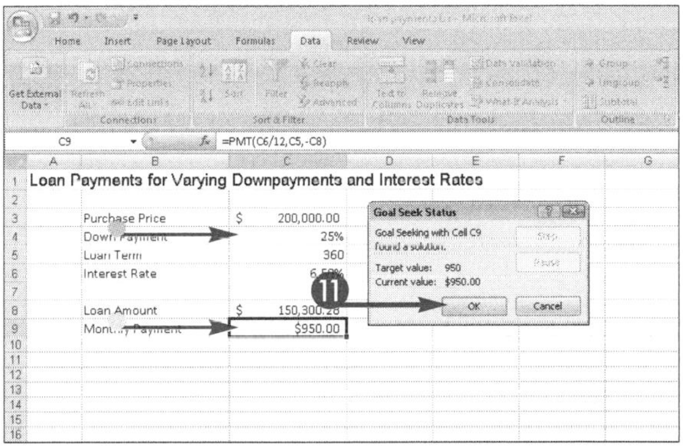

MASTER IT

I tried to use the steps in this section and Excel reported that it could not find a solution. What did I do wrong?

▼ Possibly nothing. There are some problems for which there simply is no solution. And, when Excel cannot find a solution, the goal Seek Status dialog box informs you of that fact. It is also possible Excel needs more iterations to solve the problem.

Although the Goal Seek Status dialog box reports no solution to my problem, I am fairly certain there is a solution. What should I do?

▼ Try modifying the value you supply in the To Value field of the Goal Seek dialog box; if you change the value to something you believe is close to the solution you seek, Excel may be able to solve the problem.

Is there a way to make Excel use more iterations when solving?

▼ Yes, you can try adjusting the Maximum Iterations setting. Click the Office button and click Excel Options. Click Formulas on the left. Under Calculations Options, try changing Maximum Iterations from 100 to 200 or some larger number. Setting the value to a higher number makes Excel try more possible solutions, but do not get carried away, or Excel may take a long time to calculate.

Use Solver to Maximize Profit

You can use the Excel add-in Solver to help you solve problems that are more complex than the Goal Seek feature and data tables can handle. While the Goal Seek feature and data tables can be powerful in their own right, they have a few limitations. In particular, neither feature allows you to specify constraints. And there are many problems in the world where you need to specify constraints.

Suppose, for example, that you run the warehouse for a company that produces four products. Each product uses five different materials in varying quantities. You know the quantities you have on hand of each of the raw materials and you know the amount of profit you make on each unit sold. Your job is to determine how to allocate raw materials when producing products to maximize profit based on production. You can use the Solver add-in to calculate the number of each product you should produce based on the quantities of raw materials you have on-hand as well as the profit associated with each product.

The Solver add-in is not available by default in Excel; to use it, you must enable it.

Use Solver to Maximize Profit

Install Solver

1. Click [icon].
2. Click Excel Options.

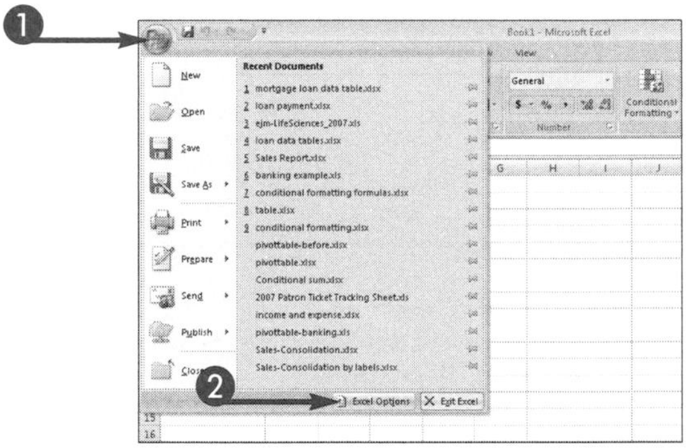

The Excel Options dialog box appears.

3. Click Add-Ins.
4. Click Go.

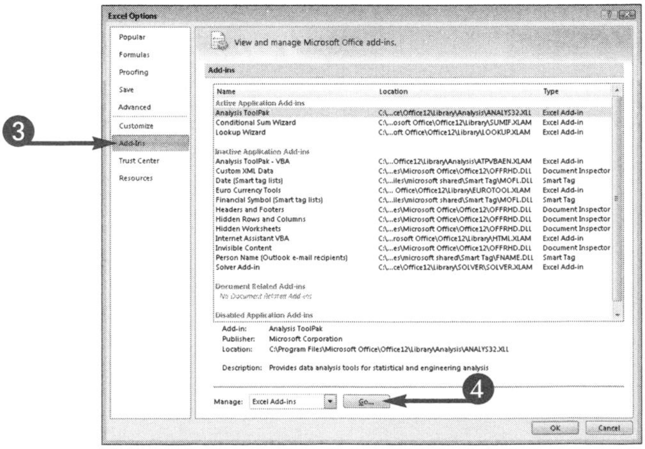

The Add-Ins dialog box appears.

5 Click Solver Add-in (☐ changes to ☑).

6 Click OK.

Note: *Excel may ask if you want to install the add-in; click Yes.*

- Excel adds Solver to the Analysis group on the Data tab.

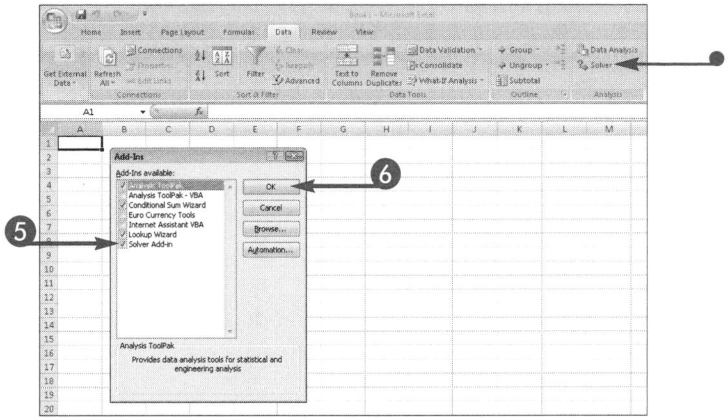

Maximize Profit

1 Enter the values needed to make calculations.

2 Set up the formulas Excel needs to calculate.

- In this example, formulas appear in Column I.
- Formulas also appear in Rows 8 and 9.

3 Click the cell you want to maximize.

Note: *In this example, click cell I11.*

4 Click the Data tab.

5 Click Solver.

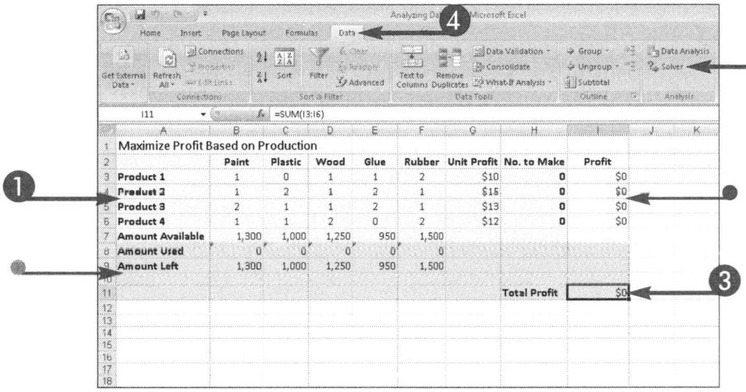

PART V

Does the arrangement of the worksheet matter?

▼ No. You can place the information in any arrangement you want. In this example, the raw materials could have appeared in the rows and the products in the columns. The Unit Profit, No. to Make, and Profit columns appear together to make setting up the Profit formula easy.

What formula appears in the Amount Used row and the Amount Left row?

▼ The SUMPRODUCT function calculates the amount used. In cell B8, the following formula appears:

=SUMPRODUCT(B3:B6,$H$3:$H$6).

Using absolute cell references for the values in column H enables you to copy the formula from cell B8 to the range C8:F8. In cell B9, =B7-B8 appears.

When I finish using the Solver add-in, can I hide it again?

▼ You can, but you do not need to do so unless you really want to hide it. To hide the Solver add-in, repeat the steps in the subsection, "Install Solver." When you perform Step 5, ☑ changes to ☐. When you perform Step 6, Excel removes the Solver add-in from the Analysis group on the Data tab.

continued

Use Solver to Maximize Profit *(Continued)*

To use the Solver add-in, worksheet setup is important. You display the values used in the calculations and the formulas to calculate. And, you optionally specify constraints.

In this example, you need to establish the products you produce and the amounts of each of the raw materials required to make each product. You also need to identify the amount of each raw material available for production and the profit you make per unit. These values do not change.

You need to establish formulas for each product that calculate profit, which would be the number of units produced multiplied by the profit per unit. You also need to sum the profit of each product — your goal is to maximize this value. And, you need to calculate the amount remaining of each raw material, which would be the amount available minus the amount used. Finally, you need a formula to calculate the amount used, which is based on the number of each raw material needed multiplied by the number of each product produced.

Last, you need two constraints for this problem: You cannot use more of any raw material than you have available, and the number of products made must be positive.

Use Solver to Maximize Profit *(continued)*

The Solver Parameters dialog box appears.

6. Make sure the cell you selected in Step 3 appears here.
7. Click Max (◎ changes to ◉).
8. Click here and select the cells Excel should adjust while solving.
9. Click Add to display the Add Constraint dialog box.
10. Click here and select a cell range to constrain.
11. Click ▾ and select a comparison operator.
12. Click here and type the comparison value.
13. To add more constraints, click Add.

Note: *Step 13 is optional. If you do not add more constraints, skip to Step 15.*

Repeat Steps 10 to 13 for each constraint.

14. Click OK.

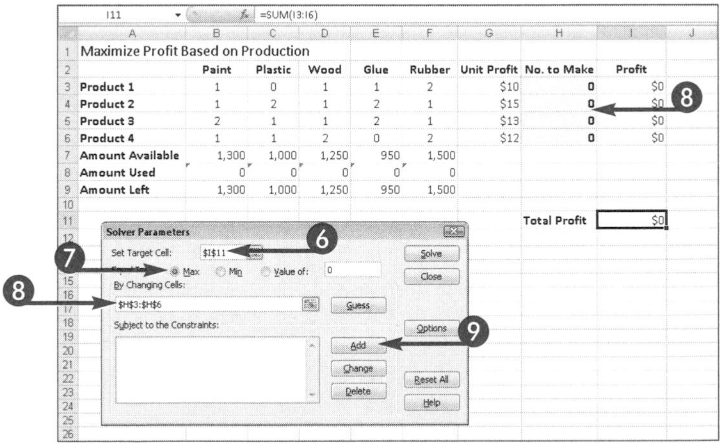

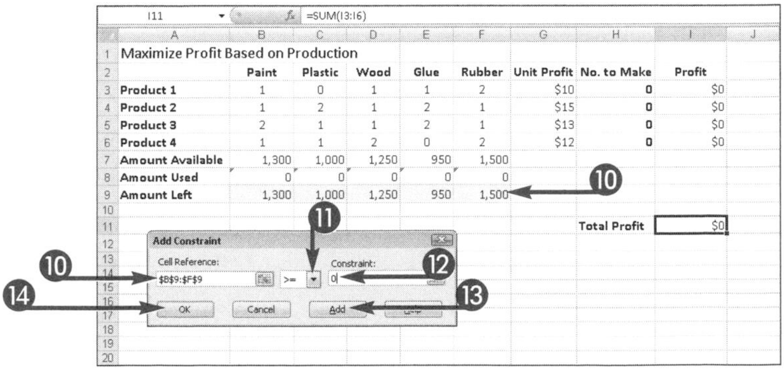

- The Solver Parameters dialog box reappears, showing all the constraints you defined.

⓯ Click Solve.

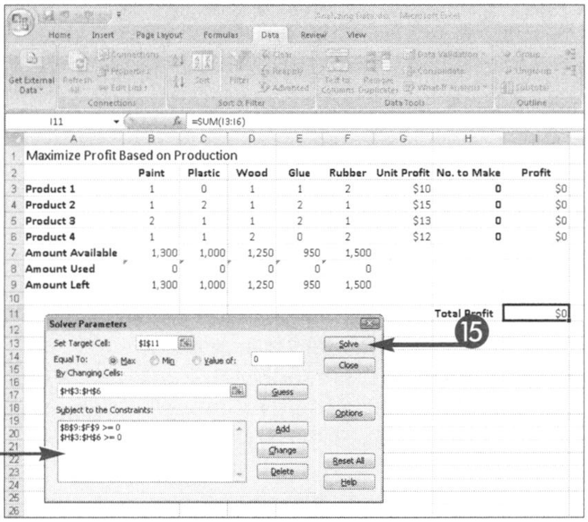

The Solver Results dialog box appears.

- Solver displays the solution.

⓰ Click Keep Solver Solution to retain the Solver solution, or click Restore Original Values to restore the original values (◎ changes to ◉).

⓱ Click OK.

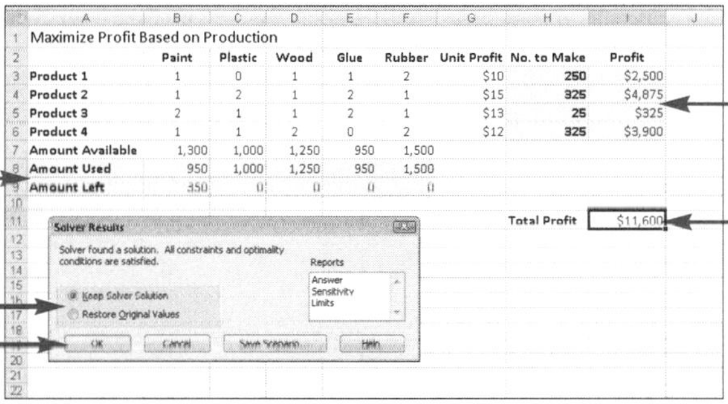

PART V

MASTER IT

Is there a way to pause the calculation before it is completed?

▼ If your calculation is complicated enough that you have the time to stop it before it finishes, press the Esc key. Excel displays the Show Trial Solution dialog box, which informs you that the process has been paused. To continue solving, click Continue. Otherwise, click Stop.

Can I undo the results if I accept the Solver solution?

▼ No, you cannot. If you want to be able to switch between your original values and the Solver solution, click Save Scenario in the Solver Results dialog box. Excel displays the Save Scenario dialog box, in which you type a name for the scenario and click OK. Then, in the Solver Results dialog box, click Restore Original Values (◎ changes to ◉). To use the scenario, see the section, "Display a Scenario."

What happens if I click the Guess button in the Solver Parameters dialog box?

▼ Excel attempts to guess at the cell addresses of the changing cells. Sometimes, Excel guesses correctly, but other times, Excel guesses incorrectly. Clicking Guess cannot cause problems unless you do not double-check the range that Excel suggests. As a result, if you choose to let Excel guess, you must ensure that you review Excel's suggestion.

Create a Solver Report

Using the Solver add-in, you can review the results on-screen or you can create up to three reports that provide you with information used to produce the answer that Solver provides.

The Answer Report provides original value and final value information for the target and adjustable cells and formulas for the constraint cells in the model. Using this report, you can quickly identify the constraints Solver satisfied — these are *binding* constraints — and the constraints that have slack.

The Sensitivity Report provides information that helps describe how sensitive the model is to small changes in the values. The information shown on this report depends on whether you solve a linear or non-linear problem; this example shows the results of a non-linear problem.

The Limits Report shows lower and upper limits for each variable. To calculate these limits, Solver re-runs the model, both maximizing and minimizing each changing cell in turn without changing any other variable. The lower limit for each variable is the smallest value that the variable can take while satisfying the constraints and holding all of the other variables constant. The upper limit for each variable is the largest value the variable can take under these circumstances.

Create a Solver Report

1. Display the Solver Results dialog box.

Note: *To display this dialog box, complete Steps 1 to 15 in the subsection, "Maximize Profit," of the section, "Use Solver to Maximize Profit."*

2. Click each report you want to produce.

   Excel highlights each report you click.

3. Click OK.

   Excel creates a worksheet for each report you selected in Step 2.

4. Click the worksheet tab named Answer Report 1 to view the report.

5. Review the report results.

6. Click the worksheet tab named Sensitivity Report 1.

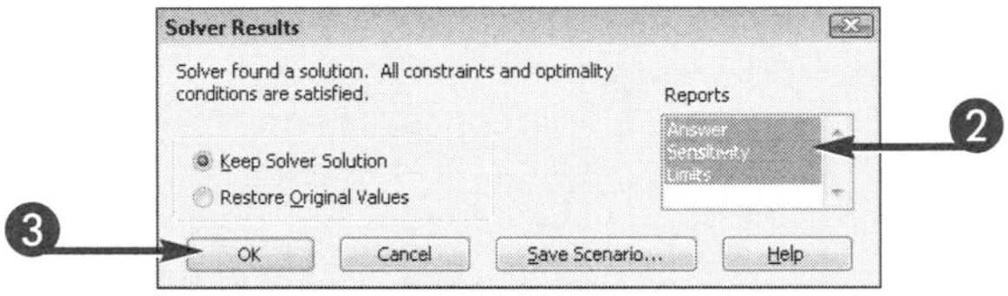

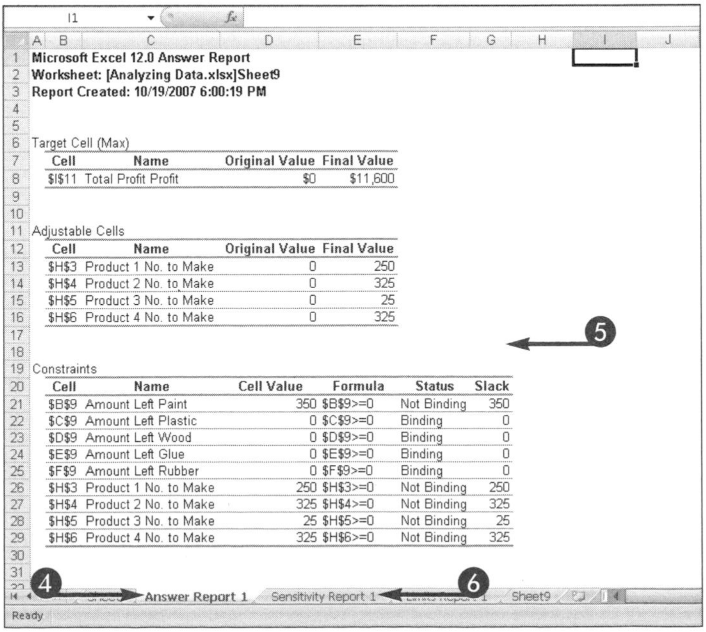

Excel displays the report.

7 Review the report results.

8 Click the worksheet tab named Limits Report 1.

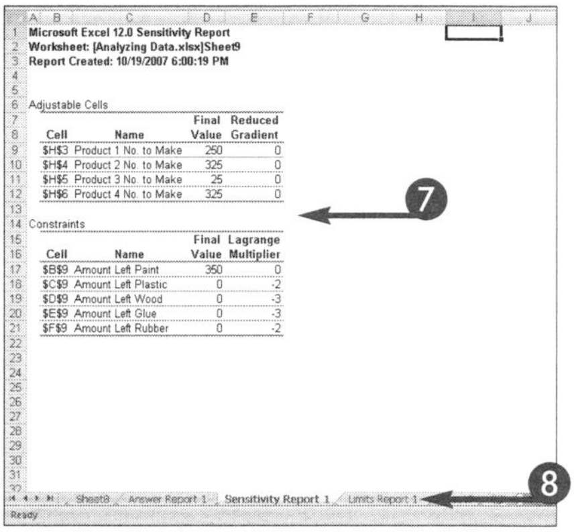

Excel displays the report.

9 Review the report results.

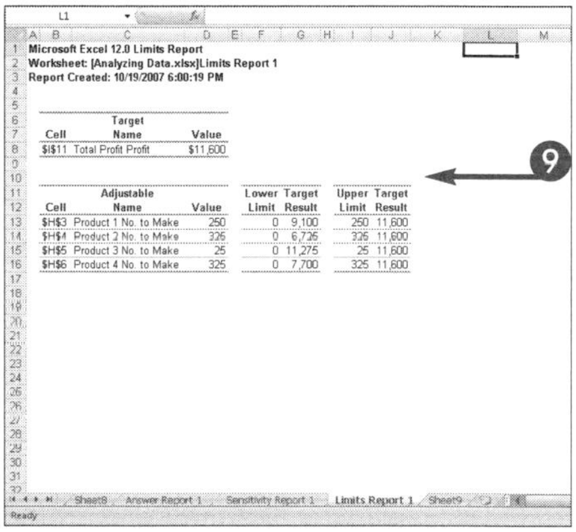

PART V

MASTER IT

Can I restore the original values before I click OK in Step 3?

▼ Yes, you can. Excel creates the reports based on the results Solver achieves, whether you save the results or restore the original values. And, the reports are not interactive, so, the values that appear on the worksheet where you ran Solver do not affect the results that display in each worksheet report.

What does slack represent on the Answer Report?

▼ Slack is the difference between the final value in the model and the lower or upper bound imposed by a particular constraint. When a constraint is binding, it always has a slack of zero except when the right-hand side of a constraint is defined as a function of the decision variables.

What does the Lagrange Multiplier on the Sensitivity Report mean?

▼ Lagrange Multipliers apply only to constraints and are not zero for binding constraints — that is, when the constraint is equal to the boundary you set. In this example, reducing the Lagrange Multiplier for plastic, wood, glue, and rubber would result in leftover raw materials. Reduced Gradient values function in a similar way for changing cells.

Save Solver Models

Although you can create scenarios to save various versions of a Solver model, you can also save the parameters you establish when solving a problem in a range you select in the worksheet. When you save a model's parameters, Excel stores the settings for the problem in your worksheet. You can click each cell to see the formulas that Excel used to solve the problem.

Saving a model's parameters has the added advantage of enabling you to easily recreate the model; you can use a Solver command to load the settings and redisplay the model's result.

When you save a Solver model, Excel suggests a range in the worksheet large enough to hold the model's parameters. The first cell in the suggested range is the cell you select when you start the process to save the model. When you designate a range where Excel can place the model's parameters, make sure that you select a location in the worksheet that contains enough empty cells to store the model's settings, because Excel overwrites any information that exists in the range you select.

Save Solver Models

1. Create and solve a model.
2. Click a blank cell in the worksheet that represents the upper-left corner of the range where you want to store the model parameters.
3. Click the Data tab.
4. Click Solver.

   The Solver Parameters dialog box appears.
5. Click Options.

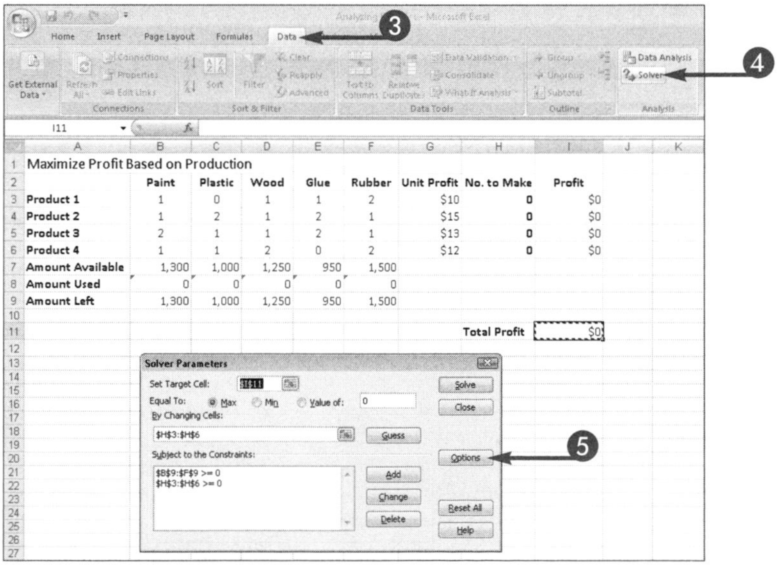

The Solver Options dialog box appears.

6. Click Save Model.

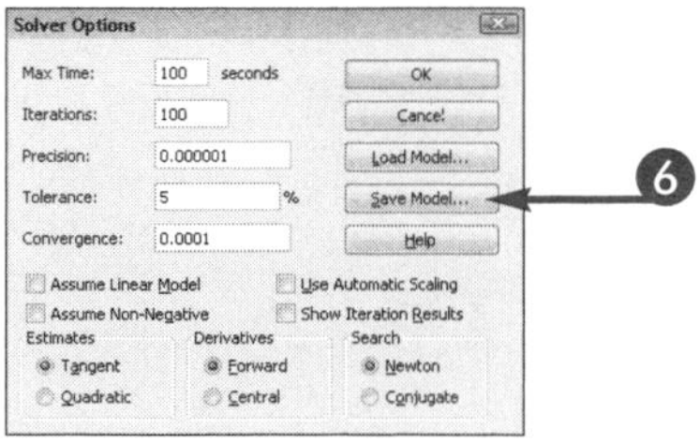

The Save Model dialog box appears.

- Excel selects a range of cells, beginning with the one you selected in Step 2, to hold the model parameters.

7 Make sure the selected range is empty.

8 Click OK.

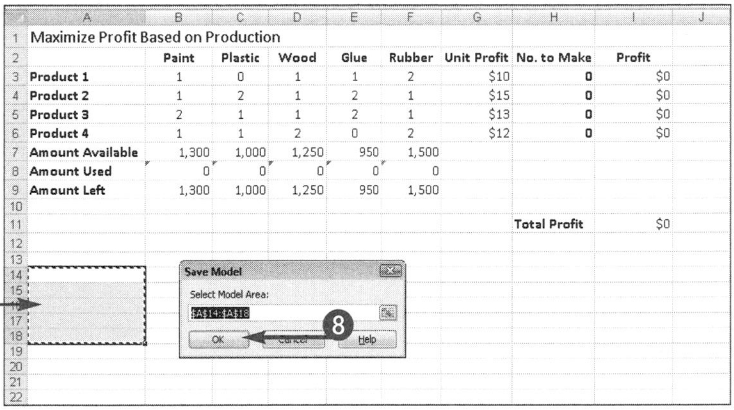
Maximize Profit Based on Production
Paint Plastic Wood Glue Rubber Unit Profit No. to Make Profit
Product 1 1 0 1 1 2 $10 0 $0
Product 2 1 2 1 2 1 $15 0 $0
Product 3 2 1 1 2 1 $13 0 $0
Product 4 1 1 2 0 2 $12 0 $0
Amount Available 1,300 1,000 1,250 950 1,500
Amount Used 0 0 0 0 0
Amount Left 1,300 1,000 1,250 950 1,500
Total Profit $0
Save Model
Select Model Area:
$A$14:$A$18
OK
Cancel
Help
8

Excel redisplays the Solver Options dialog box.

9 Click OK.

Excel redisplays the Solver Parameters dialog box.

10 Click Close.

- The model parameters appear on the worksheet.
- If you click a cell containing a parameter, you can see the formula in the Formula Bar.

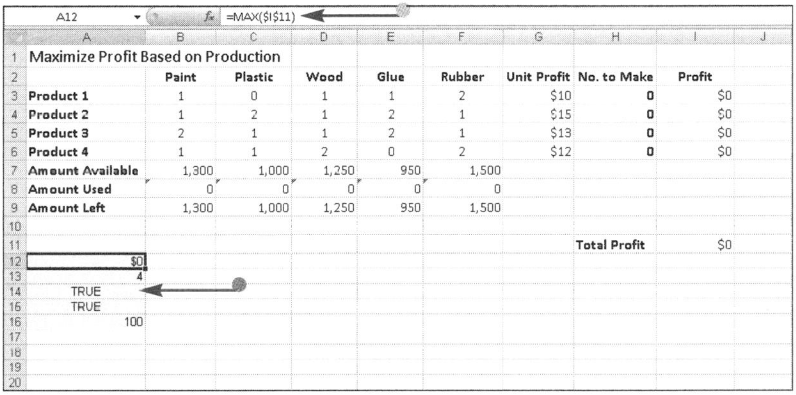
A12
=MAX($I$11)
Maximize Profit Based on Production
Paint Plastic Wood Glue Rubber Unit Profit No. to Make Profit
Product 1 1 0 1 1 2 $10 0 $0
Product 2 1 2 1 2 1 $15 0 $0
Product 3 2 1 1 2 1 $13 0 $0
Product 4 1 1 2 0 2 $12 0 $0
Amount Available 1,300 1,000 1,250 950 1,500
Amount Used 0 0 0 0 0
Amount Left 1,300 1,000 1,250 950 1,500
Total Profit $0
$0
4
TRUE
TRUE
100

PART V

MASTER IT

How do I load the model's parameters?

▼ Repeat Steps 1 to 5. In the Solver Options dialog box, click Load Model. Excel prompts you to select the Model Area, which is the range containing the model parameters. After doing so, click OK. Excel displays a message asking if it is okay to reset previous Solver cells; click OK. The Solver Options dialog box reappears; click OK to redisplay the Solver Parameters dialog box, where you see the parameters for the model you selected. Click Solve to solve the problem using those parameters. If you save multiple sets of parameters, use a nearby cell to label each set so that you can identify variations of the model.

What does the Max Time field in the Solver Options dialog box mean?

▼ Use this field to identify the maximum number of seconds you want Solver to spend trying to solve a problem. If Solver does not find a solution in the time allotted, you can increase this value to give Solver more time.

What does the Iterations setting do?

▼ This setting identifies the maximum number of trial solutions that you want Solver to consider. You can also click Show Iteration Results (☐ changes to ☑) to have Solver pause and display the results after each iteration.

Use Solver to Minimize Costs

You can use Solver to minimize a value. Suppose, for example, that you are in charge of the advertising budget for your company. You want to minimize your advertising costs while making sure that you reach 2 million people using a combination of television, radio, newspaper, and direct mail advertising. For your ads to be effective, you know that you cannot exceed a maximum number of advertising impressions, and this number varies between the mediums. You also know that advertising has varying costs on each medium and is most expensive on television. You can use Solver to help you decide how to best spend your advertising dollars to reach your target audience without exceeding the maximum number of advertising impressions.

In this example, you need to establish constants for the audience size, cost per impression, and maximum impressions for each medium.

As variables for each medium, you need to establish the dollar amount, the number of impressions, and the number of audience members reached.

The constraints for this problem are: 1) the number of impressions must not exceed the maximum impressions per medium, 2) the number of audience members reached cannot be negative, and 3) the total audience must be equal to or greater than 2 million.

Use Solver to Minimize Costs

1. Enter the values needed to make calculations.
2. Set up the formulas Excel needs to calculate.
   - In this example, formulas appear in Column F and Rows 12 and 13.
3. Click the cell you want to minimize.

Note: *In this example, click F11.*

4. Click the Data tab.
5. Click Solver.

   The Solver Parameters dialog box appears.

   - The cell selected in Step 3 appears here.
6. Click Min (◎ changes to ◉).
7. Click here and select the cells Excel should adjust while solving.
8. Click Add to display the Add Constraint dialog box.

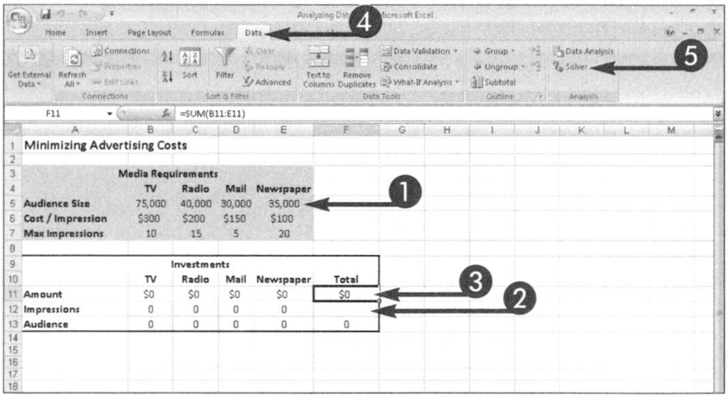

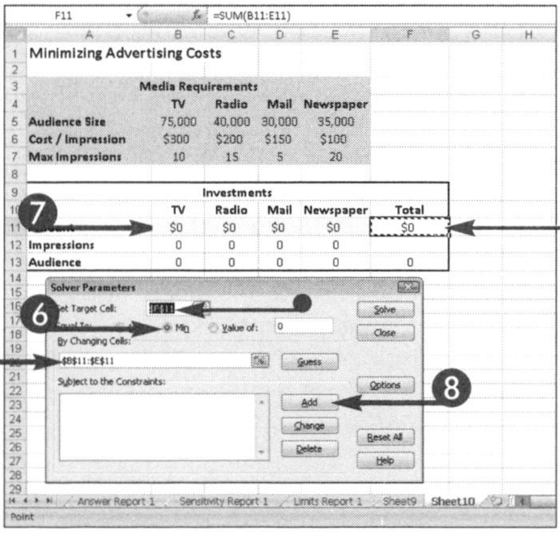

9 Click here and select a range to constrain.

10 Click ▾ to select an operator.

11 Click in the Constraints box and type the comparison value or select it in the worksheet.

12 Click Add and repeat Steps 9 to 11 for each constraint.

13 Click OK to redisplay the Solver Parameters dialog box.

14 Click Solve.

The Solver Results dialog box appears.

- Solver displays the solution.

15 Click Keep Solver Solution to retain the Solver solution or click Restore Original Values to restore the original values (◎ changes to ◉).

16 Click OK.

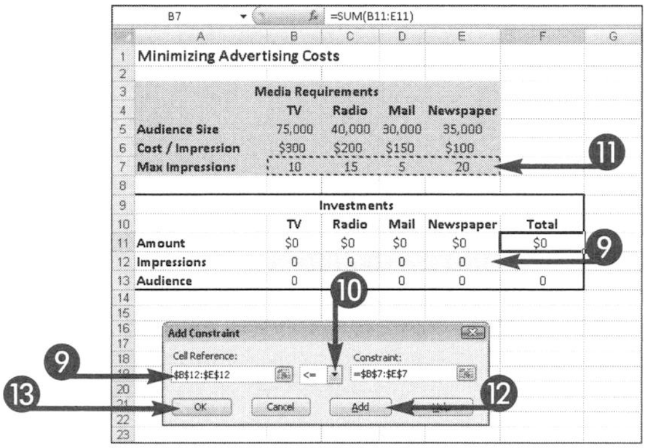

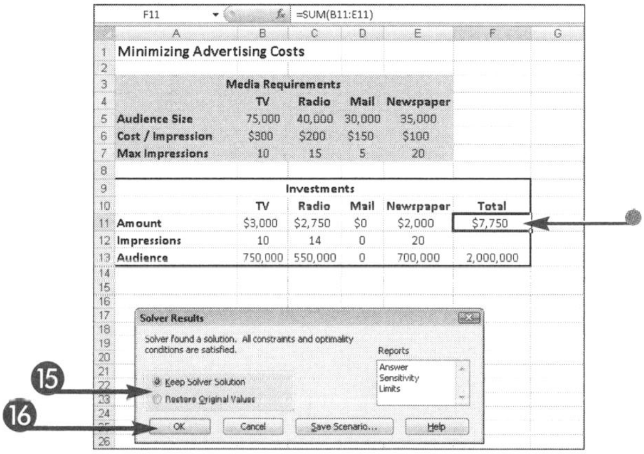

MASTER IT

How does Solver arrive at a solution?

▼ The Solver add-in uses a trial-and-error method using linear or non-linear equations or inequalities. Essentially, Solver substitutes values, finding solutions but continuing to try other possibilities in an effort to find the "best" solution within the values you provide, the constraints you impose, and the desired solution — that is, minimizing, maximizing, or achieving a goal.

Does Solver always find the best solution?

▼ The term "best" is relative. Solver finds the best solution given the starting values, the variables, and the constraints that you define. However, the solution Solver offers may not be the best solution for you. You may want to run Solver several times, adjusting the starting values you provide, to look at other possible solutions.

Is there any reason for me to change the default options Solver uses?

▼ In most cases, the default options work just fine and there is no need for you to change them. On occasion, though, you may want to change some of the options. For example, you may want to increase the number of iterations if Solver does not find a solution the first time you try solving the problem. Increasing iterations allows Solver to try more possible combinations.

Calculate Anova

You can calculate single-factor Anova, two-factor Anova with replication, and two-factor Anova without replication using tools available in the Analysis ToolPak add-in that comes with Excel. To perform any of these calculations, you need to install the Analysis ToolPak add-in; see "Enable Excel Add-Ins" in Chapter 30 for more details.

Anova is the 'analysis of variance' tool that performs a statistical test to determine whether two or more statistical samples were drawn from the same population. If you are comparing only two samples, you can use the TTEST function, but, if you are comparing two or more samples, you can use the Anova tools in the Analysis ToolPak. This section assumes that you understand the type of statistical analysis the tool calculates.

This section provides an example of calculating single-factor Anova for three samples of test scores that were collected to compare three methods of studying. In this example, the independent variable, also called the *factor*, is the study method. Each occurrence of the independent variable is called a *level*, and this example has three levels — three different study methods. In this example, to evaluate the teaching methods, you tested thirty students — ten using each study method.

Calculate Anova

1. Set up the data in a worksheet.
2. Click the Data tab.
3. Click Data Analysis.

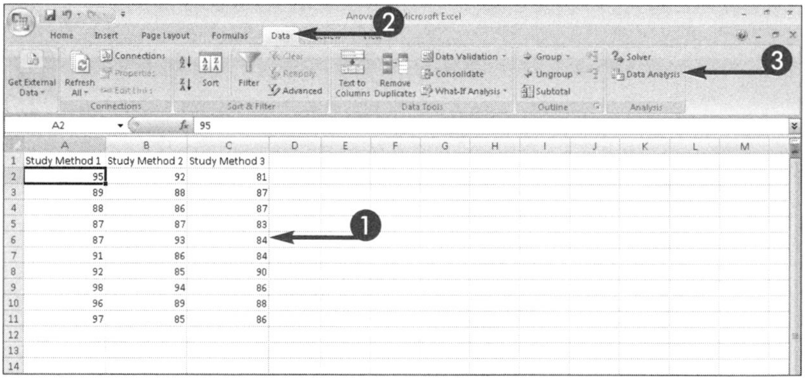

The Data Analysis dialog box appears.

4. Click Anova: Single Factor.
5. Click OK.

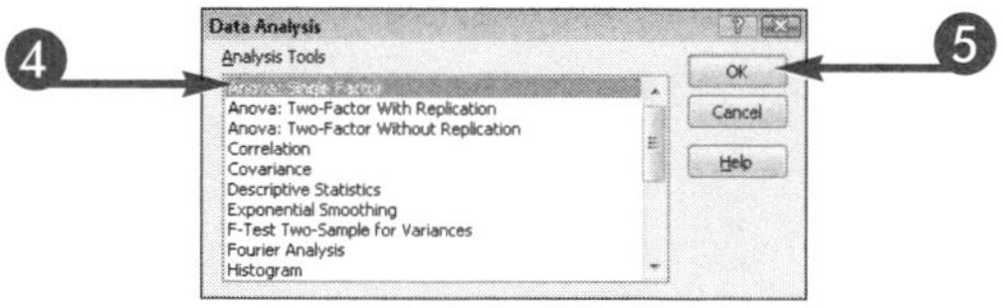

The Anova: Single Factor dialog box appears.

6. Click here and select the range containing the data you selected.
7. Click the "Labels in first row" option if the range you selected in Step 6 contains labels in the first row (☐ changes to ☑).
   - You can click here to change the Alpha value.
8. Click here to select an output location.
9. Click OK.
   - The results of the Anova Single Factor analysis tool appear.

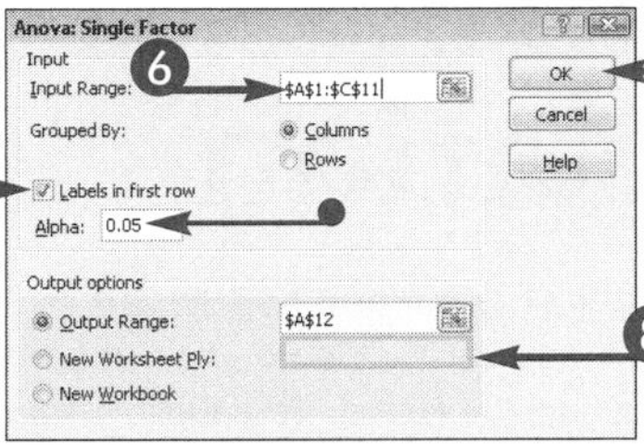

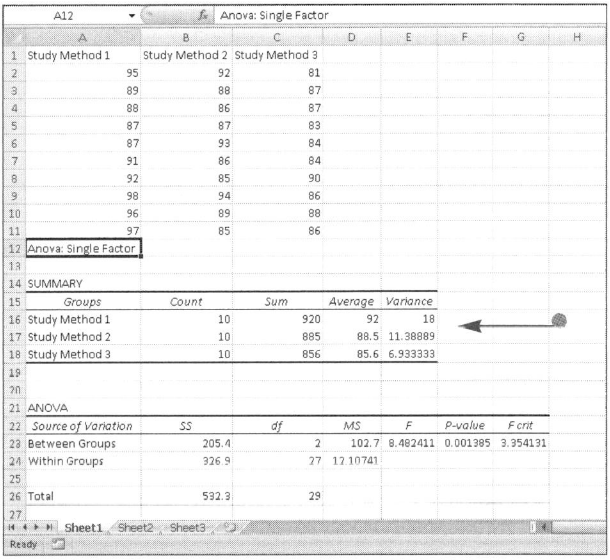

	A	B	C	D	E	F	G
1	Study Method 1	Study Method 2	Study Method 3				
2	95	92	81				
3	89	88	87				
4	88	86	87				
5	87	87	83				
6	87	93	84				
7	91	86	84				
8	92	85	90				
9	98	94	86				
10	96	89	88				
11	97	85	86				
12	Anova: Single Factor						
13							
14	SUMMARY						
15	*Groups*	*Count*	*Sum*	*Average*	*Variance*		
16	Study Method 1	10	920	92	18		
17	Study Method 2	10	885	88.5	11.38889		
18	Study Method 3	10	856	85.6	6.933333		
19							
20							
21	ANOVA						
22	*Source of Variation*	*SS*	*df*	*MS*	*F*	*P-value*	*F crit*
23	Between Groups	205.4	2	102.7	8.482411	0.001385	3.354131
24	Within Groups	326.9	27	12.10741			
25							
26	Total	532.3	29				
27							

MASTER IT

When would I use the Anova: Two-Factor With Replication tool?

▼ You would use this tool when you have data with two independent factors and you have more than one level of data for each independent factor. Suppose, for example, that you want to evaluate comprehension when material is presented with humor or without humor. You also want to measure comprehension when the material is written or spoken. You would use this tool to analyze the variance considering all information.

When would I use the Anova: Two-Factor Without Replication tool?

▼ You would use this tool to analyze data with two independent factors and only one level of data for each independent factor. For example, you may grow three plants using three different fertilizers and watering schedules. You assign one fertilizer/watering schedule to each plant. In this case, your tests do not overlap — or *replicate* — variables, and so you would use the Anova: Two-Factor Without Replication tool.

What does the New Worksheet Ply Output option do?

▼ When you select this option, the output for the Anova Single Factor analysis appears on a new worksheet in the same workbook where you placed the input data.

What does the Alpha value represent?

▼ The Alpha value represents your statistical confidence level for the test. A value of .05 is the default and usually works well, unless you have other information that indicates you should change the Alpha value.

Measure Correlation

You can use the Correlation tool in the Analysis ToolPak to measure the degree to which two sets of data vary together. To perform this calculation, you need to install the Analysis ToolPak add-in; see "Enable Excel Add-Ins" in Chapter 30 for more details.

Correlation is the analysis tool that performs a statistical test to determine whether two statistical samples vary together. The correlation value you calculate using the Correlation tool is called the *correlation coefficient* and is a value between -1 and 1; the higher the correlation coefficient, the more likely it is that the two data sets vary together. For example, if rainfall occurs more often in higher dew point conditions, the rainfall data is said to have a positive correlation to the dew point data, and the correlation coefficient will be a positive number. This section assumes that you understand the type of statistical analysis the tool calculates.

When you use the Correlation tool to calculate the correlation of two data sets, you identify an input range, which contains the values you want to analyze, and an output range, where Excel should display the results of the analysis. You also specify whether the first row of the input range contains labels.

Measure Correlation

1. Set up the data in a worksheet.
2. Click the Data tab.
3. Click Data Analysis.

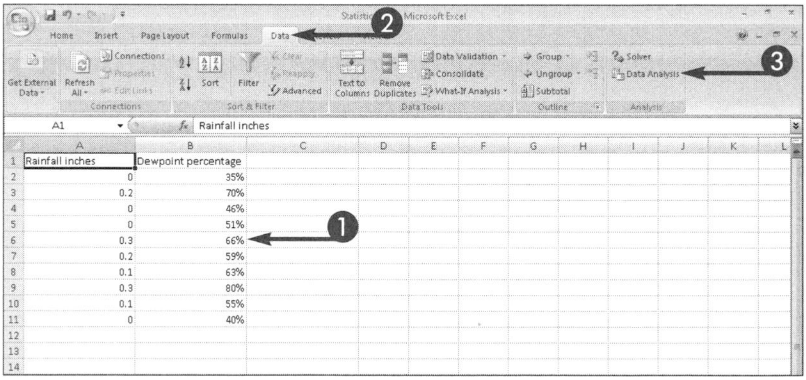

The Data Analysis dialog box appears.

4. Click Correlation.
5. Click OK.

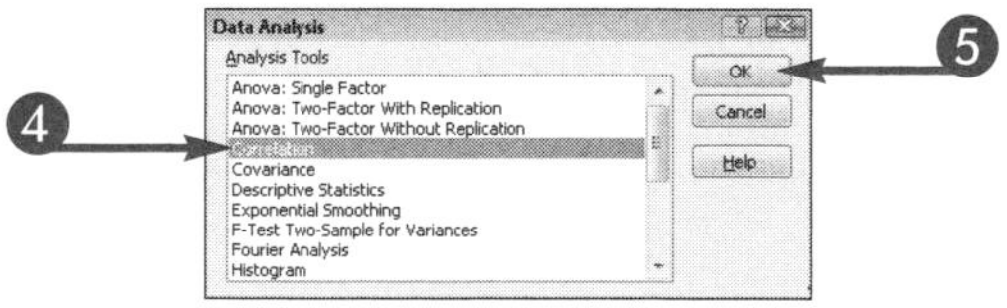

The Correlation dialog box appears.

6 Click here and select the range containing the data you selected.

7 Click the "Labels in first row" option if the range you selected in Step 6 contains labels in the first row (☐ changes to ☑).

8 Click here to select an output location (◎ changes to ◉).

9 Click OK.

- The results of the Correlation analysis tool appear.

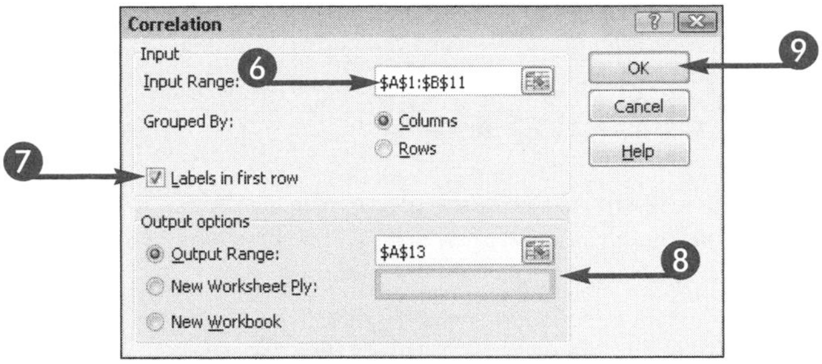

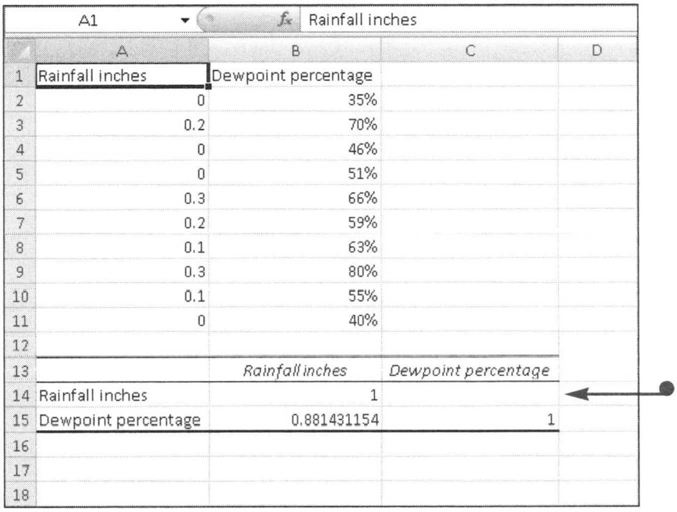
A1
Rainfall inches
A
B
C
D
Rainfall inches
Dewpoint percentage
0 | 35%
0.2 | 70%
0 | 46%
0 | 51%
0.3 | 66%
0.2 | 59%
0.1 | 63%
0.3 | 80%
0.1 | 55%
0 | 40%
Rainfall inches
Dewpoint percentage
Rainfall inches | 1
Dewpoint percentage | 0.881431154 | 1

MASTER IT

How do I know which Grouped By option to select?

▼ You use the Grouped By option to identify whether your data points appear in rows or in columns. If you have a label at the top of the data, your information appears in columns. If you have a label at the left edge of the data, your information appears in rows.

In your example, does a higher dew point mean more rain?

▼ No. It means that rainfall occurs more often when the dew point is higher. It does not necessarily mean that a higher dew point causes rain. It is important to understand that the data does not indicate that one factor causes the other. Correlation examines the relationship between data sets but does not address cause and effect.

What does a 0 correlation coefficient mean?

▼ It means that the two data sets do not have any relationship. If the correlation coefficient is a positive number, higher values in one data set are associated with higher values in the other data set. If the correlation coefficient is negative, then higher values in one data set are associated with lower values in the other data set. The closer the correlation coefficient is to 1 or -1, the stronger the correlation between the data sets.

Measure Covariance

You can use the Covariance tool in the Analysis ToolPak to measure the degree to which two sets of data vary together. To perform this calculation, you need to install the Analysis ToolPak add-in; see "Enable Excel Add-Ins" in Chapter 30 for more details.

Covariance, like correlation, performs a statistical test to determine whether two statistical samples vary together. You can use both tools under the same conditions. When considering several pairs of data points, covariance is the average of the product of the deviations of each pair of data points from their respective means. The Covariance tool in the Analysis ToolPak computes the Excel COVAR function for each pair of variables. While the correlation coefficient is a value between -1 and 1, the covariance is not scaled to fit within a range of values. This section assumes that you understand the type of statistical analysis the tool calculates.

When you use the Covariance tool to calculate the covariance of two data sets, you identify an input range, which contains the values you want to analyze, and an output range, where Excel should display the results of the analysis. You also specify whether the first row of the input range contains labels.

Measure Covariance

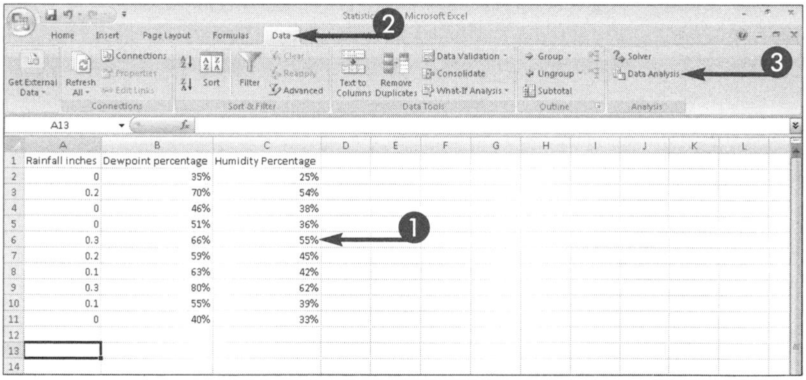

1. Set up the data in a worksheet.
2. Click the Data tab.
3. Click Data Analysis.

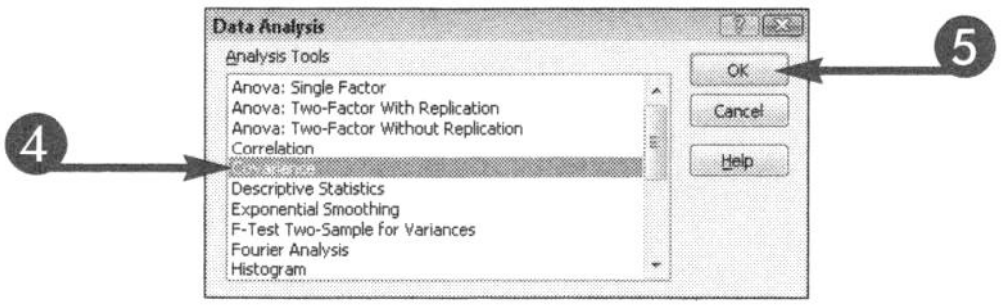

The Data Analysis dialog box appears.

4. Click Covariance.
5. Click OK.

The Covariance dialog box appears.

6 Click here and select the range containing the data you selected.

7 Click the "Labels in first row" option if the range you selected in Step 6 contains labels in the first row (☐ changes to ☑).

8 Click here to select an output location (○ changes to ◉).

9 Click OK.

The results of the Covariance analysis tool appear.

- The Covariance analysis tool calculates the VARP function for each value on the diagonal of the covariance matrix.
- The formula appears here.

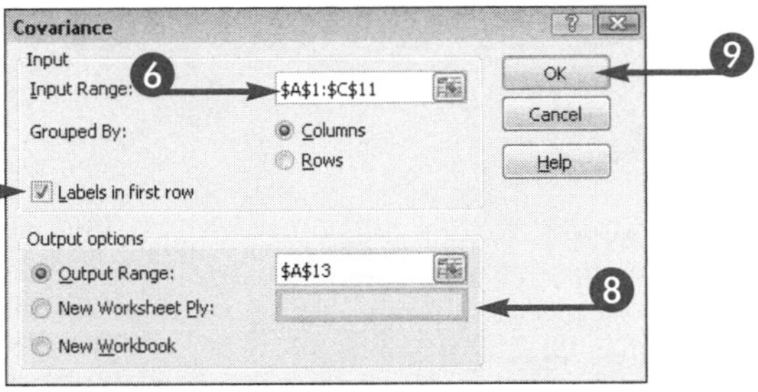

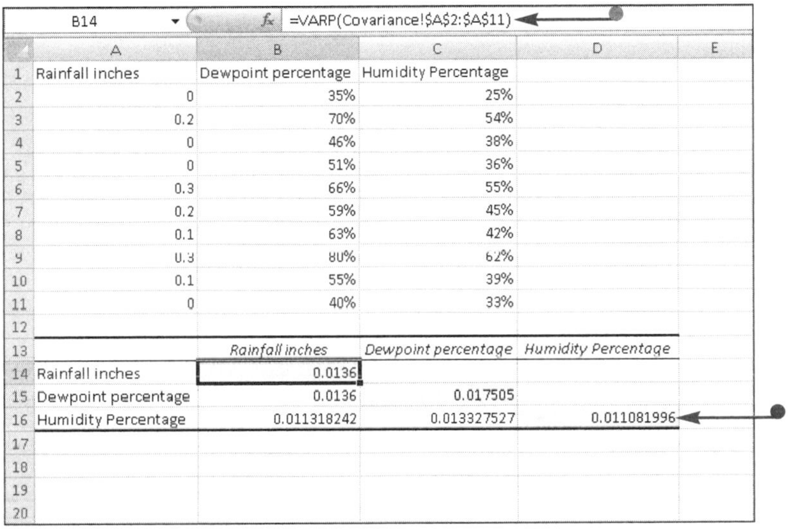

B14
=VARP(Covariance!$A$2:$A$11)
A B C D E
1 Rainfall inches | Dewpoint percentage | Humidity Percentage
2 0 | 35% | 25%
3 0.2 | 70% | 54%
4 0 | 46% | 38%
5 0 | 51% | 36%
6 0.3 | 66% | 55%
7 0.2 | 59% | 45%
8 0.1 | 63% | 42%
9 0.3 | 80% | 62%
10 0.1 | 55% | 39%
11 0 | 40% | 33%
13 Rainfall inches | Dewpoint percentage | Humidity Percentage
14 Rainfall inches | 0.0136
15 Dewpoint percentage | 0.0136 | 0.017505
16 Humidity Percentage | 0.011318242 | 0.013327527 | 0.011081996

MASTER IT

Do I care that the covariance is unscaled?

▼ Because the covariance is unscaled, the value of the covariance changes if you change the unit of measurement for sample values. For example, if one of your variables is time and your sample units are in minutes, then converting the sample units to hours affects the covariance value. The same conversion does not affect the correlation coefficient, which remains a value between 1 and -1.

When should I use the COVAR function instead of using the Covariance tool in the Analysis ToolPak?

▼ You can use the COVAR function when you are calculating covariance for only two variables. You can use the Covariance tool in the Analysis ToolPak any time you want to calculate covariance, but you will find it more useful when you are calculating covariance for more than two variables.

Can you explain the output matrix?

▼ Each cell in the matrix presents the covariance of the variable shown in the row and the variable shown in the column. The main diagonal in the matrix — B14, C15, and D16 in this example — shows the variance of each variable, which is equivalent to the covariance of a variable with itself. In this case, the variance is the result you get when you use the VARP function, which appears in each cell in the diagonal.

Produce Descriptive Statistics

You can use the Descriptive Statistics tool in the Analysis ToolPak to produce some standard statistics about sample data. To perform this calculation, you need to install the Analysis ToolPak add-in; see "Enable Excel Add-Ins" in Chapter 30 for more details.

You can select the statistics to display; the summary statistics include the mean, standard error, median, mode, standard deviation, sample variance, kurtosis, skewness, range, minimum, maximum, sum, and count for the ranges you select. None of the values are calculated using Excel functions, and so, if your data changes, you need to rerun the tool.

You can also display the *nth*-largest and *nth*-smallest values. For example, you can display the third-largest and third-smallest values in the ranges. You can also have the Descriptive Statistics tool display the confidence level for the samples. This section assumes that you understand the type of statistical analysis the tool calculates.

When you use this tool, you identify an input range, which contains the values you want to analyze, and an output range, where Excel should display the results of the analysis. You also specify whether the first row of the input range contains labels.

Produce Descriptive Statistics

1. Set up the data in a worksheet.
2. Click the Data tab.
3. Click Data Analysis.

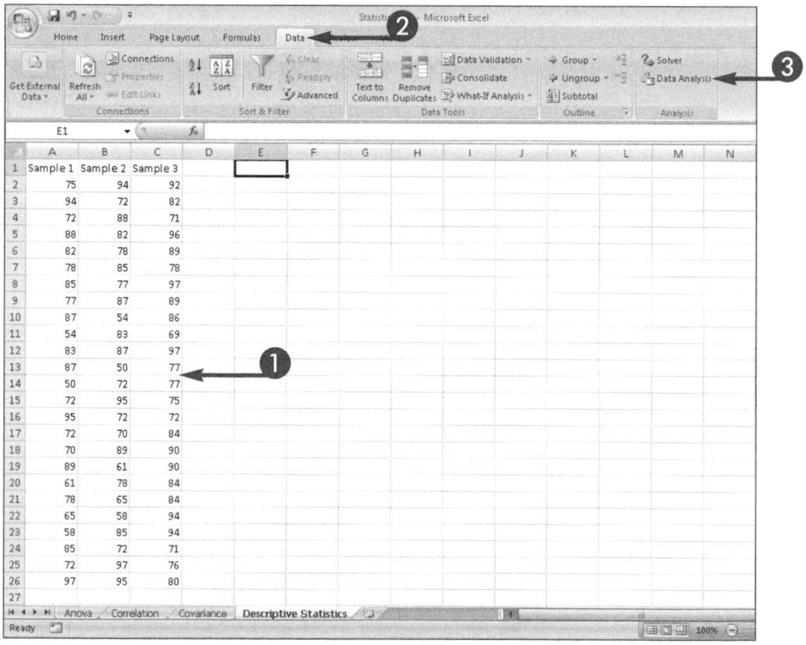

The Data Analysis dialog box appears.

4. Click Descriptive Statistics.
5. Click OK.

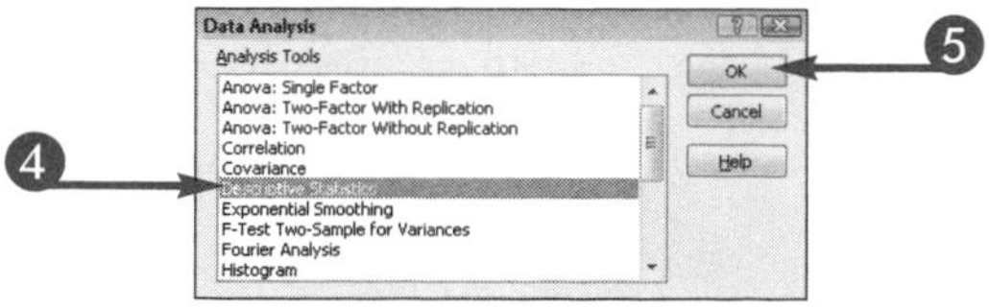

The Descriptive Statistics dialog box appears.

6. Click here and select the range containing the data you selected.
7. Click the "Labels in first row" option if the range you selected in Step 6 contains labels in the first row (☐ changes to ☑).
8. Click here to select an output location (○ changes to ◉).
9. Click here to select the statistics you want to see (☐ changes to ☑).
10. Click OK.

- The results of the Descriptive Statistics analysis tool appear, showing the same statistics for each range of data.

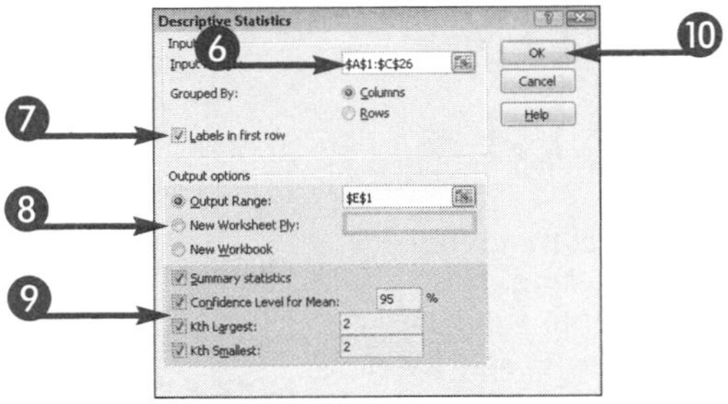

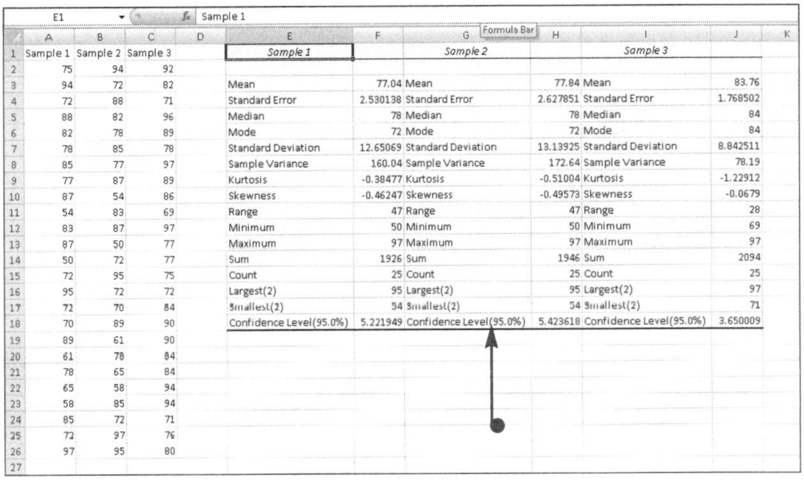

	A	B	C	D	E	F	G	H	I	J
1	Sample 1	Sample 2	Sample 3		*Sample 1*		*Sample 2*		*Sample 3*	
2	75	94	92							
3	94	72	82		Mean	77.04	Mean	77.84	Mean	83.76
4	72	88	71		Standard Error	2.530138	Standard Error	2.627851	Standard Error	1.768502
5	88	82	96		Median	78	Median	78	Median	84
6	82	78	89		Mode	72	Mode	72	Mode	84
7	78	85	78		Standard Deviation	12.65069	Standard Deviation	13.13925	Standard Deviation	8.842511
8	85	77	97		Sample Variance	160.04	Sample Variance	172.64	Sample Variance	78.19
9	77	87	89		Kurtosis	-0.38477	Kurtosis	-0.51004	Kurtosis	-1.22912
10	87	54	86		Skewness	-0.46247	Skewness	-0.49573	Skewness	-0.0679
11	54	83	69		Range	47	Range	47	Range	28
12	83	87	97		Minimum	50	Minimum	50	Minimum	69
13	87	50	77		Maximum	97	Maximum	97	Maximum	97
14	50	72	77		Sum	1926	Sum	1946	Sum	2094
15	72	95	75		Count	25	Count	25	Count	25
16	95	72	72		Largest(2)	95	Largest(2)	95	Largest(2)	97
17	72	70	84		Smallest(2)	54	Smallest(2)	54	Smallest(2)	71
18	70	89	90		Confidence Level(95.0%)	5.221949	Confidence Level(95.0%)	5.423618	Confidence Level(95.0%)	3.650009
19	89	61	90							
20	61	78	84							
21	78	65	84							
22	65	58	94							
23	58	85	94							
24	85	72	71							
25	72	97	76							
26	97	95	80							
27										

PART V

MASTER IT

What is kurtosis?

▼ Kurtosis is a statistical measurement that is related to mean and variance, two measures that describe your data in relation to the center data point. The *mean* identifies the center of your data and the *variance* tells you how spread out from the center your data points are. Kurtosis shows you whether your data points are distributed with a peak somewhere near the center value.

What is skewness?

▼ Like kurtosis, skewness is also a statistical measurement related to the mean and variance, the two measures that describe the center of your data. Skewness shows you how symmetrical the data points are in relation to the center of the data. Skewness can be positive or negative; when your data points are perfectly symmetrical, skewness is 0.

What is the confidence level?

▼ The confidence level is the probability value associated with a confidence interval. A confidence interval provides the upper and lower boundaries of values within which the mean of a sample might lie. If you set the confidence level to 95 percent, then you are saying that you are 95 percent confident that the confidence interval contains the mean.

Exponentially Smooth Data

You can use the Exponential Smoothing tool to forecast data points using existing data points. To perform this calculation, you need to install the Analysis ToolPak add-in; see "Enable Excel Add-Ins" in Chapter 30 for more details.

Using exponential smoothing is similar to calculating a moving average, but you work with a series of actual values to calculate a moving average. When you use exponential smoothing, you also take into consideration previous predictions. This section assumes that you understand the type of statistical analysis the tool calculates.

When you use the Exponential Smoothing tool, you identify an input range, which contains the values you want to analyze, and an output range, where Excel should display the results of the analysis. The input range can consist of only one row or one column of data. You also specify whether the first row of the input range contains labels, and you can specify a damping factor, also called a smoothing constant. The *damping factor* is a number between 0 and 1 and determines the weight the tool assigns to previous predictions for error corrections. You can also produce output in chart form and a column of standard errors.

Exponentially Smooth Data

1. Set up the data in a worksheet.
2. Click the Data tab.
3. Click Data Analysis.

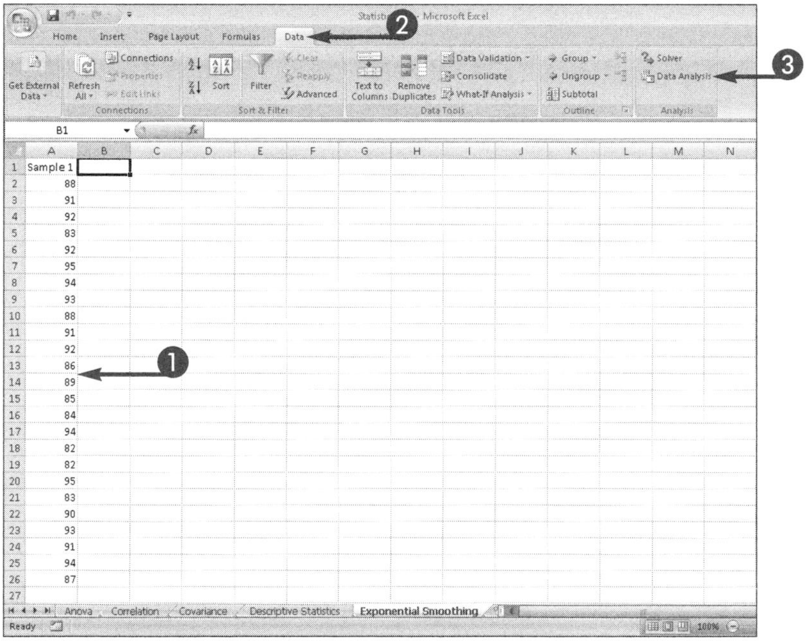

The Data Analysis dialog box appears.

4. Click Exponential Smoothing.
5. Click OK.

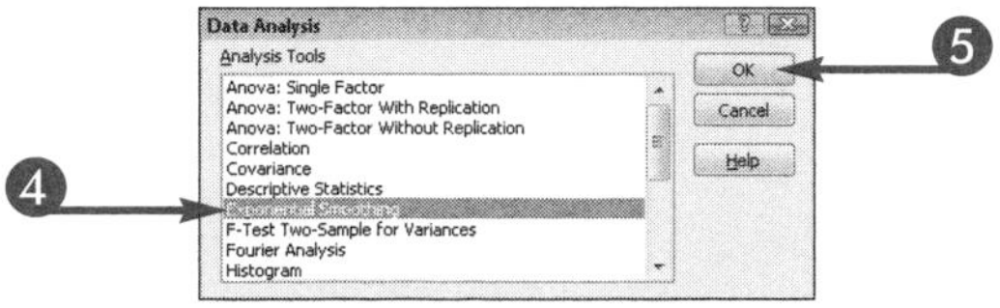

The Exponential Smoothing dialog box appears.

6. Click here and select the range containing the data to analyze.
7. Click here to provide a damping factor.
8. Click the "Labels" option if the range you selected in Step 6 contains labels in the first row (☐ changes to ☑).
9. Click here to select an output range.
10. Click OK.
    - The results of the Exponential Smoothing analysis tool appear.
    - The results in each cell are formulas that calculate predicted values based on prior values.

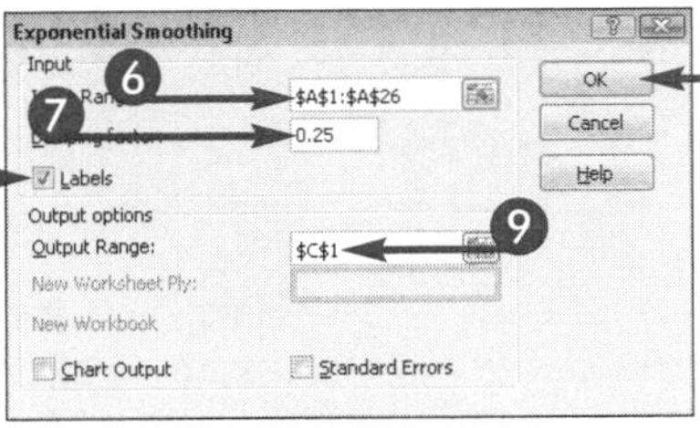

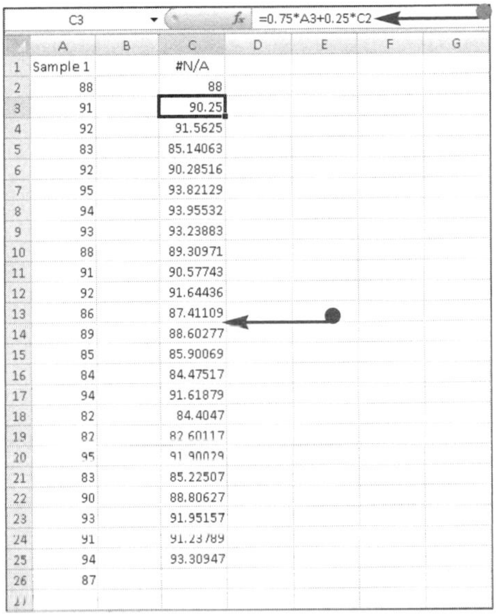

	A	B	C	D	E	F	G
1	Sample 1		#N/A				
2	88		88				
3	91		90.25				
4	92		91.5625				
5	83		85.14063				
6	92		90.28516				
7	95		93.82129				
8	94		93.95532				
9	93		93.23883				
10	88		89.30971				
11	91		90.57743				
12	92		91.64436				
13	86		87.41109				
14	89		88.60277				
15	85		85.90069				
16	84		84.47517				
17	94		91.61879				
18	82		84.4047				
19	82		82.60117				
20	95		91.90029				
21	83		85.22507				
22	90		88.80627				
23	93		91.95157				
24	91		91.23789				
25	94		93.30947				
26	87						
27							

MASTER IT

How do I know what damping factor to use?

▼ The default damping factor is .3. During calculation, the Exponential Smoothing tool applies the damping factor to each value, adjusting the value being calculated by 30 percent for error in the previously calculated value. If you examine the values in the output, you find that each contains a formula that refers to the previous cell and also adjusts the current cell by the damping factor. Reasonable damping factors are .2 to .3.

What kind of chart does the Exponential Smoothing tool produce?

▼ The Exponential Smoothing tool produces an embedded column chart that presents the forecast values shown in the output table. The X axis displays a number that represents each data point — that is, if you have ten data points, the X-axis scale runs from 1 to 10. The Y-axis scale runs from 0 to just over the value of the largest predicted data point.

What does the standard error output look like?

▼ The forecast values are essentially mean values, and when working with means, including the standard error of the mean helps the viewer to understand the spread of values around each mean. The standard error column contains a series of formulas that are a combination of the SQRT function, which calculates square root, and the SUMXMY2 function, which calculates the sum of squares of differences between two arrays.

Perform a Two-Sample "F-Test"

You can use the F-Test Two-Sample for Variances tool to compare the variances of two sample populations. To perform this calculation, you need to install the Analysis ToolPak add-in; see "Enable Excel Add-Ins" in Chapter 30 for more details.

Suppose that you need to purchase a machine to make a part that must meet very precise specifications, with little room for variability. To choose between two machines that produce the part, you obtain samples created from each machine, measure them, and find the variance for each sample. Now you need to compare the variances.

To compare variances, you use the F-test — named for its inventor, Sir Ronald Fisher — to calculate the F-ratio. You can use the F-Test Two-Sample for Variances tool to make the calculations and produce several common statistics. This section assumes that you understand the type of statistical analysis the tool calculates.

When you use the F-Test Two-Sample for Variances tool, you identify two input ranges, which contain the values you want to analyze, and an output range, where Excel should display the results of the analysis. You also specify whether the first row of the input range contains labels, and you can specify a confidence level between 0 and 1.

Perform a Two-Sample "F-Test"

1. Set up the data in a worksheet.
2. Click the Data tab.
3. Click Data Analysis.

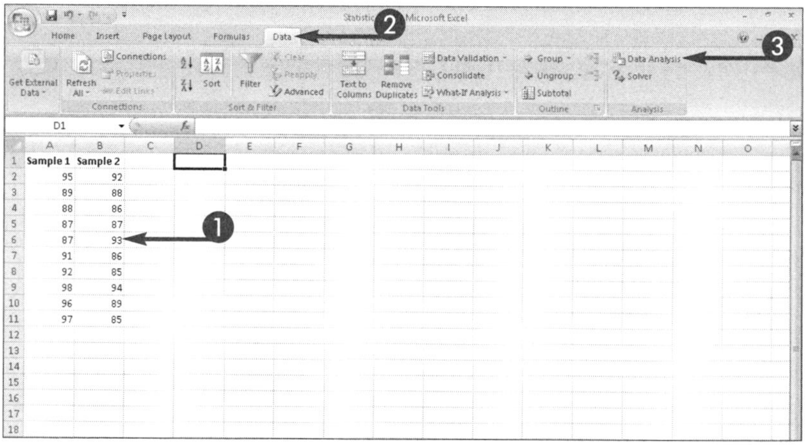

The Data Analysis dialog box appears.

4. Click F-Test Two-Sample for Variances.
5. Click OK.

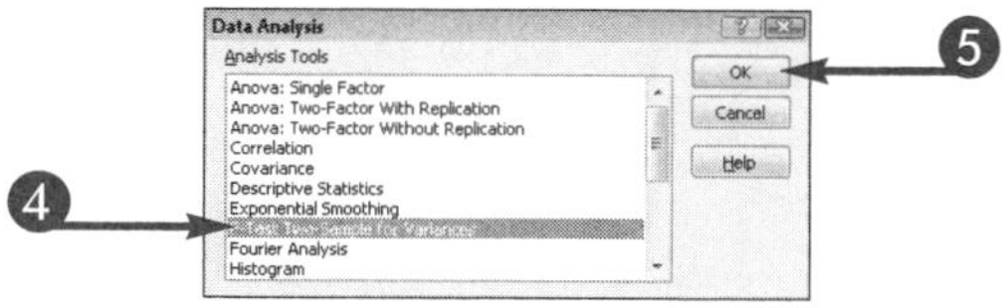

The F-Test Two-Sample for Variances dialog box appears.

6. Use these two fields to select the two ranges containing the data to analyze.
7. Click the "Labels" option if the range you selected in Step 6 contains labels in the first row (☐ changes to ☑).
8. Click here to select an output range (◯ changes to ◉).
9. Click OK.

- The results of the F-Test Two-Sample for Variances analysis tool appear.

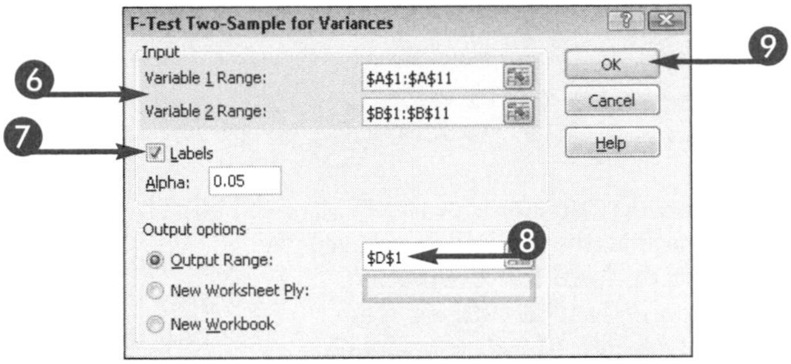

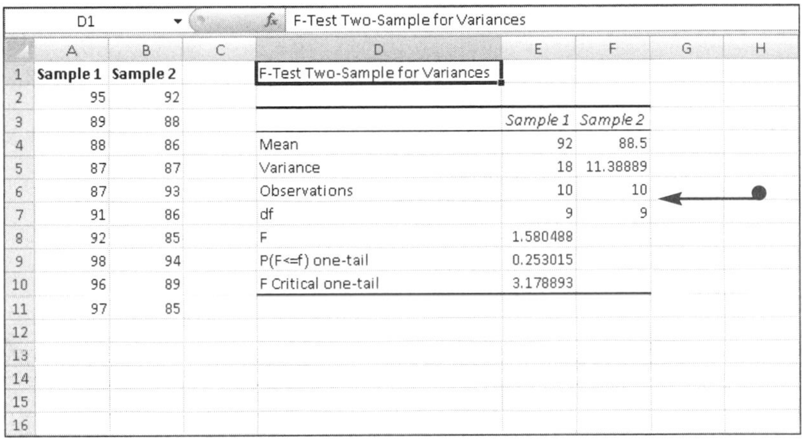
D1
F-Test Two-Sample for Variances
Sample 1 Sample 2
95 92
89 88
88 86
87 87
87 93
91 86
92 85
98 94
96 89
97 85
F-Test Two-Sample for Variances
Sample 1 Sample 2
Mean 92 88.5
Variance 18 11.38889
Observations 10 10
df 9 9
F 1.580488
P(F<=f) one-tail 0.253015
F Critical one-tail 3.178893

PART V

MASTER IT

What does *df* stand for?

▼ The acronym *df* is commonly used in statistics to represent "degrees of freedom." Degrees of freedom are used when calculating variances in small-sized samples to attempt to compensate for the small sample size. The value of df is generally expressed as N – 1, where *N* is your sample size.

How do I interpret F?

▼ When F is close to 1, you can assume that the underlying population variances are equal. You only see one F value because F represents a relationship between the two samples. If F is greater than 1, as in this example, the value of P(F <= f) one-tail shows you the probability of observing a value of the F-statistic greater than the one shown when population variances are equal.

What does F Critical one-tail tell me?

▼ In statistics, when you test a hypothesis, you calculate a sampling distribution curve and you reject a region of that curve that falls outside the accepted distribution. When the area you reject is one-tailed, you are rejecting a portion of the curve on one end of the curve. The F Critical one-tail value gives you the proportion of the area that is rejected.

Calculate a Moving Average

You can use the Moving Average tool to smooth out data points among which you see ups and downs. To perform this calculation, you need to install the Analysis ToolPak add-in; see "Enable Excel Add-Ins" in Chapter 30 for more details.

Investors often collect stock price information over time to try to identify trends within the stock's price. As you might expect, the price information varies over time, and you can use the Moving Average tool to help smooth the data to make trends more apparent. This section assumes that you understand the type of statistical analysis the tool calculates.

When you use the Moving Average tool, you identify an input range, which contains the values you want to analyze, and an output range, where Excel should display the results of the analysis; by default, the output is a series of numbers calculated using the AVERAGE function. In addition to the raw numbers, you can chart the values and display the standard errors for the values. You also specify whether the first row of the input range contains labels, and you can specify an interval, which is the number of values in the range that you want Excel to use when calculating the average.

Calculate a Moving Average

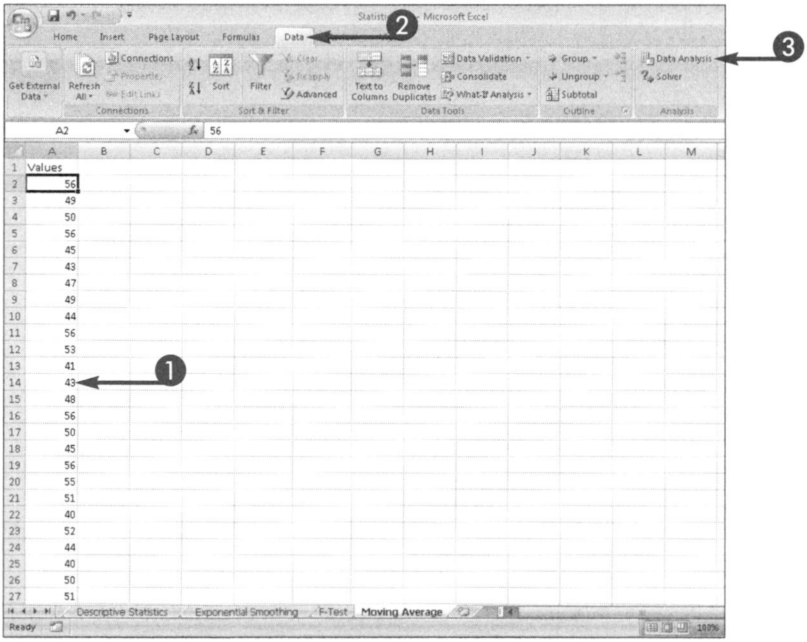

1. Set up the data in a worksheet.
2. Click the Data tab.
3. Click Data Analysis.

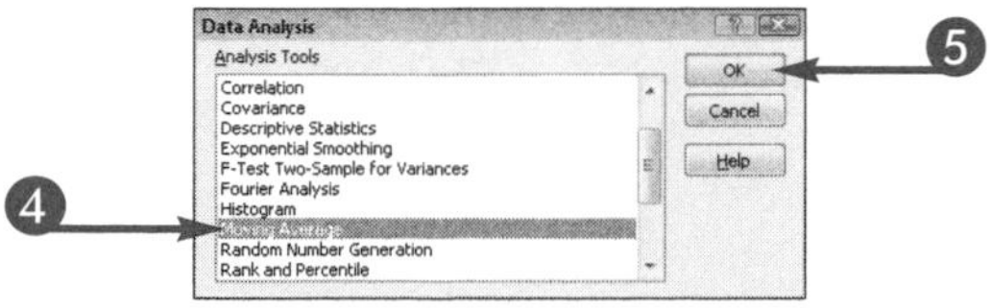

The Data Analysis dialog box appears.

4. Click Moving Average.
5. Click OK.

The Moving Average dialog box appears.

6 Click here to select the range containing the data to analyze.

7 Click the "Labels in first row" option if the range you selected in Step 6 contains labels in the first row (☐ changes to ☑).

8 Click here to select an output range.

9 Click the "Chart Output" option to create a chart (☐ changes to ☑).

10 Click OK.

The results of the Moving Average analysis tool appear.

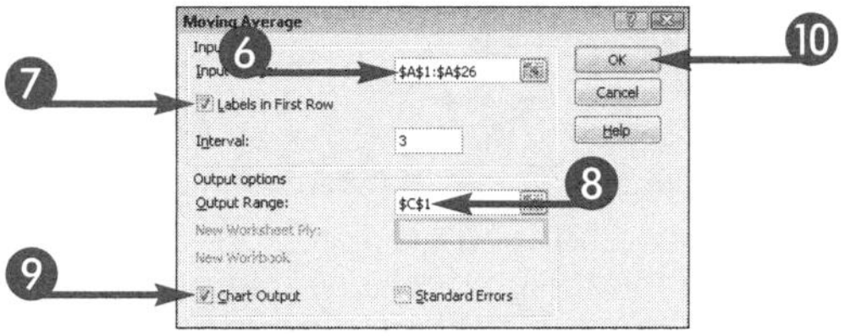

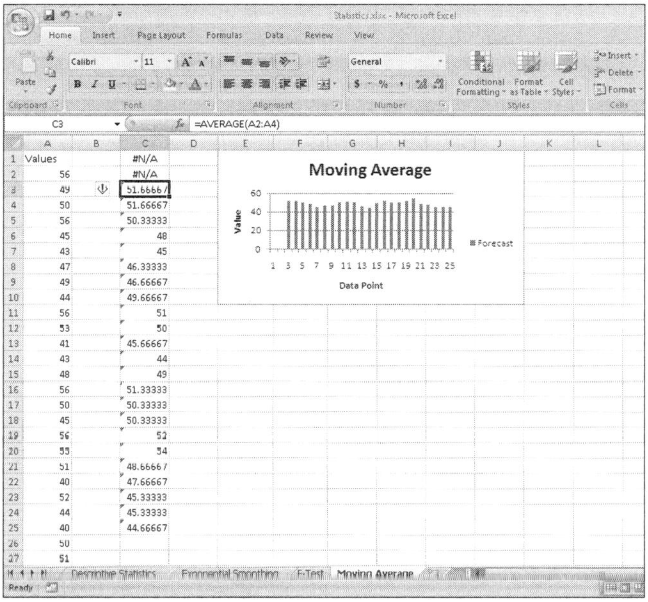

How do I know what interval to use?

▼ The default interval is 3, which tells the Moving Average tool to average three values at a time. If you click an output cell and look at the Formula bar, you see that the formula in the cell uses the AVERAGE function to average the number of cells you specified as the interval. The larger the value you set for the interval, the fewer data points the Moving Average tool generates and, if you create a chart, the fewer the data points on the chart. Also, the resulting output chart, which creates bars for each generated moving average data point, typically shows smoother data when you use a higher interval.

Why does #N/A appear?

▼ You may notice that #N/A appears only at the top of the range of moving average data points that the Moving Average tool calculates. The #N/A message appears when the Moving Average tool does not have enough data points to average. In this example, which uses 3 as the interval, no data points are calculated for the first two values in the list because the Moving Average tool requires three data points to calculate the average. If you set an interval of 10, the Moving Average tool cannot calculate moving average data points for the first nine values in the list.

Generate a Random Number

You can use the Random Number Generation tool to generate a random number in various types of statistical distributions. To perform this calculation, you need to install the Analysis ToolPak add-in; see "Enable Excel Add-Ins" in Chapter 30 for more details.

Do you play the lottery? Are you running out of ideas for numbers to play? Or, are you planning a trip to Las Vegas? You can use the Random Number Generation tool to generate your lottery numbers or simulate throws of the dice to identify which numbers come up most often. This section assumes that you understand the type of statistical analysis the tool calculates.

When you use the Random Number Generation tool, you identify the number of variables, which corresponds to the number of columns of random numbers that you want. You also specify the quantity of random numbers you want. You identify a type of distribution you want the Random Number Generation tool to use and parameters specific to the distribution type. You can also use the Random Seed field to specify a starting value, but usually, you leave this field blank. Finally, you identify an output range, where Excel should display the results of the analysis.

Generate a Random Number

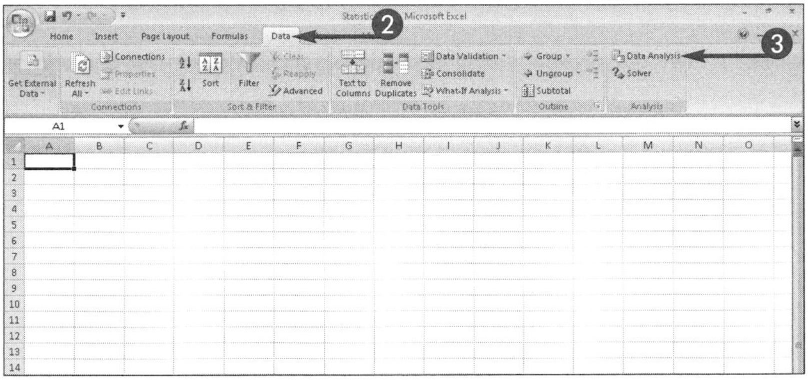

1. Display a blank worksheet or a blank area in a worksheet.
2. Click the Data tab.
3. Click Data Analysis.

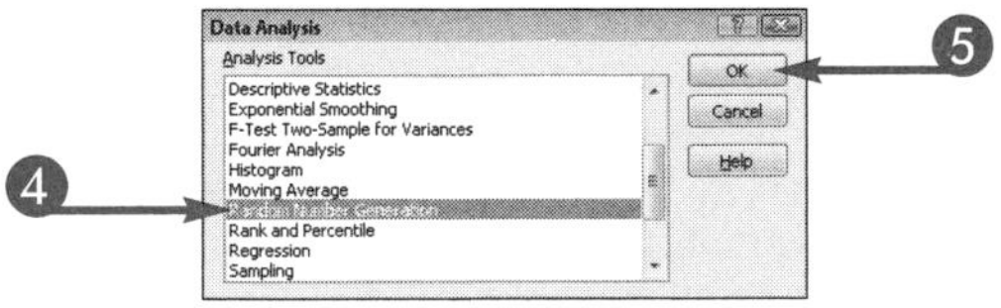

The Data Analysis dialog box appears.

4. Click Random Number Generation.
5. Click OK.

The Random Number Generation dialog box appears.

6 Click here to specify the number of columns of random numbers to generate.

7 Click here to specify the number of random numbers to generate.

8 Click the Distribution ▼ to select a distribution type.

9 Specify required parameters here.

10 Click here to select an output location (◯ changes to ◉).

11 Click OK.

The results of the Random Number Generation analysis tool appear.

Note: *Because these numbers are random, the ones you see in the figure will not match the ones you generate.*

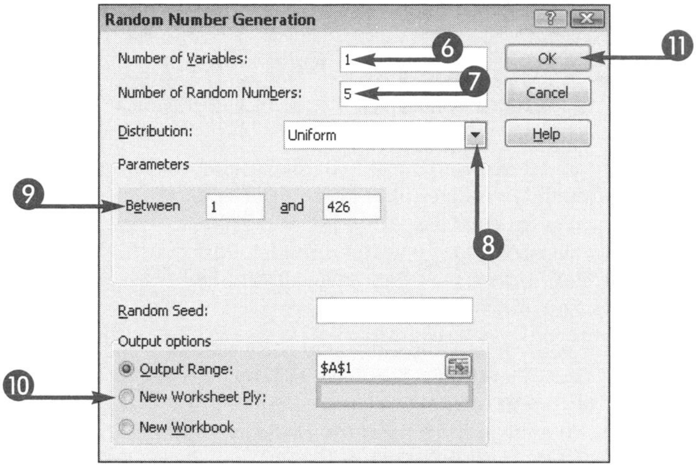

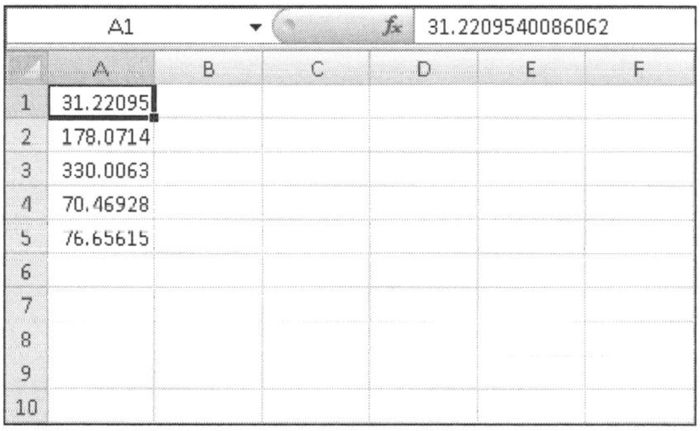

Can you tell me about the various types of distributions I can use?

Distribution Type	Description
Uniform	Using this distribution type, as the example in this section does, every random number between a lower and upper boundary that you specify has an equal chance of being generated.
Normal	Use this distribution type to generate random numbers that match a normal distribution. You specify the mean and standard deviation of the distribution.
Bernoulli	Use this distribution type to specify a probability of success and generate random numbers that are either 0 or 1.
Binomial	Use this distribution type to specify a probability of success and generate random numbers based on a Bernoulli distribution over a specific number of trials.
Poisson	Use this distribution type to generate random numbers in a Poisson distribution. You specify a lambda parameter, which is the expected number of occurrences in an interval.
Patterned	Use this distribution type to generate a pattern of numbers in step increments that you specify.
Discrete	Use this distribution type to specify the probability that certain values are chosen. This distribution type requires a two-column input range; the first column holds the values, and the second column holds the probability of each value being chosen. The sum of the probabilities in the second column must equal 100 percent.

Create a Rank and Percentile Table

You can use the Rank and Percentile Table tool to generate relative numeric and percentage rankings for the values in a list of numbers. To perform this calculation, you need to install the Analysis ToolPak add-in; see "Enable Excel Add-Ins" in Chapter 30 for more details.

Suppose that you teach a class and you track test scores in an Excel workbook. You have entered scores for the mid-term and final exams and calculated the average. You may even have used the Histogram tool to create a frequency distribution of the scores. Now, you want to determine where each student placed in relation to the rest of the class. This section assumes that you understand the type of statistical analysis the tool calculates.

When you use the Rank and Percentile Table tool, you identify an input range, which contains the values you want to analyze; the input range can be multiple columns, but this example uses only one column to make the results easier to understand. You also specify an output range, where Excel displays the results of the analysis. And, you specify whether the first row of the input range contains labels.

Create a Rank and Percentile Table

1. Set up the data in a worksheet.
2. Click the Data tab.
3. Click Data Analysis.

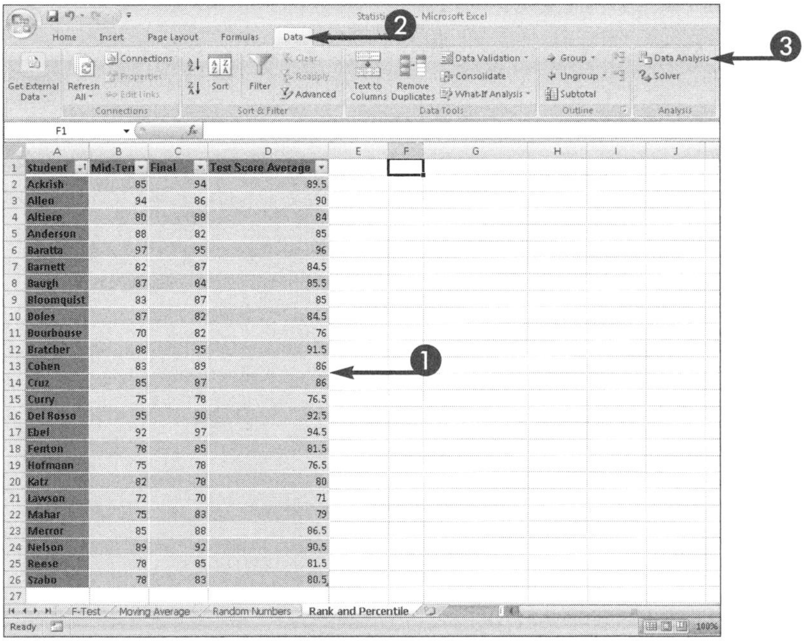

The Data Analysis dialog box appears.

4. Click Rank and Percentile.
5. Click OK.

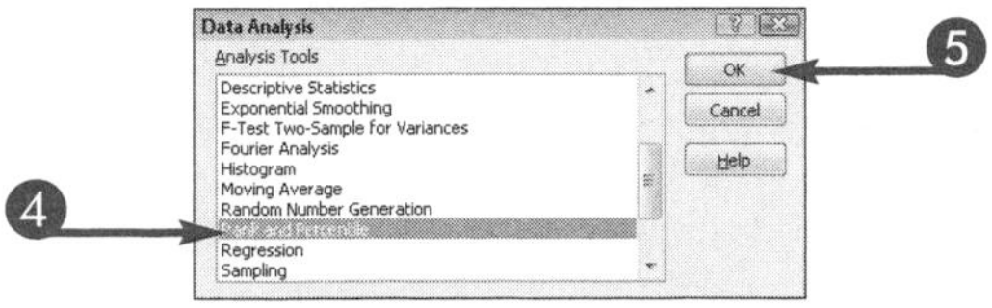

The Rank and Percentile dialog box appears.

6. Click here to select the range containing the data to analyze.
7. Click the "Labels in first row" option if the range you selected in Step 6 contains labels in the first row (☐ changes to ☑).
8. Click here to select an output location (◯ changes to ◉).
9. Click OK.

- The results of the Rank and Percentile analysis tool appear.

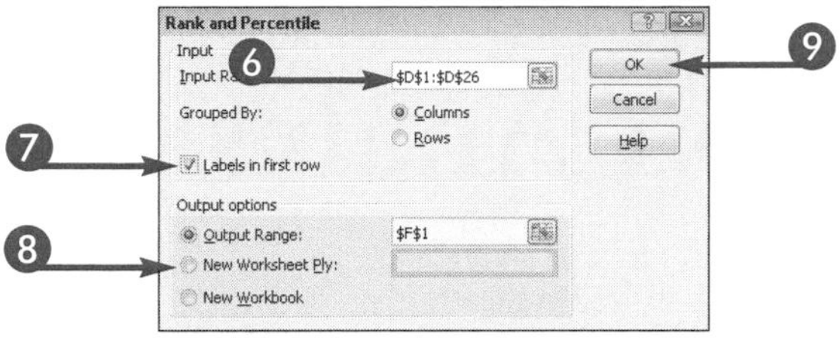

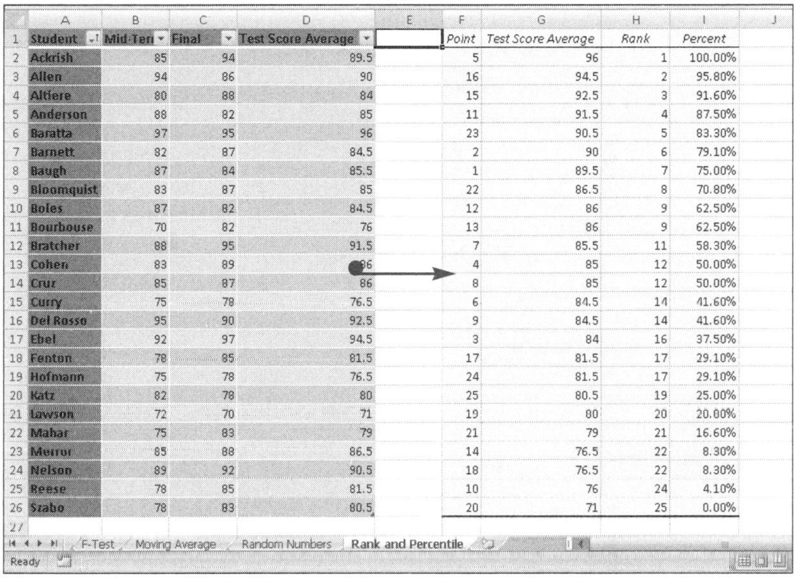

	A	B	C	D	E	F	G	H	I
1	Student	Mid-Term	Final	Test Score Average		Point	Test Score Average	Rank	Percent
2	Ackrish	85	94	89.5		5	96	1	100.00%
3	Allen	94	86	90		16	94.5	2	95.80%
4	Altiere	80	88	84		15	92.5	3	91.60%
5	Anderson	88	82	85		11	91.5	4	87.50%
6	Baratta	97	95	96		23	90.5	5	83.30%
7	Barnett	82	87	84.5		2	90	6	79.10%
8	Baugh	87	84	85.5		1	89.5	7	75.00%
9	Bloomquist	83	87	85		22	86.5	8	70.80%
10	Boles	87	82	84.5		12	86	9	62.50%
11	Bourbouse	70	82	76		13	86	9	62.50%
12	Bratcher	88	95	91.5		7	85.5	11	58.30%
13	Cohen	83	89	86		4	85	12	50.00%
14	Cruz	85	87	86		8	85	12	50.00%
15	Curry	75	78	76.5		6	84.5	14	41.60%
16	Del Rosso	95	90	92.5		9	84.5	14	41.60%
17	Ebel	92	97	94.5		3	84	16	37.50%
18	Fenton	78	85	81.5		17	81.5	17	29.10%
19	Hofmann	75	78	76.5		24	81.5	17	29.10%
20	Katz	82	78	80		25	80.5	19	25.00%
21	Lawson	72	70	71		19	80	20	20.00%
22	Mahar	75	83	79		21	79	21	16.60%
23	Merror	85	88	86.5		14	76.5	22	8.30%
24	Nelson	89	92	90.5		18	76.5	22	8.30%
25	Reese	78	85	81.5		10	76	24	4.10%
26	Szabo	78	83	80.5		20	71	25	0.00%

PART V

Master It

How do I interpret the results of the Rank and Percentile tool?

▼ The Point column refers to the data point in the input set. So, in the example, Point 5 — the first result — refers to the data point that appears on Row 6 of the input table. The Test Score Average column lists the values found in the input column selected in rank order. The Rank column lists the numeric rank of each data point, and the Percentile column lists the percentage rank of each data point. All of the output appears as values, not formulas. If your data changes, you need to rerun the tool to update the information.

When I ran the tool and placed the output beside the input range — which appears in a table, like the one in the example — I got strange results and errors. What did I do wrong?

▼ When the input range is part of a table and you place the output range in the column next to the input range, Excel attempts to include the output range in the table. Because the output for the tool displays results of calculations using the data in the input range, you get erroneous results when you do not separate the output from input stored in a table. Rerun the tool and leave at least one blank column between the table and the output range.

Perform a Regression Analysis

You can use the Regression tool to calculate a variety of regression-related statistics from worksheet data. To perform this calculation, you need to install the Analysis ToolPak add-in; see “Enable Excel Add-Ins” in Chapter 30 for more details.

Regression analysis helps you to determine the extent to which one range of information, called the *dependent variable*, changes as a result of changes to other ranges of information, called the *independent variables*. You can use regression to forecast the future and to analyze trends. Regression analysis often helps you make sense out of numbers that do not seem to be related. This section assumes that you understand the type of statistical analysis the tool calculates.

When you use the Regression tool, you identify an input range for the dependent variable and an input range for the independent variables, and you indicate whether the first row of the input ranges contains labels. The input range for the dependent variable should be one column but you can include multiple columns of independent variables; this example uses only one column for each input range to make the results easier to understand. You also specify an output range, where Excel displays the results of the analysis.

Perform a Regression Analysis

❶ Set up the data in a worksheet.

❷ Click the Data tab.

❸ Click Data Analysis.

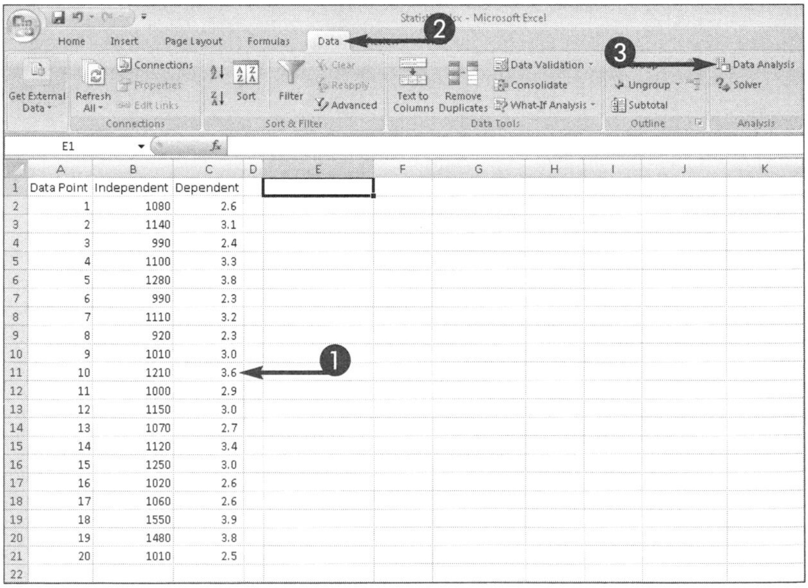

The Data Analysis dialog box appears.

❹ Click Regression.

❺ Click OK.

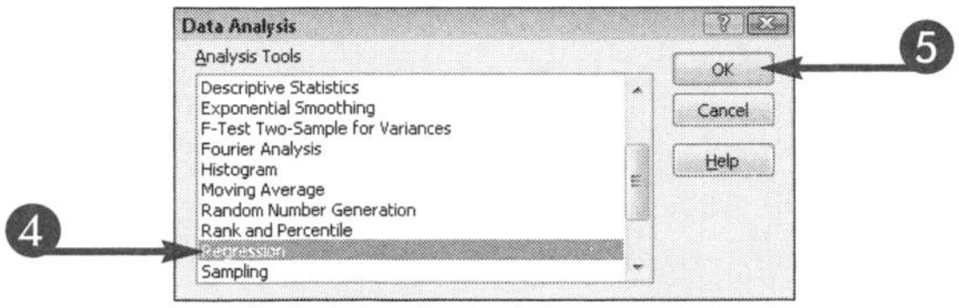

The Regression dialog box appears.

6 Click here to select the range containing the dependent variable.

7 Click here to select the range containing the independent variables.

8 Click the "Labels" option if the range you selected in Step 6 contains labels in the first row (☐ changes to ☑).

9 Click here to select an output location (◯ changes to ◉).

10 Click OK.

The results of the Regression analysis tool appear.

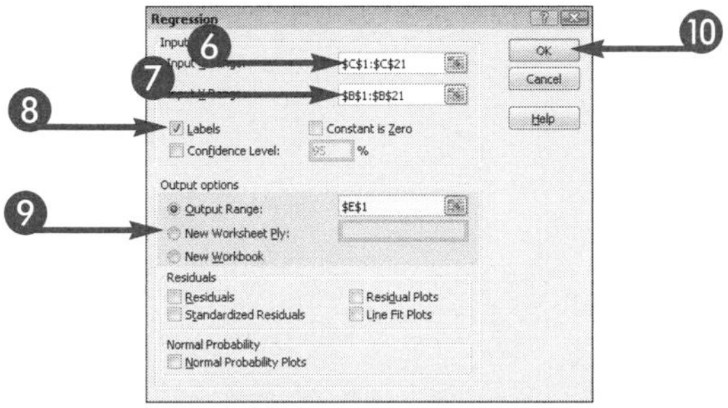

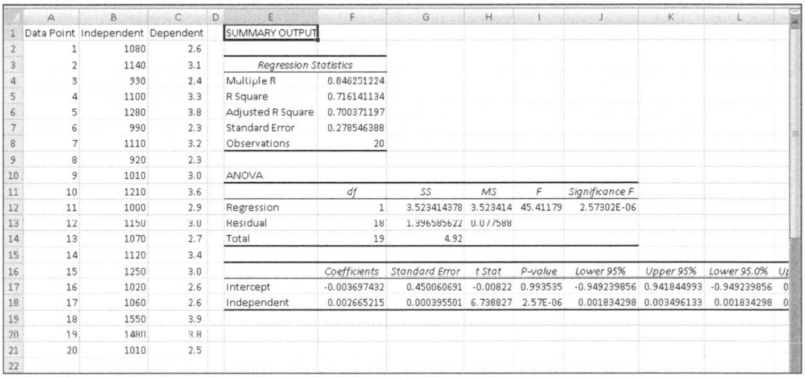

	A	B	C	D	E	F	G	H	I	J	K	L	
1	Data Point	Independent	Dependent		SUMMARY OUTPUT								
2	1	1080	2.6										
3	2	1140	3.1		*Regression Statistics*								
4	3	990	2.4		Multiple R	0.846251224							
5	4	1100	3.3		R Square	0.716141134							
6	5	1280	3.8		Adjusted R Square	0.700371197							
7	6	990	2.3		Standard Error	0.278546388							
8	7	1110	3.2		Observations	20							
9	8	920	2.3										
10	9	1010	3.0		ANOVA								
11	10	1210	3.6			*df*	*SS*	*MS*	*F*	*Significance F*			
12	11	1000	2.9		Regression	1	3.523414378	3.523414	45.41179	2.57302E-06			
13	12	1150	3.0		Residual	18	1.396585622	0.077588					
14	13	1070	2.7		Total	19	4.92						
15	14	1120	3.4										
16	15	1250	3.0			*Coefficients*	*Standard Error*	*t Stat*	*P-value*	*Lower 95%*	*Upper 95%*	*Lower 95.0%*	*Up*
17	16	1020	2.6		Intercept	-0.003697432	0.450060691	-0.00822	0.993535	-0.949239856	0.941844993	-0.949239856	0
18	17	1060	2.6		Independent	0.002665215	0.000395501	6.738827	2.57E-06	0.001834298	0.003496133	0.001834298	0
19	18	1550	3.9										
20	19	1480	3.8										
21	20	1010	2.5										
22													

MASTER IT

What do the various options at the bottom of the Regression dialog box mean?

▼ If you select these options (☐ changes to ☑), the Regression tool produces a Residual Output table and two charts. Residuals represent the differences between observed and predicted values. The table lists each data point and shows its predicted value, residual value, and standard residual value; you can use this information to analyze the variability around the regression line. The two charts help you to analyze the data visually. When you click the Normal Probability Plots option, the Regression tool produces a Probability Output table, which lists the percentiles of the dependent variable and produces a chart of the data points.

Can you explain the output of this tool?

▼ If you do not select any of the options in the Residuals or Normal Probability sections, the Regression tool produces three tables. The first table contains a series of common regression statistics, including information about R^2, which is a measure of the strength of the relationship between the dependent and independent variables. The ANOVA table shows the result of testing your hypotheses about whether the dependent variable varies due to changes in the independent variables. The last table, which is not named, provides information on the regression coefficients, the intercept, and the slope, which can help you determine whether to accept or reject your hypothesis.

Generate a Sample

You can use the Sampling tool to generate a sample. To use this tool, you need to install the Analysis ToolPak add-in; see "Enable Excel Add-Ins" in Chapter 30 for more details.

Suppose that you have a group of 100 people, divided into four groups, who are willing to participate in a test, but you want to sample only 35 of them from across all four groups. You can use the Sampling tool to help you figure out which 35 people to select.

When you use the Sampling tool, you can create a periodic sample population, where the tool chooses every *n*th person, where *n* is a number you supply.

Or, you can create a random sample, where you supply only the number you want to include in your sample, and the tool selects that number of people randomly.

You identify an input range, which contains values that represent the possible sample participants. The input range can be more than one column. If all of your input data appears in a single column, you also can indicate whether the first row of the input range contains labels. You select a sampling method, and you specify an output range, where Excel displays the results of the Sampling tool.

Generate a Sample

1. Set up the data in a worksheet.
2. Click the Data tab.
3. Click Data Analysis.

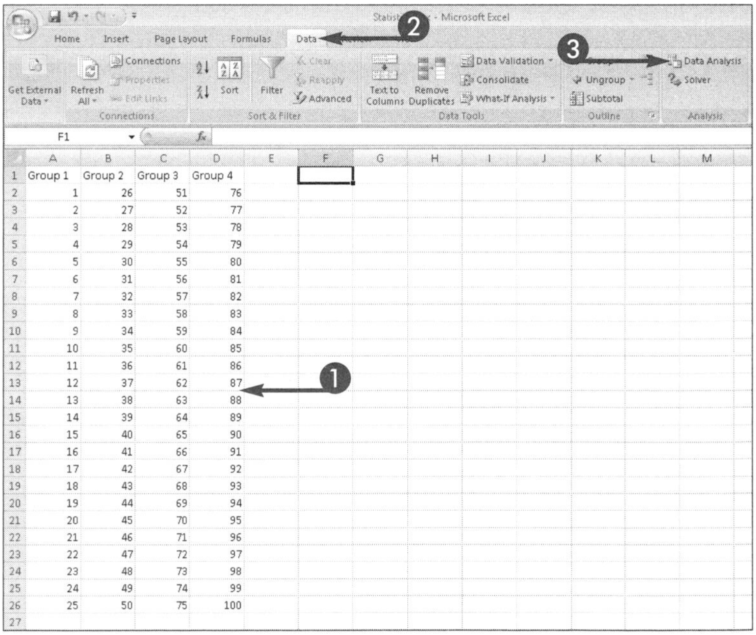

The Data Analysis dialog box appears.

4. Click Sampling.
5. Click OK.

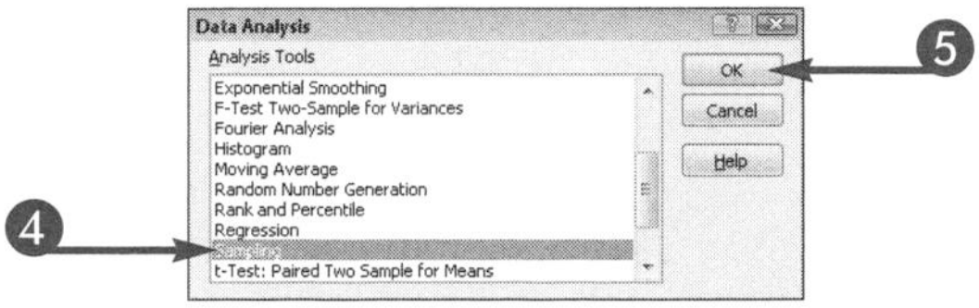

The Sampling dialog box appears.

6. Click here to select the input values.
7. Click the "Labels" option if the range you selected in Step 6 appears in a single column and contains labels in the first row (☐ changes to ☑).
8. Click a sampling method (○ changes to ◉) and supply its criterion.
9. Click here to select an output location (○ changes to ◉).
10. Click OK.

- The results of the Sampling analysis tool appear.

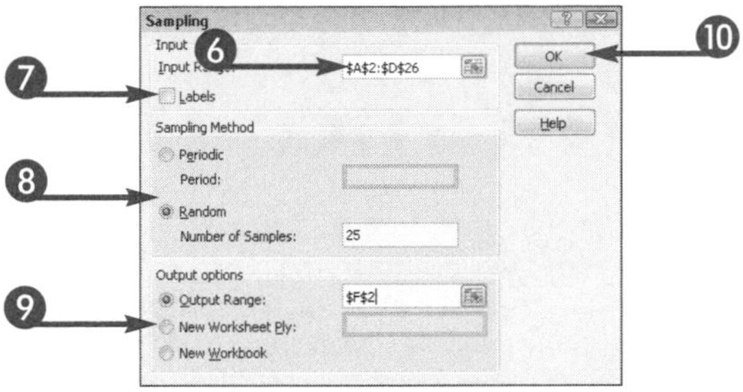

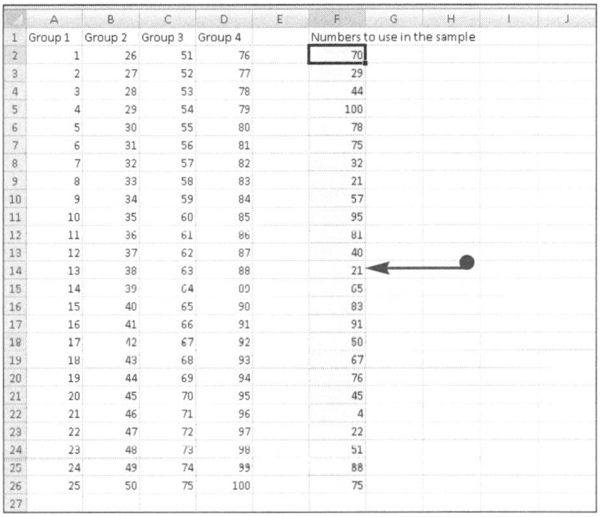

	A	B	C	D	E	F	G	H	I	J
1	Group 1	Group 2	Group 3	Group 4		Numbers to use in the sample				
2	1	26	51	76		70				
3	2	27	52	77		29				
4	3	28	53	78		44				
5	4	29	54	79		100				
6	5	30	55	80		78				
7	6	31	56	81		75				
8	7	32	57	82		32				
9	8	33	58	83		21				
10	9	34	59	84		57				
11	10	35	60	85		95				
12	11	36	61	86		81				
13	12	37	62	87		40				
14	13	38	63	88		21				
15	14	39	64	89		65				
16	15	40	65	90		83				
17	16	41	66	91		91				
18	17	42	67	92		50				
19	18	43	68	93		67				
20	19	44	69	94		76				
21	20	45	70	95		45				
22	21	46	71	96		4				
23	22	47	72	97		22				
24	23	48	73	98		51				
25	24	49	74	99		88				
26	25	50	75	100		75				
27										

Why did you not select the Labels option?

▼ Notice that the Sampling tool dialog box does not contain an option to specify if your data is grouped by columns or rows. The Sampling tool allows you to set up your input range in several columns, but it reads all of the columns as if the data were stored in only one column. In the data in this example, the labels stored in cells B2, C2, and D2 appear to the Sampling tool to be non-numeric data in the input range. The input range must contain only values. As a result, the Labels option was not selected and Row 1 was not included in the input range.

How does the Periodic option work?

▼ When you select this option, the Period field becomes available. You supply a number in the Period field; the Sampling tool uses that number to select values from the input range to become part of your sample population. Suppose that you type **15** in the Period field. The Sampling tool then selects every fifteenth value from the input range. In the example data, the Sampling tool would select 15, 30, 45, 60, 75, and 90 as your sample population. When you use this option, you do not control the number of data points in your sample population like you do with the Random option.

Analyze the Statistical Significance of Small Samples

You can use the t-Test tools to test hypotheses that compare two or more small samples and produce common statistics for the samples. To use these tools, you need to install the Analysis ToolPak add-in; see "Enable Excel Add-Ins" in Chapter 30 for more details. The Analysis ToolPak actually contains three tools to perform different types of t-Tests; this example uses the t-Test: Paired Two Sample for Means tool.

The central limit theorem, a cornerstone of statistics, states, among other things, that the sampling distribution of the mean is approximately a normal distribution if the sample size is 30 or more. As a result, you can use normal distribution tools and theories when your sample size is larger than 30. You use the t-Test tools to test whether two small samples — less than 30 data points per sample — are statistically the same or different.

You identify input ranges for two variables, which contain values that represent the two sample populations. The input ranges must each be a single column or row, and they must both be the same size. You also indicate whether the first row of the input ranges contains labels. You enter a hypothesized mean difference, and you specify an output range.

Analyze the Statistical Significance of Small Samples

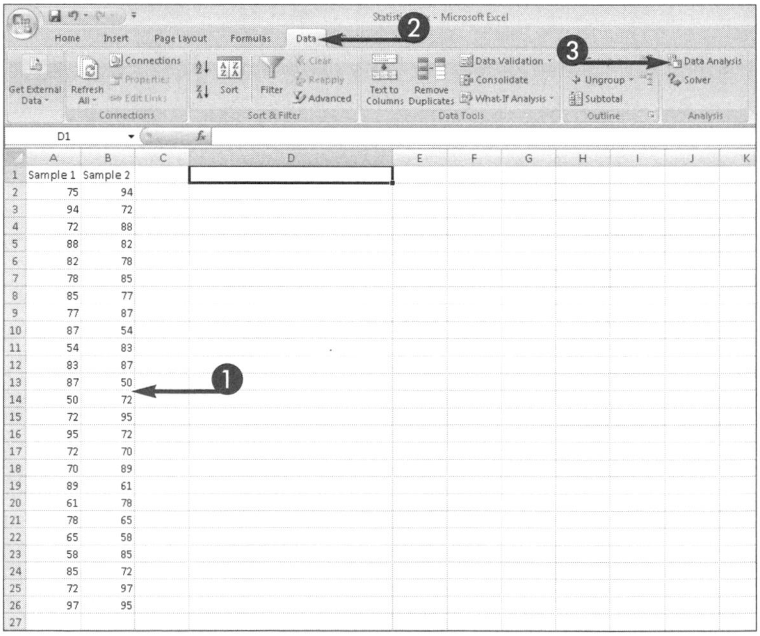

1. Set up the data in a worksheet.
2. Click the Data tab.
3. Click Data Analysis.

The Data Analysis dialog box appears.

4. Click t-Test: Paired Two Sample for Means.
5. Click OK.

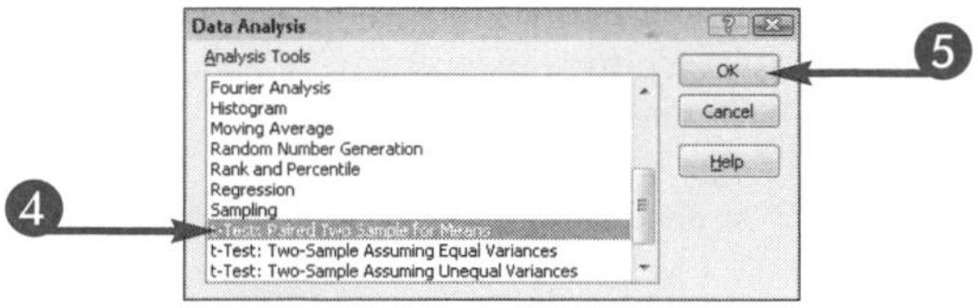

The t-Test: Paired Two Sample for Means dialog box appears.

6. Click here to select the input values for the first and second variables.
7. Click here to type a hypothesized mean difference.
8. Click the "Labels" option if the ranges you selected in Step 6 contain labels in the first row (☐ changes to ☑).
9. Click here to select an output location (○ changes to ◉).
10. Click OK.

The results of the t-Test: Paired Two-Sample for Means analysis tool appear, providing basic statistics about the two samples.

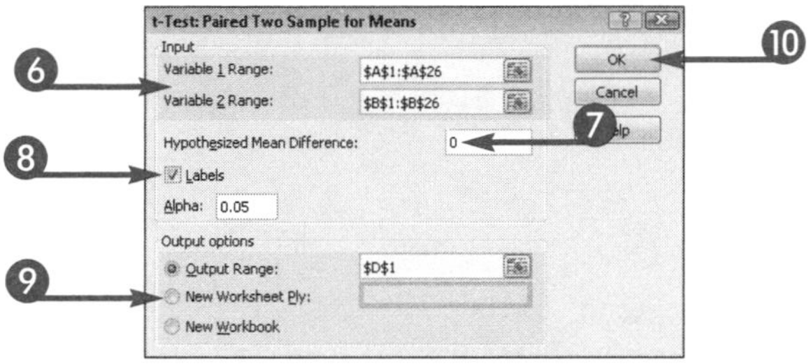

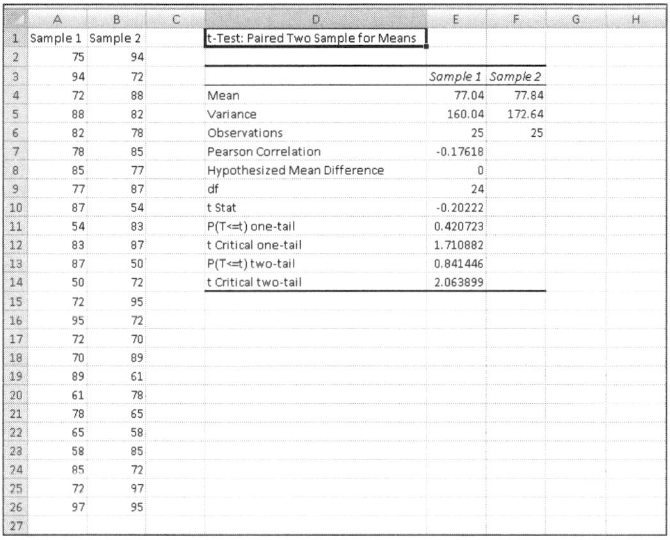

	A	B	C	D	E	F	G	H
1	Sample 1	Sample 2		t-Test: Paired Two Sample for Means				
2	75	94						
3	94	72			Sample 1	Sample 2		
4	72	88		Mean	77.04	77.84		
5	88	82		Variance	160.04	172.64		
6	82	78		Observations	25	25		
7	78	85		Pearson Correlation	-0.17618			
8	85	77		Hypothesized Mean Difference	0			
9	77	87		df	24			
10	87	54		t Stat	-0.20222			
11	54	83		P(T<=t) one-tail	0.420723			
12	83	87		t Critical one-tail	1.710882			
13	87	50		P(T<=t) two-tail	0.841446			
14	50	72		t Critical two-tail	2.063899			
15	72	95						
16	95	72						
17	72	70						
18	70	89						
19	89	61						
20	61	78						
21	78	65						
22	65	58						
23	58	85						
24	85	72						
25	72	97						
26	97	95						
27								

MASTER IT

When do I use the t-Test: Paired Two-Sample for Means tool?

- You use this tool to test for equality of the population means of each sample when you expect a natural pairing of observations in the samples. For example, suppose that you test a group's blood sugar twice — before and after eating. You would use this tool to compare the results of the two tests.

When do I use the t-Test: Paired Two-Sample Assuming Equal Variances tool?

- You use this tool to test for equality of the population means of each sample when the samples are independent and you want to determine whether the two samples are likely to have come from distributions with equal population means. This tool assumes that the two data sets came from distributions with the same variances.

When do I use the t-Test: Paired Two-Sample Assuming Unequal Variances test?

- You use this tool to test for equality of the population means of each sample when the samples are independent and you want to determine whether the two samples are likely to have come from distributions with equal population means. This tool assumes that the two data sets came from distributions with unequal variances.

29 Working with Macros

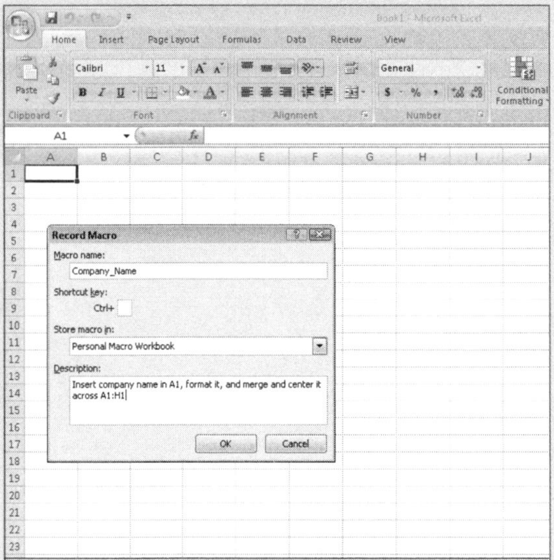

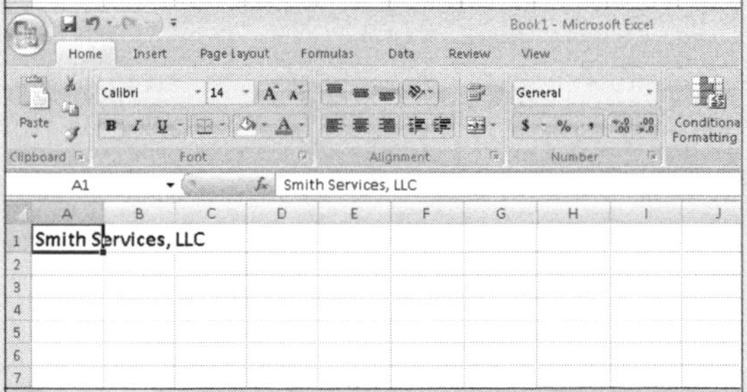

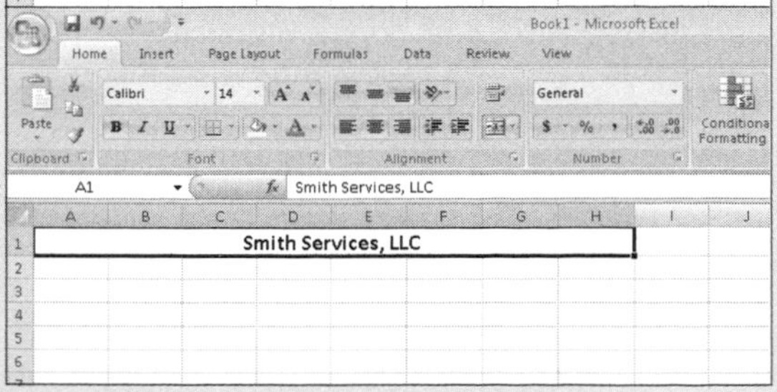

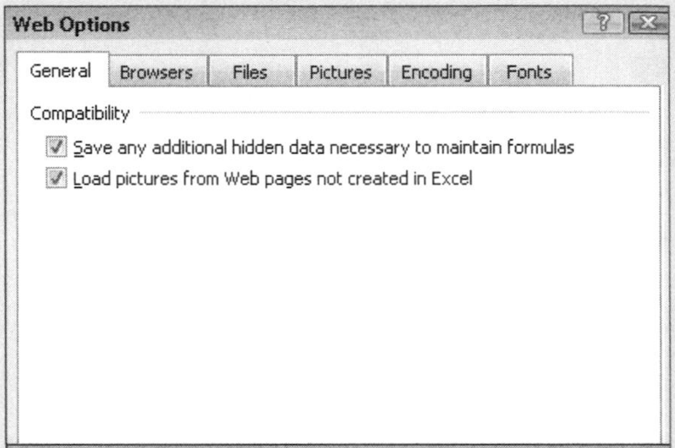

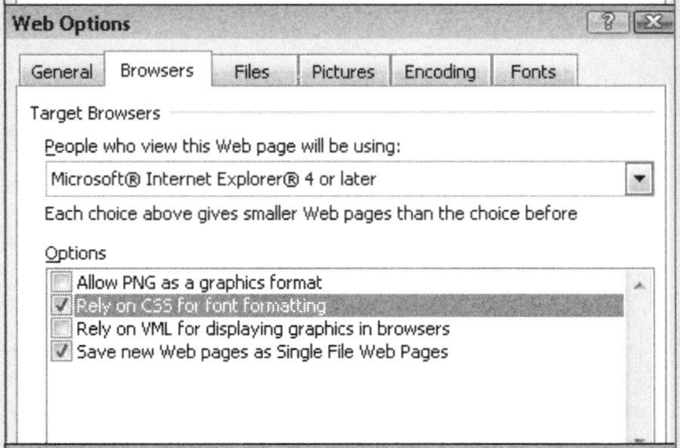

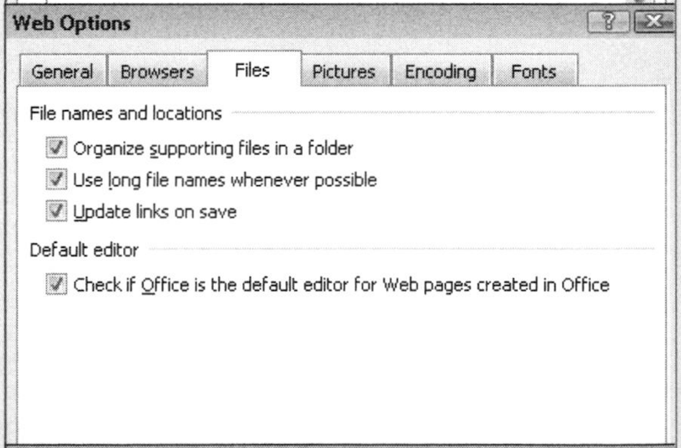

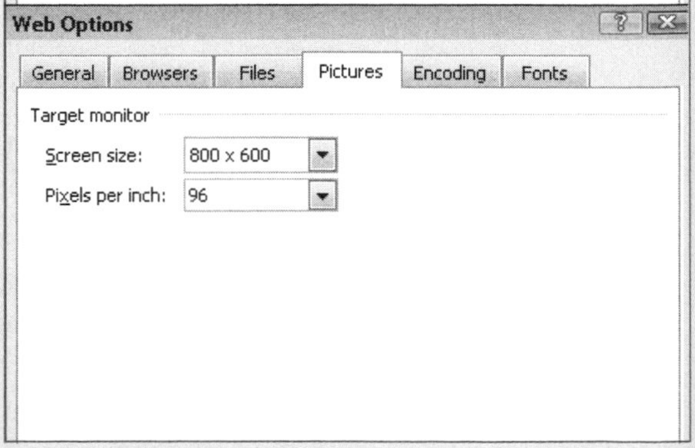

PART VI – CUSTOMIZING THE EXCEL ENVIRONMENT

30 Changing Excel Behavior

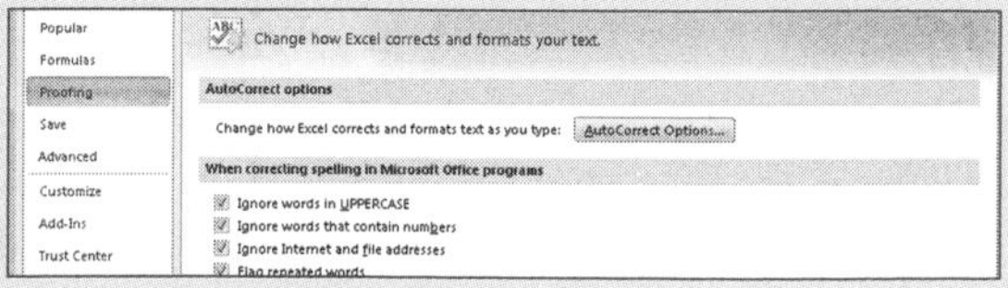

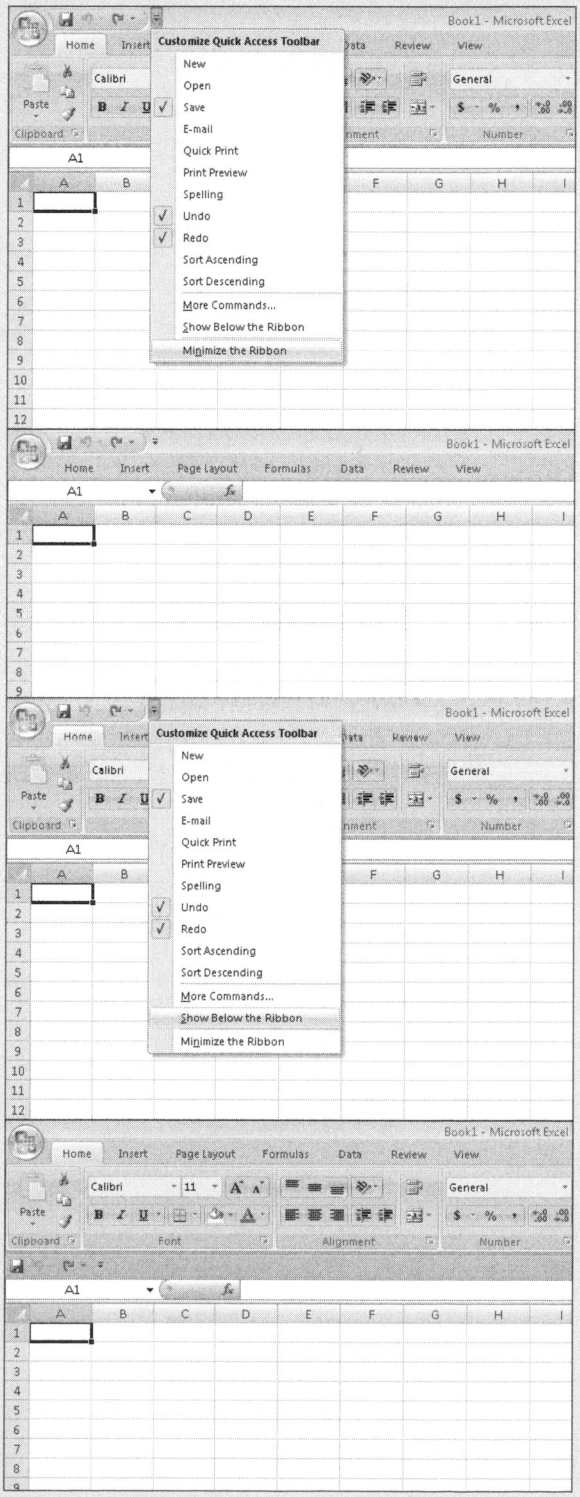

Macro Basics

A *macro* is a small program that carries out the result of a set of keystrokes and mouse clicks. Under ordinary conditions, you could simply perform the keystrokes and mouse clicks and never think about macros. However, macros become useful when the keystrokes and mouse clicks you need to perform are repetitive. When you find yourself repeating a set of keystrokes and mouse clicks in a worksheet or chart, you should consider creating a macro.

Do not let the word "program" intimidate you. You can record a macro very easily. Excel's macro feature captures your keystrokes and mouse clicks as you make them and then enables you to save the results of those keystrokes and mouse clicks. Then, you can run the macro by playing back the results of your keystrokes. Think of this process as similar to using a hand-held cassette or digital recorder; you push a button to record, speak, and then push another button to stop the recorder. Then, you push a "rewind" button to back up the recording and, finally, push a "play" button to hear the words you spoke. The process is the same to record a macro, and so, unless you really want to write program code, you do not need to do so to create a macro.

When might you use a macro? Whenever you find yourself repeating the same combination of keystrokes or mouse clicks to perform an action. Suppose, for example, that you often place your company's name in cell A1, assign the Calibri font at a size of 14 points, make it italic, and then merge the range A1:H1 and center the name in those merged cells. If you write a macro to perform these actions, Excel can enter this information for you much faster than you can do it yourself.

When you record a macro, Excel creates and stores Visual Basic for Applications (VBA) code to perform the actions. VBA is a special version of the BASIC programming language that Microsoft uses in all of the Office programs.

You can also write macros using the VBA Editor that comes with Excel if you want; and, you can record macros in Excel and then study the resulting VBA code to teach yourself how to use VBA.

When you record a macro, you can store it as part of the current workbook, a new workbook, or in a special workbook that Excel opens behind the scenes whenever you start the program. When you store a macro in the current workbook or in a new workbook, the macro is available only in those workbooks. However, storing a macro in the special workbook that Excel opens behind the scenes makes the macro available in every workbook you open. You also assign a name to the macro and decide how to run the macro. You can use a dialog box, or you can assign a keyboard shortcut to the macro and simply press those keys to run the macro. If you like to use buttons, you can assign the macro to a button that you place on the Quick Access Toolbar so that you can simply click the button to run the macro.

Macros and Security

Macros present some special security considerations because they are programs and therefore execute code on your computer. If you create a macro, you know what it does and you know that it will not harm your computer. However, if you receive a workbook from someone else that contains macros, you take a risk — possibly a considerable risk — by allowing that macro code to run, especially if you do not know the author of the code or what the macros do. It is entirely possible that macro code could infect your computer with a virus.

Digitally Signed Macros

Because macros from unknown sources can harm computers, Excel enables macro developers to digitally sign their code using a system called Microsoft Authenticode. The macro developer obtains a certificate from a reputable authority that identifies the code as coming from a trusted publisher.

To help stop unknown macros from running and potentially damaging your computer, by default, Excel checks each workbook you open for macros. If Excel finds macros, then it checks for digital signatures. If Excel does not find a valid digital signature, then it disables the macro and alerts you that the workbook contains macros.

Run Macros That Are Not Digitally Signed

There are circumstances, however, under which you may want to run macros, even if they are not digitally signed. For example, you might not have a digital signature but you might create macros. Because you created them, you know that they will not hurt your computer. You can take three approaches to handling this situation.

First, you can save macros in the Personal Macro Workbook, a global workbook that opens each time you open Excel. If you choose this approach, the macros are available each time you open Excel.

Second, you can save macros in macro-enabled workbooks, as described in the section, "Save a Workbook Containing a Macro." If you choose this approach and Excel finds unverified macros in a workbook you open, Excel displays a security alert just beneath the Ribbon. Using the security alert, you can enable the macros if you know they come from a source you trust and will not do any damage to your computer.

Third, to avoid the security warning altogether, you can store macro-enabled workbooks in a *trusted location*. When you store a workbook in a trusted location, you essentially tell Excel that it does not need to check for macros because you know the workbook is safe. In this case, when you open the workbook, Excel does not alert you about macros and simply enables them.

For more information on Excel's security and handling macros, see the section, "Handle Workbooks that Contain Macros," later in this chapter.

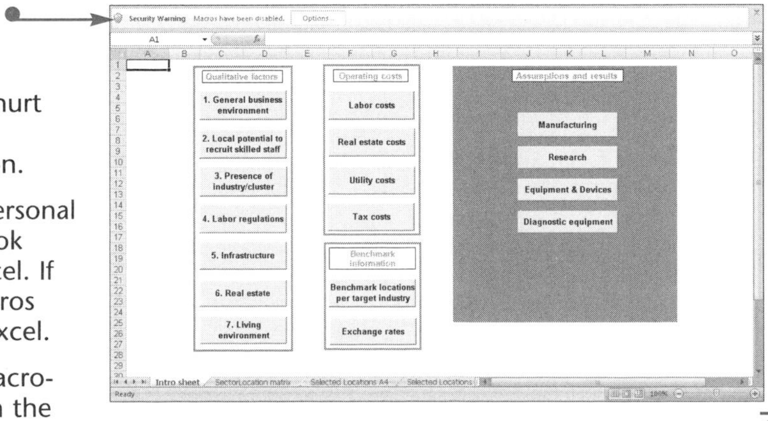

Record a Macro

You can use macros to save time performing a series of repetitive keystrokes and mouse clicks. A macro is a collection of instructions that perform the result of these keystrokes and mouse clicks. Suppose that you often place your company's name in cell A1, assign the Calibri font at a size of 14 points, make it bold, and then merge the range A1:H1 and center the name in those merged cells. If you record a macro to perform these actions, Excel can enter this information for you much faster than you can do it yourself. The example in this section shows you how to create this macro.

The Excel macro feature captures your keystrokes and mouse clicks as you make them and saves them, similar to the way you capture and then play recordings on a hand-held cassette or digital recorder.

You can store a macro in the current workbook, in a new workbook, or in the Personal Macro Workbook, a special workbook that Excel opens behind the scenes whenever you start the program. Where you save your macro determines how Excel treats the macro; for more details, see the sections, "Save a Workbook Containing a Macro" and "Handle Workbooks that Contain Macros."

Record a Macro

1. Click the Record Macro button ( ).

   The Record Macro dialog box appears.

2. Type a name for the macro that does not contain spaces.
3. Click ▾ and select a location to store the macro.
4. Type a description of the macro's purpose.
5. Click OK.

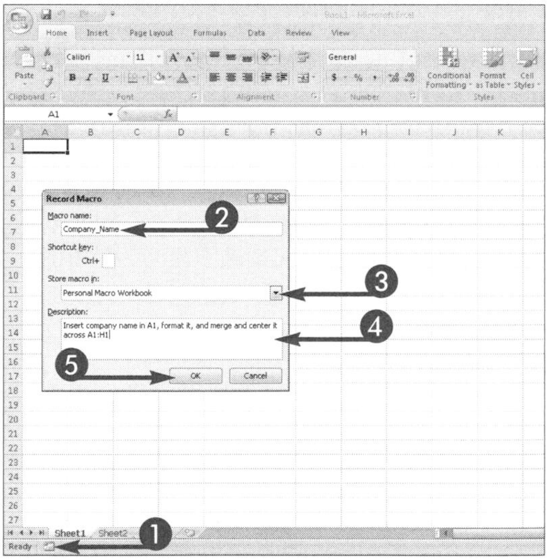

6. Perform the actions you want to record.

   This example types **Smith Services, LLC** in cell A1 and clicks ✓.

7. Click the Home tab.
8. Click **B**.
9. Click ▾ and select Calibri.
10. Click ▾ and select 14.

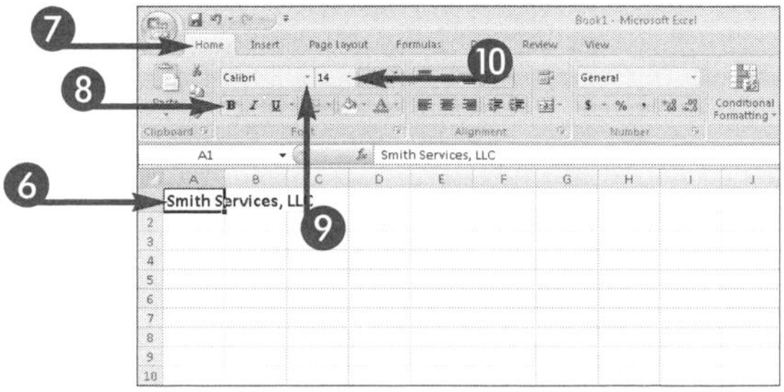

⑪ Select the range A1:H1.

⑫ Click [icon].

⑬ Click Stop Recording ([icon]).

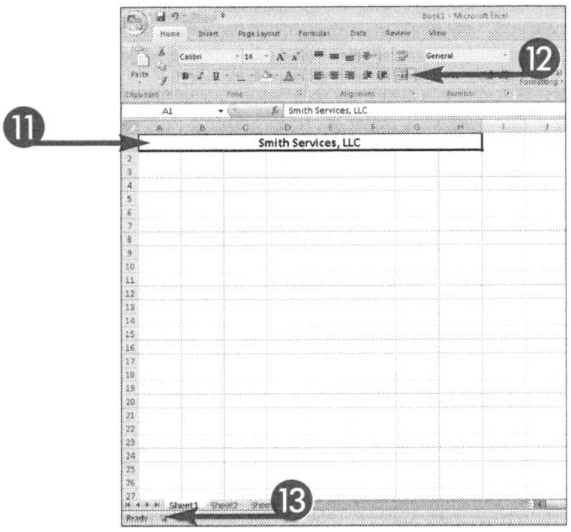

- The [icon] button changes to [icon].

Excel stores the macro.

When you close Excel, you are prompted to save the changes to the Personal Macro Workbook; click Yes.

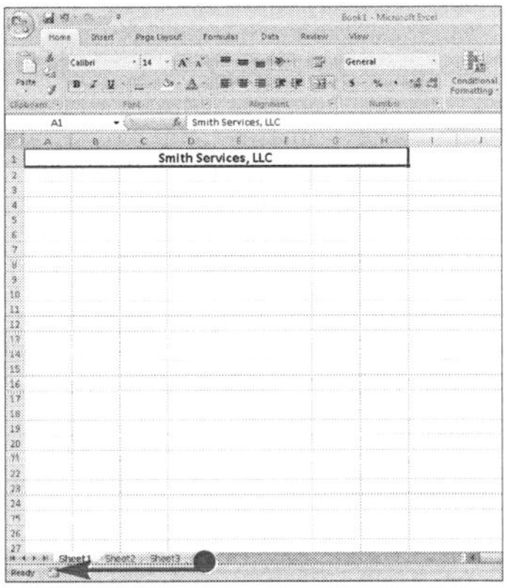

MASTER IT

The [icon] does not appear in the Status Bar. What should I do?

▼ You can right-click the Status Bar and click Macro Recording. You can also click the View tab, click [icon] below Macros, and click Record Macro. If you start recording the macro from the View tab, use the View tab to finish recording the macro. Click the View tab, click [icon] below Macros, and click Stop Recording.

Why should I store a macro in the Personal Macro Workbook?

▼ When you store a macro in the current workbook or in a new workbook, the macro is available only in those workbooks. However, when you store a macro in the Personal Macro Workbook, named Personal.xlsb, the macro is available in every workbook you open because Excel always opens the Personal Macro Workbook behind the scenes.

What is the Shortcut Key field on the Macro Options dialog box for?

▼ You can create a keyboard shortcut that you can use to run the macro; using a combination of the Ctrl key and a letter is just one way that you can run a macro. For details on setting up a keyboard shortcut, see the section, "Add a Keyboard Shortcut to a Macro," later in this chapter.

Run a Macro

You run a macro to have Excel perform the instructions stored in the macro. There are several ways to run a macro; the example in this section shows you how to run a macro using the Macro dialog box.

When you run a macro, you need to be careful about the position of the cell pointer. When you create a macro, it uses relative cell addressing by default. For most macros, you want to use relative cell addressing to make them more versatile. By using relative cell addressing, you can run a macro from any location in a workbook and the instructions in the macro still function.

However, the advantage of relative cell addressing can also be viewed as a disadvantage. Because the macro runs from any location in the workbook, it can easily overwrite information that may already exist. You should therefore position the cell pointer in a location where no worksheet data exists before you run a macro. You should also save your workbook before running a macro. You cannot easily undo the effects of a macro, and so you may want to close your workbook without saving if a macro overwrites existing information.

Run a Macro

1. Select the cell where you want the macro to start operating.

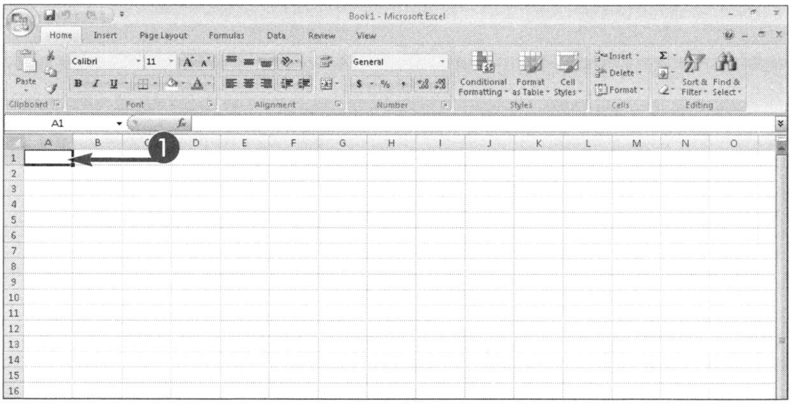

2. Click the View tab.
3. Click Macros.

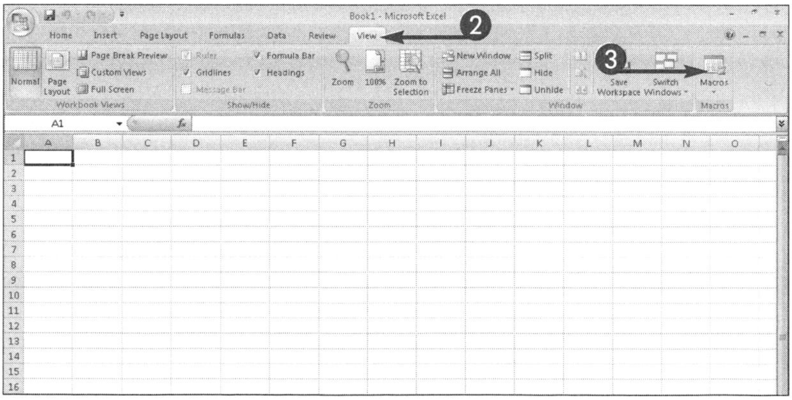

The Macro dialog box appears.

4 Click the name of the macro you want to run.

- If you provided a description when you created the macro, it appears here.

5 Click Run.

- Excel performs the steps stored in the macro instructions.

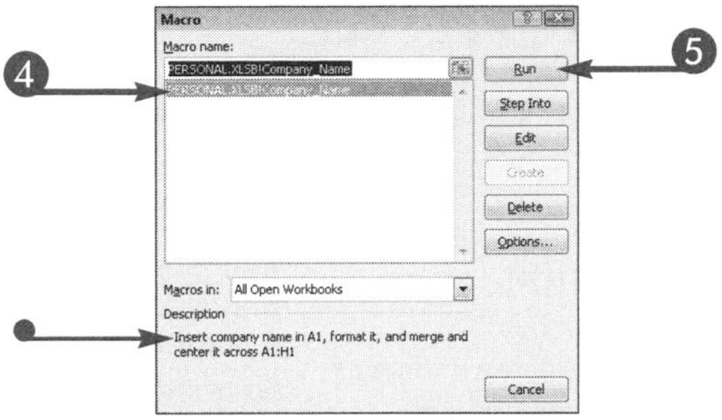

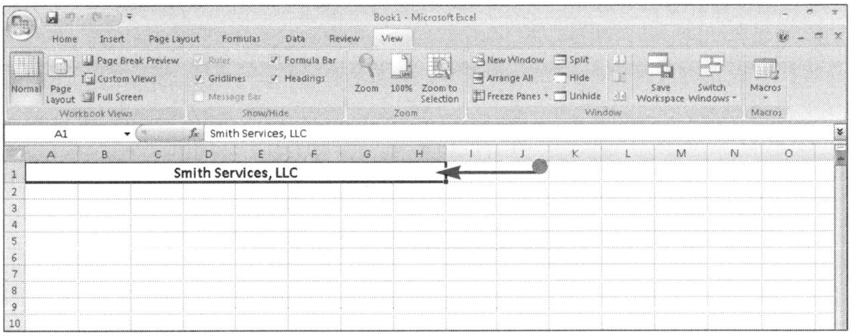

MASTER IT

I tried to edit my macro, but I get an error message. What am I doing wrong?

▼ To edit or delete a macro stored in the Personal Macro Workbook, you must work in Personal.xlsb. Click the View tab and click Unhide. In the Unhide window that appears, click Personal.xlsb and click OK; the title bar changes to display Personal.xlsb. When you finish working in Personal.xlsb, click Hide on the View tab to return to a regular workbook.

What happens if I click Step Into?

▼ Excel opens the Microsoft Visual Basic window for the open workbook and displays the VBA code for the selected macro. Using the Debug menu or the Debug toolbar, you can step through the statements in the macro code. If errors exist in the macro code, then stepping through the macro helps you to find and correct them.

What are the other ways to run a macro?

▼ You can assign a keyboard shortcut to the macro; see the section, "Add a Keyboard Shortcut to a Macro." You can also create a button on the Quick Access Toolbar, which you can click to run the macro; see the section, "Add a Macro to the Quick Access Toolbar." You can press Alt+F8 to open the Macro dialog box and select a macro to run.

Add a Keyboard Shortcut to a Macro

You can add a keyboard shortcut to a macro so that you can run the macro by pressing a combination of keys. This approach to running a macro makes the process even faster because you do not need to open the Macro dialog box and select the macro to run it. You simply select the cell where you want the macro to start, and press the keyboard combination that you assign to the macro, and the macro runs.

By default, you assign the Ctrl key as one of the keys in the keyboard shortcut. For the other keys, you can use any letter from A to Z; you can also use the Shift key. You should be cautious, because Excel may have already pre-assigned the Ctrl key combined with an alphabetic character. For example, you could assign a keyboard shortcut of Ctrl+A to a macro, but Excel has assigned that combination to the Select All command. Alternatively, you could assign Ctrl+Shift+A to a macro; this combination would not conflict with any pre-assigned combination. Before performing the steps in this section, test the combination you want to assign to make sure it does not conflict with a pre-assigned combination.

Add a Keyboard Shortcut to a Macro

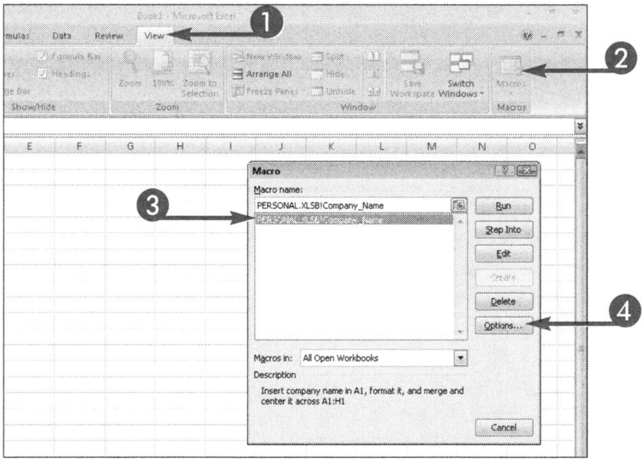

1. Click the View tab.
2. Click Macros.

   The Macro dialog box appears.
3. Click the macro to which you want to assign a keyboard shortcut.
4. Click Options.

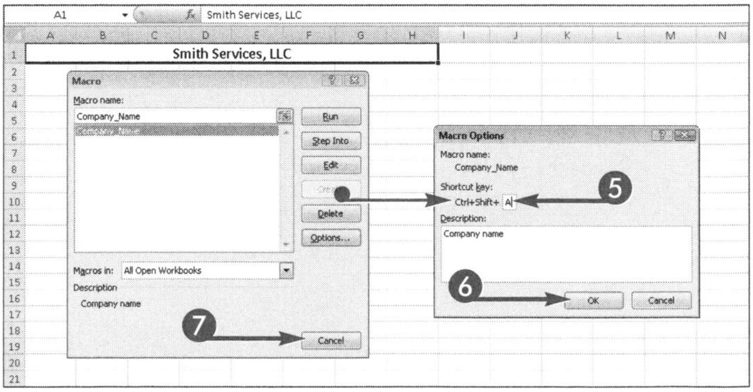

The Macro Options dialog box appears.

5. Press the keyboard combination you want to assign to the macro; exclude Ctrl, as Excel automatically assigns it.
   - Excel displays the combination.
6. Click OK.
7. Click Cancel to close the Macro dialog box.

Save a Workbook Containing a Macro

When Excel finds a macro, its behavior depends on the way you have set security. Assuming that your settings tell Excel to prompt you when it finds macros, the Excel behavior then depends on where you save macros.

If you save macros to the Personal Macro Workbook, macros are available without any prompting whenever you open Excel. For greater security, you may choose to save macros to the workbooks where you will use them. If you save macros in a workbook, then you must save the workbook as a macro-enabled workbook so that the macros will work. A macro-enabled workbook uses a special .xlsm file extension. When you create and save a macro to a macro-enabled workbook, no warnings appear when you open Excel. Instead, when you open the workbook containing the macro, Excel disables the macro but displays a security warning just below the Ribbon. From the security warning, you can enable the macros in the workbook.

To avoid warnings altogether, you can save macro-enabled workbooks to trusted locations. See the section, "Handle Workbooks that Contain Macros," later in this chapter for details on enabling the macros in macro-enabled workbooks and on establishing trusted locations.

Save a Workbook Containing a Macro

1. Click the Office button.
2. Point at Save As.
3. Click Excel Macro-Enabled Workbook.

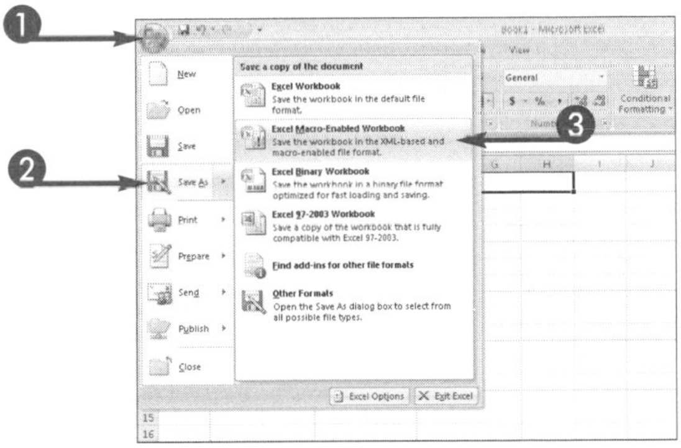

The Save As dialog box appears.

You can navigate to the folder where you want to save the workbook.

4. Type a name for the workbook.
5. Make sure that the Excel Macro-Enabled Workbook (*.xlsm) option appears here.
6. Click Save.

Excel saves the workbook.

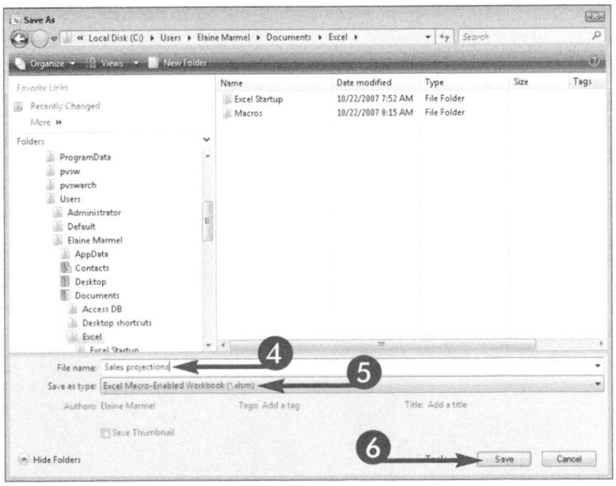

PART VI

Add a Macro to the Quick Access Toolbar

You can add a button to the Quick Access Toolbar that runs a macro of your choice. This approach to running a macro makes the macro even faster because you do not need to open the Macro dialog box and select the macro to run it. You simply select the cell where you want the macro to start and click the button on the Quick Access Toolbar that you assign to the macro, and the macro runs.

When you create a Quick Access Toolbar button to run a macro, you actually assign the macro to the button.

To assign a macro to a Quick Access Toolbar button, you customize the Quick Access Toolbar. You can place the button for the macro in any position on the Quick Access Toolbar; by default, Excel adds each button to the right end of the Quick Access Toolbar.

When you create the button, you can choose an image for the button from a list of predefined symbols that Excel displays. You can also control the tip that appears when you hover the mouse pointer over the button on the Quick Access Toolbar.

Add a Macro to the Quick Access Toolbar

1. Click .
2. Click Excel Options.

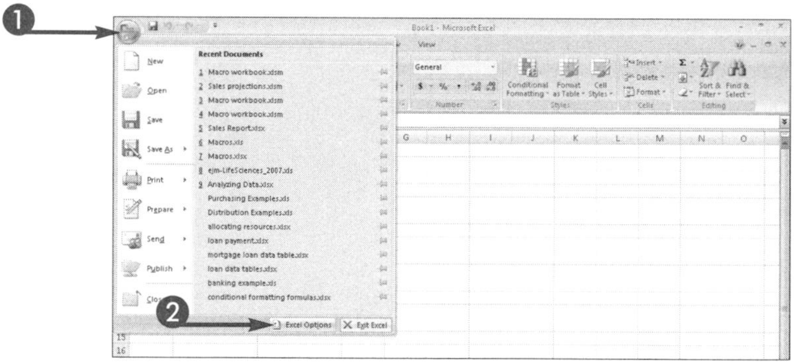

The Excel Options dialog box appears.

3. Click Customize.
4. Click ▾ and select Macros.
5. Click the macro you want on the Quick Access Toolbar.
6. Click Add.
7. Click the macro.
8. Click Modify.

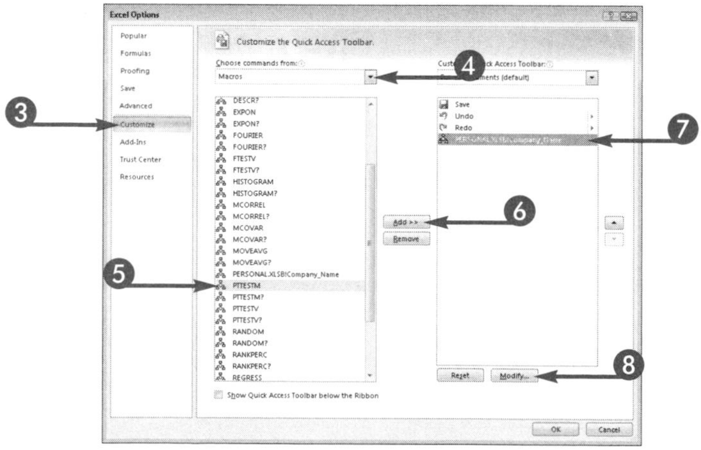

The Modify Button dialog box appears.

9. Click a symbol for the button.
10. Click here and type the name that Excel should display when the mouse pointer hovers over the button.
11. Click OK twice.

- Excel adds the button to the Quick Access Toolbar.
- The name you assigned in Step 10 appears when you hover the mouse pointer over the button.

You can click the button to run the macro.

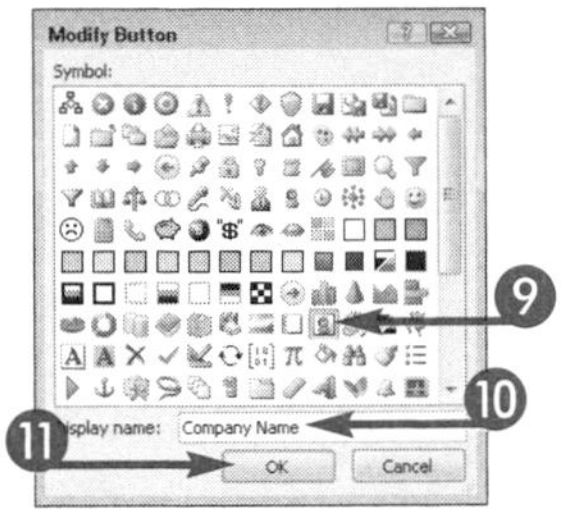

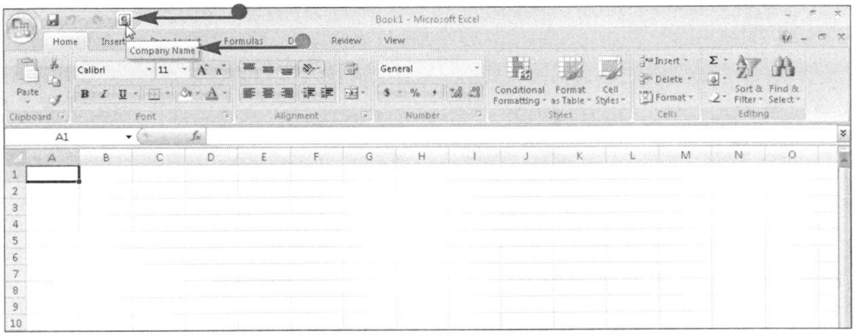

MASTER IT

Can I control the button's position on the Quick Access Toolbar?

▼ Yes, you can. By default, Excel places the button on the right edge of the Quick Access Toolbar, but you can move it. Complete Steps 1 to 3. Then click the macro on the right side of the Excel Options dialog box and click ▲ or ▼ to reposition the button. Moving the button up in the Excel Options dialog box list moves it to the left on the Quick Access Toolbar. Similarly, moving the button down in the list moves the button to the right on the Quick Access Toolbar.

When I select the Popular Commands option in the list on the left side of the Excel Options dialog box, there is a View Macros option at the bottom of this list. What does this option do?

▼ You can add this option to the Quick Access Toolbar to create a button that displays the Macro dialog box, where you select a macro to run.

If I decide I do not want a button for a macro on the Quick Access Toolbar, can I undo my action?

▼ No, but you can remove the button. Complete Steps 1 to 3. Then click the macro in the list on the right side of the Excel Options dialog box, and click the Remove button between the lists.

Handle Workbooks That Contain Macros

By default, Excel's security is set up so that Excel gives you the opportunity to enable macros. However, you can change those settings, as well as create a trusted location where you can store macro-enabled workbooks.

You can control the level of security that Excel applies to workbooks containing macros. Instead of the default behavior, you can have Excel disable macros and not notify you, disable all macros except for digitally signed macros, or enable all macros; the last setting is not recommended.

When you store macros in the Personal Macro Workbook, Excel enables those macros without prompting you each time you open the program. You may notice that Excel opens more slowly when you store macros in the Personal Macro Workbook.

For greater security, you can limit the macros you store in the Personal Macro Workbook to only those that you need to be available in every workbook, and store other macros in macro-enabled workbooks. When you store a macro-enabled workbook in a folder that Excel does not recognize as trusted, Excel initially disables the macros and notifies you. However, you can store macro-enabled workbooks in a trusted location; in this case, Excel enables macros when you open these workbooks without prompting you.

Handle Workbooks That Contain Macros

1. Click .
2. Click Excel Options.

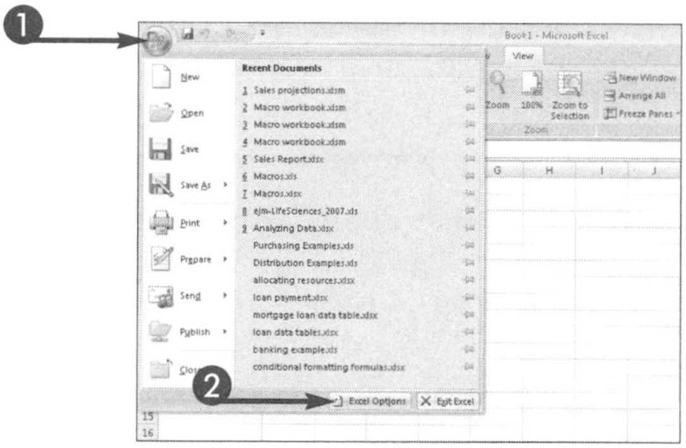

The Excel Options dialog box appears.

3. Click Trust Center.
4. Click Trust Center Settings.

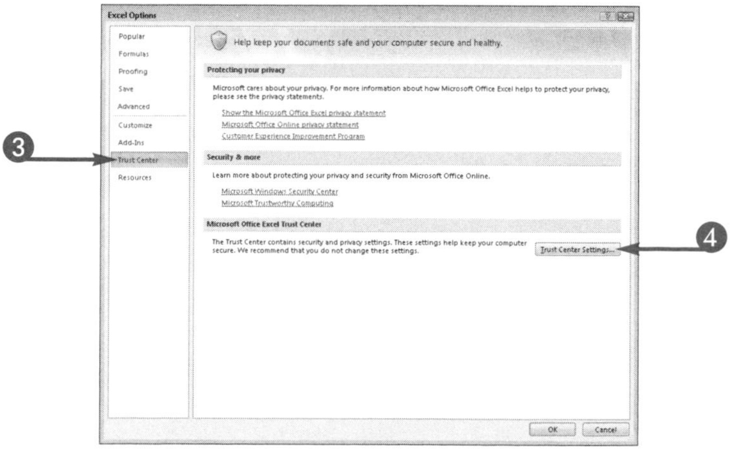

The Trust Center dialog box appears.

5 Click Macro Settings.

6 Click an option to change the security for macros (◎ changes to ◉).

Note: *The default choice gives you greatest control with protection.*

7 Click Trusted Locations.

- These locations are defined by Excel when you install the program.

8 Click Add new location.

The Microsoft Office Trusted Location dialog box appears.

9 Click Browse to navigate to a folder that you want to establish as trusted.

10 Type a description here.

11 Click OK.

The Trust Center dialog box reappears.

12 Click OK to save your settings.

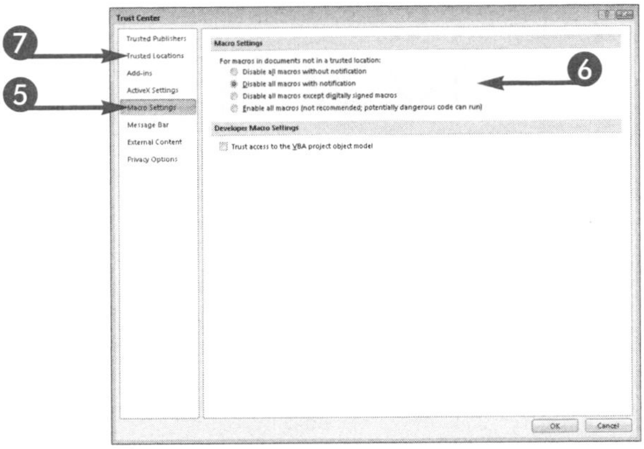

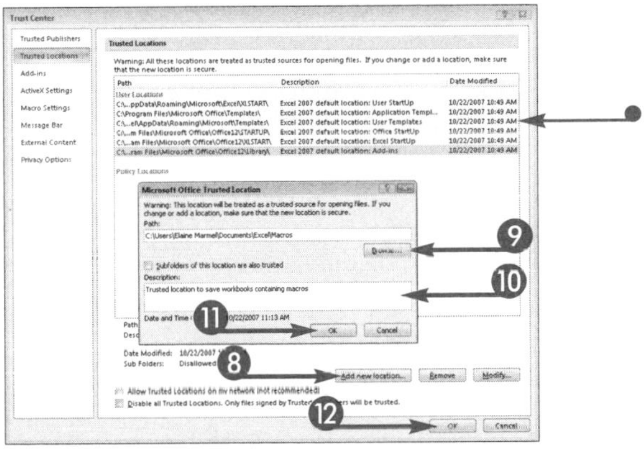

MASTER IT

How do I enable macros in a workbook that is not stored in a trusted location?

▼ When you open the workbook, a security warning appears below the Ribbon, indicating that macros are disabled. Click the Options button in that warning, and Excel displays the Microsoft Office Security Options dialog box, which contains two options. Click the Enable This Content option to enable the macros; otherwise, click the Help Protect Me From Unknown Content option to leave the macros disabled.

What do I do with the default trusted locations that already appear in the Trust Center?

▼ You do not need to do anything with them. They are already trusted locations. You can save macro-enabled workbooks in any of these locations and, when you open the workbooks, Excel does not disable the macros. Instead, they are available and functioning, and Excel does not alert you that the workbook contains any macros.

Why is enabling all macros not recommended?

▼ Macros are small programs and could infect your computer with a virus. Allowing macros to run with no controls in place is very risky. You are much better off if you store your own macro-enabled workbooks in a trusted location and place all other workbooks in a non-trusted location so that Excel prompts you if a workbook that you open contains macro code. That way, you can decide whether to allow the code to run.

Minimize the Ribbon

To save on screen real estate, you can minimize the Ribbon. The Ribbon contains the majority of commands available in Excel, organized by function onto seven tabs. Typically, you use the Ribbon by clicking the tab containing the button for the command you want, and then you click that button.

When you minimize the Ribbon, Excel displays only the names of the tabs on the Ribbon; the buttons on each tab appear to be hidden. To use the Ribbon while it is minimized, you click a tab, and Excel displays the buttons for that tab. After you click a button, Excel minimizes the Ribbon again. If you do not click a button on the selected tab but instead click a different tab, Excel displays the buttons for that tab. If you decide you do not want to click any button on the Ribbon, you can click in the worksheet. Once again, Excel minimizes the Ribbon.

The steps in this section show you how to minimize the Ribbon. If you decide that you do not like working with the minimized Ribbon, you can return the Ribbon to its original display by repeating these steps.

Minimize the Ribbon

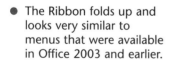

1. Click .
2. Click Minimize the Ribbon.

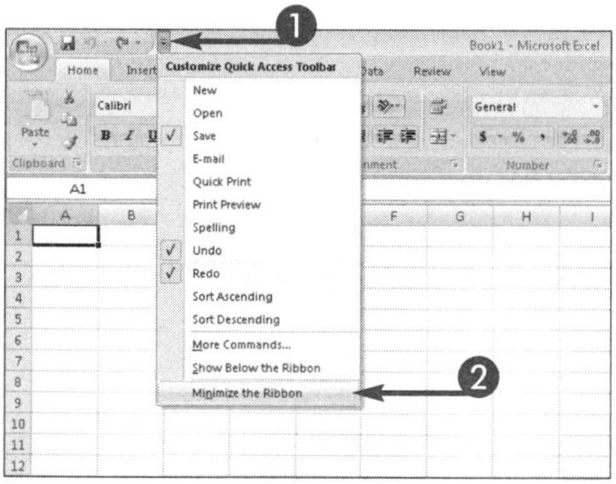

- The Ribbon folds up and looks very similar to menus that were available in Office 2003 and earlier.

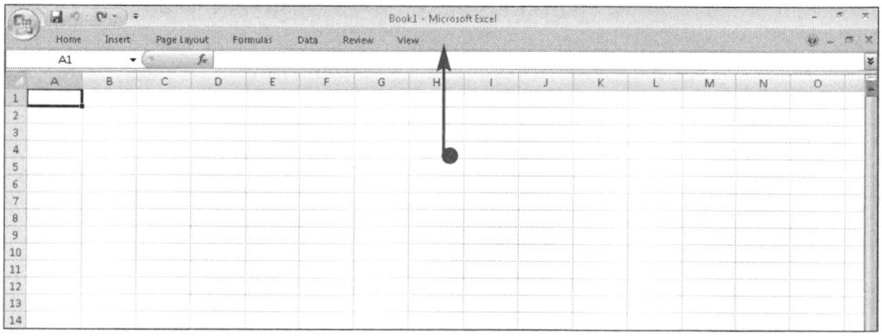

Change the Location of the Quick Access Toolbar

You can move the Quick Access Toolbar so that it appears below the Ribbon instead of above it. The location of the Quick Access Toolbar is strictly a matter of personal preference. However, if your Quick Access Toolbar contains a lot of buttons, you may prefer to display it below the Ribbon instead of above the Ribbon. By placing the Quick Access Toolbar below the Ribbon, you avoid crowding the name of the current workbook that appears, by default, to the right of the Quick Access Toolbar in its default location above the Ribbon.

For those of you who yearn for the Office 2003 and earlier interface, you can simulate the appearance of that interface somewhat if you minimize the Ribbon and then position the Quick Access Toolbar below the Ribbon. When you view the Excel 2007 interface in this configuration, the Ribbon tabs look like the menus and the Quick Access Toolbar looks like a toolbar in Excel 2003. Of course, when you click a Ribbon tab, the Ribbon reappears, and so ends the simulation. However, for a moment, you had a taste of familiarity.

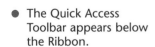

Change the Location of the Quick Access Toolbar

1. Click ▾.
2. Click Show Below the Ribbon.

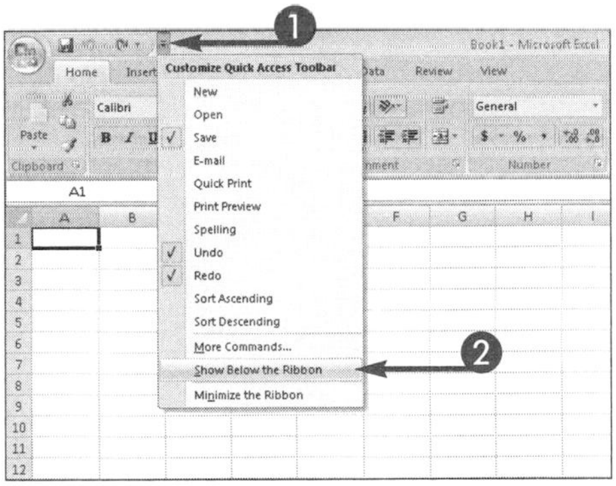

- The Quick Access Toolbar appears below the Ribbon.

Note: *You can move the Quick Access Toolbar back to its original configuration by completing these steps again, but clicking Show Above the Ribbon in Step 2.*

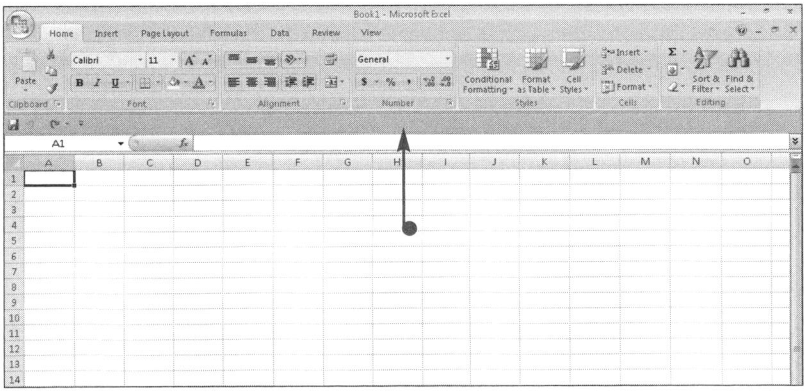

Add a Button to the Quick Access Toolbar

You can add commands that you use frequently to the Quick Access Toolbar to make them more accessible. There are commands that you use regularly in Excel that might feel like they are buried in the Ribbon. For example, if you apply boldface or italics often, you may not want to have to click the Home tab each time to access those commands. And, although you can memorize the keyboard shortcuts for commands, sometimes it is just easier to have ready access to a command that you use frequently. Placing that command on the Quick Access Toolbar meets that need.

Suppose, for example, that you work in a lot of different workbooks each day, and you find yourself closing workbooks frequently. The Close command appears on the Office menu, but you can add a button for the Close command to the Quick Access Toolbar.

When you add a button to the Quick Access Toolbar, Excel adds the button to the right end of the Quick Access Toolbar by default. You can, however, place the button in any position on the Quick Access Toolbar.

Add a Button to the Quick Access Toolbar

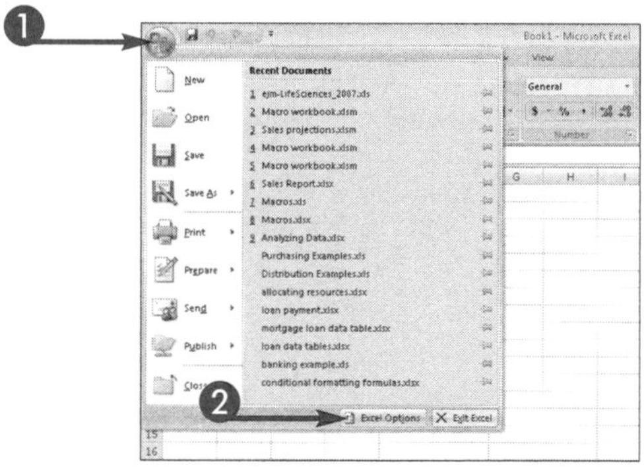

1. Click [icon].
2. Click Excel Options.

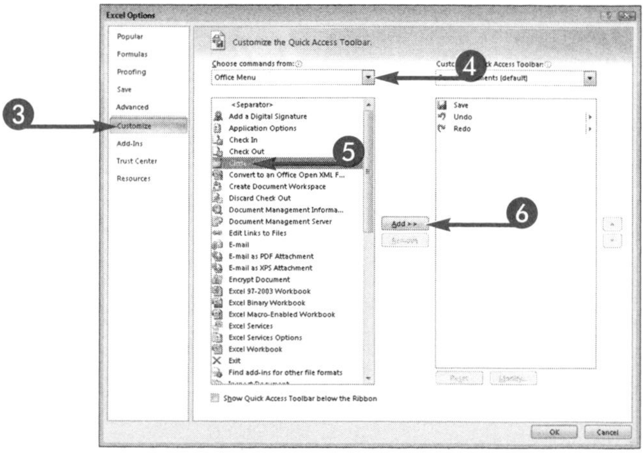

The Excel Options dialog box appears.

3. Click Customize.
4. Click [▾] to select a command group.

   Commands in each group appear in alphabetical order.

5. Click a command.
6. Click Add.

- The command appears here.
- You can use these buttons to reorder the commands on the Quick Access Toolbar.

7 Click OK.

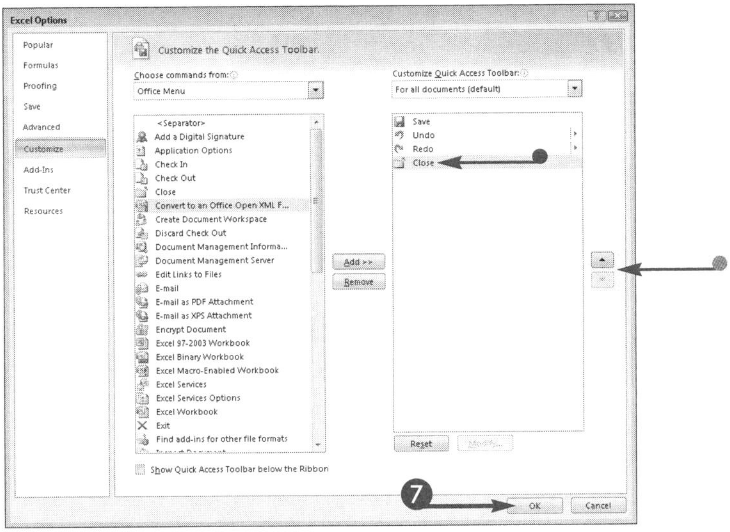

- Excel adds the button to the Quick Access Toolbar.

If you hover the mouse pointer over the button, a tip appears to let you know the purpose of the button.

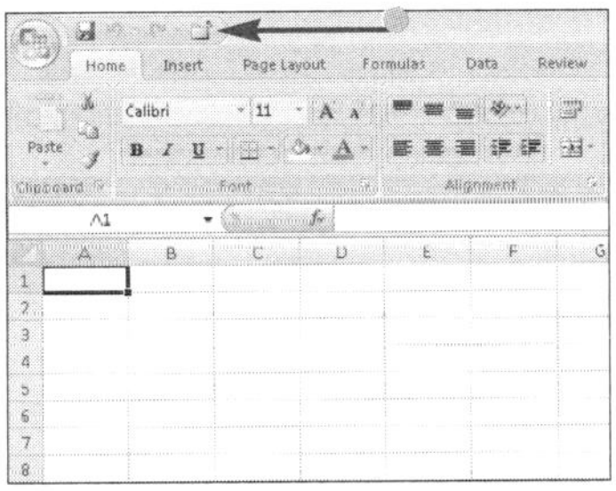

MASTER IT

If I decide I do not want a button on the Quick Access Toolbar, can I remove it?

▼ Yes. Follow Steps 1 to 3. In the list on the right side of the Excel Options dialog box, click the command you want to remove. Then click the Remove button. Excel removes the button from the list. Click OK, and Excel closes the Excel Options dialog box, saving your settings. The button you removed no longer appears on the Quick Access Toolbar.

What groups of commands are available when I click ▾ in Step 4?

▼ Four unique groups appear at the top of the drop-down menu when you click ▾: Popular Commands, Commands Not in the Ribbon, All Commands, and Macros. The other groups listed display commands based on where they appear in the program: Office Menu, the typical Ribbon tabs, and the special tabs that appear based on the action you are performing, such as the Picture Tools tab and its accompanying Format tab.

How do I reorder the buttons on the Quick Access Toolbar?

▼ Complete Steps 1 to 3. In the list on the right, click a button. Then click ▴ or ▾. Moving a button up moves it to the left on the Quick Access Toolbar, while moving it down moves it to the right.

Change Popular Options

Each time you open a new workbook, Excel applies a series of preferences to the workbook based on assumptions concerning the way you want the worksheet and chart information that you enter into the workbook to appear on-screen and in print. You can change those preferences as needed to support the way you work.

All of the options that you can control in Excel appear in the Excel Options dialog box, where you find the options grouped based on similarity. This grouping approach helps you easily find the options you want to change. Excel uses the tabs that appear down the side of the Excel Options dialog box to create the major groups for options. Then, within each group, you find additional headings that organize the options on that page.

On the Popular tab, you find three headings of options that you can change: Top Options for Working with Excel, When Creating New Workbooks, and Personalize Your Copy of Microsoft Office. Using the steps in this section, you can change any of these options to make Excel easier to work with. See the section, "Understanding Popular Options," for more information on the individual choices.

Change Popular Options

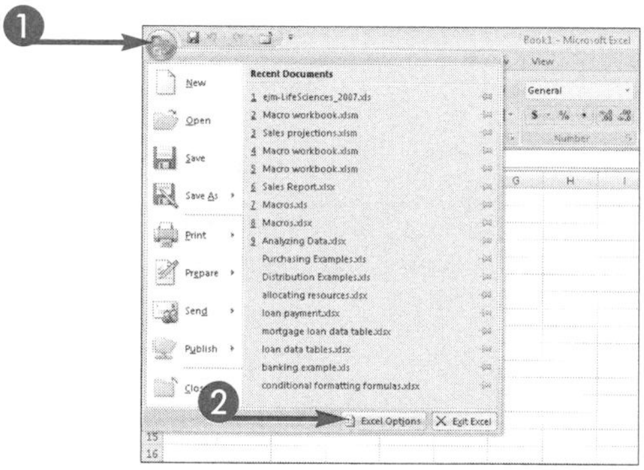

1. Click [Office button].
2. Click Excel Options.

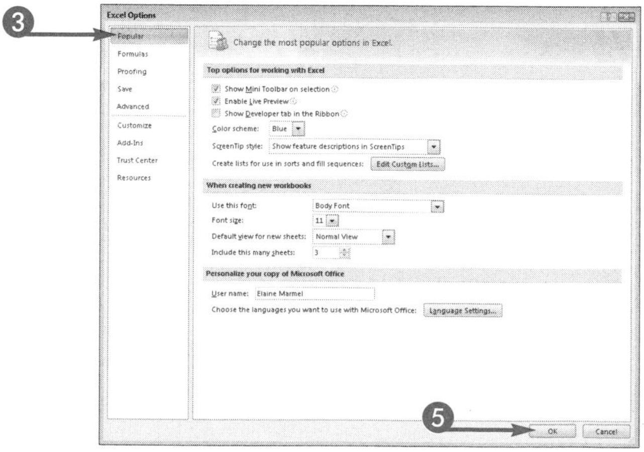

The Excel Options dialog box appears.

3. Click Popular.
4. Change any options as appropriate.
5. Click OK.

Excel saves the changes.

Understanding Popular Options

The most popular options appear in three groups on the Popular tab of the Excel Options dialog box: Top Options for Working with Excel, When Creating New Workbooks, and Personalize Your Copy of Microsoft Office. This section provides some details about the options in each group. To view and change these options, see the section, "Change Popular Options."

Top Options for Working with Excel

Option	Description
Show Mini Toolbar on Selection	Use this option to control whether the Mini Toolbar appears whenever you select text. The Mini Toolbar contains formatting options that also appear on the Home tab.
Enable Live Preview	Use this option to control whether Excel uses the Live Preview feature to show you how information will appear before you apply settings.
Show Developer Tab in the Ribbon	Use this option to control whether the Developer tab appears in the Ribbon. When displayed, this tab contains tools that you can use when working with macros, form development, or XML file formats.
Color Scheme	Use this list box to select one of three color schemes: Blue (the default), Silver, or Black.
ScreenTip Style	Use this list box to control the behavior of ScreenTips. ScreenTips display brief descriptions about the purpose of buttons on the Ribbon or the Quick Access Toolbar when you hover the mouse pointer over the button.
Edit Custom Lists	Click this button to create additional custom lists to use when AutoFilling cells. Lists exist for the days of the week and the months of the year.

When Creating New Workbooks

Option	Description
Use This Font	Use this list box to select the font you want Excel to use for all new workbooks. The default, Body Font, corresponds to Calibri.
Font Size	Use this list box to select a size, in points, for the font in all new workbooks. The default size is 11 points.
Default View for New Sheets	Use this list box to set the default view for new workbooks; the default view is Normal View, but you can also choose Page Break Preview or Page Layout View.
Include This Many Sheets	In this field, type the number of sheets you want Excel to include in each new workbook.

Personalize Your Copy of Microsoft Office

Option	Description
User Name	In this field, you can enter the name you want Excel to assign as the author of new workbooks.
Language Settings	Click this button to open the Microsoft Office Language Settings 2007 dialog box. From this dialog box, you can enable various foreign languages and set the default editing language.

Change Common Calculation Options

Each time you open a new workbook, Excel applies a series of preferences to the workbook based on assumptions concerning the way you want Excel to behave in relation to calculating workbooks. You can change those preferences as needed to support the way you work.

All of the options that you can control in Excel appear in the Excel Options dialog box, where you find the options grouped based on similarity. This grouping approach helps you easily find the options you want to change. Excel uses the tabs that appear down the side of the Excel Options dialog box to create the major groups for options. Then, within each group, you find additional headings that organize the options on that page.

On the Formulas tab, you find headings of options that you can change, but this section focuses on making changes under two of those headings: Calculation Options and Working with Formulas. See the section, "Understanding Common Calculation Options," for more information on the choices under these headings. For details on the Error Checking and Error Checking Rules sections, see the sections, "Work with Error Checking Options" and "Understanding Error Checking Options."

Change Common Calculation Options

1. Click .
2. Click Excel Options.

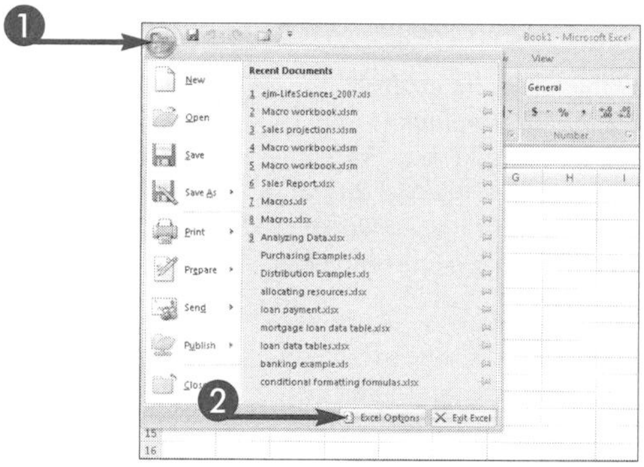

The Excel Options dialog box appears.

3. Click Formulas.
4. Change any options as appropriate.
5. Click OK.

Excel saves the changes.

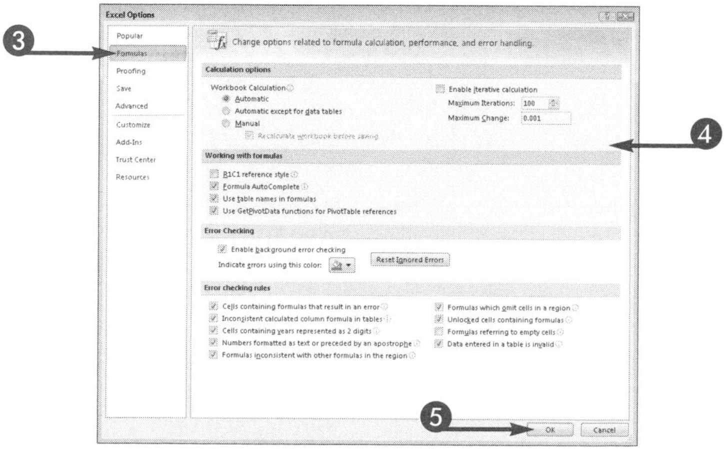

Understanding Common Calculation Options

On the Formulas tab of the Excel Options dialog box, you find four headings. This section provides some details about the options under the Calculation Options heading and the Working with Formulas heading. To view and change these options, see the section, "Change Common Calculation Options." For information on the other two headings on the Formulas tab, see the sections, "Work with Error Checking Options" and "Understanding Error Checking Options."

Calculation Options

Option	*Description*
Automatic, Automatic Except for Data Tables, Manual	Select one of these options to specify the way Excel calculates your workbook. By default, Excel recalculates everything in your workbook automatically, but you can choose to calculate data tables or the entire workbook manually if you find that Excel slows down when calculating a large workbook that contains a lot of formulas. If you choose to use manual recalculation, you can use four keyboard shortcuts to manually recalculate the workbook. The F9 shortcut recalculates formulas that have changed since the last calculation for all open workbooks. Shift+F9 recalculates formulas that have changed since the last calculation for the active worksheet. Ctrl+Alt+F9 recalculates all open workbooks, even if they have not changed since the last calculation. Ctrl+Shift+Alt+F9 rechecks formulas that depend on other formulas and then recalculates all formulas in all open workbooks, even if they have not changed since the last calculation.
Enable Iterative Calculation	Use this option to control whether Excel continues to try calculating formulas that it cannot solve on the first try.
Maximum Iterations	Use this field to set the maximum number of attempts Excel makes to solve a formula that Excel cannot solve on the first try. The number in this field applies only when you have enabled iterative calculation.
Maximum Change	Use this field to set the maximum change by which Excel increments its guesses while trying to solve a formula it cannot solve on the first try. The number in this field applies only when you have enabled iterative calculation.

Working with Formulas

Option	*Description*
R1C1 Reference Style	Use this option to control whether Excel uses numbers to refer to both columns and rows. In this cell referencing system, A1 is R1C1, and B10 is R2C10.
Formula AutoComplete	Use this option to control whether Excel attempts to complete formulas or functions that you type in cells.
Use Table Names in Formulas	Use this option to control whether Excel substitutes a table name in a formula rather than using the table's range address.
Use GetPivotData functions for PivotTable references	Use this option to enable or disable the technique Excel uses to obtain PivotTable information for a formula outside the PivotTable that refers to the PivotTable.

Set Advanced Calculation Options

Each time you open a new workbook, Excel applies a series of preferences to the workbook based on assumptions concerning the way you want Excel to behave in relation to calculating workbooks. You can change those preferences as needed to support the way you work.

All of the options that you can control in Excel appear in the Excel Options dialog box, where you find the options grouped based on similarity. This grouping approach helps you easily find the options you want to change. Excel uses the tabs that appear down the side of the Excel Options dialog box to create the major groups for options. Then, within each group, you find additional headings that organize the options on that page.

On the Advanced tab, you find two headings for calculation-related options that you can change: Formulas and When Calculating This Workbook. See the section, "Understanding Advanced Calculation Options," for more information on the choices under these headings. In most cases, you will not need to make changes to the settings under these two headings, but on occasion, you might want to make a change.

Set Advanced Calculation Options

1. Click .
2. Click Excel Options.

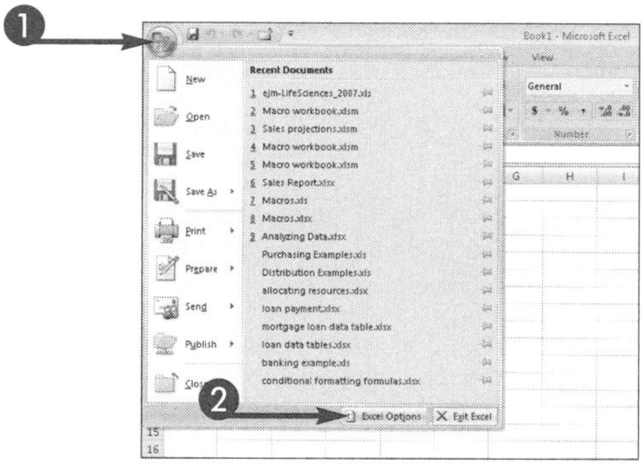

The Excel Options dialog box appears.

3. Click Advanced.
4. Change any options as appropriate.
5. Click OK.

Excel saves the changes.

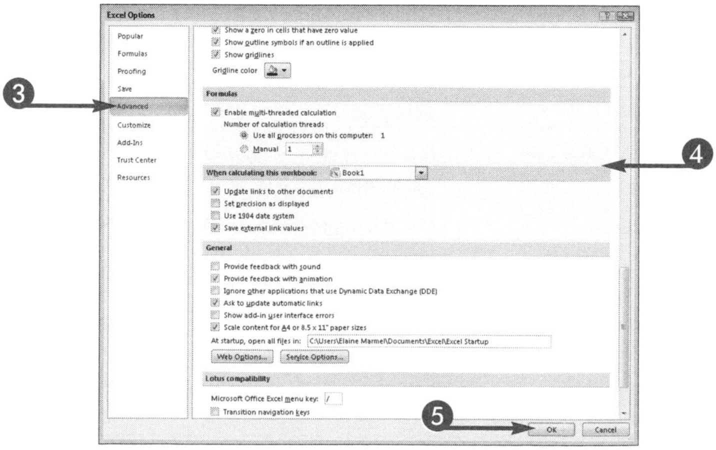

Understanding Advanced Calculation Options

You can find some options on the Advanced tab in the Excel Options dialog box that control the way Excel calculates workbooks. This section provides some details about the options under the Formulas heading and the When calculating this workbook heading. In most cases, you do not need to make changes to these options, but knowing what they do can help you in those few instances when you really do need to make a change. To view and change these options, see the section, "Set Advanced Calculation Options."

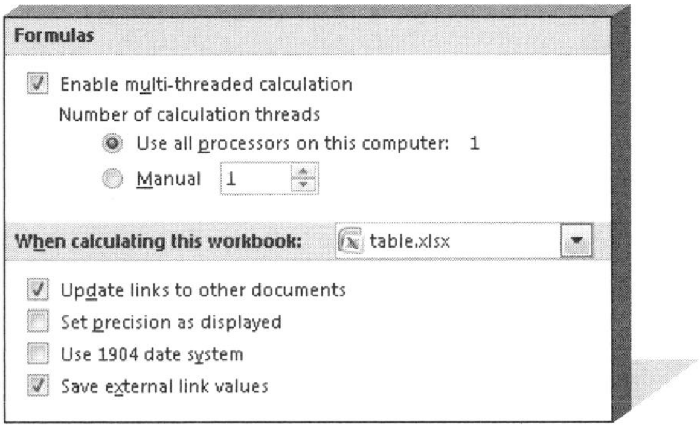

If you have multiple workbooks open, be sure to select the workbook to which you want to apply the When calculating this workbook options.

Formula options and When calculating this workbook options

Option	*Description*
Enable multi-threaded calculation	This option applies to computers that contain more than a single processor. You can select this option to have Excel use more than one processor when making calculations, and you can set the number of processors to use.
Update links to other documents	Use this option to control whether Excel updates links to other workbooks or documents when calculating the current workbook.
Set precision as displayed	You can select this option to permanently change the calculated values in the workbook to the number currently shown. Number formats change the appearance of numbers, but not the values that Excel stores in the cell. Enabling this option changes the values; most of the time, you do *not* want to select this option.
Use 1904 date system	Select this option to work with a workbook containing dates created in an older version of Excel for the Macintosh that used January 2, 1904 instead of January 1, 1900 as serial number 1.
Save external link values	Disable this option if your workbook contains links to large ranges on an external document and seems to need an unusually large amount of disk space or takes an unusually long time to open.

Work with Error Checking Options

Each time you open a new workbook, Excel applies a series of preferences to the workbook based on assumptions concerning the way you want Excel to behave in relation to checking for errors in workbooks. You can change those preferences as needed to support the way you work.

All of the options that you can control in Excel appear in the Excel Options dialog box, where you find the options grouped based on similarity. This grouping approach helps you easily find the options you want to change. Excel uses the tabs that appear down the side of the Excel Options dialog box to create the major groups for options. Then, within each group, you find additional headings that organize the options on that page.

On the Formulas tab, you find two headings related to the error checking options that you can change: Error Checking and Error Checking Rules. See the section, "Understanding Error Checking Options," for more information on the choices under these headings. In most cases, you will not need to make changes to the settings under these two headings, but on occasion, you might want to make a change.

Work with Error Checking Options

1. Click .
2. Click Excel Options.

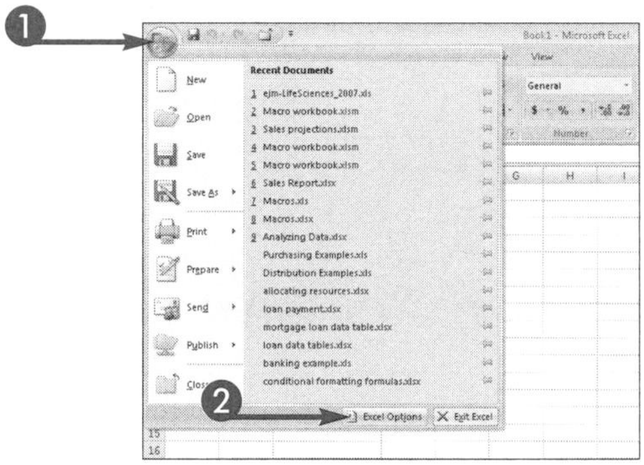

The Excel Options dialog box appears.

3. Click Formulas.
4. Change any options as appropriate.
5. Click OK.

Excel saves the changes.

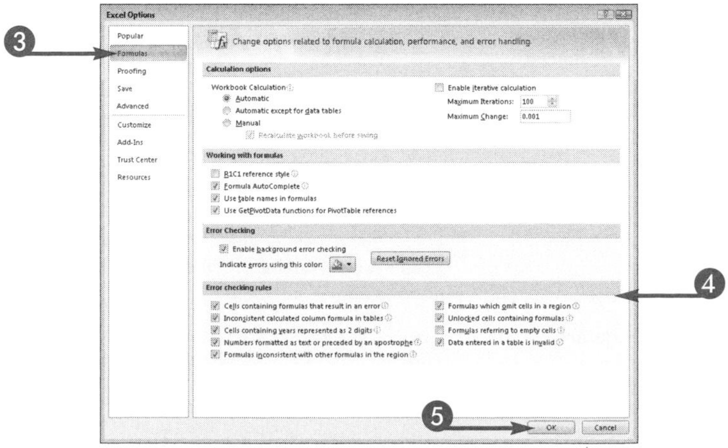

Understanding Error Checking Options

On the Formulas tab in the Excel Options dialog box, you find some options that control the way Excel handles calculation error checking in workbooks. This section provides some details about the options under the Error Checking heading and the Error Checking Rules heading. In most cases, you do not need to make changes to these options, but knowing what they do can help you in those few instances when you really do need to make a change. To view and change these options, see the section, "Work with Error Checking Options."

Error Checking

Option	***Description***
Enable background error checking	By default, Excel checks for calculation errors; if this behavior annoys you, feel free to deselect this option (☑ changes to ☐). When you allow Excel to check for calculation errors, you can select the color Excel uses to indicate that a cell contains an error. Excel identifies cells that contain errors by displaying a small green triangle in the upper-left corner of the cell.
Reset ignored errors	When correcting errors, you can choose to ignore them. If you do, you can click the Reset Ignored Errors button to redisplay errors that you chose to ignore.

Error Checking Rules

Option	***Description***
Cells containing formulas that result in an error	Use this option to control whether Excel displays an error indicator in cells that return error values.
Inconsistent calculated column formula in tables	Use this option to control whether Excel displays an error indicator in cells in a table column that contain formulas or values that are inconsistent with other formulas or values in the column.
Cells containing years represented as 2 digits	Use this option to control whether Excel displays an error indicator in cells containing dates formatted as text that display only the last two digits of the year.
Numbers formatted as text or preceded by an apostrophe	Use this option to control whether Excel displays an error indicator in cells containing numbers formatted as text or preceded by an apostrophe.
Formulas inconsistent with other formulas in the region	Use this option to control whether Excel displays an error indicator in cells containing formulas that differ from the other formulas in the same area of the worksheet.
Formulas which omit cells in a region	Use this option to control whether Excel displays an error indicator in cells containing a formula that omits cells from the range to which the formula refers.
Unlocked cells containing formulas	Use this option to control whether Excel displays an error indicator in unlocked cells that contain formulas when the worksheet is protected.
Formulas referring to empty cells	Use this option to control whether Excel displays an error indicator in cells containing formulas that refer to blank cells.
Data entered in a table is invalid	Use this option to control whether Excel displays an error indicator in cells containing formulas for which you have set up Data Validation criteria that are not valid.

Work with AutoCorrect Options

The Excel AutoCorrect feature works as you type, catching and correcting common typographical errors. The AutoCorrect feature is set up to catch hundreds of common typing and spelling mistakes, but you can add typing mistakes that you make frequently and that Excel does not catch. For example, if you consistently mistype the word "information" as "informaiton," you can create an AutoCorrect entry to tell Excel to fix this mistake for you. You can also create an AutoCorrect entry that automatically changes "pp" to "PowerPoint."

All of the options that you can control in Excel appear in the Excel Options dialog box, where you find the options grouped based on similarity. This grouping approach helps you easily find the options you want to change. Excel uses the tabs that appear down the side of the Excel Options dialog box to create the major groups for options. Then, within each group, you find additional headings that organize the options on that page.

On the Proofing tab, you find two headings related to the proofing options that you can change: AutoCorrect Options and When Correcting Spelling in Microsoft Office Programs. See the section, "Change Proofing Options," for more information on the choices under the second heading.

Work with AutoCorrect Options

Create an AutoCorrect Entry

1. Click .
2. Click Excel Options.

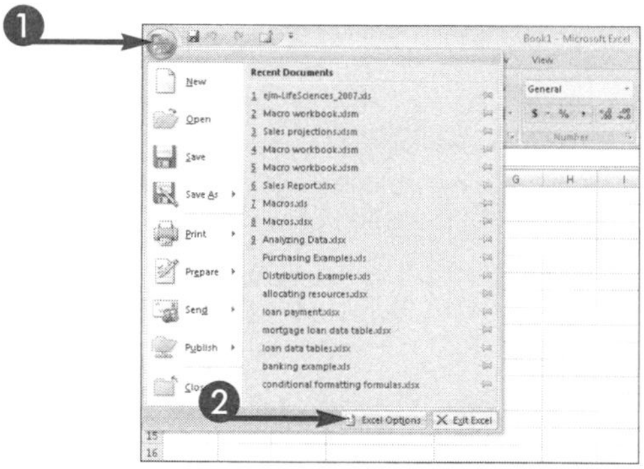

The Excel Options dialog box appears.

3. Click Proofing.
4. Click AutoCorrect Options.

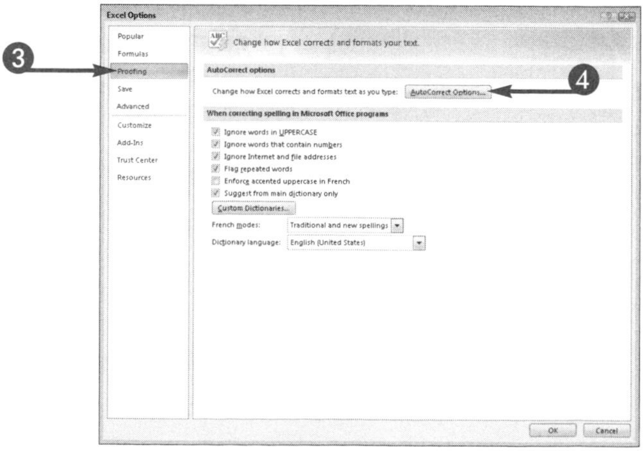

The AutoCorrect dialog box appears.

5. Type the text you want Excel to replace.
6. Type the replacement text.
7. Click Add.
8. Repeat Steps 5 to 7 for each AutoCorrect entry you want to define.
9. Click Exceptions.
   - If you do not want to set exceptions, click OK.

Set AutoCorrect Exceptions

Note: *If you closed the Excel Options dialog box, complete Steps 1 to 4 and Step 9 in the preceding subsection.*

- Click this tab to identify combinations of letters followed by a period that Excel should ignore.
- Click this tab to identify combinations of capital letters that Excel should ignore.

10. Click OK in the three dialog boxes to save your changes.

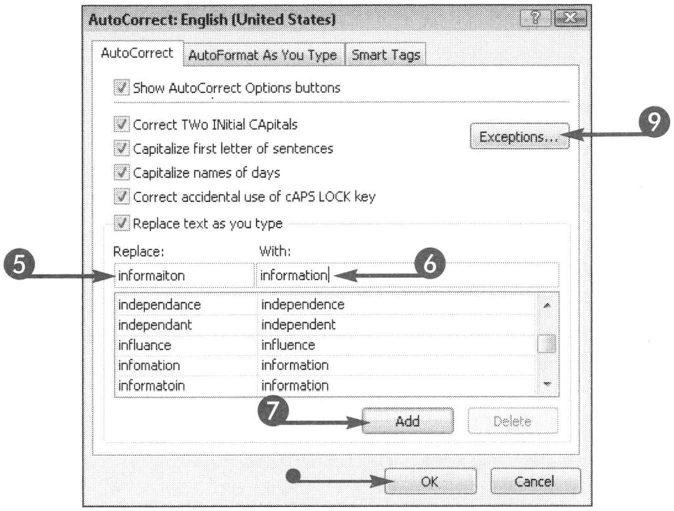

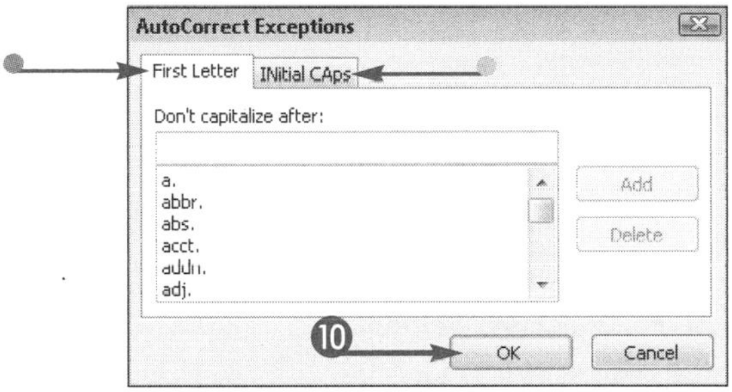

MASTER IT

What does the "Show AutoCorrect Options Buttons" option do?

▼ When Excel applies an AutoCorrect or AutoFormatting option to a cell, it displays, by default, an AutoCorrect Options button that you can use to undo the automatic change Excel made to whatever you typed in the cell. Initially, the AutoCorrect Options button appears as a flat, blue rectangle under the first letter of a cell containing an entry to which AutoCorrect options apply. When you point at the flat, blue rectangle, the AutoCorrect Options button (▣) appears. Click this button to see the available options. For more information on AutoFormatting, see the section, "Control Automatic Formatting."

When might I not want Excel to capitalize?

▼ If you are consistently using an abbreviation that does not appear at the end of a sentence, you would not want Excel to capitalize the word that follows the abbreviation's period. For example, "My appt. is at 3:00 PM."

When might I not want Excel to correct two initial capital letters?

▼ Suppose that you work in a college environment that uses teaching assistants, and you refer to teaching assistants in writing as TAs. You would not want Excel to correct this entry to Tas.

Control Automatic Formatting

You can control the way Excel behaves when automatically formatting information you enter into Excel from the AutoFormat As You Type tab of the AutoCorrect dialog box. You open the AutoCorrect dialog box from the Proofing tab of the Excel Options dialog box, which contains all of the options that control the behavior of Excel. You can change any of the following options:

The **Internet and network paths with hyperlinks** option controls whether Excel replaces Internet and network paths that you type with hyperlinks.

The **Include new rows and columns in table** option controls whether Excel adds new rows and columns to tables as you work.

The **Fill formulas in tables to create calculated columns** option controls whether Excel automatically fills formulas in tables to create calculated columns as you work.

You can also control the way Excel applies Smart Tags. Smart Tags are links from certain types of information that is entered into your workbook with other sources. For example, if you type the name of an Outlook contact, Excel applies a Smart Tag that enables you to click the contact's link and send an e-mail, schedule a meeting, open the contact's information, and perform other actions in Outlook.

Control Automatic Formatting

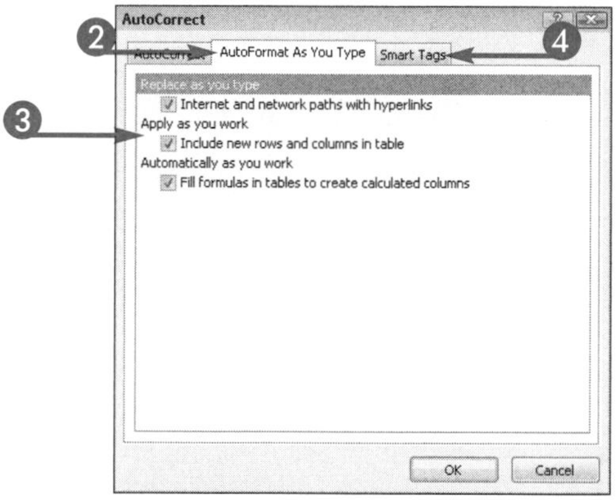

1. Display the AutoCorrect dialog box.

Note: *To display this dialog box, complete Steps 1 to 4 in the "Create an AutoCorrect Entry" subsection of the "Work with AutoCorrect Options" section.*

2. Click AutoFormat As You Type.
3. Change any options as appropriate.
4. Click Smart Tags.

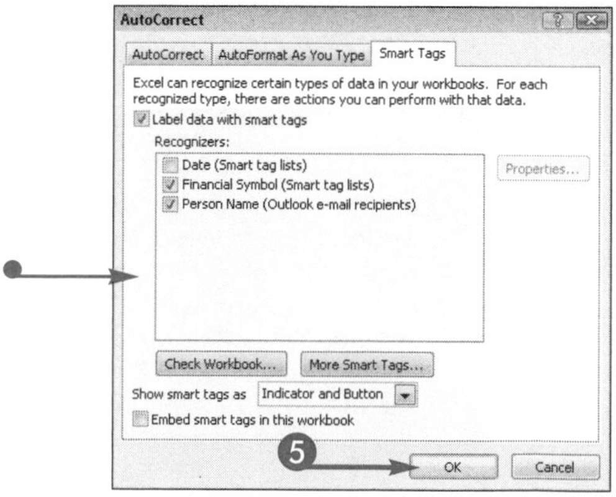

- You can use these options to control whether Excel creates Smart Tags and, if so, to what kind of information.

5. Click OK in the two dialog boxes.

Excel saves the changes and closes the AutoCorrect dialog box and the Excel Options dialog box.

Change Proofing Options

The options shown in the "When Correcting Spelling in Microsoft Office Programs" section on the Proofing tab of the Excel Options dialog box control the behavior of Excel concerning spell checking. The two French options refer to French spelling. You can change any of the following options:

Ignore words in UPPERCASE controls whether Excel marks words entered in all uppercase letters, such as acronyms, as misspellings.

Ignore words that contain numbers controls whether Excel marks words containing numbers, such as A14, as misspellings.

Ignore Internet and file addresses controls whether Excel marks Internet and file addresses as misspellings.

Flag repeated words controls whether Excel marks repetitions of the same word — such as "very very" in the sentence, "The tea was very very hot" — as misspellings.

Suggest from main dictionary only controls whether Excel uses only the main dictionary while it checks spelling.

The Custom Dictionaries button allows you to display the Custom Dictionaries dialog box. In this dialog box, you can edit the custom dictionary, which stores misspellings you identify that Excel does not recognize. You can also create new entries in the custom dictionary or create a new custom dictionary.

Dictionary language controls the language Excel uses when it checks spelling.

Change Proofing Options

1. Click .
2. Click Excel Options.

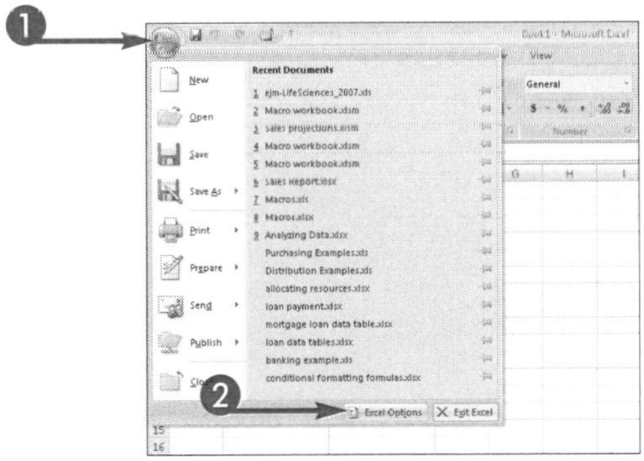

The Excel Options dialog box appears.

3. Click Proofing.
4. Change any options as appropriate.
5. Click OK.

Excel saves the changes.

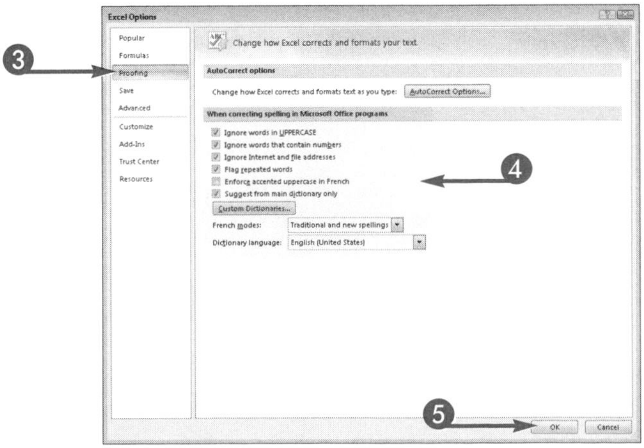

PART VI

Select Options for Saving Files

Each time you open a new workbook, Excel applies a series of preferences to the workbook based on assumptions concerning the way you want Excel to behave in relation to saving workbooks. You can change those preferences as needed to support the way you work.

All of the options that you can control in Excel appear in the Excel Options dialog box, where you find the options grouped based on similarity. This grouping approach helps you easily find the options you want to change. Excel uses the tabs that appear down the side of the Excel Options dialog box to create the major groups for options. Then, within each group, you find additional headings that organize the options on that page.

On the Save tab, you find four headings: Save Workbooks, AutoRecover Exceptions For, Offline Edition Options for Document Management Server Files, and Preserve Visual Appearance of the Workbook. See the section, "Understanding Save Options," for more information on the choices under these headings. In most cases, you will not need to make changes to the settings under these headings, but on occasion, you might want to make a change.

Select Options for Saving Files

1. Click [Office button].
2. Click Excel Options.

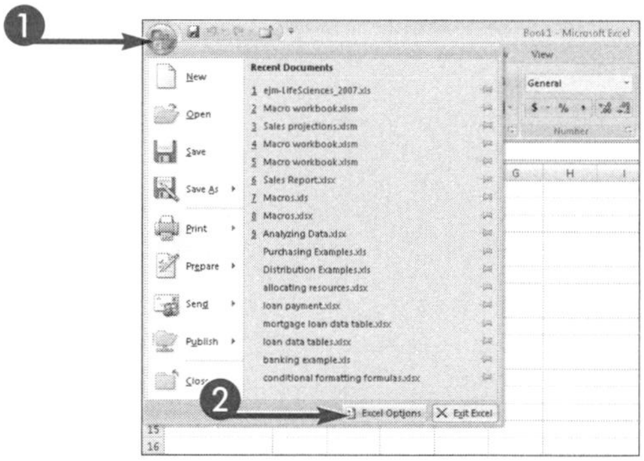

The Excel Options dialog box appears.

3. Click Save.
4. Change any options as appropriate.

   In this example, Excel Workbook has been chosen as the file format in which Excel files are saved.
5. Click OK.

   Excel saves the changes.

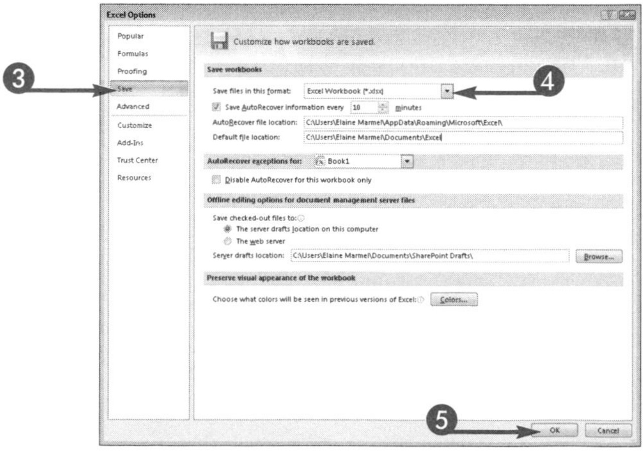

Understanding Save Options

You can use the options on the Save tab to control how Excel behaves when saving workbooks. Under the Save Workbooks heading, you can select a default file format for workbooks you save, and you can specify the folder where you want to save all of your Excel workbooks. By default, the folder Excel uses to save your workbooks depends on your operating system. In Windows XP and earlier, Excel saves workbooks to C:\Documents and Settings\Username\My Documents, where Username is the name of your account on the computer. In Windows Vista, Excel saves workbooks to C:\Users\Username\Documents, where Username is the name of your account on the computer.

Also under the Save Workbooks heading, you can control the Excel behavior with respect to the AutoRecover feature. Using the AutoRecover feature, Excel automatically saves a copy of your workbook every 10 minutes. You can control whether Excel makes AutoRecover copies and if so, how often and where Excel saves them. Under the AutoRecover Exceptions For heading, you can disable the AutoRecover feature for a specified workbook. Disabling any portion of the AutoRecover feature is not recommended; allowing Excel to make a copy of an open workbook every 10 minutes does not interfere with your work, nor does it cost you much in the way of disk space.

The AutoRecover feature also provides several advantages. For example, if your computer crashes or the power goes out or your workbook becomes corrupted, you can take advantage of the AutoRecover feature. The next time you open Excel, the AutoRecover pane appears, displaying the last copy of your workbook saved by the AutoRecover feature. This copy may contain information that you had not saved before your work was interrupted. You can open and review the copy and, if you want, you can save the AutoRecover workbook either as a replacement for or in addition to the last copy you saved.

In addition to saving a copy of your file, the AutoRecover feature also saves certain program state information. For example, if you have several workbooks open in Excel when a crash occurs, the AutoRecover feature remembers the workbooks that were open and where the cell pointer was positioned when the AutoRecover feature made the last copy. When you reopen Excel after the crash, Excel opens all of the workbooks that were open at the time of the crash and positions the cell pointer at its last known location.

The settings under the Offline Edition Options for Document Management Server Files heading apply to Excel users who use Excel Services, a part of SharePoint Services, to share workbook files. If you or your company use Excel Services, you change the location where Excel saves drafts of workbooks that you check out for editing. By default, Excel saves these drafts on your local hard drive, in a folder called SharePoint Drafts, in the Documents folder under Windows Vista or the My Documents folder under Windows XP or earlier. The options under this heading enable you to save the drafts to the Web server that contains SharePoint; to make this change, you also need the path to the Web server.

Finally, if you share Excel 2007 workbooks with users of Excel 97 to Excel 2003, you can use the Colors button to specify which color in an Excel 2007 worksheet to preserve in formatted tables and other graphics when you save the workbook file using the Excel 97-2003 file format.

Set Editing Options

Each time you open a new workbook, Excel applies a series of preferences to the workbook based on assumptions concerning the way you want Excel to behave in relation to editing workbooks. You can change those preferences as needed to support the way you work.

All of the options that you can control in Excel appear in the Excel Options dialog box, where you find the options grouped based on similarity. This grouping approach helps you easily find the options you want to change. Excel uses the tabs that appear down the side of the Excel Options dialog box to create the major groups for options. Then, within each group, you find additional headings that organize the options on that page.

On the Advanced tab, you find two headings that relate specifically to editing: Editing Options and Cut, Copy, and Paste. See the section, "Understanding Editing Options," for more information on the choices under these headings. In most cases, you will not need to make changes to the settings under these two headings, but on occasion, you might want to make a change.

Set Editing Options

1. Click [Office button].
2. Click Excel Options.

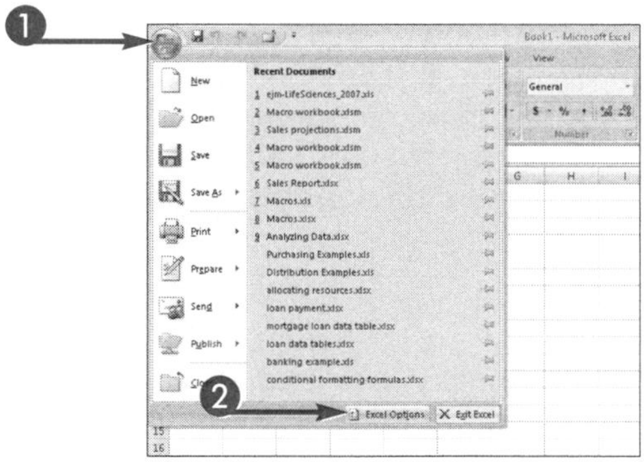

The Excel Options dialog box appears.

3. Click Advanced.
4. Change any options as appropriate.
5. Click OK.

Excel saves the changes.

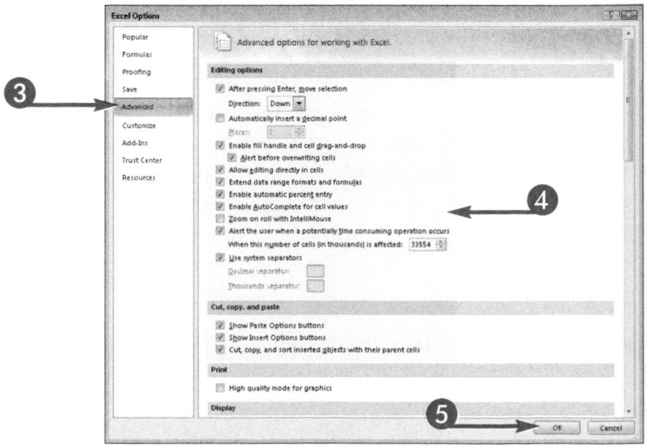

Understanding Editing Options

The options shown under the Editing heading and the Cut, Copy and Paste heading on the Advanced tab of the Excel Options dialog box control how Excel behaves in relation to editing. You can change any of the following options:

After pressing Enter, move selection controls whether Excel moves the cell pointer down, up, right, or left when you press Enter.

Automatically insert a decimal point controls whether Excel inserts a decimal point in numbers you type; if you enable this option, use the Places field to indicate where you want the decimal point inserted. You can use a positive number to move the decimal point to the left, or a negative number to move the decimal point to the right.

Enable fill handle and cell drag-and-drop controls whether you can move and copy information by dragging, as well as use the fill handle to copy information and fill adjacent cells with a series of information such as consecutive dates. If you enable this option, you must also indicate whether you want Excel to alert you if dragging and dropping or using the fill handle will overwrite information in existing cells.

Allow editing directly in cells controls whether you can edit a cell by double-clicking the cell instead of editing the cell contents in the Formula Bar.

Extend data range formats and formulas controls whether Excel automatically formats new items you add to the end of a list to match the format of the rest of the list. If you enable this option, Excel also copies formulas that are repeated in every row. Excel extends formats and formulas only if they have appeared in at least three of the five rows that precede the new row.

Enable automatic percent entry controls whether Excel multiplies by 100 all of the numbers less than 1 that you enter in cells that are formatted in the Percentage format. When you do not select this option, Excel multiplies all numbers that are formatted in the Percentage format, both less than and greater than 1.

Enable AutoComplete for cell values controls whether Excel completes text entries that you start to type in a column of data, when the first few letters match an existing entry in that column.

Zoom on roll with IntelliMouse only applies if you use the Microsoft IntelliMouse. This option controls whether the wheel button zooms or scrolls on your worksheet or chart sheet.

Alert the user when a potentially time consuming operation occurs controls whether Excel notifies you when an operation affects a large number of cells and may take a long time to process. If you select this option, you can specify the number of cells affected by an operation before Excel notifies you.

Use system separators controls whether Excel uses the default Decimal and Thousands separators for your region. Deselect this option to select alternate separators.

Show Paste Options buttons controls whether Excel displays the Paste Options button (), which you can use to select special options when you paste information.

Show Insert Options buttons controls whether Excel displays the Insert Options button (), which you can use to select special options when you insert cells, rows, or columns.

Cut, copy, and sort inserted objects with their parent cells controls whether Excel keeps graphic objects, buttons, text boxes, drawn objects, and pictures with their associated cells whenever you cut, copy, sort, or filter.

Set General Display Options

Each time you open a new workbook, Excel applies a series of preferences to the workbook based on assumptions concerning how Excel behaves in relation to displaying workbooks. You can change those preferences as needed to support the way you work.

All of the options that you can control in Excel appear in the Excel Options dialog box, where you find the options grouped based on similarity. This grouping approach helps you easily find the options you want to change. Excel uses the tabs that appear down the side of the Excel Options dialog box to create the major groups for options. Then, within each group, you find additional headings that organize the options on that page.

On the Advanced tab, you find one heading, Display, which relates specifically to the options you can set that control the overall Excel behavior when displaying information. See the section, "Understanding General Display Options," for more information on the choices under this heading. In most cases, you will not need to make changes to the settings under this heading, but on occasion, you might want to make a change.

Set General Display Options

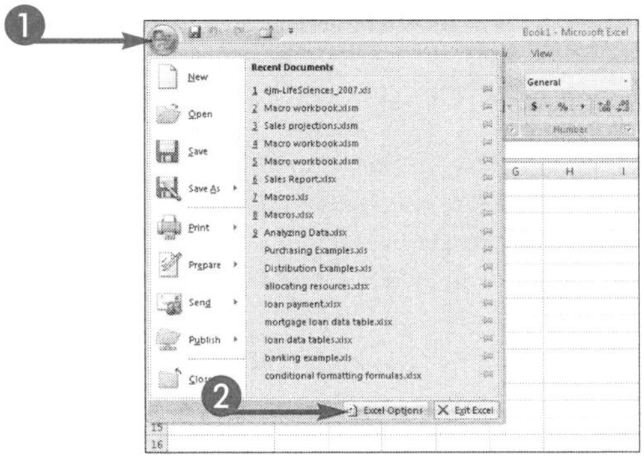

1. Click .
2. Click Excel Options.

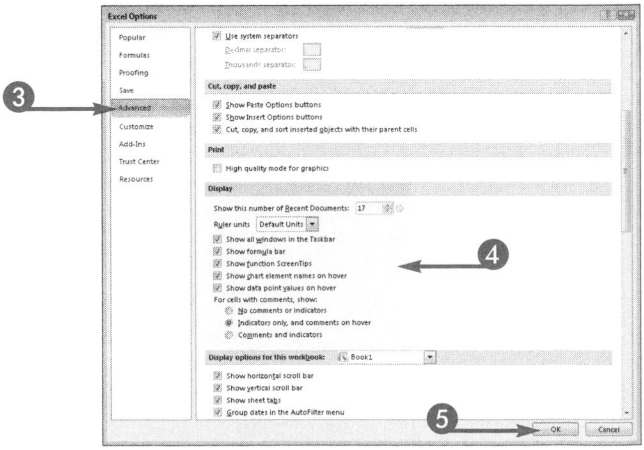

The Excel Options dialog box appears.

3. Click Advanced.

Note: *You may need to scroll down to find Display options.*

4. Change any options as appropriate.
5. Click OK.

Excel saves the changes.

Understanding General Display Options

The Advanced tab of the Excel Options dialog box contains the options you can set that control how Excel behaves when it displays various aspects of the program. These options affect the overall appearance of Excel. To set options for a particular workbook and worksheet, see the sections, "Set Display Options for the Current Workbook and Worksheet" and "Understanding Display Options for the Current Workbook and Worksheet."

Display Options

Option	*Description*
Show this number of recent documents	Use this field to control the number of recently opened workbooks when you click the Office button. You can click any workbook that appears in the list to open it. You can specify any number of workbooks between 0 and 50.
Ruler units	Use this drop-down list to control the units that appear on the ruler when you click the Page Layout button to view your workbook in Page Layout view.
Show all windows in Taskbar	Use this option to control whether Excel displays each workbook you open as a button on the Windows taskbar. If you deselect this option, only one button appears on the Windows taskbar for Excel, even if you open multiple workbooks. To switch between open workbooks, use the View tab.
Show Formula Bar	Use this option to control whether Excel displays the Formula Bar above the columns of the worksheet. When you do not display the Formula Bar, you cannot see the stored contents of the selected cell; instead, you see the cell as formatted.
Show function ScreenTips	This option works in conjunction with the Formula AutoComplete option. With Formula AutoComplete enabled, Excel suggests functions as you begin typing a function. Use this option to control whether Excel also displays brief descriptions of the functions that appear as you type a function.
Show chart element names on hover	Use this option to control whether Excel displays the name of a chart element when the mouse pointer hovers over the chart element.
Show data point values on hover	Use this option to control whether Excel displays the value of a data point when the mouse pointer hovers over the data point.
For cells with comments, show:	Use this option to control how Excel treats cells that contain comments. If you select the "No Comments or Indicators" option, Excel hides comments and comment indicators in cells that contain comments. If you select the "Indicators Only, and Comments on Hover" option, Excel displays a small triangle in the upper-right corner of a cell containing a comment. If you hover the mouse pointer over the cell, Excel displays the comment. Finally, if you select the "Comments and Indicators" option, Excel displays the comment and comment indicator, even if you do not hover the mouse pointer over the cell.

Set Display Options for the Current Workbook and Worksheet

Each time you open a new workbook, Excel applies a series of preferences to the workbook based on assumptions concerning how Excel behaves in relation to displaying workbooks. You can change those preferences as needed to support the way you work.

All of the options that you can control in Excel appear in the Excel Options dialog box, where you find the options grouped based on similarity. This grouping approach helps you easily find the options you want to change. Excel uses the tabs that appear down the side of the Excel Options dialog box to create the major groups for options. Then, within each group, you find additional headings that organize the options on that page.

On the Advanced tab, you find the sections, Display Options for this Workbook, and Display Options for this Worksheet, which relate specifically to the options you can set that control how Excel behaves when displaying information in the current workbook and worksheet. See the section, "Understanding Display Options for the Current Workbook and Worksheet," for more information on the choices under these headings. In most cases, you will not need to make changes to the settings under these headings, but on occasion, you might want to make a change.

Set Display Options for the Current Workbook and Worksheet

1. Click .
2. Click Excel Options.

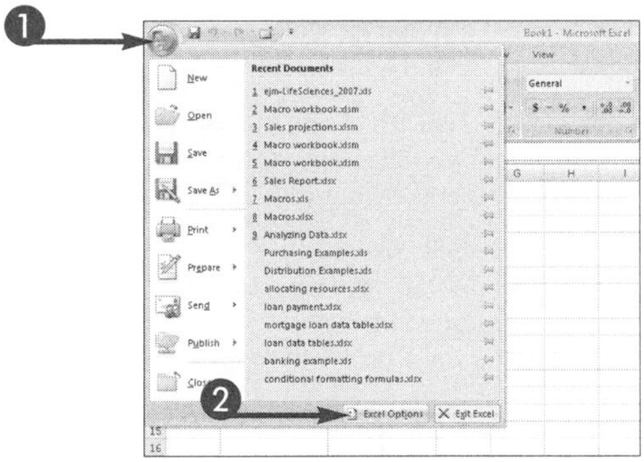

The Excel Options dialog box appears.

3. Click Advanced.
4. Change any options as appropriate.
5. Click OK.

Excel saves the changes.

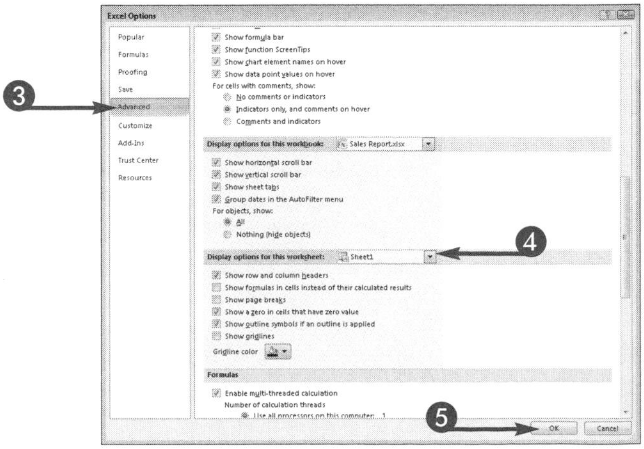

Understanding Display Options for the Current Workbook and Worksheet

On the Advanced tab of the Excel Options dialog box, you find the options you can set that control how Excel displays various aspects of a selected workbook and a selected worksheet.

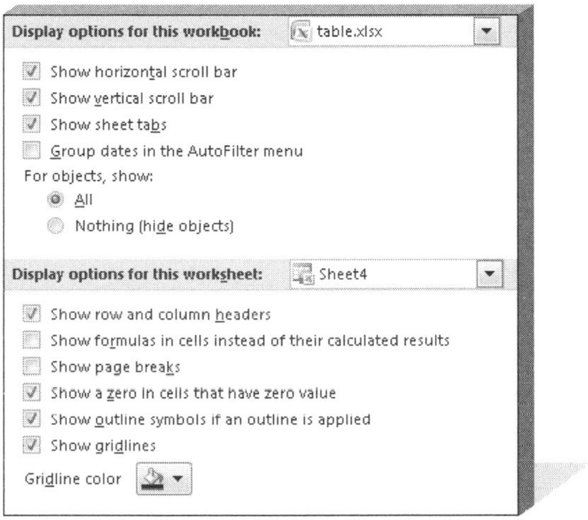

These options affect only the selected workbook or worksheet. To set display options for Excel in general, see the sections, "Set General Display Options" and "Understanding General Display Options."

Under the "Display options for this workbook" heading, you can set the options listed below. Make sure that you first select the appropriate workbook in the drop-down list above the options.

Show horizontal scroll bar controls whether Excel displays the horizontal scroll bar that appears at the bottom of the worksheet.

Show vertical scroll bar controls whether Excel displays the vertical scroll bar on the right or left side of the worksheet, depending on the language mode you use.

Show sheet tabs controls whether Excel displays worksheet tabs at the bottom of the window that you can use to switch worksheets.

Group dates in the AutoFilter menu controls whether, in a column containing dates to which you apply AutoFilters, Excel displays a hierarchical grouping of dates or a nonhierarchical list of dates on the AutoFilter menu.

For objects, show controls whether Excel displays or hides graphic objects in the workbook. If you select All, Excel displays all buttons, text boxes, drawn objects, and pictures in the workbook. If you select Nothing (hide objects), Excel hides all buttons, text boxes, drawn objects, and pictures. Excel does not print hidden objects.

Under the "Display options for this worksheet" heading, you can set the options listed below. First, make sure that you select the appropriate worksheet in the drop-down list above the options.

Show row and column headers controls whether Excel displays column letters at the top of the worksheet and row numbers on the left (or right, depending on the language mode you select) side of the worksheet.

Show formulas in cells instead of their calculated results controls whether Excel displays the formulas in cells instead of the results of the formulas. If you want to see formulas temporarily, click the Formulas tab and then click .

Show page breaks controls whether Excel displays page breaks that Excel automatically sets.

Show a zero in cells that have zero value controls whether Excel displays a 0 (zero) in cells that contain zero values. If you do not select this option, cells containing zero appear as if they were blank on the worksheet; to see their content, you must look in the Formula Bar.

Show outline symbols if an outline is applied controls whether Excel displays outline symbols when you outline a worksheet.

Show gridlines controls whether Excel displays cell gridlines in the worksheet. Displaying gridlines on-screen does not make Excel print gridlines. To print gridlines, click the Page Layout tab. In the Sheet Options group, click the Print option under Gridlines.

The Gridline Color button allows you to select the color Excel displays on-screen for gridlines.

Set General Options

Each time you open a new workbook, Excel applies a series of preferences to the workbook based on assumptions concerning how Excel behaves in general. You can change those preferences as needed to support the way you work.

All of the options that you can control in Excel appear in the Excel Options dialog box, where you find the options grouped based on similarity. This grouping approach helps you easily find the options you want to change. Excel uses the tabs that appear down the side of the Excel Options dialog box to create the major groups for options. Then, within each group, you find additional headings that organize the options on that page.

On the Advanced tab, you find one heading, General, which relates specifically to the options you can set that control how Excel generally behaves. See the section, "Understanding General Options," for more information on the choices under this heading. In most cases, you will not need to make changes to the settings under this heading, but on occasion, you might want to make a change.

Set General Options

1. Click [Office button].
2. Click Excel Options.

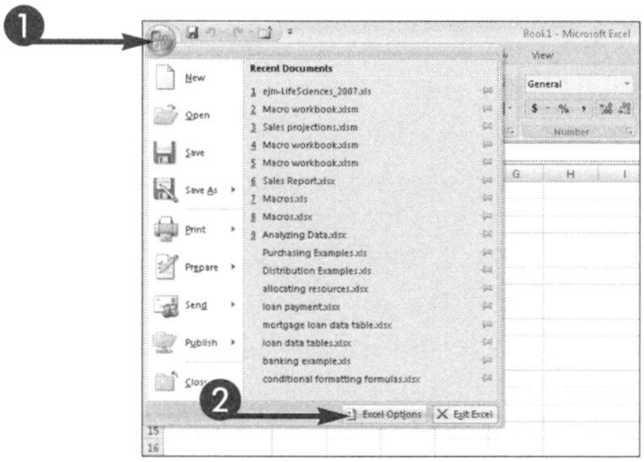

The Excel Options dialog box appears.

3. Click Advanced.
4. Change any options as appropriate.
5. Click OK.

Excel saves the changes.

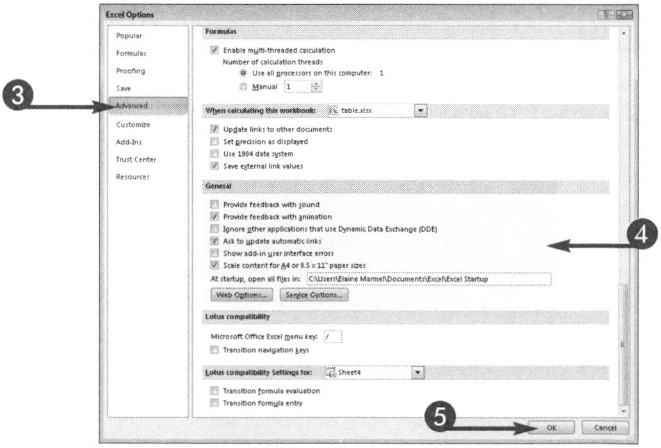

Understanding General Options

On the Advanced tab of the Excel Options dialog box, you find the options that you can set to control the general way that Excel behaves.

General Options

Option	Description
Provide feedback with sound	Use this option to control whether Excel plays sounds that are associated with Microsoft Office program events. You can change the sounds assigned to various events in the Control Panel. This setting controls sounds in all Office programs, not just Excel.
Provide feedback with animation	Use this option to control whether Excel uses animation to display worksheet movement and changes when you insert or delete cells, rows, or columns. Animation might make video performance seem slow on some computers.
Ignore other applications that use Dynamic Data Exchange (DDE)	Use this option to control whether Excel exchanges data with other applications that use Dynamic Data Exchange (DDE).
Ask to update automatic links	Use this option to control whether Excel displays a message asking if you want to update linked items.
Show add-in user interface errors	Use this option to control whether Excel displays errors in the user interface of add-ins that you install and use.
Scale content for A4 or 8.5 x 11" paper sizes	Use this option to control whether Excel automatically adjusts documents formatted for the standard paper size of another country or region so that they print correctly on the standard paper size for your country or region. This option does not affect the formatting in your document.
At startup, open all files in:	You can use this setting to specify the full pathname of a folder that contains workbooks you want Excel to open automatically when you start the program.
Web options	Click this button to set options that control how Excel data looks and responds when the data is viewed in a Web browser.
Service options	Click this button to specify a variety of document management options and shared workspace updating options, as shown in the figure.

Set Web Options

When you save a workbook or worksheet as a Web page, you can control some of the options Excel uses when saving. For information on saving Excel files as Web pages, see Chapter 32.

Although most of the time, the Web options Excel has established will work fine for you, you may occasionally have reason to make changes. On the General tab, you can set two options relating to compatibility. The first option saves any additional externally referenced data needed to make formulas functional. The second option controls whether Excel loads pictures that were created in programs other than Excel from Web pages.

The Browser tab enables you to identify the browser you believe that most people viewing your page will use. In the Options section of this tab, you can choose to display graphic files using the PNG file format, which is a compressed bitmap. You can also enable or disable the use of cascading style sheets (CSS) for font formats and Vector Markup Language (VML) to display graphics, which can speed up the downloading of Web pages. In addition, you can save new Web pages as single-file Web pages.

Set Web Options

1. Click .
2. Click Excel Options.

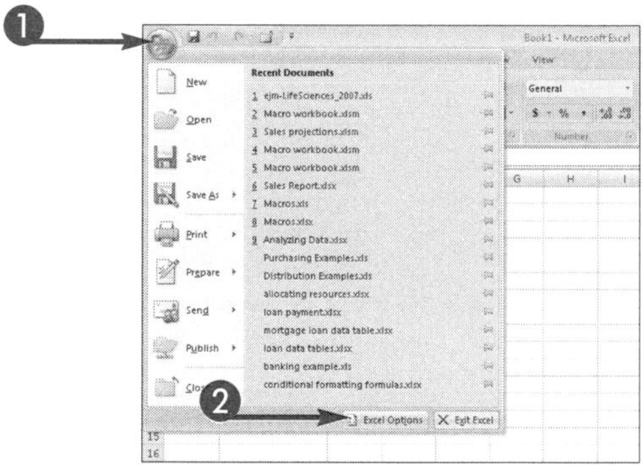

The Excel Options dialog box appears.

3. Click Advanced.
4. Click Web Options.

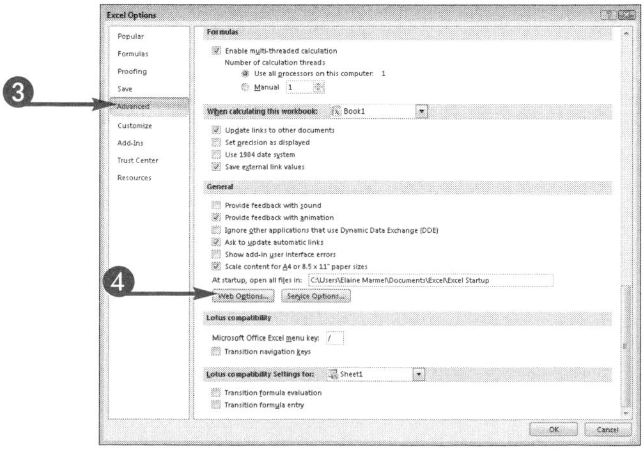

The General tab of the Web Options dialog box appears.

5 Change any options as appropriate.

6 Click the Browsers tab.

Browser-related options appear.

7 Change any options as appropriate.

8 Click the Files tab.

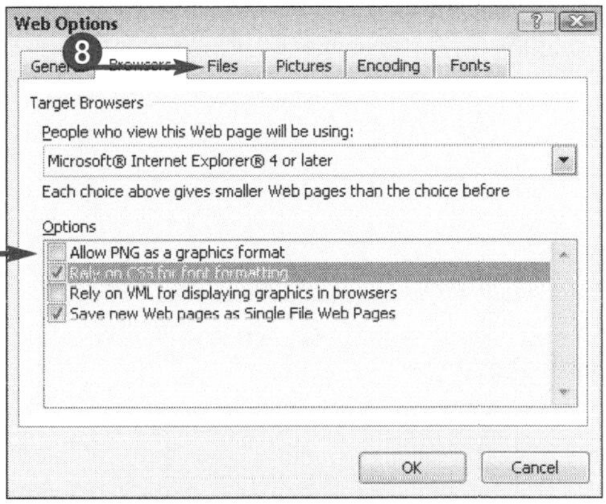

MASTER IT

Why would I disable the compatibility option that saves external data that is needed to make formulas work?

▼ This option applies only to interactive Web pages, which allow a user to make changes in a Web browser and have formulas update. The interactive Web page feature is no longer available in Excel 2007, but the option is included to preserve backward compatibility.

If I choose not to save new Web pages as single-file Web pages, what happens?

▼ Single-file Web pages embed supporting content such as bullets, background textures, and graphics embedded in the Web page. When you disable this option, Excel creates separate files for the supporting content instead of embedding the supporting content. With Excel files, single-file Web pages work better.

How do I choose which browser to use on the Browsers tab?

▼ Select the earliest version of the browser that you believe people might use; the choices are cumulative in the sense that users of later browsers can also view the content.

When should I change the CSS or VML options?

▼ You should change these options if your target browser does not support them.

continued

Set Web Options

(Continued)

From the Files tab, you can choose to store files containing supporting information, such as bullets and graphics, in the same folder as the Web page or in a separate folder. You can also choose to use long filenames if the Web server supports them. Long filenames do not follow the eight character/three character file-naming convention. You can choose whether to move or copy supporting files if you move a Web page. Finally, you can choose whether to view a message if an Office program is not the default editor when you save a Web page.

From the Pictures tab, you can set the screen size and pixels per inch of the target monitor that you expect viewers of the Web page to use.

On the Encoding tab, you can select the encoding for a Web page when Excel displays the wrong characters upon opening the Web page in a browser. You can also select the encoding language in which you want to save a Web page, or you can choose to use the default encoding language on your computer.

On the Fonts tab, you can select the character set, font, and font size that the Web page should use.

Set Web Options *(continued)*

Excel displays settings related to file management.

9. Change any options as appropriate.
10. Click the Pictures tab.

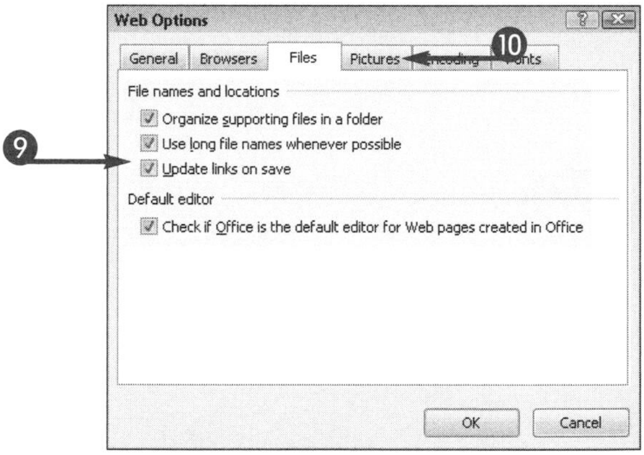

- Excel displays image-related settings.

11. Change any options as appropriate.
12. Click the Encoding tab.

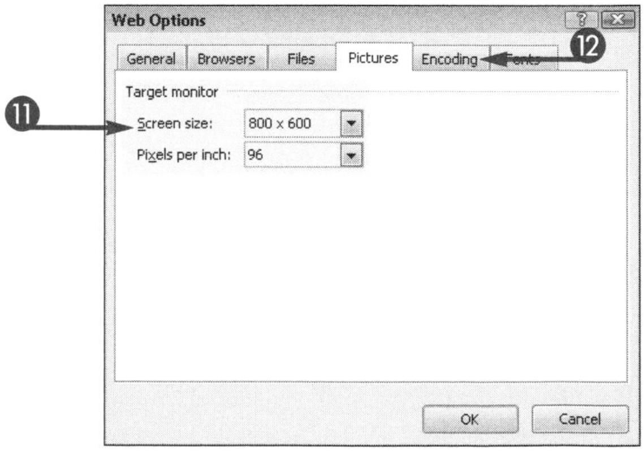

- Excel displays the Web encoding options.

13. Change any options as appropriate.
14. Click Fonts.

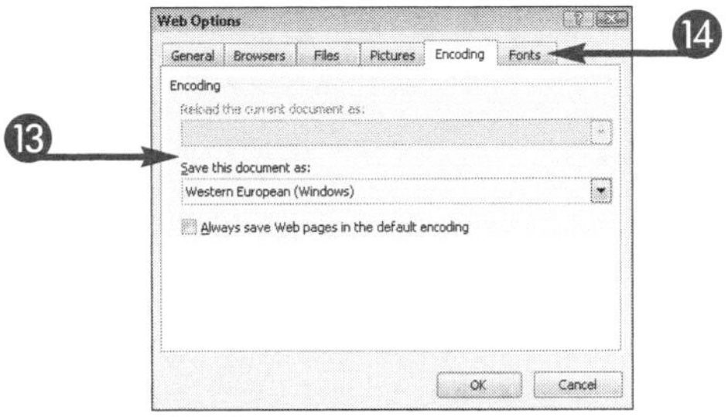

Excel displays the current font settings.

15. Change any options as appropriate.
16. Click OK to close the Web Options dialog box.
17. Click OK to close the Excel Options dialog box.

Excel saves the changes.

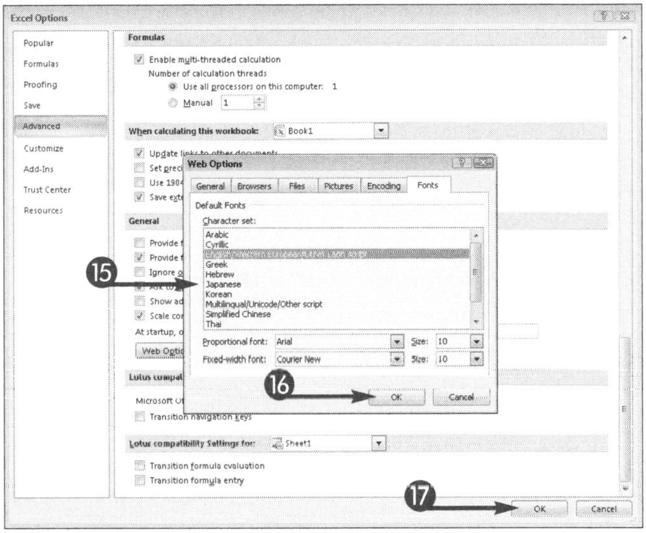

MASTER IT

What happens if I choose, on the Files tab, not to update links?

▼ When you do not update links and you move or copy a Web page, Excel also moves or copies the support files. If you choose to update links, Excel does not move the support files, but instead updates relative links on the Web page to maintain the links.

What factors should I consider when setting options on the Pictures tab?

▼ The video resolution used to view the text and graphics can affect the way that text and graphics wrap. The screen size that you select for the target monitor can affect the size and layout of images in a workbook. The pixels-per-inch setting you select affects the size of graphics relative to the size of text on the screen.

How do I decide which encoding language to use when I need to reload the document?

▼ If Excel displays the wrong characters when you open a Web page, try each encoding until you can read the text. Unicode encoding supports all characters in all languages and is readable in at least Microsoft Internet Explorer 4 and at least Netscape Navigator 4. You can also select a font from the Fonts tab.

Enable Excel Add-Ins

Excel comes with, but does not automatically enable, several add-ins that expand the Excel functionality and can help you while using Excel.

- The Analysis ToolPak supports statistical and engineering tools and adds worksheet functions; when you enable this add-in, it appears on the Data tab.
- The Analysis ToolPak – VBA provides VBA functions for the Analysis ToolPak. When enabled, these functions are not visible in Excel but are available in Microsoft Visual Basic.
- The Conditional Sum Wizard helps you create formulas that add values if the values meet specified conditions. When enabled, this tool appears on the Formulas tab.
- The Euro Currency Tools help you convert and format euro currency. When enabled these tools appear on the Formulas tab.
- The Internet Assistant VBA add-in enables VBA programmers to publish data to the Web. When enabled, this tool is not visible in Excel but is available in Microsoft Visual Basic.
- The Lookup Wizard add-in helps you create formulas to look up data in a list. When enabled, this add-in appears on the Formulas tab.
- The Solver add-in helps you use several methods to solve equations and optimize values. When enabled, this add-in appears on the Formulas tab.

You can also create your own add-in.

Enable Excel Add-Ins

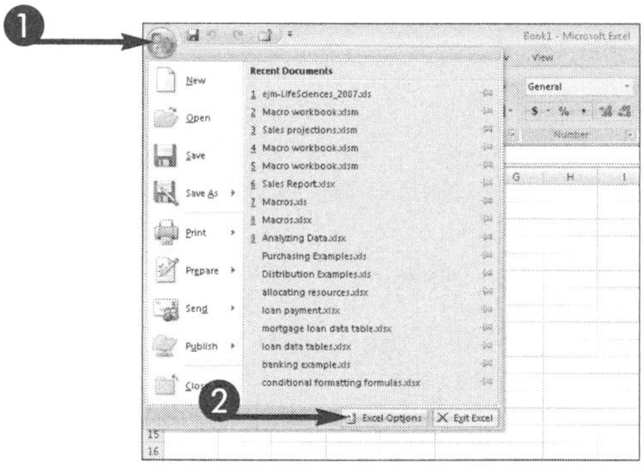

1. Click .
2. Click Excel Options.

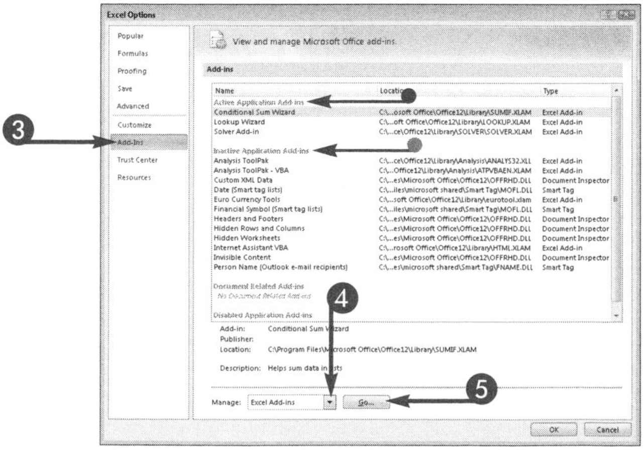

The Excel Options dialog box appears.

3. Click Add-Ins.
   - Currently enabled add-ins appear here.
   - Inactive add-ins appear here.
4. Click [▾] and select Excel Add-Ins.
5. Click Go.

The Add-Ins dialog box appears.

- If ☑ appears beside an add-in, that add-in is enabled.

6 Click each add-in that you want to enable (☐ changes to ☑).

Note: *This example enables the Euro Currency Tools.*

7 Click OK.

Excel enables the add-in.

8 Click the Formulas tab or the Data tab.

- Buttons for add-ins appear at the right edge of the Ribbon.

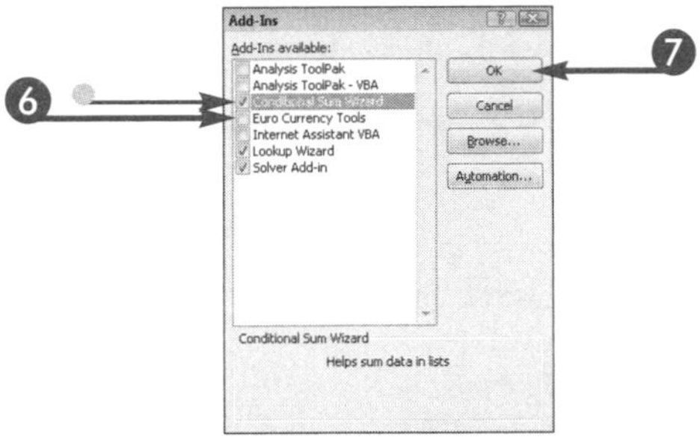

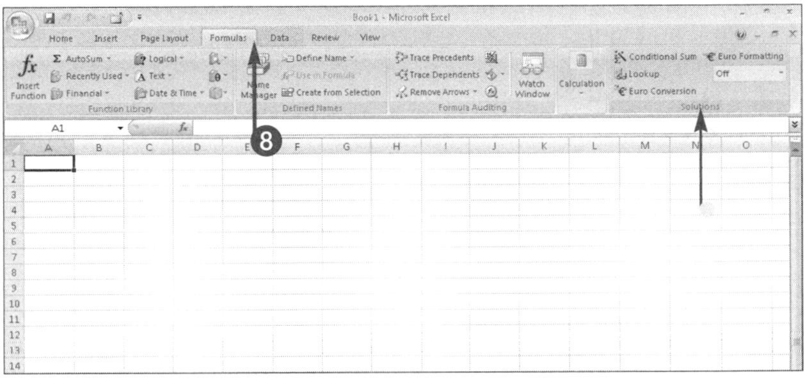

MASTER IT

Why would I want to create an add-in?

▼ Most users do not need to create add-ins; the ones that come with Excel or are available from third-party vendors are sufficient for most users. However, if you need to develop a workbook for others that contains macros, you might want to create an add-in. By creating an add-in, you can keep your macros hidden from users and avoid someone modifying your macro code in such a way that it no longer works.

How do I create an add-in?

▼ After you create the application and make sure that it works properly, save the file as an add-in by clicking [Office button] and then clicking Save As. In the Save As dialog box, provide a filename, open the Save As Type drop-down list, and click Excel Add-In (*.xlam). Excel saves the file to the default folder for add-ins. Close the workbook containing the add-in and enable the add-in by using the steps in this section.

How do I disable an add-in?

▼ Follow the steps in this section; in Step 6, click the add-in you want to disable (☑ changes to ☐). When you click OK, the add-in disappears from the Ribbon. Disabling an add-in is not really necessary; you can allow the commands to remain on the Ribbon without experiencing any performance degradation from Excel.

Control Security with the Trust Center

Using the Trust Center, you can control a variety of security and privacy settings. On the Trusted Publishers tab of the Trust Center, you can view developers that you have set up as trusted publishers of worksheets containing macros. On the Trusted Locations tab, you can view the current set of trusted locations and add, change, or delete a trusted location.

Using the options on the Add-ins tab, you can have the Trust Center check for a digital signature for the add-in and notify you when it does not load add-ins from publishers you have not trusted. If you have the Trust Center check for digital signatures, you can disable unsigned add-ins silently. You can also disable all add-ins.

You can use the options on the ActiveX Settings tab to help secure your computer from unsafe ActiveX controls. You can choose to disable or enable all ActiveX controls, or you can have Excel prompt you before enabling ActiveX controls and place additional restrictions on Unsafe for Initialization (UFI) ActiveX controls. UFI controls are ActiveX controls that have not been marked by the developer as safe for initialization.

Control Security with the Trust Center

1. Click .
2. Click Excel Options.

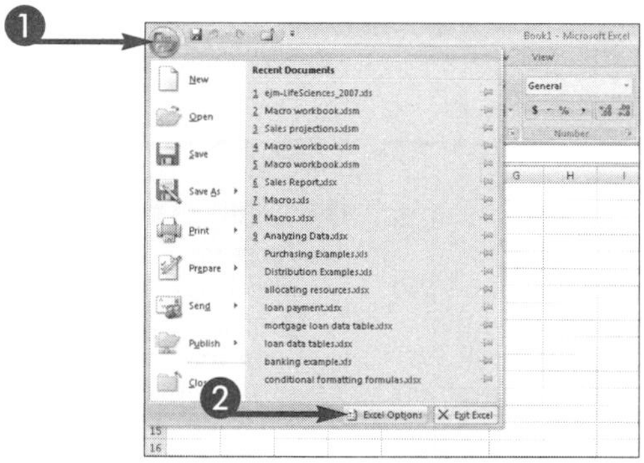

The Excel Options dialog box appears.

3. Click Trust Center.
4. Click Trust Center Settings.

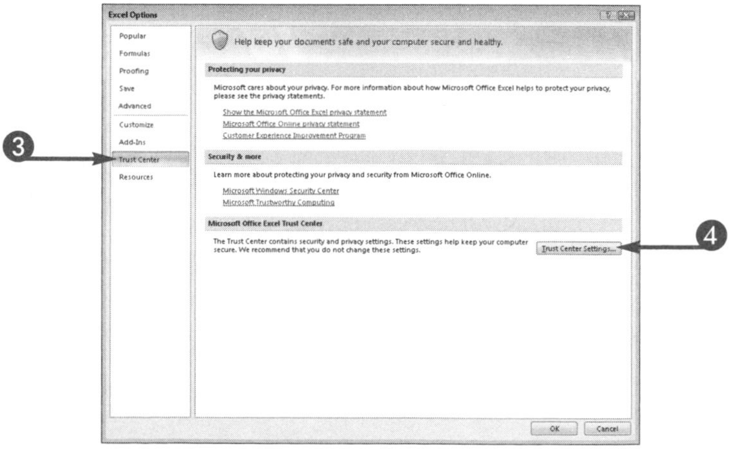

The Trust Center dialog box appears.

5 Click Add-Ins.

6 Change options as appropriate.

7 Click ActiveX Settings.

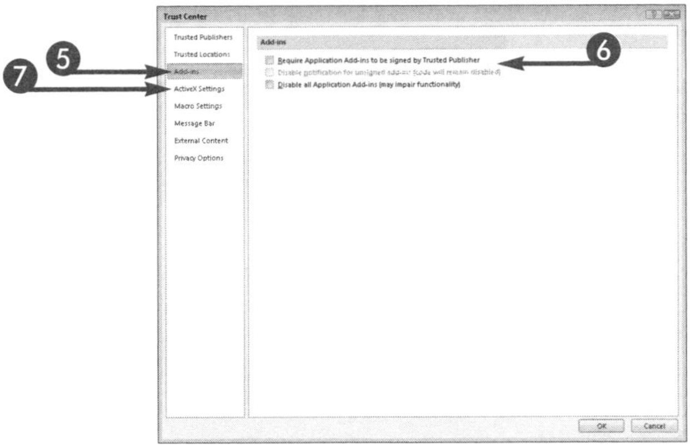

The ActiveX Settings options appear.

8 Change options as appropriate.

9 Click Macro Settings.

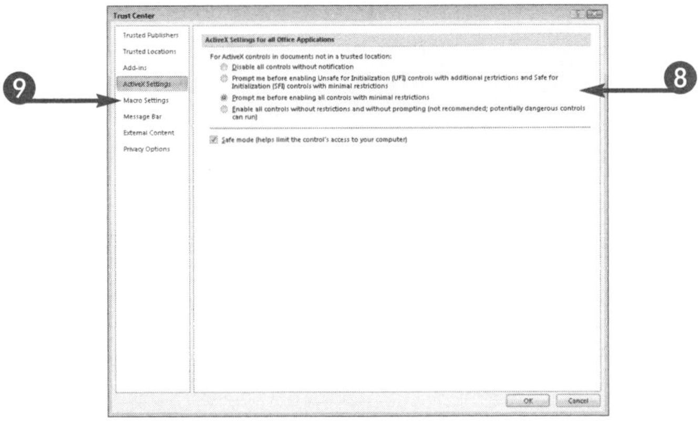

MASTER IT

What does the Safe Mode option on the ActiveX Settings tab do?

- Developers can mark ActiveX controls as Safe for Initialization (SFI). Unmarked ActiveX controls are referred to as Unsafe for Initialization (UFI) controls. By default, if you open Excel in Safe Mode — a diagnostic environment — ActiveX controls do not run. If you select the Safe Mode option, you enable SFI ActiveX controls when you run Excel in Safe Mode.

How do I establish a trusted publisher?

- When you open a workbook that contains a macro, ActiveX control, or add-in, Excel disables the code and the Trust Center checks for a valid, current digital signature from a reputable source. Select the Options button in the Message Bar to enable the content or leave it disabled. If the digital signature is valid, you can also choose to trust the publisher. When you trust a publisher, you trust all software from that publisher.

How do I use the Trusted Locations tab?

- As an alternative to trusting all software from a publisher, you can store workbooks containing macros, ActiveX controls, or add-ins that you trust in a folder you identify as a trusted location. You use the Trusted Locations tab to manage trusted folders. See Chapter 29 for details on creating a new trusted location.

continued

Control Security with the Trust Center *(Continued)*

You can use the options on the Macro Settings tab to help secure your computer from unsafe macros. You can choose to disable or enable all macros, or you can have Excel disable all macros except for digitally signed macros. You can also have Excel disable all macros and display a security alert when you open a workbook containing disabled macros.

On the Message Bar tab, you can disable the Message Bar, which displays messages whenever you open a workbook that contains ActiveX controls, macros, or add-ins that Excel has disabled.

From the External Content tab, you can control security settings for data connections and workbook links. By default, if you open a workbook that attempts to connect to an external data source using either a data connection or a hyperlink, Excel blocks the content and displays a message in the Message Bar, giving you the opportunity to enable the content. You can change the Excel default behavior to enable or disable all external content without notification.

You can use the options on the Privacy Options tab to control the information and files downloaded from or sent to Microsoft, and to help you protect your privacy when you share files with other people.

Control Security with the Trust Center *(continued)*

The Macro Settings options appear.

10. Change options as appropriate.
11. Click Message Bar.

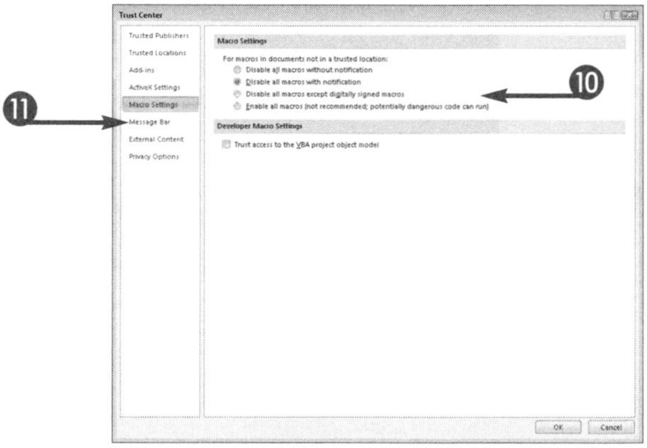

The Message Bar options page appears, showing only one option.

12. Change this option as appropriate (◎ changes to ◉).
13. Click External Content.

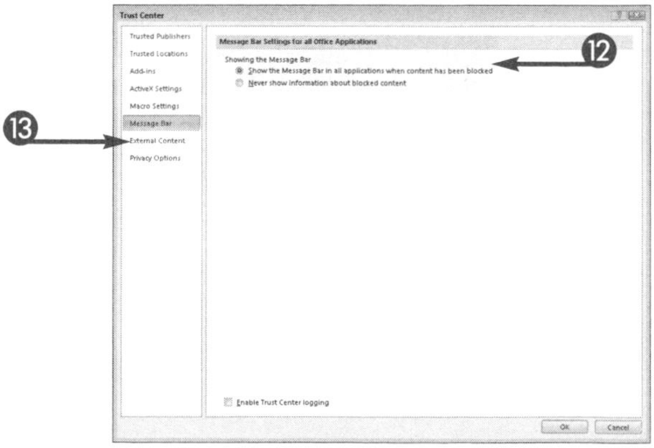

The External Content options appear.

⓮ Change options as appropriate (◎ changes to ◉).

⓯ Click Privacy Options.

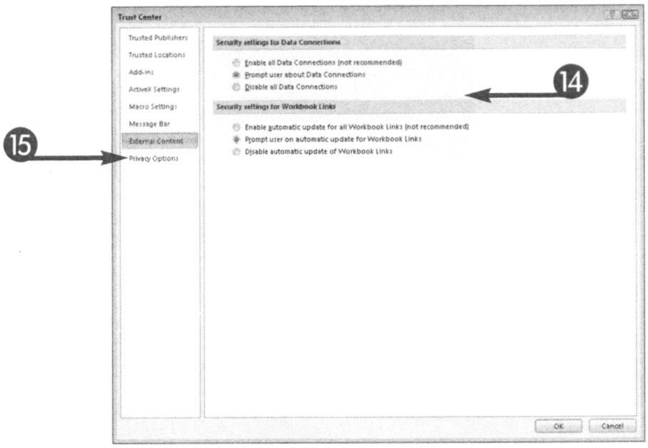

The Privacy options appear.

⓰ Change options as appropriate.

⓱ Click OK in the Trust Center and Excel Options dialog boxes.

Excel saves the settings.

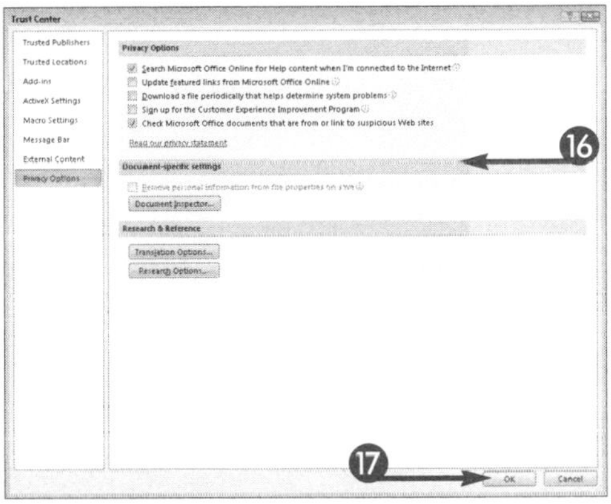

What does the "Trust Access to the VBA Project Object Model" option on the Macro Settings tab do?

▼ This setting is used by developers to allow or deny programmatic access to the VBA object model from any Automation client; by default, access is denied. If you enable this security option, unauthorized programs have a harder time building harmful code that replicates itself.

On the Privacy Options tab, is there an advantage to selecting the "Download a File Periodically that Helps Determine System Problems" option?

▼ If your computer crashes or becomes unstable, this option allows Office Online to download a file that runs the Microsoft Office Diagnostics tool automatically; this tool can help diagnose and repair the problem. In addition, you are prompted to send error reports for certain types of errors, and Microsoft uses the data to try to fix the problem.

What does the Document Inspector button on the Privacy tab do?

▼ You can click this button to inspect the current workbook for a variety of information that you might not want to share with others. If Excel finds information such as comments or hidden rows, columns, or worksheets, Excel alerts you and provides the opportunity to remove the information. For details on using the Document Inspector, see Chapter 31.

31 Using Workbooks in a Multi-User Environment

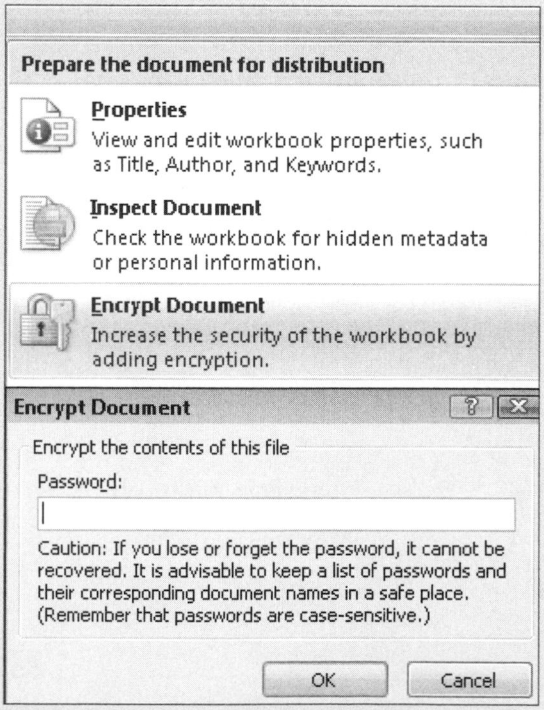

32 Sharing Excel Data with Other Programs

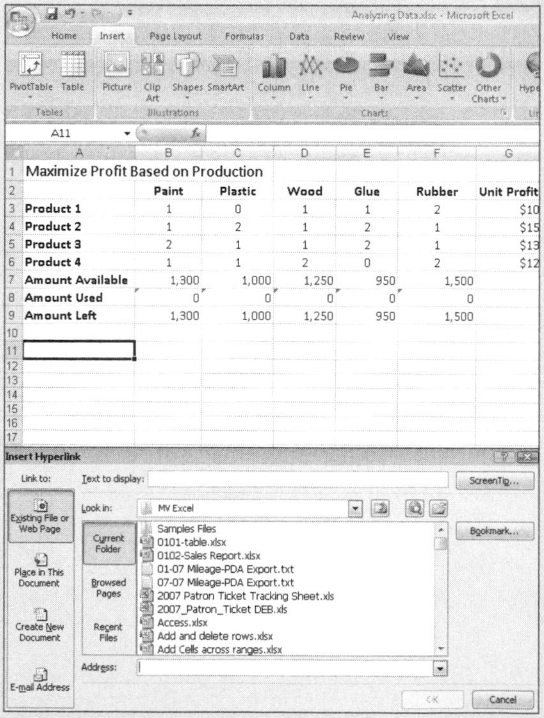

PART VII

USING EXCEL IN COLLABORATION WITH OTHERS

A Excel Functions

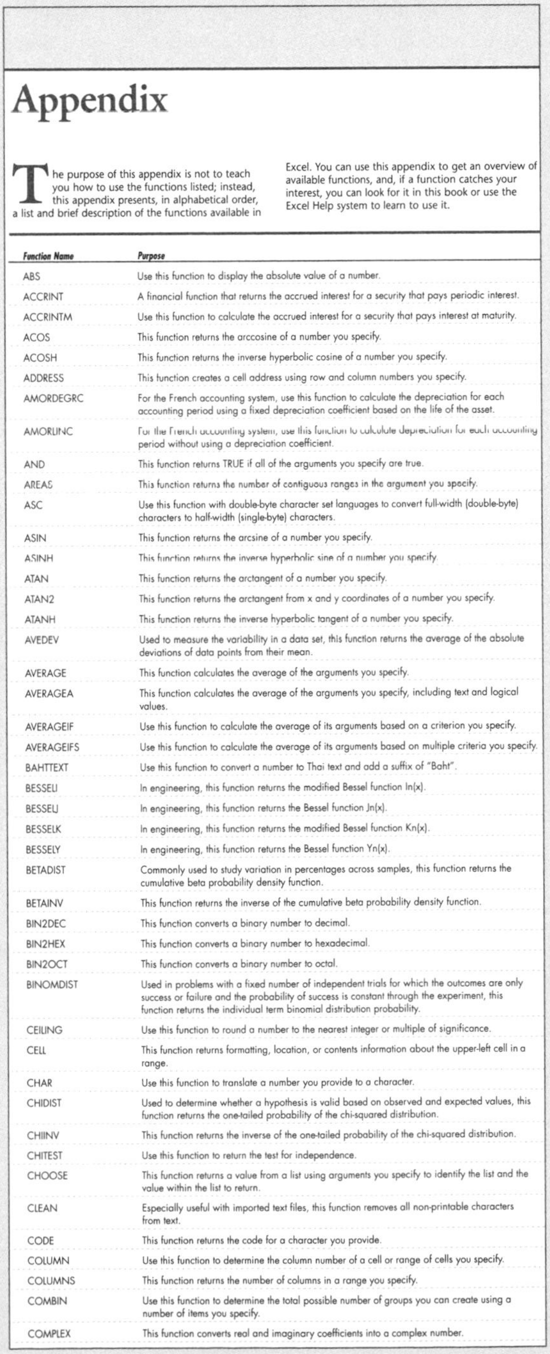

Appendix

The purpose of this appendix is not to teach you how to use the functions listed; instead, this appendix presents, in alphabetical order, a list and brief description of the functions available in Excel. You can use this appendix to get an overview of available functions, and, if a function catches your interest, you can look for it in this book or use the Excel Help system to learn to use it.

Function Name	Purpose
ABS	Use this function to display the absolute value of a number.
ACCRINT	A financial function that returns the accrued interest for a security that pays periodic interest.
ACCRINTM	Use this function to calculate the accrued interest for a security that pays interest at maturity.
ACOS	This function returns the arccosine of a number you specify.
ACOSH	This function returns the inverse hyperbolic cosine of a number you specify.
ADDRESS	This function creates a cell address using row and column numbers you specify.
AMORDEGRC	For the French accounting system, use this function to calculate the depreciation for each accounting period using a fixed depreciation coefficient based on the life of the asset.
AMORLINC	For the French accounting system, use this function to calculate depreciation for each accounting period without using a depreciation coefficient.
AND	This function returns TRUE if all of the arguments you specify are true.
AREAS	This function returns the number of contiguous ranges in the argument you specify.
ASC	Use this function with double-byte character set languages to convert full-width (double-byte) characters to half-width (single-byte) characters.
ASIN	This function returns the arcsine of a number you specify.
ASINH	This function returns the inverse hyperbolic sine of a number you specify.
ATAN	This function returns the arctangent of a number you specify.
ATAN2	This function returns the arctangent from x and y coordinates of a number you specify.
ATANH	This function returns the inverse hyperbolic tangent of a number you specify.
AVEDEV	Used to measure the variability in a data set, this function returns the average of the absolute deviations of data points from their mean.
AVERAGE	This function calculates the average of the arguments you specify.
AVERAGEA	This function calculates the average of the arguments you specify, including text and logical values.
AVERAGEIF	Use this function to calculate the average of its arguments based on a criterion you specify.
AVERAGEIFS	Use this function to calculate the average of its arguments based on multiple criteria you specify.
BAHTTEXT	Use this function to convert a number to Thai text and add a suffix of "Baht".
BESSELI	In engineering, this function returns the modified Bessel function In(x).
BESSELJ	In engineering, this function returns the Bessel function Jn(x).
BESSELK	In engineering, this function returns the modified Bessel function Kn(x).
BESSELY	In engineering, this function returns the Bessel function Yn(x).
BETADIST	Commonly used to study variation in percentages across samples, this function returns the cumulative beta probability density function.
BETAINV	This function returns the inverse of the cumulative beta probability density function.
BIN2DEC	This function converts a binary number to decimal.
BIN2HEX	This function converts a binary number to hexadecimal.
BIN2OCT	This function converts a binary number to octal.
BINOMDIST	Used in problems with a fixed number of independent trials for which the outcomes are only success or failure and the probability of success is constant through the experiment, this function returns the individual term binomial distribution probability.
CEILING	Use this function to round a number to the nearest integer or multiple of significance.
CELL	This function returns formatting, location, or contents information about the upper-left cell in a range.
CHAR	Use this function to translate a number you provide to a character.
CHIDIST	Used to determine whether a hypothesis is valid based on observed and expected values, this function returns the one-tailed probability of the chi-squared distribution.
CHIINV	This function returns the inverse of the one-tailed probability of the chi-squared distribution.
CHITEST	Use this function to return the test for independence.
CHOOSE	This function returns a value from a list using arguments you specify to identify the list and the value within the list to return.
CLEAN	Especially useful with imported text files, this function removes all non-printable characters from text.
CODE	This function returns the code for a character you provide.
COLUMN	Use this function to determine the column number of a cell or range of cells you specify.
COLUMNS	This function returns the number of columns in a range you specify.
COMBIN	Use this function to determine the total possible number of groups you can create using a number of items you specify.
COMPLEX	This function converts real and imaginary coefficients into a complex number.

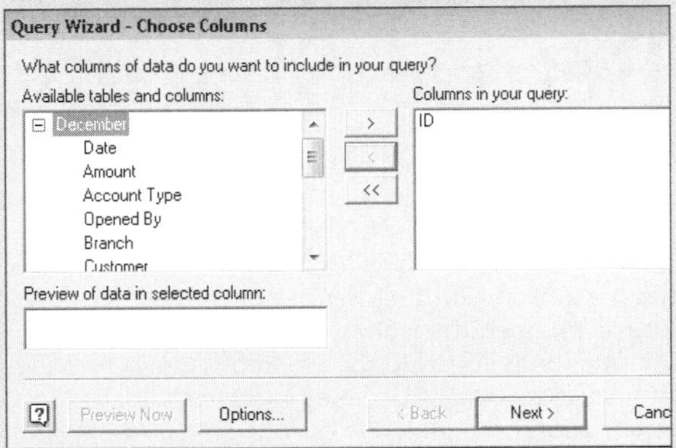

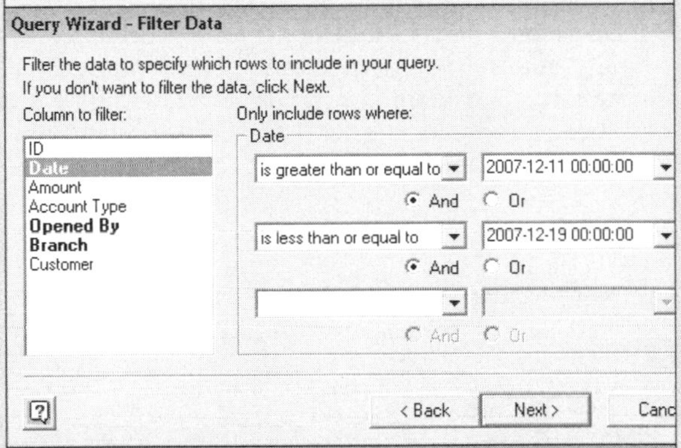

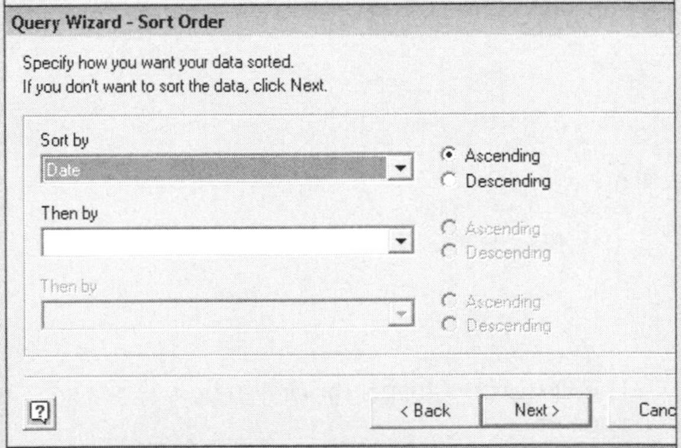

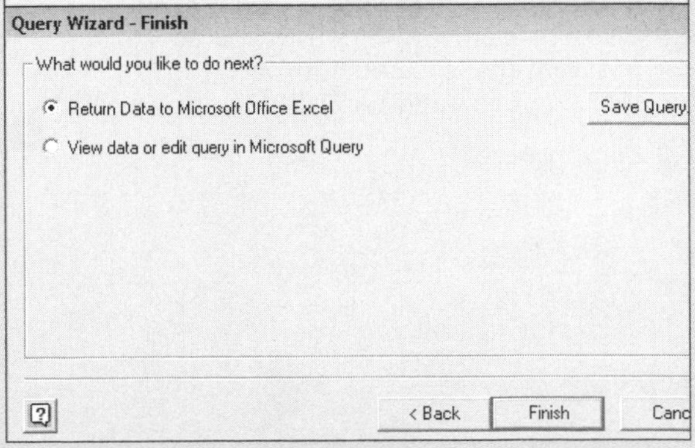

Inspect a Workbook Before Sharing

Before you distribute a workbook you intend to share, you can use the Document Inspector to help you identify and remove content you might not want to share. Your workbook can contain hidden information that might not be readily visible when you open the workbook, but, because the information is stored in the workbook, anyone viewing the workbook might be able to view or retrieve the information.

The Document Inspector searches your workbook for a variety of information, including comments and annotations, personal information, information or *metadata* stored with the workbook's properties, and document server properties. The Document Inspector also looks for header and footer information; hidden rows, columns, and worksheets; invisible objects; and custom XML data.

If the Document Inspector finds any of this information, it notifies you and offers you the opportunity to remove the information. Typically, you cannot undo the action of removing the information, and so, before you run the Document Inspector, you should save your workbook. After you run the Document Inspector and remove information, you might also want to save your workbook using a different name so that you can reopen the original to access the information you removed.

Inspect a Workbook Before Sharing

1. Click .
2. Click Prepare.
3. Click Inspect Document.

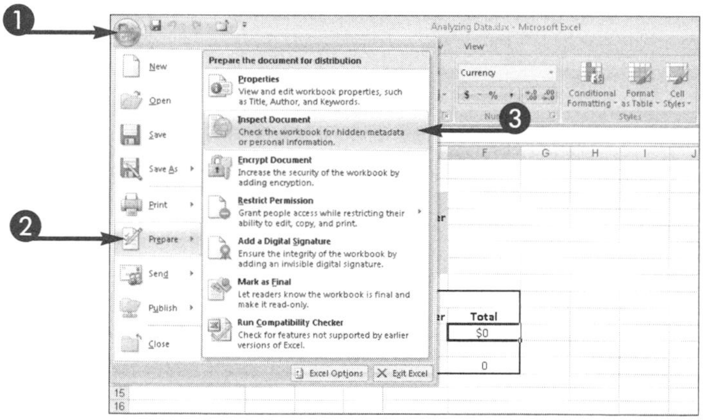

The Document Inspector dialog box appears.

4. Click any elements for which you do not want the Document Inspector to search (changes to).
5. Click Inspect.

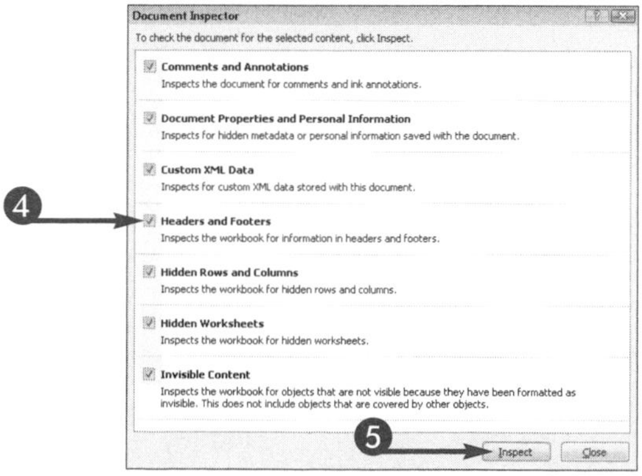

A second Document Inspector dialog box appears.

As Excel inspects the workbook, it displays a progress bar.

When Excel finishes inspecting the workbook, the results of the inspection appear.

- You can click Remove All to remove all of the elements Excel found in a particular category.
- If you remove content, you can click Reinspect to reinspect the workbook.

6 Click Close.

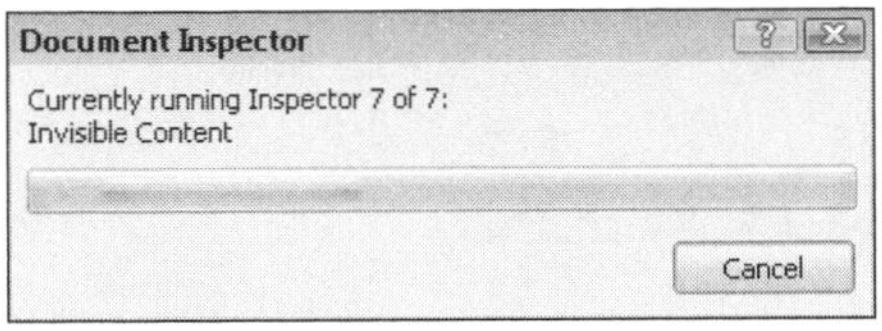

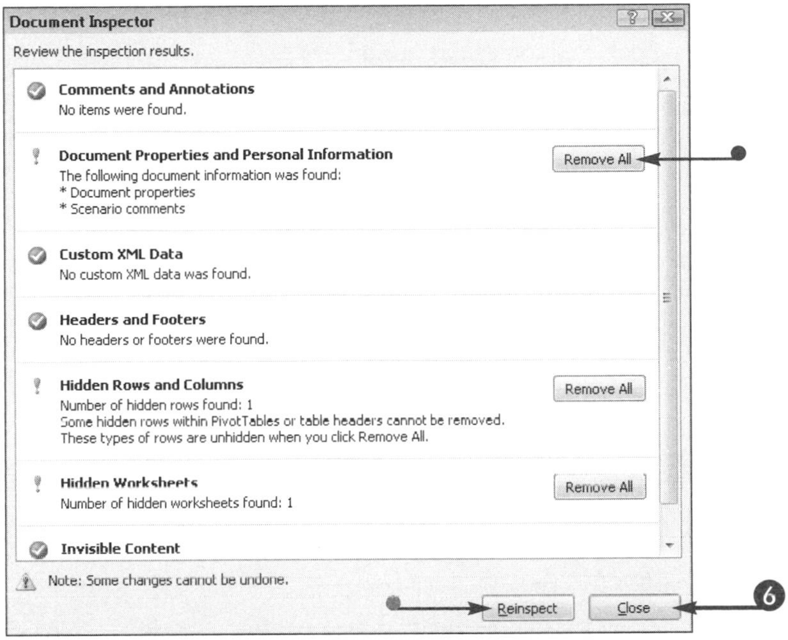

MASTER IT

I reran the Document Inspector, and a message appeared that I should save the workbook. Should I do this?

▼ Yes, particularly if you intend to remove any of the elements that Excel finds. In most cases, you cannot undo removing elements, and so the only way to recover the elements is to save the workbook before you remove them and then save the workbook using a new name after you remove them. The elements still exist in the original workbook but not in the new version.

What kind of personal information does the Document Inspector search for and remove?

▼ In addition to the information that appears when you display the Document Properties pane or the Document Properties dialog box, personal information can include e-mail headers, scenario comments, comments for tables and named ranges, printer path information, the file path information for publishing Web pages, routing slips and send-for-review information, and inactive external data connections.

Besides removing the information from the workbook, are there other possible ramifications?

▼ Yes. Exercise care when you remove hidden rows, columns, or worksheets. You might affect calculations in a workbook if you remove hidden rows, columns, or worksheets, because those hidden rows, columns, or worksheets might be referenced by formulas in visible rows, columns, and worksheets in the workbook.

Assign a Password to a Workbook

Assigning a password to a workbook is one technique you can use to secure the workbook. You can actually assign two passwords to a workbook — one password to open the workbook and another password to modify the workbook — and you can use the same or different passwords.

If you assign a password to open the workbook, Excel encrypts the workbook using AES 128-bit advanced encryption and prompts users who try to open the workbook to supply the password. If you assign a password to modify a workbook, Excel prompts users when they open the workbook for a password to save changes they subsequently make to the workbook. The password to modify a workbook is intended to help you control who makes changes to the workbook; it does not provide any other kind of security.

You can also set up the workbook without assigning a password but have Excel prompt the user to open the workbook as a read-only file to avoid accidentally making changes.

It is very important to remember the password you assign. If you forget it, Microsoft cannot retrieve it.

Assign a Password to a Workbook

1. Click ⊞.
2. Click Save As.

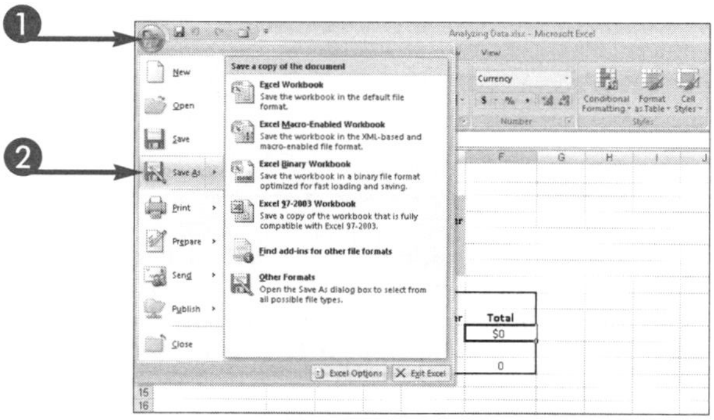

The Save As dialog box appears.

3. Click Tools.
4. Click General Options.

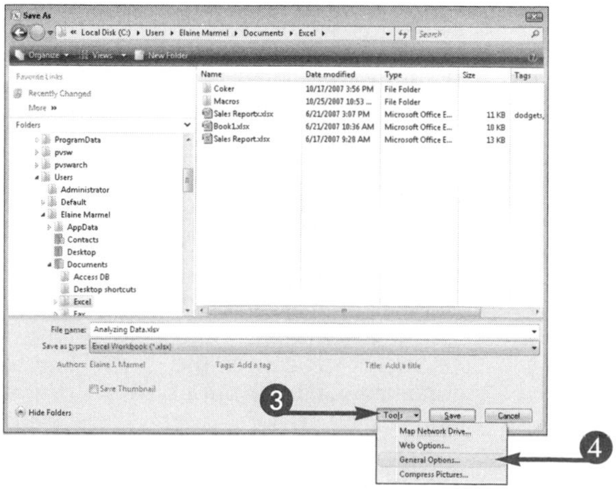

The General Options dialog box appears.

5 Click here and type a password to control who can open the workbook.

6 Click here and type a password to control who can save changes to the workbook.

- You can select the "Read-only recommended" option (☐ changes to ☑) to make Excel prompt a user to open the workbook in Read-only mode.

7 Click OK.

Excel prompts you to confirm both passwords.

8 Retype each password.

9 Click OK to redisplay the Save As dialog box.

10 Click here and type a name for the workbook.

- You can click here and select a file type.

11 Click Save.

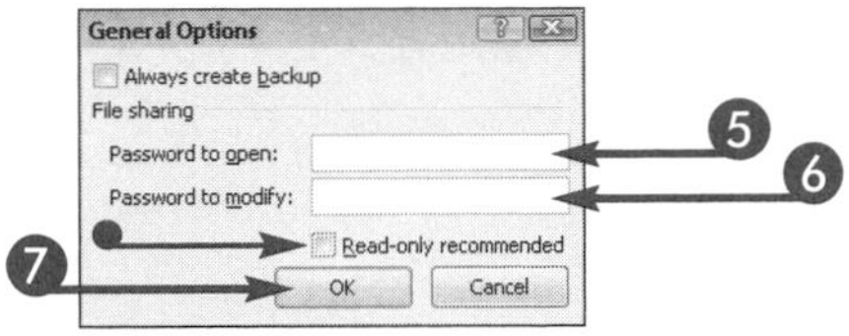

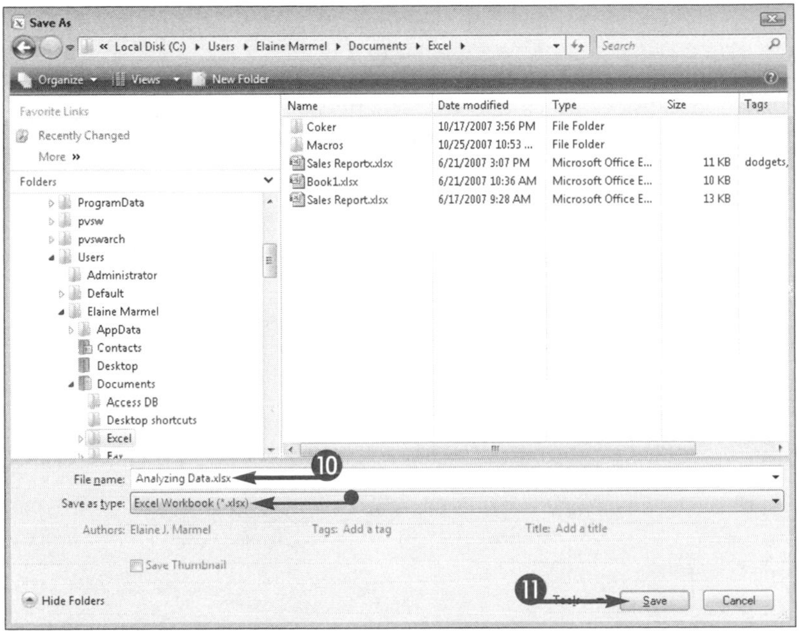

Excel saves the workbook with the password protection you applied.

MASTER IT

How do I remove a password if I do not want to password-protect the workbook anymore?

▼ Repeat the steps in this section, but, in Steps 5 and 6, remove the symbols that represent the password in the General Options dialog box. Once you click OK and save the workbook, Excel no longer prompts you for a password when you open the workbook.

How often do I need to complete the steps in this section?

▼ You only need to perform these steps once to password-protect a workbook. The password information is stored with the workbook until you remove the information. You do not need to create the password each time you save the workbook unless you want to change the password.

Are there any restrictions or recommendations for the password?

▼ A password cannot exceed 15 characters. Use a combination of uppercase and lowercase letters, numbers, and symbols, making sure, of course, that you can remember the password. The longer your password is, the harder it will be for someone to crack.

Encrypt a Workbook

Another security technique you can use is to encrypt a workbook. When you encrypt a workbook, you require a password to open the workbook. The Encrypt feature uses AES 128-bit advanced encryption to make your workbook more secure. You can assign a password of up to 255 characters, including spaces. You should use a combination of uppercase and lowercase letters, numbers, symbols such as ! or #, and spaces for your password. Also make sure that you remember your password, because Microsoft cannot retrieve it for you if you forget it.

When you encrypt a workbook, Excel prompts you for a password. After you supply the password, Excel prompts you to confirm the password by re-entering it. When someone attempts to open the workbook, they must supply the password. Any user who can open the workbook can save changes to it.

MASTER IT

Can I change the password after I assign it?

▼ Yes, you can. Open the workbook by supplying the original password. Then complete the steps in this section, replacing the existing password with the new password you want to use. Excel replaces the original password with the new one. The next time you open the workbook, supply the new password.

Encrypt a Workbook

1. Click .
2. Click Prepare.
3. Click Encrypt Document.

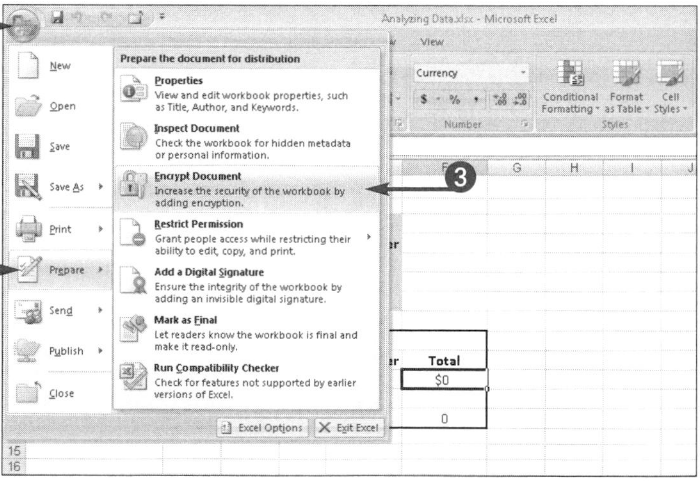

The Encrypt Document dialog box appears.

4. Type a password.
5. Click OK.

Excel prompts you to confirm the password.

6. Retype the password.
7. Click OK.

Excel saves the encryption information with the workbook.

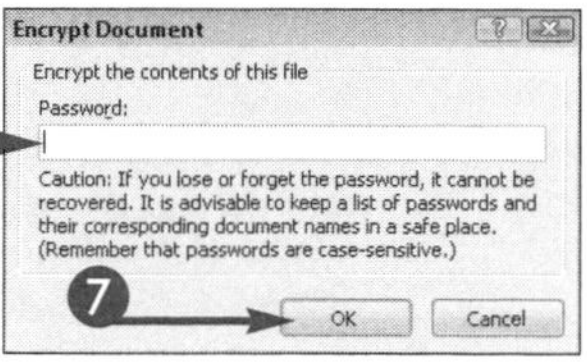

Protect Workbooks

In addition to supplying passwords to open or modify a workbook, as described in the sections, "Assign a Password to a Workbook" and "Encrypt a Workbook," you can protect a workbook's structure and window positioning. When you protect a workbook's structure, you cannot add or delete a worksheet, hide or unhide a worksheet, or rename or move a worksheet to a different position in the workbook. When you protect windows, Excel maintains the size and position of workbook windows at the time you apply protection.

When you apply workbook protection, you can supply a password; Excel then prompts for the password before permitting changes to the workbook's structure or window sizes and positions. Although you do not need to set up workbook protection and simultaneously require a password, if you do not require a password, anyone who can open the workbook can also remove your structure protection and then change the workbook's structure and window sizes and positions.

MASTER IT

What does the Restrict Access command do?

▼ This command enables you to use Information Rights Management (IRM) to restrict the printing, e-mailing, or copying of workbook information by unauthorized individuals. To use IRM, you need to purchase Microsoft's Windows Rights Management Services (RMS).

Protect Workbooks

1. Click the Review tab.
2. Click Protect Workbook.

   Excel displays a drop-down list of choices.
3. Click Protect Structures and Windows.

   The Protect Structure and Windows dialog box appears.

   - By default, the Structure option is selected.
   - You can click the Windows option to protect workbook window sizes and positions.
   - You can type a password here.
4. Click OK.

   If you typed a password, Excel prompts you to retype it to confirm it and then click OK.

   Excel protects the workbook.

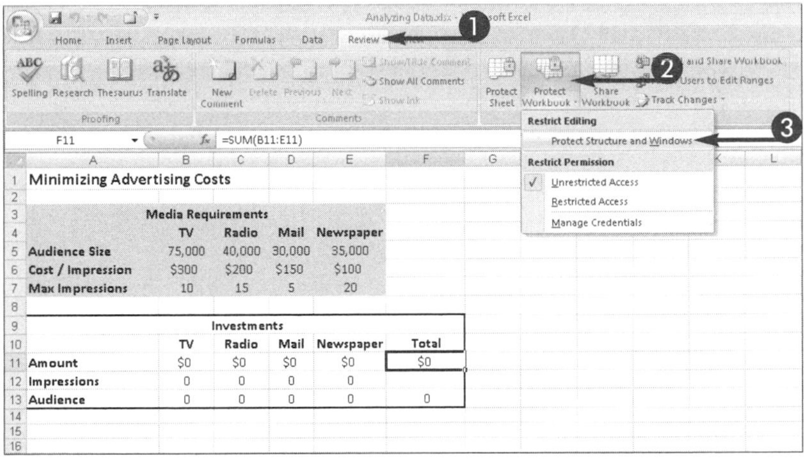

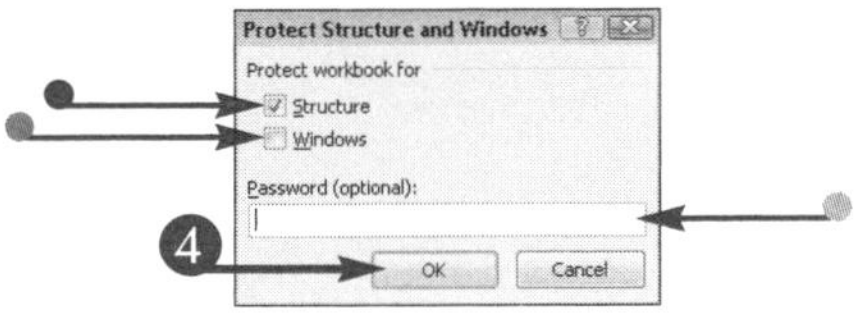

Protect a Worksheet

Using the Protect a Worksheet feature, you can allow users to change only the cells in a worksheet that you specify. For example, you can use this feature to disable changes to cells that contain formulas to prevent users from accidentally deleting or changing them.

When you work in an unprotected worksheet, you can make any changes you want. Excel formats each cell in the worksheet as a *locked* cell, but this formatting has no effect until you protect your worksheet. Once you protect your worksheet, all locked cells are protected from changes; you cannot delete or change the content or the formatting of a locked cell in a protected worksheet.

Because it is hard to imagine having any use for a worksheet that you cannot change, you identify cells that you want to allow users to change and you format those cells as unlocked instead of locked. Many people unlock cells that serve as variables on a worksheet that users need to change, but leave cells containing formulas locked.

After you protect the worksheet, users can make changes to all unprotected cells, but they cannot make any changes to the locked cells — the ones that contain formulas.

Protect a Worksheet

Designate Cells for Editing

1. Select cells you do not want protected.
2. Click the Home tab.
3. Click Format.
4. Click Format Cells.

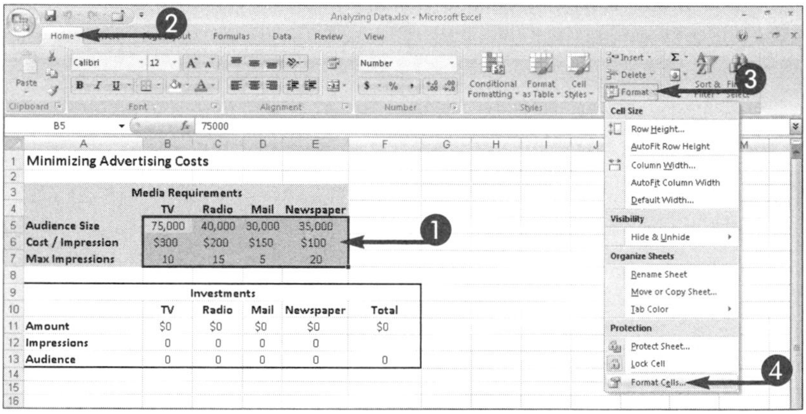

The Custom Lists dialog box appears.

5. Click the Protection tab.
6. Click Locked (☑ changes to ☐).
7. Click OK.

Excel designates the selected cells as unlocked.

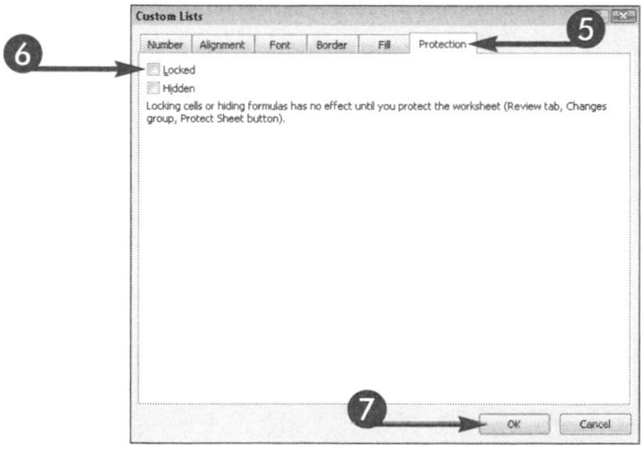

Protect the Sheet

1. Click the Review tab.
2. Click Protect Sheet.

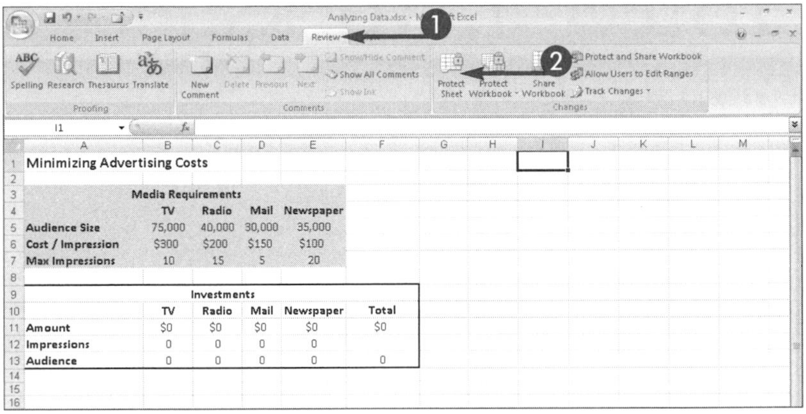

The Protect Sheet dialog box appears.

3. Type a password to unprotect the sheet.
4. Click options to identify actions that all users can take after protection is enabled.
5. Click OK.

Excel enables worksheet protection.

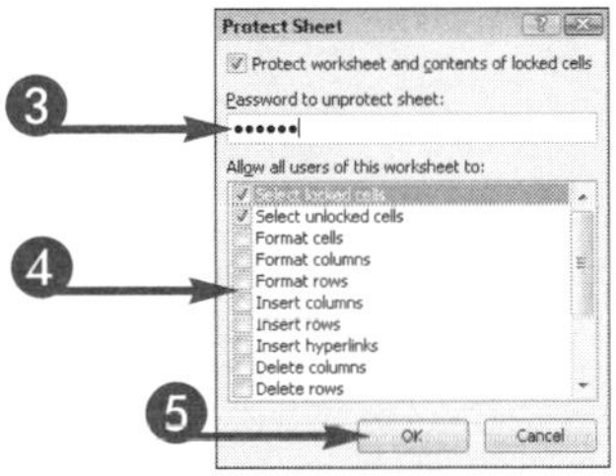

MASTER IT

I selected the Insert Rows option to disable inserting rows, but after I protected the worksheet, I could still insert a row. What did I do wrong?

▼ When you select an option in the Protect Sheet dialog box, you are identifying the actions you want to allow, not the actions you want to disable. To disable inserting rows, you need to remove the check mark from the Insert Rows option (☑ changes to ☐).

I assigned a password when I protected the worksheet, and I saved and closed the workbook. When I opened the workbook, I was not prompted for the password. What did I do wrong?

▼ Nothing. When you assign a password while protecting a worksheet, Excel stores the password and prompts for it only when you try to unprotect the worksheet. To be prompted for a password when opening a workbook, see the sections, "Assign a Password to a Workbook" or "Encrypt a Workbook."

How do I remove worksheet protection?

▼ Click the Review tab and click Unprotect Sheet. If you supplied a password when you protected the worksheet, enter that password and click OK.

What does the Hidden box on the Protection tab of the Format Cells dialog box do?

▼ If you enable this option for a cell, Excel does not display that cell's content in the Formula bar when you select the cell.

continued

Protect a Worksheet

(Continued)

When you protect a worksheet, you use the Protect Sheet dialog box to identify the actions you want to permit any user who opens the workbook to take. You can also assign a password when you protect the worksheet. The password is optional and does not control the actions that users can take; instead, it controls who has the ability to unprotect the worksheet. So, you can protect a worksheet without supplying a password, and Excel will not permit changes to locked cells. However, if a user understands worksheet protection, that user can simply remove the protection and then make changes to locked cells. To prevent this, you can supply a password when you protect a worksheet, so that only those users who know the password can remove the protection.

When you protect a worksheet and accept Excel's default suggestions to permit only selecting of locked and unlocked cells, users can select any cell on the worksheet and type new values or copy and paste values into unlocked cells, but most other Excel functions are unavailable. For details on the various actions you can enable or disable using worksheet protection, see the section, "Worksheet Actions You Can Protect."

Protect a Worksheet *(continued)*

The Confirm Password dialog box appears.

6. Retype the password.
7. Click OK.

Excel protects the worksheet.

You can make changes to any cell you selected in Step 1 of the subsection, "Designate Cells for Editing."

- If you try to edit any other cell, a warning message appears.

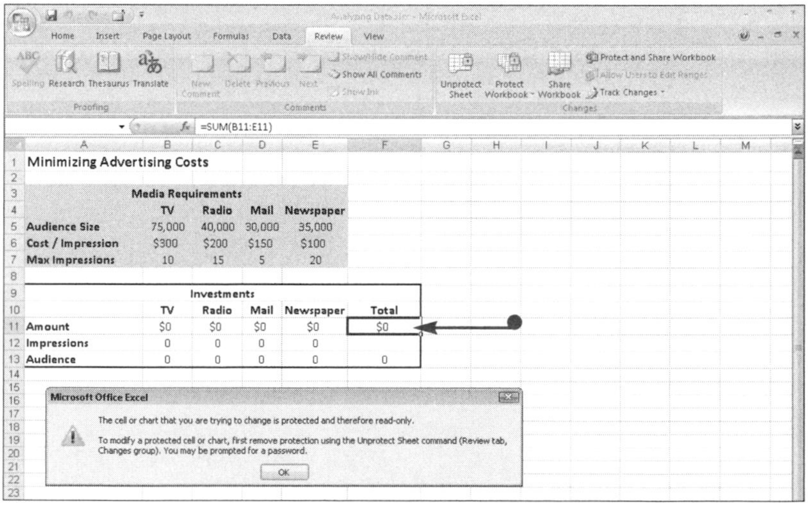

Worksheet Actions You Can Protect

You can protect a worksheet for a variety of reasons. Many people protect only certain cells within a worksheet so that no one can change the content of those cells; those cells often contain formulas that the worksheet builder wants to protect from accidental change or deletion.

When you protect a worksheet, you can choose to enable a variety of Excel features that are available even though the worksheet is protected. These features are described in the table.

Features You Can Enable in a Protected Worksheet

Feature	***What Happens When You Select This Option***
Select locked cells	Enabled by default this option allows users to select a locked cell using either the mouse or the keyboard.
Select unlocked cells	Enabled by default this option allows users to select an unlocked cell using either the mouse or the keyboard. If you enable this option, pressing Tab on a protected worksheet moves the cell pointer to the next unlocked cell, making data entry much easier.
Format cells	Click this option (☐ changes to ☑) to allow users to apply formatting to locked or unlocked cells.
Format columns	Click this option (☐ changes to ☑) to allow users to hide columns or change column widths.
Format rows	Click this option (☐ changes to ☑) to allow users to hide rows or change row heights.
Insert columns	Click this option (☐ changes to ☑) to allow users to insert new columns.
Insert rows	Click this option (☐ changes to ☑) to allow users to insert new rows.
Insert hyperlinks	Click this option (☐ changes to ☑) to allow users to insert hyperlinks in locked or unlocked cells.
Delete columns	Click this option (☐ changes to ☑) to allow users to delete columns.
Delete rows	Click this option (☐ changes to ☑) to allow users to delete rows.
Sort	Click this option (☐ changes to ☑) to allow users to sort data in a range that does not contain locked cells.
Use AutoFilter	Click this option (☐ changes to ☑) to allow users to use existing AutoFiltering.
Use PivotTable reports	Click this option (☐ changes to ☑) to allow users to change the layout of PivotTables or create new PivotTables.
Edit objects	Click this option (☐ changes to ☑) to allow users to make changes to objects and charts, as well as insert or delete comments.
Edit scenarios	Click this option (☐ changes to ☑) to allow users to use scenarios.

Add a Signature Line

You can add a signature line to a workbook file that you intend to share. By adding a signature line to the workbook, you assure the recipient that the workbook comes from you and that you have reviewed and approved its content. Adding a signature also makes the workbook read-only, and the recipient can make no changes to it.

A signature line is a graphic object that you insert in the workbook; the signature line can contain your name, the date you signed the workbook, and your title. If you use a Tablet PC or have a graphic image of your signature stored on your computer's hard drive, you can also include it so that your signature looks like your handwriting. You also have the option to add comments to the signature, perhaps to explain why you signed the workbook.

To sign a workbook, you must have a digital ID; the first time you sign a workbook, Excel prompts you to either obtain a digital ID from a Microsoft partner for a fee or to create your own digital signature; the example in this section shows you how to create your own digital signature, which has some security limitations.

Add a Signature Line

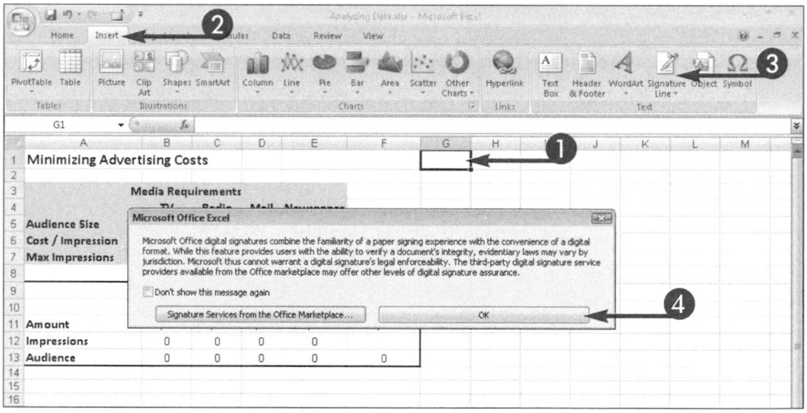

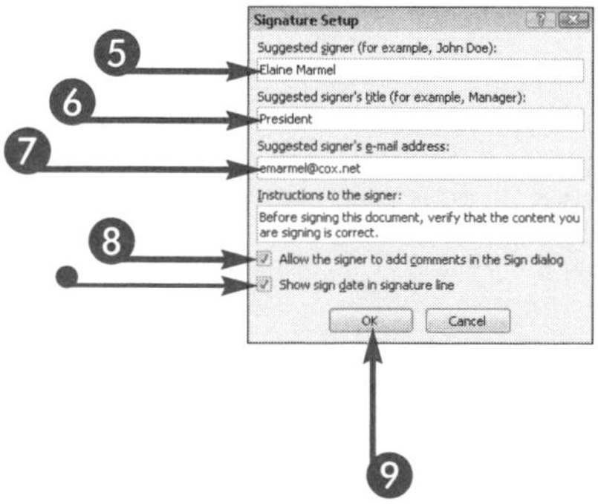

1. Click the cell that you want to display the signature.
2. Click the Insert tab.
3. Click Signature Line.

   A dialog box appears, explaining that Microsoft does not warrant the legal enforceability of the signature.
4. Click OK.

   The Signature Setup dialog box appears.
5. Click here and type your name.
6. Click here and type your title.
7. Click here and type your e-mail address.
8. Click the "Allow the signer to add comments in the Sign dialog" option to be able to add a comment to the signature (☐ changes to ☑).
   - To exclude the date from the signature, you can click the "Show sign date in signature line" option (☑ changes to ☐).
9. Click OK.

- The signature graphic object appears in the cell you selected in Step 1.

⑩ Double-click the graphic object.

The message from Microsoft, not guaranteeing the legal enforceability of the signature, appears.

⑪ Click OK.

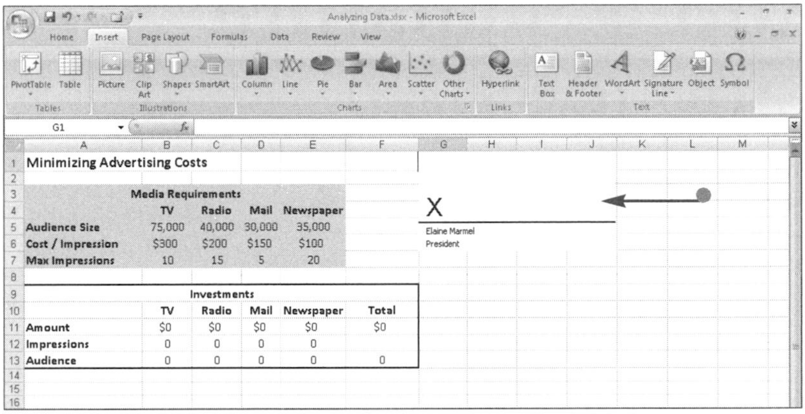

The Get a Digital ID dialog box appears if you have not previously created a digital ID.

⑫ Click the "Create your own digital ID" option (◯ changes to ◉).

⑬ Click OK.

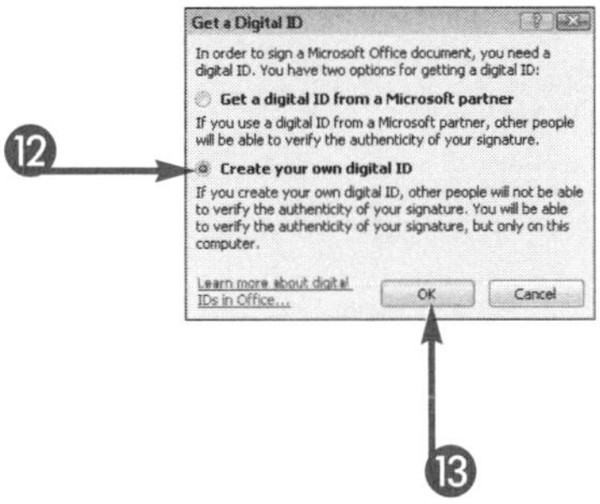

MASTER IT

What are the security limitations associated with creating my own digital signature?

▼ When you create and use your own digital signature, it cannot be authenticated on any computer other than the one where you created it because the digital certificate is stored on that computer. So, if you sign a workbook using a digital certificate that you created, those with whom you share the workbook cannot verify the authenticity of your digital signature.

What happens if I click the Signature Services from the Office Marketplace button?

▼ A Web browser opens to the Digital Signing page of the Microsoft Office Marketplace Web site. On this page, you see links to Microsoft partners who can provide you with a digital certificate, typically for a fee. Some of the vendors also offer a free trial that you can download.

How can I create a graphic image of my signature?

▼ You need a computer that has a scanner attached and scanning software. If you do not have the equipment and software, consider visiting one of the many public stores that provide printing, copying, and binding services. Sign your name on a blank piece of paper, scan the page, and save the scanned image to a picture file format such as JPEG or BMP.

continued

Add a Signature Line *(Continued)*

A digital ID, also called a digital certificate, is used to authenticate digitally signed workbooks. A signature like the one you create in this section stores a private key — a form of code — in your workbook. The digital certificate stores the public key used in conjunction with the private key to perform the authentication. Digital certificates have expiration dates, and so in addition to having a digital certificate, it must be valid.

If you want those people with whom you share your workbook to be able to authenticate your signature line, you can purchase a digital certificate or obtain a free digital certificate; you can find certificate authorities by searching the Internet or you can purchase a digital certificate from a Microsoft partner. If you choose to purchase a digital signature from a Microsoft partner when prompted, your browser opens to the Microsoft Office Marketplace Web page so that you can select a vendor.

When you sign a workbook, a disclaimer message appears as you create the signature. This message from Microsoft explains that although the signature helps to verify a workbook's integrity, laws vary from jurisdiction to jurisdiction, and Microsoft cannot guarantee that the signature can be legally enforced.

Add a Signature Line *(continued)*

The Create a Digital ID dialog box appears.

14. Click here and type your name.
15. Click here and type your e-mail address.
16. Click here and type your organization name.
17. Click here and type your geographic location.
18. Click Create.

The Sign dialog box appears.

Excel creates the digital ID.

19. Click here and type your name.

If you have a graphic image of your signature, browse to select it.

20. Click here and type a reason for signing the workbook.

Note: *This field is available only if you performed Step 8.*

21. Click Sign.

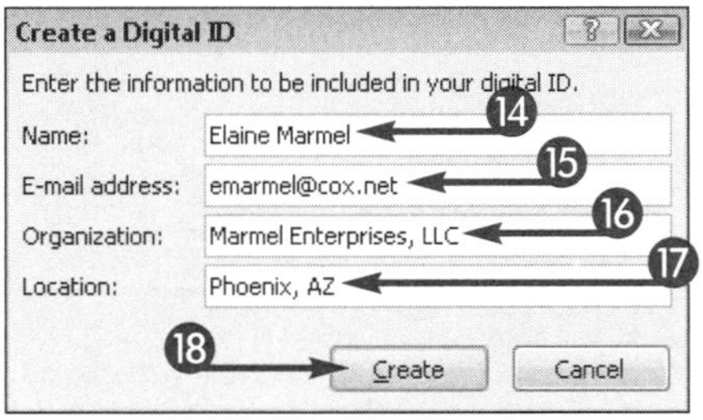

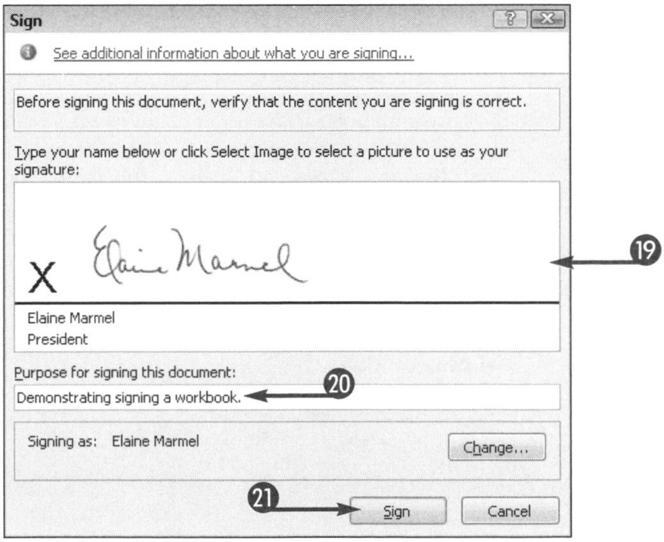

The Signature Confirmation dialog box appears.

22 Click OK.

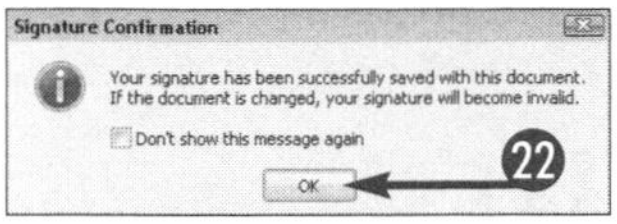

- Excel adds your signature to the workbook.
- The Signatures pane appears here.
- The workbook is now read-only.
- The Signatures button (icon) appears in the Status bar.

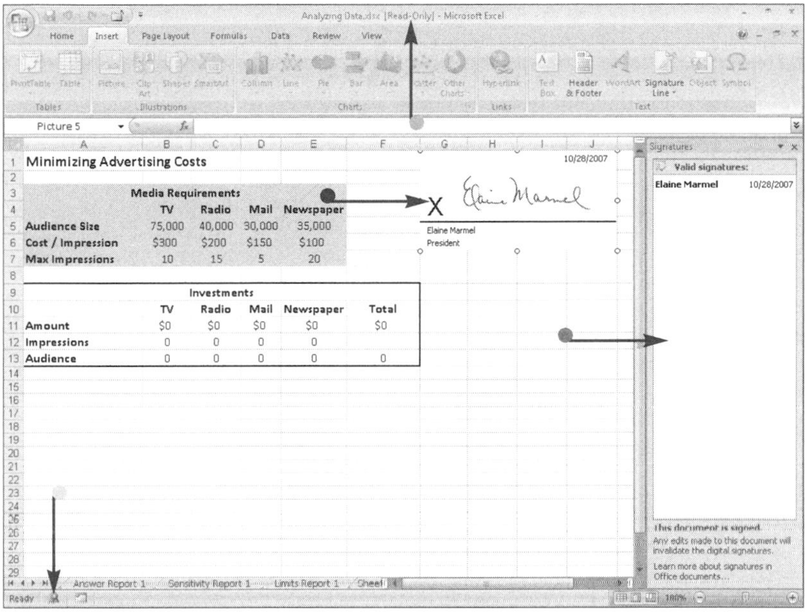

MASTER IT

Is there more validity to a signature if I purchase a digital certificate than if I create my own?

▼ In general, yes, but, from a legal perspective, the answer is "maybe." Because a certificate you create yourself cannot be authenticated on any computer except for the one on which it was created, it probably will not bear much legal weight. For a certificate you purchase, you should discuss the legal validity with the certificate authority and read the documentation provided by the certificate authority to determine whether they are selling you a digital certificate that they believe can be enforced legally.

Can I remove a digital signature from a workbook?

▼ Yes. Right-click the signature graphic and click Remove Signature. A warning appears to alert you that you cannot undo this action. Click Yes to proceed. Another message appears to tell you that the signature has been removed and your workbook has been saved; the workbook is also no longer a read-only document. The graphic containing your signature still appears in the workbook, but the signature line no longer contains your typed or written signature. To remove the graphic, click it and press Delete. Then save your workbook again.

Add an Invisible Digital Signature

You can add an invisible digital signature to a workbook. You can use a digital signature to establish that you are who you claim to be, that the content of the workbook has not changed since you digitally signed it, and that the workbook originated with you.

An invisible digital signature differs from a signature line — described in the section, "Add a Signature Line" — because when you insert an invisible digital signature, no graphic object appears in the workbook that displays a signature. Instead, Excel adds a digital signature to the workbook and makes the workbook a read-only file that no one can change unless the digital signature is removed. When you add the digital signature, Excel displays the Signatures pane, and the Signatures button appears in the Status bar at the bottom of the workbook.

To sign a workbook, you must have a digital ID; the first time you sign a workbook, Excel prompts you to either obtain a digital ID from a Microsoft partner for a fee or to create your own digital signature; the example in this section shows you how to create your own digital signature, which has some security limitations, as described in the section, "Add a Signature Line."

Add an Invisible Digital Signature

1. Save the workbook as an Excel workbook, using the *.xlsx file extension.
2. Click .
3. Click Prepare.
4. Click Add a Digital Signature.

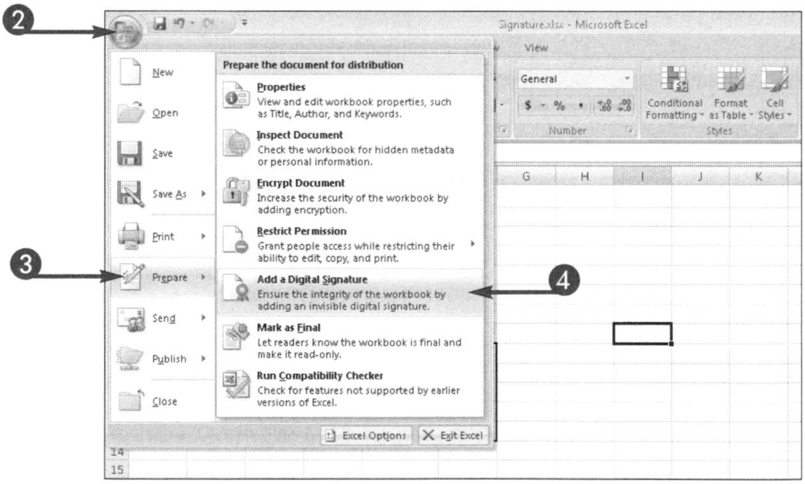

A dialog box appears, explaining that Microsoft does not warrant the legal enforceability of the signature.

5. Click OK.

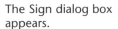

The Sign dialog box appears.

6 Click here and type the reason you are signing the workbook.

7 Click Sign.

The Signature Confirmation dialog box appears, explaining that Excel has saved the digital signature with your workbook.

8 Click OK.

- The Signatures pane appears, showing the valid signatures.
- The workbook becomes a read-only document.
- The Signatures button ( ) appears in the Status bar.

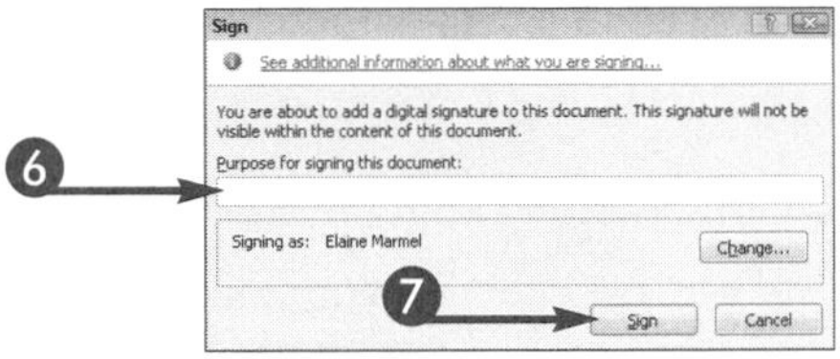

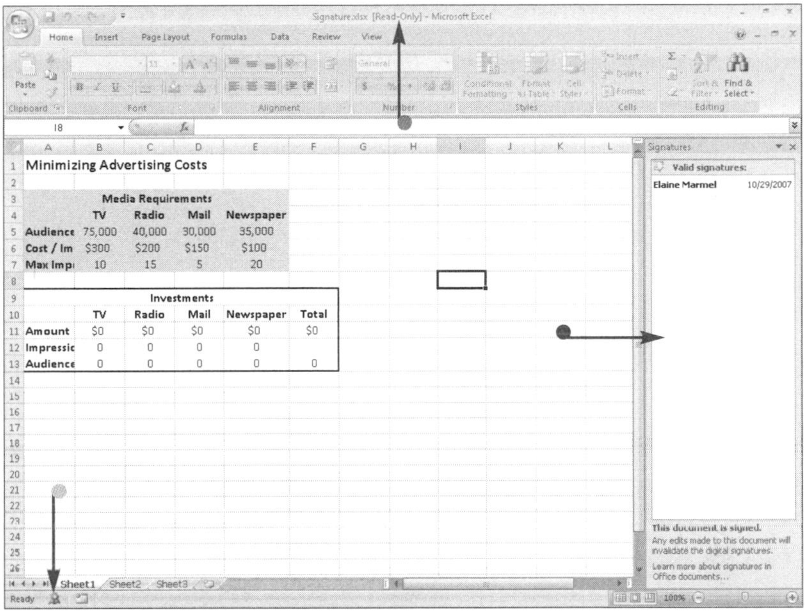

How can I tell if a digital signature is valid?

▼ Click beside the signature in the Signatures pane and click Signature Details. At the top of the box that appears, Excel displays information about the validity of the signature. If a certificate authority approved the digital signature, then information concerning the certificate authority appears in the Countersignatures section of the Digital Signature Details dialog box.

I closed the Signatures pane. How can I reopen it?

▼ You can click in the Status bar or you can click , click Prepare, and then click View Signatures (an option that appears only if your workbook contains a digital signature).

How can I determine if a workbook I received from a coworker contains a digital signature?

▼ If appears in the Status bar, the workbook has been digitally signed. To view the digital signature, click .

How can I remove a digital signature?

▼ If you are the originator of the workbook and you added a certified digital signature, you can remove the digital signature by clicking beside the signature in the Signatures pane and clicking Remove Signature.

What happens to a digital signature if somebody saves a copy of the workbook under a different filename?

▼ The digital signature is valid only for the original file, not for the copy.

Add Comments to Cells

You can add a comment to a cell in a workbook to provide clarifying information about the cell's content to your reader. If you receive a workbook to review, you can add a comment to ask for clarifying information or to suggest changes.

You attach a comment to a cell by selecting the cell before creating your comment. You can identify cells that contain comments by the red triangle that appears in the upper-right corner of the cell. When you create a comment, Excel automatically inserts your name at the top of the comment. If you are inserting a comment to clarify information in the workbook, you might want to remove your name as it could distract the reader. You can edit the text you include in a comment, including deleting your name. Using the tools on the Home tab, you can format text in a comment by selecting it and applying bold, italic, and underline formatting, and you can align the text in the comment. You cannot apply a fill color or change the font color of comment text.

Add Comments to Cells

Add a Comment

1. Click the cell to which you want to add a comment.
2. Click the Review tab.
3. Click New Comment.

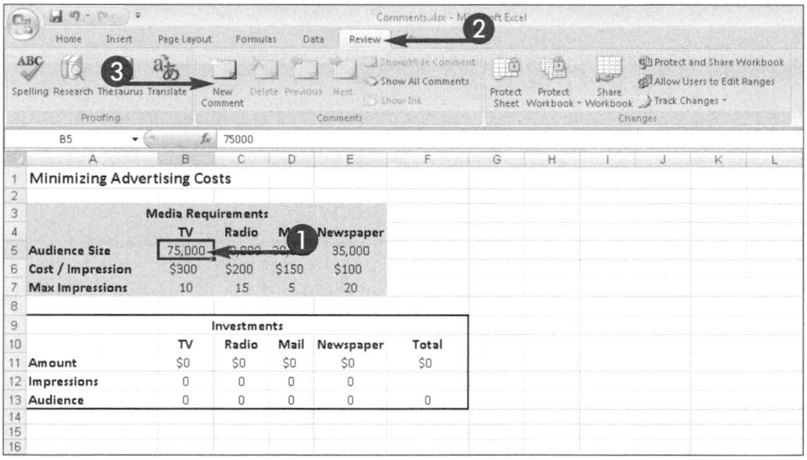

A comment text box containing your name appears on-screen.

4. Type the comment information.
5. Click outside the comment text box.

Excel stores the comment.

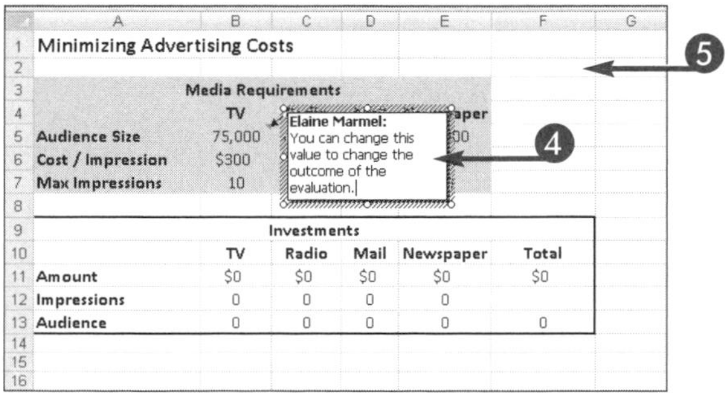

View a Comment

- You can identify cells containing comments by the red triangle that appears in the upper-right corner of the cell.

1 Move ✥ over a cell containing a comment.

Excel displays the comment.

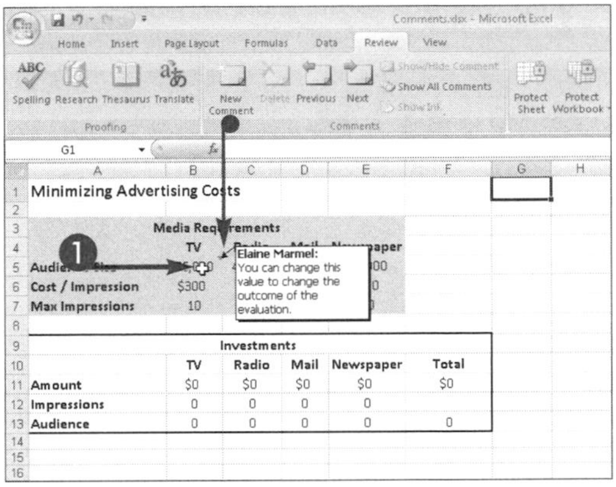

Edit a Comment

1 Click a cell containing a comment.

You can move the mouse pointer over the cell to view the comment.

2 Click the Review tab.

3 Click Edit Comment to display the comment text and make changes.

- You can click Previous or Next to display a comment and move the cell pointer to the previous or next comment.
- You can click a comment and then click Delete to delete it.

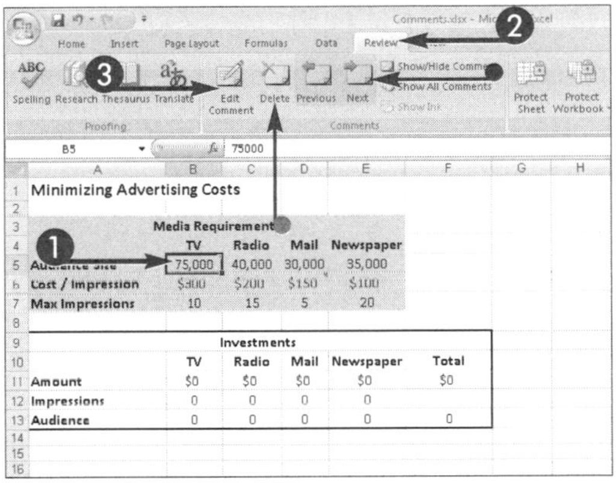

MASTER IT

Is there a way to display a comment without moving the mouse pointer over the cell?

▼ Yes. You can select the cell containing the comment and then click Show/Hide Comment. Excel displays the comment on-screen, even when you click another cell. The comment remains visible until you select the cell again and click Show/Hide Comment.

Is there a way to make all comments in the worksheet visible at the same time.

▼ Yes. You can click anywhere in the worksheet — not necessarily selecting a cell containing a comment — and click the Show All Comments button. Excel displays all comments stored in all cells of the worksheet. Be aware that comments in cells in close proximity may overlap. Click Show All Comments again to hide all comments.

Is there a way to prevent two comments from overlapping?

▼ Yes. You can click in a comment text box, and Excel displays a hatching pattern around the comment. Click the hatching pattern to select the comment text box — not the comment text — and then drag the comment text box to a location where it will not overlap another comment text box.

Print Comments

You can print comments stored in a worksheet. To print comments, you must first display them. Then you need to establish print settings to include printing comments.

When you set up the printer settings to print comments, you can choose to print comments as displayed on the worksheet or at the end of the worksheet. If you print comments as displayed, comment text boxes appear on the printed worksheet in the same positions as they appear on-screen, but the red triangles that indicate that a comment is attached to a particular cell do not appear. If you print comments at the end of the worksheet, Excel prints an extra, separate page after printing the other pages of your worksheet. On the separate page, Excel lists, on separate lines, the cell address of the cell containing the comment, the name of the person who added the comment, and the comment.

Printing comments as displayed on the worksheet gives the reader a sense of the worksheet's appearance on-screen, but this can obscure other comments or information on the worksheet. If you print comments on a separate sheet, consider also printing row numbers and column letters to help the reader identify the cell containing the comment.

Print Comments

1. Click the Review tab.
2. Click Show All Comments.

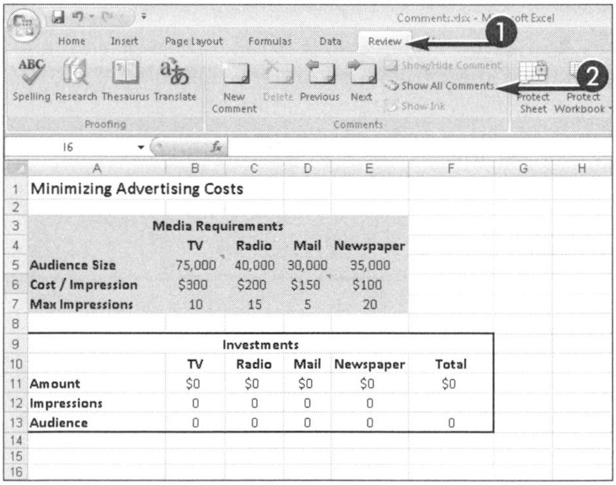

Excel displays all comments.

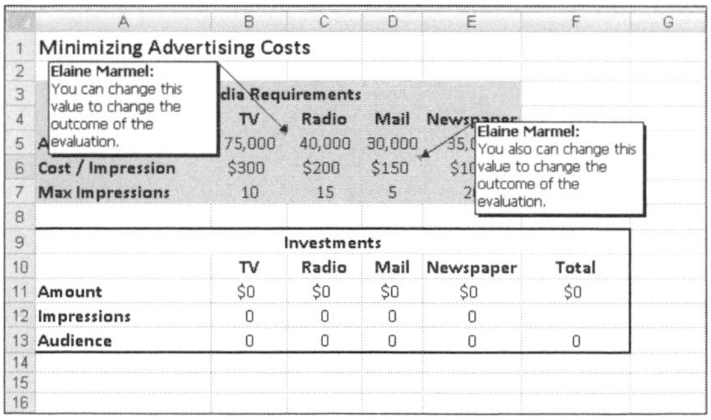

3. Click the Page Layout tab.
4. Click ▣.

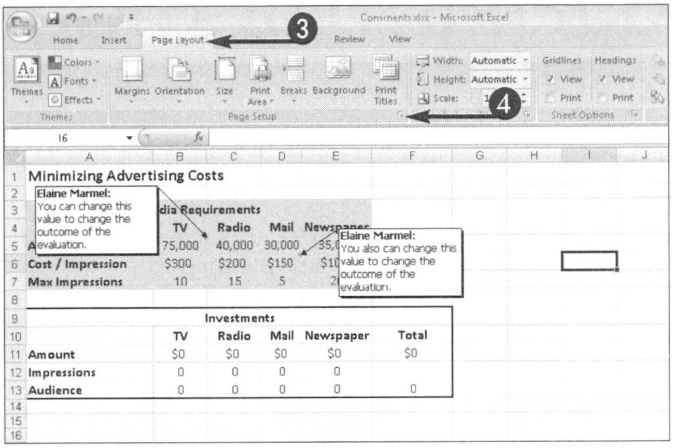

The Page Setup dialog box appears.

5. Click the Sheet tab.
6. Click the Comments ▾ and select an option.
7. Click OK.
8. Print the worksheet.

Excel prints comments according to the setting you selected in Step 6.

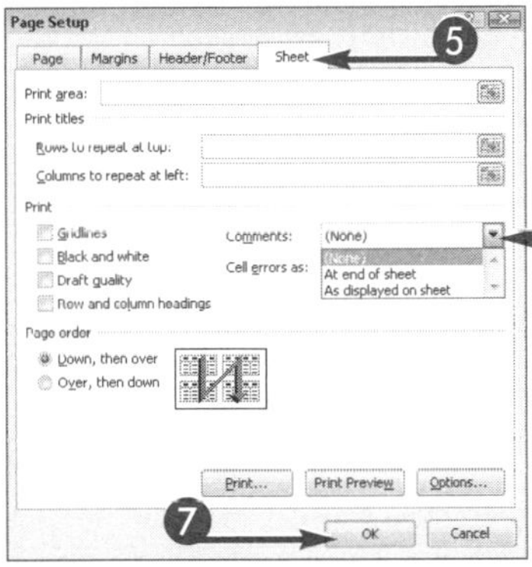

MASTER IT

Only part of my comment appears on-screen. Will all of my comment print?

▼ If you print your comments on a separate page at the end of the worksheet, Excel prints the entire comment. However, if you print comments as displayed on-screen, Excel only prints the portion that is visible on-screen. You can enlarge the comment text box to display more text; click the outside edge of the comment text box and then drag one of the round, white circles outward.

How do I print row numbers and column letters?

▼ Click the Page Layout tab and then click the Print option under Headings in the Sheet Options group (☐ changes to ☑). When you print the worksheet, Excel includes row numbers and column letters much the same way that they appear on-screen.

I have a Tablet PC. Is there a way to use digital ink to add and then print comments?

▼ Yes. Click the Review tab and then click the Start Inking button, which appears only when you run Excel on a Tablet PC. Excel then adds an Ink Tools tab to the Ribbon, and you can use the various buttons on Pens under the Ink Tools tab to highlight and mark up a worksheet.

Mark a Workbook as Final

You can mark a workbook as final to make the workbook read-only. When a workbook is read-only, you cannot make any changes to it and you cannot inspect it, as described in the section, "Inspect a Workbook Before Sharing."

Marking a workbook as final is *not* a security feature. Instead, it is a feature that helps you focus on reading rather than editing. When you mark a workbook as final, the Save command and the various editing commands become unavailable to you. In addition, Excel sets the Status field in the Document Properties box to Final. And, Excel displays an icon in the Status bar that helps you determine why the workbook is read-only.

Marking a workbook as final is not a security feature because anyone who opens the workbook can remove the final status from the workbook. If you truly want to prevent editing by others, see the sections, "Assign a Password to a Workbook" and "Encrypt a Workbook." If you want to allow some types of editing but restrict other types, see the sections, "Protect Workbooks," "Protect a Worksheet," and "Worksheet Actions You Can Protect."

Mark a Workbook as Final

Mark the Workbook

1. Click .
2. Click Prepare.
3. Click Mark as Final.

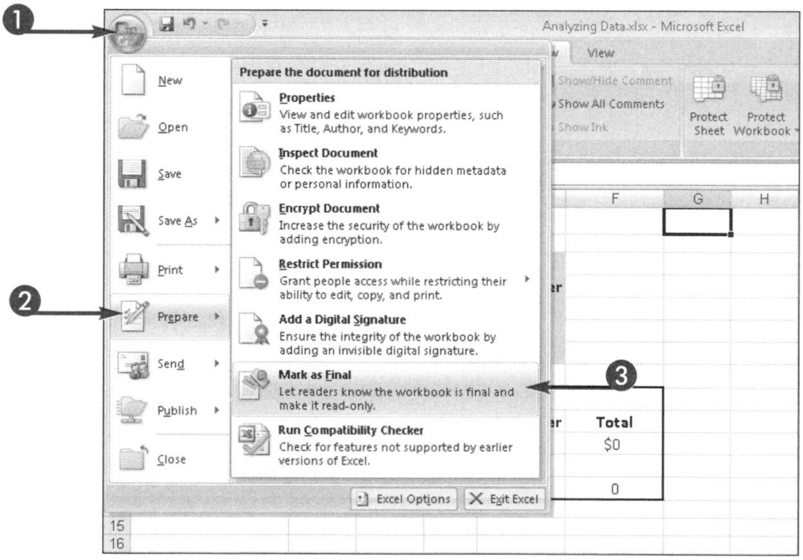

A warning message appears, explaining that Excel marks the workbook as final and saves it.

4. Click OK.

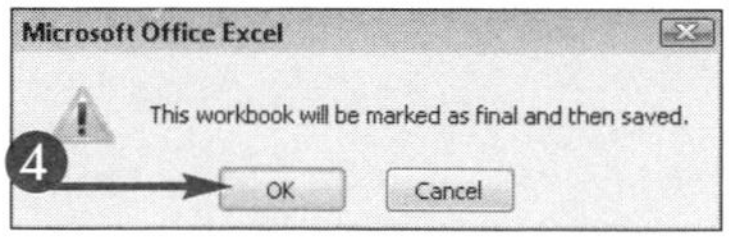

A message appears, explaining that Excel has marked the document as final and disabled typing and editing commands and proofing marks.

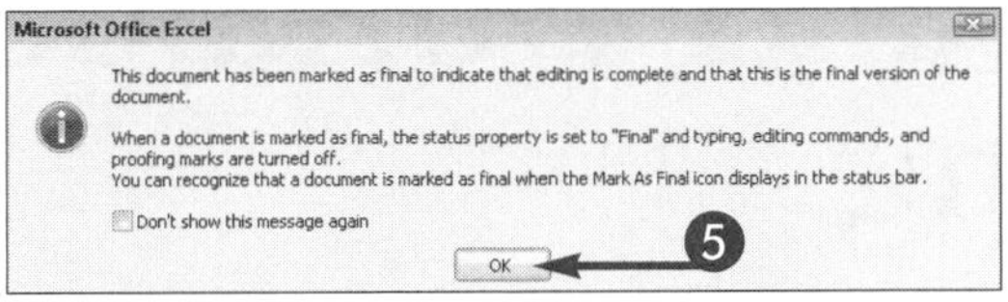

5 Click OK.

- The workbook becomes read-only.
- The Save button ( ) and various editing commands are disabled.
- The Mark as Final button ( ) appears in the Status bar.

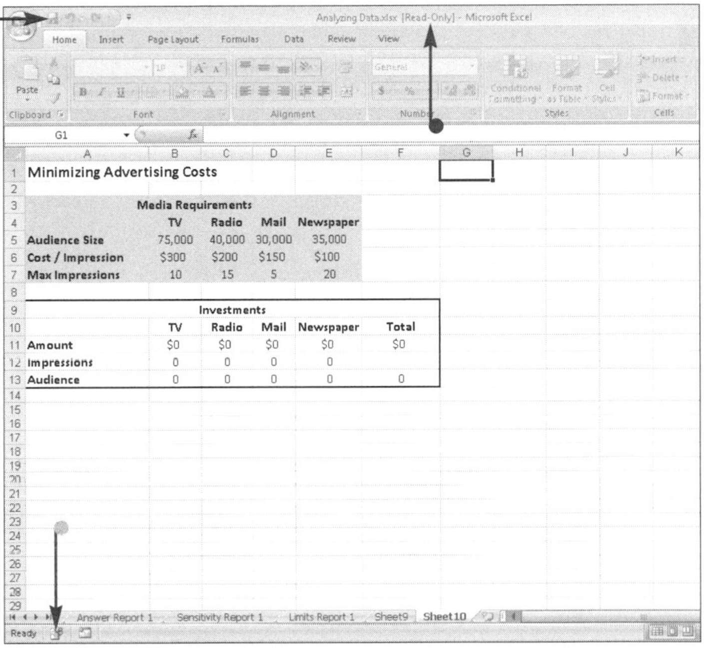

MASTER IT

Am I the only one who can change the status of a workbook marked as final?

▼ No. Anyone who opens the workbook can change its status. That is why marking a workbook as final is not a security feature. Use this feature only to give a reader the idea that editing is complete and to focus on reading. If you do not want anyone to make changes, consider using the other security measures described in this chapter.

If I need to make a change to a workbook I marked as final, what can I do?

▼ Complete Steps 1 to 3. No dialog boxes appear, but Excel removes the Final status it previously assigned to the workbook from the Document Properties box and re-enables ( ) and the various editing commands.

What happens to the Mark as Final status if I save the workbook under a new name?

▼ Excel maintains the Mark as Final status of the workbook, and ( ) and the various editing commands remain unavailable in both the original workbook and the one you created using a new name.

What happens to the Mark as Final status if I share the workbook with an Excel 2003 user?

▼ The workbook is not read-only when the Excel 2003 user opens it.

Excel and Workbook Sharing

You can share a workbook so that multiple users can make changes to it simultaneously. When you share a workbook, Excel appends "[Shared]" to the workbook title in the program title bar so that you know the workbook can be updated simultaneously. When a second user opens the workbook on another computer, that user also sees "[Shared]" in the title bar after the workbook name.

You cannot share a workbook that contains an XML map or a table. Before you share, you must remove the XML map using the Developers tab and convert the table to a range. Also, some Excel functions are not available when you edit a shared workbook. For example, you cannot delete worksheets, merge cells, draw shapes or add text boxes, group or outline worksheet data, or create data tables or PivotTables.

You also cannot set up or apply data validation, apply new conditional formats, or protect worksheets or workbooks; however, any data validation, conditional formatting, or worksheet or workbook protection already in place continues to function. You can insert or delete rows or columns, even though you cannot insert or delete ranges.

Excel and Workbook Sharing

Share a Workbook

1. Click the Review tab.
2. Click Share Workbook.

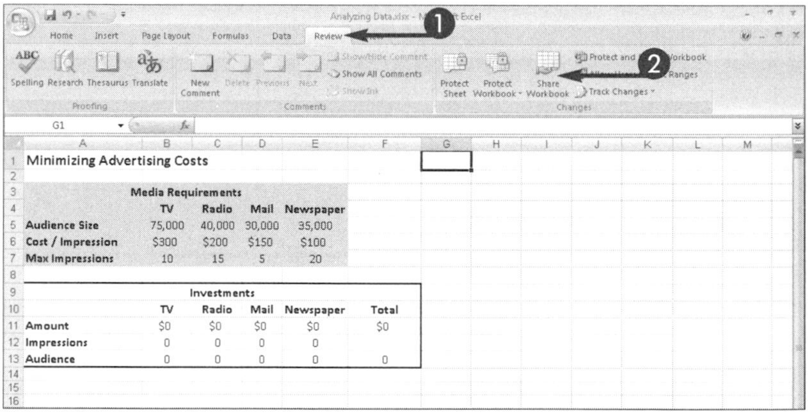

The Share Workbook dialog box appears.

3. Click here to allow changes by more than one user at the same time (☐ changes to ☑).
4. Click OK.

Excel displays a message explaining that it will save the workbook and your changes.

5. Click OK.

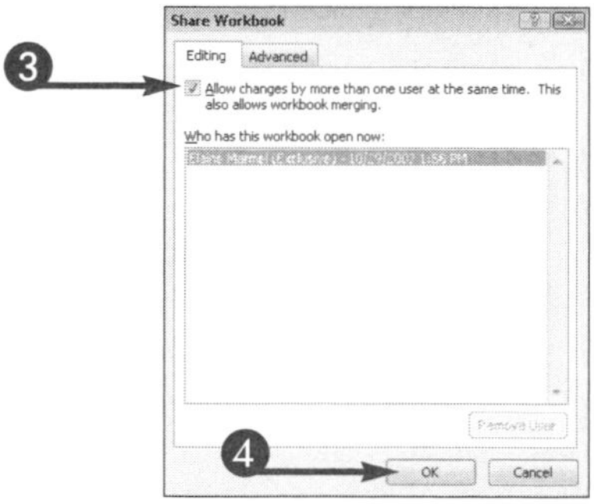

Control Share Settings

1. Click the Review tab.
2. Click Share Workbook.

   The Share Workbook dialog box appears.
3. Click Advanced.
   - Specify how long Excel keeps the change history.
   - Specify when you receive updates from other users.
   - Specify how Excel resolves conflicts caused by two users changing the same data.
   - These options enable you to use your local print and filter settings.
4. Click OK to share the file.

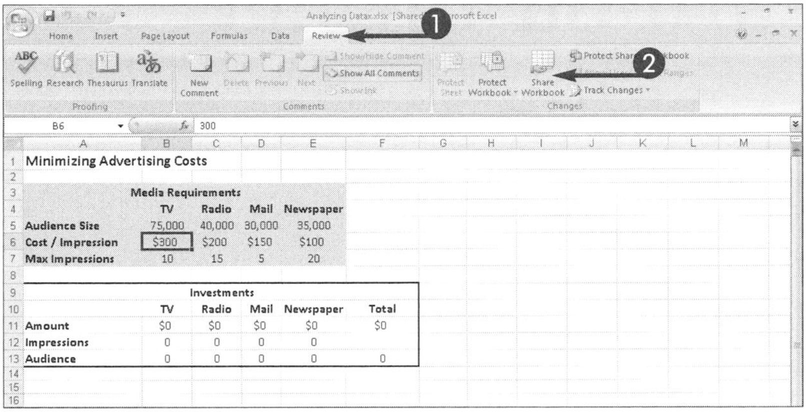

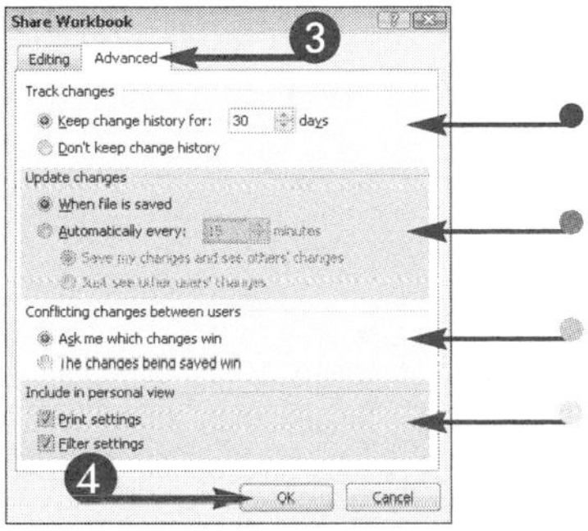

Can you explain the Update Changes options?

▼ You use these options to determine when Excel saves changes made by different users. By default, Excel saves changes when the workbook is saved. You can also set an interval to automatically save changes. If you choose this option, Excel saves your changes and shows you changes made by others. You can select the "Just See Other Users' Changes" option (◎ changes to ◉) to display other users' changes without saving your changes.

Can you explain the "Conflicting Changes between Users" options?

▼ These options control what Excel does when two or more users make changes to the same cell. By default, Excel displays a dialog box that enables you to decide which change to save. If you select "The Changes Being Saved Win" option (◎ changes to ◉), you have no choice in the matter; Excel retains the changes made by the last person saving the workbook.

Can you explain the "Include in Personal View" options?

▼ The Print Settings option controls whether Excel saves your local print settings, including the printer you use, the page breaks, and changes you make to the print area. The Filter Settings option controls whether Excel saves filter settings that you select using AutoFilters. By default, Excel saves both your print and filter settings.

How do I stop sharing a workbook?

▼ Repeat Steps 1 to 4 in the subsection, "Share a Workbook."

Turn on Change Tracking

You can use change tracking when you share documents to identify changes made by various reviewers. When you enable change tracking, Excel highlights all changes made to the contents of cells by adding comments that summarize the type of change you make. Excel displays a dark-blue box around a cell that has been changed, and a small blue triangle appears in the upper-left corner of the changed cell.

As you set up change tracking options, you can identify the changes you want Excel to highlight. You can choose to have Excel highlight all changes, changes made since you last saved, changes not yet reviewed, or changes made since a date you specify. You can also choose to view everyone's changes — including your own — or all changes except for your own. And, you can identify cells you want Excel to monitor for changes; if you do not select any cells, Excel monitors the entire workbook. You can also choose to view changes on-screen.

When you enable change tracking, Excel automatically shares the workbook, adding "[Sharing]" to the workbook name in the title bar. When you share a workbook, some Excel functions are not available when you edit the workbook.

Turn on Change Tracking

1. Click the Review tab.
2. Click Track Changes.
3. Click Highlight Changes.

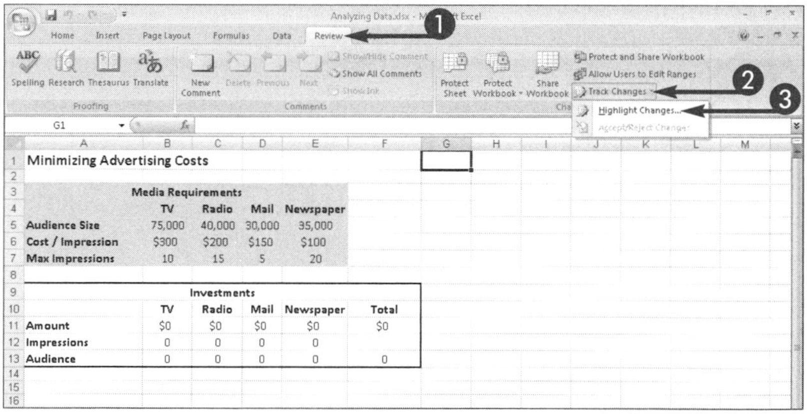

The Highlight Changes dialog box appears.

4. Click here to track changes while editing (changes to).

This also shares your workbook.

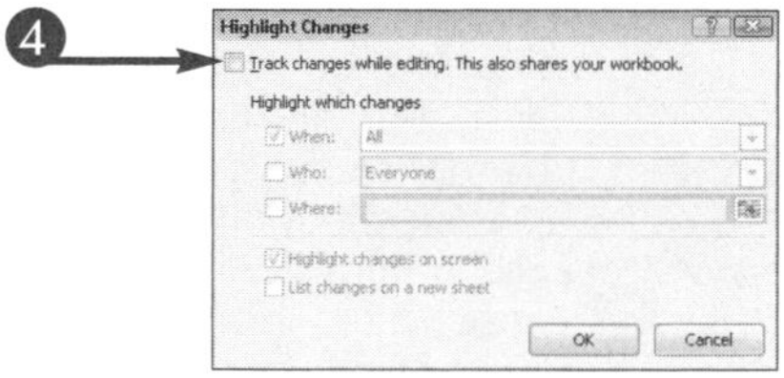

Additional tracking options become available.

5. Click the When ▾ to specify the changes to highlight (☐ changes to ☑).
6. Click the Who ▾ to specify whose changes to track (☐ changes to ☑).
7. Click the Where ▾ to specify the cells to track for changes (☐ changes to ☑).
8. Click OK.

   A warning message appears, telling you that Excel will save the workbook.

9. Click OK.

   Excel enables change tracking and shares the workbook.

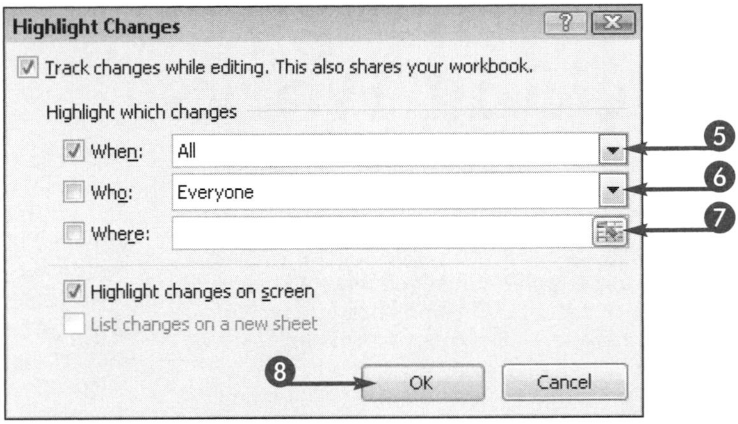

MASTER IT

What functions are not available when I enable change tracking?

▼ You cannot delete worksheets, merge cells, draw shapes, add text boxes, group or outline worksheet data, or create data tables or PivotTables. You also cannot set up or apply data validation, apply new conditional formats, or protect worksheets or workbooks; however, any data validation, conditional formatting, or worksheet or workbook protection already in place continues to function. You can insert or delete rows, columns, and cells, but you cannot insert or delete ranges.

What does the "List Changes on a New Sheet" option do and why is it not available?

▼ If you enable this option, Excel creates a History sheet in the workbook that contains changes you save by saving the workbook. You can enable this option after you enable change tracking. See the section, "Use the History Sheet to Review Tracked Changes," for more details.

What happens if I change the same cell that somebody else changes?

▼ If you have not changed file sharing options, then Excel allows you to make the change. However, when you try to save the workbook, Excel displays the Resolve Conflicts dialog box, which shows your changes to the cell and the other user's changes to the cell. You can click Accept Mine to apply your change or Accept Other to apply the change of the other user.

How Change Tracking Works

When you make changes to a workbook in which you have enabled change tracking, Excel monitors changes to the workbook or to a specified range if you set up change tracking to monitor only a range. When you make a change, Excel adds a comment that summarizes the type of change you make. In order that you can easily identify cells that were changed, Excel displays a dark-blue box around a changed cell, and a small blue triangle appears in the upper-left corner of the changed cell.

The types of changes control what you see in the changed cell's comment text box. When you change or delete a cell's content, the comment text box displays the original value and the new value; if you deleted the cell's content, Excel describes the new value as "blank." Although the Insert and Delete buttons on the Home tab of the Ribbon appear unavailable, you can insert and delete rows. If you insert or delete a row or a column, Excel tracks the change and the comment text box identifies the row or column you inserted or deleted.

How Change Tracking Works

1. Click a cell and change its content.
2. Move ✚ over the cell.
   - Excel displays the comment that describes the change.

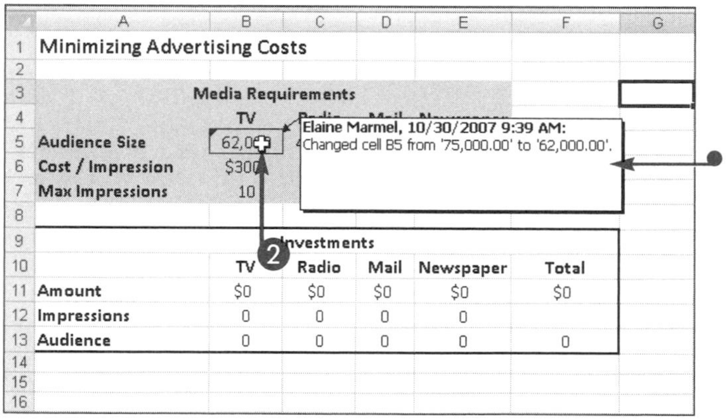

3. Click a cell and press Delete to delete its content.
4. Move ✚ over the cell.
   - Excel displays the comment that describes the change.

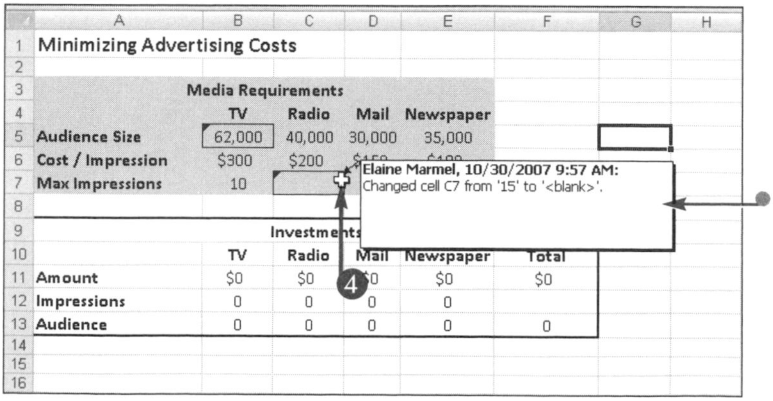

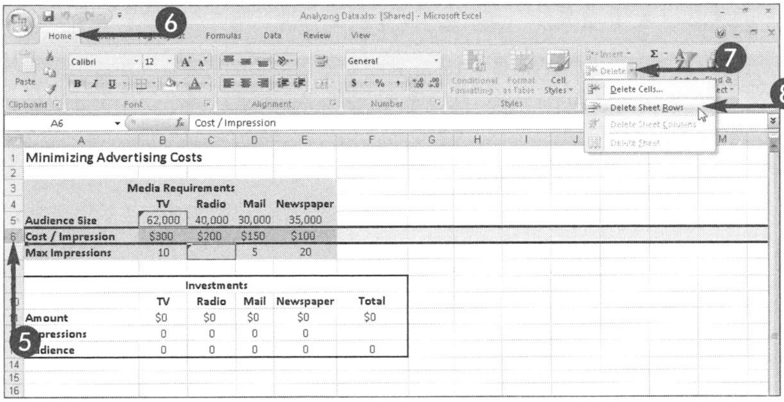

5. Select a row by clicking its row number.
6. Click the Home tab.
7. Click the Delete ▾.
8. Click Delete Sheet Rows.

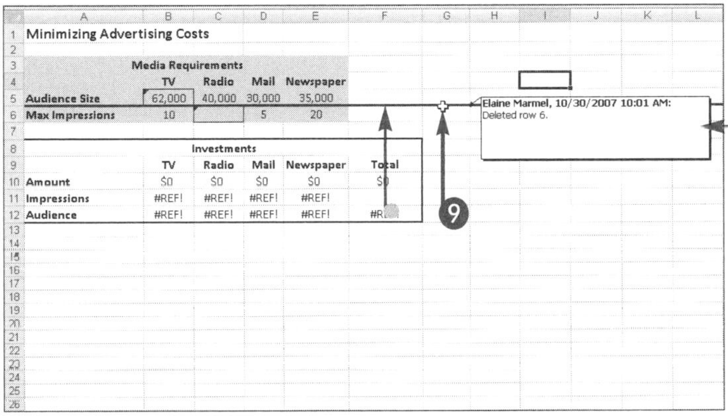

- Excel deletes the row and displays a thick blue line where the row appeared.

9. Move ✚ over the thick blue line.

- Excel displays the comment that describes the change.

MASTER IT

What happens if I copy or move cell contents?

▼ Excel displays the comment text box in the cell that received content. That is, if you copied the range D5 to I7, Excel displays a comment text box in cell I7, and the comment indicates that the content of cell I7 changed from its original value to its new value. The comment does not indicate that you copied or moved the value into cell I7, and no comment text box appears in cell D5.

I inserted a row and Excel did not track the change. What did I do wrong?

▼ You probably specified a range for Excel to monitor for changes when you enabled change tracking. In this case, Excel continues to monitor row or column deletions that you make within the range, but it does not identify row or column insertions that you make within the range. If you remove the range restriction and insert a row or column, Excel tracks the change.

Can you list the changes I can make that Excel does not track?

▼ Excel does not track changes when you apply formatting or add comments to cells, hide or unhide rows or columns, rename sheet tabs in the workbook, or insert or delete worksheets in the workbook. If you change a cell and a formula in another cell recalculates, then Excel tracks the change to the cell, but not the change to the cell containing the formula that recalculated.

Use the History Sheet to Review Tracked Changes

You can display the History sheet to review changes made to a workbook. The History sheet is a listing of changes made to the workbook up to the point at which you add the History sheet to the workbook. You can use the History sheet instead of, or in addition to, the comment text boxes that appear in various places. The History sheet can be particularly helpful if the workbook contains many sheets on which you are tracking changes, because you can review them all in one place instead of switching from sheet to sheet to review comment text boxes.

Excel does not display the History sheet by default, but you can use the steps in this section to add the History sheet to your workbook. The information that appears on the History sheet for each change includes the action number, the date and time of the change, who made the change, the type of change made, the sheet in the workbook to which the change was made, the cell or range address affected by the change, the new value, the old value, and, for actions that conflict, the action type and the action that was not saved.

Use the History Sheet to Review Tracked Changes

1. Click [save icon] to save the workbook.

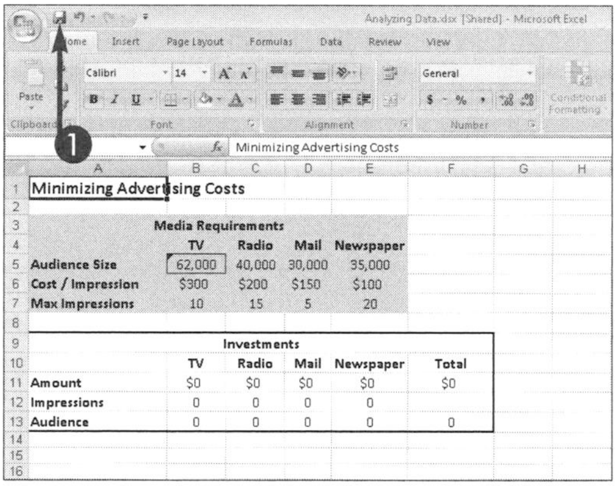

2. Click the Review tab.
3. Click Track Changes.
4. Click Highlight Changes.

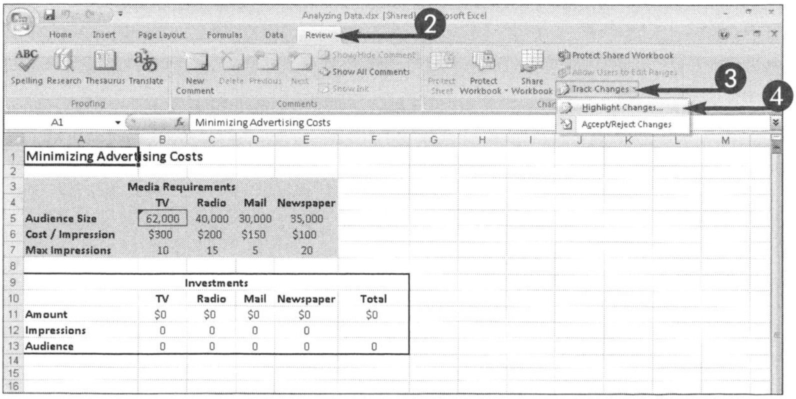

The Highlight Changes dialog box appears.

5 Click List changes on a new sheet (☐ changes to ☑).

6 Click OK.

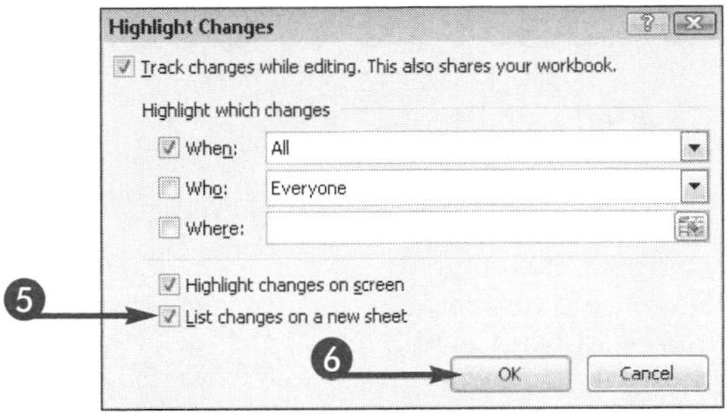

- Excel adds the History sheet to the workbook and displays it.

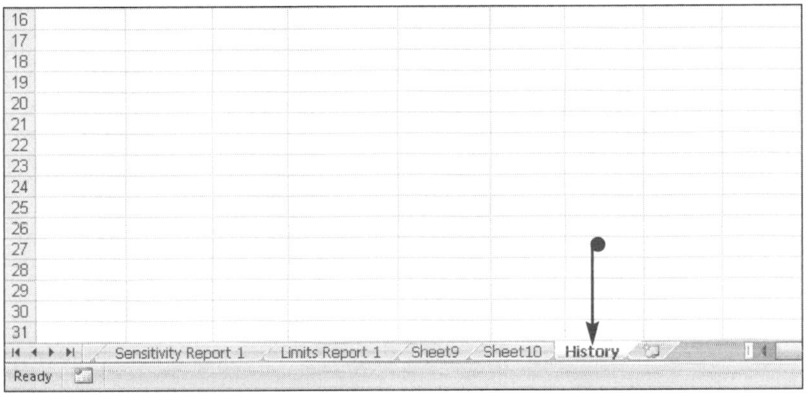

MASTER IT

What does the Action Number column on the History sheet mean?

▼ The Action Number column identifies the order of the changes you or other users made. By default, the History sheet lists the actions in the order they were made, from earliest to latest; however, by clicking ▾ beside the column title, you can reverse the order or filter to view only selected changes. You can also click ▾ beside any column title to change the order or filter.

Does Excel update the History sheet as I make changes?

▼ No, the History sheet is static and displays only those changes that have been made prior to you performing the steps in this section. To update the History sheet to display additional changes, perform the steps in this section again, and Excel will search for additional changes and display them on the History sheet.

I did not make any changes to the worksheet but I saved it. Why did the History sheet disappear?

▼ Once you save the workbook, Excel no longer considers the changes to be history, and so it deletes the History sheet. You can make the History sheet reappear if you repeat the steps in this section.

Combine Reviewers' Comments

After everybody has reviewed a shared workbook, you can combine all comments made by various reviewers and decide which comments to accept or reject. Excel displays all of the changed cells on-screen and, using the Accept or Reject Changes dialog box, Excel moves from change to change, shows you information about each change, and allows you to accept or reject a change. If one cell is changed more than once, you see each change and can select a change to apply it. If you plan to combine reviewers' changes into the workbook, you should do so before you disable sharing, and you should make a backup copy of the workbook before you start reviewing.

As you set up review options, you can identify the changes you want Excel to highlight. You can choose to have Excel highlight changes you have not yet reviewed or changes made since a date you specify. You can also choose to view everyone's changes (including your own), all changes except your own, or the changes of a particular user. And, you can identify changed cells that you want Excel to review; if you do not select any cells, Excel reviews all changes in the entire workbook.

Combine Reviewers' Comments

1. Click the Review tab.
2. Click Track Changes.
3. Click Accept/Reject Changes.

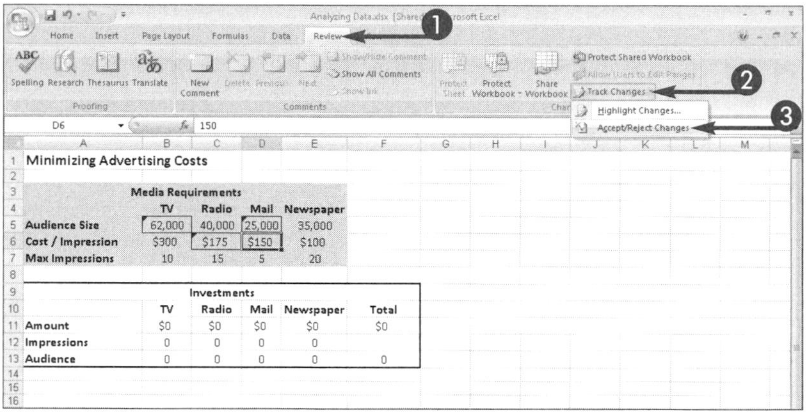

The Select Changes to Accept or Reject dialog box appears.

4. Click the When ▾ to specify the changes to review (☐ changes to ☑).
5. Click the Who ▾ to specify whose changes to review (☐ changes to ☑).
6. Click the Where ▾ to specify the cells to review for changes (☐ changes to ☑).
7. Click OK.

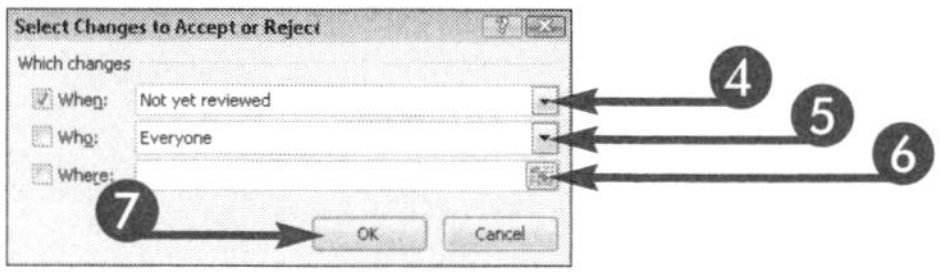

The Accept or Reject Changes dialog box appears.

- Changes made, by whom and when, appear here.

8 You can click the change you want to use.

9 Click Accept.

- Excel makes the change.
- Excel selects the next changed cell.

The Accept or Reject Changes dialog box appears with the next set of choices.

10 Repeat Steps 8 and 9 until you have reviewed all changes.

Excel automatically closes the Accept or Reject Changes dialog box after you review all changes.

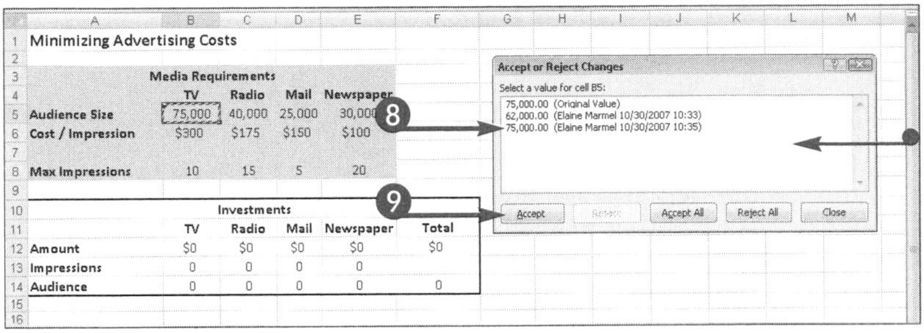

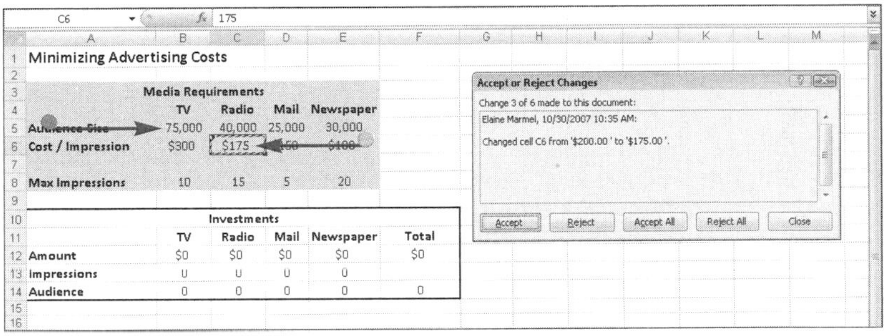

MASTER IT

When would I want to limit whose changes I review?

▼ You might want to limit the changes you review if you are responsible for certain people in the organization and have authority to review their changes. If you review all changes under these circumstances, your review will take longer. If you review a limited set of changes, click Close in the Accept or Reject Changes dialog box after you complete your review.

I am responsible only for certain cells in a shared workbook that was distributed for review. Can I review changes only to those cells?

▼ Yes. Perform Steps 1 to 5 and, in Step 6, click [icon] so that you can select just the cells you want to review for changes. After you select the cells, Excel redisplays the Select Changes to Accept or Reject dialog box, and you can continue with the steps in this section.

Why should I make a backup copy of the workbook before reviewing?

▼ If you have not saved the workbook before you start reviewing, Excel saves it before it walks you through reviewing changes. If you make a mistake concerning a particular change, you cannot undo the mistake, and the only way to recover the information is to open the backup copy and use the information that it contains.

Collaborate through E-mail

You may decide to collaborate by e-mailing a workbook instead of sharing it on a network. You can attach the workbook to an e-mail message directly from Excel without opening your e-mail program. Once you create the message, you then send it using your e-mail program.

You can send the workbook to multiple users simultaneously for review and, when they return the workbook to you, you can merge the changes. For this procedure to work properly, you need to share the workbook and turn on change tracking. See the section, "Turn on Change Tracking," for details; turning on change tracking automatically shares the workbook.

When you send out the workbook through e-mail, you instruct each recipient to make changes and return the workbook to you. As you receive the workbook back, you should change its filename so that you can identify the recipient from whom you received it. You should save the original workbook and all copies of it to the same folder. You can then use the Compare and Merge Workbooks button to select workbooks containing changes and merge the changes into the original workbook. You need to add the Compare and Merge Workbooks button to the Quick Access Toolbar because no button for the command appears on the Ribbon.

Collaborate through E-mail

1. Open the shared workbook you want to e-mail.
2. Click [Office button].
3. Click Send.
4. Click E-mail.

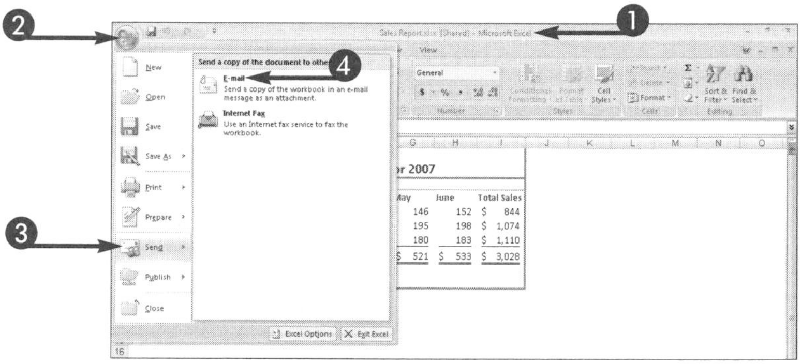

Your default e-mail program opens a new e-mail message.

5. Click in the To field and type the e-mail address of a recipient.
6. Click in the Cc field and type the e-mail address of a recipient to whom you want to send a copy.

Note: *To send the message or copies to multiple recipients, separate each e-mail address with a semicolon (;) and a space.*

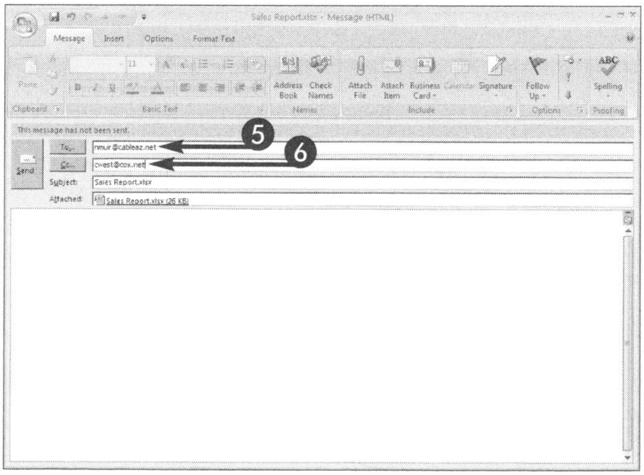

Excel supplies the workbook filename as the e-mail subject by default.

7. Type a new subject here.

Note: *Subjects are not required, but including one is considerate.*

- Excel automatically attaches the workbook to the e-mail message.

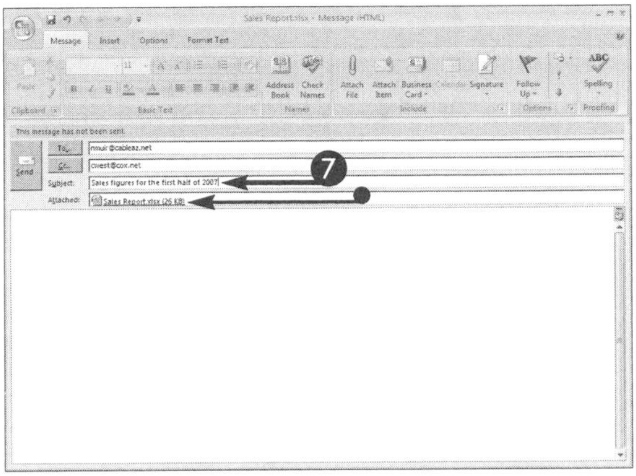

8. Ttype the message body here.

9. Click Send.

   Excel places a message in your e-mail program's Outbox and closes the e-mail message.

10. Use your e-mail program to send the message.

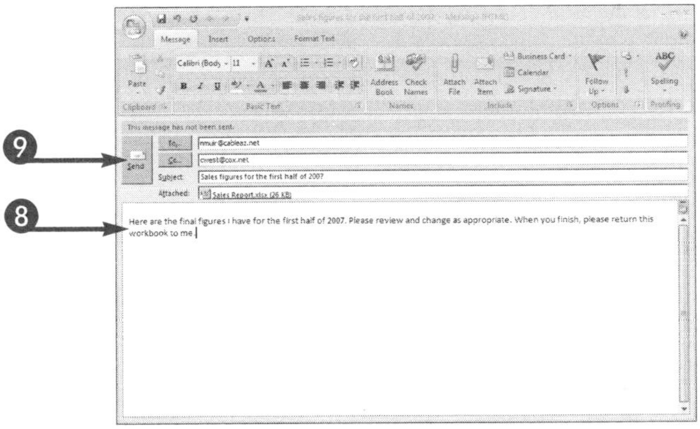

MASTER IT

How do I add the Compare and Merge Workbooks button to the Quick Access Toolbar?

▼ To add the Compare and Merge Workbooks button to the Quick Access Toolbar, click [button] and then click Excel Options. Click Customize and then click All Commands from the list on the left. Click Compare and Merge Workbooks and click Add. Then click OK. The button appears on the right end of the Quick Access Toolbar.

How do I compare and merge changes?

▼ Assign a unique name to each workbook you receive back from reviewers and store the original and the copies in the same folder. Open the original workbook. Click the Compare and Merge Workbooks button to display the Select Files to Merge Into Current Workbook. Click the files you received back from reviewers — do not select the open workbook — and click Open. Excel merges the changes from each workbook into the open workbook.

What happens if I do not share the workbook before I e-mail it?

▼ Excel displays a message that explains that you should share the workbook before e-mailing it if you intend to merge the information you receive from recipients. In the same message, Excel offers to save a shared version of the workbook and turn on change tracking. Click Yes and continue with the steps in this section to complete the e-mail message.

Create a Hyperlink in a Workbook

Hyperlinks help the user navigate. You can create a hyperlink in a workbook to link your workbook to another workbook, a document of any kind, an e-mail address, a graphic file, or a Web page. When you click a hyperlink, the link opens the file or Web page to which you linked.

Hyperlinks encode the destination file or Web page as a Uniform Resource Locator (URL). The URL identifies the location of the file or Web page by listing a protocol, a Web server or network location, a path, and a filename. An *absolute* hyperlink contains a full pathname to the destination file or Web page. A *relative* hyperlink, usually used for Web pages, has one or more missing parts that are taken from the current Web page. If you create a relative hyperlink in a workbook, Excel assumes that the missing parts of the hyperlink are associated with the location of the active workbook.

In Excel, you can create links to files or Web pages, or you can create links to other sheets in the same workbook, typing the link to a specific cell, as shown in this example.

Create a Hyperlink in a Workbook

1. Click the cell in which you want to store the hyperlink.
2. Click the Insert tab.
3. Click Hyperlink.

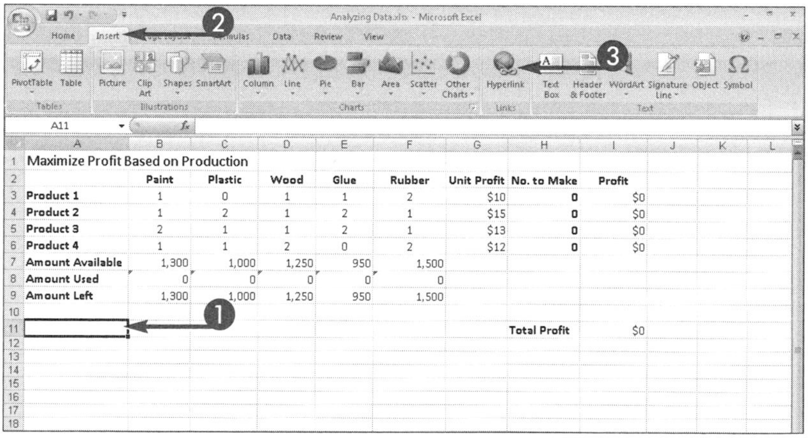

The Insert Hyperlink dialog box appears.

- You can use these buttons to identify the file, worksheet, or e-mail address to which you want to link.

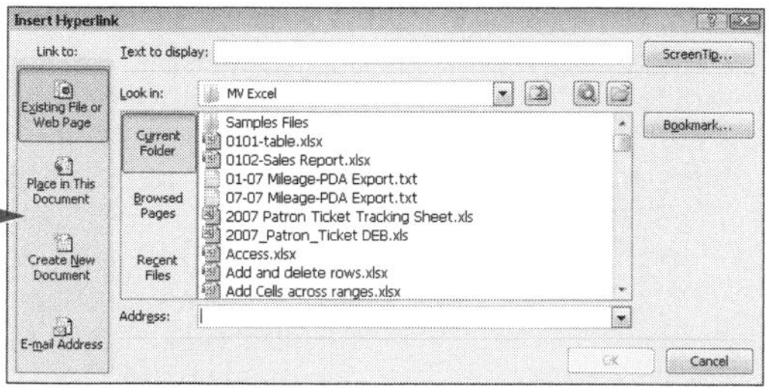

4. Click Place in This Document.
5. Click an entry in this list.
6. Click in the "Text to display" field to type the text Excel should display as the link.
   - When linking to a worksheet, you can click in the "Type the cell reference" field to specify a cell address.
7. Click OK.

Excel inserts the hyperlink in the cell you selected in Step 1.

You can click the hyperlink to display the file, Web page, or worksheet and cell to which you linked.

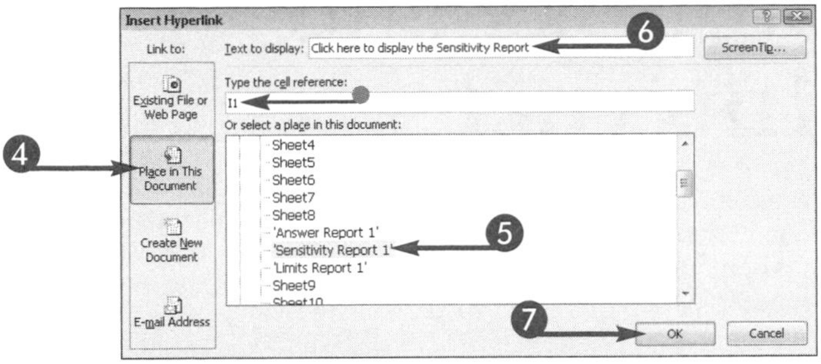

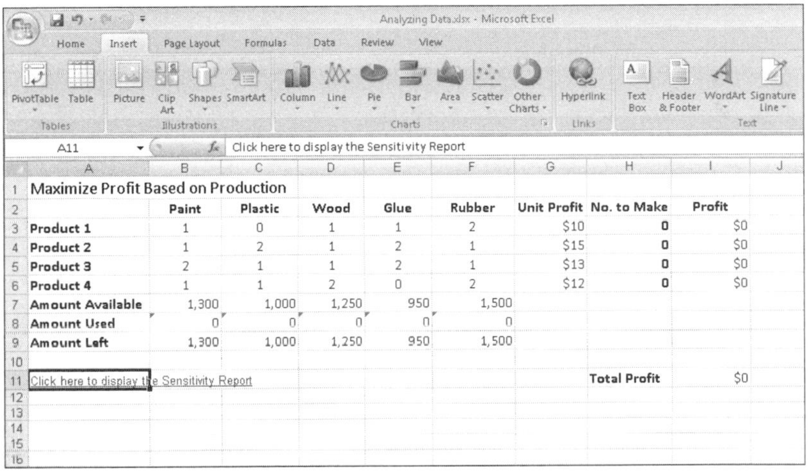

Master It

Is there a way to select a cell containing a hyperlink without activating the hyperlink?

▼ Yes. You can use the arrow keys on the keyboard. You can also use the mouse by clicking the cell containing the hyperlink, and pressing and holding the mouse button until the mouse pointer changes to . When you release the mouse button, Excel leaves the cell pointer in the cell containing the hyperlink without switching to the destination.

My hyperlink no longer works. What have I done wrong?

▼ If the file or Web page to which you link is deleted or changes locations, a hyperlink might not work any longer. To solve the problem, edit the hyperlink and change the destination to match the new location of the file or Web page. If the destination no longer exists, remove the hyperlink. To edit the link, select it without activating the link and repeat the steps in this section.

How do I remove a hyperlink?

▼ Select the cell containing the link without activating the link and then press Delete.

Can I move or copy the hyperlink to a different cell without changing the link?

▼ Yes. Right-click the hyperlink and click or . Click the cell where you want the hyperlink to appear, click the Home tab, and then click Paste.

Workbooks and the Internet

You can create a Web page from an Excel workbook. To enable users to make changes to a workbook using a browser, you need to publish the workbook. Otherwise, you can create a static Web page so that users can view your workbook information in a browser and do not need to open it in Excel. Users cannot make changes to a workbook saved to a static Web page.

Publishing a Workbook

If your organization uses Excel Services, you can publish your workbook to your company's intranet. Excel Services is a server that runs Microsoft Office SharePoint Server 2007 and is capable of running Excel Calculation Services. Once you publish a workbook, users can view the workbook using a browser through Excel Web Access. Although you publish the entire workbook, you can define the parts of the workbook that you want displayed in Excel Web Access. You can then use Office SharePoint Server 2007 permissions to identify authorized users who can refresh, recalculate, and make changes to the viewable data.

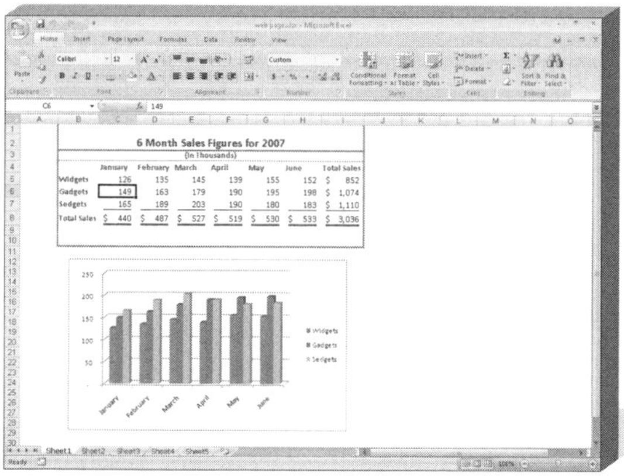

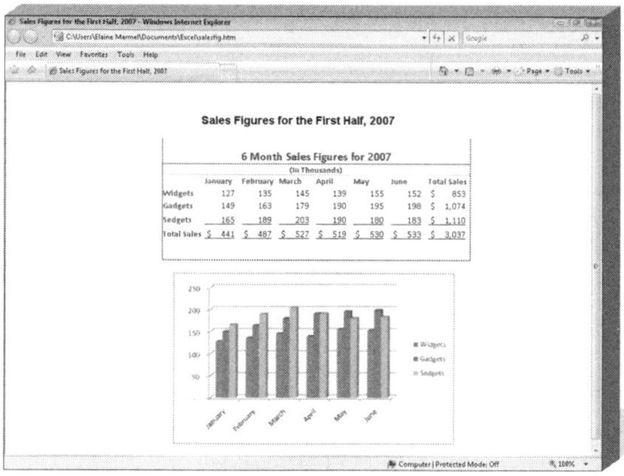

Saving a Static Workbook

You can save an entire workbook or portions of a workbook as a static Web page that users can view on the Internet or on your company's intranet. Suppose, for example, that you have a workbook that contains sales figures for the last six months, along with a chart showing trends. You can save the information to a static Web page, and users can view the information using a Web browser.

When you create a Web page from an Excel workbook, the Web page may have supporting files, such as graphic objects like charts or bullets, and hyperlinks. Excel offers two ways to store the supporting files: First, you can choose to store the supporting files in a separate folder that appears inside the folder where you store the Web page. Second, you can tell Excel to embed the supporting files in the Web page, making them part of the Web page.

You can open a Web page that you create in a browser; if you want to edit the Web page, you can open it in Excel, but some Excel features may not be available while you edit the Web page. So, if you anticipate that you will want to make changes to your workbook, you should save the workbook as a workbook before you create the Web page. That way, you can open the original workbook, make the changes, and then save it again as a Web page to incorporate the updates.

Each time you save your workbook, you can have Excel automatically republish it as a Web page using the AutoRepublish feature. However, you may not want to automatically republish the workbook as a Web page when you save the workbook; for example, if you are working on a computer that is not currently connected to your network or Web server, you really do not want Excel to try to republish the workbook.

Save a Workbook as a Web Page

You can save workbook information as a static Web page that others can then view using a Web browser. When you create a static Web page, others cannot edit the information; they can simply view it.

During the process of saving an Excel workbook as a Web page, you identify the portions of the workbook that you want to save. You can save the entire workbook, including tabs for navigating worksheets, or you can save a portion of a single worksheet, such as a range or chart.

You can also specify a title that will appear in the title bar when you view the Web page in a browser, and you identify the location where you want to store the Web page and any supporting files. You can set options for automatically republishing the Web page if you modify the workbook, and you can choose to view the Web page that you create when you are finished.

When you create a Web page from Excel workbook information, the Web page may contain supporting files, such as hyperlinks and graphic objects like charts or bullets. The type of Web page you save determines how Excel saves the supporting files.

Save a Workbook as a Web Page

1. Open the workbook you want to save as a Web page.
2. Click .
3. Click Save As.

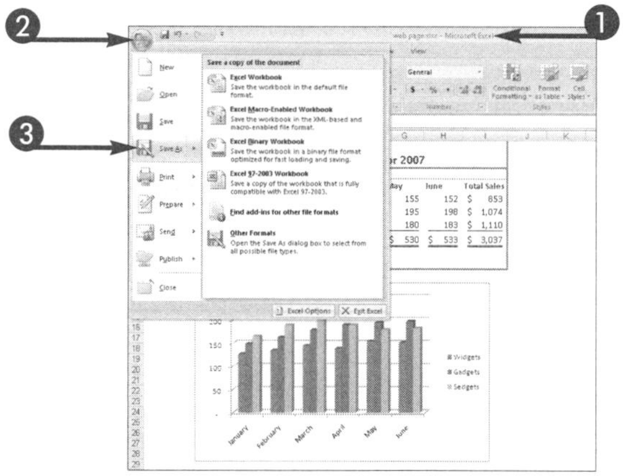

The Save As dialog box appears.

4. Navigate to the folder where you want to store the Web page files.
5. Click the "Save As Type" drop-down arrow and select Web Page.
6. Click in the "File Name" field to type a name for the Web page file.
7. Click Publish.

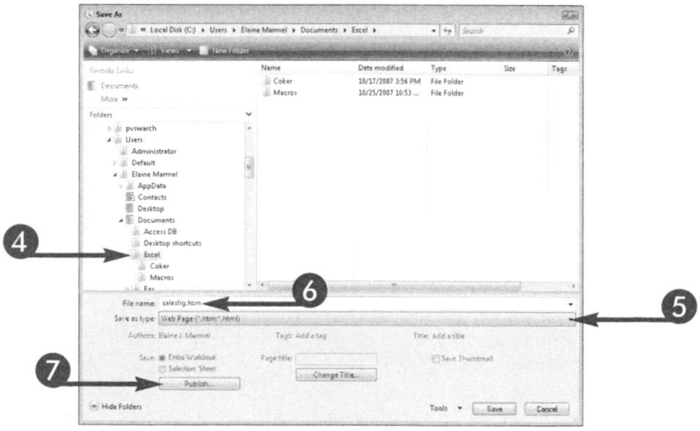

The Publish as Web Page dialog box appears.

8. Click the Choose ▾ to select what you want to publish.
   - You can click Change to display the Set Title dialog box, and type a title for the Web page.
   - The path where Excel stores the Web page files appears here.
9. Click here to preview the Web page in a browser.
10. Click Publish.

Excel saves the information as a Web page and displays it in your default browser.

- The title you set appears here.
- The path to the Web page file appears here.

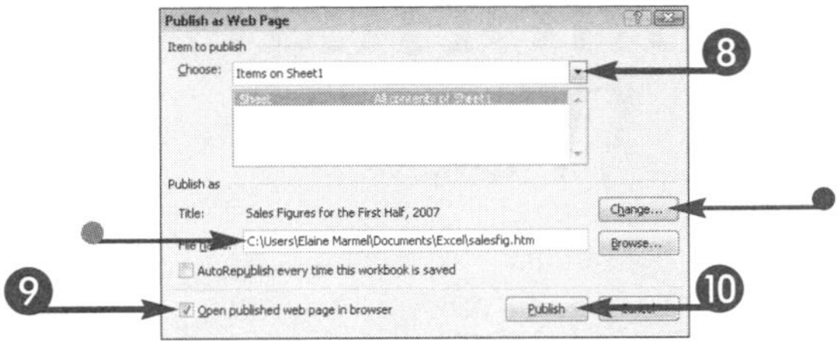

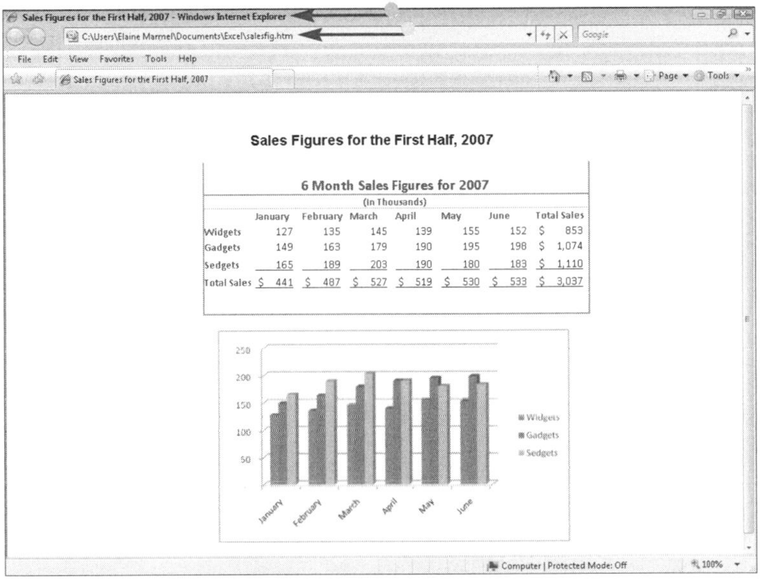

MASTER IT

Do I need to choose between the entire workbook or just a selection before clicking Publish?

▼ Regardless of the choice you make for these options, Excel displays the Publish As Web Page dialog box, where you can choose to publish the entire workbook or some portion of the workbook, using Step 8 in this section. So, the option you choose here does not matter.

What does the "AutoRepublish every time this workbook is saved" option do?

▼ If you select this option and make a subsequent change to the workbook, Excel displays a message each time that you save the workbook, asking if you want to republish the workbook as a Web page. From this message box, you can enable the AutoRepublish feature to republish the workbook, or you can temporarily disable the AutoRepublish feature and not republish the workbook.

What is the difference between the Web Page option and the Single File Web Page option?

▼ When you use the Web Page option, Excel places supporting files for the Web page, such as graphics and hyperlinks, in a separate folder. The supporting files folder appears inside the folder where you store the Web page. When you create a single file Web page, Excel embeds all supporting files into the Web page and does not place them in a separate folder.

Import Information from the Web

You can use an external data query to obtain information from a Web site and display it in your Excel workbook. The information that you bring into your workbook is not necessarily static. Suppose that you import stock market index data. The values you import are the values of the indices at the time you import them, and in your Excel workbook, they do not change. However, from within Excel, you can update those values at any time to obtain new, updated information.

When you set up a Web query, Excel opens the New Web Query dialog box, and, in that dialog box, you initially see the Home page of your default browser. Using the Address bar provided in the New Web Query dialog box, you can navigate to any Web site to import information.

As you view Web sites, you notice that small boxes containing yellow arrows appear; these yellow areas identify tables of information on the Web page, and you can import any or all of the tables on the page.

Excel keeps track of each external data query you establish so that you can reuse a query at any time in any workbook.

Import Information from the Web

1. Click the Data tab.
2. Click From Web.

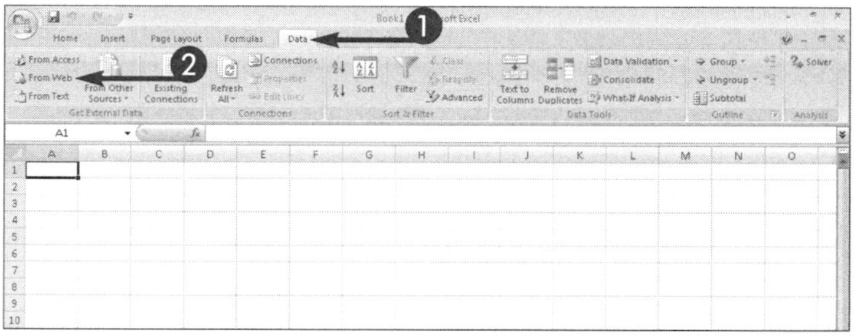

The New Web Query dialog box opens.

3. Click here and type a Web address.
4. Click Go.
5. Click a table selection button (→ changes to ☑).
6. Repeat Step 5 for each table you want to download.
7. Click Import.

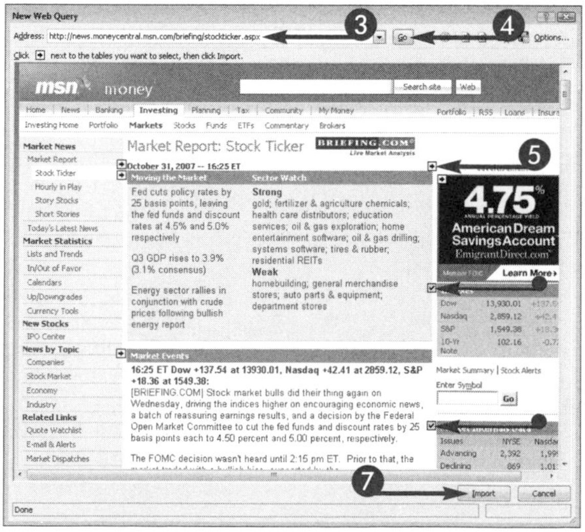

The Import Data dialog box appears.

8 Select the cell where you want the information to appear.

9 Click OK.

- Excel downloads the information into the workbook.

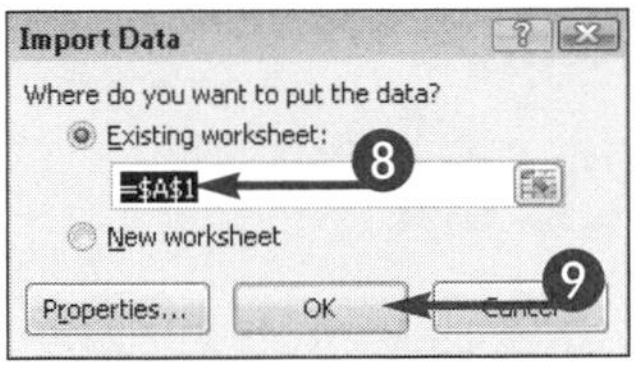

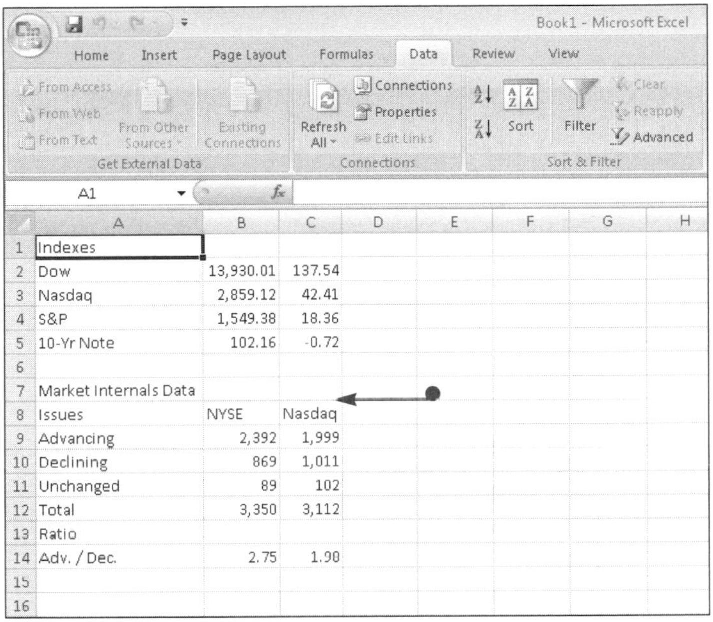

MASTER IT

What happens if I click the Properties button in the Import Data dialog box?

▼ The External Data Range Properties dialog box appears. In it, you can choose to save the query definition, and control how Excel refreshes the data, how Excel formats and lays out the data, and how Excel handles a change in the number of rows when you refresh the data.

I see a security warning when I open the workbook. What should I do?

▼ The security warning indicates that Excel has disabled data connections, and an external data query to a Web page is a data connection. If you need to update the information you imported, click the Options button and then click Enable This Content (◎ changes to ◉). Click OK, and Excel enables the connection.

How can I refresh the information I imported?

▼ Click the Data tab and then click Refresh All. If your workbook contains more than one external query and you want to refresh information for only one query, click anywhere in the range containing that information and then click ▾ at the bottom of the Refresh All button. From the menu that appears, click Refresh.

Import a Text File into Excel

You can import lists of related information from CSV text files and TXT text files into Excel. Most text files consist of rows of information, and, if you examine a text file using a tool such as Notepad, you find that each row contains the same information at the same position on the row. Each new row marks the beginning of a new record. For example, in a text file containing names and phone numbers, each row contains one name and phone number, and the phone numbers appear in the same relative position in each row.

Most text files separate fields on each row by a common character, such as a comma. Files set up this way are *delimited* files. In delimited files, you can identify missing information in a row whenever you see two successive separator characters. The implication is that information between the separators is missing. The example in this section uses a delimited file.

In some cases, you might find that a text file contains data that appears to be aligned in columns with an equal number of spaces between each field but no special character separating the fields. Files set up this way are *fixed width* files.

Import a Text File into Excel

1. Click the Data tab.
2. Click From Text.

   The Import Text File dialog box appears.
3. Click the file you want to import.
4. Click Import.

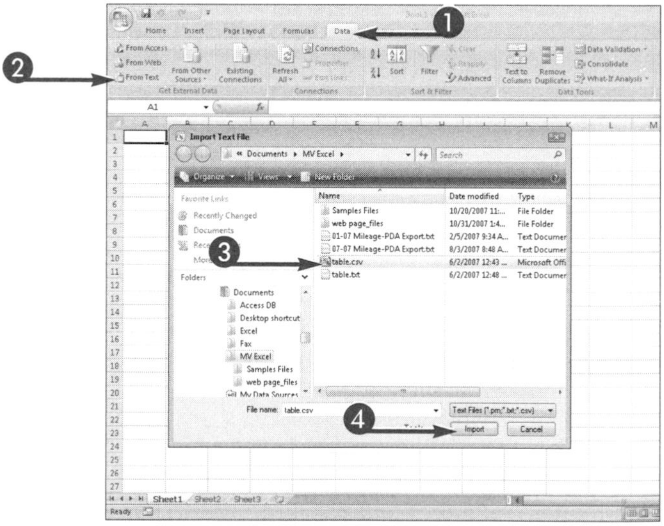

The Text Import Wizard - Step 1 of 3 dialog box appears.

5. Click here to describe the type of file you are importing.
   - You can designate the first row of data to import here.
6. Click Next.

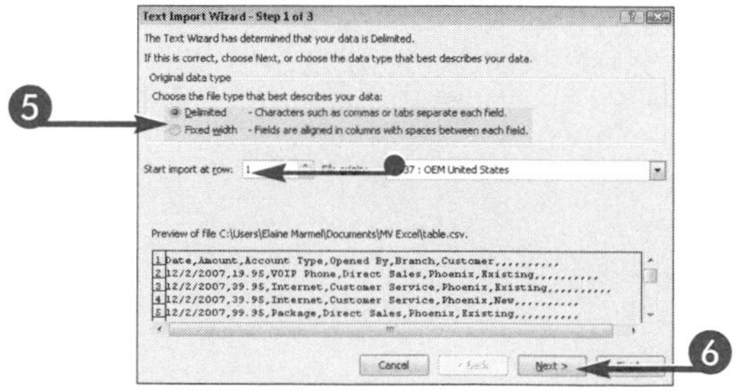

The Text Import Wizard - Step 2 of 3 dialog box appears.

7. Click all delimiters that apply (☐ changes to ☑).
   - Your data will import properly when each field appears in its own column.

8. Click Next.

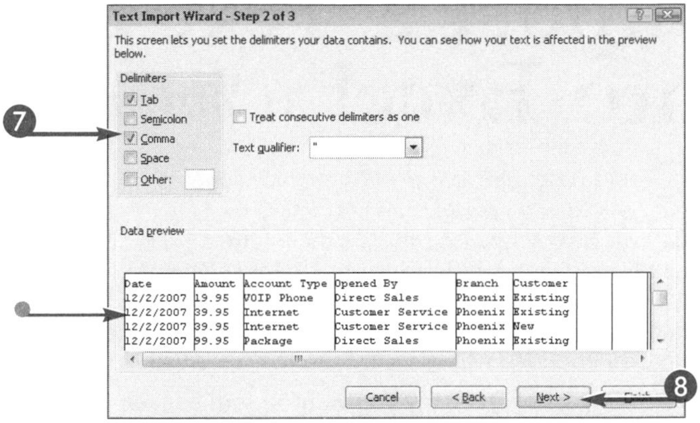

The Text Import Wizard - Step 3 of 3 dialog box appears.

9. Click a column.

10. Click here to describe the type of data in the column.
    - For dates, you can click ▾ to select the date format.

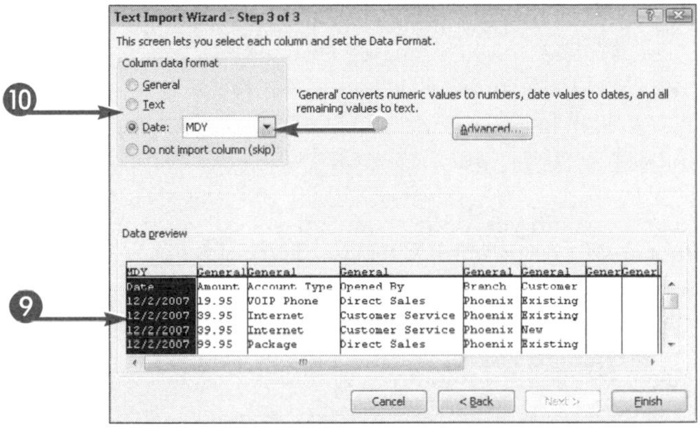

MASTER IT

How do I import a fixed width text file?

▼ Complete Steps 1 to 4. In Step 5, click the Fixed Width option (◯ changes to ◉). Click Next and, in the dialog box that appears, click in the Data Preview area to designate where each column should begin; Excel inserts vertical break lines at each location. Click Next and complete Steps 9 to 22.

If I import a fixed width text file and click in the wrong spot on the Data Preview area, what should I do?

▼ You can correct mistakes by either deleting a vertical break line or by moving a vertical break line. You can delete a vertical break line by double-clicking it. You can move any break line by clicking and dragging it to the new location.

What does the "Treat Consecutive Delimiters as One" option do?

▼ Suppose that your text file contains two successive delimiters in the same position in every row. This means that the data that should have appeared between those delimiters is missing from the entire file. In this case, there is no reason to import what would effectively be an empty column, and so you would click the "Treat Consecutive Delimiters as One" option (☐ changes to ☑).

continued

Import a Text File into Excel *(Continued)*

The Text Import Wizard uses the facts you provide about a text file's structure to determine how to separate the information in the text file into columns in Excel. You identify whether the fields in the rows of the text file are delimited or separated by a common character, or whether the information appears in columns that have a fixed width.

You also can identify the way you want to format each column of information that you import. For example, you can format a column that contains dates using a date format. If you apply a general format to a column, Excel treats numeric values as numbers, recognizes date values as dates, and recognizes any other kind of information as text.

When you import the information, you can choose where the information should appear. You can place the information in a new worksheet or in the current worksheet, and you designate the cell you want to use as the upper-left corner of the range for the imported information. Excel imports the information, using as many cells as necessary. Importing information overwrites any existing information, and so you should select an area with enough empty cells to accommodate the information.

Import a Text File into Excel *(continued)*

11. Click a column you do not want to import.
12. Click the "Do not import column (skip)" option (☐ changes to ☑).

    Excel identifies the column as one to skip.
13. Click a column containing numbers.
14. Click the General option (☐ changes to ☑).
15. Click Advanced.

    The Advanced Text Import Settings dialog box appears.
16. Click the Decimal separator ▾ to select a decimal separator.
17. Click the Thousands separator ▾ to select a thousands separator.
    - You can control whether negative numbers display a trailing minus sign by selecting this option.
18. Click OK.
19. Repeat Steps 10 to 18 as needed.
20. Click Finish.

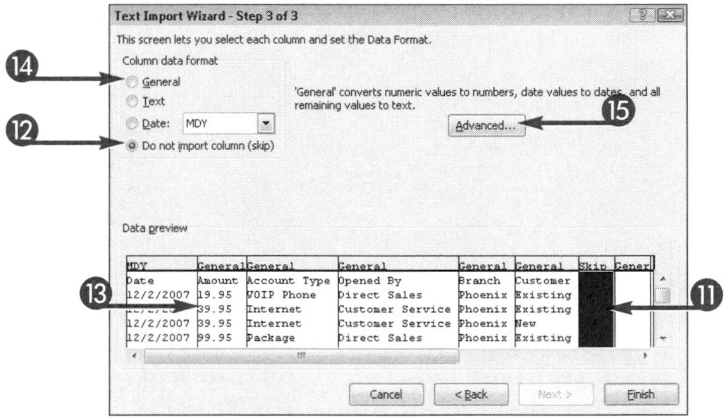

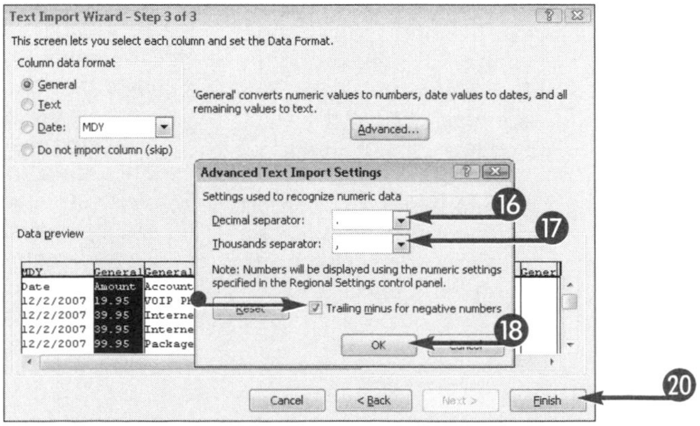

The Import Data dialog box appears.

21. Identify where Excel should place imported data.

22. Click OK.

- Excel imports the data.

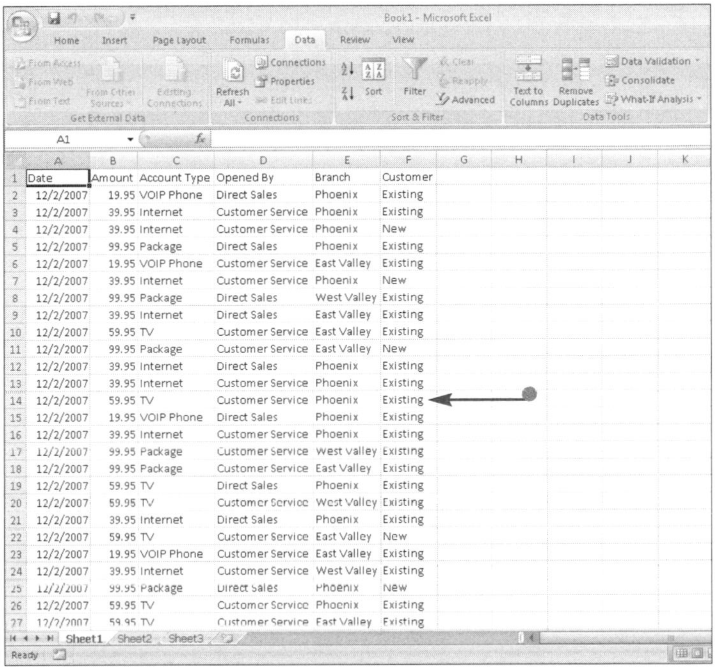

MASTER IT

What does the File Origin field do?

▼ Excel takes a guess at the type of information that appears in the text file. If Excel seems to be far off the mark when guessing, try changing the selection in the File Origin field to help Excel identify the type of data in the file. By selecting the correct origin for the file, Excel may have better luck recognizing the information and parsing it properly.

What does the Text Qualifier drop-down list box do?

▼ By default, the Text Import Wizard treats any set of characters in the text file that are enclosed in quotation marks as text entries. If your text file encloses text entries in apostrophes instead of quotation marks, you can use the Text Qualifier drop-down list box to select the correct character to enclose text entries in your text file.

Why are fields on the Data tab unavailable after I import information from a text file?

▼ Excel establishes an external data query when you import information from a text file, and, whenever you click in the range created from the text file, many commands on the Data tab become unavailable. You can click in the imported range and click the Refresh All button to update the information in your workbook if the information in the text file changes.

Copy Excel Data into Word

You can copy Excel information into a Microsoft Word document in two different ways: First, you can copy Excel data into a Word document as static information that you do not want to update, even if the Excel data changes. Second, if you expect the Excel information to change and you want to keep the Word document up-to-date, you can copy the Excel data and simultaneously link the information in the Word document to the Excel data. When you link the information and then make a change in the Excel workbook, the Word document updates automatically, and you do not need to recopy the information.

When you do not care if the information in your Word document updates due to changes made in the Excel workbook from which you copy it, you can copy and paste the information using the same technique you use to copy information from one range in a workbook to another. When you copy the information in Excel, Excel places the information on the Windows Clipboard, making it available to any program. Follow the steps in the subsection, "Static Information," to see how this approach works.

Copy Excel Data into Word

Static Information

1. In Excel, open the workbook containing the information you want to copy to Word.
2. Open Word and the document that should contain the information.
3. In Excel, select the information you want to copy to Word.
4. Click the Home tab.
5. Click .

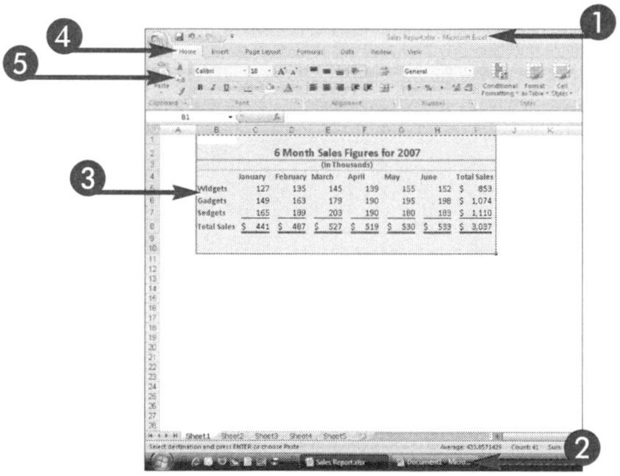

6. Click here to switch to Word.
7. Position the insertion point where you want the information to appear.
8. Click the Home tab.
9. Click Paste.

- The information from Excel appears in the Word document as a Word table.

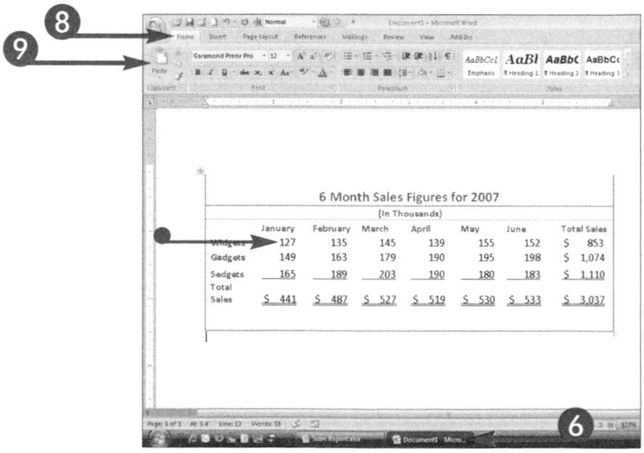

10. Click here to switch to Excel.
11. Make a change to the information.

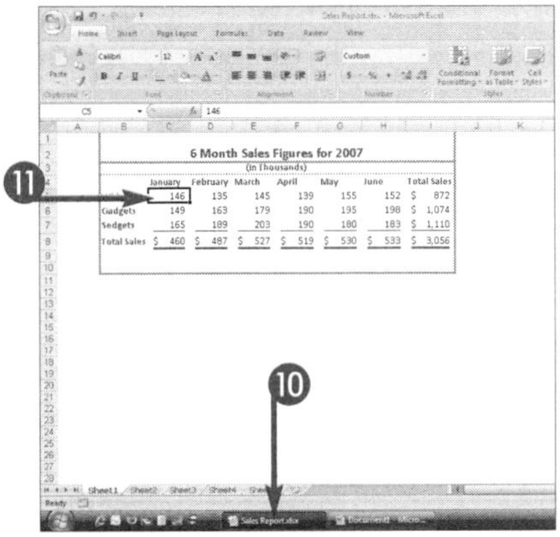

12. Click here to switch to Word.
    - The information does not change.

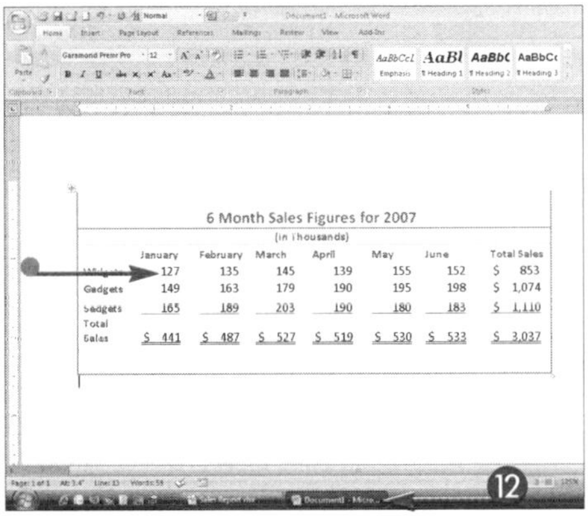

MASTER IT

What is the difference between the Formatted Text (RTF) option and the Unformatted Text option in the Paste Special dialog box?

▼ The difference lies in the result you get when you paste. When you select the Formatted Text (RTF) option while pasting an Excel range into a Word document, Word formats the pasted information as a table and retains some of the formatting that you might have applied in Excel. When you select the Unformatted Text option while pasting an Excel range into a Word document, Word pastes raw information with no formatting, and separates cells using a Tab character.

In Word's Paste Special dialog box, when would I choose the "Microsoft Office Excel Worksheet Object" option?

▼ You use this option when you want to insert an Excel object into a Word document and have the ability to edit the Excel object using the Excel Ribbon without leaving Word. See the section, "Embed an Excel Workbook into Word," for more details.

What happens if I choose the Picture (Enhanced Metafile) option in Word's Paste Special dialog box?

▼ Regardless of whether you choose the Picture (Enhanced Metafile) option, the Bitmap option, or the Picture (Windows Metafile) option, Word pastes the range into the Word document as a picture.

continued

Copy Excel Data into Word *(Continued)*

Suppose that you copy information from an Excel workbook into a Word document and you anticipate that the information in the Excel workbook will be changing in the future. Further suppose that you want the information in the Word document to change whenever the information in the Excel workbook changes. In this case, you can link the information contained in the Excel workbook to the copy you place in the Word document.

To create this link, you copy the information in the Excel workbook that you want to place in the Word document, and Excel places the information on the Windows Clipboard. When you paste the information into Word, however, you use the Paste Special dialog box, where you indicate that you want to both paste and link the information. You select the format to use when Word pastes the information; by default, Word suggests HTML as the format, and that format usually works best.

When you subsequently make a change in the Excel workbook to the data you copied into Word, Word updates the information in the Word document immediately if the Word document is open at the time of the update.

Copy Excel Data into Word *(continued)*

Changing Information

1. Complete Steps 1 to 8 in the subsection, "Static Information."
2. Click the Paste ▾.
3. Click Paste Special.

The Paste Special dialog box appears.

4. Click Paste Link (◎ changes to ◉).
5. Click HTML Format.
6. Click OK.

- The information from Excel appears in the Word document as a Word table.

7. Click here to switch to Excel.

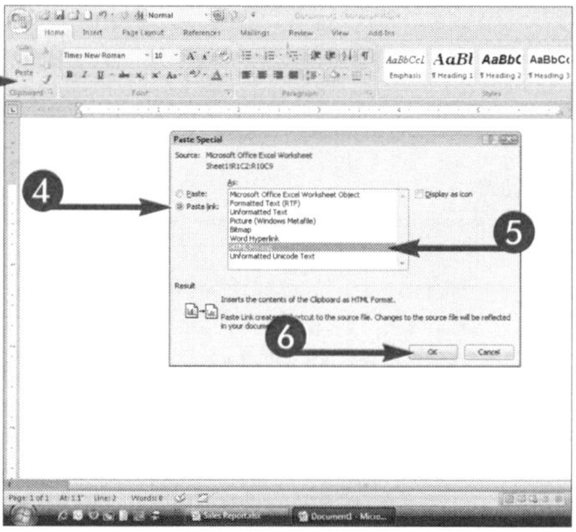

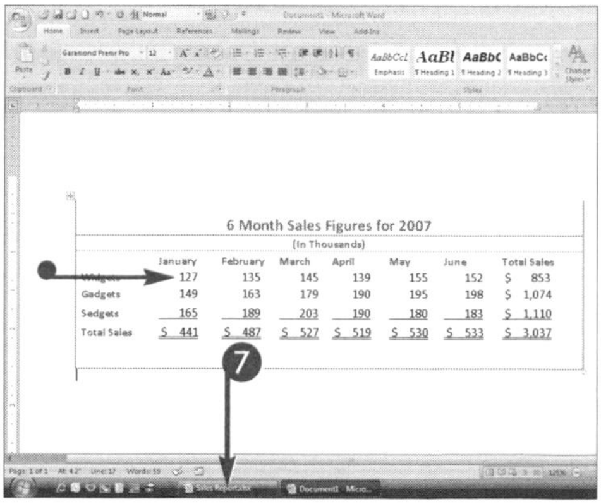

8. Make a change to the information.
9. Click here to switch to Word.

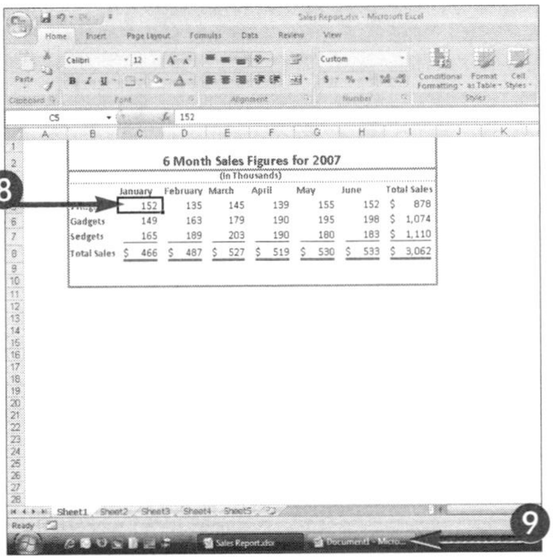

- The information changes.

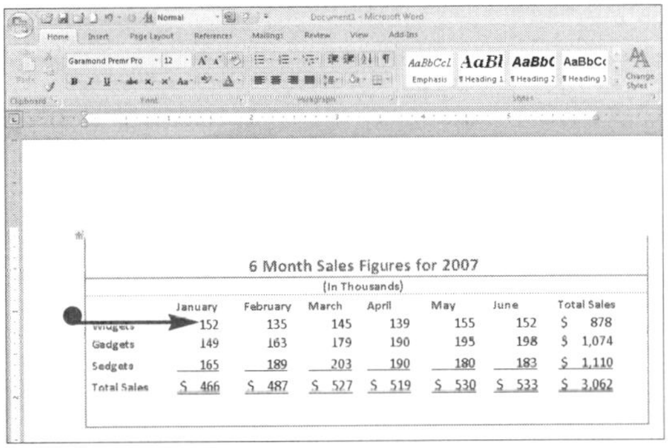

MASTER IT

What happens if I update the information in the Excel workbook, but I do not have the document open in Word?

▼ The link still functions, but you will not see the document update until you open the document in Word. Each time you open the document in Word, Word uses the link to determine what information to display in the Word document.

Can I update linked information in the Word document to update the Excel workbook?

▼ No. When you copy information in Excel and paste it into Word and create a link, the link works in one direction only. Changing the information in the Word document has no effect on the information stored in the Excel workbook, but changing the information in the Excel workbook updates the Word document.

Can I create a table in Word and use the techniques described in this section to copy it to Excel?

▼ Yes, you can. If you copy the table as static information, changes that you make to the information in either program do not affect the information in the other program. If you link the information, you can update the information in Word and it will also update in Excel.

Copy an Excel Chart into Word

You are not limited to copying Excel ranges into a Word document; you can also copy an Excel chart into a Word document. Copying a chart can be particularly useful. Suppose that you are preparing a report on product sales for the first half of 2007. If you show the data in a chart format, relationships between the data are much easier for the reader to comprehend. And, if you already have the data in Excel, creating a chart from this data is a quick and easy process; see Chapters 19, 20, and 21 for details on creating and formatting charts in Excel. Once you have created the chart in Excel, copying the chart to Word is also very easy.

By default, when you copy a chart from Excel and paste it into Word, Word creates a link to the chart. So, if you make changes in the Excel workbook that contains the chart to the data that you used to create the chart, the changes also appear in the Word document into which you pasted the chart. You can break the link between the Excel workbook and the Word document if you want the chart to remain unaffected by any changes you make to the Excel workbook.

Copy an Excel Chart into Word

1. Open the workbook in Excel containing the chart you want to copy to Word.
2. Open Word and the document that should contain the chart.
3. In Excel, select the chart.
4. Click the Home tab.
5. Click .

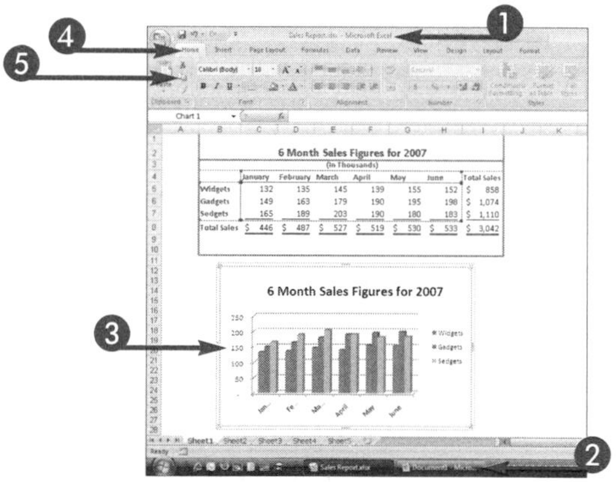

6. Click here to switch to Word.
7. Position the insertion point where you want the chart to appear.
8. Click the Home tab.
9. Click Paste.

- The Excel chart appears in the Word document as a Word chart.

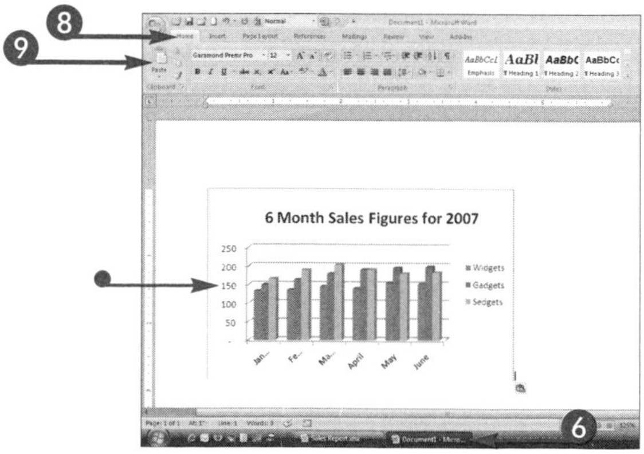

⑩ Click here to switch to Excel.

⑪ Make a change to the information you used to create the chart.

- Excel updates the chart.

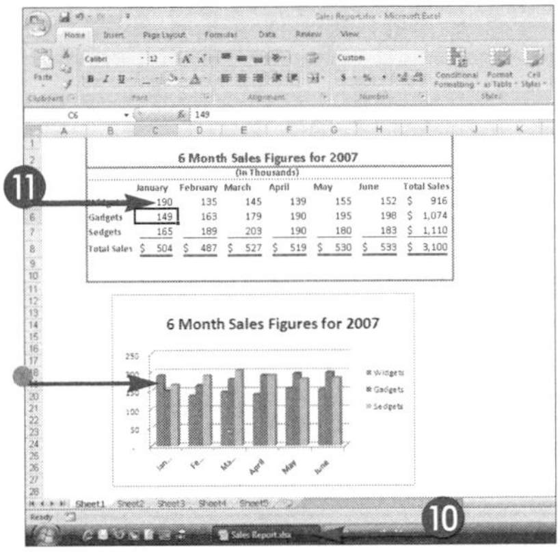

⑫ Click here to switch to Word.

- The change you made to the chart in Excel also appears in Word.

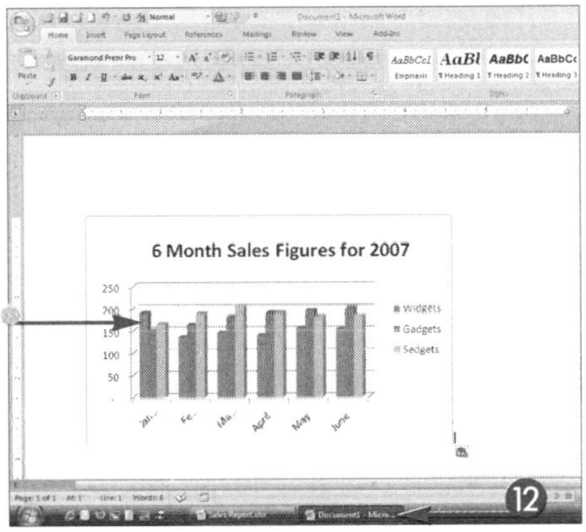

MASTER IT

How do I break the link between the Excel workbook containing the chart and the chart I paste into a Word document?

▼ When you paste the chart into Word, [icon] appears beside the chart. To break the link between the chart in the Excel workbook and the chart in the Word document, click [icon] and click Paste as Picture. Word breaks the link and converts the chart to a picture; when you select the picture, the Word Picture Tools become available.

If I know in advance that I do not want to link the chart in the Excel workbook to the chart in the Word document, what should I do differently?

▼ Complete Steps 1 to 8. In Step 9, click [icon] beneath the Paste button and click Paste Special. In the Paste Special dialog box, select any of the available picture formats: Picture (Windows Metafile), Bitmap, Picture (Enhanced Metafile), Picture (GIF), Picture (PNG), or Picture (JPEG).

In the Paste Special dialog box in Word, I see two other choices besides the picture formats. What do these options do?

▼ When you use the "Microsoft Office Graphic Object" option, Word inserts the Excel chart as a Word chart that is linked to the Excel workbook containing the chart. When you use the "Microsoft Office Excel Chart Object" option, Word pastes the chart as an object that is not linked to the Excel chart.

Embed an Excel Workbook into Word

You can share information between Excel and Word in two different ways: You can either copy ranges of information or charts from Excel to Word, or you can copy an entire Excel workbook into Word — a process called *embedding*.

When you copy a range of information from Excel to Word, you can link the information so that, if you make a change in the Excel file, the change also appears in the Word document. You can also copy a range of information from Excel to Word without linking the information; in this case, a change to the Excel file has no effect on the Word document. You can read about copying a range of information from Excel to Word in the section, "Copy Excel Data into Word."

When you copy a chart from Excel to Word, you automatically create a link between the Excel workbook and the Word document; you can read about copying a chart from Excel to Word in the section, "Copy an Excel Chart into Word." This section describes how to embed an entire Excel workbook into a Word document.

Embed an Excel Workbook into Word

1. Open the workbook in Excel containing the information you want to copy to Word.
2. Open Word and the document that should contain the information.
3. In Excel, select the information you want to copy to Word.
4. Click the Home tab.
5. Click .

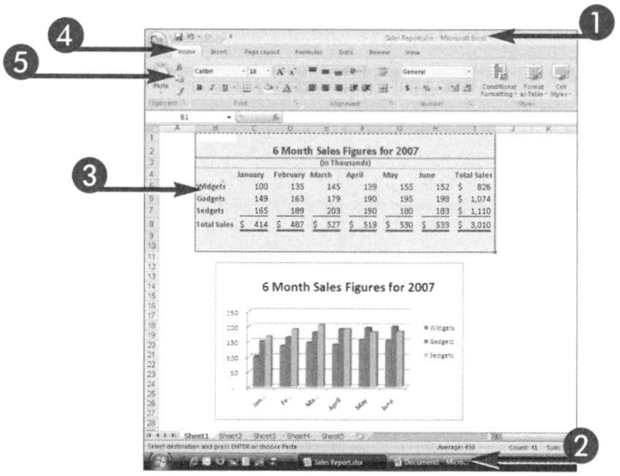

6. Click here to switch to Word.
7. Position the insertion point where you want the information to appear.
8. Click the Home tab.
9. Click the Paste .
10. Click Paste Special.

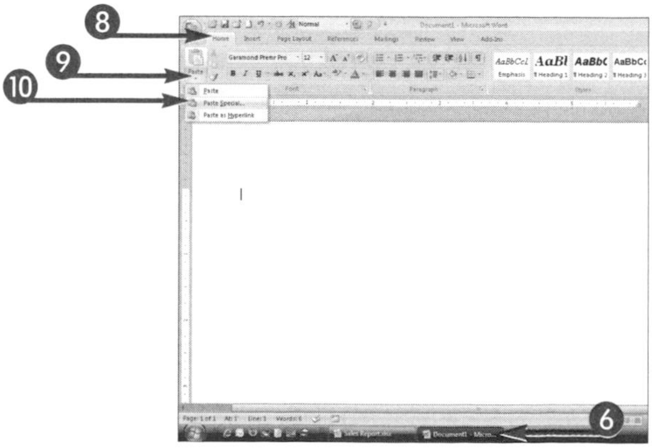

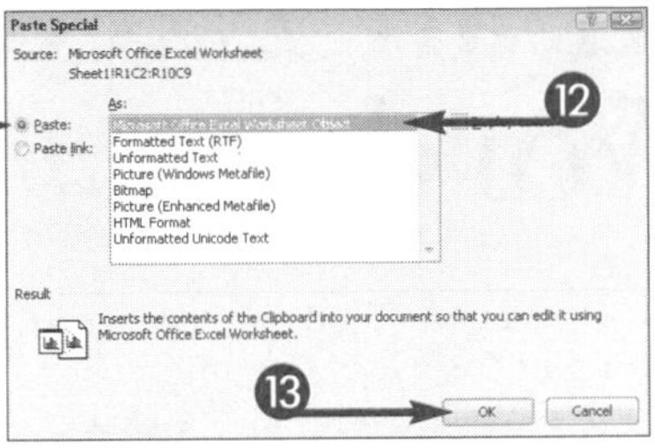

Word displays the Paste Special dialog box.

11. Click Paste (◎ changes to ◉).
12. Click Microsoft Office Excel Worksheet Object.
13. Click OK.

- The information from Excel appears in the Word document as an object.

14. Double-click the object.

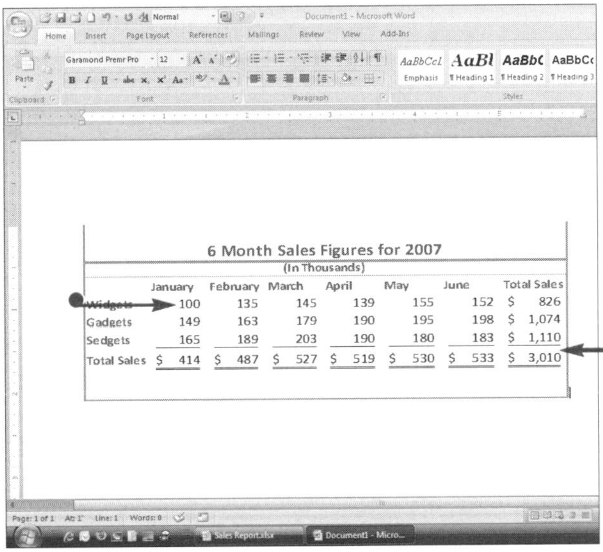

Document1 - Microsoft Word
Home
Insert
Page Layout
References
Mailings
Review
View
Add-Ins
6 Month Sales Figures for 2007
(In Thousands)
January February March April May June Total Sales
Widgets 100 135 145 139 155 152 $ 826
Gadgets 149 163 179 190 195 198 $ 1,074
Sedgets 165 189 203 190 180 183 $ 1,110
Total Sales $ 414 $ 487 $ 527 $ 519 $ 530 $ 533 $ 3,010
14

MASTER IT

What happens if I click the "Microsoft Excel Worksheet Object" option that is available when I click the "Paste Link" option in Word's Paste Special dialog box?

▼ You insert an object into the Word document, but the object is not embedded in the Word document. Instead, you create a link between the Word document and the Excel workbook. When you double-click the object, Excel displays the workbook. That is, you do not see the Excel Ribbon replace the Word Ribbon, as shown in this section. Instead, you switch to Excel. If Excel is not open when you double-click the object, Excel opens and opens the workbook to which you linked. You do your editing in Excel, and the object updates in Word.

What are the advantages and disadvantages of embedding a workbook instead of linking it?

▼ When you embed a workbook in a Word document, the Word document is complete. You can move the Word document to any computer anywhere, open it, and all of the information you want in the document appears. If you link and move the Word document but not the Excel workbook, the Word document will be incomplete when you open it. So, when you move files, you must remember to move both the Word document and the Excel workbook. The disadvantage to embedding concerns file size: Because the embedded workbook is actually part of the Word document, embedding creates a larger file size than linking.

continued

Embed an Excel Workbook into Word *(Continued)*

When you embed an object, you do not create a connection between the Excel workbook that contains the original information and the Word document where you copy it. If you make changes in the Excel workbook after you embed it into a Word document, the Word document does not update to reflect the changes. This is because the embedded information in the Word document is not part of the Excel workbook from which you copied it.

When you embed an Excel workbook in a Word document, you select worksheet data and copy it to the Windows Clipboard. However, when you paste it, you paste more than just the worksheet data that you selected; you paste the entire workbook. You can edit the embedded object in Word without switching to Excel, and, when you edit the object, you use the Excel Ribbon, not the Word Ribbon. In addition, all of the worksheet tabs contained in the Excel workbook appear when you edit the object in Word.

If you make changes to the embedded object in Word, those changes do not appear in Excel. This is because there is no link between the embedded object in the Word document and the Excel workbook from which you copied the information.

Embed an Excel Workbook into Word *(continued)*

- The Excel column letters and row numbers appear.
- Sheet tabs appear.
- The Excel Ribbon replaces the Word Ribbon.

⑮ Drag here to enlarge the window.

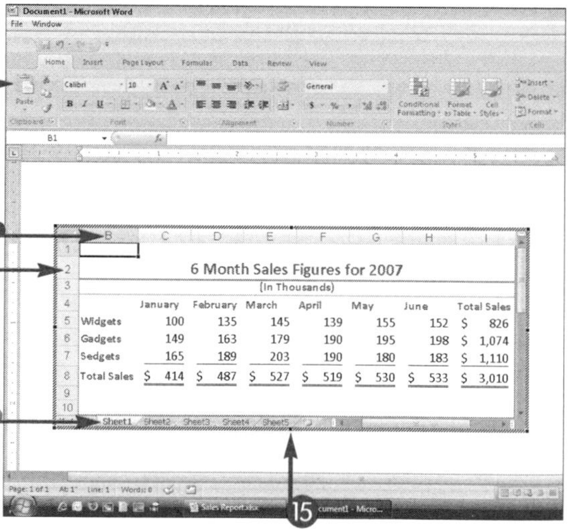

- More of the current worksheet becomes visible, and you can see that you brought in more information than you copied.

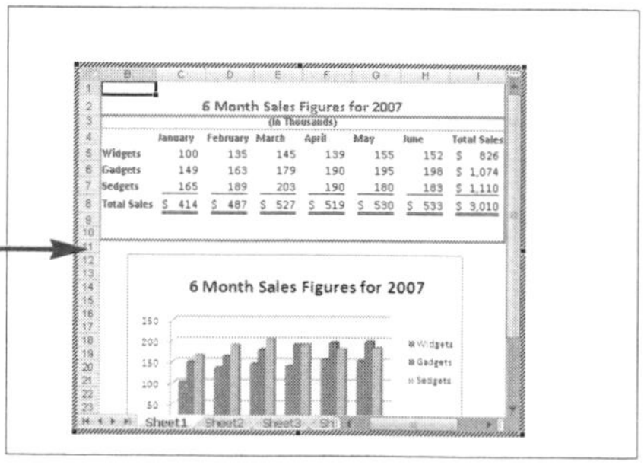

16 Make a change to the worksheet information.

- If it is affected by the change, chart information also updates.

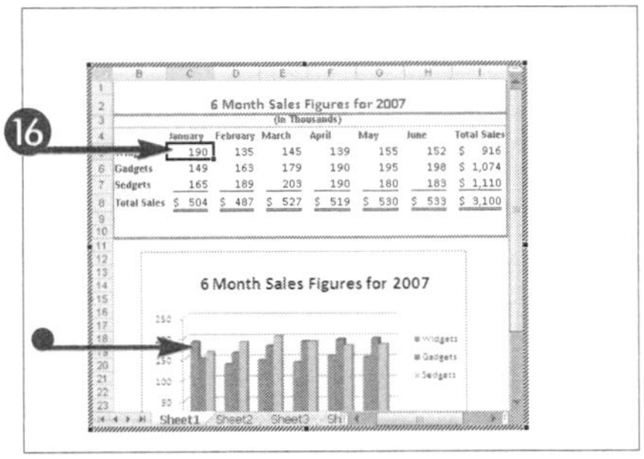

17 Click here to switch to Excel.

- The cell information does not change.
- The chart information does not change.

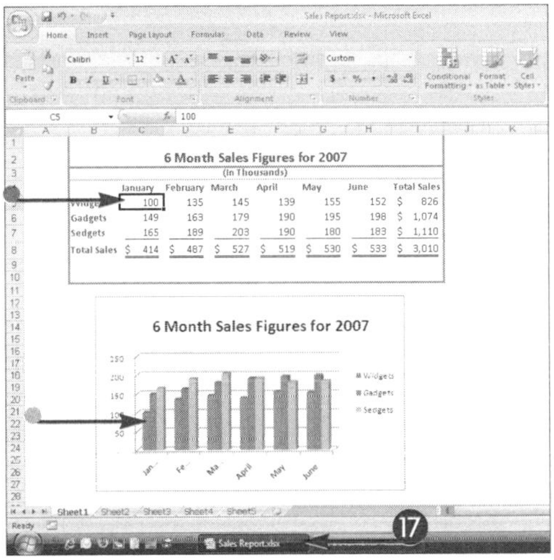

Is there a way to embed an Excel workbook into Word but start the process in Word?

▼ Yes. Open the Word document into which you want to embed an Excel workbook and position the insertion point where the workbook object should appear. Click the Word Insert tab and then click the Object button in the Text group. In the Object dialog box that appears, click the Create from File tab. Click Browse and navigate to the Excel workbook that you want to embed. Click Insert and then click OK. The Excel workbook is embedded in the Word document; if you double-click it, you can expect the same behavior that you see in this section.

Can I embed using "drag and drop"?

▼ Yes, if you set up the windows so that you can see the Excel information that you want to embed in a Word document at the same time that you view the Word document. In Windows Vista, right-click the Windows taskbar and click Show Windows Side by Side or Show Windows Stacked. In Windows XP, you can right-click the Windows taskbar and then click Tile Windows Vertically or Tile Windows Horizontally. With both windows visible on-screen, select the Excel information, and then press and hold Ctrl as you click and drag the border of the range from Excel to Word. Release the mouse button, and a copy of the Excel range appears in the Word document.

Create an Excel Worksheet in Word

While working in Word, you can create an Excel worksheet. Although Word contains a Table feature, creating an Excel worksheet gives you the benefit of using the formulas and functions that you are familiar with, while you work in Word to create your tabular information. For example, suppose that you are preparing a report and you need to set up a short, quick worksheet to sum product sales numbers and calculate the percentage of total sales for each product. You certainly could create the worksheet in Excel and then embed or link the information in your Word document, but why leave Word? Instead, you can create a new Excel worksheet while you work in Word. You do not even need to open Excel to create an Excel worksheet in a Word document.

While you work in the worksheet, the Excel Ribbon replaces the Word Ribbon, and so all of the familiar Excel commands are available to you. The Excel column letters and row numbers also appear in the worksheet to help you identify the position of the cell pointer. You can use any Excel command as you work in the worksheet.

Create an Excel Worksheet in Word

1. Open the Word document in which you want to create an Excel worksheet.
2. Position the insertion point where you want the Excel worksheet to appear.
3. Click the Insert tab.
4. Click Object.

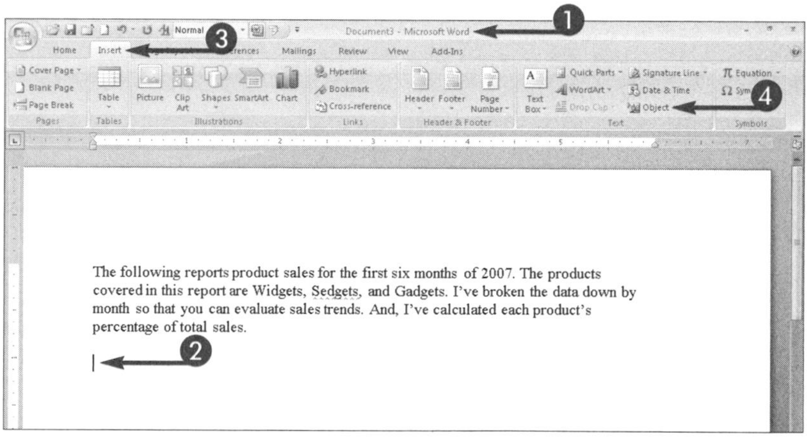

The Object dialog box appears.

5. Click the Create New tab.
6. Click Microsoft Office Excel Worksheet.
7. Click OK.

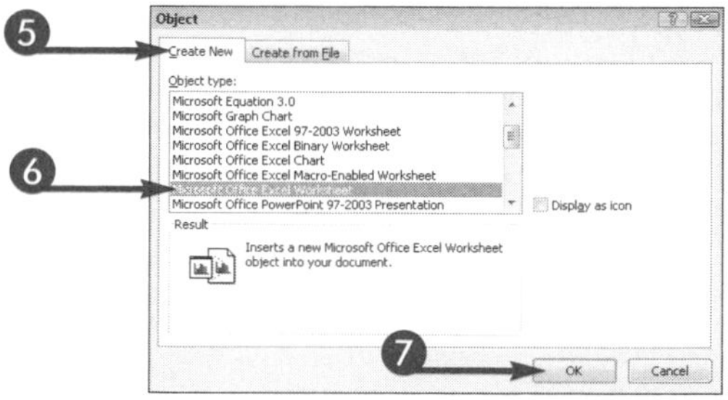

An Excel worksheet appears.

- Column letters and row numbers appear.
- The Excel Ribbon is available.

Note: *The worksheet appears off-center, but that appearance is temporary.*

8 Type your information into the worksheet.

9 Click anywhere outside the worksheet in the Word document.

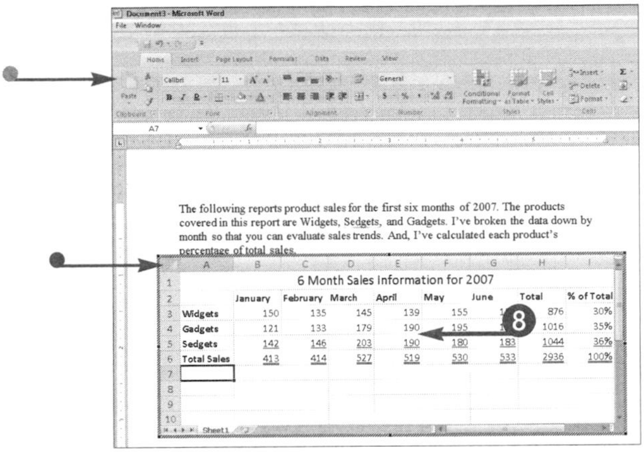

- The worksheet takes on the appearance of an object.
- The Word Ribbon reappears.

The Excel features, including column letters, row numbers, the Excel Ribbon, and the sheet tab, disappear.

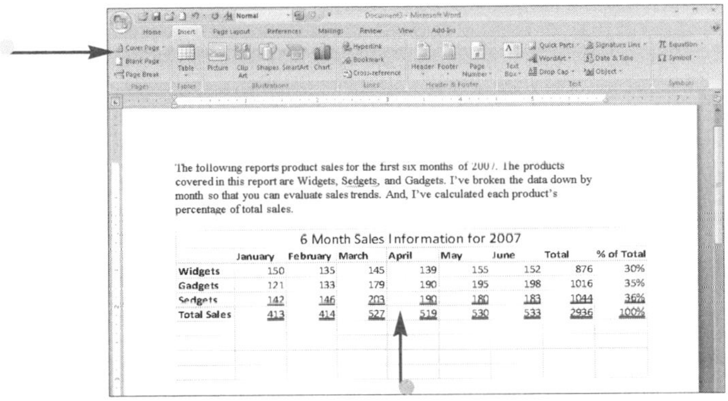

MASTER IT

How can I see more of the Excel worksheet as I work?

▼ Drag any small black square around the edge of the worksheet outward to enlarge the visible area of the worksheet. The number of rows and columns that appear after you click outside the worksheet is determined by the number of rows and columns that are visible while you work in the worksheet. So, you can remove empty rows and columns using the same technique, but dragging inward.

What should I do if I need to use a command that is not available on the Ribbon in Excel?

▼ As you work on the worksheet in Word, you use the Excel Ribbon and the Excel Quick Access Toolbar. You can add a command to the Quick Access Toolbar in Excel, and this command also appears as you work on the worksheet in Excel.

Do I need to save the Excel worksheet, and, if so, how do I save it?

▼ When you use the steps in this section, you embed an object in Word that happens to be an Excel worksheet. When you save the Word document, you also save the Excel worksheet object. However, you do not save the Excel worksheet as a separate Excel file.

Use Excel Data to Create Mailing Labels in Word

You can use an Excel workbook that contains name and address information to create mailing labels in a Microsoft Word document.

To create mailing labels in Word using an Excel file as the source of the address information, you perform a mail merge operation using the Mail Merge feature in Word. Before you start working in Word, make sure that your Excel workbook contains the information needed by the mail merge operation in a format the Mail Merge feature can recognize. The name and address information for each addressee should appear on a single row, and each piece of information over which you want independent control — a field — should appear in a separate column in the workbook.

Performing a mail merge is actually a multi-part process. In addition to setting up your Excel workbook, you select the mailing label that corresponds to the one you plan to use so that Word can format the mail merge document properly. Word displays a dialog box where you can select the vendor whose mailing labels you purchased and then select the product number of the mailing label. If you do not find your mailing label listed, you can create a custom label.

Use Excel Data to Create Mailing Labels in Word

Set Up the Mailing List Workbook

1. Set up an Excel worksheet that contains name and address information, placing each recipient's information on a single row.

Note: *Once you confirm the structure of the worksheet, you can close the workbook and Excel if you want.*

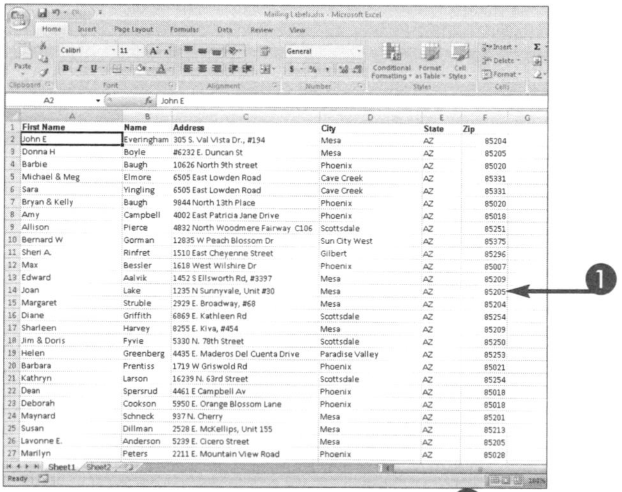

Select a Mailing Label

1. Open Word and start a new blank document.
2. Click the Mailings tab.
3. Click Start Mail Merge.
4. Click Labels.

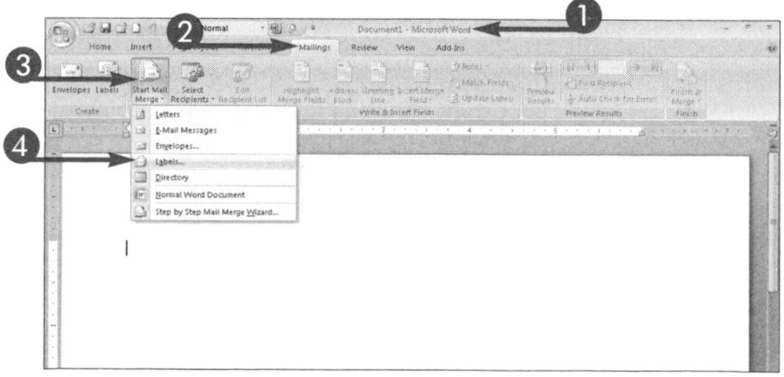

The Label Options dialog box appears.

5 Click an option to select the type of printer you want (◯ changes to ◉).

6 Click the Label vendors ▾ to select a label vendor.

7 Click the label's product number.

- Information about label dimensions appears here.

8 Click OK.

Word sets up the document for the labels you selected.

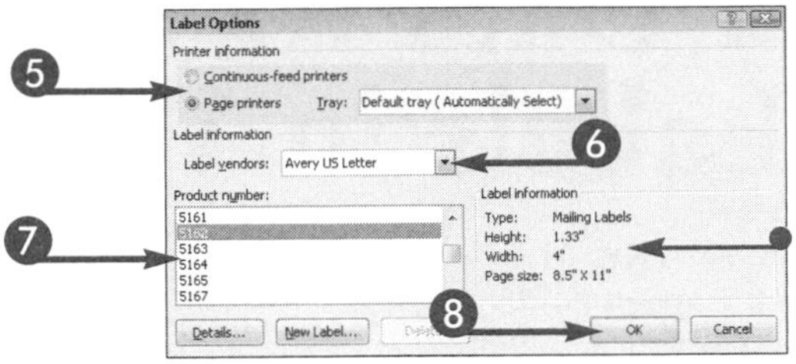

Attach the Mailing List Workbook

1 Click Select Recipients.

2 Click Use Existing List.

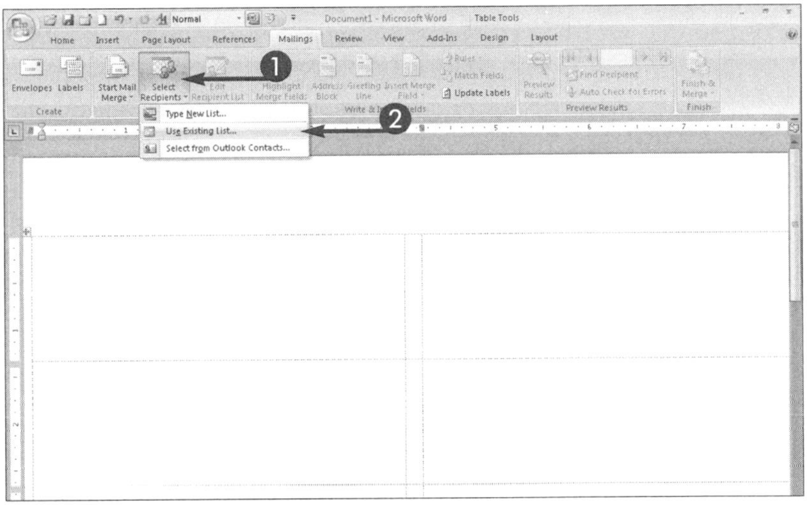

What should I do if I do not see my label vendor or the product number I need?

▼ You can create a custom label. Use the label information in the lower-right corner of the Label Options dialog box to find a label that is close in size to your labels. Then click the New Label button to display a dialog box that you can use to establish settings, such as the margins, height and width, and number across or down, to describe your labels. In the Label Name field, type a name for your custom label. When you click OK, Word displays the label vendor as Other/Custom, and the name you assigned appears in the Product Number list box.

What happens if I click the Details button in the Label Options dialog box?

▼ Word displays the Mailing Labels Information dialog box, specific to the label you selected in Step 7. You see the paper size and the number of labels that appear across and down the page. You also see the top and side margins, and the vertical and horizontal label dimensions. Although you can change this information, you typically do not.

My document does not show lines that demarcate each label. What did I do wrong?

▼ Nothing. To display lines, click the Layout tab under Table Tools and then click View Gridlines.

continued

Use Excel Data to Create Mailing Labels in Word *(Continued)*

After you select or create a mailing label format, Word formats the document to match the labels you are using. You then attach your workbook to the mail merge document that Word creates. Attaching your workbook is not difficult; Word prompts you to navigate to the folder where you stored the workbook and select it. If the workbook contains more than one sheet, Word prompts you to select the sheet containing the mailing label information.

After you connect the Word document to your Excel workbook, some editing restrictions come into play concerning your Excel workbook. If your Excel workbook is closed when you connect it to the Word document, you cannot open the Excel workbook as long as the mail merge document is open in Word. You can, however, open the Excel workbook before you start the mail merge in Word and still successfully connect the two files. If your Excel workbook is open when you connect it to the Word document, you can make changes to the Excel workbook and, because you have created a connection between the two files, you can update the Word document to reflect the changes.

Use Excel Data to Create Mailing Labels in Word *(continued)*

The Select Data Source dialog box appears.

3. Navigate to the folder containing the mailing list workbook, and click the workbook to select it.
4. Click Open.

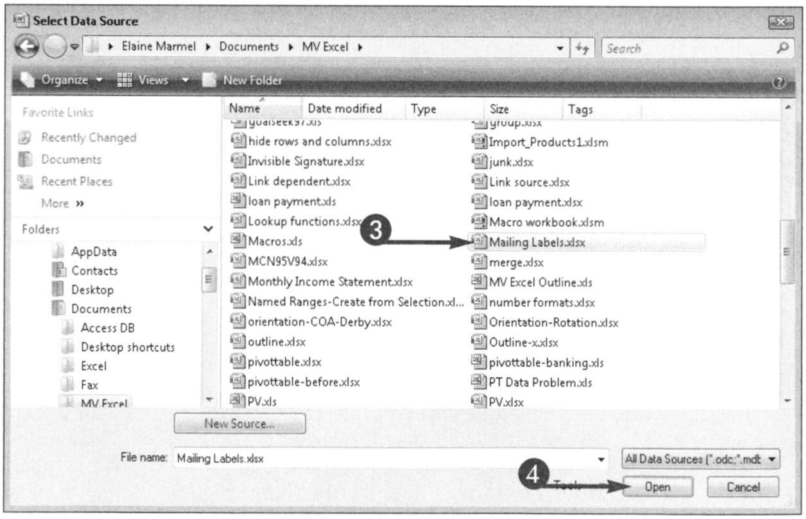

The Confirm Data Source dialog box appears.

5. Click OLE DB Data Base files.
6. Click OK.

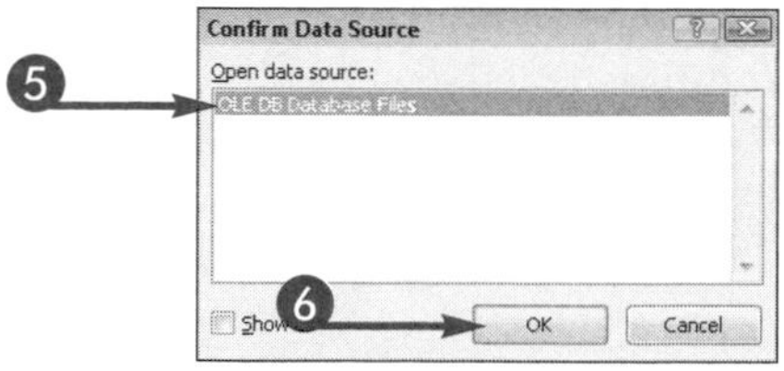

The Select Table dialog box appears, displaying the sheet names of each worksheet in the workbook.

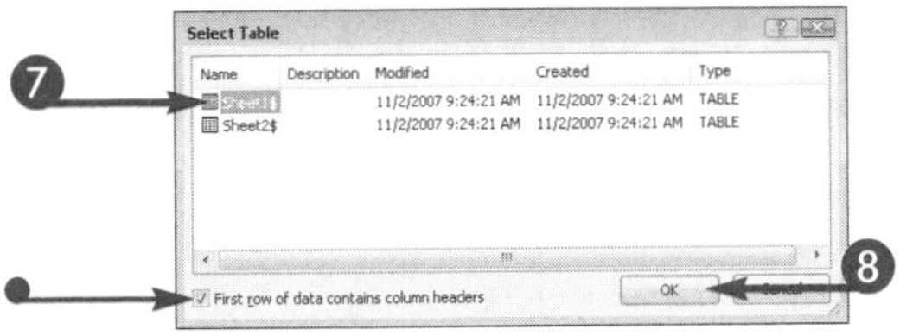

7 Click the worksheet containing the mailing list.

- If the first row of the worksheet does *not* contain headings, click the "First row of data contains column headers" option (☑ changes to ☐).

8 Click OK.

Word adds <<Next Record>> merge fields to all labels except for the first label.

Add the Address to the Label

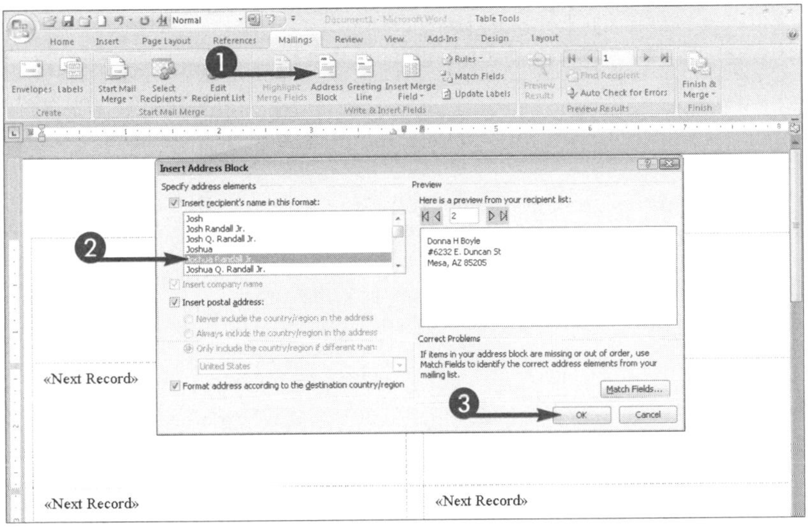

1 Click Address Block.

The Insert Address Block dialog box appears.

2 Click a format to use for the recipient's name.

3 Click OK.

MASTER IT

Can I create mailing labels for only some of the recipients stored in the Excel workbook?

▼ Yes. After completing the steps in "Attach the Mailing List Workbook," click the Edit Recipient List button on the Mailings tab of the Word Ribbon. The Mail Merge Recipients dialog box appears. A check box appears beside each person's name. Deselect any addresses for whom you do not want to create a mailing label and click OK.

Should I save a merge document that I create in Word?

▼ If you expect to print the labels frequently, saving the label document can save you time. If you expect to change the Excel workbook, save the document you use to set up the mail merge instead of saving the result of the merge. Word can update this document with changes from the Excel workbook.

What does the Auto Check for Errors button on the Mailings tab of the Word Ribbon do?

▼ When you click this button, Word gives you the opportunity to determine whether you have correctly set up the merge. The Checking and Reporting Errors dialog box appears; click an option (○ changes to ◉) and click OK. Depending on the option you choose, Word reports errors as they occur or in a new document.

continued

Use Excel Data to Create Mailing Labels in Word *(Continued)*

In the Word document, you add a merge field to the mailing label to represent the address block. A *merge field* is a placeholder for the information that changes as Word performs the mail merge; in the case of the mailing label, the changing information is the address block. You can then preview the way your mailing labels will look with your address information on them.

After you confirm that the information is laid out correctly, you complete the merge by selecting a destination for the merged information. You can merge to an individual document, as shown in this example; Word creates one document that contains as many pages as needed to merge all of the information. So, for example, if you have 100 names and addresses for which you want to create mailing labels and the labels you use are formatted 14 to a sheet, the merged document will contain eight pages.

If you prefer, you can merge directly to the printer and avoid creating a Word document. You can also merge to e-mail messages; you typically use this option when you are merging information for a letter that you want to send electronically rather than when you are creating mailing labels.

Use Excel Data to Create Mailing Labels in Word *(continued)*

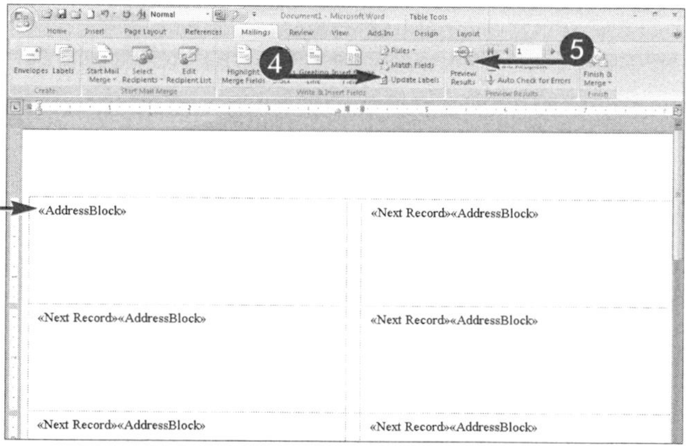

- Word adds the Address Block merge field to the first label.

4. Click Update Labels.

   Word adds the Address Block merge field to all of the labels.

5. Click Preview Results.

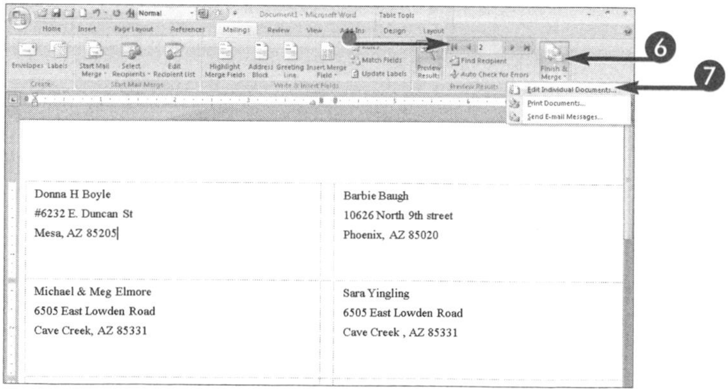

Word displays a preview of your labels, replacing the merge field with information from the mailing list workbook.

- You can click these buttons to preview the next label and previous labels.

6. Click Finish & Merge.
7. Click Edit Individual Documents.

The Merge to New Document dialog box appears.

8 Click an option to identify those for whom you want to create mailing labels (◎ changes to ◉).

9 Click OK.

- Word creates the mailing labels in a new Word document named Labels1.

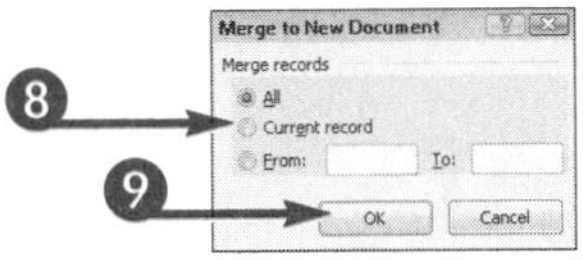

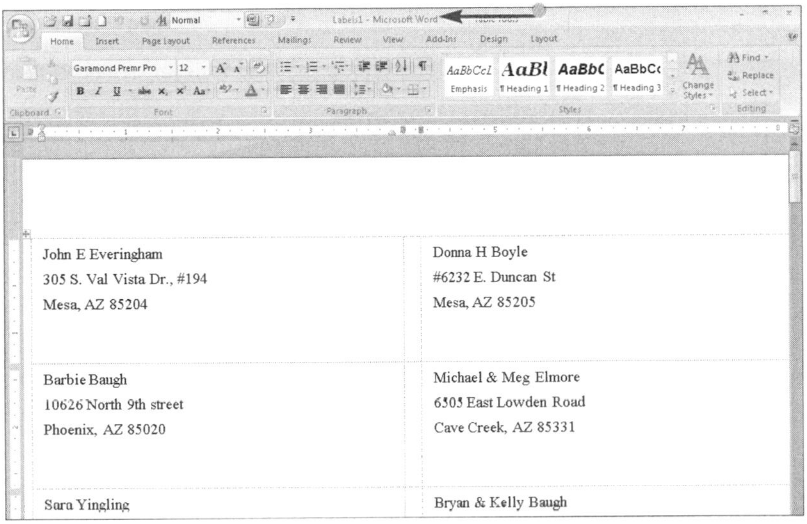

MASTER IT

What do the various choices in the Merge to New Document dialog box do?

▼ Click the All option (◎ changes to ◉) to create a mailing label for each entry listed in the Excel workbook. Click the Current Record option (◎ changes to ◉) to create mailing labels for the page of labels you are previewing. Click the From option (◎ changes to ◉) and supply numbers to specify pages of labels to create.

How do I print the labels?

▼ Load the labels into your printer. Click ▾ beside the Quick Access Toolbar and click Quick Print to add the Quick Print button to the Quick Access Toolbar. When you click this button, the labels print immediately; you do not have the opportunity to select a printer. To select a printer, click the Office button and click Print to display the Print dialog box, where you can select a printer and make other printing adjustments.

Can you explain the Send E-mail Messages option in the Finish & Merge drop-down list?

▼ You use this option if you selected E-mail Messages in Step 4 of the subsection, "Select a Mailing Label." Suppose that you want to send a standard message to each of your customers, but you want to personalize the messages. You can create a mail merge e-mail message that addresses each recipient by name and is sent separately to just that recipient.

Copy Excel Information into PowerPoint

You can copy a range of Excel information from an Excel workbook to a PowerPoint slide. You can embed Excel information onto a PowerPoint slide if you do not want to update the information even if the Excel data changes. Or, if you expect the Excel information to change and you want to keep the PowerPoint slide up-to-date, you can copy the Excel data and simultaneously link the information on the PowerPoint slide to the Excel workbook. When you link the information and then make a change in the Excel workbook, you can update the PowerPoint slide without recopying the information.

When you do not care if the information on your PowerPoint slide updates due to changes made in the Excel workbook from which you copy it, you can copy and paste the information using the same technique you use to copy information from one range in a workbook to another. When you copy the information in Excel, Excel places the information on the Windows Clipboard, making it available to any program. When you link information on a PowerPoint slide to an Excel workbook, you use a slightly different technique. This example shows you how to embed Excel information on a PowerPoint slide.

Copy Excel Information into PowerPoint

1. Open the workbook in Excel containing the information you want to copy to PowerPoint.
2. Open PowerPoint.
3. In Excel, select the information you want to copy to PowerPoint.

Note: *Format your Excel data to match the PowerPoint slide formatting for a more attractive slide.*

4. Click the Home tab.
5. Click .
6. Click here to switch to PowerPoint.
7. Display the slide that should contain the information.

Note: *Use a blank slide or a slide with just a title.*

8. Click the Home tab.
9. Click the Paste .
10. Click Paste Special.

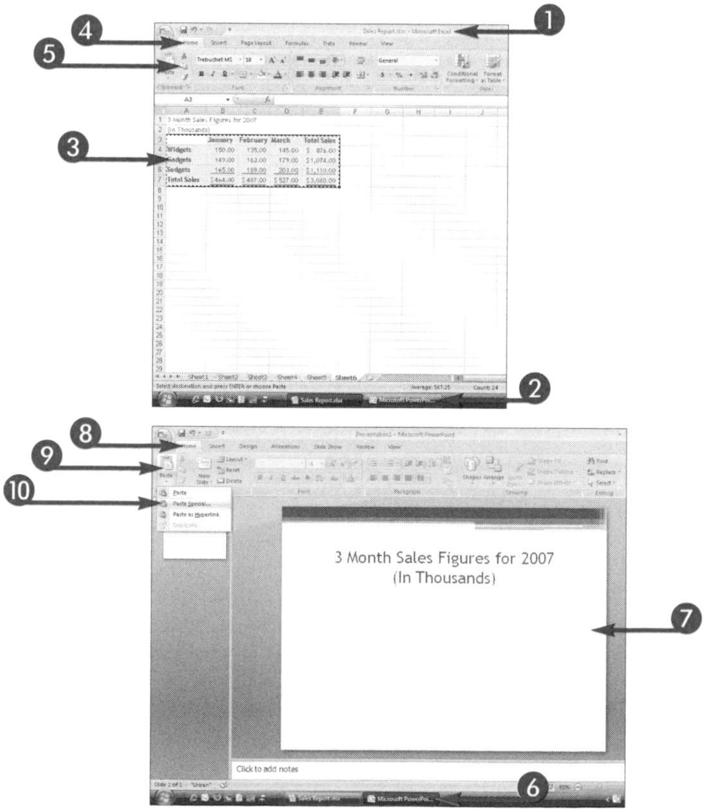

The Paste Special dialog box appears.

⓫ Click Paste (◎ changes to ◉).

⓬ Click Microsoft Office Excel Worksheet Object.

⓭ Click OK.

- The information from Excel appears on the PowerPoint slide as a graphic object.

You can move or resize the graphic object as necessary.

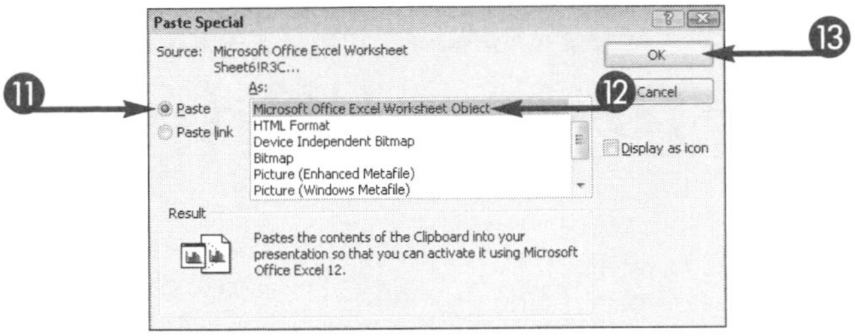

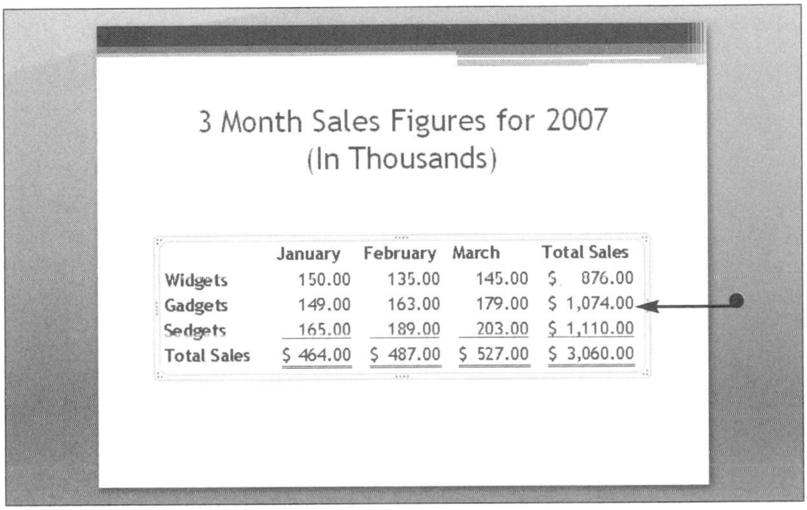
3 Month Sales Figures for 2007
(In Thousands)
January February March Total Sales
Widgets 150.00 135.00 145.00 $ 876.00
Gadgets 149.00 163.00 179.00 $ 1,074.00
Sedgets 165.00 189.00 203.00 $ 1,110.00
Total Sales $ 464.00 $ 487.00 $ 527.00 $ 3,060.00

MASTER IT

How do I move or resize the graphic object?

▼ To resize it, position the mouse pointer over any set of three dots on the graphic's border. When you see ⇔, ⇕, or ⤢, drag. If you drag a corner, PowerPoint resizes both the length and width of the graphic at the same time. To move the graphic object, position the mouse pointer over the border anywhere you do *not* see three dots. When the mouse pointer changes to ✥, drag.

Can I edit the information I copied into PowerPoint?

▼ Yes, you can. Double-click the graphic object; the PowerPoint Ribbon is replaced by the Excel Ribbon, and Excel column letters and row numbers appear. The entire Excel workbook is actually available to you, including sheet tabs. Make your changes and click anywhere on the PowerPoint slide outside the Excel graphic. Any changes that you make do not affect the original Excel workbook from which you copied the data.

If I want to be able to make changes that update the PowerPoint slide, what should I do differently?

▼ In Step 11, click Paste Link. After you save the PowerPoint presentation, you can make changes to the Excel workbook — not the graphic in PowerPoint — and the slide should update. If it does not, right-click the Excel object on the slide and click Update Link.

Place an Excel Chart in a PowerPoint Slide

You can copy a chart that you create in an Excel workbook to a PowerPoint slide. Copying a chart can be particularly useful in a PowerPoint presentation in which it presents numeric information graphically.

Suppose that you are preparing a report on product sales for the first quarter of 2007. If you show the data in a chart format, relationships between the data are much easier for the reader to comprehend. And, if you already have the data in Excel, creating a chart from the information is quick and easy; see Chapters 19, 20, and 21 for details on creating and formatting charts in Excel. Once you have created the chart in Excel, copying the chart to PowerPoint is very easy.

By default, when you copy a chart from Excel and paste it into PowerPoint, PowerPoint creates a link between the Excel data and the PowerPoint chart. So, if you make changes in the Excel workbook to the data that you used to create the chart, the changes appear on the chart in Excel and also on the PowerPoint slide where you pasted the chart.

Place an Excel Chart in a PowerPoint Slide

1. Open the workbook in Excel containing the chart that you want to copy to PowerPoint.
2. Open PowerPoint.
3. In Excel, select the chart that you want to copy to PowerPoint.
4. Click the Home tab.
5. Click [icon].

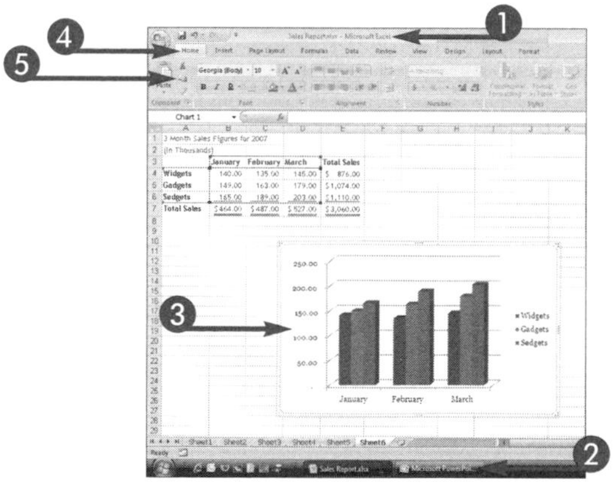

6. Click here to switch to PowerPoint.
7. Display the slide that should contain the information.

Note: *Use a blank slide or a slide with just a title.*

8. Click the Home tab.
9. Click the Paste [▼].
10. Click Paste Special.

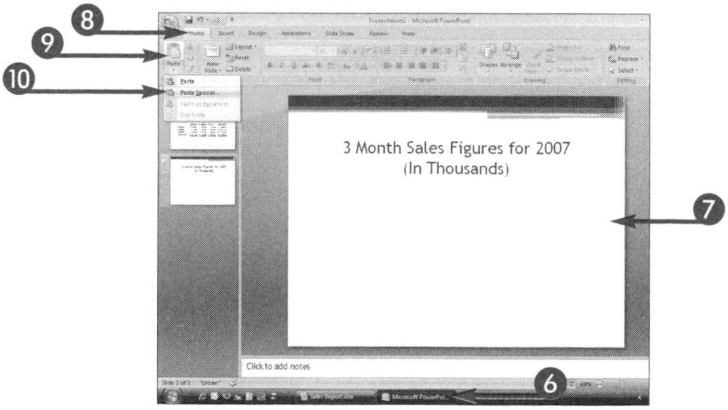

The Paste Special dialog box appears.

⑪ Click Paste Link (◯ changes to ◉).

⑫ Click Microsoft Office Excel Chart Object.

⑬ Click OK.

- The information from Excel appears on the PowerPoint slide as a graphic object.

You can move or resize the graphic object as necessary.

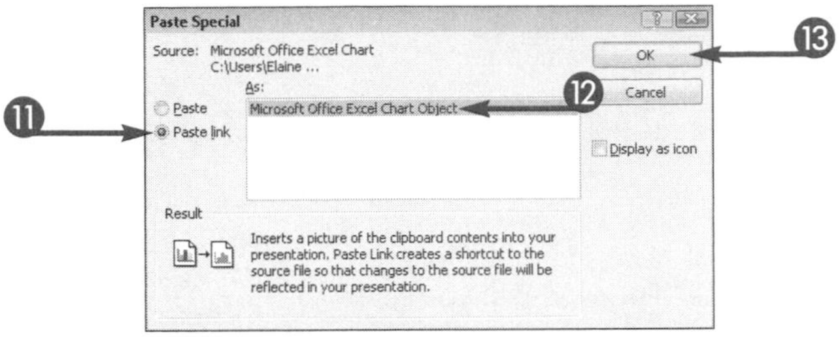

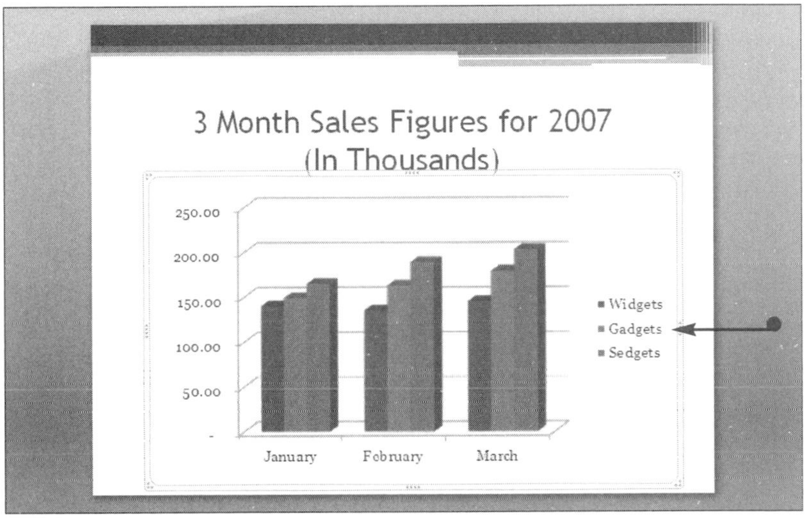

MASTER IT

My chart in PowerPoint has a light-gray line surrounding it. How can I get rid of this line?

▼ You need to edit the chart's format. In Excel, select the chart and click the Layout tab under Chart Tools. Make sure that you see Chart Area in the Current Selection box at the left end of the Ribbon. Click Format Selection and, in the Format Chart Area dialog box that appears, click Border Color. Click the No Line option (◯ changes to ◉) and click Close. The chart in Excel no longer has a light-gray line surrounding it. Next, in PowerPoint, right-click the chart and click Update Link. The light-gray line disappears from the PowerPoint slide chart.

What happens if I just click the Paste button in PowerPoint?

▼ The Excel chart appears in PowerPoint and is linked to the chart in the Excel workbook; you can make a change in Excel and the change is reflected on the PowerPoint slide. When you use this approach, the chart in PowerPoint is actually a chart object, and you can use the Chart Tools tabs that appear when you select the chart in PowerPoint to make changes to the chart's appearance. Any changes that you make do not affect the chart in the Excel workbook. When you use the approach described in this section, the object inserted in the PowerPoint presentation is a drawing object, not a chart.

Import Excel Information into Access

You can import an Excel worksheet into Access to take advantage of Access features that are not available in Excel. For example, you might want to create Access reports or forms using data you originally set up in Excel. You can import the information you have already set up in Excel into a new or existing table in an Access database without affecting the Excel workbook. You can import a named range or an entire worksheet. If you want to import a workbook that contains multiple worksheets, you must import each worksheet separately using the steps in this section. The worksheet or range can contain headings in the first row.

You should use the technique described in this section when you anticipate importing the same Excel information into Access on a regular basis. This technique does not create a connection to the information stored in Excel. Changes to the information in Excel do not appear automatically in the Access table.

You do not need to open the Excel workbook when you import it into Access. You can import the worksheet or range into a new or existing Access database. This example imports an Excel worksheet into a new table in an empty Access database.

Import Excel Information into Access

1. In Access, create a new database or open the database into which you want to import the Excel worksheet.
2. Click External Data.
3. Click Excel.

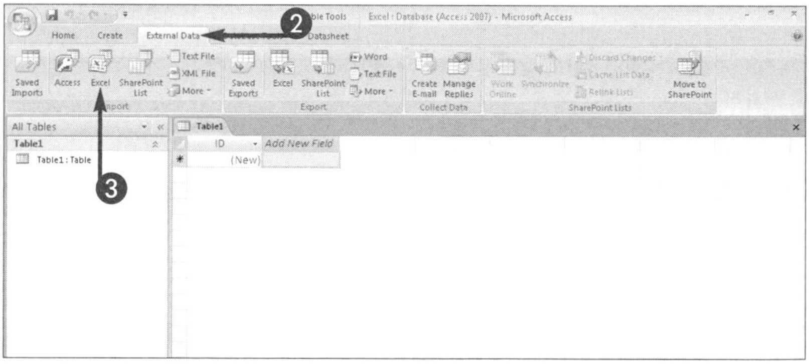

The Get External Data dialog box appears.

4. Click the "Import the source data into a new table in the current database" option (◯ changes to ◉).
5. Click Browse.

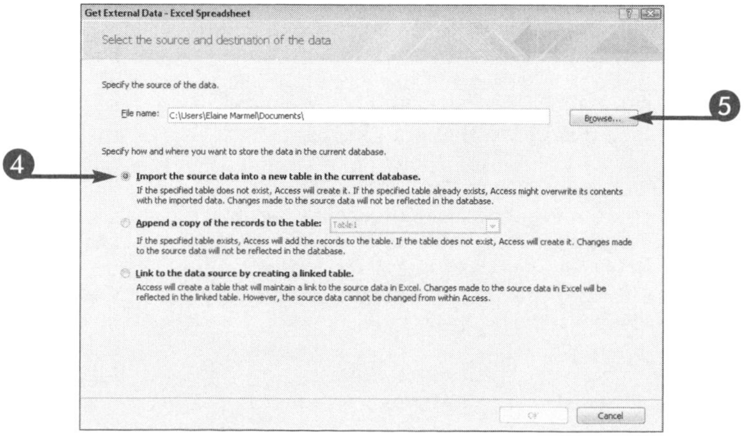

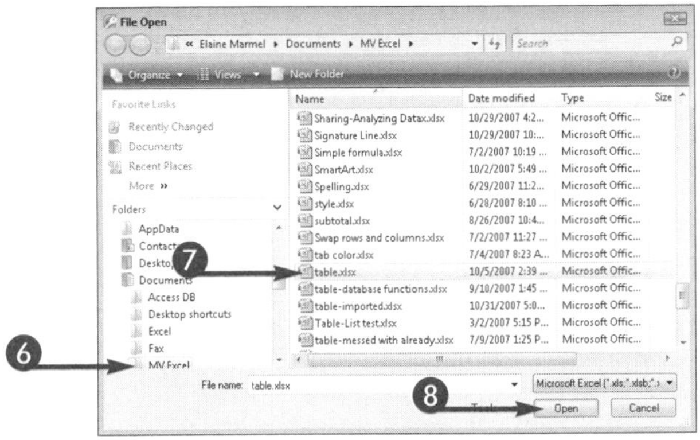

The File Open dialog box appears.

6. Navigate to the folder where the Excel workbook is located.
7. Click the workbook containing the table you want to import.
8. Click Open.

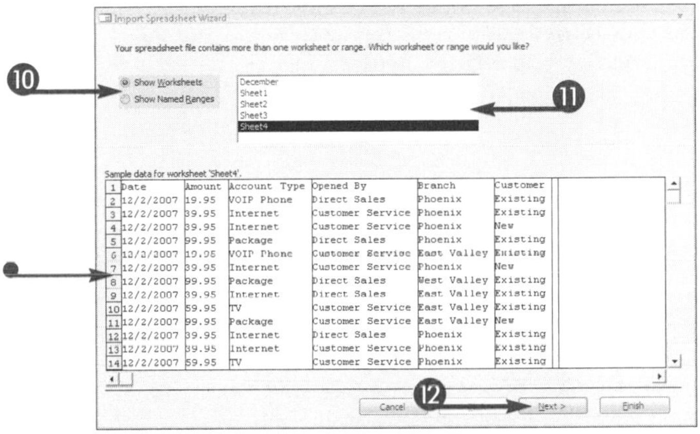

The Get External Data dialog box reappears.

9. Click OK.

The Import Spreadsheet Wizard appears.

10. Click an option to import a worksheet or range.
11. Click the worksheet or range you want to import.
    - A preview of the worksheet or range appears here.
12. Click Next.

I do not anticipate needing to import the Excel information into Access very often. What should I do?

▼ You can copy and paste the information from Excel to Access. In Excel, select the information you want to use in Access. Click the Home tab and click . Switch to Access and create a new table by clicking the Create tab and then clicking Table. Access displays the new table in Datasheet View. Click the Home tab and, in the Find group, click Select; from the menu that appears, click Select All. Then click Paste. Access displays a message asking if you are sure you want to paste the selection; click Yes.

In the Get External Data dialog box, what does the "Append a Copy of the Records to the Table" option do?

▼ You can use this option to add the Excel information to an existing Access table that you select. The structure of the Excel information must match the structure of the Access table, or you will not be able to successfully import the information. For example, if the Access table contains a primary key, you must ensure that the Excel information contains a field for the primary key and that each value is unique. Similarly, you must ensure that any column headings in the worksheet exactly match Access table headings, and add to the Access table any Excel fields that are missing.

continued

Import Excel Information into Access *(Continued)*

As you set up an import, you answer a series of questions. You identify the workbook containing the information you want to import and whether you want to import the information into a new table or an existing table. You select the worksheet or named range in the workbook that you want to import. You can indicate whether your worksheet contains field headings in the first row of the data, and, if the headings are valid in Access, Access uses those headings in the Access table. If they are not valid, Access adjusts them for you.

You can describe the type of information stored in each column; for example, if a column contains dates, you can make sure that Access recognizes the dates. You also can choose to skip importing certain fields.

You can specify how to handle the primary key for the table, and you can assign the Excel sheet or range name to the Access table, or create a new name. And, finally, you can save the settings you create during the process so that you do not need to set up the import the next time you want to bring the table information into Access.

Import Excel Information into Access *(continued)*

The next Import Spreadsheet Wizard screen appears.

13 Click the "First Row Contains Column Headings" option if the worksheet contains headings in the first row that you want Access to use.

Note: *You may see a message explaining that some of the names are not valid and that Access will replace them with valid names. Click OK.*

14 Click Next.

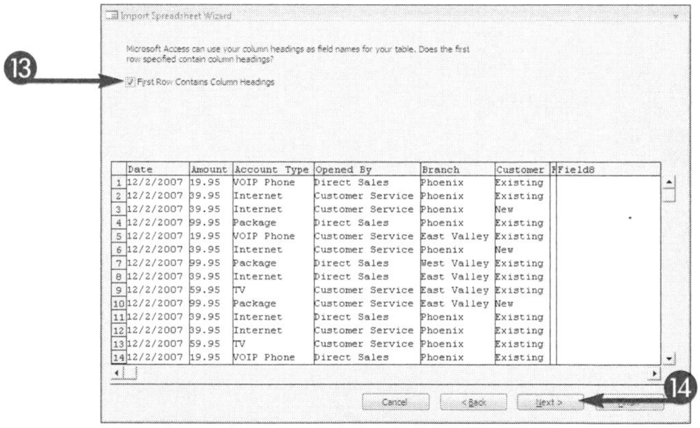

The next Import Spreadsheet Wizard screen appears.

15 Click each column and make sure that Access correctly identifies the type of information.

- You can select a column and click the "Do not import field (Skip)" option to tell Access not to import a column (☐ changes to ☑).

16 Click Next.

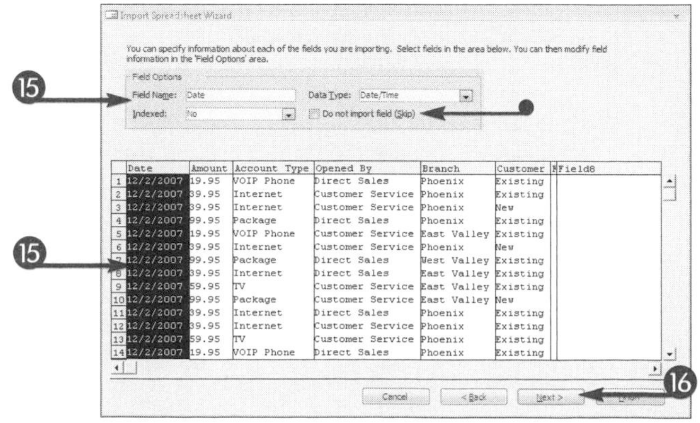

The next Import Spreadsheet Wizard screen appears.

⑰ Click an option to specify how to define the primary key for your table.

Note: *If you let Access create a key, Access adds an ID column to the table. If you choose your own key, you can select any column in the table.*

⑱ Click Next.

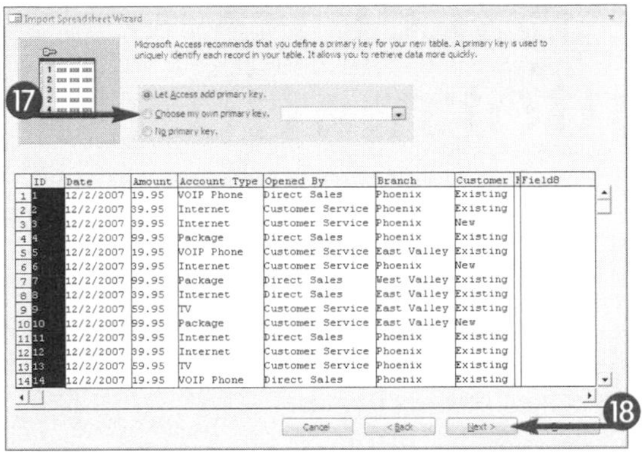

The next Import Spreadsheet Wizard screen appears.

Note: *You can accept the sheet name as the table name or you can rename the table.*

⑲ Click Finish.

A screen appears, enabling you to save the import steps.

⑳ Click Close.

- The table appears in the Access database.

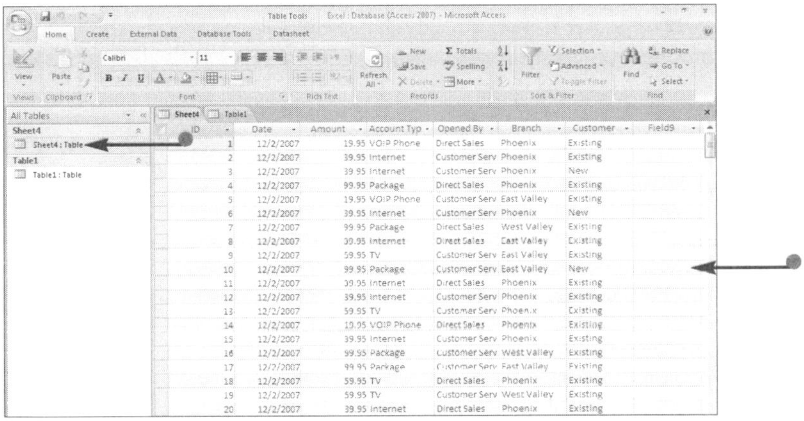

What are the choices concerning a primary key?

▼ A primary key uniquely identifies each record in the table; using a primary key helps you to retrieve information quickly from the table. You can let Access add a primary key or you can choose your own primary key from the column headings in the range or worksheet that you import. You can also choose not to include a primary key.

How do I save the steps to import this table?

▼ On the last screen of the Import Spreadsheet Wizard, click the Save Import Steps option (☐ changes to ☑). Provide a name that describes the import and, if you want, a description. If you regularly perform this import and you use Outlook, you can click Create Outlook Task. Then click Save Import.

If I save the import steps, how do I use them again?

▼ In Access, click the External Data tab and then click Saved Imports. The Manage Data Tasks dialog box appears. Click the name you assigned when saving the import steps, and click Run. Access does all the work for you and displays a message that the import completed successfully. Click Close, and the new table appears in Access.

Connect Excel to Access Information

You can use information stored in an Access table to create an Excel worksheet, a PivotTable report, or both a PivotChart and PivotTable report. When you create an Excel worksheet, PivotTable, or PivotChart and PivotTable from an Access table, you create a connection between the Access database and the Excel workbook. Because the two files are connected, you can make changes in the Access database and then update the Excel workbook to reflect the changes. You do not need to reconnect the files to make sure that the Excel workbook version is up-to-date with the latest information in the Access database.

When you create the connection between Excel and Access, you can select the Access table to bring into Excel. You cannot, however, select specific records in the table to bring into Excel. During the connection process, you navigate to the folder containing the Access database, and then, when prompted, you identify the table you want to bring into Excel. You also specify whether to place the table in the existing worksheet or on a new worksheet. If you choose to place the table on the existing worksheet, you select the location on the worksheet.

Connect Excel to Access Information

Connect Excel to Access

1. Click the Data tab.
2. Click From Access.

   The Select Data Source dialog box appears.

3. Navigate to the folder containing the Access database.
4. Select the Access database.
5. Click Open.

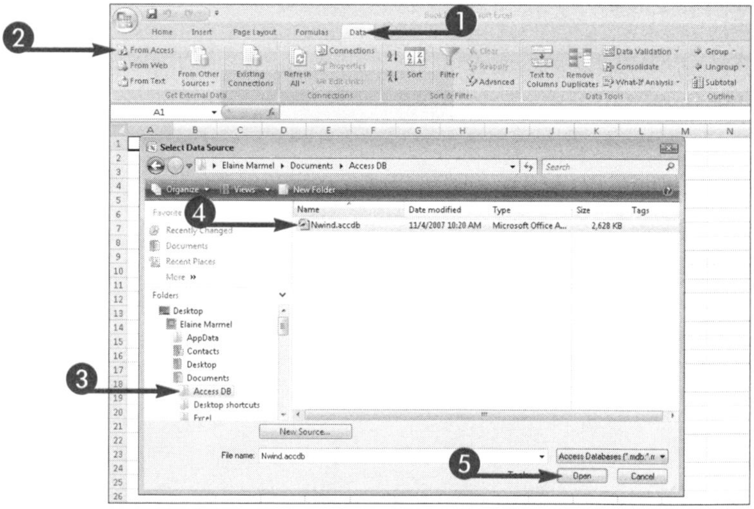

The Select Table dialog box appears.

6. Click the Access table you want to import.
7. Click OK.

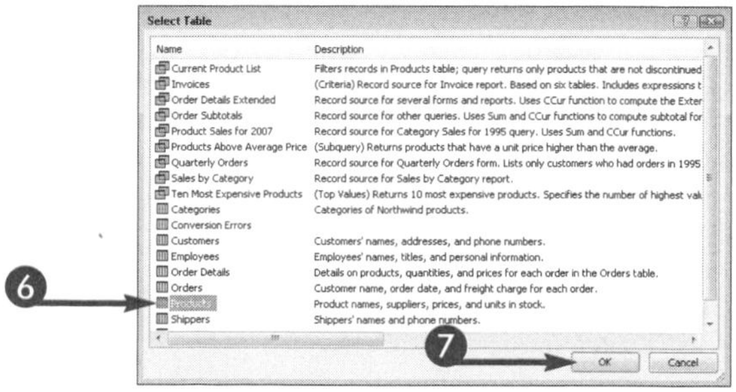

The Import Data dialog box appears.

8. Click an option to indicate how you want to view the data in Excel.

9. Click an option to indicate where to place the data in the workbook.

   - If you select the existing worksheet, select the cell representing the upper-left corner of the range where data should appear.

10. Click OK.

   - The Access table appears in Excel, formatted as a table.

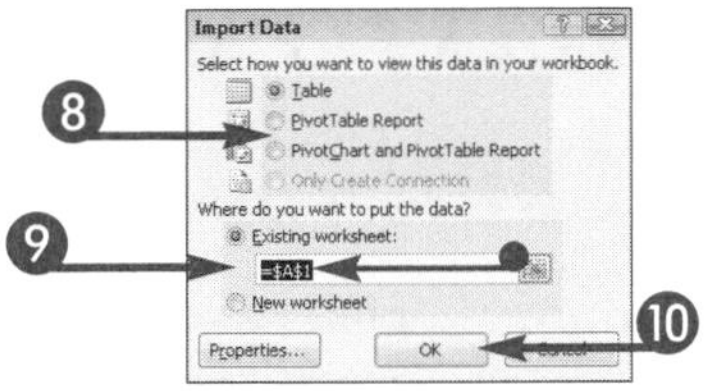

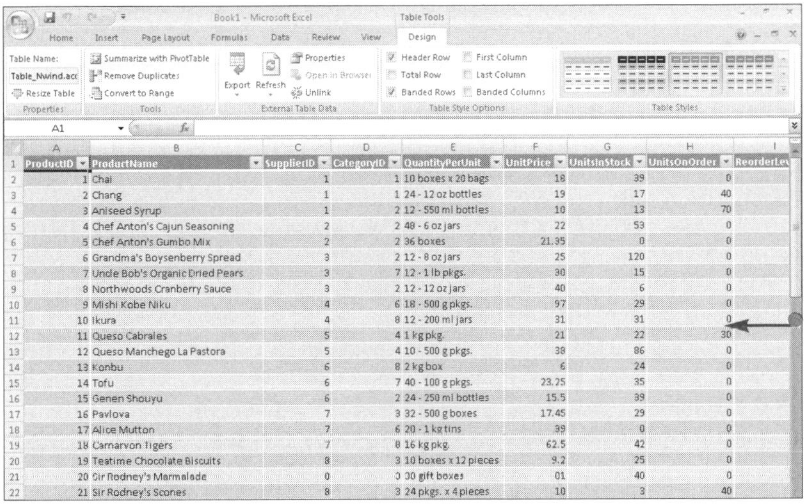

When I tried to connect to the Access database, I saw the Data Link Properties dialog box after I selected the database. What did I do wrong?

▼ Nothing. The database to which you want to connect is open. Because it is open, you need to confirm the information shown in the Data Link Properties dialog box. If you accept the defaults and click OK, the "Please Enter Microsoft Office Access Database Engine OLE DB Initialization Information" dialog box appears. Accept the default settings and click OK in this dialog box; the Select Table dialog box appears, and you can continue with Step 6.

If I choose to create a PivotTable, how does Excel arrange the information?

▼ Excel does not arrange the information. Instead, a blank PivotTable appears and Excel displays the PivotTable Field List down the right side of the screen. In the top portion of the PivotTable Field List, all of the Access table fields appear. You drag and drop them into the PivotTable areas at the bottom of the PivotTable Field List. For details on working with PivotTables and PivotCharts, see Chapter 24.

Can I connect two tables in the same Access database to the same Excel workbook?

▼ Yes. Click outside the first table, and the From Access button becomes available. Repeat the steps in this section.

Connect Excel to Access Information *(Continued)*

Once you have connected an Excel workbook to an Access database, you can easily keep the workbook up-to-date with any changes made to the Access database. You simply open the Excel workbook and refresh the data.

When you connect an Excel workbook to an external source of data such as an Access database, the default Excel security settings do not automatically enable the connection each time you open the workbook. Instead, you see a security warning in the Message bar above the workbook that indicates that the data connection is not enabled. However, you can use the Message bar to enable the connection.

After you re-enable the connection, you can update the content in the Excel workbook by refreshing. If the database is not open, Excel refreshes the data when you request a refresh. If the database is open and in use by someone else, you may see a message that tells you to try refreshing later; when you close that message, you may see another message that asks you to confirm the database initialization information. When you close that message, the Excel workbook updates with the most current Access database information.

Connect Excel to Access Information *(continued)*

Refresh After Updating

1. Open the database and table in Access.
2. Make a change to the table.
3. Save the database.

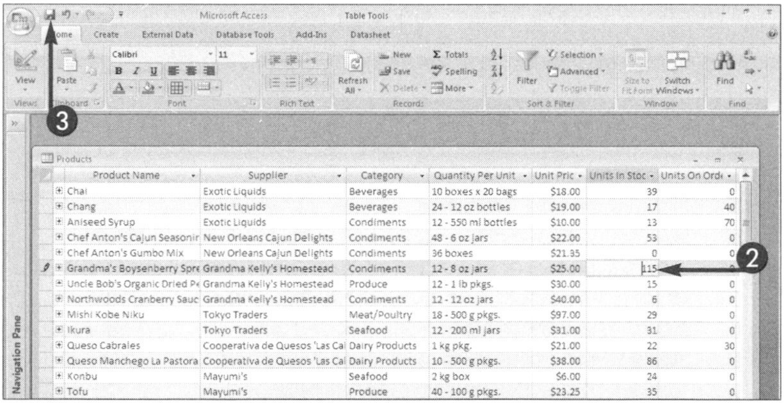

4. Switch to the workbook in Excel.
   - The changes you made in Access do not yet appear in Excel.
   - A security warning appears.
5. Click Options.

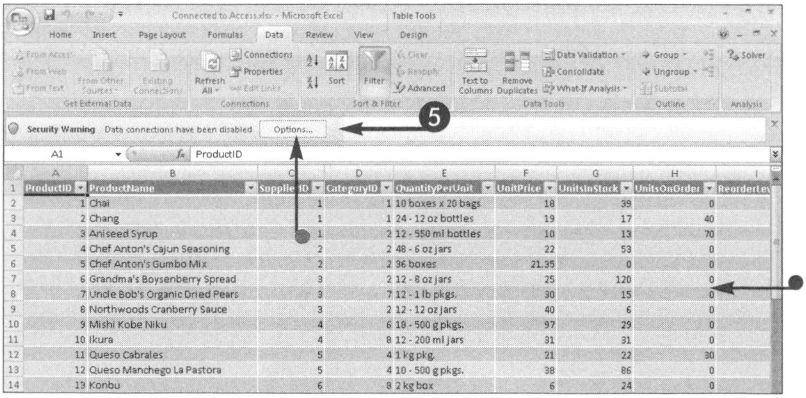

The Security Alert - Data Connection dialog box appears.

6 Click the "Enable this content" option (◯ changes to ◉).

7 Click OK.

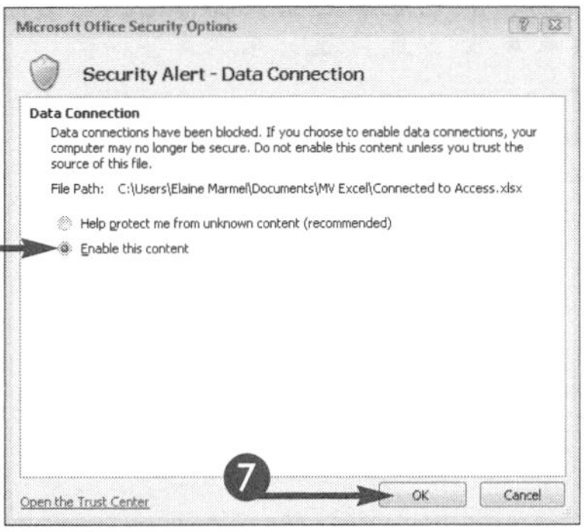

The security warning disappears.

8 Click the Data tab.

9 Click ▾ under Refresh All.

10 Click Refresh All.

- The changes you made in Access appear in Excel.

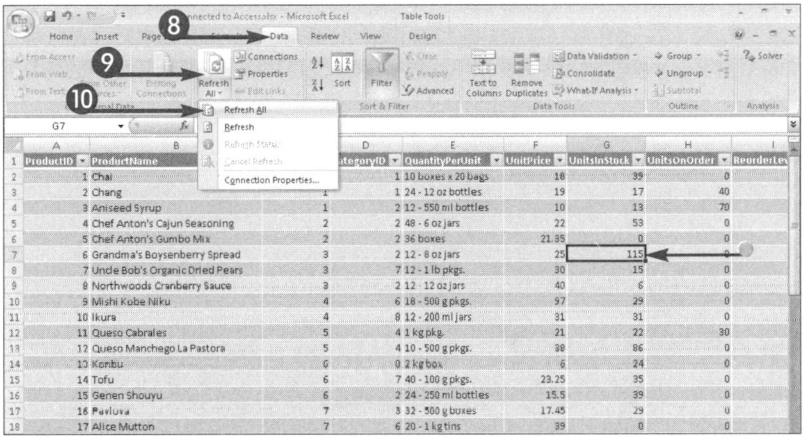

What happens if I click Connection Properties in Step 10?

▼ The Connection Properties dialog box appears. It contains two tabs: Usage and Definition. From the Usage tab, you can control the way Excel refreshes. By default, background refreshing is enabled. You can also control how often Excel refreshes and whether Excel refreshes as you open the workbook, which may cause opening the workbook to take longer than opening the workbook without refreshing. If you are retrieving data from an OLAP server, you also find settings to control the way the information is retrieved. On the Definition tab, you find settings that describe how the connection is defined.

How would I use the Definition tab?

▼ You can use the Definition tab to switch the connection to a different database. You can change the connection to a different database of the same type, but you cannot connect to a different type of database. For example, you cannot switch from a non-OLAP PivotTable to an OLAP PivotTable. You can control the command type and text; for example, when you select Table from the Command Type list, Excel displays the table name in the Command Text text box. If you connect to a data source that is displayed in Excel Services, you can click Authentication Settings to select an authentication method.

Query Data in an External Source

Suppose that you want to bring into an Excel workbook a subset of information stored in an Access table. Although you could bring in the entire table and use Excel to filter the data, it is conceivable that the table may contain more records than Excel can hold. You can therefore create a connection to an external data source and bring in only the information you need. The example in this section uses Microsoft Query, an application that ships with Excel, to create a connection to an Access database and then import into Excel a subset of the information stored in one of the database tables.

You may wonder why you would not use the steps in the section, "Connect Excel to Access Information," instead of the steps in this section. The section, "Connect Excel to Access Information," describes how to connect an Excel workbook to an entire table in an Access database, and that type of connection works well when you need all of the information in the table.

To establish this type of connection, you go through a two-part process. First, you establish the connection, and then you create and run the query.

Query Data in an External Source

Set up a New Data Source

1. Open a new workbook or the workbook you want to use to connect to the external data source.
2. Click the Data tab.
3. Click From Other Sources.
4. Click From Microsoft Query.

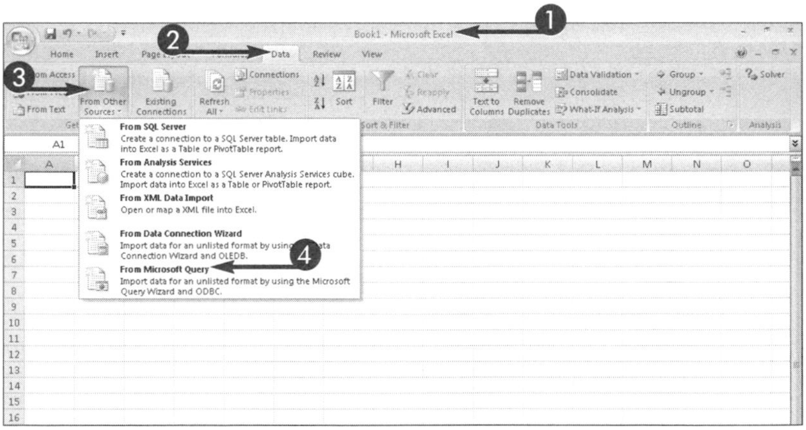

The Choose Data Source dialog box appears.

5. Click <New Data Source>.
6. Click the "Use the Query Wizard to create/edit queries" option (☐ changes to ☑).
7. Click OK.

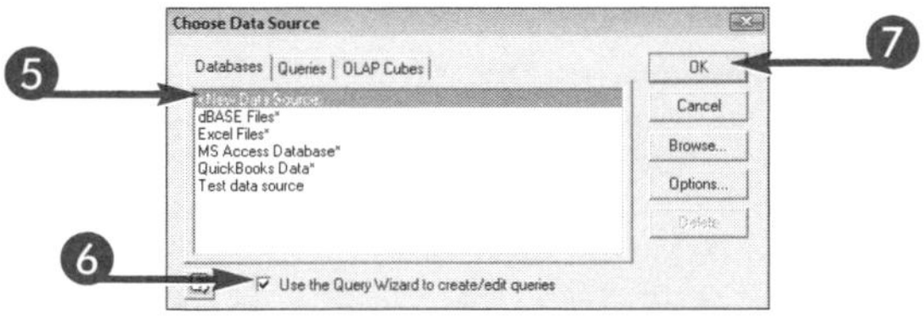

The Create New Data Source dialog box appears.

8. Type a name for the data source.
9. Click ▾ and select a driver for the type of database.

   This example uses Microsoft Access Driver (*.mdb, *.accdb).

10. Click Connect.

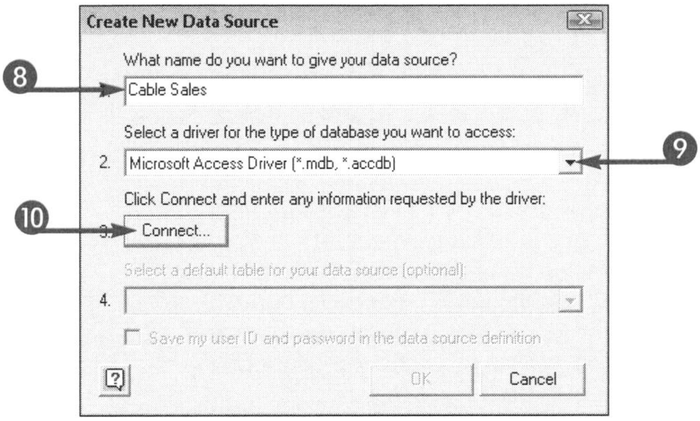

The ODBC Setup dialog box appears for the type of database that you selected.

11. Click Select.

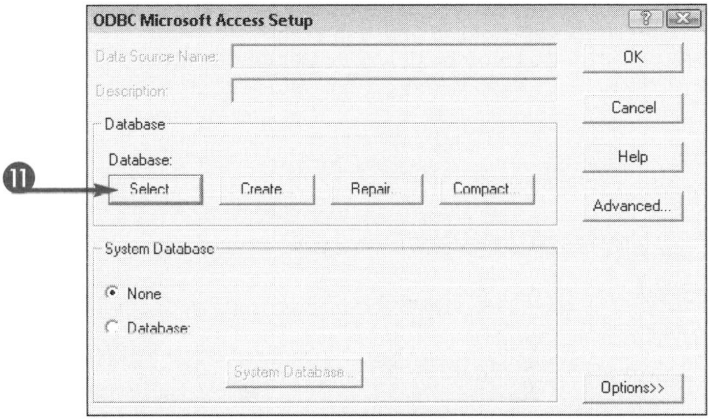

MASTER IT

To use this connection again for another query, what do I do?

▼ Complete Steps 1 to 4 in the subsection, "Set Up a New Data Source." In the Choose Data Source dialog box, click the name of the connection you created previously using the steps in this subsection, and click OK. The Query Wizard starts. Complete the steps in the subsections, "Select Columns to Include in the Query," "Set Query Filters," and "Set Sort Options," to set up and run your query.

What do the entries on the various tabs in the Choose Data Source dialog box represent?

▼ On the Databases tab, you see data sources that are known to Microsoft Query. It is possible that this tab might be empty; its content depends on the data sources that are defined on your computer. On the Queries tab, you see a list of saved queries. On the OLAP Cubes tab, you see a list of OLAP databases that are available for query.

What happens when I click the Options button in the Choose Data Source dialog box?

▼ The Data Source Options dialog box appears. From this dialog box, you can add path names for Microsoft Query to search for data sources. In most cases, you do not need to make changes to any listed paths or add any paths. To add a path, click the Browse button and navigate to the folder you want to include when searching for data sources.

Query Data in an External Source *(Continued)*

You can use the information in this section to not only connect to an Access database, but also to import data stored in other types of external sources, such as XML data or data on an SQL Server or an SQL Server Analysis Services cube. Or, to import another type of data, you can use the Excel Data Connection Wizard to create the connection.

Before creating a query, you create a connection to the external data source that remains available to you to use over and over; this means that you only have to go through the steps to create the connection to the data source once. To create the data source, you provide a name for the data source, using a name that will help you remember the data source for future use. You also select a driver that is appropriate for the type of external data source you will query; the example in this section uses an Access driver. You then connect to the external data source by navigating to it using a typical navigation dialog box that enables you to select a drive, a folder, and a database file. After you connect to the database, you can, optionally, select a default table to query.

Query Data in an External Source *(continued)*

The Select Database dialog box appears.

12 Navigate to the folder containing the database, and select it.

13 Click OK.

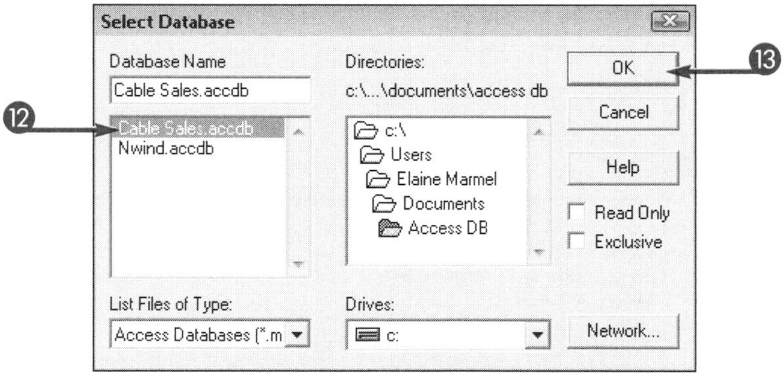

The Create New Data Source dialog box reappears.

14 Click ▾ to select a default table.

15 Click OK twice to start the Query Wizard.

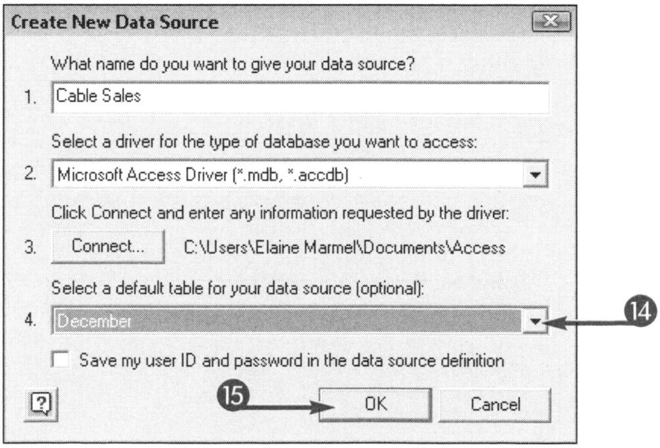

Select Columns to Include in the Query

1. Click a column that you want to include in the query.
2. Click here (>) to include the column in the query.
3. Repeat Steps 1 and 2 for each column you want to include in the query.

Note: To include all columns, click the table name and click >.

4. Click Next.

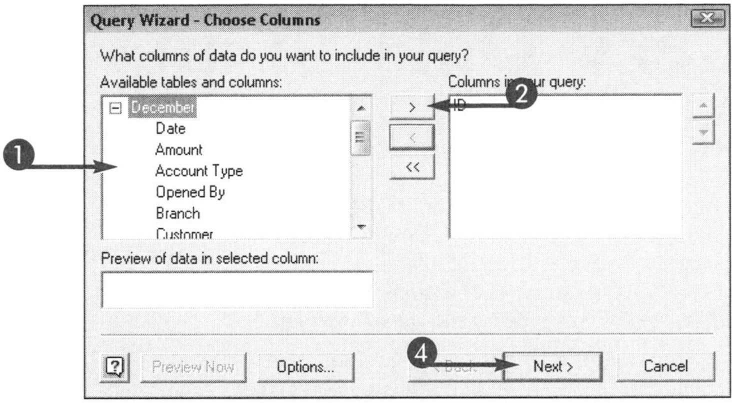

Set Query Filters

The Query Wizard Filter Data screen appears.

1. Click a column.
2. Click ▾ and select an operator.
3. Click ▾ and select a value.
4. Repeat Steps 1 to 3 for each filter you want to set.
   - Each filtered column appears in boldface.
5. Click Next.

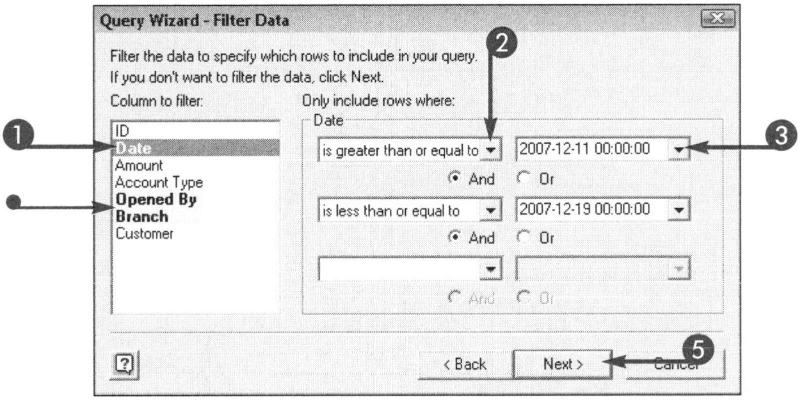

MASTER IT

Should I add all columns to the query or only selected columns?

▼ You determine the columns to add to the query based on the information you want to view as a result of the query. For example, if you are importing records from the cable company sales database and you do not care whether the sales were made to new or existing customers, you have no need to include that column in the query.

How do I use the Preview field in the Choose Columns screen of the Query Wizard?

▼ Click a column in the Available Tables and Columns list and then click the Preview Now button. You do not need to add the column to the query to preview it. When you preview a column, you see a list of the data stored in that column of the table.

What happens if I click Options in the Choose Columns screen?

▼ The Table Options dialog box appears. In this dialog box, you can select the types of information to show on the Choose Columns screen; for an Access database, you can show tables, views, system tables, and synonyms. You can also choose to list tables and columns in alphabetical order instead of the order in which they appear in the table.

continued

Query Data in an External Source *(Continued)*

After you create a connection to the external data source, you use the Query Wizard to create the query. If you are familiar with Microsoft Query, you can write the query directly, but the Query Wizard makes writing the query very easy.

You identify the columns of data on which you want to report; you can select certain columns or you can easily include all of the columns in the table.

Next, you filter the data in the table by selecting a column and specifying records to return. Suppose that your table contains December sales records for an Arizona cable company and you want to see sales for the Phoenix branch office. To set the office filter, you select the Branch field, a comparison operator such as "equals," and a value for the field — in this example, Phoenix.

As the last query option, you can select sort fields for the information that the query returns. Then you identify the location in the workbook where you want to view the query results; you can place the query in Microsoft Query or your Excel workbook. If you place the query in Excel, you can select the worksheet where the query results should appear.

Query Data in an External Source *(continued)*

Set Sort Options

The Query Wizard Sort Order screen appears.

1. Click ▾ and click a column by which to sort.
2. Click an option to sort in ascending or descending order.

Note: *You can repeat Steps 1 and 2 to set additional sort order options.*

3. Click Next.

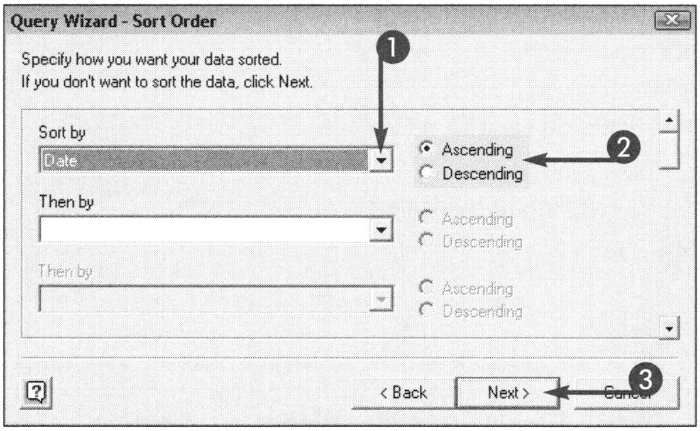

The Query Wizard Finish screen appears.

4. Click an option to specify where you want the query results to appear.

This example returns the query results to Excel.

5. Click Finish.

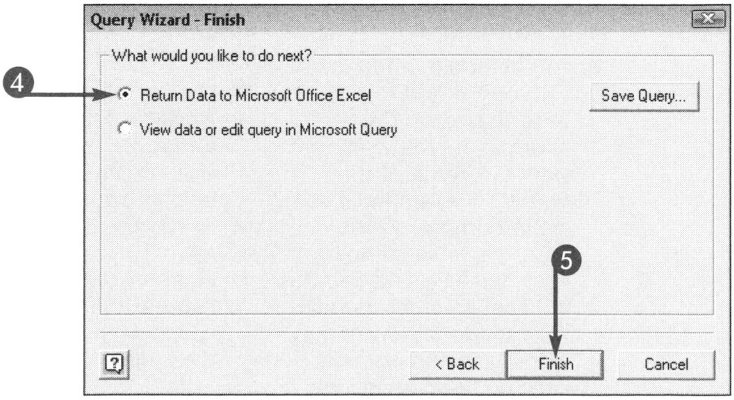

The Import Data dialog box appears.

6 Click an option to specify how you want to view the query results in Excel.

This example displays the results in a table.

7 Click an option to specify whether the data should appear in the current or a new worksheet.

Note: *If you click Existing worksheet, select a cell for the upper-left corner of the query result range.*

8 Click OK.

- The query results appear in your workbook.

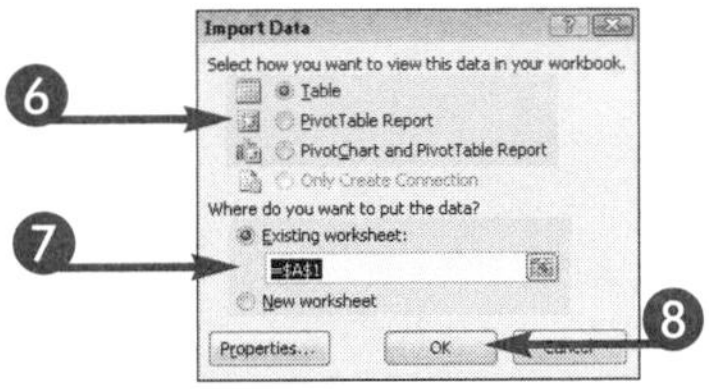

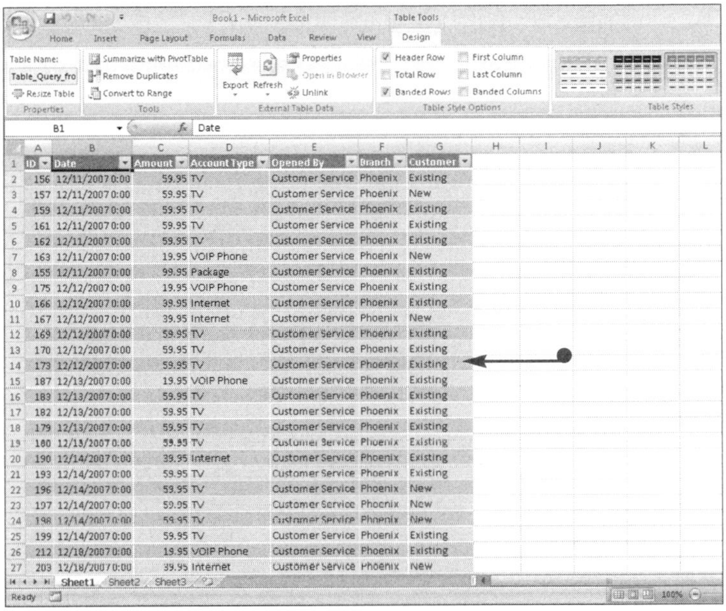

Can you explain what the And and Or options mean when setting up filters?

▼ You use both options to set two or more conditions for the same column. Using the And option usually results in limiting the amount of data returned by the query. In this example, the date range filter used an And condition to select dates greater than December 11 and less than December 19. You use the Or option when you want to see data that meets either of the criteria you set. For example, you could use the Or option to indicate that you want to see records where the Branch equals Phoenix or Flagstaff, and the query returns records that meet either criteria.

When should I choose to return the query results to Microsoft Query?

▼ If you know how to use Microsoft Query, then you can return the results of the query to Microsoft Query. If you do not know how to use Microsoft Query, return the results to Excel.

What happens if I click the Save Query button on the Finish screen of the wizard?

▼ The Save As dialog box appears, offering you the option of saving the query in a format that is readable by Microsoft Query. In addition, the query appears on the Queries tab of the Choose Data Source dialog box. If you plan to rerun the same query many times, you can save yourself time and effort by saving the query.

Excel Functions

The purpose of this appendix is not to teach you how to use the functions listed; instead, this appendix presents, in alphabetical order, a list and brief description of the functions available in Excel. You can use this appendix to get an overview of available functions, and, if a function catches your interest, you can look for it in this book or use the Excel Help system to learn to use it.

Function Name	*Purpose*
ABS	Use this function to display the absolute value of a number.
ACCRINT	A financial function that returns the accrued interest for a security that pays periodic interest.
ACCRINTM	Use this function to calculate the accrued interest for a security that pays interest at maturity.
ACOS	This function returns the arccosine of a number you specify.
ACOSH	This function returns the inverse hyperbolic cosine of a number you specify.
ADDRESS	This function creates a cell address using row and column numbers you specify.
AMORDEGRC	For the French accounting system, use this function to calculate the depreciation for each accounting period using a fixed depreciation coefficient based on the life of the asset.
AMORLINC	For the French accounting system, use this function to calculate depreciation for each accounting period without using a depreciation coefficient.
AND	This function returns TRUE if all of the arguments you specify are true.
AREAS	This function returns the number of contiguous ranges in the argument you specify.
ASC	Use this function with double-byte character set languages to convert full-width (double-byte) characters to half-width (single-byte) characters.
ASIN	This function returns the arcsine of a number you specify.
ASINH	This function returns the inverse hyperbolic sine of a number you specify.
ATAN	This function returns the arctangent of a number you specify.
ATAN2	This function returns the arctangent from x and y coordinates of a number you specify.
ATANH	This function returns the inverse hyperbolic tangent of a number you specify.
AVEDEV	Used to measure the variability in a data set, this function returns the average of the absolute deviations of data points from their mean.
AVERAGE	This function calculates the average of the arguments you specify.
AVERAGEA	This function calculates the average of the arguments you specify, including text and logical values.
AVERAGEIF	Use this function to calculate the average of its arguments based on a criterion you specify.
AVERAGEIFS	Use this function to calculate the average of its arguments based on multiple criteria you specify.

Function Name	Purpose
BAHTTEXT	Use this function to convert a number to Thai text and add a suffix of "Baht".
BESSELI	In engineering, this function returns the modified Bessel function In(x).
BESSELJ	In engineering, this function returns the Bessel function Jn(x).
BESSELK	In engineering, this function returns the modified Bessel function Kn(x).
BESSELY	In engineering, this function returns the Bessel function Yn(x).
BETADIST	Commonly used to study variation in percentages across samples, this function returns the cumulative beta probability density function.
BETAINV	This function returns the inverse of the cumulative beta probability density function.
BIN2DEC	This function converts a binary number to decimal.
BIN2HEX	This function converts a binary number to hexadecimal.
BIN2OCT	This function converts a binary number to octal.
BINOMDIST	Used in problems with a fixed number of independent trials for which the outcomes are only success or failure and the probability of success is constant through the experiment, this function returns the individual term binomial distribution probability.
CEILING	Use this function to round a number to the nearest integer or multiple of significance.
CELL	This function returns formatting, location, or contents information about the upper-left cell in a range.
CHAR	Use this function to translate a number you provide to a character.
CHIDIST	Used to determine whether a hypothesis is valid based on observed and expected values, this function returns the one-tailed probability of the chi-squared distribution.
CHIINV	This function returns the inverse of the one-tailed probability of the chi-squared distribution.
CHITEST	Use this function to return the test for independence.
CHOOSE	This function returns a value from a list using arguments you specify to identify the list and the value within the list to return.
CLEAN	Especially useful with imported text files, this function removes all non-printable characters from text.
CODE	This function returns the code for a character you provide.
COLUMN	Use this function to determine the column number of a cell or range of cells you specify.
COLUMNS	This function returns the number of columns in a range you specify.
COMBIN	Use this function to determine the total possible number of groups you can create using a number of items you specify.
COMPLEX	This function converts real and imaginary coefficients into a complex number.

continued

Excel Functions

(Continued)

Function Name	Purpose
CONCATENATE	Use this function to join several text strings into one text string.
CONFIDENCE	This function returns a value that you can use to construct a confidence interval for a population mean.
CONVERT	Use this function to convert a number from one measurement system to another.
CORREL	This function returns the correlation coefficient between two data sets you identify.
COS	Use this function to return the cosine of a number you specify.
COSH	Use this function to return the hyperbolic cosine of a number you specify.
COUNT	Use this function to count the number of cells in a range that contain numbers.
COUNTA	Use this function to count the number of cells in a range that are not blank.
COUNTBLANK	Use this function to count the number of cells in a range that are blank.
COUNTIF	This function counts the number of cells in a range that meet a criterion you specify.
COUNTIFS	This function counts the number of cells in a range that meet multiple criteria you specify.
COUPDAYBS	This function calculates the number of days from the beginning of the coupon period to the settlement date of a security.
COUPDAYS	Use this function to calculate the number of days in the coupon period that contains the settlement date of a security.
COUPDAYSNC	This function calculates the number of days from the settlement date to the next coupon date of a security.
COUPNCD	This function returns the next coupon date after the settlement date of a security.
COUPNUM	Use this function to calculate the number of coupons payable between the settlement date and the maturity date of a security.
COUPPCD	This function returns the coupon date prior to the settlement date of a security.
COVAR	This function returns covariance, which is the measure of how much two random variables vary together.
CRITBINOM	Use this function to find the smallest value for which the cumulative binomial distribution is less than or equal to a criterion you specify.
CUBEKPIMEMBER	This function returns a key performance indicator name, property, and measure.
CUBEMEMBER	Use this function to determine whether a member or cubetuple exists in a cube.
CUBEMEMBERPROPERTY	Use this function to determine that a member name exists within a cube.
CUBERANKEDMEMBER	Use this function to identify a cube member with a ranking you specify.
CUBESET	This function defines a calculated set of members or tuples.
CUBESETCOUNT	This function returns the number of items in a set.

Function Name	Purpose
CUBEVALUE	This function returns a cumulative value from a cube.
CUMIPMT	This function calculates the cumulative interest paid on a loan between two periods.
CUMPRINC	This function calculates the cumulative principal paid on a loan between two periods.
DATE	Use this function to determine the serial number of a particular date.
DATEVALUE	This function converts a date in the form of text to a serial number.
DAVERAGE	This function returns the average of values in an Excel database that meet conditions you specify.
DAY	Use this function to convert a serial number to its corresponding day of the month.
DAYS360	This function calculates the number of days between two dates using a 360-day year.
DB	Using the fixed-declining-balance depreciation method, this function calculates the depreciation of an asset for a period you specify.
DCOUNT	This function counts the cells in an Excel database that contain numbers and meet conditions you specify.
DCOUNTA	This function counts the nonblank cells in an Excel database that meet conditions you specify.
DDB	Using the double-declining balance depreciation method or another depreciation method you specify, this function calculates the depreciation of an asset for a period you specify.
DEC2BIN	This function converts a decimal number to binary.
DEC2HEX	This function converts a decimal number to hexadecimal.
DEC2OCT	This function converts a decimal number to octal.
DEGREES	Use this function to convert radians to degrees.
DELTA	Use this function to test whether two values are equal.
DEVSQ	This function calculates the sum of squares of deviations.
DGET	This function returns a value from an Excel database that meets conditions you specify.
DISC	This function returns the discount rate for a security.
DMAX	This function returns the largest value in an Excel database that meets conditions you specify.
DMIN	This function returns the smallest value in an Excel database that meets conditions you specify.
DOLLAR	This function applies currency formatting to a number and then converts the number to text.
DOLLARDE	This function converts a dollar price expressed as a fraction into a dollar price expressed as a decimal.
DOLLARFR	This function converts a dollar price expressed as a decimal into a dollar price expressed as a fraction.
DPRODUCT	This function multiplies values in an Excel database that meet conditions you specify.

continued

Excel Functions

(Continued)

Function Name	Purpose
DSTDEV	Use this function to estimate the standard deviation of a database based on a sample of selected database entries that meet conditions you specify.
DSTDEVP	Use this function to estimate the standard deviation of a database based on all database entries that meet conditions you specify.
DSUM	This function adds values in an Excel database that meet conditions you specify.
DURATION	Use this function to calculate the annual duration of a security with periodic interest payments.
DVAR	Use this function to estimate the variance of a database based on a sample of selected database entries that meet conditions you specify.
DVARP	Use this function to estimate the variance of a database based on all database entries that meet conditions you specify.
EDATE	This function returns the serial number of the date that is a specific number of months before or after a start date you provide.
EFFECT	This function calculates the effective annual interest rate of an investment.
EOMONTH	This function returns the serial number of the last day of the month that is a specific number of months before or after a date you provide.
ERF	In engineering, this function returns the error function integrated between a lower and upper limit you specify.
ERFC	In engineering, this function returns the complementary ERF function integrated between *x*, a value you specify, and infinity.
ERROR.TYPE	This function returns a number that corresponds to one of the error values in Excel.
EVEN	This function rounds a number up to the nearest even integer.
EXACT	Use this function to compare two text strings and determine if they are exactly the same.
EXP	This function returns the constant *e* raised to the power of a number you provide.
EXPONDIST	This function returns the exponential distribution.
FACT	This function returns the factorial of a number you specify.
FACTDOUBLE	This function doubles the factorial of a number you specify.
FALSE	This function displays the logical value FALSE.
FDIST	Use this function to calculate the F probability distribution.
FIND	For single-byte character sets, use this function to find a text string within another text string when case sensitivity matters. Use FINDB for double-byte character sets.
FINV	Use this function to calculate the inverse of the F probability distribution.
FISHER	This function returns the Fisher transformation.
FISHERINV	This function returns the inverse of the Fisher transformation.

Function Name	Purpose
FIXED	This function rounds a number to the number of decimals you indicate, formats the number using a period and commas, and returns the results as text.
FLOOR	Use this function to round a number down to the nearest multiple of significance.
FORECAST	This function predicts a future value using existing values.
FREQUENCY	This function returns a frequency distribution as a vertical array.
FTEST	This function returns the result of an F-test, which measures the two-tailed probability that the variances in two arrays you specify are not significantly different.
FV	This function calculates the future value of an investment.
FVSCHEDULE	This function calculates the future value of an initial principal amount after applying a series of compound interest rates.
GAMMADIST	This function returns the gamma distribution, which is commonly used in queuing analysis.
GAMMAINV	This function returns the inverse of the gamma distribution.
GAMMALN	This function returns the natural logarithm of the gamma function, G(x).
GCD	Use this function to return the greatest common divisor of a number you specify.
GEOMEAN	This function returns the geometric mean.
GESTEP	Use this function to test whether a number you provide is greater than a threshold you specify.
GETPIVOTDATA	Use this function to return data stored in a PivotTable report.
GROWTH	Use this function to predict exponential growth based on existing data.
HARMEAN	Use this function to calculate the harmonic mean of data you specify.
HEX2BIN	This function converts a hexadecimal number to binary.
HEX2DEC	This function converts a hexadecimal number to decimal.
HEX2OCT	This function converts a hexadecimal number to octal.
HLOOKUP	This function looks up data in a list by horizontally matching a value in the top row and then finding a value in the matched column from a row you specify.
HOUR	Use this function to convert a serial number to an hour.
HYPERLINK	This function creates a shortcut to a document on your hard drive, a server, or the Internet.
HYPGEOMDIST	This function returns the probability of a given number of sample successes, given the sample size, population successes, and population size.
IF	Use this function to perform a logical test.
IFERROR	This function returns a value you specify if a formula calculates to an error; otherwise, this function returns the result of the formula.
IMABS	This function returns the absolute value of a complex number.

continued

Excel Functions

(Continued)

Function Name	Purpose
IMAGINARY	In engineering, use this function to calculate the imaginary coefficient of a complex number.
IMARGUMENT	This function returns the argument theta, an angle expressed in radians.
IMCONJUGATE	This function returns the complex conjugate of a complex number you specify.
IMCOS	This function returns the cosine of a complex number you specify.
IMDIV	This function calculates the quotient of two complex numbers you specify.
IMEXP	This function returns the exponential of a complex number you provide.
IMLN	This function returns the natural logarithm of a complex number you provide.
IMLOG10	This function returns the base-10 logarithm of a complex number you provide.
IMLOG2	This function returns the base-2 logarithm of a complex number you provide.
IMPOWER	This function returns a complex number you provide raised to an integer power you specify.
IMPRODUCT	Use this function to calculate the product of two complex numbers you specify.
IMREAL	This function returns the real coefficient of a complex number you provide.
IMSIN	This function returns the sine of a complex number you specify.
IMSQRT	This function returns the square root of a complex number you provide.
IMSUB	This function calculates the difference between two complex numbers you provide.
IMSUM	This function calculates the sum of two or more complex numbers you provide.
INDEX	This function returns a value or cell reference from an array or a range you specify.
INDIRECT	This function returns a reference indicated by a text value.
INFO	Use this function to return information such as the current folder or the number of active worksheets in open workbooks.
INT	Use this function to round a number down to the nearest integer.
INTERCEPT	Using existing *x* and *y* values, this function calculates the point at which a line will intersect the *y*-axis.
INTRATE	Use this function to calculate the interest rate for a fully invested security.
IPMT	Use this function to calculate the interest payment for an investment for a period you specify.
IRR	Use this function to calculate the internal rate of return for a series of cash flows.
ISBLANK	This function returns TRUE if the specified cell is blank.
ISERR	This function returns TRUE if the specified cell contains any error value except #N/A.
ISERROR	This function returns TRUE if the specified cell contains any error value.
ISEVEN	This function returns TRUE if the specified cell contains an even number.

Function Name	Purpose
ISLOGICAL	This function returns TRUE if the specified cell contains a logical value.
ISNA	This function returns TRUE if the specified cell contains the error value #N/A.
ISNONTEXT	This function returns TRUE if the specified cell does not contain text.
ISNUMBER	This function returns TRUE if the specified cell contains a number.
ISODD	This function returns TRUE if the specified cell contains an odd number.
ISPMT	Use this function to calculate the interest associated with a loan payment you specify.
ISREF	This function returns TRUE if the specified cell contains a cell reference.
ISTEXT	This function returns TRUE if the specified cell contains text.
KURT	This function returns the kurtosis of a data set, which compares the curve of the data set with the normal distribution curve.
LARGE	This function returns a value based on its relative largeness within an array using a relative largeness position you specify.
LCM	Use this function to determine the least common multiple of a number you specify.
LEFT	For single-byte character sets, this function returns characters at the left edge of a character string, and you specify the number of characters to return. Use LEFTB for double-byte character sets.
LEN	For single-byte character sets, use this function to determine the number of characters in a text string. Use LENB for double-byte character sets.
LINEST	This function uses the "least squares" method to calculate a straight line that best fits your data, and then returns an array that describes the line.
LN	Use this function to calculate the natural logarithm of a number you specify.
LOG	This function returns the logarithm of a number to a base you specify.
LOG10	This function returns the base-10 logarithm of a number you specify.
LOGEST	Used in regression analysis, this function calculates an exponential curve that fits your data and returns an array of values that describes the curve.
LOGINV	This function returns the inverse of the lognormal distribution.
LOGNORMDIST	This function returns the cumulative lognormal distribution.
LOOKUP	Use this function to return a value from a one-row or one-column range.
LOWER	Use this function to convert uppercase letters in a text string to lowercase letters.
MATCH	Use this function to determine the relative position of an item in an array.
MAX	Use this function to find the largest number in a list of numbers.
MAXA	Use this function to find the largest value in a list of values that might include logical values or text representations of numbers.

continued

Excel Functions

(Continued)

Function Name	Purpose
MDETERM	Use this function to return the matrix determinant of an array.
MDURATION	This function returns the Macauley modified duration for a security with an assumed par value of $100.
MEDIAN	Use this function to find the middle value in a list of numbers.
MID	For single-byte character sets, use this function to extract characters from a text string starting at a position within the string that you specify. Use MIDB for double-byte character sets.
MIN	Use this function to find the smallest number in a list of numbers.
MINA	Use this function to find the smallest value in a list of values that might include logical values or text representations of numbers.
MINUTE	Use this function to convert a serial number to a minute.
MINVERSE	Use this function to return the matrix inverse of an array.
MIRR	Use this function to calculate the internal rate of return when you finance positive and negative cash flows at different rates.
MMULT	Use this function to multiply two arrays.
MOD	This function returns the remainder from a division operation.
MODE	This function identifies the most frequently occurring value in a range or an array.
MONTH	Use this function to convert a serial number to a month.
MROUND	This function returns a number you specify rounded to the multiple you specify.
MULTINOMIAL	Use this function to return the multinomial of a set of numbers you provide.
N	Use this function to convert a value you specify to a number.
NA	Use this function to display the error value #N/A.
NEGBINOMDIST	This function returns the negative binomial distribution.
NETWORKDAYS	This function calculates the number of whole workdays between two dates you provide.
NOMINAL	Use this function to calculate the annual nominal interest rate of an investment.
NORMDIST	Use this function to return the normal cumulative distribution for a mean and standard deviation you provide.
NORMINV	This function returns the inverse of the normal cumulative distribution for a mean and standard deviation you provide.
NORMSDIST	This function returns the standard normal cumulative distribution using a mean of 0 and a standard deviation of 1.
NORMSINV	This function returns the inverse of the standard normal cumulative distribution.
NOT	This function returns TRUE when its arguments evaluate to FALSE, and FALSE when its arguments evaluate to TRUE.

Function Name	Purpose
NOW	This function returns the serial number of the current date and time.
NPER	Use this function to calculate the number of periods for an investment.
NPV	This function calculates the net present value of an investment using a series of periodic cash flows and a discount rate.
OCT2BIN	This function converts an octal number to binary.
OCT2DEC	This function converts an octal number to decimal.
OCT2HEX	This function converts an octal number to hexadecimal.
ODD	This function rounds a number up to the nearest odd integer.
ODDFPRICE	Use this function to calculate the price per $100 face value of a security with a short or long first period.
ODDFYIELD	Use this function to calculate the yield of a security with a long or short first period.
ODDLPRICE	Use this function to calculate the price per $100 face value of a security with a short or long last period.
ODDLYIELD	Use this function to calculate the yield of a security with a long or short last period.
OFFSET	This function returns a reference to a range that is a specific number of rows and columns from a range you include as an argument to the function.
OR	Use this function to return TRUE if any of the function's arguments are true.
PEARSON	Used to reflect the extent of a linear relationship between two data sets, this function returns the Pearson product moment correlation coefficient.
PERCENTILE	This function returns a value based on its relative percentile within an array using a relative percentile position you specify.
PERCENTRANK	Use this function to determine the rank of a value in a data set as a percentage of the data set.
PERMUT	This function returns the number of permutations given a number of objects and the number of objects in each permutation.
PI	Use this function to return the value of *pi*.
PMT	Use this function to calculate the periodic payment for an annuity.
POISSON	Use this function to return the Poisson distribution.
POWER	This function returns the result of a number you specify raised to a power you specify.
PPMT	Use this function to calculate the payment on the principal of an investment for a period you specify.
PRICE	This function calculates the price per $100 face value of a security that pays periodic interest.
PRICEDISC	This function calculates the price per $100 face value of a discounted security.

PART VII

continued

Excel Functions

(Continued)

Function Name	Purpose
PRICEMAT	This function calculates the price per $100 face value of a security that pays interest at maturity.
PROB	This function calculates the probability that values in a range you specify fall between two limits you provide.
PRODUCT	This function returns the result of multiplying its arguments.
PROPER	Use this function to capitalize the first letter of each word in a text string.
PV	Use this function to calculate the present value of an investment.
QUARTILE	This function returns the quartile of an array based on a quartile value you specify.
QUOTIENT	Use this function to return only the integer portion of a division operation, discarding the remainder.
RADIANS	This function converts degrees to radians.
RAND	This function returns a random number between 0 and 1.
RANDBETWEEN	Use this function to return a random number between two values you provide.
RANK	Use this function to determine the rank of a number within a list of numbers.
RATE	Use this function to calculate the interest rate per period of an annuity.
RECEIVED	This function calculates the amount received at maturity for a fully invested security.
REPLACE	For single-byte character sets, use this function to replace one text string with another text string, starting at a position within the original text that you specify and replacing the number of characters in the original text string that you specify. Use REPLACEB for double-byte character sets.
REPT	This function repeats, within a cell, characters you specify the number of times you specify.
RIGHT	For single-byte character sets, this function returns characters at the right edge of a character string, and you specify the number of characters to return. Use RIGHTB for double-byte character sets.
ROMAN	Use this function to convert an Arabic numeral to a Roman numeral, which is then treated by Excel as text.
ROUND	Use this function to round a value to a number of digits you specify.
ROUNDDOWN	Use this function to round a value down to a number of digits you specify.
ROUNDUP	Use this function to round a value up to a number of digits you specify.
ROW	Use this function to determine the row number of a cell or range of cells you specify.
ROWS	This function returns the number of rows in a range you specify.
RSQ	This function returns the square of the Pearson product moment correlation coefficient.
RTD	This function returns real-time data from a program that supports automation using a COM add-in.

Function Name	*Purpose*
SEARCH	For single-byte character sets, use this function to find a text string within another text string when case sensitivity does not matter. Use SEARCHB for double-byte character sets.
SECOND	Use this function to convert a serial number to a second as part of a time value.
SERIESSUM	This function returns the sum of a power series, using arguments you provide for an input value, an initial power to which you want to raise the input value, a step by which to increase the initial power, and a set of coefficients.
SIGN	This function returns the sign, positive or negative, of a number you specify.
SIN	Use this function to display the sine of an angle you specify.
SINH	Use this function to display the hyperbolic sine of an angle you specify.
SKEW	Use this function to calculate how asymmetric a distribution is around its mean.
SLN	Using the straight-line depreciation method, this function calculates depreciation of an asset for one period.
SLOPE	Use this function to calculate the slope of the linear regression line.
SMALL	This function returns a value based on its relative smallness within an array using a relative smallness position you specify.
SQRT	Use this function to calculate the square root of a number you specify.
SQRTPI	This function returns the square root of *pi*.
STANDARDIZE	This function normalizes a value in a distribution using the mean and standard deviation of the distribution.
STDEV	This function estimates the standard deviation of a sample, ignoring text and logical values.
STDEVA	This function estimates the standard deviation of a sample, including text and logical values.
STDEVP	This function estimates the standard deviation of an entire population, ignoring text and logical values.
STDEVPA	This function estimates the standard deviation of an entire population, including text and logical values.
STEYX	Use this function to determine the standard error of the predicted y-value for each x in the regression.
SUBSTITUTE	Use this function to replace one text string with another text string without specifying a starting position or a number of characters within the original text.
SUBTOTAL	Use this function to calculate a subtotal in a list.
SUM	This function adds the arguments you specify.
SUMIF	This function adds the cells that meet a criterion you specify.
SUMIFS	This function adds the cells that meet multiple criteria you specify.

continued

Excel Functions

(Continued)

Function Name	Purpose
SUMPRODUCT	This function multiples corresponding components of arrays you specify and returns the sum of those products.
SUMSQ	Use this function to calculate the sum of the squares of the arguments you specify.
SUMX2MY2	This function returns the sum of the difference of squares of corresponding values in two arrays you specify.
SUMX2PY2	Commonly used in statistical calculations, this function returns the sum of the sum of squares of corresponding values in two arrays you specify.
SUMXMY2	This function returns the sum of the squares of differences of corresponding values in two arrays you specify.
SYD	Using the sum-of-years' digits depreciation method, this function calculates depreciation of an asset for a period you specify.
T	This function converts the argument you supply — a number — to text.
TAN	Use this function to determine the tangent of a number you specify.
TANH	Use this function to determine the hyperbolic tangent of a number you specify.
TBILLEQ	This function calculates the bond-equivalent yield for a Treasury bill.
TBILLPRICE	This function calculates the price per $100 face value for a Treasury bill.
TBILLYIELD	This function calculates the yield for a Treasury bill.
TDIST	This function returns the Student's t-distribution.
TEXT	This function applies a numeric format you provide to a number you supply, and converts the number to text.
TIME	This function returns the serial number of a time you specify.
TIMEVALUE	This function converts a time in the form of text to a serial number.
TINV	This function returns the inverse of the Student's t-distribution.
TODAY	This function returns the serial number for today's date.
TRANSPOSE	This function converts a vertical range into a horizontal range, or a horizontal range into a vertical range.
TREND	This function returns values along a linear trend.
TRIM	Use this function to remove excess spaces from a text string.
TRIMMEAN	Used to exclude outlying data points from analysis, this function calculates the mean by excluding a percentage of data points at the top and bottom of the data set.
TRUE	This function displays the logical value TRUE.
TRUNC	This function truncates a number you specify to an integer by removing the fractional portion of the number.

Function Name	*Purpose*
TTEST	Use this function to calculate the probability associated with a Student's t-test.
TYPE	Use this function to display a number that corresponds to the type of data stored in a cell.
UPPER	Use this function to convert uppercase letters in a text string to lowercase letters.
VALUE	This function converts text you supply to a number.
VAR	Use this function to estimate variance based on a sample while ignoring logical values and text.
VARA	Use this function to estimate variance based on a sample, including logical values and text.
VARP	Use this function to estimate variance for an entire population while ignoring logical values and text.
VARPA	Use this function to estimate variance for an entire population, including logical values and text.
VDB	Using a declining balance depreciation method, this function calculates depreciation of an asset for a period you specify, including partial periods.
VLOOKUP	This function looks up data in a list by vertically matching a value in the left column and then finding a value in the matched row from a column you specify.
WEEKDAY	This function converts a serial number to its corresponding day of the week.
WEEKNUM	Use this function to determine the number of a particular week in a year.
WEIBULL	This function returns the Weibull distribution, which is used in reliability analysis.
WORKDAY	This function returns the serial number of the date before or after a number of workdays you specify.
XIRR	This function calculates the internal rate of return for a set of cash flows that may or may not be periodic.
XNPV	This function calculates the net present value for a set of cash flows that may or may not be periodic.
YEAR	This function converts a serial number to a year.
YEARFRAC	This function returns the year fraction that represents the number of whole days between starting and ending dates you provide.
YIELD	Use this function to calculate the yield on a security that pays periodic interest.
YIELDDISC	Use this function to calculate the annual yield for a discounted security.
YIELDMAT	This function calculates the annual yield of a security that pays interest at maturity.
ZTEST	This function calculates the one-tailed probability value of a z-test.

Symbols

A

B

C

D

continued

G

H

O

P

continued

S

T

U

V

W

X

Y

Z

Read Less–Learn More®

Visual®

There's a Visual book for every learning level...

Simplified®

The place to start if you're new to computers. Full color.

- Computers
- Creating Web Pages
- Mac OS
- Office
- Windows

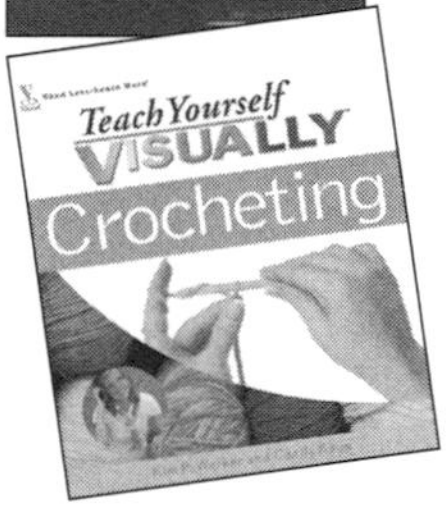

Teach Yourself VISUALLY™

Get beginning to intermediate-level training in a variety of topics. Full color.

- Access
- Bridge
- Chess
- Computers
- Crocheting
- Digital Photography
- Dog training
- Dreamweaver
- Excel
- Flash
- Golf
- Guitar
- Handspinning
- HTML
- Jewelry Making & Beading
- Knitting
- Mac OS
- Office
- Photoshop
- Photoshop Elements
- Piano
- Poker
- PowerPoint
- Quilting
- Scrapbooking
- Sewing
- Windows
- Wireless Networking
- Word

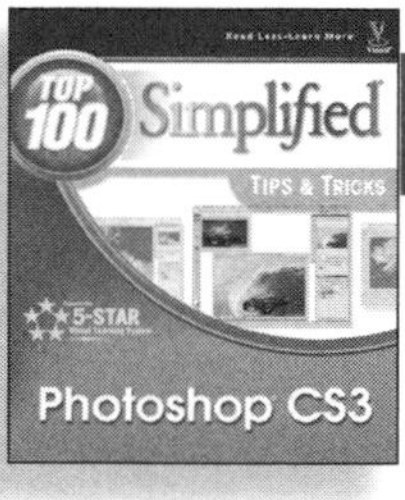

Top 100 Simplified® Tips & Tricks

Tips and techniques to take your skills beyond the basics. Full color.

- Digital Photography
- eBay
- Excel
- Google
- Internet
- Mac OS
- Office
- Photoshop
- Photoshop Elements
- PowerPoint
- Windows